Advance praise for the second edition

"*The Cambridge Companion to the Bible* was a remarkable contribution when it was first released in 1997, which only makes the achievements of this thoroughly updated second edition all the more impressive. The abundance of stunning new photos from Todd Bolen, the additional sidebars of useful, contextualized information, the new maps in each section, and the revised bibliographies and main text all make the second edition an essential book for serious students, clergy, and general readers alike."

–Desmond Tutu, Archbishop Emeritus of Cape Town

"This resource book offered by Cambridge University Press is a rich, accessible, and reliable reference. It provides state-of-the-art scholarship that connects each of the Biblical books to its socio-historical context. Its offer of 'social history' is broad and deep. Such a perspective is crucial in the current 'battle for the Bible,' and the work here is exceedingly well done. Its publication will immediately make it a primary reference for serious students of the Bible."

–Walter Brueggemann, Columbia Theological Seminary

"A clear, up-to-date, and authoritative account of the Bible by the leaders of the field, the new edition of the *Cambridge Companion* defines the context in which the Bible is read for history, literature, religion, and theology, the best path into Scripture now in print."

–Jacob Neusner, Bard College, Distinguished Service
Professor of the History and Theology of Judaism

"For those readers of Scripture who want a broader and deeper glimpse into the forces and factors which shaped the Biblical community, it is hard to imagine a tool more convenient and accessible than *The Cambridge Companion to the Bible.*"

–The Rt. Rev. Mark S. Sisk, Fifteenth Episcopal Bishop of
New York

"An excellent update of a masterful work! *The Cambridge Companion to the Bible, Second Edition,* is packed with indispensable information of understanding the world's best-selling and most influential book. It somehow manages to be both studious and exhilarating, thorough yet remarkably concise. No other Bible companion is as competently informed by modern archaeological research or by historical analysis of the societies for which the biblical writings were produced. The main text, trustworthy and illuminating in its own right, is supplemented by more than 250 sidebars that render the volume ripe for browsing and provide a wealth of information on intriguing topics. As a bonus, the Companion also treats the significant apocryphal works that did not come to be numbered among the 'sacred sixty-six' books of the Christian canon but that are revealing of Jewish and Christian religion nevertheless."

–Mark Allan Powell, Trinity Lutheran Seminary

Praise for the first edition

"A truly wonderful book. Clear, concise, illuminating. It will be useful for all of those of us who preach every week, and for the educated person who wants to learn more about the sacred scriptures without being overwhelmed by academic detail. Everyone should have a copy."

> – Father Andrew M. Greeley, The University of Chicago and the University of Arizona

"The Bible, the greatest of all books, is half-closed to those who cannot identify the innumerable names and places which are central to almost every chapter. *The Cambridge Companion to the Bible* answers this need in a learned, and very accessible, way. It is indispensable to the general reader and to the student."

> – Arthur Hertzberg, Professor Emeritus of Religion, Dartmouth College

THE CAMBRIDGE COMPANION TO THE BIBLE, Second Edition

Written by an international team of experts, *The Cambridge Companion to the Bible*, second edition, provides in-depth information and analysis on the canonical writings of the Hebrew Bible and New Testament, as well as the apocryphal works produced by Jewish and Christian writers. Throughout, the book offers an expanded focus on the ever-changing social and cultural worlds in which the biblical authors and their original readers lived. Bruce Chilton served as the general editor of the second edition, synthesizing revisions from the authors, information on the most recent archaeological discoveries, and the new secondary literature. Improvements to the *look* of the book include 107 stunning new photographs, a new color section, and nine newly created maps (for a total of 21). In addition, all of the 250 sidebars have been updated, and 22 of them are new to this edition, collectively illuminating the book's main narrative. The result is an indispensable resource for anyone interested in fully encountering the Bible and its world.

Bruce Chilton is Bernard Iddings Bell Professor of Religion at Bard College. His most recent books include *Rabbi Jesus: An Intimate Biography* (2000), *Redeeming Time: The Wisdom of Ancient Jewish and Christian Festal Calendars* (2002), *Rabbi Paul: An Intellectual Biography* (2004), and *Mary Magdalene: A Biography* (2005).

Howard Clark Kee is William Goodwin Aurelio Professor of Biblical Studies, Emeritus, at Boston University. He is the author or editor of more than twenty books, including the first edition of *The Cambridge Companion to the Bible*, *Understanding the New Testament* (fifth edition), and *Jesus in History* (third edition).

Amy-Jill Levine is E. Rhodes and Leona B. Carpenter Professor of New Testament Studies at Vanderbilt University. Her numerous publications address Christian origins; Jewish-Christian relations; and sexuality, gender, and the Bible. Her most recent books (as author or editor) include *The Misunderstood Jew: The Church and the Scandal of the Jewish Jesus* (2006), *The Historical Jesus in Context* (2006), and *The Feminist Companions to the New Testament and Early Christian Writing*.

Eric M. Meyers is Bernice and Morton Lerner Professor of Judaic Studies at Duke University. He has authored or coauthored nine books, edited many others, and published widely in the fields of Hebrew Bible, biblical archaeology, and Second Temple Judaism. He also served as editor in chief of the five-volume work *The Oxford Encyclopedia of Archaeology in the Near East* (1997).

John Rogerson is the author of *The Atlas of the Bible* (1984); *The Study and Use of the Bible,* volume 2 (1988); and *The Bible: A Cultural Atlas for Young Children* (1993) and coauthor of *The Old Testament World* (1989).

Anthony J. Saldarini was at the time of his death in 2001 Professor of Biblical Studies at Boston College and a leading scholar of Second Temple and Rabbinic Judaism. His books include *The Fathers According to Rabbi Nathan* (1975); *Jesus and Passover* (1984); *Pharisees, Scribes and Saducees in Palestinian Society* (1989); and *Matthew's Christian-Jewish Community* (1994).

THE CAMBRIDGE COMPANION TO THE BIBLE

Second Edition

**Bruce Chilton,
General Editor**

Bard College

Howard Clark Kee

Boston University, Emeritus

Amy-Jill Levine

Vanderbilt University

Eric M. Meyers

Duke University

John Rogerson

University of Sheffield, Emeritus

Anthony J. Saldarini

Late of Boston College

CAMBRIDGE
UNIVERSITY PRESS

CAMBRIDGE UNIVERSITY PRESS
Cambridge, New York, Melbourne, Madrid, Cape Town, Singapore, São Paulo, Delhi

Cambridge University Press
32 Avenue of the Americas, New York NY 10013-2473, USA

www.cambridge.org
Information on this title: www.cambridge.org/9780521869973

First edition published 1997
Reprinted 1997, 1998 (twice), 1999
Second edition published 2008

Printed in the United States of America

A catalog record for this publication is available from the British Library.

Library of Congress Cataloging in Publication Data
The Cambridge companion to the Bible / Howard Clark Kee . . .[et al.].
p.   cm.
Includes bibliographical references and index.
1. Bible – Introductions.   2. Bible – History of contemporary events.
3. Bible – History of Biblical events.   I. Chilton, Bruce
BS475.2.C26   1997
220.9 – dc20   96 – 43914

ISBN   978-0-521-86997-3 hardback
ISBN   978-0-521-69140-6 paperback

CONTENTS

Color plates follow page 38

EDITOR'S FOREWORD

Contributions from Cambridge University Press have stood out for several decades among introductions to the Bible and works of biblical reference. In *The Cambridge Companion to the Bible*, serious students as well as general readers have enjoyed access to critical discussion of the Scriptures with appropriate reference to the secondary literature. In terms of judicious balance, theological sensitivity, and historical accuracy, the Press has set the standard within this sector of publishing.

This second edition revises and updates the brilliant investigations developed in the first edition of key historical and exegetical issues within the study of the Bible. Two principles have been applied consistently to the task of revision.

The first principle involves understanding the social histories of Israel and the early Church as they shaped the biblical texts. This approach identifies the constituencies for which the sources of the texts were produced. By "sources" we do not mean the documents as they stand (Genesis, Exodus, Leviticus, and so on), but rather the traditions that fed into those documents. The final, editorial moment when traditions were crystallized in writing is a vital juncture in the literary formation of the Scriptures but is not solely determinative of their meaning. The unfolding of meanings within texts during the whole of their development explodes the claim of a single, exclusive meaning in biblical exegesis. The *Companion* attends to the variety of meanings inherent within the Scriptures – without limitation to a particular theory of interpretation, and with constant attention to issues of historical context.

The second principle concerns reference to archaeological discoveries, already an important feature of the first edition. The archaeological aspect of any work in the Bible has been severely complicated since the appearance of the first edition. Accusations of fraud and forgery, including warrants of arrest issued by the Israel Antiquities Authority, have emphasized the necessity of disciplined care in this field. In addition, new electronic communication permits images and maps to be produced that improve on the illustrative value of the first edition. Finally, the interpretative interface between archaeology and exegesis has seen renewed discussion within the last decade, which is reflected in this second edition.

My involvement in the second edition of the *Companion* comes at the suggestion of Howard Clark Kee (William Goodwin Aurelio Professor of Biblical Studies, Emeritus, Boston University), who served as General Editor of the first edition, and with the agreement of Eric M. Meyers (Bernice and Morton Lerner Professor of Judaic Studies, Duke University) and John Rogerson (Professor of Biblical Studies, Emeritus, the University of Sheffield), Professor Kee's colleagues in that project. They have been helpful and patient in consulting on the second edition, a process that was greatly facilitated by Andrew Beck (Commissioning Editor, Religion and Anthropology, Cambridge University Press). A great deal of the work that the late Anthony J. Saldarini (Professor of Biblical Studies, Boston College) contributed to the first edition remains; with the permission of his estate his section of the *Companion* was revised initially by Amy-Jill Levine (E. Rhodes and Leona B. Carpenter Professor of New Testament Studies, Vanderbilt University). I worked on the basis of revisions, my own contributions, and the original work, giving all my colleagues access to any part of the manuscript they asked to see in addition to their own sections.

Collaborative projects are notorious for occasioning unanticipated and inadvertent disagreements. Owing to the high level of engagement on the part of my colleagues, I am happy to note that any disagreements in preparing the second edition have been professional and substantive; these scholars have also been extremely cooperative in implementing my policy of attempting to explore possible consensus, while letting a range of opinions become explicit, as appropriate. The *Companion* focuses on exegesis and interpretation with close reference to texts and encourages readers to pursue issues of scholarly debate as they may wish.

Todd Bolen (Associate Professor of Biblical Studies, The Master's College, Israel) consulted with my colleagues and me on archaeological work and provided a number of illustrations, so that the images differ substantially from those in the first edition. (Consultation with staff of the British Museum, the Cairo Archaeological Museum, the Department of Antiquities of Jordan, the Hellenic Republic Ministry of Culture, Heritage Malta, the Ministry of Culture in Ankara, the Rockefeller Museum in Jerusalem, the Soprintendenze Archeologica di Roma, and the Soprintendenze per i Beni Archeologici delle province di Napoli e Caserta resolved issues of authenticity and of the fair use of images.) In addition, maps for the second edition expand on the initial presentation and take greater account of physical features as a result of the work of David Cox.

It remains for me only to thank my colleagues, to acknowledge the support extended to the project by the Press and by Bard College, and to wish our readers well in assessing the literatures of the Bible within the contexts that produced them while enjoying the enduring significance of their messages.

Bruce Chilton
Bernard Iddings Bell Professor of Religion
Bard College

Introduction

Howard Clark Kee

I. PREFACE

No other book has exerted the depth and range of influence that the Bible has. Judaism and Christianity both claim the Bible in different forms as their own, but other religious sources – most notably the Qur'an – as well as literary works from Chaucer to Dostoyevski develop much of its force and content. The Bible tells the story of God's people, shapes their identity through prophecy, and informs their understanding with a rich variety of writings. The Torah (or "Law"), the Prophets, and the Writings are the three main divisions of the Hebrew Bible. Christians recognize as the Bible not only the Scriptures of Israel but also twenty-seven documents that describe or that derive from the persons and events that gave rise to faith in Jesus. Christians designate this second group as "the New Testament" and refer to Israel's writings as "the Old Testament."

In addition to the writings included in the canons of the Bible, there are a number of writings that some communities, past and present, have regarded as of equal value, or as essential supplements to the biblical sources. The Wisdom of Solomon and 1 and 2 Maccabees, for example, appear in some Christian Bibles, and the *Book of Enoch* acquired the authority of a sacred text at Qumran. Many early churches used Gospels other than the four now found in the New Testament. In this new edition of the *Companion to the Bible* we shall examine the writings widely accepted as authoritative, but also look at a number of the texts associated with the Bible within Judaism and Christianity. An awareness of this penumbra of literatures around official canons helps us to appreciate the diversity of belief and practice within Judaism and Christianity, and to see the links between the biblical tradition and the religions of antiquity.

Biblical influence on other literatures, on views of human history and society, and on personal and social ethical norms, has been profound, especially – although by no means uniquely – in Western culture. Accordingly, study of the Bible has typically involved historians, archaeologists, philologists, theologians, and ethicists, as well as philosophers, experts in interpretation, and literary critics of various kinds. Since the biblical writings were written in several different languages (Hebrew, Aramaic, and Greek) across the better part of two millennia and in a variety of circumstances, this

COVENANT/TESTAMENT

The Hebrew word *berit* is used for formal agreements reached between two parties, each of whom assumes certain obligations. In the Scriptures of Israel and in documents from the ancient Near East, such contracts are instanced between nations, between rulers and their subjects, and between individuals (e.g., Genesis 31:43–54; 2 Samuel 5:3; 1 Kings 5:26). Antecedents for the covenant between Yahweh and the twelve clans at Mount Sinai (Exodus 19–24) include God's covenant with Abraham, in which God promises Abraham many descendants and vast territory (Genesis 15). Initially, God puts no conditions on Abraham, but obligations became apparent (Genesis 17, 22), and the same is true of God's covenant with David, which promises him an unending line of successors to the throne of Israel (2 Samuel 7). When divine judgment on God's people drives them from the Promised Land and places them under foreign rule, the prophet Jeremiah voices the assurance of a "new covenant" (Jeremiah 31:31–4) by which the people of Israel will be inwardly transformed and their knowledge of God will become personal and direct. It is this expectation that is taken up in the early Christian tradition and is seen as in the process of fulfillment through Jesus (1 Corinthians 11:23–5; also in some manuscripts and in ancient versions of Mark 14:24).

The Greek word *diatheke*, which means "contract" or "compact" and thus matches the Hebrew term well, was also widely used for "last will and testament." Hence it came to be translated in the early Latin versions of the New Testament as *testamentum*. When the phrase "New Covenant" was used as the title of the whole collection of early Christian writings, with the implicit claim that Jesus had fulfilled the prophecy of Jeremiah, it too was translated into Latin as "Novum Testamentum" and thus into English as "New Testament."

wide range of approaches has proven crucial to appreciating the rich variety of literatures that the Bible presents.

In view of the complexity of the Bible itself, and the variety of approaches to its study, informed readers will wish to orient themselves with an awareness of how biblical texts were produced. Understanding that generative process reveals how the Bible grew and evolved over many centuries within different historical contexts. The distinctive keys and strains of biblical language and thought emerge, as do patterns of influence from one biblical community to another.

The cumulative effect of these different communities, each distinctive and vibrant, produced the Bible. Multiple constituencies – sometimes at odds with one another, sometimes forging compromises, sometimes influencing or replying to competitors, and sometimes building on each other, but also willing to set off in new directions – generated the world's most influential book. However we might interpret these texts today, from whatever theological, philosophical, or literary perspectives, an appreciation of the people and of the processes and social worlds that lie behind the documents is indispensable to informed reading.

For that reason, this *Companion* does not engage in a discussion of methods of interpretation, which may be approached in *The Cambridge Companion to Biblical Interpretation* edited by John Barton (Cambridge: Cambridge University Press, 1998). Regardless of the approach one develops – in accordance with recent trends or on one's own, from the standpoint of religious faith or from an atheist perspective – critical reading involves developing both an awareness of the content of the Bible and an appreciation of how its various documents took shape. For that reason, the contributors to this *Companion* have devoted their attention to that preliminary but indispensable task.

II. PURPOSE

Information on the changing circumstances in which the biblical writers and their original readers lived guides critical, informed reading. This *Companion to the Bible* seeks to provide basic knowledge of the cultural contexts in which the biblical books were produced, including the history, languages, and religious beliefs and philosophical insights of the writers, the people they wrote about, and the audiences for whom they wrote. The *Companion* is largely chronological in its organization, moving from the earliest historical and cultural circumstances depicted in the biblical accounts, through the changing conditions of the history of Israel, down to the destruction of the Second Temple by the Roman armies under Titus in 70 C.E., and on to Christianity's emergence out of its Jewish matrix and its development into the second century C.E. The biblical writings, broadly defined, are examined in their respective contexts. Maps, images, and descriptions of the various lands and peoples of the Bible are designed to help the reader understand the geographical contexts involved. Illustrations feature cultural contexts; boxes throughout provide definitions of terms and descriptions of individuals, movements, and practices of basic importance to the biblical writers, as well as chronological orientation. Indexes of subjects and of references to the biblical and related writings enable the reader to trace themes, to locate passages relevant to particular lines of inquiry, and to correlate features of the biblical writings with their specific contexts.

This book is written mostly in the form of continuous narratives, in which the successive stages of the biblical writings and their context are described with an eye on the present order of the Bible. In this regard the editors have compromised the principle of following the chronological development of the texts. Had they followed that principle strictly, they would, for example, have begun with Judges, by common agreement the biblical book composed at the earliest stage of Israel's history. There is much to be said for tracing the phases of the biblical literatures rigorously through their generative development, but the *Companion*'s purpose would not be served if readers could not easily follow the sequence of the books in their printed Bibles, similarly, we have kept familiar translations in view, while introducing our own for the sake of accuracy.

In the analysis of the biblical texts, which constitutes the major portion of this book, we move through the literature by two coordinated modes of organization: (1) chronological sequence, and (2) type of literature. Within each part there is a balance between the descriptions of the successive epochs in which these documents were produced, and the various aims and literary styles of the documents. The documents analyzed include not only those writings recognized today as authoritative by various religious traditions but also associated works that have been regarded as "biblical" by some religious groups. The examination of these documents of disputed authority enables us to see concretely the diversity of the biblical traditions and the special interests that led certain groups to include these works on their authoritative lists. Following a convention of long standing, titles of noncanonical works are printed in italics. Readers seeking information about a particular book, concept, or event might consult the indexes.

III. THE CONCEPT OF GOD'S PEOPLE

A. Who Are God's People? How Does God Speak to Them?

Those who contributed to the Bible, whether in writing or in the oral traditions that eventually achieved written form, shared two convictions: that God speaks to his people in particular circumstances of human experience, and that the divine message, though spoken through individuals, concerns the identity and welfare of the members of the whole community. Even when reports are given of some private disclosure by God to an individual, the communication is not intended for that person alone. Rather, it is addressed to the group of which this single intermediary between God and his people is a representative.

The conviction that God addresses his people in the circumstances of their common history permeates the biblical tradition and requires the reader of the Bible to give careful attention to the social, cultural, and historical contexts in which it is claimed that the word of God was heard by his people. Throughout the whole range of the biblical writings, however, those who saw themselves as God's people lived in circumstances that changed, sometimes radically. The changes occured in both the inner structures of the group (its values and goals) and the social and cultural conditions in which it lived.

The earliest traditions of the origins of the people Israel portray them as a group of clans joined in a loose association based on common ancestry and identification with the religious experience of their ancestor Abraham. The migration to Egypt in a time of threatening famine led to their enslavement by the pharaoh. They discerned direct divine intervention in their successful flight from Egypt and in being led through the wilderness of Sinai to the borders of Canaan, the Promised Land. On arrival they were once more a confederacy of clans, sharing (in addition to their common ancestry) the belief that their God was in their midst, present in the portable shrine (the ark of the covenant) that they brought with them out of the wilderness. The founding principles of their group identity were given to them by revelation through Moses, their leader, at Mount Sinai. To this code they jointly committed themselves.

Ram in a thicket. Found in a cemetery at Ur, on the Euphrates River midway between Baghdad and the Persian Gulf, and dating to 2600 B.C.E., this image of a ram eating leaves recalls the story of Abraham finding a ram caught in a thicket by its horns (Genesis 22:13). (BiblePlaces.com)

In the land of promise they lived more or less separate – and sometimes competing – social existences, bound by their common history and their devotion to the God who dwelt in their midst in the shrine, which on occasion was moved from place to place. Leaders arose in times of crisis to settle internal disputes or to defend tribes from external enemies. The decision to erect the Temple in Jerusalem as a permanent house for Yahweh, their God, coincided with the designation of a national leader, a king chosen from one of the clans. The monarchy lasted only a few generations and ended with two nations and two cultic centers – in Jerusalem and on Mount Gerizim in Samaria – competing for the claim to be Yahweh's residence among his people. First the northern and then the southern nation was taken off into captivity in Mesopotamia, and their shrines lay in ruins until the decision by Cyrus, the Persian ruler of the Middle East, to allow the tribes of Judah to return to their ancestral land. From the rise of the monarchy down through the period of the exile in Babylon and the return, certain figures came forth in Israel to utter predictions and protests and to call the ruler and the people to account before God. These were the prophets of Israel. After the monarchy was gone, leadership and identity for the Jews were provided increasingly through their priests. Traditional aids for individual and group worship were brought together to form the Book of Psalms. The wisdom traditions were edited in such books as Proverbs and Ecclesiastes.

Mount Gerizim, looking east with Mount Ebal to the left. Mounts Gerizim and Ebal are on opposite sides of the valley where Shechem and Jacob's well were located, in what came to be known as Samaria. When the northern clans broke with the southern, Judean tribes, they not only formed a separate monarchy but also, both then and after the Samaritans were allowed to return from exile in Babylon in the sixth century B.C.E., built altars that competed with the Temple in Jerusalem. (BiblePlaces.com)

HELLENISTIC

From the Greek word meaning "Greek" – *Hellen* – came the verb "to hellenize," or to convert to Greek culture and style of life. Alexander the Great and his successors as rulers of the Middle East – especially the Ptolemaic monarchs in Egypt and the Seleucid rulers in Syria – saw this process of "Greek-izing" as a central goal of their rule over these non-Greek territories. They thought of themselves as bringing true culture to benighted peoples. In addition to rebuilding the cities in the Greek style, they promoted Greek education and culture, and devotion to the Greek gods among their subjects. The term "Hellenistic" has been applied by historians to the period lasting from the rise of Alexander during the fourth century B.C.E. to the time of the coming of the Romans to the eastern Mediterranean in the mid-first century B.C.E.

With the takeover of the land by Alexander the Great and his Hellenistic successors, the people of Judea were subjected to enormous pressures to conform to Greek-style culture. Their resistance was led by a priestly family, the Maccabees (or Hasmoneans), and resulted in the establishment of a dynasty that became increasingly objectionable to many Jews because its kings were from the priestly line rather than descended from David, the model king whose dynasty had been a covenantal mandate. Further, the Hasmonean rulers became increasingly secular and harsh. As a result, there arose various Jewish groups whose members sought fulfillment of their sense of unique relationship with God outside the frameworks provided by either the Temple priesthood or the political establishment. In this context movements emerged from within Judaism that were to have such profound importance for the subsequent history of biblical religion: the Pharisees, the Essenes (or Dead Sea community), and the Christians. In all these changing circumstances the twin convictions remained that God addressed his people through chosen instruments and that it was obligatory for his people to confirm their special relationship to God.

Closely linked with the changing context of revelation was the constant modification of what historical communities understood to be the nature of their relationship to the God who spoke to them about his

Relief from a sarcophagus from the late fourth century B.C.E. This probably depicts Alexander's most important battle, when his defeat of the Persian army at Issus, in a narrow stretch of land in southern Turkey, gave him access to all the lands to the east, including Syria and Mesopotamia, and as far as India. (BiblePlaces.com)

Cliffs overlooking Qumran. After local Bedouins discovered the first of the scrolls in a cave overlooking the Dead Sea in 1947, other manuscripts were found here and in nearby sites, and the ruins of a community center were excavated. The oldest extant copies of the Hebrew Scriptures and related writings, as well as previously unknown texts in Hebrew and Aramaic, have been found preserved in the caves. (BiblePlaces.com)

THE DEAD SEA SCROLLS AND THE QUMRAN COMMUNITY

Khirbet Qumran is the modern name for the ruins at the site of the Jewish community that withdrew in the first century B.C.E. from life in Jerusalem and the mainstream of Jewish society to live together in what their anonymous founder and his followers were convinced was the pure life of devotion to God, until – as they were convinced – God would intervene in their behalf and grant them the priestly role in a renewed Temple in Jerusalem.

The community was located on a bluff overlooking the northwestern end of the Dead Sea. The Wadi Qumran ("wadi" refers to the rocky bed of a seasonal stream), just below their sacred site, provides a runoff for water from the Temple site in Jerusalem.

According to Ezekiel 47, through this channel a mighty stream would flow from the renewed Temple and would transform the salty Dead Sea into a freshwater lake. The community had a central building where they gathered to study, to prepare copies of their writings, and to eat common meals. There are also ruins of other structures, including pools (possibly for baptisms), caves where some members appear to have lived, and tombs for their deceased. The Dead Sea community lived on this site awaiting the divine renewal of God's people, of Jerusalem and the Temple (with themselves in charge), and of the land of Israel.

The documents found there include the oldest surviving copies of the Jewish Scriptures, in addition to commentaries on the Prophets of Israel, predicting the imminent fulfillment of the prophecies for and through this community. Basic writings describing the origins, organization, rules, and destiny of the community were also found, of which the most revealing is the *Scroll of the Rule*.

purpose and their destiny. At the same time, the perception of who the human instrument was through whom God had addressed them – a king, a clan leader, a prophet, a priest, someone especially gifted to interpret the tradition – varied dramatically from time to time and place to place. There is no uniform pattern of divine communication in the biblical writings, nor is there a single view of how one was to define the people of God addressed by him. The two persistent themes running throughout the biblical writings are that (1) there is a people of God, and (2) they have been spoken to by God. The content of the message and the community context in which it was heard changed throughout the centuries of the biblical period. But in every case, the authority of what was uttered is traced to God. The responsibility for and the consequences of the response rested with those who, by various criteria, saw themselves as God's people.

B. The Biblical Writings and the Cultural Setting

As the social and political setting of the covenant people changed over the centuries, so did both the linguistic and the literary styles of scriptures. The oldest Hebrew literary traditions included in the Bible, which consist of epic accounts of the origins of the people Israel, seem to have originated from earlier, oral traditions in about the year 1200 B.C.E. During or after the exile of 587 B.C.E., they were incorporated with later materials into what we know as the Pentateuch. The oldest surviving inscriptions and documents in the Hebrew language – which is akin to Akkadian (the language spoken in ancient Babylonia) but is even more closely related to the Semitic languages spoken in Palestine (Canaanite and Phoenician) – date from around the tenth century B.C.E. By the eighth century B.C.E., however, Aramaic (which was spoken by a Semitic group that invaded Palestine and Syria from Mesopotamia) had become the major language of the Middle East. In the sixth century B.C.E. the Persians made Aramaic the official language of their empire, which included the land of Israel. Hebrew continued as the traditional religious language of Israel, but Aramaic was increasingly used by the Israelites for oral and written communication. Parts of Ezra and Daniel are in Aramaic, and it later became necessary to provide translations and paraphrases of the Scriptures of Israel in Aramaic in order for readers and worshippers to understand them. By the fifth century C.E., the Aramaic versions were officially recognized by the Rabbinic leaders as suitable for religious and devotional purposes. Meanwhile, a revived form of Hebrew also served the rabbis, along with Aramaic, in the works known as the Mishnah and the Talmud, which were written in the period from the second to the sixth centuries C.E.

The biblical writers used the literary styles and forms that were employed in their own era as media for communicating to their contemporaries. In many cases, these literary patterns were adapted or modified, but the

PENTATEUCH

Taken literally, the term "penta-teuch" indicates any book in five parts, and is widely used in biblical scholarship to refer to the first five books of the Bible: Genesis, Exodus, Leviticus, Numbers, and Deuteron-omy. These books have been tradi-tionally attributed to Moses. In Jew-ish usage, these writings are often referred to as Torah ("instruction"), or the Law of Moses. It seems likely that the Pentateuch is the end prod-uct of a period of development and modification that extended from the second millennium B.C.E. to as late as the fifth century B.C.E. Details of this development and analyses of the contents of the Pentateuch are pre-sented in Part 1 of the *Companion*.

underlying structures and strategies used by other religions and cultures remain readily recognizable. Epic narratives were an important feature of the literatures of various ethnic and cultural groups in the ancient Middle East. The biblical writers used this genre for their own purposes, both in the Pentateuch (especially in Genesis) and in the historical writings. Forms of poetry, and especially of hymns and liturgical passages, are also similar to those found in other ancient Semitic literatures of comparable periods. The biblical legal codes have their counterparts in contemporary legal traditions of other societies. In various ways, the wisdom traditions of Israel resemble the proverbs and oracles of contemporary cultures. Similarly, the prophetic oracles have their rough equivalents in other Semitic cultures.

From the late fourth century B.C.E. on, more and more Jews were reared in a Greek-speaking environment. By the third century B.C.E. thousands of Jews lived in Egypt, which accorded them welcome as mercenaries, merchants, and loyal subjects, and they were powerfully influenced by Hellenistic culture and learning. Their basic language was Greek, and they were schooled in Greek literature and philosophy. Since many of these Jews were unable to read the Bible in the original Hebrew and Aramaic, the pagan ruler of Egypt reportedly collaborated with the priestly leader-ship in Jerusalem to have a Greek translation made of the Pentateuch, which in subsequent centuries was followed by translations of the other books of the Bible. A legend arose about the miraculous agreement among seventy translators working independently, and the translation in its final form came to be known as the Septuagint, from the Greek word for "sev-enty." It was widely used throughout the Greco-Roman world, by Jews and later by Christians, becoming the basis of the Christian canon in Greek.

Books such as *4 Maccabees* not only were first written in Greek but also retell the story of Judas Maccabaeus's triumph over the idolatrous rulers in terms that show the direct influence of Greek philosophy, including the Stoic philosophical notion of virtue triumphing over adversity. The book variously known as the Wisdom of Ben Sira, Sirach, and Ecclesiasticus shows another kind of Hellenistic influence in that it counters the older biblical writings' uniform denunciation of physicians as magicians and agents of evil powers. Instead, Ben Sira honors physicians as instruments of God, reflecting Greek medicine's rise under Hippocrates and its promi-nence and increased respect during the Hellenistic period.

Just as in Egyptian mythology the goddess of knowledge, Ma'at, came to be seen as the instrument through whom the world was created, as well as the agent for conveying divine knowledge to the true seekers, so in Israel Wisdom became personified as the divine consort and aide in creation and the one through whom the knowledge of Yahweh is conveyed to his people. In Egypt during the Hellenistic period, the creative and revelatory role of Ma'at was transferred to Isis, who was portrayed in the mythology of the period as personally concerned for her worshippers and as revealing herself to them in mystical communion. The functions of Isis as intermediary

STOICISM

Stoicism is the philosophical school of thought that grew out of the work of Zeno of Citium (ca. 333–264 B.C.E.), who taught publicly in the porticoes – or stoa – of the market-place in Athens. His teaching empha-sized reason as the pervasive force that sustained the universe. He insisted on the material nature of the universe, as contrasted with the ideal realm of reality in the philosophy of Plato. Cleanthes (331–232 B.C.E.), who developed Zeno's ideas further, pictured God as the unseen force that gave life and purpose to the universe. The life of virtue for human beings was to live according to that law of nature. If the universal law were per-ceived and obeyed, human society could achieve peace and prosperity. The Stoic movement went through three phases: Old, Middle, and Later Stoicism. In the Middle period, his-tory, philosophy, and the natural sci-ences were studied with the aim of discerning the connection between logic and natural law. The divine pres-ence is described as *pneuma*, which means "spirit." Later Stoicism is rep-resented by the Roman philosopher Seneca (4 B.C.E.–65 C.E.). He discussed human suffering, which was a problem for those who stressed the divine presence and action, and depicted it as the divinely intended process by which humans were tested and puri-fied. Epictetus (50–120 C.E.) empha-sized that it was the human capacity for understanding and responding to the divine purpose – that is, con-science – that made possible human conformity to the law of nature.

between God and humans are paralleled in other writings of the Hellenis-tic period. This model of divine communication and relationship was taken up and transformed by the author of the Gospel according to John. Further, he assigns them to a male figure, the *Logos* (or Word), which he identifies with Jesus. During the Hellenistic and Roman periods, the styles for composing letters, for making speeches, for telling popular stories about religious persons and their experiences with the gods, and for writ-ing history strongly influenced the biblical writers as well.

In at least one case – that of the Gospels – biblical writers seem to have created a new literary type. Features of the Gospels resemble contempo-rary literary forms, including the biography and what anthropologists call a "foundation document," that is, a writing that presents an account of the circumstances under which a religious movement began and that indicates the basic pattern of life and thought that the movement's followers are to observe. The specific forms in which these elements are combined in the Gospels produced a unique contribution to world literature.

C. The Literary Evolution of the Biblical Writings

In most cases biblical writings evolved from oral forms. Individual epics, for example, were woven into a sequential narrative. Hymns of praise and prayers of petition were over a period of time incorporated into other doc-uments, legal or historical, or arranged into a body of liturgical material, such as the Book of Psalms. Legal materials grew from simpler to more complex forms as the circumstances of Israel's historical existence changed and its needs varied with changing cultural conditions. The same is true of prophetic oracles, which were supplemented by later material and organized into the collections in which we now read them. Similarly, the Wisdom

The Ptolemaic temple of Edfu was built between Aswan and Luxor during the period 237–57 B.C.E. Remarkable for the state of its preservation, it houses this relief of the sky god Horus (symbolized by both the sun and the falcon) who is suckled by his mother, Isis, goddess of fertility and wife of Osiris. Although Egyptian mythology is no more static than any such narratives from the ancient period, the associations among Horus, Isis, and Osiris seem to have been well established during much of the biblical period. (BiblePlaces.com)

tradition was expanded from its older forms as speculation grew about the role of Wisdom in the creation of the world and as efforts were made to correlate what pagans claimed about wisdom (philosophy) with the Wisdom the biblical tradition asserted had been revealed by God to his people. The oral components of the Gospels may also be identified through careful analysis.

The change from oral to written forms involved extensive editing of traditional materials, as well as arranging them into the patterns presented in the biblical books. In addition to the weaving of narratives into a consecutive epic form, the form of the first five books of the Bible shows clearly that materials were compiled and expanded over a period of centuries and in a variety of circumstances. Within this complex development, the Law – given in expanded and variegated form – features centrally together with narratives and genealogical lists tracing Israel's origins back to the ancestors.

"GOSPEL" AND SYNOPTIC GOSPELS

The word "gospel" is a translation of the Greek noun *euangelion*, which means "message of triumph." Most frequently used in the Christian Scriptures with reference to the message about Jesus as God's agent to renew his people and establish his rule on earth, it appears commonly in Paul's letters. The Hebrew verb *basar* has connotations similar to the Christian term "gospel." It is used in the Scriptures of Israel to announce the new things that God is about to do on behalf of his people and of the created order (Isaiah 40:9, 41:27, 52:7, 61:1). It is not surprising that (1) the early Christians claimed that this hope was being fulfilled through Jesus (Luke 4:16–21), and (2) the equivalent noun, *euangelion* (*besor/ta'* in Aramaic), was applied to the basic documents in which the message and activities of Jesus were reported.

Perhaps because the word appears in the opening phrase of Mark, it came to be used for the first four documents to be included in the Christian Scriptures. The first three of these documents have a roughly similar format and have long been designated as the Synoptic Gospels (or the Synoptics), because they have the same basic literary approach to the story of Jesus and follow much the same order. John's more discursive Gospel is quite different from the others in form and content.

The heavy underscoring of the ritual aspects of the Law in the period covered by the Pentateuch is an unequivocal sign that in its final editing the hand of the priestly leaders of Israel was at work reshaping the tradition.

At least two major motivations were at work in this recasting of older biblical traditions: (1) the desire to bring the tradition up to date, so that its relevance for the contemporary situation in the life of Israel would be immediately apparent; and (2) the desire to harmonize or at least blend diverse traditions to impute an overall unity to the tradition as finally recorded. This process is also evident in the historical and prophetic materials. The Books of Chronicles, for example, when compared with the accounts of the same events in the Books of Kings, show that the values and point of view of the priests in the period after Israel's return from exile in Babylon had an influence on the Chronicler's version of Israel's history. Also in the period after the exile, traces of Persian ideas appear in the biblical writings, such as the notion of Satan as God's adversary. In the case of the prophets of Israel, their earlier predictions that did not take place as expected are balanced in the present versions of the writings of the prophets by the addition of later material. For example, the prophecies of the eighth-century B.C.E. prophet Isaiah that predict God's punishment of his disobedient people are supplemented by predictions about the end of the age (Isaiah 24–7) and then by later reports and celebrations of Israel's deliverance in the land (Isaiah 36–9) and hopes for the future fulfillment of God's purposes for his renewed people (Isaiah 40–66). Less obviously, but just as significantly, other prophetic writings received later supplements, as happened with Amos, Zechariah, and Malachi.

D. The Issue of Authority

In Judaism and Christianity, documents addressing the issues of the identity and destiny of the people of God continued to be produced long after the documents that are included in the Bible had achieved the forms in

Qumran manuscript. The relative stability of temperature and humidity at this site almost thirteen hundred feet below sea level was a major factor in the survival of the Dead Sea manuscripts. They provide direct knowledge about the group based at Qumran, which was critical of the priestly establishment and which looked forward to divine vindication of the group and its elevation to power in a renewed Jerusalem. (H. C. Kee)

which we know them. Official lists emerged of those writings that were to be considered authoritative for the various constituencies that used the Bible. Called "canons," from the Greek word meaning "norm" or "standard," these lists were not uniform among Jews or Christians. Many Jews, for example, recognized as authoritative all the writings included in the Septuagint, whereas others around the end of the first century C.E. adopted a list of books that had been originally written in Hebrew or Aramaic, not in Greek. Christians also have disputed which books compose their canon, and that disagreement continues to this day as a major difference among Catholic, Orthodox, and Protestant believers.

Many of the books that Jewish or Christian groups tried to get accepted as authoritative were modeled after those that did find a place on the official lists. Other writings purported to be essential supplements to the canonical books. The supplemental books for the Scriptures of Israel included writings claiming to be the "last will and testament" of one or another of the figures of ancient Israel, such as Abraham or the sons of Jacob. Other writings not generally recognized by Jews as official include collections of psalms attributed to Solomon, and prophetic oracles in the style of the later prophets and priestly leaders such as Ezra. Although a modern sense of historical authenticity and trustworthiness might deplore such spurious claims of authorship, one must remember that part of the aim of these writings was to show how these ancient figures and their insights into the ways of God were crucial for later times. Certain small groups that broke away from the recognized authorities of their traditions, whether Jewish or Christian, also offered writings that supplemented or gave a distinctive interpretation to the older scriptural writings. In Judaism of the late first century B.C.E., for example, the Dead Sea community had its own explanations of the Scriptures and its own guidebooks on the origins, aims, and destiny of the group. Beginning in the second century C.E., groups now known as Gnostics (which means, roughly, "those who are in the know") had their own versions of the Gospel tradition and their own additions to what Jesus was supposed to have taught his inner circle of followers.

Parallel with the development of official lists of the Scriptures, writings that claimed to offer the true and proper interpretation of the canonical writings appeared within both Judaism and Christianity. At the site of the Dead Sea sect in Qumran, for example, extensive commentaries on books of the Bible, such as Habakkuk, were found. Their characteristic purpose was to show in detail how what the sacred writer wrote directly related to, and was fulfilled within, the present experience of this group. Beginning informally

ALEXANDRIA

In 332 B.C.E., on an ancient site in the delta of the Nile along the shore of the Mediterranean, Alexander the Great began to plan for a city that would serve to fulfill three objectives: provide a naval base for his fleet, a commercial base for exchange between his native Macedonia and the wealth of the Nile Valley, and a center for implanting Hellenistic culture in this conquered land. He died before his plans were completed, but his successors followed through on the project and created one of the great cities of the Hellenistic era, in which study was carried out and an incomparable library assembled, covering the fields of philosophy, natural science, history, and medicine. Down into the early centuries of the Christian Church, Alexandria was a major center of cultural and intellectual life.

PLATO

During his long life (427–348 B.C.E.), Plato founded and lectured at the Academy, a school in Athens, and wrote dozens of works in various forms: laws, letters, dialogues. His work concerned the whole range of human action: political, ethical, psychological, logical, physical, metaphysical, and religious. The basic concepts in his mature work are that there is an eternal, divine mind whose purpose and power shape the structure of the universe and the destiny of its inhabitants; that all phenomena, whether tangible objects or abstract ideas and principles, are only imperfect copies of the heavenly paradigms or ideal forms of reality; that these ideas exist eternally, whereas all the earthly copies are subject to decay; that in all creation, only human beings possess the capacity to discern this ultimate reality of the universe and come to understand it through reason. To live the good life is to sharpen this grasp of reality and to guide one's personal and social existence by means of these eternal principles.

in the first century B.C.E., and taking distinctive shape in the period from the second to the sixth centuries C.E., the Rabbinic method of offering interpretations of Scripture relevant for the present covenant community produced documents known generically as Midrash. The Rabbis developed their own style of and process for training leaders for this interpretive task. Prior to this development, Philo appeared in Alexandria at the turn of the eras. Philo's many writings interpret the Torah allegorically, seeking to demonstrate the basic kinship between the inner meaning of Scripture and the philosophical insights of Plato and the Stoics. That same approach was adopted by those who established the Christian catechetical school in Alexandria. In the third century C.E. this school was headed by Origen, whose interpretation of the Gospel of John follows a method similar to that of Philo. This technique was not regarded as a distortion but as a means of demonstrating the relevance of the sacred writings to the interpreter's own day.

E. The Historical Value of the Writings

With the development of the Christian creeds in the second century C.E. and subsequently, Scripture was turned to as an authoritative basis for

ORIGEN OF ALEXANDRIA

Born in the latter part of the second century, Origen's intellectual brilliance and discipline were such that at age eighteen he was appointed head of the Christian catechetical school in Alexandria. His eloquence and his mastery of classical Greek and Hellenistic philosophical literature were such that non-Christian scholars came to hear his lectures and to engage him in learned conversation. His extensive writings (many of which have not survived to the present) included debates with the critics of Christianity (especially in his late work, *Against Celsus*), detailed studies of Old and New Testament texts (for which he used allegorical methods like those of the earlier Jewish scholar Philo of Alexandria), and detailed comparative analyses of various copies and versions of the Jewish Scriptures (the Hexapla). Opposition from certain Christians and the threat of persecution by the Roman authorities led Origen to move to Caesarea in Palestine, where his skill as a writer and his popularity as a lecturer continued to attract many believers as well as pagan intellectuals.

documenting and confirming the creedal affirmations. In the Protestant Reformation of the sixteenth century, Scripture was understood to be a mode of direct address by God to his people, and in many quarters, texts of Scripture were appealed to as necessary proof of what theologians affirmed in their doctrinal systems. Those strategies were sharply challenged, however, beginning in the seventeenth century, when ancient documents, including the Bible, began to be studied by academics, who had two scholarly objectives in mind: (1) to determine what the original wording of the ancient texts had been, and (2) to reconstruct the historical origins of these writings.

The first undertaking involved examining and comparing the earliest copies of the various parts of the Bible to reconstruct, as nearly as possible, the original text. At the beginning of this critical quest, the oldest copies of the books of the Hebrew Bible were relatively modern: from the tenth century C.E. In the middle of the twentieth century, however, copies of parts of the Bible going back to the turn of the eras were discovered among the Dead Sea Scrolls, including complete texts of Isaiah. The tenth-century standardized text of the Hebrew Bible matched remarkably well, however, with the text used by ancient Christian biblical scholars, such as Origen (185–254 C.E.) and Jerome (347–420 C.E.). Further attestation of the text of the Hebrew Bible came from other ancient sources. After the ninth-century B.C.E. split in ancient Israel between the northern and southern tribes, what is known as the Samaritan version of the Pentateuch developed. The oldest copies of this antedate those of the standard Hebrew Bible of late antiquity, but its text resembles that of the Septuagint, and both these forms of the Scriptures of Israel are remarkably close to the traditional Hebrew text.

The oldest copies of the complete New Testament go back to the fourth century C.E., although the majority of the surviving New Testament manuscripts represent a fairly late, standardized version of the Greek text, which includes additions and adjusts differences between the Gospel accounts. Extant fragments of the Gospels, however, go back to the third and even to the second century. These manuscripts bring the scholar within a few decades of the time when these early Christian writings were originally composed. Based on the details of their contents, ancient copies of Christian biblical writings have been classified into the Common Text (which is found in the majority of the Greek manuscripts, most of them late), the Fourth-Century Text (which survives in only a few copies, but which may be closest to the original), and a group usually known as the Western Text (which was influenced by oral traditions and seems to lie behind the Latin version in use in western Europe from early medieval times onward). Complete copies of the Fourth-Century Text include a manuscript found at Saint Catherine's monastery on Mount Sinai in the nineteenth century and one at the Vatican library. Each of these manuscript traditions also shows some affinity with copies of ancient translations of the Christian Bible into such languages as Coptic (in Egypt), Syriac, and Armenian.

The second scholarly task was the effort to recover the historical origins of the biblical writings, as contrasted with the times and circumstances that they claim to be reporting. As early as the third century C.E., the pagan philosopher Porphyry (233–304) had shown that the Book of Daniel did not date from the time of Israel's exile in Babylonia (sixth century B.C.E.), as its narrative suggests, but from the reign of Antiochus IV Epiphanes (early second century B.C.E.), in the Hellenistic era. By the seventeenth century, Thomas Hobbes, in his *Leviathan* (1651), tried to prove that the Pentateuch had been written after the time of Moses. In 1753 the French Catholic physician and scholar Jean Astruc advanced the theory that there were multiple sources behind the Books of Genesis and Exodus, and that they could be distinguished by whether they referred to God as Yahweh (God's special name, revealed only to Israel) or simply as God (for which the Hebrew word is *'elohim*). This proposal was expanded and refined in the nineteenth century by K. H. Graf (1865) and J. Wellhausen (1878), so that there emerged a widely held theory that there are four literary strands behind the Pentateuch in its present form: J (Yahwist; abbreviated as J, rather than Y, following the German *Jahwist*), E (Elohist), P (Priestly), and D (Deuteronomist). The last two strands represent respectively the priestly and the legal-revisionist reworking of the Pentateuchal traditions in the period during or just after the exile in Babylon. The first two strands, J and E, are the oldest strata of the tradition. Also in the nineteenth century, scholars sought to show that the earlier prophetic utterances in the books of the Prophets had been worked over, expanded, supplemented, and otherwise edited at the end of, or after, Israel's return from exile, and only then achieved the form that we now possess.

In studies of the historical and literary origins of the Christian biblical writings, the most significant challenge to the traditional views came from John Locke (1632–1704). He portrayed Jesus as the spokesperson for natural law and rational religion. Locke saw as a perversion of the real aims and methods of Jesus both the supernatural claims made by the New Testament writers in Jesus' behalf and the notion that his wisdom was available only to the inner circle of his followers. Matthew Tindal (1657–1733) took this approach a major step further in his work *Christianity as Old as Creation; or, The Gospel a Republication of the Religion of Nature* (1730). In this essay he raised serious questions about the integrity of the disciples and implied that they had misunderstood and distorted Jesus' intentions. H. S. Reimarus (1694–1768) followed up on this interpretation of the Gospel evidence and claimed that Jesus had actually preached nationalistic hopes of an uprising against Rome but that his disciples had pictured him as a universal savior whose realm was solely within the life of the human spirit.

By the middle of the nineteenth century, efforts were made to show that the supernatural aura surrounding the figure of Jesus was the construct of pious imagination or the result of mythical interpretation of Jesus and his activities (in the *Life of Jesus* by David Friedrich Strauss in 1835). Attempts to strip away the mythical and to disclose the true historical Jesus were strongly influenced by eighteenth- and early-nineteenth-century philosophical ideas, such as those of Immanuel Kant (1724–1804) and G. W. F. Hegel (1770–1831). In this perspective, Jesus was represented as the embodiment of the highest moral ideas, and the stories of his exorcisms and miracles, as well as his predictions of the end of the age, were dismissed as regrettable later additions. His announcement of the coming of God's rule was seen by some interpreters, however, as a timeless invitation to attain to spiritual obedience within the self.

F. Aims of the Biblical Writers

Throughout the nineteenth century, concurrent with the attempt to discern and distinguish the literary sources behind the Pentateuch, scholars sought to discover the particular aims and interests of those who edited the biblical traditions into the texts that have come down to us. The same sort of inquiry was under way for the prophetic, Wisdom, and poetic writings. The question was not simply, What do the documents tell us? but, For what purposes and with what assumptions were they written? Meanwhile, since the eighteenth century scholars had been giving attention to questions concerning the sources of the Gospels and concerning literary relationships among such groups of early Christian writings as those attributed to Paul, John, and Peter. Questions about authenticity as well as about authorship were raised, often producing controversy. In the first quarter of the twentieth century, scholars sought to discover not merely the possible literary sources behind the Gospels as we have them but the oral forms in which the tradition had been passed on before the Gospels were written. The "form critics," as they came to be called, were interested in determining both the original forms of these traditions and what functions they served in the life of the early Christian communities that preserved them. These functions included preaching, instruction, and worship. Similar questions about the forms of the oral tradition were also raised by those studying the Scriptures of Israel.

In the period after the Second World War, interest shifted away from what the oral or literary components of the biblical writings were toward what the final writer or editor did with this material. This mode of analysis has been applied to the legal, prophetic, poetic, Wisdom, Gospel, and rhetorical traditions of the Bible. The questions are: What purposes are served by the biblical material as we have it? How did the editor see his role in relation to the community for which he prepared the material, and what role did he foresee for the community in the overall purposes of God? From the way in which the tradition has been modified, what can one infer about the social and cultural context of the community to whom it was addressed in the form in which we now have it? What are the values and ethical norms explicit or implicit in these writings? What did the community for whom the writing was prepared fear, and what did it hope for? Who were its leaders, and what was the ground of their authority? It is with these sorts of questions in mind, together with a renewed interest in recent decades in history and in underlying traditions, that critical reading of biblical writings may proceed.

FORM CRITICISM

"Form" refers to the shape and structure of a communication, which affects how the hearer understands its meaning. Knowledge that a given set of words constitute, for example, a poem or a chronicle or a philosophy or a law will influence how those words are evaluated.

By the end of the nineteenth century, biblical scholars had long been sorting out the forms in which the texts of the Bible appeared, to avoid the misconception of the texts as uniform. "Form" could refer, as "genre" did, to the shape and structure of an entire document of the Bible. Increasingly, however, "form" came to be used for the oral traditions incorporated within the written biblical texts. This distinction became determinative for the development of form criticism during the twentieth century, with great emphasis placed on the social situation or "setting in life" (*Sitz im Leben*) in which the forms originally arose. Today the belief that the original settings must have been oral is not as strong as it once was, although form criticism (as the analysis of the underlying structures of tradition within a text, however they arose) continues to be pursued.

Their studies of the sources of the Hebrew Bible and the New Testament had sensitized scholars to the possibility of oral traditions behind the texts, so that discrete forms of oral communication came to be referenced. Typically, forms involving law (Exodus 20:1–17 and Matthew 5:17–48), announcement (1 Kings 17:1 and Mark 1:15), prayer (1 Kings 8:12–54 and Luke 11:1–4), proverb (Proverbs 9 and Matthew 25:31–46), poetry (Song of Songs 2 and Colossians 1:12–20),

instruction (Genesis 17:9–14 and Galatians 4:1–11), epic (Judges 5 and Hebrews 11), and philosophical argument (Wisdom 2 and Romans 9–11) were readily identified. All of these involved patterns of speech, and such forms (along with others, with variations of nomenclature as well as of categories, and debates regarding the usual size of forms) were fairly well agreed on.

Study of the Hebrew Bible had long been friendly to the hypothesis of a long period of oral development prior to the development of the sources that eventually fed the received texts, but the New Testament's formation, between the time of Jesus and the emergence of the texts, simply did not allow for centuries of development. That led to the strong suspicion that the histories of formation of the two canons differed profoundly. In addition, the case of the Hebrew Bible, especially as compared to other traditions' literatures (e.g., Greek, Indian, Icelandic, and Roman), suggested that forms of traditions were usually woven together prior to their inclusion within the written texts that emerged later.

These considerations, as well as bifurcation in study of "the Old Testament" and "the New Testament," resulted in marked contrasts in the craft of form criticism. For the Hebrew Bible, investigators stressed the similarity of its forms to those of other literatures and their progressive incorporation within the texts. Scholars of the New Testament, especially in the wake of the work of Rudolf Bultmann, took a different tack. They posited the existence of autonomous, individual forms of tradition that were taken up

directly within the Gospels and, to a lesser extent, elsewhere in the canon.

Bultmann's approach to form criticism agreed with his theology, according to which the New Testament, composed by the Christian community, did not provide evidence of Jesus himself, but rather evidence of faith in Jesus. For Bultmann, study of the historical Jesus was strictly speaking impossible and in any case beside the point of faith, since the issue of faith was whether one accepted Jesus and his death on the cross, not whether specific facts about his life could be settled. The picture of the Gospels collecting anonymous Christian traditions supported such a view.

But after the Second World War, study of Jesus as a figure in history resumed, and today is thriving at the expense of curiosity about how the texts concerning Jesus emerged. During the same period, study focused more on whole documents, within redaction-critical, rhetorical-critical, structuralist, deconstructionist, and postmodern approaches, so that form criticism was accorded a less central role than it once enjoyed.

Although form critics were quick to identify different types of spoken tradition, and comparison within the Bible and outside facilitated that process, the description of narrative proved especially contentious. Bultmann himself distinguished between legends (i.e., stories designed to teach faith) and miracles (distinguished between healings and prodigies of nature). But those categories broke down on analysis. All stories have some sort of instructional value, an issue Bultmann attempted to address by referring to the allegedly "kerygmatic" content of many stories in the Gospels (his target documents, although form critics attempted to generalize to the Bible as a whole). That understanding, however, requires that an external factor, the "preaching" (the *kerugma*), determines the form, rather than forms being genuinely comparable from culture to culture. Similarly, the category of "miracle" imports a post-Enlightenment definition (namely, of miracles as abrogations of natural law) into the study of ancient texts.

Yet since the rise of new understandings of history, beginning with the work of R. G. Collingwood prior to the Second World War, form criticism has seen a revival. Collingwood stressed the vital connection between history as narrative and the meaning attached to events by those who referred to them (not only the events in and of themselves). History on Collingwood's understanding appears as perspective as well as record, and that view has emerged with new force with the ebb of postmodernism. The shape of traditions prior to the written text of the Bible has accordingly resurfaced as a productive interest. The distinction between "written" and "oral" forms, always problematic when asserted as a rigid difference, has been softened by the many examples of both traditions existing and enriching one another that have come to light in the study of Rabbinic literature. By the same token, the symbiotic relationship between forms and sources has been acknowledged, as well as the capacity (as in the case of the Mishnah) for a tradition that is oral in principle to reach written form quickly.

Perhaps most important, form criticism as presently practiced assumes neither that only the faith of communities is reflected in traditions (as Bultmann claimed) nor that there must be a one-to-one correspondence between every statement in the Bible and what actually happened in the past. Accordingly, Bultmann's form of "miracle" can be refined so as to be a genuinely literary tool, comparable to the other forms, rather than a predisposition toward a finding. What the Enlightenment called miracles were in ancient texts (not only the Bible) stories of exorcism, healing, visions, and signs. Similarly, the idea of the "legend" need no longer obscure the underlying issue of form or prejudge historical judgment: stories from the ancient world commonly exert paradigmatic value, illustrating the power of a given teaching, or of exorcistic, therapeutic, or visionary practices. With such corrections, form criticism appears poised for a return to a central position in critical reading of the Bible.

G. The Lands of the Bible

Before beginning our study of the context, contents, and intent of the biblical material, we must consider carefully the lands in which these insights arose and these events occurred. Physical context can be as important as the cultural context for understanding how the literatures of the Bible unfolded. Our initial focus is on the lands stretching from the valley of the Nile in Egypt, and across Canaan and Syria to the Land between the Rivers – known variously as Mesopotamia or Babylon or, in modern times, Iraq – and to Persia beyond the rivers. Also important in the later biblical records are those centers of civilization that extend westward from the upper end of the Persian Gulf across the mountain ranges and plateaus south of the Caspian Sea to the Mediterranean Sea. From the sixth century before our era onward, we shall also be concerned with the mainland of Europe, from the north of the Greek peninsula across the Adriatic Sea to Rome.

The peoples who inhabited these lands have been classified by the languages they used, although several of their languages do not fit the traditional classifications. In Genesis 10, the nations of the Middle East are grouped on the basis of their alleged relationship to the sons of Noah. The descendants of Ham were the Egyptians, Cushites (Ethiopians), and Libyans. The descendants of Shem were the Assyrians, Babylonians (Akkadians), Canaanites, Phoenicians, Arameans, Amorites, Moabites, Edomites, and Hebrews. Not included in the biblical list, but figuring importantly in the biblical story, are the linguistic groups known as the Indo-Europeans: Greeks, Romans, Lydians, Medes, Persians, Scythians, Hittites, and Philistines. Although the traditions of Genesis 10 attempted to order all these peoples within an Israelite account of human origins (through Japheth), many of them developed civilizations and empires that dwarfed Israel by comparison at the time.

1. Egypt

The Nile Valley not only is the central physical feature of Egypt but also offers the less than 4 percent of the land that was and is susceptible of development. The rest of Egypt is mostly desert or wilderness, except for some areas along the seacoast. The waters of the Nile come from the high country of east-central Africa; rainfall in Egypt outside the Nile Valley is negligible. After passing over a series of cataracts, the last of which is at modern Aswan, some 400 miles from the Mediterranean, the river winds gently between limestone cliffs that rise mostly well back from the river channel itself. Its tributaries arise 350 miles south of Aswan. Near the sea, its silt has formed an enormous delta (about 100 by 150 miles), which is fertile and has been highly cultivated since antiquity. From there the Nile used to flow out into the Mediterranean through a series of mouths, but in modern times these have been reduced to two.

The Western Desert is a limestone plateau, broken by depressions, some below sea level. The best known of these is Lake Moeris, which was apparently watered by a natural runoff from the Nile perhaps dating back to about 2000 B.C.E. The lake has been mentioned by this name in Greek since the fifth century B.C.E. The Eastern Desert (Arabian Desert), on the other hand, includes a series of mountains that reach to heights of 7,000 feet. There are some springs and some scanty vegetation in this region, which extends to the Gulf of Suez and the Persian Gulf.

Upstream from Egypt proper lie the districts known as Cush (Ethiopia) and Nubia, both of which figure in the ancient literature. Ethiopians were among the early converts to Christianity, and the Scriptures seem to have been translated early into Ethiopic, a South Semitic language. The seasonal rains in the upper (southern) Nile Valley caused flooding in Egypt, which resulted in the annual cycles of crops in that country. The worship of Osiris, the god of the Nile, was directly linked with this pattern of fertility in the upper river valley.

The two major centers of Egyptian civilization were Thebes, which is downstream from the first cataract, and Memphis, which is upstream from the delta. After the fourth century B.C.E., the dominant political and cultural center in Egypt was in the Nile Delta, where Alexander the Great founded a city to promote Greek culture and named it for himself:

Alexandria. In the vicinity of Thebes are the ruins of some of the great temples of ancient Egypt, while at Giza (on the site of Memphis, near modern Cairo) are the great pyramids.

Historians have traced the course of twenty-six Egyptian dynasties, dating from about 3000 B.C.E. to the sixth century B.C.E., when Egypt was conquered by the Persians. In the period known as the New Kingdom (1550–1070 B.C.E.), the Egyptians controlled the territory from some distance south of the cataracts of the Nile across Palestine to Syria and parts of Mesopotamia. In diplomatic correspondence from the fourteenth century B.C.E. there appear references to a people called Habiru, who were causing difficulties for tribal rulers in Syria–Canaan, who were subject to Egypt. Some scholars have sought to link these people with the tribes of Israel. From the Nineteenth Dynasty (1293–1185 B.C.E.) have survived records of Egyptian military victories in Palestine and Syria, including the section known as Canaan. Rameses II (1279–1212 B.C.E.) is reported to have used Israelite slaves in the construction of cities in Lower Egypt (Exodus 1:11). From the story of Abraham's stay in Egypt (Genesis 12:10) through the account of the Exodus (told in Genesis and Exodus) to the tale of Jesus being taken to Egypt by his family (Matthew 2:14–15), this land figures importantly in the biblical narratives.

2. Sinai

Today Sinai designates a triangular land bridge joining Africa and Asia. The northern limits front on the Mediterranean, where a sea-level land route was a major commercial link in this part of the world. The east and west sides of the peninsula abut on what in modern times are known respectively as the Gulf of Aqaba and the Gulf of Suez. The latter now gives access to the Suez Canal. From the sandy shores and inlets of the Mediterranean coast, Sinai slopes upward in elevation toward the south. The northern plateau is a plain of flint, limestone, and sand dunes. The southern half, however, rises steadily and is crossed by many wadies (seasonal watercourses, which drain the land during bursts of rain) and culminates in mountain peaks. The highest of these is Gebel Musa (Mountain of Moses; also known as Mount Sinai and Mount of Saint Catherine), the mountain where some traditions say God gave the Law to the people Israel through Moses, although many ancient authors place the site much further east. Abundant evidence of commercial and military passage through the Sinai exists, but there seems to have been chiefly nomadic population there throughout the millennia.

3. The Negev and the Lands West and East of the Jordan

Beginning to the north of the Sinai peninsula and extending north as far as Syria, the land divides roughly into a series of north–south strips. The coastal plain varies in width, broken only by the mountain ridge of Carmel, which juts out into the sea and forced traders inland to find passes over the mountains. To the east of the sea plain is a range of low hills, reasonably well watered during the annual rainy season and suitable for cultivation. Farther east still is the main ridge of the mountains, reaching elevations of more than two thousand feet above the Mediterranean. Valleys among these hills make north–south travel possible as does the Jordan Valley. The eastern slopes of these hills are desolate. They drop off rapidly into the Jordan Valley proper, which at its southern end goes down to more than 1,200 feet below sea level. The Jordan River itself begins in the mountains north of the Sea of Galilee and then descends gently to the south. From ancient times the valley has been paralleled by major travel routes. The area east of the Jordan is agriculturally marginal, but from Greek times onward the region supported substantial Greek-style cities, for which water was provided by aqueducts from the eastern mountains. The rain-laden clouds coming in off the Mediterranean provide seasonal rains for the western slopes of the mountains on both the east and west banks of the Jordan. Beyond these mountains, and in other areas where rainfall is minimal, the land is barren and suitable for nomadic economies.

Among the various peoples mentioned in the Bible as living in the land between the Mediterranean and the Arabian Desert on both sides of the Jordan Valley, some are linked (Genesis 25) with place-names in Arabia or with persons who figure in the narratives: Midianites and, in the area south and east of the Dead Sea, Moabites, Edomites, and Ammonites. These all seem to have been Semitic-speaking peoples who lived as semi-nomads or settled in small city-states. A later group of this type, the Nabateans, provided the Romans with puppet rulers, such as Aretas, who is mentioned in 2 Corinthians 11:32 as ruler of Damascus while Paul was being persecuted there. The spectacular remains of their capital city, Petra, are still visible in southern Jordan, a development made possible by the Nabateans' mastery of irrigation. The Israelites passed through this region on their way into the land of Canaan, following the Exodus from Egypt. Another group, the Edomites (or Idumeans), seem to have been crowded out of their copper-mining territory on the southeast side of the Dead Sea and to have moved to the southwest side in Roman times. It was from the Idumeans that the Romans chose Antipas, the father of Herod the Great, as their regional administrator or client king.

To achieve the Roman objective of conforming the local populace in the territory east of the Jordan to Hellenistic culture, an elaborate effort was made to build or rebuild cities in the area after the Greek style. This meant constructing pagan temples, theaters, hippodromes, gymnasia, baths, and other features of the Hellenistic cities of Greece and Asia Minor. In the first half of the first century B.C.E., ten of these cities formed a loose union called the Decapolis (meaning "ten cities"). Of these cities, one lay west of the Jordan (Scythopolis, known in earlier times as Bet She'an), and one was in Syria (Damascus). Of the others, the following appear in early Christian literature: Gerasa; Gadara; Pella (named for the city of the father of Alexander the Great); and Ammon, east of the Jordan, which became Philadelphia. These places demonstrate the extent of exposure of people of biblical lands to Hellenistic culture, although this exposure was at most sporadic in Galilee during the biblical period.

Farther east are the regions identified simply as "Arabia," from which tribute was paid to Solomon (1 Kings 10:25) and where Paul fled following his vision of the risen Christ (Galatians 1:17, 4:25). One of the oracles in Isaiah (Isaiah 21:3–17) is against Arabia.

4. Canaan

The land of Canaan, as it is often referred to in the Scriptures of Israel, is a narrow strip of land between the mountains east of the Jordan Valley and the sea. Because of the dominant role played in this part of the world by the Philistines, who entered this region around 1200 B.C.E. and who figure importantly in ancient accounts of wars and diplomatic dealings, the region has been referred to as Palestine since the time of Roman administration. The distance from the southern end of the Dead Sea to the Mediterranean coast is approximately 75 miles. The distance from the sources of the Jordan in the north to the Mediterranean is about half that. The Jordan flows from sources on the slopes of Mount Hermon (which reaches an elevation of 9,100 feet) down to the Sea of Galilee, around 695 feet below sea level, and then on down the valley to the Dead Sea, which is 1,290 feet lower than the Mediterranean. The Jordan rift extends to the south of the Dead Sea in the form of an arid valley known as the Araba. Throughout the valley of the Jordan, and especially in the section adjacent to the Sea of Galilee, there are agriculturally productive lands. Jericho, near the southern end of the valley, has springs that have been used from prehistoric times to water crops, which can grow in that warm and sheltered place throughout the year. Some archaeologists surmise that it is the oldest continually inhabited place on the face of the earth.

The mountains and rolling hills that form the western slope of the Jordan rift range in height from a 4,000-foot peak in the Galilee region to the 3,000-foot peaks of Mounts Ebal and Gerizim (in the region that came to be known as Samaria) and then to 2,500 feet at Jerusalem. These mountains are barren on the east, since the winter rains that come in off the Mediterranean fall on the western slopes. Most of the towns and villages of the land were on the western slopes of north–south ridges around Jerusalem, in Samaria, and in Galilee, or in the upland valleys and plains that extend westward toward the sea. The coastal region is relatively narrow, and, except for the region around Acco and Mount Carmel, lacks natural harbors. In Greek and Roman times, harbors were constructed along the coast, and cities in the Greco-Roman style flourished there, including Ashkelon, Ashdod, and Caesarea. Ptolemais (formerly Acco) and, north of Palestine, Tyre, Sidon, and Antioch became model centers of Hellenistic culture in their social, cultural, and architectural styles. The Phoenicians, whose economic

THE CLIMATE OF PALESTINE

The diversity of the weather patterns in Palestine is the result of the convergence of three factors: (1) the latitude of the location; (2) the different kinds of air masses that cross the region during the year; and (3) the variations in terrain and elevation.

The latitude of Palestine (between 31°15′ and 33°15′ N) places it on the northern edge of the subtropical zone, but the intrusions of air masses from the temperate zone to the north result in a considerable range of heat, humidity, and precipitation. The summers are warm with little rain, and the winters are cool and often stormy. The transitional periods between the seasons bring rains and sometimes extremely hot, dry, dusty periods caused by air masses from the desert (called *khamsin*).

The dominant forces in the summer are the warm, calm air masses over the eastern Mediterranean, but in the winter, cold air from the Atlantic and northern Europe, as well as from Central Asia, clashes with warm tropical systems arising in Africa, and the result is severe storms of wind and rain. The rains come in mostly from the sea and fall chiefly on the coastland and the western faces of the main north–south ridges and mountains in the interior, while decreasing sharply in the desert areas of the south and east. Along the coastal plain there is also heavy dew, summer and winter.

The major topographical features in Palestine are the coastal plain; the ridges and mountains west of the Jordan River; the Great Valley, in which are the Jordan River, the Sea of Galilee, and the Dead Sea; the desert areas; and the east Jordan Plateau. Humidity, precipitation, and heat level vary widely in these different regions. Humidity and rainfall are high along the Mediterranean coast, and even higher in the hilly districts of the interior. Along the coast, temperatures range from summer maximums of over 100°F to winter lows in the upper forties. The ridges and hills are cooler in the summer, but in the winter the temperature frequently hovers in the fifties and forties, and occasionally there are days of frost, especially in January. Much colder temperatures occur in the higher elevations in the north, but are milder in the Great Valley from Galilee south to the lower Jordan and Dead Sea, where there is little rainfall and the temperatures are predominantly warm. East of the Jordan the land is higher, and mountains there attract rainfall from the clouds that drift in from the Mediterranean, although the fertile land there is a relatively narrow strip, giving way to true desert in the east. The seasons do not change abruptly, and even in the winter, periods of rain alternate with clear stretches, although there are occasional snows. Early rain in the spring softens the soil for planting, and late rains in the early fall improve the harvests. But in some years there is a severe decline in precipitation, which may extend over several years, so that the resultant drought brings on a famine in the land, as was the case when Jacob and his family had to move to Egypt (Genesis 41:53–7). There the abundant water flow was dependent on conditions in central Africa at the sources of the Nile and not on the variable factors of the eastern Mediterranean region.

and military skills enabled them to control territories in other parts of the Mediterranean, dominated these northern coastal cities. In the days of the patriarchs, however, the culture was predominantly Semitic.

Archaeological excavations in Palestine and Syria have provided extensive knowledge of the Semitic groups that settled in this area, or that moved through in their nomadic wanderings. These include the Amorites, who seem to have alternated between settling in certain sites, where they seized power (in places ranging from Babylon to Aleppo in north Syria), and nomadic existence. The latter is apparent in Jericho, where, during their period of occupation of the city, they seem not to have built houses or city walls but to have lived in tents.

The Canaanites or their predecessors settled in Jericho during the Neolithic period, dating back to the eighth millennium B.C.E. They

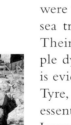

Jericho, Neolithic tower from the north. Excavations at Jericho uncovered building work from before the time of the oldest pottery in the area, that is, from some six thousand years before the Israelites settled the land under Joshua ca. 1200 B.C.E. (BiblePlaces.com)

continued to occupy various sections of the region in subsequent centuries. They seem to have engaged in a considerable amount of merchant activity and to have attained a high level of cultural achievement. Included among the subgroups of the Canaanites mentioned in the Bible are the Kenites, Perizzites, Kadmonites, Jebusites (who occupied the city that was later to be known as Jerusalem), and the Hivites.

Other important residents, especially north and west of Palestine, were the Phoenicians, or Sidonians as they later were called. They were sea traders, with commercial connections around the Mediterranean. Their exports included cedar from the mountains in Lebanon and purple dye, which they extracted from sea snails. Their cosmopolitan style is evident from those of their cities that have been excavated, including Tyre, Sidon, Ugarit, Gebal, and certain levels at Ashdod. They provided essential aid to Solomon in the building of the Temple of Yahweh in Jerusalem. In time, their territory was taken over by the Persians, and later by Alexander the Great. In Hellenistic times, shrines, theaters, baths, and other manifestations of Greek culture were erected in cities along the coast and in Galilee but also in such traditional centers as Samaria, Jericho, and Jerusalem.

5. Syria

Instead of modest hills and low mountains, as in Canaan or Israel, southern Syria is divided by a twin range of very high mountains, known in modern times as Lebanon and Anti-Lebanon, that reach elevations of more

Excavation from a city gate in Shechem from the Middle Bronze period. This excavation evidences urban habitation at a time prior to Israelite settlement. According to the Book of Genesis (33:18–20), Jacob bought a plot of land near here, and this is where the well associated with him is located. Shechem later became a principal site of the ark of the covenant. (BiblePlaces.com)

Aerial view of Jericho taken from the south-east. This view gives an impression of the richness of the remains of millennia of human habitation, and of the inherent difficulty of balancing contemporary development with archaeological investigation. (BiblePlaces.com)

than 9,000 feet. Between these formidable ranges lies the Beqaa, a lofty valley where shrines to various deities have been erected for millennia. The Beqaa rises in the north to a plateau 8,100 feet above sea level. The road linking Damascus and Beirut crosses the Beqaa farther south at an elevation of more than 5,000 feet. These ranges are the source of the water that forms the Litani River to the south and feeds the Orontes to the north. The Litani Valley is fertile, while the Orontes flows through more barren territory, reaching the sea at the point where the Hellenistic rulers of Syria in the third century B.C.E. built the city of Antioch. Damascus is on the eastern side of the Lebanon range and was a major center of Hellenistic culture in the same period that Antioch was the capital of Syria.

The coast of Syria varies widely: sandy beaches around Tyre in the south, more rugged coast between Beirut and Tripoli, rocky cliffs and headlands north of Latakia. The northeastern limits of Syria are formed by the Taurus Mountains, which extend eastward from Turkey. A narrow coastal strip at Issus provides access from the east to Tarsus and the upland country of Asia Minor. The northwestern sections of Syria are part of the broad valley of

Baalbek. Located in the Beqaa Valley in what is now eastern Lebanon, Baalbek was a center for the worship of the Near Eastern fertility god Baal-Haddad. In Hellenistic times the deity honored there was Helios, the god of the sun, and the city became known as Heliopolis. The Romans under Augustus established a Roman colony and garrison there, and Antoninus Pius (reigned 138–61 C.E.) launched the construction of a great temple to Jupiter Heliopolitanus, which was not completed until the reign of Caracalla (211–17). Some of the enormous stones in the surrounding wall measure more than 60 × 14 × 11 feet. In the sixth century the great court of the temple was converted into a church. (Library of Congress, Prints & Photographs Division, LC-DIG–matpc – 01175/ LifeintheHolyLand.com)

the Euphrates, which rises in the mountains north of Syria to begin its long, slow flow into the Persian Gulf. A triangular section historically linked with Syria reaches across the Euphrates to its twin stream, the Tigris, farther to the north and east. On the eastern border, which is marked by lower mountain ranges stretching north and east from beyond Damascus, one of the chief cities is Palmyra. South and east of Damascus is the rocky, volcanic region known as the Hauran, which reaches its highest point in the mountain known since Islamic times as Jebel Druse (5,900 feet). Eastward from this section is the Arabian Desert. The major trade routes from the east followed the course of the twin rivers from Mesopotamia, passing through the valleys of Syria on the way to Palestine and Egypt.

6. Mesopotamia

Mesopotamia refers to the land that lies between the Tigris and Euphrates Rivers in the central part of modern Iraq. This region can be divided into three distinct sections: (1) the wilderness area south and west of the line at which the desert plain drops off to form the valley of the Euphrates; (2) the central lowland, which includes the area between the rivers and the delta at the point where the rivers join, from which the combined stream flows into the Persian Gulf; and (3) the land north and east of the Tigris that extends up to the mountain ranges of Turkey in the north and Persia in the south.

The central lowland is itself divided into three different segments: (1) the northern part, south of the Turkish mountains and largely desert; (2) the plain along the northern Tigris (which extends to the foot of the Persian mountains), where Assyria rose to a place of dominance in the Middle East; and (3) the well-watered section of the valley, beginning north of Baghdad and reaching down toward the gulf. In the biblical period, the center of power shifted back and forth from the cities of the lower valley (Ur, Nippur, Babylon) to those in the Assyrian plain (Asshur and Nineveh). This region of the ancient world formed the natural link, culturally and economically, between the civilizations of the Mediterranean region and those to the south and east along the Indian Ocean. The history of Israel is involved with this part of the world from the times of the patriarchs, when Abraham came from Ur, through the experience of the Babylonian exile, to the development of the Babylonian Talmud in the second to sixth centuries of our era.

7. Persia

The area known in modern times as Iran, and in antiquity as Persia, includes four topographical regions: (1) The so-called Zagros fold consists of a series of mountain ranges reaching from the area west of the lower end of the Caspian Sea, southward and eastward above the valley of the

Ziggurat at Ur. Given the lack of mountains in the Tigris-Euphrates Valley, this mass of clay was erected to serve as a high place where the god could be worshipped appropriately. Pottery jars were embedded in the sides of the structure for decoration but also to offset erosion. The shrine proper was located at the top of the edifice, which dates from the fourth millennium B.C.E. (University Museum, University of Pennsylvania)

Stela of Ur Nammu. The fragments of this pillar have been reconstructed in various ways. The stela measures 5 × 10 feet and depicts the building of a sacred mountain (ziggurat) between 2112 and 2095 B.C.E. Also portrayed are King Ur Nammu in prayer, with angels descending; the god (Nanna) and goddess (Ningal) present as the work begins; and the king with the tools of architect and builder. Ur Nammu also promulgated a code of law that is a precursor of the more famous code of Hammurabi. (University Museum, University of Pennsylvania)

Tigris, along a series of lower mountains extending eastward along the Arabian Sea to the borders of India. (2) The northern highlands overlook the Caspian Sea from the south; between these peaks (which reach elevations of 18,000 feet) and the sea is a plain varying in width from 70 to 10 miles. It is the best-watered part of Iran and is now the most densely populated. (3) The eastern mountains are barren and subject to violent wind- and sandstorms. They form part of the range that includes the Himalayas to the east. (4) The central plateau includes high mountains and many lakes, some of which have dried up. Across it are strings of oases, so that travel in this region was relatively simple even in antiquity. It was in the area where this plateau adjoins the southern stretch of the mountains that Darius built his capital city, known as Persepolis, in 515 B.C.E. The peoples who lived in these regions were numerous and competitive. Among those who rose to the dominant position in the biblical period were the Persians, the Medes, and the Parthians. Their rise and fall, and those of the Mesopotamian powers – and later of the Greek and Roman powers – were closely interconnected. Certain features of Persian religion – especially an emphasis on good and evil as metaphysical realities – influenced biblical culture as well.

8. Asia Minor (Anatolia)

Asia Minor, or Anatolia, is a huge peninsula more or less rectangular in shape, extending about 900 miles east and west, and 300 miles north and south. It covers roughly the same territory as modern Turkey. It is bounded on the north by the Black Sea, on the south by the eastern Mediterranean, and on the west by the Aegean Sea, which separates it from the mainland of Greece. The central part of the land consists of a plateau, which averages 3,000 feet above sea level and is surrounded on each side by mountains, which slope sharply down to the sea on the west and south. On the east, they form a great natural barrier extending from the southern border with Syria up to the area between the Black and Caspian Seas.

The Black Sea coast is about 750 miles long, consisting mostly of a narrow strip of irregular width between the sea and the mountains. In some areas, however, there are fertile valleys and forests. Here were located a number of provinces that figure in the literature of the Roman Empire and of early Christianity, including Bithynia, Pontus, and Paphlagonia. Western Anatolia is an area that slopes upward from the sea to the central plateau. In the western part of the central plateau was the province of Galatia, named for the Celtic people who had migrated there from western Europe (although some of them also settled further south and east). Along the western coast of Anatolia are deep indentations where many natural harbors were developed into important commercial centers. Parts of the west coast consist of fertile valleys and plains, with the result that many of the important cities of Asia Minor arose in this part of the land. The mountain peaks range in height from 5,000 to 8,000 feet. One of the most fertile sections is near Pergamum, which was an important center politically. It was also significant religiously, in that it was a center for honoring the healing god Asklepios, as well as a major location for divine honors to the Roman emperor and for the production of manuscripts.

The steep Taurus Mountains to the east of Anatolia extend northeast from the seacoast and form natural boundaries with Syria, Mesopotamia, and Iran. The rugged ranges, cut by steep valleys and winding rivers, rise to peaks of around 13,000 feet. From the Anatolian plateau, an ancient route leads southward to the sea, through a valley long known as the Cilician Gates. To the south lies a coastal plain, on which was located the city of Tarsus, which served as a major center for Greek philosophical study in the Greco-Roman period. Just to the east is the narrow coastal plain of Issus, where Alexander defeated the Persians and began his conquest of the lands from Egypt to India.

Links with Europe were made easy by the narrow stretches of water that pass through the Bosporus and the Dardanelles, where the Black Sea empties into the Mediterranean. To the southeast of this isthmus lay the cities of Troy and Ephesus. To the west was to rise Constantinople, from which in the fourth century C.E. Constantine tried in vain to join the eastern and western segments of the former Roman Empire.

9. Greek Lands

Of the various ethnic and cultural regions into which Greece was divided in antiquity, the most significant for our purposes were Thrace, Macedonia, Illyrica, and Achaia.

Cilician Gates. Cilicia is a district in southeastern Asia Minor that includes the southern section of the Taurus Mountains and the hills and plain reaching down to the Mediterranean coast. The great highway that led from the western part of Asia Minor and the central Anatolian plateau to Syria passed through the rock-lined Cydnus River valley, which was known as the Cilician Gates. Nearby on the Cilician Plain was the city of Tarsus, important for commercial and military (especially naval) activities and a major intellectual center for Stoic philosophy. Acts 9:11, 21:39, and 22:3 identify Paul as a citizen of Tarsus. (H. C. Kee)

The Tholos at Delphi. A famous temple and oracle of Apollo were located in Delphi, six miles north of the Gulf of Corinth. According to legend, Apollo slew Pytho, a female snake who was probably the earth goddess, at Delphi. From all over the world came supplicants, whose questions to the god had to be submitted in writing. The messages from the god were given by priestesses (called Pythians) who, after having chewed sacred leaves and drunk from the spring that was channeled into the temple, sat on the sacred tripod. When the priestess had uttered the god's response, it was edited and put in verse form by the resident prophets and holy men affiliated with the oracle. This circular building (*tholos* in Greek) was erected between 380 B.C.E. and 360 B.C.E. (BiblePlaces.com)

Thrace, which included the area west of the Dardanelles and the Black Sea that now comprises northeastern Greece and parts of western Turkey, Bulgaria, and Romania, was separated from the rest of Greece by a range of mountains, which established its southern limits. The southern sections of Greece seem to have regarded the Thracians as little more civilized than barbarians, as contrasted with the sophisticated culture of Athens and its surrounding region.

Macedonia included parts of northern Greece bordering Thrace, but it extended to the Adriatic Sea in the west. Its terrain consisted of mountain ranges, valleys, and plateaus, with the Via Egnatia crossing through it to the Adriatic. This highway was of major importance militarily and commercially in the Roman period. Macedonia was the home of Philip, the monarch who took over Greece and the Greek cities of Anatolia during the fourth century B.C.E., and of his even more famous son, Alexander. Plains line the rivers that flow in Macedonia, so the region was well suited for agriculture. Its cities included Thessalonica, Neapolis (modern Cavalla), and (in ancient times) Philippi, named for the local monarch.

The center for the Eleusinian Mysteries, reconstruction. Located north and west of Athens overlooking the bay, Eleusis was famed as the locus of the enactment of mysteries in the Hall of Initiation (Telesterion). The myth on which these ceremonies were based told how Hades, the god of the underworld, had taken to that region Kore, the daughter of Demeter, the goddess of grain. During her sorrowing search for her daughter, the fertility of the earth languished. On finding her, Demeter learned that her daughter had eaten some seeds in the underworld and therefore could never be wholly free from that place. The compromise was that she would spend half of each year with her mother and half with her captor. The enactment of the myth in dance and drama was understood as ensuring the fertility of the crops but also as providing initiates with assurance of participation in the life of the world to come. The sanctuary was destroyed in 396 C.E. by Alaric and the Visigoths, but some of the rituals involved (some from better than a thousand years earlier) are well documented. (Department of Archaeology, Bryn Mawr College)

West of Macedonia lay Illyrica (or Illyricum), which included part of what is now known as northwestern Greece, Albania, and southwestern Yugoslavia. The western terminus of the Via Egnatia was located in Illyrica. Excavations in this region show the extent and high level of Greek civilization there.

The main part of modern Greece, including the Peloponnesus, was known in Roman times as Achaia. Its upper limits began south of Thessalonica and Epirus. It included two major cities: Athens and Corinth. Athens was of major cultural importance, as represented by the philosophical schools of Plato and Aristotle that arose there. But it also had religious significance, since it was the seat of the goddess Athena, and within the province were the centers of devotion to the gods Apollo (at Delphi), Dionysus (at Eleusis, just west of Athens), and Askiepios, whose healing shrine was at Epidauros, not far from Corinth. Corinth was of major economic importance, since it sat astride the narrow neck of land that connects the mainland of Greece with the Peloponnesus and thus was the channel through which much of the east–west trade passed in the Mediterranean. It was famous in classical times for the shrine of the fertility goddess Aphrodite, located on a mountain just outside the city.

10. Major Mediterranean Islands

The following mediterranean islands are mentioned in the biblical narratives (here identified from east to west): Cyprus, Crete, Malta, and Sicily. Cyprus lies south of Anatolia and west of Syria. It is 140 miles long and 60 miles at its widest point. Two prongs project eastward from the main part of the island; between these lies Salamis, the principal city of the island in ancient times. The terrain ranges from sandy beaches to the southwestern mountains, which reach a height of 6,500 feet. The forests that covered the island in ancient times have now largely disappeared. Paul and other apostles and apostolic associates paid visits to the island or had connections there.

Crete lies off mainland Greece and is 160 miles long and ranges from 7 to 36 miles in width. The northern coast is indented with natural harbors, whereas the southern coast has none. Near the southernmost point of the island is a small harbor, known as Fair Havens, where Paul's ship is reported to have stopped briefly on his journey to Rome (Acts 27:8).

Malta consists of a group of small islands, the chief of which measures 17 by 9 miles. Most of the coast of this island is lined with steep cliffs, but there are some bays to the east, one of which is traditionally linked with Paul. The hills are no more than 750 feet high, and there are no rivers or lakes on the island.

Just off the southern tip of Italy lies Sicily. The strait between them is only two miles wide. Much of the main island is taken up by a plateau about 900 feet above the sea. But Mount Etna, an active volcano, rises to more than 10,000 feet. Sections of the island are well watered by springs and streams. The island early became a center of Greek culture and continued to participate in this culture, even though in the fifth century B.C.E. it was taken over by the powerful Carthaginians, who came from North Africa. By the late third century B.C.E., however, Sicily was under Roman control, and Carthage was finally defeated in 146 B.C.E.

11. Italy

The great peninsula of Italy extends from the Alps southward more than 700 miles into the Mediterranean. The central part of the peninsula is dominated by the Apennine Mountains, of which the watershed is closer to the Adriatic on the east than to the sea on the west. The peaks range from 4,000 to 9,500 feet in height. Among the rivers flowing to the west from this ridge, the best known is the Tiber, on which Rome is located, and which flows into the sea at the port of Ostia, about 15 miles southwest of Rome.

The Tiber, with the Castel Sant'Angelo behind. Beginning in the Apennines at an elevation of more than 4,000 feet above sea level, the Tiber flows about 250 miles through ravines and valleys until it crosses the plain where Rome is situated on its way to the sea. From prehistoric times, silt has extended the land at its mouth to form the coastal plain. Emperor Claudius opened another mouth for the river by building a canal at Fiumicino. Emperor Antoninus Pius completed what is now called the Castel Sant'Angelo in 139 C.E. (BiblePlaces.com)

More than 100 miles south of Rome, two mountain ranges branch out from the main ridge and extend to the sea, forming the Bay of Naples and the Bay of Salerno. Overlooking the Bay of Naples is Mount Vesuvius, and near the base of the mountain are the ruins of Pompeii and Herculaneum, both destroyed when the volcano erupted in the late first century C.E. The peninsula branches into two smaller parts, representing what are commonly known as the heel and toe of the boot of Italy. On the heel lies Brundisium (Brindisi), which was a major port for trade to and from the eastern Mediterranean and was the southern terminus of the Appian Way, the major north–south highway in Italy.

BIBLIOGRAPHICAL ESSAY

In the two centuries before and the two after the turn of the eras, the literature now known as the Bible was brought together – some of it to constitute the Scriptures of Israel and some to form what came to be known as the Old and New Testaments. To understand these writings it is essential to be informed about the historical developments, the geographical and ethnic settings, and the changing cultural features of the contexts in which these documents – and others akin to them – were produced.

Excellent surveys of the lands of the Bible in terms of their historical developments include Yohanan Aharoni, *The Land of the Bible: A Historical Geography,* rev. and enl. ed. (Philadelphia: Westminster, 1979), and John Rogerson, *Atlas of the Bible* (Oxford: Phaidor, 1989; New York: Facts on File, 1985). For a fine summary of archaeological finds illuminating biblical history, see Jerome Murphy-O'Connor, *The Holy Land: An Archaeological Guide from Earliest Times to 1700* (Oxford and New York: Oxford University Press, 1992), and Jonathan L. Reed, *Archaeology and the Galilean Jesus: A Re-examination of the Evidence* (Harrisburg, PA: Trinity Press International, 2000). Useful studies of the history of Israel include John Bright, *A History of Israel* (Louisville: Westminster John Knox, 2000); J. Alberto Soggin, *A History of Ancient Israel: From the Beginnings to the Bar Kochba Revolt, A.D. 135* (Philadelphia: Westminster, 1985); and the comprehensive, multivolume work *The Cambridge Ancient History,* vol. 1, pts. 1 and 2, *Early History of the Middle East* (Cambridge: Cambridge University Press, 1980); vol. 2, pt. 1, *The Middle East and the Aegean Region, 1800–1350 B.C.* (1973); vol. 2, pt. 2, *The Middle East, 1350–1000 B.C.* (1975); vol. 3, pt. 2, *The Assyrian and Babylonian Empires, 8th to 6th Centuries* (1991); vol. 4, *Persia, Greece, and the Western Mediterranean* (1988).

Broad studies of ancient religions, including those of the ancient Near East, are offered in Mircea Eliade, *The Sacred and the Profane: The Nature of Religion* (New York: Harper Torchbook, 1961); Rudolf Otto, *The Idea of the Holy,* 2d ed., trans. J. W. Harvey (London: Oxford University Press, 1950); Helmer Ringgren, *Religions of the Ancient Near East,* trans. J. Sturdy

(Philadelphia: Westminster, 1973); and *The Biblical World,* ed. John Barton (London: Routledge, 2002).

A fine set of translations of texts from the ancient Near East is that of James B. Pritchard, *Ancient Near Eastern Texts Relating to the Old Testament,* 3d ed. (Princeton: Princeton University Press, 1969), to which was added a volume of pictures, *Ancient Near East in Pictures with Supplement* (Princeton: Princeton University Press, 1969). Abbreviated editions were published by Princeton University Press in paperback in 1975.

A comprehensive study of the Scriptures of Israel, including extensive bibliography, is offered in Bernhard W. Anderson, Steven Bishop, and Judith Newman, *Understanding the Old Testament* (Englewood Cliffs, NJ: Prentice-Hall, 2006). Two very different approaches to this literature are developed in Brevard S. Childs, *Introduction to the Old Testament as Scripture* (Minneapolis: Fortress Press, 1979), and Norman K. Gottwald, *The Hebrew Bible: A Socio-literary Introduction* (Philadelphia: Fortress Press, 1985). For a fine survey of critical scholarly methods for the study of the Hebrew Scriptures, see Douglas A. Knight and Gene M. Tucker, eds., *The Hebrew Bible and Its Modern Interpreters* (Philadelphia: Fortress Press, 1985).

In the period following the return of the Jews from exile in Babylon, the dominant cultural and political impact on them came from the Persian and then the Hellenistic and Roman rulers who controlled the region: first the Ptolemies of Egypt, then the Seleucids of Syria, and finally the Romans. The period from the exile to the first Jewish revolt against the Romans is surveyed in the essays found in John H. Hayes and J. Maxwell Miller, eds., *Israelite and Judaean History* (Harrisburg, PA: Trinity Press International, 1994). Details of developments within Judaism in the latter period are offered in E. Schurer, *The History of the Jewish People in the Age of Jesus Christ, 175 B.C. – A.D. 135,* 3 vols. (Edinburgh: T. & T. Clark, 1973–87), and Oskar Skarsaune, *In the Shadow of the Temple: Jewish Influences on Early Christianity* (Downers Grove, IL: InterVarsity, 2002).

Introductions to the literature produced in the postexilic period are offered in George Nickelsburg and Robert A. Kraft, eds., *Jewish Literature between the Bible and the Mishnah* (Minneapolis: Fortress Press, 2005). A survey of scholarly assessment of that literature and of historical reconstructions of the period is available in G. W. Nickelsburg and R. A. Kraft, eds., *Early Judaism and Its Modern Interpreters* (Atlanta: Scholars Press, 1985). For a perceptive study of the origins of apocalyptic – the Jewish phenomenon that was to have a significant impact on the origins of Christianity – see Paul D. Hanson, *The Dawn of Apocalyptic* (Philadelphia: Fortress Press, 1975). A fine edition of the Dead Sea Scrolls is available in Michael O. Wise, Martin G. Abegg, Jr., and Edward M. Cook, *The Dead Sea Scrolls: A New Translation* (New York: HarperSanFrancisco, 2005). Jacob Neusner's study of the origins of the Pharisees offered a major insight concerning the context of early Christianity and has had an enduring and widespread impact: *From Politics to Piety: The Emergence of Pharisaic Judaism* (New York: Ktav, 1970). Translations and analyses of noncanonical Jewish writings from the period before and after the turn of the eras are offered with introductions and annotations in H. C. Kee, ed., *Cambridge Annotated Study Apocrypha* (Cambridge: Cambridge University Press, 1994), and in J. H. Charlesworth, ed., *The Old Testament Pseudepigrapha,* 2 vols. (New York: Doubleday, 1983–5). Orientations in the study of the New Testament are developed in Bruce Chilton, *Beginning New Testament Study* (London: SPCK, 1986), and Raymond E. Brown, *An Introduction to the New Testament,* Anchor Bible Reference Library (New York: Doubleday, 1997).

Ein Gedi and Cliffs on the western side of the Dead Sea. Excavations at the oasis and surrounding area called in Hebrew Ein Gedi (Kid Spring) evidence extensive human building since the fourth millennium B.C.E. Ein Gedi features as a place of vineyards in the Song of Songs 1:14 and as a refuge to which David resorted in his flight from Saul in 1 Samuel 23:29–24:22. Cliffs and caves provided ideal hiding places for caches of ancient documents, including (much further north) the Dead Sea Scrolls. (Todd Bolen/Bible Places.com)

Hezekiah's Tunnel. As he prepared his city for Assyrian invasion and siege at the end of the eighth century B.C.E. King Hezekiah arranged to give Jerusalem access to water from within its walls and to deny the invaders easy provisions (2 Kings 20:20; 2 Chronicles 32:30; Ecclesiasticus 48:17). The identification of his project in relation to arrangements already in place prior to Hezekiah and to those that followed him is a matter of continuing discussion among archaeologists. (Todd Bolen/Bible Places.com)

Jerusalem from the East. Even in the midst of considerable modern development, the Temple Mount as constructed by Herod the Great remains the dominant feature in the Old City. The destruction of the Second Temple by Roman armies in 70 C.E. and 135 C.E. removed the immense sacred structures from the top of the Mount, but today the gold-covered Dome of the Rock, a Muslim holy site since the seventh century C.E., is reminiscent of Josephus's description that pilgrims approaching the city had to avert their eyes from the light flashing from the gold and bronze of the Second Temple as they would from the sun (*The Jewish War* 5.222-23). (Todd Bolen/Bible Places.com)

Theater in Ephesus. This theater predates the New Testament, but was renovated and enlarged considerably after the time of Paul. Spectacles accommodated here included plays, gladiatorial combat, executions, and therefore martyrdoms. Acts 19:29 describes the public interrogation of Paul's associates in the theater, and Paul himself refers to engaging in "beast-combat in Ephesus" (1 Corinthians 15:32), although it is not necessary to take his statement literally. (Todd Bolen/Bible Places.com)

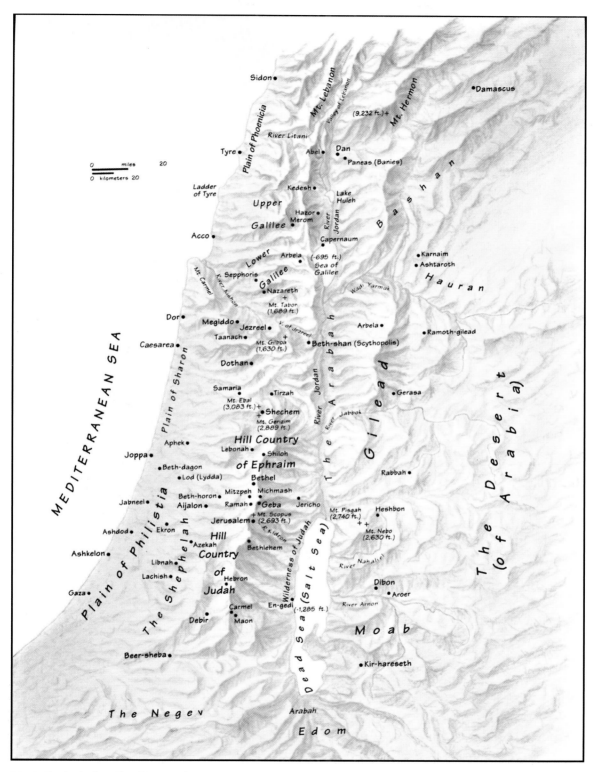

Map I. The land of Israel in the time of Jesus.

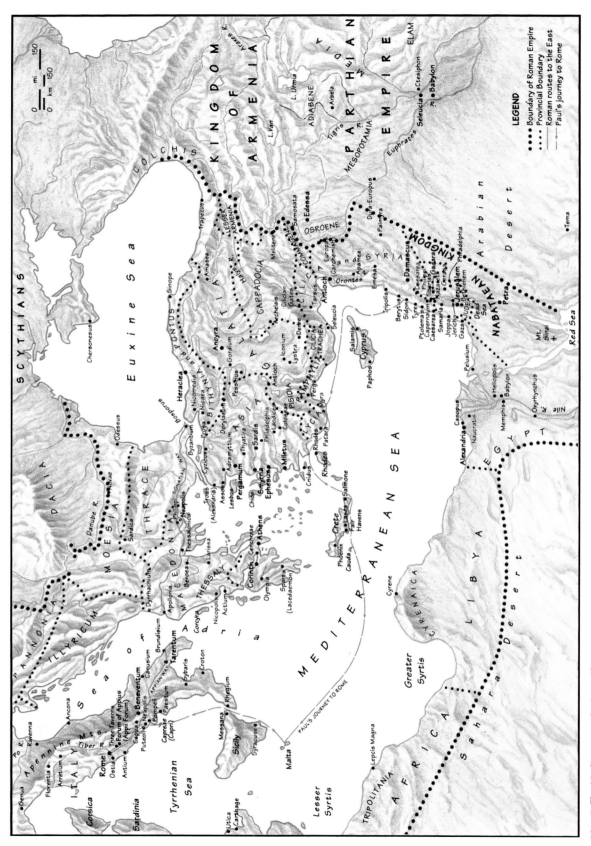

Map II. The Mediterranean Basin, c. 65 C.E.

PART ONE

The World of the Hebrew Bible

Eric M. Meyers and John Rogerson

I. THE WORLD OF ISRAEL'S ANCESTORS (THE BOOKS OF GENESIS THROUGH DEUTERONOMY) AND OUR WORLD

The first five books of the Bible describe the creation of the world (Genesis 1–2) and the earliest history of humanity including the destruction of the inhabited world by a flood, before they tell the story of the ancestors of Jacob, who came to be called "Israel," which means "he struggles with God." The story includes the call of Abraham to come to the land of Canaan (Genesis 12) and continues with the lives of Isaac and Jacob. Jacob is named Israel as the consequence of his physical struggle with God (Genesis 32), and he gives that name to the people called Israel. The twelve sons of Jacob/Israel go down to Egypt; after their descendants become a sizable people, they are forced into slavery by a pharaoh. Moses, one of the "Hebrews" (as the Egyptians call these foreigners with their strange, West Semitic language) brought up at the Egyptian court, leads the Hebrews out of slavery and through the wilderness of Sinai to the threshold of the land of Canaan. On the way, Moses gives the people, on behalf of God, civil, religious, and ceremonial laws that identify the Hebrews as the people of Yahweh, who first called Abraham, Isaac, and Jacob and who delivered the Hebrews from slavery. Deuteronomy caps the entire saga with an address by Moses to the people Israel as they stand poised to cross the river Jordan and take possession of Canaan, the land promised to Abraham and his descendants.

Until the eighteenth century most scholars assumed that the history contained in these books was generally accurate, and that its account of the creation of the world could be shown to be in harmony with science. Yet even by that time, voyages of discovery from the fifteenth century onward had shown biblical geography (as reflected in Genesis 10, for example) to be inadequate. The world had proven to be bigger and more diverse than any reading of the Bible had suggested. John Calvin, the greatest systematic thinker in the Protestant tradition, argued during the sixteenth century that Genesis 1 did not reflect the facts of physics and astronomy, but described the creation of the earth for the benefit of ancient Hebrew observers who had no understanding of science. Arguments over the accuracy of biblical cosmology nonetheless raged among theologians for much of the nineteenth century, and have continued to our own day in the United States.

In modern scholarship, two questions posed during the late eighteenth century have set the modern agenda for interpreting the Books of Genesis through Deuteronomy: (1) When and by what process did these books come into being? and (2) How do their stories about the creation and Flood relate to similar stories that circulated among Israel's neighbors in the ancient world? Section A deals with how the Books of Genesis through Deuteronomy were composed. Section B discusses the question of ancient Near Eastern stories similar to those in Genesis.

A. Oral Tradition and the Documentary Hypothesis

Writing was invented during the fourth millennium B.C.E., and by 2500 B.C.E. writing systems involving complex pictographs and symbols recorded laws and narratives. The stories of the Hebrews, from Abraham onward, could theoretically have been written down at the time. In a conservative critical view, Abraham lived around 1800 B.C.E., although as we shall see the very existence of the patriarchs has been challenged in some recent discussion. Yet the fact that writing existed does not prove that it was a commonly acquired skill. Until the invention of the phonetic alphabet, literacy involved the ability to write and read hundreds of different signs; it was a skill confined to a small profession in the service of rulers and temples in relatively developed and wealthy societies. Generally speaking, literacy never became a common attainment in ancient societies, but was restricted to a tiny proportion of the population.

The invention of the phonetic alphabet around 1500 B.C.E. reduced the number of signs needed for writing from hundreds to around thirty; the Hebrew alphabet eventually made do with twenty-two signs. Once that happened, literacy could be acquired more easily than before, and was probably no longer confined to an exlusive minority of the royal and ritual elite (although it remained restricted to a specialist class of scribes). The

Egyptian scribes at work, from the tomb of Mereruka (vizier at the end of the reign of Teti, founder of the Sixth Dynasty from 2345 B.C.E.) at Saqqara. Village headmen are depicted being brought before local tax officials and flogged at a whipping post for nonpayment of taxes. Scribes record the proceedings.

THE ORIGIN OF WRITING

Writing probably began as a way of recording economic activity and establishing ownership. The earliest attempts, appearing around the middle of the fourth millennium B.C.E., were pictographic. As scripts developed, they became ideographic; that is, a word-sign came to represent a whole range of ideas.

Sumerian is the oldest language directly relevant to study of the Hebrew Bible. The Sumerians invented a pictographic cuneiform script sometime before 3000 B.C.E. Cuneiform (meaning "wedge shaped," from the shapes created on wet clay with a stylus) evolved from a pictographic script into a system of about one thousand ideographic and syllabic phonetic signs, and became the principal writing system of the ancient Near East. The Akkadians, another Mesopotamian people, adopted cuneiform during the third millennium B.C.E. By the fourteenth century B.C.E., their language, Akkadian, had become the lingua franca of the ancient Near Eastern world and was used, along with their cuneiform script, by such diverse peoples as the Elamites, the Hittites, the Hurrians, and the Urartians. Ugaritic, a very early dialect of the Northwest Semitic family of languages (to which Hebrew also belongs), was also written with cuneiform signs, but it was an alphabetic rather than a syllabic script and was originally written with about twenty-nine signs.

Writing in cuneiform suited the Mesopotamian conditions because its characters were easily inscribed on tablets and cylinders made from the region's abundant clay. After being inscribed, the moist clay was sun- or oven-dried to harden and preserve it. Stone was in relatively short supply, so only important records merited inscription on commemorative monuments (known as *stelae*). Many letters, business documents, and literary texts relevant to the study of Hebrew exist in cuneiform.

Hieroglyphics rather than cuneiform emerged as the writing system of ancient Egypt. Hieroglyphs arose as pictographs, and about seven hundred of them are known, although they were not all in simultaneous use. These characters were inscribed in stone on numerous pyramids, tombs, obelisks, and temples from as early as 3000 B.C.E. The papyrus plant, which grew freely in the Nile Valley, was easily prepared for writing, and texts written on this medium were well preserved by Egypt's arid climate. Egyptian hieroglyphics had a seminal influence on the development of the Semitic alphabet.

Both the Egyptian and Mesopotamian writing systems eventually utilized the principle of phonetization. Pictures or wedge shapes came to represent phonetic syllables (consonant + vowel or vice versa). From there developed alphabetic writing systems, in which one symbol stood for one consonant or vowel.

invention of the alphabet did not result in anything like general literacy in ancient Israel. Most people needed to write things down very rarely, and — absent educational systems for the population as a whole, as in modern societies — they had recourse to paid scribes when they had such needs. The fact that the term "scribe," (*sopher*, a "book person" or "letterer" in Hebrew), refers to a class of professionals shows that the ambient rate of Israelite literacy was never high.

Written documents recorded the ownership and sale of land, the adoption of children, and other pressing legal matters. Writing was not designed for popular consumption or entertainment. Rulers and priests had recourse to written records on a regular basis, for treaties and correspondence, laws, accounts and inventories, calendars, court chronicles, and sacred texts. People outside those privileged circles relied on storytellers for education, entertainment, and guidance in their lives. These tellers of tales preserved oral accounts of heroes of the past that brought the folk wisdom of Israel alive for their audiences. Later in this section the nature

LATIN (ENGLISH)	ORIGINAL NAME	GRAPHIC PICTURE	EARLIEST KNOWN FORMS	SOUTH SEMITIC (SABAEAN)	MODERN ETHIOPIC	N. WEST SEMITIC (EARLY HEBREW)	PHOENICIAN	MID-EARLY GREEK	ARAMAIC (MODERN HEBREW)	ARABIC
A	'alf	ox-head							א	
B	bēt	house							ב	
C, G	gaml	throw-stick							ג	
D	dāg	fish							ד	
E	hē	man calling							ה	
U, V, W	waw	mace							ו	
Z	zēn	?							ז	
H	hēt	fence							ח	
I, J, Y	yad	hand w/closed fist							י	
K	kapp	palm							כ	
L	lamd	ox-goad (whip)							ל	
M	maym	water (waves)							מ	
N	nahāš	snake							נ	
O	'ayin	eye							ע	
F, P	pēh	mouth/corner							פ	
Q	qu(p-)	?							ק	
R	ra'š	head							ר	
S, X	tann	composite bow							ס ש	
T	taw	cross-marker							ת	

Origins of the Hebrew script. (E. Isaac, Institute of Semitic Studies, Princeton, NJ)

THE FIRST ALPHABETS AND FIRST SCRIPTS

The first alphabetic script appeared in the area of Syria (including ancient Canaan) around the beginning of the second millennium B.C.E. The earliest known alphabetic inscriptions were found in the ancient Egyptian turquoise-mining town of Serabit el Khadim on the Sinai peninsula. In these proto-Sinaitic inscriptions (as they are called), each pictographic sign represented the consonant with which the object it symbolized began. This ingenious development doomed the elaborate writing systems of Egypt and Mesopotamia to obscurity, for a system of thirty or fewer signs ultimately made writing more accessible. Professional scribes now found the art of writing easier to pass on.

These very early symbols evolved into the proto-Canaanite (or Old Canaanite) script. By 1200 B.C.E. the letters had been simplified and they became more abstract than pictorial, while their names and order had evolved by the fourteenth century B.C.E. By the mid-eleventh century the twenty-two letters, their individual forms, and the direction in which they were written had also been stabilized. This proto-Canaanite script received its classic expression in the Phoenician alphabet of the Early Iron Age (ca. 1000 B.C.E.)

From either this Phoenician script or its proto-Canaanite precursor the great national scripts of Hebrew developed. The national scripts of Moab, Ammon, and Edom are closely related to the Hebrew of this early period, although they were influenced heavily by Aramaic, embraced as the language of Assyrian kingdoms and empires, in later centuries (i.e., between 900 and 320 B.C.E.). The Greeks also borrowed the Phoenician alphabet, which they had fully adapted to the needs of their own language by the ninth century B.C.E.

By the ninth century B.C.E., Aramaic, Hebrew's linguistic cousin, had become the diplomatic and commercial language of Syria and Israel. After the termination of ancient Israel's political existence in 587 B.C.E., Hebrew continued to be used as a language of ritual, liturgy, tradition, and scholarship, but Aramaic predominated as the common language. The archaic Hebrew characters in which much of the Hebrew Bible was probably first written also fell gradually under the influence of Aramaic script.

of the oral tradition and its study will be discussed. For the moment, however, our concern is: When did the stories about Abraham and his descendants make the transition from oral telling to written documents? This question involves assessing when conditions in Israel favored the writing down of traditions, as well as detecting signs in the books from Genesis to Deuteronomy that reflect their time and their mode of composition.

1. The Hypothesis of Sources within the Pentateuch

According to a broad consensus of scholarship since the end of the eighteenth century, the first five books of the Bible (the Pentateuch) were based upon varied sources. The most obvious sign of different sources is that, at the beginning of the Pentateuch, sometimes Israel's deity is called *'elohim* (God), and at other times *yhwh* (Yahweh). A single narrator would presumably not change divine names with no apparent sign of purpose or logic.

The Bible itself intimates that the Pentateuch came into existence by means of an evolutionary process. Second Kings 22:8–10 tells of a lawbook discovered in the Temple around 622 B.C.E., and, since the time of Saint Jerome (during the fifth century C.E.), that scroll has been identified with the Book of Deuteronomy. In 1805, W. M. L. de Wette argued further that Deuteronomy had been produced during the seventh century B.C.E., near the time 2 Kings says it was found. De Wette pointed out that while Deuteronomy commands that sacrifice to God must be offered only at the single sanctuary in Jerusalem (see Deuteronomy 12:4–14), Israelite leaders such as Samuel (ca. 1030 B.C.E.) had used a number of sanctuaries. He concluded that Deuteronomy innovated the single-sanctuary command during the time of King Josiah, and that prior to the seventh century there had been no such restrictions on where sacrifice could be offered. If Deuteronomy, which commanded a single sanctuary, was composed during the seventh century, it followed that stories that describe Abraham and Jacob building altars at sanctuaries such as Shechem, Bethel, and Mamre were written before the seventh century. This relative dating of sources has been a recognized principle of research for two centuries.

During the second half of the nineteenth century attention focused on one ancient source that used the divine name *'elohim* and contained much priestly legislation. Scholars such as the missionary Anglican bishop J. W. Colenso (1814–1883) and the Dutch professor Abraham Kuenen (1828–1891) carried out fundamental research that enabled the German scholar Julius Wellhausen (1844–1918) to set out a documentary hypothesis for the composition of the Pentateuch that is widely taught to this day.

According to Wellhausen's synthesis, first proposed in 1878, four ancient sources formed the basis of the collection of documents from Genesis through Deuteronomy. Two of them, "J" (which uses the divine name Yahweh, transliterated with an initial "J" in German) and "E" (which uses *'elohim*), were written during the period of the monarchy between the tenth and eighth centuries B.C.E., when Israelites still sacrificed at local sanctuaries. These

THE DOCUMENTARY HYPOTHESIS

From the late nineteenth century until the present day, most scholars of the Hebrew Bible have agreed that the five books of Moses represent an editorial compilation of four distinct sources, usually labeled in their chronological order as J, E, D, and P.

The abbreviation J denotes the so-called Yahwistic source (after the German spelling *Jahveh*), consisting of traditions of the southern kingdom of Judah and dating from the tenth century B.C.E. The Elohistic source (E) is closely interwoven with J, although it betrays special concerns of its own. The E source particularly conveys concerns of prophetic groups in the northern kingdom of Israel, and scholars usually assign it a date within the ninth (or perhaps eighth) century B.C.E. D stands for Deuteronomy. The Deuteronomistic source is for the most part limited in the Pentateuch to the book from which its name is derived. It is associated (at least in part) with the work found in the Temple at Jerusalem during the last quarter of the seventh century B.C.E., which served as the basis of the reforms of King Josiah (2 Kings 22). The Pentateuch's Priestly source is designated P and makes up the largest portion of the Pentateuch. It dates in its present form to the sixth and fifth centuries B.C.E. and is concerned with traditions of Israel's cultic worship.

These Pentateuchal strands are no longer thought to represent discrete, unified documents as they were when this theory was first formulated. The history of any one of these four major streams of tradition may well be as complicated as the history of the Pentateuch as a whole. Scholars disagree about the exact extent and influence of each source. However, the "JEDP" hypothesis provides a conceptual framework that accounts for the broad patterns and developmental history of the complicated literature in the Pentateuch.

Early Israelites adopted the Canaanite alphabetic script, shown here on a calendar incised on a tablet from the tenth century B.C.E. found at Gezer (between Jerusalem and Tel Aviv on the western slopes of the Judean Hills). This is the earliest Hebrew text of significant length. It records the seasons of the year and the agricultural activities associated with them. (BiblePlaces.com)

documents, as well as the Books of 1 Samuel and 2 Samuel, presuppose decentralized worship in different cultic centers within ancient Israel, both in Judah and in the northern kingdom, which revolted against the rule of Davidic monarchs in Jerusalem. Deuteronomy (D) reflects, as De Wette showed, Josiah's program of reformation during the seventh century B.C.E. His reform closed all sanctuaries except for the Temple in Jerusalem and reformulated J and E in the light of the ideal of centralized sacrifice and worship in Jerusalem. The document containing the priestly traditions (P) was written later, during and after the exile of 587 B.C.E. Its stress on the details of ritual and sacrifice developed what had begun with Deuteronomy, when the first attempts were made to regulate the freer, more spontaneous worship presupposed in J and E.

Wellhausen's grand synthesis, called the documentary hypothesis, begged many questions as he formulated it. For example, it is risky to assume that "spontaneous" worship must come earlier than prescribed ritual, and many scholars would date the sources of the Pentatuch considerably later than Wellhausen did. But debates over specifics of this theory cannot detract from its overall explanatory power. Wellhausen established a framework for the identification and dating of the sources of Genesis through Deuteronomy that, despite much criticism and modification, remains massively influential. It implies that the stories about Abraham, Isaac, and Jacob, the Exodus from Egypt, and the journey of the Hebrews to Canaan were first put into something like the written form we know no earlier than the tenth to ninth centuries B.C.E., that most of Deuteronomy was written in the seventh century B.C.E., and that the form of the Pentateuch as we know it was not completed until the sixth or fifth century B.C.E.

2. The Composition of Genesis through Deuteronomy

According to the theory of sources in its classic expression, the Pentateuch first reached written form with the emergences of J and E during the tenth and ninth centuries B.C.E. That would mean that from the time of King David and King Solomon (during the tenth century B.C.E.), conditions existed in Jerusalem to make transcriptions of traditions possible and likely. As rulers of a small kingdom only lately (and as it proved, briefly) emerged from intertribal rivalry, David and Solomon needed literate administrators. They may have been recruited from Egypt, or from any of the greater kingdoms and empires that surrounded Israel initially, but probably one of their duties was to arrange for training local, Israelite scribes.

This view has recently been challenged by scholars who hold that there is no archaeological evidence for even a small Davidic or Solomonic kingdom, and that neither the need nor the resources for a scribal school existed. P. R. Davies has supported this view, arguing that the sociological conditions for the growth of Hebrew literature did not exist until well after the exile (in 587/6 B.C.E.), and therefore dating many of the Pentateuchal stories to the Persian period (between the sixth and fourth centuries B.C.E.). In recent years, controversy has pitted "biblical maximalists," who favor an early dating of the sources of the Penteuch, against "biblical minimalists," who insist that the Pentateuch is a literary production from after the period of the exile of 587 B.C.E. Neither "maximalists" nor "minimalists" should be confused with those who insist that the Bible is infallible, but this dispute has also drawn the participation of those who support this position of Fundamentalism.

Archaeology has helped shed light on a debate that often seems ideologically driven. D. W. Jamieson-Drake (1991), for example, has produced computer-generated models that trace the social development of ancient Israel on the basis of archaeological evidence. A number of important criteria suggest that Judah was sufficiently centralized during the monarchy to employ a scribal administration. These criteria include the location of settlements and land use, the number of public works, the probable extent of literacy, and the distribution of luxury items. In each case, Jamieson-Drake's charts show a dramatic increase in these criteria during the eighth century B.C.E. compared with previous centuries, an increase sustained or exceeded in the seventh century and followed by a dramatic decline during the sixth century.

A cautious conclusion from these findings is that the conditions for scribal schools and literacy existed in eighth-century B.C.E. Judah, and that by the time of Hezekiah (toward the end of the eighth century) scribal activities flourished. Can we push the capacity for literary production back to the time of Solomon? We can if we grant the accuracy of the biblical tradition that Solomon built a temple and palace in Jerusalem as well as fortifications in the land, and that he used foreign and forced labor to do so. Accounts had to have been kept and labor carefully organized to achieve anything like the results described in 1 Kings (4–9), where administrators are in fact named.

Even if he did not preside over a small, centralized kingdom, Solomon at least needed an in-house group of literate administrators, just for purposes of constructing and governing Jerusalem. The conditions for the beginnings of Israelite literature would have existed, then, even if they made only a small impact upon the criteria used in Jamieson-Drake's study.

This brings us back to the tenth century B.C.E. as a plausible period for the transcription of traditions about Israel's ancestors. That dating, and the interaction of earlier sources within the complete edition of the Pentateuch, accounts for what "minimalist" theories cannot explain: the wide diversity of materials included within the collection, which far exceeds what a single narrator or a small group of narrators could invent many centuries after the events. Even so, of course, the gap in time between the tenth century and the epoch of Israel's ancestors is enormous, so that no argument for biblical infallibility is implied within the theory of sources.

On the Bible's own chronology (1 Kings 6:1; Exodus 12:40–1), Abraham lived around 1950 B.C.E., although even conservative critical estimates generally fall between 1800 and 1450 B.C.E. If we take the lowest figure, 1450, we still have a gap of over 500 years between the time of Abraham and the writing down of stories about him. How much do we know about what was happening in our own countries 500 years ago, when we have the advantage of written records and history books about the time? Yet any sense that Israelites had no real memory of their primordial past needs to take account of another reality, distant from most modern cultures: the deep, formative influence of oral tradition.

IBN EZRA, EARLY CRITIC OF THE PENTATEUCH

Prior to critical study of the Bible during the late eighteenth century, predominant belief held that Moses was the author of the entire Pentateuch. The New Testament reflects this assumption (Matthew 19:7, Mark 12:26, Acts 15:21, Romans 10:5), and the tradition of Mosaic authorship has its roots in the Hebrew Bible itself, when Moses writes down the divine revelation in order to explain it before the people (Exodus 24:4; Numbers 33:2; Deuteronomy 31:9, 24) and serves as the pivotal agent in the transmission of Israel's law (Malachi 3:22, 2 Chronicles 25:4, Ezra 3:2).

The first real criticism of the notion of Mosaic authorship came in a veiled remark by the eleventh-century Spanish rabbi Abraham Ibn Ezra, in his commentary on Deuteronomy. Ibn Ezra pointed to five cases in the Torah (the Pentateuch) that clearly seem to be additions or expansions that originated after Moses' time – the account of Moses' own death and burial in Deuteronomy 34 being the most obvious instance. Ibn Ezra also correctly noted that the mention of the "mount of Yahweh" (i.e., the Temple Mount in Jerusalem) in the story of Isaac's binding (Genesis 22:14) is anachronistic, because the Temple did not exist before King Solomon's time.

No one ventured along the challenging path Ibn Ezra charted until scholars began employing new critical skills forged in the Enlightenment. But his work evidences the close, careful study of Scripture in the Jewish tradition that seeks to understand the complicated process by which the Bible came into being. Nineteenth-century scholars, most of them Christian, took Ibn Ezra's lead and continued to note anachronisms, repetitions, discrepancies, and different styles and linguistic usages in the Pentateuch. From their observations emerged modern theories about the formation of the Pentateuch, especially the widely held hypothesis of sources championed by Julius Wellhausen in both its original and its more sophisticated expressions.

3. Oral Tradition

Biblical scholars first became interested in oral tradition at the end of the eighteenth century, and a breakthrough in study came during the first part of the nineteenth century. Classical scholars such as B. G. Niebuhr and K. O. Müller assessed the legends and myths of ancient Greece and Rome for their historical value, and two brothers, Jacob and Wilhelm Grimm, collected German myths and folktales. Heinrich Ewald produced the first scholarly history of Israel (with publication beginning in 1843). Ewald had been a colleague of Müller and the Grimm brothers, and he concentrated on the capacity of oral tradition to preserve information about Israel's ancestors. Ewald held that the stories of the ancestors preserved memories of the interactions of groups of people, and that characters such as Abraham and Jacob had become stereotypes embodying the virtues, character, and culture of these groups. Ewald fully appreciated that oral tradition has a tendency to shape and idealize the characters whom it portrays even when it may preserve memories of actual events.

At the end of the nineteenth century, Hermann Gunkel applied the study of oral traditions within his commentary on Genesis (1901, 1902, 1910). Gunkel became convinced as he worked that the folktale, as compared to myth and legend, was the earliest among the genres of oral tradition, and that examples of folktale motifs in Hebrew literature evidenced ancient Israel's generation of an oral legacy. Gunkel's research did not answer the question of the historical value of oral traditions, but it did establish that oral tradition was a vital part of ancient Israelite life. This tradition evidently did not cease when literacy began to spread in Israel and Judah. In all probability written and oral versions of stories of the ancestors existed side by side, exerting profound influences on one another. The written versions available in the present Hebrew texts were most likely intended to serve both religious and political ends in claiming that God had guided and inspired the ancestors so that the people as a whole were the people of God.

Oral traditions probably do preserve genuine memories, such as that the original homeland of the Israelites' ancestors was not Canaan but northern Mesopotamia, and that the ancestors were originally city dwellers who became pastoralists without fixed abode. The Exodus story recalls slavery in Egypt and an escape attributed to divine intervention. The wilderness stories recollect groups living in or traveling through the wilderness of Sinai.

Why were these stories told, preserved, and retold? In many cases the aim may well have been entertainment. Typically humorous folklore motifs, such as that of the younger brother (Jacob, say) getting the better of his elder brother (Esau), supports this understanding. But the stories also make claims that were vital to the Israelites. The story of Abraham's purchase of a burial ground near Hebron (Genesis 23) establishes a literal claim to land. Perhaps

THE SOURCES OF THE PENTATEUCH AND BIBLICAL HISTORY

There is an inherent problem of applying a modern definition of history to ancient sources of most kinds. Those who produced those sources simply did not accept the standards of evidence and proof that became conventional from the time of the Enlightenment during the eighteenth and nineteenth centuries, which emphasizes empricism in understanding history.

Before one can make any judgment about what events the biblical sources might reflect, one needs to have a clear sense of what those sources are and what purposes they embody. The "Chart of Biblical Literature, and Inferred Chronology" (on p. 52) sketches the development of the documents and the timing of some events implicit within them. Because debates in interpreting biblical sources have typically turned on the Pentateuch (the first five books of the Bible, attributed to Moses), that is a good point of access to the issue of biblical history.

A consensus of scholarship – not universal, yet very broad – places the Pentateuch's final composition during the fifth century B.C.E., with the addition of a specifically Priestly source, which provides direction for the conduct of sacrificial worship. The Pentateuch projects an ideal Israel, according to the regulations of Moses, which became a canonical standard. Torah was now written, and it offered the key for the constitution of Israel.

The materials within the Priestly source were not invented only during the fifth century. Earlier sources had already been composed. During the tenth century B.C.E., the Temple constructed by Solomon had become a new center of the understanding of Israel and therefore a focus of the codification of tradition. In addition to the "Court History," an account of David's reign produced shortly after his death (2 Samuel 9-1; Kings 2), the source within the Pentateuch known to scholarship as "J" was produced. J (named after its putative author or authors, the "Yahwist" [earlier spelled with a J in the Latin and german manner]) first linked, in literary form, the people of the Davidic kingdom with creation, the patriarchs, the Exodus, and the possession of the land. From the outset, God is known as "Yahweh" in this source.

Shorter books had been compiled earlier to be recited at cultic centers, so that a treaty, or regulations of purity or ethics, or alleged genealogical connections, or victories and other formative events might be remembered in association with sacrifice at any cultic center. But Jerusalem became the preeminent sacrificial center under the protection of the Davidic dynasty, and that involved the collection of these materials during the tenth century, and an early attempt to present them more coherently, for use in the Temple (and the royal court) during feasts that were primarily celebrated there.

After Solomon's death, united Israel was divided in 922 B.C.E. into Israel in the north and Judah in the south. 1 Kings lays the blame for that division on Solomon's apostasy (1 Kings 11:29–40), and there is a thematic link in Scripture between marriage to non-Israelite women and idolatry. But the kings, both north and south, undermined their own authority by their recourse to slavery and by their conspicuous consumption, not only by their idolatry. This last aspect is nonetheless an especial feature in the careers of the worst kings. During the ninth century B.C.E., Ahab in the north with his Phoenician wife Jezebel fomented the worship of Baal, and was opposed by the prophet Elijah (1 Kings 16:29–22:40); and in the south during the eighth century, Ahaz renovated the Temple to look like the one in Damascus, and may even have practiced human sacrifice (2 Kings 16:1–20). It is evident that the alliance of Ahab with Tyre and of Ahaz with Damascus proved a formative influence in the respective religious policy of each ruler.

Prophecy found its voice as a movement in its opposition to the monarchs it regarded as apostate. Prior to the crystallizing impact of that opposition, prophets appear to have been identified as those who spoke for God, often in association with worship in particular sanctuaries. Their prophetic ministry might, to a greater or lesser extent, involve unusual states of consciousness or atypical behavior, or both, sometimes accompanied by music and dance. But first the association with David, and then the antagonism of kings in the north and south, made of prophecy a surprisingly coherent movement. The emergence of prophecy as a literary genre is to be dated to the eighth century B.C.E. and the message of Amos. Fundamentally a prophet of doom against the northern kingdom, Amos foretold judgment against Israel's apostate kings, and Hosea vividly generalized that theme to include the nation as a whole. Micah and Isaiah followed them in the south, and an urgent appeal for social justice became a hallmark of prophecy there.

The doom announced against the north by an Amos or a Hosea must have appeared an idle prophecy during periods of prosperity, but when, in 722/1 B.C.E., the capital of the north was taken by the Assyrians, climaxing in the subjection of Israel to a policy of subjugation and exile, the prophetic message appeared to be vindicated. The works of the northern prophets were preserved in the south, together with another source of the Pentateuch, known as "E" (for the "Elohist," after the Hebrew name for "God"). That source also tells the story of Israel's beginnings, but with a northern slant.

God is portrayed as revealing his personal name to Moses alone in E, so that beforehand he was known as 'elohim, "God". The mountain of Moses' revelation is known as Horeb, rather than Sinai, and there are alternative versions of stories known in J, and some new stories; in addition, the conception of God is markedly less anthropomorphic. Clearly, there

were those in the north, priests and prophets and scribes, who opposed the royal attempt at syncretism. Nonetheless, the attacks the canonical prophets direct against other, deceitful prophets and against the cultic hypocrisy of some priests is eloquent testimony to the power of the opposition, and its support among both prophetic and priestly groups.

Spurred on by the demise of Israel in the north, whose people were largely lost to history, the prophets in Judah attempted to purify the life of their people. Isaiah urgently argued against foreign alliances and insisted that fidelity to God alone would save Jerusalem; Jeremiah ceaselessly denounced faithlessness, and was prosecuted for his trouble; Ezekiel's enactments of coming disaster won him a reputation as a crank. But in the reign of Josiah, a royal reformation backed much of the critique of the prophets (cf. 2 Kings 22:1–23:30; 2 Chronicles 34:1–35:27).

Josiah changed worship in the Temple to accord with covenantal norms; he centralized sacrifice, even of the Pesach (Passover), in Jerusalem; he tolerated no foreign incursions. In his program, he was guided by a scroll of the law, which was found in the Temple during the restoration. That scroll has, since antiquity (and the scholarship of Saint Jerome in particular), been associated with the present Book of Deuteronomy, which presses an agenda of radical centralization and separation from foreign nations such as impelled Josiah. But in 609 B.C.E., Josiah was killed in battle in an attempt to thwart a military expedition by

Pharaoh Necho II and the Assyrians at the strategic location called Megiddo. The effect of his death may be gauged by the impact of that name upon the apocalyptic tradition, in the form "Armageddon" (Revelation 16:16, cf. Zechariah 12:11).

The end of the kingdom of Judah came quickly after the death of Josiah. Culminating in 587/6 B.C.E., the Babylonian Empire, which had succeeded the Assyrian (cf. the Book of Nahum), implemented a policy of exile, subsequent to their siege of Jerusalem and their destruction of the Temple. Had events then followed what had happened to Israel in the north, there would today be no Judaism to study. Paradoxically, however, just the forces that must have seemed sure to destroy the religion of the covenant with Yawheh instead assured its survival and nurtured its international dimension. During the Babylonian exile, the priestly and prophetic movements joined forces to form a united program of restoration that put a form of Israel back on the map within a generation. Of even greater influence, they memorialized their vision of that Israel in a book and made it classic for their successors.

The Josian reforms had already allied some priests with some prophets, and the priests played a central part in the formation of "classic" Israel. Priestly/prophetic scribes redacted "D," the source of the Pentateuch in tune with the message of Deuteronomy, together with J and E. That work, probably completed during the sixth century B.C.E., was shortly later combined with what is known as the

(continued)

THE SOURCES OF THE PENTATEUCH AND BIBLICAL HISTORY (continued)

"Deuteronomistic History," a relation of events between Moses and the exile that explains success or failure according to the nation's adherence to the program that drove Josiah. The Pentateuch as we know it was completed during the fifth century, with the addition of "P," the specifically Priestly source that provides direction for the conduct of sacrificial worship. With the emergence of the Pentateuch, an ideal Israel, attributed to the regulations of Moses, emerged as a truly canonical standard.

The dispossession of Judah to Babylon, then, set up the priestly and prophetic hegemony that made restoration possible. But just as P sets out particularly priestly concerns, the prophetic movement also brought a distinctive message to the canon. The prophets generally agreed with their priestly confederates that the land was to be possessed again, and postexilic additions to the Books of Isaiah (40–55), Jeremiah (23:1–8; 31), and Ezekiel (40-8) constitute powerful visions of (and incentives to) return. But the previous abuses of sacrificial worship by the kings made the prophetic movement insist on righteousness as the prerequisite for sacri-

fice and that the events of the recent past were a warning.

A Zechariah might be happy to set out the hope of a priestly Messiah beside the Davidic king who was to rule (chapters 3 and 4), but even so the predominant emphasis fell upon the crucial necessity of loyalty to the worship of God (see Zechariah 14). Moreover, eschatology became characteristic of the prophetic movement, both in additions to biblical prophets, such as Isaiah and Ezekiel, and in fresh works, such as Joel and Malachi: the contemporary governance, whether Persian (from 539 B.C.E.), Alexandrine (from 332 B.C.E.), Ptolemaic (from 323 B.C.E.), or Seleucid (from 200 B.C.E.), and the present Temple were provisional, until an anointed king and an anointed priest would rule properly. The image of a priestly orientation redefined by the prophets is projected into the career of Ezra in the Books of Ezra and Nehemiah: prophet, priest, and scribe become one in their insistence on the vision of classic Israel, centered upon the restored Temple.

Obviously, the Pentateuch is deliberately idealized and might accurately be described as propaganda in the sense that its concern is more to realize its

vision of Israel than to describe Israel as it really was in the past. Before critical judgments can be made about what events and persons produced the literature, the perspectives embodied in each of the sources need to be acknowledged, the sort of literature (poem, psalm, song, epic, narrative, parable, sacrificial manual, prayer, creed) has to be appreciated, and the relationship of a source to the events it refers to needs to be taken into account. All biblical history begins with literary history, that is, with an assessment of how the literature was generated over time. Necessarily, that involves critical inference so that we may understand the interplay of sources that led to the documents as we can read them today. Then, to address the events that generated those sources, a second level of inference is necessary. That second stage should be informed by the literature of cultures surrounding Israel, as well as by archaeology and by the insights of social anthropology, but the history that results will always remain at the level of inference (and, indeed, inference upon inference) because in the texts as they stand we have no direct access to "objective" reports by firsthand observers or even to public records.

the persistent reference to the origins of the ancestors in Haran in northern Mesopotamia served a similar interest. These stories also helped listeners to identify themselves as members of clans and lineages named after heroes such as Abraham and Jacob and the latter's sons. In other cases, such as the Exodus story, the traditions were preserved and shaped during the liturgical celebration of deliverance from slavery.

In the form in which we read them, the stories of the ancestors have been idealized, shaped, and stereotyped, sometimes to the point that stories about one character are repeated and even retold with another character in

HERMANN GUNKEL AND FOLKLORE RESEARCH

Early in the twentieth century many scholars began to apply the findings of folklore studies to their understandings of the Bible. In *Das Märchen im Alten Testament* (*The Folktale in the Old Testament;* 1917) Hermann Gunkel examined the role oral tradition played in the formation of the Hebrew Bible.

Folklore researchers had identified certain basic forms, conventions, and themes used in a variety of cultures to transmit their collective stories orally from one generation to the next. Gunkel argued that folktales were the most primitive expressions of a people's unique history. He studied the motifs that folktales employed and the conventional beliefs associated with them, using this knowledge to analyze and classify Hebrew narratives.

Gunkel believed that many biblical stories had undergone an extensive process of oral transmission and shaping prior to reaching their written form, and he showed how Hebrew narratives had been influenced during that process by motifs common to oral traditions around the world. A classic characteristic of folktales is that they ascribe human personality to the forces of nature; ghosts and magic likewise play an important role. Gunkel found residues of these characteristics and beliefs in many parts of the Hebrew Bible, including stories about haughty brambles (1 Kings 14:9), clever snakes (Genesis 3), and sassy donkeys (Numbers 28). In addition, giants stalk the land (Genesis 6:4); strange men appear at tents (Genesis 18); cloaks mysteriously part the water (2 Kings 2:13); staves turn into serpents and back again (Exodus 4:3); and men speak from beyond the grave (1 Samuel 28). Gunkel also noted that the Hebrew Bible utilizes storytelling motifs that were common among many cultures, including traditions about exposing children to die (Exodus 2, the story of Moses in the bulrushes) and the recurring theme of the poor lad who becomes king (as in the case of the central biblical characters Joseph, Saul, and David).

Gunkel envisioned using his knowledge of folklore to assess the historical reliability of biblical narratives. He tended to assume that any story that employs folktale conventions is unhistorical. Further research, however, has shown that many folktales contain elements of historical reality, so that folklore studies cannot be used to reject the historical value of oral traditions as a whole.

The real value of Gunkel's work is in its contribution to our understanding of how the narratives of the Hebrew Bible were shaped and passed down before they reached their final written form. Gunkel spelled out the interplay between historical events, folktale motifs, and oral transmission, and reaffirmed the principle that accurate historical records are only one way of revealing truth.

---

the principal role (see, for example, Genesis 12, 20, 26). Although they are not the *creations* of the time at which they were written down, they reflect political, religious, and cultural *influences* of the time when they were transcribed, that is, during the early monarchy (tenth and ninth centuries B.C.E.), through to the period when the stories received their final form (the sixth or fifth century B.C.E.). Yet these traditions also sometimes distinguish between their historical settings and the later periods of Israelite history. For example, there is no mention of priests in the stories of the ancestors. Patriarchs typically offer sacrifices themselves, although the services of priests were required at the time when the stories received their final form.

In reading the Hebrew Bible, we must be aware that these stories functioned in a world different from our own, which originated and shaped them during the course of both oral and literary transmission. Their purpose was not to record history according to modern standards,

but to inform, entertain, and express identity. As the storytellers of
ancient Israel conveyed the wealth of their memorized traditions, they
also interpreted the circumstances of their own times, and celebrated
their belief in the promises of God and the purposes of Israel in God's
creation of humanity.

CHART OF BIBLICAL LITERATURE, AND INFERRED CHRONOLOGY

PATRIARCHAL AGE (2000–1300
B.C.E.)
  Oral production of patriarchal
    stories, cultic legends, and
    foundation epics
AGES OF MOSES, JOSHUA,
JUDGES: Clan period (1300–1000)
  Early poems (e.g., Exodus 15,
    Judges 5, Psalm 29,
    Deuteronomy 33, Genesis 49)
UNITED MONARCHY: Saul, David,
Solomon (1010–922)
  Early poems in 1–2 Samuel
  Some Davidic psalms
  Earliest versions of Court History
    (2 Samuel 9–1 Kings 2)
DIVIDED MONARCHY (922–587/6)
Tenth and Ninth Centuries
  Oldest prose of Pentateuch:
    J (920), E (850)
EIGHTH CENTURY (fall of northern
kingdom, 722/1)
  Amos (760–740); Hosea
    (750–720)
  Early prose parts of Former
    Prophets
  First edition of Isaiah [chapters
    1–39] (742–700)
  Micah (740–690)
SEVENTH CENTURY (Josiah,
640–609)
  More psalms produced
  Zephaniah (640–625)
  First edition of the source D,
    principally parts of Deuteronomy
  Most of Jeremiah (627–582)

Nahum (612–610)
Habakkuk (610–598)
EXILIC PERIOD (587–539)
  Parts of Jeremiah
  Early edition of D
    (Deuteronomy–Kings) by 586
  Ezekiel (593–565)
  Compilation of Peutateuchal
    materials, including P, as well as
    Proverbs (between 560 and 450)
POSTEXILIC PERIOD (538
B.C.E.–70 C.E.): Return from exile,
538–516 B.C.E. (restoration with the
beginning of Persian period)
  Second Isaiah (chapters 40–55)
    (538–522)
  Haggai (520)
  First edition of Zechariah (chapters
    1–8, and including the earlier
    prophecy of Haggai)
    (520–518)
PERSIAN PERIOD (516–332)
  Third Isaiah (chapters 56–66)
    (500–450)
  Malachi, Joel, Obadiah (fifth
    century B.C.E.)
  Second edition of Zechariah
    (chapters 9–14) (fifth century, or
    later according to many scholars,
    some of whom locate chapters
    12–14 during the Hellenistic
    period)
  Ezra/Nehemiah and Chronicles
    (450–350)
  Final shaping of Proverbs (400)
  Job (fifth or fourth century B.C.E.)

Jonah, Ruth, Song of Songs,
  Lamentations (fourth century B.C.E.)
HELLENISTIC PERIOD (332–164)
  Former and Latter Prophets
    collected together, with
    composition of the second half
    of Joel, and canonization of the
    Pentateuch
  Ecclesiastes (fourth or third
    century)
  Beginning of the Enochic tradition
    (third century), Esther (third
    century)
  Translation of Pentateuch into
    Greek (beginning in 250)
  Ben Sira or Ecclesiasticus (ca. 200)
MACCABEAN PERIOD: In 164
B.C.E. Judas Maccabeus sees to the
restoration of the cult of Yahweh
in the Temple and establishes a
dynasty nationally allied with the
Romans in 161 B.C.E., which extends
the borders of Israel to cover the
greatest territory ever by the end
of the century
  Daniel (ca. 165)
  Final compilation of Psalter, and
    canonization with the Prophets;
    composition of 1 Maccabees
    (during the second century B.C.E.)
ROMAN PERIOD (63 B.C.E., when
Pompey claimed Jerusalem and
Israel for Rome, until the fourth
century C.E.)
  Close of canon of Hebrew Bible,
    by 200 C.E.

B. The World and Its Inhabitants (Genesis 1–11)

1. The Nature and Functions of Myth

Within ancient cultures stories explained the origins of the world and humanity; these were "myths" – not in the popular sense today of something that is not true, but legends that enabled people to understand who they were and what their purpose was. Israel's mythic narrative is similar to those of its neighbors in the Near East, and in all cases the traditions in the Bible were written down later than similar writings in neighboring countries. Because Genesis 1–11 contains material attested elsewhere in ancient mythology, study of this nonbiblical material enhances our understanding of how comparable Israelite traditions emerged.

Origin stories in the ancient Near East helped societies in those times to cope with the difficult and puzzling world in which they lived. In their harsh physical environment, water, although vital for food production, sometimes came in the sudden, destructive abundance of floods. At other times water's absence brought the prolonged agony of drought. The human world was filled with violence between neighboring peoples and even within close-knit social groups. Sickness and death were everyday mysteries, and the preservation of the species through the bearing of children was uncertain and often mortally dangerous for mothers.

Ancient Near Eastern myths – mostly stories set at the beginning of time about gods and goddesses or heroes and heroines – sought to explain and reflect on the dangers and mysteries of existence. Some myths proposed that the lot of humanity was hard because the gods had created humans to perform tasks that the gods wished to avoid doing themselves. In others, humanity suffered by being the innocent victims of quarrels and fights among gods, especially between those personifying water and drought. Another theme was the fruitless quest of humanity to gain the secret of immortality, so that humans could, like the gods, be freed from the fear of death. The prevalence of flood stories evidences the importance of water in daily life, as well as expresses the anxiety humans had about the power of water to destroy their attempts to tame the forces of nature.

Flood stories were linked with creation stories in many ancient societies; narratives juxtaposing order (creation) and chaos (floods) expressed the paradox of life. Survival involved a constant struggle to discover order in the natural world and to impose order upon human activities, because that order was believed to preserve human existence. Attempts to order life and to understand the world as ordered were threatened by disruptive forces, both human and natural. Myths reflect a way of life in which order and security were longed for but all too rarely enjoyed. These motifs from the myths of the ancient Near East are used in varying ways in the literature of the region; they served as building blocks with which differing attempts to explain the origin and significance of life could be constructed. This accounts for why Genesis 1–11 have much in common

WATER, LAND, AND LIFE IN THE ANCIENT NEAR EAST: EGYPT AND MESOPOTAMIA

Civilizations that flourished in the sometimes arid climate of the ancient Near East were strongly influenced by the role of water in their environment. From June to September of every year, the Nile in Egypt swelled beyond its banks and brought an inundation of fresh, fertile silt to parched and barren land. Human effort was required to utilize the Nile's floodwaters, and the amount of the annual flow was subject to some fluctuation, but the Nile's regularity inspired ancient Egyptians with confidence in the order and stability of the world. Life was seen as reliable and renewable. Many Egyptians believed that their good existence would not end with death. Just as the Nile brought life-giving water in the new spring, so could humankind awaken to new life in the world to come.

Mesopotamian civilization also grew up around an important watershed area, the floodplains of the Tigris and Euphrates Rivers. On the whole, this environment was less friendly than the Nile's. Nature contained an element of force and violence in Mesopotamia that was missing in Egypt. The Tigris and Euphrates Rivers, unlike the Nile, rose unpredictably, and were prone to change their courses and turn villages into swamps.

Mesopotamians also endured an irregular climate. Seasons of torrential rains swept away hard-earned human accomplishments in agriculture and irrigation with destructive floods; devastating droughts smothered crops with dust. Faced with such an environment, Mesopotamian civilization developed a skepticism about the power and ultimate significance of human beings. Life's tragic potential was caught in an interplay of giant forces over which people had no power. The Mesopotamian cosmos was ordered, but not with the safe and reassuring order of Egypt's. Nature showed the world to be a seething cauldron of powerful, conflicting wills. Order had to be achieved, not taken as a given, and immortality remained the prerogative of the gods.

with other ancient Near Eastern traditions and yet present a unique reflection upon the origins and purpose of the world.

Genesis 1–11 are set in a time completely different from that of the readers, a typical indication of the mythical function of the material. The following phrases act as markers, dividing the time and the setting of the narratives from the experience of those who heard the stories recited:

1:1   When God began to create [in modern translations, this rendering – which captures the sense of the Hebrew – is either in the main text or in a footnote] . . .

2:4b In the day that the LORD made the earth and the heavens . . .

2:25 And the man and his wife were both naked and were not ashamed.

3:1   Now the serpent was more subtle . . .

6:1   When the people began to multiply on the face of the ground . . .

6:4   Nephilim [giants] were on the earth in those days . . .

11:1 Now the whole earth had one language and few words . . .

These markers not only set the time of the narratives as primordial reality but also indicated how the narratives were to be read and related to the world of the readers and hearers. The stories explained their world, but on the basis of a world that no longer existed as described. Nature and society in the present found their significance in the supernatural forces of the primordial past.

Although Israelite readers no doubt accepted the stories of Genesis 1–11 as true, they did not expect in their everyday lives to meet serpents that would converse with them, fruit trees that would confer immortality, or people who lived to be hundreds of years old. They believed that a flood had once covered the earth, but they did not expect that to happen to them now, even if local floods could be destructive. After all, God had promised by a solemn covenant that there would be no more cataclysmic floods (Genesis 9:8–17), just as he had banished the primal man and woman from his garden (Genesis 3:22–4)

The narratives spoke of a time different from that of the readers, and yet realities basic to Israelite existence were rooted in that primordial epoch.. These included the Sabbath (Genesis 2:2–3), marriage (2:24), clothing (3:7), the pain of childbirth (3:16), death (3:22–4), murder (4:8), sacrifice (8:20), different languages (11:7), and peoples well known to the Israelites, such as the Egyptians, the Philistines, the Canaanites, and the inhabitants of Assyria and Babylon (Genesis 10). Genesis grounded the familiar world in a time when God literally walked the earth. These myths gave Israelites confidence in the ability of their divinely mandated institutions to cope with the circumstances of their own world. The narratives served the same purpose as the myths of surrounding peoples, even as they expressed religious beliefs unique to ancient Israel.

BABYLONIAN FLOOD STORIES

The biblical Flood story represents a narrative genre that was widespread in the ancient world, bearing closest resemblance to the literature of Mesopotamia. Mesopotamian Flood stories date from at least the time of ancient Sumer and were widely disseminated in the ancient Near East (ca. 2500 B.C.E.); copies from the seventeenth century B.C.E. and later have been discovered.

The Atrahasis Epic recounts the creation of humankind from clay composed of divine blood mixed with dust. These human creatures were created to relieve the gods of their mundane duties. The human population swelled beyond control, however, and their noise was bothersome to the gods. A coalition of gods threatened the offending creatures with a number of punishments, culminating with a plot to drown all of them. But a friendly god warned the hero, Atrahasis, in a dream that he should build a boat to escape the coming flood.

The most famous and most complete Mesopotamian Flood story is a later addition to the well-known Epic of Gilgamesh. The original story concerns the adventures of Gilgamesh, the king of Uruk, and his companion Enkidu. The two friends set out to gain immortality through their memorable deeds, one of which brings fatal wrath from the gods upon Enkidu. A bereaved Gilgamesh then goes in search of the secret of personal immortality – above and beyond the afterlife of reputation – from his ancestor Utnapishtim, who once learned the secret of eternal life. After a series of fiery trials, Gilgamesh arrives at his destination, only to be disappointed. Utnapishtim, it seems, had become immortal by virtue of an unrepeatable circumstance: he and his wife had survived a great flood and by a special dispensation had been granted the divine prerogative of life eternal.

A number of interesting similarities between the Genesis acount of Noah, and the Flood story as narrated by Utnapishtim in the Epic of Gilgamesh continue to fascinate scholars and general readers alike. In both, the deluge comes by divine decree, and one individual is warned of the impending disaster and told to build a boat according to exact specifications. Both traditions include instructions about what is to be taken aboard the vessel, and in both the flood destroys the people and the beasts that are left behind. Both Noah's ark and Utnapishtim's boat come to rest on high mountains, and both characters send birds out to determine if the land has again become livable. In a final striking parallel, both heroes build altars and offer sacrifice to their gods.

Such parallels do not imply that the collectors of the Genesis traditions simply borrowed a Mesopotamian story to frame their own narrative. The Hebrew and Babylonian texts are each consonant with their culture's worldview, and the biblical version is clearly written from the perspective of ethical monotheism. The biblical authors thoroughly revised Mesopotamian and other traditions to create their own highly distinctive version.

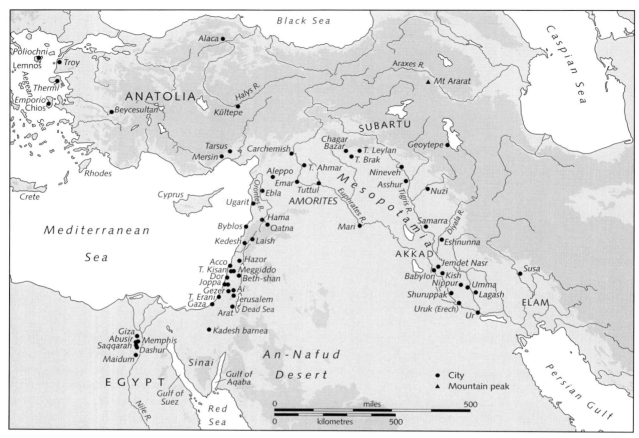

Map III. The ancient Near East in the third millennium B.C.E.

2. Ancient Near Eastern Cosmologies

The narrators who produced Genesis 1–11 were familiar with the great mythological traditions of the ancient Near East, and a comparison with the literature of surrounding cultures reveals the particular character of Israel's myths.

Genesis 1:1–2:4a

Ever since its discovery in 1875, the Babylonian creation story (written around 1120 B.C.E.), called after its opening words Enuma Elish, has been compared with Genesis 1. The Enuma Elish is a narrative about a struggle among many gods in which the god Marduk becomes the champion of some against the goddess Tiamat, defeats her, and creates the world out of her dismembered carcass (Pritchard, *Ancient Near Eastern Texts Relating to the Old Testament,* 1969, pp. 60–72; hereafter *Ancient Near Eastern Texts*). That, of course, seems a very far cry from Genesis 1. Although the Enuma Elish articulates the wish for order to prevail over chaos, its theology differs from that of Genesis, quite apart from its political function to exalt Marduk, the god of Babylon. Nonetheless, striking comparisons remain:

Enuma Elish	Genesis 1:1–2:4a
Divine spirit and cosmic matter are coexistent and coeternal	Divine spirit shapes cosmic matter and exists independent from it
Primeval chaos: Tiamat (a goddess of watery chaos) enveloped in darkness	The earth is a desolate waste, with darkness covering the deep (*tehom*)
Light emanates from the gods	Light created
Creation of the firmament	Creation of the firmament
Creation of dry land	Creation of dry land
Creation of the luminaries	Creation of the luminaries
Creation of humanity	Creation of humans (especially males)
Gods rest and celebrate	God rests and sanctifies the seventh day

One of the greatest differences between the texts is that there is no struggle between the gods prior to creation in Genesis 1. Israelite belief in the supremacy of the God of Israel ruled that out, although some scholars have seen allusions to the motif of the divine struggle in passages such as Psalm 89:9–12:

> You rule the raging of the sea;
> when its waves rise, you still them.
> You crushed Rahab like a carcass,
> you scattered your enemies with your mighty arm.
> The heavens are yours, the earth also is yours;
> the world and all that is in it – you have founded them.

Genesis 2:4b–25

Genesis 2:4b–25 speaks of the creation of humanity and of people's lot in the world. The man (called *Adam,* "man" in Hebrew) is made from the earth (*adamah* in Hebrew) to tend a garden that is abundantly watered and without thorns or thistles. The Lord makes animals to support the man and creates woman to be his partner. The whole picture contrasts sharply with other ancient Near Eastern texts. Both Sumerian and Akkadian texts assert that humans were created so that they could perform manual labor for the gods, such as building canals and cities. In the Enuma Elish humanity is created from the blood of an executed traitor god:

> Kingu it was who created the strife,
> And caused Tiamat to revolt and prepare for battle.
> They bound him and held him before Ea;
> Punishment they inflicted upon him by cutting (the arteries of) his blood.
> With his blood they created mankind.
> (Heidel, *The Babylonian Genesis,* p. 47)

This passage provides an explanation for the willful and destructive tendency in human beings; humans are made from the blood of a god who instigated rebellion against order and who was executed for treachery.

A closer parallel to Genesis 2 comes from the Epic of Gilgamesh (written ca. 1600 B.C.E.), where the uncivilized man Enkidu is also created from earth:

> The goddess Aruru, she washed her hands,
> Took a pinch of clay, threw it down in the wild.
> In the wild she created Enkidu, the hero,
> Offspring of silence, knit strong by Ninurta.
> (George, *The Epic of Gilgamesh*, p. 5)

Genesis 2 shares its conception of humanity with both the Enuma Elish and the Epic of Gilgamesh. The LORD crafts Adam from the earth and yet animates him with his own breath; the breath (Hebrew *neshamah*) that God breathed into him is an endowment (Genesis 2:7), an inherent part of people.

Genesis 3

The ancient Near East produced a literature that lamented the losses of paradise and immortality. A Sumerian writing, Enki and Ninhursag (probably from the first half of the second millennium B.C.E.; see *Ancient Near Eastern Texts*, pp. 37–41), speaks of the land of Dilmun, which is "pure, clean and bright" and where

> The lion kills not.
> The wolf snatches not the lamb,
> Unknown is the kid-devouring wild dog,
> . . . its old woman [says] not "I am an old woman";
> Its old man [says] not "I am an old man."

This ideal state, similar to that in Genesis 2 and surfacing again in Isaiah 11:6–9 and 65:20–5, is disturbed when the divine ruler of Dilmun, Enki, cuts down and eats eight plants created by the goddess Ninhursag. She curses Enki, he apparently begins to experience pain, and Ninhursag creates eight deities from the parts of Enki's body where he experiences pain. Thus sickness and possibly death come into a world that previously did not know them, all as the result of the cutting down and eating of some plants.

The search for immortality is a main theme of the Epic of Gilgamesh, which went through several versions in antiquity. In the earlier Sumerian story "The Death of Bilgames" (from the first half of the second millennium; George, *The Epic of Gilgamesh*, pp. 195–208), Bilgames has to content himself with the pale immortality of knowing that, because he had been a great king, his memory would live on. The Akkadian Epic of Gilgamesh is even more pessimistic. The death of his friend Enkidu plunges Gilgamesh into despair. His quest for immortality fails, and his failure is all the more tragic because he comes near to success. Gilgamesh journeys far to visit Utnapishtim, who survived the Flood by building a ship and who was granted immortality. From him, Gilgamesh learns of a plant at the bottom of the sea that restores people's youth. Gilgamesh obtains the plant but, on his return journey, while bathing in a pool, he loses it to a serpent.

Another text that connects the loss of an idyllic world with human rebellion is the Egyptian myth of the heavenly cow. A time when there is harmony between the gods and humanity is disrupted when the humans rebel. This ideal world is subject to decay followed by regeneration, a process that affects Re, the creator god. Humanity is punished by the destruction of the world by fire; but the creator god rescues some humans and establishes a new, but inferior world. Access to the former world is now possible only by death.

Genesis 6–9

Several versions of Flood stories, in which various heroes survive, appear in the literature of the ancient Near East. In a Sumerian version the hero is Ziasudra, and he survives a seven-day flood by building a boat. An Akkadian hero named Atrahasis is warned by a god to prepare for a flood sent because the human race had become too numerous and too noisy! Atrahasis is instructed to take into his ship not only his family and relatives but animals as well. In the Flood story that appears in the Epic of Gilgamesh the hero, Utnapishtim, is warned by a god to make preparations, and he takes craftsmen on board his ship together with his family and animals. This version contains themes familiar from the Genesis stories (chapters 6–9): as the flood subsides, Utnapishtim sends out a dove and a swallow, both of which return. A raven does not return, showing that the earth is fruitful once again. On leaving the ship, the party offers sacrifices to the gods, who gather like flies at the delicious smell.

The Worldview Implicit in Genesis

These examples illustrate attempts in the ancient Near East to explain the origin of the world, of humanity, and of humanity's worst fears, including death, sickness, hard labor, and floods. Genesis 1–11 not only fits into this milieu but also shares the view of the composition of the physical world implicit in these ancient stories. As set out in Genesis 1, the basic element on which everything else in the world rests is water. Even dry land rests on water, so that when the Flood lets loose in Genesis 6, the subterranean waters burst up through the earth (Genesis 7:11). Over the earth and waters, like a turned-over bowl, is the firmament. This dome protects the area of the sky, but above it are other waters (Genesis 1:7), which also fed the Flood when the windows of the heavens were opened (Genesis 7:11). Water features as the key of this cosmogony. The land of Israel was not greatly blessed with reliable rainfall; famine punctuated Israel at every stage in its development. The precious element that was vital to life was also the principal substance of the world's makeup. Its unreliable availability and occasional overabundance was not due to chance or to the whim of God but to Israel's unwillingness to obey God's laws.

Tablet of cuneiform found at Late Bronze Age Megiddo (fifteenth or fourteenth century B.C.E.). This tablet contains a portion of the Mesopotamia Flood story from the Epic of Gilgamesh. Discovery of this tablet in ancient Palestine is a reminder that the Bronze Age inhabitants of the land had copies of the literary masterpieces of Mesopotamia. Formal literary texts like this were written on both sides of the tablet. (Biblical Archaeology Slides, no. 112)

3. The Nature of the World and of Its Inhabitants

Ancient Near Eastern myths employed a variety of common motifs to produce differing accounts of the world's origins; Genesis provides an example of that in chapters 1–11. During the sixth or fifth century B.C.E., priestly editors put the stories in Genesis 1–11 into a framework that expressed the distinctive religious beliefs of ancient Israel.

The contrast between Genesis 1:26–30 and 9:1–7 provides insight into the conception of the Priestly source. In the first passage humanity (including male and female together) is created in God's image and given a shepherding role in relation to the rest of the creation. It is noteworthy that this is a vegetarian culture in which animals are not ferocious and humans do not exploit them. In Genesis 9:1–7, when the mandate to the human race is renewed after the Flood, things are different. Meat is allowed to humans so long as it is not eaten with its blood still in it, because blood constitutes life itself (Genesis 9:4–6) and belongs to God alone. Accordingly, the role of humanity in relation to the animals is strengthened. Animals will now fear humans, who must act more as police than as shepherds in a world where violence is endemic.

Why has the world changed, necessitating the revised mandate to accommodate a more brutal life and the loss of a better, peaceable existence? The answer is given in Genesis 3–8, developing a theme deeply embedded in ancient Near Eastern mythology: creation is order, and human attempts to disrupt this divine order undermine and injure the creation. Genesis 1 sets out the physical categories of God's creation: the world is divided into water, earth, and sky; plants, animals, sea creatures, and even stars are assigned their proper places. Genesis 2 continues this theme. By naming the animals, the first human orders and classifies them; and his partner comes, not from the animals, but from his own substance. The command not to eat the fruit of the tree of knowledge introduces a moral boundary. Not only do objects and animals occupy particular places in the order of things, but human actions, too, occupy their proper spheres, which people ignore at their peril.

From Genesis 3 on there are repeated violations of the boundaries that maintain the order of creation. The serpent encourages Eve to disobey God's command so that she and her husband will become like God (or, "the gods," since the Hebrew phrasing can be taken either way), knowing good and evil. This is an incitement to cross the boundary that divides the human from the divine, and God responds by making that divide uncrossable. In Genesis 4, Cain transgresses the bonds of family obligations by murdering his brother, Abel; the ground consequently loses some of its fertility (4:12), because moral law and nature's order both stem from God. At the beginning of Genesis 6, a cryptic reference in which the "sons of God" marry the daughters of men and beget giants – monstrous hybrids that once stormed around the earth – suggests another violation of the boundary between the human and divine beings (which the Bible elsewhere calls angels). When the Flood narrative begins, one reason for the divine decision to send the deluge is that "all flesh had corrupted their way upon the earth" (6:12). Put in other words, humans had destroyed the integrity of creation by violating the moral boundaries that were part of its order.

Because the human inhabitants of earth have undermined the created order, it is necessary for the world to be wiped clean and for an order commensurate with destructive human tendencies to be established. The Flood does not destroy the earth completely, but allows a new start to be made, with a revised mandate that recognizes that the creation cannot be vegetarian and at peace with itself. Further, humanity is given a warning, in the form of the rainbow that appears from time to time. We today think of the rainbow as a symbol of peace, but Genesis conveys a richer symbolism. Extensive iconographic studies by Othmar Keel show that the bow was a symbol of war, and the broken bow a symbol of peace (Psalm 46:9). Seen from that perspective, the bow mentioned in Genesis 9:12–16 is the sign of a promise that the earth will not again be destroyed by a flood, as God promises, but also a warning to the human race. Their misconduct caused the Flood, and God will defend with the powers at his command his created order against the attempts of humanity to undermine it.

The narratives of Genesis 1–11 show, as they continue beyond 9:1–7, that humanity remains rebellious and destructive in the world as it has come to be after the Flood. One of Noah's sons fails to observe decency and respect toward his father, and his descendants are cursed (Genesis 9:18–27). In Genesis 11 the human race seeks to invade the divine sphere again by building a tower that will reach to the heavens. They do not want to accept their allotted place in God's world, but to achieve divine standing without God. Their scattering abroad as peoples separated by the barrier of language is the prelude to the next part of the story in Genesis 12, the call of Abraham.

Genesis 1–11 is no open-ended reflection upon the inscrutable lot of humanity, in the vein of the Sumerian version of Gilgamesh, where the hero must simply learn to accept his fate. Chapters 1–11 are part of a larger story in which God takes the initiative with a view to producing a humanity that will gladly accept their divinely appointed place in the world. This story has been described as an education of voluntary creatures to make them free. With the hope that a humanity worthy of the world may emerge, Genesis intimates that the original creation might after all be regained. A restored vegetarian and peaceful creation is envisioned in passages such as Isaiah 65:17–25, which conclude with the words:

> The wolf and the lamb shall feed together,
> the lion shall eat straw like the ox;
> but the serpent — its food shall be dust!
> They shall not hurt or destroy in all my holy mountain, says the LORD.

These words, reminiscent of the Sumerian myth Enki and Ninhursag, bring us full circle. The materials in Genesis 1–11 are deeply rooted in those myths of the ancient Near East that attempt to explain and come to terms with the paradoxes of human existence in stories about gods, goddesses, and heroes. In the Hebrew Bible, however, these myths have been pressed into

THE MAXIMALIST–MINIMALIST DEBATE

Scholars of the Hebrew Bible have recently engaged in intense and some-times acrimonious debate between "maximalists" and "minimalists." The former group sees a great deal of actual history behind scriptural accounts of such formative events for Israel as the exodus, the giving of Torah to Moses, and the entry into the promised land. The latter group conceives the appar-ent history of the Hebrew Bible as a convenient literary construction of a much later period, perhaps as late as the second century B.C.E.

The controversy originated in the early 1990s, with the publication of a series of books and articles (including Philip Davies, *In Search of Ancient Israel*) that questioned the viability of the Hebrew Bible as a source for the reconstruction of ancient Israel's his-tory. Within a few years, scholars from Europe and England also began to ask whether even archaeological data could be used to reconstruct Israelite origins prior to the period of David and Solomon. When viewed from the perspective of the history of biblical scholarship, this debate is a nat-ural outgrowth of the tension that has built for generations between archae-ologists working in Israel for many years and biblical scholars since the time of Julius Wellhausen who dated the redaction of the Hebrew Bible as during the exile or later. Most biblical archaeologists during the twentieth century, including William Foxwell Albright, George Ernest Wright, and Nelson Glueck, accepted the historicity of the patriarchs, dating them to the beginning of the second millennium B.C.E. By the 1970s, however, scholars not only began to doubt the existence of the patriarchs and matriarchs, but they also sought out Israel's origins within the indigenous population of Canaan at the very end of the Late Bronze Age (during the thirteenth cen-tury B.C.E.) and the beginning of the Iron Age (ca. 1200 B.C.E. and later).

The Israeli archaeologist Israel Finkel-stein became an unlikely ally in the deconstruction of the history of early Israel; his surveys and excavations led him to doubt whether there had been an occupation of the central hill country prior to the eleventh century B.C.E., and to wonder whether some key archaeo-logical data used to support the exis-tence of a strongly centralized kingdom (such sites as Beersheba, Dan, Hazor, Gezer, Jerusalem, and Megiddo) had been correctly dated. In lowering the ceramic chronology for dating these sites, he questioned the existence of monumental remains from the tenth and ninth centuries, consequently undermining the case for a strong, urban Jerusalem and key cities prior to the eighth century.

More extreme elements in biblical scholarship began to suggest that the Persian and even the Hellenistic peri-ods were when Israel's history was com-posed (not just edited), and that the biblical materials could be used only with the greatest of caution in respect of ancient Israel. The strident tone of some exchanges has created confusion in the field, and while archaeologists are now generally in agreement about the existence of a united monarchy under David and Solomon (*pace* Finkel-stein and his few followers), their con-ceptions of Israelite origins are diverse. Biblical scholarship remains deeply divided concerning the use of relatively late, postexilic sources to reconstruct preexilic history.

service to help express Israel's faith in a God who is not withdrawn from creation but who is constantly involved in it, a God who has chosen to work through a special people in order to bring to the whole human race that perfect freedom that comes from joyful recognition of his sovereignty.

C. The Ancestors of Israel (Genesis 12–50)

1. The Period of the Patriarchs

During which archaeological period did Abraham, Isaac, and Jacob live? For decades scholars favored the Middle Bronze Age (more precisely MB IIB–C; ca. 1800–1550 B.C.E.), but support has recently grown for set-ting the patriarchs in the Late Bronze Age (LB; ca. 1550–1200), or even at the beginning of the Iron Age.

At first sight biblical chronology seems to support a Middle Bronze dating. First Kings 6:1 puts the Exodus from Egypt 480 years prior to the building of Solomon's Temple, and Exodus 12:40 gives a figure of 430 years for the duration of the sojourn in Egypt. If the Temple building began in 957 B.C.E., that brings us back to 1867 B.C.E. for the latter part of Jacob's life, when he went to Egypt in his old age (Genesis 47:27–8). The stories of the ancestors refer to customs that have parallels in texts of neighboring peoples in the Middle Bronze Age; Abraham adopts a son because he had no heir (Genesis 15:2), for example. Although the Hebrew Bible is otherwise silent about adoption as a feature of ancient Israelite life, tablets from Nuzi in northern Mesopotamia indicate that adoption was practiced there, and according to Genesis, Abraham's family came from northern Mesopotamia (Genesis 11:31–2). Further, names similar to those of the ancestors are attested in northern Mesopotamia. Striking examples are Abamram and Jacob-el, and these are Amorites, that is, Semitic immigrants to northern Syria and Mesopotamia around 2000 B.C.E. Amihai Mazar has defended the setting of the ancestors in the Middle Bronze Age, making the additional argument that most of the cities named in the Genesis narratives were occupied and fortified during MB IIB-C.

The last forty years have seen fierce controversy over this Middle Bronze dating, which runs into trouble even if biblical chronology is accepted. The figures given in 1 Kings 6:1 make the Exodus too early (i.e., fifteenth century B.C.E.), because the genealogy of Moses (Exodus 6:16–20) indicates that there were only four generations from Jacob to Moses, a length of time impossible to square with the 430 years of sojourn given in Exodus 12:40. Moreover, the occurrence of names and customs in MB IIB-C texts does not prove anything about the date of the stories in Genesis, since names and customs often persist long after the period in which they originated.

Perhaps the strongest argument against setting the ancestors in Middle Bronze Canaan is the fact that the land was replete with cities and settlements at that time, which conflicts with the biblical portrait of how Israelites made Canaan their home. The archaeologist Israel Finkelstein (1988) has summarized the situation in Canaan in MB II, when an unprecedented number of settlements thrived in the central hill country in addition to the cities found in the usual places of occupation – the fertile parts of the coastal plain, the Shephelah, and the northern valleys. Around two hundred sites of the MB IIB-C period have been reportedly found in the central hill country, with more discoveries expected as surveying continues. In the Late Bronze Age there was a dramatic decline in the number of settlements; clear evidence points to the existence of nomadic peoples in Canaan during this period, and the Israelites may well have numbered among them.

The stories about the ancestors depict a largely uninhabited land that accommodated their herding-based economy. When the flocks and herds of Abraham and his nephew Lot become so numerous that their pasturage cannot support them both there is, according to Genesis, enough land available that they can agree to separate, with Abraham

MARI

The Middle Bronze Age (ca. 2200–1550 B.C.E.) ushered in a period of major social and political development in the ancient Near East. A number of Mesopotamian city-states were overrun by a Semitic people known to the native inhabitants as Amurru (from the Akkadian word meaning "westerner"), the biblical Amorites. These seminomadic invaders were the dominant power in northern Mesopotamia in the latter half of the eighteenth century B.C.E., ruling from the impressive city-state of Mari.

Mari was situated along the southern bank of the middle Euphrates in today's Syria. A river port located along two major caravan routes, Mari grew to be a city of considerable importance. Excavations at the ancient city have revealed a rich Amorite culture. Researchers uncovered a temple to the goddess Ishtar, a ziggurat (temple tower), and an eight-acre palace containing almost three hundred rooms and housing some twenty-five thousand cuneiform tablets dating from the nineteenth to the eighteenth century B.C.E. The tablets preserve economic, administrative, and legal texts as well as the royal correspondence of Mari's last king, Zimri-Lim. The Mari texts bear witness to a civilization that developed extensively irrigated agriculture and long-distance trade. Busy commercial traffic provided the city with extraordinary wealth. Mari flourished until it fell to the Babylonians under the great Hammurabi during the eighteenth century.

Texts from Mari illustrate the history and environment of northern Mesopotamia, and also refer to several well-known locations in Syria and Canaan. In addition, Mari has provided a rich resource for understanding the prehistory of Northwest Semitic languages, the linguistic family to which biblical Hebrew also belongs. Some visionary-cultic figures referred to on artifacts from Mari may also help in identifying an early form of prophetic activity.

Some scholars have linked the migration of the patriarchs to the great Amorite movements, roughly contemporary with the golden age of Mari (eighteenth century B.C.E.). They have bolstered their case by noting personal names in the Mari texts parallel to the biblical Abraham, Laban, and Jacob. Some have also drawn parallels between the sociological world of the patriarchs and the way of life in ancient Mari. But neither names nor social conditions are exclusive to any particular era, so the importance of the Mari texts for dating the patriarchs must not be exaggerated. The Mari documents most certainly help fill out the history and early customs of the Amorites, cousins of the Hebrew people, who later spread throughout Syria and Canaan.

The Mari archives provide vital information about upper Mesopotamia, the region traditionally associated with biblical ancestors. The city of Haran, to which Abraham migrated from his home in Ur of the Chaldees (Genesis 11), was a trading center in the cultural orbit of Mari and also played a significant role in its politics. These archives have also illuminated the movements of various ethnic groups at around the beginning of the second millennium. Perhaps most important, they shed light on a type of society where city dwellers coexisted with partially settled pastoralists – an arrangement likely to have been practiced in early Israel several centuries later.

choosing Canaan and Lot going into the Jordan Valley (Genesis 13:5–12). These biblical narratives were never designed to provide precise information about land use, but inferring a plausible setting for the stories involves taking into account what they say about conditions in their times, and they do not fit well into the developed and well-settled Canaan of MB IIB-C.

The Late Bronze Age offers better agreement with the conditions described or assumed in the stories of the ancestors. In the central hill country, where a number of the stories are set, there was a drastic reduction of settlements. As opposed to 116 MB II sites in the tribal area of Manasseh, there were at most 31 LB sites (Finkelstein 1988, pp. 339–40); Ephraim, Benjamin, and Judah were also sparsely occupied from the point of view of permanent

NUZI

During the seventeenth century B.C.E. an Indo-European people called the Hurrians began pushing into Mesopotamia from the north. They eventually settled throughout Asia Minor (and also in Canaan, where they are known in the Hebrew Bible as Horites or Hivites). Their greatest concentration was in northern Mesopotamia, where they established the kingdom of Mitanni (ca. 1500–1370). In this solidly Hurrian area lay the city of Nuzi.

Nuzi is best known for the collection of some five thousand private and public cuneiform legal texts uncovered there. Situated far to the northeast of Syria in modern-day Iraq, Nuzi's apparent remoteness did not undermine its ancient standing as a major center linking east and west. The region of Haran, where Israel's ancestors lived before arriving in Canaan, was controlled by Hurrians. Although little is known directly about the region, scholars have been able to reconstruct a great deal about its social and political customs from the records of the Hurrian community at Nuzi. Many enigmatic biblical concepts and practices have been traced back to Hurrian society through the documents at Nuzi. For example, some compare the Hurrian practice of establishing birthright by parental decree (rather than chronological priority of birth) to the biblical patriarchs' freedom from the rules of inheritance (Genesis 27, 49). Others note similarities of Nuzi marriage contracts and adoption procedures to events in the ancestors' narratives.

For some historians these parallels are indicative of the accuracy with which Israel remembered the culture of its founders. But even those who infer a direct relationship between Nuzi and the biblical ancestors are forced to note significant disparities between the two kinds of materials they left behind. The Nuzi documents remain valuable for comparing Hebrew and Hurrian social practice and family life, although many of the explanations of patriarchal customs derived from these materials are no longer accepted. In some cases it is not even clear whether the texts reflect a uniquely Hurrian culture or simply testify to common Mesopotamian practice.

settlements in the LB period. Sparse settlement is consonant with the stories of the ancestors, in which the heroes – living in a land that seems to be little occupied – come into contact with other peoples only occasionally. A drastic decline in the number of settlements need not have entailed a precipitate decline in total population. Some people may have abandoned their permanent settlements under economic, military, and/or political duress to become pastoralists, moving from place to place. The presence of a significant nomadic element in a Canaan with a few main cities corresponds well to the picture implied in the stories of the ancestors.

References in Egyptian texts to the nomadic *shasu* between the time of Thutmosis II (1482–1479 B.C.E.) and that of Rameses II (1279–1212 B.C.E.) confirm this conclusion. The *shasu*, tent dwellers and pastoralists who organized themselves into lineages presided over by leaders, occupied parts of Canaan, Transjordan, and the northern Negev south of Judah – the setting of the stories of Isaac, Jacob, and Esau. To the Egyptians they posed the usual threat that "civilized" people perceive when encountering "nomads": they seemed anarchistic, violent, and dangerous. Some of the *shasu* who were subdued by the Egyptians became slaves; others became soldiers.

Although the uncertainties involved leave room for argument, it is a reasonable inference that the Israelites we encounter in the twelfth century B.C.E. had their roots in the people whom the Egyptian texts call the *shasu*. Egyptian iconographic material details their appearance. They wore short beards and had a distinctive hairstyle, with the hair combed up and back and held in place with a headband. They wore a knee-length tasseled garment, bringing to mind the command in Numbers 15:38–9 that Israelites must wear tassels on the corners of their garments. Other peoples, among them Canaanites, may well have joined later with this distinctive group to form the nucleus of Israel.

The description "nomad" or "seminomad" is often used of people such as the *shasu* and the Israelites. These somewhat imprecise terms

Modern Bedouin tent. This tent, erected on Tell Hesban in modern Jordan, illustrates the possibilities of tension between seminomadic and urban cultures. Tell Hesban has been plausibly identified with biblical Heshbon (Numbers 21:26; 32:37; Isaiah 15:4; 16:8–9). (BiblePlaces.com)

describe peoples who combined two, at first sight different, activities: herding and traveling. Stories of the ancestors describe pastoral nomads, whose degree and frequency of movement would have depended upon the kind of herding they engaged in, since the amount and type of pasturage required varies from one sort of animal to another. The movement necessary to nurture herds corresponded to seasonal changes, producing a cycle pattern of travel through the year that also encouraged the development of agriculture.

Although camels are mentioned among the animals possessed by the ancestors (e.g., Genesis 12:16), that statement is probably anachronistic. The key issue for consideration is not the date of the domestication of the camel as such, but of the use of the camel in and around Canaan, and the evidence of iconography tells against the use of camels in Canaan in the Late Bronze Age. The ancestors must have had flocks primarily of sheep and goats. The Joseph stories (Genesis 37) give a good description of the ancestors' typical way of life. Although we are not told in the story exactly where Jacob was living, reference to the valley of Hebron (Genesis 37:14) indicates the general area. From Hebron, Joseph is sent by his father to seek out his brothers, who are pasturing flocks near Shechem, sixty miles to the north as the crow flies. On arriving in Shechem, Joseph finds that his brothers have moved nearly twenty miles further to the north, to Dothan. These geographical terms of reference accurately reflect the conditions of pastoralists in ancient Canaan. Shechem is situated at a point in the central hill country where small fertile valleys begin to merge with larger ones, until the broad plain of Dothan is reached, with the great triangular Jezreel Valley only a little farther to the north. The farther north one goes, the greater becomes the annual rainfall. The picture conveyed, then, involves pastoralists traveling many miles from their home base to find grazing, and ending up in the fertile and wetter valleys of the northern hill country.

Other features of the story also reflect their social setting. Joseph's dream, in which he and his family bind sheaves in the field (Genesis 37:5–8), indicates that Jacob's group farmed in addition to keeping animals. Yet agriculture did not provide a permanent base. When famine becomes severe, Jacob and his family leave the Hebron area and travel to Egypt. The Joseph stories overall present a vivid and realistic picture of a group practicing mixed agriculture and pastoralism, ranging a hundred miles from their base in search of pasturage, and being forced to abandon their base when the ecological balance tips against them and famine ensues.

All this may seem to imply a peaceful world, but the Late Bronze Age in Canaan was in reality a turbulent period. For much of that time Canaan was subject to Egypt, to which the rulers of the city-states looked for protection. The iconographic evidence shows that the art of the period featured warlike and political gods, and portrayals of humans emphasized battle, domination, loyalty, and legitimation. This evidence comes, of course, from the cities; nomadic peoples have left no such remains apart from the Bible. The pressure of conflicting demands for loyalty imposed upon villages may help explain why many settlements were abandoned by their inhabitants in favor of different forms of nomadism.

Scenes from the tomb of the feudal lord Amenemhet at Beni Hasan. They illustrate the importance of slave labor to the Middle Kingdom during the second millennium in Egypt, even prior to the enormous projects of Rameses II during the New Kingdom. (BiblePlaces.com)

One group responsible for contributing to the violence and tension of the period were the Habiru, probably more of a social class than an ethnic group. The El-Amarna letters, written during the fourteenth century B.C.E. by Canaanite city rulers to Pharaoh Amenophis IV, pleaded for help against this group. Whether the names "Habiru" and "Hebrew" are etymologically connected and whether the ancestors of Israel were part of the Habiru are topics that have generated heated debate. Although the etymological similarity has never been convincingly demonstrated, the Habiru question may well illuminate one otherwise puzzling chapter in the stories of the ancestors, Genesis 14. Here Abraham uncharacteristically engages in warfare against kings who, according to this unusual chapter of Genesis, invaded the Jordan Valley, the Dead Sea region, and parts of Transjordan and the Negev. In an implausible military exploit, Abraham pursues them as far as north of Damascus (Genesis 14:15). The names of these kings are curious, suggestive of invading forces, and the references to the Habiru in the El-Amarna letters show that landless warrior groups in Late Bronze Age Canaan disrupted

---

THE "HABIRU" PROBLEM

The people known as Habiru have featured prominently in scholarly discussion regarding the origins of the Hebrew people. The term "Habiru" (more properly 'Apiru, or its cuneiform equivalent) occurs in over two hundred texts that date to the second millennium B.C.E. and that come from every part of the ancient Near East. The term appears to refer not to a specific national or ethnic group but rather to a class of individuals. In some texts 'Apiru appear as vagrants who raid and otherwise harass resident populations; sometimes they are apparently mercenaries whose services are available to the highest bidder. Some 'Apiru seem to have been more like migrant workers who occasionally entered into voluntary servitude. Wherever the 'Apiru appear, they are foreigners or resident aliens, a rootless outsider class relegated to an inferior social status.

Defining the word "Habiru" etymologically is difficult. The term has been related to Semitic linguistic roots meaning "to provide," in the sense that the 'Apiru were ones who depended on the rations provided by their patrons to survive; or "dust," in the sense that they were dusty people, Bedouins from the desert sands; or "earth," in the sense that the 'Apiru dwelled in a political no-man's-land away from urban population centers. The cuneiform designation means either "aggressor" or "bandit," and may be applied simply to any rebellious or marauding people. The resemblance between the words 'Apiru and "Hebrew" has led some scholars to suggest that the patriarchs belonged to this social class.

Recent theories about the Israelite settlement of Canaan have identified the 'Apiru with socially disaffected inhabitants of the land who took part in a broad egalitarian revolution from which the nation of Israel was formed. These revolutionary groups are conceived as being composed of anyone occupying the lower levels of Canaan-

ite society who threatened the established order. This ready identification of the 'Apiru with the founders of Israel has also been criticized as an oversimplification.

The words 'Apiru and "Hebrew" cannot be equated linguistically. Moreover, the term "Hebrew" is always used in the Hebrew Bible to designate Israelites as opposed to other ethnic groups, while the term 'Apiru appears to be more of a social category than an ethnic designation. A direct correlation between the 'Apiru and the ancestors of Israel is thus unlikely. Still, the patriarchs belong to the same historical era and seem to have shared a similar lifestyle with the 'Apiru to a limited extent, and they perhaps belonged to the same broad social stratum of the ancient Near East. The two terms may be connected insofar as the biblical Hebrews could also be seen as an element marginal to society, that is, as one example of a people who could be called 'Apiru.

the affairs of even powerful city-states. Although Genesis 14 portrays Abraham rather like one of the Habiru (Genesis 14:13: "one who had escaped came and told Abram the Hebrew . . ."), it is probably safer to locate Abraham and the other ancestors among the *shasu*, remembering that, according to the Egyptian iconography and texts, these so-called nomads could also be warlike, quite capable of defending themselves against the Habiru as occasion demanded. Over time the oral traditions produced by both *shasu* and Habiru might well have coalesced in the portrayals of the patriarchs, so that Abraham represents an amalgam of heroic presentations, among which his military foray in Genesis stands out as unusual.

In the narratives of Genesis 12–50 God displays an intimacy with the ancestors not paralleled elsewhere in the Hebrew Bible. For example, in Genesis 18 God appears to Abraham in the form of three men (or as one of those men), and in Genesis 32:22–32 Jacob wrestles with an angel who either manifests God or really is God. The religion of the ancestors centered on the God of the fathers (e.g., Genesis 31:52–3). It was a religion in which a supreme God, who is not identified with a particular sanctuary, initiates a personal relationship with a leader or ancestor, and is worshipped by his descendants as the God of that person. We need to be cautious about how we use the narratives of Genesis 12–50 for information about the historical Abraham, Isaac, and Jacob, yet their picture of ancestral religion as one of intimate piety, focused on the patriarch and radiating through his clan, fits well into what is known of the religion of Late Bronze Age Canaan.

2. Stories of the Ancestors

Genesis 12–50 may conveniently be divided into three narrative cycles: the Abraham-Lot cycle (12–25:11), the Jacob cycle (25:12–36:43), and the Joseph cycle (37–50). A broad consensus of scholarship has held that the first two cycles were based on oral traditions collected during the early monarchy in both the southern kingdom, Judah (producing the J source), and the northern kingdom, Israel (producing the E source), and that these sources were later combined by a redactor. Attempts to divide up the Joseph stories into J and E (as first tried by K. D. Ilgen in 1798) commanded less agreement. Internal literary links within each of the three cycles have prompted doubts in a mechanical view of an assemblage of stories from sources. These literary connections are most obvious in the Joseph cycle, one of the most polished pieces of narrative in the whole Hebrew Bible (the latter part of 1 Samuel and 2 Samuel 1–20 representing another example). But even though the Abraham and Jacob cycles are less homogeneous than the Joseph stories, this does not mean that they lack literary unity or artistry. A shift away from seeing Genesis 12–50 as compilations from oral tradition to seeing them as literary compositions has sometimes led to exaggerated estimates of the fictional nature of the stories and a lack of sensitivity to the varied perspectives and materials represented within each of the cycles. Although literary approaches have unquesitonably shed valuable light on the composition history of Genesis, perceiving the literary design of the assembled traditions does not make them any less representative of oral reminiscences of the premonarchic period. In fact, the more acute one's literary observation, the more apparent the influence of sources and early traditions becomes.

Literary sensitivity helps explain a puzzle: why, when Jacob is the father of the twelve tribes of Israel and the ancestor whose name is changed to Israel (Genesis 32:28), does the story of the Hebrew people begin with Abraham? The answer to that question probably lies in the history of traditions about Jacob. These grew toward their present form in the northern kingdom of Israel, while those about Abraham had a separate genesis in the southern kingdom of Judah. The dominant position of Abraham reflects the political realities of the period when the cycles were joined together. This was probably after the fall of the northern kingdom in 722–721 B.C.E., when Judah alone remained and was able to lay claim to represent the whole of the promise and the territory of Israel. The Judean Abraham was thus pictured as prior to, and more prominent than, the Israelite Jacob. Abrahamic traditions center primarily on the Judean capital Hebron, whereas those concerning Jacob feature the Israelite cities of Bethel and Shechem.

In their edited form these stories date from the sixth to the fifth centuries B.C.E. and reflect many of the realities of the period of the monarchy, but it remains likely that Abraham and Jacob were indeed ancestors of the groups of Israelites that later constituted the kingdoms of Judah and Israel. Traditions about them were preserved among their descendants, because they justified claims upon land and permitted families to know who was related to whom. Genealogies facilitated key social activities as varied as arranging marriages, parceling out land, and determining allies who would join in mutual defense against threats or perceived threats from enemies. The stories of Joseph were more likely composed in the northern kingdom of Israel than in Judah; their hero, Joseph, is the father of the tribes of Ephraim and Manasseh, the two tribes that occupied most of the central hill country and were the backbone of the kingdom of Israel. The Joseph stories were probably developed to supplement the Jacob cycle in the north so as to complete a story that initially ranged from Jacob's birth (Genesis 25:21–6) until his death (Genesis 49:33).

The sixth- or fifth-century editors of Genesis 12–50 went out of their way to present the era of the ancestors as a time different from their own. We have already noted customs such as adoption that do not appear to have been common in Israel at the time the stories grew into their present literary forms. Abraham's begetting a son by his wife's servant (Genesis 16:1–4) and Jacob's begetting sons by the maids of his two wives (Genesis 30:3–13) find no parallel in Israel's later customs, although they form crucial junctures in the story of Genesis as a whole.

The ancestors' religion is also presented as different from that of later Israel. Absent the arrangements for a priesthood at the time of the Temple, Abraham builds altars at Bethel (Genesis 12:8) and Hebron (13:18), Isaac builds an altar at Beersheba (26:25), and Jacob builds altars at Shechem (33:19–20), Bethel (35:3–7), and Beersheba (46:1), and offers sacrifice on the mountain where he made a pact with Laban (31:54). The ancestors as heads of the families approach God directly in Genesis 12–50, building altars and sacrificing without the need for priestly mediation.

Even as these stories maintain a distance between their world and the ancestral world, they also reflect political realities of later periods. Many of the narratives deal with relationships between the ancestors and peoples who were part of Israel's political world during the extensive period when the stories were being written down. Lot is the ancestor of the Transjordanian peoples of Ammon and Moab, and Ishmael personifies the nomadic peoples known to have inhabited north Arabia (located in the Paran in Genesis 21:21). Esau personifies Edom (36:1), and Laban represents the Aramean states to Israel's north. These ethnic references perhaps reflect conditions during the eighth century B.C.E. A more persistent theme differentiates the ancestors from the indigenous Canaanites. Abraham even sends his servant to Haran in northeast Mesopotamia to seek out a wife for Isaac from among his own kinsfolk, while Esau is implicitly condemned for marrying Canaanite women (26:34–5, 36:2–3). There is no reason to doubt the tradition that the roots of the ancestors were in northern Mesopotamia, and it is likely that the narratives functioned to define Judah and Israel as separate from the peoples of Canaan, among whom they had lived for generations.

This theme of what made Judah and Israel unlike neighboring peoples involves more than social distinctions: God, it is claimed, chose the ancestors to bring his blessing to all peoples (Genesis 22:15), but also required of them an obedience that separated them from other peoples. Ammon, Moab, nomadic groups, Edom, and the Aramean states are presented as being related to Judah and Israel, yet they are not chosen by God. Ammon and Moab come into being through Lot's incest with his daughters (19:30–8), and Edom through Esau's marriage to Canaanite women. Jacob (Israel) outwits Laban (the Aramean states) after having served him. Ishmael (representing nomadic populations) is expelled by Abraham but is treated favorably by God. The narratives thus show how God is at work among various peoples, testing and refining them, and choosing to work through the ancestors in particular. Nowhere is this theme more strongly stressed than in the Joseph stories: at the climax, when Joseph reveals himself to his brothers, he says that it was God who sent him to Egypt and that his brothers were merely the instrument through whom God worked (Genesis 45:4–8).

While the narratives portray God as guiding the ancestors so as to achieve his purposes, they also portray the ancestors' keen sense of danger and their reluctance to cooperate with or to trust in God entirely. In Genesis 12, Abraham – having been promised the land of Canaan and that his descendants will be a great nation – goes to Egypt because of famine and is not prepared to admit that Sarah is his wife. In a similar story in Genesis 26, Isaac does not go down to Egypt, thus obeying God's command, but he still tries to pass Rebekah off as his sister rather than his wife.

Abraham, having been promised that he will sire a great nation, tries to bring this about by his own initiative, first by adopting Eliezer (Genesis 15:1–6) and then by having a son by his wife's Egyptian maid, Hagar.

The theme of danger from God himself is exemplified in strange and profound stories, such as the binding of Isaac (Genesis 22) and Jacob's wrestling with the angel (32:22–32). In the first story God appears to command Abraham to destroy the divine plan – because Isaac, who is to be sacrificed, is the child promised by God to Abraham to realize the divine purposes. In the story of Jacob's wrestling, we are not told that the assailant tried to kill Jacob, but he did disable him. Had Jacob been completely defeated, that would have prevented his reconciliation with Esau and presumably even his settlement in the land that came to be called Israel after him. Intentionally or not, these stories express an awareness that the divine plan to bless the nations through God's choosing of the ancestors and the peoples they personify had a rough and ambiguous passage in the world described in Genesis.

D. From Egypt to Canaan

1. The Exodus in History and in Tradition

The narrative of Genesis 46 through Exodus 15 describes how, as a result of famine, the whole of the Israelite people left Canaan to sojourn in Egypt, where Joseph became regent of the land. The families of Jacob and of his twelve sons became so numerous that after an abortive attempt to restrict their numbers, the pharaoh organized them into slave labor groups. They were delivered only when Moses led them out of Egypt and on through the wilderness to the threshold of the land of Canaan. For many reasons modern scholarship has not accepted this account at face value.

The biblical picture of the conquest of Canaan does not seem plausible. The occupation of the land was much more likely to have been a process in which wandering pastoralist groups established settlements. Those settlements were almost entirely in the northern hill country, with little penetration into Judah. Indeed, as reconstructed by modern scholarship Judah plays no part in the history of Israel until the late eleventh century B.C.E.; the biblical narratives idealized events, as is only to be expected of accounts written hundreds of years after the fact.

The biblical portrait of six hundred thousand men who left Egypt on foot at the time of the Exodus – apart from women, children, and their flocks (Exodus 12:37) – has aroused skepticism. The German orientalist H. S. Reimarus, whose work was published between 1774 and 1778 after his death (1768), estimated that the total number of Israelites leaving Egypt would then have been over three million, requiring six thousand carts, one hundred thousand horses, three hundred thousand oxen, and six hundred thousand sheep. One estimate of the length of the column crossing the Red Sea put it at over eight hundred miles! The view that six hundred thousand is a scribal error cannot be sustained, since this figure is implied in other passages, such as Exodus 38:26 and Numbers 1:46.

Another difficulty arises from the ritual of Passover, which the Israelites allegedly observed in all its detail as they were leaving Egypt (Exodus 12), although that would have involved several days of preparation and a week to hold the Feast of Unleavened Bread – just the kind of autonomy and free time that Israel is portrayed as not having under the circumstances of their flight. Aside from the reference in Exodus 12, the narratives of the Hebrew Bible are strangely silent about the Passover until the reign of Hezekiah of Judah (during the eighth century B.C.E.; see 2 Chronicles 30). The inference that the Passover ritual evolved considerably is confirmed by the instructions about observing the Passover in Deuteronomy 16:1–8: here Israel is settled in its own land and must worship and sacrifice at only one place in all Israel – the single sanctuary in Jerusalem. Whereas Exodus 12 tells the Israelites to kill the Passover lamb family by family, in their households wherever they are, Deuteronomy 16:1–8 prescribes that the lamb be killed and eaten at the central sanctuary. Because a much larger contingent of worshippers is envisaged, people offer Passover bulls as well as Passover lambs.

Many considerations have caused scholars to conclude that the picture of all Israel going to Egypt and experiencing the Exodus, Passover, and wilderness wanderings is an idealization. But idealization should not be confused with invention: some group of people that later became a central part of Israel must have experienced what they believed to be a miraculous deliverance from Egypt in order for the Exodus tradition to have been generated. If, as has been suggested here, some Israelites were part of the pastoralist *shasu* peoples, many of them almost certainly had become slaves in Egypt and escaped to freedom. In the process they had what they believed to be an encounter with God, which became the basis of a powerful theology. The figure of Moses in the tradition is too dominant, and represented in too many independent sources, to be a complete fabrication. In some details, the portrait of Moses seems much more realistic than idealized: for example, he grows up in the Egyptian court rather than with the Israelites (Exodus 2) and is hampered by an impediment of speech (Exodus 4:10).

When did these proto-Israelites who produced the Exodus tradition enter Egypt, how long did they stay, and under what conditions? If we assume that the ancestors lived during the Middle Bronze Age (although the question of the historicity of the ancestors remains in dispute), it would be tempting to put their entry into Egypt during the period when the Hyksos ruled Egypt (ca. 1730–1552 B.C.E.). The Hyksos were Semitic invaders, and it has been suggested that the story of Joseph's rise to power would be credible during the period when Semitic kings ruled Egypt. But this hypothesis probably does not allow sufficiently for the fact that the biblical stories of the ancestors are literary creations of the tenth to fifth centuries B.C.E. in Israel. We have already seen in section C that the Late Bronze Age or Early Iron Age provides a more plausible setting for the ancestors, and if we connect them with the *shasu* "nomads," we have plenty of evidence for such groups entering Egypt and staying there. A famous reference occurs in Papyrus Anastasi VI at the end of the thirteenth century B.C.E. It is the report by a frontier official that

> we have finished letting the *shasu* tribes of Edom pass the Fortress of Mer-ne-ptah . . . which is (in) Tjeku, to the pools of Per-Atum . . . to keep them alive and to keep their cattle alive. . . . (*Ancient Near Eastern Texts*, p. 259)

The region to which these *shasu* were being admitted is the region in which the Israelites of the sojourn in Egypt are located in Exodus 1–15, to the east of the Nile Delta.

THE HYKSOS

Hyksos, a contracted form of the Egyptian words meaning "rulers of foreign peoples," refers to an ethnically composite group that dominated Syria, Canaan, and Egypt during part of the Middle Bronze Age (ca. 2200–1550 B.C.E.). The Second Intermediate period of Egyptian history saw Hyksos dynasties controlling much of northern Egypt. This period of non-native rule encompassed the reign of six kings, spanning some 108 years.

The origins of the Hyksos are widely debated, although most scholars agree that the group was a mixture of Asiatic peoples among whom Semites predominated. The Hyksos first infiltrated the Nile Delta region from the northeast during the politically unsettled period at the close of Egypt's Twelfth Dynasty (ca. 1792 B.C.E.). Their advance is often understood as a part of the great Amorite migrations of the Middle Bronze Age. The Hyksos began assuming power in Egypt by 1730 B.C.E., founding their first dynasty at the capital city of Avaris in 1670. They extended their dominion throughout Lower Egypt, as far south as the ancient capital of Memphis. Their rulers adopted the traditional style and bureaucratic organization of the indigenous pharaohs, gradually replacing native Egyptians with officials of their own. Joseph's rise to power (Genesis 40–1) and his kinsmen's migration to Egypt has in the past been associated with this historical period, although that dating seems too early to the majority of scholars today.

Deepening dissatisfaction with these foreign rulers spawned a burst of nationalism that culminated in the formation of Egypt's New Kingdom in 1552 B.C.E. Kamose began expelling the Hyksos from Egypt around that time, but he did not capture their capital. That task fell to his brother, Amose, who took Avaris after a ten-year struggle. Amose pursued the remaining Hyksos into Canaan, where they sought refuge. After a siege of three years, their fortress city of Sharuhen also fell to the Egyptians. When Exodus 1:5 speaks of "the new king over Egypt who knew not Joseph," it could conceivably be commenting on the return to power of native Egyptians, who held the Semitic Hyksos in contempt. The early New Kingdom was also marked by an exclusivistic, militant spirit that might have formed the background for many of the events in the biblical portrayal of the Israelites and their escape from Egypt.

Later Egyptian tradition portrayed the Hyksos as barbarians and destroyers of culture. A century after they had expelled the Hyksos, Egyptians were still bemoaning the ruin brought by those "foreigners." Even in the fourth century B.C.E., an Egyptian historian described the Hyksos as a "smiting blast of God." Although the Hyksos certainly damaged Egypt's pride and sense of national security, they were hardly the brigands later generations made them out to be. From architectural remains in Syria, Canaan, and the Egyptian Delta we know them to be representatives of the highly urbanized Phoenecian-Palestinian cultures of the Middle Bronze Age. They seem to have adapted quite well to the Egyptian world. Their skill in metallurgy and jewelry making shows that they developed advanced crafts.

The Hyksos were mighty warriors, credited with introducing the horse-drawn chariot to the ancient world's armory. Some historians also date the introduction of the composite bow to their era. The importance of military power to Hyksos culture is reflected in both their massive urban fortifications and their characteristic burials, in which the warrior and his horse were interred together in the same grave. These practices, and the level of development evidenced among the Hyksos, tell against their direct identification with the Israelites, but their history illustrates the turbulence that newly arriving and departing groups could cause in Egypt.

If we assume that proto-Israelite *shasu* entered Egypt at a time of famine elsewhere, say during the thirteenth century B.C.E., what sort of country did they enter? Egypt stretched along the course of the Nile; its governance was less secure along the river's southern extent, but sometimes its hegemonic reach was truly imperial. Even with its periods of relative weakness, ancient Egypt achieved continuity of culture and supported considerable advances in civilization for more than three thousand years. The Nile made Egypt a fertile and prosperous country. During some periods Egypt controlled areas as far as northern Mesopotamia. During the fourteenth century B.C.E. Pharaoh Amenophis IV (ca. 1358–1340) tried to introduce a radical religious reform that abolished the worship of all gods save one, the god Aten. Aten was the manifestation of the sun in rays of sunlight; and he could not be represented in human or animal form. He was praised in hymns as the creator of the earth and its inhabitants, and as the lord of foreign lands. The lofty monotheism of hymns praising Aten has been likened to that in Psalm 104. Amenophis's religious reform failed, partly because the new religion was abstract and remote from ordinary people. In its place there emerged the religion of Amun-Re, a god who combined something of the universal power of Aten with greater approachability. At the same time, iconographic evidence indicates that Amun-Re was regarded as a hidden god despite being accessible (Keel and Uehlinger, 1992, pp. 124–5). The Egyptian religion of the thirteenth to twelfth centuries B.C.E. provides a plausible context for the emergence of Israelite belief in a God of universal power who was not amenable to artistic representation by humans but who was active on behalf of his chosen people.

During the thirteenth century B.C.E. Pharaoh Rameses II began to build a new city, called Pi-Rameses, in the northeastern part of the Nile Delta near the modern city of Qantir. This was a huge site, and there were a number of other building projects in the vicinity. Exodus 1:11 records that the Israelites in Egypt were forced to build the cities of Pithom and Raamses, and although the identifications of these sites is not certain, they have been located at Tell el-Maskuta and Tell el-Daba, respectively, in the northeastern part of the Nile Delta. The building projects of Rameses II seem the likely historical occasion of the enslavement of a group of proto-Israelites and of their escape to freedom, although Tell el-Daba has also been identified with Avaris, the Hyksos capital.

Johannes De Moor (1990), from the Kampen Theological University in the Netherlands, has gone further, suggesting that on the basis of Egyptian sources Moses should be identified with a Canaanite who rose to a position of great power in Egypt at the beginning of the twelfth century B.C.E. The Egyptian name of this Canaanite meant "Rameses-Is-the-Manifestation-of-the-Gods," the first part of which contains an element reminiscent of the name "Moses." His Semitic name was Beya, and De Moor argues that he was a trained scribe with scant regard for the gods of Egypt. On the death of Seti II in 1197 B.C.E., Beya became, in effect, the ruler of Egypt, since Pharaoh Siptah was a boy. In his third year of rule, Siptah gave permission to Beya to build a tomb in the Valley of the Kings – a signal honor. When civil war followed the death of Siptah in 1192, Queen Mother Tausret, Beya, and their supporters fled from Egypt. De Moor points out that the building of the stone city of Raamses continued after the death of Rameses II in 1212 B.C.E. and suggests that, in this case, the slavery and Exodus might be brought down to the time of Beya, thus making possible his identification with Moses.

The biblical account, of course, differs significantly from this scenario. Moses is never portrayed as a ruler of Egypt, and he flees from the Egyptian court after killing an Egyptian who was ill-treating a Hebrew. He returns from his Midianite place of exile when God commissions him to lead the Hebrews to freedom. In any case, the attempt to identify Moses with a historical figure who was a literate Canaanite prominent in the Egyptian court goes against much recent scholarship, which has been dubious about finding historical veracity behind the legendary material of Exodus 1–15. Whether or not the historical Beya is the reality behind the stories of Moses, what does seem to be secure is the inference that sometime in the thirteenth century B.C.E. and most likely during the reign of Rameses II, a group of proto-Israelite *shasu* escaped from slavery, linked up with other pastoralists and disenfranchised Canaanites, and formed what was later to be Israel.

Faith, History, and the Uses of Narrative

God's freeing of Israel from slavery was a powerful theological conviction that shaped Israelite law, prophecy, and worship. In Deuteronomy's version of the Ten Commandments (Deuteronomy 5:6–21), the Sabbath is given to enable slaves to rest. This text continues:

> Remember that you were a servant in the land of Egypt, and the LORD your God brought you out from there with a mighty hand and an outstretched arm; therefore the LORD your God commanded you to keep the Sabbath day.

Appeal to the Exodus deliverance as the motive for keeping God's commandments is found many times in the Books of Exodus and Deuteronomy. Among prophetic texts Hosea 11:1 represents the most famous reference to the motif:

> Israel is young, and I have loved him,
>   and out of Egypt I called my son.

In Isaiah 40–55, imagery from the Exodus and wilderness wanderings is used to describe how God will bring back his people from their exile in Babylon (e.g., Isaiah 43:15–21, 51:9–11). Among the Psalms, 105 and 106 recall the deliverance from Egypt and the wilderness wanderings (see also Psalms 135 and 136).

The powerful influence and detail of the Exodus narrative contrasts strikingly with the little that can be said about what may actually have happened. The nearest that we can get to the events may be to surmise that some proto-Israelites among the *shasu* were forced into the building gangs of Rameses II and that they believed they escaped with divine help. This gap between literary and historical events widens when we add the difficulty that the narratives undoubtedly contain inaccuracies, as is evident from the discrepancies from text to text (see, for example, the description of routes of the Exodus in Exodus 13:17–18 and in Numbers 33:5–8). All the clans of Israel did not take part in the Exodus, a factor that needs to be taken into account when considering how Israel occupied Canaan and eventually formed a nation. The origin of Passover poses another difficulty. Many scholars hold that the ceremony of killing a lamb and of daubing its blood on the door of the tent is something done by nomads when they move from their winter pasture in wilderness closer to more populated areas. The blood wards off the evil and danger they associate with movement to more occupied land. In this view (which is itself not free of difficulties), the Passover did not originate at the time of the Exodus, but was a ceremony observed annually by nomads that was gradually historicized and became part of the Exodus story. One puzzle in the Passover story might be resolved on this reading. Why did the angel who killed the first-born need to see the blood on the door to know whom not to destroy? In the stories of the plagues, God afflicted the Egyptians while sparing the Israelites (e.g., Exodus 9:7, 22–6). Why was an extra sign needed at the Passover? Perhaps the answer is that the blood was a primitive aspect of the ritual that was then accommodated to the story of the Exodus.

The escaping Israelites believed that God had shaped events to make the Exodus possible. Their religious beliefs made them certain that their escape, against all the odds, was not something that they could have achieved on their own. What others might have seen as fortunate coincidences in their favor, they saw as the work of their God on their behalf. The remarkable feature of their faith is not only how they understood the events at the time but how their story about the meaning of those events began to shape their understanding of who they were and what their obligations were to God and to each other. This story was not just a remembrance of the past: it defined who the Israelite hearers of the story were century after century as they heard the narrative. It did not articulate simply what God had done in the past; it made faith in God possible in the present, a faith that had and has far-reaching moral obligations.

As the narrative was told and retold and celebrated in worship, people who had not personally experienced the escape accepted the story as their own story too. The narrative became the way in which they could believe and trust in the God who had set the captives free. For them, the Exodus articulated the character and nature of God, helping people to have faith. Naturally, the story was embellished in order to leave hearers in no doubt that God had acted "with a mighty hand and an outstretched arm." The miraculous element in the stories of the plagues and the crossing of the Red Sea was heightened (as may be seen by comparing Exodus 14:21-31 with Psalm 77:15-20), and in the ceremony of the Passover, whatever its origins, a means was provided whereby the deliverance could be celebrated annually. No doubt in this process many features of the story were elaborated in ways neither literally accurate nor plausible. Yet this elaboration was not an exercise in deceit; it was part of a process in which the story grew as it expressed faith in God generation after generation. Ultimately, the truth of the story of the Exodus is not to be assessed solely according to its approximation to modern scholarly reconstructions of history. Its truth has to be seen in moral terms as well. The Exodus story constantly challenged the Israelites to self-criticism. It condemned slavery within Israel and enjoined the gracious treatment not only of the poor, the weak, and the oppressed but also of domestic animals, fields, and vineyards. In its fullest sense, then, the story of the Exodus was not just a story about a past event. It was a narrative that helped God and Israel interact down through the generations, making known the divine character and how the redeemed people were to live responsibly in God's presence. None of this helps us to know whether the story is true in the sense that there really is a God who helped some proto-Israelite escape from slavery in Egypt. This is a matter for readers to judge as they follow the story for themselves and see how it affects them. There is one certain datum, however. Israel had this faith, and its influence upon their literature was far-reaching and pervasive.

A monumental seated statue of Rameses II of Egypt (who ruled from 1279 B.C.E. until 1212 B.C.E.) in the first court of the Luxor temple and colonnade. Rameses, identified by some scholars as the pharaoh of the Israelite oppression, was a great builder of palaces, temples, and colossal statuary. (BiblePlaces.com)

2. The Story of the Exodus

Exodus 1–15 is not the only place in the Hebrew Bible where the Exodus is recalled; Psalms 105 and 106 also commemorate the events in some detail. Yet the Book of Exodus is well named, providing the classic account with rich literary and theological themes.

The narrative begins by naming the sons of Jacob who had entered Egypt. These eleven men personify eleven clans, and their number is brought up to twelve by reference to the death of Joseph (1:6). The story therefore concerns all Israel, and the introduction helps later Israelite readers to see this story as their story. The two following sections (1:8–13, 15–22) are, at the level of fact, contradictory. A ruler who needs slaves to work on building projects would be unlikely to want to restrict their numbers. Even if he wishes to keep their numbers down while exploiting their labor, killing girls rather than boys at birth would logically be his policy. In any case, having mentioned the use of Hebrews to build the pharaoh's cities in verses 8–13, the narrative shifts to a new goal: that of the birth and Egyptian upbringing of the future deliverer.

The incident of the midwives (vv. 15–22) is a valuable clue to the type of literature we are dealing with. In the story the women converse directly with the pharaoh, an obvious anachronism in the absolute monarchy of Egypt. The godlike Egyptian ruler was shielded from his subjects by an impenetrable bureaucracy. But in a folk narrative common people can converse with and defy the highest earthly rulers. By the same token, only two midwives are needed to deal with all the pregnant women of Israel! Whether the midwives were Hebrew women or Egyptians acting as midwives to the Hebrews remains unclear. The fact that they have Hebrew names is irrelevant in a type of literature that accommodates its story to the customs and language of a later time. If the women *were* understood to be Egyptians, then there is a contrast between a ruler who is doing wrong, and two of his subjects who are defying him because they fear God and intend to do what is right.

The next section (chapters 2–4) concentrates on Moses' birth, his Egyptian upbringing, his solidarity with his people, and his flight to Midian after he kills an Egyptian who has been beating a Hebrew. Here two important themes emerge. The first is that of Moses' problematic standing among his own people. His direct intervention on behalf of a fellow Hebrew brings him no praise or gratitude; the next day another Hebrew reminds Moses of the killing, as if his act has weakened his stature rather than augmenting his authority. Moses' ambiguous identity features strongly when, having arrived in Midian and having helped the daughters of a Midianite priest, he is described by the maidens to their father as an Egyptian. The second, and related theme, arises from the name of Moses' son, Gershom, borne by one of these maidens. Gershom's name is explained as meaning "I have been a sojourner [Hebrew *ger*] in a foreign land" (2:22). The question is, which land? Of the two possibilities, Midian and Egypt, the latter would indicate that although Moses is seen by others as an Egyptian, in his heart he feels like an exile in Egypt. Yet if Moses felt like an exile in Midian, that would imply that Egypt were somehow his home, the only other land he knew. Either way, a theme of persistently being out of place is conveyed.

Chapters 3–4 present the call of Moses in terms comparable to the vocations of prophets (Isaiah 6:1–10; Jeremiah 1:4–10; Ezekiel 2:1–10; cf. Amos 7:14–15). The parallels with Isaiah's call are clearest; common themes include the manifestation of God's presence, the feeling of inadequacy to carry out the task, and the uncertainty about whether the people of Israel will listen to the message. For Moses, obstacle after obstacle is placed in the way of the divine commission. He says he is not important enough to speak to the pharaoh (3:11; although the midwives spoke to the pharaoh and they did not grow up in the Egyptian court!). Moses complains he does not know God's name (3:13), so the people will not believe that God appeared to him (4:1). Even after God has given Moses the secret of his personal name (3:14) and the power to perform signs to convince the people of his commission (4:2–9), Moses argues that he lacks the necessary eloquence to be a spokesperson for his people. The narrative undoubtedly expresses the harsh lesson learned by many prophets: mediating between the initiative of a gracious yet demanding God and the indifference or hostility of people intended to benefit from prophecy involves suffering. Initially, Moses need not have worried. The people accept the news of God's intention to set them free without demur (4:31). Later, matters will prove different.

A strange and difficult passage, Exodus 4:24–6, needs at least brief comment. Here as Moses is on his way back to Egypt, God meets and seeks to kill him. Moses' Midianite wife, Zipporah, saves her husband by circumcising their son and touching Moses' "feet" (a term that can also refer to genitals) with the boy's foreskin. This passage has provoked many differing interpretations, but two observations seem securely based. God's anger is directed against the halfhearted way that Moses has accepted his commission. In contrast, a foreign woman, the Midianite Zipporah, has faith that Moses will prevail and the foresight to defend Moses with the ritual of circumcision that he should have initiated himself, in accordance with the covenant with Abraham. The second and related observation is that Moses' symbolic circumcision resolves the ambiguity of his identity. He is now a circumcised Hebrew, not an Egyptian liable to be killed in the future as a firstborn son (cf. 4:23).

Chapters 5–11 relate a series of meetings between Moses and Aaron and the pharaoh in which the petitions of the Hebrews escalate from a request to go into the wilderness to sacrifice (5:3) to a demand that they be released from slavery to pharaoh altogether (9:1). These demands are reinforced by plagues, and the interviews are punctuated by alternating agreement and refusal on pharaoh's part. The narrative ascribes this vacillation both to pharaoh's obstinacy (e.g., 8:15) and to God's hardening of pharaoh's heart (e.g., 9:12).

As integrated by their editors, the materials in these chapters form a literary masterpiece, heightening the expectations of the reader and bringing the narrative to the climax of the final, tenth plague that follows the others: the death of the firstborn. Attempts to divide the plague stories into the three sources J, E, and P on the basis of who initiates the plague (Moses, God directly, or Aaron at Moses' behest) are not wholly convincing. Yet a priestly tradition with a distinctive vocabulary, in which Aaron acts on Moses' instructions, can be identified, and it is instructive to separate out this material and to compare it with the nonpriestly traditions in Exodus and those in Psalm 105. Adding the distinctive plagues of P (the gnats and the boils) to the earlier list produces the ten plagues when the death of the firstborn is included.

Priestly Plagues	Nonpriestly Plagues	The Scourges of Psalm 105
water into blood (7:19–24)	water into blood (7:14–18)	darkness (v. 28)
		water into blood (v. 29)
frogs (8:5–15)	frogs (8:1–4)	frogs (v. 30)
gnats (8:16–19)		
	flies (8:20–4)	flies and gnats (v. 31)
	cattle plague (9:1–7)	
boils (9:8–12)	hail and thunder (9:22–6)	hail and lightning (vv. 32–3)
	locusts (10:12–15)	locusts (vv. 34–5)
	darkness (10:21–23)	

This breakdown suggests that there were varying and to some extent overlapping traditions about the plagues and that the total of ten plagues is the result of the final composition of the narrative.

The chapters dealing with the plagues lead into the account of the institution of the Passover (chapter 12), into which the tenth plague is dovetailed. In its present form chapter 12 envisages the celebration of the Passover in the land of Israel, although the action is set in Egypt. Verses 14–20 add details about the Feast of Unleavened Bread, a festival that lasts seven days and was originally an agricultural feast associated with the barley harvest (March/April) in Israel (see Chilton 2002). The number of Israelites leaving Egypt after God had destroyed the firstborn of Egyptian children and animals (600,000; see 12:37) has already been discussed. Within this type of literature, the historical problems created by such numbers are irrelevant, of as little concern as the absurdly low number of midwives active among the Hebrews.

The Israelites' departure from Egypt brings about pharaoh's last change of mind and, consequently, his downfall in the Red Sea. With his army he chases the departing Israelites, and after the Israelites get across the sea, pharaoh and his army are overwhelmed by it. There has been much discussion about how to translate the Hebrew words conventionally rendered "Red Sea," as well as about the location of this body of water. The translation "Red Sea" goes back to the Greek translators of the Hebrew Bible, who understood by the designation what we today call the Gulfs of Suez and Aqaba. A suggestion that has found much favor is that the Hebrew *suph* is the equivalent of the Egyptian *twf(y)* (papyrus) so that the correct translation is "Sea of Reeds." This opens up the possibility, if one is inclined to attempt a high degree of specification, of locating the Israelites' deliverance either at one of the lakes along the line of what is now the Suez Canal or at a lagoon on the Mediterranean, Lake Sirbonis.

But what did those responsible for the edited text of Exodus understand by the Hebrew words? Although the term *suph* is used at Exodus 2:3, 5 to mean the rushes in the Nile, the accounts in chapters 14 and 15 do not give the impression that the storytellers had in mind a lake of reeds or rushes. At 1 Kings 9:26 the Hebrew *suph* is used in reference to the Gulf of Aqaba, and it is probably safest to assume that the Book of Exodus envisages a large, uncrossable sea such as that, and that no one at the time of writing had sufficient knowledge of the geography of Egypt to know precisely where the crossing had taken place. This does not rule out a small lake to the east of the Qantir region or Lake Sirbonis as possible stretches of water crossed by escaping proto-Israelites. But if the question is, what did the narrators have in mind, any reasonable answer must involve a miracle on a large scale.

The presentation of the events in the Book of Exodus cautions against trying to rationalize the account, for example by attributing the Israelites' deliverance to a change in the tide. The narrative as it stands intentionally invokes a supernatural explanation. God is miraculously present as a pillar of cloud by day and a pillar of fire by night (13:21–2), and the sea is divided by a wind that is strong enough to separate it and dry a path, without at the same time harming the Israelites. The Israelites' deliverance is, in effect, the Egyptians' eleventh plague, with engulfing waters brought upon the pharaoh and his army in the same way that many plagues are initiated – by Moses stretching out his hand at God's command. The emphasis of chapter 14 lies not so much on how the miracle is presented as on two themes, one of which becomes a common feature of the wilderness narratives. The first is that of the people's regret that they have been delivered from slavery (14:11–12), and the second insists that God alone can give salvation (14:13–14), which his people must accept in faith.

The Exodus story is rounded off by the poetic hymn of 15:1–19, whose date and original setting have prompted much debate. Feminist interpreters have convincingly suggested that the song was originally composed and sung by Miriam (see v. 21) as a victory hymn and that male editing has ascribed the song to Moses and made it seem as though Miriam and the women simply imitated the men.

3. Israel in the Wilderness

About half the material Exodus 15:22–19:25 deals with involves the discontent of the people at conditions in the wilderness and their regret at having left their security in Egypt, even though it came at the price of slavery. In their present form, these chapters (15:22–17:7) are designed to instruct Israelites long after the Exodus in the proper observance of God's laws. Exodus 16:13–30 provides a conspicuous example: the gift of the *manna,* which the Israelites are to gather each day, and just enough for that day. If kept longer, *manna* goes bad, except on the sixth day, when a double amount is gathered to suffice for the sixth day and the Sabbath. Since the Israelites have yet to be commanded to observe the Sabbath (Exodus 20:8–11), all this makes for an obvious anachronism, but such discrepancies do not matter in a type of literature more concerned with commandments regarding the Sabbath than with verisimilitude. The provision of the quails and the *manna* corresponds to some actual conditions in the region. Quails (*Coturnix coturnix*) cross the northern part of the Sinai desert on their way to the Sudan in August/September and then again in March on their way back north. *Manna* may be a resin, secreted by the tree or shrub *Tamarix mannifera,* that falls to the ground, forming a small edible disk. Although both sources of food can be found in the Sinai desert naturally, in Exodus 16 the provision is miraculous, and on that basis the *manna*'s collection is coordinated with the Sabbath, as a food that obeys the cycle of creation because it comes from the creator himself.

4. Israel at Sinai

Covenant in the Ancient Near East and in Israel

Once the Book of Exodus has the Israelites arrive at Mount Sinai, God promises them that if they keep his covenant, they will endure as his own possession among all peoples (Exodus 19:5). After the giving of the Ten Commandments (20:1–17) and the "ordinances" (21:1–23:19), there is a solemn ritual in which the Israelites agree to obey what is contained in the "Book of the Covenant" (24:7), and during which they are consecrated by the "blood of the covenant" (24:8).

This is not the first time that the word "covenant" (Hebrew *berit*) occurs in the Torah (i.e., the "Law," or Pentateuch) as it stands. After the Flood, God makes a covenant with Noah (Genesis 9:8–17), and after the call of Abraham, God makes covenants with him, with Isaac, and with Jacob (Genesis 15:18, 17:2–21; Exodus 2:24). There are also various covenants between the ancestors and local peoples. (In Genesis 14:13, for example, the Amorites are described as allies, literally, "possessors of a covenant with Abram.") The history of the concept of covenant in the Hebrew Bible is complex, and interwoven with social relations in the ancient Near East that are only partially understood.

Comparisons of Hittite suzerainty treaties from between the fifteenth and thirteenth centuries B.C.E. with the Ten Commandments, the Sinai narrative, and the Book of Deuteronomy have proven helpful. These Hittite treaties were published in the early part of the twentieth century; a

SINAI

The Sinai peninsula is a large, wedge-shaped block of land forming a major land bridge, with a total area of some twenty-four thousand square miles, between Africa and Asia. Sinai's borders are clearly defined by the Mediterranean Sea in the north, the Red Sea in the south, the Gulf of Suez in the east, and the Gulf of Aqaba in the west. Sinai is actually a part of the Saharo-Arabian Desert, and its climate is quite arid. Annual rainfall averages from 2.5 inches in the north to less than 1 inch in the south. Geographically, Sinai is divisible into three regions – the north, a low, sandy plateau marked by expansive sand dunes dotted with oases; the central region, a high limestone plateau with little rainfall and sparse vegetation; and the south, covered by rough granite mountains whose highest peak reaches an elevation of 8,660 feet.

Sinai's climate is difficult, but the area is not uninhabitable. Archaeological evidence suggests that the peninsula has been intermittently occupied for over thirty thousand years. Egypt began exploiting the southern region's lode of turquoise no later than 2650 B.C.E., and copper mining was common throughout the second millennium B.C.E. The coastal zone especially has served through the ages as an important military thoroughfare.

Biblical references to Sinai concern distinct tracts of territory within the larger Sinai peninsula. The wildernesses of Shur, Sin, Paran, and Zin are the biblical designations for desert regions of the peninsula. The wilderness of Sinai is commonly located in the south-central part of the peninsula. In this region Moses is said to have seen the burning bush; there the Israelites were encamped when they received the Law. The Hebrew Bible uses the word "Sinai" to designate a range of mountains (Deuteronomy 33:2) and, more specifically, to indicate the single mountain peak on which Moses received the Law.

This "Mount Sinai" is known to biblical writers by several names ("the mountain," Exodus 19:2; "mountain of God," Exodus 3:1; "Mount Horeb," 1 Kings 19:8), but its exact location remains a mystery. As many as a dozen mountains in Sinai and western Arabia have been designated as the sacred place, and scholars still debate the location of Mount Sinai in relation to the continuing controversy over the route of Israel's Exodus from Egypt and subsequent travels. Some suggest a location near Kadeshbarnea in the north, based on other areas sometimes mentioned in close proximity to Mount Sinai. A majority prefer a candidate farther south. Since the fourth century, Christian tradition has held Mount Sinai to be modern-day Gebel Musa ("Mountain of Moses"), a 7,363-foot peak situated in the mountain ranges of the Sinai peninsula's southern tip. But the apostle Paul believed, along with many of his contemporaries, that Sinai was "a mountain in Arabia" (Galatains 4:25), east of the Gulf of Aqaba (see Martin Hengel, "Paul in Arabia," *Bulletin for Biblical Research* 12.1 [2002]: 47–66).

Communities of Christian monks have lived at the foot of Gebel Musa since at least 373 C.E. Early in the fourth century Emperor Constantine's mother, Helena, built a small church on its northwestern slope. The Byzantine emperor Justinian founded the present Monastery of Saint Catherine at its base in 527. Gebel Musa received new attention in 1859 when Constantine Tischendorf discovered a fourth-century C.E. Greek manuscript of the Old and New Testaments in the monastery (called the Codex Sinaiticus), one of the earliest in existence.

Whatever its precise location, Mount Sinai became a significant focus and symbol of divine revelation (Exodus 43:16; Deuteronomy 33:2). The memory of Mount Sinai was inextricably linked with the history of the covenant made there between Yahweh and the people of Israel (Nehemiah 9:13), and with the commandments associated with the covenant (Malachi 4:4). The Lord's presence on this peak came to stand for the reality of divine protection (Judges 5:4–5; Psalm 68:8). Thus the prophet Elijah sought Mount Sinai/Horeb in a time of distress, hoping for a fresh revelation from God there, and Saint Paul made his way to Arabia – where he believed the mountain of Moses' revelation was located – following his conversion.

selection can be found in *Ancient Near Eastern Texts,* pp. 201–6. Although there are some variations, the treaties share a basic structure:

1. Preamble
2. Historical prologue
3. Stipulations
4. Provisions for the text to be deposited and read publicly
5. List of divine witnesses to the treaty
6. Blessings and curses

The treaty between a king named Mursilis and Duppi-Tessub, who became his vassal, instances several of these features (*Ancient Near Eastern Texts,* pp. 203–5). The preamble establishes Mursilis's identity as the major party:

These are the words of the Sun Mursilis, the great king . . .

The historical prologue recalls that

Aziras was the grandfather of you, Duppi-Tessub. He rebelled against my father, but submitted again to my father . . .

Then come clauses that deal with future relations between the two parties, in which Mursilis demands the exclusive loyalty of Duppi-Tessub. Clauses on military arrangements likewise stress Duppi-Tessub's need to be absolutely loyal, and that same theme governs the issue of relations with foreigners. Throughout, Mursilis and Duppi-Tessub stand for their people and their progeny as well as for themselves, and their relationship is embedded in the divine order as well as in the human order. Dozens of gods are named as witnesses to the treaty, and the text closes with blessings and curses:

. . . should Duppi-Tessub not honour these words of the treaty and the oath, may these gods of the oath destroy Duppi-Tessub. . . . But if Duppi-Tessub honours these words of the treaty. . . . may these gods of the oath protect him. . . .

A stipulation about depositing and reading the treaty is not extant, although this record was to be carefully preserved and its provisions were evidently designed to be promulgated so as to govern the behavior of Duppi-Tessub and his successors.

At first reading this treaty may not seem anything like the Sinai story; but as its individual elements are enumerated, similarities begin to emerge. The Ten Commandments also begin with words identifying the major party, "I am Yahweh your God," and continue with a historical reference: "who brought you out of the land of Egypt" (Exodus 20:2) In the commandments that follow, the need for Israel's exclusive loyalty to Yahweh is also stressed.

It is true that the Ten Commandments do not contain explicit provisions for depositing and reading them, invocations of gods, or blessings and curses. Yet in Exodus 24:7 the Book of the Covenant is in fact read to the people, and Exodus 25:21–2 mentions the ark as a box that will contain the testimony that God gives. In Exodus 23:22–33 blessings are promised Israel: if they serve God unswervingly, then he will drive out the Canaanites and

ANCIENT NEAR EASTERN COVENANTS

Covenants were promises made between two parties, who were bound by formal oaths, concerning their future actions and relations. In the ancient Near East, covenants were made within recognized legal communities and between different sociopolitical groups, and sometimes formed the basis of international treaties.

The earliest remains of covenant-treaties, although fragmentary, come from ancient Sumer during the middle of the third millennium B.C.E.. Covenants are also mentioned in the Mari archives (which date between the nineteenth and eighteenth centuries B.C.E.), but with insufficient detail to form a useful basis of comparison. By far the most useful and extensive documentation of ancient covenant forms comes from the Hittite Empire of the Late Bronze Age (ca. 1450–1200 B.C.E.).

These Hittite treaties document a highly developed form available to many societies of the ancient Near East. There are two types of Hittite covenants: suzerainty treaties and parity treaties. In suzerainty treaties a firm relationship of support is established between two parties of unequal status: the sovereign and his vassal. The vassal is obligated by the treaty to abide by the stipulations of his overlord (in this case, the Hittite king). In parity or bilateral treaties, two parties of equal status are bound to obey identical stipulations.

The broad similarities between the written Hittite treaties and the major covenant traditions of the Hebrew Bible, as well as the dating of the treaties within the time frame normally assigned to Moses, have prompted some scholars to use them as evidence for the Mosaic origin of Israel's legal traditions. However, the differences between the two are great enough that any direct influence seems unlikely. The Hittite covenants nevertheless add to our understanding of an important social convention of the ancient Near East that played a key role in the origin and formation of biblical traditions.

other peoples from the land of Canaan and make Israel a great nation; curses may easily be inferred from these blessings, should Israel fail to serve Yahweh.

Moreover, the Book of Deuteronomy represents an even closer fit with the form of Hittite treaty:

> Historical prologue (chapters 1–4)
> Stipulations of the covenant (chapters 5–26)
> Command to write the words of the law (27:8)
> Blessings and curses (chapters 28–9)
> Heaven and earth called as witnesses (30:15–20)

Similarities of this kind led some scholars early in the twentieth century to conclude that in the period before the monarchy, Israel took and used the model of a treaty between two nations to express its covenantal relationship with Yahweh. The idea of the covenant was thus seen to be a primitive feature of Israel's religion, and this argument was buttressed by the belief that only the second-millennium treaty forms provided parallels to the Hebrew texts.

Two emerging factors in discussion have for the most part disposed of this theory. First, the discovery of Assyrian treaties from a much later period (the seventh century B.C.E.) established that the same structure represented by the Hittite treaties persisted for many centuries. Second, the literary growth of the Books of Exodus and Deuteronomy has been shown to have involved a complex interaction among traditions, ancient forms, contemporary circumstances, and their editors' theologies. Whether by design or by chance, ancient elements sometimes appear in relatively late literary forms, as with the similarities between the Hittite treaties and the Book of Deuteronomy.

The earliest material in relation to the covenant is probably contained in Exodus 34:10–26. This passage (especially in vv. 17–26) reflects foundational features of Israelite religion, beginning with the command, "You shall not make cast idols," which is followed by instructions about observing the Feast of Unleavened Bread during the month of Abib, the month of the Exodus. There is no reference at this point to the Passover; apparently, the full ritual and nomenclature had not emerged at the time these instructions were formulated. (An out-of-place reference to the Passover in verse 25 appears to be a later gloss.) Next there are instructions about dedicating to God all firstborn sons, as well as all firstborn cattle and other domestic animals. A Sabbath command appears in the following form:

> Six days you shall work, but on the seventh day you shall rest; even in plowing time and in harvest time you shall rest.

The observance of two other agricultural festivals is also enjoined: the Feast of Weeks (the wheat harvest), which later entered the Christian calendar as Pentecost, and the Feast of Ingathering (the fruit harvest in the autumn; also known as the Feast of Booths). The final instructions are that leaven must not be added to sacrifices, that first fruits must be brought to the sanctuary, and that the Israelites must not boil a kid in its mother's milk.

These injunctions represent the raw material that was later developed into the now more familiar presentations of the Ten Commandments and the full story of the Exodus. The command to dedicate firstborn sons and animals, coming after the mention of Egypt, is reminiscent of the tenth plague, while the commandments not to make cast gods and to rest on the seventh day reflect an embryonic form of the Ten Commandments. The agricultural setting of this early covenantal code also indicates its primitive origin; the practices stipulated would evidently have distinguished Israelites from their Canaanite neighbors. Not working on the seventh day, not adding leaven to sacrifices, and not boiling kids in their mothers' milk constituted markers of social, ritual, and dietary separation from the surrounding culture, as well as emblems of devotion to Yahweh. This is a rudimentary covenant that binds to God a group of people who had been delivered from Egypt and who were living among Canaanites in the land of Israel. Their identity as a separate people bound to their God is articulated both negatively and positively: negatively by avoiding certain Canaanite practices, and positively by treating the principal agricultural festivals as occasions for acknowledging dependence upon and connection with God. This passage is probably the closest we can get to ancient Israel's initial understanding of the covenant, although it is far from easy to suggest a date – any period between the eleventh and ninth centuries B.C.E. seems possible.

The reign of Josiah (640–609 B.C.E.) saw a major new phase in the development of the covenantal idea. Josiah was able to gain considerable autonomy for Judah after a long period of subjugation to Assyria (from around 700 until 627 B.C.E.). Instead of the vassal treaties that had been imposed upon Judah by successive Assyrian kings, Josiah expressed Judah's independence in terms of being the vassal of Yahweh, bound to him alone

THE DIVINE NAME

The *tetragrammaton*, a Greek term meaning "writing in four letters," refers to the sacred name YHWH, and appears some sixty-eight hundred times in the Hebrew Bible. It is deliberately written without vowels, although many scholars believe the correct pronunciation to be something like "Yahweh." According to the Elohist source in the Pentateuch, this personal covenant name of Israel's God was revealed to Moses at the time of the Exodus (Exodus 3). However, some of the most ancient Pentateuchal traditions trace the use of the name to long before Moses, and the source aptly called the Yahwist has people calling on Yahweh from the time of Enosh, the grandson of Adam (Genesis 4:26). *Enosh* means "man" in Hebrew, and the use of the name from the creation story onward in the Yahwist source represents an attempt to view all of human history in light of the historic events of the Exodus. A theological point is being made:

YHWH is the God not only of Israel but also of all humanity.

The precise meaning of the name YHWH is obscure. A shortened form, "Yah," occurs about twenty-five times in the Hebrew Bible, as, for example, in the cultic cry "*hallelu-yah*," which means "praise Yah!" Theophoric names often also commonly use a shortened form of the divine name: for example, "Joel" means "Yo is God," and the name "Isaiah" tells us, "Yahu is salvation." But the complete form of the divine name YHWH is attested in early biblical narratives and in extrabiblical documents from the sixth century B.C.E., a good indication that this longer form is original. Moreover, the commandment prohibiting any trivial use of God's name (Exodus 20:7; Deuteronomy 5:11) led the Israelites to limit use of the full tetragrammaton, until in Rabbinic practice only the high priest uttered this secret, and then but once a year, on the Day of Atonement. For this reason, manu-

scripts of the Hebrew Bible spell YHWH without the vowels necessary for pronunciation. As for its meaning, linguists have suggested that YHWH might be derived from words meaning "to act passionately," thus emphasizing the divinity's loving concern; or "to speak," stressing God's revelatory function; or "to blow" or "to cause to fall," indicating that YHWH was originally a storm god. More likely, as the Book of Exodus attests (3:14), YHWH should be linked with the verb *hyh*, "to be." Although some scholars have attempted to trace the use of the divine name to Mesopotamia or Syria, its origin more likely lies in the Sinai peninsula. There Moses came in contact with Jethro (also called Hobab or Reuel), the high priest of Midian, and married Jethro's daughter, Zipporah. If, as the Elohist source insists, Moses was the first Israelite to call on YHWH by name, perhaps Jethro and Zipporah mediated the name to him.

by a covenant that he had sworn to the ancestors. This view of Judah's relationship to Yahweh was incorporated within the Book of Deuteronomy, with its insistence that the people should be absolutely loyal to Yahweh and worship him at one sanctuary only. The covenant as formulated in Deuteronomy warns of the curses that will fall upon Israel if God's commandments are ignored.

When Jerusalem fell in the sixth century B.C.E. and the Judean upper classes were exiled to Babylon, it appeared that the curses threatened in the Deuteronomic covenant had in fact been visited upon Israel. But the view that the exile was the occasion to discharge these curses helped Judah to survive that catastrophe. A later addition to Jeremiah (31:31–4) promised that God would make a new covenant with his people, not like the old one at the time of the Exodus, which the people broke. The priestly historical work, written in the sixth or fifth century B.C.E. and found in parts of Genesis, Exodus, and Numbers, expresses the view that God's covenant cannot be broken, despite Israel's disobedience. The covenant is now taken back to the time of Noah – a covenant with the whole human race – and to Abraham (Genesis 17:1–7).

Law in the Ancient Near East and in Israel

Written laws in the ancient Near East predate those in the Hebrew Bible by more than a thousand years (see *Ancient Near Eastern Texts*, pp. 160–98 and 523–8). The earliest extant Sumerian laws date from around 2100 B.C.E. Such written laws presuppose centralized authority in a society sufficiently diverse that customary relationships once guided by local, for the most part oral, traditions – as basic and as varied as the family, property, commerce, slavery, prices, and wages – need to be regulated formally. The rulers of the empire of the Third Dynasty of Ur in southern Mesopotamia (ca. 2100–2000 B.C.E.), for example, presided over twenty-three city-states, each with its civil and military rulers responsible to pay monthly taxes to the king. The administration of this empire required scribes and scribal schools so that laws could be written and records of court proceedings kept. Yet it is generally agreed that the collections of laws that kings caused to be written were not complete or comprehensive. Sometimes their purpose was propagandistic: to convince the gods and posterity that the king had fulfilled his role as the upholder of justice.

ISRAELITE LAW IN ANCIENT NEAR EASTERN CONTEXT

Israel's ancestors probably lived by legal conventions they learned in their native Mesopotamia. Centuries later these ancient traditions found their way into the laws of the Hebrew Bible. Several other collections of Mesopotamian laws have survived, the oldest of which date from the end of the third millennium B.C.E. (e.g., the collections of Ur-Nammu of Ur, ca. 2050, and of Lipit-Istar of Isin and Bilalama of Eshunna, ca. 2000). The most famous and best-preserved collection was promulgated by Hammurabi, king of Babylon in the first half of the eighteenth century B.C.E.

The Code of Hammurabi (much as the legal material in the Hebrew Bible) did not encompass the full range of regulations and procedures that governed Hammurabi's society. His code is rather a collection of selected legal guidelines valid in certain carefully pre-scribed circumstances. These laws are usually cast in a casuistic form that describes specific prohibitions and penalties. The standard formulation is "If a person commits this crime, then this will be the punishment"; subclauses often make exceptions for extenuating or exacerbating circumstances.

Similarities between ancient Near Eastern laws and the collection of laws known as the Book of the Covenant (chapters 20–3 in Exodus) have drawn considerable interest. Most scholars date the Book of the Covenant well after Israel's entrance into Canaan, since it presupposes a settled people living in an agricultural society and having close relations with foreigners. Yet this collection no doubt reflects earlier material. It is structured in the traditional form of ancient Near Eastern law codes, including prologue (20:22), the laws themselves (20:23–23:19), and epilogue (23:20–3). Most of its laws are in the casuistic form, which was dominant in the ancient Near East. Many laws in the Book of the Covenant share identical or nearly identical formulations with those found in Mesopotamian law codes.

Yet there are also significant differences between Israelite law and Mesopotamian law. Ancient Israelites evidently modified the traditions they received in light of their own religious and ethical sensibilities. Some biblical decrees address the same problems that Mesopotamian laws do (an indication of shared cultural background) but offer a different legal treatment. As a whole, Israelite law was more concerned with personal than with property rights, and it ventured beyond Mesopotamian law to give religious and cultic instruction as well. Penalities in Israelite law were, generally speaking, more humane than their ancient Near Eastern counterparts, although capital punishment – typically by stoning – featured strongly. Finally, Israel gave prominence to legal traditions whose form stressed categorical imperatives and prohibitions (of the type, "Thou shalt not . . . ") rather than conditional statements. Although this apodictic form (from a Greek term that means "pointing out [a command]") was not unique to Israel, Israelite law emphasized its usage because it conveyed the absolute character of Yahweh's covenantal demands upon his people.

Laws in the Hebrew Bible appear similarly incomplete. A simple contrast illustrates their partial character: the laws of Hammurabi (1792–1750 B.C.E.), themselves far from comprehensive, deal with marriage, divorce, adoption, the rights of prisoners of war, redress against a physician for injuries received during medical treatment, and reparations from the builder of a faulty house, whereas the oldest Israelite legal material either ignores these matters completely or barely alludes to them. Moreover, some laws in the Torah, especially in Deuteronomy, do not specify details but appeal simply to a person's generosity. A good example is the law on the release of slaves (Deuteronomy 15:12–18). Instead of prescribing that a released slave be given a precise number of sheep and a specific measure of wheat, the injunction is "Provide him liberally out of your flock," followed by the imperative "thus giving to him some of the bounty with which the LORD your God had blessed you." In practice, this could have amounted to a miser's charter! Collections of laws in the ancient Near East and in the Torah, then, represent only a selection of the laws that must have existed to regulate social relations; the Torah is as much an indication of Israelite ethics and theology as of Israelite legal practice. Moreover, some ancient codes of law may be the result of professional scribal activity removed from or only tangentially related to the actual practice of law.

Collections of law as presently written in the Hebrew Bible presuppose conditions in which central authorities make laws and courts enforce them. But in Judah and Israel those conditions probably did not reliably exist until the ninth or the eighth century B.C.E. The texts themselves also attest less formal legal arrangements prior to centralization, arrangements that in fact survived alongside the establishment of courts by kings. Michael Fishbane (1985) has suggested thinking in terms of four stages of legal process: (1) direct appeal to God, often with the use of an oracle or trial by ordeal; (2) decisions ad hoc under the authority of charismatic arbitrators; (3) the collection, systematization, and administration of laws by established authorities; and (4) professional interpretation and lawmaking by lawyers or scribes.

In the absence of witnesses and adversarial or investigative procedures, the first stage of justice prevails. In 1 Samuel 14:40–2 and Joshua 7:16–19, the divine lot (probably a form of dice) identifies Jonathan and Achan as culprits. At Exodus 22:7 and 10, where property entrusted to someone to look after has been lost or stolen, that person can take an oath that he has not misappropriated the property. The assumption is that if he is guilty, he will not dare to take an oath that will include imprecations such as "May God do to me and more also if I have stolen this property." At the second stage we find characters such as Deborah, Samuel, David, and Solomon, who dispense justice in an ad hoc manner. One reason why Absalom was able to stir up a revolt against David was that David was not hearing cases brought to him for arbitration, nor appointing a deputy to do so (2 Samuel 15:2–4). In the previous chapter (2 Samuel 14) a woman is procured to bring a bogus case for David's decision as a means of getting him to recall Absalom to court. We also read of cases being decided by village elders meeting "in the gate." In addition, local customs of crime prevention and law enforcement appear, such as the right of a relative of a murdered person to seek out and kill the murderer (Numbers 35:9–34). These first two two stages are necessarily more concerned with *how* to administer justice than with what laws to administer, because decisions have to be made in particular cases that threaten to fracture small communities. The larger and more complex any group of communities becomes, the greater the tendency toward centralization.

According to 2 Chronicles 19:4–11, the Judean king Jehoshaphat (ca. 871–848 B.C.E.) placed judges in the fortified cities of Judah and charged them to administer justice impartially. Whenever these courts were established, they probably administered laws that existed as local oral traditions, taking them into account as they formulated their own decisions. Written collections of customs, decrees, and decisions eventually made possible the interpretation and extension of the scope of existing laws. In Exodus 23:11b, the words "you shall do the same with" extend the law about leaving fields fallow to include vineyards and olive orchards; in Exodus 22:9, the words "or any other loss" extend the scope of a law about entrusting animals to another's care. As scribal administrative activity increased in Judah and Israel,

JUSTICE IN THE GATE

The Hebrew word *sha'ar* refers to the entire gate complex of a walled city and the open area adjacent to it. Gates controlled access to the city, shutting out marauders and wild animals at night. As the weakest point in a city's defensive wall system, gates were often fortified with towers, equipped with multiple doors, secured with great bars of iron, and protected by guard rooms within the complex. But the gate served an important role in community life beyond its utility for protection and defense.

City gates also became preferred sites of many social, administrative, and business transactions in the ancient world. Much like the Greek agora or the Roman forum, the Near Eastern city's gate was the center of public discourse, where communal issues could be negotiated. Abraham bargained at the Hittites' city gate for the cave at Machpelah (Genesis 23); the fugitive requesting admission to a

city of refuge was first interrogated by the community's leaders at the gate (Joshua 20:4). The gate served as the place where legal transactions took place (Ruth 4:1) as well as the site where some public punishments were administered (Deuteronomy 17:5, 21:19). The square (oftentimes a threshing floor) inside the city gate was a natural place to congregate, functioning as a central marketplace. By metonymy, the gate has the connotation of "community" or "assembly" (see Ruth 3:11, *kol sha'ar 'ammi*, "all the gate of my people").

Especially in Canaanite cities, the gate was the seat of the community's elders. A text from Ugarit refers to the hero Dan'el, who "sits in front of the gate, by the dignitaries who are on the threshing floor" (2 Aqhat 5:6–7). Those who "go in at the gate" (Genesis 23:10, 18) are city fathers, who have an authoritative voice in the affairs of the community. According to 1 Kings

22:10, Jehoshaphat, king of Judah, and the king of Israel also sat, "each on his throne, at the threshing floor at the entrance of the gate of Samaria."

From the gate, kings and elders meted out justice to the people (Deuteronomy 21:9; Joshua 20:4). The gate was the place of judicial decision making, analogous to the modern-day courtroom. Prophets often launched their invectives against official corruption from vantage points near the city gate, that is, near the site of the offense in the hearing of those being indicted. Proverbs 22:22 warns against robbing the poor and crushing the afflicted at the gate. Amos lashes out against leaders who despise honest judgment. He says, "They hate him who reproves in the gate, and they abhor him who speaks the truth" (5:10). The prophet calls for his listeners to "hate evil, and love good, and establish justice in the gate" (5:15).

drafting law became an end in itself, a way for scribes to exercise their craft and broaden their influence apart from the practicalities of legal proceedings. Moshe Weinfeld (1972), of the Hebrew University in Jerusalem, has argued that, in their final form, the collections of laws in Deuteronomy come from a wisdom school of scribes who were attempting to articulate a particular ideology rather than engaging in legal practice.

Israel's Laws: The Ten Commandments, the Book of the Covenant, and the Holiness Code

The Hebrew Bible presents the Ten Commandments, as they are traditionally known, in two versions (Exodus 20:1–17 and Deuteronomy 5:6–21) that differ from one another. For example, Exodus 20:10–11 and Deuteronomy 5:13–15 give two different reasons why Israelites should observe the Sabbath (or seventh day). In Exodus, God's rest on the seventh day after creating the world demands a like response from his people. Deuteronomy, however, says that because God freed the Israelites from slavery in Egypt, Israelites must treat their own servants humanely by allowing them to rest on the Sabbath. There are many smaller differences as well; comparing the two texts, side by side, quickly reveals interesting deviations.

To this day, religious traditions disagree over how the commandments should be numbered. Orthodox Jews take the first commandment to be Exodus 20:2: "I am the LORD your God"; and the second to be 20:3: "you shall have no other gods before me." Christians take 20:3 as the first commandment, with the previous verse as a preamble. But Christians disagree about whether verses 4–6 (which concern idolatry) continue the first commandment (as the Catholic and Lutheran traditions maintain) or whether verses 4–6 are the second commandment (the Reformed Protestant position). (The basic issue in the Christian dispute turns on whether the word "them" in verse 5 ["you shall not bow down to them"] refers back to the idols of verse 4 or to the other gods of verse 3.) These disagreements caution against taking the Ten Commandments in any one form as a distillation of the Torah. After all, in Exodus 34:38 Moses does not write "the Ten Commandments" on tablets, but "the words of the covenant, ten words." Furthermore, the commandments at issue in Exodus 34 (vv. 14-26, probably from the Yahwist source) are different again from what are traditionally called the Ten Commandments in content, order, and enumeration.

Differences among versions of commandments within the Torah itself and disagreements about how to number them in later traditions suggest that they had a long history before reaching their present form (one embedded within material from the Elohist source, and the other within material from the Deuteronomist). The Ten Commandments of Exodus 20 and Deuteronomy 5 naturally fall into two sections. The first (Exodus 20:2–11; Deuteronomy 5:6–15) deals with Israel's duty to God: his exclusive claim upon them, the prohibition of idolatry and of making wrong use of God's name, and the commandment to observe the Sabbath. The remaining commandments concern interhuman relationships, enjoining the honor of one's parents while forbidding murder, adultery, theft, giving false evidence, and coveting.

Scholars do not agree regarding the origin and date of the Ten Commandments, although there is a consensus that they evolved over a long time. A precise chronology is not likely to be agreed on in view of the dearth of information concerning the specific issues the commandments address. For example, although we know that the Sabbath was observed after the exile (in the sixth century B.C.E.), we do not know to what extent it was kept or how it was viewed prior to the exile. Does this mean that there was no Sabbath commandment until the sixth century B.C.E.? That possibility has seemed likely to some scholars, yet the "ten words" of Exodus 34:38 include a version of the Sabbath commandment, albeit in a form and order different from the other versions (34:21), so uncertainty remains. Then again, Exodus 20:4 forbids the making of idols, but idols have been found in ancient Israel from the ninth century B.C.E. onward, and 1 Kings 7:23–39 carefully describes images near the altar of Solomon's Temple. Does this mean that the commandment against idolatry did not exist prior to the exile? If kept by a few Israelites, was it otherwise unknown or ignored? Were the idols archaeologists discovered used only by non-Israelites? Were idols prohibited only when *worship* of them, rather than of the God of Israel, was involved? Or did official religion differ from popular religion, and did both exist independent of Israel as portrayed in the Scriptures? All those possibilities need to be kept in mind when grappling with what the texts meant and how far they influenced behavior on the ground at any given time.

By virtue of their lack of specificity the commandments address Israel in many different situations, and that helps account for their centrality in biblical tradition as well as in Judaism and Christianity. They remind the people Israel of their delivery from foreign bondage, enjoin them to be loyal to Yahweh in the manner of ancient suzerainty treaties, and lay down basic rules for maintaining religious and social life. The commandments fit the time of Moses (although they presuppose settled agricultural life and the possession of servants) and also comport with the relative independence of Judah from Assyria in the reign of Josiah (640–609 B.C.E.) and offer guidance for the return from exile (around 520 B.C.E.).

The so-called Book of the Covenant (whose decrees appear in Exodus 20:23–23:19; for the name, see Exodus 24:7) is generally regarded as among the oldest collection of laws in the Hebrew Bible and is divided into two main parts: (1) 21:1–22:20 (22:19 in the Hebrew Bible), and (2) 22:21 (22:20 in the Hebrew Bible)–23:19. The first part deals with three main subjects: slavery (21:2–6 and 7–11), injuries to persons (21:12–17 and 18–32), and injuries to property (21:33–22:15 [22:14 in the Hebrew Bible] and 22:16–20 [22:15–19 in the Hebrew Bible]). The second part consists of categorical commandments, that is, commandments that apply to all persons and situations regardless of circumstances. These are in contrast to the presentation of the first part, in which the commandments are mostly casuistic, carefully defining the circumstances in which the laws apply.

Exodus 22:28 (22:27 in the Hebrew Bible) provides an example of a categorical law from the second part of the Book of the Covenant:

You shall not revile God, nor curse a leader of your people.

Exodus 21:33–4 represents a typical casuistic law from the first part of the Book of the Covenant:

> If someone leaves a pit open, or digs a pit and does not cover it, and an ox or a donkey falls into it, the owner of the pit shall make restitution.

While the first part of the Book of the Covenant is almost entirely secular, the second part introduces cultic regulations, mixing them with injunctions that are designed to protect the weak. Exodus 23:12 presents a good example, a striking version of the command to rest on the seventh day:

> Six days you shall do your work, but on the seventh day you shall rest; that your ox and your donkey may have relief, and your homeborn slave and the resident may be refreshed.

Editorial activity is apparent within the first part of the Book of the Covenant. Exodus 21:22 prescribes the penalty for a man who accidentally injures a pregnant woman, stating that he should be fined "what the woman's husband demands." An editorial addition brings this penalty under the scope of the court: "paying as much as the judges determine." Three verses (Exodus 21:15–17) stand out prominently in the first part, because they are categorical laws surrounded by casuistic laws:

> Whoever strikes father or mother shall be put to death.
> Whoever kidnaps a person . . . shall be put to death.
> Whoever curses father or mother shall be put to death.

The most likely explanation for this placement of hybrid materials is that an editor inserted an independent group of categorical laws into a context dealing with injuries against persons.

The two parts of the Book of the Covenant, with their quite different emphases, probably originated as separate collections. The first part contains examples of Israel's secular law, reflecting a legal tradition common in the ancient Near East. These regulations are reminiscent of the laws of Hammurabi (see *Ancient Near Eastern Texts*, p. 176, laws 245–53), which dealt with dangerous oxen, damage to property, and property entrusted to another's care. The second part (along with Exodus 34:17–26) defines the life of a group of people in relation to belief in a God who freed his people from slavery. They are not to follow the religious practices of their neighbors, and their common life should be characterized by compassion for anyone or anything that can be exploited (including domestic animals, wild beasts, fields, vineyards, and olive orchards). This compassion will imitate the compassion shown by God in freeing Israel from slavery.

Although these two parts of the Book of Covenant may not have been combined and incorporated into the Sinai narrative until the seventh century B.C.E., they are certainly older than that in their constituent elements. Hints of local adjudication rather than court-administered justice (e.g., Exodus 21:22) may suggest the period of the early monarchy for the first part, while the second part could be even earlier. In their present context, however, these

DIVINATION

Divination, the practice of seeking information from superhuman powers by physical means, was a common feature of life in the ancient Near East. Diviners examined the progression of heavenly bodies or meteorological events and engaged in deliberative procedures such as shooting arrows and reading the significance of how they fell, casting lots, and seeking communication with the dead (necromancy).

Ancient Babylon developed the art of soothsaying until it became a widespread, socially important, and quasi-scientific discipline. In classical antiquity, the name "Chaldean" (an ethnic designation for citizens of the Neo-Babylonian Empire) became synonymous with "magician" (see Daniel 1:4, 5:11). Babylonian diviners excelled mainly in the field of hepatoscopy, that is, the examination of livers from sacrificial animals. In Mesopotamian thought, the liver was considered the seat of life, an ideal vehicle for discerning the will and intentions of the gods. Large collections of model livers have been discovered from every time and place in which Babylon and Assyria held sway in the ancient world. These aids were designed for the training of novices,

as well as for the discussion of difficult cases among experts. They attest the extent, importance, and professionalism of hepatoscopy. This branch of divination was also a common practice in ancient Mari, in both state and private affairs.

As was the case with magical practices generally, divination came to be forbidden to the Israelites (Leviticus 19:26; Deuteronomy 18:11). Israel's refusal of magic and divination became an important marker of its unique status and belief among other peoples of the area (e.g., Canaanites and Philistines) and the great surrounding nations of the ancient Near East (Egypt, Babylon, and Assyria). The Israelites believed that Yahweh communicated his will to them, but only through carefully prescribed channels. Israel's developing theology drew a sharp contrast between attempts to foretell the future by artificial means and legitimate, divinely inspired prophecy (Deuteronomy 18:14–15). Prophets become the chief opponents of divination, tireless in their battle against magical practices, which were often widespread in the land of Israel (Micah 3:7; Isaiah 44:25; Ezekiel 12:24).

Nonetheless, an earlier epoch in Israelite history – when divination was freely practiced – has left its mark on the Hebrew Bible. Shaking and dropping lots or shooting arrows as a means of discerning God's will appears to be the background for incidents in the lives of David and Jonathan (1 Samuel 20) and of Joash (2 Kings 13). Specific locations were associated with the practice of divination, especially sacred trees (for example, the diviners' oak, Judges 9:37, which is perhaps reflected also in the story of Abraham at Mamre, Genesis 12:6). Isaiah 57:3 suggests that Israel's soothsayers were eventually organized into a professional caste. No less a personage than King Saul resorted to the medium at Endor to summon the dead prophet Samuel when there had been no answer from the LORD in dreams, divination by Urim and Thummin, and prophecy (1 Samuel 28).

Israel's cult also involved communication from God by means of the obscure Urim and Thummim, a form of divination by lots with wide precedent throughout human history. The ephod and teraphim, whose exact identification is also unclear, were also used to obtain information from God (Zechariah 10:2; Hosea 3:4).

traditions are not meant to be a comprehensive version of Israel's laws. They are illustrative; even the secular first part begins with laws about slavery in order to make the point that Israel is to be a free people, and that when slavery occurs (usually because of debt), its effects must be limited.

Leviticus 17–26 represents another collection of laws, usually called "the Holiness Code." The scholarly designation "code" gives the false impression of an official law code that was centrally enforced throughout Israel. By content, style, and purpose, this "Code" appears much more to be a programmatic – sometimes utopian – vision than a book of case law; its similarity to visionary parts of the Book of Ezekiel confirm that impression. These chapters were, in all probability, composed during the fifth century B.C.E. and betray a priestly origin. In contrast, the Book of the Covenant never mentions priests. Another signal difference is that Exodus 22:31 (22:30 in the Hebrew Bible) says that the flesh of an animal corpse found in open country may not be eaten by humans, while Leviticus 17:14–16 prescribes a ritual for anyone who eats the flesh of an animal that died naturally or was killed by other animals. Several sections of Leviticus (e.g., 21:1–22:9) deal with priests and the special regulations that govern their lives. The two collections overlap where they deal with respect for parents, the treatment of slaves, and the observance of festivals. However, the emphasis of Leviticus 17–26 differs from that of the Book of the Covenant (Exodus 21–23). In Leviticus, the purpose of regulated order is for God's blessing to rest upon the land: God's holiness requires a strict separation between priests and the people, and between Israel and other peoples.

Chapters 19 and 25 of Leviticus deal with social matters. The core of chapter 19 is verses 11–18 and 26–36; in them we find the concern about protecting those who are vulnerable that has already been noted in the Book of the Covenant. One of the two great commandments in the New Testament – "you shall love your neighbor as yourself" – is found at verse 18, another example of material from an ancient collection whose purpose was to order the life of a group as the people of Yahweh.

Leviticus 25 begins with the charge to let the land lie fallow in the seventh year – a theological ideal enshrining the number seven (as in the days of the week) rather than an agricultural necessity, because to be effective fallowing needs to take place much more frequently than once in seven years. Regulations about the seventh year then lead to laws about the fiftieth year (following the multiple of seven times seven), the Jubilee, the year in which all property purportedly reverted to the original owners, and all slaves were supposedly released. There are also regulations designed to ease the hardship of those obliged to raise loans (by prohibiting interest) or to become hired servants. Whether or not the Jubilee was ever really observed, and if so, over how much territory within Israel, its importance as a theological statement remains. This chapter recognizes that, with time, inequalities caused by such accidental factors as variation in climate, illness, and vermin, as well as by economic conditions, made some people dependent upon others, sometimes losing their land and then their freedom in the process. The Jubilee is there to counteract these inequalities. The loss of freedom that they bring is not tolerable over the long term in a society that was once enslaved and then delivered by God. Israel's law made a statement about the kind of common life that God requires as it regulated legal practice.

5. From Sinai to the Land

In Numbers 10:11–33:48 Israel makes its epic migration from Mount Sinai to the plains of Moab, where Moses later in the narrative speaks to the Israelites the words known to us as the Book of Deuteronomy. Prior to that journey, the people remain encamped at Mount Sinai (Exodus 25:1–Numbers 10:10), where they receive priestly legislation (principally, although not entirely, contained in Leviticus), as well as instructions about

---

TENT AND TABERNACLE

The "Tent of Meeting" is mentioned some one hundred thirty times in the Hebrew Bible. Known also as the "Tent of the Testimony," the "Tent of Yahweh," or simply "the Tent," this is where Yahweh was thought to meet Moses and Israel in the desert after the revelation on Mount Sinai or Horeb. In some accounts this portable sanctuary is called the "tabernacle" – mishkan, from the Hebrew verb shakan, meaning "to dwell" – since it was the structure in which Yahweh dwelled among his people.

Exodus 25–31 contains an elaborate description of the desert tabernacle, specifying its pattern and placement, as well as the mode of and timetable for erecting this portable sanctuary. Exodus 35–40 reports the successful completion of these instructions (although there are some differences here in the details of assembly). These chapters in Exodus portray the tabernacle as an ornate portable sanctuary whose overall dimensions were 45 × 15 × 15 feet. The tabernacle was a tent consisting of ten embroidered linen curtains covered by layers of dyed animal skins and supported by a series of forty-eight frames made of acacia wood. The final covering was dyed an unusual red. Inside, the tabernacle was partitioned into two rooms, forming an outer and an inner chamber. The latter was known as the "holy of holies" and was separated from the outer chamber by a thick veil. In the outer chamber stood the table of presence ("shewbread" in the King James Version), the golden lampstand with seven branches, and probably an altar of incense. The inner sanctuary held the ark of the covenant, covered by the mercy seat and guarded by two griffinlike cherubim with outstretched wings.

The biblical text provides no detailed description of the tabernacle between the time Israel entered the land and David decided to bring the ark to Jerusalem. During that long period, the ark of the covenant had remained temporarily at Shechem, between Mount Gerizim and Mount Ebal (Joshua 8:30–5, 24), and later in a more permanent structure at Shiloh (Psalm 78:60; Joshua 18:1; 19:51), although other texts have God speak of moving around "from tent to tent," as if several more locations were involved (1 Chronicles 17:5; cf. 2 Samuel 7:6). The priestly tabernacle in Exodus 25–31, then, may well represent a projection into the past of the details of the tent that David built to house the ark of the covenant in his new capital. In that case, David's tent would symbolize his attempt to integrate Mosaic traditions within elements from the culture of Jerusalem. This tent, as described in Exodus 25–31 and 35–40, was a transitional structure, intermediary between the simple, portable container that held Israel's most sacred artifacts and Solomon's more permanent and elaborate Temple.

---

making a portable sanctuary (Exodus 25–7, 35–40), the arrangement of the clans into parties for the journey, and the organization of the Levites (Numbers 1–4). The material from Exodus 25 to the end of Numbers has a complex literary history and reached its final form during and after the exile (between the sixth and fifth centuries B.C.E.). This tradition articulates key theological statements, especially by means of narrating archetypal incidents: the golden calf (Exodus 32, 34), the mission of the spies (Numbers 13–15), the people's rejection of Moses (detailed in various passages), the bronze serpent (Numbers 21:4–9), and the stories of Balaam (Numbers 22–4).

In the story of the golden calf, Moses lingers on Mount Sinai so long that the people ask Aaron to make gods "who shall go before us." Aaron tells the people to give him their golden jewelry, which he melts down to make a statue of a calf. The people cry out:

These are your gods, O Israel, who brought you up out of the land of Egypt. (Exodus 32:4)

Aaron builds an altar and proclaims a feast to Yahweh (32:5), completing the narrative image of surreal idolatry.

This story provokes many questions. How does it relate to the setting up of golden calves at Bethel and Dan by Jeroboam (931–910 B.C.E.) when he revolted against the house of David, together with his proclamation that these were the gods that delivered Israel from Egypt (1 Kings 12:28)? Does the proclamation of a feast for Yahweh reflect a time in Israel when Yahweh was believed to be enthroned on a bull? Given the prominent role of Aaron in the apostasy, does the narrative imply that the priesthood of Israel tends inevitably toward idolatry? Tentative answers to these questions may be provided by iconographic evidence, which shows a marked falloff in the representation of calves during Iron Age II (ninth century B.C.E.) compared with the Late Bronze Age and Iron Age I (1350–900 B.C.E.; see the data collected by Keel and Uehlinger, 1992). This suggests that Jeroboam during the tenth century B.C.E. was appealing to traditional religion, rather than introducing something new to Israel, when he set up his northern alternative to the Temple in Jerusalem. The story of the golden calf probably does have Jeroboam in mind, and so denounces the rebellious northern kingdom and the idolatry it embodied. Priesthood is therefore criticized to the extent that it tolerates or endorses the kind of deviation from the worship of Yahweh that Jeroboam and other kings who attempted to introduce idolatry represented.

The theological message of the story is pointed. The people of Israel are portrayed as unreliable recipients of divine redemption. This apostasy does not involve the turning away from God by the children or grandchildren of those delivered from slavery long ago. Rather, recently freed slaves who should have been grateful for their deliverance – and who had themselves said, "All that the LORD has spoken we will do, and we will be obedient" (Exodus 24:7) – rebel against God. The whole incident reflects the experience of Israel's leaders that the people's loyalty to God could prove fragile. Yet the fact that the covenant is renewed despite having been broken so quickly holds out hope for later Israelites faced with crises such as the exile. (And the story as edited may well be in part a response to the exile.) Exodus 34 appears to renew the Ten Commandments as the basis for the covenant, although commentators continue to dispute how some of these commands (e.g., Exodus 34:17–28) can be reconciled with the traditional listing (which derives, as we have seen, from Exodus 20 and Deuteronomy 5). Be that as it may, the covenant is renewed, but not before three thousand men have been executed by Moses and the Levites (Exodus 32:25–35).

The mission of the spies (Numbers 13–15) continues to explore the theme of the fragile loyalty of the freed Israelites. The spies, one from each clan group, visit the land of Canaan and bring back a gloomy report:

> The land that we have gone through as spies is a land that devours its inhabitants; and all the people that we saw in it are of great size . . . and to ourselves we seemed like grasshoppers, and so we seemed to them. (Numbers 13:32–3)

The people respond to this disheartening news with a renewed outcry that expresses their regret that they had left Egypt. They even plan to choose someone who will lead them back to Egypt (Numbers 14:4). Only Moses' intercession persuades God not to disinherit the people. Nonetheless, God resolves that none of the generation that left Egypt will enter Canaan – except for Joshua and Caleb, two spies who brought back good reports. Here again a classic narrative brings hope to Israelites in situations where the obstinacy of the people seems to annul the purposes of God. Yet the section ends with a sting in its tail. The people suddenly decide that they will, after all, try to occupy Canaan. But they try to do so without God's help and against Moses' advice (Numbers 14:35–44); their subsequent defeat ironically bears out what the gloomy report of the spies had warned.

Moses himself features among those condemned not to enter the Promised Land because the people turned from God. He suffers a double rejection: by the people and by God. The first rejection begins early (Exodus 2), when a Hebrew reminds Moses that he killed an Egyptian. The plague stories involving the pharoah (e.g., Exodus 5:20–1) and the journey to Sinai see that pattern deepen. The making of the golden calf constitutes yet another rejection, while at Numbers 12, Aaron and his sister Miriam reprove Moses, and in Numbers 16, Korah, Dathan, and Abiram rebel against Moses. The theme of the rejection of the servant of God also figures prominently in prophetic literature, especially in Jeremiah and in the song about the Servant of God in Isaiah 52:13–53:12. This literary pattern no doubt reflects the experience of those who tried to be faithful to God and to guide Israel toward faithfulness. The fact that Moses also suffered in this endeavor gave hope to subsequent prophets. Further, Moses – like the prophets – undergoes suffering in a way that at least partially deflects the divine judgment against the people who had been unfaithful. Not only is Moses denied entry to Canaan, but he also wishes he could die (Numbers 11:15). His prayers are full of urgency and pathos (Numbers 11:11–15, 14:13–19), and all that he endures serves to fulfill the promise made to Abraham of his territorial inheritance.

The story of the bronze serpent (Numbers 21:4–9) begins with the complaint of the Israelites; once again they regret that they ever left Egypt. The setting marks a new phase of the journey; the king of Edom having denied them passage through his territory, Israel travels east of Edom (Numbers 20:14–21). In response to the people's complaint, God sends fiery serpents (Hebrew *nehashim seraphim*) among them. The bites of these snakes are fatal, and the people repent and ask for help. God commands Moses to make a fiery serpent and put it on a pole. When the bronze serpent has been made, it brings healing to any person who has been bitten and who looks at it.

This passage has evident links with 2 Kings 18:4, where King Hezekiah destroys the bronze serpent that Moses had made because the people burned incense to it. Similar imagery also appears in Isaiah 6:1–3, where the heavenly attendants of God are described as winged *seraphim*. Winged serpents, in origin an Egyptian symbol of protection, are found on seals in both Judah and Israel from the eighth century B.C.E. The relationship between this evidence and the biblical passages is a matter for surmise, but it does seem that a bronze serpent, pagan in origin, had been venerated in

Jerusalem. Hezekiah destroyed this image during his reform at the end of the eighth century in order to remove an incitement to idolatry from the context of worship. Yet this measure obviously did not eliminate the representation of this protective symbol on personal seals; it had become a part of centuries-old traditional practice. The Numbers 21 story must date from before this reform, and provided an Israelite justification for worshipping an object that was originally a pagan cultic figure.

Within the context of Numbers 21:4–10, this narrative makes several points. The punishment of the people is reminiscent of the plagues in Egypt that were occasioned by pharaoh's obstinacy. Their deliverance, when granted, is not a blanket remedy. The story implies that Israelites who did not look at the bronze serpent died as a consequence of bites from the *nehashim seraphim*. The people who lived were those who trusted in Moses, in God's commandment, and obeyed.

KUNTILLET 'AJRUD

Archaeological excavation in 1975 of a small site in the Negev near what would have been the southern border of the Judean kingdom uncovered a building complex that was occupied for a short time during the mid-ninth century B.C.E. Nearby roads connecting Kadesh-barnea in southern Judah with Elat and the lower Sinai suggest the reason for this installation at Kuntillet 'Ajrud. Some finds underline the importance of trade: shells from the Red Sea and the Mediterranean, branches of cedar and sycamore wood, and the wood of pistachios, which grow only in southern Sinai. Unlike any other known Negev fortress of the Israelite period, Kuntillet 'Ajrud ("the solitary hill of the water wells") does not seem to have served a military purpose. The site appears to have been a commercial and religious center that may have had some connection with journeys by the Judean kings to Ezion-geber, the Israelite port on the Red Sea. The center is somewhat reminiscent of the Israelite traditions concerning Sinai. Travelers could pray at the holy place, each to his own god, asking a divine blessing for his journey.

Material unearthed at Kuntillet 'Ajrud bears witness to the close association of Israelite religion with the cultic beliefs, practices, and artistic representations of the wider region. The site includes the remains of two structures. The more important building measures approximately 25 × 15 meters. Its walls were apparently painted with colorful floral motifs. An entryway led from a small court into a long room that provided the site's most important finds. The room had benches along the walls that took up most of the floor space, indicating that they represented the room's main function. At each end this "bench room" was connected by a small passageway to compartments that served as *favissae*, depositories for the sacred offering vessels that had initially been placed on the benches and had then been removed and replaced by new gifts.

The finds at Kuntillet 'Ajrud are especially important because they included a large number of inscriptions from the biblical period – a time frame from which the remains of written records are otherwise scanty. The few writings that survive elsewhere in Palestine from the time of the first Temple deal with political and administrative matters. The inscriptions from Kuntillet 'Ajrud include dedications, prayers, and blessings that were incised on pottery and stone or written with ink on plaster. Among the inscriptions is an enigmatic reference to Yahweh and to his consort ("Asherah").

Several large storage jars that were found bear a variety of drawings and designs. Figures of gods, people, and animals appear. Among the crudely drawn pictures are representations of male and female deities, a cultic procession, a tree of life flanked by two ibexes, and a cow licking the tail of a suckling calf. Such designs were common in art in the region. They suggest a large degree of integration of the traditions and practices of Israel within wider Iron Age culture.

About a hundred cloth fragments (mostly linen, with some wool) were also found at Kuntillet 'Ajrud, the only regional remains of textiles from the monarchic period available to date.

Chapters 22–4 of Numbers narrate the Balaam stories. Their setting is the plains of Moab on the east side of the Jordan opposite Jericho, where the presence of the Israelites puts fear into the Moabites and causes their king, Balak, to send for the pagan oracle Balaam to come and curse the Israelites. The implication is that Balaam is a powerful seer whose oracles convey genuine visionary perception. His location "near the River" (i.e., the Euphrates), some four hundred miles away, indicates that Balak went to enormous lengths to acquire Balaam's services. Balaam will not make the journey until he is sure that it is God's will. On arrival he delivers four oracles, three of which bless the Israelites instead of cursing them, and the fourth of which curses the enemies of Israel, including Moab. References to Israel's neighbors raise the question of the oracles' date. The fourth oracle (24:15–24) mentions Moab, Edom, Amalek, and the Kenites, and refers to an Assyrian captivity suffered by Kain as well as ships from Kittim afflicting Asshur and Eber. Proposed dates for this speech range from the twelfth century B.C.E. (De Moor seeing a reference to the invasion of the Sea Peoples) to the postexilic period (sixth to fifth centuries B.C.E.).

Possible light on the stories of Balaam has been shed by the discovery of an inscription at Tell Deir Alla (biblical Succoth in Transjordan). Dated around 700 B.C.E., it clearly mentions Balaam the son of Beor (cf. Numbers 22:5), although its fragmentary nature and its language make interpretation difficult. As translated by Hans-Peter Müller, the opening lines read:

> This is the inscription of [Balaam the son of Beor], the man who sees the gods. See [?], the gods came to him by night [. . .] and they spoke to Balaam the son of Beor as follows.

The remainder of the inscription (another 23 lines) tells of the gathering of an assembly, but its purpose is not clear. The opening has similarities with Numbers 22:20 ("That night God came to Balaam") and perhaps explains the problematic Hebrew phrase at 24:3, "the man whose eye is clear." An expression toward the end of the inscription, which speaks of cosmic disruption, is reminiscent of the enigmatic words of Numbers 24:17: "a star shall proceed from Jacob." A reasonable assumption is that the Balaam stories are based on traditions about a non-Israelite prophet, an example of which has come to light in the Deir Alla finds. In context, the Balaam oracles show how even a non-Israelite prophet is sensitive to the word of the God of Israel, and how his words assure future blessing for Israel on their way to the Promised Land. Numbers 32 then tells of the conquering of those parts of Transjordan that were to be occupied by Reuben and Gad.

6. The Deuteronomic Law

The Social and Religious World of the Deuteronomists

The identity, origin, and history of the Deuteronomists are probably the most complex and keenly argued subjects in Hebrew Bible scholarship. The controversy involves not only the Book of Deuteronomy, but also the Deuteronomistic History (in English Bibles, the Books of Joshua to 2 Kings minus Ruth, so called because of the vocabulary and ideas distinctive to the Book of Deuteronomy that occur in Joshua through 2 Kings). In what follows, the term "Deuteronomists" will be used, as in the heading, to describe successive generations of Israelites whose literature and outlook received classical expression in the Book of Deuteronomy and in the definitive form of the Deuteronomistic History. The debate turns on the following questions: How did the Deuteronomistic History reach its present form? Was it composed by a single author in the exilic period (sixth century B.C.E.), or did a substantial first draft exist by the time of King Hezekiah (late eighth century B.C.E.) or of King Josiah (late seventh century B.C.E.)? How did the Book of Deuteronomy reach its present form; how and when was it linked to the Deuteronomistic History? Did the Deuteronomistic History receive the attention of several editors in the postexilic period (sixth to fifth centuries B.C.E.)? The sketch that follows draws on the views of scholars of differing opinions.

The Deuteronomists were probably first active in the northern kingdom of Israel. Deuteronomy itself envisages a ceremony of blessing and cursing on Mounts Ebal and Gerizim (Deuteronomy 27) and, although the relation of this material to the rest of the book remains a matter of debate, the intention of the text comes through clearly: on entering the land of Canaan the people are to assemble at or near Shechem, in the heartland of what became the northern kingdom. The Deuteronomistic History provides other indications of northern origins. The Book of Judges makes virtually no mention of Judah and concentrates mostly on northern leaders. In the Books of Kings, stories about the northern bands of prophets led by Elijah and Elisha dominate the text from 1 Kings 17 until 2 Kings 10. References of this kind do not amount to proof of the northern origins of the Deuteronomists; but if the Deuteronomists were Judahites, their recourse to so many northern traditions would pose an anomaly.

Yet inferring a northern origin for the Deuteronomists creates a problem of its own. To what social group would these determined editors have belonged? Did they start among a group of prophets comparable to the adherents of Elijah? If so, how did they – unlike the groups around Elijah and Elisha – acquire the ability to record traditions and produce literature? Were they Levites, in which case where did they fit into the religious setup in Israel with its anti-Judahite alternative to the Temple in Jerusalem? Could they have represented prominent members of the Israelite administration such as Obadiah, who, according to 1 Kings 18:3–16, sided with the prophets against Ahab and Jezebel?

The last suggestion would explain why there were written traditions about leaders and prophets in the northern kingdom. But how would such administrators or their supporters have been able to come to Judah, as we must infer they did for their written work to survive, after the destruction of the northern kingdom by the Assyrians in 722–721 B.C.E.? We can do no more than make informed suppositions, although by coordinating other evidence with the biblical texts, our inferences increase in their plausibility. Archaeology has shown there was a large increase in population in Jerusalem at the end of the eighth century B.C.E.; if that was due to people moving down to Judah from the former northern kingdom, we may suppose that the guardians of the northern traditions were among them. If they were connected with the scribal, administrative class from the northern kingdom, they would have linked up with the Jerusalem scribal elite. There they began a literary enterprise whose aim was to describe the history of Israel from presettlement times to the time of Hezekiah from the point of view of those loyal to Yahweh and Moses. This history aimed to show that Judah now represented Israel as a whole, and to press the claims of Jerusalem to be the capital of Israel and of the Davidic ruler to be king of all Israel. That design demanded recourse to a strong view of prophetic rather than political authority, because Judah had in fact been only marginally significant in the story of Israel, for most of the ninth and part of the eighth centuries B.C.E. amounting to a mere vassal state of the stronger kingdom of Israel ruled from Samaria.

Hezekiah's bold policy (ca. 727–698 B.C.E.) asserted the independence of Judah, rather than dependence upon Assyria, which had been the policy of Ahaz, Hezekiah's father. The arrival of the Deuteronomists in Judah, with their strong teaching of devotion to Yahweh alone, encouraged Hezekiah's religious reform, as well as the articulation of Judah's identity as the true heir of all Israel in literature and storytelling. Yet at the close of his reign, Hezekiah was defeated by the Assyrians; although Jerusalem itself escaped capture, Judahite independence was lost for much of the seventh century (from around 700 until 627 B.C.E.). During this period, Assyrian influence upon Judahite iconography is demonstrable, for example in a noticeable increase in astral imagery that represented divine powers with symbols derived from the night sky. There was also a tendency to represent gods in human form; Asherah, in the previous period a life-giving object in the form of a tree, took on human characteristics. The Deuteronomists must have kept a low profile for a couple of generations, waiting for the time when they could influence the whole nation with their particular type of faith in Yahweh.

Their opportunity came after the death of Manasseh (in 642 B.C.E.), the accession of his grandson Josiah (in 640 B.C.E.), and the waning of Assyrian power. According to 2 Kings 22:8, "the book of the law" was discovered in the Temple during its repair under Josiah's orders (in 622 B.C.E.). As a result of this discovery the king gathered the representatives of the nation, and a covenant between the people and Yahweh was solemnized (2 Kings 23:1–3). There then followed a reform in which the Temple was cleansed of vessels made for Baal, Asherah, and other gods; places of worship other than Jerusalem were destroyed; and the Passover was celebrated as a national festival rather than as a household feast. It has long been held that the scroll of the law found in the Temple was Deuteronomy, or part of it; but the "discovery" and its implications need to be considered further to appreciate the impact of the Deuteronomists on the whole shape of the Hebrew Bible.

The correspondence between Deuteronomy's demand for the centralization of worship and the actions carried out as Josiah's reform is too close

THE CULT OF ASHERAH

Some forty references to the cult of the old Canaanite fertility goddess Asherah appear in the Hebrew Bible. This deity is known from mythological texts at Ugarit as the consort of El, chief god of Canaan's pantheon. In the Bible, her appearance often seems confusing. Because Semitic gods were conceived of in generally flexible terms, Asherah sometimes appears to be fused with other personifications of a universal mother goddess (e.g., with Anath, consort of the storm and fertility god Baal; or with Ashtar/Astarte, an astral deity also involved in the fertility cycle). Disapproving ancient scribes further confused the situation by deliberately misvocalizing the deity's name, retaining the consonants but substituting the vowels of the Hebrew word *boshet* ("shame") – resulting in the Hebrew "Ashtoreth" (1 Kings 11:5, 33). These terms are slippery, sometimes referring to an enigmatic cult image (perhaps a wooden pole or a tree), sometimes to the goddess herself, and sometimes to the general practice of Canaanite religion. Often the name occurs in a plural form (Hebrew *'ashterot, 'asherim*), suggesting that the goddess was worshipped in various local manifestations. To some of those sites she gave her name (Ashtoroth-Karnaim in Gilead, for example).

Throughout the region archaeologists have unearthed large numbers of small female statuettes that are probably related to the worship of Asherah. Molded of clay, the goddess is usually represented as a naked woman with long hair who holds her breasts, which are exaggerated along with her pudenda. These images have been associated mostly with private residences, suggesting that they are symbols of prayers or vows to the goddess of fertility. Perhaps they were made on the principle of imitative magic, to influence the deity and thus achieve conception.

Some scholars argue that the widespread evidence for the cult of Asherah in the Hebrew Bible is simply another expression of the persistence of Canaanite religious practices among the common folk of early Israel. Far into the later periods of the monarchy, the worship of fertility deities like Asherah even enjoyed official sanction: furnishings for Asherah's use in the Temple of Jerusalem are mentioned in 2 Kings 21:7. Solomon patronized the cult of Asherah (1 Kings 11:5), and she enjoyed a worship place in the Judean royal capital throughout most of the monarchy (2 Kings 23:13). A typical Hebrew blessing found on a tomb inscription at Khirbet el-Qom and similar blessings and some cultic drawings discovered at Kuntillet 'Ajrud suggest that Asherah was even worshipped as Yahweh's female consort. At least in some circles, the Israelite national God Yahweh merely succeeded the Canaanite god El and appropriated El's consort for himself. Apparently this cult was so thoroughly suppressed by the Yahwistic reformers of the eighth to sixth centuries B.C.E. that later interpreters had difficulty understanding allusions to this fertility goddess in the Old Testament.

Because devotion to Asherah is decried in the biblical text, archaeological data become all the more important in illuminating and clarifying the history of worship in Israel. The worship of female fertility deities was common in many cultures of the ancient world (e.g., Ishtar in Mesopotamia, Ashtarath from Phoenicia, Qodshu of Egypt, and Aphrodite and Venus in later Hellenistic and Roman tradition). It is likely that throughout the Judean monarchy, and well into Second Temple times, Israel participated in this rich history of fertility worship.

to suggest that finding the law scroll was a matter of pure happenstance or that 2 Kings 22:3–10 represents a disinterested account of this discovery. The fact is that 2 Kings 22:3–10 is itself part of the Deuteronomistic History and therefore part and parcel of complex interrelationships among the Deuteronomists, the Deuteronomistic History, and the Book of Deuteronomy. There is no reason to doubt that a scroll of the law was found in the Temple during Josiah's program of reform. But it is difficult to believe that the lawbook was hidden by scribes centuries before who had no idea whether or when the scroll would be found, and that, only because it was

THE PRIESTLY BENEDICTION AND THE KETEF HINNOM AMULET

Excavations during the 1970s on a plot of land behind St. Andrew's Church in Jerusalem – overlooking the Hinnom Valley and facing Mount Zion – brought to light one of the most important archaeological discoveries of the modern period. In a burial cave hewn out during the later part of the Judean monarchy a silver amulet was found, inscribed in Hebrew with a fragmentary text virtually identical with Numbers 6:24-6 (known as the priestly benediction).

This amulet or plaque and the finds from the tomb, all of which were excavated in situ, date to the latter part of the seventh century B.C.E. and constitute the earliest text of the Hebrew Bible so far discovered. The next oldest fragments are the Nash Papyrus, which includes a version of the Ten Commandments, and the Dead Sea Scrolls, all of which date to the late Second Temple period.

The amulet text reads: "The Lord bless you and keep you; the Lord make his face shine upon you and be gracious to you; the Lord lift up his countenance upon you and grant you peace." A second silver plaque combines the second and third benedictions of the biblical text with a shortened version of Psalm 67:2.

Aside from the obvious importance of the discovery in itself, it also represents irrefutable evidence that parts of the Hebrew Bible were known in preexilic times and circulating in written form.

accidentally found at precisely the right moment in history, a religious reformation ensued that was guided by this scroll's content.

A more probable reading of the Deuteronomists' triumph takes account of conditions at the time. As Assyrian power weakened during the early part of Josiah's reign, the Deuteronomists began to prepare for independence. By 622 B.C.E. conditions were suitable for reform, including the repair of the Temple and the destruction of idols, actions that featured crucially in a national program in which subservience to Assyria was repudiated and the covenant with Yahweh reigned supreme. This covenant took the form of a loyalty oath, also instanced in international agreements of the period. As part of this process, the scroll of the law was produced from the Temple.

Of what, then, did this scroll of the law consist? Deuteronomy 12–16 and 26 probably represent the nucleus of the book. A new section begins in 12:1, which states, "These are the statutes and ordinances," and the text proceeds with characteristically Deuteronomic provisions. Chapter 16 contains regulations about celebrating the Passover at the central sanctuary (and ends with material comparable to Exodus 34:10–27). It is noteworthy that Deuteronomy 16:21 forbids the planting of "any tree as a sacred pole [Asherah] beside the altar that you make for the LORD your God." The Asherah as a tree symbol was an eighth-century B.C.E. feature, whereas in the seventh century Asherah was more often represented in human form. Deuteronomy 16:21 might therefore be an eighth-century composition and part of the book that was found in the seventh century in the Temple.

If part of Deuteronomy was produced from the Temple and later edited during Josiah's reign, how did the book reach its present form? It probably did so in several stages. First, chapters 12–26 were cast into the form of a lawbook, broadly following the sequence of the Ten Commandments and perhaps intended as a commentary on them. Second, the material was given the form of a loyalty oath by the addition of the historical prologue (chapters 5–11) and the material about making the covenant (chapters 27–8). This version of the book may have been the basis of the covenant between the nation and Yahweh during the time of Josiah.

There is no reason to suppose that the covenant ceremony described in 2 Kings 23:1–3 happened immediately after the discovery of the lawbook. The scroll could have been expanded and used as the basis for the covenant. The correspondence between what was done in the reform and what we find in Deuteronomy does not prove that the reform was based upon Deuteronomy exactly as we know the book. Deuteronomy in its present form is likely based upon the reform, just as an earlier version provided the incentive and pattern for the reform. The final stages of Deuteronomy's growth were a response to the crisis of the falls of Jerusalem to the Babylonians in 597 and 587/6 B.C.E. and their aftermath; the book continued to be written and edited in the sixth century B.C.E. during the exile.

In their present form, both Deuteronomy and the Deuteronomistic History presuppose the fall of Jerusalem and the exile. Deuteronomy is presented as a speech by Moses to the Israelites on the eve of entering the land of Canaan; but it is clear from passages such as Deuteronomy 30:1–4 that the exile has occurred in the experience of those who composed the book:

> When these things have happened to you . . . if you call them to mind among all the nations where the LORD your God has driven you, and return to the LORD your God . . . then the LORD your God will restore your fortunes . . . and gather you again from all the peoples among whom the LORD your God has scattered you . . . and the LORD your God will bring you into the land that your ancestors possessed, and you will possess it.

The Israelites here are either poised to return to the land of Israel or they have returned. Deuteronomy sets out the supreme covenant by which they are to live (the covenant of the plains of Moab), while the Deuteronomistic History is an account of and explanation for the faithlessness that led to the fall of Jerusalem. It was as a result of the exile, then, that Deuteronomy received its framework of chapters 1–4 and 30–34, that the Deuteronomistic History reached its final form, and that Deuteronomy was linked to the Deuteronomistic History, by showing, for example, how Joshua fulfilled the instructions of Deuteronomy 27:1–8 (see Joshua 8:30–5).

The Book of Jeremiah also received its final edition at the hands of Deuteronomists; this finding, together with recent discoveries, sheds new light on the Deuteronomists. On being discovered in the Temple, "the book of the law" was given to Shaphan, the secretary, for transmission to the king. The family of Shaphan clearly extended crucial support to Jeremiah. The prophet's letter to the exiles in Babylon was delivered by Shaphan's son Elasah (Jeremiah 29:3), and when the scroll that Jeremiah had dictated to Baruch was read to the state officials, it was read in the chamber of another of Shaphan's sons, Gemariah. Still another son, Ahikam, protected Jeremiah when he was accused of treason (Jeremiah 26:24), and it was Ahikam's son Gedaliah – appointed governor of Judah by the Babylonians after 586 B.C.E. – who extended his protection to Jeremiah (Jeremiah 40:6-12). The family of Shaphan, then, was an elite group within Judah's administration that remained in close sympathy with Jeremiah, suggesting how the Deuteronomists made their way into positions of influence during the most critical period in the history of Israel.

The Deuteronomists evidently included elite administrative groups in Judah during the seventh and sixth centuries B.C.E., people who were connected to the "discovery" of the lawbook in 622, who supported Jeremiah, and who were not all deported to Babylon after 586. This would explain the elevated, courtly style of Deuteronomy, and its apparent knowledge and use of international forms of agreement such as the oath of loyalty. The Deuteronomists influenced the literature of the Hebrew Bible and shaped the Israelite conception of faith in ways that have only begun to be understood.

The Structure and Theology of Deuteronomy

Deuteronomy divides by topic and content into a number of sections.

DEUTERONOMY 1:1–4:43. This section is the introductory address of Moses to the Israelites, who are assembled on the plains of Moab. Moses rehearses the journey of the people from Mount Horeb (the northern name for the mountain called Sinai in Judah) to the threshold of the Promised Land. It is based on material from Exodus and Numbers, and emphasizes the lack of faith of the people despite God's provision for them. A key verse is 1:27:

> You murmured in your tents, and said, "Because the LORD hated us he has brought us forth out of the land of Egypt, to give us into the hand of the Amorites, to destroy us."

DEUTERONOMY 4:44–11:32. This section places the Ten Commandments in a prominent position (5:1–22) and then combines other injunctions with incidents from the period of the wilderness wanderings to serve as object lessons. Among the incidents related are the worship of the golden calf (9:6–21), the miracle at the Red Sea (11:2–4), and the rebellion of Dathan and Abiram (11:6).

Within this section a theology of grace emphasizes that God did not choose Israel or deliver the people from bondage because they were deserving, but saved them because of his love for them and because of his oath to their fathers (7:6–10). On this view God did not enable Israel to enter Canaan because of Israel's righteousness but to punish the wickedness of the nations already there (9:4–5).

> Know, therefore, that the LORD your God is not giving you this good land to possess because of your righteousness, for you are a stubborn people.

At the same time, this rebellious people whose standing before God is dependent on his grace is called upon to love him in response and unconditionally. The opening words of the classic prayer, the Shema (because in Hebrew *shema'* means "hear!") are taken from Deuteronomy 6:4–9:

> Hear, O Israel: The LORD our God, the LORD is one; and you shall love the LORD God with all your heart, and with all your soul, and with all your might.

Nevertheless, this section is permeated with warnings about the curses that will come upon the people if they forsake God.

DEUTERONOMY 12:1–26:19. The heart of the book is a collection of laws, to some extent based upon laws from the Book of the Covenant (Exodus 21–3) or a similar collection; but its outlook is very different from that of the material in Exodus. The theme of exclusive loyalty to God is prominent. The images and altars of the gods of the "nations" in the land of Israel are to be destroyed (12:1–3), and sacrifices are to be offered only at the

THE SHEMA

Deuteronomy 6:4 holds an unparalleled place in the liturgy, literature, theology, and practice of Judaism. From ancient times this verse featured as an important part of the regular service of sacrifice at the Temple and as a call to religious meeting and worship in ordinary communities far from the Temple. The Shema (from the first word of Deuteronomy 6:4 in Hebrew, the imperative "Hear!") appears in the daily liturgy, although in classical times the exact passages added to Deuteronomy 6:4 varied. In its definitive form today the Shema consists of Deuteronomy 6:4–9 and 11:13–21, Numbers 15:37–41, and appropriate benedictions. The faithful are enjoined to recite the text twice each day, upon rising in the morning and before falling asleep at night (Deuteronomy 6:7), so that Jesus' reference to the content of the Shema as the "first" commandment (see Mark 12:28–30) reflects Judaic practice in his time.

In an ancient Judaic practice, the biblical passages with the Shema and the Ten Commandments (Exodus 20:2–17) were written on parchment, and the rolled-up parchment slips were put inside phylacteries, or prayer capsules (*tefillin* in Hebrew). Pious Jews bound phylacteries on their left arms and foreheads when they prayed. The custom of praying daily with phylacteries finds its scriptural basis in Deuteronomy 6:8 and 11:8, and Exodus 13:9 and 16. Archaeological evidence suggests that *tefillin* were already used during the time of the Second Temple (515 B.C.E.–70 C.E.).

Deuteronomy 6:4–9 is also one of the two passages written on the mezuzah, a tiny parchment scroll inserted into a case and affixed to the doorpost of a Jewish home. The practice is enjoined in Deuteronomy 6:9 and 11:20. The earliest evidence for the fulfillment of the commandment to place such a scroll on the doorpost also comes from the Second Temple period.

In addition to its devotional importance, the Shema has in modern times come to be regarded as the Jewish confession of faith, expressing the fundamental doctrine of Judaism. These interpretations are associated with classic Rabbinic expressions of the Shema's meaning, which can be summarized in two phrases: accepting the yoke of the kingdom of heaven, and proclaiming the indivisible unity of God's name. The first, a more ancient interpretation, confesses God's preeminent sovereignty, unrivaled power, and providence, and calls for the citizens of God's kingdom to be bound together in their own corporate identity, free from the lesser, political kingdoms of the world. The second phrase represents a response to competing claims about God (including Christianity's) and to persecution, by articulating the immutable oneness of the single divine being, the God of Israel.

Copper inkwell from Qumran. This inkwell, although from a period much later than the Book of Deuteronomy, illustrates the technology of writing. The discovery of scrolls near Qumran include the earliest extant texts of the Hebrew Bible. (BiblePlaces.com)

place that God chooses (12:4–14). Any prophet, kinsperson, or "base fellow" who incites the people to follow other gods is to be put to death, and any city that serves other gods is to be destroyed (13:1–18). These laws are directed to the integrity of the entire nation. That is why apostate cities must be destroyed, why the Passover is to be celebrated at the central sanctuary in Jerusalem (16:1–8), why judges must be appointed in every town (16:18–20), why the king must write out and learn the laws (17:18–20), why there are rules about the nation going to war (20:1–20), why there is a ceremony for cleansing the land from bloodguilt when there is an unsolved murder (21:1–9), and why Deuteronomy excludes foreigners and those of suspect parentage along with those who are physically or genealogically defective from the "assembly of the LORD" (23:2–8).

Provision for the poor and defenseless also features as a national obligation. Indeed, Deuteronomy 15:4 declares that "there will be no poor among you." Released slaves must be generously endowed with provisions (15:12–18), the sojourner, the fatherless, and widows must be provided for at the great festivals and at harvest times (16:11, 14; 24:19–22), female prisoners of war are to be protected (21:10–14), runaway slaves must not be given back to their masters (23:15–16), and the poor and needy who have become day laborers must be protected (24:14–15, 17–18). While Exodus 21:7–11 envisages freedom for female slaves only if they marry a master or his son, Deuteronomy 15:12 extends to female slaves the same right of release as male slaves, after six years of service.

An apparent paradox within the laws in Deuteronomy is that they detail religious observances but emphasize how ordinary Israelites rather than priests alone are to fulfill them. Chapter 12 concerns the location of the central place of worship and how to deal with the killing of meat. Chapter 14 regulates clean and unclean food; chapter 16 prescribes how the Passover is to be celebrated; chapter 18 deals with the Levites; and chapter 21 has a ceremony for atoning for an unsolved murder. As Weinfeld (1972) has pointed out, the purpose of Deuteronomy is not to advance the Levitical cult, but to curtail it. In the ceremony in Deuteronomy 21:1–9, in which a heifer's neck is broken as an atonement for an unsolved murder, although Levitical priests are present it is the *elders* who carry out the killing. The Israelite who brings his offerings of first fruits to the sanctuary is the central figure in the ceremony and liturgy of the offering (26:3–11), while the priest plays a largely passive role. The section about sacrifice and about the slaughter of meat not intended for sacrifice (12:15–28) works out the logic of the centralization of the cult so as to limit the range of its influence. Priestly legislation had once required that the slaughter of all animals, apart from game, was to be considered to be a sacrifice that needed to be carried out by a priest at a local sanctuary (Leviticus 17:1–7). Whether or not that restriction was ever widely practiced, Deuteronomy certainly labored the point that recognizing a single sanctuary entailed dispensing with the need for a priest to undertake routine slaughter. Instead, ordinary Israelites could slaughter animals for their food, provided they disposed of the blood correctly (Deuteronomy 15:23). A collection of laws closely connected with a religious reform therefore carries with it a paradoxical, secularizing tendency, together with a movement from an institutional to a more personal form of religion in which social concern is urged upon individuals as they reflect on the deliverance from slavery that God achieved for the people.

There is another paradox to be noted. The laws combine a heightened concern for the poor and needy with a heightened insistence upon *intol-erance*. The images of other gods must be utterly destroyed (12:1–3), as must apostate cities (13:12–18), the cities of the "nations" in the land of Israel (20:16–18), and all the males in cities outside the land that are defeated by the Israelites (20:10–13). Such requirements convey the need for Israel to show exclusive loyalty to Yahweh.

DEUTERONOMY 27. This chapter contains the so-called Shechemite Dodecalogue (Twelve Commandments), which may reflect primitive tradition. It extends the legal section to the important chapter 28, which articulates the blessings and curses connected with the covenant, and which presumably concluded the book at one stage in its composition.

DEUTERONOMY 29–30. These chapters contain a farewell speech by Moses, similar to farewell speeches in the Deuteronomistic History, such as those of Joshua (Joshua 23) and Samuel (1 Samuel 12), in which brief summaries of Israel's history are set forth. This speech addresses Israel's exilic or postexilic situation.

DEUTERONOMY 31–4. These chapters link Deuteronomy with the Book of Joshua (especially the account of Moses' death in chapter 34) and include two poems: the Song of Moses (chapter 32) and the Blessing of Moses (chapter 33). These may well be ancient poems in origin, and it is noteworthy that, in the blessings of the clans (chapter 33), Judah receives only one verse whereas the Joseph tribes of Israel's northern heartland receive five verses. A northern origin is suggested by this fact.

II. THE WORLD OF ISRAEL'S "HISTORIANS" (JOSHUA, JUDGES, SAMUEL, KINGS, CHRONICLES, EZRA, NEHEMIAH)

Is it correct to speak at all about Israel's "historians"? The answer is both no and yes – beginning with the negative. The books in the English Bible called historical belong to categories quites different from history in the biblical canon of Judaism: the "Former Prophets" (works from Joshua to 2 Kings, except Ruth) and the "Writings" (Chronicles to Song of Solomon and Ruth, Lamentations, and Daniel). This canon does not separate historical books out from prophetic and poetic works. From the point of view of modern historiography, it has been denied that *any* of the the authors of the Hebrew Bible were historians on the grounds that historians can write about the past only from the perspective of human events and motives, a perspective that has no place for God (or for the gods in general) within the processes of history.

When scholars write history today, even biblical or religious history, they try to explain what happened in human terms; for example, they explore the subject from social, economic, and political standpoints. Even historians who believe in God leave the divine out of their attempts to understand the past, for the simple reason that it is impossible to verify the mind or the workings of God in the same way one can verify historical facts. Those who composed the Hebrew Bible felt no such difficulty. They believed that God had communicated his laws to Israel and that he had informed prophets concerning what he had done, what he intended to do, and why. In this sense it is entirely appropriate that most of the so-called historical books should have been classified as the Former Prophets in ancient Judaism. What we call history was for the Israelites who contributed to the Bible the equivalent of prophecy, only looking backward instead of into the future.

Yet the difference between the biblical authors and modern historians should not be exaggerated. Although ancient scribes lacked the resources of modern historians, such as reference libraries (although there were libraries in the ancient world, for example, that of the Assyrian king Ashurbanipal in Nineveh), they did keep records of major events, and later historians drew on these when writing their accounts of Israel's past. Where there were gaps in their knowledge they drew inferences or made informed guesses, much as modern historians do. Although they had their biases and interests, in regard to the necessity of surmise they were no different from modern historians. Our approach aims to avoid two extremes. We do not suppose that biblical writers wrote history with the same resources, and standards of accuracy, that apply to modern historians. Efforts to place their work above criticism or improvement only diminishes their theological achievement. But neither do we automatically dismiss the historical achievements of the biblical writers. They displayed genuine historical instincts within the resources available to them, and if their results now seem more like story than history, we keep in mind that all history writing is narrative and, to that extent, a form of story.

A. The Deuteronomists' History

Although the Deuteronomistic History did not reach its final form until after the exile (during the sixth century B.C.E.), substantial parts had certainly been completed by the time of Josiah's death in 609 B.C.E. This history tells the story of Israel and Judah from the entry to the land of Israel to the destruction of the Temple in Jerusalem in 587/6 B.C.E. and the early days of the subsequent exile. In what follows, we will examine each biblical book from the point of view of its literary history and of what we can gather of the period described by each book.

THE CENTRAL HILL COUNTRY

Deuteronomy portrays the Israelites who settled in Canaan as taking possession of an extensive countryside that was fruitful and productive – a land "flowing with milk and honey" (Deuteronomy 7:7–8). Archaeological evidence and other biblical narratives make that portrait appear highly idealized. The original area in which the Israelite clans settled seems to have been limited in both size and agricultural potential.

The earliest Israelite settlements in Canaan were made in the "hill country" of Judea, Samaria, and Galilee. This region amounts to a strip of rugged, mountainous land located between the Jordan Rift Valley and the coastal plain. Sparsely populated prior to Israelite occupation, the area consists of an irregular configuration of rocky hills and valleys that were heavily forested during the Early Iron Age (see Joshua 17:18). Evergreen oaks (*Quercus calliprinos*, 'elon in Hebrew)

and deciduous terebinths (*Pistacia palaestina*, 'elah in Hebrew) were scattered among dense thickets of tall shrubs known as maquis. Isolated from each other and from the urban life of nearby Canaanite city-states, settlements in the central hill country remained generally inaccessible. Often they were built on high crags – improving their defensibility but further increasing their isolation. These settlements were also far enough away from the established routes of intercontinental commercial and military traffic to be largely unnoticed.

With trained armies and superior military technology, including chariots, Canaanites held the fertile plains and valleys of the land during the Late Bronze Age and Early Iron Age. Hill country settlements took up only unwanted land that was marginally productive. Most soils in the region were poor, rocky, and easily eroded. Fields for orchards and crops had to

be artificially constructed. This mountainous area also provided few perennial sources of water. Great seasonal and annual variations in rainfall made a constant water supply even more problematic. Intense rainfall in the winter months led to high rates of runoff, and that water was consequently lost for agricultural purposes, while groundwater evaporated quickly during the hot, dry summer.

Still, the picture was not bleak in every part of the hill country, where ecosystems were remarkably diverse. Topographers today divide this small area into no fewer than seventeen subregions. Some sites enjoyed far better agricultural circumstances. Places like Hazor and Shiloh were near to continuous springs and situated on hills astride fairly level, small plateaus. Yet in the Early Iron Age the highlands were still frontier territory. In this complex, often inhospitable environment Israel made its first home.

1. Joshua

The "Conquest" of Canaan

As described in the Book of Joshua, the conquest of Canaan was the action of the twelve clans led by Joshua, whom Yahweh guided step by step. After the Israelites crossed the Jordan – miraculously parted by the power of the ark of the covenant borne by priests (Joshua 3) – they established their camp at Gilgal (Joshua 5:2–12), a site usually considered to be to the north of Jericho in the Jordan Valley. After destroying Jericho, the Israelites pushed up on to the hill country of Bethel, eventually capturing Ai and moving to the west. There they defeated a coalition of kings of cities in the Jerusalem saddle and the Shephelah in the valley of Aijalon. This was followed by a campaign against the city of Hazor in lower Galilee. Joshua 12:7–24 presents a list of defeated kings, which includes those named in previous chapters as well as kings of cities whose defeat is not otherwise described. Joshua 13 outlines the division of the land among the tribes, and the book ends with Joshua gathering the tribes together at Shechem, where they make a joint covenant that expresses their allegiance to Yahweh.

Current remains at Et-Tell, biblical Ai. These remains suggest the spectacle that might well have produced stories of Ai's cataclysmic destruction. Archaeological study has indicated a gap in the city's habitation between 2400 B.C.E. and 1000 B.C.E. (BiblePlaces.com)

This account of the conquest actually covers little of the land that eventually became Israel's. Summary statements such as Joshua 10:40–2 indeed say that Joshua smote the whole land and left no one alive in it; but these passages belong to the latest additions to the book. Moreover, unequivocal references (such as Joshua 16:10 and 17:12–13) show that sometimes clans were unable to conquer cities within the areas allocated to them.

Excavations of Jericho and other cities early in the twentieth century initially seemed to confirm the biblical account of Joshua's conquest. But

The original ark that held the tablets of the law did not survive into the Second Temple period. This sculpted decoration from the Byzantine synagogue at Capernaum shows an early ark as a wheeled chest in the shape of a Greek-style temple. The doors on the front of the temple chest would have opened to give access to the scrolls stored inside. (BiblePlaces.com)

as more sites were excavated and those earlier excavations were reassessed, the picture became ambiguous. Archaeological evidence supported the claim that Lachish, Hazor, and Debir (if Debir is to be located at Tell Bet Mirsim, a debated issue) had been destroyed, although Joshua's role in any such destruction cannot be proven. And no evidence could be found that Jericho and Ai were inhabited at the time of the Israelite settlement (during the late thirteenth century B.C.E.). The debate between those who held that archaeology supported an Israelite conquest and those who ascribed the destruction of towns such as Lachish and Tell Bet Mirsim to the Philistines or to inter-Canaanite feuding remained inconclusive. Those denying the conquest theory argued that the Israelite migration entailed the relatively peaceful settlement of seminomadic peoples without the coordinated campaign of subjugation described in the Book of Joshua.

These views, however, seem to have been overtaken by the evidence of the dramatic increase in settlements in Israel during the Iron Age. Toward the end of the Late Bronze Age only 25 or 30 cities were settled in the area from the Beersheba Valley in the south to the Jezreel Valley in the north, and only seven or eight sites were occupied in upper and lower Galilee. During the Early Iron Age the situation changed dramatically. The number of sites between the Beersheba and Jezreel Valleys increased to 240, and there were 68 in Galilee. Because these figures refer to sites that happen to have been discovered, they cannot be regarded as actual totals. But even allowing for this uncertainty, a spectacular change in settlement pattern from the thirteenth century B.C.E. onward is evident. Neither the theory of peaceful settlement nor an alternative theory first suggested by George E. Mendenhall (1962) – who proposed that the "conquest" was an internal revolt of peasants against their Canaanite overlords – can easily explain the evidence that the number of settlements grew by a factor of nearly ten.

Plowed field in eastern Samaria illustrating the continuing fertility of the lowland, despite centuries of deforestation. (BiblePlaces.com)

JERICHO

In the biblical account, the Israelites' first contact with the people inhabiting the land of Canaan took place at Jericho. According to chapters 2, 4, and 6 in the Book of Joshua, Joshua sent two spies, who reconnoitered the city with the help of Rahab the harlot. Based on their intelligence, the Israelite clans prepared an army of forty thousand soldiers for the attack. But the city was shut tight against the Israelites' campaign; they proved incapable of breaching its defenses. Then, following Yahweh's instruction through Joshua, the children of Israel marched around the city once a day with the ark of the covenant for six days. On the seventh day they performed seven circuits followed by the famous trumpet blast, and Jericho's walls collapsed. The city was stormed and put to the torch. Only Rahab was saved, while Joshua placed a curse on anyone who undertook to rebuild the troublesome city.

From the earliest days of biblical archaeology researchers have attempted to find the walls of Jericho that crumbled during the Israelite conquest of Canaan. An 1868 investigation at Tell es-Sultan, which corresponds to ancient Jericho, proved uneventful. But during the 1930s the archaeologist John Garstang found a Canaanite city on that mound of Tell es-Sultan that had been destroyed by earthquake and fire. He proclaimed that city to be the Jericho conquered by Joshua, and many were pleased that the relatively new science of archaeology had validated the historicity of the biblical narrative.

Kathleen Kenyon showed by a series of innovative excavations in 1950 that Garstang had been mistaken. She identified over six millennia of occupation at Tell es-Sultan, stretching back to a layer from the eighth millennium B.C.E. that may well represent the first city in the world. That city, with its massive fortifications, impressive public works, and extensive irrigation system, had been destroyed around 6800 B.C.E. During the Early Bronze Age (ca. 3300–2300 B.C.E.) the city was rebuilt no fewer than fourteen times. Kenyon showed that the tumbled walls that Garstang had attributed to biblical Jericho actually belonged to the final phase of Early Bronze Age Jericho, which was destroyed around 2300 B.C.E. (fully a thousand years before the era in which Israel settled in Canaan). A third major period of occupation ended when a city that had flourished during the Middle Bronze Age (between 1900 and 1500, the Hyksos period) was destroyed in a great conflagration around 1500. Garstang's ashes proved to have been from this destruction, still several centuries before Israel began to occupy the highlands of Canaan. At the time when Joshua should have been campaigning through the Promised Land, Kenyon found that the site of ancient Jericho had been unfortified. There was only meager evidence of any occupation at all during that period.

Various suggestions have been offered to explain the apparent discrepancy between the biblical narrative and the archaeological evidence concerning Jericho. The upper strata of Tell es-Sultan were badly eroded; some scholars insist that structures that might have corroborated Joshua's account of the fall of Jericho vanished long ago as rainwashed debris. Others understand Joshua 6 as an imaginative way of explaining the ruins of Tell es-Sultan, which would have been impressive during the time the Israelites settled in Palestine. Then again, perhaps the biblical story is simply a logically necessary chapter in Israel's national history of its "conquest," since Jericho is the most likely geographical location from which to begin an invasion of the land from the east.

These suggestions remain speculative, since the vital evidence from 1400–1250 B.C.E. (the period many scholars think most likely for the beginning of Israel's occupation of Canaan) is incomplete at Jericho. Still, scholars generally view the excavations at Jericho as evidence against a conquest model of Israel's settlement – an example of how Israelite traditions were inflated, transposed, and compressed in the complex process of constructing a cohesive history of the unified nation of Israel.

The new data might seem to confirm that an Israelite invasion took place after all, but that would be a hasty conclusion. Most of the Iron Age settlements were in those areas of Israel — the central hill country later known as the territory of Ephraim and Manasseh — about which the Book of Joshua says almost nothing. Another geographical oddity in the Book of

Joshua has long been recognized: although Joshua assembles the tribes at Shechem, located in the Bethel and Samaria hill country, the book lacks an account of the conquest of that area. The new evidence about the settlement patterns only serves to make this anomaly appear more acute.

To account for the archaeological evidence, Israel Finkelstein (1988) suggests that settlement took place incrementally over some two hundred years. People who were initially pastoralists, dependent mainly on sheep and goats, at first settled in areas most suited to a combination of pastoralism and cereal growing in the dry fringes to the east of the Bethel and Samaria hills. From there they spread to the west and the south, at first occupying the valleys, which had long since been cleared of trees, and then settling in and beginning to clear the wooded parts of the central hill country. Settlement in Judah seems to have been small compared with that in the Bethel and Samaria hills.

But were these settlers Israelites? The answer given to this question will depend on one's view of the nature and development of Israelite religion and identity. Scholars who hold that Israel's religion was primarily the creation of prophetic groups from the ninth century B.C.E. onward often maintain that the settlers of the thirteenth century B.C.E. were "Canaanites," from among whom "Israel" gradually developed a separate identity. Scholars who maintain that faith in Yahweh before the land was settled under the name of Israel bound together social groups that claimed common ancestors, and that these groups believed that Yahweh had delivered at least some of them from slavery in Egypt, are inclined to argue that the settlers were indeed Israelites or their ancestors.

Whatever the answer given, for several reasons the question remains crucial. It reminds us that we cannot accept uncritically the picture presented in Joshua of Israelites invading a land already occupied by Canaanites. Finkelstein's reconstruction involves large-scale occupation of a land mostly *devoid* of settlements, raising the additional question: where did the biblical Canaanites come from? Archaeological and sociological explanations have their limitations when ancient peoples are concerned. They can neither prove nor disprove that the settlers were Israelites. A mediating position would conceive that the settlers included Israelites in sufficient numbers for the reference to Israel in the victory stela set up by the Egyptian pharaoh Merneptah prior to 1203 B.C.E. (see *Ancient Near Eastern Texts*, pp. 376–8) after invading Canaan to be understood in its commonly accepted sense – that Merneptah was referring to a people called Israel, probably in the Bethel and Samaria hill country, whom he had defeated.

Where had these settlers come from? Some no doubt *had* escaped from slavery in Egypt and linked up with relatives on the fringes of Israel and Transjordan. But claims of genealogical relationship in the ancient world often expressed social alliance more than genetic kinship: many settlers who took the name Israel were pastoral seminomads descended from people who had lived in Canaan in the Late Bronze Age and whose adoption of a semi-nomadic way of life corresponded to the dramatic decline in the number of

The pharaoh Merneptah succeeded his father, Rameses II, ruling until his death in 1203 B.C.E. This stele eulogies his accomplishments, among them: "Hatti is pacified; Canaan is plundered with every evil; Ashkelon is taken; Gezer is captured; Yanoam is made non-existent; Israel lies desolate, its seed is no more." (BiblePlaces.com)

AI

Joshua's campaign against the cities of Canaan next targeted the city of Ai, according to the biblical account. As at Jericho, the Israelite military leader sent men to spy out the objective. The spies reported that a force of only two or three thousand could take the city. Yet when Israel attacked, their forces were routed. At Yahweh's prompting, Joshua identified Achan, a tribesman of Judah who had violated the ban on taking booty from the captured city of Jericho, as the cause of this unexpected defeat. Achan's defilement having been removed by his execution, Yahweh, speaking to Joshua (Joshua 8:1), planned a second attack on Ai. The battle plan of deception and ambush is recorded with realistic detail in Joshua 7–8. Ai's army was wiped out, its inhabitants were killed, its buildings were burned, and its king was executed – buried under a mound of rocks.

Yet Khirbet et-Tell (the site of ancient Ai) provides no evidence of human occupation during the period when the Israelites were most likely to have been settling in Canaan. Extensive excavation from the mid-1960s through the early 1970s uncovered a settlement dating from the Early Bronze Age (ca. 3100 B.C.E.) that had grown to a major walled city of almost thirty acres by the early third millennium. That city was destroyed around 2000 B.C.E. The site then remained unoccupied for eleven hundred years, including the Late Bronze Age (1400–1250 B.C.E.), the period during which most scholars conjecture that the Israelite tribes began to occupy the Palestinian highlands.

Excavators did uncover an Early Iron Age settlement (1250–1000 B.C.E.) at Khirbet et-Tell that many scholars adduce as among the first indications of Israelite occupation in Palestine. This small, unwalled Iron Age village was the setting for a new culture of farmers and shepherds, who built cisterns and used characteristic pillars to support the roofs of their usually four-room houses. Many similar installations appeared throughout Palestine at about the same time, some at new sites and others at sites such as Ai that had been occupied before. These cultural remains do not appear distinctively Israelite, however, because they share characteristics common among many Iron Age settlements in the wider region.

Even if the Iron Age settlers at Ai could be identified as Israelites, the archaeological remains show that these settlers did not establish their new dwelling by military conquest, as described in the Book of Joshua. They occupied a site that had been abandoned for fifty generations. Then what of the biblical story of Ai? Does it have any historical basis that archaeology can complement?

A few scholars insist that et-Tell is not the site of ancient Ai and that the real location of Joshua's victory has yet to be unearthed, but a consensus of scholarship maintains that et-Tell has been correctly identified. Another proposal to vindicate the account in Joshua argues that Iron Age Ai, which indeed existed at et-Tell, went through two phases of building: Canaanite and Israelite. On this view the Israelite takeover has left its mark in a remodeling of the first phase, representing a minor raid that became the Bible's exciting story through generations of retelling. Unfortunately for this theory, ceramic and structural evidence does not support such an interpretation. The distinguished biblical scholar and prominent archaeologist William F. Albright suggested that the biblical story of Ai was really the report of a battle at nearby Bethel (modern-day Beitin) – a site that does offer evidence of complete destruction during the Late Bronze Age. He proposed that somewhere in its transmission across the generations confusion arose about the story's setting. Other scholars propose that the account of the conquest in the Joshua story represents an early form of historical speculation, an etiological narrative that gives a colorful explanation for the rock-heaped ruin of Ai that the Israelites encountered when they settled in Palestine. Finally, some understand Joshua 7–8 as a tale created to make a theological point rather than a historical assertion.

On the whole, archaeology has eliminated the historical underpinning of the biblical account of Ai's destruction by an army of conquering Israelites. How the remains at Ai are interpreted beyond that consensus depends as much on the excavator's model of Israel's settlement in Canaan as it does on the material evidence. Careful investigation at Ai and other sites like it has served the important purpose of challenging long-standing assumptions about the history of Israel, and it has forced scholars to look for new perspectives from which to understand Joshua and the alleged conquest of Canaan.

settlements in the Late Bronze Age. If we take a period of four hundred years between 1600 and 1200 B.C.E., we can suppose that, for reasons unknown to us, a majority of people in Canaan adopted a lifestyle in which they abandoned their settlements and depended mainly on sheep and goats, living on the fringes of the areas still occupied by prosperous city-states. During the thirteenth century B.C.E. the trend started to reverse, and the land began to be settled once more, with social tensions and sporadic violence the predictable result.

HAZOR

Joshua 11:10–13 records the Israelite defeat of the city of Hazor. Located in northern Galilee, Hazor was the premier settlement in Palestine during the Middle and Late Bronze Ages (2300–1200 B.C.E.). This magnificent city of perhaps forty thousand people occupied some two hundred acres in two major fortified areas. Unlike Jericho, which is not mentioned in any extrabiblical document, Hazor is known to us from the Egyptian Execration Texts (a collection referring to places to be cursed, and dating to ca. 2000 B.C.E.), the Mari archives (ca. 1900 B.C.E.), and the Amarna letters (ca. 1400 B.C.E.). It was an important center of commerce. Tell el-Qedah, the mound on which the ancient upper city of Hazor was located, was a key control point for the principal military and commercial routes that passed nearby. The Bronze Age city was a center for Canaanite culture, its temples and palaces featuring centrally in the cultural prehistory of ancient Israel's religious and political institutions.

All the glory that was Hazor came to an abrupt and violent end late in the thirteenth century B.C.E. Sacked and burned to the ground, the city was resettled shortly thereafter by a small group of culturally less advanced, seminomadic people. The new set-

tlers lived much more modestly, with a less secure and more austere lifestyle. Dwelling in an unfortified area, they made their homes in tents and huts, each with its own storage pits and cooking installation.

This archaeological reconstruction meshes well with the biblical account of Hazor's ruin by the advancing Israelites if we accept the traditional dating: violent destruction of the impressive Canaanite city comes before the settlement of new people. (Another report, in Judges 4, where the defeat of "Jabin, king of Hazor," comes *after* the Israelite settlement in the land, would still remain unexplained in that case.) Along with cities in the Judean highlands like Lachish, Eglon, and Kiriath Sepher, Hazor has been cited as corroborating the historicity of the Bible's account of how Israel took possession of the land of Canaan by force. The takeover seems to have been by means of systematic, or at least generally organized, military conquest. Evidence from the Iron Age resettlement of Hazor has also been added to the catalogue of remains said to represent a uniquely Israelite material culture during the eleventh century B.C.E. More recent excavations, however, have proposed lowering the chronology for the destruction or settlement, which would make corrobora-

tion with the biblical account much less straightforward.

The data from Hazor are in any case difficult to correlate with the Book of Joshua. There is no way to know if the destruction of Hazor can be unequivocally attributed to one or more of the Israelite clans. Political ambitions in Egypt's Nineteenth Dynasty and wide-ranging unrest in the Canaanite city-states during the Late Bronze Age make it possible that invading Egyptians or rival Canaanites destroyed Hazor. And Hazor's destruction may not necessarily have resulted solely from military attack; natural disaster or internal conflict might have played a role. Some scholars even doubt the existence of a distinctive Israelite material culture. In any case, there is no definitive evidence that requires Hazor's Iron Age inhabitants to be identified as Israelites.

However scholars may interpret the destruction of Canaanite Hazor, its Iron Age resettlement contributes to a larger picture that shows an era of great change and unrest during the twelfth to eleventh centuries B.C.E. New players enter the stage of history, probably at Hazor, and many scholars – rightly in our view – identify the new settlers as among those who would later join together to form the nation of Israel.

The precise reasons for these reversals are a matter for surmise. They may have been related to the attacks of the Habiru upon cities in the fourteenth century B.C.E. or to pressures exerted by Egypt or to both. Another possible explanation – for which evidence is not available – is that changes in climate such as prolonged droughts had forced settled communities to become seminomadic, and that these conditions later eased. The reversal toward renewed settlement may also have depended on changed political circumstances, such as the inability of city-states to provide the seminomads with grain in return for animal products. This would have forced the seminomads to become their own grain producers, requiring them either to establish or to take over permanent settlements.

Two new factors significantly affected the lives of those who settled (or resettled) in the land. First was the arrival of the Philistines as part of the migrations of the Sea Peoples in the twelfth century B.C.E. They would later try to conquer Israel. Second, some of the settlers in the Bethel and Samaria hills were bound together by faith in Yahweh, who had liberated his people from slavery in Egypt. These two new factors would be decisive for the subsequent history of Israel and Judah.

Iron Age settlements in the Bethel and Samaria hills varied in population size from one hundred to a thousand inhabitants. Many of these settlements took the form of an elliptical circle of broad-roomed houses, with each house enclosing a central courtyard. In areas where the growing of cereals predominated, small silos for storing grain were commonly found within the courtyards; in olive-growing areas produce was stored in collared-rim jars. The shape of the settlements imitated the shape of settlements of tent dwellers, suggesting that the settlers in Iron Age Israel were making the transition from seminomadic to permanent settlement. The broad-roomed houses probably developed into the four-roomed

In about 1175 B.C.E. Rameses III successfully stopped the Sea Peoples (including the Philistines) from invading Egypt. This account is recorded on the walls of his mortuary temple at Medinet Habu. The Philistines are known by their use of feather headdresses, swan decorations, two-edged swords, spears, and rounded shields. The majority of the Sea Peoples are clean-shaven, but a few Philistines are depicted with beards. (BiblePlaces.com)

ISRAELITE FARMING AND TECHNOLOGY

Early Israel's economy was based on agriculture and supplemented by animal husbandry. Communities were generally self-sufficient, passing along skills in ceramics, textiles, and metallurgy from generation to generation. Those who farmed the highlands during the Early Iron Age were faced with formidable challenges. In addition to the day-to-day activities necessary for survival in a preindustrial society, Israelite settlers had to perform a range of pioneering tasks specific to their hill country environment. Before crops could be planted, land had to be cleared of its dense overcoat of trees and shrubs. In many places rocks that cluttered cultivatable land also had to be removed. In other places artificial fields had to be constructed by building terraces along steep slopes that in their natural state were agriculturally useless.

More than any other Iron Age technology, agricultural terracing opened up the highlands to productive farming. Terraces transformed inhospitable gradients into a series of level fields suitable for crop production. Walls of dry-laid fieldstone held these artificially level surfaces in place. Terracing reduced erosion and increased groundwater retention, but also proved costly and time-consuming, because terraces required great expenditures of cooperative labor to maintain. Without regular attention, terraces deteriorated rapidly, and the combined weight of unanchored soil and tumbled walls could produce devastating landslides.

The first Israelites did not irrigate, but relied on rainfall to sustain their crops through the cycle of germination and growth. Rain was plentiful during the cool, wet winter months. But high rates of runoff and evaporation meant that water could not be conserved in sufficient quantity to assure growth throughout the hot summer growing season. Consequently, the rainfall pattern made highland farming precarious.

Nonetheless, the widespread use of cisterns – a vital technology for early highland farmers – did make it possible for humans and animals to carry on during the dry summer months. Many cisterns were lined with waterproof lime plaster. Scholars have often credited the opening of the highland frontier to the widespread use of these facilities, coupled with the introduction of iron tools that facilitated the pioneer tasks of clearing forests, plowing fields, and hewing cisterns. Yet the technology for building slaked-lime cisterns had been available before the Iron Age, and in some areas local geological conditions provided highland farmers with impermeable bedrock that made waterproofing their cisterns unnecessary. Further, iron did not come into widespread use in the hill country before the tenth century B.C.E. – well after the time of the Israelite settlement. Recent research suggests that the early Israelite farmers adapted to their precarious environment by more subtle means than widescale technological change.

To conserve soil resources and maintain fertility, hill country agriculturalists probably employed a variety of procedures. Fields were allowed to stand fallow at regular intervals. Flocks and herds grazed on the fallow grounds, their manure providing excellent fertilizer. These methods proved only marginally effective, however, so that farmers had to be satisfied with low crop yields (perhaps no better than 1:15 or 1:20), which decreased as local soils were depleted by prolonged use.

Communities of farmers in the Early Iron Age highlands adapted to their irregular environments by planting multiple crops in order to avoid depending on a single pattern of rainfall, since there could be great variety from year to year, as well as from season to season. Staple cereals and vegetables were mainstays in the highland diet, although tree and vine crops were part of the mix as well. Deuteronomy 8:8 lists wheat, barley, grapes, figs, pomegranates, olives, and dates among the fruits of the land. Archaeological investigation would add nuts (e.g., almonds) and legumes (e.g., broad beans, lentils, chickpeas) to this list. This diversity helped farming communities avoid becoming dependent on a single crop that might fail during a given year.

Highland farmers further reduced the risk of their difficult venture by storing the abundance of a good year against future agriculture disasters. Many crops could be preserved; fruit was dried or made into juice, and olives were pressed into oil. Large storage jars and household grain pits of the early Israelite period attest to these common practices.

Flocks and herds also served as a way of storing food reserves. Subject to a different set of environmental constraints, these animals put on weight in years of plenty and could be culled when annual crops were inadequate for the community's survival. Sheep and goats contributed to the farm diet by also providing dairy products (especially milk for making curds and butter). Livestock husbandry made use of marginal lands and provided much-needed fertilizer. Wool and hides were also important household commodities.

Israelite farming was a corporate venture with labor demands that often went beyond what a single nuclear family could provide. The challenging, risky environment in which the early highland farmers eked out their existence was instrumental in the development of inter-household and intervillage systems of cooperation and exchange networks. Those systems may well have facilitated the formation of the Israelite nation and its socially conscious religion.

houses that are a feature of Iron Age architecture in Israel and elsewhere in the region. The average size of a household was five; families probably consisted of from three to eight persons. It appears that limited local trading among settlements took place, with settlements using surplus grain to buy olives, and vice versa.

The Literary History of Joshua

In its present form the Book of Joshua is part of the Deuteronomistic History, dating from the sixth or fifth century B.C.E. Its content is closely linked with Deuteronomy. The command in Deuteronomy 27:1–8, that an altar should be built at Mount Ebal after the Israelites have crossed the Jordan, is carried out at Joshua 8:30–5. This literary link produces the historical and geographical anomaly that Joshua and the Israelites occupy the heartland of Israel without first having conquered it. As a result, early Christian attempts to identify Mounts Ebal and Gerizim, such as in Eusebius's fourth-century C.E. *Chronikon,* located them in the Jordan Valley to the north of Jericho. (These two erroneously identified peaks can be seen clearly today by anyone standing on Tell es-Sultan, the site of ancient Jericho). Other links between Joshua and Deuteronomy include Deuteronomy 19:1–10, whose command to designate three cities of refuge is carried out at Joshua 20:1–6; Joshua 11:21, where the sons of the Anakim mentioned at Deuteronomy 9:1–3 are destroyed by Joshua; and the mention of hornets in both Deuteronomy 7:20 and Joshua 24:12.

By means of these links, Joshua is portrayed as the true successor to Moses, carrying out the divine mandates given to his master that applied to conditions in the Promised Land. A summary of this view is found at Joshua 8:35: "There was not a word of all that Moses commanded that Joshua did not read before all the assembly of Israel." This portrayal, however, raises questions about the identity of the historical Joshua and the origin of the stories about the conquests attributed to him.

A notice about Joshua's death and burial at Joshua 24:29–30 locates his inheritance at Timnath-serah in the hill country of Ephraim. If this is correctly located at Khirbet Tibnah, then Joshua's home was a large village on an elongated hilltop with an adjacent spring in the southwestern part of Ephraim. That is not more than ten miles away from the valley of Aijalon, where the battle in defense of Gibeon took place and where, it is said, Joshua exhorted the sun to stand still (Joshua 10:6–14). The story of this miraculous and bloody victory is attributed to a prior souce, the Book of Jashar (Joshua 10:13) – possibly an ancient war epic or collection of poems. Joshua must have been an inspired local leader whose successful military exploits against neighboring Canaanites made him the ideal figure to be portrayed in Israelite storytelling as Moses' successor and the single spearhead of the conquest. History writing and storytelling alike abhor a vacuum; where there are gaps the roles of figures prominent in tradition are expanded to fill them.

The literary history of the Book of Joshua suggests that, although the settlement of the Israelites in Canaan may have been relatively peaceful, conflicts developed between the Israelites and the other settlers, the "Canaanites" referred to in the text. In some cases the Canaanites made common cause with, or formally allied themselves under, powerful city-states in the land. Joshua emerged as a prominent and successful warrior at this early stage of Israel's development, when the people defined themselves by common lineages, a common deliverance from slavery in Egypt, and their common rejection of the city-state ethos. Stories of the conquest of cities naturally began to gather around Joshua. Archaeological excavations have shown that some cities mentioned in these stories were indeed destroyed, although the dates of destruction cannot necessarily be linked to the time of Joshua, nor can the destroyers be identified as Israelites. Yet genuine historical reminiscences are clearly woven into these stories. The Book of Joshua may have been composed as a continuation of the story about the ancestors and the Exodus begun in the Pentateuch and written down during the time of Hezekiah (ca. 727–698 B.C.E.) from earlier sources such as the Book of Jashar. The Book of Joshua at this stage related how all the Israelites entered the land of Israel after journeying through the wilderness following the Exodus from Egypt. This early version of the book possibly jumped from what is now the beginning of chapter 13 (which deals with the allotment of territory) to what is now the beginning of Judges by way of the notice of Joshua's death in 24:29–30. Joshua 13:1 speaks of Joshua as "old and advanced in years" and states that much land remained to be possessed. Judges 1 begins with the question, after the death of Joshua, of who will go up to fight against the Canaanites.

The substance of Joshua 1 to 13:1 was linked firmly to Deuteronomy by the passages already mentioned. At this stage certain passages were added, such as those that show Joshua carrying out Moses' instructions and those that claim that the whole of the land was subdued and cleared of inhabitants (Joshua 10:40–2). How much of this was composed during the reign of Josiah (640–609 B.C.E.), when the first major draft of the whole Deuteronomistic History was written, we cannot say. But it is likely that chapters 13–21, which record the partition of the land among the clans, date from

Josiah's time, although some scholars date the material in these chapters to the early monarchy (during the tenth century B.C.E.). Joshua's speech to the assembled Israelites in chapter 23 is similar to other key speeches and passages in the Deuteronomistic History (1 Samuel 12; 1 Kings 8; 2 Kings 17), and seems to be later than Joshua 24, which in turn is closer to Samuel's speech in 1 Samuel 12 than is Joshua 23. Joshua 24 may thus belong to an earlier, and Joshua 23 to a later, Deuteronomistic editing of Joshua.

The Literary Structure and Function of Joshua

The literary structure of Joshua is simple. Chapters 1–11 describe how the Israelites crossed the Jordan and set up camp at Gilgal, and how they defeated Jericho before advancing to the eastern fringe of the Bethel hill country, where they campaigned against Ai and a coalition of kings from the Jerusalem saddle and the Shephelah. An account of a campaign against Hazor in lower Galilee and of fighting in the hill country of Judah (chapter 11) leads to a list of the kings whom the Israelites defeated (chapter 12). From chapters 13–21 we have the account of the allocation of the land to the clans. Chapter 22 deals with the special problem of the Transjordanian clan groups, and chapters 23–4 are accounts of Joshua's gathering all such groups together and of his speeches to them.

The best way to describe the book's function is to address the problem that most obviously confronts modern readers: the barbarity of a narrative that enjoins the wholesale slaughter of populations in God's name. That the Israelites fought wars in which they believed that God was on their side, much as modern nations have assumed during the twentieth century, cannot be doubted. However, in describing war in terms of a campaign to exterminate whole populations, the biblical writers were not depicting reality but were following literary conventions. We also find outside the Hebrew Bible the same claim of having destroyed whole populations, for example, in the ninth-century B.C.E. inscription of Mesha (*Ancient Near Eastern Texts*, pp. 320–1).

In Joshua, this literary convention of the "holy war" is used to present object lessons about what happens when the Israelites obey God and what happens when they disobey him. This is clearly to be seen in the stories of Jericho and Ai (chapters 6–8), which are notable in Joshua for their literary construction and artistry.

In the story of Jericho's conquest, the Israelites do nothing except march around the city once a day for six days, carrying the ark of the covenant and blowing trumpets, but otherwise maintaining silence. On the seventh day they march around the city seven times, and then, on Joshua's command, the Israelites shout and the city's walls fall down. This successful, if unorthodox, method of warfare contrasts with what happens in chapter 7, where a conventional assault upon a minor town (whose Hebrew name, Ai, means "a ruin") results in disaster for the Israelites. Why? Because the Israelite Achan had disobeyed the command that no spoil of Jericho was to be kept as a personal possession. Once Achan has been identified as the

Inscription (carved during the middle of the ninth century B.C.E.) on behalf of Mesha, king of Moab. This inscription shows that the ideology of holy war was not limited to Israel. Mesha relates that his god, "Chemosh said to me, 'Go, take Nebo against Israel.' And I went by night and fought against it from the break of dawn until noon, and I took it and slew all, seven thousand men and boys and women and girls and female slaves; for Ashtor-Chemosh I had devoted it. And I took from there the vessels of Yhwh and brought them before Chemosh." (BiblePlaces.com)

HOLY WAR

In many texts, Yahweh appears as a mighty master of war; sometimes he is explicitly the Divine Warrior (e.g., Exodus 15:3). Israel's earliest national traditions portray the flight from Egypt into the land of Canaan as a grand march accompanied by a heavenly army arrayed around the children of Israel and guided through the desert by their divine commander in chief. During the period of Israel's settlement of the Promised Land, the idea of a warrior God continued to play an important role. One of Israel's earliest collections of poetry, now lost but mentioned in the Hebrew Bible, contained a record of the "wars of Canaan" fought during the settlement (Judges 3:1). This collection contained Israel's songs of praise to the great Divine Warrior who had driven out the inhabitants of the land before them. Israelites thought of their success as dependent not so much on their own military prowess, as on their uncompromising trust in Yahweh's ability to give them victory.

This ideology received an early expression in the Israelite institution of "holy war," the complete submission (*cherem* in Hebrew) of a non-Israelite city to Yahweh by means of its utter destruction. This ideology of formative Israelite society reached its fullest development and greatest influence in the settlement period, although the extent to which it was put into practice is a matter of debate. Some detailed instructions on how to conduct holy war have been preserved in the Hebrew Bible. Information about the preparation, personnel, conduct, and outcome of holy war is tantalizing, often specific, and yet incomplete and sometimes self-contradictory. The constant factor nonetheless remains that holy war was conducted with the full support of Israelite religious institutions, including the priesthood and the sacrificial cult. The army apparently underwent a ritual cleansing before a battle (Joshua 3:5), regulations for which included abstention from sexual intercourse (2 Samuel 11:11).

Deuteronomy 20 pictures three possible outcomes of a holy war, in a refinement of the practice of the *cherem*. (1) A city about to be attacked had to be offered terms of surrender. If its inhabitants accepted, their lives were spared, but the entire population was enslaved. (2) If surrender terms were rejected, the soon-to-be victorious Israelites were to kill all the city's adult male citizens, taking the city's women, children, and possessions as the spoils of war. (3) The exception to these rules of engagement were cities that lay within the boundaries of the Promised Land. When any of those cities was captured, Israel was to destroy them completely, offering them as a sacrifice to Yahweh.

Holy war ideology was by no means confined to ancient Israel. Archaeological remains such as the Mesha inscription make it clear that other peoples held ideas very similar to those of their Israelite neighbors. Ancient warfare was often cast in terms of an ultimate power struggle between the gods of warring nations. During monarchical times holy war traditions from the conquest and the period of the Judges were transformed into instruments of national policy. The declaration of war became a royal prerogative rather than a divine imperative, and ad hoc armies were replaced by a professional army and organized conscripts. As the *institution* of holy war faded away, however, the *ideology* of sacred warfare continued to influence Israel's prophets and its priestly establishment. This ideology forms the background for many biblical presentations and reworkings of themes from the Exodus and conquest, and became a standard judgment motif in later prophetic and eschatological writings.

culprit and has been stoned to death, the fight against Ai is resumed and meets with success.

These stories take us into the realm of religious instruction rather than of detached historical description. It is notable that, after the punishment of Achan, the Book of Joshua does allow Israel to keep some booty (Joshua 8:1–2), so that the ideal of a complete "devotion" (*cherem*), or destruction of city-states in the Promised Land, can eventually be honored in the breach as well as by the observance. The *cherem* regulations show that obedience to God is necessary if the people are to enjoy peace and security, and that divine commandments are calibrated within Israel's capacity to perform them (see Deuteronomy 30:11–14). The whole conquest is not a triumph of military strength or skill but the work of God, made possible in particular by Joshua's scrupulous adherence to the Law and instructions given to him by Moses. If one of the purposes of the Deuteronomistic History is to present Israel's history as a story of obedience and disobedience and their consequences, for the benefit of those who had returned to Judah from exile, we can see how Joshua plays its part in that scheme.

2. Judges

The Settlement of Canaan

The Book of Judges presents a more plausible account of the Israelite conquest than does Joshua in the opinion of many scholars. Judges 1 portrays the clans attempting individually to possess the lands allotted to them and enjoying only limited success. In a typical example, Judges 1:27 states that

> Manasseh did not drive out the inhabitants of Beth-shean and its villages, or Taanach and its villages, or the inhabitants of Dor and its villages, or the inhabitants of Megiddo and its villages; but the Canaanites continued to live in that land.

This account of the occupation appears more realistic than those passages in Joshua (e.g., 10:40–2) that claim that the whole land was subdued by Joshua and that the indigenous population was destroyed.

Yet Joshua and Judges 1 also agree to a remarkable extent, with Joshua 13:1 even acknowledging that the conquest did not completely succeed. Joshua's account of the division of the land among the clans also emphasizes the imperfections involved: the men of Judah could not drive out the Jebusites who lived in Jerusalem (Joshua 15:63), nor could the men of Ephraim drive out the Canaanites from Gezer (Joshua 16:10). Joshua 17:11 goes on to list cities that the men of Manasseh were unable to possess, and Joshua 17:16–18 indicates that Ephraim and Manasseh had to deal with Canaanite cities whose armies had chariots, which the Israelites could not match.

However much historical or archaeological investigation might refine the presentation in the Book of Joshua, it does not in fact envisage a complete and successful conquest at variance with Judges 1. Although a little of the material in Judges 1 repeats what we read in Joshua (most notably the account of the conquest of Hebron and Debir in Joshua 15:13–19 and Judges 1:11–15, 20), Joshua and Judges as a whole complement one another as a continuous narrative. In Joshua the land is subdued to the extent that it is by all twelve clans acting together. In Judges, after the death of Joshua, the "tribes" go individually into their allotted territories, which still contain pockets of resistance to Israelite rule. But how far does Judges relate to what we can surmise about what actually happened?

CHARIOTS

Chariots dramatically advanced the development of ancient warfare, playing a vital role in the military history of ancient Israel. Moses is pictured leading the children of Israel across the Red Sea with pharaoh's chariots in pursuit (Exodus 14), and the Canaanites' chariots of iron prevented the Israelites from claiming what they considered to be their divine patrimony (Judges 1:19). Only when David's army acquired competence in chariotry did the fledgling nation finally secure its existence against the Philistines (2 Samuel 8:4). The Solomonic golden age of Israel was measured in terms of its horses and charioteers (1 Kings 4), while the superior chariot power of Assyria and Babylon finally put an end to Israel's independent existence.

Wheeled vehicles drawn by asses first appear in Mesopotamian art around 3000 B.C.E. By the time of Hammurabi during the eighteenth century B.C.E., chariots equipped with spoked wheels (which greatly reduced the weight and enhanced the maneuverability of vehicles) had become standard in the art of war. Drawn by people or oxen, chariots were effective military weapons on smooth, dry ground but were notoriously slow, unstable, and clumsy on rough terrain. The great innovation in chariot warfare came via the Hyksos, the Asiatic people controlling Syria–Palestine and much of Egypt during the Middle Bronze Age (ca. 1600 B.C.E.): they introduced the horse-drawn chariot.

The speed and versatility of this new war vehicle made for great tactical advantage. Horse-drawn chariots for two or three warriors provided the key to military dominance in the ancient Near East. The advent of equine chariotry made possible the rapid extension of the New Kingdom in Egypt, of the Hittite kingdoms, and of the Neo-Assyrian Empire. Tribute lists and victory memorials from Egyptian and Assyrian kings show that horse-drawn chariots proved decisive in victory. Because chariots formed an integral part of every powerful king's arsenal, chariot inventories became an index of political power.

The Hebrew Bible records the use of chariots by foreign rulers (Exodus 14:25; Joshua 11:6; Nahum 3:2), and the rise of the Judean monarchy brought Israel's own use of chariot technology (1 Samuel 8:11). Chariots came to symbolize royalty and political sovereignty, and even emerged as the master symbol of divine omnipotence (Zechariah 6:1–8). Yahweh, the God of Israel, was himself portrayed as a mighty king riding his terrifying chariot (Isaiah 66:15; Habakkuk 3:8). A fiery chariot came to symbolize the awesome presence of God (2 Kings 2:11). In his magnificent first vision, the prophet Ezekiel employs a stylized throne-chariot to portray Yahweh's supreme sovereignty (Ezekiel 1:4–28). Ancient Near Eastern gods were commonly pictured riding on powerful beasts or in fearsome war vehicles, and Ezekiel, imitating Near Eastern models, combined the two modes of transportation in his vision of a chariot made, not of wood or metal, but of surreal living creatures.

Social History of Israel during the Period of the Judges

Recent archaeololgical research suggests there was a relatively peaceful occupation of the Bethel and Samaria hill country, probably during the latter part of the thirteenth century B.C.E. (as we have discussed in our treatment of the Book of Joshua). Settlement succeeded mostly in unpopulated areas, where villages with between one hundred and a thousand inhabitants established themselves. Did the settlers call themselves Israelites at this stage, or did they later divide into the two groups that we call Israelites and Canaanites? Those remain difficult and often contentious questions.

The Book of Judges may help to provide at least some answers. Apart from the struggle the Israelite leaders Deborah and Barak engaged in with the Canaanite commander Sisera (discussed shortly), the oppressors of Israel in Judges are invaders from *outside* the land. Ehud resists the Moabites (Judges 3); Gideon, the nomadic Amalekites and Midianites (Judges 6–7);

Jephthah, the Ammonites (Judges 11–12); and Samson, the Philistines (Judges 13–16). This pattern, as well as what we now know about Israelite settlement, suggests that Israelite villages were subjected to localized threats from groups from outside the land wanting either to take the villages' best land or to force the Israelite villages to pay tribute in the form of agricultural produce. The "judges," whose stories form the core of the book, were local heroes who led the Israelites against these oppressors. This picture can be commended as plausible rather than as probable, but it appears best to fit the textual and archaeological evidence as a whole.

The two accounts of *internal* conflicts, the exceptions to the pattern just observed, also become explicable within this general picture. The first concerns a coalition of Canaanite city-states led by Sisera against the tribes of Naphtali and Zebulun in lower Galilee and the Jezreel Valley (Judges 4). That provides evidence of a struggle between Canaanites and Israelites for mastery after settlement in the land, probably during the twelfth century B.C.E., that the Israelites eventually won. The other exception is Abimelech's attempt, described in Judges 9, to gain control over the Israelite villages, possibly with the help of non-Israelites in Shechem. The twelfth-century groups of clans that would ultimately comprise Israel were far from immune to violence and oppression, and the picture in Judges of recurrent invasion by groups from outside and of internal attempts to gain power is, unfortunately, consistent with the historical experience in the region.

The Book of Judges says remarkably little about the clan of Judah. Judah does lead the clans in possessing its territory (Judges 1) and furnishes a "judge" in the person of Othniel (Judges 3:7–11). But apart from these passages (and Judah is not mentioned *explicitly* in 3:7–11) and the obvious gloss at 20:18, Judah plays no part in Judges. This accords well with the evidence from archaeological surveys, which shows that settlement in Judah was sparse compared with the Bethel and Samaria hills.

How were these villages organized socially? We know less than is often supposed. Over the years, various theories have been put forward about Israel's organization in the period of the judges. A very influential view, given classic expression by the German scholar Martin Noth in the 1930s, held that Israel was a twelve-"tribe" amphictyony, that is, a confederation of semiautonomous peoples (rather than clans) bound together by mutual obligations and centered on a particular sanctuary. This view rested partly on Judges 20–1, in which the tribes unite to punish Benjamin for a moral outrage. Recently, it has proven popular to argue that Israel was an egalitarian segmentary society: a society in which there was no central source of power or authority and in which power was distributed horizontally among groups of equal status rather than vertically downward from rulers to subjects. The segmentary theory is probably closer to the truth than the amphictyony theory, provided we remember that the Israelites had powerful local leaders during the period of the judges without having one single seat of absolute power.

Judges 10:1–5 and 12:8–15 give brief details regarding lesser-known judges. We learn that Jair the Gileadite had thirty sons and thirty cities (Judges 10:3–4), and that Abdon had forty sons and thirty grandsons who rode on seventy asses (12:13–14). The conclusion of the story of Gideon (8:29–30) claims that he had seventy sons born to his many wives. Even allowing for evident exaggerations, these passages show that the judges were leading men in their local communities who, in return for the responsibilities that they had assumed for their people, enjoyed privileges such as a multiplicity of wives. Their responsibilities probably included the coordination of activities that needed the resources of more than one village (such as clearing forests and building terraces) and the settlement of disputes. Their families were or became dominant in their localities. Whether or not we can call them leaders of "tribes" is a difficult question because that term has been applied in different ways in scholarship. In the case of ancient Israel we do not know whether we are dealing with descent groups or with territorial areas or with both. We also do not know whether these groups took their names from or gave their names to the geographical areas in which they settled.

On the basis of these considerations we can characterize the emergence of Israel in the period of the Judges (ca. 1200–1010 B.C.E.). Territorial Israel consisted of a number of villages in the Bethel and Samaria hills and in lower Galilee. Leading members of dominant families exercised local control over these villages, heading up small armies in war and adjudicating disputes. These local leaders dealt with threats from groups from outside the land, and the leaders' exploits were preserved in traditional stories. Sometimes, different Israelite groups united to face a common enemy, such as Sisera (Judges 4–5); but Israelite clans also quarreled and fought with one another, as in Gideon of Manasseh's dispute with Ephraim and the men of Succoth and Penuel. The Gileadites under Jephthah also had a bitter dispute with the Ephraimites (12:1–6). The attempt of Abimelech to establish centralized control only exacerbated intra-Israelite strife (Judges 9).

Religious attitudes and actions featured in Judges often contradict commandments found elsewhere in the Hebrew Bible regarding religious practice (especially those emanating from the Deuteronomists during the seventh century B.C.E and later). Jephthah sacrifices his only daughter in fulfillment of a vow to God (11:29–40). Samson's involvement with foreign women, corpses, and unclean animals in chapters 13–16 conflicts with the Nazirite vow he had allegedly undertaken from before his birth, because Nazirites abstained from alcohol and uncleanness (see Numbers 6). In Judges 18 the men of Dan enlist a Levite to be their priest and use force to acquire household gods and a graven image to be part of his cult. If Judges 18–20 reflects the conditions of this chaotic period, then the "tribes" were pledged not only to provide mutual help against a common enemy but also to punish any tribe that violated the customs of hospitality and the protection of travelers.

FAMILY LIFE IN EARLY ISRAEL

A typical Israelite household during the Early Iron Age consisted of four to five persons. Infant mortality rates were so high that six births per couple were necessary to ensure the survival of the average family's two children. This typical family lived with their livestock in a two-story stone house with about fifty square meters of livable floor space. Their home was located in a cluster of similar domestic buildings that housed other families to whom they were closely related. Families lived crowded together in open settlements, not on individual farming plots. Each day, workers walked to the fields early in the morning and returned at night. From ten to twenty extended family units made up the small highland villages. An average village would have been home to fewer than a hundred people.

These figures derive from estimates based on archaeological and ethnographic investigation, not from any actual census of Israelite settlements in the twelfth to eleventh centuries B.C.E. Yet archaeology, anthropology, and biblical history can provide some insight into what family life was like in early Israel.

Iron Age dwellings in the highlands commonly had stone walls, plastered floors, and ceilings of mud and straw reinforced with wooden beams. A door led into the most spacious of the house's rooms, a living area often used for food preparation, household crafts, and storage. A narrow room to one side, often separated by stone pillars that supported low partitions of masonry fill, was used as a stable. The back end of the house formed a broad room running the length of the building.

On the ground floor of these typical "four-room houses" archaeologists have found countless storage jars (called *pithoi*), kitchenwares (cooking pots, for example), and implements for processing food (stone hand mills, chopping blocks, and flint sickle blades), along with evidence of small craft production (such as spinning and sewing). Animals shared the first floor with human inhabitants. Livestock, mainly sheep and goats, were brought into the house at night to the flagstone-paved side room through a small passage in the principal domestic quarters. Warmth radiating from them up to the second-story living quarters provided an inexpensive (albeit malodorous) source of heat. The second-story rooms built across the timber-supported ceiling of the ground floor accommodated dining, sleeping, and small-scale social activities. The design was a successful adaptation to farm life by rural families who grew crops and raised livestock.

Early Israelite farmhouses were normally built in clustered compounds. Common walls sometimes linked two or three private houses, presumably to accommodate families as they grew by marriage and procreation, and to permit multiple familes to reduce the labor required to erect a house. Each house in the compound had a separate entrance, usually approached through a shared courtyard enclosure. Compounds of multiple families and extended families constituted the basic socioeconomic unit in ancient Israel. Households cooperated to procure, process, store, preserve, prepare, and serve food. Sometimes they shared an open-air workshop for metallurgy. The group collectively held land and shared labor needs.

In biblical terminology this social unit was the *bet 'ab*, "house of the father." An ideal household consisted of a senior couple, their children, and the families of their married sons or daughters. Sometimes even after a father's death married brothers continued to live in the same compound, working together cooperatively as a single household, and provision was made for daughters to inherit in the absence of surviving sons. Authority was held by the eldest male member, although the household's primary female probably wielded power by virtue of her decision making in allocating the family's resources. Life in such farming villages would have been consumed with meeting the everyday needs of survival for their inhabitants. Agricultural and domestic tasks required long hours of hard work. The routine seasonal pattern of plowing, sowing, pruning, harvesting, threshing, and gathering set the rhythm for life in each family and in the entire village. Men, women, and children shared household and farm responsibilities as these early Israelite families scratched out an existence on the highland frontiers.

The Literary History of Judges

The Bible incorporates an edition of the Book of Judges that claims to describe what happened to the whole Israelite nation from the death of Joshua to the eve of the rise of the monarchy. The narrative is guided by the schema that "all" Israel had traveled from Egypt to Israel and had fought against the Canaanites before the clans separated to occupy their allotted land. Local leaders seem to lead the whole nation, and local enemies become the enemies of the whole people. The final edition of the work, whenever the various stories originated, anticipates the rise of the monarchy and assumes that moral chaos is the result of failing to appoint a king acceptable to God.

Twelve judges span the period from Joshua to the eve of the birth of Samuel:

Othniel	3:7–11
Ehud	3:12–30
Deborah	4:1–23
Gideon	6:1–8:35
Abimelech	9:1–57
Tola	10:1–2
Jair	10:3–5
Jephthah	11:1–12:7
Ibzan	12:8–10
Elon	12:11–12
Abdon	12:13–15
Samson	13:1–16:31

This list reflects two types of material: longer stories about the judges who deliver Israel from oppressors (Ehud, Deborah, Gideon, Abimelech, Jephthah, and Samson) and brief notices about powerful local strong men (Tola, Jair, Ibzan, Elon, Abdon, and probably Othniel). These traditions have been joined to fill the gap from Joshua to the time of Samuel, so as to produce a master narrative of Israel's acquisition and settlement of the promised land.

Judges sets up a theological framework that interprets the events of the period in terms of disobedience, punishment, repentance, and restoration. The people of Israel turn from Yahweh to serve other gods. God then gives them into the hand of one enemy or another, who oppresses them. When the Israelites return to God and cry for help, he raises up a deliverer who defeats the enemy and gives the Israelites rest for a period, until the whole process begins again. In some cases this framework appears to be a later addition to stories about individual deliverers. The saga of Samson, for example, begins with a statement of the theological framework (Judges 13:1, 5b), but the Philistines only gradually appear as the enemy. This suggests that the Book of Judges went through several editions before reaching its present form.

The initial editions probably lacked the theological introduction in chapters 2:1–3:11, as well as regular references to the cycle of disobedience, oppression, repentance, and deliverance. Although the precise forms of stories in their various stages cannot be reconstructed, they probably became part of a larger work that included the stories of the ancestors and the conquest, and that culminated in the establishment of David's kingship. A date for this edition is hard to establish; a plausible time would be the reign of Hezekiah (727–698 B.C.E.). Probably during the time of Josiah (640–609 B.C.E.) this edition was adapted into the Deuteronomistic History, where it began to receive its theological framework and Deuteronomistic comments. This process was not completed until the exile (during the sixth century B.C.E.). Two sections of Judges have provoked debate among specialists from the point of view of dating them: the Song of Deborah in chapter 5, and the so-called epilogue to the book, chapters 19–21 (or 17–21, in the view of some scholars).

The date of the Song of Deborah is much disputed. Many scholars take the song to be among the most ancient materials in the Bible, notable for its description of God marching from Edom (5:4), its attribution of Israel's victory to the stars of heaven (5:20), its lack of reference to Judah, and its complaint that some of the peoples of Israel did not join with Deborah in the victory (5:15c–17). On this understanding, the song offers evidence of the situation of the clans in the period between 1200 and 1010 B.C.E. Alternative views date the song's completion within the eighth or the seventh century B.C.E. A subsidiary question is the relationship of chapter 5 to chapter 4. Chapter 4 names only two tribes, Zebulun and Naphtali, as involved in the battle, whereas chapter 5 aligns Issachar, Zebulun, Ephraim, Benjamin, and Machir (perhaps a poetic name for Manasseh, or a subsidiary clan) with Deborah and Barak. The failure to name Judah, the apparent location of Dan near the coastal plain rather than in the far north, and the unusual name for Manasseh tell in favor of the view that the Song of Deborah includes ancient material whatever the time of its composition in its present form.

If Judges originally ended at 16:31, with the death of Samson, the book would have been an excellent prelude to the story of the birth of Samuel in 1 Samuel. Chapters 17–21 interrupt this sequence and, with their recurring refrain that there was no king in Israel and that everyone did what was right in his own eyes, they seem to address a different agenda from that of the rest of the book. They have often been treated as having been added at a late stage in the book's composition. On the other hand, as mentioned earlier, some of the religious practices described in chapters 17–21 seem to be at odds with later practice. Further, if Judges looks forward to and promotes David's kingship, then chapters 17–21 could well have been part of an early edition of Judges, serving to show how necessary it was for a king chosen by God to rule the people.

The Literary Structure and Function of Judges

Judges consists of an account of the clans entering their territories after Joshua's death (chapter 1), followed by reflection upon the unfaithfulness

THE TWELVE "TRIBES" OF ISRAEL

The final editors of Israel's national religious history present what seems to be a clear picture of early Israelite social organization. From the very moment of the Exodus the people of Israel are said to have been divided into twelve "tribes," or clans, each descended from one of the sons of their common ancestor, Jacob. Leah bore Reuben, Simeon, Levi, Judah, Issachar, and Zebulun; Rachel bore Joseph and Benjamin; Bilha bore Dan and Naphtali; Zilpah bore Gad and Asher. Because a direct genealogical relationship is asserted, the term "tribe" is used with a greater claim to familial connection than that term term usually conveys, so "clan" might also be used, and is increasingly seen as preferable.

According to Judges 13–22, these tribes were apportioned adjoining territories in Palestine and the Transjordan. A close examination of the biblical text, however, suggests that this twelve-tribe system oversimplifies the social realities in early Israel. The tribal designations sometimes reflect the possession of land, rather than genealogical divisions. Groups that were bound by similar histories and who shared lifestyles and territories often expressed their relationship in terms of their belief that they descended from a common ancestry. But even understanding the twelve tribes as inhabitants of twelve separate territories would be simplistic. The tribal society of Israel before the monarchy was marked by vague and fluid divisions. Identities and relationships between social units changed from time to time; claims of clan affinity served to weld these complex variations into a coherent order and sense of social identity.

Social (and later, administrative) needs imposed a twelve-tribe system on the complicated and sometimes competing concerns of genealogy, land, and alliance in early Israel. In the north, Manasseh – descended from Joseph (Genesis 48–1) – settled with the associated and perhaps subordinate groups known as Ephraimites, Benjaminites, and Gileadites. Asher, Zebulun, Issachar, and Naphtali settled in the region of Galilee and Jezreel. Calebites, Kenizzites, Jerahmeelites, Kenites, and Simeonites – groups that would come to compose the social entity of greater Judah – lived in the south. The tribes of Reuben and Gad apparently had no fixed territory but roamed about with their herds and flocks. At some point the Danite tribe seems to have migrated under Philistine pressure from its coastal territory to the region near the springs that feed the Jordan north of the Sea of Galilee. This picture, drawn from close inspection of narratives in Joshua and Judges, takes account of the independence and interrelatedness of various tribes and/or clans. Although they cooperated loosely and sporadically, for the most part in the face of military threats, these groups by and large lived autonomously.

For centuries scholars reconstructed the history of premonarchic Israel along more formal lines, specifically on analogy to sacred tribal leagues that existed in the Mediterranean world among the Greeks and Old Latins. Israel's tribes were thought to have existed in a close alliance that exhibited many of the same characteristics as these amphictyonies (from the Greek term for "inhabitants of the neighboring district"). An amphictyony was an association of autonomous groups organized into multimember confederations. The groups worshipped a common deity at a common shrine (cf. Yahweh's ark at Shechem and later Shiloh), accepted binding sacred law (cf. the Sinai covenant), and submitted to the rule of a body of officers delegated from the member groups (cf. the Israelite judges). Biblical evidence for such a confederacy in Israel is at best uncertain. The twelve-tribe system is a relatively late phenomenon in premonarchic Israel, if it is not a construct from the period of the monarchy itself; worship in early Israel was certainly not limited to a single shrine, and the biblical judges were seldom national leaders.

Yet before the nation of Israel was established by Saul and David, military cooperation and social bonds did link various Israelite groups. The formation of the Israelite monarchy itself presupposes preliminary tribal association, and even an early text like the Song of Deborah (Judges 5) assumes a degree of pan-tribal organization, although the list of tribes in that passage differs in number and content from the classic formulation of Israel's twelve tribes.

Recently scholars have suggested that the twelve-tribe system familiar to us took shape just prior to the formation of the monarchy. David apparently expanded and reconstituted earlier groupings to incorporate the Canaanite populace of his growing territories. David's roster of tribes represents administrative districts organized around traditional social groups from which the king drew his monthly quotas of military personnel and supplies (2 Samuel 5:1–5). Solomon utilized this system in his program of redistricting the nation, which was designed to increase administrative efficiency. In doing so, however, Solomon stretched the old designations, since his boundaries were drawn according to practical needs rather than traditional social divisions (1 Kings 4:7–19). After the separation of the northern and southern kingdoms, the twelve-tribe system became a traditional concept that expressed the unity of all those who worshipped Yahweh rather than social realities.

This reconstruction helps explain an anomaly in the biblical presentation of the twelve tribes. The Hebrew Bible actually preserves two different lists with twelve tribes each. One list includes Ephraim and Manasseh as separate tribes, omitting the Levites; the other includes the tribe of Levi and telescopes Ephraim and Manasseh into the single tribe of Joseph. Most scholars think that the Ephraim–Manasseh list is older. When the system of twelve tribes became more symbolic than actual, it became necessary to include the priestly Levites as one of the original twelve tribes. To retain the traditional number of twelve tribes, two closely related tribes in the north were conflated and given the name of their common ancestor, Joseph.

The "twelve tribes" of Israel became an encompassing conception read back into the earliest days of Israel's history. It symbolized the unity of the Israelite people from the days of Moses onward, and it was even retrojected into the grand genealogical design of the patriarch Jacob and his twelve sons. In that way a system that took shape in the days of the united kingdom became a way of expressing the cooperation among traditional "proto-Israelite" groups during the time Israel was first settling into the land of Canaan.

of the people to God, and how God both punished and delivered them (2:1–3:11), leading to the stories of the deliverer-judges, whose numbers are made to add up to twelve by means of the brief notices of minor judges (3:12–16:31). The epilogue (chapters 17–21) describes the unsatisfactory moral and religious state of affairs when there was no king in Israel.

The most obvious function of the book is indicated by the Deuteronomistic introduction in chapters 2 and 3 and by the passages that show the persistence and consistency of the disobedience—punishment—repentance—deliverance cycle. Within the Deuteronomistic history the function of this material is clear. If the History is addressed to the Jews who stand poised to return, or have just returned, to Judah and Jerusalem, Judges is telling them that their exile to Babylon was the result of their disobedience to God. Their return has been God's gracious act of deliverance. If they wish to remain in the land in the future, they must heed the warnings contained in Judges and not turn away from Yahweh.

Whether or not Judges once existed in a version without its Deuteronomistic trappings, the book serves another function: to exalt the house of David, particularly in its implicit contrast with the settled system of courts that Solomon presided over. By looking forward to David's kingship and ending with the observation that there was no king in Israel and that moral chaos was the result, the narrative structure presents the ancient leaders before David as deeply flawed – and none of them establishes a dynasty.

Ehud is left-handed – a defect in Israelite society, although this trait gives him his triumph over Eglon, king of Moab (Judges 3:12–30); Barak is not prepared to lead his people unless accompanied by Deborah (Judges 4:8–9); and Deborah herself cannot become a king or founder of a dynasty because she is a woman. Gideon is offered the kingship and rightly refuses, on the grounds that Yahweh alone is Israel's king; he nonetheless makes an

Map IV. Territorial allocations to the clans of Israel

idol that entraps Israel (Judges 8:22–7). Gideon's son Abimelech does try to become king in chapter 9, but the attempt is a disaster and he is killed while attacking one of his own cities. Jephthah has only one child, a daughter, and she is sacrificed in fulfillment of Jephthah's vow to sacrifice the first person he meets on returning home if God grants him victory (chapter 11). Samson is hardly a suitable candidate to establish permanent leadership given his lust for foreign women who connive at his defeat.

After these stories of brave but defective heroes and heroines, the final chapters of the book portray religious and moral chaos in a leaderless, rudderless Israel. Although the Israelite clans unite to punish the tribe of Benjamin for the outrage perpetrated in one town on a traveling Levite and his concubine, the outcome is out of all proportion to the original crime, heinous though that crime is (chapters 19–21). Losses in the battle between Israel and Benjamin amount to tens of thousands of warriors, and that is not the end of the slaughter. Benjamin lies at the edge of extinction. Although the other clans will not give their daughters in marriage to Benjaminite men, wives need to be found if the life of Benjamin as a clan is to go on. Jabesh-gilead provides the solution. Allegedly because the men of Jabesh-gilead (in Transjordan) did not join the rest of Israel in fighting Benjamin, all its males are slaughtered and four hundred virgins are brought from Jabesh-gilead to Benjamin. The book closes with its most gruesome portrait of self-destructive chaos in Israel, a chaos ascribed to the lack of a king. The Books of Samuel narrate how that lack was to be met.

Early Iron Age pillar house at Beersheba, also known as a four-room house. Typical of the ancient Near East, this is the kind of house wealthy Israelites inhabited. (BiblePlaces.com)

3. First and Second Samuel

Israel before and during the United Monarchy

As the eleventh century B.C.E. drew to a close, Israel consisted of a number of villages in the Bethel and Samaria hills and in lower Galilee. No Israelite urban center had yet emerged to exercise hegemony. Rather, what we may call chiefs – leading members of dominant families who were accorded privileges in their roles as leaders in battle and judges in disputes – exerted local rule. Judah was less densely settled than Israel and witnessed a slow increase in population during the twelfth and eleventh centuries, so that the arrangement of local chiefs prevailed there as well. A social and religious identity linking the Israelites (and possibly Judeans) nonetheless formed and consolidated during the period of the judges. How this identity was expressed politically remains difficult to specify. It is going too far to speak of a confederation with officials and a common law, such as was demanded by the old scholarly theory of the Israelite amphictyony. Yet there was at least a sufficient sense of a common interest for Israelite villages to unite locally and perhaps even nationally on occasion in the face of threats from outside and to frame the most ancient traditions in the Books of Judges and Joshua. This common interest included an element of kinship along with religion, with the latter focused on the ark of the covenant. This portable sacred box attested that Yahweh, the God who had freed his people from slavery and who accompanied them in their battles on his movable throne, was present with Israel.

As the eleventh century B.C.E. ended, the last and most serious threat to Israel from an outside group emerged in the form of the Philistines. They figured among the Sea Peoples, who had traveled by sea and by land from Crete or Asia Minor and had attempted to settle in Egypt a little after 1200. Some succeeded in settling in the coastal plain in the ancient cities of Ashkelon, Ashdod, and Gaza. They then began to expand into the Shephelah, where they founded or occupied Gath and Ekron (whose exact locations remain uncertain). Around 1040 B.C.E. they began to exert pressure on the tribe of Dan, which was situated on the coastal plain, in the valley of Aijalon, and in the Shephelah to the north of the Philistines. The stories of Samson belong to this period.

Having forced the Danites to migrate to the far north, the Philistines set out to conquer inland around 1020 B.C.E., and they defeated the Israelite forces in two battles in the foothills of Ephraim (1 Samuel 4). The Shephelah is a transitional zone between the coastal plain and the Judean hill country, so that a movement into Judah would have made sense. Why did the Philistines turn their attention to the Ephraim hills instead of moving immediately eastward against Judah? Judges 15:9–13 tells a story about the Philistines invading to make the Judeans capture and hand over Samson, implying that part of Judah, at least, was subject to such raids. The famous story of David and Goliath (1 Samuel 17), ignoring its later political and theological elaboration, also represents the memory of a time when the Philistines and the men of Judah fought each other in the Shephelah and

Distinctive pottery, found at sites along the coast of Palestine and inland from the twelfth and eleventh centuries B.C.E., produced by the Philistines. This example from Gezer show the influence of the Mycenean painted pottery traditions, which the Philistines encountered on the way to Canaan. (BiblePlaces.com)

THE ARK OF THE COVENANT

Mentioned some two hundred times in the Hebrew Bible, the ark of the covenant became ancient Israel's most important religious symbol. In Exodus 25 the ark is described as a box made of acacia wood, measuring 4 × 2½ × 2½ feet and covered with gold. Golden rings were attached through which poles could be inserted to carry the ark about. Over the ark was a plate of gold called the *kipporet*, the place of appeasement or "mercy seat" (as it is called in the King James Version). Two cherubim, winged sphinxlike creatures, stood at the ends of the *kipporet*, covering it with their wings as a canopy. According to priestly tradition, the ark was the throne of Yahweh. Similar imagery, and its associated ideology, run throughout the religious art of the ancient Near East. An elaborate tent or "tabernacle" was built to accommodate the ark, which was central to the worship of the Israelites from the days of their wanderings in the desert until the end of Israel's independent existence.

Like the description, of the tabernacle, which the Book of Exodus also details, this picture of the ark probably represents a retrojection into an earlier age of arrangements in Solomon's Temple, where the ark stood in the sanctuary's holiest place. The ark seems to have played a key role in some of Israel's earliest national traditions, but it is likely at first to have been a simple wooden box designed as a receptacle for an abstract or a copy of the covenant with Yahweh (Deuteronomy 9:9). Ancient covenants were often deposited in special locations related to the presence of the gods in whose names they were made. The ark became the visible sign of Yahweh's presence, an extension of his divine personality (see Psalm 132). The ark also plays an important role in military contexts, as a symbol of divine protection in war and adversity (Numbers 10:33–6). The ark is said to have led Israel over the Jordan and to have figured prominently in the stories of the Israelite settlement of the Promised Land (e.g., at Jericho, Joshua 5–6).

The precise location of the ark of the covenant becomes obscure during the period of the Judges until it reappears at Shiloh under the protection of Eli and his family. Its place in Israel's worship before the monarchy is uncertain. Although the ark may have been important for some groups, it most likely did not serve – as once was thought – as the focal point of any tribal confederacy during the days of early Israel. The ark does play a central role again in the Samuel narratives, which culminate with the story of how David brought the ark to Jerusalem. A variety of narratives celebrate the power and grandeur of the ark long before it achieved its final place of glory in Solomon's Temple. The Philistines experienced its effects when a plague of boils struck them after they had captured the ark (1 Samuel 5); seventy men were struck down for not rejoicing when the ark appeared (1 Samuel 6:19); and Uzzah's death came when he inadvertently touched the ark during its grand procession to the new capital (2 Samuel 6:7).

By moving the ark to Jerusalem, David ensured that his new southern-based kingdom was heir to the religious and political traditions of the north. The move symbolized Jerusalem's new role as the religious center of the nation, and David claimed for himself the role of protector and patron of the national cult. The ark was placed in a tent built especially for that purpose until Solomon completed work on its final resting place, the Temple of Yahweh. The ark of the covenant probably disappeared during the invasion of Nebuchadnezzar in 587/6 B.C.E., although it may have been taken along with the Temple's other treasures when the Babylonians exacted tribute from King Jehoiachin ten years earlier or even when Shishak of Egypt plundered treasures from the Temple centuries before that (1 Kings 14:25–6). No new ark was made for the Second Temple (Jeremiah 3:16), though some scholars understand the *kipporet* – the seat of the divine presence – to be a substitute for it in the postexilic tradition (1 Chronicles 28:11; cf. Leviticus 16:2, 3).

their champions met in combat. David is even introduced into the entourage of Saul as a man of war (1 Samuel 16:18).

Yet there is no explicit information in 1 Samuel about a Philistine campaign in Judah. This may be accidental, but there is another way of looking at the matter. Philistine expansion was no doubt inspired by a desire for power and territory. Their campaign needed food supplies to sustain it: fertile land was a likely target of takeover for practical reasons as well as in consideration of its value. In regard to fertility, the region of Israel (the northern "tribes") was richer than Judah. Rainfall becomes more reliable the further north one goes, and the broad valleys of the Samaria hills and lower Galilee were more suitable for producing grain than the Judean hill country. The move against Israel therefore made long-term strategic sense, and after defeating the Israelite armies, the Philistines established themselves in key ancient cities such as Megiddo and Bet She'an, as well as in small garrisons in the central hill country.

The traditional Israelite response to threats from outsiders – a campaign led by a local warlord – failed on this occasion. The principal local leader of the time seems to have been Samuel. Although he is credited with victories over the Philistines (1 Samuel 7:5–14), any respite was temporary, and Israel looked to a more powerful type of leadership, that of a "king," to deliver them from the Philistines. Recent discussion of the monarchy in Israel has concluded that it is more accurate to describe Saul and David as chiefs rather than as kings, and to regard Solomon as the first Israelite ruler to put into place the administrative infrastructure that would make the description "king" appropriate. This scholarship also points to the importance of the personalities of Saul and David and to the role of their families in establishing their power. Nonetheless, the terminology of "king" will be retained here, while bearing the preceding points in mind, because Saul and David do mark a significant national departure from the pattern of rule reflected in the Book of Judges.

Saul, from the tribe of Benjamin, emerged as a chief, although the accounts of his leadership in 1 Samuel 8–15 leave much that is unclear. We do not even know how long he reigned. No doubt as a result of textual corruption, 1 Samuel 13:1 says two years, but gives Saul's age at accession as one year old! How he became king is also obscure, apart from the story of Samuel's grudging agreement to anoint Saul on behalf of Yahweh (1 Samuel 9–10). First Samuel has its sights set so firmly on the establishment of David's rule that it truncates the story of Saul's leadership. But 1 Samuel does indicate that Saul was associated with the prophetic groups led by Samuel (1 Samuel 10:12), that he was a zealous adherent of Yahweh (1 Samuel 28:3; 2 Samuel 21:1–6), and that he delivered the men of Jabesh-gilead from the Ammonites (1 Samuel 11:1–11), all probably prior to becoming Israel's supreme chief in the struggle with the Philistines.

Why did this new form of leadership arise? The Philistine threat, taken by itself, is probably not a sufficient explanation; underlying social and economic causes should be also factored in. According to one view, the change of leadership was allied to the inability of the existing structures of production and distribution to provide adequate food for a growing population. Of the two possible responses to this situation – the emigration of surplus population or the adoption of new, more centralizing structures of production – the latter won the day. Although such explanations are helpful, it remains likely that the Philistine threat was the principal catalyst for the move to a new type of leadership.

KINGSHIP IN THE ANCIENT NEAR EAST

Kingship was the foundation of civilized life in the great cultures of the ancient Near East, and the focus of the ancient world's hopes for security, peace, and justice. The king stood at the center of religious reality in ancient Near Eastern cultures, because sacred power and secular power were considered to derive from divine mandate and to be intimately related. The monarch provided the vital contact point between this world and the otherworldly realm of the gods. Human society was viewed as an integral part of the larger cosmos, and it was the king's function to maintain the harmony of that integration.

The precise concept of kingship varied extensively, however, within specific cultural contexts. An Egyptian monarch was conceived of as a divine being actually descended from the gods. Although living among mortals, he or she remained an important part of the divine world, a continual reincarnation of the god Horus, who lived in mysterious communion with his predecessor, Osiris. To the rulers of Egypt were attributed superhuman physical powers, qualities characteristic only of the gods. Egypt's rulers enjoyed a status that embodied the community's freedom from fear and uncertainty. When pharaoh ruled on the throne, the world was seen to be functioning as it should; established order was holding back the onslaught of the powers of chaos. The pharaoh enjoyed absolute power, yet he was not to wield it capriciously, but to exercise it within the bounds of order, justice, and right (Egyptian *ma'at*). In the early dynasties the Egyptian ruler frequently represented the entire society and embodied the hopes of the members of that society for life beyond death.

In Mesopotamian cultures, the conception of the divine essence and status of the monarch, which was fundamental to Egyptian civilization and religion, was not developed. Kings in the "Land between the Rivers" were mortals. The Mesopotamian word for "king" literally means "great man." Although the king was a heroic person and leader of his people, he was not essentially different from his fellows. Mesopotamian rulers were elected by the gods, but they did not necessarily enjoy the benefit of special divine counsel. Kings and commoners alike in Mesopotamia were forced to seek knowledge from rites, dreams, and omens in order to perform their respective duties in accordance with the often capricious will of the gods. Kings in Mesopotamia served three functions: to administer the realm faithfully, to represent the people prayerfully before the gods to ensure prosperity and well-being, and to serve the gods regularly by building temples for them and by officiating at their state festivals. Society and nature were not as seamlessly integrated in Mesopotamia as they were in Egyptian ideology; the harmony between the world of the gods and the world of humankind was by no means assured. Since the ruler was himself only a mortal, he too stood anxious before the unpredictable will of the gods. As a consequence of this lack of divine status, in Mesopotamia the community maintained considerable independence from the king.

Israel's monarchy developed in the context of these and other ancient Near Eastern conceptions of kingship. The uniquely Israelite religious and social traditions that were to emerge were characterized by a peculiar royal institution that emphasized the king's dependence on Yahweh and his responsibility to the people and their traditional allegiances. The conception that the king became a "son" to Yahweh (Psalm 2:7) may reflect the royal ideology of the Canaanites, who also referred to their monarch in this way, mediating between the Egyptian and Mesopotamian models. In Israel the monarchy took shape at the prompting of the community and under the strain of a national emergency, rather than developing as the society's original mode of organization. Still, Israel designed its unique form of kingship by drawing on a common stock of ideas and forms current in other ancient Near Eastern cultures. It is not surprising to find hints of Israelite belief and practice that represent beliefs and practices originating in Mesopotamia and Egypt.

Several competing concepts of kingship existed in Israel, some more favorably disposed toward foreign models than others, although the Hebrew Bible downplays these similarities between Israel and its contemporaries. The final editors of the biblical narratives are also likely to have colored historical accounts with their own perspectives, which developed in a time when the monarchy had been generally discredited and was no longer a viable political institution.

Whatever the reasons Saul rose to power, his leadership provided only temporary respite from the Philistine threat; it was left to David to turn a desperate situation to the advantage of Israel and Judah. Fragments of genealogy, such as 2 Samuel 17:25 (with 1 Kings 14:31; 1 Chronicles 2:16–17) suggest that David was related through his mother to the rulers of the Ammonites of eastern Jordan. The group to which David was related may have settled in Judah during the twelfth century B.C.E., traveling from Ammon via Moab. Judah probably became formally allied with Israel against the Philistines when David, the son of a chief in Judah, joined Saul's entourage (1 Samuel 16:14–23). David soon became close friends with Saul's son Jonathan, and married Saul's daughter Michal, but Saul's suspicions of his motives led to a breach with David, forcing the latter to become the leader of a powerful group of guerilla fighters before eventually deserting to the Philistines. After Saul's defeat and death at the hands of the Philistines, David consolidated a power base in Judah until he was strong enough to defeat the Philistines, to establish his rule over Israel and Judah, and to inflict defeats upon neighboring peoples such as those in Damascus, Ammon, Edom, and Moab.

Just as there has been debate over use of the term "king" to describe Saul and David, so it has been doubted whether we should speak of a Davidic state or empire. The question turns on the extent of infrastructure necessary to make it meaningful to speak of king, state, or empire. According to the indices of public works, the size of the urban center, literacy, and the availability of luxury items, "Judah was a small state in the 8th–7th centuries, but not before" (Jamieson-Drake 1991, p. 139). Using these indices, not even Solomon could properly be called a king, although according to Jamieson-Drake, he "should be credited with setting in motion the institutional forces which eventually resulted in state bureaucratic controls accompanied by an intensity of settlement and levels of regional economic activity appropriate to a state" (1991, p. 144).

It seems, then, that we must look at David's achievements in a new way: his power in Israel was that of a chief to whom loyalty was forthcoming because he had freed the people from Philistine domination. His war against the Ammonites was probably on behalf of Israelites living in northern Transjordan, but his other victories did not result in the establishment of his rule over other territories outside Israel so as to establish an empire. The personal nature of David's rule is intimated by the fact that, according to 2 Samuel 14–15, the king was expected to adjudicate legal disputes, as the "judges" once did (and in some locales no doubt continued to do). Further, there were two revolts against David, and his commander and nephew Joab was able to disregard David's instructions and to wield power over him (2 Samuel 3:20–39).

Standard descriptions of Israel's history from 1200 to 1000 B.C.E. once depicted a transition from tribal confederacy to dynastic state. Recent research makes these labels inappropriate, because the local power of the clans resisted central authority, whether in the form of confederation or monarchy. Yet David's reign did achieve the temporary takeover of Israel by Judah. Under Solomon, that takeover was defended as Yahweh's will, with deep implications for the form and content of the biblical writings.

The Literary History of the Books of Samuel

First and Second Samuel reached their final form as part of the Deuteronomistic History during the exile, as a broad consensus of scholarship maintains,
but experts differ strongly over the antiquity of the material contained within
the books. Thirty years ago it was generally agreed that 2 Samuel 9–20 was
part of a court chronicle written during the reign of Solomon. Although
scholars debated the purpose of this composition – whether it intended, for
example, to tell the triumphant story of the succession to David's throne or to
mount a religious and prophetic critique of David's misdemeanors – the date
was not disputed. Today, some scholars believe that 2 Samuel 9–20 was written after the exile. These chronological issues remain contentious, but 1 and 2
Samuel do seem to contain at least some material from the period of David
and Solomon and to include fragments about Saul's leadership (1 Samuel
9–11, 13–15). The story of David's rise to power, which begins in 1 Samuel
16, is intertwined with stories about David and Jonathan before emerging as
a clear story line in the closing chapter of 1 Samuel, and it continues through
to 2 Samuel 20, with some insertions in chapters 2 and 8. The final chapters
of 2 Samuel also contain what looks like ancient material.

Written material did not circulate widely in premonarchic Israel; why was
the story of David's rise written down? It is possible, of course, that the material is a written version of stories about David and Saul that circulated orally
and were intended to entertain as much as to inform. One line of approach
takes its bearings from how the story of David's rise from 1 Samuel 16 insists
on absolving David of guilt in the failure of Saul's rule. For example, David's
desertion to the Philistines is presented as a last, desperate move by David to
get out of reach of Saul's manic quest to destroy him. David's nonparticipa-
tion on the Philistine side in the battle in which Saul and Jonathan are killed
is stressed, and David's elimination of Saul's family in 2 Samuel 21:1–14 is
described as necessary to avert famines that are God's punishment for Saul's
unlawful slaying of the Gibeonites. Yet this is not an attempt to present David
as a generally exemplary character: 2 Samuel 10–12 narrates David's adultery
with Bathsheba critically, as well as his cynical maneuver to get her husband
killed in battle, and the disastrous consequences of such actions.

It is difficult to imagine that these attempts to vindicate David in his dealings with Saul, while vilifying David's personal behavior, were first penned
during the exile (in the sixth century B.C.E.). After all, by that time the
northern kingdom had not existed for nearly two hundred years. A more
likely period of composition is when Judah took over Israel's identity following the demise of the northern kingdom during the reign of Hezekiah
(ca. 727–698), or during the time of Solomon (961–922 B.C.E.), when the
northern tribes were uneasy about being ruled from Jerusalem by a dynasty
known to have Ammonite connections. Indeed, 1 Kings 14:31 notes that
Solomon's son and successor, Rehoboam, had an Ammonite mother.

Of these two alternatives, the time of Solomon and shortly thereafter
appears more plausible as the period when stories of David's rise were circulated orally and then written down. Their purpose was to make David
and his son acceptable to the northern tribes, while later, during

SOLOMON'S REORGANIZATION OF THE KINGDOM (961–922 B.C.E.)

The Kingdom of David and Solomon was no simple, self-contained nation-state. The ruling dynasty of this volatile, short-lived, and difficult to manage kingdom affected imperial power, although in size, infrastructure, and hegemony Israel could never compete with the traditional empires that held sway in the ancient Near East. David emerged as a charismatic warrior who brought the tribes together under unified rule and extended his influence into surrounding territories. In order to maintain this miniature empire, Solomon imposed strict administrative and economic controls over the interior relations of his kingdom. He implemented a redistricting plan for Israel that cut across traditional tribal boundaries (1 Kings 4:7–19). The new system attempted a more even distribution of the cost involved to provision the expanding Jerusalem court and fulfill the labor demands of royal programs of construction. Solomon showed more concern for bureaucratic rationality rather than age-old tribal affiliations. Court-appointed administrators who were loyal to the crown rather than to traditional authorities of village or clan assured royal control of the districts.

Solomon also reorganized the royal cabinet, elaborating the civil bureaucracy and streamlining the military establishment. The list of Solomonic officials in 1 Kings 4:1–6 in comparison with similar rolls from the time of David indicates a consolidation of the royal armies and a decrease in con-

cern for immediately military affairs. New officers were added to aid the king with the growing complexity of administering his empire.

These efforts by Solomon to reorganize the kingdom of Israel aimed to keep control of the labor force and the economic resources that had been captured by David's military exploits. Solomon was faced with the task of maintaining the loyalty of his own bureaucracy and sustaining the tributary status of vassal states. His ability to exact taxation and tribute rested upon belief in his dynastic supremacy. Solomon therefore fashioned Jerusalem into the center of his aspiring empire and set about developing the small Davidic city into a symbol of his dynasty's splendor, might, and right to rule.

Solomon also recast intertribal Yahwism in nationalistic terms, a move with international implications. The worship of Yahweh became the celebration of a dynastic as well as of a national, ethnic, and cultural deity. As such, worship emerged as a useful symbol for differentiating Israel from its conquered peoples. Solomon's construction of the elaborate Temple complex symbolized Yahweh's presence in Jerusalem. To the people dominated by the short-lived united monarchy, the Temple served as the visible focus of Israel's identity as the people of Yahweh.

Enhancing the grandeur of Jerusalem provided a further dramatic symbol, available for all to see, that Yahweh

legitimated Solomon's rule. Solomon's reputation in international trade, however exaggerated it may be in the Scriptures of Israel, is related to the role of Jerusalem as both the political and the symbolic center of the empire. The eclectic styles of royal construction, along with the accumulation of costly and exotic goods in the royal Temple treasuries, portrayed the empire's center as the dominating microcosm of all the peripheral areas around it.

Maintaining Jerusalem as the center of an empire and demonstrating the strength necessary to legitimate this right to rule demanded that Solomon extract heavy taxation, tribute, and forced labor from his kingdoms. The mechanics of empire also depended upon the construction of store cities, administrative centers, and military outposts throughout the land. Solomon executed a successful plan of reorganization and capital improvements that met the needs of empire after the Davidic conquests had exhausted the supply of captive workers and expended the spoils of war. But the cost to Israel and its conquered peoples was considerable. Most of the territories they inhabited were not naturally suitable for yielding economic surpluses, and after Solomon's reign the royal heirs were no longer able to exploit the overextended resources necessary to maintain Israel's imperial status. Both central control and the united nation fell apart from its center.

Hezekiah's reign, this material was joined with an early edition of the material in Judges and narratives of the ancestors, the Exodus, and the wilderness wanderings to show how God's promise to Abraham that his descendants would possess the land of Israel had been fulfilled in David, and to argue that David was the leader chosen by God to establish a

This beautiful monumental gateway at Gezer comes from the time of Solomon, and is similar to those at Hazor and Megiddo. The date of this gate is confirmed by the presence of a destruction level underneath it (from the unnamed pharaoh who gave the city to Solomon) and a destruction level (corresponding to the invasion under Shishak) not long after its construction. (BiblePlaces.com)

dynasty over Israel. In Josiah's reign, 1 and 2 Samuel then became part of the Deuteronomistic History. During the exile, passages such as 1 Samuel 8, expressing a very negative view of the kingship; the story of the loss and recovery of the ark in 1 Samuel 4–6; and the present form of 2 Samuel 7, with its qualified promise that God will maintain the Davidic dynasty, were added (although some of them may well rest on ancient tradition). This view of the literary history of the Books of Samuel explains why David is presented as what we now call a chief rather than a king, hearing and adjudicating cases and ruling through his family. It also explains the fragments of genealogy with Ammonite overtones (2 Samuel 17:25), as well as the important material in 2 Samuel 23 about David's heroes.

Samuel as Prophet: An Introduction to Prophecy

Section III of Part One in this *Companion* deals specifically with the world of Israel's prophets with particular reference to the literatures involved – the three major prophetic books (Isaiah, Jeremiah, and Ezekiel) and the Twelve Minor Prophets. But these books are not the only evidence that documents prophetic activities in the ancient Israel. Abraham is described as a prophet at Genesis 20:7 by Abimelech, Aaron is called a prophet at Exodus 7:1, and

Solomon saw to the construction of this gate at Hazor at the same time that he fortified Gezer (1 Kings 9:15). (BiblePlaces.com)

his sister Miriam is accorded the title of prophetess at Exodus 15:20. In Deuteronomy 18:15–22, Moses promises that "God will raise up for you a prophet like me," and in an earlier section we discussed the non-Israelite prophet Balaam. There is also an interesting incident in Numbers 11:16–17, 24–30, in which God takes some of the spirit that is upon Moses and puts it upon seventy elders who are to assist Moses in his governing of the people. When the spirit rests upon them, they prophesy, which means that they speak in a state of ecstasy. Two men who are not with the seventy elders also receive a share of Moses' spirit and they, too, "prophesy." When this is reported to Moses, he replies, "Would that all the LORD's people were prophets, that the LORD would put his spirit upon them."

This passage shares a conception of prophecy with 1 Samuel, where bands of ecstatic prophets appear, led by Samuel. If the Hebrew Bible is read from front to back as literature, without regard to scholarly conclusions about the dates of the individual books and the history of Israelite religion, then the appearance of ecstatic prophets in 1 Samuel is not a surprise, since they have already appeared in Numbers 11:24–30. But in the history of religion in Israel, it seems that ecstatic prophets first became prominent during the eleventh century B.C.E., and that both Samuel and Saul were connected with such groups. Although the material in Numbers 11:24–30 was probably written later than 1 Samuel, it articulates a view of what prophets were that is similar to what we find in 1 Samuel, namely, that they are zealous followers of Yahweh, whose spirit causes them to enter ecstatic states in which their speech and behavior depart from what is usual. There is no immediate indication that this "prophesying" involved passing formal messages from God to third parties, in the manner of the literary prophets of a later period, although we must not rule out this possibility. In 2 Samuel we meet a prophet, Nathan, who *does* speak in the name of Yahweh, and even the story of the birth and youth of Samuel in 1 Samuel 1:1–2, 26, and 3:1–4 describes how Samuel passed on messages from Yahweh.

A question of method, as well as a problem of nomenclature, inevitably arises when prophecy is at issue. A number of different types of person in the Hebrew Bible are traditionally described as prophets. There are the ecstatics of Numbers 11:24–30 and 1 Samuel, the court prophets such as Nathan and Isaiah, the "provincial" prophets such as Micah, the opponents of kings and rulers such as Elijah, and figures such as Amos who deny that they are prophets at all. From the point of view of the editors of the received form of the Bible, these diverse figures were all prophets – men and women inspired by the spirit of God to perform a special task. From the point of view of religion in ancient Israel, however, we should regard them as representing distinct phenomena, and the texts in fact use varying terminology in referring to them. Recognizing this diversity will prevent us from assuming that there was a single coherent religious institution in Israel called "prophecy." If we did assume this, we would then wonder how the ecstatic type of prophecy met in 1 Samuel suddenly became the oracular type of prophecy exemplified by Nathan in 2 Samuel. We might draw faulty conclusions about the dates of material by inferring that the political, oracular prophecy of Nathan must be a highly developed, and therefore much later, form of what we meet in the ecstatic bands of prophets. The fact is that they are different and separate phenomena, which can exist side by side.

This diversity is recognized within the terminology in the Hebrew Bible. In 1 Samuel 9:9 we are informed that a man who was formerly called a seer (Hebrew *ro'eh*) is now called a prophet (Hebrew *navi'*). But we also find the designations "seer" (a different Hebrew word, *hozeh*) and "man of God." It is safest to assume that in Israel there were various types of what have been called, with deliberate generality, "intermediaries" between God and humans. In some cases these were groups of people who lived on the margins of society, such as those led by Elijah and Elisha (2 Kings 1). Other groups were ecstatics. Some intermediaries were thought to possess powers of insight into the future or of divination. Some were employed at court in large numbers, such as the four hundred at Ahab's court (1 Kings 22:6). Some were part of the establishment, and others were opposed to the establishment. Some were closely connected with sacrificial centers. This diversity can be matched elsewhere in the ancient Near East. For example, texts from Mari dating from the eighteenth century B.C.E. provide evidence of intermediaries known variously as answerers, cult functionaries, ecstatics, and diviners.

For the purposes of reading the Books of Samuel and Kings, we can say that the prophetic groups were zealous adherents of Yahweh and were prepared to oppose – and if necessary depose – kings who were unfaithful to God. In 1 and 2 Samuel, Saul is made king and then disowned as king by Samuel, whom we should not regard as an isolated individual but as the leader of prophetic bands. The saying "Is Saul also among the prophets?" (1 Samuel 10:11–12) indicates that even Saul, however temporarily, was considered a member of such a group. Perhaps for this reason he instituted religious reforms in Israel (1 Samuel 28:3) and attacked the Gibeonites in an attempt to cleanse the land of foreigners (2 Samuel 21:2).

In 1 Samuel we meet the prophetic groups for the first time as a significant political and military force. Led by Samuel they probably contributed to the initial success in resisting the Philistines. When they failed, they designated Saul to do the job but were quick to switch to David when it was clear that Saul could not succeed. In the ninth century B.C.E. they would lead the opposition to the dynasty of Omri and Ahab, and in that role emerge as a principal force in the shaping of the Hebrew Bible.

The Literary Structure and Function of First and Second Samuel

The Books of Samuel may be considered in three unequal sections from a literary point of view: (*a*) 1 Samuel 1:1–15:35, (*b*) 1 Samuel 16:1–2 Samuel 20:25, (*c*) 2 Samuel 21:1–24:25. The first section contains four blocks: the birth and youth of Samuel (1:1–4:1a), the story of the ark (4:1b–7:2), the ministry of Samuel (7:3–8:3), and the story of Saul (8:4–15:35). Although the four blocks are self-contained (and probably once existed independently), they are linked to form a continuous narrative. For example, the story of the ark's capture by the Philistines and its return after causing death and panic stands alone and without reference to Samuel, but the account in it of the death of Eli and his two sons links it to the story of Samuel's birth and youth, since Eli is the priest who brings up Samuel.

Characteristic themes appear in the first two blocks. First Samuel 2:27–36, concerning an unnamed "man of God," introduces a perspective that resonates through the remainder of Samuel and Kings: that events are shaped by God, especially as God brings disaster in response to the wickedness of leaders. The destruction of Eli's house is foretold, and it is promised that God will raise up a faithful priest. Second Kings 2:27, in which Abiathar is thrust out from the priesthood, refers back to this promise in 1 Samuel 2:35, binding Samuel and Kings together in the Deuteronomistic History. In the story of the loss and recovery of the ark, which was edited during the exile, it is hard not to see an anticipation of the future fall of Jerusalem and therefore a hope that it will be restored, just as the captured ark was returned.

The brief third block, dealing with Samuel's ministry, casts Samuel as similar to the judges, crediting him with victories over the Philistines that are historically plausible. Yet like the judges, Samuel's line does not amount to a dynasty; his sons are described in 1 Samuel 8:1–3 as judges who perverted justice, and the way is prepared for the story of Saul.

The fourth block is confusing because it contains several independent stories that have been woven together in a rough manner. (Biblical editors preserved and presented the material at their disposal without resort to footnotes or bibliographies.) These individual stories within First Samuel are (*a*) 9:1–10:16, 13:8–14; (*b*) 8:4–22, 10:17–27, 15:1–33; (*c*) 11:1–15; and (*d*) 14:1–52. It is possible that story *c* was once part of story *a*, but if so it has been edited to fit the sequence of the narrative as a whole. The first two stories describe Saul's elevation to and deposition from the kingship. Story *a* implies that Saul was king for only a period of days before Samuel deposed him (cf. 10:8 with 13:8) because he wrongly offered burnt offerings. In story *b* the deposition results from Saul's refusal to destroy the Amalekite king, Agag. Thus, although chapters 8–15 jumble the events of Saul's reign, the biblical account articulates a generally negative view of kingship (8:10–17) and a hostile attitude toward Saul in particular. The one narrative of a brave deed (apart from Saul's rescue of the men of Jabesh-gilead in 11:1–11) is that of Saul's son Jonathan in chapter 14.

The extensive story of David begins in 1 Samuel 16. Initially, the interwoven tale of David and Jonathan obscures the main lines of the saga of David, but from 1 Samuel 25 it is recognizably a single narrative that then extends to 2 Samuel 20, with a few additions such as 2 Samuel 8. For literary artistry it is matched only by the story of Joseph (in Genesis 37–47). For example, in 1 Samuel 31 Saul's death in battle against the Philistines at Mount Gilboa is related. Saul asks his armor bearer to kill him and takes his own life when the latter refuses. In 2 Samuel 1 David is in Ziklag waiting for news of the battle. News is brought by an Amalekite, who says that he killed Saul at Saul's request, bringing Saul's crown and armlet to David as proof.

This vignette displays literary artistry at several levels. The reader knows that the Amalekite is lying. The reader also knows from 1 Samuel 30 that while Saul and the Philistines were fighting at Mount Gilboa, David was pursuing Amalekites. They had raided Ziklag while David was on his way back from Mount Gilboa, the Philistines having decided that they could not trust him to fight with them against Saul. Amalekite treachery has therefore been established as a theme, and this particular Amalekite forfeits his life by his own false testimony. David has him killed for having done what Saul's armor bearer declined to do — strike dead the Lord's anointed. What about the detail of the crown and armlet? Although an Amalekite might conceivably have been close enough to Saul in battle to take his crown and armlet when he fell, it is more likely that a biblical storyteller has used his imagination to symbolize the passing of the kingship from Saul to David by narrating that the crown and armlet were brought from the battlefield to David.

The theme that the kingship has passed finally to David drives the next part of the narrative as David becomes, first, king over Judah in Hebron,

and then, king over Israel following the collapse of the attempt to preserve
Saul's kingdom by his cousin and military commander, Abner. Here as elsewhere, the narrative emphasizes that David is innocent of any complicity
in the downfall of Saul and his house. The next landmarks are the capture
of Jerusalem (2 Samuel 5), the bringing of the ark to Jerusalem (chapter 6),
and the dynastic oracle (chapter 7), in which God promises to preserve
David's house forever. Second Samuel 9–20 represents the court chronicle,
a marvelously crafted narrative that describes David's adultery with Bath-
sheba, the plot to ensure that her husband falls in battle, the denunciation
of David by Nathan the prophet, and the account of the consequent frat-
ricide within David's family and the two revolts against him, one led by his
son Absalom. Themes and subplots become intricate and are skillfully
woven. The ambiguous character of Joab emerges, for example, either as
blindly loyal to David (to the point of disobedience when it is in David's
interest), or as calculating and ambitious to the point of wielding power
over David. What remains remarkable on any reading is that soon after the
promise to David that God will preserve his dynasty, an unflattering narrative depicts the chosen servant of God with many human failings.

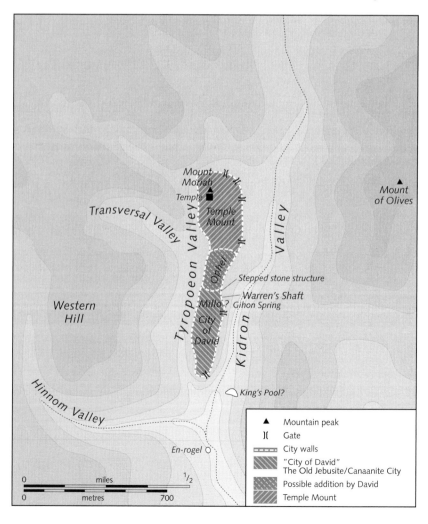

Map V. Jerusalem in the time of David and
Solomon, with later extension of the Temple
Mount

JERUSALEM BECOMES THE CAPITAL

The enigmatic story of how David captured the Canaanite city of Jerusalem from the Jebusites is told in 2 Samuel 5:6–10. With that masterstroke, David set in motion a course of events that would transform a relatively unimportant walled village in the Palestinian highlands into the booming capital of a small Levantine kingdom. From its humble beginnings Jerusalem grew to enjoy wealth and prestige as the organizational and administrative hub from which David and Solomon supervised their expanding territories and consolidated the power of their fledgling monarchy. In time, Jerusalem also became the religious, cultural, and political center of the Israelite nation – and was indisputably such after the fall of Samaria in 721 B.C.E.

The original Jebusite settlement was limited to the southern spur of Jerusalem's eastern hill, below the Temple Mount (or Haram es-Sharif) of the modern-day Old City. The first Israelite occupants of the city simply appropriated the fortifications and town plan that had existed from the Late Bronze Age (during the fourteenth century B.C.E.). Their impressive defenses made the Jebusite rulers believe they could repel David

and his forces with only the blind and the lame among them. That hope proved ill-founded, but only because David sent his raiding party through a water conduit (2 Samuel 5:6–8). Extensive archaeological investigation in this area, properly known as the City of David, has indicated that those responsible for transforming Jebusite Jerusalem into the Israelite capital reused many Canaanite defense walls and support structures.

Surrounded on three sides by deep valleys and provided with a perennial supply of water, Jerusalem enjoyed an excellent strategic location. But its uneven togography of hills and valleys required the construction of artificial platforms along the side of the hill to provide sufficient area for extensive building activities on its crest. The Canaanite city boasted a series of terraces with stone support walls that served as the substructure of a massive fortress built to overlook the Kidron Valley. After David captured that fortress (the "stronghold of Zion," 2 Samuel 5:7), he rebuilt it as his own citadel. The terraced walls that supported the Canaanite fortified precincts were covered with an immense structure of stepped stones, perhaps the biblical *millo* (see 2

Samuel 5:9; 1 Kings 9:15). Over two hundred square meters of this stepped-stone structure have been excavated, qualifying it as one of the most impressive monuments of the Iron Age in Israel.

On top of the stepped-stone structure was located a fortified district that became the heart of the monarchy's new capital. The area can be identified as the Ophel (Citadel) of Jerusalem (see Isaiah 32:14; 2 Chronicles 27:3). The Ophel quarter housed the royal palaces, administrative buildings, military bunkers, and other public structures.

When David acquired it as his capital Jerusalem was a small city with an area of only some twenty acres. The residential districts of the lower city were home to no more than a few thousand people. But Solomon annexed a large area north of the main city to build a monumental palace and temple complex. The new capital was becoming the focus of power and the repository of wealth associated with the increasing prominence of the royal household and the national cult. Within a few centuries future expansions and a growing population would transform Jerusalem into the most important urban center in the region.

Second Samuel ends with scenes of David the poet, David the commander of a band of heroes, and David the initiator in building the Temple (by buying the site where it will be built). When he reappears in 1 Kings, David is a feeble old man whose approaching death occasions wrangling for the succession. David's legacy is preserved in 2 Samuel with a portrait of David that accords with what the tradition claims for him – that he brought Israel from a disaster that threatened its disappearance to a future full of hope.

4. First and Second Kings

Israel and Judah during the Period 961–560 B.C.E.

The Books of Kings deal with the time from the accession of Solomon around 961 B.C.E. to the thirty-seventh year of the captivity of the last

Excavations of the City of David, looking toward the Temple Mount, built a thousand years after David by Herod the Great, suggesting the relatively small scale of the Jerusalem that David conquered. (BiblePlaces.com)

Solomon's kingdom. An aerial view from the east of the mound of Megiddo, originally excavated by the Oriental Institute of the University of Chicago (1935–9). Renewed excavations by American and Israeli scholars were begun in 1994. (BiblePlaces.com)

Tenth-century B.C.E. cult stand found at Tell Taanach, eight miles southeast of Megiddo. It stands three feet high. The nude female holding two lions by the ear on the bottom register may represent a female deity. Two sphinxes flank the doorway on the next register, and a tree of life stands above. The calf on top may represent Baal. (American Schools of Oriental Research)

surviving Davidic king, Jehoiachin, in 560, a period rich in archaeological evidence. The results of archaeologists' analyses, which plot public works, the area of walled cities, and the spread of literacy and of luxury items in Judah show that in the eighth century the work put into constructing walls and public buildings far exceeded that of preceding or following centuries. The seventh century predominated in the presence of luxury items and in the spread of literacy, but these indices of prosperity and development plummet during the seventh and the sixth centuries.

From the time of Solomon (or following other reconstructions, the reigns of Omri and Ahab during the ninth century) there is also evidence

From the latter half of the ninth century B.C.E., an inscription and image from a monument of Shalmaneser III of Assyria called the Black Obelisk showing Jehu, king of Israel (see 2 Kings, chapters 9 and 10), paying tribute to his Assyrian overlord. (BiblePlaces.com)

of construction of new city walls and gates at Hazor, Megiddo, Beersheba, and Gezer, as well as other indications that Solomon undertook extensive fortification within his kingdom. Around 918 B.C.E. the land was invaded by the Egyptian pharaoh Sheshonq 1, called Shishak in the Bible (1 Kings 14:25). A list of towns that Sheshonq claims to have conquered has been preserved at the Amun temple in Karnak (see *Ancient Near Eastern Texts*, pp. 242–3), and a fragment of a stela found at Megiddo appears to be part of a victory monument erected by this pharaoh. Although Sheshonq's list is scarcely a full historical account, it seems that his purpose was to destroy fortified towns rather than to occupy territory. First Kings 14:25 says that he came up against Jerusalem, although it is possible that he received tribute from Jerusalem on condition that he spare the city. Some scholars have recently suggested that this invasion reduced the already residual power of the Canaanite city-states, opening the way for the dynasties of Omri and Ahab.

The inscription of Mesha, king of Moab, dating from about 850 B.C.E., mentions Omri, the king of Israel from 885 to 874 B.C.E., who built Samaria as the northern kingdom's capital. It relates how Omri had subdued Moab and how Mesha turned the tables on the Israelites after Omri's death. From the same period (885–853 B.C.E.) we have archaeological evidence from Megiddo and Hazor that impressive water systems were constructed that tapped the deep water table.

The latter part of the ninth century B.C.E. brought Israel and Judah into conflict with Assyria, as shown by the portrayal of the Israelite king Jehu (or his representative) on the Black Obelisk of Shalmaneser III presenting tribute to the Assyrian king. Jehu is described on the obelisk as the "son" of Omri, although in fact he had destroyed Omri's dynasty and taken over the kingship at the urging of the Israelite prophet Elisha. The remembrance of Omri outlived his dynasty – even outside Israel.

From the eighth century B.C.E. the famous seal of "Shema the servant of Jeroboam" bears what today is called the Megiddo lion, named after the place where it was found. The "Jeroboam" concerned is King Jeroboam II (782–747 B.C.E.); Shema must have been a high officer in his administration. Potsherds or ostraca from Samaria during the same period record receipts of wine and oil made to the capital from surrounding districts. Assyrian records chart the rise of Tiglath-pileser III (745–727 B.C.E.) and his campaigns into Israel – still referred to as the "house of Omri" nearly a hundred and fifty years after Omri's death! The conquest of Samaria in 722/1 B.C.E. and its takeover by Sargon II are reported in that king's annals (*Ancient Near Eastern Texts*, pp. 284–5); likewise, the siege of Jerusalem mounted by the Assyrian king Sennacherib in 701 B.C.E. is reported in Sennacherib's annals (*Ancient Near Eastern Texts*, pp. 207–8). This account mentions "Hezekiah the Jew (that is, the Judean)," who would not submit and who was made a prisoner inside Jerusalem "like a bird in a cage." This reference is to King Hezekiah of Judah, and the large tribute he paid is recorded. From the Jerusalem of this time there are indications that the city

SIEGEWORKS IN ANCIENT NEAR EASTERN WARFARE

Powerful armies commanded by the great empires of the ancient Near East left small kingdoms such as Israel little recourse for their defense beyond seeking protection behind fortified city walls. By the middle of the Iron Age these fortifications encircled entire cities at a height of up to twelve meters. Sometimes six meters thick, the walls were further strengthened by bastions and outcropping salients. They were crowned with balconies and crenellated parapets from which soldiers defended the city when it was under attack. The city was often protected by a sloping stone glacis, which made any approach to the wall's lower reaches difficult at best. Yet these fortifications were still vulnerable to assault and siege. Enemies mounted attacks by storming the ramparts, breaching the walls and gates, scaling, tunneling, and resorting to psychological warfare.

The Assyrian army apparently introduced battering rams, the scourge of fortified cities, to the ancient arsenal. The first machines were heavy objects with limited mobility. Typically the ram was mounted on a six-wheeled body built over a wooden frame, with wicker shields covering the sides. At the front of the body stood a tall, round-domed turret. The battering beam could swing like a pendulum from a rope hung from this turret. Warriors who kept the ram in motion and aimed its clumsy power offered nice targets for defending archers

above. For that reason, attackers often had their own bowmen who, perched on mobile towers nearby, covered the attacking soldiers with volleys aimed at the defenders from below. In time, advanced types of battering rams were developed, light-bodied and with four wheels rather than six. Metal ramming rods were attached that could be manipulated to wedge out chunks of the wall weakened by the battering beam. Sennacherib's battering rams, covered with leather, were made of materials that could be assembled and dismantled. His machines were relatively maneuverable and could be used alone or in formations.

The city gate was an attacking army's focal point. The gate was usually the wall's weakest point, and battering rams could be wheeled up the path that led to it without requiring construction of a special ramp. But in some situations ramps had to be constructed to overcome a city's natural strategic setting when the preferred point of breach lay somewhere along the wall itself.

Aggressive warfare was costly in human and material terms, so passive siege was often used as a method of weakening a walled city. Starved for water and food, besieged cities were often forced to capitulate (see the account of the fall of Samaria after a siege of three years in 2 Kings 6:25). A city's ability to withstand siege depended on its ability to feed and

provide water for its inhabitants. To that end the kings of Judah built store cities and in several sites engineered impressive underground systems that could provide a constant supply of water should those cities fall under siege. But loss of morale among defenders was also a problem during a prolonged engagement. Throughout the siege the attacking army might engage in ruses and stratagems designed to draw the defenders out of the city or to gain access for their own forces. They also employed threats and psychological manipulation to undermine the confidence of the besieged defenders, inciting the people and army to overthrow their leaders by threatening severe action if they refused and promising great rewards if they acquiesced (see the account of Sennacherib's siege of Jerusalem in 1 Kings 18–19).

The Assyrian and Babylonian Empires perfected the art of siege and captured the fortified cities of Iron Age Israel. Lachish and other important cities of Israel and Judah were destroyed by Assyria late in the eighth century B.C.E., a campaign remembered in the great reliefs from the palace of Sennacherib. Jerusalem was besieged but miraculously spared, but only for a time. Lachish rose again only to fall a little more than a century later, this time together with Jerusalem, to the siege and attack of Nebuchadnezzar of Babylon.

was considerably enlarged, presumably to contain Israelites who had come south to Judah after the fall of Samaria. Hezekiah also may have constructed the shaft known as Warren's shaft, bringing water from a spring outside the eastern walls into the city. The tunnel that today is often called Hezekiah's tunnel was probably built five hundred years later.

Seals and bullae from the seventh century B.C.E. show that paganism flourished during the time of Manasseh, whose reign is described in 1 Kings 21. The goddess Asherah, who had previously been represented as a tree, now took on female form. This striking evidence for the syncretistic religion of the time is to be contrasted with the equally striking fact that seals bearing the names of men known to be associated with Josiah's reform of the cult during the last quarter of the seventh century are aniconic, that is, without representations of human or animal figures.

A letter written on a sherd, most of the pieces of which were discovered in 1960 at Mesad Hashavyahu (Yavneh Yam), sheds light on an aspect of social conditions during the seventh century. It is usually dated to 630 B.C.E., a time when Judah was establishing control over the area as Assyrian power collapsed (see *Ancient Near Eastern Texts*, p. 568). The letter represents a complaint from someone whose name is not preserved to a local military ruler or high official. The complainant is a member of a gang of conscripted laborers whose job is to harvest a quota of grain. He claims to have fulfilled his allocation, despite which the overseer, Hoshiah (or Hashabiah), has taken his garment. Hoshiah's action is presumably designed to make the complainant return and do more work in order to get his garment back. The complainant insists that his fellow workers will back up his story, and he appeals to the high official to see that his garment is returned. This sad text shows how far Israelite society had changed from being an association of cooperative villages ruled by local chiefs to a society in which free men were conscripted to do public work and put at the mercy of overseers and officials. Prophetic denunciations of the abuse of power by those in authority become easily understandable in the light of such evidence.

The Babylonian Chronicles of the seventh to sixth centuries B.C.E. record Jerusalem's capture on 16 March 597 B.C.E. by Nebuchadnezzar, the exile of its king into captivity, and the installation of a new king who met Nebuchadnezzar's requirement (*Ancient Near Eastern Texts*, p. 564). The last period of Judah's independence, before the destruction of Jerusalem and of the Temple in 587/6, is illuminated by the Lachish letters. These are messages, written on broken sherds, sent from observation posts to the defenders at Lachish. One mentions that the observers are looking for the fire signals of Lachish because they can no longer see those of Azekah. This latter town was on the main route through the Shephelah to Lachish, and the letter vividly intimates that it had just fallen to the Babylonians. Another letter complains that the words of the princes are weakening the hands of the people, that is, undermining morale (*Ancient Near Eastern Texts*, p. 322). This is reminiscent of the charge made against Jeremiah, who advocated surrender to the Babylonians as the will of God (Jeremiah 38:4). Babylonian records listing the provision of food for prisoners of war dependent on the royal household mention provisions for Jehoiachin, some of his sons, and eight men of Judah (*Ancient Near Eastern Texts*, p. 308). The Books of Kings end with Jehoiachin still a captive in Babylon in 560 B.C.E.

Archaeological evidence in the form of excavated remains in cities, inscriptions and letters, and seals and bullae indicate that urban centers became more dominant in Judah during the eighth century B.C.E. The same is probably true in the northern kingdom until the Assyrian invasion, with Samaria dominating the surrounding area. Old patterns of confederated villages broke down in the face of increasing centralization, conscription, and imposition of taxes in the form of food products to supply an increasing number of state officials. With such taxes came the inability of some to pay if, for example, there was a bad harvest. Failure to pay carried grievous consequences, first indebtedness, then becoming a day laborer on land one had been forced to sell, and finally complete loss of freedom. Wealth became concentrated into fewer families, and families who saw their status slipping away formed opposition parties.

The rise of powerful and competing families is especially evident in the time of Jeremiah prior to the fall of Jerusalem in 587/6 B.C.E. The Books of 2 Kings and Jeremiah indicate that one powerful family, that of Shaphan, was involved in Josiah's reformation of 622 B.C.E. This family also protected Jeremiah from his opponents and read Jeremiah's words of warning to the assembled people. Gedaliah, the governor of Judah, to whom Jeremiah was entrusted after the fall of Jerusalem, was a member of the Shaphan family. Opposed to the family of Shaphan was that of Elishamah, whose grandson Ishmael murdered Gedaliah, probably in 582 B.C.E.

The Literary History, Structure, and Function of Kings

The preceding section has shown how much archaeological evidence is available to scholars who wish to reconstruct the history of Israel and Judah between 961 and 560 B.C.E. A historical outline of the period not only places this extrabiblical evidence into perspective but also shows how much modern reconstructions differ from the biblical accounts. That, in turn, will enable us better to appreciate the particular perspectives fashioned in 1 Kings and 2 Kings.

Solomon evidently consolidated his father's conquests, although scholarly estimates of his reign (ca. 961–922 B.C.E.) differ widely. The new king made treaties with surrounding peoples according to the biblical account, fortified cities in key areas, developed trade, and built the Temple and palace in Jerusalem. While scholars continue to dispute the extent to which Solomon created a centralized state with an administrative apparatus and public buildings in key cities, unrest did clearly develop because his steps toward such centralization undermined the relative independence that Israelite villages had enjoyed. Taxes were imposed, and villagers were conscripted into gangs of construction workers. To pay for his schemes, Solomon also gave away territory and cities to the king of Tyre (1 Kings 9:10–14). Prophetic opposition to Solomon gained strength in Israel, and and prophets encouraged Jeroboam to revolt. He was unable to mount a rebellion until Solomon's death, but at that time he led ten tribes in a breakaway to form the northern kingdom of Israel, leaving Solomon's son

ROYAL ZION THEOLOGY

When David established Jerusalem as the capital of his kingdom, he set in motion the development of a theological tradition found throughout the Bible. This royal Zion theology grew up in Jerusalem, the political and religious center of the Israelite realm during the time of the united kingdom, and the seat of David's dynasty. Royal Zion theology appears first in the context of oracles about the regal installations of David and Solomon (2 Samuel 7:8–17, 23:1–7; 1 Kings 8:46–53, 9:2–9), and may be summarized in five points:

1. Yahweh chose Jerusalem as the place of his own special presence and as the chief city of his people.
2. Yahweh designated David and his descendants to rule from Jerusalem in an unending dynastic succession.
3. The Jerusalem Temple was to be the nation's central religious shrine, since it was there Yahweh would "cause his name to dwell."
4. David and his successors were to play a key role as mediators between Yahweh and his people.
5. Jerusalem was secured against the threat of natural or supernatural forces as long as (a) a descendant of David sat on the throne and (b) the people were faithful in their allegiance to Yahweh.

These convictions, all centering on the royal city, developed over several hundred years, principally through the reign of Solomon and the tumultuous history of the Judean monarchy. Scholars disagree, however, about the tradition's exact origin. Some consider it a continuation of ideas current in the Jebusite city of Jerusalem that David captured, while others understand the concepts as original creations of the Davidic court. A few scholars emphasize the continuity between royal Zion theology and earlier Israelite religious traditions, especially beliefs associated with the ark of the covenant and the cult at Shiloh. These scholars suggest that the complex of ideas surrounding Jerusalem that developed during the monarchy represent a transfer of older Israelite theology to a new geographical and political context. Aspects of all three suggestions are probably correct. Royal Zion theology most likely developed as a unique combination of ancient traditions from Israel, modified to meet new historical circumstances and colored by religious ideology drawn from the larger world of the ancient Near East.

Several psalms express royal Zion theology, cast in the mythological imagery of religions practiced by Israel's neighbors. Rich in Canaanite symbolism, these psalms (especially 46, 48, 76) emphasize Zion as the highest mountain of the north, on which the gods dwell, although the actual size of Zion was and is comparatively modest. From the beginning, this theology functioned symbolically, so that the power of various mountain myths was ascribed to Jerusalem. Jerusalem became the center of the world, from which the river of paradise flowed, the place where Yahweh conquered the watery chaos monster and then triumphed over the heathen nations. Primordially and eternally, Zion stood on the axis of heaven and earth.

Royal Zion theology played a vital role in the traditions that grew up around the deliverance of Jerusalem from the Assyrians in 701 B.C.E. Although Hezekiah probably capitulated and paid tribute to spare the city from Sennacherib's vindictive destruction, the fact that Jerusalem avoided battle and military defeat was later interpreted as a sign of the city's inviolability. This interpretation, emphasizing the special divine providence that attached to Jerusalem, was later invoked in times of national crisis by those who wished to portray the city as safe from any danger of invasion or siege. Ultimately, the prophets castigated individuals who were more committed to a belief in an inviolable Jerusalem than they were firm in their loyalty to Yahweh.

When the city subsequently fell to the Babylonians, belief in royal Zion theology as applied literally to Jerusalem was shattered. Yet its underlying hope was projected into the eschatological future. These Jerusalem traditions continued to be reinterpreted. Jerusalem in time became the focus of prophetic and apocalyptic hopes for the restoration of Israel in history and beyond history. It would be the place to which

all nations shall flow,
and many peoples shall come
 and say,
"Come, let us go up to the mountain
 of the LORD,
to the House of the God of Jacob."
(Isaiah 2:2–3)

TRADE DURING THE EARLY MONARCHY

In the ancient Near East a country had to have good land-and-sea communications with other peoples and surplus industrial or agricultural products for trade in order to become a commercial center. The fledgling kingdom of Israel barely fulfilled these criteria, but during the early monarchy the country evidently began to share eagerly in the commerce of the Near East. Israel lacked good seaports in first Temple times, but the country lay across the main land routes between the major economic powers of Egypt, Phoenicia, Persia, and Mesopotamia. Both the Way of the Sea and the King's Highway, the most important overland routes of the age, crossed Israelite territory. References to trade and traders in the Bible suggest that in the early period of Israelite history trade was conducted by foreign merchants passing through the country along these caravan routes (see Genesis 37:25 and 28, for example). During the years when Israel had just begun to settle the land, trade in small imported goods and the purchase of local wares for export apparently still lay in the hands of the indigenous people of Canaan. But with the establishment of the monarchy, trade became a significant element in the Israelite economy.

Trade took place under royal monopoly in the ancient Near East, and Solomon seems to have been successful in developing a network of merchants and trading partners (1 Kings 10:28–9). The Solomonic kingdom, although relatively small and weak, maintained economic and diplomatic ties with many of the important rulers of the era, not the least of whom was the Egyptian pharaoh. Solomon also arranged with Hiram, king of Tyre, to build and equip a fleet of ships that could exchange the copper of Ezion-geber for the gold and precious stones of Ophir. The Temple of Yahweh in Jerusalem was constructed with labor and materials from Phoenicia that were exchanged for Israelite agricultural products. First Kings 10 details the quantity and variety of valuable goods that Solomon is said to have imported into his kingdom, although the list probably exaggerates.

Solomon is also credited with establishing a monopoly in the trade of horse-drawn chariots in his region. In the biblical narrative he emerges as a "middleman" within the ancient arms trade, putting together imported horses from Cilicia with chariots from Egypt to outfit the most advanced military equipment of his day. Solomon built up his own chariot army and exported his surplus of these essential armaments to rulers of petty kingdoms in Syria and Anatolia. The traditional story of the Queen of Sheba's visit to the Solomonic court (1 Kings 10) perhaps indicates how the early Israelite kingdom also shared in the lucrative commercial interests of South Arabia. Frankincense and myrrh, Arabian luxury exports used for a variety of medical, cosmetic, and cultic purposes in the ancient world, are listed among the gifts that this mysterious queen gave to King Solomon.

Exactly how Solomon paid for all his imported goods remains unclear. The region's most valuable exports were agricultural: oil, wine, and grain. Tyrian merchants sometimes bought these commodities and sold them throughout the Mediterranean. Tyre, a city whose wealth flowed from its fabled harbors and its expertise in dyemaking, may also have bought timber from the northern part of Israel to build ships and make oars (Ezekiel 27:17). Solomon provided wheat and oil in exchange for Hiram's assistance in building the Temple (1 Kings 5:6, 10–11). Oil was also sold to Egypt (Hosea 12:1). Some references suggest, however, that Israel's production of agricultural goods and revenues did not provide a sufficient basis for external trade. In 1 Kings 9:11–13, for example, twenty Israelite cities are said to have been leased to the king of Tyre.

Most scholars agree that the biblical accounts of Solomon's reign are exaggerated. Yet these narratives suggest that with the development of the monarchy, Israel took its place among the small kingdoms of the region in a flourishing environment of international trade. The young kingdom exchanged its meager surpluses for the accoutrements of empire, eventually overextending its resources in an attempt to prove its importance in the international scene. Yet after Israel and Judah divided, trade continued between the separate Israelite kingdoms and the larger ancient Near Eastern world. Archaeological data have demonstrated continued economic exchange among Judah and Israel and the cultures of Egypt, Syria, Persia, Phoenicia, Africa, and Mesopotamia. The development of urban life during the monarchy provided an expanding market for such trade. From the tenth century B.C.E. onward, this process was accelerated by increased international contacts, the alternation of military campaigns with periods of peace, and the opening up of international trade routes throughout the Near East.

Rehoboam with Judah and Benjamin. Whatever else motivated the revolt, it attempted to reestablish Israel as religiously separate from Judah, with its innovative Jerusalem Temple and Davidic dynasty, and the result was the politically independent kingdoms of Israel and Judah.

Relations between the two kingdoms were affected by external factors. The invasion of the Egyptian pharaoh Sheshonq seems to have damaged the larger Israel more than the smaller Judah; even so, Judah needed to make an alliance with the Syrians north of Israel in order to curb the ambitions of Israel, the more powerful of the two kingdoms. In 885 B.C.E. the accession of Omri as king of Israel after a bitter civil war enabled Israel to gain control over Judah, Moab, and possibly even Damascus. Omri built a new capital at Samaria, and his son Ahab built and fortified many cities. Elijah and Elisha focused prophetic opposition to Omri's dynasty during Ahab's reign. The dynasty ended with a revolution when Jehu seized the throne and destroyed the house of Omri. This internal strife weakened Israel's ability to withstand invasions from Damascus; with the appearance of the Assyrian Shalmaneser III, Jehu was forced to pay heavy tribute, leading to impositions on the population as a whole.

Around 800 B.C.E., Damascus was crushed by the Assyrians; Israel and Judah suddenly enjoyed a period of relative peace and prosperity, although the rich and powerful benefited at the expense of the poor. Around 750, the prophets Hosea and Amos began to warn the people of approaching judgment. The second half of the eighth century B.C.E. saw the reassertion of Assyrian power under Tiglath-pileser III (745–727 B.C.E.). In 734/3, the Assyrians annexed large parts of Israel, leaving only the rump of the northern hill country with its capital Samaria. In 722/1 Samaria itself fell, and the northern kingdom came to an end. Many people loyal to Yahweh fled south to Judah, where, during the reign of Hezekiah (727–698 B.C.E.), the traditions of Judah and Israel began to be combined.

Hezekiah tried to extend the influence of Judah over parts of the former kingdom of Israel. His ambitions brought him into conflict with Assyria, however, and at the end of his reign he was forced to pay heavy tribute to Sennacherib following an Assyrian invasion of Judah. Under the long reign of Hezekiah's son Manasseh (698–642 B.C.E.), Judah became a vassal of Assyria; the religious reforms that Hezekiah had attempted were undone. Local paganism, no doubt reinforced by Assyrian religious practices, became rife, and those loyal to Yahweh saw their influence eclipsed. When Manasseh died in 642 B.C.E., his son Amon reigned for less than two years before being assassinated. The "people of the land" (2 Kings 21:24) – apparently powerful landowners who favored opposition to Assyria – put the assassins to death and made Amon's son Josiah king. Josiah was eight years old, and during his reign, as Assyrian power waned, Judah began to extend control into the former northern kingdom. The "discovery" of the book of the law in the Temple in 622 B.C.E. was the occasion for a far-reaching religious reform that included closing down sanctuaries other than Jerusalem and elevating Jerusalem to the status of a national sanctuary.

Sennacherib's invasion of Judah in 701 B.C.E., and specifically his successful siege of Lachish, which he made a base of operation (2 Kings 18:14, 17; Isaiah 36:2; 37:8; 2 Chronicles 32:9), is memorialized in reliefs from his palace in Nineveh. The first image shows typical weapons of war: slings, and bows and arrows. Other panels depict chariots and siege engines. The second image pictures the obeisance that Sennacherib compelled. (BiblePlaces.com)

The hopes generated by Deuteronomic reform were short-lived. Josiah was killed in battle at Megiddo by the Egyptian pharaoh Necho II in 609 B.C.E., his policies collapsed, and Judah faced the menace of the expansion of Babylon, which had taken Assyria's place as the greatest power over that part of the world. In 597, Nebuchadnezzar captured Jerusalem and exiled the king, the nobility, and key craftsmen to Babylon. King Jehoiachin was eighteen years old and had been king for only three months at this time, and the Babylonians replaced him with his uncle Zedekiah. When Zedekiah rebelled in 589/8, the Babylonians invaded once more, capturing and destroying Jerusalem in 587/6. The history covered by the Books of Kings ends here, except for reference to the favorable treatment of the exiled Jehoiachin in 560.

The themes and patterns of the Books of Kings to some extent came from their sources, named as "the Book of the Acts of Solomon" (1 Kings 11:41), "the Book of the Chronicles of the Kings of Israel" (1 Kings 14:19), and "the Book of the Chronicles of the Kings of Judah" (1 Kings 14:29). These sources do not survive except for such references, but we can detect excerpts of them in 1 and 2 Kings. The first of these sources probably included an account of the building of the Temple (1 Kings 6) and may have been contemporary with the events described. It is noteworthy that, in two places, it uses Canaanite names for months of the year (Ziv and Bul in 1 Kings 6:1 and 37–8); later compilers added explanatory glosses for later readers, in whose time these names were no longer used. Material such as the long list of Solomon's officials and of his administrative districts (1 Kings 4:1–19) may also come from this source. The books of the chronicles of the kings of Judah and Israel were probably administrative archives compiled and preserved in Jerusalem and Samaria.

These were independent works on which the biblical authors relied and from which they occasionally quoted in producing their own narrative. In addition to these "official" sources, there is a large block of material from 1 Kings 17 onward dealing with the prophets Elijah and Elisha. We suggested (earlier) that there was a link in the northern kingdom between the prophetic groups led by Elijah and Elisha and the scribal high official Obadiah. The Elijah and Elisha stories may have been preserved by the circle of Obadiah and brought to Judah together with the Chronicles of the Kings of Israel after the fall of Samaria in 722/1 B.C.E.

The most striking feature of the Books of Kings is the presence of Deuteronomistic material and a Deuteronomistic scheme (see earlier

A chamber from a gate at Megiddo that may be associated with Solomon's fortifications. (BiblePlaces.com)

discussion of the Deuteronomists). Scholars disagree whether the Books of Kings were composed in several stages – the main part during the reign of Josiah and the rest during and after the exile – or in one stage during and after the exile. However, it is generally agreed that the Books of Kings in their present form are a Deuteronomistic compilation, although a pre-Deuteronomistic first draft completed in Hezekiah's reign (727–698 B.C.E.) cannot be ruled out.

The Deuteronomistic material is of two main kinds. First, there is a scheme of prophecy and fulfillment that provides a basic framework from 1 Kings 12 onward. Second, two extended reflections (1 Kings 8:12–53; 2 Kings 17:7–23) articulate the theology of the final form of Kings. These two types of material are not unique to Kings. A brief appearance of the prophecy and fulfillment pattern is found in 1 Samuel 2:27–36, with a sequel in 4:12–22, and 1 Samuel 12 presents an extended reflection of a Deuteronomistic type. Nonetheless, the impact of these two types of Deuteronomistic material is greater in the Books of Kings than elsewhere.

The prophecy-and-fulfillment scheme in the Books of Kings can be set out as follows:

1. 1 Kings 11:29–39. Ahijah prophesies that Jeroboam will rule over ten tribes in the divided kingdom. The narrative sequel is 1 Kings 12:1–20.
2. 1 Kings 13:1–3. A man of God prophesies that Josiah will tear down the altar at Bethel. The narrative sequel is 2 Kings 23:15–20.
3. 1 Kings 14:4–16. Ahijah prophesies the destruction of Jeroboam's dynasty and the exile of the northern kingdom. The narrative sequels are 1 Kings 15:27–30 and 2 Kings 17:1–6.
4. 1 Kings 16:1–4. Jehu, son of Hanani, prophesies the destruction of the dynasty of Baasha. The narrative sequel is 1 Kings 16:8–13.
5. 2 Kings 14:25. Jeroboam II restores the borders of Israel in accordance with the prophecy of Jonah, son of Amittai.
6. 2 Kings 21:10–15. God's prophets prophesy the exile of Judah because of Manasseh's wickedness. The narrative sequel is 2 Kings 25.
7. 2 Kings 22. Huldah prophesies that God will punish Jerusalem and that Josiah will "be gathered to his grave in peace." The narrative sequel for Jerusalem is 2 Kings 25, although Josiah was killed in battle (23:29–30).

A long gap in this scheme intrudes between sections 4 and 5 and a smaller one between sections 5 and 6. This is because the stories centered on Elijah and Elisha occupy much material between 1 Kings 17 and 2 Kings 10, and because Isaiah is prominent in 2 Kings 19. When taken with the prophecy-and-fulfillment scheme, these chapters show that the history presented in Kings as a whole is bound up with the word of God as spoken by his prophets.

History in the view of 1 Kings and 2 Kings is not determined or driven by the prophetic word, however; nor do these books portray an inexorable, impersonal law of retribution at work. Rather, the prophets testify that God is revealed within historical experience and that the obedience or self-will of

Horned incense altar from the high place in Dan. (BiblePlaces.com)

kings leads to blessing or punishment. For example, Jeroboam is promised that if he walks in God's ways and observes his statutes, God will build a sure house for him (1 Kings 11:38). Evil does not come upon the northern kingdom as a direct consequence of God's will, but results from Jeroboam's disobedience.

Modern readers might well object that these writers projected their own ideology back onto the past. They wrote from the perspective of Judah and with its interests in mind; they knew that the northern kingdom had been destroyed and that Jeroboam's dynasty had lasted only briefly; they rationalized events to make history a part of the pattern of prophecy. There is much truth in this criticism, but that does not imply that the narrative of 1 Kings and 2 Kings was invented out of whole cloth. There can be little doubt but that prophetic groups under Elijah and Elisha in fact waged a bitter war against the dynasty of Omri in the name of the God of Israel, who stood for justice in the minds of the prophets. In these groups, the word of God shaped opposition to the religious and political establishment that glorified power and oppressed the weak. The overthrow of Omri's dynasty by the prophetically backed Jehu (2 Kings 9) was a victory for faith in the God of liberation and justice. The compilers of the final version of Kings sought to show that the experience of Israel and Judah was the history not of a secular people, but of the people of God. Because they were chosen for God's purposes, they could not opt out of his covenant by trying to go their own way.

While Israel and Judah existed politically as independent kingdoms with powerful rulers, this perspective probably offered little interest to most Israelite and Judahite monarchs. But when 1 and 2 Kings reached their completed form during the exile, neither nation existed politically any longer, and this perspective took on a new significance. If Israel and Judah really were the people of God and could not opt out of God's purposes, then perhaps there was hope for the future, especially a future when the people of God would learn from the mistakes of the past. In their postexilic form the Books of Kings articulated hope for the future combined with warnings about the past.

The extended reflection at 1 Kings 8:12–53, Solomon's prayer at the dedication of the Jerusalem Temple, powerfully articulates this hope for the future based on past warnings. (The other such passage of extended reflection, 2 Kings 17:7–23, is concerned mainly with why the northern kingdom was destroyed by the Assyrians.) Probably composed after the Temple's destruction by the Babylonians, this speech spells out the theology of the Books of Kings.

The prayer in 1 Kings 8 begins by summarizing why the Temple was built (vv. 15–21) and extols God's faithfulness (vv. 22–6), but it then goes on to speak of the inadequacy of the Temple in comparison to the grandeur of God:

> Even heaven and the highest heaven cannot contain you; much less this house that I have built! (v. 27)

THE TEMPLE OF SOLOMON

During his reign, Solomon launched an extended building campaign across the kingdom of Israel. His efforts were nowhere more impressive than in Jerusalem, and none was more significant than the Temple of Yahweh that Solomon erected in a complex of royal buildings that took altogether twenty years to construct (1 Kings 7:1–12, 9:1). Work on the Temple itself spanned seven years according to 1 Kings 6:37. Begun in the fifth year of Solomon's reign (ca. 957 B.C.E.) during the first month of the dry season, a period suitable for building, the first Temple served basically as a royal chapel. However, the Temple also had public and national significance, increasingly so as Israelite political and religious institutions developed.

Solomon's Temple, like other temples in the ancient Near East, was intended for ritual activities that were the exclusive domain of a special priestly order, although the ruling monarch also played a significant role in the cult. Common worshippers were not allowed to enter into the most sacred areas. The Temple's religious services, described in Leviticus, included the acceptance of tithes and offerings to support the needs of Temple personnel and to accomplish the daily sacrifices. Also a focus for public worship, the Temple became a pilgrimage center where masses of people assembled, prayed, and offered sacrifices on key holidays and other ritually prescribed occasions. The Temple also seems to have served as the royal treasury.

No archaeological remains of the Solomonic Temple have been recovered, so modern conceptions of its appearance must be drawn by examining the biblical text and by inferring features from analogous structures. Extensive descriptions of the Temple are given in the Hebrew Bible, the most detailed in 1 Kings 5–8. A parallel account in 2 Chronicles is more exaggerated but contains a few important additional details. Ezekiel's description of the Temple is a visionary depiction of a future temple following the first Temple's destruction in 587/6 B.C.E., yet some scholars argue that his narrative also contains relevant information about the actual preexilic structure. Most experts agree that the description of the desert tabernacle in the Priestly source ("P") also reflects some features in the Solomonic house of worship. From these diverse sources archaeologists have attempted to reconstruct an accurate picture of Solomon's Temple.

The building's exterior measurements are said to have been 60 x 20 x 30 cubits (about 90 x 30 x 45 feet). The Temple was constructed of hewn stone and cedar, the masonry locked together by beams – a common, archaeologically attested building method. Structurally, Solomon's Temple was divided into three parts: the 'ulam (rendered in English by such terms as "porch," "portico," "vestibule," and "entrance hall"), the hekhal ("main room," "holy place," "temple proper," or "nave"), and the devir ("holy of holies," "shrine," "most holy place," "inner sanctuary," or "adytum"). Such a tripartite division was a common feature of worship structures in the region, and is familiar to archaeologists from Hazor, Megiddo, Bet She'an, Arad, Lachish, Shechem, and Tell Tayinat (ancient Hattina, located in northern Syria). In general, the Solomonic Temple was constructed according to this "Phoenician," or Canaanite, plan. Biblical texts preserve the memory of how Solomon relied on craftsmen from Tyre to construct and decorate the building (1 Kings 5:5), and their designs came with their craftsmanship.

Like most Semitic sanctuaries, the Temple stood in the middle of an enclosed courtyard used for public assembly and sacrifice. A small porch ('ulam) separated the sacred Temple grounds from the profane world. In the main hall (hekhal), lit by means of recessed frame windows, most of the priestly rituals were performed, (the most sacred of which were reserved for the devir). All along the outside of the building (except the porch) ran a three-storied structure (the yaziq, "side building") that buttressed the Temple's external walls and provided storage space for cultic paraphernalia (pots, shovels, sprinkling bowls, lamps, tongs, snuffers, etc.) and the Temple treasury. The Temple's gates and interior were lavishly decorated with fine sculpture, metalwork, and embroidery. Appointments were made from rare woods, expensive metals and jewels, and fine fabrics. Remains from other monumental buildings of the Iron Age and common oriental imagery give modern artists some idea of how the Temple was decorated.

In front of the Temple stood two tall (nearly 40 feet each) bronze pillars

(continued)

THE TEMPLE OF SOLOMON (continued)

enigmatically named Jachin and Boaz. A horned altar made of bronze or stone stood in the courtyard along with the great "Molten Sea," a fantastically immense bronze basin that held water for the priests' ritual purifications. According to the biblical account, this huge tank held about ten thousand gallons and was supported by twelve bronze bulls arranged in groups of three, each group facing a cardinal point of the compass.

Many of the Temple's auxiliary features reflect the rich sacramental symbolism that Israel shared with other cultures of the ancient Near East. The bronze pillars hearken back to the common erection of sacred stone pillars (*matztzebot*) by the Canaanites. In the context of Solomon's Temple, they probably symbolized the power supporting the Davidic dynasty and the Jerusalemite religious establish-

ment. The size of the Molten Sea suggests it had a deeper symbolic significance, representing the great primordial waters of chaos that Yahweh conquered when he created the earth. Bulls usually symbolized virility and fertility among the peoples of the Mediterranean world, and those that supported the basin probably did, as well. The Canaanite storm god Baal, by no means unfamiliar to the Israelites, was often pictured as a bull. Solomon's Temple was most likely oriented toward the rising sun, perhaps indicative of solar elements in the religions that influenced the Israelite cult. All in all, the Temple was conceived of as the abode in this world of the God who dwelled in the heavens – a microcosmic earthly representation of Yahweh's heavenly dwelling place.

However Solomon's Temple may have looked originally, it did not remain

that way for very long. In the course of Israel's history various kings altered and, at least according to their own judgment, improved it. Some utilized it for the worship of deities other than Yahweh. A few were forced to convert its wealth to tribute money for foreign kings (as in the case of Ahaz's payment to Tiglath-pileser of Assyria, 2 Kings 16:7–8); sometimes foreign kings plundered it for themselves (e.g., Pharaoh Shishak/Sheshonq, 1 Kings 14:25; King Jehoash of Israel, 2 Kings 14:11–14). These historical developments are not clearly detailed in the Bible's pastiche of Temple descriptions, because they contradict the prophetic paradigms of loyalty to Yahweh and of the inviolability of the Temple. Yet despite the promise of an eternal sanctuary, the first Temple was emptied of its treasures and finally destroyed by Nebuchadnezzar and the Babylonians in 587/6 B.C.E.

The Temple will function as a place toward which people pray. There then follow a series of possible situations in which people will pray toward the Temple. Apart from verse 31, where the example is of someone coming to swear an oath before the altar (something that could be also done in the ruined Temple), there is no mention of any ceremony or service taking place in the Temple, nor of sacrifices, which in postexilic Judaism could be offered only in the rebuilt Temple. All the examples (save for v. 31) concern praying toward the Temple; and they conclude, significantly, with the example of the people taken captive to a foreign land.

> . . . if they come to their senses in the land to which they have been taken captive, and repents. . . . then hear in heaven your dwelling place their prayer and their plea, maintain their cause and forgive your people. (vv. 47, 49–50)

The prayer reminds God that they are his people, whom he delivered from Egypt (v. 51).

This dedication prayer, then, holds out hope to the people whose history is described in the Books of Kings, a history that had come to an apparent end when these books reached their final form. Even in captivity, the editors insisted, there is hope for the future. True repentance and the desire for God, expressed in prayer toward the ruined Temple, will bring a response from the God whose word was active in Israel's history, even to the point of being responsible for the very destruction of the Temple.

B. The Books of Chronicles, Ezra, and Nehemiah

1. History and Sources of the Works

Although the events described in 1 and 2 Chronicles precede those in Ezra and Nehemiah, the latter two books were written before Chronicles; the Books of Ezra and Nehemiah are the principal source of evidence for the history and the social conditions that led up to the time of the composition of Chronicles. For that reason, we begin here with Ezra and Nehemiah, and then deal with Chronicles. The term "Chronicler" is widely understood to describe the person or persons responsible for the composition of 1 and 2 Chronicles. Sometimes Ezra and Nehemiah are also attributed to "the Chronicler" in critical discussion, although under scrutiny that convention appears problematic.

Map VI. Powers of the Mediterranean and Near East at the beginning of the sixth century B.C.E.

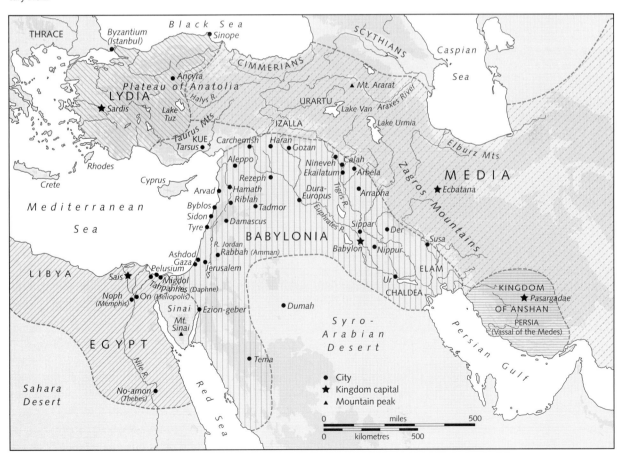

Memorial cylinder of Cyrus celebrating his triumphs, which he attributes to the god Marduk. At the same time, the "Cyrus Cylinder," as it is called, sets out an imperative that "all the gods whom I have placed within their sanctuaries address a daily prayer in my favor before Bel and Nabu, that my days be long." (BiblePlaces.com)

The Books of Ezra and Nehemiah present some of the most difficult questions in the critical study of the Hebrew Bible, and scholarly agreement has proven difficult to achieve. Treated as a single work in the earliest canons of Judaism, Ezra and Nehemiah overlap in period and in the events they deal with, and yet sometimes they stand in an inharmonious, even contradictory relationship to each other.

The Book of Ezra begins with the decree of Cyrus the Great (in 539 B.C.E.) that allowed Jews in exile in Babylon to return to Jerusalem and rebuild their Temple. Led by Sheshbazzar – a leader mentioned only in Ezra, and about whom nothing is otherwise known – a first group of exiles returns, bringing with them more than five thousand vessels of gold and silver (chapter 1). According to chapter two, almost fifty thousand people returned (Ezra 2:64–5), a no doubt exaggerated figure. Chapters 3–6 (of which 4:8–6:18 is in Aramaic, the official language of Cyrus's Persian Empire, which became the principal spoken language among Jews) tell of efforts to rebuild the Temple under the leadership of the priest Jeshua (the Aramaic form of the Hebrew name Joshua) and a ruler named Zerubbabel. The "adversaries of Judah and Benjamin" frustrated and stalled these efforts, however, and the work was achieved only after a search of the imperial archives confirmed Cyrus's decree during the reign of Darius (522–486 B.C.E.). The Temple was finally completed in Darius's sixth year (515 B.C.E.; Ezra 6:15) and then dedicated. Yet Jeshua and Zerubbabel are not explicitly mentioned in connection with this completion and dedication.

Ezra 7 introduces us to the person Ezra, the "scribe skilled in the law of Moses" (Ezra 7:6), and dates his journey from Babylonia to the seventh year of Artaxerxes, king of Persia, probably a reference to the first of several kings of that name (reigning from 465 until 424 B.C.E.). Ezra's mission is authorized by a letter from this king (Ezra 7:11–26), and the book gives a first-person account of Ezra's work (7:27–9:15), including a description of those who accompanied him (8:1–14), how he journeyed with his party (8:15–31), his arrival in Jerusalem (8:32–6), and his shame at what he found there (9:1–15). The cause of his shame was that Jews in Jerusalem, including priests and Levites, had intermarried with non-Jews. Chapter 10 is a third-person account of how Ezra assembled the people and had them make a covenant to "put away" their foreign wives and children. A list of those who did so concludes the book (10:18–44).

The Book of Nehemiah begins with a long first-person account of how Nehemiah obtained permission from Artaxerxes to go to Jerusalem as governor in that king's twentieth year, after learning that Jerusalem's wall was broken down, that its gates were destroyed by fire, and that the Jewish returnees were in great trouble (Nehemiah 1:3). Chapters 1–6 describe Nehemiah's journey, his inspection of the city, and his rebuilding of its walls despite the opposition of Sanballat (governor of Samaria), Tobiah the Ammonite, and Geshem the Arab. In chapter 7, Nehemiah decides to enroll the people by genealogy, in the course of which he discovers the list of those who first returned from exile. This list (Nehemiah 7:6–69) is almost identical

CYRUS THE GREAT AND THE EDICT OF RELEASE

During the middle of the sixth century B.C.E. a new ruling power arose in the ancient Near East. The Persians, an Indo-European people whose homeland lay to the northeast of the Fertile Crescent, speedily established the most comprehensive empire in the Near Eastern world until that time, the forerunner of the later empires of Alexander the Great and the Roman Caesars. Cyrus ("the Great") of Anshan was the architect of this new empire. Taking advantage of the weakness of Babylon, Lydia, Media, and Egypt, Cyrus appealed to those who favored international power in place of the limited ethnic kingdoms that had held sway since the demise of the Assyrian Empire. Cyrus was the founder of a powerful dynasty that eventually controlled most of Anatolia, the Fertile Crescent, and the Mediterranean basin. He proclaimed himself "king of the world, great king, legitimate king, king of Babylon, king of Sumer and Akkad, king of the four rims (of the earth)." Cyrus's son, Cambyses, added Egypt to the Persian holdings. His grandson, Darius I, further expanded an already huge empire and improved its internal organization. Syria-Palestine and the Jewish community in Judah were a part of this Persian hegemony for more than two centuries, from the capture of Babylon in 539 B.C.E. until the fall of Tyre to Alexander the Great in 332 B.C.E.

During the reign of Cyrus the Great, Jewish exiles started to return to Palestine from their captivity in Babylon, to construct the Second Temple and to refortify the city of Jerusalem. Persian policy, instituted by Cyrus, permitted these key events in the life of Israel to take place, exhibiting tolerance and benevolence to this subject people as to others. In the age-old royal tradition of the Near East, Cyrus promoted himself as "gatherer of the dispersed" and "restorer of the gods and their sanctuaries." Cyrus played the role of liberator, accepting and acknowledging the patronage of the gods worshipped by those capitulating to and supporting him. This Persian policy of permitting relative cultural autonomy among the separate peoples of the realm proved to be an excellent method of political control. Contented regions were less likely to rebel.

Both the biblical picture of Cyrus and ancient historical portraits of this great ruler are idealized. His treatment of groups that had been deported and settled throughout the empires of Assyria and Babylon probably varied from case to case. When it was politically expedient, the Persians did not hesitate to take harsh measures against their subjects or against the cultic centers in which they participated. Nonetheless, Cyrus's edict in 539 B.C.E. allowed Jewish exiles to return from Babylon, and he was hailed by the prophecies of Deutero-Isaiah as the savior and redeemer of Israel, chosen by Yahweh. Here Cyrus is even called "messiah," the one "whose right hand [Yahweh] has grasped, to subdue nations before him and ungird the loins of kings" (Isaiah 45:1).

The Hebrew Bible relates this edict in two versions. Persian records do not refer to it directly, although the Cyrus Cylinder celebrates a general policy of permitting resettlement and a return to ancestral religion. The edict recounted in Ezra 1:2–4 is in Hebrew, perhaps representing the original message of Cyrus's new policy related to various Jewish communities by official heralds. Ezra 6:3–5 is preserved in Aramaic, the official language of diplomatic relations in the Persian period and the lingua franca of the whole region both during and after the empire. Focusing on details of the Temple's reconstruction, this version may represent an official memorandum stored in the royal Persian archives. The edict describes the Temple's dimensions, provides for Persian support in defraying the cost of rebuilding, and assures the return of the Temple's cultic vessels from their storage in the treasuries of Babylon.

These decrees do not represent any Persian favoritism toward the Jews. Such actions were typical of Cyrus when he judged they were in the best interest of his empire. The political realities of Cyrus's conflicts with Egypt on his southwestern border made it expedient to allow the emergence of a Jewish vassal-city and buffer-zone. The biblical records of Cyrus's edict of release portray him as a devotee of Yahweh, to whom Cyrus attributed his good political fortune. But Cyrus himself (in his Cylinder) made similar affirmations about the Babylonian god Marduk. In the end, the edict of release was more Persian propaganda – of which Cyrus was a master – than historical reality. It did not require or allow a massive ingathering of the Jewish Diaspora scattered throughout the Persian Empire. No return en masse was envisioned, and it would be many years before the Jews of Palestine would be able to establish firm political, religious, and economic foundations in the postexilic period.

with Ezra 2:1–67. In Nehemiah 8 a narrative about Ezra suddenly appears; he formally reads "the book of the law of Moses" to the assembled people while Levites and other named teachers help to explain the meaning of the Torah. The main outcome is the observance of the Feast of Booths (8:13–18), after which the assembly confesses its sins (9:1–2) and Ezra utters an extended prayer and meditation on Israel's past history (9:6–37), concluding with the moving, tormented words: "Here we are, slaves to this day – slaves in the land that you gave to our ancestors. . . . Its rich yield goes to the kings whom you have set over us because of our sins" (9:36–7).

Nehemiah 10 lists those who made a covenant to abstain from marriage with foreigners, to observe the Sabbath and the Sabbatical year, not to exact debts, and to make various offerings for the support of the priests and Levites. In chapters 11–12 there are further lists of people, especially Temple officials, after which Nehemiah's first-person account resumes at 12:31. This relates how Nehemiah organized a sacrifice of thanksgiving and made provision for the support of priests and Levites. Chapter 13 relates how, after returning to Jerusalem in the thirty-second year of Artaxerxes, Nehemiah had to deal with covenantal abuses: nonprovision of support for the Levites and singers (13:10–14), nonobservance of the Sabbath (13:15–22), and marriages with foreigners (13:23–7).

Even this basic outline illustrates several problems posed by the Books of Ezra and Nehemiah: the "disappearance" of Sheshbazzar in connection with rebuilding the Temple, the appearance of Jeshua and Zerubbabel in connection with that effort and their absence from the account of the Temple's dedication, the repetition of the list of returnees in Ezra 2 and Nehemiah 7, the meager description of Ezra's reforms in the Book of Ezra and the fuller account of his work in the Book of Nehemiah, and the remarkable overlap in the reforms carried out by Ezra and by Nehemiah (with Nehemiah 13 listing precisely the issues that Ezra had already dealt with: the Sabbath, provision for Temple officials, and mixed marriages). Troublesome anachronisms also emerge; for example, in Ezra 4–5, letters from the reign of an Artaxerxes (465–424 B.C.E.) are placed between the reigns of Cyrus (559–529 B.C.E.) and Darius (522–486 B.C.E.). An explanation of these difficulties, together with a tentative history of the period 539–420 B.C.E. will now concern us.

The authors of Ezra and Nehemiah probably worked during the fourth century B.C.E. Even if they gathered and composed and edited their material starting in 400 B.C.E., that would have been one hundred forty years after the beginning of the return from exile. That delay would be the equivalent of a historian in 2014 describing events that started in 1874. Difficulties posed by a considerable delay were compounded by the meager sources that informed the authors. These sources included (a) the prophetic Books of Haggai and Zechariah 1–8, (b) miscellaneous official documents from the reigns of Cyrus, Darius, and Artaxerxes (presumably Artaxerxes I), (c) various lists of citizens and Temple officials, and (d) the first-person narrative in Nehemiah 1:1–7:5 and 12:31–13:31, commonly called the Nehemiah memoirs. Some scholars also believe that Ezra 8–9 incorporate Ezra's memoirs, but the existence of that source is widely disputed.

From official Persian documents the authors knew that Cyrus had authorized a return of Jews to Jerusalem to rebuild the Temple and that Sheshbazzar was entrusted with the task. This royal decree was consonant with Cyrus's policy toward subject peoples, as expressed in the official cuneiform text called the Cyrus Cylinder. From the Books of Haggai and Zechariah 1–8 the authors of Ezra and Nehemiah knew that the project of rebuilding had not gone well. Haggai records that, in Darius's second year (520 B.C.E., some nineteen years after Cyrus's authorization of the rebuilding), the people were saying "the time has not yet come to rebuild the house of the LORD" (Haggai 1:1–2). From the two prophetic books the authors learned that the principal leaders in Jerusalem were Zerubbabel and the high priest, Joshua (as spelled in its Hebrew form in Haggai and Zechariah). Nothing was known about who had appointed them or whether or how they had replaced Sheshbazzar. The authors also had official documents from a much later period (the reign of Artaxerxes), which concerned attempts to rebuild, not the Temple, but the city walls of Jerusalem, a project that was halted by offical action (Ezra 4:7–23). In composing Ezra 1-6, the authors freely adapted official documents and used correspondence about stopping the building of the city walls in the fifth century B.C.E. to explain why building some of the Temple had taken so long in the sixth century! They also used a census list from a later period to detail the names and numbers of those who returned with Sheshbazzar in 539 B.C.E.

Gaps, anachronisms, and confusions resulted from the authors' attempts to reconstruct the past with the usual tools of history: incomplete (sometimes fragmentary) sources, logical inferences, surmise, and hopeful guesses. They did their best with the material and knowledge available to them, lacking a contextual sense of Persian history, for example, but dedicated in their faith that the Torah would sustain the restoration of Jerusalem. In chapter 7 of the Book of Ezra the authors introduce Ezra himself, who was known to them only from a document from the reign of Artaxerxes that commissioned Ezra to go to Jerusalem and teach the people the Jewish law. Having no other information about Ezra, the authors liberally composed an account of Ezra's mission by basing it on what Nehemiah claimed to have done in his memoirs, together with some of the census lists that were available. This explains the overlap in the characterizations of the activities of the two men. At the time the Books of Ezra and Nehemiah were compiled, Nehemiah's memoirs had already been composed. Into this material the authors freely inserted material relating to Ezra (chapters 8–10), as well as various other lists of civic and religious functionaries (11:1–12:26).

Social History during the Period 539–420 B.C.E.

The Judah to which the decree of Cyrus permitted Jews to return in 539 B.C.E. was smaller than the Judah that the Babylonians had conquered in

597 and then gutted in 587/6. To the north it included the territory of Benjamin, as had preexilic Judah; but its southern boundary ran only to the north of Hebron. This had been Judah's capital prior to the conquest of Jerusalem, but now it was occupied by Edomites. Because those deported to Babylon in 597 and 587/6 were the nobility and the skilled classes, those left behind eked out a living on farms supported by semiskilled and unskilled laborers; the settlements that remained to them did not include areas where grain was best grown, so it is likely that they concentrated on the production of oil and wine.

How many Jews returned we cannot say (much as the population of Judah prior to the exile is a matter of speculative estimate). There were flourishing Jewish communities in Babylonia, some of whose inhabitants were well integrated within the larger society (as is indicated by the Murashu tablets); many of them probably did not wish to return. Those who did return with Sheshbazzar in 539 B.C.E. evidently had insufficient resources to accomplish much with the Temple, which would explain why little work was done on the rebuilding between 539 and 520.

The prophetic Books of Haggai and Zechariah 1–8, which date from this period, attest new activity on behalf of the Temple under Zerubbabel

---

THE MURASHU ARCHIVE

Uncovered at the Babylonian city of Nippur in 1893, the Murashu archive represents the single most important source available for understanding the life of Jews living beyond the borders of Palestine during the exilic and postexilic periods. The collection includes some 730 clay tablets inscribed with cuneiform Akkadian. The tablets belonged to the non-Jewish banking family of Murashu, but they include records of commodity transactions with Jews. The family records date from the reigns of Artaxerxes I (465–424 B.C.E.) and Darius II (424–404 B.C.E.).

Little is known about how the exiled Jews fared after the destruction of Jerusalem, which is why the indirect evidence offered by the Murashu tablets is crucial. Jeremiah urged the exiles to make a good home for themselves in Mesopotamia (Jeremiah 29:4–7), and some cuneiform records list rations sent to the exilic community. But the Murashu archive yields more than just confirmation of Jewish presence in Babylon; they also reflect a vibrant, cosmopolitan city with many different national or ethnic groups engaged in cooperative trade. Personal names in the Murashu archive reflect Babylonian, Persian, Median, Egyptian, and Semitic ancestry. Some of these names can be identified as specifically Jewish in origin.

Records of transactions between the Murashu family and persons clearly bearing Jewish names reveal interesting social realities. Jews at Nippur engaged in the same kinds of commerce that occupied the lives of non-Jews. Interest rates were no different for the banking family's Jewish customers, and no group seems to have suffered discrimination on religious grounds. At least two Jews mentioned in the archive appear to have obtained prestigious positions in Nippur's financial community.

The personal names attested in the Murashu archive provide clues to beliefs and customs in the Jewish community in Nippur, as well as an idea of the social pressures that Jews faced. Many Jews in the Babylonian Diaspora gave their children Babylonian names (the royal governors Sheshbazzar and Zerubbabel, for example). Analysis of the changes in Jewish name giving in Nippur, in Judah, and in the narrative literature of the Hebrew Bible suggests that the Jewish community was increasingly assimilated to the culture of Babylon. By the fifth century B.C.E., the Jews at Nippur seem to have fully integrated themselves into the life of a foreign city that had initially been a place of exile. The community appears to have heeded Jeremiah's advice – perhaps even more than the prophet intended.

and Joshua in 520 B.C.E., and suggest that a series of agricultural disasters were partly to blame for the early lack of progress. Zerubbabel is credited in Zechariah 4:9 with laying the foundation of the Temple, and the prophet promises that he will complete it. The perspective of both these prophetic books is eschatological, such that the rebuilding of the Temple is expected to usher in a new era of the fulfillment of divine promise, with implications for the whole earth. Nations will be overthrown, and Zerubbabel will be given a position of great power (Haggai 2:23; Zechariah 3:6–10). These hopes were disappointed. If Ezra 6:15–18 is to be taken literally, Zerubbabel was not even present at the Temple's rededication. He may have been removed from his position as governor by the Persians, or he may have left Jerusalem or died.

Events in Judah, or Yehud (as the Persians called the province), between 515 B.C.E. and 458 B.C.E. are not recorded. Ezra'a mission, which began in the seventh year of Artaxerxes I (465–424 B.C.E.) according to Ezra 7:7, represents the next major happening. Much has been written on the question of the respective dates of the missions of Ezra and Nehemiah. Some scholars have argued that Ezra came to Jerusalem in the seventh year of Artaxerxes II (404–359 B.C.E.), and others have argued – by emending "seventh" to "thirty-seventh" at Ezra 7:7 – that he came in the thirty-seventh year of Artaxerxes I (i.e., in 428 B.C.E.). The main reason for proposing these later dates is that such hypotheses ease the problem of Ezra and Nehemiah's overlapping activities, however slightly. But if, as seems probable, the accounts of Ezra's activities in Ezra 8–9 and in Nehemiah 8–10 are free compositions based on Nehemiah's memoirs, then we know nothing of the exact nature, length, or outcome of Ezra's mission. Ezra is less a person than a symbol of the Torah's centrality.

Nehemiah as a person comes through more clearly, because his memoirs tell of events from his own point of view. But in his case, as in Ezra's, unanswered questions remain. For example, why were the city walls of Jerusalem broken down nearly a century after the return from exile (Nehemiah 1:3)? Correspondence between the governor of Samaria and the Persian court provides a partial answer. (This correspondence has been preserved, but misplaced, at Ezra 4.) The rebuilding of the walls had been officially stopped because, from the Persian perspective, Jerusalem was a rebellious city and rebuilding defenses would only encourage further disobedience (Ezra 4:13–16). Perhaps there had been a rebellion in Judah that made local officialdom regard Jerusalem with such suspicion that they kept the once great city in a defenseless state. How Judah was being administered when Nehemiah arrived in Jerusalem in 445 B.C.E. is not known. In the Book of Nehemiah, Sanballat of Samaria opposed Nehemiah's appointment as governor of Judah and his work of rebuilding, and that picture has led to the widely held belief that Judah was ruled from Samaria. One of the Elephantine papyri (letters to Judah from a Jewish colony at Elephantine on the upper Nile) by its address to the sons of Sanballat, governor of Samaria, as well as to Bagoas, governor of Judah, may seem to support this finding (see *Ancient Near Eastern Texts*, p. 492). Yet Judah did

BULLAE FROM POSTEXILIC JUDAH

Bullae are small lumps of clay used to seal letters and other documents. They were pressed on the knotted string or cord that tied up a rolled papyrus or leather scroll and then stamped with a seal. A collection of seventy such bullae came to light in 1974. Scholars obtained them from an antiquities dealer who could identify them only as having been found in a pottery vessel somewhere in the region around Jerusalem. More than likely, the documents that they sealed had disintegrated long ago. When such ancient artifacts are removed from their archaeological context, much information is lost. Nonetheless, scholars have been able to identify these bullae as the remains of a late-sixth-century B.C.E. archive of official documents from the Persian sub-province of Yehud (Judah).

The bullae are inscribed in the Hebrew language using an Aramaic script that became widely used following the return of the Jewish exiles from Babylon. They record activity by fourteen persons with twelve different names. Most of the names also appear in the Books of Ezra and Nehemiah and may refer to the same people in at least some cases. Among the persons named on the bullae is Elnathan, who bears the title "governor." Some scholars suggest that Elnathan held office between the administrations of Zerubbabel (ca. 520 B.C.E.) and Nehemiah (445–432 B.C.E.). The name of Elnathan's "maidservant" (possibly his wife), Shelomith, also appears on one of the bullae. Her high position of responsibility is unusual for a woman in the biblical period. Whether she held such a position by virtue of office or of her personal relationship with the governor is unclear. The bullae also record activity by a professional scribe and various other officials or private individuals. Some of the people represented may have been owners of estates, who affixed their seals to legal documents, records of commercial transactions, or important public communications.

Many of the bullae bear the official provincial stamp "Yehud," the name by which the land of Judah was known to the Persian administration. The bullae present further evidence that Judah existed as a separate Persian subprovince beginning in the sixth century B.C.E., a distinct administrative unit with its own autonomous internal rule. Other archaeological evidence corroborates this conclusion. Storage jars found at a variety of sites in the country bear similar stamps. The stamp gave official sanction to the jars, whose contents were used to pay taxes in kind. One name, Hanana, actually appears both on one of these jars and on one of the sixth-century bullae. Small silver coins stamped with the "Yehud" legend also testify to Judah's provincial administrative autonomy under Persian rule.

indeed have its own governors, including the biblical Sheshbazzar and Zerubbabel as well as Bagoas in the papyrus from Elephantine, and that list can be supplemented by bullae, jars, and jar handles that have on them "Yehud" (Judah), the word for "governor," and a personal name.

The exile produced a new and basic form of social organization among the Jews: the *bet 'avot*. Literally translated, the phrase means "house of fathers," signaling the importance of male descent in restored Israel. In practice the *bet 'avot* was probably a descent group named after a particular ancestor. The list at Ezra 2 (and Nehemiah 7:6–73) refers to the sizes and progenitors of many such groups:

> sons of Parosh, 2,172
> sons of Shephatiah, 372
> sons of Arach, 652
> sons of Pahat-Moab belonging to the sons of Joshua and Joab, 2,818 . . .

This new social pattern was probably the result of the destruction of old kinship and territorial ties when the exiles were scattered in Babylon.

Under this new organizing principle, people belonged to groups initially headed by prominent leaders and later named after them. When these groups returned to Judah, they retained their new social identities, apparently in contrast to those who had not gone into exile and who were identified by the names of the villages in which they lived (see Ezra 2:27–8). The postexilic community of the fifth century B.C.E. and later was dominated by the life and organization of the Jerusalem Temple, as well as having a new concern with genealogy. Judging from the lists in Ezra and Nehemiah, up to a third of the entire community (at least as those two books reckoned its true numbers) were priests, Levites, and other Temple officials.

Nehemiah 5 reflects a situation in which some landholders forced other landholders into debt and even slavery. Poorer Jews had borrowed money from their brethren during times of famine and to pay the Persian king's tax on land (Nehemiah 5:3–4); having fallen into arrears, they sold their sons and daughters as slaves. Successive years of drought and perennial Persian bureaucracy exacerbated vicious inequality. The complaint made to Nehemiah in his capacity as governor was that, far from helping one another, some Jews profiteered to the detriment of fellow Jews. Nehemiah deals with the problem by ordering all fields, vineyards, and olive orchards to be returned to their owners, and for loans to be free of interest. Unfortunately, we do not know whether those who were losing their lands were descended from returnees or from those who had remained, or whether both groups were affected.

One clear aim of Nehemiah's policies was to dissolve marriages between Jews and non-Jews and to give the Jewish community in Judah a clearer identity. The Books of Ruth and Jonah show that some people were more ready to accept non-Jews as members of the community; and passages in Isaiah 56–66 imply a conflict between those hostile to and those in favor of non-Jews (e.g., Isaiah 56:3–8, 63:15–19). What motivated the more negative attitude? Perhaps the writers and compilers of Ezra and Nehemiah (as distinct from, but not necessarily in opposition to, the historical Nehemiah) believed that abolishing mixed marriages would lead to more faithful observance of the Jewish law, which in turn would bring blessings upon Judah and free the people from subservience to Persia (see Nehemiah 9:36–7). If this was also the view of the historical Nehemiah, the opposition of people such as the governor of Samaria, Sanballat, becomes understandable since they would desire a less religious regime that accepted non-Jews. The rebuilding of the city walls and the consolidation of the Jewish religious community of Judah would have been threats to their position.

The Literary Purpose of Ezra and Nehemiah

The writers of Ezra and Nehemiah probably lived at a time when Nehemiah's reforms were beginning to produce a more exclusively religious community, but without removing the Persian yoke. The writers' attitude toward the Persian Empire was ambivalent. On the one hand, Persian kings had facilitated a return to Jerusalem and the rebuilding of the

Temple, and had authorized Ezra and Nehemiah to reform the community. On the other hand, the same Persian king who authorized Ezra and Nehemiah had ordered a stop to the rebuilding of Jerusalem's walls; and Persian kings levied a tax on the land, which sometimes caused grievous hardship to farmers. Moreover, foreign possession of the land was a sore point for those who believed that God had given the land to the Israelites as a permanent possession (Nehemiah 9:24–5).

The tone in Ezra and Nehemiah is one of penitence before God – who is in control of nations, who has worked to bring about a partial restoration of his people's fortunes, and who will also, it is hoped, restore their fortunes completely. This tone is struck particularly in Nehemiah's memoirs, with appeals to God "to remember for good" what Nehemiah has done, and in the extended prayers composed by the writer and attributed to Ezra. Here, then, is the literature of a people penitently and expectantly waiting upon God to restore their fortunes completely. They have rebuilt their Temple, restored and repopulated the city, dissolved mixed marriages, and arranged for the Sabbath to be observed and the Temple officials to be supported. It is now up to God to exert his sovereign power on their behalf.

The Books of Chronicles

Chronicles may most easily be understood within the setting just described, which shaped their distinctive account of Israel's history. These books, written in the fourth century B.C.E., are unique in the Hebrew Bible, in that we possess many of the sources on which they are based. The writers made use of the Books of Samuel and Kings in versions not completely identical with Samuel and Kings as we now have them, but very close to them indeed. The standard view conceives of the direct accessibility of versions of Samuel and Kings to the Chroniclers, but it has recently been argued that we should rather think in terms of a source to which the writers of Samuel and Kings also had access. The Chroniclers also used parts of Psalms 96, 105, and 106; a list from Nehemiah 11; and genealogical material based on Genesis.

Chronicles begins, one might say, at "the beginning," with Adam, and the first eight chapters are genealogies, with the family of David bringing the descent line from Adam to close to the time of the writing of Chronicles. In 1 Chronicles 3:10–24 the genealogy of descendants of Solomon lists seven generations following King Jehoiachin, who was exiled to Babylon in 597 B.C.E. and was still living in 560 (2 Kings 25:27). If we reckon 25 years for a generation, seven generations add up to 175 years and brings the seventh generation into the fourth century B.C.E. This genealogy may have been intended to keep hopes of a restoration of the Davidic dynasty alive. Yet given their emphasis on cultic arrangements, the Chroniclers' greater concern might have been the belief that David had been responsible for instituting arrangements for worship in the first Temple. First Chronicles portrays David as careful about sacrifice (1 Chronicles 16:40), as receiving the spectacular intervention of fire from heaven in the manner of Elijah (1 Chronicles 21:26), as avoiding the altar at Gibeon (1 Chronicles

21:29–22:1), and as progressing far in preparations for constructing the Temple (1 Chronicles 28:18). The continuance of the line of David after the exile helped to stress the continuity between the first and the second Temples – a pivotal issue for a small community dominated by the Temple.

Chapters 1–8 of 1 Chronicles also contains genealogies of tribes from the northern kingdom, although in territorial terms they had ceased to exist nearly four hundred years before the book was written. The authors evidently had no information about Dan and Zebulun, but the other tribal clans are represented, including Reuben (a tribe that had been absorbed into other tribes well before the Assyrian invasion) and the east Jordan tribe of Gad. The writers' motivation for including northern (and eastern) tribes was their belief that the Judah of their day represented the whole of Israel as it had once been, a belief that reflects the power of the genealogies of the period to convey social and religious identity. The Chroniclers largely ignored the material in the Books of Kings about the northern kingdom in later Israelite history and yet claimed at the same time to represent the heritage of Israel as a whole.

From 1 Chronicles 10 the story of Israel as a nation begins to be told, starting with Saul and concentrating, from chapter 11 to the end of 1 Chronicles, on the reign of David and his ordering of worship in the Temple. Much of the material from chapters 11–21 is based on the Books of Samuel, and portions of Psalms are also used. Material unique to Chronicles appears in chapter 12, with its claim that although David was a Philistine vassal in Ziklag, he received support from men from the tribes of Benjamin, Gad, Manasseh, Issachar, Zebulun, Naphtali, Dan, Asher, and Reuben. As in the case of much of the innovative material in Chronicles, it is disputed whether the writer was composing freely or using an ancient source not otherwise known to us. Although scholars have not agreed on this point, the tendency to launder David's reputation is manifest in Chronicles. One interesting feature of 1 Chronicles 12 is the inspired utterance by a leader of the Benjaminites as they come to pledge loyalty to David. He proclaims (1 Chronicles 12:18):

> We are yours, O David;
> and with you, O son of Jesse!
> Peace, peace to you,
> and peace to the one who helps you!
> For your God is the one who helps you.

Because we can compare passages in Samuel and Kings with how they have been used in Chronicles, we can arrive at secure conclusions about the author's outlook and intentions. The following themes and patterns emerge.

1. Chronicles gives an explicit "all Israel" flavor to the narratives. This becomes evident in a comparison of the narratives of the bringing of the ark to Jerusalem in 2 Samuel 6 and in 1 Chronicles 13. In the former, David simply goes with "all the people who were with him" to bring the ark up

from Baale-judah. In the latter, David consults with all the commanders and leaders in Israel as well as with the "assembly of Israel," resolving to summon all Israelites, especially priests and Levites, "in cities that have pasturelands" to come together to bring up the ark.

2. Where it suits the writers, the order of presentation in the sources is disregarded. Thus 2 Samuel 6 (the bringing up of the ark) is placed before 2 Samuel 5:13–25 (which refers to David's wives and concubines in Jerusalem and the defeat of the Philistines).

3. The Chroniclers present David's character in a more favorable light than the writers of 2 Samuel by omitting the whole of the narrative about David's adultery with Bath-sheba, his successful plan to have her husband, Uriah, killed in battle, and the subsequent turmoil in his family and kingdom.

4. From 2 Chronicles 13 onward, speeches made before battles and other incidents are prominent in the narratives. In 2 Chronicles 13:4–12 Abijah speaks before encountering Jeroboam; in 14:11 Asa prays to God before defeating the Ethiopians; in 15:2–7 the prophet Azariah encourages Asa to carry out a reform. In 20:6–12 Jehoshaphat prays before the assembly prior to fighting the Moabites and Ammonites and is further encouraged by an inspired utterance from the Levite Jahaziel (20:15–17). The people go into battle fortified by a further brief exhortation from the king (20:20) and by singing

> Give thanks to the LORD,
> for his steadfast love endures forever.

In these and similar passages, the writers of Chronicles let us see and hear their community at worship. It is a community that draws upon its spiritual heritage of psalms and is encouraged by inspired outbursts of Levites and others. It has a firm belief in the sovereignty of God, who, having delivered his people in the past in response to their faithful obedience to the Law and their trust as expressed in worship, will do the same in the present and the future.

5. One of the most striking aspects of the Chroniclers' perspective is the way in which they reverse the verdict upon kings of Judah as compared with the account of them in the Books of Kings, most blatantly for kings considered bad in the Books of Kings.

Abijam, as portrayed in 1 Kings 15:1–8, deserved punishment: "He walked in all the sins which his father did before him; and his heart was not wholly true to the LORD his God" (15:3). Yet, as we have just seen, Abijah (as he is called in Chronicles) gives an address before defeating Jeroboam. In the address he claims that he and his people have not forsaken God and that God is with them (2 Chronicles 13:10); no negative verdict is passed on Abijah in Chronicles.

Manasseh represents the most surprising reversal of reputation. Chapter 21 of 2 Kings has such a negative view of him that, in verses 10–15, God's prophets warn that his evil reign will be the reason why Jerusalem will be destroyed as Samaria was destroyed. Chapter 33 of 2 Chronicles begins in a similar vein but then, unexpectedly, tells us that when Manasseh was taken by the king of Assyria to Babylon, he humbled himself and prayed to God, and that God, hearing his prayer, brought him back to Jerusalem (vv. 10–13). The Chroniclers' Manasseh subsequently carried out a reformation in which foreign gods and idols were removed from the Temple and destroyed (v. 15). Manasseh's repentance and reform seem to reflect the Chroniclers' theology rather than the facts of the case; this portrayal successfully conveys the Chroniclers' conviction that God will honor the sincere repentance of even the most wicked offender.

Whereas Chronicles is generous to wicked kings who repent, it is also hard on some of the "good" kings in the accounts of the Books of Kings and in its own material. We have seen how Asa prayed to God and was encouraged by a prophet (2 Chronicles 14:11; 15:2–7). But at the end of the narrative concerning him, he is condemned by a prophet for making an alliance with Damascus instead of relying on God. This prophet is imprisoned for his utterances (16:10), and Asa's reign ends under a cloud.

The account of Jehoash's reign in 2 Kings 11:21–12:21 is favorable, but a different perspective is given in 2 Chronicles 24. After the death of the priest Jehoiada, Joash (as he is called in Chronicles) forsakes God, and the son of Jehoiada is stoned to death on Joash's orders because he warns the people, in an inspired utterance, that they have forsaken God. Joash's assassination is described as retribution for this act.

Changes are also made in the case of Josiah, the hero of the Deuteronomistic History. In 2 Kings 22–3 he is given an outstanding portrait as a good king, ending with the words:

> Before him there was no king like him, who turned to the LORD with all his heart, with all his soul, and with all his might . . . nor did any like him arise after him. (2 Kings 23:25)

In 2 Chronicles, however, a sour note is introduced. When Josiah goes up to his fatal encounter with the Egyptian pharaoh Necho, the latter is inspired by God to warn Josiah off (2 Chronicles 35:21–2). Josiah takes no notice. Thus Chronicles describes his death as the result of his refusal to listen to God's word. Even a nearly ideal king can be flawed in his attention to God and suffer the consequences.

In Chronicles, the past history of Israel is perceived and presented from the viewpoint of a worshipping, Temple-based community. The sense of the all-encompassing sovereignty of God is such that there is a scaling down of human achievements and an exaltation of what God can do with even the most unpromising material. Thus Josiah can err, and even Manasseh can repent.

The community's hope that, in due time, God will reward their faithfulness and trust is best summed up in two of the prayers uttered by two kings. In 2 Chronicles 20:12 Jehoshaphat, faced by overwhelming enemy armies, prays:

we are powerless against this great multitude that is coming against us. We do not know what to do, but our eyes are on you.

At 1 Chronicles 29:14–15, David prays:

But who am I, and what is my people, that we should be able to make this freewill offering? For all things come from you, and of your own have we given you. For we are aliens and transients before you, as were all our ancestors; our days on the earth are like a shadow, and there is no hope.

This piety, the outcome of Nehemiah's attempt to reconstitute Judah as a community faithful to God's laws even at the price of abolishing mixed marriages and the contention that that produced, reflects the promise inherent in Israelite identity that the Books of Ezra, Nehemiah, and Chronicles articulate.

III. THE WORLD OF ISRAEL'S PROPHETS

A. The Organization of the Prophetic Writings

1. Prophetic Forms of Speech

By origin and in their continuing intent, prophets were primarily speakers rather than writers. Theirs was not the power of the pen; the spoken word was their principal resource as they confronted kings, princes, priests, and other people of their time with oracles often prefaced by the phrase "thus says (or said) the LORD." Written books in the Bible attributed to named prophets such as Amos, Isaiah, or Jeremiah contain material that did not emanate directly from the prophet after whom the book is named, because the form of a book was actually foreign to prophetic discourse, and editors were required so that prophets could make the transition to the medium of writing.

In ancient Israel prophecy was not a uniform or typical discourse; neither did prophets necessarily belong to a distinctive guild or profession. They were different types of people from diverse backgrounds. Ezekiel was a priest, Isaiah was close to the Davidic entourage, and Micah was a provincial leader, evidently hostile to the establishment in Jerusalem. Amos denied that he was a prophet at all (Amos 7:14); because scholars have been determined to see prophecy as an identifiable institution within ancient Israel, they have often refused to take his disclaimer seriously. They have argued that Amos was saying that he was not a *professional* prophet or guild member, and even that the words "I am no prophet" were a way for Amos to say that he really was a prophet after all! The only thing that people whom we now call prophets had in common during the preexilic period was their conviction that God had spoken to them and

that they were impelled to communicate to the king or the people what
God had said:

> The lion has roared;
> who will not fear?
> The Lord GOD has spoken;
> who can but prophesy?
> > (Amos 3:8)

If we ask how the prophets believed that God had spoken to them, the
texts do not tell the whole story, but they do provide a few clues. Several
passages suggest by their use of puns that seeing an ordinary object triggered an association and therefore a message in the prophet's mind. For
example, Amos sees a basket of summer fruit (*qayits* in Hebrew) and thinks
of the similar word for "end" (*qets* in Hebrew; Amos 8:1). Jeremiah sees an
almond tree (*shaqed* in Hebrew) and thinks of the word for "watching"
(*shoqed;* Jeremiah 1:11–12). The observation of everyday happenings could
also trigger a message, as when Jeremiah saw a potter at work (Jeremiah
18:1–4) or when Amos saw locusts eating grass (Amos 7:1–3). Prophets
were clearly people who, in prayer and visions as well as in daily experiences, believed that they were being given a message to proclaim because
of their intimate relationship with God.

Prophets used a variety of devices to get their messages across. A famous
example is the messenger formula that was used by kings and other rulers
to convey messages to each other. A messenger would stand in his king's
presence while the king spoke the message to be conveyed to another
ruler. The messenger would go to that ruler and repeat exactly what he
had heard. There is an example of this formula in Judges 11, when Jephthah
sends messages to the king of the Ammonites. His message in verse 14
begins "Thus says Jephthah." When the prophets delivered a message that
began "Thus says (or said) the LORD," they implied that they had stood in
God's presence and had heard him say words that they repeated. They had
stood in God's court in a visionary state, or perhaps metaphorically; whatever the case, they claimed to speak on behalf of a power greater than that
of any human king, so that the impact of their use of the messenger formula must have been very great, representing a message that had to be
embraced or fiercely rejected, but which could scarcely be ignored. The
messenger formula became stylized and took the form of an introduction
describing how a state of affairs had developed, followed by a statement of
what the king who sent the emissary demanded or was about to do, preceded by the word "therefore."

Another common form was that of legal accusation. The prophet called
heaven and earth, or the citizens of surrounding nations, to hear an accusation that God brought against his people. The beginning of Isaiah presents a good example of this form:

> Hear, O heavens, and give ear, O earth;
> for the LORD has spoken:

"Sons have I reared and brought up,
but they have rebelled against me.
The ox knows its master,
and the ass its master's crib;
but Israel does not know,
my people does not understand."
                              (Isaiah 1:2–3)

Another device was to use the type of lamentation with which death was mourned. Prophets often spoke in poetry, and lamentation had a distinctive pattern: a line of three stressed syllables followed by a line with two stresses. This is not easy to reproduce in English, but Amos 5:2–3, where the poem is even introduced as a lament, makes the pattern evident even in translation. The stresses are marked here:

Fállen, no móre to ríse,
is the vírgin Israél;
forsáken ón her lánd,
with nóne to raise hér up.
                              (Amos 5:2)

In contrast, the prophet of Isaiah 5:1–2 used the form of a love poem to convey his message:

Let me sing a song for my beloved
a love song concerning his vineyard.
                              (Isaiah 5:1)

At the end of the same passage there is yet another device – the use of similar-sounding words with different meanings:

and he looked for justice [*mishpat*]
but behold, bloodshed [*mispah*];
for righteousness [*tsedaqah*],
but behold, a cry [*tse'aqah*].
                              (Isaiah 5:7)

In Micah 1 there is an extended speech in which puns are made on the names of cities in order to warn their inhabitants. The poem is badly preserved, but the following modernization conveys its flavor:

1:10b   In Dust-ville, roll yourselves in the dust.
1:11b   Do not go out, citizen of Out-town.
1:13a   Harness the chariot to the horse, citizens of Horse-ville.
1:14c   The homes of Deceit-ville are deceitful.

Mention must also be made of what has been called "prophetic symbolism," when prophets engaged in gestures that included both an oracle and a physical performance designed to give dramatic expression to the words spoken. One of the best-known examples of prophetic symbolism is recorded in 1 Kings 11:29–39. The prophet Ahijah meets Jeroboam on the road and takes his own new garment and tears it into twelve pieces, giving Jeroboam ten of them. This dramatically symbolizes his words:

> Behold I am about to tear the kingdom from the hand of Solomon, and will give you ten tribes. (1 Kings 11:31)

In Isaiah 8:1–4 the prophet writes on a large tablet the name to be given to his son: Maher-shalal-hash-baz, meaning "the spoil speeds, the prey hastes." This dramatically reinforces the prophet's warnings to Damascus about its imminent fate. It is also possible that the difficult first chapter of Hosea is to be understood as prophetic symbolism, in which case the prophet deliberately acts out the divine command by marrying a prostitute and fathering children by her. This, however, is only one of several ways of interpreting this intriguing prophecy.

Prophetic gestural symbolism is met dramatically in Ezekiel. In chapter 4 the prophet draws a picture on a brick of Jerusalem surrounded by siege works. He is instructed to lie on his left side for 390 days, symbolizing the years of the punishment of Israel (the northern kingdom), followed by 40 days on his right side, representing the years of the punishment of Judah. Whether Ezekiel actually lay in public view on his left side for a year and a month we will probably never know. (In any case, would his viewers have kept count?) It has been plausibly suggested that Ezekiel was performing the equivalent of street theater, and that in this way, in the example given, he acted a part as though he was lying on his side for 390 days. Whatever the literal truth of this narrative, the fact remains that prophetic utterance not only drew upon many oratorical devices but in some cases backed these up with dramatic actions.

From Oral to Written Prophecy

We have practically no direct information regarding how the spoken (and enacted) words of prophets reached the form in which we have them in the prophetic books. During the eighteenth century the idea that prophets wrote the books that bear their names began to be abandoned, largely because passages or sections demonstrably later than the time of a given prophet were identified. For example, in the 1770s chapters 40–66 of Isaiah were ascribed to a prophet who lived two hundred years later than the prophet of Isaiah 1–39. Further research indicated that sections of Isaiah 1–39 were also later than the time of Isaiah of Jerusalem (the "author" of Isaiah 1–12, who lived in the second half of the eighth century B.C.E.). In the nineteenth century the prophets were rediscovered as speakers rather than writers, as inspired figures who proclaimed "thus saith the LORD" to their contemporaries. So how did these spoken words come to be written down?

Jeremiah 36 describes how Jeremiah dictated his oracles to the scribe Baruch son of Neriah. Attempts to discredit this claim have been weakened by the publication by Nahman Avigad in 1986 of a seal bearing the name "Barachiah son of Neriah the scribe." We seem, therefore, to know one way in which oracles were written down. It would be wrong to conclude that all prophetic books were produced in the same way, but the example of Jeremiah indicates that prophets (even difficult prophets) were not solitary figures, that they had supporters and disciples. In most cases the sources are silent about who these followers were; but studies by social anthropologists of intermediaries between the divine and human realms show that support groups, whether they function at the center or at the periphery of a society, are important for prophets. The involved stories concerning Elijah and Elisha, which stretch from 1 Kings 17 through 2 Kings 13, indicate that they presided over groups called "sons of the prophets," and Isaiah 8:16–18 hints that Isaiah also had a substantial number of disciples. Obviously, we must not overlook the diversity that existed among those we call prophets, but it is safe to assume that none whose words have come down to us was a completely isolated individual.

Although it is not an easy passage to understand, Isaiah 8:16–20 suggests that prophetic oracles were written down, sealed, and kept by disciples so that they could be used on subsequent occasions to discern the word and will of God. This amounts to an indication of how and by whom oracles were initially recorded and transmitted. But how were they later arranged into a collection? Various organizing principles prevailed, the most obvious being thematic; when blocks of oracles target foreign nations, for example, they might be aggregated (Isaiah 17–19; Jeremiah 46–51; Ezekiel 24–32). In other cases, short collections such as Amos 3, 4, and 5, each begining with the formula "hear this word," were put together to form a larger block. Another organizing principle was the "catchword," whereby an oracle beginning with a particular word, name, or phrase would be linked to an oracle with a similar term. Not many clear examples of the catchword arrangement can be found in the Hebrew Bible (although they are common at a later period in Rabbinic literature as well as in the New Testament and in Gnostic writings).

The work of the collectors did not stop with arranging the material available to them. Critical commentators on most prophetic books have agreed that original oracles were reworked and expanded. The word from God that the oracles contained was believed to be relevant, not only for its original occasion of speaking but also for later situations, so that this attempt to extend the meaning of what a prophet had said was only natural. Prophecy was a living tradition, begun by individual prophets but sustained by generations of disciples engaged in the interpretation of the initial words.

The Babylonian exile of the sixth century B.C.E. proved a decisive context in the transcription of prophetic books. Prophetic groups who saw the fall of Jerusalem as God's punishment of his people's unfaithfulness and who believed in a restoration of Jerusalem enabled Israel to survive an unthinkable catastrophe. The influence of the exile seems eventually to have brought all the existing prophetic traditions under the control of a combination of priestly and scribal authorities in postexilic Judah. Such an alliance had not been natural prior to the exile, and as we shall see, it was not achieved without protest (cf. the discussion of Malachi in Section P). The prophetic books nonetheless reached their final form under the auspices of this new coalition, and the diversity that had once existed among prophets and their followers was molded toward literary uniformity.

One result of the new homogeneity was that prophets whose original words had been hostile to Israel and Judah, to the point of offering nothing beyond God's annihilating judgment, had oracles of hope added to the books attributed to them. The concluding verses of Amos (9:1–15) speak of raising up the booth of David that is fallen, presupposing the fall of Jerusalem. Because this happened one hundred and fifty years after the time of Amos, these verses seem an addition designed to mitigate the book's uncompromising message of judgment. Micah was treated even more drastically, with oracles of salvation interspersed among oracles of destruction. As they worked their material, the literary editors of the prophetic traditions articulated their belief that the history of Israel and Judah should be viewed from a larger and longer perspective than was possible for any individual prophet at an earlier period. Amos and Micah had been proved correct in their warnings of coming judgment, but there had also been a restoration, and the final editors set the messages of Amos and Micah in that context. This process was a vital part of the move from oral to written prophecy.

The Organization of the Prophetic Books

In the English Bible, the prophetic books are Isaiah, Jeremiah, Ezekiel, Daniel, and the Twelve Minor Prophets. They come at the end of the Old Testament, so that the closing words of Malachi, which speak of the coming of Elijah, form a fitting prelude to the New Testament and the Elijah-like activity of John the Baptist. But in the Hebrew Bible, Daniel belongs to the section known as the Writings, and the remainder of the prophets are designated Latter Prophets and follow the Former Prophets (Joshua, Judges, Samuel, and Kings). In the Rabbinic Bible there are four Latter Prophets – Isaiah, Jeremiah, Ezekiel, and the Twelve Minor Prophets (regarded as one book). Perhaps the length of each corresponds to what could be written on a single scroll. A traditional enumeration in Judaism gives the following numbers of verses: Isaiah, 1,295; Jeremiah, 1,365; Ezekiel, 1,273; the Twelve, 1,050. Of the three "larger" prophets, the Book of Isaiah is unique, perhaps representing the work of an Isaian "school" over many generations, in that it consists of three blocks of material from three quite different periods: chapters 1–39 (with later additions) from the eighth century B.C.E., chapters 40–55 from the sixth century, and chapters 56–66 from the fifth century.

There has been much speculation over the order and arrangement of the Twelve Minor Prophets. One influential theory has seen them as arranged according to the putative dates of the prophets after whom they were named. Hosea, Amos, and Micah (eighth century B.C.E.) preceded Nahum, Habakkuk, and Zephaniah (seventh century B.C.E.), who in turn preceded the fifth-century B.C.E. Haggai and Zechariah (chapters 1–8) and the fourth-century Malachi. Later, chapters 9–14 were added to Zechariah, and Joel and Obadiah were composed during the third century. The positions of Jonah, Joel, and Obadiah were determined on inferential grounds. Jonah was placed before Micah because of the reference in 2 Kings 14:25 to a Jonah who prophesied during the reign of Jeroboam II (during the eighth century B.C.E.). Joel was placed between Hosea and Amos because Joel 3:16a (Hebrew Bible, 4:16a) was similar to Amos 1:2, and Joel 3:18a (4:18a) was similar to Amos 9:13. Obadiah was placed after Amos because it concerned Edom and thus followed naturally from the end of Amos (before the addition to Amos of 9:13–15) at 9:12, where Edom is mentioned. In other words, we have both a chronological and a "catchword" principle operating in the arrangement of the Twelve.

A striking difference between the three major prophetic books and the Twelve is that, apart from Jonah, we are told almost nothing about the prophets named in connection with the Twelve, whereas the Books of Isaiah, Jeremiah, and Ezekiel contain at least some biographical material. It has been suggested, although anything like proof is impossible, that the biographical information about the prophets in the Twelve was omitted in the redaction process for two reasons: to shorten the material so as to occupy one scroll, and to remove historical details so that the oracles would be applicable to situations beyond their original setting.

2. Prophecy in Israelite History

The Monarchical Period (from the Eleventh to the Sixth Centuries B.C.E.)

Prophets did not belong to a recognizable "institution" in ancient Israel, and they varied widely in the classes and groups they represented and in the methods they used. As 1 Samuel 9:9 indicates, different kinds of intermediaries (to use the neutral term favored by anthropologists and sociologists for "prophets") were recognized:

> Formerly in Israel, when a man went to inquire of God, he said, "Come, let us go to the seer"; for he who is now called a prophet was formerly called a seer.

The setting of 1 Samuel 9 is Saul's search for some lost asses, and the purpose of consulting the seer is to obtain supernatural information about the journey that Saul and his servant have undertaken. Saul's servant assures his master about the seer Samuel, saying that "all that he says comes true" (1 Samuel 9:6). As presented in 1 Samuel 9–10 and 19:18–24, Samuel is the head of a group of "prophets" whose distinctive characteristic is their ecstatic behavior, which included lying naked on the ground for hours on end. Samuel is also presented as a powerful figure in his society, with authority both to anoint a king and to reprove him. This authority no doubt derived from popular belief that he was in direct communication with God.

Elijah and Elisha seem to have continued the type of prophecy repre-sented by Samuel. They, too, preside over groups of prophets, although we are not told that these groups were ecstatic, and the Elijah and Elisha sto-ries celebrate these men as wonder-workers who can restore the dead to life (1 Kings 17:17–24; 2 Kings 4:18–37), cause vessels never to be empty (1 Kings 17:8–15), and make iron ax heads float on water (2 Kings 6:1–7). These prophets also resort to supernatural violence. Elijah destroys men seeking to arrest him by calling down fire from heaven (2 Kings 1:9–12), and Elisha curses small boys who taunt him by saying, "Go up, you bald-head" – a prank for which they are killed by two she-bears (2 Kings 2:23–5). Elijah and Elisha were also active in national affairs, opposing Ahab and Jezebel, and anointing Jehu to carry out a revolution by over-throwing Ahab's dynasty. The account of Elijah's contest with the prophets of Baal (1 Kings 18:17–40) shows that prophets were not peculiar to the worship of Yahweh. The narrative describes Baal's prophets as cutting themselves with swords and lances, and limping and raving in order to pre-vail upon their god.

While Elijah and Elisha (and Samuel, although in different circum-stances) operated from the margins of society in championing traditional faith in the God of Israel, albeit with support from powerful sympathiz-ers at the center of power (see 1 Kings 18:3–4), there were also prophets employed officially by kings. Nathan was apparently a prophet at David's court; from that position he reproved David's adultery with Bath-sheba and his orchestration of Uriah's death (2 Samuel 12:1–15), and played an important part in the succession of Solomon to the throne (1 Kings 1:22–40). In 1 Kings 22:5–12, four hundred prophets gather to advise Ahab whether to fight at Ramoth-gilead. They apparently resorted to ecstatic prophecy, if this is a correct inference from verse 10: "All the prophets were prophesying before them [i.e., Ahab and the Judean king Jehoshaphat]." Other prophets mentioned in the period from Saul (eleventh century B.C.E.) to the end of the ninth century B.C.E. include Ahijah, who encouraged Jeroboam's rebellion against Solomon's son Rehoboam (1 Kings 11:29–39), and Micaiah, who foretold the death of Ahab, contradicting the view of the four hundred prophets who foresaw Ahab's success (1 Kings 22:13–23). The picture that emerges from this is a diversity of Yahwistic prophets who, whatever their other differences, opposed the prophets of Baal and other gods, claimed supernatural pow-ers, and played an active role in the religious and political affairs of Judah and Israel, helping to set up and to bring down kings and zealously defending faith in the God of Israel.

The eighth century B.C.E. saw the first of the prophets to whom prophetic books are attributed; they continued the tradition of prophetic diversity. Isaiah seems to have been a court prophet in Jerusalem, whereas Amos and Micah were from small provincial towns in Judah, with Amos denying that he even was a prophet (Amos 7:14). We know nothing directly of Hosea, but presume he came from the northern kingdom,

Israel, since his oracles concern Israel specifically. (But for that matter, so do most of Amos's, and he came from the southern town of Tekoa; Amos 1:1). These eighth-century prophets did not try to overthrow kings, as far as we know, but their oracles were often concerned with God's coming judgment upon Israel and Judah because the people *and* their rulers had forsaken God. The seventh-century B.C.E. prophets – Zephaniah, Nahum, and Habakkuk, all of whom are anonymous in everything but name – adhere to this pattern and show how influential the models of their eighth-century predecessors had become. Nahum stands out from the rest in that the oracles of his book are directed not against Judah but against Nineveh. Jeremiah's ministry dates from the end of the seventh century to the beginning of the sixth and was concerned with Jerusalem's impending destruction. He exemplifies the type of prophet who operated from the margins of society but who nonetheless had supporters close to the seat of power.

Scholars have debated two main questions regarding prophets during the period of monarchy. The first is: Did they actually create the faith of Israel? The view that they did so became influential during the second half of the nineteenth century. The prophets were seen as the originators of ethical monotheism, who preached this religion to an Israel that had been barely distinguishable from their Canaanite neighbors. Prophetic religion was, in this view, embodied in the Deuteronomistic law and enacted in the reforms of Josiah, only to be swamped in the postexilic period by an emergent priestly-scribal religion that gave preeminence to the law.

There is some truth in these contentions. The Law did not reach its present form until after the exile, when priestly-scribal religion predominated, and a link between prophetic witness and the Deuteronomistic tradition is very likely. Further, the contribution of preexilic prophecy to upholding and developing Israel's religion must have been crucial. Yet to see the prophets as the inventors of Israel's faith in Yahweh is probably a serious exaggeration. Some of the traditions preserved in Deuteronomy have their origin in the premonarchical period and imply a prior, albeit simple, form of agreement that bound Israelite groups to Yahweh. If, as appears likely, Jeroboam's revolt against Solomon and his son was supported by prophets of the "old" faith against the novel Temple cult in the lately elevated Jerusalem, this shows that prophets preserved – and did not only invent – traditions that expressed the people's faith in Yahweh.

The second question that has exercised scholars is: How did the prophets relate to institutions such as the Temple cult? Inference is our only guide, and in this instance scholars have inferred quite differently. That Isaiah received his call as part of a Temple vision (Isaiah 6:1–10) and that Jeremiah preached in the Temple court (Jeremiah 7:1–4) may mean little or a great deal – depending upon one's perspective. Discussion has centered on the theme of the "Day of Yahweh," which is found in Isaiah, Amos, and Zephaniah and possibly (by implication) in Nahum and Habakkuk. This "day" is one of judgment and wrath for the ungodly in Judah, Israel, and elsewhere, when God acts to assert his sovereignty. Whether the Day of

THE DAY OF THE LORD

Reference to the Day of the LORD (i.e., the Day of Yahweh) occurs frequently in the Hebrew Bible, especially in the prophetic canon, having originated much earlier in Israel's history. Scholars have long debated the exact origins of the concept, and several theories have been proposed. The eminent scholar Gerhard von Rad argued that the prophets' Day of Yahweh, understood as a moment of victory, grew out of Israel's historical and theological experience of holy war, described vividly in Joshua and Judges. Von Rad's distinguished Scandanavian colleague, Sigmund Mowinckel, suggested a more cultic origin, locating the concept as part of a hypothetical Israelite celebration of the New Year when Yahweh was ritually reenthroned as divine king each year. Others have contended that the idea of an awesome divine epiphany is a holdover from Canaanite mythology. In any case, the Day of Yahweh began with the promise that Israel would be vindicated by Yahweh. When Yahweh appeared, the enemy would flee, the universe would return to order, and peace and security would be assured for the whole people of Israel by means of Yahweh's just judgment.

By the time of the eighth-century B.C.E. prophets, the Day of Yahweh had taken on entirely new meaning. In the speeches of Amos (5:18–20), Isaiah (2:9–19), and, later, Zephaniah (1:7–16, 2:2–3), the Day of Yahweh is anticipated as a day of destruction for Israel and Judah. When Yahweh appears, his purpose is to punish the people for their sins and bring them to repentance. Although warnings about the impending Day of Yahweh often paint its coming in fearful poetic images, the classical prophets refer on the whole to real catastrophes that were about to befall their people, with agricultural and military disasters featuring most commonly. Some prophets found the fulfillment of oracles about the Day of Yahweh in the sixth-century B.C.E. destruction of Jerusalem. Ezekiel (34:12) and Lamentations (1:21) understand the Day of Yahweh as an event that had already come to pass.

Apocalypticism influenced the theological conception of the Day of Yahweh in the Hebrew Bible's later writings. In Zechariah (14) and Joel (English translation, 1–2, 3:14–15), the Day of Yahweh is depicted as a period of cosmic cataclysm that marks the end of all history. The final battle between good and evil is fought on that terrible day in the midst of universal upheaval and natural destruction. On this apocalyptic Day of Yahweh, the people of God will triumph over all their enemies, and every surviving nation will worship the king, Yahweh of Hosts.

The exact phrase "Day of Yahweh" disappears from Jewish literature in the postbiblical period, although the idea it expresses remained important in the thought of Judaism. The rapidly approaching Day of Final Judgment holds an important place in apocryphal, pseudepigraphic, and Rabbinic works. These eschatological expectations influenced the New Testament profoundly. The Day of the Lord is recast in christological terms and taken up by the Gospels (Luke 17:24; cf. John 8:56), the Pauline epistles (1 Thessalonians 5:2; 2 Corinthians 1:14), and the Apocalypse (Revelation 16:14).

Yahweh is to be associated with the Temple cult and connected with an annual or periodic celebration of the universal kingship of God, or whether it derives from the institution of holy war, is a matter of scholarly disagreement. This disagreement arises partly from a dearth of evidence; but the fact that three prophets invoke the theme of the Day of Yahweh indicates that they were operating in the context of traditions or institutions, even if we can say little more than that. We are on firmer ground with the prophetic Zion theology, which does presuppose some connection with the Temple. This theology identifies "Yahweh of Hosts" as the divine protector of Zion (Isaiah 6:3) and stresses the righteousness that God possesses and requires of his people. Articulated in Isaiah, this theology also appears in Psalms (e.g., Psalms 24, 46), and so cannot be considered to have belonged to prophets alone.

The Exilic Period (Sixth Century B.C.E.)

The exile produced two dominant prophetic works: Ezekiel and the unknown prophet of Isaiah 40–55. These two substantial writings bring to a high point Israel's faith in the sovereignty of God. Ezekiel's certainty that God must destroy Jerusalem before there can be any hope of national restoration is expressed in visions of Jerusalem's abominations and of God's judgment against nations that might come to Judah's help, especially Egypt. Only when news reaches Ezekiel that Jerusalem has fallen does he begin to speak of restoration. In Ezekiel 37 the prophet has a vision of dry bones being clothed with flesh and becoming an army of living people, a powerful metaphor of how a situation that seems utterly hopeless from a human standpoint can be redeemed by the power of God.

Isaiah 40–55 (known as Second Isaiah) articulates two main themes: the lordship of God over historical events, and the power of vicarious suffering to bring repentance to wrongdoers. The prophet sees the victorious march of the Persian king Cyrus toward Babylon as God's action prior to restoring his people. But these chapters also speak of the sufferings of the mysterious "Servant of the Lord" (the prophet himself or the prophet and his disciples, who are the true remnant of Israel), sufferings that make the people recognize their wrongdoing and the possibility of renewal. Both Ezekiel and Second Isaiah immeasurably deepened the biblical understanding of the nature and ways of God in the midst of a calamity that might easily have destroyed the faith of Israel.

The Restoration Period (Late Sixth to Fifth Centuries B.C.E.)

The restoration period (begining in 539 B.C.E.) brought great changes in prophetic activity without eliminating its diversity. The earliest restoration prophets are Haggai and Zechariah (chapters 1–8), who encouraged the rebuilding of the Temple. This fact at once separates them from Micah during the eighth century B.C.E., who envisaged Jerusalem's desolation, from Isaiah (chapters 1–12), who fervently participated in the cult of the Temple, and from Jeremiah, who foretold the Temple's destruction. Haggai and Zechariah comport well with the final chapters of Ezekiel, which foresee a restored Temple, although Ezekiel was also unsparing in his denunciations of the cult in the first Temple. Surprisingly, prophets emerge to support the cult, rather than denounce it, in the Books of Chronicles. For example, 1 Chronicles 25:1 has David appoint "certain of the sons of Asaph, and of Heman, and of Jeduthun, who should prophesy with lyres, with harps, and with cymbals." This seems an attempt to absorb prophets within the Temple personnel responsible for leading worship and reflects the changed circumstances of postexilic Judah – a small community dominated by the Temple.

Isaiah 56–66 nonetheless sounds a note of dissent from any uncritical call to loyalty to the Temple. While chapters 60–2 express positive sentiments in regard to the restoration of Jerusalem, nothing is said in these passages about the Temple itself, and elsewhere there are sharp attacks on the cult. Chapter 58 contrasts religious observance unfavorably with the practice of social justice, while 66:11–12 seems to deny the need for a Temple. Chapters 56–66 oppose redrawing of the boundaries of the Jewish community in narrow, exclusive terms (see especially 63:15–19 and 56:6–8, which calls the Temple "a house of prayer for all peoples").

Isaiah 56–66 are difficult to position within postexilic Judah. The same is true of passages such as Zechariah 13:2–6. This remarkable piece, which includes a parody of Amos's denial that he is a prophet (Zechariah 13:5; cf. Amos 7:14), envisages a period when God will *remove* "the prophets and the unclean spirit" from the land. That is an extreme response to a problem that is already wrestled with in Deuteronomy (13:1–5) and in Jeremiah (28:1–16), as well as in the Micaiah incident in 1 Kings 22 – the problem of false prophecy and of how to distinguish it from true prophecy. In the radical solution of Zechariah 13, any person who claims to be a prophet is suspect. Similarly, Joel and Malachi imply that prophecy is something not to be expected now, although it will occur in the Latter Days. Thus Joel 2:22 (Hebrew Bible, 3:1) looks forward to the time when God will pour out his spirit on all flesh and when "your sons and your daughters shall prophesy." Malachi anticipates not so much the renewal of prophecy as the coming of a particular prophet, Elijah, who will prepare the people for the coming Day of Yahweh (Malachi 4:5–6; Hebrew Bible, 3:23–4).

However these diverse elements are to be related theologically, the fact is that they were gathered together and formed into the prophetic collections as we have them. In this process, a pro-Temple view triumphed, but without severe criticicism of the cult being excised. Thus, as we have seen, the most uncompromising critic of the Temple, Micah, was edited in such a way that his polemic was softened. Nonetheless, apocalyptic literature represents hostility to the status quo in the Temple and may well have originated from circles such as those represented by Isaiah 56–66. Although the origin and stance of apocalyptic are treated in this *Companion* in a separate section, apocalyptic elements (such as Isaiah 24–7 and Zechariah 9–14) undeniably found their place in the prophetic corpus.

B. Isaiah

1. Isaiah 1–39

The Prophet and His Period

The division of the Book of Isaiah into three blocks (1–39, 40–55, and 56–66) might create the false impression that chapters 1–39 as a whole belong to the eighth-century B.C.E. "Isaiah of Jerusalem." In fact, chapters 12–13, 15–16, 19, 21, 23–7, and 33–9 were all written later than the eighth century. If we concentrate on what can be determined about the original Isaiah (a concentration that goes against the fashion of interest in the "final" form of the text alone), we can characterize both the prophet and the history of his period.

Isaiah was called to be a prophet in the year of King Uzziah's death (ca. 739 B.C.E.) and was active during the reigns of Jotham, Ahaz, and Hezekiah. (An alternative has it that Isaiah was active also during Uzziah's reign and that chapter 6 concerns not a call to be a prophet but a special commission.) The latest date that can be associated with Isaiah's work is 701 B.C.E., the time of Sennacherib's invasion of Judah. Thus, Isaiah lived through the collapse and destruction of the northern kingdom, the influx of refugees who settled in Judah after 722/1, Hezekiah's attempts to establish Judah's independence from Assyria, and the failure of that effort when the Babylonian king Sennacherib invaded in 701 and devastated Judah.

Isaiah's work as reflected in his oracles can be divided into five main periods. First is the period of Jotham (perhaps overlapping with Uzziah's time), from 739 B.C.E. (or, possibly, 745) to 734 B.C.E. In this period Isaiah attacked the social injustice that had emerged during the long and (for some) prosperous reign of Uzziah. Powerful landowners had dispossessed their poorer neighbors, basic equity had not been practiced, and the rich had followed an indulgent lifestyle (see Isaiah's description of the wealthy "daughters of Zion" at 3:16–26). In this situation Isaiah looked for a coming Day of Yahweh, when human achievements would collapse before God's majestic intervention (chapter 2).

The second period concerns the crisis of 734–3 B.C.E., when the kings of Israel and Syria declared war on Judah and evidently besieged Jerusalem. Isaiah 7:1–2 describes this "Syro-Ephraimite" onslaught (as scholars often call it), whose purpose was perhaps to force king Ahaz (ca. 734–727 B.C.E.) to join an anti-Assyrian coalition, although no direct evidence supports this hypothesis. In any case, Isaiah confronted Ahaz and urged him to put his trust in God for deliverance (7:3–16), giving him the sign of a child called "Immanuel" (meaning "God-with-us" in Hebrew). A young woman would become pregnant and give birth, the prophet said, and the land would be free from the two kings before the child could choose between good and evil (7:14–16). Despite the prophetic warning, Ahaz turned to the Assyrian king Tiglath-pileser III for help (2 Kings 16:5–16), and that king attacked Syria and Israel, leaving to the latter only the rump of Samaria. During the third period, before 722/1, Isaiah prophesied against the northern kingdom, warning of its fate. Material pertinent to this period includes 9:8–21, 17:3–6, and 28:1–4.

The fourth period is defined by the rebellion of Ashdod against the Assyrian king Sargon in 711 B.C.E. Isaiah 20:1–6 and 18:1–2, among other passages, reflect this period. The fifth period is that of Sennacherib's invasion of 701 in response to Hezekiah's rebellion. Jerusalem survived the siege, thanks to Hezekiah's fortifications and the construction of "Warren's shaft" to secure the water supply; but the rest of the land suffered grievously. The conquest of Lachish, Judah's second city, was recorded by Sennacherib on famous reliefs now in the British Museum in London, and Hezekiah was forced to pay heavy tribute. This incident is reflected in chapters 28–32 (especially where dependence on Egypt is denounced), as well as in 1:4–8 and 22:1–14. Chapters 36–9 also tell of this time, in material directly comparable to 2 Kings 18–19.

The Literary Structure and Contents of Isaiah 1–39

Isaiah 1–39 may be divided into five sections: 1–12, 13–23, 24–7, 28–32, and 33–9.

ISAIAH 1–12. Chapter 1 begins with a complaint about the nation's faithlessness (vv. 2–3) and then describes the nation's situation at the time of Sennacherib's invasion (vv. 4–9). The catchwords "Sodom" and "Gomorrah" (vv. 9–10) introduce a section that castigates Jerusalem's failures in worship and justice and that looks forward to the city's cleansing (vv. 10–31). This hope is endorsed by the famous vision of an exalted Jerusalem as a place of pilgrimage of the nations (2:1–4[5]; see also Micah 4:1–4[5]):

> In days to come
>   the mountain of the LORD's house
> shall be established on the highest of the mountains,
> and shall be raised above the hills;
>   all the nations shall stream to it.
> Many peoples shall come and say:
> "Come, let us go up to the mountain of the LORD,
> to the house of the God of Jacob;
> that he may teach us his ways
>   and that we may walk in his paths."
>
> (Isaiah 2:1–2)

The theme of judgment returns, articulated in terms of the Day of Yahweh (2:6–22). Future judgment will totally destabilize a corrupt society, including the rich women of Zion (3:1–4:1), but there will still be hope for Zion and its women (4:2–6). Later editors layered oracles of hope (e.g., 2:1–4 and 4:2–6) into these oracles of judgment. Isaiah 5:1–30 denounces social injustices, a theme continued in 10:1–4. Isaiah 9:8–21 denounces Israel, using a refrain found also in chapter 5 (cf. 5:25b; 9:12b, 17b, 21b – possibly originally one passage), while 10:5–34 both summons Assyria to be God's instrument of punishment of Israel and Judah, and speaks of punishment of Assyria on account of its pride.

Chapters 6–8 deal with Isaiah's call (or perhaps his special commissioning) as prophet and describe the Syro-Ephraimite crisis. (These chapters have been inserted into the section consisting of chapters 5 and 9–10.) Isaiah 9:1–7 (Hebrew Bible, 8:23–9:6) contains the words "For a child has been born for us." Whether this passage and 11:1–9 represent Isaiah's own prophecy or were produced at a later period remains disputed. Isaiah 11:1–9 seems to imply that the tree of the house of Jesse (David's father) has been cut down, that is, that the fall of Jerusalem in 587/6 B.C.E. has occurred, so that chapter 11 and the hymn of praise in chapter 12 are probably exilic or postexilic. Isaiah 9:1–7 is harder to date. Verse 1 looks forward to the restoration to Israel of areas lost to Tiglath-pileser III; verses 2–7 may or may not be connected to verse 1. Isaiah 9:2–7 combines two themes: a holy war of restoration of God's people, and the birth (or coronation) of a prince of five names (of which the last is not fully preserved, because the Hebrew text appears incomplete). If these verses come from Isaiah, who is the prince? The lack of precise detail, which may be deliberate, allows for various candidates (e.g., Hezekiah or Josiah), but commentators have not agreed on the prince's identity.

ISAIAH 13–23. These chapters contain oracles against the nations: Babylon (13, 14:1–23), Assyria (14:24–7), Philistia (14:28–31), Moab (15–16), Damascus and Israel (17), Egypt and Ethiopia (18–20), Edom (21), Jerusalem (22), and Tyre (23).

ISAIAH 24–7. Often called the "little apocalypse," this section in fact does not represent a calendar of the final events of history, such as characterizes works that are thoroughly apocalyptic. Yet these chapters do contain apocalyptic motifs, such as that the heavenly host will be punished and imprisoned for many days, that the sun and moon will be confounded and ashamed (24:21–4), that the dead will be raised (26:19), and that the primordial sea dragon Leviathan will be slain (27:1) – but without specifying when those ultimate events are to occur. Chapter 24 envisages the punishment of earth and heaven before God reigns in glory in Jerusalem, while chapters 25–6 incorporate hymns of praise to God for what he has done and will do for those who are faithful to him. Chapter 27 also expresses hope for the future, using the theme of the vineyard that God protects (possibly forming a deliberate contrast with the Song of the Vineyard at 5:1–7).

ISAIAH 28–32. These chapters date mostly from the time of Sennacherib's invasion in 701 B.C.E., although they begin with an oracle against the northern kingdom to be dated around 722. These oracles include condemnations against trusting in help from Egypt, as well as oracles of hope and encouragement (e.g., 29:13–14, 15–16, 17–21, 22–4).

ISAIAH 33–9. This section parallels 2 Kings 18–20, and some commentators consider these prose chapters to be earlier than those in 2 Kings. They relate Hezekiah's rebellion against Sennacherib, the siege and deliverance of Jerusalem (36–7), Hezekiah's illness and recovery, and the embassy from the Babylonian king Merodachbaladan (38–9). Chapter 33 includes a prayer to God for salvation (vv. 2–4) and a divine response (vv. 10–12), followed by a summons of encouragement to those who hope for a purified

Jerusalem (vv. 13–24). Chapter 34 is an oracle against Edom, and chapter 35, which is strongly reminiscent of chapters 40–55, envisages the return of the exiles to Jerusalem.

Is this whole collection haphazard or coherent? The answer is: something of both. Readers looking for logical development will find Isaiah 1–39 an incongruent collection of inspiring and puzzling passages. Yet on further reflection, Jerusalem emerges as a recurrent theme throughout. Chapter 1 introduces the unfaithful city; and in Ahaz it has an unfaithful king. But there are also hopes for a restored and cleansed city, hopes that center in part on a faithful king, Hezekiah. Those who threaten Jerusalem, such as Israel and Damascus, will be punished, as will the chosen instrument of God's judgment upon Jerusalem (Assyria). Judah's dependence upon God, rather than upon other nations such as Assyria and Egypt, is enjoined; Hezekiah's virtue, as opposed to Ahaz's vice, was just such dependence on God. Where there is trust in God, there is sure hope of restoration.

Although it is customary to see a break between chapters 39 and 40, it is arguable that 39:5 – "Days are coming when all that is in your house . . . shall be carried to Babylon" – is an introduction to the restoration theme, with which chapters 40–55 are concerned.

2. Isaiah 40–55

The Social Situation of the Period

Isaiah 40–55 (often referred to as Second Isaiah or Deutero-Isaiah) represents the work of an unknown prophet who lived in exile in Babylon toward the end of the reign of Nabonidus (556–539 B.C.E.) and into the early part of the reign of the Persian king Cyrus (who conquered Babylon in 539 B.C.E.). The book addresses an audience that lives far from Jerusalem, and promises a return to the city. Babylon's religious processions are described in chapter 46, and its fall is anticipated in chapter 47. The freeing of the people will be accomplished by Cyrus, whose victories over the Babylonians are described as God's work (41:2–4), and Cyrus is called God's messiah, his "anointed" (45:1), with the task of subduing kings.

The setting of chapters 40–55 in sixth-century B.C.E. Babylon has long been recognized, but as long as scholars believed that prophets predicted events centuries in the future, they had little difficulty ascribing these chapters, concerned with sixth-century Babylon, to the eighth-century Isaiah of Jerusalem. During the Enlightenment, however, a profound shift in critical study of the Old Testament among Christian interpreters took place, and scholars first suggested that these chapters were actually written in the sixth century B.C.E., and in Babylon. (The emergence of this approach corresponds to the analysis of the Pentateuch according to its sources, which also developed during the eighteenth and nineteenth centuries.) Some Christians object that this finding denies God's power to inspire prophets to foretell the future. Such objections ignore clear indications that, in these chapters of Isaiah, a prophet spoke God's word to the exiles in sixth-century Babylon by addressing their conditions directly. Nothing in the Book of Isaiah suggests that an eighth-century prophet set out to provide a social description of a future community that had no relevance to his own circumstances.

The social setting implicit in Isaiah 40–55 corresponds to what exilic and postexilic texts say of the condition of the exiles in Babylonia as a whole. There are names of places where the exiles are located in Ezra 2:59 (Tel-melah, Tel-harsha, Cherub, Addan, Immer), and Ezekiel mentions Telabib by the "River" Chebar (which was probably a canal). Reference should also be made to the Murashu documents, which date to about 455–404 and are from an archive of a business in Nippur, some of whose senior members were Jews. They contain information about where Jews were settled in the Nippur region and what trades they practiced. But what seems most pertinent to the background of Isaiah 40–55 is Babylon itself. This great city formed a focus of the unknown prophet's concern.

Under Nabopolassar (625–605 B.C.E.) and Nebuchadnezzar II (604–562 B.C.E.) Babylon was restored as a capital worthy of a great empire. The Euphrates River flowed through its center, dividing the western from the eastern part of the city. Moats devised by diverting water from the river enclosed the city, which walls and gates protected further, defining an area of five square miles. Babylon's celebrated achievements included "the hanging gardens," towers with parks on top that seemed to dangle from heaven, and the Ishtar Gate, through which passed the processional way from the temple of Marduk to the *ahitu* temple. There the symbolic sacred marriage of the king, who represented the god, to the goddess Ishtar (better known as Astarte in the West) took place during the *ahitu* festival, celebrated at the New Year. The glazed-brick walls of the processional way portrayed lions over three feet high; bulls and dragons incorporating features of lions, snakes, and eagles decorated the Ishtar Gate.

Exiles from Judah who lived near or visited Babylon must have been overwhelmed by what they saw. Some would have despaired, seeing evidence of a mighty empire that had crushed their own nation and of mighty gods superior to their own. Jerusalem seemed a tiny irrelevance compared with Babylon's size and magnificence.

For all its splendor, the city of Babylon remained Babylonian for but a few years. After Nebuchadnezzar's death, his son Amel-Marduk (called Evil-Merodach in the Bible at 2 Kings 25:27–30) reigned from 561 B.C.E. only until 560 B.C.E. Two kings reigned between 560 and 556, and the second of them was assassinated after only two months. The end of the Babylonian Empire came with Nabonidus (556–539 B.C.E.), a deeply religious man who worshipped the god Sin and rebuilt the temples of Sin in Ur and Haran. His loyalty to Sin brought him into conflict with the priests of Babylonia's holy cities, such as Babylon itself, Nippur, and Ur. Possibly in obedience to a dream or an oracle, Nabonidus spent a long period (possibly ten years) at Taima in northwest Arabia. During this time his son Belshazzar ruled in Babylon. By the time Nabonidus returned from Taima to

Babylon (between 544 and 540 B.C.E.), his kingdom was doomed. In 559 B.C.E. Cyrus became ruler of the Persians, who were at that time vassals of the Medes. Around 550 Cyrus overcame the Medes and ruled over a vast empire to the north of Babylonia. In 539, after defeating the Babylonian army at Opis, the Persian army entered Babylon without a fight (to some extent because the priests of the traditional god Marduk took Cyrus's side), and Nabonidus was taken prisoner. Having been hopeless exiles, the Jews now became the recipients of Cyrus's benevolent treatment of some captives of Babylonia, and they were allowed to return home. For the prophet of Isaiah 40–55, this was the work of the God of Israel, the Lord of creation and of history.

Literary Structure and Contents of Isaiah 40–55

Second Isaiah begins with the words "Comfort, comfort my people" (40:1), which set the tone for a series of passages from which denunciation, and threats of imminent judgment – familiar from the preexilic prophets – are absent. The prophet reassures his people that the time of punishment is over (40:2). God has not forgotten or forsaken them; they are to be afraid no longer, but must trust in the power and in the word of the incomparable Lord of creation. This word will accomplish its purpose as surely as rain and snow allow plants that provide food to grow (55:10–11). Because there is so much stress on comfort and reassurance in Second Isaiah, as well as hymnic passages celebrating God's lordship in creation, readers will inevitably be reminded of passages in those psalms that offer reassurance to those who seek God when they are in trouble and that rehearse how God is Lord of creation. Yet Isaiah 40–55 and the Book of Psalms do not seem to be in a relationship of literary dependence one way or the other.

Literary structure is not easy to specify in Second Isaiah. The work probably begins with a prophet's call when he hears a voice (presumably in the heavenly court) say, "Cry," and he responds, "What shall I cry?" in words perhaps deliberately reminiscent of Isaiah 6:8–11. The work ends with an assertion of the power of God's word. Some commentators have suggested a change in mood between 40–48 and 49–55, with the second section postdating Cyrus's decree permitting exiles to return, but that suggestion remains quite hypothetical. An important question is whether the Servant Songs (42:1–4, 49:1–6, 50:4–9, 52:13, 53:12) are later additions to the text or are fully integrated within it. The fact that both positions can be advocated shows that no clear literary scheme is apparent. This being so, the material is best approached through some of its main themes.

GOD'S SUPERIORITY OVER OTHER GODS. In these chapters, the belief that other gods are at best powerless, and at worst nonexistent, is strongly articulated. The idol maker's work is parodied in 40:18–20, 41:7, and 44:9–20, emphasizing that idols are no more powerful than their human makers. In 46:1–7, in a possible allusion to processions in which the images of gods were solemnly carried on carts through Babylon, the prophet contrasts gods that need to be carried around with the true God, who carries his people.

GOD, THE LORD OF HISTORY. The events involved with Cyrus's victories are seen as God's doing, bringing new things to pass. The setting of a trial is invoked in Isaiah 41:1–4. Not only has God stirred up Cyrus, but he has also declared what will happen before it occurs (41:25–9). Nations and their gods cannot match this (41:21–4). In 44:24–45:7 the coming victories of Cyrus are connected with God's power over nature and human events, and with God's determination to restore Jerusalem, reform its Temple, and rebuild the cities of Judah. A lament over the imminent fate of Babylon, pictured as a virgin daughter, shows how powerless human greatness is in the face of God's action (chapter 47).

GOD THE CREATOR. Second Isaiah contains the most sublime language in the Hebrew Bible about God as creator and Lord of nature. Powerful nations are like a drop in a bucket, and compared with God "who sits above the circle of the earth, its inhabitants are like grasshoppers" (40:12–17, 21–4). Human questioning of the creator's actions is like clay questioning the potter (45:9–13). God the creator is the incomparable one, the first and the last (48:12–13).

GOD'S PURPOSES EMBRACE THE NATIONS. Because God is the incomparable Lord of creation and history, his purposes, although centered on Jerusalem, affect other nations. They will recognize that Cyrus's victories are God's doing and will fear (41:5–6), and when Israel is saved, nations will do homage to God's people (45:14–17). They will bring back to God's people those scattered in exile (49:22–6).

ISRAEL'S PAST TRADITIONS. Second Isaiah's references to Abraham (41:8, 51:2), Sarah (51:2), the Exodus (43:16–17), the wilderness wanderings (43:19–21), and the Flood and deliverance of Noah (54:9–10) embed Israel's experience of exile in the primordial past. For example, during the wilderness wanderings: "they did not thirst when he led them through the deserts; he made water flow for them from the rock" (Isaiah 48:21; see Exodus 17:2–7 and Numbers 20:2–13). This reference to the creation and calling of Israel is part of a contrast between old things and new things. The guarantee of God's promise to restore the people is grounded not only in the new things God is doing, such as the victories of Cyrus, but also in what he did of old. The return of the people to Jerusalem will be, in effect, a new Exodus (51:9–11).

THE SERVANT SONGS. The term "servant" occurs many times in Isaiah 40–55. The servant is identified as Israel (41:8), who is now a worm but will become a threshing sledge (41:14–16) when God vindicates him. The servant is reassured when he believes that God has forgotten or forsaken him (40:27–31; 49:14–21). He has sinned (42:21–5), but is now forgiven (43:25–8).

In the Servant Songs (42:1–4; 49:1–6; 50:4–9; 52:13–53:12) we have a different picture, which is why scholars have treated these passages separately from the rest of Isaiah 40–55. If the servant remains Israel (49:3 is the only direct identification within the Servant Songs proper), this identification is not prominent. The servant is passive (42:2–3) and has a mission *to* Israel (49:6) and possibly to the nations (49:6). If he needs reassurance, it is not because he thinks God has forgotten him, but because he fears he has labored in vain (49:4). Rather than having been justly punished and now forgiven, the servant has suffered innocently (50:6), and his suffering will bring about forgiveness for others (53:3–6).

Given that the songs are not collected together in a single section, but are distributed throughout the chapters, it could be argued that the editor or author intended readers to connect the servant in the songs with the servant elsewhere in the chapters. Israel, then, as a complete entity, consisting of a faithful remnant that suffered vicariously and the larger body that had been justly punished and that is now reassured, would be at issue. However, even if this is the case, we are still justified in asking the identity of the remnant, that is, the identity of the group or individual that suffers vicariously.

A widely held view, accepted here, is that the servant in the Servant Songs is the prophet himself and that the songs describe this prophet's ministry. We can surmise, from 50:6, "I gave my back to those who struck me," and 53:4, "we accounted him stricken, struck down by God and afflicted," that the prophet had some physical wound or disability and that his mission was badly received. Opinions are divided about the interpretation of 53:9, "they made his grave with the wicked." Does this indicate an actual death (in which case the fourth song was composed by a disciple after the prophet's death), or should we compare it to one of the psalms (e.g., 22 or 130) in which the psalmist came close to death, regarded himself as in the grave, and yet survived? In either case, the prophet's mission succeeded when his rejection and suffering brought his detractors to the realization that he truly was God's servant (see 53:4–11). Although an understanding of the servant as an individual provides the most convincing reading, there is also an argument for a corporate identity. Just as the servant-prophet was, outwardly, an unlikely vehicle for God's work (see 53:2–3), so the servant-people were, in the eyes of the nations and perhaps in their own eyes, an unlikely vehicle for God's work. This was why the people needed constant reassurance of God's concern for them. This symmetry between the servant-prophet and the servant-people vividly incorporates the biblical theme that God "raises the poor from the dust" (1 Samuel 2:8).

The way in which the oracles about the servant-prophet are woven into those about the servant-people is characteristic of Second Isaiah as a whole. The continual juxtaposition of recurring themes brings about a rich and exciting kaleidoscopic effect. The chapters should be read through, not to discover a plan or structure, but to experience the shifting patterns of its uniquely rich material.

3. Isaiah 56–66

A New Social Period

As we move from chapters 40–55 to 56–66, we find ourselves in a different world. Gone is the continual interplay between doubt and reassurance, and confident, hymnic affirmation in response to the uncertainty of the people. Instead, we find denunciations of leaders, of injustice, and of insincere worship. If the people complain, it is directly about their present plight, rather than because of the fear that God has abandoned or forgotten them in their suffering. There are, of course, also passages of divine reassurance and, at 61:1–4, an oracle that is reminiscent of the Servant Songs of chapters 40–55, as well as passages similar to those in chapters 40–55 that speak of God's lordship over the universe and history. Yet the overall cultural or social impression is quite different from that in chapters 40–55.

The diversity of the material involved has left scholars divided over whether these chapters are the work of one prophet at one period or of several prophets over a time span of two hundred years. For example, 64:10–11,

> Your holy cities have become a wilderness,
> Zion has become a wilderness,
> Jerusalem a desolation.
> Our holy and beautiful house,
> where our ancestors praised you,
> has been burned by fire,

implies that the Temple is still in ruins. A date of 539–520 B.C.E. is therefore implicit. Material in chapter 56, however, could fit in the situation described in Nehemiah (the latter half of the fifth century B.C.E.), when foreigners who have joined the community must not say, "The LORD will surely separate me from his people" (56:3). Membership in the community will *not* depend on birth but on faithfulness to God's covenant (54:6) – a view contrary to that in Ezra and Nehemiah, possibly representing the perspective of a prophetic group opposed to policies of Nehemiah that were hostile to non-Jews.

Even if these chapters are ascribed to one prophet and one period, the historical setting they imply is impossible to determine with certainty. Is it a situation similar to that implied in Haggai and in Zechariah 1–8, in which a small, dispirited community copes with economic hardship and is ambivalent about rebuilding the Temple? Or are those scholars correct who have envisaged a deep split in the community between a priestly, Temple-centered group and a prophetic-apocalyptic group whose views came to expression in support of faithful foreigners (56:3–8), in criticism of the Temple cult (58:1–9), and in doubting the need for a Temple at all (66:1–4)? Yet another possibility is that these chapters are to be read, not in the context of an assumed social and historical setting, but in the light of Isaiah 1–55, on which they to some extent constitute a commentary.

On the whole, the chapters make most sense if set in the period between 539 and 520 B.C.E. The prophet has returned from Babylon with a group who had been encouraged by the prophecies of chapters 40–55. The reality that the community faces is different from what they expected. The Temple is still in ruins, there is social injustice, and the leadership is ineffective. Moreover, there is uncertainty about who is entitled to membership in the covenant people. In this situation the prophet affirms his commission to "build up the ancient ruins" (61:4), enjoins the people to practice social justice, and gives hope to the people on the basis of God's sovereign power.

Literary Structure and the Contents of Isaiah 56–66

Chapters 60–2, with their words of hope and consolation, form the core of chapters 56–66 (sometimes called the Third Isaiah, or Trito-Isaiah). This core appears between two communal laments: 59:9–20 and 63:7–64:12. An outer framework is provided by 56:9–59:8, 65:1–16, and 66:1–16, which are oracles of judgment. The overall scheme may be represented as follows:

56:9–59:8	oracles of judgment
59:9–20	lament
60:1–62:12	oracles of hope
63:7–64:12	lament
65:1–16, 66:1–16	oracles of judgment

Some passages simply fall outside this scheme: 56:1–8 (concerning faithful foreigners), 63:1–6 (God's wrath against the nations), 65:17–25 (vision of a new heaven and earth), and 66:17–24 (a seemingly miscellaneous collection).

ISAIAH 60–2. Isaiah 61:1–4 features centrally in the core of the Third Isaiah, beginning with the words "The Spirit of the Lord GOD is upon me." Here, the prophet speaks of his commission to set the people free so that the ancient ruins may be rebuilt. The section begins with the encouragement "Arise, shine; for your light has come" (60:1). God will bring back Zion's captives, and the nations will serve God's people. The glory of the people will be restored (60:17–18), and they will possess the Promised Land forever (60:21–2). In chapter 62 Zion is promised that she will be called "married" and "sought out." The theme of hope and confidence is strongly maintained throughout and is emphasized in bridal imagery.

ISAIAH 59:9–20 AND 63:7–64:12. The first lament complains that though the people look for light, all they see is darkness. Is there an allusion here to 60:1? The sins of the community are confessed: transgression of the law, denying God, prevention of justice, lack of truth. Divine action is promised.

The second lament (63:7–64:12) draws on Israel's past history, including the Exodus and wilderness wanderings (63:11–14). God did mighty things in the past and "no eye has seen any God besides you" (64:4). Will you restrain yourself, and keep quiet, ask the people (64:12).

ISAIAH 56:9–59:8. These oracles of judgment condemn the leaders (described as watchmen and shepherds in 56:9–11) and imply that the sons of sorceresses and adulterers are in charge (57:1–4) and that idolatry is rife (57:4–10). Isaiah 58:1–9 condemns fasting that is merely an outward observance, and coexisting with injustice and strife. God will hear his people only if they practice social justice. Isaiah 59:1–8 condemns the perversion of justice.

ISAIAH 65:1–16 AND 66:1–16. The first passage condemns those who perform religious perversions such as eating swine's flesh and burning incense (presumably to idols: 65:3–4). These unfaithful people will starve and suffer (65:13–16). The second condemnation is also about worship, but implies that formally correct worship can also be an abomination, when offered insincerely: "he who presents a cereal offering [is] like him who offers swine's blood" (66:3). It ends with words of consolation to Zion based on God's indignation against his enemies.

ISAIAH 56:1–8, 63:1–6, AND 66:18–21. These passages deal, in different ways, with non-Israelites. In the first, there are promises for foreigners who are faithful to God's covenant. The second, using the figure of a man treading the grapes of wrath, vividly describes God's judgment on the neighboring nations. The third passage speaks of the nations' acknowledging God's glory and giving up Jewish captives, some of whom God will take for priests and Levites (66:21).

ISAIAH 65:17–25. This magnificent passage is a vision of the future when God creates a new heaven and a new earth. All pain and ambiguity will be removed from creation. The closing verse, very similar to Isaiah 11:6–9, reintroduces the vegetarian creation implied in Genesis 1:26–30 – a creation different from that of our experience.

4. The Book of Isaiah as a Whole

Previous sections have shown that Isaiah did not reach its present form in three simple stages consisting of composition of 1–39, addition of 40–55, supplementation with 56–66. Chapters 1–39 contain much material that is later than "Isaiah of Jerusalem," for example, while 66:24 echoes 1:6–9. Although we can only estimate the actual process of edition, the person or persons who put the book into its present form apparently intended certain themes to run through the whole. The most prominent among them include the following motifs. Each could easily be elaborated; but basic familiality with them shows how many of the themes of Isaiah 1–11 run through the whole book and indicates the value of a thematic reading of the whole.

THE DAUGHTER OF ZION. In 1:8 the daughter of Zion is described as an isolated booth in a vineyard and as a besieged city. In 49:11–26, Zion complains that she has been forsaken. Her consolation and restoration are dealt with several times in chapters 56–66 (e.g., in 62:1–12, 66:12–14).

JERUSALEM, THE CITY OF INJUSTICE AND JUSTICE. Isaiah 1:21–8 explores the theme of Jerusalem's lost justice and the restoration of its righteousness. Establishment of justice is promised at 54:14, and 60:21 states that Zion's people will be righteous.

GOD'S GLORY. At Isaiah's call or commissioning, he hears the seraphim praising God's glory (6:3). The glory of God will be made clear for all to see (40:5), and the people are promised that "the glory of the LORD has risen upon you" (60:1).

COMFORT. At 12:1 Israel is told that they will say, "you comforted me." Isaiah 40:1 begins with the famous words "Comfort, comfort my people."

INSINCERE WORSHIP. This theme figures extensively in Isaiah 1:12–20. Sacrifice without social justice is an abomination to God. The theme returns strongly in 56–66. Thus 58:1–9 speaks of the uselessness of fasting without social justice, and 66:3–4 (reminiscent also of 1:10–11) says that formal worship by those who do evil is no better than murder or idolatry.

C. Jeremiah

1. Social History of the Prophet's Period

Jeremiah 1:2–3 dates the prophet Jeremiah's ministry from the thirteenth year of Josiah (627 B.C.E.) until the eleventh year of Zedekiah (587/6 B.C.E.). However, chapters 39–44 record Jeremiah's activity in the period after Zedekiah's final capitulation to the Babylonians in 587/6, and describe how Gedaliah was appointed governor of Judah, how he was assassinated, and how Jeremiah was taken unwillingly to Egypt. A final date for Jeremiah's ministry can only be conjectured, although 585 B.C.E. has become generally accepted. The period delineated by the Book of Jeremiah overall includes the reigns of Josiah (640–609 B.C.E.), Jehoahaz (609 B.C.E.), Jehoiakim (609–598 B.C.E.), Jehoiachin (598–560 B.C.E., almost all of which was spent in exile in Babylon), and Zedekiah (597–587/6 B.C.E.), and part of the exile (to ca. 585 B.C.E.).

When Josiah ascended the throne in Judah at the age of eight, Ashurbanipal, king of Assyria, was in the second half of his long reign (668–627 B.C.E.). By 640 B.C.E. Ashurbanipal had quelled the civil war initiated by his brother (who was king of Babylon) and had dealt with other rebels in a huge empire that stretched from Egypt, through Syria and Palestine, and on to the Persian Gulf. Ashurbanipal had also established a library in

Nineveh, which he stocked with texts collected from temples and scribal schools throughout Babylonia. He claimed to be able to read texts in Sumerian and Akkadian. When he died, probably in 627 (although the date is not certain), civil war again broke out between Assyria and Babylonia, which hastened the demise of the Assyrian Empire and saw the emergence of a new Babylonian Empire. Nabopolassar became king of Babylon in 625 B.C.E., and by 616 he had secured Babylon's independence from Assyria and began to threaten Assyria. In 612, in alliance with the Medes, the Babylonians captured and destroyed the Assyrian capital, Nineveh. A last stand was made by the Assyrians at Haran, but they were defeated in 609.

Assyria's decline gave Egypt the opportunity to expand. The Egyptians had been the allies of Assyria, and in 610–609 B.C.E. they came to Assyria's aid. Josiah tried to block their progress at the strategic pass at Megiddo, but he was killed by the Egyptian Necho II, who also deposed Josiah's heir, Jehoahaz, replacing him with Jehoiakim. The Egyptians now occupied Syria and Israel as far as Carchemish, but in 605 they were defeated at Carchemish by the Babylonian crown prince, Nebuchadnezzar. Soon after this, Nebuchadnezzar succeeded to his father's throne and resumed his campaign against the Egyptians. By 601 he was in control of Syria and Israel and was fighting on Egypt's frontiers, but in that year one frontier battle proved indecisive, and perhaps even constituted a defeat for Babylon. This probably encouraged Jehoiakim to rebel; as a result the Babylonian army invaded Judah and captured Jerusalem on 16 March 597 B.C.E. Jehoiakim's son Jehoiachin, who had been king for only three months, was deported to Babylon, together with nobles and craftsmen. His uncle Zedekiah was placed on the throne by Babylon. When Zedekiah later rebelled, the Babylonians attacked yet again, and this time they destroyed Jerusalem. The year was 587/6. The Babylonians then appointed a Judahite, Gedaliah, governor of Judah in Mizpah, but he was assassinated by Judahites who were sympathetic to Egypt. These Judahites fled to Egypt, taking Jeremiah along with them.

Against this general background, the social history of Judah emerges in its main outlines. In 627 B.C.E., the likely year of Ashurbanipal's death, Josiah "began to seek the God of David his father," at least according to 2 Chronicles 34:3. He set in motion a reform that involved closing down Judah's high places and destroying the altars of Baal and other cult objects offensive to the worship of Yahweh alone. A different view emerges in 2 Kings 22:3–23:14. According to this account, it was only *after* the discovery of the "book of the law" in the Temple during Josiah's eighteenth year (622 B.C.E.) that the reformation began to be carried out. The main difference between the two accounts is that in Chronicles, Josiah initiated the reform, whereas in Kings he merely ordered the repair of the Temple and then carried out the reform after the book of the law was found. In either case, the reign of Josiah saw a religious reformation whose effects have been confirmed by the iconographic remains of Israel and Judah. Bullae bearing the names of men connected with the reform, such as Gemariah son of Shaphan (Jeremiah 36:10), are aniconic, in contrast with seals earlier in the seventh century, which bear visual religious symbols. The reform was supported by the powerful family of Shaphan, with whom Deuteronomistic groups were also connected.

After Josiah's death in 609 B.C.E., a split developed between the Shaphan family, which supported Jeremiah and became pro-Babylonian, and the family of Elishama (36:12), who looked instead to Egypt for help. In the immediate aftermath of Josiah's death, the pro-Egypt party seems to have gained the upper hand. After the battle of Carchemish and until 597, when the Babylonians first captured Jerusalem, the struggle between the two sides was fairly equal. When Zedekiah rebelled against Nebuchadnezzar, the partisans of Egypt gained strength with the prospect of a relief army against the besieging Babylonians (Jeremiah 37:6–12). Their temporary ascendancy enabled them to arrest and imprison Jeremiah (37:12–38:16).

Messages discovered in a guardroom at Lachish shed light on the final days of Judah. These letters represent reports from lookouts who could evidently observe fire signals from both Lachish and Azekah. These letters are usually dated immediately before the siege of Lachish in 589 or 588 B.C.E., and they present some intriguing similarities with the Book of Jeremiah. Letter 3 from Lachish even speaks of a letter that came "through the prophet." Although that prophet's name has not survived in these texts, letter 3 does indicate that prophets played an active role in the events of Judah's demise, though whether for or against the "establishment" in Jerusalem (such as it was) no one can say. The same letter mentions a commander who has "come down in order to go into Egypt" (*Ancient Near Eastern Texts*, p. 322). Jeremiah 37:3–10 agrees that there was support for Judah from Egypt. Letter 6 contains a complaint that the words of the princes "weaken our hands" (i.e., bring down morale) and "slacken the hands" of others (*Ancient Near Eastern Texts*, p. 322). A similar charge is brought against Jeremiah (Jeremiah 38:4), using the phrase "weakening the hands of the soldiers" (or, as the New Revised Standard Version renders the Hebrew, "discouraging" the soldiers). In letter 4 the observers say that they can no longer see the fire signals of Azekah. At Jeremiah 34:7 we are told that, apart from Jerusalem, only Azekah and Lachish remained of Judah's fortified cities following the Babylonian attack on Judah. Lachish letter 4 evidently derives from the moment when Azekah, too, fell. When Lachish itself was captured by the Babylonians, they destroyed the city by fire.

2. The Literary History of Jeremiah

The Book of Jeremiah, uniquely within the Hebrew Bible, provides details of its composition. Chapter 36 records that Jeremiah dictated all the words he had spoken against Israel and Judah to Baruch the scribe. King Jehoiakim had this scroll burned, but Jeremiah dictated his words again, adding new material to them at the same time (36:32). At 51:60–1 Jeremiah is depicted as personally writing the oracles against Babylon and giving them to Seraiah (apparently Baruch's brother) to read in Babylon when he accompanied Zedekiah thence in the latter's fourth year of his reign (605 B.C.E.).

Scholars have differed in their assessments of this information. One view accepts that Jeremiah had learned the scribal arts and that he wrote parts of his book. This view links the prophet strongly with the scribal family of Shaphan and also accepts that Baruch played a role in the genesis of the Book of Jeremiah. (It is to be noted that chapters 1–25 are mainly in poetry, and chapters 26–45 are mostly in prose. Whether or not this indicates that the scroll dictated to Baruch included much of chapters 1–25 is debated.) An opposite view observes that, if Jeremiah were himself a scribe, he would scarcely have needed Baruch's services to write his words down. When barred from entering the Temple (Jeremiah 36:5–8) and needing Baruch to read his words for him in the Temple, why would Jeremiah – if he were a scribe – not *write* the scroll himself and then get Baruch to read it in public? The Seraiah incident creates the further difficulty that Jeremiah publicly condemns Babylon in 605 B.C.E., but then spends the remainder of his ministry proclaiming that God has given Jerusalem into the hands of Nebuchadnezzar, king of Babylon! The conclusion often drawn is that the materials relating to Baruch and Seraiah reflect a period when the Jeremiah of legend was being created, and say little directly about Jeremiah himself.

Another matter of dispute concerns the Deuteronomistic style of prose speeches within the Book of Jeremiah (e.g., in chapters 7–8). Are they the work of Jeremiah himself, so that their style might be attributed to Jeremiah's close links with Deuteronomistic circles; or are they the work of exilic Deuteronomists who put the book into its present form in Jeremiah's name? Discussion is further complicated by the two distinct versions of Jeremiah: the traditional Hebrew text, and the Greek translation of the third century B.C.E., the Septuagint. The order of the material differs significantly in the two versions. Although the literary variations that result are highly complex, in general the Greek version places the oracles against the nations earlier than does the Hebrew version (so that chapters 46–51 in the Hebrew become chapters 26–32 in the Greek, and at the same time, chapters 26–45 in the Hebrew become chapters 33–51 in the Greek). The Hebrew text contains many expansive glosses as compared to the Greek, raising the suspicion that the version in the Septuagint is closer to the original. The discovery of fragments of a Hebrew text of Jeremiah at Qumran that support the shorter, Greek readings indicates that the Greek translation was indeed made from a shorter and earlier Hebrew text.

The existence of the two versions has occasioned various solutions to the question of the literary development of Jeremiah. If – as seems likely – the Greek translation was accomplished in Egypt, would this mean that Jeremiah took an almost complete Hebrew text with him to Egypt (or put an almost complete text together while in Egypt), which was then translated into Greek? If, on the other hand, the Deuteronomists compiled the shorter Hebrew text (found at Qumran), at what stage was this version taken to Egypt, and where and when was this shorter text expanded into the longer, traditional Hebrew text?

The shorter Hebrew text, reflected in the Septuagint, suggests by the style of its prose speeches that it was compiled by the Deuteronomists. These included members of the Shaphan family, who supported Jeremiah. They esteemed him because he predicted the coming destruction of Jerusalem and yet also insisted that the God who was about to punish his people also had a future in mind for them. Preserving Jeremiah's sayings and telling his story helped to cope with the shock and upheaval of the fall of Jerusalem, and the Shaphan family exerted enough influence to mount a scribal program for the survival of the people despite the exile. No doubt, they idealized the figure of Jeremiah in the course of their program, as is in the nature of tradition looking back to a hero. But it does not follow that the man Jeremiah is entirely the creation of the tradition or the scribal program. The bullae of the period and the Lachish letters amount to circumstantial confirmation of the conditions Jeremiah confronted, and there is no reason to doubt he could have dictated some of his oracles and written others, although the exact processes involved seem unrecoverable.

Three types of material appear in Jeremiah in the assessment of many scholars: (*a*) oracles and first-person narratives, which may be the work of Jeremiah (mainly in chapters 1–26 but incoporated with other material); (*b*) narratives about Jeremiah in the third person, perhaps the work of Baruch (comprising 19:1–20:6 and chapters 26–9 and 36–45); and (*c*) Deuteronomistic prose speeches (including 7:1–8:3, 11:1–14, 18:1–12, 21:1–10, 22:1–5, 25:1–11, 34:8–22, and chapter 35). The provenience of chapters 30–3, commonly called the Book of Comfort, remains disputed. They probably consist of material that derives from Jeremiah but that has been expanded by postexilic editors.

3. The Literary Structure and Contents of Jeremiah

The three main blocks of Jeremiah are chapters 1–25 (mostly in poetry), 26–45 (mostly in prose), and 46–51 (oracles against the nations). Chapter 52 is an appendix. These blocks may be subdivided as follows:

JEREMIAH 1:1–10:25. These chapters begin with Jeremiah's call and consist mostly of oracles of coming judgment marked by an intensity hardly matched elsewhere in the Hebrew Bible. The prophet "sees" the ruined city of Jerusalem, "hears" the sounds of its destruction and subsequent despair, and himself experiences the population's anguish. These passages are often dated to 627–622 B.C.E.; according to this chronology, the vivid portrayals of Jerusalem's imminent doom would have led to the prophet's becoming totally discredited when no "foe from the north" (Jeremiah 1:14) materialized. (It used to be argued that the foe did come, in the form of Scythian hordes as described by the Greek historian Herodotus; but few experts now credit this hypothesis.) But it also remains possible that all or much of this material belongs to a later period, such as following Josiah's death.

JEREMIAH 11:1–20:18. This section differs from the preceding section, containing much more third-person material (e.g., 19:1–20:6), some of which (e.g., 11:1–14, 18:1–12) is probably Deuteronomistic. But it also includes personal laments that have been called the Confessions of Jeremiah (11:18–20, 15:10–21, 17:14–18, 18:19–23, 20:7–18). The Confessions are unique within prophetic literature, revealing Jeremiah's existential fear, anguish, and even bitterness about being a servant of God. The most poignant poem is in 20:7–18, where the speaker agonizes over unenviable alternatives before him: either speaking in the name of God and thereby evoking derision from his fellow citizens, or keeping quiet and feeling the unspoken word of God like a burning fire shut up in his bones. The poem concludes, in words similar to those in Job 3:3–13, with a curse upon the day the speaker was born.

JEREMIAH 21:1–24:10. The oracles in this section are mostly warnings to officials and leaders in Judah of coming judgment. The material comes from various periods: 21:1–10 from the time of Zedekiah (597–587/6 B.C.E., probably toward the end of that period), 22:11–12 probably from soon after Josiah's death in 609 B.C.E. and the deposition of his son, 22:24–30 and 24:1–10 probably from soon after Jehoiachin's exile to Babylon in 597.

JEREMIAH 25:1–38. This is the conclusion of the first main section (1–25) and is a declaration of impending judgment not only on Judah but also on the surrounding nations and empires.

JEREMIAH 26–9 AND 34–45. These chapters present a third-person narrative relative to Jeremiah's work from the beginning of Jehoiakim's reign (609–598 B.C.E.) to when the prophet was taken to Egypt after the assassination of Gedaliah. The material is not entirely in chronological order, but chapters 37–44 are a consecutive narrative from the last two or three years before the fall of Jerusalem in 587/6 B.C.E. The narrative provides an important supplement to the bare account of the events leading up to the fall of Jerusalem found in 2 Kings 24:18–25:2. The story of the dictating and burning of Jeremiah's prophecies is also recounted here (chapter 36).

JEREMIAH 30–3. The Book of Comfort is a mixture of poetry and prose, with emphasis upon hopes of restoration. Some of the oracles (e.g., 30:10–11, 18–22; 31:2–6, 7–9, 10–14) are reminiscent of material in Isaiah 40–55. A famous passage promises that God will make a new covenant with Israel (31:31–4). Scholars are divided as to whether the passage derives from Jeremiah or from exilic editors, but this decision hardly affects the important content of the verses. Chapter 32 is the story of Jeremiah buying a field in Anathoth to demonstrate, at the time of the siege of Jerusalem (588–587 B.C.E.), that "houses and fields and vineyards will again be bought in this land" (32:15).

These chapters occupy an important position in the book as a whole. There are earlier promises of restoration (e.g., 16:14–15), but chapters 30–3 set the grim story of the following chapters in a context of hope: the God who is about to execute judgment has already promised restoration.

JEREMIAH 46–51. Oracles against the nations concern Egypt (46:1–12, 13–24), Philistia (47:1–7), Moab (48:1–47), Ammon (49:1–6), Edom (49:7–22), Damascus (49:23–7), Kedar (i.e., inhabitants of the desert, 49:28–33), Elam (49:34–9), and Babylon (50:1–51:58). Whatever the exact circumstances that occasioned each of these oracles, their collection together and placement here reinforce the theme that the God who destroyed Jerusalem is the sovereign Lord of the nations, not merely a local god. Promises of restoration (e.g., 48:47, 49:39) also feature within these oracles of judgment.

JEREMIAH 51:59–52:34. This appendix to the Book of Jeremiah repeats much of 2 Kings 24:18–25:30 and is an account of the destruction of Jerusalem (already given at 39:1–10), ending with the release of Jehoiachin from captivity in 560 B.C.E.

D. Ezekiel

1. Social History of the Period

At first sight, the background to the Book of Ezekiel might seem identical to that of Isaiah 40–55. Like the unnamed prophet of Second Isaiah, Ezekiel was also an exile in Babylonia, living within an expatriate community (Ezekiel 1:1). Yet Ezekiel's circumstances and background differed markedly from those of the Second Isaiah prophet, quite apart from the fact that Ezekiel's prophecies ended some forty years before those of Isaiah 40–55. Whereas the prophet of Isaiah 40–55 seems to have been an unrecognized (or even excluded) figure, Ezekiel belonged to a priestly family that was exiled in 597 B.C.E. along with other noble, skilled, and influential people; the elders of his community consulted him regularly (Ezekiel 8:1, 20:1). By genealogy, status, and expertise, Ezekiel was poised to guide those who listened to his prophecy through the crisis of the Temple's destruction. Although his location, near the "river" (probably a canal) called Chebar (Ezekiel 1:1), cannot be precisely identified, it seems possible that he conducted, or spoke in the context of, the worship of his exiled community.

THE DIASPORA

During no period of Israelite or Jewish history have all Jews or their predecessors been resident in the territory called Israel. During the great expansion of the united monarchy, David and Solomon sent Israelites to various parts of Asia and Africa as government colonists or private traders. Some of them undoubtedly settled in those places permanently. A minor deportation of prisoners of war may have taken place during the invasion of Pharaoh Shishak (Sheshonq; ca. 918 B.C.E.). But, of course, the greatest cause of dispersion was the series of exiles imposed on Israel and Judah by the Assyrian and Babylonian Empires.

The Hebrew term for large-scale dispersion is *galut*, "exile." Greek translations of the Hebrew Scriptures render this term, and several similar nouns referring to Jewish people living outside the borders of the land of Israel, with the word *diaspora*, which means "scattering." After the destruction of Jerusalem in 587/6 B.C.E., this Diaspora became one of the distinguishing features of Jewish life, growing geographically and numerically as people were displaced from Israel. Political and religious pressures there, together with economic prospects emerging in other, more prosperous countries, added to the Diaspora's extent and population.

Babylon became the most heavily settled Jewish center outside of Palestine during the Persian and Greco-Roman periods. The text of the Bible was first redacted in Babylon, and antecedents of synagogue Judaism appeared there. The very long-term impact of this Diaspora on Rabbinic Judaism is evident in the formative influence of the Babylonian Amoraim ("interpreters"; literally, "speakers"), the successors to the great Galilean sages (the Tannaim, or "repeaters"). The Babylonian Talmud became the authoritative interpretation of the Jewish legal tradition preserved in the Mishnah. Next in importance to the Babylonian *galut* was the dispersion to Egypt, which hosted an early (sixth century B.C.E.) and well-settled center of Jewish population. By the beginning of the Common Era, Philo Judaeus reported that the Jewish population of all Egypt, from the border with Libya on the east and with Ethiopia to the south, was "no less than one million." Two of Alexandria's five districts were predominantly Jewish. At the height of the Greco-Roman period, the Diaspora reached to such farflung territories as Phoenicia, Syria, Pamphylia, Bithynia, Greece, Italy, Cyprus, Crete, Egypt, and almost every country west of the Euphrates.

The Diaspora brought Jews into close contact with Greco-Roman civilization, which played a powerful role in the development of Judaism during the Hellenistic period. Where their numbers and influence permitted, the Jews of the Diaspora participated in the political life of their adopted countries. They were accorded religious tolerance in many instances, permitted to organize their own communities, and allowed to maintain contact with the religio-political center in Jerusalem. Most scholars suggest that the Diaspora gave birth to the Jewish synagogue and was responsible for the translation of the Hebrew Scriptures into Greek. During the early centuries of the Common Era, the Diaspora facilitated the early and rapid spread of Christianity, hosting a network of people who were familiar with the Scriptures and who shared messianic expectations that the Christian teachers claimed had been fulfilled by Jesus of Nazareth.

Many of the exiles (an estimated three thousand people) had supported Jehoiakim's rebellion against Nebuchadnezzar; they hoped that their fortunes would soon be reversed and that Egypt would defeat Nebuchadnezzar. (Whether the Babylonians would have concentrated, rather than dispersed, these potential rebels remains an open question.) Such a situation would explain the number of anti-Egyptian oracles in the Book of Ezekiel, since the prophet believed that no human agency or nation could save Jerusalem from punishment and destruction.

Ezekiel uniquely describes abominations in the first Temple that one would not have expected to find: the "image of jealousy" north of the altar gate (8:5), portrayals of "creeping things, and loathsome animals," on a wall

(8:10), women weeping for Tammuz (8:14), and men worshipping the sun (8:16). Is this an exaggerated picture of Judah's provocations against God, or an accurate reflection of what was happening in the Temple between 597 and 587 B.C.E.? If the latter, Ezekiel's description would suggest that Josiah's religious reformation in 622 had hardly touched the "folk religion" of the ordinary people, the innovations of priests, or the cultic architecture of the nation. Josiah's had been a "top–down" reformation; the suppression of local shrines meant that Jerusalem became the unrivaled religious center of Judah, but the religion actually ensconced there evidently transgressed the standards of the Deuteronomist or anything Josiah would have authorized. The worship of the sun, for example, can be attributed to continuing Egyptian influence, which was reasserted after Necho II defeated and killed Josiah in 609.

Othmar Keel's research has shed light on Ezekiel's visions of God in chapters 1 and 10. In particular, two pieces of artwork found in Arad and Bethlehem depict a deity in human form shrouded by a lotus plant, in concentric circles, giving a chariot-wheel effect. Ezekiel's visions clearly owed something to the iconography of his times; and his apparent knowledge of the mythology of foreign nations (as in the oracles against Tyre and Egypt in chapters 28 and 31) suggests that, within intellectual circles, such mythologies were learned as part of one's education.

2. The Literary History, Structure, and Contents of Ezekiel

Ezekiel is unique within the Hebrew Bible in the number of dated oracles that it contains. From their position in the book, much can be deduced about the book's literary history. The following table is based on the analysis and reconstruction developed by Bernhard Lang (1981). All dates are B.C.E.

Reference	Date in Ezekiel (day/mo./yr.)	Modern date (day/mo./yr.)	Subject
1:1	5/4/30	24/7/568	opening verse
1:2	5/unknown/5	593–2	opening vision
8:1	5/6/6	17/9/592	address to elders
20:1	10/5/7	14/8/591	address to elders
24:1	10/10/9	5/1/587	against Jerusalem (see 2 Kings 25:1; Ezekiel 24:1 is dated to the beginning of the siege of Jerusalem in the reign of Zedekiah)
26:1	Perhaps 1/11 (Septuagint: 12)	586 or 585	against Tyre, which was besieged ca. 12 (585–572)

29:1	12/10/10	7/1/587	against Egypt
29:17	1/1/27	26/4/571	against Tyre
30.20	7/1/11	29/4/587	against Egypt
31:1	1/3/11	21/6/587	against Egypt
32:1	1/12/12 (Septuagint: 11)	3/3/586 or 585	against Egypt (after the fall of Jerusalem but before the news reached Ezekiel)
32:17	15/unknown/12	27/4/586–17/3/585	against Egypt
33:21	5/10/12	8/1/585	against Israel (immediately after receiving news of Jerusalem's fall)
40:1	10/1/25	28/4/573	vision of restored Temple

The table shows that the oracles are not collected in their chronological order. In particular, the two oracles against Tyre (26:1 and 29:17) appear in their inverse sequence in time. As with the Books of Isaiah (13–23) and Jeremiah (46–51), the Book of Ezekiel artificially aggregated oracles against foreign nation, which suggests that the book reached its present form at the hands of editors.

Chapters 38–9 break the connection between 37:28 and 40:1, and they appear to date from a period when the hopes of restoration expressed in Ezekiel had not been fully realized. They envisage a future conflict, when Gog of the land of Magog will be brought by God against the Israelites reassembled in their land (38:8). The attack of Gog against Israel will cause God to defend his people, and in so doing he will manifest his glory among the nations (39:21). God's people will also recognize his power and understand his purposes (39:25–9). Although visions of Ezekiel consisted overwhelmingly of assurances of the destruction and eventual restoration of Israel (particularly Jerusalem), Ezekiel 40–8 present details of a visionary temple and its cult. These chapters manifest an affinity with "the Holiness Code" (Leviticus 17–26) within the Pentateuch, as well as with the later *Temple Scroll* from Qumran, but they also set out a program for the priestly dominance of the Zadokite group that is distinctive. The remainder of the book may be set out in a tabular form:

Section A	Transition	Section B
(*a*) 1–3; the call of the prophet		(*a*) 33:1–20, 21–33; the call of the prophet

(b) 4–7, 12–15; prophecies of judgment against Jerusalem and its leaders

(c) 8–11; visions in Jerusalem of its abominations, "glory" departs (11:22–3)

(d) 16–19; parables of judgment and hope

(e) 20–32; prophecies of judgment against Jerusalem, Samaria, Ammon, Moab, Edom, Philistia, Egypt

(b) 34–7; prophecies of judgment against and hope for Jerusalem and its leaders.

(c) 40–8; visions in Jerusalem of its restoration; the "glory" returns (43:1–5)

This scheme may be of help for the modern reader and intimates the concerns of the editor. The departure of the "glory" (God's presence) from the Temple and city at the end of chapter 11 is balanced by its return at 43:1–5. Also, the gathering together of the oracles against the nations into chapters 20–32 yields the result that, after the renewal of the call to the prophet in chapter 33, the final section (34–7, 40–8) is able to concentrate on the theme of the restoration of Jerusalem without interruption by oracles against foreign nations.

Only a few oracles of hope appear in Ezekiel until after he received the news of Jerusalem's fall (33:21–2; the few exceptions appearing in chapters 16–19). From that point onward, oracles of hope and restoration abound. This pattern probably corresponds to Ezekiel's actual activity: as long as people hoped that a foreign power (Egypt, in particular) would defeat Babylon and restore them to Jerusalem, Ezekiel's oracles against foreign powers were insistent. (Some against Tyre were given much later, of course; see 26; 29:17–18.) From the time he knew that the Temple had been destroyed, however, Ezekiel began to speak predominantly in terms of hope. Once it was no longer possible for people to resort to the false hope of a human intervention to save Jerusalem, Ezekiel could speak of the restoration that God alone could provide.

Ezekiel presents several unique features. The prophet's strange actions in lying on his side with a model of Jerusalem for long periods (4:1–17), in shaving his head and beard, in burning some of his hair (5:1–4), in carrying his possessions with him (12:1–7), and in his dumbness (3:26–7; 24:25–7; 33:21–2) have prompted theories about his behavior ranging from a hypothetical illnesses (such as catalepsy) to the proposal that he was indulging in street theater. His visionary shifts from Babylon to Jerusalem and back have led some to argue that some of his ministry was actually spent in Jerusalem. His visions of the glory of God in the form of a chariot supporting a throne are remarkable in their own right.

Some of Ezekiel's "parables" are also remarkable. In chapter 16 Jerusalem is likened to an abandoned female baby, whom God saved from death and married when she was physically ready for love. Her subsequent harlotries are an illustration of Israel's turning to other gods; the thought and imagery, although to some extent precedented in the Book of Hosea, are daring in their application. Again, the vision of the valley of dry bones in chapter 37 is a powerful statement of God's power to bring hope to the most impossible situation.

Another famous passage is at 28:11–19, an oracle against Tyre in which its king is said to have been placed in the garden of Eden and to have been blameless until pride and violence caused a guardian cherub to drive him from the garden. The similarities with Genesis 3 have long been noted, occasioning speculation regarding the literary or conceptual interdependence of the two passages.

When Ezekiel is compared with his younger fellow prophet of the Babylonian exile, Second Isaiah, the diversity of Israelite prophecy becomes apparent. The one is a respected priestly visionary given to strange behavior and insistent that there is no hope of restoration apart from God. The other is a prophet of consolation, probably persecuted and despised in his lifetime and recognized as God's servant only by way of hindsight.

E. Hosea

1. Social History of the Period

According to Hosea 1:1, the prophet of that name was active during the reigns of Uzziah, Jotham, Ahaz, and Hezekiah (kings of Judah) and of Jeroboam II (king of Israel). The Judahite kings concerned reigned between 767 and 698 B.C.E. while Jeroboam's reign was from 782 until 747 B.C.E. Taken together, these reigns cover more than eighty years, far too long a period to be plausible. But scholars generally agree that echoes may be heard in Hosea of the anti-Assyrian coalition between Israel and Damascus (733/2 B.C.E.) and its aftermath (Hosea 5:8–14), and that there are possible references to the period from the death of Tiglath-pileser III (727 B.C.E.) and the fall of Samaria (722/1 B.C.E.), when there was hope of help from Egypt (Hosea 11:5, 12:1 [Hebrew, 12:2]). Some oracles, such as those in Hosea 2 and 4:4–5:7, derive from the period before the anti-Assyrian coalition of 733, but it is hard to say how much earlier than this Hosea's work began. On the evidence of the book apart from 1:1, Hosea's period of activity was roughly between 750 and 720 B.C.E.

Hosea, as a prophet of the north, concerned himself almost entirely with the northern peoples who constituted the kingdom of Israel after Jeroboam's revolt against Rehoboam. Hosea began his prophecy during Jeroboam II's reign, a time of peace and prosperity some two centuries after Israel's separation from Judah. According to 2 Kings 14:28, Jeroboam II greatly extended the boundaries of the northern kingdom, and we can infer that Israel also enjoyed increased trade, economic activity, and political influence. Although that led to an increase of wealth for the rich and of oppression for the poor (cf. the Book of Amos), the emphasis of Hosea is religious. Hosea (4:2) does complain of "swearing, lying, killing, stealing, and committing adultery" (a vocabulary that may reflect knowledge of the Ten Commandments), but these terms of reference are not typical of the book. The overwhelming focus is upon Israel's *religious* apostasy: its

EZEKIEL AT DURA-EUROPOS

In 1932 an extraordinarily well-preserved synagogue, dating from the third century C.E., was uncovered at Salahiyeh in Syria. This site, on the upper Euphrates River, was identified as the ancient city of Dura-Europos, which was established by the Seleucid ruler Nicator I around 300 B.C.E. Although occupied by several different invading armies, the city retained its Hellenistic character until it fell to the Sassanids in 256 C.E. Only a few years before the city's destruction, at least two artists decorated the upper story of a small synagogue with two-tiered panels of exquisite paintings depicting mostly biblical scenes. These scenes were often supplemented with details drawn from the rich world of Jewish homiletical tradition, some of which have been preserved in the Talmud and in early Christian works that incorporated (or were influenced by) Jewish tradition. The paintings also used figures, forms, and symbols from the Greek and Persian worlds. Scenes from the life of Moses, Elijah, and David were combined with pictures of Greek gods and goddesses to present a Jewish–Hellenistic fusion of Eastern and Western art.

On the lower panel along the synagogue's northern wall is the longest painting, depicting a pageant of events from the life of the prophet Ezekiel. He is presented in three great scenes, separated by two large mountains. The painting is designed to be read from left to right, away from the west wall, where it adjoins the scene of the infancy of Moses. At the painting's extreme left is a tree drawn in a familiar, classical style. To the tree's right is a row of three bushy-haired, lightly bearded figures in different poses but in identical dress. Clad in Persian costume, the figures wear soft white boots, reddish brown smocks covered with elaborate embroidery, and green trousers. All three men have been taken to be the prophet Ezekiel. At their feet are a number of human heads, arms, and legs. A heavenly hand lifts the first Ezekiel by the hair of his head into this place of human fragments. The artist thus portrays God bringing Ezekiel into the famous valley of dry bones (Ezekiel 37) by the means described in an earlier vision (Ezekiel 8:2–3). The second Ezekiel is prophesying to the bones, and the third points to a strange mountain beside him.

A second mountain, topped by a fruit tree, divides this scene of heavenly triumph from the final panel, which depicts the legendary execution of Ezekiel. This panel shows a figure in Persian clothing who has been dragged by his hair away from an altar. He stands at the mercy of a royal military figure who is about to behead him. Jewish–Christian tradition suggests that Ezekiel may have been martyred at the request of the head of the Babylonian Jewish community, a descendant of the Davidic line, whose apostasy the prophet had continually upbraided.

The Dura-Europos Ezekiel cycle was constructed from various details as an original series of scenes from the prophet's career. Mountains, for example, repeatedly appear in Ezekiel's prophecies (e.g., Ezekiel 6:2–7, 32:5, 35:1–8, 36:1–7, 38:20, 40:40–1). The Dura-Europos paintings present selections from the legend and text of Ezekiel according to an established iconographic tradition of the postbiblical period. Little other tradition about Ezekiel himself has survived, so interpreting these paintings is difficult. Nonetheless, the paintings probably reflect the prophet's ascent into the heavenly regions (the central panel), followed by a return to the sorry world of earthly reality and death, which has been cast in terms of Ezekiel's description of the valley of dry bones. This cycle of earth, heavenly glory, and then return to earth, though ostensibly inspired by the prophet's life, was also a prominent theme in some strands of early Jewish mysticism. To the person or persons who designed the wall, Ezekiel seems to have been a great mystic guide of the soul, able to lead humankind to the highest perfection. In any case, the Ezekiel cycle is eloquent testimony to the continuing vitality of Israelite traditions toward the end of the Greco-Roman era, both in Judaism and in Christianity, which shared many of the same interpretations and iconographic conventions.

desertion of Yahweh and its predilection for the Canaanite god Baal. Nonetheless, Hosea 1:4–5 seems to condemn the revolution (or at least the tactics) of Jehu, who was anointed by one of Elisha's servants in order to destroy the dynasty of Omri and Ahab (2 Kings 9), a dynasty that favored Baal over Yahweh.

Third-century C.E. reconstructed frescoes from the ancient synagogue at Dura-Europos. The niche to the left is where the scroll of the Torah was displayed during worship.

Othmar Keel argues, on the basis of his iconographical research, that in the Israel of this period Yahweh and Baal fulfilled identical functions for the people and thus became interchangeable. (Although Keel stoutly maintains that, while Baal had a female consort, Yahweh did not, we shall see that in view of the Book of Proverbs, even this general distinction seems risky.) Whatever the prophetic guardians of "pure" faith in Yahweh might have wanted, the religion of Israel's sanctuaries appears to have been syncretistic. No doubt this was encouraged by the ruling dynasty, which legitimated its power with reference to a variety of religious traditions. In this regard, there is a link between Hosea and the guilds of prophets led by Elijah and Elisha during the ninth century B.C.E.; they, too, opposed the official encouragement of the cult of Baal and waged a religious war with political weapons. On the other hand, as just noted Hosea 1:4–5 appears to condemn the revolution of Jehu, who was appointed by one of Elisha's servants to destroy the dynasty of Omri and Ahab (2 Kings 9).

An interesting feature of Hosea is its references to the ancient traditions of Israel. Possible allusions to the Ten Commandments have been mentioned

KNOWLEDGE OF GOD

The concept of the "knowledge of God" (*da'at 'elohim*) occurs throughout the prophetic literature of the Hebrew Bible. The phrase is particularly important in the Book of Hosea (see, for example, the famous statement that "knowledge of God is better than sacrifice," Hosea 6:6). The Hebrew Bible presents knowledge of God as deriving from momentous historical events through which God has revealed himself to the chosen people, Israel. Individuals display this knowledge by their proper conduct – doing justice, performing God's commandments, judging the cases of the poor and needy, remaining upright of heart, trusting in divine wisdom. In some passages, knowledge of God appears cognate with the virtue "fear of Yahweh" as a description of authentic Israelite religion (Isaiah 11:2; Jeremiah 22:16).

Hosea identifies knowledge of God as a constitutive element of covenant faith. The phrase appears alongside the central concepts of faithfulness (*'emet*) and of mercy (*chesed*). In this context, knowledge of God refers to understanding the ways of God as revealed in the covenant. When the Israelite community did not possess this knowledge (i.e., when they did not uphold the covenant), religious decline and apostasy resulted. Theft, adultery, murder, perjury, and blasphemy were the inevitable accompaniments, leading to the people's eventual destruction (Hosea 4:1–6).

Some texts suggest that the absence of knowledge of God can be the result of inexperience (Genesis 17). Other texts imply that, outside the community of Israel, knowledge of God cannot exist at all. In their ignorance, Gentiles could not enjoy a right relation to Yahweh (Psalm 79:6, Jeremiah 10:25). The technical term *da'at 'elohim* nonetheless retains a less exclusive connotation; *'elohim*, the creator, is God of the whole world.

already. In addition, Exodus traditions (2:15; 8:13; 9:3, 10; 11:1–4; 12:9, 13–14; 13:4–5), as well as the story of the Israelite hero Jacob (12:3–4, 12:12), resonate in this book. Such allusions support the theory that, in prophetic circles in Israel, the Jacob and Exodus traditions were known or being composed prior to their being brought south after the fall of Samaria in 722/1 B.C.E.

2. The Literary Structure and Contents of Hosea

Hosea can be divided into distinct sections: (*a*) 1–3, (*b*) 4:1–5:7, (*c*) 5:8–6:6, (*d*) 6:7–9:9, (*e*) 9:10–13:16 (Hebrew, 14:1), and (*f*) 14:1–9 (Hebrew, 14:2–10).

HOSEA 1–3. Chapters 1–3 begin with God's command to Hosea to "take a wife of whoredom and have children of whoredom" (1:2). The prophet marries Gomer, and two sons and a daughter are born to them; each child is given a symbolic name. The elder son's name, Jezreel, is a sign that God will soon bring an end to the dynasty of Jehu, whose descendant was Jeroboam II. The connection between Jehu's dynasty and the name Jezreel is that it was in the city of Jezreel that Jehu received the heads of seventy sons of King Ahab slaughtered on Jehu's instructions (see 2 Kings 10:1–11). The daughter is named Lo-ruchamah, which means in Hebrew "not pitied." The younger son is named Lo-ammi, meaning "not my people." The whole passage (1:2–9), with its declaration that God will destroy his people without pity, is followed (vv. 10–11; Hebrew, 2:1–2) by a prophecy of the restoration of Israel and Judah.

Chapter 2 (Hebrew, 2:3–25) is a complex poem that is difficult to summarize. A speaker in the first person commands at least two people (the Hebrew imperative form used is for two or more people) to tell their brother, now called Ammi "my people," and sister, now called Ruhamah "pitied," that they must plead with their mother, telling her that the speaker is no longer her husband. She has committed adultery, and he will expose and punish not only her but her children. Further, she will be punished when she tries to pursue her lovers. Then, in a tender passage, the speaker promises to win his rejected wife back so that their relationship will be as it was when she was young, when she came out of the land of Egypt. These verses indicate that the speaker is God himself, and that the wife is Israel as a whole. The passage contrasts Israel's faithfulness to God in the wilderness after the Exodus with their unfaithfulness after entering the land of Canaan. (In contrast, the wilderness wanderings stories in the Books of Exodus and Numbers mostly stress Israel's unfaithfulness during the wilderness period!) Chapter 2 ends with a promise of future blessing when Israel will be completely faithful to God.

In chapter 3 the prophet is commanded to "love a woman who has a lover and is an adulteress" (3:1). The prophet buys a woman for fifteen pieces of silver plus measures of grain and wine. He tells her that she is to have no intercourse with any man, including him, symbolizing a period when Israel will have no king or sacrifices.

These very difficult chapters have given rise to a number of interpretations. The best known of them understands the passage as reflecting Hosea's personal experience, postulating that he married a woman who became a prostitute and was sold into slavery, and that Hosea bought her back from slavery and made her his wife once more. Another view is that when Hosea was commanded to marry "a wife of whoredom," he and his wife and children were to act out a dramatization, in which they took the parts of a prostitute and her children. Many interpreters have asked whether God is likely to have ordered the prophet to engage in an immoral act such as marrying a prostitute (1:2) or loving an adulteress (3:1). Another difficult question is whether the prostitute and the adulteress are the same woman, or two different women. Given all these uncertainties, it is probably best not to speculate about whether the chapter reflects Hosea's personal experiences. What is clear is that chapter 2 uses the *imagery* of prostitution and divorce to describe Israel's apostasy from God and his determination to win his people back to faithfulness after he has punished them. In its development of an extended metaphor whose meaning is much more certain than its initial point of departure, the Book of Hosea marks a major literary attainment in the evolution of Israelite prophecy.

HOSEA 4:1–5:7. This section presents a series of oracles of judgment in the form of legal accusations. God has a controversy with his people (4:1), and he is the one who will press the case (4:4). Among those singled out for condemnation are the leaders: the priests (4:4–6, 5:1) and the king (5:1).

HOSEA 5:8–6:6. This material is usually connected with the Syro-Ephraimite war of 733/2 B.C.E., when Judah appealed to the Assyrian king, Tiglath-pileser III, for help when threatened by Israel and Damascus.

HOSEA 6:7–9:9. Here Hosea denounces the corruptions of human leadership and false worship. Wickedness gladdens the king and his nobles (7:3), and the current royal leaders are not approved by God (8:4). The nation seeks help from foreign countries (7:11; 8:9–10) and false gods (7:16, 8:5b). Not only do the people not seek God, but they reject the prophets whose task it is to warn them of the consequences of their deeds (9:7–9).

HOSEA 9:10–13:16. Allusions to Israel's patriarchal and Exodus traditions emerge in this section. Those traditions are a continuous story of Israel's backslidings despite being freed from slavery and guided through the desert to the accompaniment of signs and wonders. The story provides rich allusions for this part of Hosea, central to which is 11:1–9, in which God declares that he cannot and will not abandon the child he called out of Egypt, despite that child's apostasies.

HOSEA 14:1–9. Hosea ends with a plea to the people to return to God, even to the point of providing them words with which to seek God's mercy (14:2–3). An assurance that mercy will be forthcoming is concluded with a verse in the wisdom traditions of Israel (14:9).

F. Joel

The Book of Joel contains no reference that enables it to be linked with any known event or to be placed within any specific historical or social context. It is not even clear whether the book was written mainly by one author, or whether there were two authors from different periods whose work was joined together, or whether a second, later author composed the second half of the book in deliberate response to the first part. In view of these uncertainties, it is not possible to treat separately the matters of historical and social setting, literary history, and structure and content.

The division of material in Joel differs in the Greek translation from that in the traditional Hebrew text. The differences are straightforward:

Hebrew chapter 1 equals Greek chapter 1
Hebrew chapter 2 equals Greek 2:1–27
Hebrew chapter 3 equals Greek 2:28–32
Hebrew chapter 4 equals Greek chapter 3

The standard English translations follow the Greek numbering, which is accepted here for the sake of clarity.

Joel may naturally be divided into two parts: 1:2–17 and 2:20–3:21. Verses 2:18–19 form a bridge between these two parts. The overwhelming message of part one is of imminent disaster, which repentance on the part of the people may possibly avert. After the opening verse, which names (but does not date) Joel, there is a devastating account of the effects upon the land of a plague of locusts (1:4–7). The impact is so comprehensive that crops, vines, and fruits are ruined, and even the Temple service has been deprived of cereal and drink offerings (1:8–13). The situation demands a national fast and a solemn assembly (1:14). Further, it heralds the "Day of Yahweh" – that awesome day when God will bring his armies to execute justice on his people (1:15–20).

Chapter 2 warns the people of the approach of the Day of Yahweh and pictures its arrival in apocalyptic language. There will be gloom and thick darkness, the enemy will be preceded by fire, the earth will tremble, and the sun and moon will be darkened (2:1–11). This grim prospect is the occasion for a call for repentance, to be accompanied by fasting and weeping and led by the priests in the Temple. God, who is gracious and merciful, must be implored to spare his people (2:12–17).

Devastating plagues of locusts descended on Israel from time to time, even into modern times. In Joel 2, the imagery of the advancing army of locusts describes the advent of the armies that God will summon to be part of his "Day." Older commentators understandably identified this imminent army with the Syrians of the ninth century B.C.E. or with the Assyrians and Babylonians of the eighth and seventh centuries, respectively. But other considerations suggest a postexilic setting: there is no mention of a king, the prophet's attitude toward the priests and the Temple cult is positive (in contrast to the severe criticisms of the preexilic prophets), and the oracles would fit well within a small community dominated by the Temple. Part one may therefore be dated sometime between 450 and 400 B.C.E.

The bridge to part two is a declaration that God responded to his people's prayers and answered them favorably (2:18–19). The remainder of the book, in contrast to part one, is characterized by consolation for God's people. Even the Day of Yahweh is transformed from a day of judgment for God's people to a day of deliverance (3:9–21). Whereas part one speaks of the devastation caused by the locusts, 2:23–7 speaks of the abundance of produce that the land and the people will enjoy. The sense of promise is so great that Peter's speech in Acts 2:17–21 quotes Joel 2:28–9, a resonant passage about the outpouring of the Spirit of God:

> Then afterward
> I will pour out my spirit on all flesh.

A reference in 3:4–8 might suggest a period for this part of the book. Tyre, Sidon, and Philistia are accused of selling God's people to the Greeks. This could date the passage to the late fourth century B.C.E., although many scholars see 3:4–8 as an even later addition to Joel.

A prominent feature of part two is its apparent usage of earlier prophecies. The words

> beat your plowshares into swords
> and your pruning hooks into spears (3:10)

immediately recall Micah 4:3 and Isaiah 2:4. But there are other allusions, too. "The LORD roars from Zion" (Joel 3:16) recalls Amos 1:2, while Joel 3:18 seems to combine themes from the closing verses of Amos (9:13) and Ezekiel (47:1–12). For this reason, Joel has been called in German a *Schriftprofet*, that is, a user and interpreter of earlier written prophecies.

Despite its complicated history of composition, Joel has been fashioned into a literary unity. The fears of coming judgment engendered by the plague of locusts are transformed into hope for Jerusalem and Judah. Because God is faithful to his people, their want will be turned to plenty, and the judgment they fear will become their vindication in the eyes of their enemies.

G. Amos

1. Social History of the Period

According to the Book of Amos 1:1, Amos was active during the reigns of Uzziah in Judah (ca. 767–739 B.C.E.) and of Jeroboam II in Israel (782–747 B.C.E.). This places him within the eighth century B.C.E. prior to the fall of Israel's capital, Samaria, in 722/1. There is also a reference to an earthquake in 1:1, and Amos is said to have spoken two years, or during the two years, before this event. Evidence of a massive earthquake has been found at Hazor; but this does not really help us to date Amos, because archaeologists have used Amos to date the earthquake!

Archaeological investigations in the northern kingdom of Israel, where Amos was active, indicate that his period during the eighth century B.C.E. witnessed little, if any, building activity. Massive works of fortification had already been undertaken during the ninth century in major cities, and these served their cities through the eighth century, until the Assyrians began to conquer the land around 734. In the case of Hazor, where the earthquake caused buildings to collapse, they seem to have been rebuilt along the same lines as before; and we may surmise that this was also true of other cities affected by seismic damage.

According to 2 Kings 14:25 Jeroboam II "restored the border of Israel from Lebohamath as far as the Sea of the Arabah"; verse 28 adds that he recovered Damascus and Hamath for Israel (citing as a source the Book of the Chronicles of the Kings of Israel). All this implies an enormous extension of Israelite power to the north, and most commentators suppose that the claims are exaggerated, or speak of ideal boundaries rather than actual borders. The credibility of the passage is not helped by verse 26, which describes the bitter distress of Israel, claiming that "there was no one left, bond or free, and no one to help Israel." How this is supposed to square with the usual view of Israel at this time, as enjoying unparalleled prosperity, is hard to fathom. Yet even if this description is exaggerated (and confused), the summary of Jeroboam's reign plausibly insists that the king fought his enemies, and that affects our estimate of the sociology of the period: war inevitably entailed the conscription of labor and the levying of taxes to support soldiers who were no longer productive agriculturally.

The Samaria ostraca feature among the archaeological discoveries of this period; these accounts record the receipt of jars of oil or wine sent to Samaria from a number of towns, most of them between four and eight

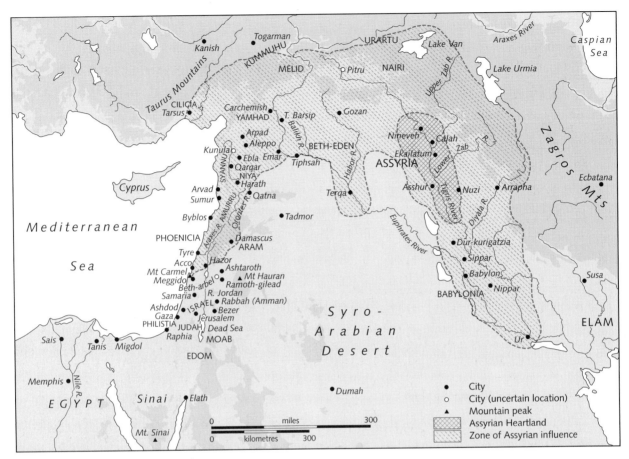

Map VII. Israel, Judah, and the surrounding empires and nations during the eighth century B.C.E.

miles from Samaria. Usually dated during the reign of Jeroboam II, they are believed to indicate, not a nationwide system of taxation, but sources of wine and oil that were used to supply the needs of the capital city. These supplies amounted to a kind of local tribute that supported the luxurious lifestyle of those who lived in Samaria, a lifestyle that Amos condemned (4:1).

A disputed point among experts is whether Jeroboam's reign was one in which general prosperity enabled the rich to grow more powerful at the expense of the poor, or whether, as decreasing rates of construction might suggest, it was a period of declining wealth in which the attempt by the rich to retain their standard of living during a time of warfare bore heavily on the poor, causing them greater hardship. Whichever model is more accurate, the poor certainly suffered, and this is reflected in passages such as Amos 2:6–8 and 8:4–6. These texts indicate that justice was being perverted, that pledges taken in lieu of loans were not being properly honored, and that there was dishonest trading. Yet it must be noted that these accusations are general rather than specific and give no information that would allow us to reconstruct the sociology of the period.

SAMARIA

Samaria was the capital of the northern kingdom of Israel. Although archaeological excavations at the site show some signs of very ancient occupation, the city owed its construction primarily to the collapse of the united monarchy following the death of Solomon. David's capital, Jerusalem, was retained by rulers of the southern territory of Judah, and the kings of Israel needed an administrative center of their own in the north.

Samaria was built during the Early Iron II period (900–800 B.C.E.), during the reigns of Omri and Ahab. Located on a hill overlooking fertile valleys, it was from the outset a carefully designed, beautiful city, becoming a showcase for the wealth and power of Israel. Most of the city's remains have been destroyed by later quarrying and construction, but archaeologists have found more than five hundred fragments of ivory inlay near the city's summit, where the royal palaces were located (see the reference to Ahab's house of ivory in 1 Kings 22:39). The city's riches drew the wrath of prophets like Amos, who protested against rulers amassing wealth at the expense of those they ruled (Amos 6:4–7).

Samaria survived revolution, assassination, and prophetic protest – but not the Assyrian army. The city fell in 722/1 B.C.E. and was burned to the ground by the army of Sargon II. Yet it took the powerful Assyrian military machine three years of hard fighting to capture Samaria, eloquent testimony to the effectiveness of the city's strong, three-ringed defense system. The people of Israel were deported, in accordance with the Assyrian policy of transplanting the populations of captured territories to prevent future nationalistic revolt. The northern kingdom of Israel disappeared from history, its remnants ("the lost tribes of Israel") fruitful topics of legend.

The city of Samaria nevertheless outlasted the kingdom of Israel. Assyrian captives from Babylon, Ananth, Ava, and Hamath settled in the city, and these new Samaritans gradually adopted a modified form of Yahwism and worshipped at a temple on Mount Gerizim. The enmity that developed between them and the inhabitants of Judah extended well into the Common Era (see, for example, John 4:9). The city itself went on to serve as a provincial capital for the Persian, Greek, Roman, and Arab rulers of Palestine.

The social history of the period nonetheless emerges in general terms. Jeroboam II inherited a kingdom that was recovering from the hard times of the latter part of the ninth century B.C.E. when both Assyria and Damascus had pressed Israel. A period of relative peace and freedom from Assyrian interference enabled Jeroboam to settle some old scores against Damascus. Possessions in the area of Transjordan south of Damascus were always in dispute between the two kingdoms, and Jeroboam either seized several that had been lost to Israel or allowed them to remain in Syrian hands in return for trading concessions in Damascus. Even small-scale wars, together with the demands of supplying food and drink to Samaria, bore heavily on small landowners. Although rainfall was more secure in Israel than in Judah, droughts and bad harvests remained a problem. Such natural disasters, added to conscription for military service and to royal taxes, could reduce small landowners to hired laborers on their own landholdings. The gap between rich and poor thus became greater and greater.

Samaritan ivory showing sphinx in lotus thicket, ninth century B.C.E.

2. The Prophet Amos and His Book

Amos is usually regarded as a "prophet" from the town of Tekoa in Judah, on the edge of the wilderness that slopes down to the Dead Sea (Amos 1:1). Yet this identification raises questions. If he was a man of Judah, why did he prophesy as persistently as he did in Israel? How did he become familiar with conditions in Israel and in its capital, Samaria? A further problem is that, while Amos described himself as one who tended and harvested sycamore trees (Hebrew *shiqmah;* plural, *shiqmim;* Amos 7:14), these trees did not grow near Tekoa in Judah.

Accordingly, a northern, Galilean location for Tekoa has been suggested – at Khirbet Shema', not far from Meron, several miles northwest of Tsephat. The fig sycamore (*shiqmah*) grew in lower Galilee (in the north of Israel) according to the Mishnah (second century C.E.; *Sheviith* 9:2). This northern location for Tekoa has not found great favor among scholars, however, and the southern location still finds defenders for several reason. First, the fig sycamore grew in Jericho according to a discussion in the Babylonian Talmud (*Pesachim* 56, a–b), and Amos could easily have traveled there from Tekoa. Further, as a shepherd (1:1) Amos would be likely to move with his flocks and would thus be aware of events in the northern kingdom. But these considerations still do not address all the outstanding questions. In particular, if Amos was an owner of cattle as well as of sheep (cf. 7:14), would he have traveled extensively with his animals? Was it possible for shepherds from Judah to move freely into the northern kingdom and use pasturage there? Perhaps we should admit that we know less about Amos than has often been assumed.

Another question concerns whether or not Amos regarded himself as a prophet. In the incident in 7:10–17, in which he was reproved for speaking against (or at, as another view would have it) the sanctuary of Bethel, Amos averred that he was not a prophet. However, verse 14 can be translated in two ways:

1. I was not a prophet . . .
2. I am not a prophet . . .

The first would imply that, before his call, Amos was not a member of a prophetic guild or family, and that he owed his status as prophet uniquely to his call from God. The second would imply that he had never been, and was not now, a prophet in the technical sense. If the second approach is followed, this still does not mean that Amos was a solitary speaker of God's words. After all, someone must have preserved what he had said or written; and presumably, the belief that he had spoken shortly before the earthquake must have been a tradition within a circle of followers or friends. Indeed, their support of Amos made him the first known prophet whose oracles were collected in writing and therefore the pioneer figure of literary prophecy.

The following parts of the book are usually attributed to the historical Amos (although this list is by no means exhaustive):

1. The oracles against Damascus, Gaza, Ammon, Moab, and Israel (1:3–8, 13–15; 2:1–3, 6–16)
2. The five visions of 7:1–3, 4–6, 7–9; 8:1–2(3); 9:1–2
3. Three collections of sayings beginning with "hear this word," at 3:1–15, 4:1–13; 5:1–6
4. Three small collections beginning with the word "woe," at 5:7, 10–17, 18–24; 6:1–7

The book is based upon a number of collections of Amos's prophecies with formal, rhetorical features. Thus, the opening oracles against the nations begin

For three transgressions of X,
and for four, I will not revoke the punishment.

Three of the visions begin with the phrase "This is what the Lord GOD showed me." In Amos 3:1–6 and 8, a series of questions expecting the answer "no" leads to a climax.

Although we can at best surmise the literary history of the book, a plausible account would begin with chapters 3–6 (excluding the hymnic passages at 4:13 and 5:8–9) as the first main collection. The oracles against the nations were added at the beginning, and the visions at the end. The series of visions was interrupted by the addition of the story of Amos's reproof by Amaziah (7:10–17) and a passage of social critique at 8:(3)4–14, which is extended in 9:2–4 and 7–10. The second stage of the book's growth involved the addition of the oracles against Tyre, Edom, and Judah (1:9–12; 2:4–5), perhaps during the early exilic period (sixth century B.C.E.). At some stage the three hymnic passages at 4:13, 5:8–9, and 9:5–6, which have a distinctive style in Hebrew, were added. The final addition was 9:11–15, and this gave the book a different flavor. While the message of the rest of Amos is almost entirely without hope, the epilogue, set in a time when the "booth of David" is fallen (i.e., the southern kingdom had collapsed), looks forward to a time of restoration. As in the case of Micah, the postexilic community was able to set grim words of judgment into a new context. The judgment had indeed come; but, they insisted, so had a restoration, through God's mercy.

We can thus perceive three main stages in the composition and sense of the book. The first stage was a collection of oracles of judgment delivered by a man who was not a professional prophet, but who had been commissioned by God to warn the northern kingdom of Israel of impending doom. In the second stage the words of judgment were seen to be applicable to Judah as well as Israel. The third stage, following the fall of both nations, expressed hope for a future restoration.

3. The Literary Structure and Contents of Amos

The content of Amos can be considered from several angles. If it is divided into two very unequal parts, 1:1–9:10 and 9:11–15, it follows a pattern, found elsewhere in the Minor Prophets, of oracles of judgment followed by words of hope and restoration. Another view is that Amos uniquely places its oracles against the nations at the beginning, the usual place being the middle or toward the end. In the present treatment Amos will be considered under the following headings: (*a*) oracles against the nations (1:2–2:16), (*b*) material concerning prophecy (3:1–8; 7:10–17), (*c*) general words of judgment (3:9–6:14, 8:[3]4–14; 9:2–10), (*d*) the five visions (7:1–3, 4–6, 7–9; 8:1–2[3]; 9:1–2), and (*e*) the epilogue (9:11–15).

Oracles against the Nations

The oracles that derive from Amos himself condemn Damascus (1:3–5), Gaza (1:6–8), Ammon (1:13–15), Moab (2:1–3), and Israel (2:6–16). The first four have a formal, recurrent structure. The opening mentions three and four transgressions for which punishment will not be revoked, but in fact only one offense is detailed. God then threatens to send a fire against the nation that will destroy the strongholds of a king or principal city, after which more general punishment will fall on the people. In each instance, the offense mentioned is what we would today call a war crime: drawing threshing sledges across the backs of prisoners (1:3), exiling whole communities (1:6), ripping open pregnant women (1:13), and denying burial to a defeated king (2:1).

The significance of these passages is twofold. First, their opening and closing words, "Thus says the LORD" and "says the LORD," place them in a religious context, asserting that cruel acts by people, including people outside Israel, against other people, are an affront to God and punishable by him. God is concerned not only with Israel but with all nations – humanity as such. Second, the prophet is appealing to what we can call "natural morality" and assumes that there are international principles of right and wrong that should not only be accepted by all people but are standards that God expects them to observe.

The oracle against Israel, with which the series originally concluded, was intended to shock Amos's listeners. It differs from those that precede it in that it presupposes a special relationship between God and Israel rather than a general standard of morality. The Exodus and wilderness wanderings are appealed to (2:10), and God addresses Israel in the first person. The offenses include the corruption of justice, the affliction of the poor, and the disregard of holy things (2:2–8). The coming judgment mentions that the strong and powerful, in particular, will not escape (2:13–16). The implication here, as elsewhere in Amos, is that the God of the nations expects an appropriate loyalty to his laws from the nation that he has specially chosen and that it will not be exempted from judgment.

The oracles against Tyre (1:9–10), Edom (1:11–12), and Judah (2:4–5) do not entirely reproduce the form of the other oracles against the nations and do not mention fire devouring a principal city. Regarding Judah there is no hint of a special relationship with God, and the offense is that Judah rejected God's law and has not kept his statutes. In context, these three oracles apply God's concern for justice to people outside Israel and in this constitute a proper extension of Amos's message. The first two chapters set the tone for the remainder of the book.

Material Concerning Prophecy

Chapter 3 begins with two verses that sum up chapters 1–2: knowledge of God entails his judgment rather than his indulgence. A passage regarding prophecy follows. A series of rhetorical questions, expecting the answer "no," leads to a verse (3:8) that gives a poetic but unambiguous answer to the implied question: Is it possible to be silent if one is spoken to by God?

> The lion has roared;
> who will not fear
> The Lord GOD has spoken;
> who can but prophesy?

This passage represents Amos's justification for his prophetic activity, and it is of a piece with 7:10–17, in which Amos denies that he is, or has been, a prophet in the professional sense. He owes his work entirely to the call of God and rejects the idea (7:16) that any human has the authority to tell him to be silent. The God who has called Amos, we must note, is the awesome God of the opening chapters, who judges the nations. A verse inserted during editing at 3:7 interrupts the sequence of rhetorical questions leading to the climax at 3:8 and has the effect of claiming Amos as a prophet after all! In a sense, of course, the verse is correct.

General Words of Judgment

These oracles, in chapters 3–6, 8, and 9, amplify the words against Israel in chapter 2, condemning perversion of justice (5:7, 10; 6:12), oppression of the poor (3:10, 5:11, 8:4–5), and abuse of worship (4:4–5; 5:21–4). A new theme is the trenchant denunciation of the rich in Samaria (4:1, 6:1b–6), and the message is presented with great artistry. In 4:6–12, a poem with the refrain "yet you did not return to me" at the end of each of five verses leads to the climax "Prepare to meet your God!" The poem details various setbacks faced by Israel: famine, drought, blight, illness, and war (raising here, and at 5:3, the question of how peaceful Amos's times really were). The background to the poem may well be the covenant promises and curses as we find them now in passages such as Deuteronomy 28:20–7, with the implication that the curses are now coming upon Israel.

In Amos 5:1–2, words of judgment are introduced by a dirge, such as might be sung at a funeral. Amos 5:18–20 famously portrays the Day of the Lord, not as a day on which God's armies will fight *for* Israel, but as a day of gloom and darkness. Amos 9:2–44 represents a poem that reads like a negative version of Psalm 139 and that may have been a deliberate parody of that psalm or a similar passage. The idea that God's presence is everywhere, even in Sheol (the underworld), is given a sinister twist: there is no hiding place from God's judgment. The material is punctuated by three hymnic passages (4:13, 5:8–9, and 9:5–6), which, if they are later additions, have been superbly placed. They celebrate the might of God the creator and complement the opening two chapters. The other material in this section consists of various descriptions of coming judgment.

The Five Visions

Of the first four visions, two are of ordinary events that Amos sees and are shown to have deeper meaning. In the first, the threat of locusts to the harvest indicates coming judgment that Israel will be too weak to withstand (7:1–3). In the fourth, the similarity between the Hebrew words for "summer fruit" (*qayits*) and "end" (*qets*) yields the message that the end of Israel is near (8:1–3). Visions two and three are more mysterious, involving a fire that consumes the deep (7:4–6, with Hebrew *tehom;* cf. Genesis 1:2) and a vision of God holding a plumb line against a wall (7:7–9). Yet despite the more mysterious nature of these two visions, there is none of the exotic imagery of Zechariah 9–14 or Daniel, and no angelic interpreter. God himself shows the visions and questions Amos. In the first two visions (7:1–3, 4–6) there is a hope that God will relent; but this is not to be, and the fifth vision (9:1–2) involves no dialogue with the prophet. God commands judgment to be carried out, and no one will escape.

The Epilogue

The book ends on a note of hope, with the promise that David's fallen booth (his kingdom and dynasty) will be raised up. This unexpected Judahite perspective is, as already noted, a later addition. It places the Book of Amos in the context of the community that is now on the yonder side of the judgment that Amos foresaw for Israel and that his editors extended to Judah.

H. Obadiah

The Book of Obadiah, only twenty-one verses long, concerns Edom, the kingdom in Transjordan roughly south and east of the Dead Sea (Obadiah 1, 6, 8, 18, 19, 21). The first nine verses envisage the coming devastation of Edom. Its cities built upon high and inaccessible rocks will not escape, nor will its fabled wisdom avail. The reason for the coming disaster is given in verses 10–14. Edom (descended from Esau; see Genesis 25:19–34) was not loyal to its brother Jacob when Judah and Jerusalem were plundered. Indeed, instead of aiding its brother, Edom gloated over the disaster and joined in the looting.

Verses 15–16 are a transition to the final verses, which describe a time when the dispossessed Israelites will return and will repossess their land. Edom will be destroyed, and Israelites will occupy the land from Edom and the Negev north through the Shephelah to Ephraim, Samaria, and Gilead (northern Transjordan), and as far as Phoenicia. This is roughly the extent of David's empire as described in 2 Samuel 8. According to verses 15–16, this time of reversal is near, when those nations that wronged Jerusalem and Judah will receive due punishment.

The lack of specific historical detail in Obadiah makes it difficult to identify the occasion of Edom's complicity against Jerusalem, although most scholars believe that the most likely event was the destruction of Jerusalem in 587/6 B.C.E. Indeed, on the basis of Obadiah scholars have supposed that the Edomites joined in the plundering of Jerusalem and Judah; although they may be correct, we must note that Jeremiah 40:11 says that after Jerusalem's fall, some men of Judah *took refuge* in Moab, Ammon, and Edom. If so, we may well ask why Judahites went to shelter in a country that had attacked Judah and Jerusalem. Perhaps verses 10–13 refer to the occupation of the southern part of Judah by the Edomites during the postexilic period, and this movement has been telescoped into the fall of Jerusalem in 587/6.

Of the prophet Obadiah and his circumstances we know nothing, and any surmise is complicated by the fact that parts of the book echo other texts in the Hebrew Bible. Verses 1b–9 follow parts of Jeremiah 49:7–16, which is also an oracle against Edom. Verses 1b–4 are close to Jeremiah 49:14–16, and verse 5 resembles Jeremiah 49:9. In these examples, the verbal agreement is very high. Other parallels, with less extensive but significant verbal agreement, include Obadiah 8 with Jeremiah 49:7, where there are references to Edom's wisdom, and Obadiah 16 with Jeremiah 49:12, where the common theme links drinking and its relation to punishment. Parallels can also be drawn between Obadiah and Joel (see especially Obadiah 15, 16, 17, and 18 with Joel 1:15, 3:17, 2:32, and 2:5).

What are we to make of these parallels? Has Obadiah (assuming him to have been an actual prophet) drawn upon a common stock of ideas used also in Jeremiah 49 and Joel, or was he dependent on Jeremiah and Joel? Or is it possible, advancing the most extreme point of view, that the Book of Obadiah was compiled by the editors of the book of the Twelve Minor Prophets out of already existing material in order to bring the number of Minor Prophets to twelve? We cannot answer these questions; but they indicate how this short book, which expresses the hope of a bright future arising from the ashes of disaster, presents the reader and the interpreter with an intriguing set of problems.

I. Jonah

The Book of Jonah is unique among the Minor Prophets in that it is a narrative incorporating a psalm. Although the well-known story of Jonah seems simple, its interpretation raises many questions.

The book opens with God's command to Jonah, son of Amittai, to go to Nineveh, the capital of Assyria, and to prophesy against the city. The same prophet is named in 2 Kings 14:25; he was active during the reign of Jeroboam II of Israel (782–747 B.C.E.) and appears to have prophesied that Jeroboam would restore Israel's borders to their fullest extent. But most scholars hold that the Book of Jonah is to be dated much later, and that the writer has constructed his narrative and his psalm using the name of a prophet from the distant past.

The story unfolds with great skill and irony. Jonah disobeys God by setting off by boat to Tarshish instead of traveling over land to Nineveh. A dreadful storm arises, during which Jonah sleeps while the crew desperately tries to save the boat. Lots are cast to see who is to blame for the storm. Jonah is identified as the cause, and he confesses that he worships the "God of heaven, who made the sea and the dry land" (1:9). The irony that he had hoped to evade the command of this God is apparent. He requests that he be cast into the sea, where he is swallowed by a great fish. Another irony of chapter 1 that anticipates what is to come is that the non-Israelite seamen fear and sacrifice to Yahweh.

Chapter 2 represents Jonah's psalm while in the belly of the fish. Even if added later to the book, the psalm has the dramatic effect of bringing the first main scene to an end with great skill. It echoes the Book of Psalms, in particular, in metaphors that speak of God's anger in terms of being overcome by floods or being taken down to the grave. In Jonah they receive a new, existential content without losing their metaphorical power. Indeed, the psalm powerfully proves the truth of what Jonah confessed when the casting of lots identified him as the cause of the storm: he indeed worships the God who made the seas and the dry land. Even while he is in the depths of the sea, he is not cut off from God, who hears his prayer and grants him deliverance.

Deliverance, however, means the resumption of duty, and the command to go to Nineveh comes a second time (chapter 3). The result of Jonah's preaching of imminent judgment is that the people of Nineveh (who are Assyrians) repent, from the king on down. God decides not to bring judgment upon them. Again, the irony is profound, bordering on bitter. If Jonah had been preaching in the capital of Israel, for instance, would the result have been the same? Chapter 4 records Jonah's anger that God did not punish Nineveh. The book closes with God making the point, by means of the parabolic story of Jonah and the plant that gave Jonah shade, that he cares for the people and also the animals of Nineveh and would not delight in their needless destruction.

This simple story can be read at many levels. Older scholarship, taking the Book of Jonah as a protest against the nationalistic policies of Ezra and

Nehemiah, dated it during the fourth century B.C.E., which is quite plausible chronologically (and is the view taken here). But God's willingness to be gracious to non-Israelites is probably not the book's main point, even though the importance of this theme is evident. The central problem of the book seems to be that of true and false prophecy. Jonah turns out to be a false prophet according to the criterion of Deuteronomy 18:22, where a prophet is false if what he says does not take place. Told by God to say that Nineveh would be overthrown in forty days, Jonah feared that this would not come to pass, and he refused to go to Nineveh (4:2). And as a matter of fact, Nineveh was *not* overthrown (at least, not in connection with Jonah's prophecy). The narrative presents the Deuteronomistic criterion as too simplistic and as inadequate to account for the inner conflict and pain experienced by prophets. In that it portrays the conflicted inner life of a prophet, Jonah as a book is similar to Jeremiah, and refuses to treat prophets as though they were merely mouthpieces without feelings or emotions.

The Book of Jonah asserts that God does not delight in destruction, but rather in repentance, and it generously develops this theme in respect of non-Israelites. Indeed, the choice of Nineveh as the recipient of mercy is remarkable, given the harsh words about Nineveh in Nahum and Zephaniah, although the fact that the book was written well after the destruction of Nineveh makes it something of a thought experiment. (Implicitly, the Book of Jonah asserts that Nineveh's destruction, when it finally came, must have been just.) Within the collection of the Twelve Minor Prophets, however, Jonah articulates a key principle that clarifies why later editors added oracles of hope to prophetic words of doom. By the criterion of Deuteronomy 18:22, Micah was a false prophet if he envisaged the destruction of Jerusalem and that it would not be rebuilt (Micah 3:12). Amos was a false prophet if he saw no hope for Israel. Yet in both these books (and also at the end of Zephaniah) oracles of hope were added by the postexilic editors to show that after judgment came restoration.

Jonah shows us the pain and anxiety involved in responding to the divine call to prophesy. It warns against oversimplifications and conveys the message to its readers that God responds graciously to repentance, and it explains why prophetic books originally concerned mainly with judgment had oracles of hope added to them by editors living at the time of the restoration that followed Jerusalem's fall.

J. Micah

1. Social History of the Period

According to Micah 1:1, the prophet – a native of Moresheth in Judah – was active during the reigns of Jotham, Ahaz, and Hezekiah, that is, between 739 and 698 B.C.E. The full name of Micah's town is usually taken to be

Presently at the museum in Iconium, this carving of a fish swallowing a man from Derbe in Asia, dated to 157 C.E., is reminiscent of the story of Jonah and its application within Christianity. (BiblePlaces.com)

JONAH IN JEWISH AND CHRISTIAN TRADITION

Artists and storytellers have long been attracted to the colorful tale of Jonah and the "whale" (although the text speaks of a "big fish"). The reluctant prophet occupies a place in the folklore, theology, art, and liturgy of Jews and Christians alike.

Classical Judaism provided a setting for fantastic embellishments of Jonah's story. According to one tradition, Jonah was the son of the widow of Zarephath whom Elijah restored to life (1 Kings 17). His flight from God at the beginning of the book and his fury at the worm that destroyed the plant that shaded him at the end notwithstanding, Jonah came to be thought of as one of the few perfectly righteous men the world had ever known. A Rabbinic haggadah preserves the tradition that when Jonah fled toward Tarshish, he was acting in the best interests of his people. Were the heathen Ninevites to repent at the words of one lone prophet, surely God would punish recalcitrant Israel, since the chosen people had remained impenitent despite the many holy men from God who preached repen-

tance to them. The Rabbis understood Jonah as one who sacrificed his life for the sake of his fellow Israelites.

The New Testament mentions two events from the life of Jonah: his stay in the belly of the great fish (e.g., Matthew 12:40) and his successful preaching of repentance in Nineveh (e.g., Luke 11:32). The Gospels also seem to cast the story of Jesus' stilling the storm (e.g., Mark 4:35–41) in language that recalls Jonah's adventures on the stormy sea. Teachers in the early church portrayed Jonah as prophetic proof that God had indeed intended that Gentiles should be saved. Jonah's tale also found a place in the early Christian polemic against Judaism. The repentance of the Ninevites became a symbolic warning and threat to the Jews: at the Day of Judgment, the men of Nineveh would accuse and condemn those who would not heed the words of Jesus – a prophet even greater than Jonah (Luke 11:32).

Both Matthew and Luke mention "the sign of Jonah," a concept that played an important role in early

Christian theology. This enigmatic phrase may refer to Jonah's miraculous deliverance from the great fish and to his effectiveness in persuading Gentiles. The miracle confirmed Jonah's message. The early Christian community understood that God had also authorized Jesus as a divine messenger by similarly delivering him from death. The Gospel writers were quick to draw a parallel between Jesus' time in the tomb and Jonah's three days in the great fish. Accordingly, scenes from the life of Jonah became a key feature of Christian funerary art. Jonah's theme of human repentance and divine mercy found a significant place in the liturgies of both church and synagogue. Jews read Jonah at the afternoon service of the Day of Atonement (Yom Kippur). According to the Mishnah, the Book of Jonah was chosen for that occasion because it illustrates the power of repentance and shows that there is no escape from God. The traditional liturgy for Ash Wednesday, the beginning of the Christian season of Lent, also includes a reading from Jonah.

Moresheth-gath (Micah 1:14), meaning "possession of Gath." But if scholars are correct in identifying Moresheth with Tell ej-Judeideh (Tel Goded), why should such a large and prominent settlement be named as though it was a mere suburb of Gath? Perhaps the equation with Moresheth-gath, or the location at Tell ej-Judeideh, is wrong. Yet if we accept that location, then Micah's home was a large site overlooking the important route through the Shephelah from Bet Shemesh to Lachish. (Today it is to be found on the left-hand side of the road just north of Bet Guvrin.) Even if this precise location is erroneous, the poem of Micah 1:10–16 locates Micah's home *somewhere* on the Bet Shemesh–Lachish route, since the following identifiable sites in that area are mentioned in the poem: Gath, Adullam, and Lachish.

Micah's location influences an understanding of his context and his message. He was not a Jerusalemite, but a provincial, possibly an elder of his

Aerial view of Moresheth-gath from the east.
(BiblePlaces.com)

town. He lived in an area that was fertile and also strategic, in that anyone invading Judah would use the route from Bet Shemesh to reach Lachish, Judah's second city after Jerusalem. In 701 B.C.E. the Assyrian king Sennacherib besieged and captured Lachish and recorded his triumph on reliefs now in the British Museum. The poem in Micah 1:10–16 implies an impending attack along the route to Lachish, although the date of the passage cannot be fixed, and seems to be prior to Sennacherib's destructive campaign. In 2:1–11 there may be reference to the militarization of the towns along the route, involving the seizing of houses and fields (2:2) and the eviction of inhabitants (2:9). This poem may, however, refer to the acquisition of property by the imposition of taxes that could not be paid, resulting in the indebtedness and ultimate dispossession of the landholders; but the forcible militarization of the area would also explain the bitterness that Micah felt toward Jerusalem.

If Micah 5:2–5a (Hebrew, 5:1–4a) in fact was written by the prophet (and many scholars would deny this attribution), his prophecy represented an important alternative to the view manifested in the many parts of the Hebrew Bible that glorify Jerusalem. At the end of chapter 3, Micah announces that Jerusalem will be destroyed and never rebuilt (becoming a wooded height). If his words originally continued in 5:2–3, then the prophet was looking for a new beginning that would switch the center of God's activity from Jerusalem to Bethlehem. Because the line of David had become corrupted in Jerusalem, it would be replaced by a new line, issuing from the small village of Bethlehem. Just as a leader from Bethlehem (David himself) had once delivered his people, so a new leader from that town would deliver them anew. Although this reading attributes more of the Book of Micah directly to the prophet than much scholarship would accept, Micah 1–3 is all but universally accepted as original. Those chapters establish that Micah was a provincial champion of oppressed small farmers in Judah, who protested their treatment by the central government in Jerusalem at a time when Judah was threatened with invasion from Assyria.

2. The Literary History of Micah

Scholars disagree on the material in Micah that should be attributed to the prophet, and sometimes the criteria of authenticity they invoke seem subjective. A common convention accepts only chapters 1–3 as original, while a maximalist view contends that, in addition to chapters 1–3, chapters 5:2–6 (Hebrew, 5:1–5), 10–15 (Hebrew, 9–14), 6:9–16, and 7:1–7 may also derive from Micah. If this was the original core of the book, additional material was added that reflects the exile and the exilic period (during the sixth and fifth centuries B.C.E.). The oracle of 4:1–5 approaches very closely to wording to Isaiah 2:2–4 and was probably added to soften the prediction about Jerusalem's fall in 3:12 and to reflect the fact that Jerusalem and its Temple had been rebuilt at the end of the sixth century B.C.E. Micah 4:6–5:1 (Hebrew, 4:6–14) implies that the Babylonian exile is imminent or has happened. The command to Zion to thresh her enemies is similar to Isaiah 41:15. In 5:7–9 (Hebrew, 5:6–8) the people are described as a remnant surrounded by the Gentile nations. This evokes the setting of the exilic or postexilic community.

    Micah 6:1–8 contains the famous passage in which God tells his people "to do justice, and to love kindness, and to walk humbly with your God" (6:8). Whether this whole passage is Micah's or not depends on the judgment about whether the references to Moses, Aaron, Balak, and Balaam (6:4–5) imply that the Pentateuchal traditions had reached something like their final form (which may not have happened until the fifth century B.C.E.) and were quoted here. The critical attitude toward the cult in 6:6–8 favors attribution to the prophet, because Micah's opposition to Jerusalem, whose "priests teach for a price" (3:11), reflects the prophetic stance prior to the destruction of the Temple. Yet the conclusion of the book implies that Jerusalem has fallen, an event that occurred long after Micah's death, and warns its enemies not to rejoice at its fate (7:8–10). There follows a prophecy of restoration (7:11–17) and an assertion (7:18–20) of God's pardoning love. The implied setting and the sentiments of the conclusion are appropriate to the situation of the exile rather than to Micah's complaint against Jerusalem.

3. The Structure and Contents of Micah

The Book of Micah as it stands is structured in alternate layers of judgment and promise of salvation:

Judgment	Promise of Salvation
1:1–2:11	2:12–13
3:1–12	4:1–8
4:9–5:1 (Hebrew, 4:9–14)	5:2–9 (Hebrew, 5:1–8)
5:10–6:16 (Hebrew, 5:9–6:16)	7:1–20

The book puts the words of the prophet into a form that makes the work into a dramatic whole, opening with a striking picture of the majestic coming of God to judge Samaria. The mountains and valleys are obliterated, and the magnificent buildings on the hill of Samaria are tossed into the valley below. However, it is not only Samaria that is targeted; Jerusalem is also under the threat of judgment, and this is bad news for the towns of the Shephelah along the road that has been fortified to protect the hill country of Judah. The poem of 1:10–16 is full of wordplays that the following rendering attempts to convey:

in the house of Aphrah [*bet le 'aphrah*]
roll yourselves in the dust [*'aphar*] (1:10)
Harness the chariots to the steeds [*rekhesh*]
inhabitant of Lachish [*lakhish*] (1:13)
The houses of Akhziv [*'akhziv*]
will be a deception [*'akhzav*]
to the kings of Israel (1:14)

Chapter 2 condemns those who dispossess the inhabitants from their lands (2:1–5) and includes a poem about an attempt to prevent the prophet from speaking, which opens and closes with the verb "to preach" (2:6–11; cf. vv. 6 and 11). After a small postexilic addition (2:12–13), chapter 3 introduces some of the toughest language condemning injustice found anywhere in the Bible. The rulers are depicted as cannibals, cooking the flesh and bones of the people to devour them (3:2–3); Zion is built on blood (3:10); Jerusalem will be destroyed and never rebuilt (3:12).

Micah's harsh words are then softened by the oracles concerning the exaltation of Jerusalem in the Latter Days (4:1–5) and a promise of gathering together those who have been scattered from Zion (4:6–7). A new deliverer from Bethlehem is promised (5:2–6; Hebrew, 5:1–5), and Jacob is described as a lion among its enemies.

Passages in the first person dominate chapters 6–7. God asks his people why they have become weary of him (6:3–5), and a representative of the people replies (6:6–7). God cries out that he cannot tolerate injustice (6:9–16). At 7:1–10 desolate Zion speaks, and after being reassured that she will be vindicated (7:11–17), rejoices in God's pardoning love (7:18–20).

The drama of the book moves from the awesome description of God's coming in judgment to the moving affirmation of his graciousness, from the detached description of the divine judgment on injustice to the personal and intimate discourse of God and Zion. This elegant literary development from exterior to interior and from judgment to hope no doubt added nuances to the original sentiments of the historical Micah, who expressed a more primal outrage at the unjust treatment of his people. The tradition and literary editing gave this outrage a deeper dimension that has not suppressed the words of Micah, but has created new ways of appreciating them.

K. Nahum

The Book of Nahum is a collection of prophecies usually said to be directed against Nineveh, the capital of Assyria, which fell in 612 B.C.E. Nineveh is mentioned at 2:8 (Hebrew, 2:9) and 3:7; reference to Assyria appears in 3:18; and the heading of the book reads, "An oracle concerning Nineveh." Were it not for this heading, however, readers might well be disposed to see the book in a different light.

Nahum 1:2–14 presents a poem that is an awesome statement of the avenging majesty of God. Not only does it draw upon stock imagery, such as God's coming in the whirlwind and storm (1:3), with resultant terror on the part of the mountains (1:5), but it is also an acrostic poem (i.e., a poem in which the first word of each verse follows an alphabetical sequence), although incomplete. Verses 2, 4, 5, 7, and 10 begin with the Hebrew letters *aleph*, *gimel*, *he*, *tet*, and *kaph*, and the intervening letters *bet*, *vav*, *zayin*, and *het* appear at 3b, 5b, 6a (the second word), and 6b. (The complete sequence would be *aleph*, *bet*, *gimel*, *dalet*, *he*, *vav*, *zayin*, *het*, *tet*, *yod*, and *kaph*.) If we were not predisposed by 1:1 to read this poem in connection with Nineveh, we would see it as a general warning of God's coming in judgment and the impossibility of human resistance.

After this first poem, how the material is divided proves crucial to its interpretation. The Hebrew numbering of chapters and verses begins chapter 2 at 1:15 in our English Bible. This contains a reference to Judah; and if what immediately follows is a continuation of 1:15, then the country being addressed in chapter 2 appears to be Judah rather than Assyria. It is true that Nineveh is mentioned in 2:8 (Hebrew, 2:9), but the Hebrew of this verse is very obscure ("and Nineveh is like a water pool, she is from the days; and they flee. Stand! Stand! But no one turns"), and it is not obvious that Nineveh's destruction is being described or predicted, although a case can be made for reading the material in that way.

In view of these ambiguities, some commentators have doubted whether chapters 1–2 were composed with the destruction of Nineveh in view. An attempt has even been made to argue that oracles originally addressed against Judah and Jerusalem have been reapplied to Nineveh.

In chapter 3, the material seems to be directed more toward Nineveh, and verse 7 reads:

> Nineveh is devastated;
> who will bemoan her?

There is also a reference to the sleeping shepherds (i.e., rulers) of Assyria in verse 18. Yet even in chapter 3 there is not any detail that connects the material with Assyria and Nineveh in such a way as to rule out other possible identifications.

All this implies that the interpretation of Nahum concerns more than just the fall of Nineveh in 612 B.C.E., so that the only critical question is whether the book was composed before or after 612 (or, in other words, whether it is a forecast or a subsequent description of the fall of Nineveh). On a cautious view, chapters 2–3 do forecast Nineveh's fall, including a reference (3:8) to the fall of Thebes, which was finally captured by the Assyrians in 661. In this case, chapters 2–3 would predate 612. To these poems, it could be argued, was added a part or the whole of an acrostic poem describing the awesome vengeance of God. This could have been added before or after 612. The heading then made it clear that the whole book concerned the fall of Nineveh.

Even if this cautious view is accepted, it must be noted that the book shows signs of reaching its final form during the Babylonian exile (in the sixth century B.C.E.). The words of comfort to Judah at 1:15 (Hebrew, 2:1),

> Look! On the mountains the feet of one
> who brings good tidings,
> who proclaims peace!

have been compared with Isaiah 40:9 and 52:7 (from Second Isaiah, during the sixth century B.C.E.), and this raises the possibility that 1:2–15 was originally addressed to Judah to promise deliverance from the Babylonian oppressor.

Within the book of the Twelve Minor Prophets, Nahum presents an interesting contrast to Jonah. The latter book used Nineveh as an object lesson to show how unresponsive Israel had been to the preaching of the prophets. It portrays a God of compassion who desires not to destroy Nineveh if he can possibly avoid it – for the sake of the animals as well as the humans. In Nahum, God's vengeance must be worked out upon a people that is, by implication, unrepentant, and who use animals as instruments of war. It is interesting that, in the Greek Bible, Nahum follows Jonah.

In the context of the book of the Twelve, then, Nahum is an example of the variety and creativity within Israelite tradition. Its poetry ranks among the most vivid in the Hebrew Bible, especially at 2:3–5 and 3:3–4, articulating a sublime view of the majestic power of God over a mighty foreign nation. Its explicit references to Nineveh require it to be read together with the completely different Book of Jonah, and the relationship between those two books supports the growing opinion among scholars that the individual Minor Prophets must be taken together as a single book.

L. Habakkuk

Among the other Minor Prophets, Habakkuk presents an unusual degree of similarity to the Book of Psalms. Chapter 3 is mainly a psalm (headed "A prayer of the prophet Habakkuk"), complete with a musical direction ("to Shigionoth"), and 1:2–4 and 12–17 are comparable to individual laments. Chapter 2 features some difficulties, especially at verses 6–17. This is a poem with four sections, each introduced by the word "alas" and containing a criticism of social abuse. The obvious reference is to abuses in Jerusalem such as those summarized in 1:2–4. Yet as each section continues, it seems to refer not to Jerusalem but to an imperial nation. Some commentators have consequently argued that 2:6–17 was originally a denunciation of social abuses in Jerusalem that was expanded to apply it to Babylon. This view helps to explain how Habakkuk reached its present form.

The book begins with a complaint of the prophet in the form of a lament (1:2–4), grieving that the law is slack, that justice is not effective, and that the wicked surround the righteous. Such a complaint could have been voiced on many occasions in the history of ancient Israel; but a possible clue for dating Habakkuk emerges in 1:5–11 when God's reply says that he is rousing the Chaldeans (i.e., the Babylonians), with the implication that this is his way of addressing the situation. This suggests that the prophet was a contemporary of Jeremiah and that, like Jeremiah, he regarded the Babylonians, initially at any rate, as God's instruments for justice. A date between 610 and 600 B.C.E. might therefore be intimated.

The language of the prophet's reply to God (1:12–17) and of the oracle in 2:6–17 does not make it clear whether these are renewals of the complaint about injustice in Jerusalem or complaints about the Babylonians. Modern translators have disagreed. The Hebrew word "he" in 1:15 (which is not expressed separately but is included in the verb form) is translated as "the wicked" in the Revised English Bible and as "the enemy" in the New Revised Standard Version. In other words, the Revised English Bible translators think that the complaints are against wicked people in Jerusalem, and the translators of the New Revised Standard Version think that the complaints are against the Babylonians. A solution to the difficulty is that the prophet initially welcomed the Babylonians in 610–600 B.C.E. as God's punishment for injustice but then was appalled at their brutality. He then reapplied to the Babylonians his original complaint about the behavior of wicked people in Jerusalem. It is also possible that a later editor reapplied Habakkuk's words.

In reply to Habakkuk's complaint in 1:12–17 God tells him to write down on tablets a vision for the end time, in which pride and wealth will perish and those who are righteous will be sustained by their faithfulness (2:2–5). There follows the powerful poem of 2:6–17, which condemns creditors, those who profit unlawfully, those who build by means of bloodshed, and those who make their neighbors get drunk (a metaphorical description of despoiling them). These accusations are applied implicitly to Babylon. This assessment is reinforced at 2:18–20, which condemns idols and their makers in terms very similar to Isaiah 40:18–20 and 42:17, where Babylonian idolatry is attacked.

Chapter 3 is entirely different. It is a psalm in the tradition of Psalm 68, speaking of God's coming from the south (Teman and Mount Paran) in warlike majesty to rescue his people. It is similar to other passages in the Hebrew Bible that celebrate God's warlike deeds in the past (e.g., Judges 5; Psalm 68). Its implications are clear for the book as a whole (whether or not it is a later addition): God's justice executed through human agency will be less than perfect and may bring no improvement, in which case God's own assertion of his just rule is required and will happen in the future as it did in the past. This brings the response that climaxes the book's expression of hope:

> Though the fig tree does not blossom,
> and no fruit is on the vines;
> though the produce of the olive fails,
> and the fields yield no food;
> though the flock is cut off from the fold,
> and there is no herd in the stalls,
> yet will I rejoice in the LORD;
> I will exult in the God of my salvation.
>
> (3:17–18)

M. Zephaniah

According to the heading in Zephaniah 1:1, the prophet Zephaniah was active during the reign of Josiah (640–609 B.C.E.). The contents of the book are largely consistent with this information, if we assume that Zephaniah's ministry fell within the early part of Josiah's reign, before the king began to reform his nation's religion in 622. Judah and Jerusalem are portrayed as places where there were idolatrous priests and where the Canaanite god Baal (1:4) and the host of heaven (i.e., sun, moon, and stars) were worshiped. Zephaniah addresses conditions in which officials adopt foreign (probably Assyrian) dress (1:8) and wealthy trading classes act unjustly (1:10–13). A particularly strong

HABAKKUK AT QUMRAN

One of the most interesting sectarian documents found at Qumran is the *pesher*, a Hebrew term meaning "commentary" or "interpretation," on Habakkuk. Among the first of the Dead Sea Scrolls to be published, the *Habakkuk Pesher* consists of twelve columns of running commentary on nearly the whole text of Habakkuk 1–2. The scroll has illuminated the textual development of the Hebrew Bible, the literary study of Habakkuk, and the history and practice of the Qumran community.

Text critics who have studied the *Habakkuk Pesher* have found nearly 135 distinct occurrences where the Qumran scroll's text varies from the received text of the Hebrew Bible. Some of the discrepancies resulted from simple scribal errors. However, many differences seem to indicate that the biblical text represented in the Qumran scrolls is based on a textual tradition separate from the traditional Masoretic Text. (The Masoretic Text was established around 800 C.E. by a group of Jewish scribes who added vocalization to the consonantal Hebrew text.) Scholars have used material like the *Habakkuk Pesher* in their attempts to unravel the complicated textual traditions of the Hebrew Bible in the period before the traditional text became standardized.

The *Habakkuk Pesher* does not include the text of Habakkuk's third chapter, a fact that some scholars have used to support the hypothesis that the liturgical poem in Habakkuk 3 was a later addition to the book. Biblical critics have long suspected that Habakkuk's third chapter was not original, but specialists in the literature of Qumran are hesitant to use information drawn from the *Habakkuk Pesher* as evidence in this ongoing debate. They speculate that while the textual tradition from which the Qumran sectarians drew their Scriptures may not have included the third chapter, it is also possible that the Qumran interpreters simply did not care to comment on the third chapter since it did not lend itself well to the style of exposition they had used for chapters 1 and 2, in which they systematically related Habakkuk's prophecies to the history of their own group.

The *Commentary on Habakkuk* is only one example of the literary genre *pesher*, which the group at Qumran embraced. Researchers have also found extensive *pesharim* (plural of *pesher*) on Nahum and the Psalms, as well as fragmentary texts with running commentary on parts of Isaiah, Hosea, Micah, and Zephaniah. These scrolls and fragments are verse-by-verse commentaries on lengthy blocks of biblical text. Usually they quote a passage from the Bible and then follow with explanatory remarks formally introduced by the words "the interpretation of the passage is" (*pesher haddabar*). The purpose of *pesharim* was to disclose historical and eschatological events in biblical prophecies. A gap existed between the biblical text's literal meaning and the community's interpretation of it. Thus the Qumran community used a series of hermeneutical devices to extract from ancient texts predictions relevant to their own historical existence. The leaders at Qumran tried to interpret "mysteries" that had come to pass at "the end of time," in which they believed they were living. With divine revelation, they thought themselves able to understand cryptic references to contemporary events that had been hidden in prophetic texts.

Three historical persons — or groups – play a prominent role in the *Habakkuk Pesher*. The central figure is the Teacher of Righteousness, apparently the leader of the sect. Much of the scroll relates the conflict between him and his opponent, the Wicked Priest. Scholars have attempted to draw a portrait of the Qumran congregation's early history from this conflict. Sometime during the rule of the Wicked Priest, the Teacher of Righteousness spawned a religious controversy over the interpretation of Scripture and *halakah* (legal material from the Scriptures or from postbiblical Jewish literature), as well as over the conduct of worship in the Temple. In the midst of this ongoing political rivalry, the Teacher of Righteousness and the community gathered around him endured persecution at the hands of the Wicked Priest. The text creates a typology of good and evil characteristic of the Qumran sectarian mentality: the archvillains, the Wicked Priest and the Man of Lies, head a "congregation of falsehood," while the poor, persecuted, but just Teacher of Righteousness leads the community chosen by God, "the congregation of his elect."

This scroll also describes the appearance of the Roman army in Israel under the name "Kittim," a fearful, warlike people who come from the islands of the sea to subjugate Israel cruelly. The term "Kittim" is taken from Balaam's prophecy in Numbers 24:24, where it designates a group that will play a major role in the Last Days. The Kittim are sent by God to punish the wicked priestly establishment in Jerusalem. The *Habakkuk Pesher* vividly characterizes the irresistible Roman legions, which ground out their victories with merciless ferocity.

The *Habakkuk Pesher*'s description of the Roman army bears the marks of fresh memory, and most scholars date the document to around 30 B.C.E., the period when Rome gained political control of Palestine. Identifying the Wicked Priest has proven a more controversial endeavor. Most specialists of Qumran literature nominate either Jonathan or Simon Maccabee, the first two Hasmonean priests (152–134 B.C.E.). In light of the existing data from published texts, an identification of the Teacher of Righteousness does not seem possible.

Excavation at Qumran showing what is usually identified as the sciptorium, where manuscripts would have been produced. Daniel Gebhardt/(BiblePlaces.com)

attack on those in authority occurs in 3:3–5. The officials and judges are described as lions and wolves, the prophets as faithless, and the priests as having profaned what is sacred. All this fits well with what the Hebrew Bible tells us elsewhere about the reign of Manasseh (698–642 B.C.E.), which preceded Josiah's (with Manasseh's son Amon reigning for only two years, 642–640 B.C.E.). This was a time when paganism and injustice were rife (2 Kings 21:1–18), to some extent as a result of Judah's subjugation to Assyria, against which there is an oracle of judgment in Zephaniah at 2:13–15.

The bulk of the book fits plausibly into the period when the boy Josiah had begun to reign, but when many abuses from Manasseh's rule persisted. It is also apparent that Zephaniah contains some postexilic material. In particular, 3:14–20 has strong echoes of Isaiah 40–66, and this section's command to Zion to rejoice because God's judgments against her have ceased provides Zephaniah with an optimistic ending.

The remainder of the book has a quite different thrust. Chapter 1 contains, in verses 14–18, an important passage about the imminent Day of Yahweh, normally understood as a time when God will defeat the enemies of his people. The idea that the God of Israel commands heavenly armies that fight against Israel's enemies can be found in poems such as Judges 5 and Psalm 68, and it helped to shape the final form of the accounts of Joshua's battles. For example, in Joshua 6 the Israelites did almost no fighting against Jericho; they merely obeyed God's instructions, and he ensured the victory. But in the hands of the prophets, the idea of the Day of Yahweh, when God would defeat Israel's enemies, was turned on its head to become a day of judgment against Israel. In Zephaniah 1:14–18 the military imagery is unmistakable and follows a passage that also portrays the coming judgment of God in awesome terms. This poem is directed against Judah and Jerusalem, as is the passage in 3:1–7.

Zephaniah includes a series of oracles against foreign nations that is more comprehensive than is usual among the Minor Prophets: Gaza, Ashkelon, Ashdod, and Ekron (2:4), other parts of the coastal plain (2:5–7), Moab and Ammon (2:8–11), Ethiopia (2:12), and Assyria (2:13–15). The details in these oracles are vague, so that it is impossible to link them with specific historical events. For example, Moab and Ammon have "made boasts" against Israel's territory (2:8), as must have happened on many occasions.

In chapter 3, God expresses the vain hope that Jerusalem will turn to him to accept correction (3:7). Is there a contrast here with Nineveh's repentance in Jonah? Zephaniah 3:8–13 speaks of a coming judgment of nations that will herald a new order. All nations will speak one language and will worship Yahweh, who will leave in Jerusalem a purified remnant worthy of the new order.

In the variety of the book named after him Zephaniah, about whom we know nothing except that he was possibly a descendant of King Hezekiah

(1:21), stands for the diversity of those servants of God to whom we apply the blanket term "prophet."

N. Haggai

In contrast to most of the Minor Prophets, Haggai (like Zechariah 1–8) is furnished with precise dates. According to 1:1, God's word came to Haggai on the first day of the sixth month of Darius's second year (i.e., 520 B.C.E.). Further datings at 2:1, 10, and 20 take us to the twenty-first day of month seven and the twenty-fourth day of month nine. There is also a date at 1:15 (the twenty-fourth of the sixth month) that is not easy to fit into the context. Thus, Haggai's recorded oracles fit into a period of about four months in 520 B.C.E.

The book mainly concerns the rebuilding of the Temple that the Babylonians had destroyed. Haggai 1:2 cites the opinion of the people that "the time has not yet come to rebuild the LORD's house." The prophet insists in reply (1:4–6, 7–11) that recently the people have suffered through bad harvests because they have been more concerned with their own houses than with rebuilding God's house. As a result of Haggai's prophecy, the people, led by the Davidic descendant Zerubbabel and the high priest Joshua, begin work on the Temple (1:12–14), and God encourages this work (2:1–9). Despite apparently disappointing results (2:3), God promises that he will shake the heavens, the earth, the sea, and the nations, and that the latter splendor of the Temple will be greater than the former.

The mood changes in Haggai 2:10–14. Here Haggai asks the priests for a ruling on the relative potency of clean and unclean objects, a request that presupposes the increasing power of the priesthood. The answer is that unclean things can defile holy things but that clean things cannot purify defiled things. The application is then made to the people's situation. Their holy task – presumably, rebuilding the Temple – can become defiled if what the people offer is unclean. Some scholars have seen this cryptic passage as a reference to the involvement of "outsiders" such as Samaritans in the rebuilding work, but such an interpretation requires reading into the text references that are not apparent. Two other interpretations are more likely: first, that the unclean work by the people is their lack of justice (cf. Isaiah 1:12–17); second, that their offerings (e.g., of grain) are ritually impure. Haggai 2:15–19, which links bad harvests to the failure to rebuild the Temple and draws attention to the immediate benefits following the beginning of work on the Temple, is probably an expansion of the sentiment of chapter 1. The prophet Haggai's larger point is that, because God's spirit is active within Israel (Haggai 2:5), despite the current state of uncleanness, the Temple *can* be sanctified, because divine Spirit can cleanse what no human agency can. As a result, blessing will come and the line of David can be continued (Haggai 2:14–23). The book concludes with another promise of imminent divine

ZERUBBABEL AND THE DAVIDIC LINE

Zerubbabel, whose name means "the offspring of Babylon," was a leader of the Jewish community in Babylon during the reign of Darius I. His ancestry and achievements are variously reported in historical sources from the early postexilic period. Zerubbabel most likely led a second wave of settlers back to Jerusalem from the Babylonian exile. Zerubbabel was closely associated with the program of his elder brother (or perhaps uncle) Sheshbazzar. By the year 520 B.C.E., Zerubbabel had assumed complete leadership.

Zerubbabel owed his prominence to his royal lineage. He was the grandson of Jehoiachin, the Judean king who had been exiled to Babylon in 597 B.C.E. The prophets Haggai and Zechariah allude to messianic hopes associated with Zerubbabel as the Davidic scion (Isaiah 11:1; cf. Haggai 2:20–3; Zechariah 3:8, 6:12). To Zerubbabel belonged the mantle of David's ideal kingship. Some scholars have understood Zerubbabel as the focus of Jewish nationalistic hopes during the early postexilic period, suggesting even that his followers were a threat to the Persian Empire's control of Palestine (cf. Haggai 2:21–2; Zechariah 4:6–7). More likely Zerubbabel, like Nehemiah, was groomed for his position within the Persian court. Zerubbabel may well have been named governor in order to conciliate the citizens of Yehud (Judah), who were hoping for the restoration of the Temple. It was in the Persians' best interests not to give full independence to the population occupying the strategically vital land between Asia and Africa.

For the prophets Haggai and Zechariah, Zerubbabel's essential role was as the monarchical representative necessary for the laying of the foundations of the Temple. The notion of an ideal Davidic king sitting on the throne in Jerusalem was only a future hope in their view. Zerubbabel's limited authority had only the *potential* to become, at some later time, the legitimate kingship of an independent state.

Zerubbabel may not have been the last of the Davidic line to be associated with the governor's office in the Persian subprovince of Yehud. Elnathan, Zerubbabel's successor, apparently strengthened his position as governor by marrying into the Davidic line. A recently discovered seal identifies Elnathan's presumed wife (literally, "maidservant") as Shelomith, a name known from 1 Chronicles 3:19 as a daughter of Zerubbabel.

cosmic action when nations will be overthrown and Zerubbabel will be made "like a signet ring" (2:23).

Haggai (and Zechariah 1–8, which shares a common editorial framework) is usually interpreted in terms of Ezra 2:2, 3:1–13, 4:1–3, 5:1–2, and 6:13–15. According to the context established in Ezra, Zerubbabel and Joshua had returned from exile in Babylon and were encouraged by Haggai and Zechariah to rebuild the Temple, and that task was completed in the sixth year of Darius (515 B.C.E.; Ezra 6:15). However, this comparative approach is not without difficulty. According to other information in Ezra, the exiles returned from Babylon in 539 B.C.E. and were led by Sheshbazzar, who laid the Temple's foundation (Ezra 1:8, 11; 5:16). No doubt it is possible to harmonize Ezra and Haggai; but it still needs to be asked why nearly twenty years elapsed between the return from exile and the surge of building activity inspired by Haggai and Zechariah. A further question is whether Ezra 3 implies that Zerubbabel began work immediately (i.e., in 539/8 B.C.E.), and how we can reconcile the impressive contribution to the rebuilding described in Ezra 3 with the meager progress by 520 implied in Haggai 2:1–9.

In view of these questions it has already been argued that the writers of Ezra (which was composed around 400 B.C.E.) used Haggai and Zechariah (which were written around 520 B.C.E.) as sources for a general reconstruction of the period. Although the reconstruction in Ezra was in no sense a deliberate falsification, it was nonetheless inaccurate.

Even if we accept that the writer(s) of Ezra made mistakes in working out what had happened on the basis of the information available, we must agree that the use made of Haggai was not unreasonable. Haggai says nothing about a return from exile; but a change in the political circumstances of Judah must lie behind the prophet's activity. To have attempted to rebuild the Temple while Judah was part of the Babylonian Empire would have been regarded as rebellion. Only with the defeat of Babylon by Persia in 540 B.C.E. did rebuilding become an option. The existence and encouragement of that option needed to be made known to those living in Judah. This would most likely come from returnees from Babylon or from a newly appointed governor.

Questions remain. Why was Joshua, the high priest, apparently content to be priest of a ruined (or, at any rate, unbuilt) Temple? Why were the people satisfied with this situation? Even if these questions must remain unanswered, Haggai contains sufficient information for us to glimpse this situation. A series of catastrophic harvests enabled Haggai to counter the general view that the time was not right for rebuilding the Temple. In a situation where self-interest had concentrated people's attention on their own welfare, perhaps to the neglect of social justice for the poor, the prophet was able to urge the people to turn to God by way of joining in the work of rebuilding the Temple. The result was that the harvests improved, and Haggai senses a renewal of hope that would lead swiftly to divine action to crush the nations and restore the glory of the Temple. Even if these hopes were not immediately realized, they played their part in the reestablishing of the Jewish community in Judah in the late sixth century B.C.E.

O. Zechariah

Zechariah includes more chapters (fourteen) than any of the other Minor Prophets, and the book consists of two quite distinct parts. Scholars see the dates given at 1:1, 1:7, and 7:1 as a continuation of the scheme in Haggai. In Haggai, the oracles were dated between the sixth and ninth months of Darius's second year (520 B.C.E.). Zechariah's visions are dated to the eighth month of 520 B.C.E. (1:1), the twenty-fourth day of the eleventh month of 520 (1:7), and the fourth day of the ninth month of 518 (7:1). With chapter 9 we have a complete change. The material is not dated and is introduced by the heading "An Oracle," as is the material in chapter 12.

These indications have led to the view that Zechariah should be divided into two "books," chapters 1–8 and 9–14 (or even into three, chapters 1–8, 9–11, and 12–14). The presentation of the text supports this division into two books, although the material included was no doubt generated through a more complex process than two simple stages of edition.

1. Zechariah 1–8

The core of Zechariah is a series of seven visions, whose original form was probably as follows:

1. Four horsemen who have patrolled the earth and found it at peace (1:8–12)

2. Four horns that scattered Judah, and four blacksmiths come to strike them down (1:18–21 [Hebrew, 2:1–4])

3. A man measuring Jerusalem with a measuring line (2:1–5 [Hebrew, 2:5–9])

4. The lampstand with seven lamps, and two olive trees (4:1–6a [to "he said to me"], 10b [from "these seven"]–14); the anointed son of David and the anointed priest

5. The flying scroll, which is a curse (5:1–4)

6. The woman in the basket taken to Shinar (5:5–11)

7. Four chariots representing four winds or spirits patrolling the earth (6:1–8)

A symmetrical pattern is probably implied:

1. Four horsemen patrolling the earth
  2. Judah's enemies defeated
    3. Jerusalem restored
      4. The two anointed ones
    5. The wicked cut off from the land
  6. The land's guilt removed
7. Four chariots patrolling the earth

Taken in this way the visions center on the two anointed leaders. The two preceding visions concern the defeat of Judah's enemies and the rebuilding of Jerusalem, and the two following visions depict the spiritual and moral cleansing of the land. The visions set the events in the context of God's universal rule.

We do not know whether the date of the visions given at 1:7 (the twenty-fourth of the eleventh month of Darius's second year, i.e., 520 B.C.E.) is the date on which the visions were seen or conceived. If so, then the year 520 B.C.E. would perhaps be late for visions of restoration, since at least some Jews had already returned to Jerusalem from Babylon in 539. No doubt, however, further incentives for return proved necessary over the years, and Zechariah's visions might well have fulfilled that need. We might also surmise that the visions were composed in Babylon shortly before Cyrus of Persia conquered the city and released the Jews from captivity in 539. In that case, the visions would have been written slightly later than Isaiah 40–55; and it is noteworthy that a passage such as 2:6–12 (Hebrew, 2:10–16) has many similarities with Isaiah 40–55.

In the form in which we have Zechariah, the visions (whenever they were initially conceived) have been set in the context of the events of 520 B.C.E., when the prophets Haggai and Zechariah encouraged Zerubbabel and the high priest Joshua to rebuild the Temple. The Temple as such does not have the prominence in Zechariah that it does in Haggai; instead, the main themes are restoration and cleansing. Whoever the two anointed figures in Zechariah 4:14 were originally understood to be, in the edited form of Zechariah they are Zerubbabel (explicitly) and Joshua (implicitly).

In the central vision of the seven visions, an expansion refers explicitly to Zerubbabel (4:6b–10a). But it is also possible that, by the time the book reached its final form, Zerubbabel had disappeared from the scene and only Joshua remained. This possibility is suggested by chapter 3, which breaks the sequence of the visions (taking the form of a vision, but differing from the seven in that no interpreting angel appears). Joshua alone appears and is promised that God's servant, "the Branch," *will* come (3:8). "The Branch" is probably a future royal figure. In 6:9–14 the prophet is told to collect silver and gold in order to make a crown, according to the Greek and Syriac versions, or crowns, according to the Hebrew. However, only one crown is used in the narrative and is placed on the head of Joshua, the high priest. But the high priest is not the focus of the passage. The focus is again "the Branch" (6:12), who has royal honor and will sit on his throne with a priest at his side.

The obscurity of this passage has led to much speculation. Was there an attempt to crown Zerubbabel as king, and was he removed or executed by the Persians? Was the passage reworked when Zerubbabel simply died or moved away before the hoped-for glory had materialized? We do not know, and Zechariah 1–8 remains a tantalizing text as a result.

The visions are confined to chapters 1–6. Chapters 7–8 are different in content and possibly serve as a bridge to the material in chapters 9–14. Zechariah 7:1–7 concerns a question to priests about fasting, and the answer given there and in 7:8–14 appears to condemn insincere fasting and to command social justice, and to link up with the concerns of Haggai 2:10–14. The similarity of this theme with Isaiah 58 is also striking. Chapter 8 continues the theme of fasting (8:18–19) and justice (8:16–17), and looks forward to hopeful days for the Jerusalem community. The strong impression gained from this chapter is that although the foundation of the Temple has been laid, times are still hard for the people of Judah.

2. Zechariah 9–14

Chapters 9–14 contain much strange and fascinating material, especially interesting to Christian readers because it influenced the presentation of the Passion of Jesus in the Gospels. In 9:9 a king rides into Jerusalem on a donkey, as Jesus entered into Jerusalem (cf. Matthew 21:5). Zechariah 11:12 is part of an involved series of prophetic actions in which a "shepherd" is paid his wages: thirty shekels of silver. An identical sum of money is paid to Judas for betraying Jesus (Matthew 26:15). In the narrative of Jesus' Passion, Matthew 26:31 quotes Zechariah 13:7:

> I will strike the shepherd,
> And the sheep of the flock will be scattered.

It is also noteworthy that in Zechariah 12:10–14, in the context of the promise of God to "pour out a spirit of compassion and supplication on the house of David," there is an obscure reference to "one whom they have pierced." This is reminiscent of the piercing of the side of Jesus in John 19:34, and the connection with Zechariah is explicitly made in John 19:37.

Weaving such vivid images together, Zechariah 9–14 articulates the following main themes:

1. The restoration of Judah and the gathering of exiles (9:11–17, 10:7–12)
2. Battles of the nations against Jerusalem (12:1–9, 14:1–15)
3. Divine condemnation of the "shepherds" (i.e., leaders; 10:3–5, 11:4–17, 12:7–9)

These themes are plain, but they involve difficulty in dating and interpreting the chapters. On the one hand, the passages about gathering the exiles and restoring Judah could be exilic, and thus earlier than the dates given for Zechariah 1–8 (520–500 B.C.E.). On the other hand, the material about the nations warring against Jerusalem gives the impression of being later in the postexilic period, perhaps during the fourth century B.C.E. But there is a further factor, and that is that Zechariah 9–14 seems to include echoes, perhaps deliberate allusions, of others parts of the Hebrew Bible.

The theme of the "shepherds" is one that appears in Ezekiel 34; and the passages about the wars against Jerusalem have the same flavor as Ezekiel 38–9, the threat of Gog of Magog. Another hint of Ezekiel surfaces at 14:8, which reads, "On that day living waters shall flow out of Jerusalem" (cf. Ezekiel 47:1–5). A remarkable allusion features at 13:5, in a passage that promises the removal of prophets from the land (and idols and unclean spirits). Any who prophesy must be pierced through by their parents (13:3), and there is a promise that on the day that God acts decisively, prophets will no longer deceive but will say, "I am no prophet; I am a tiller of the soil" (13:5). This is a clear reference back to Amos 7:14, where that prophet declares that he is not (or has not been) a prophet.

These allusions raise the possibility that Zechariah 9–14 is a collection of disparate material dating from the exile (during the sixth century B.C.E.) to as late as Hellenistic times (i.e., from the fourth century B.C.E. onward). One of the oracles about gathering in the exiles seems to date from the Greek period in the view of some scholars, given its explicit reference to Greece (9:13). Attempts have also been made to see a reference to the split between Jews and Samaritans at 11:14, where the prophet breaks the staff named Unity. But we do not know exactly when this split took place.

Can anything be said about the community or circle that produced Zechariah 9–14? Some scholars have argued that the "apocalyptic" nature of the material indicates its setting in an antiestablishment, eschatological group, but these chapters do not fit the profile of such circles. The strictures against the "shepherds" could indicate an antiestablishment perspective, but then many prophets, even such obviously "establishment" figures as Isaiah, condemned rulers (see Isaiah 1:10–15). The polemic against prophets in chapter 13 is of more specific interest in this context. Might this indicate a setting in an established, literary, possibly priestly circle devoted to interpretation of what is written, as opposed to the unscripted words of prophets? Meyers and Meyers (1993) do not accept this suggestion. They attribute Zechariah 9–14 to individuals who spoke within the framework of earlier prophecy and who emerged in the shadow of the prophet of Zechariah 1–8. The prophetic discourse of Zechariah 9–14, focused on the final pilgrimage of all the survivors of the nations to the Temple (14:16–21), is so consumed with the promise it envisions that its context remains elusive.

P. Malachi

"Malachi" is Hebrew for "my messenger," rather than the name of any actual person, as virtually all critical commentators agree. The opening verse (1:1) picks up the beginning of 3:1, "See, I am sending my messenger," and this designation was taken up as a heading. The beginning of the Book of Malachi ("An oracle. The word of the LORD to Israel by Malachi") is similar to headings in Zechariah (9:1 and 12:1).

Malachi takes on a unique literary form within the Hebrew Bible, citing and answering a series of questions that were important to the people or their priests. These questions refer to God in either the second or third person:

1:2	How have you [God] loved us?
1:6	How have we despised your name?
1:7	How have we polluted [the altar]?
2:14	Why does he [God] not [accept our offering]?
2:17	How have we wearied him?
3:8	How are we robbing you?
3:13	How have we spoken against you?

In some cases, further statements from the people or their priests implicitly answer the questions, or explain God's attitude toward those who question him. At 1:13, for example, the priests have said, "what a weariness this is," concerning the exact observance of the regulations about offering pure animals to God in sacrifice. At 2:17, in turn, God has been wearied by people. Likewise, God takes up the taunt against him that it is vain to serve him (3:13–15).

From these words spoken against God we can build up a picture of the community in Malachi. Their main concern was that evil and injustice had not been punished, whether by their leaders or by God. Malachi 3:5 lists as wrongdoers, soon to be judged by God, sorcerers, adulterers, those who swear falsely, and those who oppress hired workers, widows, orphans, and aliens. If this list accurately reflects wrongdoing at the time (although the catalog may be conventional), then the period concerned is most likely to be a little known period, the first part of the fifth century B.C.E., prior to the reforms of Nehemiah.

TEMPLE BUILDING IN THE ANCIENT NEAR EAST

A temple in the ancient world was not conceived of principally as a place of worship for the general public, but as the residence, house, or palace of a deity. As befits a divine dwelling, a temple contained all the furnishings that a royal resident might require. As the abode of a god, the temple had to be constructed of materials suitable to its exalted inhabitant. Furthermore, the needs of the resident deity had to be met. Temple sacrifice and other cultic acts in Near Eastern religions can be explained, at least in part, as the ritual provision for all the needs of the god.

Yet it would be a mistake to assume that the temple's role was confined to its cultic functions. Temples were central to the existence and vitality of political states in the ancient world, and were typically bound up with the founding of cities and with legitimating nations. No human king could claim authority to execute justice, levy taxes, or conscript armies without approval from the stronger forces of the cosmos, often conceived of as the king's divine "father." Building a temple in which the god took up residence was a powerful symbolic statement, signifying that the god sanctioned the dynastic power. The local citizenry could not oppose the dictates of rulers who had the approval of the resident deity. Erecting a temple in an administrative center was

therefore an integral part of establishing the authority of a political regime.

Once erected on its specifically prepared spot in the capital city, the temple became the hub of the economic, political, and legal life of the nation and dynasty that were responsible for its existence. The king was the chief officer of the state, but the officers of the temple were also important administrators. Palace and temple together constituted the administrative core of the realm. Thus a decision to build a temple was generally thought of as a monarchic prerogative. Building a temple was of momentous national importance.

In view of the structure's key role in ancient societies, invading armies typically destroyed the temple of a conquered territory. Refounding a temple that had been destroyed made a bold statement that a nation was once again claiming for itself at least a semiautonomous existence. Physical continuity between the old and new orders was expressed symbolically when a temple was refounded, if possible on the same site. Sometimes great effort was necessary to prepare a devastated site for new construction. In addition, a unit of building material removed from the former temple ruins might become a symbolically important part of the new building. (This foundation stone

is known by the technical term "first brick," or "premier stone.") Placing the foundation stone marked the completion of the preparatory labors mandated for the reconstruction of a ruined building. A deposit of metal nails or tablets (the "tin stone" of Zechariah 4:10a) was also laid in the new temple's foundation. This "peg deposit" was the symbol of the temple's future existence, as well as of its continuity with the past – a statement of optimism that the structure would endure for many years.

Ancient Near Eastern kings and queens were directly involved with the construction of temples in their realms. In Mesopotamian practice the king carried the bricks to be used in the new building and even formed some of them. The actual ceremony of refoundation was a joyous occasion. It was a celebration filled with much ceremonial rejoicing by the priestly establishment and the temple's professional musicians. The public also participated by expressing their support with loud exclamations of approval during the ceremony.

Zechariah 4:6–10 and Ezra 3:10–12 recount this occasion in the life of the postexilic community of Judah. The refounding of the Temple of Yahweh shares extensively in the heritage of temple-building practices common throughout the ancient Near Eastern world.

The lack of justice and fairness led to disillusionment: "It is vain to serve God" (3:14). The offering of animals as sacrifices was performed in a grudging manner that disregarded the regulations of the Temple (1:6–14). The expansion of Edom into southern Judah (if this is the background of 1:2–5) produced despair. Divorce laws, intended to protect wives, were being ignored (2:13–16). There was a refusal to pay tithes to the Temple and to give offerings to support the priests (3:8–12). This tableau of despondency was depicted against the background of bad harvests (3:10–12).

In the midst of disillusionment and frustration, the prophet whom tradition has called Malachi proceeds on two fronts. First, he insists in various ways that the people are in the wrong in their attitude toward God and the proper worship of him. Second, he promises that God will send his messenger, who will be like a refiner's fire; he will both purify the service of the Temple and put right social injustices (3:2–3). This emphasis on the messenger coming to the Temple reminds us how much of Malachi is concerned with cultic matters. The text is clearly the product of a Temple-based community in which both religion and justice had become corrupt. The identity of the messenger who will come and cleanse the Temple and society is not revealed in the earliest edition of Malachi (although we are about to discuss the addition that makes a full identification), and there is no way for us to know what or whom the writer intended.

Those who put the book into its present form, however, were explicit. The famous closing words about God sending the prophet Elijah (4:5–6; Hebrew, 3:23–4) belong to a later, editorial phase, and indicate a time when legends about Elijah began to multiply, putting him alongside Moses (mentioned in the previous verse) as an archetypical prophet.

> Lo, I will send you the prophet Elijah before the great and terrible Day of the LORD comes. He will turn the hearts of parents to their children and the hearts of children to their parents, so that I will not come and strike the land with a curse.

The account of Elijah being taken up into heaven in 2 Kings 2 led to the belief that he did not die, and that he would be sent back to earth to herald the coming Day of the Lord. The enigmatic reference to "my messenger" in 3:1 has been elaborated in terms of the Elijah legend.

IV. THE WORLD OF ISRAEL'S WORSHIP

A. Worship, Sacrifice, and Ritual

A temple-based community living in and around Jerusalem between the fifth and second century B.C.E. gathered together and systematized in the Hebrew Bible traditions related to worship and sacrifice that predate by many centuries the compilation of the texts as we know them. This material originated not only from Jerusalem but also from the northern kingdom of Israel, and derived from the activities of towns and villages at great occasions such as harvest festivals as well as from specifically religious centers. The editors of the Hebrew Bible effected their systematization by designating Moses as the founder of the priestly and sacrificial cult, and David as the founder of the musical and liturgical organization of the Temple. Any attempt to describe the historical development of worship in Israel and Judah has, therefore, to take account of the way in which the relevant material has been generated and assembled. Complete agreement among scholars in their resulting reconstructions cannot be expected, but a consensus has begun to emerge in broad outline.

WORSHIP IN EARLY ISRAEL

The biblical narratives present an idealized picture of the religious beliefs and practices of the Israelites who first settled in the land of Canaan, eleven clans led in worship by the priestly tribe of Levi. According to the texts in their presently received form, the Levites championed the faith of Yahweh, which contrasted sharply with the native Canaanite religions; Shechem and Shiloh served as the central cultic shrines where the twelve tribes joined together to worship the national God of Israel.

Archaeological evidence as well as the earliest sources incorporated in the Hebrew Bible suggest that the situation was not as clear-cut, that there was a large degree of continuity between the early Israelite cult and the religions practiced by the indigenous population of Syria–Canaan. The age-old practices and symbolism of Canaan became popular in the worship of early Israel. Numerous shrines, high places, and altars were scattered throughout the territories of the Israelite clans. Although some would have been of greater renown than others, enjoying a broader constituency, no one exclusive cultic center existed in premonarchic times. Some sites (such as Shiloh) incorporated structures, others were open-air sanctuaries, and

some (Hazor and Dan, for example) involved shrines and installations.

Moreover, no single priestly family seems to have had a monopoly on cultic leadership. In fact, priestly families and guilds probably competed against each other. Perhaps most important, the early religion of Israel is likely to have been syncretistic, a combination of the influences of surrounding cultures with the growing dedication to Yahweh. Even late in the history of the Israelite kingdoms, those who championed the worship of Yahweh alone faced a considerable challenge, sometimes from the royal establishment and almost always on a popular level. Yahwistic religion played some role in the settlement period, but no uniform faith held the allegiance of all Israel in the days before the monarchy.

Israelites probably worshipped Yahweh along with other gods from the pantheon of Syria–Canaan (e.g., Baal, El, and Astarte) and in a similar fashion. Local groups or families of priests oversaw cults that were organized around making sacrifices, celebrating ritual meals, and seeking divine oracles. Religious celebrations often involved music and solemn processions. Several narratives in Judges mention sacred objects associated with this kind of worship: the ephod (Judges 8:27),

teraphim, and various molten and graven images (cf. Judges 18:14).

In addition to the more elaborate sanctuaries adapted from the Canaanite world, the early tribes of Israel probably worshipped in open-air holy seats known in the Hebrew Bible as *bamot* (from the singular *bamah*, meaning "high place"). These country shrines were usually built on a height or a mound, sometimes on a natural outcropping of rock. They were used for making seasonal offerings and sacrifices similar to those of the fertility cults of the Canaanites and for ceremonies connected with clan memories of revered ancestors. Often marked by a tree or a group of trees, high places were generally provided with altars. A sacred wooden pole (*'asherah*) and stone pillar (*matztzebah*) were associated features.

In general, early Israel's worship was pluralistic. On the level of popular religion, and sometimes with official endorsement, this pluralism continued well into the period of the monarchy. But the increasing importance of monotheistic Yahwism in the later kingdom left its impression on the texts concerning the beliefs and practices of Israel during the settlement period. The orthodoxy those texts imply is more a later ideal than a historical reality.

1. Worship and Sacrifice in Israel and Judah prior to the Reforms of Hezekiah (727–698 B.C.E.) and Josiah (640–609 B.C.E.)

Prior to the seventh century B.C.E., many different holy places hosted the worship of Israel's God. Abraham and Jacob are described as building altars at Shechem (Genesis 12:7; 33:20) and Bethel (Genesis 12:8, 35:1–2), and Jacob exclaims after his dream at Bethel, "This is none other than the house of God" (Genesis 28:17). Saul and Samuel sacrifice to God at Shiloh, Gilgal, Mizpah, and Nob. In the story of Absalom's revolt against David, Absalom offers sacrifices at Hebron (2 Samuel 15:7–12) to signal his assumption of kingship, and David pauses at the summit of the Mount of Olives, "where God was worshipped" (2 Samuel 15:32). Prior to building the Temple in Jerusalem, even Solomon offered many sacrifices at Gibeon (1 Kings 3:4). Amos condemns the insincere worship offered at Beersheba in addition to that at Bethel and Gilgal (Amos 5:5). The Hebrew Bible (Judges 18:27–31; 1 Kings 12:29) refers to a famous Israelite sanctuary at Dan in the north, and excavations at Arad far to the south have uncovered an Israelite temple that was originally thought to date to the tenth century but is now considered to be somewhat later.

Texts and excavations together yield a picture of many sanctuaries serving the needs of local populations, although little detail emerges concerning what went on at these sanctuaries. Perhaps they mainly served the particular needs of families and individuals, who could offer their sacrifices locally in time of illness or give thanks for the birth of a child. These sanctuaries provided places where a slave might affirm his lifelong loyalty to his master (Exodus 21:5–6), and where people took legal disputes that could not otherwise be settled. We gain a glimpse of what went on at a local sanctuary in the opening chapters of 1 Samuel. Elkanah used to go up each year to offer sacrifice at Shiloh (1 Samuel 1), and other worshippers also brought sacrifices, from which the priests (wrongly) profited (1 Samuel 2:12–17). Yet these glimpses provide little hard information.

Israelite worship did not take place exclusively at local sanctuaries, as the history of Passover illustrates. The origin of Passover can only be surmised, but it seems clear it was observed as a family celebration in the northern kingdom of Israel until Hezekiah (2 Chronicles 30) and Josiah (2 Kings 23:21–3) made it a national festival for Judah (and, by implication, Israel). Yet this centralization of worship was only possible because the festal calendar of Israel already implied a strong degree of coordination among local sanctuaries. Each major festival in the Hebrew Bible represents a week of harvest: in the spring, in the summer, in the autumn. Spring brings early grain, especially barley, and is also time to move the flocks on from one pasture to another. Summer sees the larger grain-harvest of wheat. Autumn is the last time of gathering for the cycle, and the grapes and olives and nuts of that season make it the most joyous time of all.

The calendar of ancient Israel developed profoundly theological explanations of these recurring festivals: Passover was associated with the Exodus from Egypt, Weeks or Pentecost with the solemnization of the covenant,

Inside the Iron Age fortress at Arad, where archaeologists found remains of a temple used for several centuries during the time of the divided monarchy. Though worship centers outside of Jerusalem were forbidden by the Law of Moses (Deuteronomy 12), high places flourished throughout the land according to the Bible. The sacrificial altar is visible in the outer courtyard. (Bible-Places.com)

and Booths (or Tabernacles, as it is also known) with the sojourn in the wilderness. Nonetheless, the primacy of agricultural practice and experience needs to be recollected throughout, if one is to appreciate the sense of the calendar and the genuine enjoyment involved in the festivals. The fundamental importance of the three great agricultural festivals is signaled by the requirement that every male of Israel appear before the Lord every year in Jerusalem at these times (so Exodus 23:14–17, 34:23; Deuteronomy 16:16–17), making them occasions of pilgrimmage. That is, of course, an idealized expectation, but it enables us to appreciate how deeply felt was the connection between the rhythm of the fields and the rhythm of God's choice of Israel. It could be felt in city, town, and country, wherever the biblical calendar was known. These harvest festivals, originally times of communal celebration and thanksgiving in towns and villages, were also, the Book of Ruth (Ruth 3) suggests, a time for wooing.

Other occasions of worship included an annual festival at Shiloh at which young women danced in the vineyards (Judges 21:19–21), a new moon feast presided over by Saul (1 Samuel 20:18–24), and a family sacrifice in

SANCTUARIES IN EARLY ISRAEL

The typical sanctuary of the Israelite tribes was a local operation serving one or more clans or villages, or at most one or two larger clan groups (or tribes). Individual families could even set up their own shrines, altars, or temples. Although the compilers of Genesis through 2 Kings present Shiloh as the principal religious and political center of premonarchic Israel, important sanctuaries seem to have been located in several towns during the settlement period. These early cultic centers included Shechem, Shiloh, Nob, Kadesh, Beersheba, Dan, Penuel, Bethel/Mizpah/Gilgal, Hebron, Gibeon, and Ophra.

Israel's first sanctuaries were likely patterned after the Bronze Age worship places of the land's indigenous peoples. Archaeological evidence suggests, for example, that the Canaanite sanctuary at Shechem was also used by the Israelites during the Iron Age. In Near Eastern culture the sanctity attributed to holy places frequently outlasted the physical structures constructed on them. Built originally around 1600 B.C.E., the temple-fortress at Shechem contained a massive earthen altar flanked by a pair of sacred pillars.

The altar was positioned to be visible from almost any place within the city. In the Late Bronze Age (ca. 1500 B.C.E.) the temple was renovated. A new pillar was erected in the front of the structure, which had been rebuilt so as to be oriented toward the rising sun. Another change came in about 1150 B.C.E., when a new stone altar replaced the earlier earthen construction. This newly modified structure is probably to be identified with the "House of Baal Berith" (the temple of the Lord of the covenant) mentioned in Judges in association with the story of Abimelech. The standing stone of Joshua 24:26 is also likely to be related to these structures in Shechem.

Stone pillars of this kind, known in Hebrew as *matztzebot* (from the singular, *matztzebah*), featured centrally in early Israelite sanctuaries. *Matztzebot* have survived in a wide variety of archaeological sites related to the period of Israelite settlement, and were common constructions in the sacred architecture of the area. The Gezer High Place, for instance, dates to around 1600 B.C.E., and its impressive arrangement of ten enormous stone stelae could well have been known to the early Israelites. The stones, some more than nine feet high, were set in a north–south line just inside the city wall. *Matztzebot* were central cultic objects that may have served as memorials for important ancestors, as witnesses to an experience of theophany, or as remembrances of a solemn covenant. They were sometimes set up on hallowed ground in the countryside, especially in association with sacred trees.

Commemorative stones appear in many geographical and cultural contexts. Sometimes the *matztzebah* served as an object of worship, especially in early Israel, when the cult of Yahweh would have been but one of many religious traditions sharing the same symbols and practices. Orthodox Yahwism rejected that particular understanding of the *matztzebot*, though such conceptions persisted on a mostly popular level. The Bible depicts Israelites as often erecting *matztzebot*, but not as ascribing divine power to them (Exodus 24:4; Genesis 35:14). Nevertheless, in Israelite tradition the *matztzebah* continued to be a monument to Yahweh's actual presence and as such a sacred object.

Bethlehem for David's family (1 Samuel 20:27–9). New moon and Sabbath festivals might bring the visit of a holy man (2 Kings 4:23). The point at which the Sabbath became a day of communal rest and worship cannot be specified, but the number seven, of course, stands out as basic to the entire calendar that coordinates the feasts, each of which was to last a week. The weeks of a month mark out the quarters of the lunar month, and each week ends with the Sabbath, which is itself a regular feast. (The timing of each major feast in the middle of its month corresponds to the full moon, as is appropriate for a feast of harvest.) The Sabbath year and the Jubilee Year (the Sabbath of Sabbaths) fit into the scheme that makes seven a basic unit of measurement. There seem to have been national festivals, especially

Early Bronze Age sacrificial altar, at Megiddo.
(BiblePlaces.com)

Horned altar from Beersheba, probably the
first of its kind now extant within the setting
of ancient Israel. (BiblePlaces.com)

in the northern kingdom, at which the covenant law was read to the
assembled people. Traces of this may be seen in Deuteronomy 27:11–26,
where the Shechemite Dodecalogue (Twelve Commandments) is rehearsed,
and Deuteronomy 31:7, where a reading of the law every seventh year at
the Feast of Booths is enjoined.

2. Worship and Sacrifice from the Reforms of Hezekiah (727–698 B.C.E.) and Josiah (640–609 B.C.E.) to the Exile (597/6 B.C.E.)

During 722/1 B.C.E. the northern kingdom of Israel fell to the Assyrians
and ceased to exist as an independent entity. Refugees from the former
northern kingdom made their way south to Jerusalem. Among them were
the prophets and guardians of Israelite traditions concerning the Torah. The
introduction of these traditions into Jerusalem changed how Israel's religion and worship were understood in Jerusalem. Hezekiah, king of Judah,
used his power to effect a reformation intended to free the worship of the

Tel Dan high place. This site covers nearly a half acre and dates from the tenth to eighth centuries B.C.E. (BiblePlaces.com)

people from practices that were now regarded as abuses. Worship by many ordinary Israelites at local sanctuaries had not been "pure" from the point of view of the new orthodoxy. The worship of the God of Israel was accompanied by popular superstitious practices, including fertility rites intended to assist the growth of crops and the birth of children, as well as consultation with mediums. Biblical condemnations of such practices (e.g., 1 Samuel 28:3–25; Isaiah 8:19; Micah 1:7) show how deeply entrenched they were, and iconography also yields impressive evidence for these folk practices. We must not overlook, either, the prophetic criticism of an official religion that offered sacrifice while ignoring the requirements of justice (Amos 2:6–8; 5:21–4; Hosea 6:6; Micah 6:6–8).

Hezekiah attempted to suppress all holy places other than Jerusalem (1 Kings 18:4–5, 22) and commanded the observance of the Passover as a national festival (2 Chronicles 30). His aim was to remove the "abuses" of local sanctuaries by closing them down altogether. How far he was successful reamins unknown; in any case, his reforms were short-lived, because during the long reign of his son Manasseh (698–642 B.C.E.) many local pagan and foreign religious practices reasserted themselves. Josiah (640–609 B.C.E.) tried again to centralize and control worship in Jerusalem. No doubt this reformation consolidated his own power and brought economic advantages, but it would be unfair to say that the reformation was motivated by purely political considerations. It was also the work of religious reformers.

One effect of these reformations was to begin the process of producing a coherent story out of the diverse elements that constituted Israel's worship in the preexilic period. Unfortunately, we do not know whether any of the psalms, liturgical practices, or rituals of sanctuaries other than Jerusalem were preserved during this process (although that seems likely), or whether it was only Jerusalem practice that was used as the basis for the regulations for worship and sacrifice in books such as Chronicles and Leviticus. Attempts have sometimes been made to see some psalms (e.g., 42–5) as originating in sanctuaries other than Jerusalem, but there can be no certainty in that regard. After the return from exile there was only one sanctuary, Jerusalem, so that the history of the Israelite cult was written from that perspective.

3. Sacrifice in Ancient Israel

According to the received form of the Hebrew Bible, Moses instituted a complete system of priesthood and sacrifice, and Exodus 25 through Leviticus, along with parts of Numbers, provide his instructions about these matters. Moses is not said to have commanded the building of a temple, although the account of the construction of the tabernacle and its appurtenances in Exodus 25–30 and 36–40 is written in the light of the arrangements in the Second Temple, which was completed in 515 B.C.E. after the return from exile, as well as in the Temple of Solomon. The history of worship in Israel was filled with more twists and turns than the final form of the biblical text suggests, and the same is true of the history of sacrifice.

The Hebrew Bible acknowledges that non-Israelites and Hebrews before the time of Moses offered sacrifices. Thus, Cain and Abel made offerings (Genesis 4), Noah sacrificed burnt offerings of all clean birds and animals after the Flood (Genesis 8:20–1), and Abraham and Jacob built several altars. The non-Israelite Job made burnt offerings for his children in case they had sinned (Job 1:5). The Moabite king's offering of his firstborn son as a burnt offering upon the wall of Kir-hareseth is said to have brought great wrath down on the invading Israelites (2 Kings 3:26–7). The Hebrew Bible recognizes, then, that sacrifice in the ancient world did not originate with Moses. Rather, the designation of Moses as the founder of Israel's cult situates the sacrificial system within the story of Israel's election as the covenant people.

The whole burnt offering ('olah in Hebrew), which reduced an entire animal to ashes, was a widespread type of sacrifice in the ancient Near East and practiced for a variety of reasons. Job, as we have seen, availed himself of the 'olah in case his children had sinned; but we must recognize the sin concerned probably refers at least as much to ritual as to moral acts. Armies before going to war might offer the 'olah (1 Samuel 13:8–12), as well as during war as a desperate measure (2 Kings 3:26–7). In the story of Noah the burnt offerings feature as a thanksgiving after the Flood.

Exodus, Leviticus, and Numbers attempt to present offerings as a coherent whole. Although in its present form this material dates from the fifth century B.C.E., priestly tradition about rituals, especially in oral form, was very robust, and the information that we have about sacrifices in the

Hebrew Bible almost certainly goes back to a time long before the exile, however much reshaping and reuse after the exile came into play.

Keeping in mind the main types of offering helps to rationalize the complex interactions that Israelite sacrifice involved. Leviticus 1 details the *'olah*, showing that any clean animal or bird could be offered. The sacrifice is described as providing a "pleasing odor" to God, a phrase that probably reflects the antiquity of this type of offering, since it is unlikely that the final editors of the Hebrew believed that God had a sense of smell such that he enjoyed the odor of burning flesh. The name of the burnt offering in Hebrew (*'olah* means a "going up") signals its exceptional status among sacrifices: the whole of the animal went up in smoke in order to give pleasure to Yahweh, and Yahweh alone.

Peace offerings (Hebrew *shelamim*, perhaps referring to "sharings" of the sacrifice) are described in Leviticus 3 and 7:11–34 and constitute another principal class of animal sacrifice. Only certain parts of the animal are burnt in this sacrifice, to which unleavened cakes or wafers may be added. Most of the flesh of the animal is shared and eaten by the worshippers. This class of offering appears to be connected with acts of thanksgiving, followed by a communal meal, and it occasioned lavish celebrations during the principal festivals of the year.

Sin offerings, meticulously described in Leviticus 4:1–5:13, 6:24–30, 8:14–17, and 16:3–22, represent a special case of peace offerings, because the parts of the animals ordinarily eaten are given away, consigned to priests or consumed by the flames, rather than eaten by the worshipper. These sacrifices are required when commandments are unintentionally broken (Leviticus 4:2), and the type of animal offered depends on the status of the offender. If the offender is the high priest or the whole congregation, a young bull is offered. For a leader of the people the offering is a male goat; for an ordinary person it is a female goat or sheep, and a poor person may offer a dove or a pigeon. In cases of deep poverty, a measure of fine flour suffices. The offender's status also affects how and where the animal is used. The higher the status, the more holy are the objects in the tabernacle to which the blood of the sacrifice is applied. Thus, in the offering for the congregation, the blood is sprinkled in front of the curtain and applied to the "altar that is before the LORD" (Leviticus 4:17–18), whereas in the offering of an ordinary Israelite, the blood is applied to the altar of burnt offering, which is farther from God's presence in the holy of holies. These operations with the blood of the offering were considered crucial, in order to sanctify afresh the sacrificial continuity that sin in Israel had vitiated.

A fourth type of offering, usually called a guilt offering but better regarded as a restoration offering, is described in Leviticus 5:14–6:7 (Hebrew, 5:14–26), 7:1–6. This offering deals with deliberate moral offenses among the actions it seeks to remedy; examples (Leviticus 6:1–6; Hebrew, 5:20–5) involve fraud and robbery. The offerings, of a ram or a lamb, the flesh of which is eaten by the priests (Leviticus 7:6), are made only after the damage incurred by the fraud or robbery has been made good, plus one-fifth.

For many offenses that we regard today as serious moral offenses, no sacrifices were prescribed in the Hebrew Bible, because the penalty prescribed was death. Capital offenses included intentional murder, striking or cursing a parent, kidnapping, adultery, and raping a betrothed woman (see Exodus 21:15–17 and Deuteronomy 22:23–7). To what extent these penalties were actually carried out we do not know. David survived after committing adultery and arranging for the offended husband, Uriah, to be killed in battle, although he did not escape consequent disasters (see 2 Samuel 12–20). When the death penalty was carried out for the prescribed offense, it was believed to purge evil from the people (see Deuteronomy 13:5), somewhat as sacrifice did.

How were sacrifices believed to be effective? Scholars have proposed various explanations, some of which have been influenced by general theories of sacrifice put forward by social anthropologists. Sacrifice has been seen as a gift, given in the mistaken hope that a god might be bought off, so that evil might be warded off and good produced. That suggestion of a payoff is ancient: the expression *do ut des* ("I give that you might give") is in the stock and trade of Greco-Roman expressions of disaffection with anthropomorphism. During the nineteenth century, Edward Burnett Tylor spelled out this idea as a general theory, that sacrifice is a bribe offered to a deity. Tylor was willing to admit that sacrifices might be offered and accepted in a symbolic sense, but he concerned himself only with the examples he could find of people giving so that deities might give in return. Yet the majority of known instances of sacrifice, which are far more routine, are simply not explained by this theory.

Before there were gifts, there was food, and William Robertson Smith attempted to explicate the consistent link between sacrifice and eating. He found that in the most ancient Hebrew sacrifices, the animal victim was presented at the altar and devoted by the imposition of hands. But apart from the fraction of the offering given to God, the greater part of the flesh was returned to the worshipper, so that God and worshipper were joined in the communion of eating the same flesh. Robertson Smith understood sacrifice as a communal act, and he argued with such force that the earlier, unreflective emphasis upon the individual in religious life, which predominated during the nineteenth century, was overcome. Rather, he correctly appreciated that sacrificial activity is irreducibly communal. Moreover, he recognized the social dimensions involved in all aspects of sacrifice, its celebration and consumption of the fruits of common labor. Sadly, however, Robertson Smith concluded that the god was in some sense eaten in sacrifice, and evidence for this theory is very thin. As a result, in biblical study the theory of sacrifice as a gift has all but eclipsed the model of communal eating that Robertson Smith developed.

James George Frazer's *The Golden Bough* was first published in 1890, just after the posthumous appearance of Robertson Smith's lectures, and has been through many incarnations. Frazer believed that the purpose of sacrifice was to free immortal spirit from the impairment and inevitable decay of being tied to a mortal being. Sacrifice is a form of liberating violence (from the point of view of the preservation of spirit), or of destructive violence (from the point of view of the victim destroyed). More recently, René Girard has argued an interesting variant of this theory. He maintains that the central problem of society is how to deal with envy, which is as endemic as it is potentially violent. The answer is to find a scapegoat, to whom social problems are attributed. The victim is then lynched, and the release of envy results in a replication of this sacrifice. Another view suggests that sacrifices were offered in order to cope with and to prevent violence within the postexilic community (Lohfink 1983).

Two French sociologists, Henri Hubert and Marcel Mauss contended that sacrifice is intended to maintain a balance between the divine world and the human world. The rite as a whole is one of either "sacralization," where the purpose is to increase the sanctity of the sacrificer, or "desacralization," where the purpose is to transfer the sanctity of the sacrificer to the victim. The purpose of the sacrifice is to protect or empower those who offer sacrifice.

For Tylor, sacrifice is tribute; for Robertson Smith, it is a communal consumption of deity. Frazer sees the death of the victim as the destruction of an envelope of power in order to release that power. Hubert and Mauss portray sacrifice as the knife's edge that balances the sacred and the profane. None of the paradigms just sketched is negligible: the simple fact is that each is based on some evidence. The problem for modern understanding is that no single one of them explains the others, nor can it account for the wide range of sacrificial activities in which worshippers do not deploy any particular theory of sacrifice.

The Book of Leviticus presents sacrifice in a way that is close to part of Robertson Smith's explanation, especially regarding the peace offering, or "sacrifice of sharings" (Leviticus 3:1). The notion that a sacrifice might involve worshippers in a meal is a commonplace in ethnographic studies, and it is specifically attested in patriarchal and Mosaic narratives. Jacob formalizes his treaty with Laban on that basis (Genesis 31:51–54), and Jethro celebrates both the Lord's greatness and the presence of Aaron and the elders thereby (Exodus 18:9–12). In 1 Samuel 1:3–5, it is recounted as a matter of course that Elkanah should distribute sacrificial portions in his own household. At the time of the sacrifice to solemnize the covenant, Moses, Aaron, Nadab, Abihu, and the seventy elders are particularly said to behold God while they eat and drink, and that festive communion is an example of a sacrifice of sharings (Exodus 24:4–11). The association is persistent in royal provision for feasts to be held together with sacrifices, whether the king involved be David (2 Samuel 6:17–19), Solomon (1 Kings 3:15; 8:62–5) or Hezekiah (2 Chronicles 30:22).

In Leviticus 3 the animals offered are the focus: they must be unblemished cattle, sheep, or goats, male or female (vv. 1, 6, 12). The offerer lays his hand on the animal and kills it in front of the tent of meeting (vv. 2, 8, 13). The priests take up their duties of throwing the blood and receiving the fat of the entrails, the kidneys with their fat, and the remainder of the liver that comes off with them (vv. 3, 4, 9, 10, 14, 15). Following the logic that the fat as well as blood belongs to God, the whole of the lamb's tail is also taken (v. 9). The priests offer these fatty portions for "an odor of pleasantness to the LORD" (v. 5; cf. vv. 3, 16), or as God's "food" (vv. 11, 16). While the "peace offerings" involved a fellowship meal with God, the eating of the flesh of the "guilt offering" by the priests meant that the worshippers were forgoing the meat they usually would have enjoyed. In the case of the sin offering, the offense was thought to pollute the sanctuary, hence the need to cleanse the most sacred parts of the tabernacle if the offender was the high priest or the congregation as a whole. In the rituals for the consecration of a priest or for the readmission of a cured "leper" (i.e., a person with a chronic condition of broken skin, resulting from one of several skin diseases) to the community (Leviticus 8:22–35, 14:2–32), certain common acts suggest that the ritual enabled the person to change status. The priest is removed from the sphere of the everyday into that of the holy, whereas the "leper" is brought back into the community from which he or she had been excluded. Noteworthy in both instances is the transitional period of seven days spent in the camp at the entrance of the tent of meeting (Leviticus 8:33–5, 14:11). This transitional period, together with the other offerings, effects a crossing of boundaries: in the one case into the sphere of the holy, in the other case into the sphere of the everyday. A similar use of the spatial categories of holy, everyday, and outside the community is evident in the ritual for the Day of Atonement (Leviticus 16). The goat chosen to bear the sins of the community is led from the holy place, through the camp, to the wilderness outside the camp (Leviticus 16:21–2), thus symbolizing the removal from the community of the sins that have been confessed.

Rituals such as that of the red heifer (for providing ashes that will transform water into a powerful agent of purification; see Numbers 19) obviously played an enormously important role in ancient Israel. Scholars and theologians continue to debate the balance between such practices and what has been called the spiritualization of sacrifice (the tradition that true sacrifices are the inward offering of heart and soul; see, for example, Psalms 50–1).

The Altar

The word "altar" renders *mizbe-ach*, a place for sacrifice in Hebrew; the term derives from the verb *zabach* (meaning "to slaughter"). There offerings were sacrificed and the people of God joined in celebrating the divine pleasure in this sacred and communal meal, a feast that they also shared with one another. In Greek the term *thusiasterion* bears the same relationship to the verb *thuo*. The English term "altar" derives from the Latin designation of a high place.

"LEPROSY," AN OLD CONFUSION

The noun *tsara'at*, whose basic meaning is "outbreak," appears over thirty times in the Hebrew Bible, predominantly in Leviticus, referring to a state of ritual defilement manifested as an interruptive skin or pigment condition, as well as a problem in cloth, leather, and the walls of houses. In the Septuagint, the Greek translation of the Hebrew Bible, *nega' tsara'at* ("strike of outbreak") was translated as *aphe lepras* ("scaly condition"); in the Latin Vulgate, this became *plega leprae*. The Greek and Latin phrases were drawn from medical language, implying a condition that spread over the body, rather than simply ritual impurity.

Tsara'at has continued to be translated as "leprosy," even though this term is not appropriate; leprosy as we call it (referring to the condition caused by Hansen's bacillus) was not prevalent in the Near East during the time the Hebrew Bible was written. Many scholars have suggested that the proper translation of *tsara'at* is "mold." Prior to its deforestation, Israel was damper than it is now, so that the problem of discolored, leaky, and bulging walls must have troubled ancient Israelite householders, especially since the principal building materials were not stone, stucco, and brick, but mud, wood, and thatching. Use of those materials to build structures with few openings for ventilation must have made "outbreak" a frequent result of variations of temperature and humidity, affecting walls, cloth, and human skin. The identification of a specific mold (Stachybotrys) that contaminates buildings and causes respiratory distress, memory loss, and rash, and the fact that mold has been present for millennia, gives support to the understanding of *tsara'at* as an outbreak of mold.

"Outbreak" continued to be a problem long after the time of the Book of Leviticus and its sources, as can be seen by the way in which Jesus is portrayed as dealing with the problem – in specifically Levitical terms – within the New Testament. The Synoptic Gospels agree in presenting the story of what is known as Jesus' cleansing of a leper early in their portrayals of his ministry (Matthew 8:2–4; Mark 1:40–4; Luke 5:12–14). In the story, a "leper" approaches Jesus, and for no stated reason, asserts that Jesus is able to cleanse him. Jesus assents, pronouncing the man clean, and ordering him (*a*) to show himself to a priest, and (*b*) to offer the sacrifice prescribed by Moses for cleansing. The only sense the pericope has within the literary texts is christological; by a variety of devices, all of which are obvious (cf. Matthew 8:17; Mark 1:45; Luke 5:15, 16), the link is made between the cleansing of the leper, Jesus' fame as a healer, and Jesus' true identity. But that christological meaning is clearly not the originating sense of the story, which is developed with respect to the offering prescribed by Moses (cf. Leviticus 13, 14).

The assumption of Leviticus 13 and 14, and therefore of the story in the Synoptics, is that "leprosy," or "outbreak" (*tsara'at*), comes and goes, and that its presence or absence can be detected. In Leviticus 13, where the issue is "outbreak" in humans (as distinct from in cloth or houses), it is clear that the great concern, and the cause of uncleanness, is broken flesh (13:15). The suspicion of "outbreak" arises when the pigmentation of the skin and accompanying hair changes, but a total change signals a return to cleanness (vv. 12, 13), since the fundamental concern is broken flesh, which puts people in proximity to blood (a taboo substance in Israel's system of purity). Accordingly, sufferers are banned (vv. 45, 46).

In the happy event one is declared clean by a priest, two distinct offerings are enjoined in Leviticus 14. The first is a local sacrifice and may take place wherever there is running water. The priest kills a bird in an earthen vessel held over the water, and then dips a living bird in its blood, having beforehand attached cedar, scarlet, and hyssop to it. He then sprinkles the "outbreak" sufferer with the living bird, and releases it (14:1–8). Purification results (cf. v. 9), after which the sufferer must offer two male lambs, a ewe, cereal, and oil; together they consitute a sacrifice for guilt, a sacrifice for sin, a burnt sacrifice, and a cereal sacrifice (14:10–20). Exceptional provisions are made for instances of poverty (vv. 21–32), but the sacrificial requirement from an owner remains onerous.

Within the setting envisaged in Leviticus, the story concerning Jesus therefore refers to a specific moment. The sufferer from "outbreak" attributes to Jesus the ability to adjudicate the status of his skin, and Jesus accepts the responsibility of telling him that he may proceed directly to the sacrifice that is to occur after cleanness has been declared. Although Jesus is not portrayed as taking over any sacrificial function, he is explicitly assigned – within the story's terms of reference – the authority to pronounce on matters of purity. Pharisees evidently were similarly involved, as an entire tractate of the Mishnah (Negaim) attests, but the Synoptic tradition had apparently lost explicit reference to the principal issue involved by the time the story was construed in the texts that are to hand. Indeed, by that time Jesus was widely held to have been above issues of "mere" purity, so that the story of the cleansing of the sufferer from "outbreak" became a cipher of christology. Jesus himself appears to have been keenly concerned with purity as such, in a manner similar to the Pharisees.

THE *TEMPLE SCROLL*

Among many important documents recovered from the Qumran community, the *Temple Scroll* ranks as one of the most significant, the longest of the Dead Sea Scrolls, consisting of nineteen parchment sheets sewn together to form a rolled document over twenty-eight feet (or 8.148 m) long. The late Israeli scholar Yigael Yadin acquired the scroll in 1967, which paleographic experts date to ca. 135 B.C.E. Most scholars credit its composition to the Essenes, one of the three major sectarian groups of Jewish antiquity known to us primarily through the writings of the historian Flavius Josephus.

The scroll's state of preservation varies greatly; the first section is missing entirely. Yet plans for a new Temple in Jerusalem do survive in minute detail: its courtyards, sacrifices, cultic ritual, and purity regulations. The *Temple Scroll* makes extensive use of biblical and nonbiblical material, and the work is broadly patterned after the Books of Exodus and Deuteronomy. Surprisingly, Moses is usually referred to in the first person, as if he were intended to be understood as the scroll's author. Large sections of the scroll are simply recapitulations of canonical texts from the Hebrew Bible. Frequently,

however, scriptural portions have been modified, elucidated, harmonized, or expanded.

Some scholars believe the scroll served the Qumran community as a supplement to the canonical Torah (the Books of Genesis through Deuteronomy), legitimating the covenanters' special cultic beliefs and festal calendar. Divergences between the *Temple Scroll* and the laws set forth in the Masoretic Text of the Hebrew Bible suggest that this work represents the establishment of a *halakah* (legal prescription of behavior) unique to the sectarians at Qumran.

References to the principal altars of Israel involve thematic and ritual patterns. They are best traced by following the development of phases in the growth of the Hebrew Bible, because that resolves the many references into differing usages of altars over time. The sources involved are conventionally called the Yahwist, Elohist, Deuteronomist, and Priestly. The interest here is not in defending that model, which has already been explored, but in following the order in which narratives concerning altars were generated, collating them with the Prophets and Writings as we proceed.

Sacrifice to Yahweh, from Abraham through David

Abram builds altars near Shechem and Bethel, and calls on the name of Yahweh there (Genesis 12:6–8, 13:4), as he later does in Hebron among the oaks of Mamre (Genesis 13:18). Isaac similarly builds an altar at Beersheba (Genesis 26:23–5). For both Abram and Isaac, the building of the altar is motivated by an appearance of Yahweh to the patriarch (Genesis 12:7; 26:24). Such an appearance also results in Abram's change of name to "Abraham" (Genesis 17:5).

Abraham and Isaac make their altars in the midst of travel, using unhewn stone and earth. Destruction of more elaborate altars dedicated to other gods becomes imperative (Judges 2:1–2) to clear the way for sacrifice to Yahweh. The story of Gideon in particular links the visible presence of God with sacrifice and with the triumph of Israel, the establishment of a named altar for Yahweh, and the removal of other altars, down to the detail that sacred trees are burned on Yahweh's altar to consume a bull (Judges 6:11–28). The commandment against making covenant with the inhabitants of the land, and the injunction to destroy their altars, pillars, and sacred trees (Exodus 34:12–17, with Judges 2:1–2) follows as a matter of course.

Throughout these stories, the conception remains that Yahweh takes part in a meal, which by his participation becomes a sacrifice. His participation might be direct or by means of an emissary or angel; in either case, a simple rock can become an altar when it is the place where Yahweh enjoys an offering. In the story of Manoah (Judges 13:8–23), hospitality to Yahweh's emissary reaches its climax when "the flame went up from the altar to heaven, and the angel of the Yahweh went up in the altar's flame" (Judges 13:20). Saul builds his first altar to Yahweh (1 Samuel 14:31–5) as part of his effort to get Israelites during a military campaign to cease eating their meat with blood: the *mizbe-ach* here functions as a center of eating meat in a pure state as well as a place of sacrifice, revealing how the two are intertwined.

Gideon exercised oracular powers after his sacrifice (Judges 6:33–40), and divine guidance is also offered in proximity to the altar to Israel as a whole at Bethel in Judges 21:1–12. Abuse of the prerogatives of the altar will feature as key to the prophecy to Eli that his sons Hophni and Phinehas would die (1 Samuel 2:27–36). Samuel takes their place, eventually building an altar in Ramah as part of his role as prophet, priest, and judge (1 Samuel 7:17). David, guided by his seer Gad, offers sacrifice on an altar he builds in order to protect Jerusalem from plague (2 Samuel 24:17–25), and the result is that "Yahweh was supplicated for the land."

The Mosaic Covenant and Its Altar

Exodus 20:24–6 has God prescribe that any stone altar should not be made with hewn stone, because that would pollute the structure. In particular, stepped altars are proscribed, on the grounds that they are a pretext to show the nakedness of priests. The worship of Yahweh must be unlike that of other gods. For that reason, an altar should not be abused by a murderer as a place of refuge (Exodus 21:14). By the same logic, the altar Abraham builds near Beersheba to sacrifice his son is not used for that purpose: human offerings are rejected, not because Abraham does not obey God, but because in his fear of God he learns that Yahweh desires the ram (Genesis 22:1–19).

Jacob constructs an altar in Shechem and gives it the name, "God, the God of Israel" (Genesis 33:18–20), signaling a divine encounter. God's appearance to Jacob is explicitly the occasion of his building the altar at Bethel, which he calls "God of Bethel" (Genesis 35:7). God demands the altar to mark where he had appeared to Jacob when the patriarch fled from his brother Esau (Genesis 35:1, referring back to Genesis 28:10–22, where a rough stone monument marks the place of the vision), and Jacob responds by making preparations that involve putting away other gods from his household (Genesis 35:2–3).

As with Abraham, Isaac, and Jacob, God speaks with Moses, and Moses builds an altar in response (Exodus 17:14–16), which he names, memorializing enmity with Amalek. These themes are articulated more elaborately in Exodus 24:4 and 6, where the altar is a pivotal part of Moses' covenantal sacrifice. The God of Israel actually appears to Moses, Aaron, Nadab, Abihu, and seventy elders while they eat and drink during the course of sacrifice (Exodus 24:9–11). That caps a scene in which Moses erects twelve standing stones together with the altar, representing the twelve clans of Israel that are about to accept the covenant whose wording Moses has written.

The covenantal significance of the standing stones in this scene is beyond dispute, yet it is noteworthy that arrangements with such stones configured around altars are a part of archaeological discoveries from the Iron Age. Twelve stones arranged around an altar provided points of reference for the relative positions of the sun, moon, and other heavenly bodies, so that sacrifices could be conducted at such installations at a precise, repeatable time. Even Balaam, although in the service of an enemy of Israel, is blessed by a vision of Israel's prosperity and dominance as a result of his offerings to Yahweh on sequences of seven altars (Numbers 23, 24).

When Aaron makes an altar before the molten calf (Exodus 32), it marks the height of his apostasy. Opposition to foreign cults and to degradations of Israel's worship especially concerned the early prophets. Elijah symbolizes their confrontative stance in the context of Mount Carmel, where by supernatural means his sacrifice on the altar to Yahweh that he repairs – carefully using the twelve stones that represent Israel (1 Kings 18:30–2) – prevails over the prophets of Baal (1 Kings 18:17–40). Elijah then slays the prophets of Baal, much as Moses dealt with the idolaters of his time.

The vehemence of these attacks is rooted in prophetic opposition to the kings in the northern kingdom of Israel. Jeroboam's altars in Bethel and Dan are associated with a proclamation that echoes Aaron's apostasy: "Behold your gods, Israel, which brought you up out of the land of Egypt" (1 Kings 12:26–33; cf. v. 28 with Exodus 32:4). Ahab is compared negatively even to this in his construction of an altar (1 Kings 16:32–3) and in his destruction of Yahweh's prophets and altars (1 Kings 19:10, 14).

Prophets and Deuteronomic Lawgivers

Amos continued the prophetic attack on cultic sites opposed to Yahweh, especially at Bethel, linking that worship with social oppression (Amos 2:8; 3:14; 9:1); Hosea takes up that theme of judgment (Hosea 8:11; 10:1–2; 12:11). In Judah, on the other hand, the establishment of the Temple in Jerusalem brought about a prophetic recognition of the presence of God there, sometimes with visionary confirmation (Isaiah 6:1–10). Nonetheless, Isaiah maintains the prophetic denunciation of foreign altars and even of altars to Yahweh apart from the cult in Jerusalem (Isaiah 17:7–8; 27:9; yet compare 19:19, whose significance will concern us shortly).

This trenchant distinction between all other sites and the single authorized sanctuary in Jerusalem governed the presentation in Deuteronomy and in Deuteronomistic work associated with the last book of the Torah. Deuteronomy sets out an explicit program of the elimination of foreign sanctuaries and altars in favor of "the altar Yahweh your God" (Deuteronomy 12:2–7, 27; see also 7:5). The program includes not accommodating to styles of worship common among the peoples, such as planting a sacred grove near the altar (16:21).

Properly conducted worship permits Israelites to recite and maintain their identity as they keep the commandments and a priest offers their sacrifice at the altar (Deuteronomy 26:4–19). The words of the Torah are therefore of particular importance, and Moses instructs Israel to inscribe the words on stone and to set up an altar of whole stones on the other side of the Jordan (Deuteronomy 27:1–8). Likewise, teaching the Torah as well as offering on the altar becomes the especial blessing conveyed through the clan of Levi (Deuteronomy 33:10). Joshua is described as fulfilling Moses' instructions, including the construction of the altar on Mount Ebal (Joshua 8:30–5; see Deuteronomy 27:4). This shows that the Deuteronomistic policy of a single altar in Jerusalem did not completely efface earlier traditions. Joshua also assigns the people of Gibeon manual tasks associated with the service of the altar (Joshua 9:27).

Yet any altar outside of the place that Yahweh chooses is anathema as the site of an altar, and near civil war illustrates that (Joshua 22:9–34) when Reuben, Gad, and part of Manasseh propose to build an altar. Only their agreement to use their edifice as a monument in Yahweh's honor rather than as a true altar for sacrifice averts violence. Jeroboam's rebellion is the epitome of this problem, and the altar is the target of a prophecy that one day: "Altar, altar, thus says Yahweh: Look, a son shall be born to the house of David, Josiah his name, and he will sacrifice upon you the priests of the high places who burn incense upon you, and men's bones will burn upon you" (1 Kings 13:1–10). A sign follows, in which Jeroboam's hand withers, the altar splits, and its ashes spill away, signaling divine displeasure.

The priest Jehoiada leads a revolt centered on the altar (2 Kings 11:11, 12:9) that takes power away from the hand of the regent Athaliah and sees to the destruction of Baal's altars, idols, and priests (2 Kings 11:18). His actions are the antithesis of Ahaz's, who orders changes in the altar that accord with the design of Tiglath-pileser's in Damascus (2 Kings 16:10–16). Uriah the priest complies, including the arrangement that the bronze altar installed by Solomon (vv. 14 and 15) should be moved and reserved for the use of the king in divination. Even in Hezekiah's time, there are enough alternative sites to the Temple that the Assyrians claim that Hezekiah's removal of altars outside of Jerusalem is an affront to Yahweh (2 Kings 18:22; Isaiah 36:7).

Manasseh the king is depicted (2 Kings 21:1–18) in terms that make even Ahaz's abominations – and the Amorites' for that matter (v. 11) – pale in comparison. "He made his son pass through fire" (v. 6) and brought the prophecy that Jerusalem would be handed over to its enemies.

Just prior to the disastrous fulfillment of that prophecy, Josiah offers a brief respite of integrity, guided by a scroll found in the Temple (2 Kings 23:1–20), probably some form of the present book of Deuteronomy; he destroys the places in the Hinnom Valley, where people made their sons and daughter pass through fire to the god Molech (2 Kings 23:10), as well as cultic objects and altars constructed by Ahaz, Manasseh, and even Solomon (2 Kings 23:12–13). Particularly, he fulfills the prophecy against Jeroboam. The hope that such repentance could turn away judgment survived up until the Babylonian destruction of the Temple. Jeremiah 17:1 speaks of Judah's sin as carved on the horns of their many altars, but in context there is still hope for both the altar and the city (Jeremiah 17:24–27). Events, however, produced the exile.

Although the association of Solomon with the idolatrous kings Ahaz and Manasseh might seem strange, it is coherent within the Deuteronomistic presentation. Solomon's greatness cannot be denied, but neither can his trespass on the purview of the Temple. He has people taken from the refuge secured by holding the horns of the altar; Joab is even murdered there (1 Kings 1:50–3; 2:28–34). Solomon sacrifices and burns incense in high places, offering at Gibeon in particular, where Yahweh appears to him in a dream and Solomon makes his famous request for wisdom (1 Kings 3:1–15). That story is closed by having Solomon return to Jerusalem, stand before the ark, and offer sacrifice, but the ambivalence remains that Solomon achieves what should not be achievable by means of the high places.

The Temple itself, however, is Solomon's construction; the system of courts and the arrangement of ark and sanctuary and altars, as well as their dedication and use, are carefully described (1 Kings 6–8; 8:22, 31, 54, 64; 9:25). It is of interest that even the stone for the house was prepared before it was shipped to the site, so that it imitated the construction of the altar (1 Kings 6:7). A cedar altar covered with gold, presumably for incense, is located in the sanctuary (6:20, 22; 7:48), as well as a bronze altar that could not contain all the sacrifices Solomon offered (1 Kings 8:64), so that an additional area (implicitly, an altar of unhewn stones) was sanctified for the purpose. Although Solomon is described as offering sacrifice upon the altar three times a year and burning incense (1 Kings 9:25), he is led astray by his seven hundred wives and three hundred concubines to build high places for foreign gods, even Molech, whose devotees passed their children through fire (1 Kings 11:1–8).

Priestly Consolidation of the Prophetic Vision

The Deuteronomists characterized the process of losing the Temple as virtually inevitable: the seeds of destruction were planted even with Solomon. But the unusual circumstances after the exile that permitted Judeans to return to Jerusalem and rebuild their Temple included a visionary movement that specified the pattern according to which restoration should proceed, giving Israel its Second Temple.

The conviction that the Temple and its altar were justly lost as a result of Israel's disobedience in no way diminished the pain of that loss. Ezekiel's position as both priest and prophet made him the pivot of a visionary recovery. He insisted in terms reminiscent of the punishment of Jeroboam that the altars of Israel had been justly defiled (Ezekiel 6:4–5, 13). Yet Ezekiel's vision also includes a specification of the Temple that is to be restored and of its service. The sons of Zadok have its charge (40:46) because they alone of the Levites had not been implicated in the royal abominations that brought about the Temple's destruction (44:10–16). The "prince" (no longer called a king) is also relegated; he eats bread before Yahweh but does not offer sacrifice (Ezekiel 44:1–3). The placement, dimensions, and sanctification of altars are laid out (40:47; 41:22, here referring to the table; 43:13–27; 45:19); the promise of realizing this vision is that healing waters will issue to the south of the altar (47:1).

Similarities between Ezekiel and the "Holiness Code" (Leviticus 17–26) as well as the Priestly source generally have frequently been observed, but there is nothing like exact agreement (e.g., on the altar's measurements, which vary in ancient sources). The power of the combined prophetic and priestly perspective, however, comes through all these articulations. The altar and the whole Temple that contains the altar are God's alone; he is a reality inviolate in heaven whatever happens on earth. For that reason, the altar is a place of supernatural power as well as of communion with God.

The nature of true worship had broken through even before Israel had inherited the land and before Abraham had been called. Noah, endowed with the wisdom to offer only clean beasts, sacrifices to God on an altar (Genesis 8:20–9:17) occasioning God's favor, marked by the divine bestowal of animals for food provided that blood is not consumed, and by the covenant that permits the world to endure.

No vision can compare with Moses' in the Priestly source. God gives him specific instructions, including visionary disclosures for the altar: how it should be constructed of wood and bronze (Exodus 27:1–8), how and who can approach it without the threat of death (Exodus 28:42–3; see Leviticus 10:1–3), how its sanctity can safely be transferred to priests (Exodus 29:10–39), and how it enables Israel to dwell with God in their midst (Exodus 29:40–6). The actual layout of the altars, including a golden-covered altar for incense (Exodus 30:1–10), the relation of the principal altar to a basin for purification (Exodus 30:18, 20), and the anointing of the altars (Exodus 30:26–28) are all detailed, and the implementation of the visionary template by a craftsman named Bezazel is described (31:1–11; 37:25; 38:1–7, 30) as Moses sees to the realization of the visionary arrangement (35:15–16, 39:38–9, 40:5–33).

The Book of Leviticus specifies the sacred choreography that is to transpire within the arrangement. For that reason, the altar features persistently in chapters 1–9. As in Ezekiel, the king is called a prince, and his sacrifice for sin is under the strict control of a priest and is comparable to that of an ordinary Israelite (Leviticus 4:22–35). It is the priests who have special access to the altar (Leviticus 10:12–15), because God placed Aaron and his sons there by Moses' own hands (Leviticus 8:1–30). They render a person with an outbreak of skin clean by means of sacrifice (Leviticus 14:20), and Aaron's descendant sees to the undiminished sanctity of the altar as the place where God meets his people (Leviticus 16:20)

The Altar for the End Time

The rebuilding of the Temple did not bring the supernatural triumph envisaged by Ezekiel and enshrined in the Holiness Code and the Priestly source of the Torah. Nonetheless, the Book of Psalms, compiled during the period of the Second Temple, represents the joy experienced by worshippers around the altar, and their celebratory participation there with procession, dance, and music (Psalms 26:6; 43:4; 51:19; 84:3; 118:27). At the same time, the context of several of these references in Psalms (26:6; 51:19) makes it plain beyond dispute that innocence and righteousness, purity that reaches to the heart, were associated with sacrifice on the altar.

As compared to Solomon's Temple, however, the Second Temple was not prepossessing. The altar was established and sacrifice offered even before the foundation of the new Temple was laid (Ezra 3:2–3), and arrangements were made for service on the altar (Nehemiah 10:34), but those familiar with the first Temple wept at the dedication of the second (Ezra 3:12). The newly consecrated altar itself seemed to testify to the iniquities that had resulted in destruction. The altar proper is at issue in Lamentations 2:7, where it is said to have been forsaken, and such a lament, articulated as a rebuke for continuing corruption, features also in Joel 1:13; 2:17, and Malachi 1:7, 10; 2:13.

A powerful prophetic response to this sense of an incomplete restoration came in the form of predicting the opening of the altar to all Israel, assisted by foreigners who are included in the festivity (Isaiah 56:6–8; 60:7–14). (This expectation reversed the direction of an earlier prophecy, in which an altar to Yahweh was to stand in Egypt; Isaiah 19:18–19. The colony at Elephantine shows how plausible an extension into Egypt may have seemed.) Zechariah became the preeminent prophet of this transformation of Jerusalem, so that the whole city would serve as an altar (14:20; cf. the earlier metaphor in 9:15).

JEWS AT ELEPHANTINE

Several caches of Aramaic papyri unearthed around the beginning of the twentieth century reveal the existence during the Persian era of a thriving colony of Jews on the upper Nile River, opposite modern-day Aswan. These papyri represent legal proceedings in the life of the community at Elephantine in Egypt: loans, transfers of property, marriage contracts, divorce agreements, and writs of adoption and manumission. The texts derive principally from the archives of two families. These Aramaic-speaking Jews also left behind numerous letters, some of which have important ramifications for the study of the history of Israel and the early development of the Jewish religion.

The Jewish community at Yeb (as they called their city) may have had its origin in the sixth century B.C.E. when Israelites displaced by the Babylonian exile took up residence there. A large entourage had accompanied the exiled king Jehoahaz II to Egypt (2 Kings 23:34). Jeremiah and others fled to Egypt after the assassination of Gedaliah, and Jeremiah knew of an active Jewish community in Egypt during his days. But the Jews at Elephantine may also have been members of a military colony whose roots went back as far as the eighth to seventh centuries B.C.E., when Judean rulers traded Israelite mercenaries for Egyptian political support and military supplies. Israel had a long history of mercenary activity in Egypt (Deuteronomy 17:16; 2 Samuel 10:6; 1 Kings 15:18).

A striking feature of Jewish life at Elephantine was the existence of a temple to their ancestral God *yhw* ("Yahu" or "Yaho"). One document claims this temple had been in existence before the Persian king Cambyses's invasion of Egypt in 525 B.C.E. Priests of the Egyptian god Khnum, with the help of the local Persian commander, destroyed the temple in 410 B.C.E. A famous letter from the leaders of the Elephantine Jews to Bagoas, governor of Judah, requests his help in restoring their temple. This letter, dated 407 B.C.E., also contains reference to Sanballat (governor of Samaria) and to the high priest Johanan (Nehemiah 12:22, 13:28) – key figures in establishing dates for the work of Ezra and the Samaritan schism. The Jewish leaders in Jerusalem apparently counseled their Egyptian counterparts to rebuild the temple and resume its cultic practice, with the exception of animal sacrifice, which was to remain the sole prerogative of the main temple in Jerusalem.

Jewish religion at Elephantine seems to have veered toward syncretism. A list of temple contributors shows that the treasurer had collected funds for the gods Eshem-bethel and Anath-bethel as well as for Yahu. Epistolary salutations often refer to "the gods." In one legal text, a Jewish woman swears by Egyptian gods during a court procedure. Nonetheless, the Jews at Elephantine probably observed the weekly Sabbath festival as well as the annual feast of Passover. One papyrus from the archive is an order issued under the auspices of Darius II (ca. 419 B.C.E.) and Arsames, the governor-general of the Egyptian satrapy, which instructs the colony to observe the Feast of Unleavened Bread.

Robust though these hopes were, the proper use of the altar was also defended by looking backward, rather than forward. First Chronicles portrays David as careful regarding sacrifice (1 Chronicles 16:40), as receiving the spectacular intervention of fire from heaven in the manner of Elijah (1 Chronicles 21:26), as avoiding the altar at Gibeon (1 Chronicles 21:29–22:1), and as progressing far in preparations for constructing the Temple (1 Chronicles 28:18). Second Chronicles details the choreography and drama around the altar to serve as precedents of worship given by Solomon (2 Chronicles 5:12; 6:12–13, 8:12–15), Hezekiah (29:12–36), and Josiah (35:16–19), and repeats standard functions of the altar, such as receiving oaths as well as sacrifice (2 Chronicles 6:22–3, cf. 1 Kings 8:31–2; 2 Chronicles 7:7, cf. 1 Kings 8:64). Similarly, when Solomon besought Yahweh at Gibon, he did so by means of the bronze altar that Bezazel had made (2 Chronicles 1:5–6). Yet the drama of punishment for crime against the altar is also heightened (26:16–23).

Elephantine, on the east bank of the Nile River in southern Egypt (although it is an island today). Papyri discovered there dating from the fifth century B.C.E. open a window on a Jewish community that served as a garrison for the Persian rulers of Egypt. Among the manuscripts (known as the Elephantine papyri) are letters about a Jewish temple in Elephantine, marriage and divorce contracts, and business contracts that illustrate many facets of Jewish life under the Persians. (BiblePlaces.com)

B. Psalms

1. The Nature of Israelite Poetry

Although the psalms in the Hebrew Bible were composed as poetry, Israelite poetry is by no means confined to the psalms, nor is the type of poetry found in the Hebrew Bible peculiar to ancient Israel. Other books contain large amounts of poetry; Job, Proverbs, Isaiah, and Jeremiah, and the so-called Minor Prophets are largely poetic. Poetry can also be found in Song of Songs and Lamentations and is scattered through the remainder of the Hebrew Bible. For example, the judgment pronounced by God on Adam and Eve in Genesis 3:14–19 is in poetry, as is the Song of Lamech in Genesis 4:23–4. Notable poems outside the main poetic books include the Blessings of Jacob and Moses (Genesis 49; Deuteronomy 33), the Song of Moses (Deuteronomy 32), the Song of Deborah (Judges 5), and David's lament over Saul and Jonathan (2 Samuel 1:19–27).

A literary form called parallelism, the juxtaposition of lines crafted to be resonant in their similarity but also striking in their differences from one another, characterizes Hebrew poetry. Because this convention is not immediately recognizable to them as poetry, most readers of English need

Fragment of the apocryphal Book of Noah, found among the Dead Sea Scrolls (1Q 19). (BiblePlaces.com)

translations that set out parellelism visibly on the page in order to appreciate the poetic form. (The King James or Authorized Version of 1611 unfortunately did not do so.) Three types of parallelism have been widely acknowledged: synonymous, antithetic, and synthetic. Synonymous parallelism repeats the same sense, or nearly the same sense, in a second line using different words from those in the first line:

> For I was envious of the arrogant;
> I saw the prosperity of the wicked.
> > (Psalm 73:3)

Antithetic parallelism introduces a second line that reverses the statement of the first:

> For the LORD watches over the way of the righteous,
> but the way of the wicked will perish.
> > (Psalm 1:6)

Synthetic parallelism continues in a second line the thought of the first, without correspondence of words:

> The LORD looks down from heaven on humankind
> to see if there are any who are wise, who seek after God.
> > (Psalm 14:2)

Recent researches have proven that these basic distinctions can become complex and have also suggested different ways of describing the material. From the standpoint of transformational grammar (the theory that surface structures are transformations of kernels in the "deep structure"), a verse such as

> For he who avenges blood is mindful of them;
> he does not forget the cry of the afflicted
> (Psalm 9:12)

can be described as follows. The deep structure, "he who avenges blood remembers the cry of the afflicted," is transformed into two lines in which the parallelism is effected by contracting "he who avenges blood" to "he" and by expanding "them" into "cry of the afflicted."

Another approach is to look for pairs of words that commonly occur together and that are used in different lines. For example,

> For the *needy* shall not always be forgotten,
> nor the hope of the *poor* perish forever.
> (Psalm 9:18)

> Why do the *nations* conspire
> and the *peoples* plot in vain?
> (Psalm 2:1)

An excellent example of wordplay using a simple and frequently encountered *a-b-b-a* pattern is found in Psalm 9:19–20:

> Rise up, O LORD! Do not let *mortals* [*enosh*] prevail;
> let the *nations* [*goyim*] be judged before you.
> Put them in fear, O LORD;
> let the *nations* [*goyim*] know that they are only *human* [*enosh*].

Hebrew poetic style has generated an extensive literature in the past forty years; the approach developed here is designed to help readers to be sensitive to their own reading of Hebrew poetry.

2. The Literary History of the Psalms

In their presentation within the Hebrew Bible (of which variants will be discussed later), the psalms are divided into five books: book 1, Psalms 1–41; book 2, Psalms 42–72; book 3, Psalms 73–89; book 4, Psalms 90–106; and book 5, Psalms 107–50. There is some indication that the division resulted from the way the psalms were collected. Thus, most of the psalms of book 1 are entitled in Hebrew "David's," meaning that they were attributed to David or belonged to a collection associated with his name. Book 2 begins with eight psalms of the sons of Korah (42–9), and book 3 begins with eleven psalms of Asaph (73–83). Most of book 4's psalms have no attribution (an exception is Psalm 90, attributed to "Moses, the man of God"), and book 5 has a collection of "Songs of Ascents" (120–34) and a group of Davidic psalms (135–45).

Each book ends with a declaration of the praise of God (a doxology): book 1 with Psalm 41:13; book 2 with Psalm 72:18–19 (plus the words of

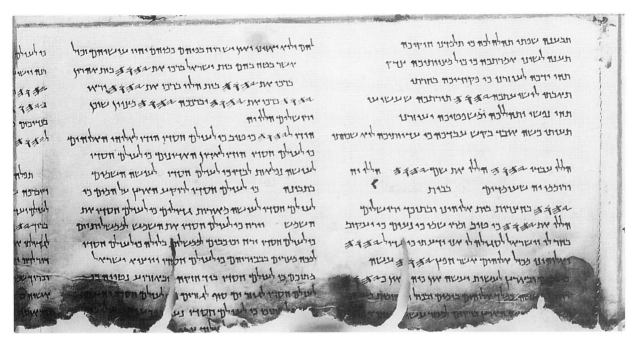

Fragment of the *Psalms Scroll* from cave 11 at Qumran. Here the name of God – the tetragrammaton (YHWH) – is written in paleo-Hebrew letters.

72:20, "The prayers of David son of Jesse are ended"); book 3 with Psalm 89:52, and book 4 with Psalm 106:48. In the case of book 5, Psalm 150 can be taken as the concluding doxology of this book and of the collection as a whole.

Some of the books show signs of having existed independently as collections before being edited into the Book of Psalms. Beginning with Psalm 42 and extending to Psalm 83, the divine name "God" (Hebrew *'elohim*) substitutes for the original "LORD" (Hebrew *yhwh*). This can be seen by comparing Psalms 14 and 53, which are nearly identical apart from the divine names, and by reading Psalms 42–83 and noticing the overwhelming preponderance of the name "God." An "Elohistic" collection (one using the Hebrew name *'elohim*) probably included most of what are now books 2 and 3, whereas Psalms 3–41 were a separate, Davidic collection.

As the whole Psalter emerged, these earlier collections of psalms were no doubt supplemented. The *Psalms Scroll* from the Dead Sea Scrolls (11QPs[a]) features an irregular order between Psalms 100 and 150. Psalms 106–8 and 110–17 are omitted, and the following deviations from the traditional Hebrew order occur: 103, 109, 118, 104, 147, 105, 146; 132, 119, 135; and 93, 141, 133, 144, 155 (one of ten noncanonical pieces in the scroll), 142–3, 149–50. In some cases, this order is the result of grouping psalms that contain the imperatives *hodu* (praise) or *hallelujah* (praise the LORD) in their superscripts or postscripts. This accounts for the grouping of 118, 104, 147, 105, and 146. Although care must be taken in drawing conclusions from this scroll, it seems to indicate that, by the first century C.E., when the *Psalms Scroll* was written, the order of books 1–3 was fixed while that of books 4–5 remained fluid.

Recent study has drawn attention to the fact that Psalm 1 is less about worship than about meditation on God's law, a theme even more prominent in Psalm 119. In its final form, the Psalter may well have been intended for private meditation as well as for use in worship. The division of the collection into five books, even though this process probably predated the final form, would make the psalms correspond to the five books of the Pentateuch, or Torah (Law).

The literary history of the psalms remains inferential, grounded in clues from the psalms themselves. We can identify separate collections and editorial processes such as the changing of the divine name in Psalms 42–83. We can note that the order of Psalms 100–150 may have been fluid as late as the first century C.E. and that the final form of the collection as a whole stresses meditation upon God's law.

There are two conventional ways of numbering the psalms. English translations in the Protestant tradition follow the system in the Hebrew Bible and is used here; but the ancient Greek translation known as the Septuagint used a different enumeration that has continued to guide the presentation of the psalms in Catholic translations. The Septuagint takes Psalms 9–10 as a single psalm, with the result that Psalms 11–113 in the Hebrew order become 10–112 in the Greek order. The material from 113–16 presents the following differences:

Hebrew	Greek
114–15	113
116:1–9	114
116:10–19	115

After this, Hebrew 117–46 equals Greek 116–45. The following final difference:

Hebrew	Greek
147:1–11	146
147:12–20	147

enables the two Psalters to agree in their enumeration of the final three psalms that they have in common. Yet there is also a Psalm 151 in the Greek (included in the Apocrypha section of the New Revised Standard Version), of which a Hebrew version has been found among the Dead Sea Scrolls.

3. The Psalms in Israelite Worship

Although the Books of Chronicles cite certain psalms in liturgical connections, on the whole the Hebrew Bible does not give much in the way of clear indications as to the use of psalms in Israel's worship. In 1 Chronicles 16:7–36, in order to celebrate bringing the ark of God to Jerusalem, David appoints Asaph and his kindred to sing a psalm made up of what we know as Psalms 105:1–15, 96:1b–13, and 106:1, 47–8 (the last verse being also the doxology that ends book 4). In the context of Solomon's

PSALMS AT QUMRAN

Like all known Jewish communities during the first century of the Common Era, the Qumran sectarians used biblical psalms as a part of their Scriptures. The Psalter played an important role in the Essenes' corporate worship and private devotions. Discoveries near the Dead Sea have unearthed many parts of the Qumran Psalter, literature that includes biblical psalms, psalms known from apocryphal collections, and some compositions that were apparently unique to the Essenes.

Archaeologists have retrieved more than thirty scrolls and fragments of psalms from eight different Qumran caves. The most important manuscript, called the Psalms Scroll (11QPsᵃ), was found by a Bedouin in February 1956, nearly a decade after the discovery of the first of the Dead Sea Scrolls. Scholars unrolled and translated the scroll in 1961. Analysis of its writing reveals that the scroll dates from the period 30–50 C.E. Together, the scrolls preserve readings from 120 of the Hebrew Bible's 150 canonical psalms.

The Psalms Scroll contains numerous variants from the traditional text of the Hebrew Bible. Among other variations, the scroll has David's poetic speech, which the Hebrew Bible preserved in 2 Samuel 23:1–7, as one more in the collection of Davidic psalms. In most early manuscripts besides those of Qumran, the sequential order of biblical psalms is quite traditional, especially in books 1 and 2 (Psalms 1–72). The Psalms Scroll contains material from only books 4 and 5 (Psalms 90–150), and the order of the compositions it preserves is quite different from that of the canonical Hebrew Bible. Scholars have used information like this to point out the complex history of the Psalter's standardization, a process not likely completed before the end of the first century C.E.

In addition to these canonical materials, the Psalms Scroll preserves eight compositions that did not come to be a part of the Hebrew Bible. Four of the ancient poems are known from ancient translations like the Greek Septuagint or the Syriac Psalter, or from medieval Hebrew manuscripts of apocryphal literature. The other four compositions were unknown before the Psalms Scroll was found. They include a prayer for eschatological deliverance addressed to the city of Zion, a prayer for liberation from evil influences, a Wisdom hymn to the creator, and a prose composition about David's wisdom and prophetic inspiration. Apparently the scribe who wrote down these psalms – and those who read and appreciated them – believed that the whole scroll was Davidic in origin and authoritative for the community.

A number of other scrolls surviving from the Qumran community contain psalm-like material. The most famous are the Thanksgiving Hymns (1QH; the Hymn Scroll). These *hodayot* (praise songs) date from the first century B.C.E. Many of them are very similar to biblical psalms, although their style is eclectic. Some of the *hodayot* are personal – almost biographical – hymns, which some scholars have attributed to the community's leader, the Teacher of Righteousness. Others seem to be expressions of the community as a whole. These psalms reflect many of the Qumran sect's fundamental ideas: dualism, predestination, election, and grace. A few specialists have suggested that the *hodayot* served a liturgical function, though most think they were more likely used for edification and reflection. Several clearly liturgical texts from Qumran also preserve hymnic material, including various supplications and expressions of praise.

prayer dedicating the Temple (2 Chronicles 6:41–2), Psalm 132:8–10 is quoted. The refrain

> For he [God] is good,
> for his steadfast love endures forever,

which occurs in Psalm 136, is referred to in 2 Chronicles 5:13 and 7:3, and evidently represents a response sung by the people, perhaps after each verse of certain psalms such as Psalm 136. The titles of the psalms say little about their original use, partly because the titles reflect the process of linking some psalms to incidents in the life of David, perhaps to assist their use in meditation. Psalm 30 is described in its title as "A Song at the Dedication of the House of David," but for most readers that psalm's meaning is deeply existential.

Given the lack of evidence within the Hebrew Bible, scholarship has resorted to conjecture to explain the use of the psalms in Israel's worship. Medieval Jewish scholars linked some psalms with worship events in the life of David and Solomon, such as the dedication of the Temple. The seventeenth-century Puritan commentator Matthew Poole noted that Psalm 2 had been connected with David's inauguration as king, while Psalms 24, 47, and 68 were reportedly composed when David brought the ark of God to Jerusalem (cf. 2 Samuel 6).

During the eighteenth century critical scholarship abandoned belief that David had composed the psalms as a whole (and many began to deny Davidic authorship of the Psalter even in part); that denial opened the way to hypothesize royal ceremonies other than those connected with David as the setting of the psalms. This possibility was exploited particularly during the twentieth century, when the royal psalms, especially Psalms 93 and 96–9, drew considerable attention. These celebrate the universal kingship of God over the world and the nations, occasioning the hypothesis of an annual New Year festival, or perhaps the anniversary of the king's coronation. Their opening acclamation (in Psalms 93, 97, and 99), "The LORD is king!" seems to have been the culmination of a ceremony that enabled worshippers to act out their belief in God's kingship in a dramatic way that reinforced their hopes and beliefs about God's kingship in the future. Precisely what form the ceremony took, we cannot know. One view, much less popular today than it was fifty years ago, is that the king, representing God, went through ritual combat, humiliation, death, and rebirth, and that the ceremony was believed to promote stability and prosperity for the following year. In this view, psalms such as 2 and 110, with their assurances of victory over enemies, preceded the ritual combat, whereas the many psalms of lamentation accompanied the combat (e.g., Psalms 3, 11, 12). This approach was deeply influenced by theories concerning the Babylonian New Year festival.

We are on firmer (although still conjectural) ground if we presume that there was a regular, possibly annual, ceremony associated with the ark that celebrated God's "coming" to Jerusalem and that proclaimed his universal rule from that city. Psalm 132 appears to describe a search for the ark followed by its triumphant entry into Jerusalem, where it is solemnly installed in its appointed place with the words,

> Rise up, O LORD, and go to your resting place,
> you and the ark of your might.
>
> (Psalm 132:8)

Psalm 47:5–7 may indicate the acclamation of God's universal kingship following the solemn installation of the ark:

> God has gone up with a shout,
> the LORD with the sound of a trumpet.

Sing praises to God, sing praises,
sing praise to our king, sing praises.
For God is king of all the earth.

Another part of the liturgy may be Psalm 24, which contains a series of challenges to the doorkeepers to admit "the king of glory." Perhaps these words were spoken as the ark was brought into the city after having been carried in procession round it (cf. Joshua 6:1–7).

Psalms such as 2 and 110 were probably used at the coronation of kings. In both of them, the king is designated as the special representative of the God among the nations. In Psalm 2 the king is given a protocol from which he reads,

You are my son;
today I have begotten you.
(Psalm 2:7)

This means that he has been adopted into a special relationship with God (see Isaiah 9:6–7, where the birth prophecy might refer to the coronation and adoption of a king). Other royal psalms may be 44, used by a king prior to a battle, and 45, used at a royal wedding.

However illuminating these suggestions may be, a word of caution is in order. If these ceremonies did take place, we do not know whether they were performed in a private royal sanctuary or to what extent Israelites as a whole joined in. Further, these royal psalms imply a date and setting in the first Temple period (ca. 957–587/6 B.C.E.), while some recent scholarship locates the use of the psalms in the second Temple period (515 B.C.E.—70 C.E.) and in communal worship apart from the Temple (Gerstenberger 1988). The history of the emergence of the Book of Psalms is complex, but four types of attitude toward the Temple have been detected. Because the Temple is the focal concern of the collection, four stages in the development of the book may be distinguished. Those stages correspond, in their turn, to four kinds of reference to God as king.

In the first stage, cultic assertions associated with worship even before the establishment of the Temple, some in connection with other gods, were brought into the sphere of the Lord's worship in Jerusalem. Although stage one is of foundational importance, it may be known only inferentially (although it seems to have left traces in Psalms 24, 29, 48). Stage two is the stage at which central sacrifice in Jerusalem is the assumed setting (see, for example, Psalms 5, 22, 93). The destruction of the first Temple in 587/6 B.C.E. provided the setting for stage three, which reflects a desire for the rebuilding of the Temple and the punishment of Israel's enemies (see Psalms 9–10, 44, 74, 95, 114, 149). The fourth and last stage is the most explicitly eschatological. It envisages the inclusion of the nations in worship on Mount Zion within the context of a cosmological renewal that will make the Temple there a new reality (see Psalms 47, 96, 97, 98, 103, 145). The force of social and historical setting within the production of the Psalter is such that we should expect that, although these different types of

MUSIC AND MUSICAL INSTRUMENTS

Music finds its place very early in the Bible, with a reference in the primeval genealogy to "Jubal, who was the father of all who play the lyre and pipe" (Genesis 4:21). This suggests that Israelites conceived of music as one of the first developments of culture, and that music played an important role in Israel's life from the beginning and served a variety of purposes. Israel's warriors and kings celebrated their victories with music, and musicians evolved as a medium in worship and prophecy, and helped those who mourned the dead.

In Israel's early history, women appear to have been the primary musicians, as is evident in Miriam's exultation over pharaoh's army (Exodus 15:20; see Deborah in Judges 5) and in women's celebration of David's victory over the Philistines (1 Samuel 18:6–7). Israel's musical traditions included a special place for women who played portable frame-drums and performed dances. Female hand-drummers accompanied and led joyous singing and dancing for many occasions, but their artistry is particularly associated with a distinctive Israelite musical genre known as the "victory song" (see Exodus 15:20; Judges 11:34; 1 Samuel 18:6; Jeremiah 31:4).

With the construction of the Temple, music became a part of Israel's official cult, and the priestly establishment controlled musical performance. The Chronicler credits David with organizing Temple musicians (1 Chronicles 15), but the consolidation of Temple music in the hands of the Levites was probably a more gradual development. By the postexilic period, Levites were almost exclusively associated with the musical service of the Temple. Music was a central component of the Jerusalem cults both before and after the exile (cf. 1 Samuel 10:5; Psalm 81:3; Isaiah 5:12). Many psalms associate the praise of God with melody and song (e.g., Psalms 33:1–3, 150:3–6). Psalm 137 suggests that even Israel's Babylonian captors knew of their captives' musical reputation.

The royal court was another musical venue. David soothed Saul's troubled spirit with song, while the aged Barzilai regretted not being able to enjoy the music of David's palace. In the eighth century B.C.E., Sennacherib carried off male and female singers from Jerusalem among his many spoils of war.

Music also played a part in the everyday life of the community. Particularly noteworthy are the associations of music with laments for the dead. David lamented Saul and Jonathan with a song (2 Samuel 1:19–27). The people similarly mourned the death of Josiah with music (2 Chronicles 35:25). Music was apparently a pastime for laborers (Isaiah 16:10) and an integral part of wedding ceremonies (Song of Solomon 5:12–16). The prophets, however, sometimes associated music with the life of luxury, which they condemned (Amos 6:5–4).

Musical instruments in the biblical period included stringed, percussive, and wind varieties. The harp and lyre are frequently mentioned, as is the drum. Musicians also employed the flute and trumpet. The sound of music in the biblical period is not recoverable, although some evidence suggests that remnants of liturgical and popular music were preserved in the chants and songs of secluded Jewish communities in Africa and Mesopotamia.

---

psalms are instanced by some of the texts, there is also an interpenetration of the differing types over time, especially as later psalmists took up the tropes of their predecessors. That leads us to consider a related topic, the form-critical study of the psalms.

In his 1811 commentary on the psalms, the German scholar W. M. L. de Wette (1780–1849) noted that over a third of the collection amounted to laments, both national (thirty-two psalms) and individual (twenty-six psalms). The laments constituted the heart of the Psalter in his view, expressing the religious doubt and struggle of the nation and its individuals. In the twentieth century scholars analyzed the forms (i.e., recurring and typical patterns) of psalms and classified them more precisely into laments, thanksgivings, and royal psalms. Attention has focused especially

Relief from Sinjerli in Asia Minor, crafted during the eighth century B.C.E. conveying a vivid sense of the importance of music within ancient worship. (BiblePlaces.com)

on typical features of the laments. They usually begin with a cry to God for assistance and continue by specifying particular troubles experienced by the psalmist before ending with an affirmation of confidence in God. But the circumstances of the psalmist's troubles are never so specifically stated as to allow their precise identification. Instead, we find general references to wrongdoers, enemies, sickness, or doubt.

Did the composers of the laments make them deliberately general so that they could be used by worshippers in a variety of situations? How were the laments preserved and made available to worshippers? Is their general nature the result of the growth of the Book of Psalms as literature, with specific details being generalized so that the psalms gain in usefulness? Did worshippers in ancient Israel use existing psalms to express their feelings, or did they compose their own psalms based on conventional patterns? Whatever the answers to these and other questions, the psalms are deeply rooted in national and individual worship and prayer in ancient Israel and have been preserved in such a way that they continue to be appropriate to the needs of worshippers in different ages, cultures, and religions.

4. The Contents of the Psalter

In the listings that follow (based on Rogerson and McKay's *Psalms: Cambridge Bible Commentary*, 1977), some psalms appear under more than one heading. This usually means that they are adaptable for use in different situations, but occasionally it means that their interpretation is open to debate.

Hymns
In praise of God because he is good, loving, faithful: 103, 111, 113, 145–6, 150
To God the creator: 8, 19, 24, 29, 104
To God the bounteous provider: 65, 84, 144, 147
To the Lord of history: 68, 78, 105, 111, 114, 117
To God both as creator and as Lord of history: 33, 89, 95, 135–6, 144, 148
To God the mighty, the victorious: 68, 76, 149
On the final victory of God and his people: 46–8, 68, 93, 96–9
"The LORD is king": 47, 93, 96–9
"Songs of Zion" (cf. 137:3): 46, 48, 76, 84, 87, 122
Suitable for use by pilgrims: 84, 121–2, 125, 127

National Psalms
Prayers for deliverance or victory: 44, 60, 74, 79–80, 83, 85, 89, 108, 126, 129, 137, 144
Prayers for blessing and continued protection: 67, 115, 125
General prayers for mercy or restoration: 90, 106, 123
Psalms that call the people to obedience: 81, 95
Royal psalms: 2, 18, 20–1, 45, 72, 89, 101, 110, 132

Other psalms that include prayers for the king: 61, 63, 80, 84
Other psalms that make reference to the king: 78, 122, 145

Prayers of the Individual in Time of Need
For protection, deliverance, or vindication in the face of persecution: 3,
    5, 7, 12, 17, 25, 35, 40–1, 54–7, 59, 64, 70, 86, 120, 123, 140–3
In times of suffering and dereliction: 6, 13, 22, 28, 31, 38–9, 42–3, 69, 71,
    77, 88, 102, 143
For justice or personal vindication: 7, 17, 26, 35, 69, 94, 109
For forgiveness: 6, 25, 38, 51, 130
Expressing a desire for the nearness of God: 22, 25, 27, 38, 42, 51, 61, 63,
    73, 77, 84, 130, 143
Expressing confidence or trust in God: 4, 11, 16, 23, 27, 52, 62, 91, 121, 131
Suitable for use in a night vigil: 5, 17, 22, 27, 30, 46, 57, 59, 63, 108, 143
The "Penitential Psalms" (in Christian tradition especially): 6, 32, 38, 51,
    102, 130, 143

Thanksgivings
For national deliverance: 118(?), 124
For personal deliverance: 18, 30, 34, 66, 116, 118, 138
For forgiveness: 32
For the knowledge of God's continuing love and care: 92, 107

Psalms Giving Instruction or Containing Meditations on Various Themes
On the law: 1, 19, 119
On the qualities required in the citizens of God's kingdom: 15, 24, 101, 112
On corruption in society: 11–12, 14, 53, 55, 58, 82, 94
On the lot of humanity, the problems of evil and suffering, the ways of
    the godly and the wicked: 1, 9–10, 14, 36–7, 39, 49, 52–3, 58, 62, 73,
    90, 92, 94, 112
On God's judgment: 50, 75, 82
On God's blessings: 127–8, 133
On God's omniscience: 139

Psalms Treated as Messianic in Christian Interpretation
The royal Messiah: 2, 18, 20–1, 45, 61, 72, 89, 110, 118, 132
The suffering Messiah: 22, 35, 41, 55, 69, 109
The second Adam, fulfiller of human destiny: 8, 16, 40
Psalms describing God as king, creator, etc., applied to Jesus in the New
    Testament: 68, 97, 102

Special Categories
Acrostics: 9–10, 25, 34, 37, 111–12, 119, 145
Songs of ascent: 120–34
Hallel: 113–18
Hallelujah: 146–50

V. THE WORLD OF ISRAEL'S SAGES AND POETS

A. The Nature of "Wisdom," and the Worldview of the Sage

Most, if not all, introductions to the literature of the Hebrew Bible today assume that the category of "Wisdom literature" includes the Books of Proverbs, Job, and Ecclesiastes. In stark contrast, most nineteenth-century introductions designated these books together with others as poetic literature. In Eduard Riehm's 1890 introduction to the Old Testament, for example, these three books were still discussed under the general heading of poetic books, but in a special section devoted to "didactic poetry" connected particularly with "the wise," and the theme of "wisdom." During the twentieth century Egyptian and Babylonian texts were published that contain material similar to that in Proverbs, Job, and Ecclesiastes. Indeed, the Egyptian Instruction of Amen-em-Opet (*Ancient Near Eastern Texts*, pp. 421–4), dating perhaps from 1100 B.C.E., is so similar to Proverbs 22:17–24:22 that many scholars believe Proverbs to be dependent in some way on the Egyptian text. Other texts that have attracted attention include the so-called Babylonian Ecclesiastes (*Ancient Near Eastern Texts*, pp. 439–40), in which a sufferer seeks comfort from a friend, and "I will praise the Lord of Wisdom" (*Ancient Near Eastern Texts*, pp. 434–7), in which a Job-like person of high rank describes his misfortunes, protests his innocence, and describes his ultimate deliverance. These discoveries suggested that "Wisdom" was an international genre, in which Israel's literature shared.

The investigation of scribal schools in the ancient Near East, in which scribes learned their craft by copying short proverbs and longer Wisdom texts, revealed a link between Wisdom traditions and royal scribal schools. Given the link in the Hebrew Bible between King Solomon and the crafting of proverbs and songs (1 Kings 4:29–34; Proverbs 1:1–4), it was natural to infer that Israelite Wisdom literature was the product of a royal scribal school dating from the time of Solomon, if not before. A distinct class of scribal sages was identified from texts such as Isaiah 29:14 ("The wisdom of their wise shall perish") and Jeremiah 8:8–9 ("The wise shall be put to shame"), which imply tension between scribal and prophetic perspectives. In this view Israelite Wisdom literature was part of a larger, international phenomenon, mediated by scribes whose profession necessitated and cultivated contact with other nations. This would explain why the literature contains no reference to the distinctive story of Israel's redemption, embraced by the prophets and connected with the patriarchs, the Exodus, and the Sinai (or Horeb) covenant.

A neat picture eventually emerged, but it has been criticized from various angles:

1. "Wisdom" was not the international phenomenon it is commonly claimed to have been. In fact, the designation "Wisdom literature" was developed from study of the Hebrew Bible and only then applied to

Egyptian and Babylonian discoveries. It is questionable whether these extrabiblical texts would have been seen as examples of ancient wisdom traditions except for the initiative that came from from biblical studies.

2. The Wisdom literature within the Hebrew Bible need not have had its setting in life in scribal or intellectual circles. Material in Proverbs has been compared with traditions among contemporary African peoples, and these comparisons have reinforced the view that there was such a thing as folk wisdom in ancient Israel – practical observations on everyday life built into a simple but robust ethical code and operating at the level of family and village circles.

3. The evidence for scribal schools in ancient Israel is slender; we cannot be sure that they existed formally in Judah prior to the time of Hezekiah (727–698 B.C.E.). In any case, we have already noticed that some of the influential families prominent in the administration of Israel and Judah, and thus involved with or members of scribal schools, were closely connected with the prophetic and Deuteronomistic movements. We obviously cannot identify such groups as interested in international culture to the exclusion of the traditions about the saving activity of God in Israel's history.

4. The books designated as constituting Israel's Wisdom literature are, in fact, so diverse that it is hard to see them as the work of a single class or group of people.

These and other observations warn us away from positing sociological classes and conditions on the basis of literary texts, and then using those sociological reconstructions restrictively to interpret the very texts from which we began. We cannot rule out the possibility that there were scribal schools in Israel and Judah that played a part in copying and transmitting proverbs of various kinds; but we must also allow that some of the Wisdom material had its origin in the folk wisdom of family and community circles, and even of prophets and priests.

If, as appears likely, many proverbs existed orally before being written down and collected together, this very process affected how they were understood. An analogy from our own culture illustrates this. If we place together the following two, apparently contradictory, proverbs: "he who hesitates is lost" and "look before you leap," their juxtaposition produces something that is greater than the sum of their parts. Benjamin Franklin illustrates just that principle (among others) in *Poor Richard's Almanack*. Something similar happened when separate proverbs were collected together and written down in ancient Israel.

In Proverbs, Job, and Ecclesiastes we find out much about daily life, including the actions of kings, of traders, of guests, and of women managing households. We hear of the enemies of ordinary, decent people – usurers, deceitful traders, oppressors, slanderers – as well as about the bad habits of laziness, greed, flattery, ill temper, and uncontrolled tongues. Common sense and experience shape the advice that is given, on the assumption that listeners and readers, scribes and editors live in the kind of moral universe in

EGYPTIAN WISDOM

With its proximity, political power, and dominant trading position, Egypt exerted a pervasive cultural influence over the whole region of and around Israel during much of the biblical period. The Egyptian traditions concerning wisdom featured prominently among these influences.

Egyptian literature provides striking parallels to the wisdom traditions of the Hebrew Bible. In both Egypt and Israel, Wisdom writings were of two general types: optimistic works that taught traditional morals and practical lessons from experience (like the Book of Proverbs), and more pessimistic works that asked weighty questions about the meaning of life and challenged established tradition (like Job and Ecclesiastes).

In the first category are the Egyptian Instructions. This body of literature, with the special title *sebayit*, "teaching," spans a period from 2800 to 100 B.C.E. About a dozen works of instructions, each known after the name of its author, have been preserved. Among the most famous is the Instruction of Amen-em-Opet, which closely resembles parts of Proverbs 22:17–24:22. These teachings are intended to train young men for court life, propounding the bureaucratic virtues of correct speech, proper relations with women, correct dealings with superiors and inferiors, rules of etiquette, diligence, reliability, self-control, and the like. These ideals have a marked similarity with the teachings of many biblical proverbs.

The Instruction pivots around the Egyptian conception of *ma'at*, the comprehensive divine reality of order, truth, goodness, and justice that created and supported both the cosmos and human society. The cosmic order and the moral order were seen as united; the goal of human activity was to live in accordance with that order through wise thought, speech, and action. Living according to the principle of *ma'at* paid off with tangible blessings, while conduct that varied from this divine order resulted in adversity.

Another branch of Egyptian wisdom literature protested earlier expressions of confidence in the natural and moral orders. This tradition ranges from pessimistic complaints about intractable social forces to a hedonistic assertion of pleasure despite the cost. Works like "The Dispute over Suicide" and "The Harper's Songs" show the same preoccupation with the central problems of life that is common to Job and Ecclesiastes. Hori's "Satirical Letter" shares the same tone of questioning that God directs against Job (38:4ff.).

Some scholars have suggested that another genre of Egyptian Wisdom literature also finds expression in the Hebrew Bible. Onomastica, or lists of name, were encyclopedic catalogues of various objects used for the training of scribes. The Onomasticon of Amen-em-Opet, for example, lists the 610 things that the god Ptah created; it is an orderly classification of divine and human beings, animate creatures, inanimate objects, natural objects, meteorological phenomena, cities, buildings, food and drink, and so on. Lists of created things in Job 38–9, Psalm 148, Wisdom of Ben Sira 43, and the Song of the Three Youths (inserted in the Greek version of Daniel 3) may reflect an Egyptian influence.

which virtue and decency will ultimately be rewarded, and vice and wickedness will be punished.

Yet this simple, one might even say simplistic, outlook is tempered with deeper realism. The Book of Job argues against the direct equation between goodness and reward, while Ecclesiastes seems to find the whole "wisdom" outlook at best boring and at worst untrue. The Wisdom texts are "humanistic" in the sense that they explore the dilemmas of life without introducing God as an easy solution to any problem. Yet this kind of humanism is set in an implicitly religious framework, and for the most part within the horizon of Israel. The world is understood as God's world; from God comes true wisdom, insight, and understanding. God is also ultimately the guarantor of justice, despite experiences that seem to contradict this truth in the short term. One of Job's contentions is that, if only he could get a fair trial before God, he would be able to prove his innocence. The Wisdom literature is also aware of the frailty and transience of humanity in contrast to the enduring nature of God's world.

In scholarship of the early twentieth century, Wisdom literature was seen as an impediment to attempts to construct a theology of the Hebrew Bible in terms of the covenant, or the history of Israel's salvation. In the past thirty years, however, the realistic humanism of this material within its wider religious context has won renewed interest among those seeking to read the Hebrew Bible in the light of wider understandings of the covenant.

B. Proverbs

The Book of Proverbs is divided into sections by a series of headingss:

1:1	"The proverbs of Solomon son of David, king of Israel"
10:1	"The proverbs of Solomon"
22:17	"The words of the wise"
24:23	"These also are sayings of the wise"
25:1	"These are other proverbs of Solomon that the officials of King Hezekiah of Judah copied"
30:1	"The words of Agur son of Jakeh"
31:1	"The words of King Lemuel. An oracle that his mother taught him."

These headings probably mark separate collections (although Agur's words are found only in 30:1–14, not the remainder of the chapter). The titles at 22:17 and 24:23, for example, correspond precisely to a section (22:17–24:22) comparable to the Egyptian Instruction of Amen-em-Opet. On the other hand, 31:10–31, an acrostic poem about the capable wife, is an appendix to Proverbs that does not have a heading. In the Greek translation, the Septuagint, some of the material is found in a different order (e.g., 30:1–14 follows 22:17–24:22) and there is additional material not found in the Hebrew text.

The first collection, 1:1–9:18, contains a series of poems that begin with the admonition, "my child" or an equivalent (usually *beni*, "my son" in Hebrew: 1:8–19; 2:1–22; 3:1–12; 3:21–35; 4:1–9; 4:10–27; 5:1–23; 6:1–5; 6:20–35; 7:1–27). They advise the child to avoid sinners, to seek wisdom in order to escape from evildoers and "loose women," to trust God and honor him with wealth, to do good to others, to learn from the example of parents, to avoid indebtedness, and to avoid temptations to commit adultery or to resort to prostitution. The address of parent to child has prompted the suggestion that some kind of formal instruction is the background here, but if so, the concentration on matters of sex suggests instruction within a family or surrogate family rather than teaching organized on a wider scale.

The remainder of 1:1–9:18 is devoted mostly to "Wisdom," personified as a woman. Proverbs 1:2–7 sets out the purpose of the book, and following the first poem addressed to "my child." Wisdom is introduced as standing in the street and calling out to scoffers and fools (1:20–33). This theme is resumed at 8:1 – "Does not wisdom call?" – where Wisdom claims that kings reign by her and rulers decree what is just by her precepts (8:15–16). The passage reaches its climax in the famous section (8:22–31) in which Wisdom claims to have been created at the beginning of God's work, before the creation of the earth. She actively created with God in the design of the earth, and delighted humanity with knowledge (Proverbs 8:22–31). This poem is clearly the result of sophisticated theological reflection concerning the nature of the world and of human experience. Virtue, industry, and faithfulness to God find their reward in personal understanding of divine power. Chapter 9 opens with the verse made famous in T. E. Lawrence's title *Seven Pillars of Wisdom:* "Wisdom has built her house, she has hewn her seven pillars." It contrasts the delights of following Lady Wisdom with the dangers of heeding Lady Folly.

With the large section 10:1–22:16 we come to material that consists mostly of individual, two-line proverbs. Among their characteristic types, antithetical comparisons are very prominent:

> A slack hand causes poverty,
> but the hand of the diligent makes rich.
>
> (10:4)

Indeed, most of chapters 10–15 are devoted to such antithetical comparisons. From 16:1 there are other forms, such as statements that contain advice:

> Casting the lot puts an end to disputes
> and decides between powerful offenders;
>
> (18:18)

and statements that imply condemnation and warning:

> A perverse person spreads strife,
> and a whisperer separates close friends.
>
> (16:28)

There are comparisons:

> Better is a dry morsel with quiet
> than a home full of feasting with strife,
>
> (17:1)

as well as statements that relate daily living to God:

> All deeds are right in the sight of the doer,
> but the LORD weighs the heart.
> To do righteousness and justice
> is more acceptable to the LORD than sacrifice.
>
> (21:2–3)

Although verses such as 21:2–3 are not in any way dominant within 10:1–22:16, they are a reminder that, in its final form, this section is far from being totally secular and has affinities with the prophetic tradition.

The section 22:17–24:22 is strikingly similar to the Egyptian Instruction of Amen-em-Opet. How similar, it is best to permit readers themselves to judge. The *order* of the material in Proverbs and the Instruction is quite different (see the table of comparison in *Ancient Near Eastern Texts*, p. 424 n. 46), but there are verbal similarities, such as:

Proverbs	Instruction (*Ancient Near Eastern Texts*, pp. 423–4)
Have I not written for you thirty sayings of admonition and knowledge? (22:20)	See thou these thirty chapters: they entertain; they instruct. (27:7–8 [chapter 30])
Incline your ear and hear my words,	Give thy ears, hear what is said.
and apply your mind to my teaching,	Give thy heart to understand them.
for it will be pleasant if you keep them within you, if all of them are ready on your lips. (22:17–18)	To put them in my heart is worthwhile, (but) it is damaging to him who neglects them. (3:9–11 [chapter 1])
Do not eat the bread of the stingy;	Be not greedy for the property of a poor man?
do not desire their delicacies;	nor hunger for his bread.
for like a hair in the throat so are they.	As for the property of a poor man,
"Eat and drink!" they say to you;	it is blocking to the throat
but they do not mean it.	it makes a vomiting to the gullet.
You will vomit up the little you have eaten,	If he has obtained it by false oaths,
and you will waste your pleasant words. (23:6–8)	his heart is penetrated by his belly.
	The mouthful of bread (too) great thou swallowest and vomitest up,
	and art emptied of thy good. (14:5–10 [chapter 11]

Although the preceding comparisons do not prove that the compiler(s) of Proverbs copied from the Instruction, it cannot be doubted that there is some form of dependence or, possibly, reliance of both texts on a common source or tradition.

The later sections of Proverbs introduce some new forms. Similes are common in chapters 25–6, for example:

> Like cold water to a thirsty soul,
> so is good news from a far country.
> (25:25)

Chapter 30 contains several numerical sayings, such as

> Three things are too wonderful for me;
> four I do not understand:

the way of an eagle in the sky,
the way of a snake on a rock,
the way of a ship on the high seas,
and the way of a man with a girl.
(30:18–19)

They have a riddle-like quality with no clear answer. Another form is the acrostic poem (each verse beginning with a successive letter of the alphabet), with which the book ends.

In its final form Proverbs dates from after the exile (and after 540 B.C.E.), but most experts allow that a good deal of the material is preexilic in origin. This is most likely true of the central collection 10:1–22:16, to which were subsequently added the smaller collections from 22:17 onward, while the whole was prefaced with the poems of 1:8–9:18 and the introduction (1:1–7).

C. Job

The questions raised by the Book of Job have generated a vast philosophical and scholarly literature, yet the book itself follows a clear structure. A prose prologue and epilogue tell a complete story. Within this prose framework poems appear in which a speech by each of Job's "comforters" is answered by a speech of Job. There are two complete series of these speeches; the third series is incomplete and is rounded off by a hymn to Wisdom (chapter 28) and a concluding speech by Job. There is then a long intervention by a previously unmentioned fourth "comforter," Elihu, before several speeches by God and a brief response by Job bring the poems to an end. The scheme is as follows:

1. Narrative framework		1:1–2:13
2. Lament of Job		3
3. First cycle	Eliphaz	4–5
	Job	6–7
	Bildad	8
	Job	9–10
	Zophar	11
	Job	12–14
4. Second cycle	Eliphaz	15
	Job	16–17
	Bildad	18
	Job	19
	Zophar	20
	Job	21
5. Third cycle	Eliphaz	22
	Job	23
	Job?	24
	Bildad	25
	Job	26–7

The narrative framework tells the story of a rich man of exemplary piety who falls victim to a wager between God and Satan. Satan is one of the heavenly beings in the divine court, and he does not believe that any human can be loyal to God for God's own sake. God puts his faith in Job's integrity and allows Satan to bring terrible disasters upon Job. In spite of everything, Job maintains his integrity, and at the end of the narrative framework his wealth is restored and seven sons and three daughters are born to him to replace those who perished at Satan's hand. As we have it now, this story is not complete. The epilogue does not mention any outcome for Satan, and it also says that the "comforters" have spoken wrongly about God – presumably a reference to the poetic sections, but the narrative does not say what exactly their error was.

In the poems we meet with a Job quite different from the submissive Job of the prologue, who had piously reproved his wife's insistence that he should curse God, saying, "Shall we receive the good at the hand of God, and not receive the bad?" (2:10). In sharp contrast the Job of the poems is combative and becomes embittered against God. He curses the day on which he was born (chapter 3) and asks God to kill him (6:8–9). He muses on the hard lot that has to be endured by human beings (chapter 7) and contrasts the nothingness of his own existence with the sovereign power of the creator (chapter 9). He appeals to God, who made him, to make allowance for his frailty, and he insists on his own innocence (chapter 10). He attacks the arrogance of his friends and accuses them of self-deception (chapter 13). Two chapters (16–17) that describe his desolation lead unexpectedly to his famous affirmation in 19:25–7 that he knows that his vindicator lives and that he will see God on his side. This is not an affirmation of life after death, but of vindication and hope based on the only ground for hope, namely, God himself. In his final speeches Job draws attention to the prosperity of the wicked (chapters 21, 24) and complains about the elusiveness of God (chapter 23). He asserts his innocence afresh (chapter 31) and contrasts his present, unfortunate state with his former prosperity (chapters 29–30).

The "comforters" offer conventional advice. Eliphaz repeats a truth attested by many generations: that wickedness is punished, so that Job's plight must be due to some evil. Bildad asserts the just nature of God, such that he will not reject a blameless person, and goes on to describe vividly the terrors of the wicked. Zophar similarly reflects upon the experiences of the wicked (chapter 20) and insists that God's ways are inscrutable (chapter 11). Elihu (chapters 32–7) summarizes what has been said and criticizes the three comforters, as well as Job. His positive contribution is to stress the redemptive aspect of suffering, which he accuses Job of ignoring (36:15–23).

When, out of a whirlwind, God himself at last speaks, he makes no attempt whatever to deal with Job's complaints. Instead, he throws out a series of rhetorical questions that concern the world in its awesomeness and mythic complexity, but also in its apparent inconsequence. Alongside the question "Where were you when I laid the foundation of the earth?" (38:4) is the question "Is the wild ox willing to serve you?" (39:9), and statements such as

The ostrich's wings flap wildly,
though its pinions lack plumage.

(39:13)

Chapters 40–1 extol the virtues of Behemoth (possibly the crocodile) and Leviathan (possibly a dolphin). (This material may be out of order, with 40:15–24 and 41:7–34 [Hebrew, 40:31–41:26] describing Behemoth, and 41:1–6 [Hebrew, 40:25–30] describing Leviathan.) This unexpected divine intervention draws the climactic confession from Job:

I had heard of you by the hearing of the ear,
but now my eye sees you;
therefore I despise myself,
and repent in dust and ashes.

(42:5–6)

In surveying the book as a whole, three main questions typically arise: what is its literary history, what is its setting, and what is its meaning? In regard to the first question, it seems that the writer of the major part of the poems composed or adapted a popular story as his context. Adaptation is more likely, because the narrative framework is somewhat dissonant with the intervening material. Whether the original author wrote three complete cycles of speeches of which the third was later disturbed when other material was added we do not know, but that seems likely. The Elihu speeches were probably added later, but their addition is skillful, their closing words (37:14–24) anticipating the speeches of God. The Book of Job, then, evidently had at least two authors, each of whom wrote on the basis of a traditional story.

The book is usually dated during the fifth or fourth centuries B.C.E., but there is little to go on in positing a date. Does the book belong to the genre of "Wisdom literature," or does it represent an attack on the teaching that God punishes the wicked and rewards the just (or "rational theodicy" in theological language)? This depends on what we understand by "Wisdom literature." It is doubtful whether a specific class of people whose worldview was that of the Wisdom books ever existed; nor, despite comparisons that can be made with Babylonian works that wrestle with the problem of suffering, can we speak with confidence of an international "wisdom" movement. Nonetheless Job certainly does attack some of the views propounded in Proverbs, and the comforters uphold some of these views.

It is possible to locate Job within the literature of the Book of Psalms. Over a third of the psalms are laments, as we have seen, and one feature of a lament is a word (or expectation) of deliverance. Job can be seen as a complex and expanded lament, with the comforters extending the words of enemies that sometimes feature in laments (see, for example, Psalm 10:5–7). The psalms also concern themselves with the problem of innocent suffering, and psalms such as 37 and 73 have been called "Wisdom psalms" on this account. Psalms also express wonder at the created order (see Psalm 104). Ultimately, it is probably going too far to locate Job entirely within the psalmic tradition, but comparisons between Job and Psalms can nonetheless prove illuminating.

Job's authors *may* have been wealthy Jews who were suffering from the hardships of postexilic Judah, and whose education and interest in philosophy made them all the more sensitive to their plight. Their lack of mention of the traditions about God's action in Israel's history since the Exodus leads to discussion of our final topic in regard to Job, the book's meaning.

On a straightforward reading, the Book of Job attacks the simplistic view that all suffering is deserved and that the universe is moral. In this context, the absence of reference to basic Israelite traditions emerges as an acute problem. Elsewhere, the Hebrew Bible reflects clear awareness that innocent people suffer. In the story of David alone, Abner is murdered by Joab (2 Samuel 3:22–34) because Abner killed Joab's brother Asahel in battle, Tamar is raped by her half-brother Amnon (2 Samuel 13:1–22), and David arranges Uriah's death in battle (2 Samuel 11:14–25). This list could easily be expanded. Further, figures such as Moses, Jeremiah, and the servant of Isaiah 40–55 suffer by being caught between God's gracious purposes and the half-hearted response of the people of Israel. In the light of all this, Job seems to be a discussion that surprisingly takes no account of an important dimension in the Hebrew Bible and stands closer to the ideology of the Book of Proverbs than to that of the Book of Psalms.

Does this mean that Job's discussion of suffering represents a new awareness of God? If so, that sets up an intriguing possibility. As Philip Davies has pointed out (Davies and Rogerson 2005, p. 192), Satan's wager with God means that whether righteousness really exists depends not on God, but on Job. If Job fails the test, Satan's view, that people do good only for the sake of reward, is vindicated; and although that does not make the world immoral, it makes human conduct cynical and calculating. If Job succeeds, then God is vindicated, but vindicated by a human being! Although the effect of the divine speeches is to move Job away from his concern for himself and to make him contemplate the creation, the narrative framework remains stubbornly human-centered.

Another question, raised by taking the narrative and the poems together, is whether the restoration of Job's wealth and family undermines

THE BABYLONIAN JOB

The problem of unjust suffering elicited early protests within the literary traditions of Mesopotamia. The Sumerian poetic essay "A Man and His God" proposed that personal suffering was the result of a basic flaw in humans, one with which the gods had burdened the human race. Nevertheless, the poem is more concerned to prescribe the proper attitude and conduct for victims of undeserved misfortune than to explain the cause of their cruel suffering. The author cites the case of an unnamed man who was wealthy, righteous, and wise, and blessed with friends and family. When sickness and suffering overwhelmed him, he did not blaspheme his god. Instead, the man came humbly before his god with tears and lamentation, praying with earnest supplication. The god was moved to compassion, heeded the man's prayers, removed his misfortunes, and turned his sufferings into joy.

The same theme recurs in a later text from Babylon entitled Ludlul Bel Nemeqi (after its opening line, "I will praise the Lord of Wisdom"). Because of its affinities with the Hebrew Bible's story of the righteous sufferer, some scholars have christened this work the Babylonian Job. The text was written in Akkadian around the year 1000 B.C.E., although its origins may be long before that date. It is a psalm of thanksgiving from a nobleman whom the god Marduk had rescued from a complete reversal of fortune. When he becomes socially ostracized and seriously ill, the hero of the story seeks the reason for his misfortune. Although he consults the gods, he finds no answer. He is convinced that evil has befallen him through no fault of his own; he recounts his exact observance of cultic regulations and his acts of pious devotion. He resigns himself to the conclusion that mortals cannot understand the gods. He gives a long and gruesome description of his disease, which leaves him incapacitated and wallowing in his own waste. He attempts a cure through exorcism, but to no avail. He confesses his trust that the gods will ultimately restore his fortunes, which they do after the hero experiences three divine visions.

The biblical Book of Job differs from this Babylonian composition in setting, literary form, and emphasis. The Akkadian poem is a poetic monologue, while Job's form is a dramatic dialogue involving several people that is placed between a prose prologue and a prose epilogue. The Babylonian sufferer emphasizes ritual, rather than moral purity. The author of Job may have been familiar with Ludlul Bel Nemeqi and other similar works from the Mesopotamian tradition. Both an acrostic poem known as the Babylonian Theodicy (also called the Babylonian Ecclesiastes) and a later composition entitled the "Dialogue of Pessimism" deal with similar themes. However, there is no evidence that Job's author or authors were directly dependent on any Babylonian literature.

the book as a whole. After all, Job's comforters had argued all along that righteousness is rewarded and wickedness is punished. Job had contradicted this position; but doesn't the close of the narrative show that the comforters were correct in the end? This is surely not the book's intent; part of its greatness is its ambiguity and the many possible answers it generates to the question of suffering. Job can also be read as the record of an experience of great, undeserved suffering whose outcome was a new awareness of God. Although many writers have stressed the universality of Job's experience and questioning, we must not rule out the possibility that the book is in some way autobiographical, as well. If this is so, it was written on the yonder side of suffering, with the conversations with the comforters representing issues that were discussed at the time. From this standpoint, the book stands for experience as opposed to theory, for the mystery of encounters with God as distinct from views of God formed by human logic, and for the importance of human honesty as opposed to attempts to coerce submission. It argues for belief in righteousness and justice in an ambiguous world, and against a superficial view of reality that produces a fatal reliance on human resources. Whatever approach we take, Job remains one of the greatest pieces of writing in the Bible and in world literature.

D. Ecclesiastes

The Hebrew name for this book is *Qohelet*, a feminine noun whose meaning and translation are greatly disputed. Traditionally rendered as Preacher, recent translations suggest Speaker, Teacher, or Philosopher. The form *Qohelet* is derived from the noun *qahal*, "congregation" or "assembly," but this provides no definitive clue about its meaning.

The claim of Ecclesiastes 1:1 that the "teacher" was the son of David, king in Jerusalem, prompted the traditional, postbiblical idea that the book is the work of Solomon. But the indirect way in which the claim is put ("son of David, king in Jerusalem," rather than an explicit reference to Solomon) alerts us to the probability that it is a literary device and not to be taken at face value. By common scholarly agreement, the book was written, not in Solomon's tenth century B.C.E., but in the fourth or third century, when Judah had become part of the Greek kingdom of Egypt, ruled by the successors of Alexander the Great's general Ptolemy. This was a period of peace and prosperity for the rich in Judah, and the author of Ecclesiastes apparently belonged to the ruling or upper class, enjoying wealth and ease.

The author's unblinking, self-assured honesty constitutes the outstanding feature of the book. He is aware of the shortcomings of his society, acknowledging its corruption: "in the place of justice, wickedness was there, and in the place of righteousness, wickedness was there as well" (3:16). He also sees oppression: "Look, the tears of the oppressed – with no one to comfort them! On the side of the oppressors there was power" (4:1). However, he does not know what he or anyone can do about these injustices. He has some hope in God as the final judge: "I said in my heart, God will judge the righteous and the wicked, for he has appointed a time for every matter and every work" (3:17). But he is also honest enough to see that this hope does not necessarily work out in practice, and he does not envisage an afterlife where justice will be done. Rather, it is death itself that is the great leveler in his mind. Death reminds humans that they are also animals (3:18–21), and it brings at least rest, if not justice, to the oppressed.

What, then, of the achievements of human culture? The writer does not deny that they are real (see 2:4–10), but he doubts whether they have any permanent value or meaning (2:18–23). They have certainly not brought him any sense of fulfillment. Indeed, even the belief in human creativity, which they may engender, is an illusion. In 3:1–8 there is a beautiful and remarkable poem in which, in each verse, two Hebrew words are contrasted with two other Hebrew words, for example:

time to-be-born	time to-die
time to-kill	time to-heal

This poem is often read today as an affirmation of the beauty of the life that God has given to the human race. But in context the poem concerns the lack of freedom that humans have in their lives. We cannot control when we are born or die. The agricultural, reproductive, and even military seasons are dictated by external or natural constraints, as are times of mourning (after a death) and celebrating (at an agricultural festival).

Along with this lack of human freedom comes the human incapacity to discern a larger purpose in life. Nature and existence are boringly repetitive (1:2–18), and a deeper purpose cannot be found (3:11). In this context, the wisdom teaching that found expression in Proverbs loses credibility, and the writer seems deliberately to parody this type of teaching:

> Dead flies make the perfumer's ointment give off a foul odor;
> so a little folly outweighs wisdom and honor.
>
> > (10:1)

> Whoever quarries stones will be hurt by them;
> and whoever splits logs will be endangered by them.
>
> > (10:9)

The author repeatedly verges on forging a disincentive to wisdom, honor, and hard work. His overall attitude toward religion is that it is better to be absolutely sincere in a small amount of observance than rash in a large amount (5:2–6).

The book's ethical stance seems in some ways fatally flawed. If the writer saw corruption and injustice in his society, why did he not try to correct them (especially since he assumed the perspective of a king or ruler)? Why retreat into a general cynicism about the impossibility of improving society and promote death as the great leveler that would in some way vindicate God? It is possible to contrast Ecclesiastes with those parts of the Hebrew Bible that – confident in the story of God's saving deeds – confess belief in a God who is intimately involved in the people's history, who is actively opposed to injustice and oppression, and who offers a vision of a renewed world and a kingdom of justice and peace.

The writer's apparent decision to tolerate injustices as well as his silence about key teachings in the Hebrew Bible raises basic questions about his location in the society of his day, but the present state of knowledge simply cannot specify his identity or his setting. Yet he could have been silent, and was not. As teacher, he at least pointed out the shortcomings of materialism, emphasized the transience of human life and achievements, and acknowledged injustice.

E. Song of Songs

The Songs of Songs is usually called the Song of Solomon because of the heading "The Song of Songs which is Solomon's" (1:1). Although Solomon is mentioned in the text (e.g., 1:5; 3:7; 8:11), few, if any, experts would maintain Solomonic authorship, but no scholarly agreement has emerged in regard to authorship or date (here surmised as the fourth century B.C.E.), or even how the book is to be divided into its component literary parts.

Just as there is little agreement on matters of date, authorship, and literary history, so there is no consensus about the book's purpose. It was once popular to see it as a dialogue between a bride and bridegroom, and the New English Bible, Revised English Bible, and New Jerusalem Bible translations actually add headings in support of this view, following the ancient Greek version in Codex Sinaiticus, a fourth-century C.E. manuscript. This, however, is a pre-emptive way of presenting the text to readers. A variation on the marriage interpretation associates the book with a cultic liturgy, possibly when the king enacted a sacred marriage on behalf of a god. Today it is usually held that the Song of Songs is a collection of love poetry, and it has been compared to Arabic love poetry or that of other ancient Near Eastern traditions. The central themes of the poem support this interpretation.

Two poems, strikingly similar, provide the core of Song of Songs: 3:1–5 and 5:2–8. Both begin with reference to sleep:

Upon my bed at night
I sought him whom my soul loves.

(3:1)

I slept but my heart was awake.

(5:2)

This introduces an element of uncertainty: is the female speaker dreaming, fantasizing, or describing real events? This uncertainty enables the incidents to hover between dream and reality, so that we do not necessarily press for the details. In the first poem the woman seeks her lover in the streets, has a neutral encounter with the sentinels of the streets, finds her beloved, and brings him to her mother's house.

In the second poem, frustration and then violence arise. The woman hears her beloved knocking to be admitted, but by the time she has dressed and opened the door, he has gone. She searches for him in the streets and encounters the sentinels, who beat, wound, and strip her. She does not find her beloved. Both poems end by binding the daughters of Jerusalem with an oath, that they should not "stir up or awaken love until it is ready" (3:5), and that they should tell the man, if they find him, that his beloved is "faint with love" (5:8).

These two central poems have echoes elsewhere in the book. The refrain of 3:5 occurs also at 2:7 and 8:4. Indeed, 2:6–7 and 8:3–4 have in common not only the oath, but the verse:

O that his left hand were under my head,
and that his right hand embraced me!

(2:6; 8:3)

Similar to the man's knocking on the door at 5:2 is his invitation to his beloved in 2:10–15 to come away with him. The phrase in 3:4

> my mother's house,
> . . . the chamber of her that conceived me,

is echoed in 8:2. Other poems amplify some of the sentiments of the core poems. Thus the man's call to the woman in 5:2, "Open to me . . . my dove, my perfect one," is amplified in the description of the woman's beauty in 4:1–11, 6:4–10, and 7:1–9.

Taking the poems together, the following themes emerge:

INNOCENCE VERSUS CONVENTION. In 8:1 the woman exclaims:

> O that you were like a brother to me,
> who nursed at my mother's breast!
> If I met you outside, I would kiss you,
> and no one would despise me.

She laments the restraints placed upon love by conventions that frustrate her natural desires. Something of this is also expressed in the two central poems, which is why it is evocative that we do not know whether the woman is actually searching for her lover at night in the streets, or whether she is dreaming or imagining that she is doing so.

NATURE VERSUS CULTURE. The frustration imposed by convention is fomented in the city, the place of culture. Here the woman is attacked by the sentinels; here the lover must come at night. In the wild, nothing of this applies. The lovers are free to express their feelings, in images drawn from nature.

THE GARDEN. The garden that each lover possesses (4:13–15; 4:16–5:1; 6:2–3) offers a haven. This theme has been compared with that in Genesis 2–3, where an at first ideal garden sees disharmony arise between man and woman and between them and God. In the Song of Songs such disharmony is dissolved. Away from the constraints imposed by the city and by the culture it represents, man and woman are equals, and their love is not sullied by shame or self-consciousness. Whether intended or not, Song of Songs stands in positive contrast to Genesis 3.

God is not mentioned in the Song of Songs, but all that is celebrated in the poems concerning the beauties of nature and the tenderness and devotion of love unspoiled by shame is arguably a reflection of the divine nature. The Song of Songs does not fear human love, but affirms it, and both Rabbinic literature and early Christian sources make this kind of love the basis on which people can join themselves to God and know God as a lover. If there is any hesitancy in the poems, it comes from the restraints of convention, a convention understandably imposed because of the way in which human relationships can be, and are, abused. In the perhaps counterfactual way in which the poems describe love, we have a vision of the future comparable to that in the prophetic literature, bearing remarkable testimony to the diversity of the literature that was admitted into the Hebrew canon.

LOVE POETRY IN THE ANCIENT NEAR EAST

The Song of Songs represents a unique genre in the Hebrew Bible, but love poetry was common in ancient Near Eastern culture. Biblical love poetry shares features with religious literature from Mesopotamia and with secular traditions from Egypt.

Early in the twentieth century scholars sought parallels to the Song of Songs in Mesopotamian liturgies of sacred marriage. Sacred erotic poetry from Mesopotamia was used in the cult worship of Ishtar, the goddess of fertility. According to the Mesopotamian myth, each year the god Tammuz (Dumuzi) descended to the netherworld. When his sister-consort, Ishtar (Inanna), went to seek him, the earth withered and died. When Ishtar and Tammuz returned to the land of the living, the earth revived. These events were annually played out in ritual dramas. Some scholars believe that during these cultic celebrations the king and the priestess of Ishtar took part in a sacred marriage, representing the god and goddess in sexual acts designed to ensure the land's fertility and abundance. Several Sumerian songs have survived from this marriage liturgy that are reminiscent of the Song of Songs. They describe the lovers' desire for one another and praise their sexual attractions. The poems share similar motifs: natural beauty, an invitation to the garden, praise of the beloved's sweetness, the brother–sister motif.

Because scholars have been unable to show that sacred marriage was a feature of Israelite culture, the secular love poetry of Egypt may provide a more appropriate comparison for the Song of Songs. Four major manuscripts and some miscellaneous pieces of Egyptian love poetry survive from antiquity. These love songs date generally from the Nineteenth and Twentieth (Ramesside) Dynasties (1305–1150 B.C.E.), a period when Egyptian hegemony over Palestine made Israelite contact with Egyptian culture likely. A thousand years elapsed between the creation of these Egyptian poems and the time when most scholars think the Song of Songs was written, and there are important differences between the two traditions. Yet the similarities between them are quite strong. The Song of Songs probably represents the Israelite flowering of a long-standing literary tradition whose roots lie, at least partially, in Egyptian love poetry.

Love poetry in Egypt did not speak of great religious or national issues. Instead, this delightful literature told of individual feelings and private concerns. Its subject matter was sexual love and the experiences of adolescent lovers, their pleasures and frustrations. It sings of the joys, desires, confusion, pain, and hope of physical love. The Song of Songs and the Egyptian love poems share this subject matter. They are also alike in their use of dramatic presentation. Their interest centers on the feelings, personalities, and experiences of dramatic characters rather than on those of the poet. Their eroticism is lush and delicate. The poems accept premarital intercourse with restraint, yet rarely with embarrassment or apology. They are fascinated by love in its infinite variety, and the world they create is bright and happy. The lovers' beauty is often projected onto the natural world. Ancient Near Eastern love poetry is an artistic exploration of lovers' emotions, seldom focusing on the larger issues of marriage, reproduction, family alliances, or national well-being.

Some scholars have suggested that ancient Near Eastern love poetry represents courting songs, or that they were used in wedding celebrations. Others have viewed this literature as love magic or as religious poetry. Whatever its original function and social setting, Egyptian and Israelite love poetry was clearly meant to entertain, to be appropriate when song, dance, and merriment were in order. Love songs have always been popular in leisure time when people seek diversion. The Song of Songs contains engaging erotic allusions, sensual language, and warm sentiments that would have diverted audiences from their everyday cares into the sensuous world of young lovers and their sexual adventures.

F. Lamentations

The Book of Lamentations consists of five poems that mourn the destruction of Jerusalem by the Babylonians in 587/6 B.C.E. Chapter 1 is divided into two equal parts: verses 1–11 and 12–22. In the first section, Jerusalem's plight is described and attributed to her sins; in the second, the city speaks and acknowledges her faults and God's just judgment. In chapter 2, only some of the verses, such as 20–2, are Jerusalem's speech. The poem stresses the action of the zealous and all-powerful God against his people. In chapter 3, the speaker is an individual male (the New Revised Standard Version's rendering, "I am the one . . ." is misleading here; the Hebrew, more accurately translated, says, "I am the man . . ."). Precisely how the speaker is to be identified is not easy to say; but what is important is that the poem is positive. God's anger will not last forever, his faithfulness is great, and he will restore his people. Chapter 4 returns to the themes of chapters 1–2, and chapter 5 is one of the most poignant descriptions in the Bible of the plight of an oppressed people.

Chapters 1–4 present different types of acrostic poems, that is, poems based on the successive letters of the Hebrew alphabet. In chapters 1–2 and 4, each stanza (or verse, in the way the text is set out in modern English translations of the Bible) begins with a successive letter of the alphabet, and thus each of these chapters has twenty-two verses. Chapter 3 has sixty-six verses, verses 1–3 beginning with the first letter of the alphabet, verses 4–6 with the second letter, and so on. Chapter 5 is not an acrostic, but, it too has twenty-two verses. The poems contain many examples of the lament (*qinah*) rhythm, in which three stressed syllables are followed by two. Indeed, it was the study of these poems in the nineteenth century that provided many suggestions about the importance of stressed syllables in Hebrew poetry.

Traditionally, the poems have been attributed to Jeremiah – although critical opinion is firmly against this attribution – and in English Bibles Lamentations follows the Book of Jeremiah as a result. In the Hebrew canon, however, Lamentations is one of the five scrolls, together with Ecclesiastes, Songs of Songs, Ruth, and Esther. It is not clear whether the five poems of Lamentations were written by one or more authors, and the place and date of composition remain obscure, although locating Lamentations within fourth-century B.C.E. Israel (with the Song of Songs) appears plausible.

The genre of a lament over the fall of a great city is well known from the ancient Near East, and a long and famous lament over the destruction of Sumer and Ur is translated in *Ancient Near Eastern Texts* (pp. 611–19). It is not surprising that these laments (including the biblical Lamentations) have elements in common: allusions to destruction, mention of enemies, appeal for divine help, and descriptions of the plight of the survivors. It is likely that any similarities between the biblical Lamentations and those from ancient Mesopotamia derive at least as much from similar circumstances as from direct influence.

These poems signally gather together much that can be found in poetry elsewhere in the Hebrew Bible. That is not to say that they are conflations or lack originality. Rather, anyone familiar with Hebrew poetry will notice allusion after allusion to images and ways of expression skillfully woven together and advanced in Lamentations.

MEGILLOT

Song of Songs, Ruth, Lamentations, Ecclesiastes, and Esther are the shortest books of the Hagiographa (one of the three main divisions of the Hebrew Scriptures, called the Writings in Hebrew) and together are known as the *hamesh megillot*, the "five scrolls." In ancient times, each book was written on a separate scroll for public reading at special seasons of the liturgical year.

Today, many congregations recite these books from a prayer book, but the Book of Esther is typically still read aloud from a separate scroll, which has come to be known as "the Megillah." Aside from their liturgical use, the five scrolls have very little in common. They represent sharp contrasts in genre, mood, and purpose.

The first scroll, the Song of Songs, is linked with Passover, being read on the intermediate Sabbath of the Jewish holiday, which recalls Israel's miraculous escape from bondage in Egypt. According to traditional interpretation, the Song of Songs is an allegory of God's love for Israel, and this book came to be associated with the spring festival (*hag ha-'abib*) because Passover is the springtime of that love. Yet the religious and historical elements of Passover were probably not the original link between the festival and this scroll. Passover is a springtime holiday with parallels in the calendars of many peoples, a celebration of nature's rebirth and renewed fertility. The Song of Songs – with its rich descriptions of natural beauty and sexual love – may have been associated early on with joyous celebrations of spring.

Ruth is read during the Feast of Weeks (*shavu'ot*), the annual celebration of the beginning of harvest, which comes seven weeks after Passover. Like the other major pilgrimage festivals (so called because they are celebrated in Jerusalem), this holiday has both historical and agricultural referents. According to Rabbinic tradition, the children of Israel received the Torah on the sixth day of the month of Sivan (the first day of the Feast of Weeks). Thus, this holiday is also *zeman matan torah*, remembrance of the giving of Torah. Ruth's association with the Feast of Weeks has several traditional explanations. The reference to "the beginning of the barley harvest" in Ruth 1:22 may explain why the book is traditionally read on the second day of the holiday. Another tradition suggests that the scroll is read at the first full harvest festival because Ruth's acceptance of the Jewish faith parallels the experience of the people of Israel, who received the Torah on the first day of the Feast of Weeks. Another explanation suggests that the scroll's seasonal association comes from the Davidic genealogy that concludes the book; according to rabbinic tradition, King David was born and died during the Feast of Weeks (i.e., Pentecost).

Lamentations, the third scroll, plays an integral role in the synagogue liturgy for the Ninth of Ab. This scroll contains an extended dirge over the destruction of Jerusalem and the Temple appropriate to the solemn fast that commemorates the saddest day of the Jewish calendar. According to Rabbinic tradition, God ordained the ninth day of the month of Ab as an especially calamitous day for the Jewish people. Because the spies sent to Canaan brought back their discouraging report on that date (Numbers 13–14), God made it an eternal day of mourning and ordained it as the date when the first and second Temples would be destroyed.

The Sabbath of the Feast of Booths (*sukkot*) is the traditional time for the recitation of Ecclesiastes, the fourth scroll. Some commentators attribute this association to the duty of rejoicing during the Feast of Booths since Ecclesiastes also enjoins the pursuit of joy and pleasure. Ecclesiastes 5:3–4 contains a warning not to neglect fulfilling vows, an injunction that some have thought appropriate to this holiday, which is the last festival of the annual cycle. Others argue that the reading of Ecclesiastes, with its somber and pessimistic outlook on life, was introduced to counteract the influence of the pagan celebrations that were common in autumn among ancient peoples.

Esther, "the scroll," is read during the festival of Purim. This strange book purports to explain the festival's origin. At both morning and evening services, the text is chanted to a special cantillation used only with the Book of Esther. The cantor chants from the scroll after it has been unrolled and folded to look like a letter of dispatch. Tradition specifies certain emphases and phrasings for the reader, and it is customary for listeners to participate by making noise whenever the name of Haman (the story's villain) is mentioned.

The customary reading of the five scrolls originated in several historical periods. The scroll of Esther seems to have been read already in the Second Temple period, and Talmudic literature mentions the reading of Lamentations. A post-Talmudic tractate records the use of Esther, Song of Songs, and Ruth (although in a different order from modern practice). Liturgical practice concerning the *megillot* probably did not reach its modern form until the medieval period.

The poems are similar to psalms of lament, as well as to laments elsewhere in the Bible over fallen cities or peoples. Thus, Amos 5:1–7 has a lamentation that begins

> Fallen, no more to rise,
> is maiden Israel;
> forsaken on her land,
> with no one to raise her up.

It may or may not be significant that the term "wormwood" (a bitter-tasting plant) is used to express the perversion of justice in Amos 5:7 and the bitterness of collapse in Lamentations 3:15, 19. Another passage that can be compared to Lamentations is Isaiah 47:1–15, which begins

> Come down and sit in the dust,
> virgin daughter Babylon.

Whether the poems in Lamentations were composed for communal use at a service of fasting and mourning, or whether they are purely literary compositions, remain disputed questions. It is easy to imagine that after the destruction of Jerusalem communal gatherings to express corporate grief were socially valuable events; and it is not impossible that even purely literary compositions were used on such occasions. Clearly, those included in the Book of Lamentations have retained their power for modern readers.

G. Ruth

In the English Bible, Ruth follows the Book of Judges in view of its opening words: "In the day when the judges ruled" (Ruth 1:1). In the Hebrew canon, Ruth is one of the "five scrolls" designed for liturgical use. The book has a simple and appealing story that has opened many possible lines of interpretation.

In the story famine forces a family consisting of a husband, wife, and two sons to leave Bethlehem and live in Moab, east of the Jordan. The husband and the two sons die, leaving the wife, Naomi, with two widowed Moabite daughters-in-law. One of them, Ruth, insists on returning with Naomi to Bethlehem (chapter 1).

On arriving in Bethlehem at the beginning of the barley harvest, Ruth goes gleaning with other young women in a field belonging to Boaz, a relative of Naomi. Boaz treats Ruth kindly, having heard of her faithfulness to Naomi (chapter 2). Naomi now advises Ruth to indicate to Boaz her willingness to marry him by lying down at his feet on the threshing floor. Because of a provision of Hebrew law (Deuteronomy 25:5–10), Boaz needs to ask a nearer relative of Naomi whether he is willing to do his duty by producing a child with Ruth for her dead husband's inheritance, since he had died childless (chapter 3). Boaz assembles the elders at the gate of the city and inquires of the nearer relative whether he will buy some land that

ANCIENT NEAR EASTERN LAMENTS

Death, calamity, and bad tidings were occasions that elicited rituals of mourning in the Hebrew Bible. Mourners wept and wailed, rent their clothing (Genesis 37:29), walked barefoot and covered their heads (2 Samuel 15:30), girded their loins with sackcloth (2 Samuel 3:31), and placed ashes on their heads (Isaiah 61:3). The Levitical code prohibited traditional mourning rites like shaving one's hair or gashing the skin (Leviticus 19:27–8), although in popular practice such customs seem to have persisted in ancient Israel (cf. Jeremiah 16:6). Professional mourners often enhanced the atmosphere of grief (Jeremiah 9:17–22) by reciting formal lamentations or elegies (Hebrew *qinot*) characterized by a stereotypical language of grief and a distinctive rhythmic pattern (see 2 Chronicles 35:25).

Mourning extended beyond situations of individual or family loss to include periods of national distress. Joshua grieved after the Israelites' defeat at Ai, as did Mordecai when he learned of Haman's plan to exterminate the Jews. Psalms 74 and 79, along with the Book of Lamentations, represent communal laments over the destruction of Jerusalem and the Temple.

In many respects these Israelite customs are in line with long-standing traditional practices in the ancient Near East. Ninth-century B.C.E. reliefs from Assyria show women with one or both hands raised above their heads, a posture that indicates mourning or weeping. This gesture of sorrow belongs to an even earlier iconographic tradition. Egyptian wall paintings depict women standing with upraised arms, weeping and tearing their hair in gestures of grief and mourning. A more ancient tradition of lamentation comes from the Sumerian civilization, which thrived in the third millennium B.C.E. The conquest of Sumer, after its revival during the Third Dynasty of Ur, left a distressing and harrowing impression on poets who wrote lengthy laments for their lost cities. Sumerologists have translated documents that preserve the laments of various Sumerian city-states, including Akkad, Eridu, Lagash, Nippur, and Ur.

Some scholars of the Hebrew Bible have argued that the Book of Lamentations relies on these very early Sumerian texts for both its form and its general content, contending that the Sumerian lamentations created a specific genre that evolved into a liturgical template used by various civilizations for over two thousand years. Bitterness, sorrow, and resignation to the divine will permeate both the Hebrew and the Sumerian compositions. Both sets of poems refer to hunger, famine, pestilence, social disintegration, the sacking of cities, the loss of valuables. and the captivity of inhabitants. Yet the literary dependence of Lamentations on Sumerian materials remains difficult to establish. Direct or indirect contact between Israel and Sumer is unlikely, and many of the alleged similarities between the two cultures' expressions of lament can be attributed to similar experiences and situations. The fate of most cities in the ancient Near East following siege and capture was usually – and tragically – quite the same.

Naomi must sell and whether he will also produce an heir with Ruth. The nearer relative refuses (to avoid reducing his own inheritance), as a result of which the duty of marrying Ruth passes legally to Boaz. A son is born to them who, according to the women, is reckoned to Naomi (4:17). He is named Obed, the grandfather of King David. The book ends with a genealogy of David including Obed, who, however, is traced through Boaz's line rather than Naomi's.

Despite its simplicity the story raises a number of difficult questions. If Naomi possessed a field (4:3), why was she so poor that Ruth had to glean to provide for them? Who had been looking after the field while Naomi was in Moab? How was the sale of the land connected with the marriage of Ruth? If the purpose of Ruth's marriage to Boaz was to produce children for Naomi's dead husband and sons, for what reason was Boaz credited with being Obed's father in the genealogy of 4:18–22?

These questions remain hard to answer. The Hebrew Bible says that a man has the duty to produce a child with his brother's widow if the marriage was childless, so that children can be reckoned to his dead brother (Deuteronomy 25:5–10). This was no doubt an important mechanism for ensuring that property was kept within the husband's family. There is also provision for a relative to buy a field if an Israelite is forced to sell it, for example, to pay off a debt (Leviticus 25:25; cf. Jeremiah 32:1–15). But these two provisions are not linked, as is done in Ruth. We do not know whether the author of the Book of Ruth knew institutions slightly different from those recorded in Leviticus and Deuteronomy, or – as seems more likely – whether the author of Ruth misunderstood these institutions.

The book can be read in many ways and at many levels. Because women dominate the story, Ruth has received many treatments from feminist scholars. These have drawn attention to the strength of purpose and loyalty of the female characters in the story, notwithstanding the constraints of a patriarchal society in which women gain justice and legitimacy only in relation to men. Another approach emphasizes the book's generous attitude toward non-Israelites. Even though Naomi's family fails to take care of Ruth and her husband and children during the famine, and the nearer relative is unwilling to marry her, Ruth is the heroine of the story – a Moabite woman who risks leaving her own country and whose loyalty to her mother-in-law produces a son who will be an ancestor of David. Only in the Book of Jonah is there a comparably generous treatment of non-Israelites.

In Ruth, God is hardly mentioned, although the book is very much concerned with how God restored Naomi from utter hopelessness in chapter 1 to the point in 4:14 where the women say to her, "Blessed be the LORD, who has not left you this day without next of kin; and may his name be renowned in Israel!" How does God restore Naomi? In various, indirect ways. Customs allowing the poor to glean in fields at harvest-time (cf. Leviticus 19:9; Deuteronomy 24:19) and specifying that relatives have to buy fields from their next of kin and produce heirs with childless widows of their brothers make Naomi's restoration possible. In addition to these customs, individual human characters prove exemplary: Ruth's loyalty, Naomi's resourcefulness, and the willingness of Boaz to pursue his interests and Ruth's within the framework of law are all praised. Such actions, in the context of institutional structures of grace, enable God to bring hope to a hopeless situation. Here is a subtle yet sincere theology.

What, then, does the story of Ruth have to do with David? Does it function as an implicit apology for David's possible foreign ancestry by exalting the loyalty of one of the representatives of that foreign strain? Or does it function as an apology for non-Israelites as a whole, by appealing to the reverence with which David was regarded in Israel and by claiming that one of his ancestors was a Moabite? The answers to these questions depend to some extent on when we think the book was written. An apology for David would have been most necessary soon after his reign and that would indicate a date in the tenth to eighth centuries B.C.E. An apology for non-Israelites would suggest a postexilic date, perhaps during the fourth century B.C.E., when the Jewish community was wrestling with problems of identity and relations with outsiders.

H. Esther

Like the Book of Ruth, Esther is a narrative about the workings of an unseen (and largely unmentioned) God, whose purpose is achieved through the strength and resourcefulness of a woman. The Jewess Esther becomes the queen of the Persian king Ahasuerus (i.e., Xerxes, who reigned between 485 and 465 B.C.E.) after the former queen, Vashti, refuses to obey her husband. Because of her beauty Esther is chosen from among many aspirants, and she uses her royal position to warn the king of a plot to assassinate him. Her informant is her cousin Mordecai, who had adopted her on the death of her parents; his part in saving the king is duly recorded in the annals. But because Mordecai refuses to bow down to the high official Haman, the latter decides to destroy Mordecai together with all the Jews. Using the lot (*pur*, a method of divination) Haman determines that the thirteenth of the month of Adar will be the date for carrying out his plan, and, under the royal seal, sends letters to all the rulers of provinces ordering them to kill all Jews on that date.

Mordecai learns of the plot and tells Esther. While the Jews in the capital, Susa, fast, the queen arranges a banquet for Ahasuerus and Haman. Meanwhile, the king discovers that Mordecai was never properly rewarded for saving him from assassination and publicly honors him. At the banquet, Esther reveals to Ahasuerus that Haman plans to kill all the Jews in the empire. The king is appalled, and Haman is executed on the very gallows he had prepared for Mordecai. The danger for the Jews is not over, however, because Haman had sent letters to all the provinces, and the enemies of the Jews are looking forward to the coming slaughter. The king empowers Mordecai to reverse Haman's instructions and to authorize the Jews to attack their enemies and plunder their goods. Thus, on 13 Adar, the Jews attack their enemies, although they refrain from plundering them. In Susa the Jews kill three hundred persons; in the provinces they kill seventy-five thousand (Esther 9:15–16). To commemorate this deliverance, the Jews are commanded by Mordecai and Esther to observe the festival of Purim on 14 and 15 Adar, and Mordecai becomes next in rank to the king himself (10:3).

The Book of Esther conveys themes found elsewhere in the Hebrew Bible. The advancement of a Jewish exile (Mordecai) to prominence at a foreign court can be compared with the stories of Joseph (Genesis 41:37–45), Nehemiah (Nehemiah 1:11), and Daniel (Daniel 1:3–21). Further, Esther shares with Daniel and his companions the distinction of being chosen for their beauty from among many non-Jewish aspirants. Daniel (Daniel 6) and his companions (Daniel 3) are plotted against by their enemies at court, as is Mordecai.

PURIM

Purim, along with Hanukkah, has the status of a minor festival in the Jewish religious calendar (when work remains allowed). Both festivals commemorate great deliverances of the Jewish people. Purim is celebrated on the fourteenth day of Adar (February/March). According to the Book of Esther (9:29), Mordecai and Esther declared the feast to celebrate the deliverance of the Jews from Haman's plot to kill them. The feast receives its name from the lots (Akkadian *puru*; Hebrew *purim*) that Haman used to determine the month when the slaughter was to take place.

Exactly when Purim was first observed remains a mystery. For various reasons, scholars have assigned the strange Book of Esther a date much later than its purported Persian setting; Jewish literature lacks any reference to the festival before the first century B.C.E. In any case, the feast was firmly established in traditional practice by the second century of the Common Era, when a whole tractate (entitled *Megillah*, "scroll") of the Mishnah was devoted to the details of its observance.

The tractate Megillah is especially concerned with rules governing the reading of the scroll of Esther (*ha-megillah*, "the scroll"). The scroll is read at both evening and morning services. Cantors customarily raise their voices at certain key points in the story, especially at the four verses of redemption (2:5, 8:15–16, 10:3). Recitation in one breath of the names of Haman's ten sons is also traditional. This practice is said to signify that all of the sons died together, though some say this hasty recitation is a reminder not to gloat over the fate of one's enemies – even if they deserve it! Children traditionally make noise with special rattles (called gragers) whenever the name of the villain Haman is mentioned as the scroll is being read.

Mordecai's instructions to the Jewish communities of the Diaspora for the celebration of Purim have engendered several customs associated with the holiday. He called on the Jews to designate and observe a day of feasting and gladness, to send food to one another, and to give gifts to the poor. The day is usually celebrated with a festive afternoon meal. The Babylonian rabbi Rava said of the celebrations, "A person should be so exhilarated [with drink] on Purim that he does not know the difference between 'cursed be Haman,' and 'blessed be Mordecai' (*b.* Megillah 7b). Later authorities tried to curtail this permissive attitude toward imbibing on Purim, but the pleasures of strong drink are very much a part of Esther's story (see Esther 1:10, 2:18, 7:1–2). Families often exchange gifts of food on Purim. It was traditional for the poor to receive extra generosity on Purim, and some congregations still collect a special offering in the synagogue vestibule.

Traditions from East European Jewry have enriched many modern observances of Purim. Carnivals, costumes, and humorous songs are now a part of many Purim celebrations. *Hamantashen*, a three-cornered pastry filled with poppy seeds, is a frequent treat during Purim. In Hebrew this pastry is called *'ozne haman*, probably from the German *Haman Ohren* (Haman's ears). This tradition may have arisen from old illustrations that depict Haman wearing a three-cornered hat. In the modern State of Israel, Purim is celebrated as a national holiday.

Many families and communities celebrate private Purim festivals that commemorate their own special great deliverances. Purim is a celebration of hope and encouragement that has provided strength for Jews through the ages. The sages took literally Esther's promise that "these days of Purim will not disappear from among the Jews, nor the memory of them perish from their descendants" (9:28), and therefore wrote, "All the festivals will cease, but the days of Purim will not cease" (*Midrash Mishle 9*).

The genealogy of Mordecai in 2:5 describes him as "son of Jair son of Shimei son of Kish, a Benjaminite." This links up with Saul's genealogy in 1 Samuel 9:1, where Kish is one of Saul's ancestors, and with Saul's relative Shimei, who, in 2 Samuel 16:5, curses David during the latter's flight from Absalom. Another connection with the story of Saul is provided by Haman's genealogy. He is said to be an Agagite (3:1), which connects him with the crucial incident during Saul's reign, when he fought against the Amalekite king Agag (1 Samuel 15:1–9, 32–3). In turn, this passage leads back to Exodus 17:8–14, where the Amalekites fought against the Israelites at Rephidim in the wilderness. Interesting as these allusions are, they are not immediately transparent, unless, for the author, Amalek is the archetypal enemy of the Jews and Saul is the archetypal deliverer. It is easier to appreciate the first of these symbols than the latter.

Research on the development of the narrative of the Book of Esther suggests that several independent stories have been woven together: the contest between Mordecai and Haman, the work of a Jewish woman in delivering her people under foreign rule, and the origin of the festival of Purim. Tracing this growth is facilitated by the existence of a Greek version of Esther (the so-called A text) that evidently represents a stage prior to the version in the traditional Hebrew text. We must also note that another Greek version (included in the Old Testament Apocrypha) adds letters, decrees, prayers, and conversations that expand parts of the story. They give the book as a whole a much more religious tenor than is the case with the Hebrew version, where the word "God" does not appear. Thus, prayers attributed to Mordecai and Esther. Greek Esther, chapters 13–14 (addition C), are utterances that recall God's saving deeds in the past and that ask for deliverance in the present.

If it is correct that the story of Esther developed from popular stories to its fullest form in the Greek version in the Apocrypha (although it has also been argued that the Hebrew version is a *shortened* form of the book as found in the Greek apocryphal text), then we should not look for one particular date or setting except that it must have been later than the time of Xerxes (485–465 B.C.E.). The original stories expressed the universal human desire for good to triumph over evil, albeit in a national (Jewish) context. Actual danger to Jews in the Persian Empire ensured the popularity of the stories and their formation into a tale of national deliverance that was told and retold into the Hellenistic period. Whether there was a national threat to the Jews during the Persian period, as Esther relates, has not been documented.

The origins of the festival of Purim, to which the story later became attached, are similarly unknown. Was this a pagan festival taken over by Jews from Babylonia or Persia, or does it commemorate a Jewish deliverance such as that during the Maccabean revolt of 167–164 B.C.E.? (The account of Nicanor's defeat [1 Maccabees 7:39–50] mentions a festival on the thirteenth of Adar to remember the occasion.) Scholars do not agree. The additions in Greek to the Hebrew version show that after the Esther story was linked to the festival of Purim, the book was used and adapted to the needs of a more specifically religious community and readership. Modern readers ought certainly to read not only the Hebrew version but also the full Greek version, as available in the New Revised Standard Version and Revised English Bible Apocryphas.

VI. THE WORLD OF APOCALYPTIC

A. The Sociology of Apocalyptic Communities

The Bible contains literature that has been called "apocalyptic"; the Greek word that underlies the word "apocalyptic" means "to uncover" or "to reveal," and in texts such as Daniel 8:15–26, the meaning of a vision or omen is disclosed to a human being by a supernatural being. In Daniel 8:15–26 Daniel's vision is explained by the angel Gabriel. The title of this section of the *Companion* obviously makes an assumption: that there are such things as "apocalyptic communities" and that we can describe their sociology. This assumption needs to be defended.

Apocalyptic literature involves certain distinctive features, such as the interpretation of dreams, visions, and omens; an emphasis on supernatural beings such as angels; a tendency toward dualism between good and evil; and the dividing up of time into epochs or periods. This literature is also concerned with the future, as well as with describing the past and present with the help of imagery and symbolism drawn from mythological literature. Yet a difficulty arises when we try to specify exactly which features must be present for a text to be considered apocalyptic. A strict view of what constitutes an example of apocalyptic literature excludes some texts traditionally included in the designation. Broadening that view adds certain characteristic features, eliminates others, and admits more candidates into the genre. In the Hebrew Bible, the texts most at issue for exclusion or inclusion are Isaiah 24–7 and Zechariah 9–14. Are these apocalypses? Isaiah 24–7 briefly mentions a mythological theme in the punishment of the fleeing serpent Leviathan (27:1), and it is concerned with God's future judgment of the world. There is even a possible reference to resurrection:

> Your dead shall live,
> their corpses shall rise.
> (Isaiah 26:19)

But do these features make it correct to call these chapters an apocalypse?

If it is not easy to delimit the genre of apocalyptic writing, what hope is there in delineating the community? But there is another assumption that has to be questioned here, the assumption that we can infer the existence of social groups from literary genres. The viewpoint of traditional sociology has been that the history and sociology of groups could be reconstructed if there was tangible evidence available; types of literature were considered to constitute such evidence. Recent sociological theory no longer accepts this assumption. Communities are constituted by many factors – historical, economic, environmental, linguistic – and literature is only a small, and perhaps unrepresentative, product of a community.

Older scholarship looked for the origins of apocalyptic in prophecy. After the return from exile (539–150 B.C.E.), it was argued, prophecy declined and its place was taken by apocalyptic, which reflected the changed conditions of life in Judah of that period. The most important change was that before the exile, Judah and Israel had been independent nations, while after the exile, Judah alone remained and was governed by the Persian Empire and successive imperial powers. Prophecy often threatened Israel and Judah with coming judgment at the hands of foreign nations, which could be both the instruments of God's judgment and themselves subject to divine judgment, but apocalyptic represented foreign nations as virtually demonic forces ranged against an innocent Jewish community, which can expect direct divine intervention to rescue it. Building on this approach, more recent scholarship tried to identify the authors of apocalyptic as antiestablishment groups in the Jewish community of this period.

A more satisfactory approach to the subject, however, is by means of mantic wisdom, defined as belief and practice in the discovery of heavenly secrets from earthly signs. Texts from the seventh century B.C.E. indicate that guilds of priests or diviners, whose profession was to interpret many types of signs, had long been established in Babylon. Their divinations enabled inquirers to know the will of the gods and to see into the future. The practice implied an understanding of reality in which the worlds of the gods and of humans were interlocked in such a way that inquiry by means of divination provided supernatural information for humans. However, we must not conclude that this understanding of reality was a *total* worldview. On the whole, humans depend on their own resources to cope with life, and they resort to

---

APOCALYPTIC

Apocalyptic (derived from a Greek word meaning "to uncover," "to reveal," "to unveil") is a chief mode of discourse in the Jewish and Christian literature of the period 200 B.C.E. to 200 C.E. The only fully developed example of apocalyptic literature in the Hebrew Bible is the second-century B.C.E. Book of Daniel, but other late biblical texts reflect the influence of early apocalypticism. For example, Isaiah 24–7 (a postexilic addition to the book) speaks of typically apocalyptic themes like the final judgment of the nations and the consummation of all things. Yahweh pronounces judgment on the earth, and the world is turned upside down (24:21). The sun and moon are darkened (24:23). The evil host of heaven are punished (24:21), and the righteous of all nations are invited to a great feast after they are raised from the dead (25:6, 26:19; cf. Zechariah 12:14; Joel 3:9–21). Many of the pseudepigraphic writings and the scrolls from Qumran take the form of apocalypses or at least share some of the characteristics of apocalyptic.

However, scholars have had great difficulty in defining clearly the literary genre, religious ideology, and social setting of this pervasive early Jewish phenomenon. In literary terms, apocalypses are usually cast in the form of visions about future events mediated to a seer through a superhuman being, in the manner of the Revelation to John in the New Testament (also called the Apocalypse, after its title in Greek), the model that scholars have used to describe the genre of "apocalyptic." These visions often employ strange mythological elements and bizarre cosmic imagery. They are generally esoteric and highly symbolic. Fantastic beasts and complicated numerologies are the codes in which this literature presents its message. Apocalyptic authors are pseudonymous.

The subject matter of apocalyptic literature usually involves the presentation of a systematic panorama of history that spans this age and the next. Apocalypses are typically attributed to seers of the ancient past; history is recounted from the perspective of the past, as if the seer were predicting events, so that his predictions of the future would be more convincing. Apocalyptic conceives this mystery as an essential ethical dualism throughout the universe, in which good (God and his angels) and evil (Satan and his demons) are engaged in a fierce battle for dominion in the world; in the eyes of apocalypticists, evil seems in the present time to be winning. The two forces are presented through their respective agents: highly developed angelology and demonology.

Apocalyptic holds a pessimistic attitude toward the present world order. The world and most of its inhabitants are considered hopelessly corrupt.

practices such as divination only in extreme circumstances, when situations such as illness or war threaten their ability to survive.

In the Hebrew Bible, of course, divination is forbidden (Deuteronomy 18:10–11), and the reliance of Babylon on enchantments and consultations is mocked (Isaiah 47:12–15). Yet Daniel 1–2 tells of a Jewish exile in the Babylonian court in the sixth century B.C.E. who does precisely what the diviners were employed to do, and does it better: interpret dreams. Daniel does this again in chapter 4, and in chapter 5 he interprets the famous omen or sign of "the writing on the wall." It is true that the biblical text emphasizes that Daniel's wisdom comes from God and is superior to Babylonian divination; but placing the Book of Daniel in the context of mantic wisdom helps to explain the origin and setting of apocalyptic in postexilic Judaism, as well as features of the Book of Daniel.

The Babylonian mantic tradition spread throughout the Greco-Roman world so that by the third and second centuries B.C.E., when the first Jewish apocalypses were written, this tradition was part of the culture in which Judah found itself. Not only priests but scribes – intellectuals engaged in teaching, administration, and writing – were imbued with this culture and its long-standing traditions and customs. In the apocryphal Wisdom of Ben Sira (also called Ecclesiasticus), written about 200 B.C.E., there is a description of the scribe who

> seeks out the wisdom of all the ancients,
> and is concerned with prophecies;
> he preserves the sayings of the famous
> and penetrates the subtleties of parables;
> he seeks out the hidden meanings of proverbs
> and is at home with the obscurities of parables.
> (Sirach 39:1–3)

In its list of famous figures from the past (Sirach 44–9), Ben Sira gives a prominent place to Enoch (44:16). It is now generally accepted that the earliest Jewish apocalypses are the *First Book of Enoch*, chapters 72–82 (the Astronomical Treatise), 1–36 (the Book of Watchers), 91–105 (the Epistle of Enoch), and 83–90 (the Book of Dreams), which date from 250 B.C.E. to 50 C.E.

Therefore we can surmise that the Babylonian tradition of mantic wisdom as diffused through and mediated by the Greco-Roman world was known among the intellectual scribal classes of Second Temple Judah. They were interested in mythical traditions, astronomical and astrological calculations, history, and philosophy. Obviously, they adapted this non-Jewish tradition to their own religion. When the events of the early second century B.C.E. began to pose a threat to Judah's existence, scribes produced the Book of Daniel, which drew upon the mantic tradition to interpret recent history and give assurance for the future. They did this, not as an antiestablishment group, but as a group intimately involved with the life – and survival – of the nation.

THE KINGDOM OF GOD

The kingdom of God is a vital concept in the Scriptures of Israel, focusing on God as the king of the universe – the fundamental force behind all that is – and on God's role in shaping human experience. The promise of the kingdom is that people will finally come to realize divine justice and peace in all that they do. Jesus made the kingdom of God the center of his preaching as well of his activity, and it remains the pivot of Christian theology.

Whether in present experience or in hope for the future, the kingdom of God was celebrated in ancient Israel in five different but closely related ways. They are all clearly represented in the Books of Psalms.

First, the kingdom of God is behind the whole of created life but is beyond the comprehension of any living thing. For that reason, the Psalms portray the kingdom as so near in time as to be present, and yet ultimate from the point of view of full disclosure (96:10):

Say among the nations that the LORD reigns.
The world is established, so as not to move:
he shall judge the peoples with equity.

All peoples are finally to know the truth that is now celebrated and sung in the Temple, but only in the future.

Second, the kingdom is transcendent in space as well as final in time. Although the usual setting of Israel's praise is in the Temple, every part of the creation will come to acknowledge what is known there (Psalm 145:10-13):

All your creatures will give you thanks, LORD,
and your faithful will bless you;

they shall speak of the glory of your kingdom,
and tell of your might,
to make your mighty deeds known to the sons of men,
and the glorious splendor of his kingdom.
Your kingdom is an everlasting kingdom,
and your rule in every generation.

All his creatures are to give thanks to the Lord, but it is his faithful in particular who are said to bless him. What is rehearsed in the Temple, the "strength of the fearful acts" of God, is to be acknowledged by all humanity (Psalm 145:6).

Third, the kingdom is an insistent force of justice that will ultimately prevail. The kingdom is ever righteous, but it attains to a consummation (see Psalm 10:15–16):

Break the arm of the wicked, and evil;
search out his wickedness until it cannot be found!
The LORD is king for ever and ever;
the nations perish from his earth!

The punishment of the wicked is the dark side of the establishment of the poor; the vindication of the meek, the fatherless, and the oppressed (in vv. 17, 18a) requires a reversal in the fortunes of those who do evil in order to be realized.

Fourth, human entry into the kingdom is contigent. Psalm 24 poses and answers a question that is central to the religion of Israel as reflected in the biblical tradition (Psalm 24:3–4):

Who will ascend the mount of the LORD,
and who will stand in his holy place?
The innocent of hands and pure of heart,

who has not lifted up his soul to vanity, and has not sworn deceitfully.

The point is that purity is affected by one's ethical behavior as well as by the practices of purification (such as bathing and abstention from sexual intercourse) that were conventionally a part of ascending the mount of the Temple.

Fifth, Psalm 47 evokes how the recognition of God is to radiate from Zion, when it identifies "the people of the God of Abraham" as "the nobles of the peoples" (Psalm 47:9):

The nobles of the peoples are gathered, the people of the God of Abraham;
for the shields of the earth are God's.
He is highly exalted!

Israel is the nucleus of the larger group of those who recognize the God of Jacob. From its center, the power of the kingdom of God is to radiate outward to include peoples beyond the usual range of Israel within its recognition.

Jesus articulated all five of these ways of seeing God's kingdom. He taught his disciples to pray to God, "Your kingdom will come" (Matthew 6; Luke 11), because he hoped for it to become fully present to all people. The dynamic quality of the kingdom's transcendence in Jesus' teaching is evident in a famous saying (Matthew 12:28; Luke 11:20), "If I by the spirit of God cast out demons, then the kingdom of God has arrived upon you." Entry into the kingdom is also the dominant image in Jesus' famous statement about wealth (Matthew 19:23–24; Mark 10:23–25; Luke 18:24): "Easier for a camel to wriggle through the eye of a needle than for a rich man to enter the kingdom of God." Jesus needed to cope with the issue of defilement as one member of Israel (with a certain set of practices) met with another member of Israel (with another set of practices). To deal with that question, a single aphorism of Jesus was precisely designed: "Nothing that is outside a person entering one can defile one, but the things coming from a person, these defile one" (Mark 7:15). Finally, in the course of Jesus' occupation of the Temple, Mark has Jesus say (Mark 11:17), "My house shall be called a house of prayer for all the nations, but you have made it a den of thieves."

In Jesus' teaching, the five coordinates of the kingdom become its dynamics: the ways in which God is active with his people. Because God as kingdom is active, response to him is active, not merely cognitive. The kingdom of God is a matter of performing the hopeful dynamics of God's revelation to his people. For that reason, his teaching was not only a matter of Jesus making statements, however carefully crafted and remembered. Jesus also engaged in characteristic activities, a conscious performance of the kingdom, which invited Israel to enter into the reality that he also portrayed in words. Once experience and activity are taken to be the terms of reference of the kingdom, what one actually does is also an instrument of its revelation, an aspect of its radiance. Jesus' awareness of that caused him to act as programmatically as he spoke, to make of his total activity a parable of the kingdom.

B. Daniel

Even on a first reading, the Book of Daniel presents a strong contrast between its first and second parts. The book begins with stories about Daniel and his three companions. Some of the stories are among the best known in the Bible: the three men in the fiery furnace, Belshazzar's feast and the writing on the wall that mysteriously appeared, and Daniel in the lions' den. These stories occupy chapters 1–6, after which there is an abrupt change. Daniel 7 presents a vision seen by Daniel in which there is a battle between beasts whose description draws upon the mythic images of the chaos that preceded creation. Its climax is the coming of "one like a son of man," to whom dominion, glory, and kingship are given. Chapters 8–12 are different again. Although they record further visions and their interpretation, the mythic imagery is subdued, and the emphasis is on events that bring divine judgment to Judah's neighbors as well as vindication and resurrection to those who are wise among God's people (Daniel 12:2–3).

Daniel is unique in the Hebrew Bible in being composed in two languages (although Ezra contains some letters in Aramaic). Daniel begins in Hebrew (1:1–2:4a) but soon has a long section in Aramaic (2:4b–7:28), which includes its best-known stories and the strikingly different chapter 7. The remainder of the book is in Hebrew again.

These facts have made the unity of Daniel a long-running debate in scholarship. Were the stories of chapters 2–6 an originally independent Aramaic book incorporated into a book composed of chapters 1 and 8–12? If so, where did chapter 7 come from, and why was it written in Aramaic? Why does the linguistic difference inconveniently extend from chapter 2 to chapter 7, instead of including the stories only? Why, if the book is the work of a single author, is it composed in two languages? In what follows, the book's sections will be discussed separately before an attempt is made to answer these more complicated questions.

1. The Stories

A fragmentary text discovered in 1952 in cave 4 at Qumram (part of the general discovery of the Dead Sea Scrolls) indicates that the stories in Daniel chapters 2–6 have their origin in legends that circulated widely in the ancient Near East. The fragment concerns the Babylonian king Nabonidus, who had prayed to "gods of silver and gold . . . wood and stone and clay" and who had been healed by a Jew from an ulcer that had afflicted him for seven years in Teiman (Taima) (Vermes 1997, p. 573). Nabonidus (556–539 B.C.E.) did indeed retreat to an oasis in the Arabian Desert, leaving Belshazzar in charge of the kingdom (*Ancient Near Eastern Texts*, p. 306), so the setting assumed in the fragment is plausible.

The Nabonidus fragment is reminiscent of two of the stories in Daniel. The first is in chapter 4, where Nebuchadnezzar is driven away from Babylon for "seven times," that is, for seven years (Daniel 4:16, 25), because of his pride; he lives with the wild animals until he comes to his senses and acknowledges that true sovereignty belongs to the God of Daniel, who has forecast the event by interpreting Nebuchadnezzar's dream. The similarities with the Nabonidus fragment are the exile of the king from Babylon and the part played by a Jew in his restoration. In Daniel chapter 4 the name of the king has changed from the less well-known Nabonidus to the more famous Nebuchadnezzar, and the unnamed Jewish healer of the Nabonidus fragment is identified as Daniel. Both of these processes (substituting a more famous person and supplying a name for an anonymous person) are well-established features of how stories change during oral transmission. The other similarity is with chapter 5, where Belshazzar and his guests praise the "gods of gold and silver, bronze, iron, wood, and stone" (Daniel 5:4; cf. the quotation from the Nabonidus fragment earlier).

Granted that we can be reasonably sure that some of the stories in Daniel 2–6 have their origins in stories that reflected events of sixth-century B.C.E. Babylon, we have to surmise their history and their development up to their incorporation into Daniel. Probably from the end of the sixth century Jews who were exiled in Babylonia and elsewhere circulated stories about how Jews had risen to prominence in the courts of foreign rulers, how rulers who had oppressed Jews had been punished by God, and how devout Jews who had maintained their faith had been delivered. These themes are found in the Book of Esther; and they have some foundation in figures such as Nehemiah, who held an important office in the Persian court (445–432 B.C.E.). Daniel 2, with its story of the statue made of various metals, may reflect the fall of the Babylonian Empire to Cyrus in 539. If this is correct, we have another of the stories whose origins go back to the sixth century.

In discussions of Daniel, scholars have been divided between those who hold that Daniel 1–6 accurately described events that took place in Babylon in the sixth century B.C.E. and those who argue that the stories were freely composed in the second century B.C.E., when Daniel was written. The truth seems to be somewhere between these positions. Although they do not record events that happened in sixth-century Babylon, chapters 2–6 are based on stories that originated at that time, some of which have a historical core, but all of which have been shaped by retelling to express the themes noted earlier. These stories were popular in the Jewish Diaspora, and when the crisis occurred that precipitated the writing of Daniel, they were incorporated into Daniel because of their popularity and relevance. That crisis was the attack upon Judaism by the Hellenistic ruler of Syria Antiochus IV (175–164 B.C.E.) in 169–167 B.C.E., a crisis implied in Daniel 5. This is the only one of the stories in which the king is punished with death for desecrating the Temple's sacred vessels, just as Antiochus desecrated the Temple and also died (Daniel 5:30; 1 Maccabees 6:1–19). In the other stories, the king repents and acknowledges the power of the God of Israel. Thus, the changing pattern of narrative reveals a centuries-long history of composition, retelling, and final use of ancient materials in the Book of Daniel. Nothing has been said about Daniel himself so far. Ezekiel 14:14 mentions three righteous men: Noah, Daniel, and Job. Ugaritic texts of the thirteenth century B.C.E. mention a hero called Dan'el. The name itself seems to be that of a popular heroic figure and was probably attached to the stories when they were being told among Diaspora Jews.

2. The Vision in Chapter 7

Many scholars have commented on the strange imagery of Daniel 7 and its resemblance to the mythology of the ancient Near East. The chapter begins with the winds stirring up the sea, from which four great beasts emerge (Daniel 7:1–8). The fourth beast is the most terrifying; at first it has ten horns, and then another, little horn grows among them and displaces three of them. In the mythology of Babylonia the sea is the place of chaos; and it has been argued that even the Hebrew Bible echoes with allusions to a primal struggle between God and the sea (e.g., Isaiah 51:9–10). The descriptions of the beasts recall the iconography of Babylonia with its strange monsters and refer in Daniel to the successive empires that had pillaged Israel and Judah.

The use of this imagery indicates that the authors were well versed in the general literature and culture of their day and supports the view that we should place Daniel in the milieu of mantic wisdom. The same consideration applies to the figure of "one like a son of man," who appears on the clouds of heaven in 7:13 and to whom is given dominion over the nations. Although it is not possible to discover any single entirely convincing analogy to Daniel's son of man in ancient Near Eastern mythology

ANIMAL IMAGERY IN APOCALYPTIC AND DANIEL

The language of apocalyptic is highly dramatic. With extravagant imagination the writers of apocalyptic embellish their message with fantastic – sometimes bizarre – imagery. Apocalyptic literature is filled with rich symbolism, which has its source in both the metaphors of the Hebrew Bible and the characters of ancient Near Eastern mythology. This strange imagery fosters the sense of secrecy and mystery characteristic of apocalyptic writings.

Particularly striking is the way that apocalypticists employed animal figures to symbolize the people and nations inhabiting their visionary portraits of history and beyond. Already during the first and second Temple periods human characteristics were depicted in symbolic terms. The ram and the horn are symbols of power and dominion (Ezekiel 34:17); the lion represents strength and ferocity (Hosea 5:14); oxen and lambs stand for domesticity and peace (Isaiah 11:6–7). This tradition is quite marked in many apocalyptic writings. In the *First Book of Enoch*, the bull stands for the patriarchs from Adam to Isaac; the righteous Moses and Aaron are sheep; Kings David and Solomon are rams; and Judah Maccabee is symbolized by a great horn. Wild beasts and

birds of prey often symbolize the Gentile nations. In the tradition of Ezekiel 39, apocalyptic literature describes the heathen under the figures of tigers, wolves, dogs, hyenas, boars, foxes, squirrels, swine, vultures, ravens, and reptiles. The Roman legions are depicted as eagles, and the Messiah, who redeems his people from them, is a mighty lion (2 Esdras 11:37; cf. Revelation 5:5).

Perhaps the most famous apocalyptic animal imagery comes from the night visions of Daniel. Daniel's four great beasts belong to no recognizable earthly species, suggesting that their origin is to be found in the world of ancient Near Eastern mythology. The general meaning of these strange creatures is more accessible than their source. The writer of Daniel uses this strange animal imagery to recount the progress of world history, depicting the four great empires: Babylonia, Media, Persia, and Greece. However, some parts of the symbolism are still lost in obscurity (e.g., the sea from which the beasts arise and the four winds that blow on it). The beasts in Revelation are similar in their origin and purpose (Revelation 12–14).

The great Leviathan also figures prominently in the animal imagery

of apocalyptic writers. The beast is known variously as Behemoth, Rahab, the serpent, and the dragon. Its origins lie in the Babylonian account of creation, where the creator god slays the sea monster Chaos and fashions the universe from the beast's carcass. This myth found its way (with significant modification) into the Hebrew tradition, and several biblical passages display reflections of it (Psalm 74:13; Job 40:15–24; Ezekiel 29:3). However, the protoapocalyptic section of Isaiah recasts God's defeat of the chaos monster from a past accomplishment into an event anticipated on the great and imminent Day of Yahweh (Isaiah 27:1). In the apocalyptic tradition related to the *First Book of Enoch*, Behemoth and Leviathan become two distinct mythical monsters. Behemoth inhabits the land, and Leviathan dwells in the sea (cf. *1 Enoch* 60:7–9; 2 Esdras 6:47–52). Some apocalyptic writings give these creatures an eschatological context and associate them with the appearance of the Messiah. According to *2 Baruch*, Leviathan and Behemoth will be the food of the righteous at the messianic banquet, which inaugurates the kingdom of God.

(comparisons having been made with the Babylonian god Marduk; the Persian Gayomart, or first man; and the Canaanite god Baal, who "comes with the clouds of heaven" and whose father, El, is called "father of years" – cf. Daniel 7:9, 13), a range of similar figures would have been recognized by the authors of Daniel. The matter of the *origin* of the son of man figure must not be confused with its use in Daniel 7, where it stands for the "holy ones of the Most High" (Daniel 7:27), who receive an everlasting kingdom and who are probably to be identified with those Jews who remained true to their faith during the persecutions initiated by Antiochus IV, the "little horn" that is judged and destroyed.

SON OF MAN

The enigmatic phrase "son of man" underwent significant changes in meaning during the course of early Jewish history. In most of the Hebrew Bible, the words *ben 'adam* (Aramaic *bar 'enash*) are simply Semitic expressions for humankind. Thus the classic anthropological question posed in Psalm 8:4 places "son of man" in poetic parallelism with the notion of "person" (Hebrew *'enosh*). In the Book of Ezekiel, the phrase occurs eighty-seven times in reference to the prophet himself.

By the second century B.C.E., "son of man" took on new connotations. Daniel 7:13 preserves a vision in which a glorious being "like a son of man" descends from the heavens to take up his dominion over the peoples of the earth. Scholars have long been divided on their interpretation of this enigmatic reference. Some believe that in this context "son of man" merely designates the strange figure as a human being who symbolically represents the saints of God. This human figure stands in contrast to the strange beasts that also inhabit Daniel's dreams. Others understand the passage as a description of an angelic being whose *appearance* seems human. A few see in Daniel the beginning of an apocalyptic tradition that introduces the "son of man" as a key figure in the events that occur at the end of the age.

Daniel's vision is the key to the meaning of the phrase in this book. The "one like a person" is an angel, standing beside God's throne. He is called the "one like a person" (traditionally translated in Daniel and the Gospels as "the son of man") because

he has a human face. His humanity stands in sharp contrast to the other angelic emanations around the throne, which are bestial. The "one like a person" vanquishes a lion, a bear, a leopard, and a horned beast from God's presence (Daniel 7:1–13). Another angel interprets Daniel's vision for him (Daniel 7:17–18):

> These great beasts that are four are four kings: they shall arise from the earth. But the holy ones of the Highest shall receive the Kingdom, and shall possess the Kingdom for the age, and for the age of the ages.

The great kings of the Assyrians, Babylonians, Persians, and Seleucids have had their day; but when Israel's angel comes to rule, Israel's sovereignty will last forever.

The visionary material in Daniel explores the cosmic battle between the "one like a person" and the angelic representatives of the great empires that had conquered Israel. It was written both as an apocalyptic prediction of the end of the world and as propaganda to promote the Jewish revolt launched in 167 B.C.E., which, to the surprise of everyone involved, actually succeeded. Daniel was written shortly after "the abomination of desolation" (Daniel 12:11), when the Seleucid king, Antiochus IV Epiphanes, ordered that swine be offered on the Temple altar (because roast pork was a favorite food of the god Zeus). Outraged Jews banded together to form an unstoppable guerrilla army, willing to go on suicide missions against a foe that greatly outnumbered them and

whose equipment dwarfed their own. The revolt succeeded in 164 B.C.E., and the Maccabees came to power. The Temple was rededicated, and the altar stones defiled by the swine were hidden until that time when a faithful prophet would arise and tell the king and high priest what to do with them (1 Maccabees 4:44–46).

Apocalypticists both combined this terminology from Daniel 7 with Near Eastern mythological traditions and vastly expanded its meaning by their own imaginations. The apocalypses of *Enoch* and 2 Esdras clearly associate the phrase "son of man" with a superhuman – almost divine – redeemer figure. The picture of this figure developed in apocalyptic literature is quite striking. This son of man is a transcendent heavenly being with no prior human existence. Indeed, he is said to have existed even before God created the world. He remains hidden until the time appointed by God, when he is revealed as an object of worship for the whole world. At the end of time, the son of man takes his seat to judge the mighty of the world. Especially in *Enoch*, the son of man comes to be identified with the Messiah ("God's Elect One," "the Lord's Anointed"), even though the two concepts have very different beginnings.

"Son of man" seems to have been the early Christian community's most frequent appellation for Jesus. Jesus himself apparently used the phrase as his own favorite self-designation. Sometimes the words are merely a way of speaking of himself as a person (e.g., Matthew 8:20). In other places, Jesus simply uses "son of man" as a traditional Semitic phrase

(continued)

SON OF MAN (continued)

that means "human being," or in reference to the angelic figure in Daniel. However, the early church invested the title "son of man" with great theological significance. In line with the apocalyptic tradition, the Gospels portray Jesus as "son of man" as a transcendent heavenly figure, the exalted Lord who will come again in glory. Matthew also portrays the son of man as the just judge, enthroned with his angels in glory, who separates the virtuous from the wicked like a shepherd divides the sheep from the goats.

But the New Testament son of man is also a suffering human figure who recalls the Servant of the Lord in Isaiah 53. The title figures prominently in Jesus' Passion predictions in Mark (e.g., Mark 8:31). It is the son of man who "came, not to be served, but to serve, and to give his life as a redemption for many" (Mark 10:45; cf. Matthew 20:28; Luke 22:27). Some scholars have argued that Jesus forged a new meaning for the traditional title "son of man" by combining and reformulating these conflicting traditions.

By the second century of the Common Era, "son of man" had lost much of its apocalyptic force. The early church fathers generally understood the phrase as biblical recognition of Jesus' human nature, in contrast to the title "Son of God," which pointed to the Savior's divinity.

3. The Visions in Chapters 8–12

The remainder of Daniel includes a number of visions and their interpretations. Chapter 8 is a vision whose interpretation (8:20–2) describes the defeat of the Medes and Persians by the Greeks (Alexander the Great, 356–323 B.C.E.) and the rise of four smaller kingdoms from the Greek kingdom. The vision (but not the interpretation) also implies the rise of Antiochus IV and his desecration of the Temple (8:9–11).

Daniel 9 is a beautiful prayer that recalls other compositions such as 1 Kings 8. The people are in exile, and Daniel requests God to look with favor on his desolated sanctuary and city (vv. 18–19). A strange passage concludes the chapter and foretells the "abomination that desolates" in the sanctuary that Antiochus will effect (9:24–7; cf. 11:31; 12:11). Chapters 10–11 continue the veiled references to the history of the fourth to third centuries B.C.E. in chapter 8, emphasizing the aftermath of the breakup of Alexander's kingdom and the struggle between his generals, especially that between the king of the south (the Egyptian Ptolemies) and the king of the north (the Syrian Seleucids). That brings the seer to his own time, and the crises brought on by Antiochus. Daniel 12 is an epilogue that introduces us to the authors, men who are among the wise who "shall shine in the brightness of the sky." It contains what is arguably the only explicit reference in the Hebrew Bible to resurrection:

> Many of those who sleep in the dust of the earth shall awake, some to everlasting life, and some to shame and everlasting contempt. (12:2)

The fate of those who are resurrected will, we presume, depend on whether or not they were faithful in the tribulations that caused the Book of Daniel to be written: Antiochus's assault on the Temple and Jerusalem in 169–167 B.C.E.

4. Conclusion

Some of the questions posed at the outset have been answered. The Book of Daniel contains material that developed over several centuries before being put into its present form during the second century B.C.E. as a result of the attack on Judaism by Antiochus IV. Its disparate material – that is, its popular stories, its mythic imagery, and its detailed allusions to the history of Babylon, Persia, Greece, and the Hellenistic kingdoms – is best explained by accepting that it was composed by "wise" scribes who were conversant with these types of literature and knowledge. The matter of the use of two languages is impossible to resolve definitively, although it is not difficult to conceive that different scribal groups would have distinctive linguistic preferences.

What must not be overlooked is the theology of Daniel. Nowhere in the Hebrew Bible do we have such striking and powerful assertions of the sovereignty of the God of Israel over the nations of the world, nor of the conviction that God will establish a kingdom that will endure forever. These hopes were expressed in the full knowledge that when it came to individuals faced by the threat of death at the hands of persecutors, there was not likely to be the miraculous deliverance implied in some of the stories in chapters 1–6. We catch a hint of this realism in the reply of the three men who were about to be put in the fiery furnace:

> If our God whom we serve is able to deliver us from the furnace of blazing fire and out of your hand, O king, let him deliver us. But if not, be it known to you, O king, that we will not serve your gods. (3:17–18)

This same realism is also implied in the passage about resurrection, promising the faithful that they will not have died in vain but would shine as the stars in a transformed existence (12:3). In the Septuagint Daniel's placement at the close of the canon in Christian usage made its themes of resurrection and the judgment of the son of man into a powerful preface to the New Testament.

Among the resources upon which the authors drew to express this hope were the past traditions of Israel, where it could be seen that, in all the challenges of their history, the people had been guided by a God who was ultimately more powerful than great empires, because he was the creator of the world. It says much for the creativity of Israelite religion that the authors of Daniel were able to write such a unique book from within their tradition in the face of a crisis that threatened their very existence. Further, their vision of hope, born out of suffering and centering on the faithful ones symbolized by "one like a son of man," produced narratives whose latent meaning gave confidence to later readers that God was with his people in the midst of persecution and suffering, and that his purposes would ultimately triumph. That meaning would help Jesus of Nazareth shape and realize his message and contribute to the Rabbis' definition of true wisdom.

BIBLIOGRAPHICAL AND BIOGRAPHICAL ESSAYS

Revised with the assistance of Matthew R. Schlimm.

A. Bibliography

1. Introductory Books

See Bernhard W. Anderson's *Understanding the Old Testament*, 5th ed. (Upper Saddle River, NJ: Pearson Prentice-Hall, 2007). Anderson's treatment of the Hebrew Bible combines an excellent historical and archaeological approach with a high standard of literary and theological analysis.

John Rogerson, John Barton, David Clines, and Paul Joyce, *Beginning Old Testament Study*, 2d ed. (London: SPCK, 1998), is designed to introduce readers to academic scholarship. It sketches the history of Old Testament study and then deals with specific issues such as methodology, the worldview of the ancient Israelites, Old Testament ethics and theology, the relation between the Old and New Testaments, and using the Old Testament in today's world.

Michael D. Coogan, *The Old Testament: A Historical and Literary Introduction to the Hebrew Scriptures* (New York: Oxford University Press, 2006), is a highly accessible introduction, covering basic issues. Frank S. Frick, *A Journey through the Hebrew Scripture*, 2d ed. (Belmont, CA: Wadsworth/Thomson Learning, 2003), offers an introduction to critical methodology, Near Eastern geography, and the literature of the Hebrew Bible. John J. Collins, *Introduction to the Hebrew Bible* (Minneapolis: Fortress, 2004), is a critical introduction with particular attention to historical and archaeological matters. C. Westermann, *Handbook to the Old Testament,* trans. R. H. Boyd (Minneapolis: Augsburg, 1967), addresses the fact that the content of the Hebrew Bible is unfamiliar to many readers today. It helps readers to become familiar with the Hebrew Bible by summarizing each book, often using diagrams, and by explaining briefly the date and purpose of each book and its sections. See also Richard Elliott Friedman, *The Bible with Sources Revealed* (San Francisco: Harper, 2003).

Philip R. Davies and John Rogerson, *The Old Testament World*, 2d ed. (Louisville: Westminster John Knox, 2005), is a comprehensive introduction to the historical, social, and political backgrounds of the Hebrew Bible as well as to its literature. Other, more specialized, introductions to aspects of the Hebrew Bible include R. E. Clements, ed., *The World of Ancient Israel: Sociological, Anthropological and Political Perspectives* (Cambridge: Cambridge University Press, 1989); Andrew D. Mayes, *The Hebrew Bible in Sociological Perspective* (London: Marshall Pickering, 1989); L. Grabbe, *Judaism from Cyrus to Hadrian*, vol. 1, *The Persian and Greek Periods* (Minneapolis: Fortress Press, 1992); C. E. Carter and C. L. Meyers, eds., *Community, Identity, and Ideology: Social Science Approaches to the Hebrew Bible* (Winona Lake, IN: Eisenbrauns, 1996); F. S. Frick, *The Formation of the State in Ancient Israel: A*

Survey of Models and Theories (Sheffield: Sheffield Academic Press, 1985); and Paula M. McNutt, *Reconstructing the Society of Ancient Israel* (Louisville: Westminster John Knox, 1999).

Brevard S. Child's *Introduction to the Old Testament as Scripture* (Philadelphia: Fortress Press, 1979) had an enormous impact on biblical studies in the 1980s in arguing for a new kind of "canonical criticism" based on the existing biblical text and the inner-biblical dialogue among the various components of the text. Norman K. Gottwald's *The Hebrew Bible: A Socioliterary Introduction* (Philadelphia: Fortress Press, 1985) had a similar impact on biblical study by applying sociological theory to the main periods of Israel's history and literary theory to the formation of the canon of Scripture. The book is best used as a reference work and supplement to biblical study. A collection of essays edited by Hershel Shanks, *Ancient Israel*, rev. ed. (Washington: Biblical Archaeological Society, 1999), provides a readable overview of recent trends in historical study. There are excellent introductions to individual books of the Hebrew Bible as well as to aspects of the Bible's history, sociology, geography, and archaeology in *The Anchor Bible Dictionary*, ed. D. N. Freedman, 6 vols. (New York: Doubleday, 1992).

One of the important features of recent interpretation of the Hebrew Bible has been the contribution made by writers committed to feminist, liberation, or postcolonial approaches. Good introductions to these interpretations are Phyllis Trible, *God and the Rhetoric of Sexuality* (London: SCM, 1992); Alice L. Laffey, *An Introduction to the Old Testament: A Feminist Perspective* (Philadelphia: Fortress Press, 1988); N. K. Gottwald, ed., *The Bible and Liberation: Political and Social Hermeneutics* (Maryknoll, NY: Orbis, 1993); and R. S. Sugirtharajah, *Postcolonial Criticism and Biblical Interpretation* (New York: Oxford University Press, 2002). Carol L. Meyers's book *Discovering Eve* (New York: Oxford University Press, 1988) enables the student of the Hebrew Bible to reread the all-important creation story in light of social-scientific and archaeological materials. In this connection, Mark Smith's *The Early History of God*, 2d ed. (Grand Rapids: Eerdmans, 2002) is invaluable since it offers a comprehensive study of Israel's concept of God in light of Northwest Semitic literature and archaeology.

2. Texts from the Ancient Near East

A book referred to frequently in the present work with the abbreviation *Ancient Near Eastern Texts* is James B. Pritchard, *Ancient Near Eastern Texts Relating to the Old Testament*, 3d ed. (Princeton: Princeton University Press, 1969). This is an invaluable collection of translations of texts from Egypt, Palestine, Syria, and Mesopotamia, covering history, law, myths, epics, Wisdom literature, letters, and inscriptions. William W. Hallo, ed., *The Context of Scripture,* 3 vols. (Leiden: Brill, 1997–2002), is a more recent collection of texts that has begun to replace Pritchard's work.

3. Archaeology

The most helpful recent guide to biblical archaeology is Amihay Mazar's *Archaeology of the Land of the Bible,* 10,000–586 B.C.E., Anchor Bible Reference Library (New York: Doubleday, 1990). Mazar's treatment is by historical period and relates the material culture of each period to the known written sources of the period. Its greatest strength is the biblical period from ca. 1200 to 600 B.C.E. Another useful guide is Amnon Ben-Tor, ed., *The Archaeology of Ancient Israel* (New Haven: Yale University Press, 1992). Detailed information on the practice of archaeology is provided in Thomas E. Levy, ed., *The Archaeology of Society in the Holy Land* (New York: Facts on File, 1995). The two most important encyclopedias focused on ancient Near Eastern archaeology are Eric M. Meyers, ed., *The Oxford Encyclopedia of Archaeology in the Near East,* 5 vols. (New York: Oxford University Press, 1997); and E. Stern, ed., *The New Encyclopedia of Archaeological Excavations of the Holy Land,* 4 vols. (Jerusalem: Israel Exploration Society and Carta; New York: Simon & Schuster, 1993).

4. Atlases

Knowledge of the geography of the ancient world is important for understanding the Hebrew Bible. A. F. Rainey and R. S. Notley, *The Sacred Bridge: Carta's Atlas of the Biblical World* (Jerusalem: Carta, 2006), is an impressive atlas that treats both the Hebrew Bible and New Testament. *The Oxford Bible Atlas,* 3d ed., ed. J. Day (Oxford: Oxford University Press, 1984), is also a handy, comprehensive, and reliable work. John Rogerson, *Atlas of the Bible* (Oxford: Phaidon, 1989; New York: Facts on File, 1985), breaks new ground by treating the subject geographically rather than historically, with emphasis on how the land looked in biblical, as opposed to modern, times. Also recommended are M. Roaf, *Cultural Atlas of Mesopotamia and the Ancient Near East* (Oxford and New York: Facts on File, 1990); and J. Baines and J. Maalek, *Atlas of Ancient Egypt* (Oxford: Phaidon, 1980).

5. Pentateuch

Two important overviews of scholarship on the Pentateuch are Joseph Blenkinsopp, *The Pentateuch* (New York: Doubleday, 1992), and E. Nicholson, *The Pentateuch in the Twentieth Century* (Oxford: Clarendon, 1998). A useful guide to source criticism of the Pentateuch is A. Rofé, *Introduction to the Composition of the Pentateuch* (Sheffield: Sheffield Academic Press, 1999). Jacob Milgrom, *Leviticus: A Book of Ritual and Ethics* (Minneapolis: Fortress, 2004), has been highly influential in understanding the cult envisioned by Leviticus.

6. Historical Books

L. S. Schearing and S. L. McKenzie, eds., *Those Elusive Deuteronomists* (Sheffield: Sheffield Academic Press, 1999), is a collection of fifteen essays that analyze many key issues pertaining to Deuteronomistic History and pan-Deuteronomism. A more general treatment of history and the Hebrew Bible is B. Halpern, *The First Historians* (University Park: Pennsylvania State University Press, 1988), which argues that the historical books were written with the intention of representing the past with fairness and accuracy. A. G. Auld, *Kings without Privilege: David and Moses in the Story of the Bible's Kings* (Edinburgh: T. & T. Clark, 1994), proposes that Chronicles did not use Samuel and Kings as sources, but that the material common to Samuel and Kings, on the one hand, and to Chronicles, on the other, represents a source used by both. This is not the same as the old theory that Samuel and Kings had used extensively, and Chronicles had used minimally, a common biographical source about the lives of David and Solomon. On Chronicles, see also the essential work of S. Japhet, *I and II Chronicles* (Louisville: Westminster John Knox, 1993).

7. Prophecy and Prophets

D. L. Petersen, *The Prophetic Literature* (Louisville: Westminster John Knox, 2002), is an excellent introduction to biblical prophecy. R. P. Gordon, ed., *"The Place Is Too Small for Us"* (Winona Lake, IN: Eisenbrauns, 1995), is a useful anthology with helpful introductory and concluding essays. Claus Westermann, *Basic Forms of Prophetic Speech* (Philadelphia: Westminster, 1967), is the classic form critical analysis of prophetic literature, whereas R. R. Wilson, *Prophecy and Society in Ancient Israel* (Philadelphia: Fortress Press, 1980), is the classic sociological analysis of the prophets.

8. Wisdom

James L. Crenshaw, *Old Testament Wisdom*, rev. ed. (Louisville: Westminster John Knox, 1998), is an outstanding and highly popular introduction to Wisdom literature. Also noteworthy is R. J. Clifford, *The Wisdom Literature* (Nashville: Abingdon, 1998).

9. Guides to Individual Books of the Hebrew Bible

Three commentary series are recommended to readers who wish to study particular books in greater depth. The Anchor Bible commentaries published by Doubleday and the Old Testament Library published by Westminster John Knox are both considered standards in the field. Meanwhile, the series of inexpensive Old Testament Guides edited by R. N. Whybray and published by T. & T. Clark (formerly by Sheffield Academic Press) introduces readers to the main issues in the academic study of each book of the Hebrew Bible and contains suggestions for further reading.

10. Books and Articles Referred to in the Text

Ancient Near Eastern Texts. *See* Pritchard, J. B.

Avigad, N. 1986. *Hebrew Bullae from the Time of Jeremiah: Remnants of a Burnt Archive*. Jerusalem: Israel Exploration Society.

Blum, E. 1984. *Die Komposition der Vätergeschichte.* Wissenschaftliche Monographien zum Alten und Neuen Testament 57. Neukirchen-Vluyn: Neukirchener Verlag.

A large and detailed work on the composition of the stories of Abraham, Isaac, and Jacob that argues that each set of traditions developed separately before being combined.

Calvin, J. 1975. *Genesis.* Trans. John King. Edinburgh: Banner of Truth Trust.

A translation of the lectures of the famous reformer that shows that he held radical views on the purpose of the creation story in Genesis 1. It was not, according to Calvin, a scientific account of the creation of the universe but a description as it would have appeared to an ancient Israelite observer.

Chilton, B. D. 1982. *The Glory of Israel: The Theology and Provenience of the Isaiah Targum.* Journal for the Study of the Old Testament, Supplement 23. Sheffield: JSOT.

—— 1996. *Pure Kingdom: Jesus' Vision of God. Studying the Historical Jesus 1.* Grand Rapids: Eerdmans; London: SPCK.

—— 2002. *Redeeming Time: The Wisdom of Ancient Jewish and Christian Festal Calendars.* Peabody, MA: Hendrickson.

Clements, R. E., ed. 1989. *The World of Ancient Israel: Sociological, Anthropological, and Political Perspectives.* Cambridge: Cambridge University Press.

Davies, G. I. 1991. *Ancient Hebrew Inscriptions.* Cambridge: Cambridge University Press.

A valuable collection of Hebrew inscriptions together with a concordance. For use by Hebraists only.

Davies, P. R. 1985. *Daniel.* Old Testament Guides. Sheffield: Sheffield Academic Press.

—— 1989. "The Social World of the Apocalyptic Writings," in Clements 1989, 251–71.

—— 1992. *In Search of Ancient Israel.* Sheffield: JSOT Press.

A stimulating and controversial book that forces readers to consider how they relate history, the Bible, and archaeology in considering Israel's origins.

Davies, P. R., and J. W. Rogerson. 2005. *The Old Testament World.* 2d ed Louisville: Westminster John Knox.

De Moor, J. C. 1990. *The Rise of Yahwism: The Roots of Israelite Monotheism.* Bibliotheca Ephemeridum Theologicarum Lovaniensium 91. Louvain: University Press and Peeters.

An attempt to identify Moses and Israelite origins with the help of biblical and non-biblical texts.

Finkelstein, I. 1988. *The Archaeology of the Israelite Settlement.* Jerusalem: Israel Exploration Society.

An important account of ancient Israel's settlement in Canaan in the light of archaeological surveys.

Finkelstein, I., and N. A. Silberman. 2001. *The Bible Unearthed: Archaeology's New Vision of Ancient Israel and the Origin of Its Sacred Texts*. New York: Touchstone.

A minimalist account of ancient Israel accessible for a nonacademic audience.

—— 2006. *David and Solomon: In Search of the Bible's Sacred Kings and the Roots of the Western Tradition*. New York: Free Press.

Fishbane, M. 1985. *Biblical Interpretation in Ancient Israel*. Oxford: Oxford University Press.

Traces biblical interpretation within the books of the Bible and applies it a discussion of the origin of Israel's legal traditions.

Frazer, J. G. 1890. *The Golden Bough: A Study in Comparative Religion*. London: Macmillan.

George, A. 1999. *The Epic of Gilgamesh*. London: Penguin.

Gerstenberger, E. 1988. *Psalms: Part I, with an Introduction to Cultic Poetry*. Grand Rapids: Eerdmans.

Dates the Psalms later (i.e., in the postexilic period) than the prevailing consensus.

Görg, M., and B. Lang, eds. 1988–. *Neues Bibel-Lexikon*. 10 vols. to date. Zürich: Benzinger.

An excellent, authoritative, concise, and up-to-date reference work.

Gunkel, H. 1917. *Das Märchen im Alten Testament*. Tübingen: Mohr.

Heidel, A. 1963a. *The Babylonian Genesis*. 2d ed. Chicago: University of Chicago Press, Phoenix Books.

This and the title that follows are standard translations and discussions of nonbiblical texts in their relation to the Hebrew Bible.

—— 1963b. *The Gilgamesh Epic and Old Testament Parallels*. 2d ed. Chicago: University of Chicago Press, Phoenix Books.

Hengel, M. 2002. "Paul in Arabia." *Bulletin for Biblical Research* 12.1: 47–66.

Hopkins, D. C. 1985. *The Highlands of Canaan: Agricultural Life in the Early Iron Age*. Social World of Biblical Antiquity 3. Sheffield: Almond/JSOT Press.

A pioneering discussion.

Houtman, C. 1986. *Exodus vertaald en verklaard: Commentaar op het Oude Testament*. Kampen: J. H. Kok.

A massive commentary for specialists and readers of Dutch.

Jamieson-Drake, D. W. 1991. *Scribes and Schools in Monarchic Judah: A Socioarchaeological Approach*. Sheffield: JSOT Press.

An important discussion of the centralization of administration in Judah based on statistical methods.

Keel, O., and S. Schroer. 1990. *Studien zu den Stempelsiegeln aus Palastina/ Israel*. Vol. 3, *Die Frühe Eisenzeit: Ein Workshop*. Freiburg: Universitatsverlag Freiburg Schweiz; Göttingen: Vandenhoeck & Ruprecht.

Keel, O., and C. Uehlinger. 1992. *Göttinnen, Götter, und Gottessymbole: Neue Erkenntnisse zur Religionsgeschichte Kanaans und Israels aufgrund bislang unerschlossener ikonographischer Quellen.* Quaestiones Disputatae 134. Freiburg-im-Breisgau: Herder Verlag.

> *This, and the title that precedes, are important contributions to understanding "popular religion" in ancient Israel based on iconography. Now available as Gods, Goddesses, and Images of God in Ancient Israel,* trans. Thomas H. Trapp. Minneapolis: Fortress Press, 1998.

Lang, B. 1981. *Ezechiel.* Darmstadt: Wissenschaftliche Buchgesellschaft.

Lohfink, N. 1983. "Die Schichten des Pentateuch und der Krieg." In N. Lohfink, ed., *Gewalt und Gewaltlosigkeit in Alten Testament,* 51–110. Quaestiones Disputatae 96. Freiburg-im-Breisgau: Herder Verlag.

> *Considers how the different Pentateuchal sources deal with the question of war.*

———. 1994. *Theology of the Pentateuch: Themes of the Priestly Narrative and Deuteronomy.* Minneapolis: Fortress.

———, ed. 1985. *Das Deuteronomium: Enstehung, Gestalt, and Botschaft.* Bibliotheca Ephemeridum Theologicarum Lovaniensium 68. Louvain: University Press and Peeters.

> *A collection of papers on the origin and purpose of Deuteronomy.*

Maurice, F. D. 1892. *The Patriarchs and Lawgivers of the Old Testament.* London: Macmillan.

> *Collected sermons by a famous nineteenth-century theologian.*

Mazar, A. 1990. *Archaeology of the Land of the Bible, 10,000–586* B.C.E. Anchor Bible Reference Library. New York: Doubleday.

> *A comprehensive survey of the material.*

Mendenhall, G. E. 1962. "The Hebrew Conquest of Palestine." *Biblical Archaeology* 25: 66–87.

Meyers, C. L., and E. M. Meyers. 1987. *Haggai–Zechariah 1–8.* Anchor Bible. New York: Doubleday.

———. 1993. *Zechariah 9–14, Malachi.* Anchor Bible. New York: Doubleday.

Müller, H.-P. 1982. "Die aramâische Inschrift von Deir 'Alla und die älteren Bileamsprüche." *Zeitschrift für die alttestamentliche Wissenschaft* 94: 214–44.

> *Translation of and commentary on the Balaam inscription from Tell Deir Alla in the Jordan Valley.*

———. 1985. "Das Motiv für die Sintflut: Die hermeneutische Funktion des Mythos und seiner Analyse." *Zeitschrift für die altestamentliche Wissenschaft* 97: 295–316.

> *An important treatment of the Flood story in Genesis.*

Pritchard, J. B. 1969. *Ancient Near Eastern Texts Relating to the Old Testament.* 3d ed. Princeton: Princeton University Press.

Riehm, E. 1890. *Einleitung in das Alte Testament.* Vol. 2. Halle: Eugen Stein.

> *One of the major nineteenth-century introductions to the Old Testament.*

Rogerson, J. W. 1978. *Anthropology and the Old Testament.* Oxford: Basil Blackwell. Repr., Sheffield: JSOT Press, 1984.

Discusses basic questions of method and approach.

——. 1984. *Old Testament Criticism in the Nineteenth Century: England and Germany.* London: SPCK.

Examines how German biblical criticism developed and was received in England.

——. 1991. *Genesis 1–11.* Old Testament Guides. Sheffield: Sheffield Academic Press.

——. 1992. *W. M. L. de Wette, Founder of Modern Biblical Criticism: An Intellectual Biography.* Sheffield: JSOT Press.

Rogerson, J. W., and J. W. McKay. 1977. *Psalms: The Cambridge Bible Commentary.* Cambridge: Cambridge University Press.

Scholder, K. 1990. *The Birth of Modern Critical Theology: Origins and Problems of Biblical Criticism in the Seventeenth Century.* London: SCM Press.

Shiloh, Y. 1986. "A Group of Hebrew Bullae from the City of David." *Israel Exploration Journal* 36: 16–38.

Staubli, T. 1991. *Das Image der Nomaden im alten Israel und in der Ikonographie seiner sesshaften Nachbarn.* Orbis Biblicis et Orientalis 107. Freiburg: Universitätsverlag Freiburg Schweiz; Göttingen: Vandenhoeck & Ruprecht.

A discussion of "nomads" in the ancient Near East based on iconography.

Vermes, G. 1997. *The Complete Dead Sea Scrolls in English.* New York: Allen Lane / Penguin.

Weinfeld, M. 1972. *Deuteronomy and the Deuteronomic School.* Oxford: Clarendon Press.

A classic study that links Deuteronomy with Israel's "wisdom" schools.

——. 1991. *Deuteronomy 1–11.* Anchor Bible. New York: Doubleday.

B. Biography

This section deals briefly with some major figures in the history of biblical research. To avoid mention of such scholars would give a false impression of the discipline and how it has developed. However, the list here is necessarily very selective.

William Foxwell Albright (1891–1971) established the discipline of biblical archaeology. He taught at Johns Hopkins University, as well as at the American School of Oriental Research in Jerusalem (now the William F. Albright Institute of Archaeological Research). His excavation sites included Tell Beit Mirsim, where he established pottery chronology for western Palestine. Albright also confirmed the authenticity of the Dead Sea Scrolls after their discovery. He wrote extensively, publishing over eleven hundred books and articles, including *The Archaeology of Palestine and the Bible* (1932), *From the Stone Age to Christianity* (1940), and *Yahweh and* *the Gods of Canaan* (1968), and tended to affirm the historical reliability of the Hebrew Bible, often using archaeology to illumine the biblical text. Albright and his students, who include G. E. Wright, N. Glueck, M. Dahood, R. Brown, J. Fitzmyer, D. N. Freedman, J. Bright, G. E. Mendenhall, and F. M. Cross, Jr., exerted great influence on the guild.

John Bright (1908–1995) was a professor of Hebrew and Old Testament interpretation at Union Theological Seminary in Virginia. Among Albright's most influential students, Bright authored *A History of Israel*, which underwent four editions (1959, 1972, 1981, 2000) and became one of the most popular accounts of Israel's past, especially in America. He defended both the historical integrity and the theological worth of the Hebrew Bible.

John William Colenso (1814–1883) was Anglican bishop of the British colony of Natal, South Africa, and a great missionary to the Zulus. He was also a pioneering biblical critic, whose massive work in seven volumes, *The Pentateuch and Joshua* (1862–79), played an important part in the development of the view given classical expression by Wellhausen. Colenso was so far ahead of his generation in Britain that attempts were made to depose him from his bishopric on account of his radical views. His work was well known on the Continent, and he corresponded extensively with Abraham Kuenen.

Roland de Vaux (1903-1971) was a professor of history and archaeology at the École Biblique et Archéologique Française in Jerusalem, eventually becoming its director. In biblical studies, he was a major figure behind the *Jerusalem Bible* (1956), and his *Histoire ancienne d'Israël* (1971) sought middle ground between Albright's optimism and Martin Noth's skepticism. In archaeology, he published many articles in *Revue Biblique* and played a key role in excavating and publishing the Dead Sea Scrolls.

Wilhelm Martin Leberecht de Wette (1780–1849) was one of the founders of modern biblical criticism. His doctoral dissertation, presented in 1804, argued that Deuteronomy must have been written no earlier than the seventh century B.C.E., and his *Beiträge zur Einleitung in das Alte Testament* of 1806–7 argued that, on the evidence of the Books of Judges, Samuel, and Kings, Moses did not institute a fully developed system of priesthood and sacrifice at a central sanctuary as implied in Exodus, Leviticus, Numbers, and Deuteronomy. These were much later developments. De Wette's writings opened up a completely new way of reconstructing the history of Israel's religion and system of sacrifice. He held posts in the Universities of Jena, Heidelberg, Berlin, and Basel.

Heinrich Ewald (1803–1875) was born in Göttingen and taught there for most of his life except for a period in Tübingen, where he went after resigning his Göttingen chair in a protest against the suspension of the constitution by the new elector of Hanover in 1837. Ewald published commentaries on many books of the Bible, but his great contribution was that, based on his study of the Bible and other relevant materials, he wrote the first truly critical history of Israel (volume 1 was published in 1843).

Hermann Gunkel (1862–1932) is best known for his commentaries on Genesis and Psalms. He used the method of form criticism, that is, the classification of each short narrative or psalm according to a particular type or genre, which he then associated with a particular social setting. He was especially interested in oral traditions and folktales, and published a small book entitled *The Folktale in the Old Testament* in 1917. He held posts in Halle, Berlin, and Giessen.

Abraham Kuenen (1828–1891) was a professor in Leiden, the Netherlands, and one of the greatest of the biblical critics of the nineteenth century. He made an important contribution by arguing that the priestly material in the Books of Genesis to Numbers was a unity and could be dated in its present form to the postexilic period. This helped to confirm de Wette's theory that the system of priesthood and sacrifice in Israel described in books such as Leviticus was a late development.

Hermann Samuel Reimarus (1694–1768) was a professor of oriental languages in Hamburg. He wrote a number of radical articles, including pieces on the history of Israel and the New Testament. These were published after his death by G. F. Lessing between 1774 and 1778, and provoked considerable controversy in Germany.

Julius Wellhausen (1844–1918) is regarded as a major figure in the history of Old Testament study. In his book *Geschichte Israels*, published in 1878, he brought together his own research and that of other scholars to present a radical view of the history of Israel's religion, which he integrated with the documentary hypothesis of the composition of the opening books of the Bible. According to this theory, the documents J and E, written in the ninth to eighth centuries B.C.E., reflected a period when there was no centralized priesthood or worship in Israel; the Book of Deuteronomy (D) was associated with Josiah's reform in 622 B.C.E. and was a move toward centralization; and the Priestly document (P) was postexilic and reflected a time when the priesthood and sacrifice were centered in Jerusalem. Wellhausen was a professor at Greifswald, Halle, Marburg, and Göttingen.

George Ernest Wright (1909-1974) taught Hebrew Bible and archaeology, first at McCormick Theological Seminary in Chicago and then at Harvard University. One of Albright's most influential students, he wrote on a range of topics, often synthesizing theological and archaeological concerns. His publications include *God Who Acts: Biblical Theology as Recital* (1952), *Biblical Archaeology* (1957), and *Shechem, Biography of a Biblical City* (1965). The leading Palestinian archaeologist of his generation, he served as president of the American Schools of Oriental Research (ASOR), founded the popular periodical *The Biblical Archaeologist*, and mentored many prominent specialists in biblical studies.

PART TWO

Jewish Responses to Greek and Roman Cultures, 332 B.C.E. to 200 C.E.

Anthony J. Saldarini as revised by Amy-Jill Levine

I. PRESERVATION AND ADAPTATION: THE ENCOUNTER WITH HELLENISM

A. Alexander and His Successors

In 333 B.C.E. Alexander the Great defeated Darius the Persian and gained access to both Egypt and Mesopotamia. A year later he took Egypt as well as the Mediterranean coast, and Jerusalem, along with all the other cities of the region, submitted. With the conquest of the eastern Mediterranean the Hellenistic period begins. Despite reports in Josephus and later Rabbinic legend, Alexander did not visit Jerusalem. But his battles did take him to Persia, which he finally subdued along with Mesopotamia and surrounding territories as far as the Indus River (in present-day Pakistan). Alexander's untimely death in 323 left his unstable and scattered conquests in the hands of his fractious generals, but the cultural and political changes that took shape in his wake prevailed. The "Hellenistic period" would last until the growing influence over and the conquest of the area by the Romans between 200 and 31 B.C.E.

One of Alexander's generals, Ptolemy, used Egypt's natural borders and wealth to consolidate his rule there and, in 305 B.C.E., declared an independent kingdom. Another general, Seleucus, who ruled Mesopotamia from Babylon, fended off numerous attacks from both indigenous populations and a third general, Antigonus, who controlled Asia Minor (modern Turkey). After surviving exile from his own kingdom, Seleucus finally consolidated his control in 301 B.C.E. when he and a coalition of local military leaders defeated Antigonus at Ipsus in western Asia Minor. Seleucus, who ruled until 281 B.C.E., and Ptolemy, who ruled until 285, established two strong empires that dominated the eastern Mediterranean for well over a century and, in weakened form, endured even longer.

During the third century B.C.E. the Seleucids secured their power by building Greek-style cities and settling loyal veterans throughout eastern Asia Minor, Syria, Mesopotamia, and Persia. Gradually, Seleucus oriented his empire toward the Mediterranean, moving his capital first from Babylon

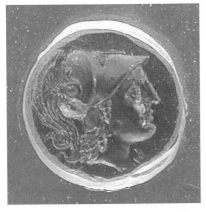

Alexander's image was literally stamped on the economic life of his empire and those that succeeded him, as this gold coin shows. (BiblePlaces.com)

to Seleucia, a new city on the Euphrates River, and then to another new city, Antioch, near the Mediterranean on the border between Syria and Asia Minor. While Seleucus faced pressures both internal and external, the Ptolemaic Empire was able to dominate the eastern Mediterranean region. The Ptolemies ruled from Alexandria, a Greek city founded by Alexander on the Mediterranean coast and a preeminent cultural and governmental center for several centuries. During the wars among Alexander's heirs, Jerusalem and other Jewish cities and towns in the region changed hands numerous times, from initial Ptolemaic rule to subsequent Seleucid control.

1. Hellenization

From Greece through Syria to Mesopotamia to Egypt, Greek practices and values came to permeate the eastern Mediterranean's governmental and cultural institutions. The native elite and retainer classes generally adapted to Hellenistic culture, while the peasantry tended toward a more conservative retention of traditional customs and beliefs. Cities were affected by Hellenization more than rural areas were, and international relations were more influenced than local politics.

Map VIII. Seleucid and Ptolemaic domains, c. 300 B.C.E.

ANTIOCH

Antioch (modern-day Antakya) was established by Seleucus I on the bank of the Orontes River fifteen miles from the Mediterranean Sea. Situated at the juncture of Asia Minor and Syria-Mesopotamia, Antioch became the capital of the Seleucid Empire. Its strategic location on caravan routes and its port at the mouth of the Orontes made it a major commercial center. The extensive plain that lay before it ensured its prosperity by providing food for its large population and exports of wine and oil. Under Roman rule it was the capital of the senatorial province of Syria and later became a center for Christian monasticism and theological inquiry.

Everyone had to adapt to new government procedures, to foreign officials, and to modified taxation systems, as indigenous populations had done for centuries in response to new conquerors. The Ptolemaic and Seleucid Empires encouraged the assimilation of local leaders who were willing to master Greek, adapt to Greek culture, and help maintain the empire. Wealthy landowners, high and low officials, military leaders, prosperous merchants, and their children benefited from a Greek education at a gymnasium, or at least from familiarity with Greek culture, which included athletics, Greek language, literature, and philosophy. Greek cities founded to provide islands of Greek culture and security helped Hellenize the local leaders and preserve for the Greek and Macedonian residents their cultural heritage.

In each conquered region, the majority of the population, who were uneducated farmers, continued to speak their native languages, follow local customs, and worship their ancestral gods. Even when new temples were built to Greek gods, these gods were often understood as local deities under another name. Intermarriage of local women with Greek settlers (mostly former soldiers) resulted in as much assimilation of the Greeks to local culture as the opposite.

EGYPTIAN AND SYRIAN RULERS

PTOLEMAIC KINGDOM	SELEUCID KINGDOM
Ptolemy I, 323–285 B.C.E.	Seleucus I, 301–281 B.C.E.
Ptolemy II, 285–246	Antiochus I, 281–261
	Antiochus II, 261–246
Ptolemy III, 246–221	Seleucus II, 246–226
	Seleucus III, 226–223
Ptolemy IV, 221–204	Antiochus III, 223–187
Ptolemy V, 204–180	Seleucus IV, 187–175
Ptolemy VI, 180–145	Antiochus IV, 175–163

GREEK CITIES

After the conquests of Alexander the Great, numerous independently governed cities were founded or recognized. These cities acknowledged the sovereignty of the emperor and paid taxes, but they controlled their own internal affairs. A city (*polis*) usually included both a walled central area and the surrounding villages and towns (often numerous) on which it depended for food. The rights of cities varied: some received exemption from certain taxes; others were authorized to mint coins. Citizenship was restricted to a portion of the population. Typically, a council (*boule*) of up to several hundred members ruled the city and was aided by various officials and judges.

Greek cities usually had a number of cultural institutions built to train the young and maintain Greek traditions; these institutions might include a stadium for races, a theater for drama and other entertainment, a gymnasium for training youth in mind and body, and the organization of youth into an ephebate. *Epheboi*, that is, Greek youth in their midteens, participated in rigorous physical and military training. They wore distinctive dress and engaged in communal activities. In the Hellenistic period the ephebate gave either equal or greater emphasis to training in literature and philosophy. Gymnasia were public institutions for physical training and sport; they included baths, dressing rooms, storage rooms, and some athletic buildings. Although open to all citizens, gymnasia were especially used by the *epheboi*, who were taught by schoolmasters, and were often associated with sacred groves.

2. Palestine under the Ptolemies

During the third century B.C.E., the Ptolemaic rulers in Alexandria governed Palestine and southern Syria. A cache of letters and documents found in the Fayum, a district in Lower Egypt, and written by Zenon, an employee of the Ptolemaic minister of finance Apollonius, shows that Egyptian officials monitored even the smallest towns. The papyri testify not only that Palestine exported grain, wine, olive oil, smoked fish, cheese, meat, dried figs, fruit, honey, dates, and slaves, but also that government monopolies and regulations provided for orderly transactions and maximum revenue.

From the beginning of the establishment of their kingdoms, the Seleucids contested the Ptolemaic claim to southern Syria and Palestine: both centers of power wanted control of the strategic and profitable coastal cities. During the third century B.C.E. these two dynasties fought five wars, which eventually led to Seleucid control of the coast and mountains in 200 B.C.E. The first three wars changed the political status little but did stimulate political unrest inside Jerusalem. After the death of Ptolemy II Philadelphus in 246 B.C.E., and during the third Syrian war, the high priest Onias II, who served as the Jewish representative to the Egyptian government and who had enormous control over political, social, and financial matters, refused to send the taxes to Ptolemy's successor; his motive was probably the desire to achieve greater independence. As the third Syrian war proceeded (245–241 B.C.E.), Onias sided with the Seleucids. His insubordination finally led Egypt to appoint the family of Tobias as official representatives of the Jewish people to the government. Although hegemony over Jerusalem shifted decisively to the Seleucids during the next two wars, rivalry between the Tobiads and Oniads continued.

Olive press at Capernaum, fashioned from basalt, representing the productivity in Galilee from which occupying powers expected to benefit. (BiblePlaces.com)

HELLENISTIC AND ROMAN TAXES

Taxes and tax collection systems varied widely by locale and period within the Hellenistic and Roman Empires. The most important tax was collected from the owners of agricultural land, who in turn collected a percentage of the crop (often 30–70 percent) from those renting the land. The other most common tax was the poll (or head) tax, either a percentage of one's worth or a flat rate for each person in a social class. Duties were collected on goods in transit and in marketplaces by local tax collectors, who paid a flat rate for their office. For example, Levi (Mark 2:1, 14) and Zacchaeus (Luke 19:1–2) collected customs in, respectively, Capernaum and Jericho, two medium-size towns on trade routes. Special taxes could be levied as needed.

Under the Ptolemies in the third century B.C.E., taxes were first paid in a lump sum by the high priest, who collected them from the people. Later, the right to collect them was sold to publicans, notably the Tobiads. In the second century, the tribute was paid to the Seleucids by the high priests Jonathan and Simon until they were "released" from this obligation, a sign that the Seleucids had lost control over Judea.

During the Roman period, independent cities and client rulers, such as Herod the Great (37 B.C.E.–4 B.C.E.) and his son, Herod Antipas (4 B.C.E.–39 C.E.), collected taxes as they wished and paid a fixed tribute to Rome. For example, Herod instituted a market tax in Jerusalem. His reign was notable for heavy taxation to finance military ventures, extensive building projects, and generous donations to imperial patrons. During the first century C.E., the prefect or procurator who ruled Judea and Samaria collected the land and poll taxes directly for Rome, whereas Herod Antipas, the client king who ruled Galilee, collected taxes there and paid tribute to Rome.

In addition, each Jew paid a traditional half-shekel tax as well as other tithes to the Temple. After the Temple was destroyed in 70 C.E., the half-shekel tax (now two drachmas and called the *fiscus Judaicus*, the "Jewish tax") was paid directly to the temple of Jupiter in Rome as a punishment for revolt.

Mosaic section of a bathhouse in Caesarea. (BiblePlaces.com)

3. The Tobiads

The Tobiad family typified the native governing class during the Hellenistic and Roman periods. According to the first-century C.E. Jewish historian Josephus, the family was recruited to serve the empire with promises of continued power and wealth, and, from a fortified palace at 'Araq el-Emir, they ruled a large area east of the Jordan River. When Onias II resisted Ptolemy III's authority, Tobias apparently seized the opportunity to have himself appointed chief representative. Later, Tobias's son Joseph had himself appointed chief tax collector by convincing Ptolemy that he could collect increased revenues if given centralized authority over the collection process and the troops to enforce his will. The politically astute Joseph maintained close governmental contacts as well as a permanent financial agent in Alexandria to manage his affairs.

That there was a Tobiad family in the Transjordan is not in doubt, for the name Tobiyah has been located in a fourth-century B.C.E. Aramaic inscription on a cave wall near 'Araq el-Emir. Further, 2 Maccabees 3:11, in the context of those who had deposited money in the Temple, mentions "Hyrcanus son of Tobias, a man of very prominent position [whose funds] totaled in all four hundred talents of silver and two hundred of gold." Unfortunately, Josephus's descriptions of this family (*Antiquities* 12.154–236) are fraught with numerous chronological impossibilities, and to some extent his story of the Tobiad Joseph is dependent on the account of the earlier, biblical Joseph (Genesis 39–47), who had great economic and political success in the Egyptian court. Hence, Josephus's recounting of this family is sometimes called the "Tobiad Romance" to indicate its somewhat novelistic quality.

4. Palestine under the Seleucids

The Seleucid ruler Antiochus III (223–187 B.C.E.) continued his assaults on the Ptolemies until finally, in 201–200 B.C.E., he had conquered almost all of southern Syria as well as the coast and defeated the Egyptian army at Paneas in northern Palestine. Two years later he established permanent Seleucid control over Palestine and the surrounding territories.

When Antiochus conquered Palestine, the pro-Ptolemaic party withdrew to Egypt, and the pro-Seleucids, led by Simon II, the Oniad high priest, were left in power. A Seleucid decree reported by Josephus notes that the Jerusalem leadership furnished supplies for the army and aided the attack on the Ptolemaic garrison left in the citadel. The decree provides for the redemption of Jewish captives and repair of the destruction suffered by Jerusalem, including duty-free imports of timber for Temple reconstruction. To give the residents of Jerusalem time to reestablish themselves, Antiochus arranged a three-year moratorium on taxes (*Antiquities* 12.138–44). Affirming the Jews' right to live by their ancestral laws, he left the high priest and council in place as the governing bodies in Judea.

LETTER OF ANTIOCHUS III CONCERNING JERUSALEM

King Antiochus to Ptolemy [the governor of Palestine], greeting. Inasmuch as the Jews, from the very moment when we entered their country, showed their eagerness to serve us, and, when we came to their city, gave us a splendid reception and met us with their senate and furnished us an abundance of provisions to our soldiers and elephants, and also helped us to expel the Egyptian garrison in the citadel, we have seen fit on our part to requite them for these acts and to restore their city which has been destroyed by the hazards of war, and to re-people it by bringing back to it those who have been dispersed abroad. In the first place we have decided, on account of their piety, to furnish them for their sacrifices an allowance of sacrificial animals, wine, oil and frankincense to the value of twenty thousand pieces of silver. . . . And it is my will that these things be made over to them as I have ordered, and that the work on the Temple be completed, including the porticoes and any other part that it may be necessary to build. The timber, moreover, shall be brought from Judea itself and from other nations and Lebanon without the imposition of a toll-charge. . . . And all the members of the nation shall have a form of government in accordance with the laws of their country, and the senate, the priests, the scribes of the Temple and the Temple-singers shall be relieved from the poll-tax and the crown-tax and the salt-tax which they pay. And, in order that the city may be more quickly inhabited, I grant both to the present inhabitants and to those who may return before the month of Hyperberetaios exemption from taxes for three years. We shall also relieve them in the future from a third part of their tribute. (Josephus, *Antiquities* 12.138–44)

During the second century B.C.E. the power of both the Seleucids and the Ptolemies steadily declined. Egypt, which became embroiled in a series of civil conflicts over dynastic succession, never again posed a serious threat to other Mediterranean powers. Antiochus III might have restored the Seleucid Empire to glory had the Romans, who were expanding eastward, not driven the Seleucid ruler out of Greece and defeated him in 190 B.C.E. at the battle of Magnesia in western Asia Minor. In the subsequent peace of Apamea (188 B.C.E.), Antiochus had to not only withdraw entirely from Greece and Asia Minor but also pay Rome a huge indemnity. A year later, he was assassinated.

B. Early Literary Responses to Hellenism

During the Hellenistic and Roman periods Jews in Palestine and the Diaspora produced an abundance of literature in Hebrew, Aramaic, Greek, and

THE ROMAN EXPANSION TO THE EASTERN MEDITERRANEAN

In the late third century B.C.E., Rome fought and won two wars to protect its colonists against the Illyrians across the Adriatic Sea to the western part of the Balkan peninsula. This began the expansion of its influence and power into the eastern Mediterranean. After gaining ascendancy over their western competition, Carthage, in 201, the Romans defeated Philip V of Macedon in the second Macedonian War (200–196 B.C.E.) and took control of Greek politics. Rome crushed any resistance. For example, it destroyed Corinth, the capital of the Achaean League, in 146. With the heirs of Alexander the Great in Macedon, Syria, and Egypt in decline, and having defeated Antiochus III in Asia Minor, Rome freely expanded its power during the next century and a half until it controlled all the lands surrounding the Mediterranean. The Roman Empire was contained only by the emerging Parthian Empire.

Latin. A number of Hebrew works, including the Torah and many texts that would eventually comprise the books of the Bible, were translated into Greek. Jewish authors revised traditional stories and materials, and they created new works based on both Greek and Jewish models. Most of these works did not become part of the Scriptures of the synagogue, since, from the second century C.E. onward, Jewish communities increasingly read the Bible in Hebrew (albeit with a translation in Aramaic) and accepted only those books found in Hebrew scrolls. Yet a number of these works did achieve canonical status for Jews in some Greek-speaking areas, and they continued to influence Judaism – and became canonical for early Christianity – well into the first few centuries C.E.

The Church accepted as inspired and authoritative several of these Hellenistic books composed by Jews for Jews, and they continue to be regarded as Scripture by the Roman Catholic, Anglican, and Eastern Orthodox communions. In the sixteenth century the Protestant reformers, regarding the Greek texts as later accretions, removed them from the canon. Thus they accepted only those Hebrew books found in what became the canon of the synagogue, although they often approved the Greek materials as pious and edifying.

The Greek translation of the books that comprise the Hebrew Bible, as well as the additional books that Greek-speaking Jewish communities accepted as canonical, is often referred to as the Septuagint, from the Greek word for "seventy," and abbreviated LXX. The name alludes to the legend, first recorded in the *Letter of Aristeas*, concerning the high priest sending seventy (or more precisely, seventy-two: six from each tribe of

---

DEUTEROCANONICAL BOOKS, APOCRYPHA, PSEUDEPIGRAPHA

Numerous Jewish books written in Hebrew, Aramaic, and Greek during the postexilic period have been imprecisely designated by the terms "Apocrypha" and "Pseudepigrapha." The Apocrypha are books and parts of books found in the Septuagint (the Greek translations of the Bible) but not in the Hebrew Bible. Roman Catholics, Anglicans, and Eastern Orthodox communions recognize some of these books as canonical. Since the term "apocryphal (= hidden) books" carries the connotation of "spurious" or "heretical," the term "Deuterocanonical" (= second canonical, as "Deuteron-

omy" means "second law"), introduced by Sixtus of Siena during the sixteenth century, is often preferred.

Different Septuagint manuscripts include several of the Deuterocanonical books in addition to the books of the Hebrew Bible. Roman Catholics recognize as canonical Tobit, Judith, Wisdom of Solomon, Ecclesiasticus (Sirach, or Ben Sira), Baruch (including the Letter of Jeremiah), 1 and 2 Maccabees, additions to the Books of Esther, and new tales connected to the prophet Daniel, such as the first "detective" story of Susanna and the Elders. The canon of the Greek Ortho-

dox community includes those books plus 1 Esdras, the Prayer of Manasseh, Psalm 151, and *3 Maccabees*, with *4 Maccabees* as an appendix.

The term "pseudepigraphical (meaning 'written with false superscription') books" designates over sixty works, composed by Jews during the third century B.C.E. through the second century C.E. and in some instances later; most are written in the names of famous biblical figures, such as Enoch, Baruch, and Ezra. Among the genres represented in this disparate collection are apocalypses, testaments, rewritings of the Bible, and psalms.

Israel) learned Jews to Egypt at the request of King Ptolemy to translate the Torah (i.e., the Pentateuch) into Greek. However, the term "Septuagint" does not designate a single translation in common usage throughout the Greek-speaking Jewish world; it is, rather, a general designation for different Greek translations of various Hebrew books done over several centuries. The Greek translation of the Pentateuch probably dates from the third century B.C.E. and was perhaps indeed composed primarily in Egypt. Other books were translated later and went through various revisions. The oldest version, the "Old Greek," is a collection of translations of various Hebrew books from different hands and times. There were multiple Hebrew manuscript traditions for the Bible, as the Dead Sea Scrolls demonstrate, and also different editions of the Scriptures of Israel in Greek, each based on discrete manuscript traditions. During the Roman period, additional Greek translations of the Bible, as well as revisions and adaptations of its books, were made to fit specific needs in the Jewish and Christian communities.

The Greek translations of the biblical books vary as to how strictly they render the Hebrew and how much they modify the text in the interests of interpretation and accommodation to local beliefs. When the Hebrew was obscure or did not fit the Hellenized culture or Jewish beliefs of the translators, adaptation and interpretation occurred. For example, the Greek version of the Book of Job omits many, though not all, anthropomorphic references to God. "I have not departed from the commandment of his lips" becomes "I have not departed from his commandments" (Job 23:12). On the other hand, the Septuagint Psalms retains references to God's body and emotions. The Greek tones down Job's attacks on God to avoid the appearance of blasphemy and to present Job as a blameless martyr. In the Hebrew, Job charges that God hid his intention to oppress him: "Yet these things you hid in your heart; I know that this was your purpose" (Job 10:13). The Greek turns Job's attack on God into an affirmation of divine omnipotence: "Having all these things in yourself, I know that you can do everything; nothing is impossible for you." Job's hypothetical admission of sin in the Hebrew text, "And even if it were true that I erred, my error remains with me" (Job 19:4), might have suggested to some readers that Job had sinned. The Greek protects his innocence by defining his hypothetical fault as a very minor failing. Thus the Christian image of "patient Job" (see James 5:11 in the New Testament) derives more from the Septuagint (and the *Testament of Job* in the Pseudepigrapha) than from the Hebrew Bible. Further, though the Hebrew Book of Job does not manifest belief in an afterlife, the Greek introduces it (Job 14:14) in order to conform the book to Jewish theology of the Hellenistic period.

1. Survival in the Diaspora

The destruction of Jerusalem and exile of its leadership in 587/6 B.C.E. stimulated a number of stories about survival in the Diaspora. These stories were

DIASPORA

In the traditional usage of Judaism, the word *diaspora* (Greek for "scattered [abroad]") sometimes translated as the "dispersion," indicates any area where Jews live outside the land of Israel; the Diaspora's origin is considered to be the conquest of the kingdom of Judah in 587/6 B.C.E., and the subsequent beginnings of the Jewish communities in Babylon as well as in Egypt. (Of course, the conquest of the kingdom of Israel in 722/1 B.C.E. also involved a *diaspora*, but the fate of those communities, "the lost tribes," is a matter of speculation.) During the Greek and Roman periods, Jewish communities could be found throughout the empire, in Europe, North Africa, Asia Minor, Egypt, Syria, and Babylon. The communities in Alexandria and Babylon were not only the earliest Diaspora settings, they were also the most prominent, and they fostered important Jewish literary activity.

revised, translated, and adapted not only by and for Jews living throughout the Hellenistic and Roman Empires but also for Jews living under foreign rulers in territorial Israel. Whether in the land of Israel or outside of it, Jews faced the same cultural pressures: to what extent would they retain their distinctive beliefs and practices, and to what extent would they assimilate into the wider Hellenistic world?

Epitomizing the problems Hellenistic culture posed to Jewish identity are the Greek additions to the Hebrew biblical materials. The Greek version of the story of Esther adds to the Hebrew text numerous notices of the heroine's Jewish practices and theological beliefs and so expresses resistance to pressures to assimilate; the folktales of Daniel were combined with visionary accounts as a response to Seleucid persecution, and later interpreters (Jewish as well as Christian) expanded the Danielic corpus even more in response to Roman conquest. The Daniel stories counsel fidelity to God, cooperation with the empire, resistance to oppression, and courage in the face of death. Since God controls the fates of foreign empires and judges their kings, Jews who pray to God for help, trust in God's care, and remain faithful to the Jewish way of life are promised divine guidance and protection.

The Book of Tobit was probably written during the third century B.C.E. in Hebrew or Aramaic and later translated into Greek; the Greek text itself went through several editions. The novella concerns the pious Jew, Tobit, who, with his wife Anna and their son Tobias, was brought to Nineveh (modern Iraq) by the Assyrians after their conquest of the northern kingdom of Israel (722/1 B.C.E.). The setting during the Assyrian captivity may have served as a model for the Babylonian, Egyptian, or other Diaspora situations.

Sleeping outside after burying an unattended corpse, Tobit is blinded by bird droppings; his unfortunate if nearly farcical fate is matched by that of his relative, Sarah, a Jewish woman in Ecbatana, a city of Media (present northwestern Iran), whose seven successive husbands had been, on their wedding night, killed by the jealous demon Asmodeus. To resolve these difficulties the angel Raphael, in disguise, guides Tobias to Media so that he can recover a deposit his father had left there, marry Sarah, exorcise the demon, and return to Tobit with a cure for his blindness. Emphasizing resistance to apostasy and assimilation, and promoting endogamy, personal prayer, and piety manifested by tithing (1:6), maintenance of Jewish dietary laws (1:10), ritual immersion (2:9), charitable giving (2:1-6), and burying the dead, the volume offers inspiration as well as instruction for Jews in the Diaspora. But the ideal remains, at least for the Book of Tobit, a return to Israel: Tobit continually speaks of devotion to the Temple and Jerusalem (1:4; 13:9–18; 14:5–7), and he expects not only the return of the captives but also that the Gentiles will acknowledge the God of Israel. Though fidelity to Judaism is encouraged, sustained hostility toward the Gentiles is absent.

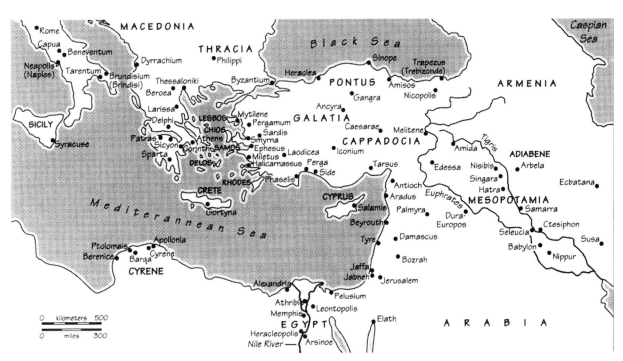

Map IX. Major centers of Diaspora Judaism.

Tobit's advice to his son epitomizes the piety, ethical code, and relationship with God that mark Jewish life. As is usually the case in the Septuagint (and the New Testament), God' personal name (YHWH) is not used or intimated; instead, he is called "Lord" (*Kurios*):

> Watch yourself, my son, in everything you do, and be disciplined in all your conduct. And what you hate, do not do to anyone. Do not drink wine to excess. . . . Give of your bread to the hungry, and of your clothing to the naked. Give all your surplus to charity, and do not let your eye begrudge the gift when you make it. Place your bread on the grave of the righteous, but give none to sinners. Seek advice from every wise man, and do not despise any useful counsel. Bless the Lord God on every occasion; ask him that your ways may be made straight and that all your paths and plans may prosper. For none of the nations has understanding; but the Lord himself gives all good things, and according to his will he humbles whomever he wishes. (Tobit 4:14–19 [New Revised Standard Version])

Other prayers and exhortations from the Hellenistic period warn against sin and encourage trust and obedience toward God. Baruch and the Letter of Jeremiah, which are part of the Septuagint and are sometimes joined together as one book, typify these imperatives. Though the former claims to have been written by Baruch, Jeremiah's secretary in the seventh and sixth centuries B.C.E., it is actually a creation by several anonymous

BARUCH

Baruch was a royal official from a highly placed Jerusalem family. Associated with Jeremiah (Jeremiah 32, 36, 42, 43), he was instrumental in the preservation of the prophet's oracles. Several later Jewish works are associated with his name because of his authoritative position as a scribe and because his experience of the loss of the Temple made him a fit speaker for authors grappling with the destruction of the first and then the second Temple. The *Second Book of Baruch* is a late-first-century C.E. apocalypse that depicts Baruch as a leader of the Jewish community, as even more authoritative than Jeremiah, and as the recipient of heavenly revelation meant to instruct and console the Jewish community, which has lost the Temple. Another apocalypse from the late first or early second century C.E., *3 Baruch*, also accords the scribe access to heavenly mysteries.

Jewish authors of the Hellenistic period. The first two sections of Baruch (1:15–2:5; 2:6–3:8) were translated from Hebrew into Greek along with the Letter of Jeremiah by the first century B.C.E. The dating of the latter two sections is uncertain; these parts may have been written originally in Greek.

In the introduction (Baruch 1:1–14) Baruch, who is in exile in Babylon, reads his book to the exilic community and arranges to send it, along with money for offerings in the Temple, to the Jews living in Jerusalem. The introduction establishes the book's concern: promoting cooperation with the empire and encouraging patience while awaiting Jerusalem's restoration. The first two sections present a beautiful and detailed confession of Israel's sin (Baruch 1:15–2:5) followed by a prayer for God's help (2:6–3:8); both parts are suffused with the Deuteronomistic theology described in Part One of the *Companion*. Affirming God's justice and attributing the sufferings of his people to their sins, Baruch asks God to forgive the people and restore them for his own sake. Repentance, obedience, and hope in God's mercy typify the attitudes suggested by this prayer.

Two poems in the second half of Baruch present solutions to Israel's dilemma. The first (3:9–4:4) affirms God's gift of wisdom and builds Israel's strength and hope on fidelity to the Torah:

> She [Wisdom] is the book of the commandments of God and the law that endures forever. All who hold fast to her will live, and those who forsake her will die. . . . Do not give your glory to another, or your advantages to an alien people. Happy are we, O Israel, for we know what is pleasing to God.

The final poem (4:5–5:9), after rehearsing the sins that led to Israel's punishment, affirming God's love, and counseling courage in the face of suffering, promises the restoration of Jerusalem and the return of the exiles, using language drawn from Second Isaiah (Isaiah 40–55). The Book of Baruch demonstrates that in the Hellenistic period Jews continued to use the experience of exile as a paradigm for understanding suffering, for affirming God's love, and for retaining their own identity.

The Letter of Jeremiah purports to be a communication from Jeremiah in Jerusalem to the new exiles in Babylon (from around 597 B.C.E.), although it is clearly a Hellenistic text. Extant only in Greek (Greek manuscript fragments from the first century B.C.E. were found among the Dead Sea Scrolls), it was probably written originally in Hebrew. A treatise against assimilation, the Letter speaks of the impotence of idols and it mocks pagan practices, using traditions found in Isaiah and Jeremiah.

> Now in Babylon you will see gods made of silver and gold and wood, which are carried on men's shoulders and inspire fear in the heathen. So take care not to become at all like the foreigners or to let fear for these gods possess you when you see the multitude before and behind them worshiping them.

Ezra the scribe, as depicted in the Dura-Europos murals from Mesopotamia. (Yale)

But say in your heart, "It is you, O Lord, whom we must worship." (Letter of Jeremiah 1:4–6; see also the later Wisdom of Solomon 13–15)

2. Greek Jewish Literature

From the third century B.C.E. through the first century C.E., Jewish authors wrote histories, stories, poems, philosophy, and apologetic works to defend Judaism against slander, encourage perseverance in the Jewish way of life, explain Jewish traditions to the Gentiles, and express Jewish piety in ways familiar to Greek-speaking Jews. Alexandria in Egypt was the greatest center of Greek Jewish culture, but Jews in territorial Israel and Syria also wrote significant works in Greek. Some of these writings seek to show that Jews can live together in mutual respect with Greeks; others reflect the violence that sometimes broke out between Jews and Gentiles.

The *Letter of Aristeas* recounts how the Pentateuch was translated into Greek at the request of Ptolemy II Philadelphus (285–246 B.C.E.) of Egypt, who wanted a copy for his library at Alexandria. The story of the embassy sent by Ptolemy to Jerusalem provides an opportunity for a detailed description of the city and the high priest, and for speeches in which Ptolemy shows great respect for Jewish wisdom, scholars, and law. When the seventy-two Jewish translators arrive in Egypt, Ptolemy entertains them at seven banquets and engages them in long philosophical discussions. Their witty and sage remarks demonstrate that they are the equals of

Roman theater in Alexandria. (BiblePlaces .com)

ALEXANDRIA

The city of Alexandria was founded by Alexander the Great on the Mediterranean coast of Egypt. It was the capital of Hellenistic Egypt and an industrial as well as a commercial center. Ptolemy II and Ptolemy III enhanced the cultural contributions of the city by constructing a library famous for its comprehensiveness, a museum, a theater, and other institutions characteristic of a Greek city. Alexandrian scholars collected, edited, and commented on Greek literature and grammar. An Alexandrian school of poetry flourished in the third century B.C.E., and succeeding generations continued to produce a variety of Greek literature. Alexandria was the home to a large and creative Greek-speaking Jewish community, but persecutions in the first and second centuries C.E. ended its power and literary productivity. Typical patterns of Alexandrian interpretation, such as discovering allegorical meanings, were developed by Christian exegetes.

any Hellenistic philosopher. For example, to the king's question, "How can one maintain the truth?" a sage responds, "By realizing that the lie brings terrible disgrace upon every man, and much more so upon kings. For if they have the power to do what they wish, what reason would they have for telling lies? It is our duty, O King, to accept this further principle that God loves the truth" (206). Finally, the seventy-two translators produce the translation in seventy-two days and are sent home with great praise and gifts.

The *Letter of Aristeas* is typical of the Jewish-Greek literature that promoted adherence to the Jewish way of life and taught the compatibility of Judaism with Hellenism, and may be dated to the third or second century B.C.E. The central institutions of Judaism – law, Jerusalem, the Temple, the high priest – are presented as ancient and laudable. The Torah in particular is reasonable and equal in dignity to Greek law and philosophy. The Jewish translators scrupulously keep the dietary laws, and the high priest explains the seemingly strange details of Jewish practice both as part of natural law and as essential to Judaism. One sage describes the Jewish laws, which contain universal ethical principles, as "unbroken palisades and iron walls to prevent our mixing with any of the peoples in any matter, thus being kept pure in body and soul, preserved from false beliefs, and worshipping the only God, omnipotent over all creation" (*Aristeas* 139). At the same time, the translators participate in a philosophical discussion of kingship, which reveals familiarity with and acceptance of Greek rather than Jewish tradition. Thus the translation of the Bible into Greek provides an expression of the common foundation of Judaism and Hellenism.

A number of Jewish writers who used Greek literary forms are known from fragments often preserved by early Christian writers. In the late third or early second century B.C.E., Philo the Poet wrote "About Jerusalem," an epic poem that describes and glorifies the city and its history. Theodotus (second to first century B.C.E.) wrote an epic poem on the Jews. The work of Aristeas the Exegete (third to second century B.C.E.) is known only through a quotation by Alexander Polyhistor (ca. 105–35 B.C.E.) preserved by the Christian historian Eusebius of Caesarea (ca. 260–341) in his *Praeparatio Evangelica* (9.25). Aristeas wrote a life of Job that, even more than the earlier Greek translation, enlarges the hero's patience and eliminates his questioning of God. In this version, Job is the son of Esau. The use of language found also in Jewish persecution and martyrdom stories marks Job's life as an edifying example for Jews who were suffering oppression. Ezekiel

ANCIENT ANTI-JEWISH LITERATURE

The third-century B.C.E. Egyptian priest Manetho was the first to write an account of Egyptian religion, customs, and history in Greek. In this work, he attacks the ancient Hebrews as aggressors against Egypt. According to him, the "Shepherds" (meaning the Hebrews) lived in a city named Auaris. They revolted and a priest of Hieropolis named Osarseph (Moses) took charge.

He made it a law that they should neither worship the gods nor refrain from any of the animals prescribed as especially sacred in Egypt, but should sacrifice and consume all alike. . . . After framing a great number of laws like these, completely opposed to Egyptian custom, he ordered them with their multitude of hands, "to repair the walls of the city and make ready for war against King Amenophis. . . . Meanwhile the Solymites [Jerusalemites] . . . along with polluted Egyptians treated the people impiously and savagely. . . ." Not only did they set towns and villages on fire, pillaging the temples and mutilating the images of the gods without restraint, but they also made a practice of using the sanctuaries as kitchens to roast the sacred animals the people worshiped. (Manetho, as quoted in Josephus, *Against Apion* 1.238–50)

the Tragedian (second century B.C.E.) wrote a play that recounts the Exodus, with stress on the Passover laws and Moses as the central hero. In each of these works, the author adapted and embellished the Bible, often employing traditions known elsewhere in Jewish and Hellenistic literature, to encourage fidelity to Jewish beliefs and practices, and connection to the land of Israel.

The Jewish philosopher Aristobulus (mid-second century B.C.E.), fragments of whose works were also preserved by Eusebius of Caesarea, explicitly affirms the antiquity and truth of Jewish traditions. The five extant fragments explain biblical anthropomorphisms as symbolic of more elevated truths. Aristobulus links the Passover festival and the Sabbath to astronomical and cosmic order, and he contends that Plato, Socrates, and Pythagoras knew parts of the Pentateuch from earlier Greek translations. He understands Greek poems concerned with the heavens and the underworld to be dependent on Jewish teaching, as are Hesiod and Homer. Succinctly summarizing his desire to reconcile Judaism with Hellenism, and echoing the themes of piety, justice, and temperance found also in Greek Stoic philosophy, he asserts:

> For it is agreed by all the philosophers that it is necessary to hold holy opinions concerning God, a point our philosophical school makes particularly well. And the whole constitution of our Law is arranged with reference to piety and justice and temperance and the rest of the things that are truly good. (Aristobulus, frag. 4:8)

Several Jewish historians retold biblical history for Hellenistic audiences, but only the writings of Flavius Josephus, the first-century C.E. military leader and priest who wrote about the war against Rome and about Jewish history, have been completely preserved. Fragments of earlier historians, such as Demetrius the Chronographer, and Eupolemus, testify to extensive Jewish participation in history writing, a popular Hellenistic genre. More than other Jewish writers, Artapanus (third to second century B.C.E.) reconciled Moses and Abraham, both of whom he presents as astrologers, with non-Jewish culture. Artapanus, whose work was summarized by Alexander Polyhistor and then recorded by Eusebius, offers a long section in his historical romance in which he claims that Moses was a leader and general in Egypt; was revered as Hermes; and was the founder of much of the Egyptian administrative system, many of Egypt's cultural institutions, and even the Egyptian worship of animals. Though Artapanus says that Moses created Egyptian religion, he also makes clear – when the Egyptian army is destroyed in the sea – that Egypt, its gods, and its culture are subordinate to the only real God. This presentation owes much to Hellenistic legends of heroes such as the Egyptian military figure and engineer Sesostris. Further, the characteristics and deeds it assigns to Moses are designed to refute anti-Jewish polemical writings, especially those of Manetho, a third-century B.C.E. Egyptian priest and historian.

ATTRACTION TO JUDAISM IN THE GRECO-ROMAN WORLD

Not only did Hellenism influence Judaism; Judaism also had an impact and influence on the Greek and Roman worlds. Significant numbers of people in the cities of the empire found aspects of Judaism attractive and were regularly drawn to the religion and to its gathering place, the synagogue – the *proseuche,* or "house of prayer." For example, both Philo of Alexandria and the Acts of the Apostles speak of non-Jews who regularly participated in the worship and life of the synagogue. Called "God-fearers" (*theophoboumenoi*), these Gentile affiliates were throughout the Diaspora a recognizable contingent in the life of the synagogue.

In *Satire* 14, the Roman author Juvenal speaks about a "Sabbath-fearing" Roman father whose son, as a result of his father's interest in Judaism, converts to Judaism and is circumcised. The Jewish historian Josephus also talks about many Greeks who came to "respect and emulate" Judaism, and archaeological remains provide substantial indication of prominent Diaspora communities comprised of both Jews and Gentile affiliates.

3. Palestinian Responses to Hellenism

By the Hellenistic period most of the books of the Bible were recognized by the Jewish community as authoritative, and their texts were substantially fixed. Because rapid cultural changes during this time required the adaptation of existing traditions, led to the creation of new customs, and fostered the development of more comprehensive viewpoints, the fixed texts of the Bible had to undergo constant interpretation. Thus a fluid and varied interpretive tradition sprang up alongside the Bible.

Palestinian Jewish writing, whether in Hebrew, Aramaic, or Greek, generally resembles its Diaspora counterparts by expanding or editing the biblical stories. Both the *Genesis Apocryphon*, an Aramaic work found among the Dead Sea Scrolls (first century B.C.E.), and the *Biblical Antiquities* (*Liber Antiquitatum Biblicarum*, also known as *Pseudo-Philo*), a work extant only in Latin but probably originally a first- or second-century C.E. Hebrew text, retell biblical history by eliminating contradictions and dramatically elaborating select stories. The *Book of Enoch*, the *Book of Jubilees*, the *Testaments of the Twelve Patriarchs* (all treated subsequently), and 1 Esdras engage in a similar rewriting of the Bible for edification.

The Wisdom of Ben Sira

Early in the second century B.C.E., a learned Jewish teacher wrote down his teachings in a book referred to as the Wisdom of Ben Sira (or Sirach; also known as Ecclesiasticus). In the mode of Greek writers, the author gives his name, which, though garbled in the manuscripts, is probably Yeshua [Jesus] ben Eleazar ben Sira (Sirach being the Greek form for Sira). His famous description of the ideal scribe (Sirach 38:24–39:11) testifies to the learned class who created the abundant Jewish literature of the Hellenistic period. The description of the scribe is so similar to the later descriptions of Israel's rulers, prophets, and priests in chapters 44–50 that Ben Sira implicitly includes himself and other scribes among Israel's leadership.

Likely from the upper classes and probably dependent on wealthy patrons, Ben Sira may have run a school in Jerusalem (see Sirach 51:23). He notes that only one who has leisure can become wise (Sirach 38:24) and contrasts the scribal life with the physical difficulty of other jobs. Many of his teachings pertain to upper-class experiences, such as the dangers of having riches and of the unscrupulous use of power; he comments on the obligation to give alms and offers instruction concerning proper etiquette at banquets. Attributing to the ideal scribe all areas of knowledge, high government station, and lasting fame, Ben Sira also insists that the scribe's wisdom is closely linked with and dependent on God because the main source of knowledge is the "law of the Most High." Because fear of the Lord is a key to wisdom and to all the other attitudes associated with right living (Sirach 1:11–2:18), Ben Sira seeks "the wisdom of the ancients" and is "concerned with prophecies" (39:1).

Though Ben Sira's teachings are based almost wholly on the Bible, especially Wisdom literature, nowhere does he quote it directly. Rather, like other Hellenistic-Jewish authors, he rewrites the biblical teaching in different literary forms. For example, the dominant form in Proverbs consists of two parallel, complementary or contrasting lines, whereas Ben Sira treats traditional Wisdom topics in units of about six to twenty verses. Toward the end of his book, lengthy hymns and reflections predominate, and at its climax, a seven-chapter review of Israel's history appears.

Like the author of Proverbs, Ben Sira begins with a hymn to Wisdom, personified as a woman who was present with God at creation. Frequently, he meditates on Wisdom's attributes and his struggles in seeking her (Sirach 1:1–10; 4:11–19; 6:18–37; 14:20–15:10; 19:20–5; 24:1–29). Strikingly, for the first time in Jewish tradition, Ben Sira defines wisdom as Torah and thus links the Wisdom tradition with the content of the Bible itself:

> Wisdom will praise herself and will glory in the midst of her people. In the assembly of the Most High she will open her mouth and in the presence of his host she will glory. . . . Then the creator of all things gave me a commandment, and the one who created me assigned a place for my tent. And he said, "Make your dwelling in Jacob, and in Israel receive your inheritance.". . . All this is the book of the covenant of the Most High God, the law which Moses commanded us as an inheritance for the congregations of Jacob. (Sirach 24:1–24)

Ben Sira thus implicitly makes the generically human wisdom common to Near Eastern culture and the Hellenistic wisdom found in Greek philosophy and literature subordinate and inferior to Jewish wisdom and the Jewish way of life articulated in a myriad of teachings concerning virtues, vices, family, nation, God, and learning.

Three hymns praising God's creation and goodness, and the order of the universe (Sirach 16:24–17:14; 39:12–35; 42:15–43:33) undergird Ben Sira's interpretation of life and explain his views on theodicy. Though Ben Sira does not seem to believe in an afterlife, he does believe that one's reputation (or "name," here italicized) continues: "The mourning of men is about their bodies, but the evil *name* of sinners will be blotted out. Have regard for your *name*, since it will remain for you longer than a thousand great stores of gold. The days of a good life are numbered, but a good *name* endures forever" (Sirach 41:11–13).

The final major section (chapters 44–50) is an epic presentation of Israel's heroes and an ideal depiction of Second Temple Jewish society (515-180 B.C.E.). The section culminates in a laudatory description of Simon, the high priest in Ben Sira's day. The sins of the nation are blamed on the monarchy, and at the end of the poem the king is replaced by the high priest and sage. Thus the text insists that, guided by Wisdom and Israel's great leaders, Jewish society has been blessed by divine favor and has preserved its glory through fidelity to the covenant, worship at the Temple, and virtuous action. Social disorders ranging from the conflicts between Ptolemaic and Seleucid parties to the rivalries that would lead to Antiochus IV's persecution of Judaism are left aside in favor of a vision of social order based on wisdom.

Unfortunately, this idealistic vision of Jewish society was soon shattered by conflict within the priesthood and assaults by the Seleucids. But Ben Sira's ideas would not be lost. In Alexandria in about 132 (or later, depending on how one dates the reference to the thirty-eighth year of Euergetes in the prologue), his grandson translated Ben Sira's book into Greek. In addition to the complete Greek text, some of the original Hebrew has survived. Though Ben Sira was never accepted into the Hebrew canon, the Talmud occasionally quotes it as authoritative. Among early and medieval Christians and among Catholic, Anglican, and Orthodox Christians today the Wisdom of Jesus ben Sira has canonical status and is revered as the "ecclesiastical" (church's) book – hence the alternative designation Ecclesiasticus – in view of its copious ethical teaching and support of community life, authority, and worship.

First Enoch

The *Book of Enoch* is a collection of revelatory materials, written from the third century B.C.E. through the first century C.E. (It is sometimes referred to as the *Ethiopic Book of Enoch* because a complete copy survives only in

A view of Masada, where part of a copy of the Wisdom of Ben Sira was found. (BiblePlaces.com)

ENOCH

Enoch is an ancient wisdom figure found in much Near Eastern literature, including the Bible. According to Genesis 5:21–4 he was in the seventh generation after Adam; at the end of his life he "walked with God and was no more." To later generations, that Enoch "walked with God" meant that he was still alive and therefore available to reveal hidden, heavenly wisdom to humans.

In the Sumerian king list, the seventh king, Enmeduranki, king of Sippar, is similar to Enoch. He is brought into the assembly of the gods and shown how to predict the future through divination. The biblical author may have drawn on these and other Babylonian traditions for the figure of Enoch.

In Jewish apocalyptic literature Enoch functions as an intermediary who receives heavenly revelations.

Along with the five independent works that comprise *1 Enoch*, texts ascribed to this ancient figure include a late-first-century B.C.E. work called *2 Enoch* (extant only in Old Church Slavonic). *Second Enoch* recounts primeval times and describes Enoch's journey to the seven heavens, where he learns about creation, the workings of the cosmos, the course of history, the wonders of heaven, and the punishments of the wicked. The work designated *3 Enoch*, or the *Hebrew Apocalypse of Enoch* (fifth to sixth centuries C.E., with earlier material included), offers an account by Rabbi Ishmael of how he journeyed to heaven, saw God's throne and chariot (the traditional objects of Rabbinic mystical contemplation), received revelation from the archangel Metatron, and witnessed the wonders of the heavenly world.

Ethiopic, and because the Ethiopic Church regards it as canonical.) Aramaic fragments have been found among the Dead Sea Scrolls, and portions of a Greek translation also exist. Enoch, who appears in Genesis 5:21–4, was chosen as a source for this revelation because the biblical circumlocution for his death, "Enoch walked with God and he was not, for God took him" (Genesis 5:24), was interpreted to mean that Enoch ascended alive to heaven where he received divine revelation. Several parts of the book are apocalypses or apocalyptic in orientation; they illustrate the mystical, speculative, and cosmic side of Jewish thought. Two such sections, the Book of Watchers (*1 Enoch* 1–36) and the Book of Luminaries (*1 Enoch* 72–82), have their origins in third-century B.C.E. Palestine.

The Book of Watchers, an expansion of the truncated account in Genesis 6:1–4 of the fall of the "watchers" (i.e., angels), addresses the origins of evil. In this recounting, a group of watchers desired the "handsome and beautiful" human women and had intercourse with them, despite knowing that this action would be considered sinful. These relationships resulted in the birth of giants, who brought evil and destruction, such that "the whole earth was filled with blood and oppression" (*1 Enoch* 6:9). The text also recounts how the watchers taught humanity magic, the art of making swords and knives, and skills in ornamentation. Enoch is enlisted to pronounce doom on the angels and those who do evil on earth (*1 Enoch* 12–16). He receives his messages in dream visions, and in chapter 14 he has a vision of God similar to those described in later Jewish mysticism.

Later in the Book of Watchers (*1 Enoch* 17–36), Enoch is taken on a journey to secret reaches of the cosmos, where he sees the origins of humanity, the world, and evil; the workings of the natural universe; the unity of heaven and earth; and the final judgment in which the good are saved and the evil punished. Founded on the premise that the end, like the beginning, will be Edenic, the account of this journey encourages its readers to recall the order of the universe and God's providential care for all life.

The Book of Luminaries, also called the Astronomical Treatise (*1 Enoch* 72–82), is a complex, mathematical account of the movements of the stars, moon, and sun. Fragments of the book found among the Dead Sea Scrolls

---

COMPOSITION OF THE *BOOK OF ENOCH*

CHAPTERS	NAME	CENTURY
1–36	Book of Watchers	3d–2d B.C.E.
	1–5 Introduction	2d–1st
	6–11 Rebellion of the Angels	3d
37–71	Similitudes of Enoch	1st C.E.
72–82	Astronomical Treatise	3d B.C.E.
83–90	Dream Visions	2d
	83–84 Vision of the Deluge	2d
	85–90 Animal Apocalypse	2d
91–108	Epistle (Letter) of Enoch	2d–1st
	93:1–10; 91:12–17, Apocalypse of Weeks	2d

---

indicate that it was once longer than the version now extant in Ethiopic. The monotonous calculations of the movements of heavenly bodies demonstrate not only universal order; they also reveal that moral and religious rectitude depend on a timely observance of Jewish seasons and festivals. Nonobservance (sin) upsets both moral and cosmic orders. The Book of Luminaries, along with the *Book of Jubilees* and other texts found at Qumran, advocates a 364-day solar calendar, rather than the traditional lunar calendar used by the Temple authorities. The solar calendar may have been promoted by those seeking a more regular and strict observance of Jewish festivals, laws, and customs based on a holistic understanding of the universe, as well as a separation from the lunar observances of Babylonian culture.

II. ANTIOCHUS IV AND THE MACCABEAN CRISIS

A. The Historical Setting

By the second century B.C.E. the province of Judea, with its capital Jerusalem, was thoroughly enmeshed within Hellenistic culture. Like most peoples in the Seleucid Empire, the Jews lived by their own laws and customs and worshipped in their traditional manner. But, without destroying the people's distinct religious character, the economy, language, arts, literature, and political institutions of the empire slowly changed Jewish ways of thinking and acting. The ruling classes were most affected by Hellenism, because members of any governing class adopted the Hellenistic way of life to promote a harmonious relationship with the sovereign and to keep peace at home. The hereditary leaders who were also the wealthy, landed aristocracy competed for the favor of various Seleucid officials and of the Seleucid king himself, on whom depended the appointment of the high priest and the attendant control of the nation. Even the Maccabean revolt

---

LUNAR AND SOLAR CALENDARS

The traditional calendar in the Near East was based on the monthly cycle of lunar phases, which took about 29.5 days. This system resulted in a year of 354.5 days and required the addition (intercalation) of an extra month every two or three years. The Egyptians had occasionally used a solar calendar of 364 days, and a similar calendar is proposed by *Jubilees, 1 Enoch*, and some other writings found among the Dead Sea Scrolls. Its attraction seems to have been its regularity: exactly 52 weeks to the year, months of exactly 30 days, and seasons of 13 weeks. The first day of the year and of each season always fell on the same day of the week, as did all the major festivals. This regularity testified to the order of the universe and to trust in divine control, themes typical of Hellenistic apocalyptic writings.

GREEK GAMES

From antiquity the Greeks had celebrated festivals, leaders' deaths, and other major events with athletic contests, of which the Olympic Games are the best known. Individual events, which predominated, included foot races, throwing the javelin and discus, long jumping, wrestling, boxing, and horse races. Greek cities in the eastern Mediterranean would typically construct an amphitheater and sponsor games. During the Roman period gladiatorial contests became common. The Greek custom of competing naked in some contests and the association of the games with the worship of the gods made these events repugnant to many Jews. Nevertheless, Herod, ever the opportunist, sponsored games in various Gentile cities to win favor in the empire.

against the Seleucids (167–164 B.C.E.) was powered by Hellenistic political and ideological concerns, as well as religious zeal.

1. Competition for Power in Jerusalem

The Book of 2 Maccabees recounts that during the reign of Seleucus IV (187–175 B.C.E.), while Apollonius was governor of Coele Syria and Phoenicia, Simon, the captain of the Temple, had a disagreement with Onias III, the high priest, over the administration of the Jerusalem market. Unable to prevail against Onias, Simon reported to Apollonius that the Temple treasury, filled with untold riches, could be brought under the king's control. Apollonius informed Seleucus about these funds, and the king sent his minister, Heliodorus, to seize the Temple treasures. Onias explained that the funds were set aside for the care of widows and orphans, and that part belonged to Hyrcanus the son of Tobias, but Heliodorus insisted on confiscating the treasury. Only a supernatural vision prevented his executing his intention. Thwarted in his plan, Simon then accused Onias of treason (2 Maccabees 3, 4). These brief notices do not give a full description of the contest for power, but the Seleucid interest in obtaining Judean money and the willingness of some Jewish officials to help set the scene for the revolt under Seleucus's brother and successor, Antiochus IV.

When Antiochus IV acceded to the throne in 175 B.C.E. by displacing his nephew, he had need for funds. Jason, the brother of Onias III, promised the king that he would use his office to collect huge revenues in exchange for being appointed high priest; he also guaranteed additional revenue from enrolling the upper class as "citizens of Antioch" and establishing key Greek institutions, including a gymnasium, an arena, and an "ephebate," that is, an official body of youth trained in Greek ways. Antiochus accepted the offer. Though the pious author of 2 Maccabees decries this abandonment of Jewish life, Jason skillfully pleased his overlord not only by producing more revenue for the Seleucid throne but also by creating a core of loyal leaders acculturated to both Greek and Jewish worlds. His own loyalty to Hellenistic society is shown by his self-identification: this new high priest replaced his original Hebrew name, Joshua (or Jesus), with that of the legendary Greek hero, Jason.

The exact nature of Jason's ploy of creating "citizens of Antioch" in Jerusalem remains unclear. He may have reorganized Jerusalem's government to conform to that of an independent Greek city (*polis*), or he may have merely arranged for the elites to be recognized as citizens of the king's capital, Antioch (as it was common practice for leading citizens in many parts of the Roman Empire to be made citizens of Rome). In neither case would the status of ordinary residents have been affected.

Three years after Jason secured the high priesthood from Antiochus, in 172 B.C.E., he was outbid for the post. Menelaus, his envoy entrusted with the task of presenting the yearly tribute (and, ironically, the brother of

Simon who had challenged Onias III), promised Antiochus a 50 percent increase, and the king promptly appointed Menelaus high priest (2 Maccabees 4:23–4). "Then Jason, who had cheated his own brother, now saw himself cheated by another man" (2 Maccabees 4:26).

Second Maccabees depicts Menelaus as tyrannical, cruel, and totally unfit for the high priesthood (2 Maccabees 4:25). Jason, who would have agreed with that description, fled to Transjordan to plot his own return to power. The financial importance of Judean revenues became apparent within a few years, when Menelaus, unable to pay the taxes he had promised to the king, was summoned to Antioch. To pay his debt and thereby preserve his position, Menelaus took gold vessels from the Temple, sold some to Tyre and other cities, and gave others to Andronicus, the king's viceroy, presumably as a bribe; during this time, the king himself was busy suppressing rebellions in Tarsus and Mallus, cities in Asia Minor that he had given as gifts to his mistress.

Onias III, the high priest ousted by Jason, exposed Menelaus's sacrilegious behavior and threatened his position. Menelaus, in turn, convinced Andronicus to have Onias murdered. "As a result, not only the Jews, but many people of other nations as well, were indignant and angry over the unjust murder of the man" (2 Maccabees 4:35). The king responded to the protests over this murder by executing Andronicus, but he continued to support Menelaus, his valued ally and financial supporter.

In 169 B.C.E., while Rome was fighting in Macedonia, Antiochus IV attacked and conquered most of Egypt and had himself briefly proclaimed pharaoh. During this time, the erstwhile high priest Jason attacked Jerusalem; hearing the false rumor that Antiochus was dead, he stormed the city, and besieged Menelaus and his supporters. Antiochus deemed Jason's incursion an act of rebellion; on his return from Egypt, he went to Jerusalem, drove Jason out, reestablished Menelaus's authority, and, according to 2 Maccabees 5:14, massacred forty thousand Jews and sold the same number of men, women, and children into slavery. In payment for his efforts, he took huge sums of money and golden vessels from the Temple (1 Maccabees 1:20–4; 2 Maccabees 5:1–23). The king also "dared to enter the holiest Temple in the world; Menelaus, that traitor both to the laws and to his country, served as guide" (2 Maccabees 5:15).

In 167 B.C.E., Antiochus IV sent Apollonius with a force of twenty-two thousand men (so 2 Maccabees; 1 Maccabees 1:29 refers to a "strong force") to attack Jerusalem. Slaughtering thousands and causing great damage to the city, he established a Syrian-controlled citadel near the Temple Mount (1 Maccabees 1:29–32; 2 Maccabees 5:24–6). Only this decisive Seleucid intervention, including the founding of this Syrian citadel, called the Akra, kept Menelaus in power and Jerusalem firmly in Seleucid hands. The Akra withstood all attempts at seizure for over twenty-five years, until Simon Maccabee finally conquered it in 141 B.C.E. Only then did Judea and Jerusalem become independent of effective Syrian control.

THE AKRA

The Greek word *akra* refers to a fortress built on high ground and dominating a city. According to 1 Maccabees 1:33–40, Jewish supporters of the Seleucids built a stronghold in the City of David overlooking the Temple. However, "City of David" often designates the hill south of and lower than the Temple – an impossible location for a fortress dominating the Temple Mount. Consequently, the location of the Akra has been disputed. To dominate the Temple the fort must have been to the north of the Temple, where the ground rose above it. Here the lack of steep slopes required extra fortification.

The term "City of David" thus must include the whole walled area on the eastern hill of Jerusalem, including the Temple and any installations north of it, not just the low hill south of the Temple (see 1 Kings 11:27; Isaiah 22:9). The garrison in the Akra was probably composed mostly of Jews sympathetic to the Seleucids and some non-Jewish Seleucid soldiers.

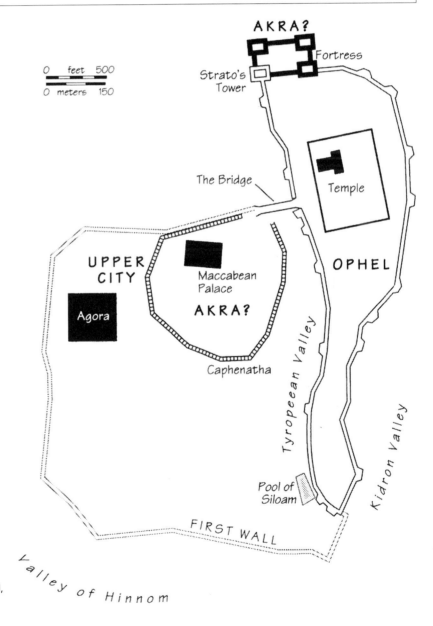

Map X. Jerusalem in the Hellenistic period, with possible locations of Akra.

Greek philosopher. Found in Sebaste in Samaria. Roman copy of an earlier Hellenistic model. (Harvard Semitic Museum)

2. Prohibition of Jewish Practice

In 167 B.C.E., Antiochus forbade the practice of numerous Jewish laws, including circumcision and observance of the Sabbath, and he destroyed all the copies of the Torah he could find. The government erected an "abomination of desolation upon the altar of burnt offerings" (1 Maccabees 1:54). In Hebrew "abomination" is a circumlocution for the name of the most popular Canaanite god, Baal. "Desolation" is somewhat similar in sound to the Hebrew phrase "of the Heavens," the epithet commonly connected to Baal. Thus, although 2 Maccabees 6:2 says that the abuses included dedicating the Temple to a Greek god, Olympian Zeus, it is possible that Canaanite worship of Baal of the Heavens was introduced and that Baal was identified with Zeus. The worship of other gods was probably introduced as well, including Dionysus (2 Maccabees 6:7) and perhaps Anath, a consort of Baal, whose presence is suggested by the charge of the practice of prostitution in the Temple (2 Maccabees 6:4). Though some have imagined that Antiochus erected a statue of Zeus in the Temple, it is likely that stone pillars, the traditional symbols for gods in Canaanite high places of worship (cf. *Matztzebot* in the Hebrew Bible), were placed on the altar and sacrifice offered on them (see 1 Maccabees 1:59, which refers to a "pagan altar" placed *on* the legitimate altar of sacrifice). Thus, when the Temple was later purified and rededicated to the God of Israel, the Jewish priests "cleaned the sanctuary and removed the defiled *stone* to an unclean place" (1 Maccabees 4:43), and then took apart the Jewish altar and stored its stones until a prophet should tell them what to do with them.

Roman theater at Sepphoris in Galilee. (BiblePlaces.com)

EASTERN MEDITERRANEAN DEITIES

The divinities of diverse ethnic groups in Asia Minor, Syria, and Mesopotamia shared numerous similarities, as did the Greek and Roman pantheons farther to the west. As mythic and symbolic patterns crossed cultures during the Hellenistic and Roman periods, many of these gods were identified with one another. Usually there was a chief heavenly god: in ancient Syria and Canaan he was El; the plural form of this term, *Elohim*, in Hebrew, principally refers to the God of Israel. In Greece the chief god was Zeus, and in Rome Jupiter. Leading the pantheon in Canaanite and Syrian religions during the biblical and Greco-Roman periods was the younger, more vigorous storm god, Baal.

In the Canaanite and Syrian systems, the consort and sister of the high god was Anath or Asherah, the queen of heaven (Jeremiah 7:18; 44:15–25). She was often identified with Athena, Zeus's daughter, the warlike and wise patroness of Athens, rather than with Zeus's consort, Hera. The Greek Aphrodite, Semitic Astarte, and Egyptian Isis frequently achieved eminence as patronesses. Also common across cultures was the worship of a younger god associated with wine and ecstatic experience, and with dying and rising. The Greek Dionysus, Roman Bacchus, Egyptian Osiris, Phoenician and Antiochene Adonis, Phrygian Attis, Mesopotamian Tammuz, and Tyrian Melqart all fill this role. In addition, in the Gentile world a plethora of local gods fulfilled various yearnings for contact with the divine.

Head of Dionysus, from Thessalonica in Greece. (Koester-Harvard Archaeological Resources for New Testament Study)

The suppression of the Jewish cult was widespread and brutal. People were forced to take part in non-Jewish rites and were executed for having their children circumcised, for possessing a copy of the Torah, or for keeping Jewish laws. The highly partisan accounts in 1 and 2 Maccabees do not make clear how many people complied with the imperial decrees and how many resisted. Second Maccabees' emphasis on the extraordinary courage of those martyred as well as First Maccabees' notice of popular resistance marked by flight into the wilderness (1 Maccabees 2:29) suggest that only a minority of Jews refused to acquiesce to or accommodate Antiochus's demands.

Zeus statue from Mount Gerizim in Samaria. (Howard C. Kee)

THE NAMES "MACCABEE" AND "HASMONEAN"

The word Maccabee probably derives from the Aramaic *mqwbh*, meaning "hammer"; it was a nickname given to Judah, the son of Mattathias, and the original military leader of the family. The nickname was then given to the books depicting the resistance to Syrian persecution and domination. According to Josephus and other sources, the family was called the Hasmoneans (from the Hebrew *Hashmonay*), a designation that was either the name of an obscure ancestor or an earlier nickname. The rulers in succeeding generations of this family are known as the Hasmoneans.

Given the long and profitable collaboration between Menelaus and Antiochus and their mutual need to preserve control and extract revenue from Judea, the decision to modify Jewish religious practices was probably undertaken for strictly political reasons. Gaining political, military, and financial control of Judea required structural changes in Jewish society, and those changes included adaptations in local law, customs, officials, and institutions. Since Antiochus and his lackey Menelaus wanted a pliant population reconciled to the new Greek ways, heavy taxation, and Seleucid rule, the Greek king and the Jewish high priest sought to institute styles of worship that were normal in Greek cities of the eastern Mediterranean and that would be considered reasonable by most inhabitants of the empire. Such a reform would fit Antiochus's predisposition to foster Hellenistic culture. The king and the high priest knew that the effort would involve violence and struggle, but they miscalculated the intensity of the resistance.

3. The Maccabean Revolt

Those who rejected imperial decrees against Jewish practice resisted by means long known in the region: they abandoned their homes and camped in uninhabited hill country, which afforded some protection and meager subsistence (1 Maccabees 2:27–30; 2 Maccabees 5:29). A coalition gradually formed of various groups including members of priestly families, Hasideans ("pious ones" known for their fidelity to Torah), and many other refugees. Establishing an organized guerilla force, they began to kill collaborators, raze altars dedicated to the pagan gods, circumcise Jewish children, and thus re-Judaize the countryside (1 Maccabees 2:42–8, 3:5–8). Though the majority of the Jewish people had passively accepted Antiochus's changes, they were generally sympathetic to the resistance and supported those who promoted it (2 Maccabees 8:1–7).

In Judea a priestly family, the Hasmoneans, aroused armed opposition to the governing forces from Syria and to those Jews who supported the Seleucid policy. Judas, or Judah, Maccabee (Maccabeus, or, "the hammer"), one of five brothers, led the initial revolt. As a popular leader, Judah rallied ill-equipped forces and won battles on his own mountainous terrain.

The Syrian response to Judah's military operations was at first mounted by the local governor, Apollonius, who used indigenous militia rather than professional troops. Judah and his followers

THE HASIDEANS

"Hasideans" (Hebrew *chasidim*, "pious ones") seems to designate people who faithfully kept Jewish law in the face of oppression. First Maccabees 2:42 speaks of a "group of Hasideans, valiant Israelites, all of them devout followers of the Law"; in chapter 7, the text mentions that the "Hasideans were the first among the Israelites to seek peace with" Alcimus, a new high priest appointed to replace Menelaus. Second Maccabees indicates that

Menelaus, who opposed the Maccabean revolt, told the new Syrian ruler, Demetrius, that "those Jews called Hasideans, led by Judas Maccabeus, are warmongers who stir up sedition and keep the kingdom from enjoying peace and quiet " (14:6). The term "Hasideans" is best seen as a generic designation for various groups of Jewish pietists notable for their fidelity to the Torah as the means to the compassion (*chesed*) of God.

Judean wilderness. (BiblePlaces.com)

easily defeated this challenge (1 Maccabees 3:10–12). The second response was a stronger army with professional soldiers led by Seron, a Syrian military commander (1 Maccabees 3:13–15). Judah and his small company ambushed and routed the larger force in a mountain pass near Beth-horon, a dozen miles northwest of Jerusalem. Finally, Antiochus IV's regent, Lysias, assembled a large force led by three experienced courtiers ("friends") of the king (1 Maccabees 3:27–39). The king himself was campaigning in Persia to collect much needed revenue; he left lesser problems, like Judea, in the hands of his subordinates. The Syrian army encamped on the plain below Jerusalem and sent a detachment of six thousand into the mountains to launch a surprise attack on Judah's forces. Judah evaded the trap and launched his own attack on the Syrian camp; he routed the main force and then the returning strike force (1 Maccabees 4:1–25).

By 164 B.C.E., Judah had gained control of the Temple Mount, except for the citadel (the Akra), whose garrison protected Menelaus and his partisans. While Judah was besieging the citadel, he ordered the Temple

Hasmonean buildings south of the Temple Mount. (BiblePlaces.com)

purified from non-Jewish sacrifices and rededicated to the worship of Israel's God. The resumption of worship was celebrated with an eight-day festival, the length of many of the major biblical festivals (1 Maccabees 4:36–61; 2 Maccabees 10:1–8).

> At the very season and on the very day that the Gentiles had profaned [the altar], it was dedicated with songs and harps and lutes and cymbals. All the

Beth-horon ridge from the south. (BiblePlaces .com)

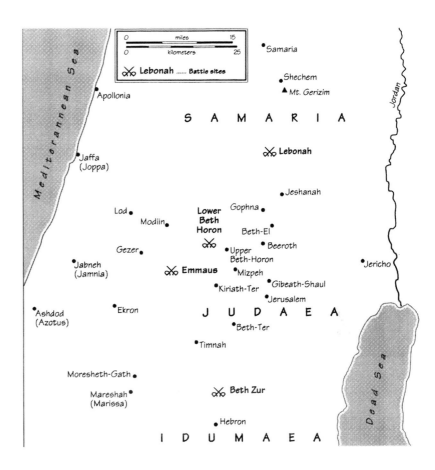

Map XI. The battles of Judah Maccabee.

people fell on their faces and worshipped and blessed Heaven, who had prospered them. So they celebrated the dedication of the altar for eight days and offered burnt offerings with gladness; they offered a sacrifice of deliverance and praise ... Then Judah and his brothers and the entire congregation of Israel decreed that the days of the dedication of the altar should be observed with joy and gladness on the anniversary every year for eight days, from the twenty-fifth day of the month Chislev. (1 Maccabees 4:54–6, 59)

The holiday of Hanukkah ("dedication"; see also John 10:22) commemorates this event. Judah also fortified the Temple Mount and Beth-zur in the south to provide security against the Syrian army.

Within a year of the rededication of the Temple, Antiochus IV died in the East, and two of his generals, Lysias and Philip, competed for control of the regency of Antiochus's young son, Antiochus V Eupator. During the disorder in Syria, Judah and his brothers Jonathan and Simon besieged and destroyed cities in Transjordan and defeated Gentile forces in Galilee. These campaigns did not result in permanent conquest but in relief of Jewish communities under attack. Both Judah and Simon brought oppressed Jews back to Judea, where they could be protected.

SIEGES

In the ancient world complex military tactics centered on well-engineered, fortified cities and siege machines capable of breaking down those fortifications. Ideally, fortified cities were built on high ground with steep approaches, an internal water source, and an ample supply of both food and defenders. The simplest siege sought to starve a city's inhabitants by blocking access to the city until food ran out. However, a wealthy, well-supplied city could hold out for years and sap the resources of the besieging army. Consequently, attack was preferable. Wealthy cities had thicker and higher walls and towers, and stronger gate buildings, as well as more ditches, outer defenses, catapults, and other means to repel enemies. To overcome these defenses, Greek and Roman engineers developed a variety of siege machines and engineering techniques. Catapults and bolt shooters could attack the walls from afar. Mobile siege towers several stories high carried catapults and battering rams up to the walls. Mobile sheds protected soldiers as they filled ditches, dug under the walls, or brought up battering rams, hooks, borers, and weaponry. Engineers built timbered tunnels under the walls and then collapsed the tunnels and walls above by burning the support timbers. Though cities with multiple walls, ditch systems, and artillery could resist attack, few could hold out forever.

4. The Hasmonean Dynasty

Judah Maccabee was able to gain only temporary victory over the Seleucids and their decrees against the Jewish way of life. Subsequent Syrian campaigns resulted in Judah's defeat and death (1 Maccabees 6:28–54; 9:1–22). After further conflict, the Seleucid general Bacchides made peace with Judah's brother Jonathan. The pro-Seleucid forces remained in control of the government in Jerusalem, but Jonathan increased his control in the countryside from a base at Michmash, several miles to the north.

The Hasmonean rulers Jonathan and then a third brother, Simon, took advantage of constant civil war among rival claimants to the Seleucid throne to gain for themselves leadership of Jewish society, the expansion of their territory beyond Judea, the fortification of their country, exemption from paying tribute to the Seleucids, and at long last control of the Akra. During these years, the Hasmonean family became the accepted leaders of Judea.

The Hasmoneans also arrogated the high priesthood to themselves. Menelaus had been replaced by the equally rapacious Alcimus, who held office from 162 to 159 B.C.E. Not only did Alcimus murder a number of the Hasideans, he also demolished the walls of the Temple's inner court. Simon drove Alcimus and his Syrian supporters out of Jerusalem, but Bacchides soon reinstated him. This reprieve ended shortly thereafter when Alcimus died.

With Alcimus dead, his allies gone or discredited, and Onias IV, the son of the murdered, legitimate high priest Onias III, having established a rival Jewish temple in the Egyptian city of Leontopolis, the Maccabees usurped the high priestly role. The Maccabees, although priests, were not from a traditional high priestly family, and they met with significant opposition. Similarly, they exercised the power of monarchy and eventually claimed royal titles, but they were not of the line of David. The Qumran texts, in their criticism of the Hasmoneans, exemplify the deep divisions over such issues during the period.

Along with their accession to the high priesthood, the other major event during the reigns of Jonathan and Simon was the cessation of tribute paid to the Seleucid ruler. In 152 B.C.E. the pretender to the Seleucid throne, Alexander Balas, appointed Jonathan high priest (and therefore ruler of Judea) in return for his support in the Syrian civil war. Ironically, the Seleucids found it economically and politically profitable to recognize the Maccabean popular leadership in Judea, whereas the originally pro-Seleucid Jewish party that had opposed the Maccabees went into decline. During ensuing Seleucid dynastic struggles Jonathan enlarged his power until finally, alarmed by the growing independence of Judea, the Syrian general Trypho, who was plotting to gain the Seleucid throne, captured Jonathan by a ruse and executed him (in 143 B.C.E.). Simon immediately switched his allegiance from Trypho back to his dynastic opponent, Demetrius II, who in 141 B.C.E. relieved Judea from any tax obligations (1 Maccabees 13:39). Although Demetrius was in no position to impose tribute on Simon anyway, this was the final and official release of Judea from foreign tax obligations.

In June of 141 B.C.E., Simon, after quickly conquering Joppa, Gazara (ancient Gezer), and Beth-zur, removed the final vestige of Seleucid control of Judea by starving out the garrison in the Akra (1 Maccabees 13:49–52). "They finally cried out to Simon for peace, and he gave them peace. He expelled them from the citadel and cleansed it of impurities" (1 Maccabees 13:50). Thus, freedom was won from the Seleucid rulers in Syria through a combination of military prowess and astute politics.

In 140 B.C.E. the assembly of priests, people, rulers, and elders approved Simon to be their high priest and leader, an office he had previously held by Seleucid appointment (1 Maccabees 14:25–49). Thus the Hasmonean dynasty, which was to endure for about one hundred years, was established. The Hasmoneans ruled Jewish society, but they did not meet with universal approval. Although 1 Maccabees treats the Maccabees as the heroes of the struggle against the Seleucids, it is clear not only from 2 Maccabees and later Jewish literature but also from 1 Maccabees itself that the Jewish community was deeply divided on how Judaism was to be lived and what response should be given to the aspiring Hasmonean empire. The new Hasmonean high priest had displaced previously powerful families, thwarted the ambitions of many leaders, and frustrated reform programs promoted by other movements and groups.

The Essenes of Qumran broke with Jerusalem, probably over the accession of Jonathan and Simon to the high priesthood. Various other parties, such as the Pharisees and Sadducees, also arose with the object of influencing or controlling Jewish society. Internal disagreements over how Jews were to live and over the appropriateness of governmental policies, as well as rivalries over who was to rule, continued until Roman rule over Judea began in 63 B.C.E.

Map XII. Alexander Jannaeus's kingdom.

B. Literary Responses to the Maccabees

Accounts of the Maccabean revolt and its aftermath appear in two partisan books, 1 and 2 Maccabees, each with its own heroes and villains. Both volumes construct their accounts under the influence of biblical parallels and are imbued with the conviction of divine providence and judgment. Although written years after the Maccabean revolt, they still breathe some of the passion and pain felt by Judean Jews during the horrors of oppression and the convulsions of war. The author of 1 Maccabees supports the activities of Judah Maccabee and his brothers and celebrates their accession to power. The author of 2 Maccabees praises Judah with restraint, ignores his brothers, and attributes the defeat of Antiochus IV and the salvation of Israel to the fortitude of the Jewish martyrs and to divine intervention.

The Book of Judith also reflects upon the Maccabean resistance, with its titular heroine (whose name is the female form of "Judah") demonstrating both military intelligence and personal piety. Other documents of the

The Qumran site from the west. (BiblePlaces
.com)

period, especially some of the apocalypses, testify to the diversity of Jewish responses to crises and to the strength of Jewish theology and way of life. Regarding the sufferings and victory of the Jewish people as part of God's plan, the apocalyptic works reduce the ambiguities and complex motives of the various conflicts to sharp contrasts between Jewish heroes and sinners or between righteous Jews and arrogant foreigners.

1. First Maccabees

First Maccabees, written to legitimate the Maccabean dynasty, begins with an unprovoked Syrian attack on Judaism and ends with the reign of Simon Maccabee, who has thrown off Syrian control and been accepted by the people as ruler of the nation (1 Maccabees 14:41; see 2:65). Although God does not directly intervene in human affairs in this account, the narrative clearly depicts the Maccabees as God's chosen instruments to deliver the people from persecution, reestablish Jewish law, and bring about peace and independence (1 Maccabees 5:61–2; 13:2–6; 14:26).

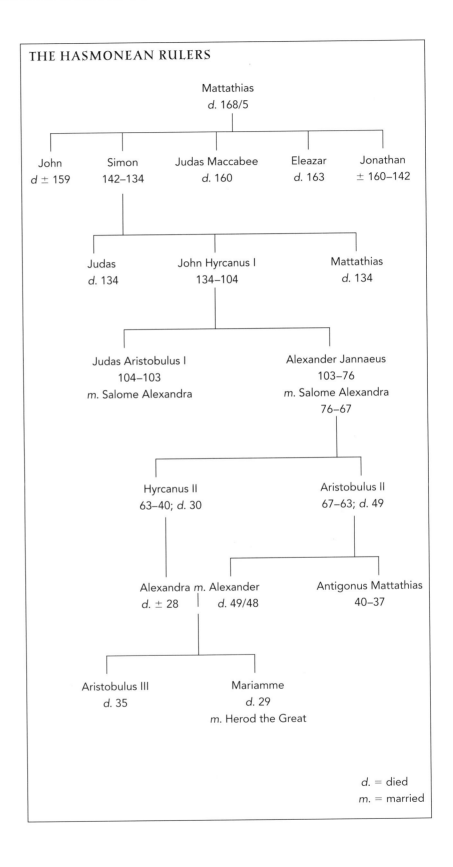

THE HASMONEAN RULERS

Mattathias
d. 168/5

John
d ± 159

Simon
142–134

Judas Maccabee
d. 160

Eleazar
d. 163

Jonathan
± 160–142

Judas
d. 134

John Hyrcanus I
134–104

Mattathias
d. 134

Judas Aristobulus I
104–103
m. Salome Alexandra

Alexander Jannaeus
103–76
m. Salome Alexandra
76–67

Hyrcanus II
63–40; *d.* 30

Aristobulus II
67–63; *d.* 49

Alexandra *m.* Alexander
d. ± 28   *d.* 49/48

Antigonus Mattathias
40–37

Aristobulus III
d. 35

Mariamme
d. 29
m. Herod the Great

d. = died
m. = married

In recounting the events of the mid-second century B.C.E. to the best advantage of the Maccabees, the author simplifies diverse social realities. Jerusalem's leading citizens who sought to balance the preservation of Jewish life with adaptation to the empire, such as through the constructing of a gymnasium, are treated as lawless sinners (1 Maccabees 1:11–15) and as a distinct minority who caused suffering for the majority. Syrian attacks on Judea and Jerusalem are presented as unprovoked initiatives caused by the malevolent Antiochus IV, who finally was punished by God through a horrible death (1 Maccabees 1:20, 29, 41; 6:1–16). No mention is made of the Jewish support for a more Hellenized life or of Jewish civil strife and resistance to the Seleucid Empire as cause for the incursions. The solution to the Syrian persecution, against which the people are helpless victims, is neither diplomacy nor compromise but Hasmonean military resistance.

The zeal of Judah Maccabee's father, Mattathias, in beginning the resistance is compared to that of the ancient Israelite Phinehas, who resorted to violence to maintain purity (1 Maccabees 2:26; Numbers 25:6–15). Maccabean leadership is personified by Judah himself, whose career is introduced by a hymn of praise (1 Maccabees 3:3–9):

> He extended the glory of his people. Like a giant he put on his breastplate; he girded on his armor of war and waged battles, protecting the host by his sword. He was like a lion in his deeds, like a lion's cub roaring for prey. He searched out and pursued the lawless. (1 Maccabees 3:3–5)

First Maccabees consistently compares Judah to a mighty biblical warrior who can call on God for help as he fights for God's law and people. Judah is like the warriors of old who fought God's battles, including Joshua (1 Maccabees 5), David (1 Maccabees 11:60–74,) and the judges (1 Maccabees 3:30 and 9:73). His death is noted with the biblical formula for the death of a king (1 Maccabees 9:20–2):

> All Israel bewailed him in great grief. They mourned for him many days, and they said, "How the mighty one has fallen, the savior of Israel!" The other acts of Judas, his battles, the brave deeds he performed, and his greatness have not been recorded, but they were very many.

Numerous allusions to biblical prophecies suggest that the author saw the Hasmonean dynasty as bringing to fulfillment God's promises to Israel. First Maccabees thus justifies Hasmonean accession to the high priesthood by depicting their service in preserving Judaism and their biblically charismatic leadership.

The poem in honor of Simon (1 Maccabees 14:4–15) presents an ideal description of peaceful life in Israel as both a sign of divine favor and the climax of the Maccabean leadership:

> The land had rest all the days of Simon.
> He sought the good of his nation;

his rule was pleasing to them,
as was the honor shown him, all his days.

....

He extended the borders of his nation
and gained full control of the country.

....

They tilled the land in peace;
the ground gave its increase,
and the trees of the plains their fruit.
Old men sat in the streets;
they all talked together of good things.

....

He established peace in the land
and Israel rejoiced with great joy.
                    (1 Maccabees 14:4–11)

This encomium is followed by the people's formal acceptance of Simon's rule, with repeated emphasis on his authority in and through the Temple:

> In the great assembly of the priests and the people and the rulers of the nation and the elders of the country, the following was proclaimed. . . . The Jews and their priests decided that Simon should be their leader and high priest forever, until a trustworthy prophet should arise, and that he should be governor over them and that he should take charge of the sanctuary and appointment over its tasks and over the country and the weapons and the strongholds, and that he should take charge of the sanctuary, and that he should be obeyed by all, and that all contracts in the country should be written in his name, and that he should be clothed in purple and wear gold. (1 Maccabees 14:28, 41–3)

The volume ends with the death of Simon in 134 B.C.E. and alludes to the chronicles of John Hyrcanus's deeds as high priest (1 Maccabees 16:23–4). These details suggest a date of composition at the end of John's reign (134–104 B.C.E.) or, after John's death, during the reign of his son and successor, Alexander Jannaeus (103–76 B.C.E.). Its positive attitude toward the Romans suggests a date prior to 63 B.C.E., when Rome conquered Jerusalem. First Maccabees was written originally in Hebrew, perhaps to counteract the criticism of the next generation of Hasmonean rulers, John Hyrcanus and Alexander Jannaeus, that the dynasty – established to preserve Judaism from destruction in the face of Hellenism – had become all too Hellenized.

2. Second Maccabees

The author of 2 Maccabees abbreviated a five-volume history of the Maccabean revolt written by a Greek-speaking Diaspora Jew, Jason of Cyrene. The absence of any account of the consolidation of power under Jonathan and Simon and the lack of mention of Judea's independence make it likely that Jason wrote before these events transpired. Further, Jason refers to Eupolemus (2 Maccabees 4:11), a mid-second-century B.C.E. Jewish-Hellenistic

THE FEAST OF HANUKKAH

Since the second century B.C.E. Jews have celebrated the rededication (*hanukkah*) of the Temple by the Maccabees for eight days during the Hebrew month of Chislev, which comes in late November or December (1 Maccabees 4:42–56; 2 Maccabees 10:1–8). Rabbinic literature calls this celebration the "Feast of Lights" because it is celebrated by the lighting of one additional candle in an eight-branched menorah each evening for eight nights, until, on the last night, all the candles are lit. The Talmud connects this practice with a legend that at the rededication a single, undefiled container of oil left in the Temple burned for eight days rather than for only one (b. Shabbat 21b). Along with light joy characterizes the feast; special prayers of thanksgiving are recited, and the Hallel (Psalms 113–18) is sung.

writer, as a contemporary. (An alternative view that dates Jason ca. 100 B.C.E. suggests he used numerous sources and government records, and thus dates 2 Maccabees to the first century B.C.E.) The author of 2 Maccabees arranged Jason's materials to argue for the centrality of the Temple and the importance of obedience to God. The Greek original suggests an audience of elite Jews in both Judea and the Diaspora.

The two letters that preface 2 Maccabees complicate the task of establishing the document's date and audience. The first (2 Maccabees 1:1–9) purports to be addressed by Jews in Jerusalem and Judea to Egyptian Jews and is dated to the year 124 B.C.E. reckoned by the Seleucid era (2 Maccabees 1:9). It refers to a previous communication on the death of Jonathan (2 Maccabees 1:7) and urges that the Egyptian Jews observe the feast of the rededication of the Temple (Hanukkah). This letter, which is probably genuine, may have been appended to 2 Maccabees after the book was written. The second letter (2 Maccabees 1:10–2:18) offers an account of Antiochus's death that is at variance with the account in the main body of the work. Though this second letter claims to have been written in 163 B.C.E., the year of Antiochus's death, most scholars date it to the first century C.E.

According to 2 Maccabees, the Temple and the fidelity of the people to God, not the Hasmonean dynasty, are crucial to Judaism's survival. Relying on the Deuteronomic understanding of divine retribution, the author teaches that arrogant leaders who attack the Temple will succeed only if the people are sinful. However, showing the increasingly popular hope in an afterlife, 2 Maccabees also insists that the pious who suffer because of the nation's sins will be rewarded through resurrection while sinners will receive a just retribution. By recounting the great defeats of three arrogant Gentiles who sought to harm the Temple and its people – Heliodorus, the Seleucid minister who attempted to confiscate Temple funds; Antiochus IV, the king who sought to outlaw Jewish practice; and Nicanor, the Syrian general who threatened that "If you do not hand Judas over to me as prisoner, I will level this precinct of God to the ground; I will tear down the altar, and erect here a splendid temple to Dionysus" (2 Maccabees 14:33) – the narrative shows divine control of history and the importance of recollecting God's righteous action. The defeats of Antiochus and Nicanor are therefore commemorated by, respectively, the festival of Hannukah and Nicanor's Day.

In the first conflict that 2 Maccabees recounts, paradigmatic for the book as a whole, the pious high priest Onias III and the people mourn the Seleucid threat to the Temple and pray to God for help. "Priests prostrated themselves in their priestly robes before the altar . . . people rushed out of their houses in crowds to make public supplication, because the Temple was in danger of being profaned; women, girded with sackcloth below their breasts, filled the streets; virgins secluded indoors ran together, some to the gates, some to the walls, others peered through the windows, all of them with hands raised toward heaven, making supplication" (2 Maccabees 3:15–20). This public display of piety brings an immediate divine response. Angels accost Heliodorus, the agent instructed to plunder the Temple, before he enters the building and beat him to the point of death (2 Maccabees 3). "Soon some of the companions of Heliodorus begged Onias to entreat the Most High, praying that the life of the man who was about to expire might be spared" (2 Maccabees 3:31). Fearing that the king would think Jewish conspirators had killed his envoy, Onias offers a sacrifice on behalf of Heliodorus, who then recovers.

The account of the conflict with Antiochus and of the consequent persecution (2 Maccabees 4–9) forms the center of the book. Chapter 6 lists the numerous abuses Antiochus perpetrated on the population: "Two women who were arrested for having circumcised their children were publicly paraded about the city with their babies hanging at their breasts and then thrown down from the top of the city wall; others, who had assembled in nearby caves to observe the Sabbath in secret, were . . . all burned to death. In their respect for the holiness of the day, they had scruples about defending themselves (2 Maccabees 6:10–11).

Differing from 1 Maccabees, this text places the responsibility for the sufferings of the Jewish people and the desecration of the Temple on both the Jewish people and the Seleucid ruler. Because many of the people (especially the leaders) sinned by deserting Jewish law for Greek ways, God brought punishment to Jerusalem. However, the fidelity of the martyrs anticipates God's reconciliation with the covenant community.

Second Maccabees values martyrdom at least as much as military resistance. Recounting the stories of the martyrs Eleazar the scribe (2 Maccabees 6) and a woman and her seven sons (2 Maccabees 7), the narrative both praises their sacrifices and encourages listeners to be equally faithful. The martyrs give speeches expressing their fidelity to God's law, confident that in the resurrection from the dead their mutilated bodies will be replaced, and desiring to set a good example. Eleazar summarizes his responsibility and the author's view: "By manfully giving up my life now, I will show myself worthy of my old age and leave to the young a noble example of how to die a good death willingly and nobly for the revered and holy laws" (2 Maccabees 6:27–8). After witnessing six of her sons being tortured to death, the mother refuses Antiochus's advice that she encourage her remaining child to transgress his ancestral traditions. "In derision of the cruel tyrant, she leaned over close to her son and said in their native language, 'Son, have pity on me, who carried you in my womb for nine months, nursed you for three years, brought you up, educated and supported you to your present age . . . do not be afraid of this executioner, but be worthy of your brothers and accept death, so that in the time of mercy I may receive you again with them'" (2 Maccabees 7:27, 29).

Only after the martyrs have died – the tortures, including the rack, dismemberment, and fire having been described in great and gory detail – does Judah Maccabee organize his army and defeat the Seleucid general Nicanor (2 Maccabees 8). God then strikes Antiochus with a "pain in his bowels for which there was no relief" and because of the king's "intolerable stench no one was able to carry the man who a little while before had thought that he could touch the stars of heaven" (2 Maccabees 9:5, 10). As

RESURRECTION

The first unambiguous evidence for belief in an afterlife among the Jews comes from the last chapter of the Book of Daniel, which was written during the Maccabean revolt:

At that time [during the final trouble] your people will be delivered, everyone whose name will be found written in the book. And many of those who sleep in the dust of the earth will awake, some to everlasting life and some to shame and everlasting contempt. And those who are wise will shine like the brightness of the firmament; and those who turn the many to righteousness, like the stars forever and ever. (Daniel 12:1–3)

Daniel's vision of the afterlife seems to involve living in the heavens like the angels, who were associated with stars and other heavenly bodies. The image of the just as stars is common in apocalyptic literature (see, for example, *1 Enoch* 104). Two other types of afterlife are commonly referred to in Hellenistic Jewish literature. One, the return to life with God through resurrection of the body, appears in 2 Maccabees and in some narratives within the Gospels. The predominant Jewish view was that the body and spirit were an integral whole, so that afterlife involved not just the survival of the spirit but also the restoration of the physical body. Thus the martyrs, who suffered extreme physical pain and mutilation, culminating in the loss of physical life, were fittingly rewarded by the restoration of their bodily integrity. At the same time, under the influence of Greek thought, some Jewish works, like the Wisdom of Solomon, affirmed the immortality of the soul, the Greek inner principle of life, thought, and will. In all cases, concern for the afterlife involves divine judgment and subsequent reward or punishment. According to the first-century C.E. Jewish historian Josephus (*Antiquities of the Jews* 18.1.4; see also Acts 23:6–8), resurrection was a fundamental Pharisaic belief, but the Sadducees did not accept the Pharisaic view.

MARTYRDOM

The value of the sufferings of the just is plainly affirmed during the Hellenistic period in 2, 3, and 4 Maccabees, the *Testament of Moses*, the Book of Daniel, the works of Philo and Josephus, and other Jewish writings as well as the New Testament. Nonviolent resistance to evil was not a sign of impotence but was part of the eschatological process that would lead to the judgment of the wicked and the vindication of the just. During the Roman period, virtuous suffering under oppression became a prime mode of testimony for both Jews and Christians. The word *martyr* itself, a Greek term, originally meant "witness" or "one who offers testimony," and thus became associated with one willing to die on behalf of a particular cause.

a result, Antiochus repents of his evils against the Jews and promises not only that he would restore their holy vessels and revenues but also that "he would become a Jew and would visit every inhabited place to proclaim the power of God" (2 Maccabees 9:17). Antiochus then dies. In the following chapter, Judah rededicates the Temple (2 Maccabees 10). So again, 2 Maccabees emphasizes divine power, not military action.

Judah Maccabee plays a major role in 2 Maccabees, but less so than in 1 Maccabees. He is presented as one among many pious Jews who resist Antiochus IV rather than in contrast with them, as in 1 Maccabees 7:12–25. In 2 Maccabees Judah does not fight on the Sabbath (2 Maccabees 12:38, 15:1; contrast 1 Maccabees 2:39–41). He believes in resurrection of the dead, an idea not mentioned in 1 Maccabees, and he offers sacrifices for those killed in battle:

He then took up a collection among all his soldiers, amounting to two thousand silver drachmas, which he sent to Jerusalem to provide for an expiatory sacrifice. In doing this he acted in a very excellent and noble way, inasmuch as he had the resurrection of the dead in view; for if he were not expecting the fallen to rise again, it would have been useless and foolish to pray for them in death. But if he did this with a view to the splendid reward that awaits those who had gone to rest in godliness, it was a holy and pious thought. Thus he made atonement for the dead that they might be freed from this sin. (2 Maccabees 12:43–5)

The text's anti-Hasmonean stance can be seen in its omission of the activities of Judah's brothers Jonathan and Simon and in the negative notice given to Simon. For example, "some of the men in Simon's force who were money lovers let themselves be bribed . . ." (2 Maccabees 10:20; see also 14:15–18).

THE GREEK HERO FIGURE

Greek literature offers ample evidence of the hero figure or the ideal wise man whose stories instruct and inspire others. For example, Plato's *Apology* and the *Phaedo* helped shape the heroic persona of Socrates, and the *Republic* and the *Laws* present wise statesmen as divinely inspired. Epicurus the Stoic, and Hercules, a favorite of Cynics as well as Stoics, both served as models of wisdom and perfection.

Jewish heroes took on some of these traits during the Hellenistic period. In his portrayals by Philo and Josephus, Moses emerges as familiar with natural law and with some of the essential Stoic doctrines. The same impact of the Greco-Roman world and the Greek hero figure can be seen in Luke's portrayal of Paul as a person acquainted with Stoic philosophy and Roman law, as well as Torah. The Pauline epistles contain some of the same Greek Stoic and Cynic influences, and Paul himself displays some of these heroic qualities. In *4 Maccabees*, which includes a retelling of the martyrdoms recounted in 2 Maccabees, Stoic traits mark even the mother of the seven sons, who urged them to embrace death rather than apostasy: "In the midst of her passionate feelings pious reason nerved her whole being with a manly courage and enabled her to transcend the immediate affections of a mother's love. . . . If then a woman and indeed a woman of advanced years, the mother of seven sons, held out while looking upon her children being tortured to death, we must concede that devout reason is sovereign over the passions" (*4 Maccabees* 15:23, 16:1).

Even Judah himself, when he has fulfilled his task of cleansing the Temple disappears; the book ends with no notice of his subsequent battles or death.

In the final sequence of events (2 Maccabees 10:10–15:36), Nicanor, the Seleucid governor, arrogantly demands that Judah be handed over to him. In threatening to tear down the "precinct of God" and build a temple to Dionysus unless the people accede to his wishes, he epitomizes the challenge to Jewish fidelity. The people, together with Judah, respond as they should: "Judas and his men met the enemy in battle with the invocation to God and prayers. So, fighting with their hands and praying to God with their hearts" (2 Maccabees 15:26–77), they defeated Nicanor. "And from that time the city has been in the possession of the Hebrews" (2 Maccabees 5:37).

Second Maccabees is written in a very literate style and follows Greek historical conventions by creating dramatic scenes and rhetorical speeches. The lurid descriptions of the suffering of the martyrs, the high emotion of the confrontations between Jews and their opponents, and the improbable repentance of Antiochus all serve to involve the hearers and arouse their emotions. The book comes from pietistic and well-educated circles that participated in the resistance to the Seleucids but did not fully support the new Maccabean political and social order.

3. Judith

The Book of Judith addresses the situation that provoked the Maccabean wars by depicting a threat to Jerusalem and the Temple in the distant past and by affirming the necessity of trust, obedience, and courage in the face of danger. Control of earthly events is left in human hands, with the "hand of a woman" (Judith 13:15; 16:5) showing the power of Israel's faithful.

A road in Samaria with pillars. (BiblePlaces .com)

The first verse of the book, which describes Nebuchadnezzar as ruling "over the Assyrians in the great city of Nineveh," contradicts what anyone could have known from 2 Kings 24–5: Nebuchadnezzar ruled *Babylon*. Thus, the narrative is clearly fictional: Nebuchadnezzar represents any threat, by any empire. Though Judith lives in an imaginary city, Bethulia, located in northern Samaria, the story is focused on Jerusalem and Judea, with Samaria seen as part of a unified homeland of Judaism. The stress on territorial integrity and freedom from foreign empires makes it likely that the story was written during the Hasmonean period, perhaps after John Hyrcanus had conquered Samaria in 107 B.C.E. Many scholars theorize that the Greek version of Judith derives from a lost Hebrew original, but no convincing argument for this view has been adduced.

The story is simple in outline, yet complex in its literary artistry. When Judea, Samaria, and other provinces in the western empire refuse the order to send troops to support his military campaigns in the east, Nebuchadnezzar sends his general Holofernes to punish them (Judith 1–3). The people respond by prayer and repentance, acknowledging their weakness and dependence upon God, and since piety and practicality are not mutually exclusive, by making military preparations. Along with fortifying their villages and storing up food, the "men of Israel and their wives and their children and their cattle and every resident alien and hired laborer and purchased slave all put sackcloth around their waists . . . they even draped the altar in sackcloth" (Judith 4:10, 12). When Holofernes then cuts off Bethulia's water supply, the people, preferring slavery to death, exhort their leaders to surrender. Uzziah, the magistrate, suggests that they "hold out for five days more" (Judith 7:30) in the hope that God will rescue them. If no rescue comes, he will agree to the people's request.

Judith, a beautiful, pious widow, at last appears in chapter 8. Her name, the feminine form of "Judah" (and so a possible allusion to Judah Maccabee) means "a woman from Judea" and, in its wider significance, "a Jewish woman." Thus Judith symbolizes the Jewish people: observant of the Law, dependent on God, courageous, resourceful, and wise. Summoning Bethulia's elders, she opposes their proposed surrender and promises to save the city (Judith 8:11–27).

Judith prays to God for help in carrying out her plan (chapter 9), beautifies herself, and leaves Bethulia for the enemy camp. Impressed by both her words and her beauty, the soldiers escort her to their general, and they say to one another, "Who can despise these people, who have women like this among them? It is not wise to leave one of their men alive, for if we let them go they will be able to beguile the whole world" (Judith 10:19). Judith succeeds marvelously in beguiling Holofernes with her looks, her promise to betray her people, and her numerous double entendres about seeking to please her "lord." Planning to seduce her, Holofernes instead drinks himself into a stupor. Judith, who had already planned her escape from the enemy camp, decapitates the general with his own sword, packs the head into her food bag, and returns triumphantly to Bethulia (Judith 10–13). Finding the decapitated corpse, Holofernes's army flees in panic; the Israelites attack the enemy, plunder their camp, and return with the spoils to celebrate in Jerusalem (chapters 14–16). Though Judith did not receive direct divine revelation or approbation, her piety, prayers, support from the people, and success leave little doubt that she had divine support.

Judith's success is based on a Deuteronomistic theology: if Israel obeys the Law, it will be safe; if not, it will be conquered. The theological scheme is expressed not only by the population of Bethulia, who speak of how God "punishes us for our sins and the sins of our ancestors" (Judith 7:28), but also by Achior, the leader of the Ammonites under Holofernes's command:

> As long as they did not sin against their God, they prospered, for the God who hates iniquity is with them. But when they departed from the way that he had appointed for them, they were utterly defeated in many battles and were led away captive to a foreign country; the Temple of their God was razed to the ground, and their cities were captured by their enemies. (Judith 5:17–18)

Achior then draws the obvious conclusion for Holofernes, even as he foreshadows Judith's victory:

> If there is any unwitting error in this people and they sin against their God and we find out their offense, then we will go up and defeat them. But if there is no transgression in their nation, then let my lord pass them by; for their Lord will defend them, and we shall be put to shame before the whole world. (Judith 5:20–1)

Because the people are faithful, Holofernes's plan is doomed. The narrative depicts a community of faithful and obedient Jews who tithe and offer first fruits (Judith 11:13). Judith observes the Sabbath especially and the discernment of the new moon; her faithful following of Jewish dietary restrictions marks her life even in the enemy camp and so provides her access to a handy food bag for carrying Holofernes's head (Judith 8:6; 11:2–4). Judith also insists on Israelite abhorrence of the major biblical sin, idolatry: "for never in our generation, not in these present days, has there been any tribe or family or people or town of ours that worships gods made with hands, as was done in days gone by" (8:18). By contrast, Holofernes declares that Nebuchadnezzar is the only god (6:2) and seeks to impose worship of him (3:8). Numerous prayers offered by the people, officials, and Judith herself acknowledge God's strength and fidelity to Israel as well as Israel's weakness and need (chapters 4, 7, 9, 15–16). The truth of this Deuteronomistic theology is borne out by the death of Holofernes at the hands of one Israelite, a woman (9:10; 13:15; 14:18; 16:6–7), and by the preservation of the nation in the face of overwhelming military might.

Judith stands in the line of biblical women such as Miriam (Exodus 15:20–1), Deborah, and Jael (Judges 4–5), but she is also cast in the role of Simeon, her ancestor, whom she evokes as having saved the "virgin" Dinah (Genesis 34) just as Judith will save Bethulia (the name of the town sounds like the Hebrew term *betulah*, "virgin"). As a literary figure, Judith both draws on and subverts conventional images of biblical women. On the one hand, she is the faithful, chaste, widow; on the other, she challenges Bethulia's elders, kills her enemy, gives orders for the Jewish attack on the Assyrian camp, and leads Israel in giving thanks to God. Although "many desired to marry her," she "gave herself to no man all the days of her life after her husband Manasseh died and was gathered to his people" (Judith 16:22). The story ends with peace and security from foreign enemies, an ideal that represents the hopes and goals of the Hasmonean fight for freedom.

4. Daniel

In the early Second Temple period Jews both in Israel and in the Diaspora had been producing "apocalyptic" literature, a type of writing whose name derives from the Greek term meaning "to uncover" or "to reveal" (hence the New Testament's Book of Revelation is also called the Apocalypse of John). Drawing on Israelite mythic, historical, and prophetic traditions, as well as on pagan motifs from the Ancient Near East and Greece, authors reported visions of the heavenly world and the end of time. The contents of these visions include phantasmagoric beasts, angelic mediators, otherworldly battles, tours of the heavens and of hell, and descriptions of the eschatological judgment in which the oppressed are redeemed and the evil punished, respond to Israel's oppression, whether by international powers or because of sectarian rivalry. The kingdom of God promised in apocalyptic works was never a vapid, internal, and purely individual state of soul but was to be a public manifestation of

THE FOUR EMPIRES

Daniel 2 describes a huge statue with parts made of four metals – gold, silver, bronze, and iron – to symbolize the four increasingly decadent and malevolent world empires: the Babylonian, Median, Persian, and Greek (although perhaps the Assyrians, Babylonians, Persians, and Seleucids are in view). These earthly powers are destroyed by a "stone [that] was cut by no human hand" (Daniel 2:34), that is, by divine power. In Daniel 7 the beasts that arise from the sea have the same symbolic meaning.

This later judgment scene describes how, when "the Ancient of Days" (God) appears, the fourth and most terrible beast, which causes great suffering, is summarily "slain, and its body destroyed and given over to be burned with fire" (Daniel 7:11). The scheme of four empires was part of Near Eastern political propaganda. Both the four empires and the four metals are found in a Persian document (the *Zand-i Vohuman Yasn*), and the mention of a Median kingdom, which ruled briefly in Persia only,

makes a Persian origin for this scheme likely. As time went on, Jewish readers and hearers of Daniel would have accommodated the list to suit the succession of empires that had ruled them. This scheme spread to the West, where it appears in the writings of the second-century B.C.E. Roman historian Aemilius Sura and in an early Greek oracle contained in the first-century C.E. *Fourth Sibylline Oracle* (49–101). This final text adds the Roman Empire as a fifth member of the scheme (102–51).

God's power on earth and in heaven. The sharply dualistic view of good and evil, God and Satan, and the proclamation of God's eventual triumph encouraged the faithful to persevere and assured them of the divine order of the universe; the openness of the symbols allowed the texts to be adopted and reinterpreted by successive generations.

The Book of Daniel, the Bible's major Hebrew apocalypse, did not originate as an apocalyptic text. The first six chapters are folktales, set in the sixth century B.C.E. in Babylonian and then Persian exile; these fanciful narratives provide instruction for living in the Diaspora and encourage trust, fortitude, and fidelity to the Law. In these adventure tales, God directly intervenes in the lives of Daniel and his associates through dreams and the gift of dream interpretation, miracles, and the manipulation of historical events in order to save the faithful.

During the persecution of the Jews by Antiochus IV Epiphanes, when Temple worship was violated and those faithful to Torah were being killed, the Book of Daniel attained its final form. With the appended chapters 7–12, the genre of the text shifts to apocalyptic. Daniel is now presented not as one who interprets the dreams of others, but as one whose dreams and visions require an angelic interpreter. Retaining the book's sixth-century B.C.E. setting, the apocalypse accords to Daniel visions of Israel's history from his time until the second century B.C.E. This form of literature is called *vaticinium ex eventu*, or "prophecy from the event": the character (Daniel, a sixth-century B.C.E. prophet) foretells what the author (a writer living in the second century B.C.E.) knows has already happened. Thus, Daniel's God-given "mantic" wisdom (the ability to interpret dreams, visions, and oracles), which played a prominent part in the stories in chapters 1–6, becomes the vehicle for understanding the Maccabean crisis. The visions in chapters

JEREMIAH'S SEVENTY YEARS

Jeremiah the prophet taught that God was using Babylon as an instrument to punish Israel and foresaw that Babylon would conquer Judea. He also prophesied that after seventy years Babylon would be punished and Israel restored (25:11–12; 29:10). Seventy, like seven, is a favorite biblical number; seventy years is almost two generations (reckoning forty years to a generation). During the Maccabean crisis (ca. 165 B.C.E.) the author of Daniel 7–12 reinterpreted Jeremiah's seventy-year prophecy in relation to his own generation. This apocalypse understands Jeremiah's prophecy to refer to seventy *weeks* of years, that is, 490 years, the period roughly equivalent to the number of years between Jeremiah's own date and the Maccabean period. (Ancient chronology was an approximate science at best.) The author of Daniel thought that sixty-nine weeks of years had passed before the persecution under Antiochus began and that one week of years of persecution would precede God's intervention in history (9:24–7).

7–8 and 10–12 and the reinterpretation of Jeremiah's prophecy of seventy years (Jeremiah 25:11–12; 29:10) into seventy weeks of years (chapter 9) reach their climax in the atrocities perpetrated by Antiochus. His plans are thwarted by divine justice, which destroys the wicked and vindicates the faithful.

The Book of Daniel was completed shortly before the rededication of the Temple and the death of Antiochus: the date is suggested by both the narrative's detailed review of Antiochus's reign and the incorrect prediction concerning Antiochus's final battle and place of death (Daniel 11:40–5). Revised dates for the coming of God's victory and judgment in the penultimate verse (Daniel 12:12) indicate that the author, writing during the turmoil itself, had to adjust the predictions to fit unfolding events. Antiochus is allied with "those who forsake the holy covenant" (11:30–2), whom he seduces with flattery. Opposing those traitors are the members of the author's group, who are wise and understanding: "The people who know their God will stand firm and take action. And those among the people who are wise will make many understand, though they will fall by the sword and flame, by captivity and plunder, for some days" (11:33). Those who understand — that is, the author and his community — conceived of their role as that of purifying the people through their suffering (see the figure of the Servant in Isaiah 53) and instructing them so that they too might embrace the group's vision of God and inherit the kingdom promised to "the people of the Saints of the Most High" (Daniel 7:27). Committed to nonmilitant resistance, they do not envision themselves fighting the Seleucids and their Hellenizing Jewish allies, as the Maccabees did (1 Maccabees 2:42). The author does not value or acknowledge the Maccabees' military efforts (unless Daniel 11:34 does so). Instead, apocalyptic expectation looks for direct divine intervention to save those who faithfully endure.

The Book of Daniel embraces suffering and persecution in a way similar to the martyrdom stories in 2 Maccabees and the *Testament of Moses* (see later). Like Daniel and his companions in exile (Daniel 1:4), the heroes of these volumes are wise in the ways of God and in the interpretation of divine purposes. Because of their knowledge of the heavenly world and their confidence in their final exaltation with God, they endure martyrdom not just to defy the Seleucids and to provide an example for their fellow Jews but also to purify themselves for union with God and his angels: "Many will purify themselves, and make themselves white, and be refined; but the wicked will do wickedly; and none of the wicked will understand; but those who are wise will understand" (Daniel 12:10). The wise, who give their lives for Judaism because they receive revelation through the apocalyptic visions and thus know how to face persecution, will live in the heavens with the other divine beings who serve God. No earthly restoration is envisioned, in contrast to the Apocalypse of Weeks in *1 Enoch* 91:13, where the just acquire houses, and to 2 Maccabees, which rejoices in a restored Temple.

5. The First Book of Enoch

First Enoch, like the Book of Daniel, is a composite text that includes material dating from different centuries. Two or three sections derive from the Maccabean period: the Animal Apocalypse (chapters 85-90), the Apocalypse of Weeks (93:1–10, 91:12–17), and perhaps the Epistle of Enoch. All three sharply distinguish the just from sinners, await God's judgment, and anticipate life after death. The first two divide history into periods and so affirm order in the universe and promote confidence in God.

The Animal Apocalypse is the second and longer of two dreams that comprise *1 Enoch*'s Book of Dreams (*1 Enoch* 83–90). This *vaticinium ex eventu* narrates the history of the world from the time of Adam, with animals representing humans and human figures used for angels. The last event in the historical account is the climactic struggle of Judah Maccabee (the "great horn of one of the sheep") against the Gentiles; the historical survey thus yields a date for the Animal Apocalypse during the Maccabean revolt (167–164 B.C.E.), the time of the composition of the Book of Daniel. *First Enoch* 90:7–8 suggests that the author was a supporter of Onias III (described as a lamb killed by raveus) early in the second century B.C.E.

The group that produced the Animal Apocalypse, like the Essenes, sought to reform or replace Jewish leadership in Jerusalem and especially in Temple administration. The postexilic, rebuilt Temple, symbolized by a tower, is seen as always polluted; the people associated with it, that is, Jews who accommodate themselves to the Gentile way of life, are imaged as blind sheep (*1 Enoch* 89:73–4). As the result of Israel's sins, God has placed the nation under the authority of seventy shepherds who are the guardian angels (and sometimes kings) of the Gentile nations, traditionally seventy in number (89:59–77). But because the shepherds' oppression of Israel is recorded for use at the judgment (90:22), the people know that justice will eventually be done, the faithful rewarded, and the wicked punished. God will reign over a new Jerusalem and a transformed people (90:28–36), including the risen martyrs. When judgment has been completed, the old Jerusalem (symbolized by a house) will be dismantled and a new one built.

> I went on seeing until the Lord of the sheep brought about a new house, greater and loftier than the first one, and set it up in the first location which had been covered up – all its pillars were new, the columns new; and the ornaments new as well as greater than those of the first, the old which was gone. All of the sheep were within it. Then I saw all the sheep that had survived as well as all the animals upon the earth and the birds of heaven, falling down and worshiping those sheep, making petition to them and obeying them in every respect. (*1 Enoch* 90:29–31)

The Apocalypse of Weeks, part of which is dislocated in the Ethiopic text (*1 Enoch* 91:12–17 belongs after 93:1–10) is, compared to the Animal Apocalypse, briefer and less detailed. It appears near the beginning of the Epistle of Enoch (the final section of *1 Enoch*), which is a long exhortation stressing the judgment of the wicked. This second form of prophecy *ex eventu* divides world history into ten weeks. Enoch was born in the first week, which was a righteous period. At the close of the fifth week, "the house of glory and dominion shall be built forever" (*1 Enoch* 93:7). Contrary to the Animal Apocalypse therefore, the Apocalypse of Weeks envisions the Temple as enduring eternally in some form. The sixth week is the period of the divided monarchy (1–2 Kings), in which "all who live in it will be blinded, and the hearts of all of them will godlessly forsake wisdom" (*1 Enoch* 93:8). This period ended with the destruction of the Temple.

The postexilic period, the seventh week, receives a judgment comparable to that given in the Animal Apocalypse. But at the end of this apostate generation the author's group arises with an unmistakable emphasis on their election: "At its close will be elected the elect righteous of the eternal plant of righteousness, to receive sevenfold instruction concerning all his creation. And they will have rooted out the foundations of violence and the structure of falsehood therein, to execute [judgment]" (*1 Enoch* 93:10 [Ethiopic]; 93:11 [Aramaic]). Like the Animal Apocalypse and Daniel, the Apocalypse of Weeks characterizes the righteous group by special knowledge.

Although the events of the eighth week (*1 Enoch* 91:12–13) have sometimes been understood as referring to the activities of Judah Maccabee, in all probability they describe God's kingdom (without a messiah) before the final judgment and the earth's destruction. Because the text does not clearly refer to the Maccabean revolt itself, this apocalypse may antedate Judah's actions. The seer envisions a time when a sword will be given to the righteous to execute judgment on the wicked and then houses (in the Aramaic text: riches) will be given to the righteous and a new Temple built for God. In the ninth week, earth and its evil will be judged and destroyed; in the tenth, the angels will be judged, a new heaven will replace the old heaven, and goodness and righteousness will endure for weeks without number (*1 Enoch* 93:14–17).

The conflict over acceptable ways of living Judaism, alluded to in the Animal Apocalypse and Apocalypse of Weeks, appears in great detail in the Epistle of Enoch (*1 Enoch* 91–108). Written as Enoch's final testament to his sons (91:1), the Epistle contains numerous exhortations that draw on both prophetic and wisdom traditions. The author condemns a number of social ills, including oppression of the poor by the rich and of the weak by the powerful, lying, theft, doing evil to fellow Jews, self-indulgence, and idolatry:

> Woe to those who build oppression and injustice!
> Who lay foundations for deceit.
> They shall soon be demolished;
> And they shall have no peace. . . .
> Those who amass gold and silver;
> They shall quickly be destroyed.
> Woe unto you, O rich people!
> For you have put your trust in your wealth.
> (*1 Enoch* 94:6, 8; see also the rest of *1 Enoch* 94–5 and 99)

THE BIBLE REWRITTEN

A number of Jewish works from the Second Temple period retell the biblical narrative through paraphrase, addition, and omission to clarify obscure passages, remove what might be perceived to be embarrassing elements, and make the material directly relevant for readers. *Jubilees* retells stories in Genesis and Exodus, with a focus on a renewed understanding of many holidays and the Sabbath, as well as on legitimating later laws and the solar calendar. The Qumran *Temple Scroll* (11QTemple) describes the regulations governing the ideal Temple and then reorganizes some of the laws in Deuteronomy 12–26. Pseudo-Philo's *Biblical Antiquities* (also known as *Liber Antiquitatum Biblicarum*) interweaves biblical and legendary accounts from Genesis to 2 Samuel to stress Israel's position as chosen and the necessity of good leaders. The Qumran *Genesis Apocryphon* reworks stories of Noah and Abraham to make them more dramatic and detailed, as well as to explain geographical terms and remove interpretive difficulties. Josephus's *Antiquities of the Jews* retells biblical history for the Greco-Roman world, using interpretations from the Jewish tradition and stressing God's providence, the necessity of morality, and the respectability of Judaism.

The righteous are promised vindication and reward, in contrast to the punishment visited on sinners in the climactic judgment scene (*1 Enoch* 102–5).

The Epistle of Enoch contains little information to help date it, for the social ills it describes existed both before and after the Maccabean revolt. Rather than picture the audiences to whom the Animal Apocalypse, the Apocalypse of Weeks, and Epistle of Enoch are addressed as a single group or an organized social movement, we should understand the groups whose traditions are presented in the *Enoch* collection as representative of a broad tendency (reflected in *Enoch*, *Jubilees*, and some Dead Sea Scrolls) to reject Temple leadership, the official (lunar) calendar, excessive Hellenization, accommodation to the Gentiles, and oppression of the poor.

6. Jubilees

The *Book of Jubilees* is an extensive elaboration of Genesis and the first part of Exodus. It expands the biblical narrative with narrative details, revisions of legal material, and indirect comments on contemporary events, and it omits offensive or "unimportant" material. The author stresses keeping the Sabbath (chapters 2 and 50, the beginning and end of the book) and festivals, the practice of circumcision, observing proper sacrificial and dietary laws, and avoiding illicit sexual practices and injustice. Great hostility to the Gentiles appears in many places (e.g., 22:16–18), especially concerning their practices of nudity when exercising (3:31), idolatry, and intermarriage (30:10):

> There is no remission or forgiveness except that the man who caused defilement of his daughter will be rooted out from the midst of all Israel because he has given some of his seed to Moloch and sinned so as to defile it. And you, Moses, command the children of Israel and exhort them not to give any of their daughters to the Gentiles and not to take for their sons any of the daughters of the Gentiles because that is contemptible before the Lord. (*Jubilees* 30:10–12)

Finally, the author connects all events and festivals to a 364-day solar calendar and thus roots all Jewish practice and history in his version of the order of the universe. This is the calendar that is found in the Astronomical Treatise of *1 Enoch* (chapters 72–82) and in some Dead Sea Scrolls.

In retelling the Genesis stories, *Jubilees* indicates that the patriarchs kept the laws and festivals that were only later revealed to Moses. *Jubilees* argues against the view of Hellenizing Jews that the laws and practices of Judaism were no longer relevant or could be changed. Rather, it insists that the laws, which came from the earliest patriarchal period and are inscribed on heavenly tablets (*Jubilees* 3:10; 31:32; 32:10), remain eternally valid (*Jubilees* 30:10). Moses is said to have received a revelation of laws, both biblical and nonbiblical, from an angel on Sinai: "And the angel of the presence spoke to Moses by the word of the Lord, saying, 'Write the whole account of creation, that in six days the Lord God completed all his work and all that he created . . .'" (*Jubilees* 2:1).

Though *Jubilees* apparently speaks only about early biblical events, it in fact alludes to the Maccabean situation before the death of Judah Maccabee. The apocalyptic review of history in *Jubilees* 23 describes the oppression and apostasy of the Maccabean period (chapters 16–25), the rise of the faithful group to whom *Jubilees* is written (*Jubilees* 26), and then God's direct, apocalyptic intervention in history (chapters 27–31). In addition, the battles against the Amorites (*Jubilees* 34) and the Edomites (chapters 37–8) – neither of which the Bible reports – allude to Judah Maccabee's battles against Nicanor (1 Maccabees 7:39–50) and against the Edomites. *Jubilees* was found among the Dead Sea Scrolls, but probably antedates the foundation of the Qumran community and so was written between 160 and 140 B.C.E.

Similarities shared among *Jubilees*, parts of the *Enoch* tradition, parts of *Daniel*, and documents from Qumran such as the *Genesis Apocryphon* suggest that Second Temple society featured circles of apocalyptically oriented Jews who shared many of the same ideas and ideals. Since *Jubilees* (31:12) prioritizes Levi (the priesthood) over Judah (the monarchy), makes Levi the custodian of the books and traditions of Israel (*Jubilees* 45:15), and places great emphasis on Israel's cultic life, the author was probably a priest.

The author's zealous fidelity to Israel and rejection of the Gentiles are based on his interpretation of Genesis 34. In the biblical account and in the retelling in *Jubilees*, Levi first rejects the Gentile Shechem's offer to marry Levi's sister Dinah, whom Schechem has raped. Then, Levi and his brother slaughter the inhabitants of the city of Shechem. For this faithful action, according to *Jubilees* 30:18-20, Levi received the priesthood. The author of *Jubilees* sees his own vocation, like Levi's, to be the protection of Israel from sexual defilement and other Gentile practices. In similar manner, the Book of Judith appeals also to Genesis 34, but Judith traces her ancestry to Simeon, Levi's brother and partner in the destruction of Shechem.

7. The Testaments

During the second century B.C.E. through the first century C.E., when apocalypses were being written, an allied literary genre, the testament, became popular. Testaments, the purported last words of a famous figure to his sons or followers, have survived in the names of the patriarchs, Moses, Job, and others. In a testament the historical figure usually tells something about his life, exhorts his descendants to virtue, and predicts his descendants' future, often in the form of an apocalypse concerning the last days and the ultimate destiny of Israel. The hortatory sections are similar to the Wisdom literature.

The *Testaments of the Twelve Patriarchs*
The most extensive collection of second-century B.C.E. testaments is the work known as the *Testaments of the Twelve Patriarchs*. These twelve testaments, in the names of the twelve sons of Jacob and tribes of Israel, are not translations of earlier Hebrew and Aramaic testaments but free Greek

BIBLICAL LAST BLESSINGS

The testament genre is modeled on the last blessings Jacob gives to his twelve sons (Genesis 49) and Moses gives to the people of Israel (Deuteronomy 33). The blessings serve as both a prediction of the heirs' future and a means of promoting particular ethical concerns. For example, Jacob's blessing of Judah, the tribe from which will emerge the Davidic line, predicts: "Judah is a lion's [symbol of royalty] whelp. . . . The scepter shall not depart from Judah, nor the ruler's staff from between his feet, until he comes to whom it belongs" (Genesis 49:9–10). Simeon and Levi, who led the attack on Shechem (Genesis 34), are cursed and condemned to be divided in Israel (49:5–7), a reflection of the fact that the tribe of Simeon was absorbed into Judah and the tribe of Levi became a landless priestly class. Yet later writers felt themselves free to redefine these concerns: the Book of Judith redeems Simeon, and the *Book of Jubilees* looks to the story of Shechem in its promotion of the Levitical priesthood. The final blessing of Moses reflects other realities of Israelite history. It praises the tribe of Levi as faithful priests: "Give to Levi your Thummim, and your Urim to the godly one, whom you tested at Massah. . . . For they observed your word and kept your covenant. They shall teach Jacob your ordinances and Israel your law" (Deuteronomy 33:8–10). Joseph, the progenitor of Ephraim and Manasseh, the two powerful tribes who held the rich central hill country, is praised extensively and called prince among his brothers (33:13–17), a reflection of anti-Davidic sentiment. The *Testaments of the Twelve Patriarchs*, the *Testament of Abraham*, and other later works such as Tobit's final admonitions to his son Tobias use the same premise of a final blessing, but tend to highlight ethical concerns over predictive elements.

NATURAL LAW

The testaments encourage the practice of Hellenistic virtues such as piety, uprightness, generosity, honesty, compassion, integrity, hard work, and self-control. Appeal is made to another Greek idea, conscience (the universal potential for responding to the natural law). Even sexual misdeeds are to be avoided through temperance, not by adherence to specifically biblical commandments. Homosexuality and idolatry are condemned because they are seen as contrary, not to biblical law, but to the law of nature. The influence of this ethical approach can be seen in the writings of Paul the apostle, who appeals to conscience (Romans 2:15) and lists virtues to be acquired and vices to be avoided (Galatians 5:19–23).

compositions loosely based on earlier models; they should not to be confused with parts of Aramaic testaments of Levi, Judah, and Naphtali found among the Dead Sea Scrolls and other manuscripts.

There are few clues to the date and place of composition of the *Testaments of the Twelve Patriarchs*. The author may have been a learned Palestinian Jew, especially given the emphasis, seen also in *Jubilees*, on the dominance of Levi and the priesthood. However, the lack of accuracy concerning place-names, the use of Hellenistic ethical exhortation that has no analogue in Semitic Jewish literature, and the fact that the sequence provided of world empires ends with the reign of the Seleucids in Syria (*Testament of Naphtali* 5:8) suggest that the author may have been living under Seleucid rule in Syria. Others have placed the work in the well-established and literate Jewish community in Egypt in view of the strong emphasis on Joseph as a model of virtue in several of the testaments (*Testament of Reuben* 4:8–10; *Testament of Benjamin* 3; *Testament of Judah* 25:1) and because the *Testament of Joseph* is elaborate in literary terms.

The date of the work is disputed. The combination of the prophetic, priestly, and kingly roles assigned to the Levitical messiah (*Testament of Levi* 18) may have been prompted by the reign of John Hyrcanus (134–104 B.C.E.). In that case, the composition would date from the same period. But if, as seems more likely, this figure developed through a number of works in the Maccabean period, the collection may have been written soon after the Maccabean crisis; this date would accord with the connections between the *Testaments of the Twelve Patriarchs* and the Dead Sea Scrolls, as well as with the *Testaments'* frequent mention of the *Book of Enoch*. The text as it now exists includes passages added by Christian copyists, although some scholars have held that the *Testaments* are substantially Christian.

All the testaments in the *Testaments of the Twelve Patriarchs*, except that of Levi, contain a narrative about the patriarch's life that serves an example either of virtue, such as integrity, self-control, courage, brotherly love, and mercy, or of vice, such as licentiousness, deceit, envy, avarice, anger, and hate. For example, after describing how he had "seen Bilhah bathing in a sheltered place" and how "so absorbed were his senses by her naked femininity that he was not able to sleep" (*Testament of Reuben* 3:11–12), Reuben exhorts his sons: "Do not devote your attention to the beauty of women . . . nor occupy your minds with their activities. But live in integrity of heart in the fear of the Lord, and weary yourself in good deeds, in learning, and in tending your flocks, until the Lord gives you the mate whom he wills, so that you do not suffer, as I did" (*Testament of Reuben* 34:1).

Though obedience to God and his laws is often mentioned the particular laws and practices emphasized in *Jubilees* do not feature here. To characterize the good Jew the author uses Hellenistic terms for ethics, virtue, and piety. Each testament ends with an ethical exhortation to copy the virtue the patriarch promoted, a prediction of the future of the tribe (or all Israel), and a recounting of the patriarch's death and burial.

In the *Testaments of the Twelve Patriarchs*, the larger world within which the struggle between virtue and vice takes place resembles that found in the apocalypses. There are two spirits, good and evil, that move humans in opposite directions. The reign of evil is under the sovereignty of Beliar, an evil spirit found in much of the contemporaneous literature. The final victory of God over evil is depicted with a variety of apocalyptic images and scenarios, including resurrection, a new Jerusalem, and paradise. *Testament of Zebulun* 10:2 records the patriarch stating: "And now, my children, do not grieve because I am dying, nor be depressed because I am leaving you. I shall rise again, in your midst as a leader among your sons, and I shall be glad in the midst of my tribe – as many as keep the Law of the Lord and the commandments of Zebulon, their father" (see also *Testament of Judah* 25:1–4).

The author's solution to the political woes and disorder in the community is communicated through frequent exhortation to obey Levi (the priesthood) and Judah (the monarchy), although the monarchy is subordinate to the priesthood (*Testament of Judah* 21:1–4). Both the biblical figure Judah and the Levitical messiah are military leaders (*Testament of Levi* 18:12) as well as cultic functionaries. They replace the Davidic messiah and the monarchy as Judaism's guiding force.

The *Testament of Levi* differs from the other testaments in the collection by being an apologetic tract that seeks to legitimate the authority of the priests. Levi is taken on a journey to heaven (2–5) and given a sword to avenge his sister Dinah's rape (5:3; cf. Genesis 34, *Jubilees*, and Judith). Because of his zeal in avenging his sister, he not only is given all power through the priesthood but also is associated with kingly rule. Levi and the priestly messiah (*Testament of Levi* 18) dominate the eschatological future and overshadow the Davidic messiah (i.e., the anointed leader from the tribe of Judah and dynasty of David; *Testament of Judah* 24–5) and the eschatological prophet promised in Scripture (Deuteronomy 18:15–19; see *Testament of Benjamin* 9:1–2).

> The Lord will raise up a new priest to whom all the words of the Lord will be revealed. He will effect the judgment of truth over the earth for many days. And his star will rise in heaven like a king. . . . And the spirit of sanctification will rest upon him . . . and there will be no successor for him from generation to generation forever. . . . And in his priesthood sin will cease . . . and righteous men will find rest in him. And he will open the gates of paradise; he will remove the sword that has threatened since Adam, and he will grant the saints to eat of the Tree of Life. (*Testament of Levi* 18)

The *Testament of Job*

Written sometime in either the first century B.C.E. or the first century C.E., the *Testament of Job* draws mainly from the shorter Septuagint version rather than the Hebrew text; in retelling the biblical story of the righteous man whom Satan tortures in order to test his fidelity to God, this testament not only develops the biblical characters but also finds humor in the story.

Told as a first-person narrative, the testament opens with Job, "having fallen ill," surrounded by his seven sons and three daughters, all of whom are named. The patriarch informs his children: "you are a chosen and honored race from the seed of Jacob, the father of your mother. For I am from the sons of Esau, the brother of Jacob, of whom is your mother Dinah, from whom I begot you. (My former wife died with the ten children in a bitter death)" (*Testament of Job* 1:5–7). This Job is even more righteous than his biblical counterpart: he "established in his house thirty tables spread at all hours, for strangers only." He "also used to maintain twelve other tables set for the widows" (*Testament of Job* 10:1–2). Not content merely with feeding the hungry, he would rouse himself "daily after the feeding of the widows, take the lyre, and play for them" (*Testament of Job* 14:2).

When Satan strikes against Job, the ailing man's (first) wife, like Anna the wife of the unfortunately blinded Tobit, is forced to support the family. "I spent forty-eight years on the dung heap outside the city under the plague so that I saw with my own eyes, my children, my first wife carrying water into the house of a certain noblewoman as a maidservant so she might get bread and bring it to me. I was stunned. And I said, 'The gall of these city fathers! How can they treat my wife like a female slave?'" (*Testament of Job* 21:1–4a). The wife, named Sitis, would eventually sell her hair to Satan. But Job is less than patient with her: "Do you not see the devil standing behind you and unsettling your reasoning so that he might deceive me too? For he seeks to make an exhibit of you as one of the senseless women who misguide their husbands' sincerity" (*Testament of Job* 26:6).

Job rebukes Satan (*Testament of Job* 27), is visited by three "kings," and finds vindication (28–44). At the end of his life Job presents his daughters with miraculous sashes or scarves, which provide them the gift of prophecy and access to the secrets of heaven (46–50).

The *Testament of Solomon*

This Greek pseudepigraphon begins "Testament of Solomon, son of David, who was king in Jerusalem, and mastered and controlled all spirits of the air, on the earth, and under the earth" (*Testament of Solomon* 1). Because the archangel Michael provides Solomon with a magical ring and seal, the king is able to harness demons and force them to help him construct the Temple. The text also details a list of demons and explains how they can be exorcised. The interest in demonology along with angelology had already begun with Tobit and with the various descriptions of the fall of the watchers (e.g., *1 Enoch* 1–36). This testament reveals that there are female demons, including one, called Onoskelis, who has an extended dialogue with the king before he condemns her to spin hemp for the Temple night and day.

Written sometime between the first and third centuries C.E., the text has been interpolated by Christian editors who added references to the Virgin Birth and the cross.

8. Sibylline Oracles

Among Jews in the Diaspora, especially in Egypt, apocalyptic prophecies of the future and political protest against the ruling empires utilized the Greco-Roman form of the *Sibylline Oracles*. The Sibyl was an aged prophetess, given long life and the power of prophecy by the gods. Various locales claimed oracles (Michelangelo placed five of them in the Sistine Chapel with the prophets). Generally, their oracles are filled with predictions of disaster for specific cities and countries. Many contain political protests and propaganda of eastern countries against their Greek and Roman conquerors. They often envision the return to a golden age under an ideal king, such as that described in Virgil's Fourth Eclogue and associated there with the Sibyl in Cumae (near Naples). Their subversive nature caused Augustus to order that copies of many oracles in Rome be destroyed.

The surviving collection of *Sibylline Oracles* derives from Jewish and Christian circles. Most oracles are composites of smaller units and modified by additions to bring them up to date. They are characterized by predictions of doom for various nations and the coming of an ideal kingdom, and by the hope of judgment, as well as by moral exhortations that condemn especially idolatry, adultery, and homosexuality.

A major part of the *Third Sibylline Oracle* (97–349, 489–829) comes from mid-second-century B.C.E. Egypt, when good relations between the Jews and Ptolemy VI Philometor (180–145 B.C.E., his second regnal period) encouraged some Egyptian Jews to hope for an ideal kingdom under a

VIRGIL'S FOURTH ECLOGUE

The great Latin poet Virgil (first century B.C.E.) was most famous for his
epic the *Aeneid*. During his lifetime,
political upheaval changed Rome
from a republic to an empire. Virgil
voices the aspirations of Rome in
one of his eclogues (poems with a
pastoral setting), in which he praises
the birth of a special child and anticipates a new, golden age. The work is
similar to other political oracles
common in Greek and Roman literature, such as the *Sibylline Oracles*
(it even references the Sibyl of
Cumae), although Virgil was writing
propaganda for rather than a
protest against Roman rule. It also
resembles Jewish apocalyptic texts,
which anticipate a golden age of justice and prosperity, and comment
on the nature of God's chosen (or
covenant) community. Some later
Christian writers took this eclogue
as a prediction of the coming of
Jesus

Now the Virgin returns, the reign
    of Saturn returns;
        now a new generation
            descends from heaven
            on high.
    ....

    ....
Smile on the birth of the
    child, under whom the
    iron brood shall first
    cease,
and a golden race spring up
    throughout the world
....
For you, child, shall the earth
    untilled pour forth
    ....

    ....
Uncalled, the goats shall
    bring home their udders
swollen with milk
and the herds shall fear not
    huge lions
....
The serpent, too, shall perish.

When the strength of years
    has made you a man,
even the trader shall quit
    the sea,
nor shall the ship of pine
    exchange wares;
every land shall bear all fruits.
    The earth shall not feel
    the harrow,
nor the vine the pruning-
    hook; the sturdy plough-
    man, too, shall now
loose his oxen from the yoke.
....
Enter on your high honor –
    the hour will soon be
    here – O dear offspring
    of the gods, mighty seed
    of a Jupiter to be.
Behold the world bowing
    with its massive dome,
earth and expanse of sea and
    heaven's depth.
Behold, how all things exult
    in the age that is at hand.

"seventh king" (193, 318, 608). The sections lack any reference to the Maccabees or the wars in Judea. Rather, the author uses a traditional scheme of
ten ages or empires, of which the last two are the Greek and Roman
Empires (the latter an increasingly menacing presence in the eastern
Mediterranean in the second century B.C.E.). Two lists of empires (156–61,
165–95) end with the Romans, and the second predicts their overthrow by
the seventh Egyptian king (191–5).

The Jewish author treats the Egyptian king, designated by the traditional
title "the king from the sun," as an eschatological figure who will be the
final ruler to precede the cosmic judgment and God's kingdom:

> And then God will send a king from the sun who will stop the entire
> world from evil war, killing some, imposing oaths of loyalty on others;
> and he will not do all these things by his private plans but in obedience
> to the noble teachings of the great God. (*Third Sibylline Oracle* 3:652–6)

The place given the Egyptian king in God's plans is like that given
Cyrus of Persia by the exilic author of Second Isaiah (Isaiah 44:28, 45:1–7).
In both cases Diaspora authors adapted Jewish expectations to local

culture. The Egyptian Jewish author of the *Third Sibylline Oracle* did not look to Palestine for deliverance but supported his local monarch, hoping that God would work through the pharaoh to bring about justice. The apocalyptic expectations of war and suffering followed by judgment and a divine kingdom, which fill the latter part of the oracle (*Third Sibylline Oracle* 601–808), were used to encourage loyalty to a good Egyptian king against invaders (be it Antiochus IV or the Romans).

Although the *Third Sibylline Oracle* alludes to neither the Maccabees nor Judea, it does puts great emphasis on the sanctity and centrality of the Temple and its holy city, Jerusalem (286–94, 564–7, 657–68, 715–40, 772–5). Warnings are given not to attack the Temple. Through this center of Judaism, the Gentiles will attain peace, and in the end they will offer sacrifice there only. The support for the Temple of the one God is consistent with the author's urgent condemnation of idolatry and sexual license, which were seen as the characteristic sins of the Gentiles.

C. Changes in Jewish Society

After the assassination of Simon Maccabee in 134, his son John Hyrcanus (134–104 B.C.E.) gained control of Jerusalem and defeated the assassin Ptolemy, who aspired to the throne. In John's first year of rule (134) the newly resurgent Seleucid monarch Antiochus VII Sidetes besieged Jerusalem and forced John to pay tribute, to demolish the city's fortifications, and to surrender his army's weapons. This final gasp of Seleucid power ended in 129 with Antiochus's death, and a series of dynastic struggles in succeeding decades left the Hasmonean dynasty free to occupy the southern region of the Seleucid Empire.

John Hyrcanus and his successors quickly enlarged Israel's borders so that it became a Hellenistic monarchy, like many others in the eastern Mediterranean, competing for territory, revenues, and influence. Mobilizing his army, Hyrcanus conquered part of the seacoast in the west, Samaria in the north, part of Transjordan in the east, and Idumea in the south. He destroyed the Samaritan temple on Mount Gerizim and razed the city of Samaria to the ground, causing a final, hostile break between Jerusalem and Samaria. He forcibly converted the Idumeans to Judaism in order to keep the country Jewish. (Ironically, an Idumean dynasty – Antipas, his son Herod, and their successors – eventually ruled Palestine.)

Hyrcanus was succeeded by two of his sons, Aristobulus I, who ruled for only one year (104–103 B.C.E.), and Alexander Jannaeus (103–76 B.C.E.). Although in ill health, Aristobulus was able to gain the conquest of the upper Galilee through the military efforts of his brother Antigonus. His domestic policies marked him as a petty despot. He imprisoned his mother and starved her to death to keep her from taking power. He then executed his brother Antigonus, whom he falsely suspected of plotting against him. Aristobulus I even took the long-unused title "king" along with that of high priest. Like other Hellenistic monarchs, he hired mercenaries to carry

THE NABATEANS

The Nabateans were a nomadic Arab tribe who gradually settled along the caravan routes running through Syria to the Gulf of Aqaba, Arabia, the Sinai, and the Red Sea. They constructed a central stronghold in Petra, halfway between the Dead Sea and the Gulf of Aqaba; their first king, Aretas I, dates from 169 B.C.E. Nabatean inscriptions are in their own dialect of Aramaic, the lingua franca of the Near East, as well as in Greek. As Seleucid power broke up in the early first century B.C.E., the Nabateans gained more control in Transjordan, clashing frequently with the Hasmonean dynasty. In 84 B.C.E. Aretas III became ruler of Damascus (Paul mentions the rule of one of his successors, Aretas IV, in 2 Corinthians 11:32). Subsequently, the Nabateans clashed with Rome and Herod. Nabatea was incorporated into the Roman province of Arabia under Trajan (105) and gradually lost power as the trade routes shifted north.

out his military policies and maintain internal security. The other rulers of the Hasmonean dynasty would follow this practice.

Aristobulus's successor, Alexander Jannaeus, who also assumed the titles of both king and high priest, engaged in constant warfare, only some of which was successful. He conquered most of the coast, the northern part of Transjordan, and areas to the north of Transjordan, including Golan, Bashan, Trachonitis, and Hauran, as well as the territory east and south of the Dead Sea. Jannaeus brought to fruition the Hasmonean goals of breaking the power of the independent Greek cities that had been set up by the Seleucids and Ptolemies, insuring that much of the population of his expanding borders practiced Judaism, and securing an economic base by collecting taxes on the extensive commerce that flowed through the region. Hasmonean expansion was contained only by the growing power of the Nabatean Arabs in the east and south and by the remnants of Seleucid power in the north. Though Jewish society prospered economically under the Hasmoneans and achieved a measure of security, constant wars brought periodic invasions by the Seleucids, Ptolemies, and Nabateans. As late as 83 B.C.E. Alexander Jannaeus had to negotiate peace with a Nabatean army that invaded Judea.

Hasmonean dynastic intrigues were frequent. Upon Jannaeus's death, the rule passed to his wife, Salome Alexandra (76–67 B.C.E.). Jannaeus's sons, Hyrcanus II and Aristobulus II, engaged in constant civil strife from 67 until 63 B.C.E., when the war-weary community leaders asked the Romans to intervene. Independent rule ceased with the Roman annexation of the Hasmonean kingdom in 63 B.C.E.

1. Pharisees and Sadducees

Many factions, coalitions, and interest groups emerged in Jewish society during the Hellenistic period. Competing priestly and aristocratic families as well as popular social movements included the activities of three groups described by Flavius Josephus, the first-century C.E. Jewish historian: Pharisees, Sadducees, and Essenes. Josephus describes them as ancient and legitimate philosophies that hold a respectable and permanent place in Judaism. The Greek word he most often uses to describe them is *hairesis* (lit. "a choice"), a term denoting a decision in regard to a way of life and referring to a philosophy or a school of thought, including its customs, dress, and activities. Although the term underlies the English word "heresy," these early voluntary associations need not be seen as sectarian in the conventional sense, that is, as subordinate groups reacting in protest against the dominant group and claiming for itself the only legitimate interpretation of the tradition. There was no single, normative belief system or practice in Second Temple Judaism, or even in the centuries after, against which these groups defined themselves.

The Sadducees left no written records, and the only evident Pharisee from whom literary texts remain is, ironically, Paul of Tarsus. Therefore,

SCHOOL OF THOUGHT (*HAIRESIS*)

The Pharisees, Sadducees, Essenes, and fourth (revolutionary) philosophy were called by Josephus *haireseis*. *Hairesis*, the singular form, is usually translated as "sect" or "school of thought." A *hairesis*, literally, "choice," was a coherent and principled decision about a way of life, and so it carried the connotation of "philosophy." People who were committed to one of the Greek schools of philosophy, such as the Stoics or the Pythagoreans, similarly lived according to a recognizable code of conduct.

to understand the programs of the Pharisees and Sadducees, scholars must sift the limited information available from Josephus, the New Testament, the Dead Sea Scrolls, later Rabbinic texts, and a few of the Pseudepigrapha.

According to Josephus, the Pharisees and Sadducees behaved like political interest groups: they sought to influence the governing class and to exercise direct power over social laws and policies. Under John Hyrcanus (134–104 B.C.E.), the Pharisees initially enjoyed political influence, but court intrigue and a trap set by the Sadducees (to make the Pharisees seem to impugn Hyrcanus's legitimacy) resulted in their falling out of favor. The Sadducees convinced Hyrcanus to follow their laws (Josephus, *Antiquities of the Jews* 13.288–98). Later, under Alexander Jannaeus (103–76 B.C.E.) the Pharisees gained a large following among people who disliked the king's authoritarianism and violence against the Pharisees, so much so that when Jannaeus was dying, he advised his wife, Salome Alexandra, to reverse his own policy and make an alliance with the Pharisees in order to secure her own position as ruler (13.399–417). She did so, and under the Jewish queen the Pharisees attained direct power over domestic policy. Their dominance did not survive Alexandra's reign (76–67 B.C.E.).

The extent to which Pharisees remained active in politics through Herodian and Roman rule and into the revolt in 66–70 C.E. remains debated: a few members of the group clearly sought political power; others gained popular influence concerning the practice of Jewish law (especially in regard to Sabbath and dietary observances). Like every other influential group, the Pharisees lost ground during the reign of Herod, though early on he patronized some Pharisaic leaders. Late in his reign, however, Herod executed many Pharisees who conspired in the intrigue of his violent family and court.

It may be that during the period from the end of Herod's reign until the revolt in 66 C.E., the Pharisees turned their attention away from politics and toward piety. Josephus is silent about their activities in Jerusalem during this period. Several sources do however suggest that the Pharisees observed biblical laws of ritual purity formerly practiced only by priests in the Temple, kept the Sabbath especially holy, and encouraged the tithing of agricultural products by all Jews. Such teachings, designed for general use, afforded fellow Jews a means of expressing their unique traditions despite Roman pressures. Some Pharisees may have been literate officials working for and seeking to influence Judea's governing class. Josephus locates several Pharisees in various leadership roles at the inception of the Great Revolt. The Acts of the Apostles (23:6), a late-first- or possibly early-second-century C.E. work, places Pharisees in the Jerusalem Sanhedrin. In the Synoptic Gospels the Pharisees in Galilee appear mainly as local community teachers.

The Sadducees, about whom little is known, were mainly drawn from the governing class; they had great economic and political power, but only a small following among the people. Their view of God as wholly transcendent and not involved in human affairs fit their task of governing the nation and managing the Temple without prophetic or other divine guidance. Similarly, their denial of resurrection as a teaching of the Torah and aversion to the apocalyptic resolution of history are consistent with the governing class's emphasis on preserving the status quo and so their own power. Perhaps they also supported a special fidelity to Israel's ancient traditions in reaction against tendencies toward Hellenization and so assimilation.

Josephus stresses that the Pharisees believed in life after death and the Sadducees adhered to the older position that required no belief in resurrection. He notes that in contrast to the Sadducaic emphasis on human responsibility, the Pharisees held a balanced view of fate and free will. Whereas he describes the Pharisees as urban and pleasant, he finds the Sadducees rude and boorish. Allowing for Josephus's biases, these descriptions generally fit the social station of each group. The Sadducees were from the governing class (*Antiquities* 18.17) – although not all the chief priests and aristocrats were Sadducees – and the Pharisees were subordinate to them. Thus the Pharisees had to seek influence and power actively and propose new interpretations of laws consistent with their program, whereas the Sadducees held onto traditional teachings and customs, which supported their dominant station in society.

2. The Essenes and the Dead Sea Scrolls

Josephus presented the Essenes as an ascetic group who emphasized God's activity in life rather than human freedom, believed in the immortality of the soul, refused to participate directly in Temple worship because they rejected the practices of the priests, cultivated virtue, and lived simply. This description received validation from the discovery, in 1947, of several complete manuscripts and thousands of fragments in eleven caves near Qumran, on the northwest shore of the Dead Sea. Most scholars now believe, after several decades of reopened discussion, that the scrolls are the library of a group of Essenes who chose to live in the desert, apart from the rest of Jewish society, and await the coming of the messianic age.

The scrolls belonged to a community centered in a settlement built on the cliffs at Qumran. The walled settlement included a tower, elaborate aqueducts and water cisterns, and numerous installations, such as a kitchen, stables, courtyards, potters, shops, and ritual baths. The community also had a scriptorium, where scrolls were copied, and an assembly hall for meetings and meals. Qumran was probably occupied by a small group of dissidents from Jerusalem in the mid-second century B.C.E.; during the next hundred years the community grew much larger. Two springs several miles to the south at Ein el-Ghuweir and Ein Feshka also show evidence of habitation by the same group.

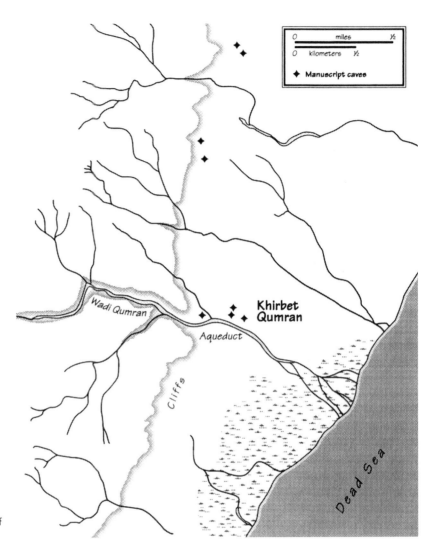

Map XIII. The location of the community of Qumran.

The Dead Sea Scrolls, written in Hebrew, Aramaic, and Greek, contain a variety of Jewish literature including Hebrew and Greek copies of the Bible (often with significantly different readings); nonbiblical, pseudepigraphical, and anonymous Jewish literature also known from other sources; writings peculiar to the Qumran community; commentaries (called *pesharim*) that connect the history of the movement to biblical prophecy; hymns and psalms; and a variety of astronomical, esoteric, apocalyptic, and mystical texts. The library contributes greatly to our understanding of Judaism from the time of the Hasmoneans (164–63 B.C.E.) through the early Roman period (63 B.C.E.–70 C.E.). Although no explicitly Christian works appear among the scrolls, the many connections between these documents and the New Testament show how deeply rooted Jesus and his first followers were in Jewish thought and practice. Communities of the followers of Jesus shared characteristics with the Qumran community, including the office of

Qumran mikveh damaged by earthquake. (BiblePlaces.com)

overseer (similar to the Greek *episkopos*, usually translated "bishop"), communal wealth (see Acts 2:44–5), lively apocalyptic and messianic expectations, and the use of biblical interpretation to establish the legitimacy of their community as the true Israel.

THE ORIGINS OF THE QUMRAN COMMUNITY

The archaeology of Qumran and allusions to the community's history in its literature suggest that the site was settled in the middle of the second century B.C.E. This date does not preclude the previous existence of the group, nor does it identify the group's origin or nature. The most widely accepted theory suggests that this priestly oriented community rejected the Hasmonean high priesthood and left Jerusalem in protest to live a sectarian existence near the Dead Sea. Since much of what has been learned of this community from Qumran literature matches descriptions of the Essenes by Josephus and Philo, the group is usually identified as Essene. Josephus and Philo also attest that Essenes lived in cities and towns.

Because some of the literature found in the Qumran collection antedates the Maccabean revolt, some scholars suggest that a dissident priestly group came into existence prior to the outrages of Antiochus IV and his Jewish priestly allies. One suggestion dates the Teacher of Righteousness and his founding of the Qumran community in the very early second century B.C.E. and dates the conflict with the Wicked Priest (Jonathan Maccabee) after 152 B.C.E., at the end of the Teacher's career. Allusions to the history of the sect are so vague and the data so sparse that no certain conclusion can be reached.

3. The Qumran Commentary on Habakkuk

The Dead Sea Scrolls place great stress on revealed knowledge as essential to salvation. In order fully to understand God's plan and will, and to separate oneself from the ordinary, sinful mode of life, a person needs special insight into Scripture. The writings of the Teacher of Righteousness and the other teachings of the community are accorded status as the only true interpretations of Scripture and the Jewish way of life. The community studied Scripture daily, and new members were allowed to learn the community's teachings only after a period of probation. The mysteries they contemplated included the

THE DEAD SEA SCROLL COMMENTARIES

The Qumran commentaries on Scripture quote a verse or short passage from a biblical book and then begin the commentary with a technical formula containing the word *pesher* ("interpretation"): "the interpretation of the matter," or "the interpretation of it." Thus these commentaries are called *pesharim*.

Pesharim use exegetical techniques found in other biblical interpretations of the period: metaphor, play on words, etymology, and development of key terms and ideas. For the most part, they relate prophecies and biblical events to the history of the Qumran community and to the events at the end of the world.

The Qumran community believed that these commentaries contained the real meaning of Scripture, revealed to the community and its Teacher of Righteousness:

> God told Habakkuk to write down that which would happen to the final generation, but he did not make known to him when time would come to an end. And as for that which he said, "That he who reads may read it speedily" (Habakkuk 2:2), interpreted this concerns the Teacher of Righteousness, to whom God made known all the mysteries of the words of his servants the prophets. (*Habakkuk Pesher*, col. 7)

apocalyptic end of the world, as planned by God, and the particular Jewish way of life needed to participate in God's victory.

Among the scrolls discovered near Qumran is a commentary on the Book of Habakkuk. The anonymous author, writing in the last half of the first century B.C.E., draws on the words of the seventh-century B.C.E. biblical prophet to describe the formation of the Qumran community in the second century B.C.E. and its subsequent history. Because the text uses the Hebrew word *pesher* ("interpretation") to introduce its interpretive comments, it is sometimes called the *Habakkuk Pesher*, abbreviated 1QpHab. (The number 1 refers to the cave in which the scroll was found; "Q" indicates Qumran, and "p" shows that the scroll is a "pesher," commentary.) The text claims that "God told Habakkuk to write down the things that are going to come upon the last generation" but did not make known to him the time of the end. It was the "Teacher of Righteousness to whom God made known all the mysteries of the words of his servants the prophets" (1QpHab 7)

Many sections of this text refer to the founder of the Qumran community (or its earliest guide), the Teacher of Righteousness (the phrase concerned might also be rendered "The One Who Teaches Rightly" or the "Righteous Teacher"), as well as to his opponent, the Wicked Priest, or Man of the Lie. The charges made against the Wicked Priest along with the rejection of present Temple worship and the formation of a community in the wilderness near the Dead Sea suggest that the Teacher of Righteousness resisted the high priesthood of either Jonathan (152 B.C.E.) or Simon (140 B.C.E.). According to 1QpHab, the Wicked Priest was originally a legitimate leader but later became corrupt:

> The Wicked Priest . . . was called by the true name at the beginning of his course, but when he ruled in Israel, he became arrogant, abandoned God, and betrayed the statutes for the sake of wealth. He stole and amassed the wealth of the men of violence who had rebelled against God, and he took the wealth of peoples to add to himself guilty sin. (1QpHab 8:8–12)

Some passages in the *Habakkuk Pesher* suggest that the Wicked Priest defeated the Teacher of Righteousness, who seems to have been a high-ranking priest, in a battle for political power and control of the Temple. The

"House of Absalom" – either the family of Absalom that supported the Maccabees (2 Maccabees 11:17; 1 Maccabees 11:70; 13:11) or a party named Absalom after David's traitorous son – is accused of abandoning the Teacher of Righteousness: "The House of Absalom and their partisans . . . were silent at the rebuke of the Teacher of Righteousness and did not support him against the Man of the Lie – who rejected the Law in the midst of all their council" (1QpHab 5:8–12).

Although the Teacher and his followers left Jerusalem, the conflict continued. The Qumran scrolls indicate that the community followed a solar calendar, which differed from the lunar calendar traditional in Jerusalem, so that their holidays fell on different days. This calendrical shift gave the high priest an excuse to attack the Teacher verbally and perhaps by military means as well. "The Wicked Priest . . . pursued the Teacher of Righteousness – to swallow him up with his poisonous vexation – to his place of exile. And at the end of the feast, during the repose of the Day of Atonement, he appeared to them [the Qumran community] to swallow them up and to make them stumble on the fast day, their restful Sabbath" (1QpHab 11:4–8). As punishment for these offenses, God gave the Wicked Priest "into the hand of his enemies to humble him with disease for annihilation in despair" (1QpHab 9:9–10). This may be a reference to Jonathan, who was killed by Trypho, or to Simon, assassinated by a family member. The Habbakuk commentary then extends its sense of divine justice by referring frequently to the coming of the Romans (called Kittim; see Numbers 24:24) as a sign of the end of days and of the eschatological punishment of the wicked. The text alludes to a fearful, warrior people from the islands of the sea who will serve as God's instrument to punish the "last priests" of Jerusalem (1QpHab 3–4, 6:1–2). The description of the Roman weight on Jewish society fits the disorder that followed Pompey's conquest, as well as Herod's authoritarian rule in the latter part of the first century B.C.E.

4. The *Nahum Pesher*

The *Nahum Pesher* appears to refer to events during the reign of Alexander Jannaeus. One well-known passage highlights the battle of Shechem in 88 B.C.E., when the Seleucid ruler Demetrius III Eucerus (95–78 B.C.E.) attacked Judea. Jannaeus, called the "Lion of Wrath" in the *pesher*, defeated the enemy and then crucified those who conspired with him. The conspirators are called the "Seekers-after-Smooth-Things" (Hebrew *dorshei halaqot*), as well as "Ephraim":

> "Where the lion went to enter, there is the lion's cub and no one disturbs it" (Nahum 2:11). The interpretation (*pesher*) of it concerns Demetrius, king of Greece, who sought to enter Jerusalem on the advice of the Seekers-after-Smooth-Things, [but God did not give Jerusalem] into the power of the kings of Greece from Antiochus until the rise of the rulers of the Kittim; but afterward she (the city) will be trampled [and will be given into the hand of the rulers of Kittim. . . .]

COVENANT

With few exceptions, Jewish documents from the Maccabean revolt to the editing of the Mishnah insist that despite Israel's persecution and suffering, God would be true to his promise and would remember the chosen community. This focus depends on three early Jewish understandings of salvation. First, the texts affirm that salvation is found not individually but collectively, through membership in the people. Second, they highlight the centrality in the self-understanding of most Jewish groups of the particular, select place the Jews hold in the divine plan as members of a covenant community. Conflict among the various communities that defined themselves as true to the covenant did erupt, but that did not diminish their covenantal focus. Third, they stress not that individuals earn salvation by following particular practices, but that the covenant is freely given by God to the community; it is a blessing to which they respond with love and loyalty, rather than a burden that they must bear. Second Temple and especially Rabbinic Jewish literature tends to emphasize the covenant made with Moses, and so the community, rather than the covenants made, according to the Bible, with Noah, Abraham, and David. The church would come to emphasize the covenants with Abraham and David, which it then saw as applying specifically to Jesus.

"The Lion tears enough for his cubs and strangles prey for his lionesses" (Nahum 2:12). [The interpretation of it concerns Demetrius, who made war] against the Lion of Wrath (Alexander Jannaeus), who would strike with his great ones and his partisans, [but they fled before him (Demetrius).

"And it fills up] its cave [with prey,] and its den with torn flesh" (Nahum 2:12). The interpretation of it concerns the Lion of Wrath, [who has found a crime punishable by] death in the Seekers-after-Smooth-Things, whom he hangs up as living men [upon the tree, as it was thus done] in Israel from of old, for regarding one hanged alive upon the tree [it] (scripture) reads, "Behold I am against you, says[s YHWH of Hosts]" (Nahum 2:13). (*Nahum Pesher* 3–4.i.1–9)

The mention of Demetrius and the explicit references to the revolt joined by Pharisees against Jannaeus in ca. 90–85 B.C.E secures the historical context. The punishment by crucifixion seems to be recounted with approval, and a passage in the Qumran *Temple Scroll* (11QTemple 64:6–13) supports crucifixion for those guilty of treason or of violating the covenant.

The Seekers-after-Smooth-Things are often identified with the Pharisees, although they could have been any group or series of groups whom the author of the *pesher* rejected. The Seekers-after-Smooth-Things are attacked for deceit, for false teaching, and for leading the people astray, and they are condemned to punishment by war, exile, and death. Because they deceived Israel, their

> wicked deeds will be revealed to all Israel at the end of time, and many will discern their sin, will hate them, and consider them repulsive on account of their guilty insolence. But when the glory of Judah is [re]vealed, the simple ones of Ephraim will flee from the midst of their assembly. They will abandon those who led them astray and will join Israel. (*Nahum Pesher* 3–4.iii.3–5)

For the Qumran community, withdrawal was the proper response to what they saw as a corrupt government, priesthood, and Temple; any accommodation or compromise meant implication in the evil system. They claimed to be the true Israel, and they awaited the final intervention of God who would punish their enemies and vindicate their faithful adherence to the covenant.

5. The *Community Rule* (1QS) and the Life of the Community

Fully conscious of what they perceived to be the corruption of Jewish society in general and of Temple worship in particular, the community sought to atone for Israel's sins and re-create a perfect society through faithful observance and worship. Their two foundation documents, expressing this worldview, give the goals, origins, and constitution of the Qumran community. The *Rule of the Community* (also known as the

Manual of Discipline and abbreviated 1QS) and the *Covenant of Damascus* (CD; also known as the *Cairo-Damascus Document* or the *Zadokite Document*) are both composites that developed over two centuries. The earliest section of the *Rule of the Community* is a manifesto calling for true Israelites to found

> a House of Perfection and Truth in Israel that they may establish a Covenant according to the everlasting precepts. And they shall be an agreeable offering, atoning for the Land and determining the judgment of wickedness, and there shall be no more iniquity. (1QS 8)

When they have formed the community, they are ordered to

> separate from the habitation of ungodly men and go into the wilderness to prepare the way of Him; as it is written, "Prepare in the wilderness the way of . . . make straight in the desert a path for our God" (Isaiah 40:3). This path is the study of the law which he commanded by the hand of Moses. (1QS 8)

The *Covenant of Damascus* envisions members of the community living both in cities and in camps (probably isolated communities such as Qumran). Josephus testifies to this dual way of life, with some Essenes living in the cities and towns of Judea, and others in separate wilderness communities. Obscure references to conflict within the community suggest that the Essenes may have divided into distinct branches. The *Rule of the Community* is written for a congregation living apart from the larger society.

Both documents detail regulations governing community organization and interpretations of biblical law. The community, whose members were male and probably committed to celibacy (at least in their wilderness settlements), was divided into hereditary priests and laypeople. The priests had precedence in ritual and governance, but an assembly of all the members had great power. Membership required a probationary period during which candidates were tested and their behavior carefully watched. They had to follow the community's interpretation of biblical law meticulously and observe ritual purity carefully. During a second year of probation a proselyte surrendered his private property to the community. In like manner, the Acts of the Apostles describes how among the early followers of Jesus "all who believed were together and had all things in common" (Acts 2:44), and a few Greek philosophical schools practiced similar forms of shared wealth.

The community was governed by a variety of officers and councils, of whom the priest, the "overseer" (a Levite), and the Council of the Community were most important. The priest presided at solemn meals and worship; the overseer taught the community and maintained community discipline. The Council of the Community, which consisted of either all the fully initiated members or a group of the senior members, met nightly to study and pray. At meetings of the community, members sat and spoke according to rank, which was presumably based on their stage of initiation, seniority, and office. The presiding officials and another community council were

ESSENE AND CHRISTIAN USES OF THE BIBLE

Both the New Testament and the *Community Rule* (1QS) cite Isaiah, chapters 28 and 40, but for very different purposes. According to Isaiah 28:16, God says: "Behold, I am laying in Zion a foundation a stone, a tested stone, a precious cornerstone, of a sure foundation." Isaiah 40:3 signals the end of the exile by a voice crying, "In the wilderness prepare the way of the LORD, make straight in the desert a highway for our God." The exhortation is for the people to construct a highway in the desert, and on that road to return to Jerusalem.

The Qumran text applies Isaiah 28:16 (paraphrased) and 40:3 to the Council of the Community and also to the community at large. According to 1QS (col. 8), the Council of the Community shall be "witnesses to the truth at the judgment, and shall be the elect of goodwill who shall atone for the Land and pay to the wicked their reward. It shall be that tried wall, that 'precious cornerstone,' whose foundations shall neither rock nor sway in their place" (Isaiah 28:16).

When the Council of the Community (probably meaning the entire community) have passed their long period of probation according to the rules,

they shall separate from the habitation of ungodly men and shall go into the wilderness to prepare the way of Him [God]; as it is written, "Prepare in the wilderness the way of . . . make straight in the desert a path for our God" (Isaiah 40:3). This path is the study of the Law which He commanded by the hand of Moses, that they may do according to all that has been revealed from age to age, and as the Prophets have revealed by His Holy Spirit.

The Qumran community and study of the law are the focus of the *Rule of the Community*.

In contrast, the New Testament looks to Jesus as the rock and the new Exodus. The Gospel of Mark begins with a composite quotation from Malachi 3:1 and Isaiah 40:3 applied to John the Baptist and Jesus (Mark 1:2–3): "Behold I send my messenger before your face, who shall prepare your way; the voice of one crying in the wilderness: Prepare the way of the Lord, make his paths straight." The focus no longer is the return of the exiles, but is John the Baptist himself, the "voice of one crying in the wilderness."

In Romans 9:33 Paul changes the point of Isaiah 28:16 concerning a secure foundation and cornerstone for Zion by combining it with Psalm 118:22 concerning a stumbling stone: "Behold I am laying in Zion a stone that will make men stumble, a rock that will make them fall; and he who believes in him [Jesus] will not be put to shame." Isaiah 28:16 and Psalm 118:22 are also combined in 1 Peter 2:4–8. There, the stumbling stone is Jesus, and the metaphor explains his rejection by Israel. Psalm 118 is also used in the Synoptic Gospels (Mark 12:10; Matthew 21:42; Luke 20:17) and in Acts 4:11; in all cases it is an apologetic explanation for the rejection by most Jews of the proclamation of Jesus' messianic identity.

responsible for imposing penalties for infractions of the rules and for investigating the conduct of new members. Infractions were punished by fasting, penance for periods of a few days to two years, and ultimately by expulsion.

The community's activity was also influenced by one other collection of rules, the *Temple Scroll* (11QTemple), which reorganized and modified many biblical regulations in order to articulate the shape of a reformed and just society. Regulations in the *Temple Scroll* cover sacrifices and festivals, the plan of the perfect temple, the sanctity of Jerusalem, ritual purity, the judicial system, idolatry, kingship, governmental institutions, and war.

The worldview expressed in the Dead Sea Scrolls shares many similarities with other contemporary Jewish documents and to some extent with early Christian literature. True to their Jewish heritage the Essenes experienced God as active in history, as just toward humans, and as merciful to those who repented and obeyed him. Joined with this confidence in God is a robust sense of human sinfulness and helplessness in the face of evil. The more than two dozen canticles in the *Thanksgiving Hymns Scroll* (1QH) contain many personal and communal expressions of the Qumran community's view of God and humanity. The early guide of the community, the Teacher of Righteousness, may have composed these hymns; alternatively, they may have evolved gradually as expressions of the community's attitudes and aspiration.

> As for me, shaking and trembling seize me and all my bones are broken; my heart dissolves like wax before fire. . . . For I remember my sins and the unfaithfulness of my fathers. When the wicked rose against your covenant and the damned against your word, I said in my sinfulness, "I am forsaken by your covenant." But calling to mind the might of your hand and the greatness of your compassion, I rose and stood, and my spirit was established in the face of the scourge. I lean upon your grace and on the multitude of your mercies, for you will pardon iniquities and through your righteousness [you will purify man] of his sin. (1QH 4)

The Dead Sea Scrolls distinguish sharply between good and evil, light and dark, the elect and the condemned, the good spirit and the evil spirit. Without denying free will or reducing the responsibility of community members to turn to God and obey him, the hymns stress the de facto division between good and evil and God's role in this mysterious conflict (e.g., 1QH 15). The overwhelming force of human evil was explained not only by malevolent human choice but also by the activities of good and evil spirits that fought for control of humans.

> (God) has created man to govern the world, and has appointed for him two spirits in which to walk until the time of his visitation: the spirits of truth and falsehood. Those born of truth spring from a fountain of light, but those born of falsehood from a source of darkness. All the children of righteousness are ruled by the Prince of Light and walk in the ways of light, but all the children of falsehood are ruled by the Angel of Darkness and walk in the ways of darkness. (1QS 3)

Both the apocalyptic resolution of history and the struggle between good and evil end with the establishment of the community's ideal life. The kingdom of God will be presided over by two messiahs, a priestly messiah and a messiah of Israel (or royal/political messiah from the House of David), who correspond to the priestly and lay sections of the community. A supplement to the *Rule of the Community* describes a messianic banquet, during which the priest messiah sits at the head of the priests and blesses the food, which is then blessed by the messiah of Israel at the head of the chiefs of the clans of Israel. Another text describes the measurements of an ideal Jerusalem in which the faithful will live. Many other descriptions of the end, collections of scriptural passages, recitations of the final apocalyptic battles, and prayers testify to the community's strong apocalyptic expectations.

The *War Scroll*, or 1QM – more fully identified as "The War of the Sons of Light with the Sons of Darkness" – depicts an eschatological battle between the angel Michael, allied with the forces of good (angelic forces and the Qumran community), and Beliar, who is joined with the forces of evil, including the Kittim (the Romans), other nations, and apostate Jews. The text imagines the battle as a holy war in which ritual purity is observed, highly symbolic banners are carried, appropriate prayers and hymns are recited, and curses hurled. The course of the battle is rehearsed in great detail, with the forces of good suffering reverses before divine intervention produces a final victory. The War Scroll, although utterly rejecting the Romans and all other unjust peoples, cannot envision overcoming them through ordinary political means; only divine help can save the righteous. The text's sense of helplessness before the Roman might is paradoxically conveyed in the use of Roman tactics and weapons by the angelic armies against the Romans themselves. The detailed military descriptions bespeak the author's vivid awareness of Roman military power, frustration with its oppressive rule, and fervent hope for its eventual destruction. Similarly, the *Melchizedek Text* (11QMelch) envisions a heavenly figure named Melchizedek (see Genesis 14:18–20; Psalms 110:4), who serves as the angelic leader in the final battle between the children of light and the children of darkness and who will both judge the good and evil humans and destroy Satan.

Perhaps the best metaphor for summing up the life and worldview of the Qumran community is worship. Many of the Dead Sea Scrolls contain hymns, poems, and prayers occupied with praise of God. The community sought to keep itself free from sin, maintain ritual purity, and commit itself firmly to God so that it could worship God as the angels did. Because the community rejected the way worship was carried out in the Temple, they turned to the angelic worship in heaven and saw themselves as a kind of temple. A set of Sabbath hymns, often called the *Angelic Liturgy* (abbreviated 4QShirShab), involves the community with angelic worship and describes the heavens in the manner of later Jewish mystical texts:

> Song of the sacrifice of the seventh Sabbath on the sixteenth of the month. Praise the God of the lofty heights, O you lofty ones among all the "gods" of knowledge. Let the holiest of the godlike ones sanctify the King of glory who sanctifies by holiness all His holy ones. O you chiefs of the praises of all the godlike beings, praise the splendidly [pr]aiseworthy God. For in the splendor of praise is the glory of His realm. (4QShirShab)

Other hymns describe the heavenly realm and locate the worshippers there in spirit:

> [And the liken]ess of living divine beings is engraved in the vestibules where the King enters, figures of luminous spirits, [… K]ing, figures of glorious li[ght, wondrous] spirits; [in] the midst of the spirits of splendor is a work of wondrous colors, figures of the living divine beings. (4QShirShab)

Other psalms collections have also been found at Qumran. One scroll contains about thirty-five canonical psalms along with several noncanonical psalms. One such text, known in the Septuagint as Psalm 151 and accepted as canonical by the Eastern Orthodox churches, appears at Qumran in a longer version. In both versions David celebrates his being chosen by God to be king,

I was small among my brothers,
and youngest in my father's house;
I tended my father's sheep.
My hands made a harp,
my fingers fashioned a lyre.
And who will declare it to my Lord?
The Lord himself; it is he who
hears.
It was he who sent his messenger
and took me from my father's
sheep,
and anointed me with his anointing
oil.
My brothers were handsome and
tall,
but the Lord was not pleased with
them.
I went out to meet the Philistine,
and he cursed me by his idols.
But I drew his own sword;
I beheaded him, and removed
reproach from the people of
Israel.

though he was smaller and less handsome than his brothers. In the shorter Greek version he celebrates his victory over Goliath; in the longer Hebrew version he praises God at greater length and focuses on God's choice of him as leader in Israel. The presence of this psalm in the Greek Bible and among the Qumran manuscripts and the presence of another psalm both at Qumran and in the Wisdom of Ben Sira testify to the variety of psalms being written, revised, and used in different contexts within Second Temple Judaism.

Finally, only in June 1994 were the six texts of the document known as 4QMMT (*Miqsat Ma'ase ha-Torah* [Hebrew], "Some [of the] Works of the Torah"]) published. Dated on linguistic grounds to an origin in the Hasmonean period, 4QMMT contains a solar calendar, a list of the legal rulings that the author believes the priests connected to the Jerusalem Temple to be violating, and a concluding exhortation that appeals to Solomon and David and warns of eschatological judgment; its language of "we," "you," and "them" suggests a polemical focus, although early conclusions that the groups could be precisely identified with Essenes, Pharisees, and Sadducees lack firm support. The document only somewhat vaguely states: "And you know that we have segregated ourselves from the rest of the people and that we avoid mingling in these affairs and associating with them in these things" (92–3). Similarly overstated are claims that the document speaks of earning one's way into the covenant and so of "works righteousness."

JEWISH MYSTICISM

Surviving Jewish mystical texts come mostly from the Talmudic period (the third century C.E. on), but the *Angelic Liturgy* at Qumran, visionary experiences and heavenly journeys depicted in numerous apocalyptic works, and several passages from the New Testament suggest that a limited but active interest in mystical topics extended back into the Second Temple period and peaked during the first century C.E. Visionary experience concerning the heavenly throne was often based on the vision of the divine chariot (*merkavah*) in Ezekiel 1; these visions are referred to as Merkavah (i.e., "chariot") mysticism. Speculation on creation and cosmogony was centered on the creation account in Genesis 1 and is referred to as the Story of Creation (*ma'ase bereshit*). Texts that speak of the heavens and God's palaces (*hekhalot*) are designated Hekhalot mysticism. Rabbinic mystical teaching stressed the dangers to the mystic and was restricted to private discussion between mature scholars. Paul, in 2 Corinthians 12:2–4, describes what appears to be his own mystical experience:

I know a person in Christ who fourteen years ago was caught up to the third heaven – whether in the body or out of the body I do not know; God knows. And I know that such a person – whether in the body or out of the body, I do not know; God knows – was caught up into Paradise and heard things that are not to be told, that no mortal is permitted to repeat.

MAJOR DEAD SEA SCROLLS

Hundreds of fragments of scrolls were found in eleven caves near Qumran and in other caves further south. A list by caves of some of these scrolls, using their most popular names, follows:

CAVE 1

Isaiah Scroll

Commentary on Habakkuk

Manual of Discipline, or Rule
of the Community

Covenant of Damascus, or
Damascus Document or
Zadokite Document

Genesis Apocryphon

War Scroll

Hymn Scroll, or
Thanksgiving Hymns

CAVE 4

Angelic Liturgy

Commentary on Nahum

Commentary on Isaiah

Commentary on Psalm 37

Messianic Florilegium

Messianic Testimonium

CAVE 11

Psalms Scroll

Targum of Job

Melchizedek Text

Temple Scroll

III. ROMAN INVASION AND JEWISH RESPONSE

A. Historical and Social Developments

For the century and a half before the Romans conquered Palestine in 63 B.C.E. they had gradually spread their influence over Macedonia, Greece, and Asia Minor by military conquest, political domination, and annexation. The threat of the Roman legions, which had prevailed in many crucial battles and through several long and stubborn wars, kept most cities and territories cooperative. In turn, Rome typically granted conquered territories internal autonomy; local governments remained, but they served at Rome's behest and for Rome's aggrandizement.

The struggle for control in Rome during the first century B.C.E. and the conflicts among powers in the East produced a series of crises. During the first century B.C.E., three powers threatened Roman influence in the East: Pontus (in Asia Minor), Armenia, and Persia. Mithradates of Pontus attacked the Roman provinces in Asia Minor and Greece, but the Roman general Sulla defeated him and halted his expansion (88–83 B.C.E.). Later, both Mithradates and Tigranes of Armenia sought to establish control over Asia Minor and Syria but, again, Roman armies drove them off (74–66 B.C.E.). During this period, Salome Alexandra, queen of Judea (76–67 B.C.E.), sent gifts to and made treaties with Tigranes while he was besieging Ptolemais (Josephus, *History of the Jewish War* 1.116).

Both Mithradates and Tigranes remained potent threats to other regional rulers and so to Rome's interests until Pompey (106–48 B.C.E.) came east in the sixties B.C.E. Pompey conquered the Mediterranean pirates and swept away Mithradates, Tigranes, and the remnants of Syria's Seleucid dynasty. He also stopped the civil war raging in Jerusalem and established the initial Roman control over Judea and Galilee.

The relatively stable rule of Salome Alexandra had dissolved amid previously suppressed internal tensions. Two of her sons, the energetic Aristobulus and the ineffective high priest Hyrcanus, fought for control. Hyrcanus was aided by the ambitious, non-Jewish Antipater, whom Jannaeus had appointed governor of Idumea. Antipater recruited Aretas, the king of Nabatea, to attack Aristobulus in Jerusalem. Hyrcanus would have taken complete control at that point had not the Roman general Scaurus, sent to Damascus by Pompey, ordered the siege lifted. After much political intrigue over who would rule – Aristobulus or Hyrcanus – Aristobulus fled Pompey's camp to Jerusalem in a bid to take control. Eventually Pompey, whom the people allowed into the city in 63 B.C.E., captured Aristobulus and fought his supporters on the Temple Mount for three months. Great loss of life ensued. Finally, Pompey sent Aristobulus and his family to Rome, breached the walls of Jerusalem, and then sacrilegiously entered the holy of holies. But Pompey neither plundered the Temple nor dismantled the Jewish leadership in Jerusalem. He reduced the power of the state by separating the cities and territories of the

Columns in the temple of Artemeis in Gerasa. (BiblePlaces.com)

Mediterranean coast, Samaria, and Transjordan from Jewish rule and leaving only Jerusalem, Judea, Idumea, and Galilee under the control of the last Hasmonean high priest, Hyrcanus. The presence of a Roman colony in Jerusalem prevented the rebuilding of the walls and discouraged revolt. Pompey's policy gained the support of Hellenistic city-states surrounding Judea, who sought both their own stability and the end to a strong Jewish state that could threaten regional peace.

The desire for independence and the popularity of the Hasmoneans did not end immediately. A few years after Pompey had set up the new order, Aristobulus and his sons, Alexander and Antigonus, who had escaped Roman custody, led several insurrections against the Romans; eventually they were defeated and recaptured (57–55 B.C.E.). Gabinius, the Roman governor in Syria, removed all political power from Hyrcanus by restricting him to Temple-based high priestly duties, and he established five districts, each with a local council charged with keeping order and collecting tribute. This more direct Roman rule resulted in further conflict between Rome and the local Jewish population in Judea. For example, Crassus, the new Roman governor, took the Temple treasure to finance his campaign against the Parthians (54 B.C.E.). In succeeding years the country needed constant pacification.

Matters were no calmer in Roman political circles. The war between Julius Caesar and Pompey for control of Rome ended with Pompey's defeat at Pharsalus in eastern Greece (49 B.C.E.) and his subsequent murder in Egypt. When Caesar had gained control of the empire, he confirmed Hyrcanus as high priest and made him "ethnarch" (i.e., leader of a nation or ethnic group), thus restoring the governing powers Gabinius had revoked. Antipater was appointed custodian (*epitropos*) of Judea, with responsibility for collecting the Roman tribute, and his son Phasael became governor (*strategos*) of Jerusalem. Judea was enlarged to include Jaffa and some villages in the Esdraelon Plain in the north. The dissolution of the Hasmonean rule in Palestine, coupled with the disorder and

THE IMPORTANCE OF PALESTINE WITHIN THE ROMAN EMPIRE

Several factors made Palestine a strategic location within the Roman Empire during the time of Pompey. First, because of Rome's ongoing struggle with the Parthians along the eastern border of the empire, Palestine and the region immediately east of it were essential military sites for Roman legions and defense. The cities of Sepphoris, Scythopolis, and Legio also functioned as Roman military garrisons. Second, during this period Palestine, and Galilee in particular, was a center of trade. The hard-stretched Roman road system from this time reflects the large amount of goods that came through Palestine from the east, from the Decapolis, and from Arabia, and then headed to the Mediterranean and on to Rome. Wine, grapes, balsam, and olive oil were but a few of Palestine's exports valued throughout the empire. Third, the Herodian family's tremendous building programs in the regions, including rebuilding or founding the cities of Sepphoris, Tiberias, and Caesarea, as well as the massive reconstruction of the Jerusalem Temple, stand even today as monuments to Palestine's importance and vitality during this period. Indeed, western Palestine and Galilee were among the empire's most densely populated rural regions at this time.

THE ROMANS AND THE PARTHIANS

During the mid-third century B.C.E., the nomadic Parni tribe migrated from the steppes of Russia, through the mountains between the Caspian and Aral Seas, and into the Seleucid satrapy of Parthia (Parthava). There they assimilated to Hellenistic culture and wavered between independence and incorporation into the Seleucid Empire. Although Antiochus III fought and defeated them in between 209 and 204 B.C.E., he had to settle for an alliance with the Parthian king as a vassal rather than assume direct rule. Seleucid control over the eastern end of Alexander's empire was tenuous and perfunctory; the vassal kingdoms there were constantly threatened by nomadic invaders from the north. Under Mithradates I and his successors (from 171 B.C.E. on) the Parthians gradually gained control of most of the territory from the Euphrates River to the Indus and kept probing westward toward Syria and Asia Minor.

Following Pompey's conquest of the remnants of the Seleucid Empire and his incorporation of Syria into the Roman Empire as its eastern border, Rome experienced a series of clashes with the expanding empire of the Parthians, who controlled the northern Iranian plateau and Mesopotamia. In 53 B.C.E. the Parthians destroyed a Roman army led by Crassus at Carrhae. In 40, during the confusion after the assassination of Julius Caesar, they briefly invaded Syria and Palestine.

The Parthians, and their Persian Sassanian successors from the third century C.E., remained a major power, a permanent threat to Rome's eastern border. Consequently, the Roman province of Syria, to which Palestine was subordinate, was kept a senatorial province, with a former consul as governor and a garrison of several legions. The security of Syria and Palestine was of the utmost importance to the Roman Empire. Mark Antony, Octavian, Tiberius, Nero, Trajan, and Septimius Severus all fought wars against the Parthians. Finally weakened in the third century, the Parthians succumbed to the rulers of the province of Persis, the Sassanians, who formed a new empire that lasted until the Muslim conquest in the seventh century.

civil war among Rome's rulers, permitted Antipater and his equally ambitious sons Herod and Phasael not only to gain power but also to erode the influence of the traditional rulers of Judaism — the priests, wealthy families, and respected officials and elders. Herod, who would emerge as the greatest politician in the family, was named governor of Galilee and later of both Coele Syria to the north and Samaria to the south.

ROMAN REORGANIZATION OF PALESTINE

In ca. 55 B.C.E., following Pompey's domination of Coele Syria ca. 66 B.C.E., Palestine was reorganized by Pompey's proconsul, Gabinius. Gabinius divided Palestine into five administrative districts, each with a capital city and a *synedrion*, or council, composed of local nobles. Galilee was one of these administrative districts, with Sepphoris as its capital. Judea proper was another, with its capital Jerusalem. Jericho, Gadara, and Amathus, three other cities along the Jordan Valley, also served as administrative capitals. This governing system deprived the Hasmoneans of any de jure authority; instead, authority in the administrative districts rested with people selected or approved by Rome. This reorganization would endure for several centuries. Pliny's letters from the second century C.E. reveal some of the provisions of the *Lex Pompeia* ("Pompeian Law"; see letter 10.112), and Dio Cassius states that this administrative system was still in force in the third century C.E.

B. Literary Responses to Roman Culture

Jewish literature from the Roman period, much of it from unknown authors or groups, reveals a variety of passionate reactions to Roman rule. Some Jews, such as Josephus and Herod, cooperated with the Romans — either out of fear of the empire's awesome power or because they benefited through such collaboration; some tried to live quietly, with as little contact as possible with Rome or its local functionaries; some fully withdrew

THE FIRST TRIUMVIRATE

From 130 B.C.E. onward, the traditional aristocratic senatorial class in Rome struggled to keep control in the face of a loose coalition of popular leaders who wanted political power, administrative reforms to deal with corruption, and increased economic benefits. The senatorial party could neither satisfy the people of Italy nor successfully manage Rome's colonies. A series of civil wars that caused enormous bloodshed, unrest, and disorder ensued.

In the sixties, Pompey, a member of the senatorial party, gained a mandate to bring order to the eastern Mediterranean, while in Rome, Julius Caesar, a high-born noble, and Marcus Licinius Crassus, who had been a consul with Pompey, dominated politics and succeeded in placating all sides. In 60 B.C.E., Pompey entered into an informal coalition with Caesar and Crassus, and for a few years they shared power peacefully. In the Roman Republic boards of three men were often appointed to govern or to administer public matters. This so-called first triumvirate consisted of Pompey, Julius Caesar, and Crassus.

During the fifties, Caesar conquered Gaul (present France), and in 53 B.C.E. Crassus was killed fighting the Parthians in the east. Meanwhile, Pompey had mismanaged Rome's government and used the resulting chaos to acquire dictatorial powers. Caesar's faction under Mark Antony fled north from Rome, where in 49 B.C.E. they joined Caesar and his army. As this coalition crossed the Rubicon and marched on Rome, Pompey and his supporters fled to Greece; there Caesar's forces defeated him in battle. Pompey was then murdered in Egypt. When Caesar came to Egypt, and a slave offered him Pompey's head, "he turned away from him with loathing, as from an assassin" (Plutarch, *Life of Pompey* 80). He also promptly deposed Ptolemy XIII, the Egyptian ruler who had planned the assassination, and replaced him with Cleopatra VII, Ptolemy's sister (and wife).

Caesar became the most powerful leader in the empire but was not officially named emperor. He was assassinated in 44 B.C.E. and replaced by the second triumvirate.

into the wilderness; some protested in word or deed; and some sought amelioration of social conditions through reform on the popular level. Many Jewish works adapted biblical and adopted Hellenistic forms of expression to condemn Roman conquest, protest foreign control of Israel, and envision the triumph of God's justice.

Tombs from the Hasmonean period in the Kidron Valley. (BiblePlaces.com)

Shop in Bet She'an with Greek inscription. (BiblePlaces.com)

1. The *Psalms of Solomon*

The *Psalms of Solomon*, a collection of eighteen psalms, respond to the Roman incursion into Jerusalem in 63 B.C.E. and subsequent control over Israel. The author (or composers) understands the shocking loss of political autonomy, as well as the profanation of the Temple by Pompey, as just punishment for the failures of the priests and other leaders. Written in the decades following the conquest of Jerusalem (with *Psalms of Solomon* 2:27–9 referring to the murder of Pompey in 48 B.C.E.), the psalms understand Rome's actions as part of a divine plan. Consequently, the events of 63 B.C.E. do not warrant despair. To the contrary, the prayer for God's mercy on faithful Israelites is coupled with confidence that God will judge and punish evil Jews and Gentiles (*Psalms of Solomon* 9–10, 13–15). The responsibility of individual Jews to resist temptation and remain faithful to God's way of life under duress depends on God's mercy (*Psalms of Solomon* 16), but those who reject God will be destroyed:

> Arrogantly the sinner broke down the strong walls with a
>   battering ram and you did not interfere.
> Gentile foreigners went up to your place of sacrifice; they
>   arrogantly trampled (it) with their sandals.
> For the Gentiles insulted Jerusalem, trampling (her) down; he
>   dragged her beauty down from the throne of glory.
> (Psalms of Solomon 2:1–2, 19)

This coded reference to Pompey's capture of Jerusalem (described also in *Psalms* 8 and 17) is closely linked with condemnation of the sins of the Jerusalem leaders:

They stole from the sanctuary of God as if there were no
    redeeming heir.
They walked on the place of sacrifice of the Lord, (coming) from
    all kinds of uncleanness;
And (coming) with menstrual blood (on them), they defiled the
    sacrifices as if they were common meat.
There was no sin they left undone in which they did not surpass
    the Gentiles.

(Psalms of Solomon 8:11–13)

Though neither the author's community nor the wicked local rulers is identified explicitly, those condemned were probably rich, influential citizens who cooperated with the Romans, compromising the Jewish way of life as the psalmist understood it, and who oppressed faithful Jews in various ways:

The words of the wicked man's tongue (are) twisted so many
    ways. His visit fills homes with a false tongue, cuts down trees
    of joy, inflaming criminals; by slander he incites homes to
    fighting. . . .
May the Lord protect the quiet person who hates injustice; may
    the Lord guide the person who lives peacefully at home.
And may the Lord's devout inherit the Lord's promises.

(Psalms of Solomon 12:2–3, 5–6)

And the children of the covenant living among the Gentile rabble
    adopted these (idolatrous practices).
No one among them in Jerusalem acted with mercy or truth.
Those who loved the assemblies of the devout fled from them as
    sparrows flee from their nest.

(Psalms of Solomon 17:15–16)

Numerous parallels in phrase and thought between this first-century B.C.E. text and the biblical Book of Psalms as well as prophetic books indicate that the author articulated the community's needs by adapting traditional literary modes and drawing on traditional theological views. The contrast between the devout and sinners in Judaism is found in 2 Maccabees and many other works, while the concern for the poor and weak, with concomitant condemnation of the strong and corrupt, extends back to Israel's prophets and to the Torah.

The power of the Romans was so great and the plight of the faithful so desperate ("When a person is tried by his mortality, your testing is in his flesh, and in the difficulty of poverty"; *Psalms of Solomon* 16:14) that the author anticipates, not a military victory over the Romans or political reform, but the coming of a ruler like David to reinstitute God's just rule, to drive out evil Gentiles and Jewish sinners, to purge Jerusalem and make it holy, and to rule over just Israelites and all the nations:

He will gather a holy people whom he will lead in righteousness;
    and he will judge the tribes of the people that have been made
    holy by the Lord their God.

MESSIAH

"Messiah" is an anglicized form of the Hebrew word *mashiach*, meaning "anointed one." The Greek translation for this term is *khristos* (in English, "Christ"). In the Bible "anointed ones" – that is, those individuals anointed as a sign of their being chosen for, and initiated into, office – include kings, high priests, and prophets. According to Second Isaiah (Isaiah 40–50), King Cyrus of Persia is God's "anointed" or "messiah" because he liberates the Jews from exile in Babylon and returns them to Jerusalem to rebuild the Temple.

Thus says the Lord to his anointed,
  to Cyrus
Whose right hand I have grasped
To subdue nations before him
And to strip kings of their robes

To open doors before him –
And the gates shall not be closed.

(Isaiah 45:1)

The figure of a suprahuman and ideal anointed leader gradually emerged in Second Temple Jewish literature. More often, however, God was the savior and ruler of Israel; no intermediary "anointed one" was needed. In some texts the transcendent leader is called by other titles, such as the Son of Man, the Elect One, or the "prophet like Moses" (see Deuteronomy 18:18: "I will raise up for them like you [i.e., Moses] from among their own people; I will put my words in the mouth of the prophet, who shall speak to them everything that I command"). Where a messiah or messianic figure appears, he has varied characteristics. In some texts he fights

against the forces of evil; in others he arrives at the end time to rule over God's kingdom; and in still others he rules over an interim kingdom and then gives the rule to God (see this tradition in Revelation 20). The Dead Sea Scrolls expect two messiahs, corresponding to the two categories of membership in the community: a priestly messiah and a Davidic (i.e., lay) messiah. By the mid-first century C.E., the title "Messiah" in certain circles had become so closely associated with Jesus of Nazareth that "Christ" seemed part of his name (e.g., 1 Corinthians 1:1–4, which begins, "Paul, called to be an apostle of Christ Jesus" and speaks of "our Lord Jesus Christ"). But at no time during the Greek or Roman periods did any single messianic expectation dominate Jewish thought.

He will not tolerate unrighteousness even to pause among them.
For he shall know them that they are all children of their God. . . .
the alien and foreigner will no longer live near them.
He will judge peoples and nations in the wisdom of his
  righteousness . . .
And he will purge Jerusalem (and make it) holy as it was even
  from the beginning. . . .
There will be no unrighteousness among them in his days,
  for all will be holy, and their king shall be the Lord Messiah.

(*Psalms of Solomon* 17:26–32)

Psalms of Solomon 17 imagines the overthrow of the Romans and the rectification of Israelite social and political life only through extraordinary leadership, beyond that of the Hasmonean high priests or of any other traditional forces in Jewish society. The author anticipates a leader anointed by God who will enable Israel to live the secure and just life promised in the Bible.

2. *Third Maccabees*

Third Maccabees was one of several texts, along with the Additions to Esther, the Prayer of Manasseh, and *Joseph and Aseneth*, that was likely composed during the first century B.C.E., probably in Alexandria.

Combining florid language and a dramatic plot, *Third Maccabees* promotes fidelity to Judaism in a Diaspora context. Gentile cruelty, the uncertainty of Jewish life in Egypt, and the allegiance of the Jews to their traditional way of life comprise the bulk of the story. Counseling peaceful coexistence with their Gentile neighbors, the Jewish elders, who are model citizens, restrain younger community members who wish to "die courageously for the ancestral law" (*3 Maccabees* 1:22–3). This position contrasts sharply with Maccabean values (1 Maccabees 2:40–1, 3:21, 13:3–4; 2 Maccabees 8:21).

The main character in *3 Maccabees* is the Egyptian king Ptolemy IV Philopater (221–204 B.C.E.), who acts arrogantly against God, is rendered insane, and finally repents of his anti-Jewish hostility. According to the narrative, during Ptolemy's triumphant tour following his defeat of the Seleucid king Antiochus III at Raphia in 217 B.C.E., he visits his Jewish allies in Jerusalem, where he wishes to inspect the Temple. Neither the people's emotional outbursts nor the prayer of the high priest can dissuade him from entering the holy of holies. Only an angelic intervention stops the king from doing so: "Then the God who beholds all, the supremely holy father among the holy, heard the prayer of supplication offered in the regular form and scourged the one who was greatly exalted by his own insolence and effrontery, tossed him to and fro like a reed on the wind until he fell impotent to the ground, with his limbs paralyzed and unable to speak, completely overpowered by a righteous judgment" (*3 Maccabees* 2:21–2; see 2 Maccabees 3 for a similar story).

Having been thwarted by the Jewish God, Ptolemy determines to punish the Jewish community. Returning to Egypt, he offers local Jews the choice of sacrificing to Egyptian gods or being registered as slaves, taxed, and branded (*3 Maccabees* 2:25–30). The author notes that the deep hostility of even the Gentiles was aroused by the king's anger (*3 Maccabees* 4:1, 16), and that Gentile hostility further stemmed from a misunderstanding of Jewish dietary practice: "But by reverencing God and conducting themselves according to his Law, they kept themselves apart in the matter of food, and for this reason they appeared hateful to some" (*3 Maccabees* 3:4). This theme of separation from the larger community reappears in *Joseph and Aseneth*, *4 Maccabees*, the Additions to Esther, and elsewhere in the Hellenistic and early Roman Jewish texts, where it is regularly accompanied by the notice that the Jews are politically loyal to the governments of the lands where they live.

The body of the story recounts with hyperbole and slapstick humor how Jews, too numerous to count, are gathered from the whole country, how God causes mental confusion in the king so that he forgets that he meant to have his Jewish subjects trampled to death by drugged elephants, and finally how the drugged elephants turn on the king's troops. As in the Books of Esther and Daniel, prayer and divine intervention avert the disaster that threatens the community. Though Ptolemy is depicted as arrogant, unstable, and vindictive, he is rehabilitated by means of imperfect repentance when he is frightened by two angels (*3 Maccabees* 6:18–23).

At the end, Ptolemy commands that the "sons of the all-conquering, living God of heaven" be released from their bonds (*3 Maccabees* 6:28). The newly enfranchised Jewish community kills apostate Jews – those who transgressed the law of God – but not the hostile Gentiles. The Jews retain their role as Egypt's loyal subjects (*3 Maccabees* 3:8; 7:11), who promote internal discipline and seek fidelity to both God and crown (*3 Maccabees* 2:31; 7:10–15). Peaceful relations with the established powers, however fragile and grudging, are maintained. The text concludes by affirming that "The great God had perfectly accomplished great things for their salvation. Blessed be the deliverer of Israel forever and ever! Amen" (*3 Maccabees* 7:23).

3. Additions to Esther

The Hebrew story of Esther is similar to *3 Maccabees* in its narrative pattern and underlying attitudes. Gentile hostility to Jews because of their customs, the threat of total destruction, the battle for the king's mind, and the royal change of heart are all present, but in a greatly different context. The Book of Esther has no direct divine intervention and does not even mention God's name. Court intrigue and competition between Jews and Gentiles are more prominent, and Esther keeps her nationality secret so that she may marry the king.

During the Hellenistic period additions were made to the Book of Esther. Some may have been added to the Hebrew Book of Esther and then translated into Greek, while others (or perhaps all) were written in Greek. Surviving only in the Greek translation of Esther, they date from either 114 or 77 B.C.E. (depending on which Ptolemy and which Cleopatra are in view), according to a translator's note preserved at the end of Greek Esther. Several verbal similarities with *3 Maccabees* suggest a literary relationship.

The additions to the Book of Esther make God's activity explicit and the narrative more dramatic and emotional. The story opens with Mordecai, the Jewish protagonist, dreaming about his struggle with his enemy Haman. The florid language and the emotive emphasis are elements of Hellenistic literature:

> And this was his dream: Voices and confusion, thunders and earthquake, tumult on the earth! Then two great dragons came forward, both ready to fight, and they roared terribly. At their roaring every nation prepared for war, to fight against the righteous nation. It was a day of darkness and gloom, affliction and great tumult on the earth. And the whole righteous nation was troubled; they feared their own evils and were ready to perish. Then they cried out to God, and at their outcry, as though from a tiny spring, there came a great river with abundant water; light came, and the sun rose, and the lowly were exalted and devoured those held in honor. (Greek Esther 11:4b–11)

The author reveals his resentment against his Greek overlords when he has the king identify Haman as a Macedonian (Greek) rather than as an "Agagite" (as the Hebrew has it in Esther 10:24). An interpretation of the dream ends the book, so that the dream functions as a summary of the story and, as in Daniel, as a witness to divine power and providence.

In another of the additions, Esther prays at length that she will succeed in convincing the king to annul the decree of destruction against the Jews. Esther explains in her prayer that she keeps the dietary laws and submits to sexual relations with the king only out of duty (14:15–18), depicting a concern for endogamy present also in Tobit and essential to Jewish survival in the Diaspora. The prayer itself is comparable to the other extended prayers that mark Second Temple Jewish literature, including a long prayer in the Additions to Esther accorded to Mordecai (Esther 13:8–17), Judith's invocation that the enemy be delivered into the hand of a woman (Judith 9), the Prayer of Manasseh, and the *Hodayot* (1QH) or *Thanksgiving Hymns* from Qumran:

> Then Queen Esther, seized with deadly anxiety, fled to the Lord. She took off her splendid apparel and put on the garments of distress and mourning, and instead of costly perfumes she covered her head with ashes and dung. . . . She prayed to the Lord God of Israel and said, "O my Lord, you only are our king; help me now I am alone and have no helper but you . . . Remember, O Lord; make yourself known in this time of our affliction, and give me courage, O King, of the gods and Master of all dominion. Put eloquent speech in my mouth before the lion, and turn his heart to hate the man who is fighting us. . . . You know my necessity – that I abhor the sign of my proud position, which is upon my head on days when I appear in public. I abhor it like a menstrous rag, and I do not wear it on the days when I am at leisure. And your servant has not eaten at Haman's table, and I have not honored the king's feast or drunk the wine of libations . . ." (Greek Esther 14:1–19)

Both the prayer and the subsequent audience with the king, a scene also expanded into a dramatic and emotional confrontation, reveal the inner attitudes and emotions of the leading characters, a dimension of the story missing in the Semitic original but literarily necessary in the Hellenistic world.

4. *Joseph and Aseneth*

Egyptian Jews displayed a variety of responses to the surrounding Gentile culture. The story of *Joseph and Aseneth*, an expansion of the biblical story of Joseph in Genesis 37–50, resolves the tensions with the Gentile world by the conversion of particularly worthy Gentiles. The Bible simply states that Joseph married "Asenath," the daughter of an Egyptian priest (Genesis 41:45). But in the Greek retelling, replete with high drama and intense emotion, Aseneth's prayers and practices leading to repentance and then conversion to Judaism, and Joseph's dialogues with her make clear the inferiority of idolatry in the face of monotheism, the importance of the sexual and dietary purity that separates Jews and Gentiles, the socially just and benevolent ethics of the Jewish community, and the ultimate promise of immortality that awaits the faithful.

Joseph and Aseneth are ideal types. Aseneth is a highborn, wealthy, and beautiful Egyptian who has carefully preserved her virginity and proudly rejected all suitors. Her only vice is an arrogant attachment to Egyptian idols and ways of life. Joseph, Pharaoh's regent, who is gathering crops for the approaching famine, arrives at Aseneth's home. Although her parents encourage her to marry him, Aseneth resists the idea until she sees Joseph; he is gorgeous, and she is smitten. But when she desires to kiss Joseph, a symbol of the union of the two cultures, he refuses her because she is impure in her worship and dietary habits.

> And Aseneth saw Joseph on his chariot and was strongly cut to the heart, and her soul was crushed, and her knees were paralyzed, and her entire body trembled, and she was filled with great fear. And she sighed and said in her heart: "What shall I do now, wretched as I am? Did I not speak, saying that Joseph is coming, the shepherd's son from the land of Canaan? And now, behold, the sun from heaven has come to us on its chariot and entered our house today, and shines in it like a light upon the earth . . . And now be gracious on me, Lord, God of Joseph, because I have spoken wicked words against him in ignorance." (*Joseph and Aseneth* 6:1–8)

The course of Aseneth's conversion includes fasting, sackcloth, visions, giving alms, rejection of luxury, rejection of unclean food and other impure items, the destruction of her idols, and an angelic appearance during which she is fed a heavenly honeycomb that symbolizes pure bread, wine, and oil as well as immortality. Her new name, "City of Refuge," and her marriage to Joseph, sanctioned by Pharaoh, suggest a political and communal stability that can be reached only through Gentile acceptance of Judaism.

This work was probably written in the first century B.C.E. (or perhaps C.E.) in Alexandria. Aseneth's name, which connects her with the Egyptian goddess Neith, the sun imagery used in the description of Joseph, the heavenly honeycomb, and many other features suggest a familiarity with Egyptian religion. The work assumes close and peaceful relations between Jews and Gentiles, yet it also promotes firm boundaries to preserve Jewish identity. The only hostilities it depicts are between Joseph and some of his brothers (chapters 22–9); Jews and Gentiles are found on each side of the struggle. This final incident, in which Pharaoh's son and four of Joseph's brothers attack Aseneth and are defeated by the other brothers' response aided by divine intervention, suggests possible opposition to the author's vision in the Jewish and Gentile communities.

5. The Prayer of Manasseh

Third Maccabees, the Additions to Esther, and *Joseph and Aseneth* are all notable for the long and emotional prayers addressed to God in times of stress, and the Prayer of Manasseh epitomizes this Hellenistic genre. The text is found in the Septuagint and is recognized as canonical in the Orthodox churches; it is included not only in Greek Orthodox and Slavonic Bibles but also in the Appendix to the Latin Vulgate.

Though 2 Kings 21 excoriates Manasseh (ca. 698–642 B.C.E.) for his idolatry and blames the eventual destruction of Jerusalem on him, 2 Chronicles (33:18–19) says that he was taken by the Assyrians into exile in Babylon, repented of his sins, and was returned to Jerusalem. The Hebrew text notes that a Prayer of Manasseh is recorded elsewhere; the Greek Prayer of Manasseh provides an appropriate prayer to supplement the note. The prayer is a simple invocation of God in his power, an appeal to his mercy toward repentant sinners, a confession of many sins, a cry for forgiveness, and a promise to praise God. In this text as well as in the other Greek-Jewish works, no matter how grave the sin or how perilous the situation, God remains near his people and will respond to the repentant sinner.

> And now, I bend the knee of my heart,
> Imploring you for your kindness.
> I have sinned, O Lord, I have sinned,
> And I acknowledge my transgressions.
> I earnestly implore you,
> Forgive me, O Lord, Forgive me!
> (Prayer of Manasseh 11–13a)

IV. HEROD THE GREAT

Herod's rise to power coincided with the end of the Hasmonean dynasty, the Roman defeat of invading Parthians, and the emergence of a single emperor in Rome. His continuance in power depended on his ability to bring stability to Palestine and to placate a succession of powerful Roman emperors. At times a decadent and arbitrary tyrant, Herod was also an energetic and courageous military commander, a ruthless and effective political leader, and an efficient economic and social administrator. Rome supported him because he collected the taxes, kept the peace, and maintained military support at the borders. Herod remained loyal to Rome because he had sense enough to know that he could not successfully revolt. He managed to carve out relative security and independence for his people, a task that his children and grandchildren failed to accomplish.

In 42 B.C.E. Mark Antony, a member of the second triumvirate, defeated Brutus and Cassius at Philippi and demanded a heavy indemnity from their supporters in the East. Herod, together with his father Antipater, had collected taxes to support Cassius's army, and so they were among the rulers from whom Antony required payment. Herod and his brother Phasael paid the tax and kept their governorships, but they

THE SECOND TRIUMVIRATE

After Julius Caesar's assassination by the Senate in 44 B.C.E., Mark Antony, his protégé, and Gaius Octavius (Octavian), his adopted son and heir, formed an alliance to gain control of Rome. Along with Lepidus, the governor of Gaul and Spain, they were given absolute power. They killed over two thousand members of the Republican faction, which had opposed Julius Caesar, and pursued his assassins to the eastern Mediterranean. Octavian ruled Italy and the surrounding areas, and Mark Antony ruled the eastern Mediterranean, where he entered into his famous liaison with Cleopatra, the ruler of Egypt. In 36 B.C.E. Octavian forced the retirement of Lepidus, and in 31 B.C.E. he defeated Antony in a sea battle at Actium and thus concentrated all power in himself. Taking the name Caesar Augustus, the new ruler ended any hope of a return to the Roman Republic and founded the Roman Empire.

incurred enormous resentment from the people from whom they exacted the money. When the Parthians took advantage of Roman disorganization on their eastern border and invaded Syria, Palestine, and the coast in 40 B.C.E., the people revolted against Herod and the other authorities. Phasael was captured and committed suicide, and Hyrcanus II, the high priest and so the nominal leader of Judaism, was mutilated so he could no longer serve as high priest. (Josephus reports that Antigonus bit Hyrcanus's ears off "with his own teeth"; see *War* 1.270). Herod escaped to Petra, and the Parthians crowned Antigonus, the son of Aristobulus and nephew of Hyrcanus, king and high priest in Jerusalem (40–37 B.C.E.).

Tomb façade at Petra. (BiblePlaces.com)

BANDITRY

English usage associates banditry with any kind of theft. But banditry in peasant societies could also function as a form of social resistance. Bandits or brigands became numerous in the Roman period. Peasants forced off the land by a combination of harsh economic conditions, politically inefficient governments, military oppression, and failed harvests typically banded together to take food and other necessities from the upper classes. Occasionally they had the support of the peasants still on the land, and they were sometimes seen as popular heroes rectifying injustices and providing a measure of security for those peasants. Since bandits threatened civic order and the social hold of the governing class, great efforts were made to suppress them. Herod made his military reputation rooting out bandits in Galilee. Bandits were also partially responsible for the revolt against Rome in 66 C.E. According to Mark 15:27, Jesus was crucified between two bandits, and Jesus rebuked the arresting officers for treating him like a bandit (Mark 14:48). Whether Mark intended to indicate that these bandits were dispossessed peasants or freedom fighters, or whether the references are meant to evoke Isaiah 53:12, "he was counted among the lawless" (see Luke 22:37; the citation also appears in some manuscripts of Mark 15: 27), remains a debated issue.

While the Parthians controlled Palestine, Herod went to Rome to seek support. In 40 B.C.E., Antony appointed him king of Judea, Idumea, Galilee, and Perea; however, he first had to recover his kingdom, and for this he had Rome's support. In 39 B.C.E. the Roman legions drove off the Parthians and Herod returned to Palestine. Yet it was not until 37 B.C.E., when Antony sent the capable general Sosius with an army from Syria to take Jerusalem, that Herod formally began his reign. Herod would spend the rest of the decade quelling resistance to his rule, including killing the bandits who were causing disruption in Galilee and defying the Jerusalem council, which wished to exercise control over him and which regarded his efforts in the Galilee as exceeding his authority (Josephus, *Antiquities* 14.163–84). The political situation also required Herod to neutralize the intrigues of Antony's Egyptian consort, Cleopatra, as well as the remnants of the Hasmonean family, both of whom sought to control Palestine. A Roman legion stationed in Jerusalem supported Herod's efforts.

Seeking to legitimate his rule in the eyes of Jewish loyalists, Herod ransomed Hyrcanus from the Parthians and then married Hyrcanus's granddaughter, the Hasmonean princess Mariamme. According to Josephus, "those who did not before favor him did join themselves to him now, because of his marriage into the family of Hyrcanus, for as he had formerly married a wife out of his own country of no ignoble blood, who was called Doris . . . so did he now marry Mariamme, the daughter of Alexander, the son of Aristobulus, and the grand-daughter of Hyrcanus, and became thereby a relation of the king" (*War*, 1.240–1).

Initially, Herod attempted to control the high priesthood by appointing a priest from Babylon who was loyal to his court. After intense political pressure, Herod yielded to local supporters of the Hasmonean faction and appointed Aristobulus III, Mariamme's brother, as high priest, but so feared his popularity that he had him drowned within the year. Offsetting the popular dissatisfaction with Herod's rule that erupted in periodic insurrections and unrest, usually involving small numbers, the people's continuing affection for the Hasmonean House manifest itself in their support of Mariamme's sons Alexander and Aristobulus.

In 31 B.C.E. Herod overcame several crises. First, when the Nabatean kingdom across the Jordan, from whom Herod collected Roman taxes, withheld payment, Herod succeeded in subduing them. In this war he proved his ability as a general and reaffirmed his personal valor in battle. That same year a disastrous earthquake destroyed the economic base in many of his cities and towns and disrupted the collection of taxes. Most critically, Octavian defeated Herod's Roman patron in the East, Mark Antony, at Actium. The empire became united under Octavian, eventually known as Caesar Augustus (31 B.C.E.–14 C.E.), and the change in leadership initially jeopardized Herod's position as king. Herod immediately shifted loyalty and so was able to secure his rule. Meeting with the new emperor on Rhodes, Herod convinced him that he would continue to be loyal and efficient in governing Judea on Rome's behalf. Octavian, pleased to have Herod in control of the crucial land bridge between Syria and Egypt, confirmed him in his office. Internally, in 30 B.C.E. Herod removed one possible rival by executing the aged Hyrcanus on the charge of conspiring with the king of Arabia to regain the throne. He would later execute many other Hasmonean descendants, whom he accused of seeking to usurp his power.

Like other dependent local rulers, Herod was expected to collect taxes and to provide military supplies and troops as needed, but to leave all foreign policy initiatives in Rome's hands. Since his position depended on Caesar's goodwill, Herod cultivated close personal relations with the emperor. He built Greek cities with temples, arenas, and baths in honor of the Caesar, most notably Caesarea on the coast (Caesarea Maritima) and Sebaste in Samaria ("Sebaste" is the Greek equivalent of "Augustus"), as well as temples and other public facilities in several coastal cities. In a number of Greek cities he sponsored the construction of public baths and temples; he also supported the Olympics and sponsored games every four years at Caesarea. His court was made up of many Gentiles and Hellenized Jews from the Diaspora, and he patronized the Greek arts and literature. Herod

Aerial view from the west of the harbor at Caesarea Maritima. (BiblePlaces.com)

acted like any other Greco-Roman leader, and consequently he was respected and accepted by the empire as part of its governing class.

Herod's kingdom was prosperous and peaceful, especially in contrast to the civil unrest in the last years of Hasmonean rule. But the peace came with a heavy price. To secure his reign Herod built numerous fortresses and palaces in a variety of cities. Herodium (east of Jerusalem) and Masada (on the western shore of the Dead Sea), the most famous, contained splendid palaces that served as refuges in times of trouble. His palace in Jerusalem had three great towers, and the one in Jericho featured beautiful decorations, baths, and pools. He supported the elaborate machinery of state by developing and settling new agricultural lands, especially in northern Transjordan, by confiscating the estates of his enemies, and by means of agricultural taxes, sales and purchase taxes, and a variety of customs duties. In his domestic policy Herod and his ruling clientele were no different from Gentile governing classes of that era.

Along with the threat – and the occasional but masterful use – of force, Herod controlled political affairs by appointing the high priest, subordinating the *synedrion* (the ruling regional council) to his wishes, and appointing family members and in-laws to all high posts. For many years his father-in-law, Simon, son of Boethus from Alexandria, was the high priest; Pheroras, his younger brother, was appointed tetrarch of Perea by Caesar Augustus; and relatives governed other districts. The independent cities in Herod's reign were attached to various districts and closely monitored. His army was drawn mostly from Gentile settlers whom he had established in new cities, such as Sebaste, and from other Greek areas, and could be counted on to control the Jewish population. Herod's Gentile

Herodium, with lower pool. (BiblePlaces.com)

Map XIV. The kingdom of Herod the Great.

settlements greatly weakened Jewish control of their homeland and led to later conflicts.

As Herod aged and his health failed in the last decade of his life (14–4 B.C.E.), his family (Herod had married at least nine wives) and followers began to plot against one another in a bid for succession. Those who plotted against him included his brother Pheroras's wife, a group of Pharisees supporting her, and other family members, all of whom Herod executed after Pheroras died. Herod condemned his three most prominent sons, including the children of Mariamme, to death. His final will, subject to the approval of the emperor, divided his kingdom among three of the few sons still alive.

To eliminate any rival, Herod had killed, impoverished, or otherwise neutralized the Hasmonean governing class and had suppressed the traditional leadership. For support, Herod depended on his family, on Diaspora Jews, and on emerging families who owed their status to him. The removal of the traditional leadership left the populace difficult to control at Herod's death. Although the high priests he appointed came from leading priestly families, they were new in this office. The gap between the governing class personally dependent on Herod and the people was filled by popular leaders who arose from traditional village society, by reform movements that responded to Roman cultural influence, by revival movements that sought to deepen the roots of the covenant among the people, and by revolutionary movements that sought immediate political change.

V. HEROD'S HEIRS

Herod divided his kingdom among three of his sons. Herod Archelaus, son of Herod's Samaritan wife Malthace, was to rule Judea, Samaria, and Idumea. Herod Antipas received two territories, Galilee and Perea (the latter being a district east of the Jordan River), which were separated by the Decapolis (a league of ten relatively autonomous, Hellenistic, and predominantly Gentile cities). Herod Philip, half-brother to Archelaus and Antipas and son of Herod's fifth wife, Cleopatra of Jerusalem, became the ruler of Ituria and Trachonitis and other districts north and east of the Sea of Galilee. Herod's wish that Archelaus be appointed king so that some semblance of unity could be maintained in his kingdom was never ratified by Caesar Augustus.

When Archelaus returned to Jerusalem from Jericho, where his father had died, crowds gathered for Passover cheered him. They also sought a reduction in taxes and the release of prisoners taken by Herod. Rejecting these demands, Archelaus had loyal soldiers massacre some in the mobs that pressed their demands. This inauspicious beginning proved an accurate harbinger of problems to come. Resentment against the Herodians increased to such an extent that while Herod's heirs were in Rome seeking Caesar Augustus's approbation, a series of peasant revolts sprang up in different parts of the country. This type of brigandage by bands of landless peasants had arisen during the transition from Hasmonean to Herodian rule, survived at the fringes during Herod's strong reign, and exploded in the chaos following his death. Led by popular leaders, some of whom claimed to be divinely anointed kings with messianic or prophetic status, the rebels were predominantly from the lower classes, which Herod had exploited and repressed. They appealed to the Bible's royal covenant traditions associated with King David, and some invoked apocalyptic expectations of divine intervention. Athronges, a shepherd, and his brothers won a series of battles in Judea and wiped out a Roman detachment at Emmaus. In Transjordan, Simon, one of Herod's slaves, led attacks on royal property, including the palace at Jericho. Another group of rebels burned down the palace in Amathus. In Galilee, Judas, the son of the bandit leader Ezekias, who had been killed by Herod, captured the capital Sepphoris and in further campaigns used the weapons he acquired there.

Map XV. Herod's divided kingdom.

To put down the unrest in Herod's territory after his death in 4 B.C.E., Varus, the Roman governor of Syria, invaded with two of his three legions stationed in Syria and with an army of Nabatean allies from Transjordan. The population of Sepphoris was enslaved, and both Sepphoris and Emmaus were burned to the ground. Varus ordered the crucifixions of over two thousand Jews, and the Nabateans looted many towns. Were Mary and Joseph in Galilee at this time, as the Gospels of Matthew and Luke indicate, they would have experienced such atrocities directly. When Sabinus, acting on Augustus's behalf to assess what remained of Herod's wealth, imprudently tried to seize Herod's treasure, the crowds at the Feast of Booths (Sukkot)

Excavation of the Pool of Siloam in Jerusalem. (BiblePlaces.com)

along with some of Herod's troops revolted and besieged the Romans in the Tower Phasael of Herod's palace. Again, Varus put down the revolt.

After order was restored, Archelaus tried to imitate Herod's grand and cruel manner of rule, but he lacked his father's political skill. After ten years, in 6 C.E., Augustus removed him from office and exiled him because of persistent protests from both Judeans and Samaritans. Though Archelaus's brothers Antipas and Philip continued to rule Jewish areas in the north, for the first time since the Persian period Jerusalem and Judea,

Excavation squares at Sepphoris. (BiblePlaces .com)

SUKKOT (THE FEAST OF BOOTHS OR TABERNACLES)

Sukkot is an agricultural festival marking the end of the fall harvest. During the festival, people celebrated with prayer and joyful processions, and in commemoration of Israel's wandering in the desert they lived in roughly made, impermanent dwellings. The name of the feast in Hebrew (*sukkot*) is usually but inadequately translated as "booths" or "tabernacles." The term actually designates huts made of branches and leaves, and refers specifically to the huts erected by the harvesters in the fields and vineyards to provide shelter at midday and sometimes at night.

Sukkot is one of the three pilgrimage festivals (along with Passover and Shavuot [the Feast of Weeks]) when Jews from throughout Judea, Galilee, and the Diaspora would travel to the Jerusalem Temple. Some biblical texts suggest that Sukkot is the most solemn of the three (Ezekiel 45:25; Leviticus 23:39; Zechariah 14:16), in keeping with the most valuable harvest of the year. According to the Mishnah, Sukkot was so popular that it was designated simply as *Hag*, that is, the festival.

The feast lasted for seven days, followed by a solemn eighth day (called Shemini Atseret); work was forbidden on the first and eighth days. Many special sacrifices were offered during the festival (Numbers 29:12–34). Other customs included carrying branches and fruit (Leviticus 23:40–1); the Mishnah specifies that participants must carry branches of palm, myrtle, and willow (*lulav*), and a citron (*'etrog*). Music, trumpet blasts, dancing, and pouring of water libations are prominently noted in the ancient sources. The "Feast of the Water Drawing," set in the Jerusalem Temple and described vividly in the Talmud (*Sukkah* 53a) was among the most joyous celebrations of the Jewish liturgical year.

Because so many Jews gathered in Jerusalem and religious and national feelings ran high, feasts were often an occasion for public unrest and rebellion. The final chapter of Zechariah assured that Sukkot would be especially associated with the expectation of the vindication of Israel. Josephus tells of numerous disturbances, especially near Passover (*Antiquities* 17.213; 18.29, 90; 20.106), and the Gospels also refer to this problem (Luke 13:1–2; Matthew 26:3–5; Mark 14:1–2).

---

the heart of Judaism, were ruled directly by a succession of foreign (now Roman) governors. The Romans left day-to-day governance, including the collection of taxes, the maintenance of public order, and the administration of the Temple, to the high priests and their council (*synedrion*), but the priests and the council were subject to the governor's wishes. High priests were replaced regularly by the Roman governors, though several came from the family of Annas (John 18:13). Though Galilee, under the rule of Antipas, was more peaceful than Jerusalem, the weight of taxation, the numbers of landless, and the pressures of Greco-Roman culture stimulated a search for national identity and new ways of Jewish life.

A. Literary Responses to Herodian Rule

1. The *Testament of Moses*

The *Testament of Moses* (sometimes called the *Assumption of Moses*) communicates Jewish confidence in God and rejection of the injustice, domestic and foreign, that marked Roman rule. The core of the book dates from the Maccabean period, but it was revised to allude to the reign of Herod and to Varus's suppression of unrest after Herod died. Like other apocalyptic writings, the *Testament of Moses* reviews Israel's history as a record of sin and punishment culminating in the salvation of a repentant remnant. The troubles of the Herodian period and Roman invasions are viewed as another painful chapter in misrule, to be followed by more intense persecution and then decisively rectified by divine intervention.

Concerning the pre-Maccabean high priests, the *Testament* has Moses predict: "They will pollute the house of worship with the customs of the nations; and they will play the harlot after foreign gods" (*Testament of Moses* 5:3). "Those who are the leaders, their teachers, in those times will become admirers of avaricious persons, accepting polluted offerings, and they will sell justice by accepting bribes" (5:5). The hundred-year rule of the Hasmoneans and their establishment of an independent principality are dismissed in one line: "Then powerful kings will rise over them, and they will be called priests of the Most High God. They will perform impiety in the Holy of Holies" (6:1). Since the Maccabees were not from legitimate high priestly families, had disenfranchised the previous governing class of Judaism, and had acted like independent Hellenistic kings, the author dismisses their achievements as destructive of Judaism.

Herod receives a little more attention: "And a wanton king, who will not be of a priestly family, will follow them. He will be a man rash and perverse, and he will judge them as they deserve.... He will kill both old and young, showing mercy to no one. Then fear of him will be heaped upon them in their land ... and he will punish them" (6:2–7). Herod's disastrous reign is concluded by Varus's invasion: "After his death there will come into their land a powerful king of the West who will subdue them; and he will take away captives, and a part of their Temple he will burn with fire. He will crucify some of them around their city" (6:8–9). Each of the details matches Josephus's account of Varus's punitive campaign.

Steps to the south of the Temple Mount. (BiblePlaces.com)

The Jewish leaders who followed Herod and his son Archelaus are attacked as avaricious, deceitful, godless men who pollute the Temple and "consume the goods of the poor, saying their acts are according to justice" (*Testament of Moses* 7:6). Their hypocrisy and destructive leadership bring a final punishment upon the nation (chapter 8). Descriptions of tortures, forced worship of other gods, and prohibition of circumcision may derive from the time of Antiochus IV, but here they relate to the final trials of Israel. The experience of waiting faithfully for God amid persecution is revealed in the story of Taxo (chapter 9), a mysterious figure who retreats to a cave to die with his sons rather than remain in society and disobey God's commands. Symbolic of the author's faithful community and evoking the martyrs in the Maccabean volumes, Taxo is the climax of the righteous suffering in the history of Israel, and his steadfastness introduces the reign of God:

> Then his kingdom will appear throughout his whole creation.
> Then the devil will have an end. Yea, sorrow will be led away with him.
> Then will be filled the hands of the messenger, who is in the highest place appointed.
> Yea, he will at once avenge them of their enemies.
> For the Heavenly One will arise from his kingly throne.
> Yea, he will go forth from his holy habitation with indignation and wrath on behalf of his sons.
>
> (*Testament of Moses* 10:1–3)

After the intervention by the angelic messenger and God, the earth will be shaken, the sun and moon will cease to give light, the waters will fail, and the nations will be punished and destroyed. Israel will be happy, will trample the necks and eagle's wings (probably a reference to Rome), and finally will be raised to the heavens (chapter 10). The description of the end is typical of apocalyptic literature and similar to some found in the Gospels (e.g., Mark 13). The compressing of the activities of the dominant political power, Rome, into a single event in the larger scheme of Jewish history affirms the ultimate power and rule of God.

2. The Revised *Third Sibylline Oracle*

The *Third Sibylline Oracle*, a political protest tract from second-century B.C.E. Egypt, was revised and updated around the time that Antony and Cleopatra ruled the East and then were defeated at the battle of Actium in 31 B.C.E. The author of the oracle and its reviser remain unknown; such oracles were numerous in the Greco-Roman world. In the section where the punishments of various nations are announced, an oracle on the Romans was added (350–80), with the prediction that Asia (meaning Egypt) would exact three times as much tribute from Rome as Rome had from Asia. The oracle lacks the historical and cosmic range of the *Testament of Moses* – and its subtlety: the identity of Rome is clear, the punishments to be visited on Rome are specific, and the agent of humiliation is a human, Cleopatra (here called "the mistress"):

> Whatever number from Asia served the house of Italians, twenty times that number of Italians will be serfs in Asia, in poverty, and they will be liable to pay ten-thousandfold. . . . Often the mistress will cut your delicate hair and, dispensing justice, will cast you from heaven to earth. (*Third Sibylline Oracle* 353–60)

The references to slavery and forced labor show how much Rome relied on coercion of its subjects and how greatly this was resented. Even so, Rome will not be destroyed but will be raised up again. After other cities are punished, Asia will rule in prosperity and peace:

> Serene peace will return to the Asian land, and Europe will then be blessed. The air will be good for pasture for many years, bracing, free from storms and hail, producing everything. . . . For all good order and righteous dealing will come upon men from starry heaven and with it temperate accord. . . . Bad government, blame, envy, anger, folly, and poverty will flee from men and constraint will flee. (*Third Sibylline Oracle* 367–78)

The utopian society pictured here and the figure of Cleopatra ruling Rome and the Mediterranean are based on prayers to and praises of the Egyptian goddess Isis. The Egyptian Jew who wrote this oracle put his trust in non-Jewish human agencies to bring about better times.

How fragile that hope was can be seen by additions near the beginning of the *Third Sibylline Oracle* that were made after the battle of Actium. Here the author, faced with the defeat and death of Antony, sees the rule of the world by a widow (Cleopatra, after the death of Antony) as an introduction to divine judgment and the destruction of the world (*Third Sibylline Oracle* 75–92). Later, with Rome fully in charge in Egypt, "the most great kingdom of the immortal king will become manifest over men" and "a holy prince will come to gain sway over the scepters of the earth forever, as time presses on. Then also implacable wrath will fall upon Latin men" (47–51). The author drew on Jewish apocalyptic themes of divine intervention, judgment, and punishment but did not envision a completely renewed world ruled by God. This Egyptian Jew still hoped for political independence for his country and a better life on earth through an enlightened ruler (see also *Joseph and Aseneth*). Egyptian Jews had not yet suffered the political and cultural oppression that motivated the apocalyptic response of Palestinian Judaism in the Seleucid and Roman periods.

VI. ROMAN RULE IN THE FIRST CENTURY C.E.

After the exile of Archelaus in 6 C.E., political, military, and judicial power in Judea and Samaria was vested in a Roman official appointed by the emperor rather than in a Jewish leader subordinate to Roman

PRAISES TO ISIS

During the Hellenistic period, the Egyptian goddess Isis became Hellenized and her worship spread throughout the Mediterranean world. As the Roman Empire expanded eastward, Isis worship extended west toward Rome.

Geographical mobility and political upheaval separated many people from their religious roots and shook their confidence in the traditional gods. For these people Isis and similar gods were patrons in the face of an unfamiliar and threatening world. In his *Metamorphoses*, Book 11, Lucius Apuleius Africanus recounts his wandering and trials (including being turned into an ass), his salvation by Isis, and his mystic experience of conversion during his initiation into the mysteries of Isis. He ends his account with a prayer to Isis that has much in common with Jewish and Christian prayers of the Greco-Roman period:

O holy and blessed dame,
the perpetual comfort of human kind,

who by your bounty and grace nourishes all the world
and bears a great affection to the adversities of the miserable as a loving mother,
you take no rest night or day,
neither are you idle at any time in giving benefits and succouring all men as well on land as sea;
you are she that puts away all storms and dangers from men's life by stretching forth your right hand,
whereby likewise you unweave even the inextricable and entangled web of fate
and appease the great tempest of fortune,
and keep back the harmful course of the stars.
The gods supernal honor you; the gods infernal have you in reverence;
you make all the earth turn, give light to the sun,
govern the world, tread down the power of hell.
By your power the stars give answer,

the seasons return, the gods rejoice, the elements serve.
At your command the winds blow, the clouds nourish the earth, the seeds prosper, and the fruits grow.
The birds of the air, the beasts of the hill,
the serpents of the den, and the fishes of the sea tremble at your majesty.
But my spirit is not able to give you sufficient praise,
my patrimony is unable to satisfy your sacrifices;
my voice has no power to utter that which I think of your majesty,
no, not if I had a thousand mouths and so many tongues and were able to continue forever.
Howbeit as a good religious person, and according to my poor estate, I will do what I may:
I will always keep your divine appearance in remembrance and close the imagination of your most holy godhead within my breast.

authority. This was the first time an empire controlling Palestine had failed to appoint a Jew as mediator between the ruling authorities and the people. The misunderstandings and hostilities created by this arrangement increasingly poisoned the atmosphere in Judea and contributed to the war with Rome sixty years later. Rather than suppressing opposition with craft and consistency like Herod, Roman officials inflamed the people by theft on a grand scale and by insults to their religious traditions and insensitivity to their needs. Provincial rulers, who were expected to enrich themselves with excess tax collections, often engaged in even less ethical practices, such as soliciting bribes and expropriating private property. Provinces where governors changed frequently could easily be bled dry as each new official stripped the population of its resources.

The Roman official in charge of Judea was at first a prefect (a military commander) and later a procurator (a civil administrator). The province's governors came from the second rank of Roman society, the equestrian order, from whom were drawn many second-level officials of the empire.

Replica of an inscription left by Pontius Pilate in Caesarea. (BiblePlaces.com)

The prefect ruled Judea, Samaria, the coast, and Idumea from his capital at Caesarea on the coast and had at his disposal non-Jewish auxiliary troops drawn from the area, including an especially loyal contingent from Sebaste in Samaria. He was responsible for keeping order, supervising tax collection, and judging major cases concerned with security. He served under the supervision of the legate of Syria, who was of the higher, senatorial order. The Syrian governor, responsible for securing the eastern border of the empire, had four legions under his control; he was not only a member of the Roman Senate but also an ex-consul (the highest military and civil magistrate in Rome).

Roman prefects left the local administration of justice to the traditional town and national authorities, usually the wealthy and hereditary community leaders. The highest authorities in Jerusalem were the high priest, the leading high priestly families of Phiabi, Boethus, Camith, and Ananus (see John 18:13), and other wealthy and established but non-priestly families who had survived the reigns of the Hasmoneans and Herod. They exercised control through a supreme council in Jerusalem, local councils, major administrative offices, and a variety of lower officials, guards, courts, and other institutions. Because their social position and prosperity were subject to Roman power and dependent on an orderly society, all provincial elites were co-opted by the Romans to keep the peace and collect taxes.

At lower levels of government and in the towns, however, scribes, some Pharisees, heads of synagogues, and the traditional leading citizens

ROMAN OFFICIALS IN PALESTINE

From the end of Archelaus's reign in 6 C.E. until the interruption of Roman rule at the inception of the revolt in 66 C.E., Judea and Samaria were ruled by Roman officials, except during the reign of the Jewish king Agrippa (41–4 C.E.). Governors drawn from the senatorial order, that is, from the leading Roman families who had a member in the Senate, administered most Roman provinces, including Syria. A few smaller provinces, like Judea (which was dependent on Syria), were governed by members of the lower, equestrian order, which was drawn from a wide range of people, many of whom were financially successful. The governor of a province had military command of

auxiliary units, financial responsibility for the district, and ultimate judicial power.

From 6 to 41 C.E. the governors were designated *prefects*, originally a military title. From 44 on, they were titled *procurators*, originally a financial officer representing the emperor on an estate or in a senatorial province. As time went on, the differences between the offices disappeared and the terms became confused, even by the Roman historian Tacitus, who calls the prefect Pontius Pilate a procurator. In the Gospels, Pilate is most often called *hegemon* (Latin *praeses*), a title most properly used for a senatorial governor.

THE ROMAN GOVERNORS OF JUDEA	
Coponius	6–9 C.E.
Ambibulus	9–12
Rufus	12–15
Valerius Gratus	15–26
Pontius Pilate	26–36 or 37
Marcellus	37
Marullus	37–41
Cuspius Fadus	44–46
Tiberius Julius Alexander	46–48
Ventidius Cumanus	48–52
Felix	52–59/60
Porcius Festus	59/60–62
Albinus	62–64
Gessius Florus	64–66

FIRST-CENTURY HIGH PRIESTS

During the reigns of Herod, his son Archelaus, and the Roman governors, the high priest, who had been the supreme authority during the Hasmonean period, lost his direct political power. He remained the highest ranking and symbolic head of Judaism, however. First Herod, then Archelaus, and finally Roman rulers appointed the high priests. Although the role had shifted from a lifetime appointment, the family of Ananus (Annas) held a prominent place (Ananus and Joseph Caiaphas are mentioned together in John 18:13). From the mid-first century C.E., high priests were appointed by the Jewish kings Agrippa I and Agrippa II. A list of the high priests through the first third of the first century C.E. (drawn mostly from Josephus, with uncertainties of dating noted) shows the political turnover:

Ananel, a Babylonian	37–36 B.C.E.
Aristobulus III, the last Hasmonean	35
Ananel (again)	34–?
Jesus son of Phiabi	?–22
Simon son of Boethus	22–5
Matthias son of Theophilus	5–?
Joseph son of Ellem	5/4
Joazar son of Boethus	4
Eleazar son of Boethus	4–1
Jesus son of See	1 B.C.E.–6 C.E.
Ananus or Annas, son of Sethi	6–15

Ismael son of Phiabi	15–16
Eleazar son of Ananus	16–17
Simon son of Kamithus	17–18
Joseph Caiaphas	18–37
Jonathan son of Ananus	37
Theophilus son of Ananus	37–41

By the time the Temple was destroyed in 70 C.E., twelve more high priests had been appointed. With the fall of Jerusalem the high priesthood lost its political influence. However, the Rabbis insisted that the priestly office and, therefore, that people of priestly descent retain special honor and privilege, most of which involved liturgical functions.

administered the law and settled disputes through local councils and courts. The Romans exercised oversight, interfering when their interests required it.

A. The Council (Sanhedrin)

The supreme legislative, executive, and judicial council in Judea met in the Temple compound. It is often called by the Hebraized form of the Greek word for council, "Sanhedrin," found in the Mishnah (200 C.E.). The powers and membership of the Jerusalem council and of other subordinate bodies varied according to the strength of the domestic or foreign ruler: under Herod the Sanhedrin was an advisory council of his family and friends; under the Romans it was Judea's major indigenous power, albeit firmly subordinated to Roman policy and the Roman governor. Differing accounts of this body in the New Testament, Rabbinic literature, and the works of the Jewish historian Josephus reflect changes over time. The Sanhedrin, like other municipal and ethnic councils, assemblies, and courts in the Greco-Roman world, was composed of the local elites. In Jerusalem the hereditary chief priests, led by the high priest, usually dominated the council; they were assisted by the heads of wealthy Jewish families as well as by learned officials and the leaders of other influential groups such as the Pharisees and Sadducees (see Josephus, *Antiquities* 14.168–76). The council's duties pertained to the overall welfare of the state, including political affairs, international relations, the maintenance and administration of the Temple, the collection of taxes, and the adjudication of important legal cases. Since religious law was thoroughly integrated into political and economic society in antiquity, any attempt to separate the council's religious from its secular authority is misguided.

We do not know the exact constitution of the Jerusalem council during the first century C.E. The Gospels indicate that the high priest, elders, and scribes (lower-ranking officials) were members. These same groups are mentioned in the Letter of Antiochus III in the early second century B.C.E. as the leaders of Judaism (Josephus, *Antiquities* 12.142). According to Rabbinic sources the Sanhedrin was led by pairs of teachers, such as Hillel and Shammai, Abtalion and Pollion, and it was a place of Torah study more than of fiscal administration. According to the Synoptic Gospels (Matthew, Mark, and Luke), the Sanhedrin (or a rump session meeting at night) investigated Jesus' activities, interrogated him, and recommended to the Roman governor that action against him be taken to keep the peace. However, John's Gospel records no Sanhedrin gathering; Jesus has only a brief hearing before Annas, the father-in-law of the high priest. Given additional discrepancies in the Gospel accounts (e.g., the Synoptic Gospels locate the Sanhedrin trial on the first night of the festival of Passover; according to John's Gospel, the Passover holiday had not yet begun when Jesus met with Annas); the questionability of the entire council's meeting regarding a popular Galilean leader; the numerous illegalities according to Rabbinic sources of a trial meeting at night, without proper witnesses; and so on, the historicity of Jesus' condemnation by the Sanhedrin remains provisional.

B. The Temple

The Jerusalem Temple was the center of Judaism, even for Jews who had never seen it. Mandated, described, and glorified in many biblical as well as noncanonical books, it served as the focus of God's presence in, and love for, Israel. Jews from throughout Judea, Galilee, and the Diaspora traveled to the Temple to offer sacrifices — for thanksgiving, for the reparation for sin — prescribed in the Bible; during the three festivals of Pesach (Passover), Shavuot (Weeks, Pentecost), and Sukkot (Booths or Tabernacles), Jewish pilgrims would fill the city. If civil unrest were threatening, these pilgrimage festivals were the likely occasion for it to erupt.

Public prayer and sacrifice in the Temple required the labor of numerous priests and Levites (i.e., a lower class of priest entrusted with keeping order in the Temple, providing for physical necessities, and leading the singing with voice and instrument). Central moments in worship were announced by trumpet blasts, and music and the singing of psalms accompanied the daily sacrifices. During the day private sacrifices were brought by the people and offered by the priests. In the case

TERMS FOR THE COUNCIL (SANHEDRIN)

"Sanhedrin," the term most commonly used for the Jerusalem supreme council, is a Hebraized form of the Greek word *synedrion*, literally a "sitting down with," which refers to a council of leaders – political, military, or organizational. The Jewish historian Josephus uses *synedrion* for various civil bodies, including the Jerusalem council. The Gospels and Acts use it in the same way. Because the Romans favored putting local affairs and tax collection into the hands of regional assemblies called *synedria*, the Greek term *synedrion* probably came to refer to the Jewish council during the Roman period. Traditionally the supreme legislative body in Greek cities had been a senate called either a *boule* (from the word for "counsel," "plan") or a *gerousia* (from the root for "elders"). The usage of these words overlaps in Greek literature, including in Josephus and the New Testament (Luke 23:50–4; Acts 5:21).

Rabbinic literature uses the Hebraized Greek term "Sanhedrin" sparingly to refer to the bodies of elders and leaders that functioned as both legislative councils and judicial courts. The more frequent Hebrew term found in the Mishnah is *bet din*, literally, "house of judgment." The great council in Jerusalem is called the *bet din hagadol*, "the great house of judgment."

of animal sacrifice, the fat and certain inner parts of the animal were burned on the altar, portions went to feed the priests, and flesh was eaten on the Temple property by the individual or family who had made the offering. Various grains and vegetables were also offered, with a small portion burned on the altar and the balance dedicated to the support of the priests. In some sacrifices wine was poured out at the base of the altar.

The Temple complex was a huge open space with the Temple building in the center, surrounded by storage and utility buildings. Around the perimeter of the Temple Mount stood colonnades and other buildings, surrounded by a massive wall with several strong gates. Thus the Temple was the last redoubt in the fortifications of Jerusalem as well as the city's administrative and judicial center. The Temple vessels, many of them made of gold and other precious metals, along with weapons for the defense of the Temple and city, a variety of foods to feed the priest, the paraphernalia of government, debt records, and the national treasury filled buildings and underground storerooms. Councils and courts met in various Temple chambers, and the leaders of the nation often conferred there, especially after the Romans took control of Herod's palace and the Antonia Fortress (at the northwest corner of the Temple compound) in the first century C.E.

The usual Roman requirement that all temples throughout the empire offer sacrifice to the emperor or to Roman gods as a sign of loyalty was adjusted to Jewish sensibilities in favor of a daily sacrifice offered for the welfare of the emperor and empire. To keep the priesthood compliant and to assert the empire's power, the Roman governor kept custody of the vestments worn by the high priest on the three pilgrimage festivals and the Day of Atonement (Yom Kippur). Only in 36 or 37 C.E. did the Roman governor of Syria, Vitellius, in order to win popular support, return the robes to Jewish custody.

C. Taxes

The Temple and priesthood were supported by biblically mandated agricultural tithes on produce of the land of Israel and by a half-shekel tax collected from every Jew in Israel and the Diaspora. The tithes

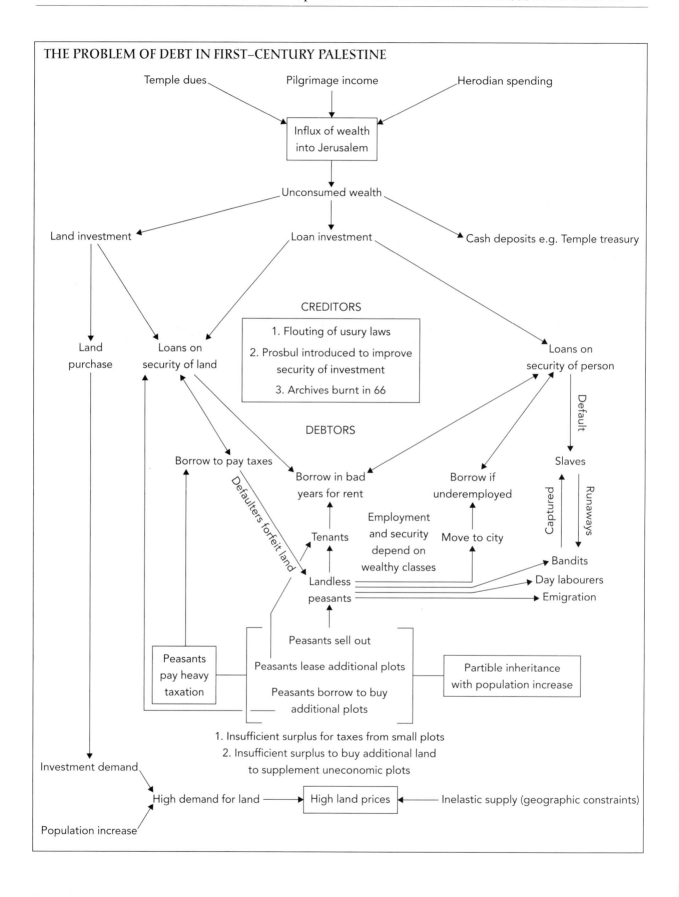

THE PROBLEM OF DEBT IN FIRST–CENTURY PALESTINE

Temple dues   Pilgrimage income   Herodian spending

Influx of wealth into Jerusalem

Unconsumed wealth

Land investment   Loan investment   Cash deposits e.g. Temple treasury

CREDITORS

1. Flouting of usury laws
2. Prosbul introduced to improve security of investment
3. Archives burnt in 66

Land purchase   Loans on security of land   Loans on security of person

DEBTORS

Borrow to pay taxes

Defaulters forfeit land

Default

Borrow in bad years for rent   Borrow if underemployed   Slaves

Tenants   Employment and security depend on wealthy classes   Move to city

Captured   Runaways

Landless peasants   Bandits   Day labourers   Emigration

Peasants pay heavy taxation

Peasants sell out

Peasants lease additional plots   Partible inheritance with population increase

Peasants borrow to buy additional plots

1. Insufficient surplus for taxes from small plots
2. Insufficient surplus to buy additional land to supplement uneconomic plots

Investment demand

Population increase

High demand for land ⟶ High land prices ⟵ Inelastic supply (geographic constraints)

Aerial view of the Temple Mount from the east. (BiblePlaces.com)

(one-tenth of the produce of a field, of new fruit, wine, etc.) were complex and changed over time. The first fruits of trees were to be brought to the Temple and the firstborn of animals were redeemed by money paid to the Temple. Proceeds from the agricultural tax were to be divided among the various levels of priests and Levites. Priests were further supported by the portions of sacrifices reserved for them, and the Temple benefited from benefactions regularly bestowed upon it by Jewish and foreign rulers. Under Roman rule, the Jerusalem leadership, led by the high priest, was responsible for collecting the yearly tribute and keeping social order.

According to Josephus (*War* 6.422), Cestius Gallus, the governor of Syria, took a census both to provide Nero with an accurate count of the population (for taxation purposes) and with the goal of encouraging the emperor to adopt conciliatory relations with his numerous Jewish subjects. Josephus does not give an explicit date for the enrollment, but the earliest date could be 63 C.E., when Gallus took office. Given the earlier census in 6 C.E., a slightly later date, suggesting a fifty-year recount, appears more likely to some scholars. Thus taxation too likely led to the outbreak of the Jewish Revolt, which resulted in the destruction of the Temple in 70 C.E., just as it did to the earlier skirmishes in Galilee. It certainly played a role during the revolt, when the Jewish population refused to surrender tax money to Rome. Agrippa II, for

"ZEALOTS" AND REBEL MOVEMENTS

First-century C.E. Palestine was rife with royal pretenders, messianic movements, prophetic figures, and rebellious brigands, many of whom are mentioned by Josephus. A shepherd named Athronges and a servant of Herod named Simon both claimed to be king and both led armed groups of bandits until finally defeated and captured (*Antiquities* 17.273–85). In the first century a prophet named Theudas (*Antiquities* 20.97–8; Acts 5:36) led followers toward the Jordan River, but Roman cavalry killed him and many of his group. In such an atmosphere, Roman and Jewish authorities who wished to keep civil order could easily see the leader of a popular movement, such as Jesus, as a threat, and decide to take steps to neutralize the threat.

The term "Zealot," as used by Josephus, refers to a coalition of popular resistance movements at the time of the revolt in 66 C.E. This coalition, which wrested control of Jerusalem from the aristocracy and priestly elders, promoted uncompromising resistance to Rome.

example, encouraged the Jews to pay the tax (*War* 2.404), and their refusal to do so explains the raiding of the Temple treasury by the governor Florus as the Jewish Revolt grew prior to Florus's removal in 66 C.E.

D. Resistance to Roman Rule

The presence of Roman garrisons in cities, the constraints created by Roman policy, the need to satisfy the Roman administration, and the burden of taxes put a severe and constant strain on Jewish society. Offensive Roman administrative practices and tactless governors frequently aggravated the situation. For example, when Judea became a Roman province in 6 C.E., the new Roman governor in Syria, Quirinius, and the new governor of Judea, Coponius, immediately conducted a census and registration of property in order to establish a tax base. This census was widely opposed, and only the mediation of High Priest Joazar son of Boethus prevented violence in Judea.

In response to the census and new taxes, a Galilean named Judas and a Pharisee named Saddok together led a revolt in which they encouraged the population to acknowledge only God as their ruler (*despotes*) and to refuse to pay tribute to Rome. This early rejection of Roman authority aroused rebellious feelings in many people and would provide the basis for later unrest (see *Jewish War* 2.119–66 and *Antiquities* 18.11–25).

According to Josephus, Judas the Galilean was "a teacher [*sophistes*] of his own school [*hairesis*]" (*War* 2.118), a fourth philosophy in addition to the three traditional "philosophies" of Judaism: the Pharisees, Sadducees, and Essenes. Because they were centuries old, nonrevolutionary, and respectable, Josephus recommended these three parties to his Roman audience and contrasted them with Judas's allegedly illegitimate innovation. Josephus describes this "fourth philosophy" as comparable to Pharisaic views regarding general beliefs but differing in its passion for liberty, its acceptance of God alone as ruler, and its revolutionary aims. Although Josephus disapproved strongly of resistance to the Romans, his account of Judas and his followers testifies to the uninterrupted tradition, dating back to the time of the Maccabees, of fidelity to God and resistance to Gentile powers that sought to limit Jewish belief, practice, and independence.

E. Sadducees and Pharisees

To establish Judiasm's dignity in the eyes of his Gentile readers, and in contrast to his description of the new fourth philosophy, Josephus describes the three traditional, ancient, and legitimate philosophies as a respectable and permanent part of Judaism. The Pharisees, Sadducees, and Essenes, along with many other groups, were active in Palestinian society during the first century C.E. The Essenes were deliberately separate from the political life of Jewish society. The Sadducees were mainly drawn from the governing class and had a small following among the people. Since the governing class acted according to Roman wishes and had great economic and political power over the people, the Sadducees' natural separation from the lower classes was intensified. Though many scholars have assumed that all the high priests and aristocrats were Sadducees, Josephus says only that the Sadducees were drawn from the upper classes. These very diverse groups such as the Pharisees and Sadducees were themselves split by factions and internal power struggles.

If Josephus is correct in presenting the Sadducees as a school of thought or philosophy, then they were probably a small group within the governing class with particular ideas about how Jewish life should be lived and the nation guided. Their view of God as wholly transcendent and not involved in human affairs may have derived from loss of confidence in the biblical promises of an active God providing security for the nation and an eternal dynasty. Continual invasion and subjugation of the governing class may have turned them from overt reliance on divine aid to dependence on human efforts in conducting human affairs, although in accordance with divine law. Such an outlook would fit their task of governing the nation in difficult times without prophetic or other divine guidance. Their denial of resurrection as a scriptural teaching and of the coming of God's kingdom is consistent with the governing class's emphasis on preserving the status quo in which they are in control and would explain their aversion to the apocalyptic resolution of history. Perhaps they also supported a special fidelity to Israel's ancient traditions in reaction against overly Hellenized and assimilationist members of the governing class. The balance between accommodating a foreign power and protecting a cultural tradition is difficult if not impossible to maintain, and it is likely that disagreements within the governing class would have spawned groups and movements, such as the Sadducees, with different understandings of Judaism.

The Pharisees had been an active political interest group from the mid-second century B.C.E. and continued to seek power and to exercise their influence during Herodian times. They encouraged the tithing of agricultural products by all Jews, observed biblical laws of ritual purity formerly restricted to the priests in the Temple, and kept the Sabbath especially holy as a way of living out their Judaism zealously. Their program required an intense commitment, which appealed to many. They had influenced John Hyrcanus's laws for a time in the second century B.C.E. and had exercised great domestic political power during the reign of Alexandra in the first century B.C.E. Like every other influential group, the Pharisees lost ground during the reign of Herod, though early on certain Pharisaic leaders were patronized by Herod and to some extent supported him. Late in Herod's reign, many Pharisees caught conspiring with Herod's sister-in-law to control the royal succession were executed.

The advent of direct Roman rule left less room for political maneuvering, so Josephus is silent about the Pharisees' activities in Jerusalem until he speaks of arrangements for war in 66 C.E., when several appear in various leadership capacities. Acts of the Apostles (23:6), a late-first-century C.E. work, places Pharisees in the Jerusalem *synedrion*. In the Synoptic Gospels the Pharisees appear mainly in Galilee as lower-level community authorities and officials, to some extent overlapping with the literate scribes. They would logically have been the ones to come in contact with Jesus, and it is their influence that he threatened. Only in Jerusalem, when Jesus was perceived as a danger by the highest authorities, did the chief priests and the rest of the governing class notice, oppose, and arrest him.

F. Governance

After the death of Caesar Augustus in 14 C.E., his stepson Tiberius, who had been exiled earlier and was made heir only after Augustus's earlier heirs had died, gained the throne. Tiberius stabilized the borders of the empire and established the empire on a sound fiscal footing. His earlier struggles with rival heirs had left him so suspicious that, in his effort to stabilize his rule, he executed many members of Rome's governing class. Spending the latter half of his reign as a recluse on the island of Capri, Tiberius ceded much of his authority to Sejanus, an equestrian whose power steadily rose until his execution in 31 C.E.

Pontius Pilate (appointed prefect in 26 C.E.), like all governors in the provinces, used his power to preserve Roman rule and to enrich himself; in both efforts he often acted with striking insensitivity to Jewish customs and laws. Since Sejanus was anti-Jewish, Pilate's challenges to Jewish customs may have been efforts to please his patron. Alternatively, they may have been typical policies reasonable to any arrogant governor unfamiliar with and uninterested in local custom.

During his first year as governor, Pilate sent his troops from Caesarea to Jerusalem for the winter and allowed them to take into their compound in the heavily fortified Herodian palace military standards depicting the bust of Caesar. Because images were forbidden in Jerusalem, especially images that were part of emperor worship, Roman governors had previously used standards without images. For several days a large number of Jews from Jerusalem protested this action in Caesarea. When Pilate surrounded the crowd with soldiers in the stadium, the faithful Jews volunteered to be martyred rather than accept the images in Jerusalem. This peaceful yet forceful demonstration finally caused Pilate to remove the images from Jerusalem.

The Cardo, or principal market street, in Jerusalem. (BiblePlaces.com)

In a more serious financial matter, Pilate refused to yield. He took money given to the Temple for sacrifices and used it to build an aqueduct to bring water to Jerusalem. Though the municipal planning was sound, the financing was blasphemous. When people thronged around Pilate's tribunal in protest, his soldiers, dressed as civilians in order to blend in with the crowd, beat the population into submission and killed many. Eventually, Pilate's insensitive policies, including his massacre of a group of Samaritans who were following their own prophet, prompted his recall to Rome in 36 or 37 C.E.

G. Galilee

Antipas successfully ruled Galilee in the north and Perea, the district east of the Jordan River, until he was removed from office in 39 C.E. Both areas were predominantly Jewish although separated geographically from one another by the Decapolis, a league of ten independent Greek cities with mostly non-Jewish populations.

Like his father, Antipas engaged in many building projects, including some that benefited the non-Jewish residents of his domain. Most significant were his rebuilding of Sepphoris as the capital of Galilee, his resettlement of the city with thoroughly Hellenized Jews as well as with non-Jews, and his construction of Tiberias. In 66 C.E. Sepphoris, loyal to Rome, refused to join the rebellion. By then Antipas's new capital, Tiberias, on the shore of the Sea of Galilee, had emerged as more important; built on a graveyard and featuring Hellensitic public buildings complete with images, the city was seen by many Jews as impure. Antipas had to settle the area with

Beth Natofa Valley, north of Sepphoris. (BiblePlaces.com)

foreigners and landless poor. Both Sepphoris and Tiberias grew to become relatively large cities of several thousand inhabitants.

Even though Sepphoris is only a few miles from Nazareth, none of the canonical Gospels depict Jesus as visiting either it or Tiberias. Instead, he is associated with small cities near the Sea of Galilee, such as Capernaum and Bethsaida. In these cities he met knowledgeable Jewish leaders such as the Pharisees, the Herodians (officials and supporters of Herod

Sheep grazing near Nazareth. This small village, founded in the third century B.C.E., was for centuries devoted wholly to agriculture. Archaeological investigation indicates that in the first century C.E. Nazareth had a probable population of several hundred. Located a few miles from Sepphoris, the Greco-Roman city that was for a time during Roman rule the governmental center of Galilee, Nazareth is mentioned neither by the Scriptures of Israel nor by Josephus. Caves and meeting rooms with Christian symbols date back to the fourth century C.E. Only in the fifth century C.E. were a large church and monastery built there; it became a Christian city of modest size and is today, with some sixty thousand inhabitants, the largest predominantly Arab city in Israel. (BiblePlaces.com)

Excavation of the foundations of basalt houses in Capernaum. (BiblePlaces.com)

Antipas; Mark 3:6), and Jewish elders such as Jairus, the ruler of the synagogue (Mark 5:22), as well as lower-level Roman officials such as the centurion in Capernaum (Matthew 8:5).

Galilean life centered on agriculture and fishing. Although only a small percentage of the population was literate, Galilee was not a rural backwater. The great Esdraelon Plain running through lower Galilee was a major trade

SYNAGOGUES

"Synagogue" represents the Greek word *synagoge* ("gathering together"), which became the term used by Josephus and the New Testament, and found in numerous inscriptions, for both the Jewish assembly and the building in which it met. Philo of Alexandria, Josephus, and Acts (16:13) also use the term "[house or place of] prayer" (*proseuche*) for Jewish assemblies. The synagogue probably began as a voluntary gathering that met in either private homes or public buildings for prayer, education, and the fostering of community life. In Judean and Galilean villages the town assembly for business and celebra-

tion was probably coextensive with the assembly for prayer on Sabbaths and holidays. The same prominent and (more or less) learned leaders and patrons who directed the community probably led the synagogue. Synagogues were led by "synagogue leaders" such as Jairus (Mark 5:22) rather than by Pharisees or "Rabbis" in the technical sense known from the Mishnah and later Rabbinic documents.

Throughout the Mediterranean world, synagogue buildings have been found in abundance from the third century C.E. on. First-century C.E. synagogues were assembly halls

but lack some of the distinctive architectural and decorative features, such as Torah niches, associated with later synagogues dedicated to worship and study.

The Rabbis gained power as synagogue leaders only during the Talmudic period (third to sixth centuries C.E.). Synagogue inscriptions from the Diaspora list the most common titles for officials as "head of the synagogue" or "synagogue leader" (*archisynagogos*; a few inscriptions present the term in the feminine, indicating that women held leadership roles in these institutions), "leader" (*archon*), and "scribe."

JOHN THE BAPTIST IN JOSEPHUS

Josephus stresses the political unrest John the Baptist caused as the reason for John's execution by Herod Antipas. His praise of John's message fits his concern to present Judaism as a virtuous way of life; his failure to condemn John's execution is consistent with his opposition to anyone who might disturb civil order.

> Herod put him to death, though he was a good man and had exhorted the Jews to lead righteous lives, to practice justice towards their fellows and piety towards God, and so doing to join in baptism. In his view this was a necessary preliminary if baptism was to be acceptable to God. They must not employ it to gain pardon for whatever sins they committed, but as a consecration of the body implying that the soul was already thoroughly cleansed by right behavior. When others too joined the crowds about him, because they were aroused [variant: *overjoyed*] to the highest degree by hearing his words, Herod became alarmed. Eloquence that had so great an effect on mankind might lead to some form of sedition [variant: *revolt*], for it looked as if they would be guided by John in everything that they did. Herod decided therefore that it would be much better to strike first and be rid of him before his work led to an uprising, than to wait for an upheaval, get involved in a difficult situation and see his mistake. Though John, because of Herod's suspicions, was brought in chains to Machaerus, the stronghold that we have previously mentioned, and there was put to death, yet the verdict of the Jews was that the destruction visited upon Herod's army [by Aretas, the Arab king] was a vindication of John, since God saw fit to inflict such a blow on Herod. (*Antiquities* 18.116–19)

route between the coast and Syria, and the Jewish villages of Galilee were within a day's walk of many local Greek enclaves as well as the great coastal trade cities. The physical evidence recovered by archaeologists shows that trade with the rest of the empire was lively and constant. Galilee exported wine and olive oil and imported luxury goods for the rich. However, the archaeological evidence also reveals that rural Galilee was for the most part thoroughly Jewish: the villages yield few if any signs of Gentile habitation (e.g., pig bones, evidence of the worship of foreign gods) and they provide clear indicators of Jewish practices, such as the presence of ritual baths, and vessels for washing hands and dishes according to Judaic custom.

The leaders of Galilee, especially Herod Antipas and members of his family and court, were members of the governing class of the empire, who traveled frequently, maintained complex political and personal relations with the emperor and his court, and engaged in personal affairs that had political repercussions. Josephus recounts (*Antiquities* 18.109–24) that Antipas, on a journey to Rome, visited his half-brother Herod, son of Mariamme, and fell in love with that Herod's wife, Herodias, who was Antipas's niece. Mark 6:17 identifies Herodias's husband as Herod Philip, the ruler of the areas to the northeast of the Sea of Galilee. Antipas and Herodias wanted to divorce their own spouses and marry each other; that caused Antipas's wife, the daughter of the Nabatean king Aretas, to return to her father. The ill will from this incident eventually prompted Aretas to sieze some boundary territory from Antipas in 36 C.E.; Antipas resisted the incursion, but Aretas defeated his troops decisively. Josephus goes on to suggest that Herod's defeat was divine punishment for his execution of John the Baptist. The emperor Tiberius ordered the Syrian governor, Vitellius, to punish Aretas, a task he reluctantly undertook and quickly dropped when Tiberius died in 37 C.E. While the Gospels suggest that Herod executed John because of the Baptist's condemnation of his marriage to Herodias, Josephus states that Herod made a preemptive strike against the popular leader, lest his teaching lead the crowd to rebellion.

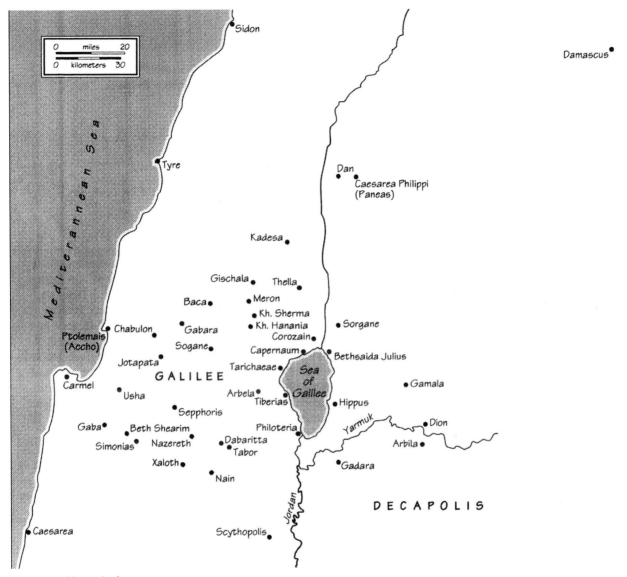

Map XVI. Galilee in the first century C.E.

The Gospels also mention that Herod Antipas was apprehensive about the growing reputation of Jesus and associated him with the movement of John the Baptist, whom he had executed (Mark 6:14). According to Luke, Herod wished to execute Jesus (13:31) and finally met him when he was arrested in Jerusalem (23:7–12). Though the reliability of Luke's account is disputed, the report of Herod's concern about Jesus as a potential threat to the civic peace is plausible.

Antipas's end as ruler came when his wife urged him to request the new emperor, Gaius Caligula, to promote him from tetrarch to king. Rivals, including Agrippa I – Herodias's brother who had attained the title "king" for himself – cast doubt on Antipas's loyalty to the emperor. Caligula banished Antipas to Gaul, and Herodias accompanied her husband into exile.

JESUS IN JOSEPHUS

Since Josephus frequently describes popular leaders who caused social unrest and were executed, his reference to Jesus is not anomalous. Unexpected, however, is his assertion that Jesus is the Messiah and that he was raised from the dead. In no other place in his copious writings, including his autobiography, does Josephus endorse or describe Christian beliefs. Complicating the authenticity of the passage further: extant copies of Josephus's *Antiquities of the Jews* were preserved by the Church (the earliest copy dating to the eleventh century); Arabic versions lack the passage (although pious Muslims might have removed the reference to the death and resurrection); and citations of Josephus from the Church fathers prior to the fourth century do not cite this passage. Consequently, it is likely that the passage in its present form, called the *Testimonium Flavianuum*

or the *Testimony of Flavius [Josephus]*, was inserted into this section of the *Antiquities* either in part or in full by a Christian copyist.

At about this time lived Jesus, a wise man, if indeed one might call him a man. For he was one who accomplished surprising feats and was a teacher of such people as accept the truth with pleasure. He won over many Jews and many of the Greeks. He was the Messiah. When Pilate, upon an indictment brought by the principal men among us, condemned him to the cross, those who had loved him from the very first did not cease to be attached to him. On the third day he appeared to them restored to life, for the holy prophets had foretold this and myriads of other marvels concerning him. And the tribe of the Christians, so called after him, has to this day still not disappeared. (*Antiquities* 18.63–4)

H. The Jesus Movement

The tenor of Jesus' teachings preserved in the Gospels suggests, with allowance made for editing as the first century went on, that Jesus stressed care for the poor and needy, reliance on God, reconciliation in social relations, nonviolent response to provocation, forgiveness of debts, and de-emphasis on human authority and honor. His followers eschewed biological and marital relations in favor of the family of faith: according to Mark 3:31–5, when Jesus' mother and brothers and sisters seek to see him, he looks at the group sitting around him and announces: "Here are my mother and my brothers. Whoever does the will of God is my brother and sister and mother." Anticipating the imminent manifestation of the kingdom of God, Jesus and this new family of disciples lived as if they were already a part of it.

A healer and exorcist as well as a gifted teacher, Jesus quickly attracted crowds, and so too the attention of Antipas and, later, of the authorities in Jerusalem. As Josephus's account of John the Baptist indicates, to gather crowds and speak about a coming kingdom would be perceived by the governing authorities as a political challenge. That some of Jesus' followers hailed him as a king, in the line of King David, confirmed for Herod Antipas in Galilee, the chief priests in Jerusalem, and the Roman governor Pilate that Jesus was a threat to the Roman-supported state, especially after he interfered in the operation of the Temple.

VII. MID-FIRST-CENTURY C.E. CRISES

After Pontius Pilate's governorship ended in 36 or 37 C.E., tensions between the Jews and Rome continued to increase over economic, political, and religious issues. The most serious crisis in the next decade was caused by the Roman emperor who replaced Tiberius, Gaius Caligula (37–41 C.E.). Gaius took emperor worship seriously, and when Jews in Jamnia, near the

Palestinian coast, tore down an altar to the emperor, he ordered a statue of himself placed in the Jerusalem Temple in reprisal. All responsible officials – including Herod the Great's grandson Agrippa I, who was in Rome at the time of the crisis; Petronius, the Roman governor in Syria; representatives of the Alexandrian Jewish community; and the Jerusalem leadership – knew that transporting the statue to Jerusalem would lead to a revolt with unimaginable slaughter. Eventually Agrippa convinced Gaius to revoke his order. However, Gaius secretly planned to bring a statue to the Temple when he visited Jerusalem. His plans were annulled only by his assassination.

Gaius's contempt for the Jews became manifest also in his dealings with the Alexandrian community. Perhaps at the emperor's instigation, Alexandrian crowds responded to a visit of Agrippa I in 38 C.E. with insults, and they bullied the governor, Flaccus, into placing statues of the emperor in Jewish houses of prayer, curtailing Jewish rights, and sanctioning a general persecution in which Jews were robbed, forced to break their laws, and killed in great numbers. Thirty-eight members of the Jewish council of elders were publicly flogged in the theater. Philo, the great Alexandrian Jewish writer, wrote extensive protests against this outrage. Flaccus, who was not in good graces with Gaius, was soon exiled and replaced by Pollio. How fiercely the Jews were oppressed in the next two years is not clear, but in 40 C.E. the Alexandrian Jewish community and government sent embassies to present their cases to the emperor in Rome. After long delays and poor treatment by the emperor, the Jewish delegation was dismissed. Only when Claudius succeeded Gaius in 41 C.E. was the situation resolved by the reinstatement of traditional Jewish privileges and by the execution of the Alexandrian officials who had instigated the strife.

Under Claudius, matters briefly improved in Judea as well. Instead of installing a Roman governor, Claudius appointed Agrippa I, who had already been appointed by Gaius ruler of Galilee, king over Judea and Samaria. Though Agrippa had been constantly in debt from dissolute and luxurious living and had gotten into various political troubles, in Palestine he observed Jewish law, governed tactfully, and was therefore remembered as a good ruler. Outside Palestine he continued the practice of his grandfather Herod in giving donations to Hellenistic temples and games. Death ended his reign in 44 C.E., and his son, Agrippa II, was too young to succeed him immediately.

After Agrippa's death, a succession of Roman procurators resumed direct control over all of Palestine. Many were bad administrators who treated the people unjustly and inflamed their passions with culturally repugnant acts. Both banditry and armed insurrection increased in Judea and Galilee. Organized bands, some sparked by messianic fervor, occasionally protested directly or symbolically the reigning governmental and social system. For example, an Egyptian claiming to be a prophet led a large group into the desert with the promise that upon their return to the Mount of Olives, the walls of Jerusalem would collapse and the Roman garrison suffer defeat; Acts 21:38 mentions this leader, and Josephus gives a fuller version of the story.

PHILO'S *EMBASSY TO GAIUS*

The Alexandrian Jewish philosopher and biblical interpreter Philo (who lived between ca. 20 B.C.E. and ca. 50 C.E.) was a member of the legation of Alexandrian Jews who presented the grievances of their community to Emperor Gaius Caligula in 40 C.E.. Gaius treated the ambassadors poorly and postponed meeting them. While waiting, they were informed of Gaius's plan to place a statue of himself as a god in the Jerusalem Temple. As described by Philo in his *Embassy to Gaius* (written shortly after Caligula's death in 41 C.E.), the ambassadors' reactions reveal how abhorrent this sacrilege was to them. The person bringing the news to the embassy asks:

> "Have you heard the new tidings?" and when he was going to report it, he was brought up short, as a flood of tears streamed from his eyes. He began again and the second time stopped short and so too a third time. . . . He managed with difficulty while sobbing and breathing spasmodically to say, "Our temple is lost, Gaius has ordered a colossal statue to be set up within the inner sanctuary dedicated to himself under the name of Zeus." As we marveled at his words and, petrified by consternation, could not get any further, since we stood there speechless and turned to water, others appeared bringing the same woeful tale. (186–9)

Gaius's motive for ordering the statue placed in the Temple is revealed in his conversation with King Agrippa I, his client and friend:

> [Gaius] said "Your excellent and worthy fellow-citizens, who alone of every race of men do not acknowledge Gaius as a god, appear to be courting even death by their recalcitrance. When I ordered a statue of Zeus to be set up in the temple they marshaled their whole population and issued forth from the city and country nominally to make a petition but actually to counteract my orders." He was about to add further charges when Agrippa in deep distress turned every kind of color, blood-red, dead pale and livid all in a moment. And by now from the crown of his head to his feet he was mastered by a fit of shuddering, every part and every limb convulsed with trembling and palpitation. With his nervous system relaxed and unbraced he was in a state of utter collapse, and finally thus paralyzed was on the point of falling. But some of the bystanders caught him and . . . took him home on a stretcher, quite unconscious in his coma of the mass of troubles which had fallen upon him. Gaius indeed was still more exasperated and pushed his hatred of the nation still further. "If Agrippa," he said, "who is my dearest and most familiar friend and bound to me by so many benefactions, is so under the dominion of its customs that he cannot even bear to hear a word against them and is prostrated almost to the point of death, what must we expect of the others who are not under the influence of any counter-acting force?" (265–8)

A. Literary Responses to Roman Oppression in the First Century

The increasing hostility toward Rome, social unrest in the face of an unjust government, and cultural frustration with corrosive Hellenistic practices fostered the mood of apocalyptic expectation reflected in early Gospel traditions and in Paul's letters as well as nourishing those traditions in Jewish literature. Apocalyptic literature looks for a solution to the massive evils of the present by direct divine intervention in the near future and by a radical and comprehensive reform in social relationships. These aspirations can be felt in the Similitudes (or Parables) of Enoch, chapters 37–71 of *1 Enoch* (the *Ethiopic Book of Enoch*). A reference to the Parthian invasion in 40 B.C.E. (*1 Enoch* 56:5–8) puts the Similitudes after the middle of the first century B.C.E. Its obsession with the powerful rulers of the earth fits well into the mid–first century C.E.

KING HEROD AGRIPPA I

Agrippa I (who lived between 10 B.C.E. and 44 C.E.), a grandson of Herod the Great, was sent to Rome to be educated with the highest echelon of Roman society. He was a close friend of the future emperor, Gaius Caligula, who made Agrippa king in 37 C.E. As a young man he was a spendthrift, constantly in debt and even jailed briefly by Tiberius. At one point, during a trip to Alexandria, Tiberius Julius Alexander (nephew of the philosopher Philo and the future governor of Palestine) provided money to Agrippa' wife to cover the future Jewish king's expenses. Agrippa would later marry his daughter Berenice into Tiberius's family.

When Gaius became emperor in 37 C.E., he gave Agrippa wealth, and the rule of Galilee and areas to the north. When Claudius replaced Gaius (41 C.E.) – Agrippa having played a substantial role in ensuring Claudius's succession – he added Samaria and Judea to Agrippa's rule. Agrippa ruled well and for the most part in accordance with Jewish law for three years; he died in 44 C.E.

According to Acts 12, Agrippa I beheaded James the son of Zebedee and imprisoned Peter. Both Acts and Josephus mention that Agrippa was hailed as a god. Acts 12:21–3 reports: "On an appointed day, Herod put on his royal robes, took his seat on the platform, and delivered a public address to [the people of Tyre and Sidon]. The people kept shouting, 'The voice of a god, and not of a mortal!' And immediately, because he had not given the glory to God, an angel of the Lord struck him down, and he was eaten by worms and died."

Josephus remarks that in Caesarea, "Herod put on a garment made wholly of silver, and of a truly wonderful texture, and came into the theater early in the morning; at which time the silver of his garment was illuminated by the fresh reflection of the sun's rays upon it. It shone out after a surprising manner, and was so resplendent as to spread a horror over those that looked intently upon it. At that moment, his flatterers cried out [. . .] that he was a god, and they added, 'Be thou merciful to us; for although we have hitherto reverenced thee only as a man, yet shall we henceforth own thee as superior to moral nature.'" Viewing an owl and recognizing it as an ill omen, Agrippa is beset with violent stomach pains and shortly thereafter dies, "being in the fifty-fourth year of his age, and in the seventh year of his reign" (*Antiquities* 19.343–50).

The Similitudes of Enoch provide hope for a society suffering continuing oppression and powerlessness. The faithful believers who were enduring economic and political evils were assured of a secure special destiny in a divinely founded society. In the face of Roman military might and undisputed sovereignty, the author turns to divine revelation derived from Enoch's journey to heaven and secret knowledge of the universe given by heavenly mediators. The three Similitudes that convey this revelation provide models for understanding the workings of the universe and human history. For example, references to the punishment of angels and Noah's flood (*1 Enoch* 39, 54) foreshadow the punishment of the earthly leaders and the overthrow of evil.

The first parable begins with the main themes of the work:

When the congregation of the righteous shall appear,
And sinners shall be judged for their sins,
And shall be driven from the face of the earth;
And when the Righteous One shall appear before the eyes
    of the righteous,
Whose works hang upon the Lord of Spirits,
And light shall appear to the righteous and the elect who dwell on
    the earth,
Where then will be the dwelling of the sinners,

THE "RIGHTEOUS" AND JEWISH FACTIONS

The years between the Maccabean revolt ca. 167 B.C.E. and the end of Bar Kosiba's bid for political autonomy in 135 C.E. can be characterized as a period of radical diversity within Jewish society. A number of competing factions, which often viewed one another with suspicion if not contempt, expressed themselves through literary polemic: the Dead Sea Scrolls, *1 Enoch*, the *Psalms of Solomon*, and the late-first-century C.E. documents *2 Baruch*, *4 Ezra*, and the Gospels according to Matthew and John are among the texts from this period that exemplify such factionalism.

This literature employs epithets such as "lawless," "hypocrites," "corrupt," and "godless" to describe the authors' enemies. Conversely, the group employing the harsh language thinks of itself as the "righteous," the "faithful and lawful," "a remnant," and "God's true people." Because of the conventionality of the language, it is often difficult to determine the exact social circumstances underlying the polemic and even more difficult to sift historical details from rhetorical hyperbole.

And where the resting place of those who have denied the Lord
    of Spirits?
It had been good for them if they had not been born.
When the secrets of the righteous shall be revealed and the sinners
    judged,
And the godless driven from the presence of the righteous and
    elect,
From that time those that possess the earth shall no longer be
    powerful and exalted;
And they shall not be able to behold the face of the holy,
For the Lord of Spirits has caused his light to appear
On the face of the holy, righteous, and elect.
Then shall the kings and the mighty perish
And be given into the hands of the righteous and holy.

(1 Enoch 38:1–5)

This view of society is fundamental to the text's understanding of the cosmos. The world is divided between the chosen, faithful, good people, and the evil majority led by society's elite. The main accusation against the opponents of the righteous, that they have denied the Lord of Spirits (a frequent title for God in the Similitudes), could pertain to non-Jews as well as assimilated Jews. The solution to the present unjust political order will be an appearance of God to effect the destruction of the mighty rulers of this world (e.g., *1 Enoch* 46, 48), so that the righteous will be vindicated (50–1) and both evil angels and evil humans punished (53–4).

In the climactic scene, reminiscent of Matthew's parable of the sheep and goats (Matthew 25:31–46), a figure called the Son of Man and identified with Enoch judges the world, rewards the righteous, and punishes the evil kings. The author envisions a resurrection of the just (61:5) and the renewal of the earth under divine rule (51:4–5).

B. Diaspora Responses to Roman Rule

1. *Fourth Maccabees*

Hostility to the Romans and conflict with Hellenistic culture were not limited to Jews living in Judea or Galilee. Jews living in other parts of the Roman Empire faced not only constant pressure to assimilate but also occasional persecution, as already noted in the case of first-century C.E. Alexandria. In several first-century Jewish works the authors express the difficulty of living as a Jew in the Diaspora even as they seek to adapt Hellenistic modes of thought and life to support and promote Jewish values, history, and practices.

Fourth Maccabees is a paean to philosophical reason that uses stories of martyrdom found in 2 Maccabees as points of illustration. The retelling of the martyrdom of Eleazar and of the mother and her seven sons reflects continuing Jewish uneasiness with the surrounding culture and keen awareness of proximate hostility. The highly detailed and rhetorically flamboyant descriptions of the tortures inflicted on the martyrs and the numerous exhortations and apologetic speeches exchanged among the characters create an intense emotional atmosphere even as they, ironically, promote the control of passion.

The thesis of *4 Maccabees*, that the passions must be ruled by reason, derives from Platonism and Stoicism and was part of popular Greek philosophy in the East. According to this philosophical perspective, reason is governed by the virtue of prudence, which in turn governs the passions through justice, temperance, and courage. The martyrs argue that fidelity to the Law accords with reason, and they refute rational arguments that urge them to abandon the Jewish way of life (*4 Maccabees* 5:7ff.; 8:16–26). Indeed, they argue for the reasonableness of Jewish tradition, including the dietary restrictions and other customs that kept Greeks and Jews apart. Thus to Antiochus's charge that the refusal to eat nonkosher meat is irrational, Eleazar answers:

> Do not suppose that it would be a petty sin if we were to eat defiling food; to transgress the law in matters either small or great is of equal seriousness, for in either case the law is equally despised. You scoff at our philosophy as though living by it were irrational, but it teaches us self-control, so that we master all pleasures and desires, and it also trains us in courage, so that we endure any suffering willingly; it instructs us in justice, so that in all our dealings we act impartially, and it teaches us piety, so that with proper reverence we worship the only real God. (*4 Maccabees* 5:19–24)

The presentation of Law as philosophy and the argument that commitment to Law is an exercise of the key Stoic virtues of self-control, courage, and justice insist that the Jewish way of life is not only acceptable but necessary for Hellenized Jews pressured by an alien environment. Though the author makes use of Stoic and Platonic ideas, the text's fundamental values are Jewish and founded on adherence to biblical law. Many particulars of the teaching remain Jewish – for example, the insistence that the passions are naturally good and to be controlled (2:22), contrary to some Stoic teaching to the effect that they are to be eradicated.

Even the final reward of the martyrs, immortality, is drawn from Greek thought: "O sacred and harmonious concord of the seven brothers on behalf of religion! None of the seven youths proved coward or shrank from death, but all of them, as though running the course toward immortality, hastened to death by torture" (*4 Maccabees* 14:4–5). In a more distinctively Jewish vein the author also notes that the martyrs atone for Israel's sins by their blood: Eleazar prays: "You know, O God, that though I might have saved myself, I am dying in burning torments for the sake of the Law. Be merciful to your people, and let our punishment suffice for them. Make my blood their purification, and take my life in exchange for these" (*4 Maccabees* 6:27–9).

The author's attitude toward Hellenistic civilization is complex. Though the stories of martyrdom bespeak hostility and estrangement between

DIVINE WISDOM

The figure of Lady Wisdom is a personification of God's wisdom, intermediate between a personality and an abstraction. In Proverbs 1–9, Lady Wisdom (Hebrew *Chokhmah*; Greek *Sophia*) plays a strong role in creation and in leading the young student to understanding and a good life. This tradition continued in Ben Sira and was picked up by the author of the Wisdom of Solomon. Along with these sources, *ma'at* in traditional Egyptian religion and Isis in Hellenistic religion seem to have influenced the Wisdom of Solomon's picture of Lady Wisdom as a wise and merciful benefactress. The figure of Lady Wisdom eventually merges with the Jewish tradition of the Shekinah, the presence (literally, "dwelling"; the term is grammatically feminine) of God among the people Israel; it also influences early Christian understandings of both the Holy Spirit ("Spirit" is feminine in Hebrew [*Ruach*], although neuter in Greek [*Pneuma*]) and the Virgin Mary.

Greco-Roman and Jewish culture, the author envisions only the punishment of the offending king, not the destruction of Hellenistic society or the apocalyptic rule of Israel over the world. According to the text, the persecutions of Antiochus were preceded by a period of friendly relations between Jews and Greeks (*4 Maccabees* 3:19–21), and a return to that state is desired. Most striking, the author defends Judaism against Greco-Roman culture and political power by writing a Greek diatribe that unites Greek philosophy and Jewish traditions into a Greek rhetorical exhortation whose purpose is to preserve Jewish identity from assimilation to Greek culture. Probably written in Syria, perhaps in the major cultural center, Antioch, in the first century C.E., *4 Maccabees* may have been recited at a yearly festival in honor of Jewish martyrs (*4 Maccabees* 1:10).

2. The Wisdom of Solomon

The Wisdom of Solomon, written in excellent Greek by an anonymous author in the later first century B.C.E. or the early first century C.E. (the intensity of the persecution in chapter 5 perhaps reflecting the Alexandrian persecutions of 38–41 C.E.), exhorts the Jewish community of Alexandria to fidelity, for "The righteous live forever and their reward is with the Lord" (5:15). Utilizing the biblical wisdom tradition as its central theme, the text draws on many other biblical traditions in its argument and exposition. It opens with an appeal to the rulers of the earth to love righteousness and with a description of Wisdom (rather than the Son of Man, as in the Similitudes of *1 Enoch*) as the judge of evil. The first five chapters employ apocalyptic traditions to portray the fate of the innocent sufferer who is persecuted by unjust and powerful men. Eventually "the righteous man will stand with great confidence in the presence of those who have afflicted him. . . . When they see him they will be shaken with dreadful fear and they will be amazed at his unexpected salvation" (Wisdom of Solomon 5:1–2). The description of Wisdom in chapters 6–9 links obedience to Wisdom's teaching with attaining immortality: "Giving heed to [Wisdom's] laws is assurance of immortality, and immortality brings one near to God" (6:19; see also 2:23). Immortality, the Greek conception that envisions the survival of the soul but not the body, functions here, as it does in 2 Maccabees and *4 Maccabees*, as an alternative to resurrection of the body and exaltation of the blessed.

Along with Greek philosophical terminology and rhetorical strategies, Greek ideas also permeate the author's discourse about fidelity to Judaism. After describing Lady Wisdom and her invitation to humanity, drawn mainly from biblical models, the Wisdom of Solomon invokes Greek categories:

> For in her [Wisdom] there is a spirit that is intelligent, holy, unique, manifold, subtle, mobile, clear, unpolluted, distinct, invulnerable, loving the good, keen, irresistible, beneficent, humane, steadfast, sure, free from anxiety, all-powerful, overseeing all, and penetrating through all spirits that

PSEUDO-PHOCYLIDES

Pseudonymously attributed to the sixth-century B.C.E. Ionic poet Phocylides, this is a 230-line Jewish-philosophical work dated sometime in the first century either B.C.E. or C.E. It is informed by both the Septuagint and by Stoic ethics, and it highlights those biblical commandments that Gentiles would find congenial. The wisdom is generally practical:

> Moderation is the best of all, and excesses are grievous. (36)
>
> The love of money is the mother of all evil. (42)
>
> Do not be harsh with your children, but be gentle, and if a child offends against you, let the mother cut her son down to size or else the elders of the family or the chiefs of the people. (208–9)
>
> Purifications are for the purity of the soul, not of the body. (228)

are intelligent and pure and most subtle. For Wisdom is more mobile than any motion; because of her pureness she pervades and penetrates all things. For she is a breath of the power of God, and a pure emanation of the glory of the Almighty; therefore nothing defiled gains entrance into her. For she is a reflection of eternal light, a spotless mirror of the working of God, and an image of his goodness. (Wisdom of Solomon 7:22–6)

This document also applies the Platonic philosophy of emanations and of type and archetype to Wisdom in order to make her the Jewish equivalent of the best of Greek thought.

In the last half of the book (chapters 10–19) history is interpreted as Wisdom's activity among humans. The author consoles fellow Jews with examples of God's mercy to Israel in contrast to the punishment meted out to the Egyptians according to the Book of Exodus. The sin of the Egyptians is dramatized by a long polemic against idolatry (13:1–15:17), which reflects a rejection of numerous aspects of the surrounding culture even while the text uses Greek language, rhetoric, and argument to make its case.

3. Philo of Alexandria

Philo of Alexandria typifies the creative tensions that beset Judaism in the Roman Empire. His family was prominent and wealthy. His brother, Alexander, was a high official in charge of customs collection; Alexander's son, Tiberius Julius Alexander, became a high Roman official, assisted Agrippa I financially, gave his son in marriage to Agrippa's daughter, held the post of governor of Judea in the years succeeding Agrippa's death, and even assisted the Romans in the siege of Jerusalem. In his old age, Philo was part of the delegation sent by the Alexandrian Jewish community to Gaius Caligula in 40 C.E. to seek relief from persecution. The Jewish community to which he belonged was very large, with numerous houses of prayer and great influence. Though Jews were not full citizens of Alexandria, the Jewish community was a recognized political entity with legal rights, an organized leadership, and substantial internal control.

Philo's voluminous writings are typical of the Alexandrian mode of philosophical thought and textual interpretation. Promoting a philosophical interpretation of the Bible and Jewish traditions, in commentary after commentary Philo used allegory to harmonize biblical materials with Greek philosophy; his philosophical treatises integrated biblical and philosophical principles, especially those of the middle Platonists and Stoics. In his apologetic writings Philo defended Judaism against misunderstandings common in the Roman world.

Philo's transposition of the biblical tradition into Greek philosophy goes deeper than the moral exhortation of *4 Maccabees*, yet it also promotes fidelity to biblical law and the Jewish way of life. The simple statement that "Abraham went [to the Promised Land] as the Lord commanded him" (Genesis 12:4) becomes for Philo the adoption of a philosophical calling:

"Abraham went as the Lord commanded him." And this is the end which is celebrated among those who study philosophy in the best manner, namely, to live in accordance with nature. And this takes place when the mind, entering into the path of virtue, treads in the steps of right reason, and follows God, remembering his commandments, and at all times and in all places confirming them both by word and deed; for "he went as the Lord commanded him." And the meaning of this is, as God commands (and he commands in a beautiful and praiseworthy manner), in that very manner does the virtuous man act, guiding the path of his life in a blameless way, so that the actions of the wise man are in no respect different from the divine commands. (*On the Migration of Abraham* 23:127–9)

This exegesis is neither arbitrary nor unreasonable. It is based on a Platonic epistemology that searches for the unseen and inner basis of visible reality. In response to God's call and blessing (Genesis 12:1–3), Abraham leaves Haran and transports his family to an alien land. In so doing he initiates a new people and a new way of life, and affirms two basic principles of Judaism: faith in God and obedience to divine commands. Implicit in Abraham's obedience is the reception of new knowledge about God and how to live, knowledge revealed subsequently to Moses. Thus, from Philo's perspective, Abraham's act is symbolic of the commitment to a philosophical way of life.

Using Greek philosophy to expound and defend Jewish tradition, Philo associates God's wisdom and activity with *logos*, a key philosophical concept that combines reason, understanding, and the rational order of the universe. Thus Philo would have agreed with the opening phrase in the Gospel of John, "In the beginning was the *Logos*." Abraham becomes for Philo an example of right reason in action.

Philo's description of the persecutions against the Alexandrian community, which testifies to his personal experience of these atrocities, rivals *3* and *4 Maccabees* in rhetorical intensity and descriptive detail. His concentration on the reward of virtue and the punishment to be visited on Flaccus, the Roman governor who conducted the persecutions, also shows views similar to those of *4 Maccabees*. Finally, Philo's description of the Therapeutae and Therapeutrides, a group of celibate Jews, male and female, who gather together for

THE THERAPEUTAE AND THERAPEUTRIDES

Philo of Alexandria's *De vita contemplativa* (On the Contemplative Life) describes an ascetic community of Jewish men and women located on the shore of Lake Mareotis outside of Alexandria. After describing the Essenes, Philo mentions a philosophical group who, "with strict regard to etymology . . . are called *therapeutae* and *therapeutrides*. . . . Out of their yearning after the immortal and blessed life, they esteem their mortal life to have already ended, and so leave their possessions to their sons or daughters, or, in default of them, to other kinsmen, of their own free will leaving to these their heritage in advance; but, if they have no kinsmen, to their comrades and friends. . . . So soon, then, as they have divested themselves of their properties, without allowing anything further to ensnare them, they flee without turning back, having abandoned brethren, children, wives, parents, all the throng of their kindred, all their friendships and companions, yes, their countries in which they were born and bred. . . ." Living in simple dwellings, they have in each house "a holy room, which is called the sanctuary and monastery; because in it they celebrate all alone the mysteries of the holy life, bringing nothing into it, neither drink, nor food, nor any other of the things necessary for the wants to the body; but only the Law and the oracles delivered under inspiration by the prophets along with the Psalms, and the other books by means of which religion and sound knowledge grow together in a perfect whole." (*On the Contemplative Life* 1.2, 2.11, 18–3.25) communal meals and common worship, resembles the descriptions of Greek philosophical groups, the Essenes, and the early church as presented in the first chapters of Acts.

VIII. THE JEWISH WORLD AFTER THE FALL OF JERUSALEM

A. The Wars Against Rome

The last third of the first century C.E. and the first third of the second century saw Jews from Judea and Galilee as well as the Diaspora engage in a series of military conflicts with the Roman government. For the Romans such periodic wars were expected crises in imperial administration, and the Jewish rebellions, like others, were put down with military might and calculated destruction. In the first war with Rome (usually dated 66–70 C.E., ignoring both the run up to and the aftermath of the conflict), Jerusalem and the Temple were destroyed and Judaism lost any vestige of priestly self-government. That this subjection to the Roman Empire was not meekly accepted is shown by the widespread uprising of Jewish communities in the eastern Mediterranean (115–17 C.E.) and the second war against the Romans, the Bar Kokhba (or Bar Kosiba) revolt (132–5 C.E.), that devastated Judea and consequently prompted the center of Palestinian Judaism to move to Galilee.

1. The First Revolt

During the venal rule of the Roman procurator Felix (52–60 C.E.) popular resentment and resistance to Roman government intensified. Felix, a freedman (a former slave, legally free but still serving his former master) of the imperial household whose brother, Pallas, was a high official, was known for his political corruption. Despite the fact that he married Drusilla, the daughter of Agrippa I and sister of Agrippa II, he was also known for his insensitivity to Jewish concerns. During his tenure, banditry and protest movements increased throughout Judea. According to the Book of Acts, Felix met with Paul, who had been arrested by the Roman Jerusalem garrison and accused by Temple authorities of fomenting unrest. Acts 24:26 notes that Felix "hoped that money would be given to him by Paul, and for that reason he used to send for him often and converse with him." Two years later, Paul was still in jail. The next governor, Festus, after consulting with Agrippa II, sent Paul to Rome for trial.

The governorship of Festus, a generally ineffective leader, was marked by the rise of the Sicarii (*sicarius* is Latin for "dagger," hence "dagger-men"). Their practice was to assassinate both Romans in Jerusalem and their Jewish

---

THE ANTONIA FORTRESS

The tower, or fortress, Antonia, was built at the northwest corner of the wall enclosing the Temple Mount. The Hasmoneans had built the original fort (the Baris) there because the level land leading up to the walls needed stronger defenses. Herod luxuriously rebuilt it and named it for his patron, Mark Antony. In the first century C.E. the Antonia was a key military installation from which the Romans could observe the activities within Jerusalem's strongest fortification, the Temple enclosure, and send in troops if necessary. For Jews the Antonia symbolized Roman domination, especially since the high priest's vestments were kept there by the Romans between festivals as another measure of control. At the beginning of the revolt against Rome in 66 C.E. the bridge between the Antonia and Temple Mount was destroyed and the Roman garrison attacked. During the siege of Jerusalem the Antonia was destroyed along with the rest of the city.

collaborators, and among their victims was Jonathan the high priest. Jose-phus recounts that "upon Festus's coming into Judea, it happened that Judea was afflicted by the robbers, while all the villages were set on fire and plun-dered by them. And then it was that the Sicarii, as they were called, who were robbers, grew numerous. They made use of small swords . . . and with these weapons they slew a great many; for they mingled themselves among the multitude at their festivals. . . . They also came frequently upon the vil-lages belonging to their enemies, with their weapons, and plundered them, and set them on fire" (*Antiquities* 20.10).

Festus was succeeded by Albinus (62–4 C.E.), who continued the guber-natorial practice of combining personal greed and unjust rule. Under Albi-nus the Sicarii took prominent Roman and Jewish hostages to exchange them for ransom and their own captured members, and Albinus conspired with both these dagger-men and the chief priests to collect the maximum amount of bribes. Albinus's successor, Florus (64–6 C.E.), plundered cities and rich individuals more openly than previous procurators and made no pretense of administering justice.

The high priests, rather than seeking to implement a just system, com-peted among themselves for power and wealth. In the interregnum between Festus and Albinus, the high priest Ananus executed numerous opponents, including James, who was the brother of Jesus and the leader of the Jerusalem Christian community. Josephus reports:

> This younger Ananus . . . was a bold man in his temper, and very insolent; he followed the party of the Sadducees, who are indeed more heartless than any of the other Jews, as I have already observed, when they sit in judgment. Possessed of such a character, Ananus thought he had now a favorable opportunity [to exercise his authority]. Festus was now dead, and Albinus was still upon the road; so he assembled the Sanhedrin of judges, and brought before them James, the brother of Jesus who was called Christ, and some others [or, some of his companions]; he accused them of having broken the Law and he delivered them up to be stoned. But those people of the city who were considered the most fair-minded and who were strict in observance of the Law were offended at this. They therefore secretly sent to the king [Agrippa II] to urge him, for what Ananus had already done was not to be justified, to order to act so no more. (*Antiquities* 20.196–208)

After only three months in the office of high priest, Ananus was deposed by Agrippa. During Albinus's tenure, the new high priest Ananias had his armed guards go to the Temple threshing floors and steal the tithes due to other priests. On another occasion the supporters of a deposed high priest battled supporters of his appointed successor in the streets of Jerusalem for control. Because both the governors and the high priests were more inter-ested in their own self-aggrandizement than in the welfare of the population, anti-Roman sentiment grew and eventually exploded, and there was no rul-ing class in Jerusalem who could compete for the respect of the crowds.

In April–May 66 C.E. Florus, the next Roman governor, took seventeen talents of gold from the Temple treasury. (A talent was a Hebrew measure

HEROD AGRIPPA II

Agrippa II, the son of Agrippa I and great-grandson of Herod the Great, was, like his father, educated in Rome; he resided there until about 53 C.E. Because he was only seventeen when his father died in 44, he did not succeed him. For a few years he nominally ruled the small kingdom of Chalcis in Lebanon and in 53 C.E. was given the areas north and east of Galilee. In the fifties and sixties, Nero gave him parts of Galilee, as well as supervision of the Temple and the right to appoint high priests.

Agrippa was both fully loyal to Rome and a supporter of Jewish causes and customs. Acts 25–6 pictures him as advising the Roman procurator Festus and interviewing the prisoner Paul. An allegedly incestuous relationship with his sister Berenice (called "Bernice" in Acts) tinged his personal life with scandal. (After the destruction of Jerusalem, Berenice engaged in a love affair with Titus, the conqueror of Jerusalem, until social disapproval in Rome forced him to send her away.)

When the revolt against Rome broke out of control in 66, Agrippa rushed back from Egypt to Jerusalem and tried to quiet the people. After he failed and his palace was burned, he aided the Romans in their war effort. He and Berenice supported Vespasian when he became emperor in 69. C.E. After the war Agrippa's territory was greatly increased; he died, without an heir, in the late nineties. Thus the Jewish kingship ended.

equal to about seventy-five pounds; when made of precious metal, it became a huge monetary unit.) This blasphemous act goaded the people to riot, so Florus had his troops put down the disorder; during their military operation, they also sacked part of the city. Florus then insisted that the people give a ceremonial welcome to his troops; when the people shouted insults instead, Florus again ordered an attack. In the ensuing battle the people gained control of the Temple Mount and cut the bridge to the Roman fortress, the Antonia. Outmaneuvered, Florus withdrew to Caesarea.

The natural mediator between Jerusalem and the Romans was Agrippa II, son of Agrippa I. Informed by a messenger when the initial riots broke out, Agrippa II returned to Jerusalem from Alexandria, where he was visiting. However, he was unable to convince the people to rebuild the connection to the Roman fortress and to pay their back taxes. Further attempts by the chief priests to take control of the city, using troops supplied by Agrippa, also failed. In a series of battles lasting until September 66, the palaces of the high priest and Agrippa were burned, the entire city fell to the rebels, and the high priest Ananias was murdered. Though the majority of the governing class opposed the revolt and feared Roman military might, Eleazar, the son of Ananias, was a leader of the insurrection. Thus along with lower-class dissatisfaction conflicts within the ruling classes contributed to the disorder. In addition, fighting between Jews and Gentiles erupted in many cities near Judea and resulted in slaughter on both sides.

Cestius Gallus, the Roman governor of Syria, who had ultimate responsibility for peace in the East, made the first coordinated military attempt to stem the revolt. Though he subdued the villages in the vicinity of Jerusalem, his force was not strong enough to take the city itself. As he withdrew, his troops were ambushed and routed in the pass at Beth-horon, as the Seleucid forces had been two centuries earlier.

During the winter of 67–8 the Judean governing class regained political control by agreeing to supervise preparations for war with Rome. Aristocrats and high-ranking priests divided up responsibility for fortifying numerous cities and towns, gathering supplies, and recruiting fighting forces. For example, Josephus, the Jewish historian, had responsibility for Galilee. Rifts in society, however, hampered military preparations for, as Josephus recounts in

THE FLAVIANS: VESPASIAN, TITUS, AND DOMITIAN

After Nero's death in 68 C.E., three Roman generals held brief tenure as emperor during 68–9, until each was assassinated. Finally, the eastern legions recognized as emperor Vespasian, who was conducting the campaign against Jerusalem. When the armies at the Danube quickly ratified this choice, Vespasian's position was ensured. After Vespasian became emperor, his son Titus completed the conquest of Jerusalem. In Rome, Vespasian instituted fiscal reforms to erase the deficit incurred by Nero, and with Titus, he reorganized the army to prevent further civil war and to build a loyal military base. Since he came from an undistinguished family, he and his sons, Titus and Domitian,

accumulated numerous offices and honors to legitimate their rule and to ensure that the dynastic principle would apply to their family. Vespasian restored the capital, built a forum and the Temple of Peace, and began the Colosseum, which Titus completed.

Titus succeeded Vespasian in 79 and after a relatively peaceful short reign, died in 81. His brother, Domitian, who ruled from 81 to 96, improved public administration and broke the power of the Senate, but he faced military and financial difficulties. The last years of his reign were marked by many conspiracies and executions, including religious persecutions, until finally with his assassination the Flavian line ended.

his *Life*, not all of the population of Galilee supported the war. When the Roman army, under the able general Vespasian, arrived in the spring of 67, Sepphoris immediately submitted and accepted a Roman garrison. Later, Tiberias, Gischala, and other towns surrendered without a siege. Others, like Jotapata and Gamla, across the Sea of Galilee, were conquered only after stiff resistance. Josephus claims that five thousand Jews threw themselves off the cliffs near Gamla rather than accept capture by the Romans (*War* 4.1–83). By the winter of 67–8 all Galilee was in Roman hands.

In the spring and summer of 68 Vespasian captured the cities surrounding Jerusalem and was preparing his attack on Jerusalem when the emperor, Nero, died. During the next two years the Roman armies proclaimed as emperor three successive generals, but each was subsequently assassinated. Finally, in late 69, Vespasian, who had been proclaimed emperor by the armies in the East, was accepted as ruler by the whole empire. Vespasian did not mount a siege of Jerusalem, although he did subdue all of Judea except for the Herodian fortresses. The new emperor left his son Titus in charge of Rome's military interests, and in the spring of 70 Titus began the siege of Jerusalem.

The two-year respite from Roman attack did not improve Jerusalem's chances for survival, because battles among factions within Jerusalem divided the city, destroyed its food supplies, decimated its leadership, killed many of its inhabitants, and weakened its defenses. A coalition of those who strongly favored revolution, the Zealots, formed around John of Gischala, who had escaped from Galilee with his forces. The Zealots, aided by an Idumean force, killed many of the pro-Roman governing class and replaced the high priest with a priest from the lower orders. Subsequently, a force of dispossessed peasants who had controlled southern Judea, were driven into Jerusalem by the Roman armies. This group, led by Simon bar Giora, fought John of Gischala's Zealots, so that the city was wracked by civil war.

Just before the arrival of the Romans, part of John's faction broke off under the leadership of Simon bar Giora's son, Eleazar; thus there were three Jewish armies in Jerusalem locked in civil war. Eleazar held the inner forecourt of the Temple, John the Temple Mount, and Simon the upper city and a large part

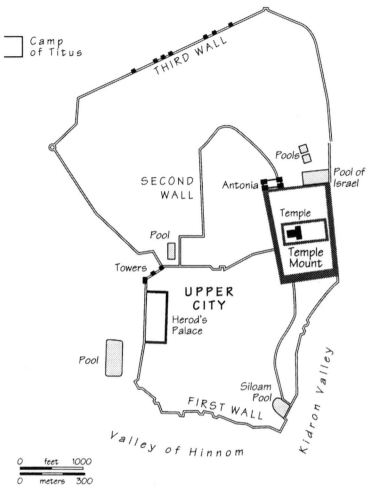

Map XVII. Jerusalem at the time of the revolt.   *Location of walls is disputed in many areas of the map.*

of the lower city. They depleted the city's defenses and population and burned much of its food to keep it from opposing factions. Even after the Roman siege had begun, John of Gischala smuggled armed men into the Temple forecourt during the Passover festival and killed Eleazar and his supporters.

The Roman assault on Jerusalem, which followed classic form, began in the north where the land was flat. Troops built several ramparts up to the walls and brought out battering rams. The defenders, who finally united, responded by strengthening the walls, sallying out against the attackers, and burning or undermining the siege works. The first wall fell in fifteen days, the second nine days later, but the fortress Antonia and the Temple Mount took over three months to be seized and the upper city a little longer. During this extended siege, the people of Jerusalem suffered grievously. The city ran out of food, and those who tried to leave were driven back in or crucified by the Romans.

MASADA

Herod the Great fortified the mountain fortress of Masada in case of a revolt, but the location became, in the first century C.E., home to a Roman garrison. In 66, the Jewish revolutionary leader Eliezer ben Jair wrested Masada from the Romans, where he was joined by fellow Jews escaping the carnage in Jerusalem. Although Rome destroyed Jerusalem in 70, the military remained at Masada to root out the last of the rebels. In 72, Lucius Flavius Silva, the Roman governor, led the legion *X Fretensis* against Masada. Josephus reports (*War* 7.389–401) that in 73, after a lengthy siege, when it appeared that the Romans would soon break through the final defenses, the 960 Jewish men, women, and children determined that suicide was preferable to either slavery or execution. They selected ten men to begin the killing, and then one of the ten put to death the other nine before killing himself. "Yet there was an ancient woman, and another who was of kin to Eleazer, and superior to most women in prudence and learning, with five children, who had concealed themselves in caverns under ground, and had carried water there for their drink, and were hidden there when the rest were intent upon the slaughter of one another."

When the Romans finally took the Temple Mount in 70 C.E., they burned the Temple and slaughtered the defenders. Josephus's claim that Titus tried to save the Temple is probably an attempt to flatter the general, who was his patron, and to exculpate him so that Jews might more easily accept Roman rule. During the battle many died, and after the Roman conquest the soldiers plundered and burned the city. Those who survived were sold into slavery or sent to the mines. Only Herod's three towers and a part of the wall were left standing.

Titus departed in triumph for Rome. Jerusalem was left uninhabitable, and Judean society, until then the center of Judaism, was shattered. The top level of the governing class had been stripped off, and all the officials, political groups, and dissidents who gave Judaism its shape were no more. The Pharisees, Sadducees, Essenes, Zealots, scribes, and (Jewish-) Christian community of Jerusalem were swept away.

2. The Diaspora Revolt

After the First Revolt, Jerusalem effectively became a Roman army camp. The Temple had been destroyed, the remaining priests had no function, the central council and the courts associated with the Temple could not be reestablished, and taxes in the form of tithes could not be collected. Rome had transformed the half-shekel tax paid by Jewish men between the ages of twenty and fifty to the Temple into the *fiscus Judaicus*, the "Jew tax," used to support the temple of Jupiter Optimus Maximus (otherwise known as the temple of Jupiter Capitolinus) in Rome. Coins depicting a mourning woman and bearing the inscription *Judea Capta* ("captured Judea") served as ongoing reminders of Jerusalem's humiliation and defeat.

Rome made Palestine into a separate senatorial province including Samaria, most of Galilee, and the coast; rule was by a higher-ranked governor and a legion of its own to keep order. Based as before at Caesarea

The Arch of Titus in Rome, erected to celebrate the conquest of Jerusalem. Successful Roman generals traditionally were awarded a triumph by the Senate. When Titus returned from the conquest of Jerusalem, he and his father, the emperor Vespasian, shared a triumph. Seven hundred handsome prisoners and the leaders Simon bar Giora and John of Gischala were brought to Rome along with the spoils of the conquest to be displayed in a parade. The seven-branched candelabrum (the menorah) and the table of showbread from the Jerusalem Temple, a copy of the Law, and many other items were carried in procession and deposited in the temple of the goddess Peace. Scenes from this triumph are sculpted on the Arch of Titus in Rome. The triumphal procession ended at the temple of Jupiter Capitolinus, where sacrifices were offered. (BiblePlaces.com)

on the coast, the Roman governor was aided by garrisons as well as by officials scattered throughout the country.

While Jews in the villages and small cites of Judea and Galilee adapted to life without a Temple or centralized priesthood, the winds of revolt spread toward the Diaspora. Whether sparked by refugees from the 66–70 C.E. revolt and their descendants, based in resentment against Rome, prompted by messianic hopes present among Jewish communities throughout the empire, or catalyzed by local persecution, Jews in Egypt and throughout the eastern Mediterranean revolted against Roman authority and their non-Jewish neighbors. This so-called War of Trajan (115–17 C.E.), also known as the Diaspora Revolt, resulted in the destruction of many Jewish communities.

The Roman governor of Egypt lost a number of battles with Jewish forces in the countryside, although in Alexandria the local citizenry slaughtered the Jewish community, a population of over one million. In Cyrene (modern Libya) the Jewish community proclaimed as king their leader, Lucuas (according to the early-fourth-century Christian historian Eusebius) or Andreias (according to the early-third-century Roman historian Dio Cassius). Archaeological evidence of destroyed temples, and an inscription concerning repopulation of the province, all testify to the seriousness of this uprising. Marcus Turbo, one of Trajan's best generals, quelled the revolt in a long series of battles that led to the death of thousands of Jews allied with the rebellion.

On Cyprus the Jewish communities killed so many thousands of non-Jewish islanders that after the revolt was suppressed, no Jews were allowed on the island. In Mesopotamia, too, Jews began to revolt at the rear of Trajan's army, which had advanced into Parthia. The unrest may also have extended to Syria and Palestine. General Lucius Quietus put down the insurrection with great loss of life.

3. The Bar Kokhba War

The Bar Kokhba War (132–5 C.E.) was more extensive and costly for both Jews and Romans than the Jewish Revolt of 66–70 and the Diaspora Revolt. The length and severity of the war suggest that it was not a sudden, popular outburst but a calculated effort on the part of the Jewish population in Palestine. Roman troop movements and the presence of two legions in the region before the war indicate that the Romans had already judged the situation to be insecure.

The causes of this second Palestinian-based Jewish war against Rome are several. Along with Jewish restiveness after the conflicts under Trajan and the deep-seated rejection of Rome's presence in Jerusalem came both changes in Roman policy toward Palestine and the influence of the charismatic leader Simon bar Kosiba himself. Roman historians mention two proximate causes: the emperor Hadrian's decision to ban circumcision and his plans to build a Roman city on the site of the destroyed Temple. Hadrian at some point did forbid castration, which was probably understood to include circumcision of converts, in order to rid the empire of what Roman culture considered "barbaric" practices. It is not certain if he did this before the revolt, however. Hadrian also constructed buildings, conducted games, and founded cities on a grand scale when he toured the eastern empire. The ruins of Jerusalem provided him with a perfect opportunity to restore its once-great magnificence; he planned for the reconstruction of the city, to be called Aelia Capitolina, with a temple to Zeus at its center. Jews could easily have seen this act of largesse as an attack on their holy places and way of life. Dio Cassius reports that "soon, the whole of Judea had been stirred up, and the Jews everywhere were showing signs of disturbance, were gathering together, and giving evidence of great hostility to the Romans, partly by secret and partly by open acts; many others, too, from other peoples, were joining them from eagerness for profit, in fact one might almost say that the whole world was being stirred up by this business."

The war began in the spring of 132 and lasted three and a half years, until late summer of 135. The Jewish revolutionaries were led by Simon bar Kosiba, who claimed the traditional title *nasi'* (prince or leader) of Israel and was proclaimed Messiah by some. The change in his name to "bar Kokhba," meaning "son of the star," has messianic connotations.

Bar Kosiba took and held the southern Judean desert and its towns for three years, though the lack of an account like Josephus's *History of the Jewish War* leaves only fragments of evidence from which to reconstruct the story. Leases, contracts, and coins from the period testify that the revolutionaries set up a complete administration in Judea and considered that a new era had begun. The new era is designated in documents as "The redemption of Israel by Simon bar Kosiba, *nasi'* of Israel," and the coins struck, which contain shortened forms of this slogan, are numbered according to the first three years of the revolt.

THE NAME "BAR KOSIBA"

The leader of the Jewish rebellion in 132–5 C.E. is often referred to by nicknames, one laudatory and the other pejorative. The most common Aramaic form of his name, Bar Kokhba (or Kokheba), meaning "son of the star," derives from Christian writings and refers to his messianic claims. Rabbinic literature, which opposed his messianic status, usually refers to him as Bar Koziba (Hebrew Ben Koziba), which means "son of the lie" (liar). Recently discovered Hebrew, Aramaic, and Greek documents from the time of the revolt record his correct name as Simon bar/ben Kosiba.

THE BAR KOSIBA DOCUMENTS

A number of cliffside caves in valleys south of Qumran and southeast of Jerusalem have yielded documents from the Bar Kokhba period. One cache contains the legal papers of a Jewish woman, Babata, daughter of Simon, including her marriage contract, a tax return sworn before a Roman magistrate, and property deeds. Other documents are letters to and from Bar Kosiba and his officials, mandating a fair distribution of resources and adherence to Sabbath observance, tithing, and the Sabbatical year. These documents are written in the three most common languages of Palestine – Hebrew, Aramaic, and Greek – as well as in Nabatean, the language of the Arabian kingdom across the Dead Sea. The texts reveal some of the workings of the Roman Empire and how integral they were to Jewish life before the revolt. The documents from 132–5 show that Bar Kosiba organized the territory he controlled into districts, appointed officials, collected taxes and supplies, and instituted a new calendar beginning with the first year of freedom from the Romans. Babata's documents demonstrate women's access to Roman courts, involvement in the administration of property and business, and personal relations with members of an extended family.

Bar Kosiba appointed a full roster of officials for various districts; refugees received care, supplies were transported, and order was maintained. The general and his supporters showed their commitment by referring to each other as brothers, by not moving caravans on Sabbath, and by laying in supplies for celebrating Jewish festivals. But not all of the population enthusiastically supported the revolt. Letters from late in the war refer to punishments meted out to those who profiteer, mistreat refugees, refuse to contribute supplies, or malinger.

Roman documents and inscriptions indicate that the threat to imperial rule from Bar Kosiba was greater than that of the first revolt. Deploying massive forces against Judea, Rome sent several legions and detachments of auxiliary troops from all over the empire, and Julius Severus, the best of Hadrian's generals, was recalled from Britain to direct operations. Letters written by Jews reveal that as the Roman forces were closing in, travel had become impossible and supplies were running out. Casualties were enormous on both sides. The end of the war was not marked by a triumph in Rome, and when Hadrian reported to the Senate, he omitted the customary opening formula that he and the legions were well.

Nahal Darga – the Wadi Muraba'at Caves – where some correspondence involving Simon bar Kosiba was discovered. (BiblePlaces.com)

BAR KOSIBA, THE MESSIAH

Rabbinic tradition records that the famous early-second-century sage Rabbi Aqiba supported Bar Kosiba, the popular messianic expectation associated with him, and the rebellion. The Jerusalem Talmud, *Taanit* 4:8 (68d), records:

1. Rabbi Simeon ben Yohai taught, "My teacher Aqiba used to expound, '*There shall step forth a star out of Jacob*' (Numbers 24:17). Thus Koziba steps forth out of Jacob."
2. When Rabbi Aqiba beheld Bar Kosiba, he exclaimed, "This is the king Messiah."
3. Rabbi Johanan ben Torta retorted, "Aqiba, grass will grow between your cheeks [i.e., you will be long dead and buried] and still he will not have come."

Paragraphs 1 and 3 are in Hebrew and represent the original dispute over the status of Bar Kosiba. Paragraph 2 is in Aramaic and is probably a later addition. Note that the text contains the later Rabbinic pejorative nickname for the general, Bar Kosiba: Koziba ("son of the lie").

Since small guerilla actions predominated during the war, destruction was widespread. Near the Dead Sea the remains of forty partisans, starved to death by the Romans, were found in their cliffside cave. Bar Kosiba made his last stand at the fort of Bethar, seven miles southwest of Jerusalem. Amid siege and starvation he and his forces fought to the end. When the war was over, thousands had been killed, all settlements in Judea had been devastated, and so many Jews had been sold into slavery that the slave markets were glutted.

After the defeat, Judea ceased to be the center of Jewish life. Hadrian built his Roman city on the site of Jerusalem and forbade Jews entry to mourn the loss of the Temple. The areas surrounding the new city, Aelia Capitolina, were annexed, and the province was officially renamed Syria Palestina in order to remove the Jewish name, Judea. The Romans put their stamp on the province by building new temples, installations, and cities. Roman roads were constructed to speed military movements in case of trouble, and two legions with supporting units were permanently stationed in the region. Hadrian made sure that security would be so firmly established and the homeland of the Jews so thoroughly transformed that there would not be a third Jewish war.

Completing what he anticipated to be the end of Jewish national hope, Hadrian both proscribed Judaism and persecuted its teachers in Palestine. Talmudic stories recount a time of desperate danger in which many were executed or fled. Rabbinic tradition says Rome forbade circumcision, Sabbath observance, ordination of Rabbis, and study of Torah. The law against circumcision was probably a continuation of a prewar policy, and the prohibition against Sabbath observance may have been a security measure banning assembly. Restrictions on ordination and the study of Torah may reflect attempts to control the activities of potentially troublesome leadership groups. Since the Rabbis were only one small, developing group in Jewish society, it is likely that other kinds of leaders were also jailed or executed.

The failure of Bar Kosiba and the devastation of Judea had several long-term consequences. First, the cultural and religious center of Palestinian Judaism shifted from Judea to Galilee. The emerging Rabbinic leaders, in Usha and then in Caesara, began to produce the traditions embodied in the Mishnah, Talmud, and midrashic commentaries that reshaped Jewish life over the next several centuries. Second, although no contemporary historical sources speak of the place of Jewish Christians in these events, later Christian historians recount that the followers of Jesus rejected Bar Kosiba's messianic claim and that this rejection at a time of war led to their persecution. Clusters of Christian communities grew in Syria, along the coast of the Mediterranean, and in Galilee. Third, Jews in Palestine and the Diaspora never again engaged in large-scale military resistance to the empire. Three costly defeats at the hands of the Romans and continued Roman vigilance led the people and their leaders to channel their efforts into strengthening their inner community life as a mode of resisting the dominant Greco-Roman, and later Christian, culture.

Triumphal Arch of Hadrian at Gerasa.
(BiblePlaces.com)

B. Literary Responses to the Wars and Destruction of the Temple

Jewish literary responses to the destruction of Jerusalem and the losses in the wars varied greatly. The Jewish historian Flavius Josephus wrote accounts of the first war and of earlier Jewish history to explain Jerusalem's loss as the fault of misguided revolutionaries, to gain recognition for Judaism, and to encourage Jewish cooperation with the empire. Several authors in Palestine wrote apocalypses that attributed the loss of Jerusalem to Jewish sin and that sought its restoration through divine intervention and a renewed commitment of Jews to God and Torah. Diaspora Jews used the traditional medium of political protest, the oracle, to predict devastation for the Roman Empire and justice for Israel. The emerging Rabbinic movement ignored political and military disasters in its writings and laid the foundation for an inwardly stable Jewish community; by describing in detail the workings of the Temple, they preserved its memory without forcefully promoting its rebuilding.

1. Josephus

Born in 37/8 C.E., Joseph ben Mattathias was a high-ranking priest with Hasmonean connections. He was well educated and had visited Rome prior to the first Jewish Revolt as part of a delegation sent to negotiate the release of priests being held by the emperor Nero. When the war was organized from Jerusalem in 66, he was placed in charge of the forces defending Galilee. Surrendering to the invading Roman forces rather than risking the massacre of his troops and the loss of his own life, Josephus became first a prisoner of the Roman general Vespasian; after presenting himself as a prophet and predicting that Vespasian was the fulfillment of an ancient oracle foretelling the rise of an emperor from Judea, he became the general's ally. When Vespasian was in fact proclaimed emperor, he not only freed Josephus but adopted him into his family, the Flavians. Thus Joseph ben Mattathias became Flavius Josephus.

During the remainder of the war, Josephus assisted Vespasian's son Titus. Following Jerusalem's destruction and Titus's victorious return to Rome, Josephus lived at the Flavian court, where he wrote two histories. The *History of the Jewish War*, which appeared first in Aramaic for Jews in the eastern empire and was later translated into Greek, supplies geographic and political detail, a brief sketch of Jewish history leading up to the first Jewish Revolt, and an integrated narrative of the major events and figures of the war. Its emotional description of Jewish sufferings was designed to overcome resentment and gain sympathy for the Jews. The *Antiquities of the Jews*, written in Greek, retells biblical history as well as covers the Hellenistic and early Roman periods up to the revolt, and it glorifies Jewish laws, institutions, and outstanding men and women. Both books are also biased toward discouraging resistance to the Romans and toward justifying the author's own actions in the war.

Josephus sought to demonstrate, to Jewish and Gentile readers alike, that Judaism was ancient and respectable and to defend Jewish rights established in previous imperial decrees. He interprets both the destruction of Jerusalem and the ascendancy of the Roman Empire, as the work of divine providence. For example, Herod's unhappy end followed from his disloyalty to Jewish tradition, and various empires rose and dominated Israel with divine acquiescence because of Israel's sin. Finally, "because God deemed the Temple to be no longer a clean place for him, he brought the Romans upon us and purification by fire upon the city" (*Antiquities* 20.166). Probably many survivors of the war, especially from the upper classes, agreed with Josephus. His initiative failed, however; a few years after his death Diaspora Jews in the East fought bloody battles with the government, and two decades after that, Palestine once again rose in revolt.

In Rome, Josephus continued to defend Judaism and to justify his own actions in the war and, later, his affiliation with the Roman court. In the 90s, he wrote *Against Apion*, an apologetic defending Jews from the accusations made by Apion, a Roman polemicist, and by the end of the decade he wrote an autobiography. The date of Josephus's death is not known.

2. Apocalyptic Literature

Three Jewish apocalypses—*4 Ezra*, *2 Baruch*, and the *Apocalypse of Abraham* — survive from the late first and early second centuries, as do expansions of the *Sibylline Oracles*. These texts, along with the Book of Revelation in the New Testament, show how Judaism and Christianity adapted traditional genres to meet the new challenges posed by the Roman Empire and the destruction of Jerusalem. All share a strong sense of loss at the destruction of the Temple, a quest for the reasons leading to the disaster, and a confidence that justice ultimately will prevail. All claim to communicate a special heavenly revelation that offers guidance to God's people as they endure until the Lord redeems the world as promised in Scripture.

Fourth Ezra

Fourth Ezra was written after the destruction of the Second Temple in 70 C.E., but, like many other works, it uses the destruction of the first Jerusalem Temple by the Babylonians in 587/6 B.C.E. (see Part One) as a paradigm for understanding present history. In the narrative, Ezra, the faithful scribe who presided over the reform of early Second Temple Judaism in the fifth century B.C.E., is pictured as receiving revelation in Babylon thirty years after the destruction of the first Temple (in the sixth century B.C.E.). Since the chronology is clearly unhistorical, the text signals that it is really speaking about the destruction of the Second Temple. The text, copied and edited by the scribes of the church, shows a number of Christian interpolations.

Faced with the loss of political independence, the dissolution of social order, death all around, and the destruction of the religious center, Ezra receives seven symbolic visions that move him, and anyone who accepts the message in this book, from discouragement and lack of confidence in God's justice to consolation and acceptance of God's plan for history. The state of Judaism without the Temple is conveyed in Ezra's lament:

> Our sanctuary has been laid waste, our altar thrown down, our Temple destroyed; our harp has been laid low, our song has been silenced, and our rejoicing has been ended; the light of our lampstand has been put out, the ark of our covenant has been plundered, our holy things have been polluted, and the name by which we are called has been profaned; our free men have suffered abuse, our priests have been burned to death, our Levites have gone into captivity; our virgins have been defiled, and our wives ravished; our righteous men have been carried off, our little ones have been cast out, our young men have been enslaved, and our strong men made powerless. And, what is more than all, the seal of Zion – for she has now lost the seal of her glory and has been given over into the hands of those that hate us. (*4 Ezra* 10:21–3)

In the first three visions Ezra engages in dialogue with his angelic interpreter, Uriel. When he complains about the prosperity of the sinful Gentiles and the punishment of Israel despite its adherence to the Law,

Ezra, like Job, is told that he does not understand God's work in the universe: "you cannot discover my judgment, or the goal of the love that I have promised my people" (*4 Ezra* 5:40). However, unlike Job, at the end of the third vision Ezra is told of the messianic kingdom, the judgment of the wicked, and the punishments of various classes of sinners:

> For behold the time will come, when the signs which I have foretold to you will come to pass; the city which now is not seen shall appear, and the land which is now hidden shall be disclosed. And everyone who has been delivered from the evils that I have foretold shall see my wonders. For the Messiah [the Syriac reads "my son the Messiah," and other ancient versions in Arabic, Ethiopic, and Georgian have variously "the Messiah" and "my Messiah," and "the elect my Messiah"; the Latin reads "my son Jesus"] shall be revealed with those who are with him, and those who remain shall rejoice four hundred years [so the Latin and one Arabic version; the Syriac read "thirty years"; the reference is absent in the Ethiopic and Armenian texts; a second Arabic version reads "one thousand years"]. And after these years my son the Messiah shall die, and all who draw human breath. And the world shall be turned back to primeval silence for seven days, as it was at the first beginnings, so that no one shall be left. (*4 Ezra* 7:26–30)

The transition from despair to hope takes place in the fourth vision (*4 Ezra* 9:26–10:59). With general questions of theodicy addressed in the first three visions, Ezra sees now the vision of a woman mourning the death of her only son on his wedding night. Ezra becomes angry with her because Jerusalem's loss is so much greater, and he encourages her to be brave and to acknowledge the justice of God's decree: "Keep your sorrow to yourself, and bear bravely the troubles that have come upon you. For if you acknowledge the decree of God to be just, you will receive your son back in due time" (10:15–16). The woman is then transformed into a renewed Jerusalem, and Ezra realizes that he has just answered his own questions and consoled himself. The final three visions establish the ground for his hope and show him communicating it to the people.

In the last vision (chapter 14) Israel is reestablished as a nation faithful to God's law. All through *4 Ezra* Israel's fault has been the rejection of God's Law (3:22; 4:23; 7:20, 24, 79, 81; 9:33–4), whereas Ezra has been granted his visions because of his knowledge and faithfulness (13:54–5). Confirming this fidelity, the final vision explicitly compares Ezra to Moses: Ezra dictates the contents of the twenty-four books of Scripture, which have been burned, plus seventy other books that will guide the newly constituted, apocalyptic community while it endures until the end. Ezra the scribe thus represents both biblical wisdom and apocalyptic traditions. His special revelation in this book and in the seventy hidden books is for the wise among the people (*4 Ezra* 12:38; 14:13, 26, 46; see Daniel 11:33), who seem to be identical with the survivors addressed after the fifth vision (12:40) and in the middle of the seventh (14:27).

LITERATURE ATTRIBUTED TO EZRA

Ezra, a priest and scribe, appears in the biblical Book of Ezra as a postexilic leader and reformer. Because of his scribal role in teaching Torah to the community, to him as well as to Jeremiah's scribe, Baruch, were accorded several books written centuries after his time. The names for the books attributed to Ezra in the Septuagint (LXX – Greek translation), Vulgate (Latin translation), and English translation of the Apocrypha/Deuterocanonical writings are confusing.

1. The Hebrew Book of Ezra: 2 Esdras in the Septuagint and 1 Esdras in the Vulgate.
2. The Hebrew Book of Nehemiah: 3 Esdras in the Septuagint and 2 Esdras in the Vulgate.

3. The English apocryphal 1 Esdras is called by the same name in the Septuagint, but called 3 Esdras in the Vulgate.
4. The English apocalyptic work 4 Ezra, which is not found in the Septuagint, is called 2 Esdras in the English Apocrypha and 4 Esdras in the Vulgate.
5. A later apocryphal work, not printed in Bibles, is sometimes designated 5 Esdras.

When distinguishing the Christian frame (chapters 1–2 and 15–16) added to the core of 4 Ezra, the following designations are sometimes used:

1 Ezra for the biblical Ezra-Nehemiah

2 Ezra for chapters 1–2 of 4 Ezra

3 Ezra for the Septuagint 1 Esdras

4 Ezra for chapters 3–14 of 4 Ezra

5 Ezra for chapters 15–16 of 4 Ezra

Fourth Ezra, the full sixteen chapters, is recognized as canonical by the Ethiopian and Russian Orthodox Churches, and it is frequently printed in collections of the Old Testament Apocrypha. Numerous translations of the text, with widely differing readings, survive not only in Latin but also in Syriac, Ethiopic, Georgian, Armenian, and Arabic. An earlier Greek version can be reconstructed; claims that the Greek was a translation of an original Hebrew or Aramaic remain speculative.

The author and his community do not expect to defeat Rome militarily and rebuild Jerusalem. The vision of Jerusalem reestablished is that of a heavenly city, far from human habitation (*4 Ezra* 10:54), and no mention is made of new priests, Temple, or cult. Rather, apocalyptic revelation, which is linked with the Law, will be the basis of the community until its vindication. Fidelity to the Law, newly understood and accepted, is common to *4 Ezra*, *2 Baruch*, the emerging Rabbinic movement, and, in a different sense, the Gospel according to Matthew.

Second Baruch

Second Baruch, also written in the aftermath of the First Revolt and the destruction of the Jerusalem Temple, shares a number of features with *4 Ezra* and dates from the same period. The document is preserved in a Syriac manuscript dating to the sixth or seventh century C.E. as well as in an Arabic version, but the Syriac text correctly indicates that it is a translation from the Greek. As with *4 Ezra*, *2 Baruch* may have originally had a Semitic (Hebrew or Aramaic) original.

According to the narrative, Baruch – the scribe associated with Jeremiah and the destruction of the first Temple (Jeremiah 32, 36, 43, 45) and to whom the Deuterocanonical Book of Baruch is ascribed – receives revelation from God, as Ezra did, and then encourages and instructs the people. Each of the text's seven sections begins with a prayer or lament, recounts a dialogue with God, and concludes with an address to the people. The audience Baruch addresses gradually widens, from the elders of the people until, in the concluding letter, all Jews are addressed. The people are gradually consoled, and they come to understand how Judaism is to be lived according to the Law but without the Temple.

Baruch, speaking as though he were writing after the destruction of the first Temple by Babylon, predicts (*ex eventu*) the destruction of the Second Temple (32:1–7). Any anxiety that might arise about the apparent lack of divine justice is assuaged by several visions that then periodize history and assure the destruction of the wicked. *Second Baruch* relativizes the trials of the present by stressing the world's corruptibility in contrast to heavenly incorruptibility (*2 Baruch* 21). Even the loss of the Temple, vividly described in the first chapters, is explained as hastening the end and as no real loss in the light of the incorruptible, heavenly Temple: "Therefore, behold the days will come and the times will hasten, more than the former, and the periods will hasten more than those which are gone, and the years will pass more quickly than the present ones. Therefore, I now took away Zion to visit the world in its own time more speedily" (*2 Baruch* 20:1–2). Eschatological comfort is even more insistent, and eloquent, at the end of the book, when the author assures the audience: "the pitcher is near to the cistern, and the ship to the port, and the course of the journey to the city, and life to [its] consummation" (*2 Baruch* 85:10).

As in *4 Ezra*, but more insistently in *2 Baruch,* Torah and wisdom become the center of Judaism. The high priests, Temple, and other institutions are gone, mired in the sins of the past, and the author proposes a renewed Israel. Those who love and keep the Law will be part of the world to come:

> When you endure and persevere in his fear and do not forget his Law, the time again will take a turn for the better for you. . . . For everything will pass away which is corruptible, and everything that dies will go away, and all present time will be forgotten, and there will be no remembrance of the present time, which is polluted by evils. . . . These are they who prepared for themselves treasures of wisdom. And stores of insight are found with them. And they have not withdrawn from mercy and they have preserved the truth of the Law. For the coming world will be given to these, but the habitation of the many others will be the fire. (*2 Baruch* 44:7–15)

Though no specific interpretation of the Torah is promoted, fidelity to Jewish practice and belief are demanded, and apostasy is condemned: "Prepare your heart so that you obey the Law, and be subject to those who are wise and understanding with fear" (46:5). When the people complain at the end that they are without leadership and guidance, Baruch's last words to them (immediately before his concluding letter to the Jews in Babylon) establish the Law as Judaism's central symbol:

> Shepherds and lamps and fountains came from the Law, and when we go away, the Law will abide. If you, therefore, look upon the Law and are intent upon wisdom, then the lamp will not be wanting and the shepherd will not give way and the fountain will not dry up. (*2 Baruch* 78:15–16)

The *Apocalypse of Abraham*

The *Apocalypse of Abraham*, like *4 Ezra* and *2 Baruch*, was probably written at the end of the first century C.E., although it is preserved only in a medieval (tenth or eleventh century) version in Old Church Slavonic and Russian redactions. Again, scholars have posited a Semitic original with a Greek translation intervening between the original Aramaic or Hebrew and the Slavonic. Though it shares some themes and the apocalyptic genre with *Baruch* and *Ezra*, it lacks their emphasis on either Torah or theodicy. On the other hand, the text shares with *1 Enoch* 1–36 a concern for the fall of the watchers; identifying the leader of the fallen angels as Azazel, it asserts that he and his companions revealed to humanity heavenly secrets and so were banished to the desert.

Rewriting God's covenantal promise to Abraham in Genesis 15, the *Apocalypse of Abraham* claims that Abraham not only hears the divine voice but also is taken on a heavenly journey, protected and guided by an angelic mediator. Abraham receives a vision of world history that firmly attributes the origin and choice of evil to human responsibility (23–4) and the loss of the Temple to corrupt worship and priests (24). Even in these evil circumstances the people of Israel (represented by Abraham, their ancestor) are not abandoned.

The *Apocalypse of Abraham*'s vision of the universe sharply distinguishes Jews and Gentiles from the beginning (contrary to *4 Ezra*), and the Gentiles' future judgment and punishment are graphically described (29–31). The solution to evil is the vindication of faithful Israelites and the reinstitution of pure worship. The coming of God's chosen one (29–30) and the final judgment will right all wrongs:

> Before the age of justice starts to grow, my judgment will come upon the heathen who have acted wickedly through the people of your seed who have been set apart for me. In those days I will bring upon all earthly creation ten plagues through evil and disease and the groaning of the bitterness of their souls. . . . And then from your seed will be left the righteous men in their number, protected by me, who strive in the glory of my name toward the place prepared beforehand for them, which you saw deserted in the picture. And they will live, being affirmed by the sacrifices and the gifts of justice and truth in the age of justice. And they will rejoice forever in me, and they will destroy those who have destroyed them. (*Apocalypse of Abraham* 29:14-20)

Prefacing the apocalyptic material of chapters 9–32 is a charming folktale, known also from Jewish and Muslim sources, concerning Abraham's childhood recognition that the idols his father makes are not gods.

The *Sibylline Oracles*

The *Fourth Sibylline Oracle* dates originally from the Hellenistic period, but it was revised in the late first century C.E., perhaps in Syria, to reflect Judaism's confrontation with Rome. The *Fifth Sibylline Oracle* comes from Egypt and dates between 80 and 130 C.E., perhaps after the debacle of 115–17. Both carry on the eastern Mediterranean tradition of anti-imperial political protest through oracles as well as the Jewish apocalyptic tradition of expecting divine intervention and judgment of the wicked. The apocalyptic punishments of the kingdoms include the destruction of evil, a conflagration, resurrection, and judgment (173–92).

Sibylline Oracle 4 divides history into four kingdoms, a periodization found in many Hellenistic Jewish and non-Jewish documents. Rome was added to the four kingdoms to bring the oracle up to date (102–51). References to the legend of Nero's imminent return (138–9), the destruction of the Temple (116), and the eruption of Mount Vesuvius in 79 C.E. (130–5), which is explained as divine punishment for the destruction of Jerusalem, all point to a late-first-century C.E. date.

Like the other *Sibylline Oracles*, this text rejects idolatry, violence, injustice, and sexual offenses (1–48). In contrast to *Sibylline Oracles 3* and *5*, it also rejects all temples and animal sacrifices (5–12, 27–30), including the Jerusalem Temple and its sacrifices. Finally, the *Fourth Sibylline Oracle* supports the kind of baptism of repentance proclaimed by John the Baptist and practiced in Syria and Palestine at the end of the first century among some Jews and Christians:

> Ah, wretched mortals, change these things, and do not lead the great God to all sorts of anger, but abandon daggers and groanings, murders and outrages, and wash your whole bodies in perennial rivers. Stretch out your hands to heaven and ask forgiveness for your previous deeds and make propitiation for bitter impiety with words of praise; God will grant repentance and will not destroy. He will stop his wrath again if you all practice honorable piety in your hearts. (*Sibylline Oracle 4.*162–70)

The *Fifth Sibylline Oracle*, in contrast to the *Third Sibylline Oracle*, manifests great alienation from Egypt's Gentile government. Whereas the author of the *Third Sibylline Oracle* hoped for an ideal Egyptian king as savior, the author of the *Fifth* looks for a heavenly savior (414–19) and an eschatological Jerusalem and Temple (249–55, 420–7) to provide a refuge for Jews against the hostile powers that rule the world. Nero is excoriated as a symbol of evil power (137–54), and the demise of Babylon and Italy is mediated by a star (possibly a metaphor for the messiah) that comes from heaven (155–61). The text reserves its strongest invective for Rome (162–78) and Egypt (179–99), and it promises its Jewish readers freedom from Gentile domination:

> No longer will the unclean foot of Greeks revel around your land, but they will have a mind in their breasts that conforms to your laws. But glorious children will honor you exceedingly, and they will attend table with devout music, all sorts of sacrifices, and with prayers honoring God. Such righteous men as endured toils will receive greater, pleasant things in exchange for a little distress. But the wicked, who dispatched lawless utterance against heaven, will desist from speaking against each other and will hide themselves until the world is changed. (*Sibylline Oracle 5.*264–73)

3. Emerging Rabbinic Judaism

Though both *4 Ezra* and *2 Baruch* promote a renewed commitment to the Torah, the interest in Torah-based piety reached its height among a group whose members referred to themselves as sages ("wise ones") and who were addressed by the title "Rabbi." These sages, with their roots among the scribes and Pharisees of the Second Temple period, emerged in the wake of the destruction of Jerusalem's governing class. Fervently devoted to the Jewish way of life and the continuation of the Jewish people, the original group of Rabbis forged their received traditions into a new amalgam that allowed Jews to commit themselves anew to Jewish life without the biblically mandated sacrificial worship; the ancient, central symbols of the Temple and Jerusalem; and the guidance of the priests. Though they began with no power or wide following among the people, their new core symbol, Torah, and their central focus – study – led to a process of reflection, articulation, and activity that allowed Judaism to adapt to changed circumstances. Their combination of practical piety, profound theology, and insistence on the sanctification of daily life ultimately won the allegiance of the Jewish community at large in Palestine and the Diaspora. By the Rabbis' own claim, and in the acknowledgment of Jews all over the world, they not only spoke about the Torah: they gave the Torah.

Between the wars of 66–70 and 132–5, these scholars taught in many Judean towns. They were led by Johanan ben Zakkai and then by Gamaliel II, probably the grandson of the Gamaliel mentioned also in the New Testament (Acts 5:34, 22:3). Their teachings and customs were strongly influenced by the prewar Pharisaic way of life, with its stress on maintaining the ritual purity proper to priests in the Temple, tithing food according to biblical law, and observing Sabbaths and festivals. In addition, they emphasized close study of the Torah and the development of detailed interpretations to guide Jewish life. Their insistence on learning as well as on practice connects them with the prewar scribal class that had maintained and taught Jewish traditions. The Mishnah (codified ca. 200 C.E.) and the Palestinian and Babylonian Talmuds recount the activities of this founding group only sporadically and episodically; their focus is on the teaching of Rabbis, often retrojecting the later roles and status of Rabbis into the first and second centuries C.E. Though picturing the Rabbis as immediately taking over the leadership of Judaism and as forming their own system in the coastal town of Jamnia (Yavneh), careful analysis of Rabbinic literature and other historical sources, including archaeological remains, shows that they only gradually developed their program for Judaism.

The leader of this school of sages was probably not recognized by Rome as the representative of Judaism until the third or fourth century C.E., nor were the sages' rules and rulings accepted by the community at large until then. Like the Pharisees, the Rabbis had no authority beyond the group that voluntarily determined to follow their teachings.

TORAH

Torah (Hebrew for "instruction" and "teaching") is used in the Bible for divine instruction given to Israel, including moral and sacerdotal laws, prophetic guidance, and popular wisdom. In Rabbinic Judaism the word "Torah" is used in several senses: (1) In its most restricted meaning it refers to the Pentateuch. (2) It is also used to refer to the whole Bible. (3) In a more comprehensive sense it refers to the "Oral Torah," that is, the teachings set down in the Mishnah, Tosefta, Talmuds, and other Rabbinic literature in the period from the second to the sixth centuries C.E. (4) Torah in its most comprehensive sense refers to the whole Jewish tradition, written and oral, text and commentary. (5) Torah is divine revelation and all that is derived from that revelation. In this sense, Torah is the central symbol of Rabbinic Judaism and includes the whole relationship of Israel with God. Fidelity to Torah includes both study and practice of Torah, and is coextensive with knowledge of, love for, and obedience to God.

The Bar Kokhba War destroyed the sages' initial achievements that helped keep Judaism intact between 70 and 132 and led to the flight or death of many Rabbis. Jewish texts recount the martyrdoms of such central teachers as Rabbi Akiva. Soon after the war, however, many survivors migrated to Galilee, living first in small towns and only later settling in the larger cities, such as Sepphoris and Tiberias. Frequent changes in the place named as their center attest to the difficulties and dislocation they faced. Initially, since they were landless and without wealth, influence, or patronage, the Rabbis worked as artisans and laborers. Slowly they rebuilt or developed their influence and gained status and prestige in Galilean society so that by the end of the second century, their leader, Rabbi Judah, called "ha-Nasi" (the prince), was wealthy enough to support some scholars and influential enough to take part in the social and political life of Galilee. The Mishnah, the body of idealized laws that he organized, appealed especially to the small landowners, the learned class of sages, and the hereditary priests. Judah ha-Nasi built a coalition of informed Jewish community leaders that would give a new and enduring shape and energy to Jewish life.

Absence of any detailed regulations in the Mishnah concerning the synagogue indicates that communal prayer was still directed by village leaders. Synagogue inscriptions from Palestine and the Diaspora during the Roman period mention a number of synagogue offices, such as president, leader, and scribe, but they do not use the title Rabbi. Nor do synagogue architecture and art follow the stipulations found in Rabbinic literature; instead, designs correspond to the cultural milieu in which they were created.

Rabbinic literature – the Mishnah, Tosefta, Talmuds, and midrashim – omits almost all mention of the loss of the Temple, political oppression by Rome, and competition from other Jewish groups and from emerging Christianity. Though the sages affirmed the resurrection of the dead and judgment of good and evil, these apocalyptic themes remain firmly in the background. The earliest Rabbinic source, the Mishnah, consists almost entirely of detailed discussions of laws affecting everyday life and the (now destroyed) Temple. Though the Mishnah and its attendant literature date from about 200 to 600 C.E. (outside the chronological scope of this *Companion*), a quick review of this literature will show the direction in which postbiblical Judaism developed.

Mishnah

Codified about 200 C.E., the Mishnah (from the Hebrew verb "to repeat," "to study") stands at the center of the development of Rabbinic Judaism. The authors of the Mishnah created an ideal Judaism that codified in words and memory much of the historical, political, and biblical Israel that had been lost, for half of the Mishnaic laws concern the Temple, priests, purity, tithes, and rituals and so were inapplicable after 70 C.E. The affirmation of the sanctity of God, the Temple, and the Jewish people countered the loss and despair of the destruction, muted enthusiastic political and apocalyptic responses, turned the attention of the Jewish spirit toward God's world, and in a subtle way rejected the Roman world by ignoring it as irrelevant.

The Mishnah's collection of sixty-three tractates is arranged in six orders: agricultural tithes, public feasts, marriage, torts, Temple sacrifices, and ritual purity. Some of the tractates, such as that on sacrifices, repeat and expand biblical law. Others elaborate new complexes of rules that go far beyond biblical concerns. An analysis of the development of Mishnah's legal traditions suggests that in the first two centuries laws concerning ritual purity, tithing, Sabbath observance, and other relatively private matters dominated. These matters are typical of a group that differentiates itself from society at large, establishes its identity by special beliefs and practices, and claims to be the true heir to the tradition. As the Qumran group had done before, the Rabbis learned to live without the Temple and to find God's presence within themselves, especially in the activity of study and zealous adherence to Torah.

However, Mishnaic laws, which presume but do not always cite a biblical antecedent, have been so thoroughly edited into a coherent structure with stereotyped rhetorical patterns that attempts to use source and form-critical analyses to isolate earlier and later strata have been only sporadically successful. Mishnaic discussions often begin in mid-argument without any explanation of the point at issue or the context from which it arose. Because it treats only a selection of subjects, gives many possible interpretations rather than definitive statements of what to do and not to do, and has no sanctions for the infractions of most of its ordinances, the Mishnah is clearly not a public law code. It is likely that the Rabbis built on earlier customs and interpretations of biblical material, but in the end they were largely governed by their own sense of what was implied or encouraged by Scripture, the logic of the subjects covered there, and their own contemporary interests. The Mishnah assumes a commitment to living a Jewish way of life and so does not refer consistently to covenant, God's love, the nation, or any of the other great biblical themes.

Though the Rabbinic movement began among a small group of learned Jews who studied and observed the Law in a particular way, the traditions they developed appealed to several sectors of the Jewish community in Palestine that had survived the two revolts against Rome. The emphasis on purity (designed to sanctify daily life) and tithing reflected the influence of the prewar Pharisees. The learned tradition of study and interpretation linked the movement with the scribes, the small group of literate officials, educators, and religious functionaries whose antecedents stretched back to the time of Ezra and before. The interest in the Temple and its laws brought into the Rabbinic movement some of the lower orders of priests who survived the wars with Rome.

After the devastation of Judea in the Bar Kokhba War, the core of the Rabbinic group migrated to Galilee and over two generations established political, social, and economic links with the landed aristocracy there. The

THE MISHNAH

The wording of the Mishnah is both very concise and elliptical. Presuming that the reader already knows the biblical and mishnaic laws applicable to the problem addressed, it specifies certain difficult or unclear cases. For example, the Mishnah tractate *Betzah*, concerned with activities on festival days, begins as follows. (Words in parentheses and brackets are added by the translator.)

> An egg which is laid on a festival day,
> the House of Shammai say,
> "It may be eaten [on that day]."
> And the House of Hillel say,
> "It may not be eaten."
> The House of Shammai say,
> "[A minimum of] leaven in the
> volume of an olive's bulk, and

> [a minimum of] what is leavened
> in the volume of a date's bulk
> [are prohibited on Passover
> (Exodus 13:7)]."
> And the House of Hillel say,
> "This and that are [prohibited
> in the volume of] an olive's
> bulk."

The Mishnah leaves numerous presuppositions unstated in order to concentrate on two precise problems. The first concerns food that may be eaten on a festival on which work is forbidden, as it is on a Sabbath. Thus the Mishnah presumes knowledge of Sabbath law, specifically, that the food to be eaten must be set aside ahead of time. Is an egg (presumably one marked for con-

sumption at the feast) part of the chicken or a new item not thus set aside? The second problem concerns Passover law (suggested by the translator's reference to Exodus). It presumes that the reader knows that both leaven and leavened products are to be destroyed before Passover. The question is how big must a piece be to come under the ban. The measures used are an olive and a date (which is considered to be bigger). With these preliminaries clear, Mishnah concisely catalogues alternative positions on these problems but does not give the reasoning behind them. One is expected to know the reasons or learn them from oral discussion.

scope of its legal interests expanded to include civil law and marriage contracts, both of which were matters of interest to the small landholders who formed the backbone of Galilean society. These larger societal interests continued to grow in the Palestinian Talmud, which is filled with case law and testifies both to the growing influence of the Rabbis as local judges and officials and to the patriarch as a national leader. At the same time, the older interest in purity laws and Temple sacrifices waned.

Tosefta

The rest of Rabbinic literature can be defined in relation to the Mishnah. The Tosefta (an Aramaic term meaning "addition") is a collection of materials arranged in sixty-three tractates parallel to those of the Mishnah. The laws, traditions, and stories expand or comment on the laws in the Mishnah, present other traditions parallel to or contradictory of the Mishnah, and gather stories and scriptural interpretations relevant to the themes of the Mishnah. The materials in the Tosefta resemble those found in the Talmud and probably date from the third or fourth century C.E.

The Palestinian and Babylonian Talmuds

Publication of the Mishnah and its acceptance as authoritative within the Rabbinic movement stimulated the growth of commentaries in Palestine and Babylon, the two great centers of Jewish life between the third through seventh centuries C.E. The Palestinian and Babylonian Talmuds comment on the Mishnah sentence by sentence. The commentary, called

Printed Talmud page. (Anthony J. Saldarini)

TANNAIM AND AMORAIM

The rabbinic designation for sages during the Mishnaic period (from the late Second Temple period until ca. 200) is tannaim. *Tanna* (pl. *tannaim*) means "teacher" and comes from the Aramaic word meaning "repeat," thus "repeat and teach a tradition." Tannaitic literature consists of the Mishnah, the Tosefta, and the tannaitic or halakhic midrashim, which quote tannaim almost exclusively.

'Amora (pl. *'amoraim*) means "speaker." Rabbinic literature designates the sages who succeeded the tannaim and are cited in the Palestinian and Babylonian Talmuds as *'amoraim*. Their literature consists of the two Talmuds and several midrashim.

the Gemara (reflecting the Aramaic usage, "to learn"), consists of an enormous variety of materials, including atomistic analyses of the words and sentences of the Mishnah, comparisons of one section of the Mishnah with another, traditions related to the Mishnah, interpretations of Scripture, stories about Rabbis and other figures, and long digressions on a variety of topics. The bulk of the Gemara is written in Aramaic, but many traditions are recorded in Hebrew. The Palestinian Talmud (completed ca. 450) covers the first four orders of the Mishnah–agriculture, feasts, marriage law, and torts – and omits the sacrificial and purity laws, which were no longer relevant. The Babylonian Talmud (ca. 600) omits some agricultural regulations, which pertained only to farmers in the land of Israel, and certain purity laws, but meditates on laws concerning the faraway and now destroyed Temple and its sacrifices, as well as on feasts, marriage law, and torts. Although both the Babylonian and Palestinian Talmuds are built around the Mishnah and quote it constantly, neither simply repeats the material. Rather, each recontextualizes Mishnaic content into its own system of thought.

The composition of the Palestinian and Babylonian Talmuds, the growth of Christian literature, and the development of Roman law all testify to the eventual power achieved by the Rabbis and their "prince" or patriarch. The prevalence of case law and practical community matters in the Talmuds is witness to the growing community involvement of the Rabbis as judges and officials. The Christian apologist Origen (mid-third century) called the Jewish prince an ethnarch and said that he had the trappings and power of a king. Finally, in the late fourth century Roman law recognized the Jewish patriarch as the official representative of Judaism. However, by the mid-fifth century, the empire no longer recognized the patriarch, and the Christian emperors and their church increasingly militated against the Rabbinic way of life

When the power of Palestinian Judaism was destroyed in the fifth century C.E. by the emerging, Christian Byzantine Empire, the most vigorous remaining center of Judaism, Babylon, became the dominant force in Jewish life throughout the world. Over the next few centuries the Babylonian Talmud was edited and expanded much more thoroughly than the Palestinian Talmud. The prestige and influence of Babylonian scholars led to the Babylonian Talmud's acceptance as the most authoritative collection of teachings in Judaism next to the Bible itself, and its rules became the rules governing Jewish communities from Mesopotamia to Europe down to modern times.

Midrashim

Midrash (from the Hebrew verb "to search," "to inquire," "to interpret") is the type of biblical interpretation found in the Talmuds and in collections of exegeses edited during the Talmudic period and after. All midrashic works organize their materials to promote a worldview in which Israel's relationship with God is preserved and fostered through the understanding of and fidelity to Israel's biblical traditions.

HALAKHAH AND HAGGADAH

"Halakhah" and "Haggadah" are somewhat general Hebrew terms used in Rabbinic literature to refer respectively to (1) legal and (2) discursive material. Whole works are sometimes characterized as one or the other, though most Rabbinic literature contains a combination of legal and nonlegal interpretations of Scripture, teachings, and stories.

Halakhah comes from the Hebrew word for "to go," "to follow," "to walk" and means a "going," or a "walking." It is used for religiously sanctioned law, whether found in the Bible or developed by Rabbinic or other authorities. Disputes over halakhah and the grounds for establishing new halakhah abound in Rabbinic and later Jewish thought.

Haggadah (aggadah in the Palestinian Talmud) comes from the Hebrew word for "to tell," "to testify," or "to announce" and means a "telling," "communication," "evidence." It is used for homiletic interpretations of biblical material, for stories in Rabbinic literature, and generally for anything not defined as halakhah.

Midrashic interpretation has much in common with New Testament and patristic biblical interpretation in that it pays close attention to the meanings of individual words and grammatical forms. It also relates words, verses, and ideas in the Bible with one another to resolve apparent contradictions and develop a coherent worldview. Finally, many midrashim seek to find a rhetorical basis for Mishnaic laws or to connect Mishnaic teachings to the Bible. Unlike the Christian materials, however, they tend not to develop extensive allegorical interpretations of biblical materials and tend to celebrate a plurality of possible interpretations rather than a single, definitive reading. For the midrashim, neither context nor the obvious sense of a passage need be determinative of meaning because biblical verses are conceived of as having many layers of significance. When juxtaposed with other verses and understood in the light of the prevailing concerns of the authors, biblical verses took on new and contemporary meanings.

A brief passage from a midrash on Deuteronomy will illustrate the nature of this genre of Rabbinic literature. The verse that prompts the interpretation is part of Deuteronomy 1:3, "Moses spoke to the children of Israel according to all which the LORD commanded him for them." The midrashic author asks what exactly Moses communicated to Israel. At stake is the whole of Rabbinic teaching, which claims Mosaic authority, and specifically midrashic interpretation.

> Did Moses prophesy only "these words" (Deuteronomy 1:1)? Where [in Scripture do we learn that he prophesied] the commandments in the Torah, [interpretations based on] a fortiori arguments, verbal analogy, [arguments from] the general and particular, and from the essentials and details? (*Sifre Deuteronomy* 2, end)

The author interprets that which God has commanded to include not just Moses' last instruction to Israel in Deuteronomy but all the commandments contained in the Pentateuch. The divine origin of these laws is expressed by the use of the verb "prophesy," which involves inspiration. But not only the explicit commands found in Scripture are included in Moses' teachings; all the interpretations developed in Rabbinic literature using various kinds of exegetical arguments are integral parts of divine revelation.

The halakhic midrashim (i.e., commentaries oriented toward practice, *halakhah*) on Exodus through Deuteronomy interpret many, but not all, sections of these books, verse by verse. A number of comments are simple explanations of the plain meaning of words and sentences. Longer passages dialectically assess all the possible meaning of a word or verse and seek to relate all postbiblical interpretations, customs, and Mishnaic laws to Scripture. When the powers of interpretive reason are shown to be inadequate for reaching a certain interpretation, the midrash subordinates reason to Scripture. Other midrashim, like *Leviticus Rabbah*, consist of homilies, each on a central theme that is developed using numerous scriptural verses. *Genesis Rabbah* combines aspects of commentary and homily.

In ancient Hebrew, Babylonian, and Persian numerology, seven represents totality – the eternally reverberating rhythm in Genesis of creation and repose. Israelite fascination with this number represents a version of Babylonian wisdom, rooted in the observation of the heavens. In the lunar calendars of the ancient Near East, the seven-day week marked the phases of the moon: four quarters waxing and waning during the month. Israel embraced this calendar, and Genesis embeds the seven-day week in the structure of nature itself (1:3–2:3), while apocalyptic thought developed its own perspective on numerological fulfillment.

Although specific details of the triumphs and failures of the seven churches cannot be recovered by modern interpreters, the central concern is very likely enunciated in 2:13, where Pergamum is described as "where Satan dwells." This is a reference to the great altar of Zeus there, which was the major center in the eastern Mediterranean world of the divine cult of the Roman emperors. As we have observed, Asia Minor yields the earliest documentation for the conflict between Church and state over this issue. The characteristics of each of the seven churches seem to have spanned the whole range of conditions and responses of churches everywhere in this period. In each case (except the Laodicean church) the faithful remnant is implicitly or explicitly described and differentiated from the wider professing group, which will renounce the faith when the pressure is applied by the state:

Ephesus (2:2 - 4)	Patience, fidelity, suffering are present, but also the need to renew love
Smyrna (2:9, 10)	The prophet gives encouragement to accept suffering, and warning against those who claim to be God's people ("Jews") and against the imperial cult
Pergamum (2:13–16)	Most have remained faithful, but some have participated in idolatry
Thyatira (2:19–20)	Patience, fidelity, and suffering are here also, but they tolerate a false prophetess (cf. 1 Kings 16:31)
Sardis (3:4)	Only a few remain pure; the rest have lost their place or have died
Philadelphia (3:9)	They have endured and are faithful, and are promised vindication
Laodicea (3:17–18)	Utterly self-satisfied, they are wholly disqualified from sharing in God's new age.

The letter section ends with a series of final warnings to the churches (3:20–1).

The main section of Revelation opens and closes with visions of the throne of God, on which the Lord of creation and Savior of the faithful community is seated in triumphant majesty. The first such vision (4:1–11) recalls the visions of Ezekiel and Daniel and emphasizes in symbolic language the brilliance, power, and purity of the divine presence. The cry of

Abot records some of Judaism's most well-known teachings, including a number of sayings attributed to Rabbi Hillel, a slightly older contemporary of Jesus of Nazareth. According to *Abot* 1.14, "Hillel used to say, 'If I am not for myself who will be for me? Yet, if I am for myself only, what am I? And if not now, when?'" *Abot* 2:5–6 offers practical wisdom:

> Hillel said: "Do not separate yourself from the community, and do not trust in yourself until the day of your death. Do not judge your fellow until you are in his place. Do not say something that cannot be understood but will be understood in the end. Say not: 'When I have time I will study' because you may never have the time."
>
> Hillel used to say: "A brutish man cannot fear sin; an ignorant man cannot be pious, nor can the shy man learn, or the impatient man teach. He who engages excessively in business cannot become wise. In a place where there are no men, strive to be a man."

The symbols, attitudes, advice, and values espoused by *Abot* became the heart of Judaism in the Talmudic period and have endured for centuries. As the Rabbinic mode of understanding and living Judaism came to dominate the Jewish community on the one hand and as Christianity developed an increasingly distinctive theology and continued to grow among the Gentiles on the other, the gap between the closely related Jewish and Christian communities of the first century gradually widened, and the two branches of the biblical tradition grew in different directions.

The Targumim

The Aramaic word *targum* by itself denotes "translation," yet the type and purpose of the rendering involved in Judaism means that the term also refers to a kind of literature. Aramaic survived the demise of the Persian Empire as a lingua franca in the Near East. It had been embraced enthusiastically by Jews (as by other peoples, such as Nabateans and Palmyrenes); the Aramaic portions of the Hebrew Bible (in Ezra and Daniel) attest a significant change in the linguistic constitution of Judaism. Even before Hebrew emerged as a distinct language, Abraham had been an Aramaean, although the variants of the Aramaic language during its extensive history are stunning. Conceivably, one reason for Jewish enthusiasm in embracing Aramaic during the Persian period was a distant memory of its affiliation with Hebrew, but it should always be borne in mind that Hebrew is quite a different language. By the time of Jesus, Aramaic had become the common language of Judea, Samaria, and Galilee (although distinctive dialects were spoken); Hebrew was understood by an educated (and/or nationalistic) stratum of the population, and some familiarity with Greek was a cultural necessity, especially in commercial and bureaucratic contexts.

The linguistic situation in Judea and Galilee demanded translation of the Hebrew Bible into Aramaic, for purposes of popular use and worship among the majority of Jews. Although fragments of Leviticus and Job in

Aramaic, which have been discovered at Qumran, are technically *targumim*, they are unrepresentative of the genre targum in literary terms. They are reasonably "literal" renderings; that is, there is a formal correspondence between the Hebrew rendered and the Aramaic that is presented. The Targumim that Rabbinic Judaism produced are of a different character.

The aim of targumic production was to give the sense of the Hebrew Scriptures, not just their wording, so paraphrase is characteristic of the Targumim. Theoretically, a passage of Scripture was to be rendered orally and from memory in the synagogue by an interpreter (a *meturgeman*) after the reading in Hebrew from a scroll; the *meturgeman* was not to be confused with the reader, lest the congregation mistake the Aramaic interpretation with the original text (see Mishnah Megillah 4:4-10 and Talmud Megillah 23b–25b). (Regulations that specify the precise number of verses that may be read prior to the delivery of a targum probably date from centuries after the period of the New Testament. The same may be said of cycles of specified lectionary readings.) Although the renderings so delivered were oral in principle, over time, traditions in important centers of learning became fixed, and coalescence became possible.

The emergence of the Rabbis as the dominant leaders within Judaism after 70 C.E. provided a centralizing tendency without which literary Targumim could never have been produced. Yet it is quite clear that the Rabbis never exerted complete control over targumic production. The Targums preserved by the Rabbis are paraphrases, yet the theological ideas conveyed are not always consistent, even within a given Targum. Although the Rabbis attempted to regulate targumic activity, the extant Targumim sometimes even contradict Rabbinic rules directly. For example, Mishnah Megillah 4:9 insists that Leviticus 18:21 ("You must not give of your seed, to deliver it to Moloch") should not be interpreted in respect of sexual intercourse with Gentiles; the Targum Pseudo-Jonathan – a late work, produced well after rabbinic authority had been established – takes just that line.

The Targumim evince such oddities because they are the products of a dialectical interaction between folk practice and Rabbinic supervision – sometimes mediated through a love of dramatic and inventive speculation – and this dynamic tension continued over centuries. Each of the extant Targumim crystallizes that complex relationship at a given moment.

The Targumim divide themselves up among those of the Torah (the Pentateuch), those of the Prophets (both "Former Prophets," or the so-called historical works in the English Bible, and the "Latter Prophets," or the Prophets as commonly designated in English), and those of the Writings (or Hagiographa), following the conventional designations of the Hebrew Bible in Judaism. The fact needs to be stressed at the outset, however, that although the Hebrew Bible is almost entirely rendered by the Targumim in aggregate, there was no single moment, and no particular movement, that produced a comprehensive Bible in Aramaic. The Targumim are irreducibly complex in dates, origins, purposes, and dialects of Aramaic. They cannot be assigned to a single epoch of ancient Rabbinic Judaism. This makes arguments based on the assumption that the Targumim as a whole predate the New Testament untenable; those that assume they are all post-Christian are equally spurious.

Among the Targumim to the Pentateuch, Targum Onqelos is a suitable point of departure because it corresponds best of all the Targumim to Rabbinic ideals of translation. Although paraphrase is evident, especially to describe God and his revelation in suitably reverent terms, the high degree of correspondence with the Hebrew of the Masoretic Text (and evidently with the Hebrew text current in antiquity) is striking. The dialect of Onqelos is commonly called "Middle Aramaic," which would place the Targum between the first century B.C.E. and 200 C.E. A better designation, however, would be "Transitional Aramaic " (200 B.C.E.–200 C.E.). This embraces the various dialects (Hasmonean, Nabatean, Palmyrene, Arsacid, Essene, as well as targumic), that came to be used during the period, and were followed by a strong regionalization in Aramaic dialects, which we can logically refer to as Regional Aramaic (200–700 C.E.). Because the dialect of 200 B.C.E.–200 C.E. was transitional between earlier Persian forms and later regionalization, various Targumim were produced in Transitional Aramaic even after its demise as a common language. For that reason, the year 200 C.E. is not a firm date, after which a Targum in Transitional Aramaic cannot have been composed. Onqelos should probably be dated toward the end of the third century C.E., in the wake of similar efforts to produce a literal Greek rendering, and well after any strict construal of the principle that Targumim were to be oral. By contrast with the later Rabbinic ethos, which permitted the creation and preservation of Onqelos in writing, one might recall the story of Rabbi Gamaliel, who is said during the first century to have immured a Targum of Job in a wall of the Temple (Talmud Shabbat 115a), scarcely a gesture of approval.

The Targum Neophyti I was discovered in 1949 by Alejandro Díez Macho in the Library of the Neophytes in Rome. Neophyti paraphrases more substantially than Onqelos. Entire paragraphs are added, as when Cain and Abel argue in the field prior to the first case of murder (Genesis 4:8):

> Cain answered and said to Abel,
> I know the world is not created with mercies,
> and it is not led in respect of fruits of good deeds,
> and there is accepting of persons in judgment:
> for what reason
> was your offering received with favor
> and my offering was not received from me with favor?
> Abel answered and said to Cain,
> I know the world is created with mercies,
> and in respect of fruits of good deeds it is led:

and because my good deeds surpassed yours
my offering was received from me with favor
while your offering was not received from you with favor.
Cain answered and said to Abel,
there is no judgment and there is no judge,
and there is no other world.
There is no giving good reward to the righteous
and there is no repaying from the wicked.
Abel answered and said to Cain,
there is judgment and there is a judge,
and there is another world,
and there is giving good reward to the righteous
and there is repaying from the wicked in the world to come.

This is no "rendering" as we understand translation, but a substantial theodicy. Abel is right according to the Targum: in this world, God's favor is a matter of justice and mercy, because it hangs on good deeds. In the world to come, all wrongs are to be righted. When the remarkable freedom to introduce a theology of this kind prevails over the text, it is impossible to predict in purely literary terms.

The dialect of Neophyti is often known as "Palestinian Aramaic," although "Tiberian" (or Galilean) is a better designation, because the Rabbis did not establish permanent academies in Jerusalem or Judea after 70 C.E. In any case, the dialect is a form of Regional Aramaic, distinct from what used to be called the "Babylonian Aramaic" of Onqelos. The distinction between "Tiberian" and "Babylonian" manifests the nascent regionalization in the Aramaic language to which we have referred. But Neophyti is produced in a frankly Regional Aramaic, whereas Onqelos appears in a Transitional Aramaic that is on the way to becoming Regional. Yet the chronology of the two Targums is about the same, although Neophyti appears somewhat later; the differences between the two are more a function of interpretative program than of dating. The Rabbis of Babylonia, who called Onqelos "our Targum" exerted greater influence over the Rabbinic movement as a whole than did their colleagues in the west, as the normative status of the Talmud of Babylonia (the Bavli) attests.

The latest representative of the type of expansive rendering found in Neophyti is Targum Pseudo-Jonathan. Its reference to the names of Muhammad's wife and daughter in Genesis 21:21 puts its final composition sometime after the seventh century C.E. This oddly designated Targum is so called because the name "Jonathan" was attributed to it during the Middle Ages, when reference to the document was abbreviated with the Hebrew letter *yod*. The letter probably had stood for "Jerusalem," although that designation is also not provably original. The title "Pseudo-Jonathan" is therefore an admission of uncertainty. Neophyti and Pseudo-Jonathan are together known as "Palestinian Targums," to distinguish their dialects and their style of interpretation from those of Onqelos. In fact, however, Pseudo-Jonathan was produced at the dawn of the period of Academic

Aramaic (700–1500 C.E.), during which rabbinic usage continued to develop the language in a literary idiom after it has been supplanted by Arabic as a lingua franca in the Near East.

Neophyti and Pseudo-Jonathan are associated with two other Targums, or to be more precise, targumic groups. The first group, in chronological order, consists of the fragments from the Cairo Geniza. They were originally part of more complete works, dating between the seventh and the eleventh centuries, which were deposited in the Geniza (i.e., a depository for work out manuscripts and scrolls) of the Old Synagogue in Cairo. In the type and substance of its interpretation, these fragments are comparable to Neophyti and Pseudo-Jonathan. The same may be said of the Fragments Targum, which was collected as a miscellany of targumic readings during the Middle Ages. An interesting feature of the Targumim of this type is that their relationship might be described as a synoptic one, in some ways comparable to the relationship among the Gospels. All four of the paraphrastic Targumim, for example, convey a debate between Cain and Abel comparable to what has been cited from Neophyti, and they do so with those variations of order and wording that are well known to students of the Synoptic Gospels.

Both the Former and the Latter Prophets are extant in Aramaic in a single collection, although the date and character of each Targum within the collection needs to be studied individually. The entire corpus is ascribed by Rabbinic tradition (Talmud Megillah 3a) to Jonathan ben Uzziel, a disciple of Hillel, the older contemporary of Jesus. (But Targum Jonathan to the Prophets is a completely different work from Pseudo-Jonathan to the Pentateuch.) On the other hand, there are passages of the Prophets' Targumim that accord precisely with renderings given in the name of Joseph bar Chiyya, a rabbi of the fourth century (see, for example, Isaiah Targum 5:17b and Talmud Pesachim 68a). As it happens, the Isaiah Targum (which has been subjected to more study than any of the Prophets' Targumim) shows signs of a nationalistic eschatology current just after the destruction of the Temple in 70 C.E., and also of the more settled perspective of the rabbis in Babylon some three hundred years later. It appears that Targum Jonathan as a whole is the result of two major periods of collecting and editing interpretations by the Rabbis, the first period being tannaitic, and the second amoraic.

Long after Targum Jonathan was composed, probably around the same time as the Fragments Targum (to the Pentateuch) was assembled, targumic addenda were appended in certain of its manuscripts; they are represented in the Codex Reuchlinianus and in a manuscript in the Bibliothèque Nationale (mis)labeled *Hébreu 75*. These represent the phenomenon of Targum upon Targum: a further interpretative extension of the Aramaic wording, not just the Hebrew original in the Bible.

Of the three categories of Targumim, that of the Writings is without question the most diverse. Although the Targum to Psalms is formally a translation, substantially it is better described as a midrash, while the

Targum to Proverbs appears to be a fairly straightforward rendition of the Peshitta (the translation of the Hebrew Bible into Syriac), and the Targum(im) to Esther seems designed for use within a celebration of the liturgy of Purim. The Targums to the Writings are the most problematic within modern study, but they are also of the least interest of the three general categories of Targumim from the point of view of understanding the New Testament, in view of their late (in several cases, medieval) dates.

BIBLIOGRAPHICAL ESSAY

The Second Temple period in Judaism extended from the return of some of the Jewish exiles from Babylon to Jerusalem in 539 B.C.E. to the destruction of the rebuilt Temple by the Romans in 70 C.E. During this time, first the Persians, then the Greeks (332 B.C.E. on), and finally the Romans (63 B.C.E. on) ruled the Near East. Historical, political, religious, and cultural changes were many and permanent. What had been the religion of the Israelites in Israel and Judea developed into what we call Judaism, originally the way of life and thought of those living in the Persian province of Judea.

Until the second part of the twentieth century, Second Temple Judaism was typically neglected in academic study. Christians regarded the development of Judaism as monolithic as well as "late," legalistic, and decadent. In the interests of emphasizing the importance and distinctiveness of Jesus' teaching, they treated the Judaism of his time as antiquated, ossified, and ready for replacement. Jewish scholars also neglected this period, moving quickly from the biblical books to the Rabbinic literature.

Since the end of the Second World War, manuscript discoveries and scholarly editions and translations have made available dozens of Jewish writings from the Second Temple and early Rabbinic periods (i.e., up until 200 C.E.). In the past fifty years numerous books and articles, both scholarly and popular, have illuminated this period and shown its critical importance for the development of both Judaism and Christianity. While earlier generations of scholars projected back into the first century C.E. (and earlier in the case of Judaism) the mature forms of orthodox Judaism and Christianity, it is now recognized that Jews in the Greek and Roman periods lived varied ways of life and had diverse viewpoints on social, religious, and political matters. Jesus of Nazareth and the early Christians were part of this creative Jewish environment, as were the Rabbis. The ancient sources indicate that it took several centuries before the majority of the Jewish communities accepted the Rabbinic vision for the Jewish world, and several decades elapsed before the followers of Jesus of Nazareth fully and consciously separated from Judaism.

Apologetics will never be absent from the scholarship, but matters have substantially improved. Historiography written from an explicitly Christian viewpoint since the Second World War shows a curtailing of overtly anti-Semitic tendencies that plagued much of that work in the past. However, problems remain. Some Christian depictions retain the tendency to portray Judaism as both monolithic and defective rather than as a richly diverse way of life that fulfilled the needs of people inside the Jewish community and attracted numerous Gentile affiliates as well as converts. Seeing Jesus as unique or "different" in his life, teachings, or purposes and Christianity as "special," they begin their understanding of the times with a conclusion already drawn. Yet such conclusions tend to clash at a practical level with the Jewishness of Jesus and the early Palestinian church. Finally, they also tend to focus on the parts of Judaism most important to Christianity and not develop a coherent and adequate interpretation of Judaism as a whole. In turn, some Jewish historiography, while now recognizing that the early Jesus movement was part of the matrix of Second Temple and early Rabbinic society, still in places retains an older, naïve view that the Rabbinic sources generally reflect pre-70 C.E. Jewish society.

The books recommended here provide accessible accounts of early Judaism and Christianity. Along with listing recent publications, the bibliography retains much of the information from the first edition of this work; a number of books listed in that first edition remain classics, and they have not disappeared from the bookshelves of students of early Jewish and Christian history.

For an older overview of the period with a selection of the literature joined by brief commentary, see D. S. Russell, *The Jews from Alexander to Herod* (Cambridge: Cambridge University Press, 1967). Russell's updated, brief survey of the period and its literature, *From Early Judaism to Early Church* (Philadelphia: Fortress Press, 1986) discusses some major topics but suffers from lack of contact with the most recent research. A slightly longer and more detailed introduction to the Jewish and Christian context can be found in A. R. C. Leaney, *Cambridge Commentaries on Writings of the Jewish and Christian World, 200 B.C. to A.D. 200*, vol. 6, *The Jewish and Christian World, 200 B.C. to A.D. 200* (Cambridge: Cambridge University Press, 1984). More than half the book attends to history and the rest to brief descriptions of the literature of Judaism and Christianity. An index makes this volume a good small reference work. Earlier volumes in this series cover Jews in the Hellenistic world, the Qumran community, Greco-Roman literature on Jews and Christians, and so on.

Several detailed, scholarly surveys of Judaism function as reference works as well as starting points for study. Lester Grabbe, in *Judaism from Cyrus to Hadrian*, vol. 1, *The Persian and Greek Periods* (Minneapolis: Fortress Press, 1991), and vol. 2, *The Roman Period* (Minneapolis: Fortress Press, 1992), combines comprehensive reviews of ancient and modern literature, balanced discussion of historical problems, and clear historical syntheses for each period of the Persian, Greek, and Roman Empires up until the defeat of Bar Kosiba in 135 C.E. For a single-volume study, Grabbe's *History of the Jews and Judaism in the Second Temple Period* (London:

T. & T. Clark, 2004) is a readable and thoughtful survey. A more detailed, and expensive, four-volume reference work is Emil Schürer, G. Vermes, F. Millar, P. Vermes, and M. Black, *The History of the Jewish People in the Age of Jesus Christ, 175 B.C.– A.D. 135* (Edinburgh: Clark, 1973–87). This thorough revision of a famous and often quite anti-Jewish, late-nineteenth-century handbook of Jewish religion and thought contains a wealth of information in its dense footnotes, reviews all the historical problems, summarizes the Jewish literature of the period, and is well indexed. A more readable but still extensively detailed account of first-century C.E. Judaism can be found in the two volumes of S. Safrai, M. Stern, D. Flusser, and W. C. van Unnik, *The Jewish People in the First Century* (Philadelphia: Fortress Press, 1974–6). Chapters by major scholars treat historical, social, economic, religious, and cultural topics. A number of chapters uncritically use later Rabbinic literature to reconstruct first-century Judaism, but a wealth of material is gathered in readable form. Finally, for a detailed study of the literature of Second Temple Judaism, see George W. E. Nickelsburg's now fully revised and expanded *Jewish Literature between the Bible and the Mishnah: A Historical and Literary Introduction, with CD-Rom* (Minneapolis: Augsburg Fortress, 2005). The CD has biblical citation hyperlinks to the NRSV and Web links to primary texts. For treatments of the Targumim, see Bruce Chilton, *The Glory of Israel: The Theology and Provenience of the Isaiah Targum,* Journal for the Study of the Old Testament, Supplement 23 (Sheffield: JSOT, 1982); *The Isaiah Targum: Introduction, Translation, Apparatus, and Notes,* The Aramaic Bible 11 (Wilmington, DE: Glazier; Edinburgh: Clark, 1987); *A Galilean Rabbi and His Bible: Jesus' Use of the Interpreted Scripture of His Time* (Wilmington, DE: Glazier, 1984; also published with the subtitle, *Jesus' Own Interpretation of Isaiah,* in London: SPCK, 1984); *Targumic Approaches to the Gospels: Essays in the Mutual Definition of Judaism and Christianity,* Studies in Judaism (Lanham, MD, and London: University Press of America, 1986); Martin McNamara, *Targum and Testament. Aramaic Paraphrases of the Hebrew Bible: A Light on the New Testament* (Grand Rapids: Eerdmans, 1972).

Martin Hengel's *Judaism and Hellenism,* 2 vols. (Philadelphia: Fortress Press, 1974) traces the early stages of Jewish adaptation and resistance to Hellenistic culture. His *Jews, Greeks, and Barbarians* (Philadelphia: Fortress Press, 1980) offers a briefer account of his position. The complex relationships and conflicts with Hellenism during the Maccabean War are clearly and briefly described in Daniel J. Harrington, *The Maccabean Revolt* (Wilmington, DE: Glazier, 1988). These various studies are advanced in the detailed studies by Eric Gruen, including *Heritage and Hellenism: The Reinvention of Jewish Tradition* (Berkeley: University of California Press, 1998) and *Diaspora: Jews amidst Greeks and Romans* (Cambridge, MA: Harvard University Press, 2002).

The Deuterocanonical texts (Old Testament Apocrypha) in their social and historical contexts are well described in David A. deSilva's *Introducing the Apocrypha: Message, Context, and Significance* (Grand Rapids: Baker Academic, 2002), which targets a Protestant Christian readership, and

Daniel J. Harrington's shorter *Invitation to the Apocrypha* (Grand Rapids: Eerdmans, 1999), which is designed for nonspecialists.

James D. Newsome's *Greeks, Romans, Jews: Currents of Culture and Belief in the New Testament World* (Philadelphia: Trinity, 1992) is a textbook written for Christians interested in Judaism as a background for the New Testament. Newsome stresses appreciation of religious content and experience; the volume offers an attractive selection of illustrative quotations. Though not all Pharisees are bad according to Newsome, many are wooden and sterile in comparison with the alleged freedom of Jesus (portrayed as a good modern individualist, if not an American). On the synagogue and many other subjects, the most current scholarship is ignored or, if noted, is slighted. Later Rabbinic sources are used inappropriately to reconstruct first-century history.

Frederick J. Murphy's *The Religious World of Jesus* (Nashville: Abingdon, 1991; 2d ed. 2005) is a readable and well-executed textbook. It explicitly corrects Christian cultural biases against Judaism and presents Judaism as a historically coherent and developing religious tradition. The major historical events and literary products of the Second Temple period are fairly and comprehensively presented. A selection of original texts are quoted, and special attention is given to topics that are relevant to Jesus and of natural interest to Christians, up to about 100 C.E. A treatment of the relationship between the ancient calendars of Judaism and Christianity is available in Bruce Chilton, *Redeeming Time: The Wisdom of Ancient Jewish and Christian Festal Calendars* (Peabody, MA: Hendrickson, 2002). Notable as well are recent volumes by two of early Judaism's most prominent scholars. James C. VanderKam's *An Introduction to Early Judaism* (Grand Rapids: Eerdmans, 2001) offers a history beginning with the Persian period not only detailing the history up until the First Revolt but also describing the Temple and the celebration of Jewish festivals. George W. E. Nickelsburg's *Ancient Judaism and Christian Origins: Diversity, Continuity, and Transformation* (Minneapolis: Fortress Press, 20003) is a theologically sensitive study that explains the relevance of Early Judaism for Christian self-understanding by detailing the place of the Torah observance in Second Temple Jewish life, the diverse views of God's interaction with humanity, and the methods by which Jewish communities negotiated with the rise of Hellenism and with Romanization.

Gabrielle Boccaccini, *Middle Judaism: Jewish Thought, 300 B.C.E.–200 C.E.* (Minneapolis: Fortress Press, 1991), attempts to redefine the relationship of Christianity to Judaism using methods from the history of philosophy and intellectual history to understand the dynamics of Judaism. His book is a preparatory study for a history of Jewish thought, not for an organic reconstruction. Offering an unusual typology, Boccaccini limits ancient Judaism to the sixth to fourth centuries B.C.E. and assigns the third century B.C.E. through the second century C.E. to "Middle Judaism," a period that encompasses several types of Judaism, including Pharisaism, early Christianity, Essenism, apocalyptic, and others. Out of Middle Judaism came four new types of Judaism: Rabbinism, Karaism, Falashas, and Christianity. Boccaccini's striking innovation, which has not received wide acceptance, is that Christianity should continue to be understood as a type of Judaism to the present day.

Sean Freyne's *The World of the New Testament* (Collegeville, MN: Liturgical Press, 1980) is a succinct, well-written description of Judaism, the Greco-Roman world, and the emergence of Christianity as a Jewish sect, and covers the essential people, events, and institutions of the period. A more scholarly study by Freyne focuses on Galilee, *Galilee from Alexander the Great to Hadrian, 323 B.C.E. to 135 C.E.: A Study of Second Temple Judaism* (Wilmington, DE: Glazier, 1980). Freyne's *Galilee, Jesus, and the Gospels* (Philadelphia: Fortress Press, 1988) is now surpassed by his *Jesus, a Jewish Galilean: A New Reading of the Jesus Story* (London and New York: T. & T. Clark, 2004). For the social roles of various Jewish groups in the first century and the structure of Palestinian society, see Anthony J. Saldarini, *Pharisees, Scribes, and Sadducees in Palestinian Society: A Sociological Analysis* (Wilmington, DE: Glazier, 1988); Bruce Chilton, *The Temple of Jesus: His Sacrificial Program within a Cultural History of Sacrifice* (University Park: Pennsylvania State University Press, 1992).

E. P. Sanders, in *Judaism: Practice and Belief, 63 B.C.E.–66 C.E.* (Philadelphia: Trinity International, 1992), attempts to describe in concrete detail Jewish life in the first centuries B.C.E. and C.E. His earlier works, *Paul and Palestinian Judaism: A Comparison of Patterns of Religion* (Philadelphia: Fortress Press, 1977) and *Jesus and Judaism* (Philadelphia: Fortress Press, 1985; see also his *The Historical Figure of Jesus* [London: Allen Lane, 1993]), correct earlier scholarship's uncritical and apologetic depictions of Judaism and demonstrate how an accurate picture of Judaism changes one's apprehension of Jesus and the New Testament. Detailed essays on the relationship between Judaism and Jewish identity are offered in Shaye J. D. Cohen's *The Beginnings of Jewishness: Boundaries, Varieties, Uncertainties* (Berkeley: University of California Press, 1999).

On the subject of Jesus and Judaism, which is enormous, see Geza Vermes, *The Religion of Jesus the Jew* (Minneapolis: Fortress Press, 1993) and *Jesus in His Jewish Context* (Minneapolis: Fortress Press, 2003); Paula Fredriksen, *Jesus of Nazareth, King of the Jews: A Jewish Life and the Emergence of Christianity* (New York: Knopf, 1999); Bruce Chilton, *Rabbi Jesus: An Intimate Biography* (New York: Doubleday, 2000); Amy-Jill Levine, *The Misunderstood Jew: The Church and the Scandal of the Jewish Jesus* (San Francisco: HarperSanFrancisco, 2006); and the various essays in A.-J. Levine, D. C. Allison, Jr., and J. D Crossan, eds., *Documenting the Historical Jesus* (Princeton: Princeton University Press, 2006).

Mark Chancey's *Greco-Roman Culture and the Galilee of Jesus* (Cambridge and New York: Cambridge University Press, 2005) and the companion volume, *The Myth of the Gentile Galilee* (Cambridge and New York: Cambridge University Press, 2002), detail the results of archaeological investigation of numerous Galilean sites, including examinations of architecture, inscriptions, coins, and art from the time of Alexander the Great to the early fourth century C.E. to demonstrate the Galilee's overwhelming Jewish presence. Chancey argues that Romanization really began in Galilee not with Antipas, but in the second century, after the placement there of a Roman garrison. Peter Richardson's *Building Jewish in the Roman East* (Waco, TX: Baylor University Press, 2004), a somewhat uneven collection of essays mostly on archaeology, reveals how well integrated Jewish communities were with their Diaspora neighbors.

For studies of the Dead Sea Scrolls, James C. VanderKam and Peter Flint's *The Meaning of the Dead Sea Scrolls: Their Significance for Understanding the Bible, Judaism, Jesus, and Christianity* (San Francisco: HarperSanFrancisco, 2002) provides a wealth of detail in an accessible format. Hershel Shanks's edited collection, *Understanding the Dead Sea Scrolls* (New York: Vintage Books, 1993) is, as its subtitle indicates, a reader from the *Biblical Archaeological Review*.

Several books from the late 1980s and early 1990s address the separation of Judaism and Christianity. James D. G. Dunn, in *The Parting of the Ways between Christianity and Judaism and Their Significance for the Character of Christianity* (Philadelphia: Trinity, 1991), analyzes the implications of the Jewish origins of Christianity and the basis for its separate identity. Reacting against A. von Harnack and R. Bultmann's earlier concept of a universal Jesus drained of Jewishness, Dunn's book is theologically oriented. Dunn builds his picture of Judaism on four pillars: monotheism, an elect covenant people, Torah, and Temple/land. When Christians questioned and redefined these pillars in the mid-second century, the ways parted. Shaye J. D. Cohen's *From the Maccabees to the Mishnah* (Philadelphia: Westminster, 1987) treats the period topically, covering its history, practices, and beliefs; Jewish institutions; various Jewish groups and sects; the scriptural canon; and the emergence of Rabbinic Judaism. Cohen concentrates on cultural and religious processes affecting Judaism, such as Hellenization, the "democratization" of religion in the Second Temple period, and the endurance of Judaism in new social circumstances. Lawrence H. Schiffman, *From Text to Tradition: A History of Second Temple and Rabbinic Judaism* (Hoboken, NJ: Ktav, 1991), moves from the Persian period to the development of the Talmud and stresses the continuities in historical experience, literary development, and religious thought. His introduction gives a full treatment of Rabbinic literature, including the Mishnah, Tosefta, Talmuds, and midrashim. For Schiffman, the diversity of Judaism flowed together into the unified, normative tradition found in the Talmud and represented by the Rabbinic sages. Thus he values the Pharisees and Rabbinic Judaism and treats other forms of Judaism during this period as background for Rabbinic literature. Finally, Alan F. Segal's *Rebecca's Children: Judaism and Christianity in the Roman World* (Cambridge, MA: Harvard University Press, 1986), a reflective and lucid narrative rather than a textbook, concentrates on the major intellectual trends and historical movements of the period and devotes considerable space to Segal's main theme, a comparison of Judaism and Christianity until they definitively separated. Segal stresses the complementarity and positive relationships between Christianity and Judaism.

Judith Lieu explores the intimate relations between Christians and Jews past the time of the writing of the New Testament. See her *Image and Reality: The Jews in the World of the Christians in the Second Century* (Edinburgh: T. & T. Clark, 1996). Daniel Boyarin's *Borderlines: The Partition of Judaeo-Christianity* (Philadelphia: University of Pennsylvania Press, 2004) is a witty, dense, and theoretically sophisticated volume that pushes the distinction between Church and Synagogue past the time of Constantine. Claudia Setzer's *Jewish Responses to Early Christians: History and Polemics, 30–150 C.E.* (Minneapolis: Fortress Press, 1994) is a good attempt at reconstructing a surprisingly overlooked subject. Stephen G. Wilson's *Related Strangers: Jews and Christians, 70–170 C.E.* (Minneapolis: Fortress Press, 1995) offers a well-written study that moves from the New Testament materials to the development of the early church. His *Leaving the Fold: Apostates and Defectors in Antiquity* (Minneapolis: Fortress Press, 2004) is the first full study to explore "conversion" from the other side.

The flourishing of women's studies has begun to illuminate the place and roles of women in antiquity. Ross S. Kraemer, in *Her Share of Blessings: Women's Religions among Pagans, Jews, and Christians in the Greco-Roman World* (New York: Oxford University Press, 1992), presents numerous testimonies to women's practice of religion and the positive and negative political and cultural consequences it had for their lives. For details on women's literary depictions and social roles, see Amy-Jill Levine's edited collection, *"Women Like This": New Perspectives on Jewish Women in the Greco-Roman World,* Early Judaism and Its Literature 1 (Atlanta: Scholars Press, 1991). Additional detailed studies appear in several works by Tal Ilan, including her *Jewish Women in Greco-Roman Palestine* (Peabody, MA: Hendrikson, 1996). For the Rabbinic period, as well as for insightful discussions of the distinctions between the Palestinian and Babylonian Talmuds, see Michael Satlow, *Jewish Marriage in Antiquity* (Princeton: Princeton University Press, 2001).

Jacob Neusner has written a number of books on Rabbinic Judaism and its relationship with Christianity. The most accessible are *Foundations of Judaism* (Philadelphia: Fortress Press, 1989); *From Testament to Torah: An Introduction to Judaism in Its Formative Age* (Englewood Cliffs, NJ: Prentice-Hall, 1988); *Midrash in Context; Messiah in Context; and Torah: From Scroll to Symbol in Formation Judaism* (Philadelphia: Fortress Press, 1983–5); *Classical Christianity and Rabbinic Judaism: Comparing Theologies,* with Bruce Chilton (Grand Rapids: Baker Academic, 2004). For a technical reference book on the complex world of the Talmud and other Rabbinic texts, see Neusner's *Introduction to Rabbinic Literature,* Anchor Bible Reference Library (New York: Random House, 1994). Neusner has also provided readable introductions to the major categories of Rabbinic literature in *The Mishnah: An Introduction*

(Northvale, NJ: Aaronson, 1989), *Invitation to Midrash* (New York: Harper, 1989), and *Invitation to Talmud* (New York: Harper, 1973). These invitations give ample examples of the original texts with explanations. Literary comparison between the development of the Gospels and Rabbinic literature is pursued in Bruce Chilton, *Profiles of a Rabbi: Synoptic Opportunities in Reading about Jesus,* Brown Judaic Studies 177 (Atlanta: Scholars Press, 1989).

Finally, a number of studies and books have grappled with the delicate question of anti-Jewish and anti-Semitic attitudes in the New Testament and early Christian literature. Four excellent collections are Alan T. Davies, ed., *Anti-Semitism and the Foundations of Christianity* (New York: Paulist, 1979); Craig A. Evans and Donald A. Hagner, eds., *Anti-Semitism and Early Christianity: Issues of Polemic and Faith* (Minneapolis: Fortress Press, 1993); Peter Richardson and S. Wilson, eds., *Anti-Judaism in Early Christianity*, vol. 1, *Paul and the Gospels;* vol. 2, *Separation and Polemic,* Studies in Christianity and Judaism 1–2 (Waterloo, Ontario: Wilfred Laurier Press, 1986); William Farmer, ed., *Anti-Judaism and the Gospels* (Harrisburg, PA: Trinity, 1999); and Paula Fredriksen and Adele Reinhartz, eds., *Jesus, Judaism, and Christian Anti-Judaism: Reading the New Testament after the Holocaust* (Louisville: Westminster John Knox, 2002).

Reading the actual Jewish writings is the most satisfying way of understanding the Second Temple period. Most of the literature can be found in several collections: James H. Charlesworth, ed., *The Old Testament Pseudepigrapha,* 2 vols. (Garden City, NY: Doubleday, 1983–5); H. D. F. Sparks, *The Apocryphal Old Testament* (Oxford: Clarendon, 1985); Geza Vermes, *The Dead Sea Scrolls in English,* 3d ed. (London: Penguin, 1987); Martin McNamara, *The Aramaic Bible* (Collegeville, MN: Liturgical Press, 1987–). Introductions to these works and their context include Michael Stone, ed., *Jewish Writings of the Second Temple Period* (Philadelphia: Fortress Press, 1984); Craig Evans, *Non-canonical Writings and New Testament Interpretation* (Peabody, MA: Hendrickson, 1992); G. Vermes, *The Dead Sea Scrolls: Qumran in Perspective* (Cleveland: Collins World, 1977); and two books by John J. Collins, *The Apocalyptic Imagination: An Introduction to the Jewish Matrix of Christianity* (New York: Crossroad, 1984), and *Between Athens and Jerusalem: Jewish Identity in the Hellenistic Diaspora* (New York: Crossroad, 1983). Each of these books summarizes the literature covered and puts it in historical, literary, and religious context.

PART THREE

The Formation of Christian Communities

Howard Clark Kee

I. JESUS AND THE COVENANT

A. Jesus and the Judaism of His Time

Jesus shared with his contemporaries a profound connection to Judaism; the covenant with Abraham, Isaac, and Jacob served for him more as the ground faith than as a particular belief. To his mind, as the Gospels show, the patriarchs were living, enduring presences that guaranteed God's eternal care for his people (Mark 12:26–7; Matthew 22:31–2; Luke 20:37–8). What God had done for Israel and disclosed to Israel in the past shaped the significance of their lives in the present and into the future. Jesus assumed, as did most Jews in his time, that Israel's Scriptures were to be interpreted and appropriated in new ways, because the present was as much in God's hands as the past. Especially given the changed circumstances in which the land promised to Israel lay under Roman dominance, much Judaic interpretation turned on the issue of how the divine promises to Abraham and the patriarchs were to be realized.

In the tradition of the prophet Jeremiah, many Israelites awaited God's renewal of the covenant (Jeremiah 31:31–4). A basic question for them became, What is the essence of belonging to God's people? In postexilic Judaism, answers to that question varied widely. The writings that came to be called the New Covenant (a more accurate rendering than "New Testament") need to be seen in the context of Jesus' distinctive attempt, along with those of his followers and successors, to understand, reclaim, and fulfill the covenantal tradition.

For the priestly establishment and those who agreed with it, the cultic system centered on the Temple in Jerusalem that uniquely maintained Israel's covenantal relationship with God. Since the Temple was believed to be the place where God was present among his people, the building and its rites ensured the continuity of Israel's place as God's special people. Daily sacrifices and other offerings had to be performed properly, and faithful Jews from territorial Israel, as well as tens of thousands from Jewish communities scattered throughout the Diaspora, arranged to take part in worship and to make contributions toward the support of the Temple and its priesthood.

Fallen stones from the Jerusalem Temple. As a result of clearing the areas adjacent to the western and southern walls of the Temple complex, the enormous size of the stones cut and positioned to form the supporting complex wall became visible. The effects of the Roman attack on Jerusalem and its Temple in 66–70 C.E., as well as in 135 C.E., are all evidenced by the fall and scattering of the massive stones. (BiblePlaces.com)

Herod the Great rebuilt the Temple in his grandiose manner, and the site became a popular cultural venue for non-Jews, so that both Jewish pilgrims and Gentile tourists made major contributions to the economy and society of Jerusalem and Judea. Because some of them lived far from Jerusalem, members of priestly families performed rituals in the Temple on a rotating basis. The priestly caste exercised considerable economic and social power. The Roman authorities not only sanctioned the performance of sacred ceremonies in the Temple, they also worked through priestly leaders to maintain social and political control over their subject peoples in what eventually was called Syria-Palestina, the Philistine coast of Syria (or "Palestine" in modern usage). As early as the first century B.C.E., any candidate for the role of high priest needed confirmation of his role from the Roman authorities if he expected to exercise his office. The mutually beneficial relationship between Roman authorities and priestly families thrived during the period after the Romans took over Palestine in 63 B.C.E. until the Jewish revolt of 66–70 C.E.

Jesus is portrayed in all the Gospels as challenging priestly control of the Temple and of worship there. He expelled from the Temple those who in the eyes of the priestly establishment made worship possible: the money changers, who exchanged various foreign currencies for the coinage accepted in the Temple, and the vendors of the sacrificial animals (Matthew 21:12–17; Mark 11:15–17; Luke 19:45–6; John 2:14–16). Jesus had organized his followers to strike against the center of Judaism in this way to protest the policies of the high priest Caiaphas. Caiaphas, as the Gospels show, permitted vendors to set up shop in the Great Court of the Temple. As a peasant from Galilee, Jesus believed that the offerings brought to the Temple should not be purchased there, but that Israelites should offer of their own produce. At the same time, Caiaphas had removed the council of local religious leaders called the Sanhedrin from the Temple to Chanuth, the market on the Mount of Olives (according to the Babylonian Talmud in Shabbat 15a; Sanhedrin 41a; Abodah Zarah 8b). Jesus' protest was to a large extent a conservative objection to innovation by the priestly elite, but he also went to the extreme of predicting the Temple's destruction in a way reminiscent of Jeremiah. Jesus contended – in the manner of many prophets before him, and with their authorization, he said – that God intended the Temple to be a place of prayer "for all nations" (Isaiah 56:7). When he said this, he was standing in the Great Court, the only part of the Temple into which non-Jews were allowed entry. The expanded people of God belonged here as far as he was concerned, not commercial operations that benefited priests. The Book of Zechariah had similarly predicted a revolutionary end-time, cataclysmic in its proportions, when God would gather people from all nations in a Temple where no merchant stood between the new people of God and their sacrificial worship (Zechariah 14). For Jesus to prophesy Gentile access could only have been regarded by the priestly establishment as a threat to the sanctity of the Temple as the place where a ritually pure Israel met their God. The priests could scarcely overlook the challenge that Jesus' utterances and actions represented, since they implied that the Temple's status quo was expendable as the point of connection between God and his people, and that access to Israel's God should be open to non-Jews. Moreover, of course, Jesus' actions directly contradicted Caiaphas's authority over the Temple on the basis of the prophetic authorization that he claimed for his actions.

The discovery of the Dead Sea Scrolls, especially the document known as the *Temple Scroll*, has made the importance of purity and Temple worship in the Judaism of this period unmistakable. Once dismissed as secondary within the religious practice of the time and at best marginal for Jesus' movement, sacrifice and purity are now recognized as central concerns. The Qumran community produced the

---

THE OSSUARY OF CAIAPHAS

In a major archaeological discovery in 1990, a bulldozer took the top off of a cave 1.5 miles south of Mount Zion, uncovering a mausoleum. An adult, even a short adult, could not have stood erect in the cave, but a pit had been dug near its entrance to allow mourners to stand while tending to their dead and praying. Corpses were laid out on a shelf, and after the flesh had decomposed, the bones were gathered and stored. Bone storage for the anonymous poor was in a pit dug in the cave's floor, and the bones of wealthier, prominent people were kept in small limestone ossuaries placed in the shafts that ran outward like spokes from the central cave.

One such ossuary had the name "Caiaphas" carved roughly into its side and back. A coin discovered in the cave is dated 42/3 C.E. (during the reign of Herod Agrippa I). If the ossuary were for Caiaphas the high priest, he would have been about sixty when he died (ca. 46), and, inside the ossuary marked with Caiaphas's name, the bones of a man aged around sixty years old were indeed found, along with the bones of an adult female, two infants, a small child, and a young adult. Death apparently came to them all from natural causes. Elegant decorative carving distinguishes Caiaphas's ossuary from most ossuaries of that place and period. It is carved with a pattern of five floral designs, for the most part in spirals, arranged around a central, spiraling flower. The palm design that surrounds the circles picks up a motif in the Temple's decoration. Placed in the tunnel to the south of the cave, the ossuary was in fact oriented to face that Temple. Caiaphas's status, and his connection to the Temple, the preeminent sacred place in Judaism, is attested by this find, and the ossuary is an eloquent witness to Judaism in the first century C.E.: a vibrant religion, centered on the Temple and passionately devoted to the worship of God through sacrifice in that holy place.

The sight of the Temple Mount from the Kidron Valley corroborates ancient descriptions of the magnificence of the entire structure. (BiblePlaces.com)

Temple Scroll during the first century B.C.E., persuaded that the priesthood in charge of the Temple was unworthy and that the ritual carried out there was not acceptable to the God of Israel. They awaited God's ultimate revelation, when their leaders would rule the Temple, which was to be rebuilt and purified as the *Temple Scroll* detailed. No portion of this new Temple was designated as the Court of the Gentiles, and there is a long list of Jews whose personal impurities disqualify even them from entering the sacred courts. This list corresponds to the identification in the Gospels of some of the people whom Jesus – in sharp contrast to the Dead Sea group – brought into the fellowship of his followers: people with broken skin (traditionally but wrongly called "lepers," as we have seen in Part One of the *Companion*, in the box "Leprosy, an old confusion"), women with flows of blood, those who had contact with the dead and who dealt with evil spirits, and children. In the *Temple Scroll*, non-Israelites are given no place in Israel's approach to God; even proselytes must wait until the fourth generation before they may enter the middle court of the Temple. Women can go no farther than the outer court. Those who violate the purity code are to be executed. Anyone considered to be a traitor to Israel or who makes a place for himself among Gentiles should be crucified, though care is to be taken that he is buried on the day of his death, so that the holy land will not be polluted by the contamination of the corpse.

Other texts among the Dead Sea Scrolls show in detail how this group of Jews (referred to in some ancient Jewish writings and by most scholars as "Essenes") were led by the founder of their movement to believe that it was no longer possible to obey God and preserve the purity of his people as long as they lived in Jerusalem under the status quo. Contact with impure people and subjection to what they regarded as corrupt religious leaders required them to withdraw to the desert or, failing that, into urban residential communities that could regulate themselves, much as Israel had done in ancient times, in preparation for its new existence in the Promised Land. The Essenes saw themselves as chosen by God to return to Jerusalem in the near future, to regulate worship in the Temple as God desired, and to purify the city and God's people. Meanwhile, their common life in and around the community center overlooking the Dead Sea required them to purify themselves regularly through immersion and to meet for common meals, which anticipated the great banquet that would take place when God restored them and sent among them the two messiahs (one priestly and one royal). Members were strictly obligated to conform to their heightened rules of purity under penalty of temporary or even permanent exclusion from the new covenant people.

Some interpreters of the Dead Sea Scrolls have sought to link Jesus with the Essenes, either directly or by supposing that John the Baptist belonged to the sect. Jesus does appear in the Gospels as one who shared with the Dead Sea group an expectation of covenant renewal, and he celebrated that future event in a characteristic meal of bread and wine. He prepared people to participate in "the kingdom of God," as he called the divinely mandated future in language also shared with the Essenes. But such similarities also linked Jesus to other Jewish communities, and he contradicted many of the Dead Sea group's standards: he welcomed out-casts, "sinners," women, and children, and approached "lepers," people thought to be dead, Gentiles, and the demon-possessed. The future of God's people, as he proclaimed it, had no place for the Temple as envis-aged by the priests, but only as anticipated by prophets such as Isaiah and Zechariah. He saw purity in terms of love of God and of neighbor – and insisted on the deep connection between God and neighbor that made loving the one equivalent to loving the other. Opponents attacked him for consorting with "tax collectors and prostitutes" (Matthew 21:31), for his acceptance of outcasts, and repeatedly his response is the same: he insisted they were fit for God's kingdom. For Jesus purity, like unclean-ness, was contagious. The crucial move in his mind was to trigger the purity that came from inside a person (Mark 7:15). Once that purity was activated, a person became an agent of God's kingdom. Through his pro-grammatic purification – of individuals and groups whom he announced forgiven of sin and ready for their encounter with the divine sovereign of Israel and the universe – Jesus extended God's kingdom meal by meal, person by person.

Jesus' prophetic perspective threatened the ideologies of both the priestly establishment and groups like the Dead Sea community. He even said that "the sons of this world are cleverer than the sons of light in their own generation" (Luke 16:8), a calculated affront to the Essenes, who proudly labeled themselves "sons of light"! The fact that Jesus claimed the support of the God of Israel and of the Scriptures for his position, even as he contradicted well-ensconced conventional views, confronted his Jewish contemporaries with a crucial question: Did this teacher come from God or from Satan, God's adversary? His challenge reached into some of the most axiomatic practices of Judaism, not only those of priests and Essenes.

During the first century C.E. the Pharisaic movement changed from an informal, largely spontaneous association into a powerful, organized group that the Romans supported after 70 C.E. (much as Rome had earlier supported the priesthood). Like the Essenes, the Pharisees were primarily concerned with the purity of their members, although they sought to maintain their cleanness while living within Israelite society, rather than apart from it. Pharisaism's major emphases were on dietary and social modes of maintaining what its constituents saw as Israel's special relationship with God. Adherents gathered for table fellowship as well as for prayer, study of the Scriptures, and memorization and interpretation of the oral traditions of their sages. The Pharisees related these gatherings to God's presence in the Temple, adapting for their meetings and households some of the ritual requirements and practices that were laid down in the Law of Moses for the Temple and its priesthood. Although daily obligations might bring the Pharisees into associations with the impure of this world, their special identity was celebrated and reinforced in their informal fellowship meals and meetings. For them, as for the priests and the Essenes of Qumran, Jesus posed a challenge and an implicit threat with his alternative, prophetic view of purity.

Christians after the time of Jesus exaggerated the intensity of antagonism between his movement and the Pharisees; in the post-70 period the Pharisees (with Roman support) moved into positions of power and influence and often opposed Christian teaching. As the pages of the New Testament show, Christians responded by making the Pharisees into archetypical villains who were directly responsible for Jesus' death and who promoted a superficial understanding of religion. Even allowing for this exaggeration, Jesus' fellowship with sinners in the name of God's kingdom flatly contradicted the Pharisees' requirements of ritually pure fellowship.

Nationalism – religious, not merely political and ethnic – also exerted a powerful influence among Jews of this period. Israel would be truly the people of God according to this view, deeply affected by the Maccabean triumphs of the recent past (when it was an autonomous state), with the divinely designated agent (king or priest or both, depending on the

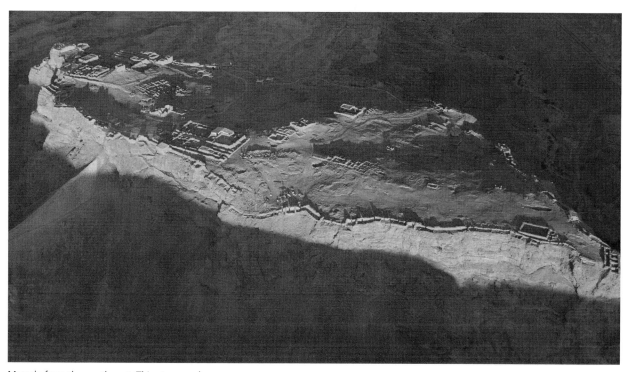

Masada from the southwest. This steep and rocky mountain, to the southwest of and overlooking the Dead Sea, was used by Hasmonean rulers in the early first century B.C.E. to site a fortress. Herod the Great, living up to his reputation as a builder, expanded the buildings, providing palaces as well as multiple bathhouses and pools served by cisterns to capture rainwater. Special facilities were built for the royal guard based there. After the destruction of the Temple in 70 C.E., Jewish revolutionaries maintained an outpost at Masada until 73 C.E., when they committed mass suicide rather than surrender to the Roman siege. At the time of the second Jewish revolt (132–5 C.E.), Masada was a major base for the Jewish revolutionaries. Beginning in 1950, extensive correspondence between Bar Kokhba (as Simon bar Kosiba called himself), the leader of the revolt, and his aides in the revolution was found in caves in canyons running down to the Dead Sea north of Masada. These provide detailed information about the course and strategies of the revolt, although no sources have survived to provide an overall picture of this unsuccessful uprising against the Romans. (BiblePlaces.com)

particular nationalism concerned) as its visible ruler. That conviction had given rise to the Maccabean revolt, and stood in tension with the Roman decision to establish Herod as king of the Jews. Herod came from Idumea, which had been forcibly converted by the Maccabees, and his mode of life sometimes contradicted Jewish law: his behavior and his pedigree (as that of his family) provoked the nationalists to revolt on several occasions. Jesus refused to take up the option of seizing power or assuming authority in a political sense. In his response to the request of James and John, that he grant them special places of honor beside him when he sat on the throne of glory in the coming kingdom of God (Mark 10:35–45), he told them that to follow him was a way of suffering and death that opened the way for the establishment of God's rule. When he was seized by the authorities and brought to trial, he was remembered as refusing either to defend himself *or* to lay claim to a political role. The Gospels portray Jesus scorned in death, labeled "King of the Jews" in cruel parody; the Roman authorities and Jewish nationalists alike understood that title as a literal claim to political and military power, and they saw Jesus as an abject failure.

Other Jews of the period were persuaded that God's self-disclosure through the Law and the Prophets gave them special insight into his nature and purposes, yet they also saw many points of contact and affinity between the scriptural tradition and the learning of the wider world. The figure of Wisdom, as we have seen, personified God's revelation to his people. For those Jews who had lived and been educated under the influence of Hellenistic philosophy, the basic harmony between revealed (Jewish) and rational (Gentile) wisdom seemed obvious and profound at the same time. There is no indication that this sort of philosophical influence was significant for Jesus personally. Wisdom did feature in his conception of the divine, but within the nonphilosophical idiom of Proverbs rather than in the intellectual terms of Philo of Alexandria. But for those who later saw Jesus as the personal disclosure of God's purpose for the whole world, the language of Greek philosophy proved indispensable. In a similar way, the practice among many Jewish intellectuals of interpreting their tradition along allegorical or symbolic lines established the precedent in early Christian teaching for appropriating the Jesus tradition in similar ways.

Jesus clearly shared with his contemporaries in Judaism the belief that, whereas for the present God allowed his faithful people to be dominated by the powers of evil (both political and demonic), he would soon act through his chosen agents – human and angelic – to defeat his enemies, vindicate the faithful, and establish his rule in the world. Insight into the divine plan and the identity of the faithful was reserved for revelation. (See the similar view in Daniel and in the Dead Sea Scrolls, as well as in other Jewish writings of the postexilic period.) Those outside the circle of revelation could not grasp this truth, which was conveyed to insiders by divine disclosure and expressed in cryptic, often symbolic language. Apocalyptic literature largely flowed from this mentality and greatly reinforced it. Within the biblical tradition (as well as in related works) this outlook caused obvious problems when the fulfillment of the hopes did not happen, or at least not on schedule. For example, the promise of Israel's renewal in the space of 70 years expressed by Jeremiah (Jeremiah 25:11, 29:10) is revised by Daniel to 70 "weeks" of years, or 490 years (Daniel 9:1–27). In the Gospels, as elsewhere in Christian writings, there is evidence that with the passage of time the expectation of an imminent end of the age had to be changed.

Jesus is addressed by the title "Rabbi," in the Gospels, which shows that he was skilled in the folk traditions of Galilean Judaism. These traditions were predominantly oral rather than written, because the majority of Jews in Galilee were illiterate. (That ambient illiteracy is what made becoming a "scribe" – a person capable of writing and therefore of reading – an unusual achievement.) That did

---

APOCALYPTIC

"Apocalyptic" comes from the Greek word *apokalupsis*, which means "uncovering," "disclosure," or "revelation." Scholars speak of "apocalyptic" in reference to a type of literature produced by religious communities in which a radical perspective is expressed that denies the reality of this world and looks forward to its supersession by a future, divinely ordered world. As a literary style, apocalyptic claims to be a revelation by God of his purpose for his chosen people and for the future of the creation. It uses visions, oracles, symbols, and cryptic language to convey this message, since the import of such writing is intended only for the inner group, the guardians of the worldview of the community involved. Symbolic descriptions of the cosmic conflict that will precede the coming of the end of the age and the establishment of God's rule in the world typify apocalyptic. The worldview implicit in apocalyptic assumes that the present age is dominated by the powers of evil, but that God is already at work to accomplish his purpose in the created order and especially for his people by making the world anew. The community of God's people is now called on to accept suffering and even martyrdom during the present period of cosmic struggle, but they are given assurance that they will be vindicated and will enjoy new life in the age to come.

not prevent Jesus from crafting a powerful and characteristic announcement of "the kingdom of God," an expectation cherished by Galilean Jews
that God would sweep away the powers of this world and install an eternal
reign of justice. His disputes with Pharisees often concerned issues of
purity, because Jesus taught that God was cleansing his people, removing
the barriers that separated them from his kingdom, as part of the process of
installing the divine reign. As a rabbi, Jesus had close followers, and he
deliberately promulgated his teaching by travel and by sending his disciples
to teach. He attempted – as did other rabbis, but with disastrous consequences in his case – to change the conduct of worship in the Temple. Several Gospels show that in Jerusalem Jesus and his sympathizers raided the
holy precincts to expel animals and their sellers, whose activities he considered unclean when introduced for purposes of trade in the Temple
(Matthew 21–5; Mark 11–13; Luke 19:28–21:38) and an obstacle to the
prophetic prediction of free access to the Temple by a vastly expanded people of God that included even non-Jews.

High priests found Jesus guilty of blasphemy for infringing on their prerogatives and denounced him to Pontius Pilate – the Roman prefect of
Judea – as a threat to public order (Matthew 26:1–27:2; Mark 14:1–15:1;
Luke 22:1–23:5). Pilate alone had the power to order Jesus' execution. From
the perspective of official Roman policies, religious conflicts among the
subject peoples of Rome were usually considered beside the point. Yet
Rome had arranged a special provision for Jews and their religion during the
time of the Republic, and they honored it. During the empire Rome even
paid for sacrifices that Israelite priests accepted and offered in the Jerusalem
Temple. That amounted to having the priests pray for Roman prosperity and
implicitly acknowledge Roman hegemony, and in exchange Jews enjoyed
liberty of worship. By this brilliant maneuver, Rome made the Temple into
a symbol of its own power while maintaining it as the center of the worship
of Israel. What the different groups did with and to one another mattered
only regarding public order, particularly in the Temple. The Roman attitude
toward internal Jewish disputes is accurately represented in the Book of Acts,
which was written around 90 C.E., in the scene where the apostle Paul is
denounced in Corinth by some Jewish opponents before the Roman official Gallio (see Acts 18:12–17). (Because Gallio left an inscription behind, we
can date this event to the year 51–2 C.E.) Gallio explicitly and firmly refuses
to adjudicate the case on the grounds that his concerns are with breaches of
the Roman law, not of the Torah. But however much the Roman officials
may have wanted to avoid the controversy caused by the emergence of Jesus'
movement, events pressed them into the center of conflict.

The emergence of a group of followers around a Galilean rabbi named
Jesus occasioned no official concern from the Romans prior to Jesus'
action in the Temple, with one big exception. Herod Antipas ruled Galilee
and Perea (east of the Jordan) as a client prince of Rome in succession to
his father, Herod the Great (who died in 4 B.C.E.). Antipas's reign was
notably stable, to a large extent because he assiduously repressed critics. For

HISTORICAL REFERENCES TO JESUS

Josephus, the Jewish historian who wrote *The Antiquities of the Jews* near the end of the first century C.E., mentions both Jesus and his brother James, both of whom he connects to national turmoil and sporadic outbreaks of violence prior to the great insurrection and war of 66–70 C.E. Although the present text of *Antiquities* (18.63) seems to have been altered by Christian copyists to make Josephus bear testimony to Jesus' resurrection and messiahship, it almost certainly included reference to Jesus' extraordinary powers, his crucifixion under Pontius Pilate, and his followers' claim that God had raised him from the dead. The Rabbinic sources, which date from much later, never refer to Jesus by name but allege the illegitimacy of his birth and denounce the heretical nature of his teachings.

The Roman historian Suetonius, in his *Lives of the Twelve Caesars*, mentions that during the reign of Claudius (41–54 C.E.), there was a disturbance among the Jews in Rome occasioned by someone named "Chrestos," a common slave's name that Suetonius mistook for the less familiar "Christos." Tensions in the Jewish community at Rome were the result of the arrival there of teachers who proclaimed Jesus' gospel, his message of triumph, whom they evidently called "Christos" (the anointed [of God]). This would mean that within two decades of Jesus' death (i.e., by 49 C.E.), the Christian message had spread to the capital of the empire. In his *Annals* (15.44), Tacitus reports that when fire destroyed Rome in 64 C.E., Nero – who had himself profited from the fire and was thought to have started the blaze or helped it along – found likely scapegoats called Christians, whose founder had been put to death by the procurator Pontius Pilate during the reign of Tiberius (14–37 C.E.). In one of his *Letters*, Pliny wrote to the emperor Trajan (98–117 C.E.) for advice in handling the religious sect of Christians, which was spreading rapidly in the province he governed (Pontus and Bithynia, in northern Asia Minor).

These sources confirm some of the basic information about Jesus that comes from the Gospels without directly contradicting it, but they do not supplement what we read in early Christian writings.

example, after John the Baptist denounced Antipas's marriage to his brother's former wife, insisting that Antipas keep the Torah of purity as any person might understand it (see Leviticus 20:21), Antipas had him beheaded (see Matthew 14:3–12; Mark 6:17–29; Luke 3:19–20; and Josephus, *Antiquities* 18.109–19). Therefore when Jesus, who had been a disciple of John's for a time, enjoyed popular success, Antipas' suspicion naturally turned to him (see Matthew 14:1–2; Mark 6:14–16; Luke 9:7–9).

The executions of John the Baptist by Herod Antipas and of Jesus by Pontius Pilate were not examples of religious oppression. In each case, the representative of Roman power was insisting (from his own point of view) on recognition of the legitimacy of the Roman settlement. Herod's marriage – challenged by John the Baptist – was a public arrangement, and the good order of the Temple – challenged by Jesus' prophetic protest – was part and parcel of the Roman recognition of Judaism as a sanctioned religion as well as of Roman hegemony. Provided routine worship in the Temple continued, and imperial sacrifices were accepted there, the old alliance from the time of the Maccabees was remembered (see 1 Maccabees 8) and Judaism enjoyed the status of *religio licita*, a legal religion.

Jesus' threat to the public order as symbolized by the Temple could not be ignored in Pilate's judgment. He alone was legally and practically responsible for the death of Jesus. But over time, as non-Jews joined Jesus' movement after his death, his followers lost the right of being considered a *religio licita* and the increasingly Gentile Christians saw Judaism as a religion separate from and hostile toward their own. That is ironic, because the first followers of Jesus all practiced Judaism and naturally assumed that their meetings were as licit as Judaism itself. After the Sabbath closed at sunset (which was seen as the end of one day and the beginning of another), followers of Jesus would continue their observance, concluding at dawn on Sunday, the day and the time of the resurrection. The rising of the heaven's sun corresponded to the rising of God's son within this practice. But these groups increasingly came to believe that non-Jews could join them in the worship of Jesus.

To these disciples, Jews and non-Jews, Pilate's execution of Jesus did not put an end to his teaching, his influence, or his life. Jesus was still alive in their midst, and they prophesied in his name, inspired by the same Holy Spirit that had moved the prophets of old (see Acts 2:1–42). They believed that as a part of this new, in-rushing power of divine Spirit, God had authorized them to include Gentiles in their community. They baptized people in water, as John the Baptist had done, but for a new purpose: so that believers, both Jews and Gentiles, could be immersed in the Holy Spirit (Acts 1:5) and become part of a new creation.

With their inclusion of non-Jews by baptism, and with their refusal to require circumcision and (in some cases) others laws of purity, followers of Jesus ran the risk of being denounced as followers of a *superstitio* (as people today would say, a "cult"), rather than accepted as practitioners of a *religio licita*. The very name given to Jesus' followers, *Khristianoi*, was a sign of coming trouble. Adherents of the movement came to be known as "Christians" (meaning partisans of Christ) in Antioch by around the year 45 C.E., and they embraced that term of intended ridicule. The use of the term by outsiders highlights the marginal status of non-Jews who accepted baptism. Without conversion to Judaism, they were not Jews in the usual understanding; having rejected the gods of Hellenism by being baptized, they were also no longer representative of the Greco-Roman syncretism that was then fashionable. By calling disciples *Khristianoi* (Acts 11:26), a term analogous to *Kaisarianoi* (supporters of Caesar), outsiders compared the movement more to a political faction than to a religion.

This perilous situation for Christians could be exploited by their opponents or by those eager to find scapegoats to deflect hostility from themselves. In the year 64 C.E., Emperor Nero used the marginal status of Christians to get out of a difficult political situation of his own. In that year, a huge fire destroyed Rome, and it was rumored that the conflagration had been set at Nero's order. There is no doubt but that the opportunity for Nero to rebuild Rome along the lines he preferred was one he exploited to the greatest possible extent. Nero attempted to deflect suspicion from himself by fastening blame for the fire on Christians. They were rounded up, interrogated, and slaughtered, often with elaborate means of torture. Nero's excesses in regard to the Christians were obvious even to those who held that their

BAPTISM

Derived from the Greek word *baptizo*, which means "to immerse," this term was used occasionally in the Septuagint for acts of purification, as in 2 Kings 5:14, where the Aramean army officer washes himself in the Jordan and is cured of leprosy. The Torah required Israelites to purify themselves following sexual activity, childbirth, contact with a corpse or other sources of impurity (e.g., animal carcasses, foreign idols, and people with skin lesions). Bathing in this way – not for hygiene, but to restore and maintain one's place in the community – expressed Israelite identity by means of a common, basic practice. But how and in what should one immerse oneself? Priestly Zadokites (the "Sadducees" of the Greek Gospels) could afford luxurious bathing pools, sometimes in their own private dwellings. The Pharisees built stepped tanks (*miqvaoth*), with a reserve tank of water the same size, that served entire communities and were financed cooperatively. The Essenes of Qumran had larger reservoirs for the exclusive use of their community. All these pools involved carving and building in rock, as well as constructing cisterns, channels, steps, and enclosures. Many Jews, however, had no access to a pool, and even when they did, the design often did not conform to the preferred pattern of the Zadokites, the

Pharisees, or the Essenes. Immersers such as John were successful because they tapped into the popular unease over attempts by factional elites to control how Israelites made themselves clean. They insisted that the God of Israel cleansed people in his own "living waters" (water flowing or collected naturally), so that artificial pools were unnecessary.

John's baptism involved a call to confession and repentance addressed to the people of Israel, including some on the periphery of Judaism (Luke 3:10–14). The first divine witness concerning Jesus' unique place in God's purpose comes at the moment of Jesus' baptism (Mark 1:9–11). In the New Testament, baptism is a symbol for the renewal of God's people by means of the Holy Spirit, of which God's provision of food and water for Israel during the Exodus from Egypt ("baptized into Moses"; 1 Corinthians 10:1–5) was a prototype. It is also a symbol for the Christian's identification with Christ in death to the old life and resurrection to the new life of faith (Romans 6:1–4). Baptism became the normal rite by which members publicly indicated their identification with the new covenant community (Acts 2:38, 41; 8:36–8; 16:15, 33; 19:5; 22:16; 1 Corinthians 1:13–15; Galatians 3:27), calling upon God as Father by the power of the Spirit (Galatians 4:6). The source of the Spirit is Jesus

as raised from the dead. In Peter's speech at Pentecost, Jesus, having been exalted to the right hand of God, receives the promise of the Holy Spirit from the Father and pours it out on his followers (2:33). The Spirit that is poured out, then, comes directly from the majesty of God, from his rule over creation as a whole. This is the Spirit as it hovered over the waters at the beginning of creation (Genesis 1:1) and not as limited to Israel. Because the Spirit is of God, who creates people in the divine image, its presence marks God's own activity, in which all those who follow Jesus are to be included. Jesus' own program had involved proclaiming God's kingdom on the authority of his possession of God's Spirit. Now, as a consequence of the resurrection, Jesus had poured out that Spirit upon those who would follow him. Baptism in the Spirit (see Acts 1:4–5) and baptism into the name of Jesus were one and the same thing for that reason. That was why believing that Jesus was God's Son and calling upon his name were the occasions on which the Spirit was to be received. In the new environment of God's Spirit that the resurrection signaled, baptism was indeed, as Matthew 28:19 indicates, an activity and an experience that involved the Father (the source of one's identity), the Son (the agent of one's identity), and the Holy Spirit (the medium of one's identity).

religion was superstitious. The result seems to have been a reduction of attacks on Christians for several decades (see Tacitus, *Annals* 15.37–44).

In Jerusalem, meanwhile, trouble of a different kind was brewing for both Judaism and Christianity. A new spirit of nationalism influenced the priestly aristocracy. Josephus, a Jewish historian of the period who himself lived during this time, began his career as a priestly nationalist, and ended

Antioch-on-the-Orontes, today in Turkey. Located on a plain between the Lebanon Mountains and the Orontes River, near where it empties into the Mediterranean, Antioch was from its founding in about 300 B.C.E. the capital of the Seleucid kingdom and, after 64 B.C.E., of the Roman province of Syria. From the early days of Antioch, many Jews lived there. The city was important commercially, with fertile lands nearby and a major seaport, Seleucia, a short distance away. It was a center of Greco-Roman intellectual and cultural life. (BiblePlaces.com)

it as Rome's protégé. He reports that James, the brother of Jesus, was killed in the Temple in 62 C.E. at the instigation of the high priest Ananus during an interregnum between the Roman governors Festus and Albinus (*Antiquities* 20.197–203). To have the most prominent leader within Christian Judaism removed was obviously a momentous event for Christianity, but this execution was also ominous for the prospects of Judaism within the empire. In response to popular opposition to his action in Jerusalem, Ananus was deposed from the high priesthood. Josephus's account of the period makes it clear that, from the time of Albinus onward, Rome had to contend with a rising tide of nationalistic Jewish violence in and around Jerusalem.

The tide rose fatefully in the year 66 C.E., when Eleazar (the *sagan*, or manager, of the Temple) convinced priests not to accept any offerings from non-Jews (*Jewish War* 2.409). That included the sacrifices paid for by Rome, so the authorities of the Temple were breaching terms basic to the Roman recognition of Judaism as *religio licita*. Jewish insurgents took the Antonia, the fortress adjacent to the Temple, and killed the Roman soldiers within. War had been irrevocably declared, and the victor could only be Rome. Consequently, the Temple itself was destroyed by fire in 70 C.E., after a protracted siege.

The strategy of the Roman Empire in the wake of the revolt was simple, direct, and punitive. Rome now demanded that the *fiscus Iudaicus*, a tax that adult males had paid for the maintenance of the Temple, be paid directly to the temple of Jupiter Capitolinus in Rome. Moreover, the Roman *fiscus Judaicus* was to be paid by *all* Jews, minors and women included, not only by adult males. It is not surprising that, in the wake of

WAS JAMES REALLY JESUS' BROTHER?

The point of departure for considering whether James was really Jesus' brother is Mark 6:3 (cf. Matthew 13:55–6), where James is actually named as Jesus' brother, along with four other men; at least two, unnamed and unenumerated, sisters are also mentioned. Until recently, Roman Catholic opinion has been dominated by the position of Saint Jerome (in his controversial work, *Against Helvidius*, ca. 383 C.E.), who argued that although "brothers" and "sisters" are the terms used in Greek, the reference is actually to cousins. Dispute has focused on whether that view can be sustained linguistically, and, on the whole, the finding has been negative. Before Jerome, Helvidius himself had maintained during the fourth century that the brothers and sisters were just what their name implies – siblings of Jesus: although Jesus had been born of a virgin, their father was Joseph and their mother was Mary. That view clearly played havoc with the emerging doctrine of Mary's virginity after Jesus' birth, and that issue occupied the center of attention. In a work that received the imprimatur, John P. Meier has endorsed the Helvidian theory, to some extent on the basis of support from second-century church fathers (*A Marginal Jew: Rethinking the Historical Jesus*, vol. 1 [New York: Doubleday, 1991], 332). Also during the second century, a group referred to as the Ebionites even denied Jesus' virgin birth in the technical sense; his "brothers" and "sisters" were implicitly that in the full sense of those words (see Irenaeus, *Against Heresies* 1.26.1–2).

Richard Bauckham has given new currency to the view of Jesus' relationship to James developed by Epiphanius during the fourth century (see "The Brothers and Sisters of Jesus: An Epiphanian Response to John P. Meier," *Catholic Biblical Quarterly* 56 [1994]: 686–700; *Panarion* 1.29.3–4; 2.66.19; 3.78.7, 9, 13), and supported by the second-century *Protoevanglium of James* 9.2 and perhaps the *Gospel of Peter* (according to Origen's *Commentary on Matthew* 10:17): Mary was Jesus' mother, not James', since Joseph had a wife prior to his marriage to Mary. Joseph's relatively advanced age is traditionally held to account for his early departure from the narrative scene of the Gospels, and that reasonable inference lends support to this theory; moreover, James' emphasis on the Davidic identity of the church (see Acts 15:16) is easily accommodated on this view. James' seniority relative to Jesus might be reflected in the parable of the prodigal (Luke 15:11–32). The story of those with Jesus seizing him in the midst of exorcism (Mark 3:21; cf. 3:31–35) reflects the kind of almost parental concern an older brother might feel for a younger brother.

Another, more pragmatic consideration supports Epiphanius's theory, although in a modified form. As mentioned, Joseph disappears from the scene of the Gospels from when Jesus was about twelve years old. His death at that time has been the traditional surmise, and such a chronology has implications for understanding Jesus' relationships with his siblings. On the Helvidian view, Mary must have given birth to *at least* seven children in twelve years (Jesus, his brothers, and two or more sisters). Assuming that not every child she gave birth to survived infancy, more than seven labors would be required during that period – all this within a culture that confined women after childbirth and prohibited intercourse with a woman with a flow of blood, and despite Joseph's age and the acknowledged prophylactic effects of lactation.

Although the consideration of a likely rate of fertility provides some support to the Epiphanian theory, in its unadulterated form it strains credulity in its own way. A widower with at least six children already in tow is not perhaps the best candidate for marriage with a young bride. A modified form of the theory (a hybrid with Helvidius's suggestion) would make James and Joses the products of Joseph's previous marriage, and Jesus, Simon, and Judah the sons of Joseph with Mary. The latter three sons have names that are notably associated with a zealous regard for the honor of Israel and they may reflect the taste of a common mother. Absent their names, or even a count of how many were involved, no such assignment of marriages can be attempted for Jesus' sisters.

On the Helvidian view, James was Jesus' younger and full brother, in a family quickly produced whose siblings were close in age. On the Epiphanian view, James was older and Jesus' half brother; it seems that, suitably modified, Epiphanius provides the more plausible finding.

those events, Judaic hopes centered on the restoration of the Temple. Works such as 2 Esdras (in the Apocrypha, also known as *4 Ezra*), written around 100 C.E., openly represent the eschatological vindication that was the object of much prayer and action. Such hopes were in cruel contrast to the political reality that the *fiscus Judaicus* was now the price of being considered a *religio licita*.

The period after the Jewish War also saw much unrest among Jews outside of geographical Israel, especially during the reign of Trajan (98–117 C.E.). Trajan had to deal as well with the question of what to do with the Christians. Although Nero's cruelty had discredited vigorous persecution, the ambivalent relationship of Christianity to Judaism raised anew the question of Christian loyalty to Rome. Even in Christian literature, there are hints of the new community's unwillingness to pay the *fiscus Judaicus* (see Matthew 17:24–7, composed ca. 80 C.E.). Moreover, the Davidic descent of Jesus and his relatives could easily be understood as a challenge to Roman hegemony, since David represented the royal line of Israel. At the same time, the growing number of Gentile Christians could not claim the legal protections that remained in place for Judaism. During the time of the Emperor Domitian (81–96 C.E.), surviving relatives of Jesus, grandsons of Jesus' brother Judas, were interrogated concerning their understanding of the kingdom preached by Jesus (see Eusebius, *History of the Church* 3.19–20). To the Romans, Christians seemed part of the problem of Jewish insurrection, which broke out yet again in Jerusalem in 132 C.E.

In a letter written in 111 C.E. to Pliny, governor of Bithynia and Pontus in Asia Minor, Trajan sets out his policy. Recognition of the gods of Rome (including the emperor as *divi filius,* son of God) is said by Trajan to be all that should be required of those denounced as Christians. The question was not their identity or their practice as such, only whether they were loyal to the empire. By this time, there is no question of simply identifying Christianity with Judaism.

Indeed, the Roman Empire may be said to have recognized a separation between Judaism and Christianity before Jews and Christians did. Nero never considered extending the rights of a *religio licita* to Christians in 64, although many followers of Jesus still worshipped in the Temple in Jerusalem as well as in synagogues throughout the Diaspora. Not until around 85 C.E. would the framers of a principal prayer of Judaism, the Eighteen Benedictions, compose a curse to be included against the Nazareans, followers of Jesus. On the Christian side the claim formally to replace Judaism only came near the end of the first century. Trajan simply takes the separation for granted, in effect treating Christianity as a passing superstition.

By the time Trajan wrote to Pliny, Christians outside Israel were reading the Gospels alongside the Scriptures of Israel in their Greek version. Each Gospel was composed in a different city of the Roman Empire in the years after 70 C.E., and in aggregate they all reflect a desire to gather the memories concerning Jesus that had earlier circulated in an oral form. The Book of Acts takes the story up from the time of Jesus' resurrection until just

TARSUS

The city of Tarsus was located at a strategic location for commerce, a port city with access to the central regions of Asia Minor through the Cilician Gates to the north, and to Syria and the East through the narrow passes between the Mediterranean Sea and the Amanus Mountains in the extreme southeastern section of Asia Minor.

Asia Minor's Judaism had its own flavor and character, venerating the memory of Noah, for example, whose ark was said to have landed locally, on Mount Ararat. Jews in Tarsus even claimed that their town was identical with the primeval city Tarshish mentioned in connection with Noah (Genesis 10:4; connected to Tarsus by Josephus, *Antiquities* 1.127). Legends of this kind express the religious sensibility of the Diaspora during the first century C.E., where the vast majority of Jews lived. The Sibyl – the premiere prophetess of Greco-Roman culture – was such a pivotal figure of prophecy that Judaism claimed her as its own. The *Sibylline Oracles* (3:809–29), a popular Diaspora book written in Greek and never included in the Bible (whether in Hebrew or Greek), present the Sibyl as Noah's daughter-in-law.

Under the Romans Tarsus became a major center for commerce and learning. Zeno and other philosophers in the Stoic tradition lived and taught there; Cicero governed Cilicia from Tarsus between 52 B.C.E. and 50 B.C.E.; and Athenodorus, the tutor of Augustus, settled in Augustus, ruling the city by imperial warrant. Although Paul does not mention the city in his letters, Antioch-on-the-Orontes (in Syria) features prominently as his base (Galatians 2:11), and he is identified with Tarsus in Acts 9:11 and 21:39. The influence of Stoicism on Paul is readily understandable if he grew up and was educated in Tarsus, which in the early Roman period rivaled Alexandria as a center of Hellenistic learning.

before Nero's pogrom against Christians in Rome. In addition, the letters of Paul, a Hellenistic Jew from Tarsus who converted to faith in Jesus, were widely read. This collection was based on what Paul himself said to early Christian communities he visited, but gradually his letters were supplemented by his followers (some of them writing as if they were Paul), and letters other than Paul's were also added to the New Testament, as Christians called their addition to the Bible of Israel.

All the writings of the New Testament were composed in Greek; many of them reveal a deep ignorance of Judaism on the part of Gentile Christians. The Gospels also began the long process of Christians blaming the Jews and their leaders for Jesus' execution, in order to ingratiate themselves to their Roman governors. Yet even Paul, the most radical thinker in the New Testament, believed that faith in Jesus was a part of God's unbreakable promise to Israel. The New Testament reflects Christianity as it was about to emerge as a religion separate from Judaism, but that process was far from complete at the time the writings were first brought together.

As a result of the extension of Jesus' Jewish movement into Hellenistic, largely Gentile populations, the early Christians grappled with basic issues of social and theological definition:

Who are the people of the covenant?

How is membership gained and maintained?

What attitude are members to assume toward nonmembers and to the cultural and social patterns in which the latter live, learn, and approach their god(s)?

Who is the agent or what is the agency through which God will achieve his purpose for the creation as a whole and for his people in particular?

How is the movement to be propagated, and who are its potential members?

What styles and structures of leadership can guide the movement?

B. Traditions about Jesus

However much historians might like to have written records of Jesus' words and deeds that were produced during his lifetime, we must acknowledge that we have none. There are also no detailed reports about him from contemporaneous non-Christian sources. The oldest of the Gospels, Mark, dates from no earlier than the late sixties, and was probably composed after the time of the Jewish revolt of 66–70 C.E. Paul's extant letters, mostly written during the decade between 50 and 60, include the oldest surviving references to Jesus, but Paul mentions only a few specific sayings and events. Jewish and Roman sources from later periods make only passing reference to Jesus, although they sometimes do confirm elements in the Gospels.

The Gospels according Matthew, Mark, Luke, and John remain our primary sources for knowledge of Jesus, but for historical purposes they can only be used with caution. As the title "gospel" (*euangelion*, which refers to a message of victory in Greek) implies, and as the opening words of Mark make explicit, these documents are not objective reports, but accounts designed to awaken and develop faith. That is, they want to convince the reader of the truth of what they describe, as Luke makes explicit: "That you may know the truth concerning the things of which you have been informed" (Luke 1:4). The authorship and the precise date of these writings are matters of inference. Each of the Gospels was written at a different time and under different circumstances, and there are significant differences among them. The first three, as they appear in the New Testament, have traditionally been called Matthew, Mark, and Luke. They share a basic narrative core and include considerable common material. Matthew and Luke include distinctive material not found in either Mark or John, presumably drawing on a sayings source (known by scholars as "Q," from the German word for "source," *Quelle*). Each of the four Gospels varies in detail in the use of material held in common; each places the whole of the tradition

---

IS MARK OUR OLDEST GOSPEL?

Since Mark is the shortest of the first three Gospels, which are very similar to one another, it has sometimes been assumed that Mark is an abbreviation of Matthew. Matthew became the most widely cited Gospel in the early church, a factor that helped this impression to thrive. Careful comparison among these Gospels shows, however, that both Matthew and Luke presuppose the contents and the order of Mark, though each of the other Gospels modifies Mark to fulfill its own particular aims. (Matthew, Mark, and Luke are so similar to one another that they are called "the Synoptic Gospels," because they can be printed side by side in columns and compared in their content, order, and wording.) For example, Matthew and Luke are completely independent of each other in their accounts of Jesus' birth and of the events following his burial; yet in narrative sequence, they closely resemble each other from the point where Mark begins (Jesus' baptism) to where Mark's account ends (at the vision of Mary Magdalene and her companions at Jesus' tomb). Passages in Mark that the Church later found difficult are either omitted or substantially modified in Matthew and Luke. An example is Mark's note that Jesus was *unable* to do many miracles because of people's unbelief (Mark 6:5). Luke completely rewrites and relocates (Luke 4:16–30) this incident, and both Luke and Matthew eliminate the mention of Jesus' relative inability (Matthew 13:58). The most plausible explanation for the relationship among the Synoptic Gospels is that Mark is closest to the original, oral message concerning Jesus. Matthew and Luke drew either on Mark or on a source nearly identical to Mark, as well as on a second common source ("Q"), and developed their structure and content independently.

APOSTLE

Derived from the Greek word *apostolos*, which means "one who is sent out," the term "apostle" was used by first-century Christians to designate the inner circle of the first followers of Jesus. The practice of sending a delegate (a *shaliach* in Aramaic), was common in the Middle East to seal a marriage or a business contract. The role of "apostle" did not emerge from the desire to establish a high ecclesiastical office or to send missionaries far away. It came out of the ordinary practice of sending a go-between or agent to settle routine transactions. Jesus adapted that custom to deal with circumstances in Galilee: knowing that Herod Antipas wanted to kill him (Luke 13:31), he sent agents to act in his place and to confuse efforts to capture him. Lists of the apostles appear in Mark 3:16–19, Matthew 10:2–4, and Luke 6:13–16; twelve in number (like the tribes of Israel), but with variations in the names. Two New Testament passages suggest qualifications for the role of apostle: Acts 1:21–6 specifies having been an eyewitness to Jesus' activity from his baptism by John until his resurrection; in 1 Corinthians 9:1 Paul mentions having "seen Jesus our Lord" after he was raised from the dead, just as the other apostles did (1 Corinthians 15:7–9). Paul refers to himself as an apostle regularly at the opening of his letters (Romans 1:1; 1 Corinthians 1:1; 2 Corinthians 1:1; Galatians 1:1) but sees his special role as an emissary of Christ (apostle) to the Gentiles (Romans 11:13; Galatians 1:16–17). Although connections with the apostles were important for second-century leaders and writers as confirming authority and correctness of doctrine, the title "apostle" was no longer used for Church officials.

that is included in a unique framework; each presents unique traditions. By the second century these writings were associated with named disciples of Jesus, or with someone closely connected with one of the apostles. The first and fourth Gospels (as they are placed in the New Testament) give no internal indication of authorship but have been associated from the early days of the church's life with two disciples of Jesus: Matthew and John. Analogously, the second and third Gospels have been accepted as the work of companions of the apostles: Mark, who is closely associated with Peter (1 Peter 5:13), and Luke, who is closely mentioned as a co-worker in letters attributed to Paul (Philemon 24; 2 Timothy 4:11).

Variations among the Gospels in their recording of Jesus' teaching suggest that traditions about him circulated orally before they were composed in written form. Later Christian writings include sayings attributed to Jesus that resemble those in the Gospels but with significant differences, in a way that supports this finding. Stories about Jesus and reports of his teachings were evidently handed down in oral form from the beginning of the Jesus movement, in a manner also instanced in Rabbinic literature. Clear support for this view may be found in Paul, who reflects Jesus' teaching that the primary commandment is to love one's neighbor (Galatians 5:14; cf. Mark 12:28–34, where Deuteronomy 6:4 and Leviticus 19:18 are linked). Paul also has an equivalent version of Jesus' words at the Last Supper (1 Corinthians 11:23–6; cf. Mark 14:22–5).

C. The "Q" Source, or the Mishnah of Jesus

Detailed analysis of the first three Gospels, focused by the scholarly practice of placing them in parallel columns for close comparison, leads to the conclusion that one of the earlier sources behind the Gospels as we know them was a collection consisting primarily of sayings of Jesus. This source was used in the composition of Matthew and Luke. There is broad agreement among scholars that both Matthew and Luke used Mark, or a source

HISTORICAL JESUS

The Gospels are the best sources for understanding Jesus, although what they have to say needs to be evaluated carefully. Between Jesus' death in 32 C.E. and the date of the first of the written Gospels (Mark, around 73 C.E.) there lies a full generation of Christian teaching activity, designed to make, initiate, and keep converts within the new faith. Each of the Gospels was written in and for a predominantly non-Jewish community in a Hellenistic city: Mark in Rome, Matthew in Damascus (in 80 C.E.), Luke in Antioch (in 90 C.E.), and John in Ephesus (in 100 C.E.). The first three Gospels follow so closely the same basic order of preaching that they are called the Synoptic Gospels: they can be laid out side by side so that they can be compared (in a layout called a "Synopsis"). Their preaching is largely based on the oral preaching of Peter, supplemented by a collection of Jesus' teaching called "Q" (an abbreviation of the German term *Quelle*, "source": the closest thing there is to a mishnah of Rabbi Jesus) and by traditions stemming from such followers as Jesus' elder brother James and the prominent Hellenistic Jew Barnabas. The purpose of the Synoptics is to prepare people, after careful training, for baptism in Jesus' name. Christians living in Rome's environment of persecution needed to be wary of the damage that informers and indiscreet admirers could inflict. Thus mastery of the materials in the Synoptic Gospels became a requirement for baptism, which assured that only serious converts joined the movement. Once they were in, they looked for more advanced, mystical teaching, which

is what the Gospel according to John provides, as well as the *Gospel according to Thomas* (about fifty years later).

Because the Gospels present either baptismal teaching (the Synoptics) or mystical teaching (John and *Thomas*), it should be obvious that they cannot be taken as objective history. A critical understanding of Jesus is possible only if we allow for the aims that produced the Gospels. In addition, we need to distinguish the urban, Hellenistic setting of the Gospels from the rural, Galilean environment of Jesus. In adjusting for both the aims and the cultural drift of the Gospels, the writings of the first-century C.E. Jewish historian Josephus are useful. Still, Josephus was no objective observer, but a Jewish general who became a famous turncoat. Because he was concerned with his own reputation and with his own, laundered, version of Judaism, Josephus's claims must be evaluated with extreme care. Bias is also evident in the famous Dead Sea Scrolls. The scrolls were produced by the Essenes, a group so sectarian that they believed that anyone who did not agree with them (including the majority of the Jewish people) would be killed in the final, holy war, when the angels would come to the Essenes' aid. So although the Dead Sea Scrolls are immensely informative about common elements of Judaism (such as the Jews' conception of God's kingdom and their usage of Aramaic), no serious scholar would try to take them as typical of Judaism or Christianity in the first century. Finally, Rabbinic literature is also helpful in assessing Jesus, but it, too,

must be used with care. The earliest document of Rabbinic literature, the Mishnah, was not produced until 200 C.E., well after Christianity and Judaism had gone their separate ways and after a prolonged period of tension, and sometimes violence, between the two. The Mishnah and later Rabbinic literature frame a new definition of Judaism, for the epoch after the Romans destroyed the Second Temple (in 70 C.E.) and after Christianity became one of Judaism's competitors. So no one should really expect that the Mishnah or the Talmud, a later commentary on the Mishnah, directly reflect Judaism in the first century.

The only access we have to Jesus critically, then, is by means of a collation of literary and archaeological and historical investigation. Investigators need to infer what the development of the literature must have been and then what events were likely involved in that literary generation. The analysis of Christian sources is much the same as developing a history of Israel – a double inference from texts to sources and from sources to events. In fact, the recent debate between "maximalists" and "minimalists" in the interpretation of the Hebrew Bible echoes more than two centuries of dispute concerning Jesus and history. In both instances, the insistence on "objective" history has distorted the discussion, because no Gospel, any more than any Israelite Scripture, was produced to make a history in the modern sense.

Two dominant relationships permit us to locate Jesus in the social history of the first century: his relationship to

(continued)

HISTORICAL JESUS (continued)

John the Baptist and his relationship to Herod Antipas. Although a full account of Jesus' life is not possible here, in addition to a chronology, we can sketch the importance of these two relationships.

Certainly the most influential figure in Jesus' life, John gave Jesus the focus on purity that, in one form or another, became an emblematic feature of his activity. Jesus did not simply meet his teacher in adulthood (as a superficial reading of the Gospels would suggest), but apprenticed himself to John as a youth. Jesus' extensive period of study and controversy with John, implied in John's Gospel, can be accommodated by this chronology. More important, it allows time for Jesus to remain in the land of Judaea *and to practice immersion* (John 3:22). Although an attempt is made slightly later in the Gospel to take this assertion back (John 4:1–3), it is an emphatic and unambiguous description: Jesus practiced a ministry of immersion comparable to John's.

John's Gospel observes that Jews did not have dealings with Samaritans (4:9), yet Jesus in the story of the Samaritan woman deals with her extensively (John 4:4–42) – and without offering any particular defense. He would later be equally matter of fact in telling the parable of the good Samaritan (Luke 10:30–7). Both the story of the Samaritan woman and the parable of the good Samaritan assume that there is a problem about consorting with Samaritans, and that the problem can be overcome. A similar perspective is represented in *The Gospel according to Thomas* (l. 60), where Jesus comments on seeing a Samaritan carrying a lamb to Judea

(presumably, in association with an offering in Jerusalem). Unlike John, with whom Jesus came into dispute over questions of purity (John 3:25–6), Jesus, at the end of his discipleship with John, believed in a principle of contagious purity, such that what was within a person could purify what was outside a person (see Mark 7:15). That difference with John assured that Jesus developed a distinctive position within Judaism, which he brought back to his native Galilee after John's execution at the hands of Herod Antipas.

The danger that Herod Antipas posed to Jesus, a former disciple of John's, helps to account for what otherwise might seem rather strange. Why does Jesus, a notably popular rabbi with a diverse following, generally stay away from cities? To a substantial extent, the answer to that question is to be found in Jesus' program of purity, which was targeted on Israelites, but as soon as we make another observation, it becomes clear that another force was also at work. The results when Jesus actually did enter the one city that he did – Jerusalem – were fatal. And Jesus was conscious of the opponent he was dealing with further north (Luke 13:31–3):

In that hour some Pharisees came forward, saying to him, Get out and go from here! Because Herod wants to kill you. And he said to them, You go, and say to that fox, Look, I put out demons and will send healings today and tomorrow, and on the third day I will be completed. Except that I must go today and tomorrow and the following day, because it is not acceptable that a prophet should perish outside of Jerusalem!

There are several indications that we are dealing with primitive material here. The Pharisees are friendly, Antipas is particularly at issue, and the Lukan Jesus does not speak in his usual, precise way about how and when he is going to die. Instead, Jesus puts himself into the general category of prophets who will be killed as a result of their prophecy.

What these verses show us is that Jesus' geographical program came over time to include an avoidance of Herod Antipas, and that it did so deliberately, until such time as confrontation with authorities might take place. And the only place for that was Jerusalem.

The threat of Antipas accounts for Jesus' crossing into Herod Philip's territory (at first in Bethsaida, where some of his disciples had relatives). In stark relief to Jesus' acceptance – albeit at a safe distance from the danger that Capernaum now posed – of the delegation from the centurion garrisoned there (Matthew 8:5–13; Luke 7:1–10), his reaction to an attempt by his own family at reconciliation was forbidding (Mark 3:31–5; Matthew 12:46–50; Luke 8:19–21). When they sent a delegation of family friends to him, he would not interrupt his teaching to greet them: "Whoever does the will of God that is my brother and sister and mother." Still more surprising is his sojourn in Decapolis. Despite some success (Mark 7:31–7; Matthew 15:29–31), his time in Decapolis proved on the whole a disaster in that Jesus' practice of purity and the proudly Hellenistic ethos of that region were as incompatible as the pure waters of the sea of Galilee proved to be with the swine that drowned therein (Mark 5:1–20; Matthew 8:28–34; Luke 8:26–39).

The fiasco of attempting to establish a base outside territorial Israel (although the attempt attests to at least the inchoate possibility of a larger Israel) led Jesus to the innovation of the Twelve, a number revelant to the theological purpose of the institution. Hunted by Herod Antipas in Galilee itself, uncertain of safety within the domain of Herod Philip, repulsed by the Gentile population east of the Sea of Galilee, where exactly could Jesus go? How could he continue to reach Galilee with his message?

His response to this dilemma was a stroke of genius that assured the wider promulgation of his message of the kingdom: he dispatched twelve disciples as delegates on his behalf. The practice of sending a delegate (a *shaliach*) was common in the Middle East to seal a marriage or business contract. The role of "apostle," from the Greek term *apostolos* (which translates *shaliach*), came out of the ordinary practice of sending a go-between to settle routine transactions. Jesus applied this custom of personal, business, and military life to spread his ideas and practices. He dispatched each *shaliach* to do what he did: proclaim God's kingdom and heal (Matthew 10:1–16; Mark 6:6–13; Luke 9:1–5).

A chronological table follows. Page numbers refer to Bruce Chilton's *Rabbi Jesus: An Intimate Biography* (New York: Doubleday, 2000), where fuller discussion is available.

Probable, Largely Inferential Dates in Jesus' Development

4 B.C.E. The death of Herod.
  Herod's death results in the division of his kingdom: his son Archelaus takes Judah, Herod Antipas inherits Galilee and Perea, and Herod Philip rules Trachonitis.

2 B.C.E.–16 C.E. In early spring of 2 B.C.E., Joseph and Mary meet and marry, prior to establishing a common residence there (pp. 6–8).

Jesus' birth in Bethlehem of Galilee; Joseph's residence, in late autumn (pp. 6, 8–9). [By October 23, for example, Mars has traveled to the west, and is in alignment with Saturn.]

Eight days later, Jesus' circumcision at Bethlehem in accordance with the Torah (pp. 3–5, 9–15).

The family moves in with Mary's family in Nazareth before the end of the year (pp. 13–14).

Just after he turns ten in 12 C.E., Jesus begins his local travel as a journeyman with Joseph (p. 20).

Joseph dies in 15 C.E. (pp. 20–2).

A year later, in the autumn of 16 C.E., Mary takes her family to Jerusalem for the feast of Sukkot, staying with Mary and Martha of Bethany (pp. 23–32).

16–21 C.E. Jesus' apprenticeship with John the Baptist.

Turning fourteen, Jesus remains in Jerusalem having parted from his family at the celebration of Sukkot in 16 C.E. (pp. 32–7).

Jesus seeks out and meets John the Baptist early in 17 C.E. (pp. 37–43).

During immersions following John's practice, Jesus increasingly experiences divine Spirit, and by 19 C.E. John begins to call him "the lamb of God" (pp. 55–8).

Jesus' new view of purity, derived from his experience of divine Spirit, puts him in conflict with his rabbi during 20 C.E. (pp. 58–60).

21 The death of John.

Herod Antipas orders John's execution in 21 C.E., on a critical reading of Josephus (pp. 60–3).

21–24 The return of Jesus to Nazareth at the age of eighteen, and his excursions out as journeyman and rabbi until his expulsion from Nazareth.

In 21 C.E., to avoid capture, Jesus returns home through Samaria to a festive reception, but his conversation with the Samaritan woman has alienated some of John's former disciples (pp. 62–71).

Beginning in 22 C.E., Jesus' journeywork from the base of Mary's house in Nazareth takes on the character of holy feasts, involving him and his family in increasingly heavy debts of honor (pp. 74–8).

By 23 C.E. Jesus' has come into contact with Capernaum and Magdala, denouncing their wealth (pp. 78–2).

Jesus' conviction that purity is a power released within people leads him to practice exorcisms that are unusually direct and abrupt (pp. 83–93).

The strain on Jesus's family from his debts of honor and his embarrassing exorcisms (pp. 93–5) leads to a break, and he makes his way to Capernaum in 24 C.E.

24–27 Jesus uses Capernaum as a base; his itinerancy makes him a major figure in Galilee by his twenty-fifth year.

(continued)

HISTORICAL JESUS (continued)

Jesus establishes his reputation in Capernaum by an exorcism in the synagogue in 24 C.E. (pp. 96–7). But his fame there leads Jesus to confront the elders in Nazareth with his claim that he has been anointed by God's Spirit. As a result, he is nearly killed by stoning late in the summer (pp. 97–106), leading to a brief retreat to Jerusalem to enjoy the hospitality of some of John's former disciples and Barnabas.

At the pool of Bethesda, Jesus heals a person for the first time, leading to his contact with Barnabas during Sukkot and with Nicodemus during the feast of Hanukkah. But increasing opposition in Jerusalem from priestly and Pharisaic authorities pushes him back to Capernaum the following year (pp. 106–23).

From 25 C.E., Capernaum became Jesus' base of support, and until 27 C.E. it is a stable haven where he enjoys his holy feasts, travels less than he had, accepts disciples, exorcises, and heals (pp. 124–48).

By the fifteenth year of Tiberius's reign, in 27 C.E., Jesus has become such a renowned figure that Herod Antipas seeks to end his life, just as he had executed John the Baptist; Jesus is forced to flee Capernaum (pp. 148–9).

27–31 Herod Antipas's threat forces Jesus to depart from Galilean territory, and to gather his followers in Syria.

During a transit to the east, to Bethsaida, formerly the home of Peter and Andrew in 27 C.E., Jesus' disciples see him still a storm (pp. 153–61).

Jesus' sojourn in Bethsaida follows his contact with a centurion, 27–8 C.E., which risked drawing Antipas's attention (pp. 161–8).

Jesus' sojourn on the eastern side of the Sea of Galilee ends with the destruction of the pigs, 28–9 C.E. [winter] (pp. 168–71).

Dispatch of his delegates or apostles, 29 C.E. (pp. 174–8).

Revival of Jairus's daughter, 29 C.E. (pp. 178–9).

Encounter with the Syro-Phoenecian woman, 30 C.E. (pp. 181–2).

Wedding at Kana, 30 C.E. (pp. 182–5).

The sign of feeding in Gaulanitis, 30 C.E. (pp. 186–8).

The Transfiguration, 30 C.E. [Sukkot], followed by the Temptations (pp. 190–7).

Walking on the water, 31 C.E. (p. 197), with Mark 7:31–7 and 8:22–6 prior.

31–32 Last year of Jesus, aged thirty, in Jerusalem.

Final drive through Galilee (with Shabbat and tax issues), 31 C.E. (pp. 197–203).

Entry into Jerusalem and raid in the Temple, 31 C.E. [Sukkot] (pp. 225–30).

The death of Sejanus in Rome on 18 October 31 C.E. (pp. 239–42).

Jesus' execution in 32 C.E., prior to Passover, and visions of him during the spring and summer having risen from the dead (pp. 254–68, 269–89).

35 The meeting of Peter, James, and Paul in Jerusalem, and the availability of the earliest sources of the Gospels: Peter's instruction for apostles such as Paul, and the mishnah of Jesus' teaching known to modern scholarship as "Q."

37 The removal of Pontius Pilate and Caiaphas from power.

40 The adaptation of Peter's Gospel by James, the brother of Jesus, in Jerusalem.

45 In Antioch, outside of Palestine, followers of Jesus are for the first time called "Christians."

53–57 Paul writes his major letters, Galatians, Corinthians, and Romans.

62 The death of James in Jerusalem by stoning, at the instigation of the high priest.

64 The deaths of Paul and Peter in Rome.

70–73 The burning of the Temple by the Roman troops under Titus; the composition of Mark's Gospel, in Rome; the end of the revolt against Rome in Palestine.

75 Josephus publishes his *Jewish War*.

80 The composition of Matthew's Gospel, in Damascus.

90 The composition of Luke's Gospel, in Antioch.

93 Josephus publishes his *Antiquities of the Jews*.

100 The composition of John's Gospel, in Ephesus.

like Mark, as the basis for structuring their narratives. Although the sayings source must be reconstructed on a hypothetical basis, by separating out of Matthew and Luke the common tradition they share that does not derive from Mark, independent analysis of the Gospels has led to clear consensus about this source – not only that it existed but also regarding its contents and form of presentation. Much of the early work done on this was by German scholars, with the result that the source came to be known by the first letter of the German word for "source," *Quelle*; hence, "Q."

More recent discussion of the source known as Q has brought about a remarkable consensus that at least some of the sayings within it were circulated a few years after the crucifixion, around the year 35 C.E. The earliest version of Q probably included a charge to Jesus' disciples (Luke 10:3–6, 9–11, 16), a strategy to cope with resistance to their message (Luke 6:27–35), examples of how to speak of the kingdom (Luke 6:20b–21; 11:2–4, 14–20; 13:18–21), curses to lay on those who reject those sent in the name of the kingdom (Luke 11:39–48, 52), and a section relating John the Baptist and Jesus as principal emissaries of the kingdom (Luke 7:24b–26, 28a, 33–4).

At the start of the tradition now called Q, Jesus' teaching was arranged in the form of a mishnah by his disciples. They took up activity in Jesus' name within Israel at large after the resurrection. The mishnaic form of Q was preserved orally in Aramaic and explained how the Twelve were to discharge their purpose. It included just the materials that have already been specified, instructions to Jesus' disciples, a strategy of love to overcome resistance, paradigms to illustrate the kingdom, threats directed toward enemies, and a reference to John the Baptist that would serve as a transition to baptism in the name of Jesus. As specified, that is probably the original, mishnaic order of Q, the closest approximation to Jesus' mishnah. It is the order that accords with Q's purpose within the redemption of Israel.

As incorporated within the Gospels, however, Q appears to have been developed with more thematic concerns and in order to address a more cosmopolitan setting (probably in Syria, where both Matthew and Luke originated). Luke appears to have preserved the Q source in a form closer to the original than Matthew's and has even approximated Q's order. Accordingly, in what follows we offer the scriptural references to the Q tradition based on Luke:

3:7–9, 16b–17	The eschatological preaching of John the Baptist
4:2b–12	Jesus' struggle with Satan
6:20–3	Beatitudes: God's blessing of the poor, the hungry, and the hated
6:27–36	Promised reward for love and forgiveness
6:37–42	Rewards of faithful discipleship
6:43–6	Parables of moral productivity
6:47–9	Discipleship must survive testing: the parable of the houses with and without foundation

NARRATIVE IN Q

The story of Jesus' healing of the centurion's servant (Luke 7:2–3, 6–10) is the one complete example of a narrative in the "Q" tradition. Like most of "Q," this passage is not in Mark but is shared by Matthew and Luke. Some parts of the Q tradition imply a narrative setting, as in the responses of Jesus to the questioners who come to him from John the Baptist (Luke 7:18–35) and to the Jewish leaders who ask him to perform a miracle to confirm that God is with him (Luke 11:29–32). The Q tradition does not represent Jesus as one who merely utters sayings, as some recent commentators associated with "The Jesus Seminar" have suggested, but as one who is engaged in public actions and social relationships. The emphasis on Jesus' sayings reflects the genre of Q; it does not reflect Jesus' activity.

7:2–3, 6–10	Healing of the centurion's servant
7:18–23	Jesus responds to John the Baptist's question
7:24–35	The place of John the Baptist in God's plan
9:57–8 (62?)	Leaving behind home and family
10:2–12	Jesus commissions his disciples to extend his work
10:13–15	Doom pronounced on unrepentant cities
10:16	The disciples share in Jesus' rejection
10:21–2	God's gift of wisdom to his own people
10:23–4	Beatitude: those to whom wisdom is granted
11:2–4	Prayer that God's rule will come on earth
11:9–13	God answers the prayers of his own people
11:14–20	Jesus' defeat of the demons as a sign of the coming of God's rule
11:24–6	The return of the unclean spirit
11:29–32	The sign of Jonah and the one greater than Jonah: Jesus as prophet and wise man
11:33–6	Parables of light and darkness
11:39–40, 42–3	Woes to the Pharisees
11:46–8, 52	Woes to the lawyers
11:49–51	Wisdom predicts the martyrdom of prophets and apostles
12:2–3	What is hidden will be revealed
12:4–5	Do not fear martyrdom
12:6–7	Parable of God's care for his own
12:8–10	The result of confessing or denying the Son of Man
12:11–12	God's support of the persecuted
12:22–31	Freedom from anxiety about earthly needs
12:33–4	Freedom from possessions
12:39–40	Parable of preparedness: the returning householder
12:42–6	Parable of the faithful steward
12:51–3	Jesus as the agent of crises
12:54–6	Signs of the impending end of the age
12:57–9	Parable of preparedness for judgment
13:20–1	Parable of leaven
13:24	Difficulty in entering the kingdom
13:25–9	Parable of exclusion from the kingdom
13:34–5	The rejection of the prophets and the vindication of God's agent
14:16–23	Parable of the banquet at the end of the age
14:26–7	Jesus shatters domestic ties and summons his followers to take up the cross
15:4–7	The joyous shepherd and the lost sheep
16:13	The inescapable choice between masters
16:16	The proclamation of the end of the age
16:17	Confidence in God's promise
17:3–4	Forgiveness within the community
17:5–6	Faith within the community

17:23–7	Sudden judgment on all who are in the world
19:12–13, 15–26	Parable of the returning nobleman; the rewards to the faithful servants
22:28–30	The promise to the faithful of a share in God's rule

These passages from Luke (with their parallels in Matthew), when viewed apart from the context and connotations that Luke and Matthew supply, convey a remarkably consistent picture of Jesus, the enterprise in which he engaged, the responsibilities that he placed on the inner core of his followers, and his expectations for them and for his people, all focused on and determined by the moment when God was to bring the present age to an end and establish his rule in the world. In this Q tradition Jesus refers to himself at times in the first person, but often by the indirect term "the Son of Man" (which in the Aramaic language refers to a human being). Since this designation is used in the biblical tradition to refer to both an individual (as in Ezekiel and *1 Enoch*) and a faithful community represented by an angel in human form (as in Daniel), it was a highly suitable expression for the role of Jesus and that of his core of followers in preparing for the coming of the kingdom of God.

Some scholars, observing the link between Jesus and wisdom in Q and the emphasis on instruction in the Q material, have concluded that this source portrays Jesus as the embodiment of wisdom in the Jewish sense of timeless, universal knowledge of God and the world. If this were the correct assessment of the Q tradition, Jesus would be pictured as a teacher of universal, eternal truths. These scholars acknowledge that there are apocalyptic features within the Q material, but they explain those elements as later intrusions into the basic picture of Jesus as a kind of philosophical rabbi. Careful analysis of the Q material, however, shows that it is pervaded by an eschatological outlook. Even Q's original form of the Beatitudes, for example, contrasts the present state of God's people with the future blessedness that will come with the new age and does not generalize about the human condition as a whole. Elements of conflict that typify the apocalyptic worldview pervade Q: both the conflicts that the elect experience in the final stages of the present cosmic struggle and the battle between the powers of evil and God's agents.

CENTURION

The Roman army consisted of large units, called legions, of approximately 5,000 soldiers each. These were divided into cohorts of 480 each, supplemented by smaller cavalry units. The cohorts were further divided into 6 "centuries," composed of 80 soldiers each, rather than 100 as the name implies. The centurions commanded the centuries and were more professional than the senior officers, who were from the upper ranks of society and usually served for short periods of time. Centurions who were especially effective in training and organizing soldiers were transferred to more prestigious legions. For security and efficiency reasons, soldiers were not usually stationed in the territories where they had originated. During Jesus' lifetime, four Roman legions were on permanent assignment in Syria-Palestine.

SON OF MAN

"Son of man" is a literal translation of the Hebrew (*ben adam*) and Aramaic (*bar ['e]nasha*) phrases used by the biblical writers to underscore human limitations, as contrasted to the sovereignty of God. Major examples of this usage are found in Psalm 8, where the splendor of God's creation is contrasted with human frailty (8:3–4), and in Ezekiel, where the prophet falls down in awe before the vision of the divine majesty, and when he is instructed to call to account rebellious Israel (from Ezekiel 1:28–2:1, and throughout the book). The term is also used to indicate one who is assigned to carry out God's purpose. In Daniel, the angelic figure who represents the faithful remnant of God's people and to whom is given the responsibility of ruling the earth in God's behalf is described as "one like a son of man" (Daniel 7:13); this figure is then associated with a group: "the saints of the Most High" (7:18, 22). In the Similitudes of Enoch, "Son of Man" is the title of the divine agent through whom the powers of evil are overcome and the rule of God is established. Assuming that this was written by the first part of the first century C.E., the term would have been known in Jesus' time. Jesus seems to have applied it to himself in this latter sense, that is, in signifying that he was God's agent or that he had an angelic counterpart in heaven.

The Q material listed earlier can be grouped under four headings that focus on Jesus' place in God's purpose and the solemn responsibilities that his followers and his hearers have as God moves to fulfill his plan for his creation. Grouped thematically, the Q materials appear coherent:

1. Discipleship: Privileges and Trials

6:20–49	The blessedness and obligations of discipleship
9:57–62	Break with home and family for the sake of the kingdom of God
10:2–16	Participation in proclaiming the kingdom in word and act
10:21–3	God's special revelation of his purpose
11:2–13	God's promise to sustain his people and grant them a role in his kingdom
12:51–3	Jesus, the divider of households
14:16–23	Those included and those excluded from the messianic banquet
14:26–7	Discipleship shatters ordinary human relations
16:13	The demands of discipleship
17:3–6	Forgiveness and faith: essentials for the life of the new community

2. Repentance or Judgment

11:33–6	Warning about light and darkness
11:39–48, 52	Woes against the religious leaders of Judaism
12:54–9	Prepare for impending judgment
13:23–9	Exclusion from a share in God's new reign
17:23–30, 33, 35, 37	Judgment will be inescapable
19:12–13, 15–26	Reward for the faithful; punishment for the lazy; the importance of perseverance

3. The Prophet as God's Messenger

3:7–9, 16–17	John the Baptist as forerunner of Jesus and as prophet of doom
11:49–51	The fate of the prophet and his emissaries
12:2–3	The promise of the revelation of God's purpose
12:4–10, 11–12, 42–6	God's care for and vindication of his messengers
13:34–5	Jerusalem's rejection and martyrdom of the prophets
16:16–17	John the Baptist as boundary of the old age; God's word is sure

4. Jesus as Revealer and Agent of God's Rule

4:2b–12	Jesus' successful struggle with the Devil
7:18–35	Jesus as agent of liberation: greater than John
10:24	Jesus as Son, agent of revelation
11:14–22	Jesus as agent of God's kingdom

13:20–1	The leaven of God's rule now at work
15:4–7	God's joy at reconciliation with a sinner
22:28–30	God grants a share in his kingdom to those for whom it has been covenanted and who have endured the struggles of its coming.

Analysis of the Q material as grouped in its topical arrangement results in a clear picture of Jesus, of his understanding of God's purpose, and of his followers and their prospects and responsibilities. The material is not neatly divided into different categories of subject matter; rather, the four major themes emerge in various parts of Q as it has been reconstructed. The analysis that follows here seeks to show how these themes are blended in the Q material.

One of the themes in the Q tradition concerns the definition of the community of Jesus' followers during his lifetime, in the near future (from the perspective of his followers), and ultimately – in the new age that God was about to establish. His followers are portrayed as those who in the present age are deprived and scorned: they are the poor, the hungry, the sorrowing, the hated, the excluded, the reviled (Luke 6:20–2). They are promised a reversal of their condition "in that day" – that is, the moment when God's purpose is achieved through the Son of Man. Their reward is already stored up in heaven in anticipation of that deliverance and vindication. Meanwhile, however, they are to love those who oppose them, to pray for their abusers, to respond generously to those who do them injustices, and to do so in the confidence that God will reward their gracious actions in the new day that is coming (Luke 6:27–36). By refusing to judge others and extending forgiveness to them, disciples will be amply rewarded by God in the future (6:37–42). Since their lives are founded on the compassion of God, they will be able to withstand the difficulties and storms that await them in the future (6:43–9), because divine compassion will be all in all.

Disciples must be prepared, however, for radical conflict with their loved ones, and they must be ready to give up traditional obligations toward the family in view of the higher demands involved in proclaiming the advent of God's kingdom in the near future (Luke 9:57–62). Their commitment to the work of the kingdom will cause violent disruptions in their domestic lives (12:51–3). What is called for in the cause of discipleship is described as hatred toward one's own family and even the willingness to abandon one's own life, as Jesus did in his fidelity to what he believed was God's will for him (14:26–7). There can be no wavering as to where one's ultimate obligations and values are directed: followers must be devoted to God and his work in the world (16:13).

Jesus' followers are to carry forward the work he launched: they must heal the sick and announce the coming of God's rule. To carry out this activity they must move from town to town, indifferent to any conventional system of support, relying only on the generosity of their hearers, but ready to move on if their message is rejected. Their responsibilities are discharged when they proclaim by word and act the triumphant message of what God is doing through Jesus. God will bring judgment in his own way on those who refuse to heed the message (Luke 10:2–16). The members of the community of Jesus rejoice in the special wisdom about God's purpose that has been disclosed to them through Jesus (10:21–3).

Q (Luke 10:5–8) instructs the disciples in Jesus' lifetime to enter any house of a village they travel to and to offer their peace. They are to accept hospitality in that house, eating what is set before them. The emphasis on eating what is provided is repeated (10:7, 8), so that it does not appear to be a later, marginal elaboration. Within Pharisaic constructions of purity, such as are reflected in the Mishnah, the foods one ate and the hospitality one offered and accepted were carefully regulated. In the tractate Demai (2:2), which concerns tithing, one who undertakes to be faithful must tithe what he eats, what he sells, and what he buys, and not accept hospitality from a "person of the land." ("Person of the land" ['am ha-aretz] is a phrase that had been used since the time of Zechariah 7:5 to refer to people whose practices could not be trusted.) Demai (2:3) further specifies that a faithful person must not sell a person of the land wet or dry produce and must not buy wet produce from him. (Wet produce was held to be susceptible to uncleanness.) The passage goes on to make the rule against hospitality more reciprocal, insofar as one who wishes to be faithful cannot have a person of land as a guest when that person is wearing his own (probably impure) garments: the person of the land must first change his clothing. These strictures clearly reflect a construction of purity among the "faithful" (chaverim) that sets them apart from other Jews by impinging on the foods one might eat and trade, and the commerce and fellowship one might enjoy.

Jesus' insistence that his disciples accept hospitality in whatever houses accept them is consonant with his reputation as a "glutton and a drunkard" (see Luke 7:34). There is a deliberate carelessness involved, in the precise sense that the disciples are not to have a care about the practices of purity of those who offer hospitality to them. They are true Israelites. When they join in the meals of the kingdom that Jesus' disciples have arrived to celebrate, when they accept and grant forgiveness to one another in the manner of the Lord's Prayer, what they set upon the table of fellowship from their own effort is by definition pure and should be gratefully consumed. The twelve disciples define and create the true Israel to which they are sent, and they tread on that territory as on holy ground, shoeless – without staff or purse.

Participation in this new Q community after Jesus' death is open to the poor who are in need and know they are, rather than primarily or exclusively to those who are in the Judaic tradition, many of whom are too preoccupied with routine affairs to respond to the invitation to take part in the new fellowship that God is establishing through Jesus. Those who do respond include those who were excluded by ritual requirements from coming into God's presence in the Temple or in the gatherings of his people. The parable of the banquet ends with the report of the complete outsiders who are brought into the new fellowship (Luke 14:16–24). An essential feature of the relationship they share within the community is an attitude of abundant forgiveness (17:3–4), and their confidence in God is to exceed all ordinary human expectations (17:5–6).

Q repeatedly sounds the solemn warning of God's judgment on the human race, especially on those who claim to be his people. All humanity will be faced with the stark alternative: repentance or judgment. Even now, however, there is a sharp distinction between those who hear God's message through Jesus and respond with faith, and those who ignore or reject it. Two sayings about light and darkness have been blended in Luke 11:33–6 to make this point: those in the light (i.e., through the knowledge of God that Jesus has brought) have no part in the realm of darkness, but have been transformed by the light. Their responsibility now is to see that the light is spread abroad to others. Changing the image to that of predicting the weather by interpreting the signs, such as clouds on the horizon, Jesus is reported as warning those who are indifferent toward his message to be alert to the indications that God is about to do something new in establishing his rule on earth (12:54–6).

The need for the faithful to remain so during the interval before the time when God's judgment will fall features centrally in the Q source. Jesus warns (Luke 17:23–30, 33, 35–7) that the end of the age, which will be dramatically demonstrated by the coming of the Son of Man, cannot be predicted but occurs in God's time – like lightning flashing across the sky. Those preoccupied with routine affairs will suffer divine judgment as did all but Noah and his extended family in the time of the Flood, and as did the wicked inhabitants of Sodom. The majority will not know what has happened until they see the vultures circling about the corpses of those who have been slain in the divine judgment that brings the present age to a close. In contrast to the indifferent masses, the followers of Jesus are called to surrender their lives – both figuratively and literally, in martyrdom – in order that they might gain the life of the age to come. This theme of proper stewardship of one's resources in the interim before the end of the age is dramatically illustrated in the parable of the absent ruler, who returns unexpectedly and calls to account those to whom he had assigned certain responsibilities. Some had used their resources effectively, while others had done nothing with them. All receive what is appropriate for their behavior, whether reward or punishment (Luke 19:12–13, 15–26).

Predictions of judgment fall most severely on religious leaders, whom Q's Jesus depicts as concerned primarily with ritual and pious ostentation rather than with true purity. They are more interested in enforcing conformity to their interpretations of Judaism than they are concerned to ease human suffering. Most serious of all is Jesus' charge that the religious leaders are like those who in earlier days rejected the message God sent to his people through the prophets, and the prophets as well. As a result, Jesus represents the entire biblical narrative as the story of the murder of God's messengers, from Abel in the Book of Genesis to Zechariah in 2 Chronicles (Luke 11:39–51). When God finally gathers his true people in the new age, many of those who had the opportunity to know and hear Jesus will be excluded, while the faithful remnant will join the men and women of faith from the days of Abraham down through the period of the prophets, sharing the fellowship of God's people.

The new community that Jesus is pictured in Q as calling into being was distinctive among those gathered around other prophetic figures of his time, as the contrast with John the Baptist makes apparent. John denounces his contemporaries for counting on their descent from Abraham rather than on their superior moral qualities and their penitence in light of God's impending judgment on his people (Luke 3:7–9, 16–17). Yet Jesus describes John as one whose role is only preparatory for the coming of God's kingdom (7:24–30). John's life was one of abstinence and strictness; Jesus' way of life is one of joy, festivity, and, above all, inclusiveness toward those excluded by way of life or occupation from participation in the community of the covenant people (7:31–5).

Jesus' own role as depicted in Q includes his being engaged in conflict with the powers of evil, as in the testing experiences in the desert of Judea, in which he resists the proposals of the Tempter by trust in God alone (Luke 4:2–12). In his public activity, the evil powers and the forces that limit or warp human life are already being overcome (7:18–23). With the insight that his disciples have received through him, they can already discern this new reality (10:23–4). Indeed, through his exorcisms, in which he defeats the prince of demons, Jesus makes the kingdom of God a present reality (11:14–22). The kingdom's powers are already at work in the midst of Jesus' contemporaries (13:20–1). The message of God's reconciliation with sinners is not merely Jesus' own idea, he insisted, but derived from God's own nature, because God takes the initiative to restore the lost sheep to the flock – which is his people (15:1–4). Those who are characterized by trust, by sharing in God's work of reconciliation, and by fidelity to Jesus in the midst of his sufferings and theirs, are promised a share in the feast that will launch the new age (22:28–30).

In aggregate, the Q tradition offers reports of Jesus' words, acts, and parables, which together represent an essential strand of the early Christian understanding of Jesus, of his relationship to God and God's purpose for the creation, and of Jesus' own portrayal of the responsibilities and destiny of his followers. Luke and Matthew have incorporated this tradition, each in its own way and with distinctive emphases. One early Christian community, however, developed its representation of Jesus independently of the Q tradition. Not content to offer a loose collection of sayings and stories, this community organized its sources into a consecutive account, which follows a narrative line in order to introduce its people to the message of Jesus and its significance. This major undertaking resulted in what we know as the Gospel according to Mark.

D. Mark: The Oldest Gospel

The oldest known theory about the origin of Mark comes from Papias of Hierapolis in Asia Minor (present-day Turkey) perhaps around the year 130 C.E. He claimed, in a passage quoted in the *Ecclesiastical History* of Eusebius, that someone named Mark had been the interpreter of Peter and that he wrote down what Peter recalled that Jesus had said or done, since Mark himself had not been one of the original followers of Jesus. This same Mark might be mentioned several times in Acts (12:12, 35; 13:5; 15:37) and/or occasionally in letters by or attributed to Paul (Colossians 4:10; 2 Timothy 4:11; Philemon 24). If so, he could have been related to one or more of Jesus' followers and might conceivably have had direct access to early traditions about Jesus through a kinsman who figured among the original disciples. But the writing that now bears Mark's name seems to have been compiled from oral and written sources that consisted of relatively short runs of tradition from several informants. This Gospel does not display the strict narrative sequence one might expect from a report from a firsthand observer of Jesus' public life such as Peter. The baptism of Jesus must have come early in the development of his public persona, and the confrontation with the authorities in Jerusalem obviously came at the end of his career; otherwise there is little firm indication of chronological order in the materials that went into making the Gospel according to Mark. (For this reason, any account of Jesus' life and development must be prepared to reassess the order of Mark, and of the Gospels as a whole.) Mark does not read as a biography would, but seems to have been composed with the broad features of Jesus' career and teaching in mind, culminating in the account of his death and the promise of meeting him raised from the dead.

The sources most immediately used by the author were apparently Greek, since quotations from the Scriptures are for the most part based on Greek, rather than Hebrew, originals. Still, from time to time Aramaic in sayings of Jesus is directly transliterated, and the version of Isaiah he cited agrees in crucial cases with the Targum (the Aramaic version) of Isaiah. That would suggest that, although some of Mark's sources ultimately reached back to Jesus and his immediate followers, they had already been rendered into Greek by the time the Gospel was composed. Mark's language is a rough and ready Greek, with occasional hints that Aramaic locutions have influenced the style. Yet some of the terms used are derived from Latin, as well.

Mark must have been written in a fairly cosmopolitan place, where Greek was the major common language, where there was exposure to Roman culture, and yet where part of the underlying culture was Semitic-speaking. Syria, where all these factors would have been present, has been proposed as a place of origin, although Papias referred to Rome as the city of origin, where a large Jewish community had existed since the second century B.C.E. The importance for Mark of Jesus' challenges to Jewish leaders – priests, Sadducees, and Pharisees – suggests that it was written with some awareness of conditions in Palestine, where these groups and issues were of major

EUSEBIUS

Born about 260 C.E., Eusebius became bishop of Caesarea (on the coast of Palestine) after 312, as Emperor Constantine brought to an end the imperial persecution of Christians launched by Diocletian (303–12 C.E.). Constantine himself convened a council of the most important bishops of the church meeting at Nicea in Asia Minor in 325. The council addressed the most controversial issue of Christian theology in that time or any other time: the relationship between Jesus and God. Should Jesus be regarded as fully equal in divinity to his Father, the creator of the universe, or should he be seen as subordinate to the Father? Eusebius was directly and deeply involved in the ensuing theological dispute within the Church concerning the relation of Jesus to God: Was Jesus coeternal with God? The so-called Nicene Creed, a confession

of Catholic, Orthodox faith recited during the Eucharist that took more than a century to produce, had its beginnings at Nicea and emerged as the first creed of the Church that had the weight of imperial authority behind it. Eusebius played a crucial role at that council as adviser to the emperor on these fundamental theological questions about the true nature of Jesus Christ.

There was an excellent library of Christian writings in Caesarea, and Eusebius drew on these in his own extensive literary output, which ranged from responses to intellectual attacks on Jesus (in *Against Hierocles*), through an elaborate effort to correlate the chronological schemes in use in the ancient world, to two elaborate defenses of the faith: *The Demonstration of the Gospel* and *The Preparation for the Gospel*. Among the

competing calendrical systems used in the ancient world, the one promoted by Eusebius placed the birth of Christ as the turning point in history and set the pattern for subsequent chronological schemes in the Western world. In his *Preparation for the Gospel* Eusebius sought to show how God had prepared the world historically and intellectually for the advent of Christ and the Christian faith. His *Ecclesiastical History* remains of profound importance, not only for its reconstruction of the origins and growth of the Church down to his time but also because Eusebius quoted at length from ancient sources – pagan and Christian – that are otherwise lost. His work is a landmark in the process of Christianity's transition from its status as a sect under attack by the empire to the official religion of the emperor.

significance. At the same time, Mark's grasp of the basics of Judaism is sometimes tenuous at best (see Mark 7:3–4). The same paradox of local knowledge expressed side by side with surprising ignorance emerges in the special attention paid in Mark's narrative to Tyre and Sidon and to the cities of the Decapolis (chief of which was Damascus, the largest of this loose confederation of Hellenistic cities and a leading city of Syria), which contrasts oddly with Mark's occasionally bizarre geography, which seems to put these very different cities in easy proximity (Mark 7:31). As a whole, Rome would seem to be this Gospel's city of origin, because it maintained sufficient contact with Judaism and Jerusalem to explain Mark's high level of information but was also sufficiently distant from them (sometimes to the point of anti-Semitism) to explain Mark's lapses into implausibility and ignorance.

The time when the Gospel according to Mark was written is also uncertain. Its specific concern with the threatened coming of armies to seize Jerusalem and destroy the Temple suggests that Mark dates from the years after the Jewish nationalists began their revolt against the Romans but before the Temple was destroyed: that is, between 66 and 70 C.E. On the other hand, some scholars have pointed to Mark's emphasis on the comprehensive defeat of Jerusalem and the destruction of the Temple to indicate that a date after the Roman campaign (ca. 73 C.E.) is more plausible.

DECAPOLIS

"Decapolis" simply means "ten cities" and refers to a loose federation of ten centers of Greco-Roman culture located from southern Syria (Damascus) to central Nabatea, east of the Jordan River (Philadelphia, which is now Amman, the capital of Jordan). Mentioned in the manuscripts of the New Testament (with many textual variants, including differences of spelling) are Gerasa, where Jesus is reported to have healed a demoniac living in a tomb (Mark 5:1–20), and Gadara, where Matthew locates this same exorcism (Matthew 8:28–34). (The actual location was probably a village.) Scythopolis (Beth She'an) was the only city of the Decapolis located west of the Jordan in the region of Galilee. Pella, which was named for the birthplace of Alexander the Great, was said by the historian Eusebius to have been the place of refuge to which the Christians fled after the fall of Jerusalem to the Romans in 70 C.E. The significance of these ten cities for biblical history and literature is that, as elaborate centers with their pagan temples, theaters, gymnasia, and other Greek institutions, they demonstrate the extent to which Jews and early Christians were surrounded by Hellenistic culture.

Mark 13, the most extensive passage in Mark that treats a unified theme and often referred to as "the Markan apocalypse," directly concerns any effort to date the composition of the Gospel. It portrays the end of the age, the sufferings of the faithful, and the destruction of the Temple. The links between this part of Mark and the Book of Daniel reinforce the impression that this final discourse of Jesus in Mark is intentionally apocalyptic. As is evident from our consideration of the Q tradition, apocalyptic involves more than a literary style in which a visionary describes the end of the present order. The seers of the apocalyptic tradition conveyed (1) a way of understanding history, (2) a belief about how knowledge of God's purpose is communicated to human beings, and (3) a set of assumptions about the community that is the recipient of this knowledge, including their immediate prospects of struggle and suffering and their long-range confidence in divine vindication. In this view of the world, history is the story of the conflict between divine forces and the forces of evil, which for the time being have seized control of the

Gerasa, city of the Decapolis. Located thirty miles southeast of the Sea of Galilee, Gerasa in the first and second centuries C.E. became one of the most impressive of the cities of the Decapolis, with colonnaded streets, temples, theaters, and a fine forum. The triumphal arch on the southern edge of the city was dedicated to Emperor Hadrian, so some of the architectural remains can be dated to the second century C.E. The distance of Gerasa from the Sea of Galilee calls into question whether "in the region of the Gerasenes" in the Gospel story of Jesus expelling the demons into a herd of swine has anything to do with the city of Gerasa. In any case, the Greek Gospel manuscripts do not accord in naming the region (see Mark 5:1 especially), and probably reflect differing points of geographical reference. (BiblePlaces.com)

human situation, subjecting both political powers and individuals to demonic control. God has disclosed to the faithful that they will have to endure suffering, even martyrdom, for some time to come, but that through his chosen agent, the hostile forces will be overcome and the divine rule established. In that new situation, the faithful will share in the rule of God and will be fully vindicated in the triumph over evil. This knowledge cannot be inferred from the course of events or arrived at by human wisdom, according to the perspective of apocalypse, but is given in veiled form only to the elect community. This outlook on God, the world, and the community of faith pervades the Gospel according to Mark.

Although Mark contains reports of the career of Jesus, it is not a biography. Rather, it resembles a type of document known from the study of other literatures and from traditions studied by anthropologists in non-Western cultures. This form of literature is known as a *foundation document*, written as a basic source of instruction for a community. A foundation document typically includes an account of the circumstances under which a community got its start, and especially how its founding figure launched the group. By anecdote and precept, the community learns what its guidelines are to be, what its aims are, and what destiny it may expect. Two closely related examples of foundation documents from the Jewish world are the *Rule of the Community* and the *Covenant of Damascus*, both prepared at Qumran near the Dead Sea for the guidance of the Essene community there. Although the details of Mark differ widely from those of these sectarian writings, the basic strategy of Mark is similar to that of these Dead Sea Scrolls.

Pella, city of the Decapolis. Evidence for occupation of the mound of Pella goes back to prehistoric times. Pella began to achieve status and wealth in the late Hellenistic period, when it was named for the birthplace of Alexander the Great. Pella was destroyed by Jewish nationalists during the time of Alexander Jannaeus for its contravention of Jewish laws. Under the Romans it joined the Hellenistic federation of cities called the Decapolis, of which Damascus was chief, and developed many of the features of Greco-Roman culture: a temple, an odeum, and baths. Christians are reported to have fled to Pella after 66 C.E., when the Romans began attacking Jerusalem and the Jewish nationalists based there. This excavation of a Byzantine church demonstrates Pella's enduring importance as a Christian site. (BiblePlaces.com)

1. Major Themes in the Gospel according to Mark

The Acts of God

John the Baptist announces the unique role that Jesus has in mediating God's rule in the world (Mark 1:7–8), and the voice from heaven at his baptism (1:11) confirms Jesus' status, as well as the role of baptism in extending Jesus' sonship to those who believe in him. Jesus' authority is evident from the outset in his teaching (1:21, 27), in his healings and exorcisms (1:23–6), and in his pronouncement of the forgiveness of sins (2:1–12).

That the authority of Jesus involves radical reinterpretation of traditions of Judaism is also explicit from the beginning of Mark. John acknowledges the contrast between his role and that of Jesus (Mark 1:7–8). This difference also comes out in the result of Jesus' baptism as contrasted with John's baptism of repentence. Whereas John practiced the traditional form of repeated immersion to achieve purity by distancing oneself from sin (1:4), in Jesus' case, the Spirit of God descended on him when he immersed during the baptism (1:9-11). The difference between Jesus and John is directly asserted by Jesus himself, in his first public statement in Mark, in which he declares the nearness of God's kingdom and the necessity for his contemporaries to change their minds about God and his ways with the world (1:14–15). Jesus claims that already in his exorcisms, God's chief adversary, Beelzebub, or Satan, is suffering defeat (3:23–7).

Quotations from and allusions to the Scriptures of Israel pervade Mark, usually based on an ancient Greek version. Hence the reader is led to anticipate the fulfillment of the purposes of Israel's God through Jesus and to expect lines of continuity with Judaic tradition. Continuity is also indicated by Jesus' actions, as when he chooses a gathering of Jews (called a "synagogue") as the setting for launching his preaching and healing activity (Mark 1:39). Yet many of his actions indicate a sharp break with the past on issues explicitly raised in the Scriptures or in subsequent Jewish tradition. For example, the people to whom he directs his healing activity are precisely those kinds of persons who would be excluded or dismissed to the periphery by the purity standards of the Qumran community (*Temple Scroll* 45–9): the deaf, the blind, the lame, those with a bloody flux, and those in occupations that compromised their ethnic loyalty or their ritual purity, such as the tax collectors. Indeed, Jesus includes one such – Levi, who collects taxes for the Romans – among his inner circle of disciples (Mark 2:13–17).

Mark frequently includes as a detail of his accounts of healing a note that the subject was in some way unclean or that Jesus' act of healing involved a violation of purity laws, such as contact with an ailing person or a corpse. Occasionally the subjects were pagans or those living in pagan territory. The first healing story concerns a "leper," that is, a person with broken or mottled skin (Mark 1:40–5), whose disease makes him ritually impure (Leviticus 13–14). When friends lower a paralytic through the roof of a house where Jesus is (Mark 2:1–12), Jesus does not immediately heal

SYNAGOGUE

The Greek verb *synago*, for which *synagoge* is the noun equivalent, means to bring people together, in the sense of gathering a group in order to achieve a meeting of minds. The meaning is similar to that of the Greek word *ekklesia*, which comes from the verb for "to call together" or "to call out [a group]," typically for civic purposes. The former term was used by Jews in Palestine and elsewhere to refer to their community gatherings for discussion, adjudication of differences, and settlement of common policies and customs, as well as for the interpretation of Scriptures and for liturgical events, including meals of fellowship. This pattern of "gatherings" seems to have flourished in Palestine under the auspices of the Pharisees in the second century B.C.E. and to have taken place in private homes or, where necessary for space reasons, in public halls. (The public buildings for prayer are already attested by this time in the Diaspora, and the institutional arrangement for such meetings may well have originated in Babylon or in Egypt long before Pharisaic practice.) By the end of the first century C.E., following the destruction of the Temple and the disappearance of the priesthood, the synagogue began to evolve into what was to become the major instrument for the preservation and fostering of Jewish life and faith. With the support of Roman authorities, the synagogue began to take on increasingly institutional and authoritative forms, developing leadership roles and establishing prescribed modes of instruction. (Concurrently, the term "rabbi" took on the meaning of established authority, as in current usage, rather than referring to teachers such as Jesus whose authority was charismatic rather than institutional.) In the later second and in the third century, distinctive architectural forms for synagogue buildings began to appear. From the New Testament (Acts 16:11–15) and from inscriptional evidence from several sites around the Mediterranean, we can infer that the gathering place for Jews was sometimes known as a *proseuche*, meaning literally "a place (or house) of prayer." Only later did the term for the gathering (*synagoge*) come to be used for the special and distinctive buildings in which the meetings took place.

him but deals with a preliminary theological question: can a person be released from the sin that produces illness? After resolving that issue by pronouncing the forgiveness of the man's sins on behalf of "the Son of Man" in heaven, Jesus proceeds to cure his disability. In another healing story Jesus is described as violating the Sabbath law against work by his act of healing a man with a withered hand (Mark 3:1–6, 10–11). Later his healing activity takes Jesus outside Jewish territory and brings him in direct contact with the dead, with unclean persons, and with those possessed by unclean spirits (5:1–20, 21–43; 6:56; 7:24–30, 31–7). On his return to Galilee and on his way to Jerusalem, he becomes involved with other people presented as on the fringe of the Jewish community (9:14–29, 10:46–52). Clearly, in Mark's presentation, the purity traditions of Israel are radically revised during Jesus' work in preparing for the coming of God's rule in the world.

Issues of purity and the Sabbath are dealt with explicitly in other parts of Mark, as when Jesus defends his disciples' action in helping themselves to grain as they move through the fields, technically performing work on the Sabbath (Mark 2:23–8). There is an extended account of Jesus' confrontation with the Pharisees in which he asserts that the essence of purity is not ritual observance but inner moral condition and right relationship with one's neighbor (7:1–23). In Mark's theology, the boundaries of the people of God are no longer to be drawn by the criteria of observance of ritual law.

Jesus also challenges Jewish convictions and institutions through the positions he adopts toward the Temple and toward the nature and destiny of historic Israel. By riding into Jerusalem on a donkey, Jesus implicitly claims Israel's kingly or messianic role, since this act fulfilled the prophecy of Zechariah 9 about the coming of the king of Zion (Mark 11:1–10). Yet after accepting the acclaim of the crowds, Jesus takes no steps toward achieving Jewish independence from Rome, as one would expect of a claimant to the role of king, but instead withdraws to the fellowship of his own intimate circle of followers outside the city (Mark 11:11). Later, the solemn covenant meal he eats with the disciples redefines for Mark the Passover celebration of Israel's tradition, replacing the death of the lamb with Jesus' own impending death, and interpreting this event as a sacrifice that would ratify the covenant, a necessary step toward the coming of God's rule (14:12–21). Similarly, Jesus' aggressive actions in the Temple are in Mark not a move toward preserving the uniqueness of Israel's access to God in this holy place, but a call for its being open to all nations, as Isaiah prophesied it would be (11:15–19). According to Mark, God's support of Jesus' claim to be the agent of covenant renewal is seen in the symbolic detail that Mark specifies (15:38): at the moment of Jesus' death, the Temple veil, which separated off the holy place and restricted access to the inner sanctuary, is said to have been torn from the top down (i.e., by God). Now, all humanity has the possibility of access to Israel's God and the Temple is marked as a thing of the past.

In addition to declaring new bases for participation in the covenant people and for access to the God of Israel, Jesus is pictured in Mark as defining his role as God's agent to establish his kingdom. We have already seen that in early Judaism there was no single, uniform understanding of the agent or agents through whom God's purpose was to be achieved. When the term "messiah" was used, it did not have a commonly agreed-on meaning, nor were the qualifications or even the role(s) of messianic figure(s) uniformly perceived. For some people, the messianic role was that of a king, whose task was to reestablish an independent Jewish state. One phrase used in this connection is "Son of God," although that designation is also broad, referring to a relationship of filial intimacy with God in a variety of contexts. For others, the messianic role was a priestly function, which would result in the purification of God's people and the establishment of the true and proper worship of Israel's God. In the Dead Sea Scrolls, both these roles are depicted, with primacy going to the priestly messiah. In Psalm 110 a royal figure, probably in the Hasmonean line that combined royal and priestly power in a way that the Essenes opposed, is called "lord" and described as ruler, and is then identified as an eternal priest. But other titles and roles were represented as well during this period, ranging from the prophet of the end-time (again, as awaited at Qumran, where Deuteronomy 18:15–22 was understood to refer to that figure) to a celestial, triumphant figure – the Son of Man – who would defeat the powers of evil and vindicate true Israel (as in the

SON OF GOD

In the Scriptures of Israel, the phrase "Son of God" is used in at least two different senses: (1) It appears as a corporate image for the historic people of Israel, especially in relation to God's action in bringing them out of slavery in Egypt and into the Promised Land. The basic text on this is Hosea 11:1, where God is quoted as having "called my son" out of Egypt. (2) It is also used in reference to David. The phrase appears in Psalm 2:7, where God addresses David as "my son" and declares, "This day have I begotten you." Further, David is specifically called God's "anointed" (i.e., messiah). Similar father/son imagery is used in Psalm 89:20–37 to depict the relationship of the Davidic royal line to God, although there David is actually addressed as "servant." These terms are linked in 2 Samuel 7:4–17, where God begets the royal line and David is called God's servant. The term "Son of God" implies a unique relationship and a central role that is to be fulfilled in the working out of God's purpose for his people, rather than expressing some form of supernatural origin or the divinization of a human being. The link between "Son of God" and "servant" underscores the obedient role that this person is to fulfill in accomplishing God's work.

Similitudes of Enoch). Although the term "servant" is not applied to Jesus in Mark, the function of serving is linked with Jesus' role as Son of Man in 10:45. As with "Son of God," the designation "servant" is used in the Scriptures with reference to both the faithful Israelites and the agent divinely ordained to achieve God's will for his people (Isaiah 42–53). The Scriptures of Israel do not consistently deploy messianic identifications of the prophet, the servant, or the Son of Man. In Mark the narratives about Jesus and the sayings attributed to him draw on a wide range of these terms and traditions, ranging far beyond any single category or categories in depicting the God-assigned purpose that Jesus is seen as fulfilling.

The lack of a common understanding of messiahship is evident in Mark when Peter acclaims Jesus as Messiah (8:29) but then rejects Jesus' announcement that, in fulfillment of that role, he must experience rejection, suffering, and death (8:31–3). That expectation is repeated in 9:30–1, with increasing detail about what Jesus' experience will be. Not only is his suffering envisioned, however, but also his vindication by God. This is specifically promised in 9:1, where his followers are told that they will live to see the triumph of God's purpose. It is also foreshadowed in the experience of Jesus and the inner core of his followers in the Transfiguration scene (9:2–13). This brief narrative recalls Daniel 10, where the seer is granted a vision of the divine that explains his purpose and is followed by assurances that he will be sustained through the hard experiences that lie ahead. The story is akin to the Jewish phenomenon known as Merkavah mysticism, in which the faithful are granted a transforming vision of God on his chariot-throne (the *merkavah*) in preparation for a time of testing that is to follow. In this scene the glistening appearance of Jesus and the divine voice affirming his special relationship to God clearly stand in the Merkavah tradition. This is wholly appropriate, as Jesus begins at this point in the Markan account to foretell his own sufferings and death – as a part of God's purpose through him.

Responses to Jesus

Mark's Gospel portrays a range of responses that Jesus elicits from his contemporaries. These include the reactions of the crowds that hear and see his marvelous acts and other signs of divine approval, initial doubts and

Sea of Galilee, looking north from Tiberias. The Sea of Galilee was also known as the Sea of Chinnereth, which may mean "harp" in Hebrew (in reference to its shape), although it may take its second name from the nearby city called Chinnereth. (Joshua 19:35). It is referred to in the New Testament as "the Sea of Galilee" (Matthew 4:18, Mark 1:16) and also as "the Lake of Gennesaret" (Luke 5:1), "the lake" (Luke 5:2), and simply "the sea" (John 6:16–25). It lies in the great geological fault that extends from the Jordan Valley, through the Dead Sea and the Red Sea, into Africa. Its surface is about 700 feet below sea level, and it is surrounded by hills of more than 1,200 feet in elevation. To the west was once a major commercial highway connecting Syria and Mesopotamia with the Palestinian coast and Egypt. Despite frequent storms, the lake provided a major source of income for fishers, who operated from the towns along its western shore, including Capernaum, where Jesus took up residence (Matthew 4:13). (BiblePlaces.com)

resistance from his family and followers, and opposition from religious and political leaders.

Mark fills the first day of Jesus' ministry with a remarkable (one might say, surreal) series of exorcisms and healings that come to a close with throngs surrounding him, including "*all*" who were sick or demon-possessed and the entire population of the towns and cities of Galilee, including Capernaum (Mark 1:14–34). As Jesus' activity of preaching and healing continued, his reputation spread so widely that, according to Mark, before he could enter a town, the crowds would flock to him in the open country or beside the Sea of Galilee (1:45, 2:13, 3:9, 4:1, 5:21; 6:45, 53–6). The crowds pack around the house where he is engaged in healings and exorcisms (2:4, 3:20), and in other places where he performs healings (5:24, 7:33, 9:14, 10:46). The crowds also witness his teachings about purity (7:14), his instruction to followers about the cost of discipleship (i.e., suffering and possibly martyrdom; 8:34), and his claim that the ultimate messiah is superior to David (i.e., Jesus is David's lord; 12:37). Crowds also see and learn from Jesus' activity in the Temple (11:18, 12:41).

MERKAVAH MYSTICISM

Jewish mysticism involves a personal encounter with God upon his throne, known as the *merkavah*, "the chariot." The throne of God is not perceived in a literal way, but as the generative point of all creation. It was called the chariot because this vortex of creative energy was conceived of as movable, so that it might be experienced in any place and at any time. The chariot was the source of God's energy and intelligence, the origin of his power to create and destroy. By focusing their minds on the chariot in meditation, sages of Merkavah mysticism sought knowledge and experience of God. This divine reality determines the significance behind any time and place in which people might live. Sensitivity to the presence of God as the chariot that makes his presence known was a powerful force in the religion of the prophets, which influenced the conception of the spiritual life in both Judaism and Christianity. The chain of tradition that teaches how to become aware of this presence is called the Kabbalah, an ancient term that resonates with mystical meaning to this day.

In its origins, the tradition of thinking of God in this way is more ancient than Israel itself. From Mesopotamia, from the twenty-third century B.C.E. and the fifteenth century B.C.E., stories are told of kings and courtiers entering the palace of heaven and receiving visions and empowerment there. Israel learned these royal traditions from Babylonia and converted them into prophetic authorization, especially during the time of Ezekiel (during the sixth century B.C.E.). Ezekiel related his classic vision of the throne of God as a chariot, a *merkavah*, and

what is usually called Merkavah mysticism derives from his vision (in Ezekiel 1). The chariots of Israel's enemies might have been impressive, but in Ezekiel's mind the greatest chariot of them all rolled through the heavens. The steeds of heaven were surreal, "Every one had four faces, and every one of them had four wings, and their legs were straight legs and the sole of their feet was as the sole of a calf's foot, and they sparkled like burnished brass. They had the hands of a man under their wings on their four sides" (Ezekiel 1:6–8). The four faces Ezekiel saw on each beast were a man's, a lion's, an ox's, and an eagle's (Ezekiel 1:10) (These faces were to be become the symbols of the four Evangelists during the second century C.E.) Magnificent wheels supported the four monsters, which propelled the chariot at the speed of lightning. After Ezekiel, the Book of Daniel (chapter 7) detailed this vision even further (during the second century B.C.E.). And by the time of Jesus, the *Book of Enoch*, found in fragments in Aramaic at Qumran, took that tradition further.

The Book of Genesis says of Enoch only that "he walked with God, and he was not" (Genesis 5:22). This disappearance is taken as a sign that Enoch enjoyed a vision by ascent into the multiple heavens above the earth and that he was authorized to relate its wisdom to Israel, indeed, to act as an intermediary to the angels who had disobeyed God. From Ezekiel, through Daniel and Enoch, and on to John and Jesus, there is a growing tradition, a *kabbalah* ("something received"), that reflects a deep commitment to the disciplined practice of the vision of God's throne. The frag-

ments of *Enoch* at Qumran are found in Aramaic, which suggests that the book was used not just by the Essenes (who tended to guard their sectarian documents in Hebrew), but by a wider audience. In fact, the *Book of Enoch* is also quoted at a later stage in the New Testament, so that there can be no doubt of its widespread use. Another work found in Hebrew at Qumran and widely attested elsewhere, the *Book of Jubilees*, also presents Enoch as a figure of revelation: he himself knows the Torah later communicated to Moses by angelic agency.

Focus on the *merkavah* is also evident in the experience of Jesus. Traces of that are perhaps plainest in the story of Jesus' baptism, which takes us back to Jesus' association with John "the Baptist" ("the immerser"; *baptistes* in Greek, from the verb *baptizo*, "to immerse"). Many people came to John for immersion, most often when they were on the way to the Temple along the well-established path of pilgrimage that followed the Jordan Valley. John offered them purification in God's own water and the assurance that this was the science of Israel's true purity. For the followers of John, this continual immersion was more than a matter of simple repentance. There was also an esoteric meaning. John conveyed a definite understanding of the final significance that his purification offered Israel. As John himself expressed it, immersing oneself in water prepared one to receive the Spirit of God, which was to drench all Israel with its sanctification. The key to John's preparation lies in the wording attributed to him, "I immerse you in water, but he himself will immerse you in Holy Spirit" (Mark 1:8; see Matthew 3:11; Luke 3:16). The link between purification with water and the vindicating presence of God's Spirit is explicitly made in the Book of Ezekiel, the same book that provides the meaning of the *merkavah* (Ezekiel 36:22–7). After all, God's Spirit proceeded from his throne, the source of all true judgment.

Jesus' skill in this vision made him one of John's most prominent disciples. The Gospels relate the particular vision of Jesus (Matthew 3:13–17; Mark 1:9–13; Luke 3:21–2). As Jesus was immersed for purification, he came to have an increasingly vivid vision, of the heavens splitting open and of God's Spirit coming upon him. And a voice: "You are my son, beloved; in you I take pleasure." Each of these elements is resonant with the Israelite *kabbalah* of the divine throne.

The heavens are conceived of in the story of Jesus' baptism (as in the Judaism of the time) as multiple, hard shells above the earth, so that any real disclosure of the divine must represent a rending of those firmaments. But once they are opened, Jesus' vision is not of ascending through the heavens, as did Enoch, but of the Spirit, as a dove, hovering over him and

descending. That image is a vivid realization that the Spirit of God at creation once hovered over the primeval waters (Genesis 1:2), as a bird. Rabbinic tradition identifies this bird as a dove, and a fragment from Qumran supports the association. The Spirit, which would one day come to Israel, in Jesus' vision was already upon him, and God took pleasure in him as a "son." The word "son" itself appears frequently in the Old Testament to refer to the special relationship between God and others. Angels are called "sons of God," Israel is spoken of as a divine son (most famously in Hosea 11:1), and the Davidic king is assured by divine voice, "You are my son, this day have I begotten you" (Psalm 2:7). All these are expressions not of a biological relationship, but of the direct revelation that God extends to angels and certain people. Jesus claims that he is of their spiritual lineage within his embrace of John's *kabbalah*.

In both Christianity and Judaism practitioners of divine presence embraced these traditions long after Jesus. Jewish mysticism, however, is better attested than its Christian counterpart because, after the Church was embraced as the religion of state during the fourth century, Christian

writings became less personal and intense than their Judaic counterparts (except in the case of monastic writings). By the Middle Ages a highly literate form of Jewish mysticism fully emerged, especially in the enriching mix of Judaic, Muslim, and Neoplatonic cultures in Spain and the south of France during the thirteenth century C.E.

Two foci of meditation were prevalent by this time. One was on the *shiur komah*, the "measure of the body." This referred to God's corporal reality, of which the human body – in the divine image and likeness – provided a reflection. The other focus involved discerning the *Sefiroth*, the emanations that vibrated outward from God and made all that is, and that resonated with the formation of the body. The Kabbalah at this stage represented the highest accomplishment of Judaic mysticism as a philosophical and personal discipline.

Conventional scholarship long sidelined the Kabbalah; even worse, commercial exploitation has trivialized its subtle teaching. But no mystical tradition better explores the intersecting mysteries of human character and divine presence than the medieval Kabbalah.

The two stories of miraculous feeding in Mark 6 and 8 are of special significance, and the presence of a crowd features centrally in them both (6:34; 8:1). These stories are told in language that points to the past of the biblical tradition and – at the same time – to the future of Mark's community. The feeding of the hungry multitude recalls biblical stories of God's providing food for Israel in the wilderness, representing the unification of God's people and God's providential care for them. The future dimension of the Gospel stories is apparent in the specific terms used by Jesus as the bread is prepared for distribution to the people: "he took, he blessed / gave thanks, he broke, he gave . . ." (6:41; 8:6). There is no mistaking the correspondence between these terms and those used in Eucharistic

EUCHARIST

Derived from the Greek word for "give thanks" (*eucharisteo*), "eucharist," which is used in the New Testament for thanksgiving to God for his benefits (1 Corinthians 14:18; 2 Corinthians 4:15, 9:11; Colossians 4:2), is also an important feature of the Lord's Supper in both the Gospel tradition (Mark 14:22–4; Matthew 26:26–8; Luke 22:17–20) and in the letters of Paul (1 Corinthians 11:23–6). The Eucharist is a solemn recalling of Jesus' death, symbolized by the broken loaf and the wine poured out, but it is also a grateful celebration in the present of the significance of that sacrificial death, as well as an anticipation of the time when God's rule will be universal (Matthew 26:29; Mark 14:25; Luke 22:17; 1 Corinthians 11:26).

These differing meanings emerged from practices of fellowship over meals in Jesus' movement both before and after his death. Like many of the prophets before him and many other rabbis in his own time, Jesus keenly interested himself in how sacrifice was offered in the Temple (Matthew 21:12–13 = Mark 11:15–17 = Luke 19:45–6 = John 2:13–17). Jesus objected to the presence of the merchants who had been given permission to sell sacrificial animals in the Temple's vast, outer court. His objection was based on his own, peasant's view of purity: he believed that Israelites should offer what they produced themselves, not things they had just bought from priests. He believed so vehemently in what he taught that he and his followers drove the animals and the sellers out of the great court, no doubt with the use of force. Jesus' interference in the ordinary worship of the Temple might have been sufficient by itself to bring

about his execution. Roman officials were so interested in its smooth functioning at the hands of the priests, whom they appointed, that they sanctioned the penalty of death for sacrilege. Yet there is no indication that Jesus was arrested immediately. Instead, he remained at liberty for some time and was finally taken into custody after one of his meals, the Last Supper. Jesus could not simply be dispatched as a cultic criminal. He was not attempting an onslaught upon the Temple as such; his dispute with the authorities concerned purity within the Temple. Other rabbis of his period also engaged in forceful demonstrations of the purity they required in the conduct of worship.

The meaning Jesus gave his meals after what he did in the Temple brought about his arrest. Jesus had, long before his final pilgrimage to Jerusalem, celebrated fellowship during meals as a foretaste of the kingdom. But now he also added a new and scandalous dimension of meaning. His occupation of the Temple having failed, Jesus said of the wine, "This is my blood," and of the bread, "This is my flesh" (Matthew 26:26, 28 = Mark 14:22, 24 = Luke 22:19–20 = 1 Corinthians 11:24–5 = Justin, *1 Apology* 66.3). In Jesus' context, the context of his confrontation with the authorities of the Temple, his words can have had only one meaning. He cannot have meant, "Here are my personal body and blood"; that is an interpretation that makes sense only at a later stage. Jesus' point was rather that, in the absence of a Temple that permitted his view of purity to be practiced, wine was his blood of sacrifice, and bread was his flesh of sacrifice. In Aramaic, "blood" and

"flesh" (which may also be rendered as "body") can carry such a sacrificial meaning, and in Jesus' context, that is their most natural meaning. The meaning of "the Last Supper," then, actually evolved over a series of meals after Jesus' occupation of the Temple. During that period, Jesus claimed that wine and bread were a better sacrifice than what was offered in the Temple: at least wine and bread were Israel's own, not tokens of priestly dominance. No wonder the opposition to him, even among the Twelve (in the shape of Judas, according to the Gospels) became deadly. In essence, Jesus made his meals into a rival altar, and we may call such a reading of his words a ritual or sacrificial interpretation.

The sacrificial interpretation has two advantages over the traditional, autobiographical interpretation as the meaning Jesus attributed to his own final meals. The first advantage is contextual: the sacrificial interpretation places Jesus firmly with the Judaism of his period and at the same time accounts for the opposition of the authorities to him. The second advantage is its explanatory power: the sacrificial interpretation enables us to explain subsequent developments in the understanding of Eucharist within early Christianity and to appreciate the ongoing importance of sacrificial thinking within modern culture.

In the practice of the circle around Peter represented in Acts, the blessing or breaking of bread at home, the *berakhah* of Judaism, became a principal model of Eucharist. A practical result of that development was that bread came to have precedence over wine. More profoundly, the circle of Peter conceived of Jesus as a new

Moses, who gave commands concerning purity as Moses did on Sinai, and who also expected his followers to worship on Mount Zion. But the Eucharist was also seen as a Seder by some followers of Jesus, in terms of both its meaning and its chronology. So understood, only Jews in a state of purity could participate in Eucharist, which could be truly recollected only once a year, at Passover in Jerusalem.

The Synoptic Gospels insist by various wordings that Jesus' blood is shed in the interests of the communities for which those Gospels were composed: for the "many" in Damascus (Matthew 26:28) and Rome (Mark 14:24), and on behalf of "you" in Antioch (Luke 22:20). The Synoptic tradition also provided two stories of miraculous feeding that symbolized the inclusion of Jews and non-Jews within Eucharist, understood as in the nature of a philosophical symposium (see Mark 6:32–44, 8:1–10, and parallels).

The feeding of the five thousand – understood as occurring at Passover – is taken up in John 6 in a fully paschal sense. Jesus himself is identified as the *manna*, miraculous food bestowed by God upon his people. The motif was already articulated by Paul (1 Corinthians 10:1–4), but John develops it to construe the Eucharist as a Mystery, in which Jesus offers his own flesh and blood (carefully defined to avoid a crude misunderstanding; John 6:30–4, 41–58). That autobiographical reading of Jesus' words – as giving his personal body and blood in Eucharist – had probably already occurred to Hellenistic Christians who followed Synoptic practice. The Johannine practice made that meaning as explicit as the break with Judaism is in the fourth Gospel.

accounts given by Mark (14:23–4, and by Paul in 1 Corinthians 11:23–5). The symbolic meaning of these stories is evident: both accounts anticipate the establishment of a covenant people, membership in which will be open to all who come to Jesus seeking insight and renewal of life. The fact that one of these stories is described as taking place in predominantly Jewish territory (Mark 6) and the other in a Gentile district (Mark 8) underscores that neither social, ethnic, nor ritual factors are prerequisite for participation in God's people.

In the latter parts of Mark, allusions appear to wider responses to Jesus after his death and resurrection. The scene in 14:3–9, in which Jesus is sitting at table in the home of Simon the "leper" and allows a woman to anoint him, anticipates the openness that was to characterize the early church, and especially the Markan community. There is also a double prediction that the new people of God will include men and women from all over the earth (13:10, 27). The responses to Jesus of the centurion (15:39) and of Joseph of Arimathea (15:42–6) symbolize that both the Jewish and the Gentile worlds will provide leadership for the people of God. The latter part of Mark also strikes an ironic note concerning the crowd (14:43, 15:8–11), because they join the religious leaders in seizing Jesus and in the successful effort to persuade Pilate to have Jesus put to death. The "crowd" has potential for both faith and unfaith.

The parables of Mark 4 also assert that the response to Jesus was mixed, and yet produced astonishingly results. There the seed (i.e., the message of the kingdom) is sown in a variety of soils, producing varied but ultimately very fruitful results (4:1–9). The point that the seed is sown everywhere underscores the fact that there are no ethnic or religious preconditions as to who is an appropriate hearer of the Gospel. The impressive response to Jesus' proclamation is also implied in the parables of the seed growing by itself

The fishing village of Magdala, after which Mary Magdalene was named. (BiblePlaces.com)

(4:26–9) and of the mustard seed (4:30–2). This same point is made in Mark's reports of Jesus' healing activity primarily among those who were socially marginal or ritually excluded from the circles of Israelite piety in this period.

A second mode of response to Jesus in Mark consists of evidence of divine approval. The voice from God on the occasion of Jesus' baptism acclaims him as the divine Son and expresses pleasure in him (1:11). Jesus' departure to the desert is under the power of the Spirit of God, and during his time of trial angels minister to him (1:12). The divine empowering by which Jesus carries on his activities is evident in the cosmic control by which he calms the storm (4:35–41) and in his walking on the water (6:45–52). A paradoxical aspect of his miracles is that he performs them to meet human need, but he refuses to do them when challenged to offer a sign to corroborate his claim to have been sent and empowered by God (8:11–13). Divine compassion through Jesus, in Mark's view, responds to mortal weakness and resists any human tendency to sit in judgment of God (9:23–4).

Jesus' special relationship to God is disclosed in his prayer in the garden of Gethsemane (Mark 14:32–43) and in his claim that he expects divine vindication in the presence of God (14:62, quoting a mixture of Daniel 7:13 and Psalm 110:1). The overt evidences of God's support of these claims appear in the tearing of the Temple veil (15:38), in the darkness that falls at the time of his death (15:33), and in the opening of his tomb (16:4–6).

The third kind of response to Jesus that Mark describes is that of his family and of the inner core of his followers, the disciples. Ambivalence is characteristic of both these groups in Mark. The first emphatic indication of this inability to understand who Jesus is and how he fits into God's plan appears in Mark 3:20–1, where Jesus has gone to his home, and certain

Gethsemane. On the western slope of the Mount of Olives, across the Kidron Valley from the Jerusalem Temple mount, was an area called in Aramaic *geth-shemenayya*, which refers to a place for pressing oil from olives. The olive groves in this area were destroyed by Titus and the Roman troops during the Jewish revolt of 66–70 C.E., so the exact site cannot be determined. Churches honoring Jesus' struggle in Gethsemane as he faced death (Mark 14:32–42) have been erected in the vicinity since the fourth century. (BiblePlaces.com)

persons come to take him out of public view because they say he is crazy. Who they are is disclosed in 3:31–5: his mother and his brothers (and possibly his sisters). The reaction of Jesus to this misguided, though well-meaning act by his family is to redefine the family to mean those who are united with him in commitment to doing the will of God (3:34–5). (This Markan perspective resulted in locating this story in Capernaum, although it is likely based on an earlier event in Nazareth.) Since the family was the primary ground of personal identity and obligation in Jewish society, as in nearly every other culture, Jesus' teaching here is as socially radical as his stance against ritual purity was radical for religious identity.

The inability of Jesus' disciples to grasp his understanding of the role God had assigned to him – with its emphasis on suffering and death – led them to dream up various kinds of power roles for themselves, which in turn elicited stern rebukes from Jesus (Mark 8:32–3, 9:33–7, 10:35–40). His disciples expressed horror at his warnings that they would deny, betray, and abandon him, but his predictions proved to be accurate, as the stories about Judas (14:17–21, 43–6) and about Peter's denial and consorting with the

SCRIBE

The Hebrew and Greek terms for "scribe" carry the same connotations as does the English word "writer." The functions of scribes included keeping military records and fulfilling administrative roles in finance and government (2 Kings 22:3–14; Jeremiah 36:10). By the time of Israel's return from exile, however, when the law code was the dominant factor in reorganizing the nation, "scribe" became the designation of those skilled in the interpretation of the Law of Moses, as Ezra 7 and Ben Sira 38–9 attest. This role in the first century C.E. seems to have involved both administrative and interpretive functions, which earned scribes a place of power in local affairs. It seems that only after 70 C.E., with the destruction of the Temple and the establishment of more direct political control by the Romans, did the scribes become primarily religious functionaries, devoted to debate over and interpretation of the Mosaic Law.

enemy (14:26–31, 54, 66–72) demonstrate. As Jesus agonized over his fate in Gethsemane and the agents of the religious authorities were coming to seize him, all the disciples were asleep (14:37–42). The details of the young man and then all the disciples fleeing when Jesus was arrested (14:50–1) show that they had not grasped or been willing to accept his basic understanding of his role as the suffering son of man. Only a group of women remain faithful at the cross and the tomb (15:40–1, 47; 16:1–8). Yet even they keep silent rather than report the young man's announcement at the tomb that Jesus had been raised from the dead.

The fourth kind of response to Jesus in Mark's account is that of religious and political leaders. From the outset, Jesus' authority in interpreting the purpose of God for his people is contrasted with that of the scribes (Mark 1:22). Jesus' authority puzzles scribes, Pharisees, and even followers of John the Baptist, who question the basis of his ability to cast out demons (2:6–10). They are shocked by his eating with tax collectors and sinners (2:13–17) and by the failure of his disciples to fast (2:18–22). Pharisees and leaders of the synagogue challenge his contradiction of their teaching about Sabbath observance (2:24, 3:1–6). Later, Pharisees and other religious leaders pose test questions, addressing when divorce is permissible (10:1–12), what the source of his authority is (11:27–33), whether Jews should pay tribute to Caesar (12:13–17), how resurrection can be reconciled with Scripture (12:18–27), and which is the chief of the divine commandments (12:28–34). With the exception of the last question, his answers range from the controversial to the radical, and intensify the opposition of the religious leadership toward Jesus. In response, he warns his disciples against the prideful religious ostentation of the scribes.

TAX COLLECTOR

Roman policy for collecting revenues was to arrange contracts with local citizens for gathering tolls and taxes. Candidates bid for the post on the basis of what they expected to collect each year, and the job went to the bidder who offered Rome the best terms. Both local sales and the transit of goods from one province to another were subject to tax. Those who gathered the tax money were under obligation to pay to Rome the amount for which they had contracted and could keep an agreed amount above that, a system obviously open to abuse. Because in the course of their work they had contact with unclean substances and with ritually unclean people, tax collectors were shunned by many pious Jews, and even as traitors to their own people, since the money they collected from local sources went to maintain the alien, pagan power of Rome. Jesus' initiative in associating with tax collectors to the extent of including one among his inner core of followers would have been abhorrent to Jews of traditional piety and evoked hostility toward him from religious leaders (Matthew 9:11, 11:19; Luke 15:1, 19:1–10).

Yet Mark pictures Jesus as participating in much of the religious tradition of Israel: Jesus takes part in the voluntary gatherings known as the synagogue (Mark 1:39), recommends that a cleansed "leper" fulfill the law by showing himself to the priest and offering sacrifice (1:44; cf. Leviticus 13:49, 14:22), and makes pilgrimage to the Temple in Jerusalem (11:11). At least one leading figure in a synagogue comes seeking Jesus' help to restore his ailing daughter (5:22–43). Nonetheless, Jesus' challenge to Jewish traditions was so severe that to plan for his destruction "the Pharisees," according to Mark, joined with the Jewish group that backed Herod Antipas (3:6). (Luke 13:31 shows that some Pharisees remained sympathetic to Jesus; Mark is evidently generalizing here.) Even worshippers in a synagogue are offended by Jesus' claims and actions (6:1–6). The report of the interest in Jesus expressed by Herod Antipas, who linked him with John the Baptist and the prophets (6:14–16), is followed by the gruesome account of John's cruel execution (clearly out of chronological order). This serves to notify the hearer or reader of the Gospel that Jesus will suffer a comparable fate through the combined actions of Jewish and secular leadership.

At the midpoint of Mark, Jesus begins explicitly to announce his own fate: suffering, death, and resurrection (8:31, 9:31, 10:33), including his being turned over to the Gentiles. The conspiracy of the religious leaders to be rid of him is confirmed in 11:18, following his action in the Temple. Hostility only intensifies when Jesus predicts this Temple's destruction (13:1–4), and he does so by an appeal (13:14) to the precedent described in Daniel 9:27 and 12:11 of the desecration of the sanctuary under Antiochus Epiphanes – the event that triggered the Maccabean revolt. At the same time, Jesus warns his followers that they should expect persecution in the synagogues (13:9). The division of Jesus' movement from emergent, synagogue-based Judaism of the later first century is sharply drawn in Mark and makes for a distinct contrast with Jesus' location within, rather than apart from, the Judaism of his day.

The closing chapters of Mark (14–16) describe the combination of forces that resulted in Jesus' crucifixion. A coalition of leading priests and scribes, mentioned earlier in Mark (and anachronistically, since priests and scribes held sway in Jerusalem, rather than in Galilee), goes into action to arrest Jesus "by stealth" and kill him (14:1). This stealth is an effort to avoid any popular uprising of support for Jesus. Judas offers to help the coalition, according to 14:10–11. The role that Judas plays in the plot is apparently to lead the guards to where Jesus is staying outside the city and in the dark of night. Once that objective is achieved (14:43–6), Jesus is taken before the council (in Greek, *sunedrion*, which is transliterated into Aramaic as "Sanhedrin"), which by Roman law is qualified to make decisions affecting local problems and to recommend the execution of an offender against local customs. The membership includes three power groups: chief priests, elders, and scribes. When the guards come to seize Jesus, he asks if they have come to seize him as a militant thug (often misleadingly understood

SUNEDRION, SANHEDRIN

In the Hellenistic period, and subsequently in the Roman Empire, the Greek term *sunedrion* was used for local councils given responsibility for establishing and enforcing regional policy on a range of issues. Under Roman rule, councils of local religious, economic, and social leaders were brought together to order and stabilize communities and were given power to adjudicate local issues. The evidence from the Gospels and from Josephus indicates that in Palestine in the first century C.E. the membership of a council included priests, elders (honored because of their wealth, prestige, or learning), and scribes. Councils needed to interpret local law and custom within the terms of reference of Roman hegemony, assuring both community support and Rome's continued favor. During the Rabbinic period, the designation for these councils was transliterated into Hebrew and Aramaic as "Sanhedrin," and the councils' function became the defining and adjudication of more purely religious issues based on emerging norms for promulgating the Law of Moses.

as a common "robber," as if the issue were petty criminality). That is, indeed, the case they want to make against him, in order to shift responsibility for him to the Roman authorities.

The climax of the hearing before the council comes when the high priest asks Jesus if he is the Messiah, the Son of God (14:62), obviously referring to the king of Israel in the Davidic tradition. Jesus affirms that he is the Messiah but goes on to link his role with the coming vindication by God at the end of the age, in the apocalyptic tradition of Daniel 7:13 (Mark 14:62). His point gets through to his examiners, who mockingly demand of him that he begin to prophesy (14:65). The council's decision to turn him over to Pilate (15:1) and his subsequent interrogation by Pilate in Mark take place to determine whether he is claiming to be the king of the Jews – understood in a political sense that would challenge Roman authority. The murkiness of this issue is depicted by Mark as the reason for Pilate's reluctance to execute Jesus, although that portrayal reflects Mark's interest in portraying faith in Jesus as compatible with acceptable conduct in the Roman Empire. The crucifixion of noncitizens by prefects such as Pilate was summary, a matter of military authority rather than careful juridical procedure. Mark dramatizes these events, as they would be remembered liturgically, as the accusations by the religious leaders continue (15:3), supported by the crowd (15:11–14), as well as by the soldiers, who in mockery treat Jesus as a royal figure, with crown (of thorns) and kingly robe (14:16–32). The charge is made explicit in the inscription placed on the cross, "The King of the Jews" (15:26), and is echoed once more by the religious leaders (15:31–2a) and by the real revolutionaries who are crucified with Jesus (15:32b). This mockery continues down to the moment of his death; then he is hastily buried in a tomb outside the city (16:8).

The Mystery of the Kingdom of God

In keeping with the apocalyptic tradition that characterizes Mark, Jesus' understanding of what God is doing and will accomplish in the future is disclosed only to the circle of his followers (4:11–12, 33–4). For those outside that group, everything that Jesus says and does is an enigma (literally, "a parable," but the underlying Semitic term includes the meaning "riddle"). This pattern of public statements and private explanations is repeated in 8:14–21, where the meaning of the (Eucharistic) loaves is reserved for the insiders, and even they are challenged by Jesus' explanation.

This restriction of full understanding of who Jesus is and what God is doing through him to the inner circle of his followers results in Jesus' repeated orders to those whom he healed, and especially to the demons that he expelled, not to publicize the news of what he had done (Mark 1:34, 3:12, 5:43, 7:33, 36; 8:26). An exception to this call for secrecy occurs when Jesus tells the demoniac from Gerasa to report to his friends "how much the Lord has done for you," and to do so in the Gentile territory in which he lives, rather than in territorial Israel (5:19–20): for Mark this

INSURRECTIONIST

In Mark 15:27 and Matthew 27:38, we read that Jesus was crucified along with two others, who are described in most English translations as "thieves" or "robbers." The Greek term, *lestes*, can carry that meaning. A careful analysis of the socioeconomic conditions of Palestine in the first century C.E., however, indicates that the wealth of the land had become concentrated in the hands of a small elite, which included Roman landlords, those persons who were connected with the Temple (the chief source of revenue in the land), and those individuals who served in the administrative group established by the family of the Herods with the support of the Roman governors. Tenant farmers, whose absentee owners could expel them if they failed to produce what the owners regarded as adequate revenue, tilled much of the land.

When deprived of legitimate income and residence, they often resorted to robbery to survive, taking money and marketable objects from travelers passing through their district. Although Jesus did not condone theft, he identified with deprived and unjustly treated people in his mission to preach "triumph to the poor" (Luke 4:18). Some scholars have suggested that those crucified with Jesus were revolutionaries attempting to overthrow Roman rule, and Josephus indicates that Galileans were involved in such efforts even before the time of Jesus. But the best evidence of organized political revolt against Roman rule is from the second half of the first century, just prior to the Jewish revolt of 66–70 C.E. Jesus befriended the poor and forgave those who violated the law, but he did not side with or promote political revolution.

shows that the time will come, following Jesus' death and resurrection, when the triumphal message about him and the new community will be disseminated everywhere. This will specifically include the mission to the Gentiles, which the disciples are to take up after Jesus' resurrection, in preparation for the end of the age (13:10). The coming of the new age is sure, as the parable of the fig tree implies (13:28–9), and will occur during the generation of Jesus' disciples (13:30), although the exact time is a secret known only to God (13:32–7).

The theme of the hidden nature of the divine purpose is implied in the strange ending of Mark (16:8), where the women who have seen the young man at the tomb say nothing to anyone but are filled with astonishment, fear, and trembling. Those reactions, however, are precisely the ones attributed to Daniel (Daniel 10:7–12) after God has granted him visions of the end-time and of the throne of God. The very terms used here by Mark are the same as those found in one of the ancient Greek versions of Daniel at this point. The framework in which Mark portrays Jesus, and the revelation of God and his purpose that came through him, is that of apocalyptic.

The Responsibilities of the Markan Community

From the beginning of his public activity, Jesus charges his followers with carrying forward his work: preaching the message of divine victory, healing the sick, expelling demons (Mark 3:13–19). They are to call people into the fellowship of God's people, just as they once caught fish in their nets (1:16–19). Relying on the authority that Jesus gave them to accomplish these goals, and on the hospitality of the towns they visit for their daily sustenance, they are sent forth by Jesus (6:6–13).

At the same time, they are to be prepared for violent opposition, persecution, even martyrdom, because of their association with Jesus (Mark 8:35–8, 9:38–41, 10:35–45). As God's people, they face the prospect of conflict and resistance, from the personal to the international level (13:5–8), and hostility from both religious and political powers (13:9–11). They are promised that God will sustain them through these times of suffering, and they are called on to persevere until the end of the age (13:12), especially in light of the appearance among them of false messiahs and false prophets (13:21–3). The whole of humanity will undergo turmoil of unprecedented intensity (13:17–20), and there will be cosmic disturbances (13:24–5). The culmination of all this will be Jesus' appearance as the triumphant agent of God to establish God's rule on the earth – the Son of Man (13:26) – and the consequent assembling from all over the world of the new covenant people (13:27).

Meanwhile, the community has guidelines by which to regulate the lives of its members on a range of subjects: divorce and marriage (Mark 10:1–11), the place of children in the group (10:13–16), and attitudes toward wealth (10:13–16) and toward the pagan state (12:13–17). Guidelines about such theological issues as the resurrection (12:18–27), the most important commandment (12:28–34), and the traditional expectation of a royal messiah (12:35–7) are all sketched. The virtues that are to characterize the community include true obedience to God's will rather than pious evasion (7:9–13), genuine purity (7:17–23), generosity (12:41–4), and – above all – unrelenting personal discipline (9:42–50). Clearly, Mark is written to serve as the foundation document for his community, building on the example, the precepts, and the promises of Jesus.

Emperor Vespasian. Following the murder of Nero in 68 C.E. and a succession of unsuccessful emperors (Galba, Otho, and Vitellius) in a single year, Vespasian was declared emperor by the army, part of which he was leading in the successful effort to put down the Jewish revolt in Israel. Leaving Titus in charge of the troops, he returned to Rome and began to rebuild the city and its financial and administrative structure. He authorized construction of the Colosseum, completed by Titus, where many Christians were to die. (BiblePlaces.com)

II. PAUL: THE JESUS MOVEMENT IN THE ROMAN WORLD

Paul was the single most important figure in spreading the movement that began with Jesus and came to be known as Christianity (a term Paul himself did not use) to the wider Roman world. His deepest influence was largely literary (and postmortem); no fewer than thirteen documents in the New Testament were written by him or are attributed to him. In the Book of Acts Paul also features as a central figure, although there are crucial differences between what he says or implies in his letters and what is said about him in Acts. Yet Acts does preserve valuable information about Paul's career and about the strategy of other apostles and leaders to bring Jesus' message to the Mediterranean basin.

In reconstructing and analyzing the career of Paul and the subsequent spread of Christianity across the Roman Empire, it is useful to have in mind the chronology of the successive emperors from the time of Jesus' birth to the emperor under whom the Jews suffered defeat in the second revolt (Bar Kokhba's War):

Augustus	31 B.C.E.–14 C.E.	Vitellius	69
Tiberius	14–37	Vespasian	69–79
Gaius Caligula	37–41	Titus	79–81
Claudius	41–54	Domitian	81–96
Nero	54–68	Nerva	96–8
Galba	68	Trajan	98–117
Otho	69	Hadrian	117–38

A. The Cultural and Geographical Sphere of Paul's Career

Paul's letters reflect how much he had in common with other Jews of the Diaspora during the first part of the first century C.E., and how much his thought remains faithful to the biblical heritage. Yet in many details his writings also show substantial influence from the Hellenistic culture that permeated the eastern Mediterranean world. Fortunately, Paul includes in his letters some details of his own background in Judaism, as well as of his conversion experience. In Philippians 3:5–6 he describes his heritage in historical and linguistic terms – the people Israel, the tribe of Benjamin, and Aramaic-speaking parents. He also insists on his ancestral fidelity to Jewish practices, as evidenced by his parents' having circumcised him on the eighth day and by his own commitment to the Torah. The approach to the Law with which he identified was that of the Pharisees in their commitment to maintain the ritual boundaries, transferred from the Temple cult to personal life, that mark off the people of God as pure and obedient. It is wholly in keeping with this outlook that he traveled as a young man to Jerusalem, the center of the Pharisaic movement, and that after his conversion to Jesus' movement two of his major letters, Galatians and Romans, involve an extended argument to define the covenant people.

The scene of Paul's conversion is near Damascus, the largest of the cities of the Decapolis and the oldest city in Syria. Acts has him traveling to that city from Jerusalem on behalf of the high priest; Paul himself reports that he tried to destroy the Church in Judea (Galatians 1:13–17). He must have regarded the Church as a threat to what he, as a Pharisee, was persuaded was the purity of God's people, and he had aligned himself with Caiaphas, the high priest who continued to target Jesus' movement for persecution after the crucifixion. Acts 9:1–2 pictures Paul (under his Pharisaic name, Saul) proceeding to Damascus to see to the arrest of Jesus' followers. Given the legal circumstances of Roman rule, it is more likely that Caiaphas sought to encourage a continuing Roman campaign against Jesus' movement. His intervention in the Temple had put Jesus at odds with the priestly administration, and Acts plausibly portrays Paul as a supporter of the high priest, and therefore as an opponent of those who, like Jesus, believed the prophetic teaching that the Temple was to be a house of prayer for all people.

To an outsider, the "church" (*ekklesia*) and the "synagogue" (*synagoge*) in Damascus – and most anywhere else, for that matter – seemed very much alike: both were voluntary, unstructured gatherings of monotheists who believed that the tradition of Israel, as set forth in the Scriptures, was best realized among them. To understand and to enter into the purposes of God for his people, both groups met regularly for the study of Scripture, for prayer, and for table fellowship, in which they celebrated their common life as God's chosen people. One main difference was that, as a result of the activity of Jesus and of what his followers taught after they said he had been raised from the dead, the Church relaxed some ritual and cultic

EKKLESIA, ECCLESIA

In Greek culture, the term *ekklesia* means an assembly of persons convened for political or entertainment purposes. Greek-speaking Jews came to use the term to refer to the gathering of the covenant community in any place, for purposes of information, instruction, and worship (a meeting such as those described in Deuteronomy 31:30 and 1 Kings 8:14). The early Christian community took over *ekklesia* as a group designation (1 Corinthians 11:18; 14:4, 19, 28, 35). Usually translated as "church," in most cases each "assembly" met in private homes or tenements (Romans 16:5; 1 Corinthians 16:19; Philemon 2; Colossians 4:15). In Acts (14:23) and in the letters of Paul (1 Corinthians 16:1) rules are laid down to be observed within each of the individual "assemblies." Assemblies of Christians in metropolitan areas or districts could be referred to collectively as "the churches of" that area (Galatians 1:2, 22; 2 Corinthians 8:1). Occasionally, Paul uses the term in a comprehensive way to refer to the whole body of God's people (e.g., in 1 Corinthians 10:32, 12:28; Philippians 3:6; and probably Galatians 1:13). This usage leads to the global designation of Christians as a whole constituting "the Church." Even when Paul addresses the "church of God," he sometimes adds "which is at (or in)" followed by the name of the city or province involved (2 Corinthians 1:1, 1; Thessalonians 2:14). The combined meanings of local assembly and comprehensive membership of God's people is explicit in 1 Corinthians 1:2, where the letter is addressed to "the church of God which is at Corinth," but also to "all those who in every place call on the name of the Lord."

In later writings attributed to Paul, *ekklesia* grew to mean the whole body of Christians with Christ at its head, as in Ephesians 1:22. Accordingly, the Church is described in structural, organizational terms in Ephesians 2:19–22, where the metaphors used are those of hierarchy, foundation, and temple. The most familiar reference to *ekklesia* in the gospel tradition, Matthew 16:16, is also universal in scope: "On this rock I will build my church." The generalized force of the term "church" is highlighted by the description of the totality of the first Christians in the period after Pentecost as "the church throughout all Judea and Galilee and Samaria" (Acts 8:31). What began as a designation for a local fellowship of Christians had become by the end of the first century a title for the body of believers across the Roman world.

requirements for membership, welcoming marginal Jews and even Gentiles into its common life. This is probably one reason Saul was persuaded that loyalty to the tradition required him to take the initiative in destroying the church.

It may seem paradoxical that someone with Paul's set of values should become convinced that God had called him to take the initiative in carrying the Christian message to the Gentiles. While Acts gives a circumstantial account of Paul's conversion experience, in his letters Paul tells us only that God was pleased "to reveal his Son in me" (Galatians 1:16). Elsewhere he notes simply that, like the other apostles, he has "seen Jesus our Lord," risen from the dead (1 Corinthians 9:1, 15:8). What was important for Paul were not the circumstances or details of his vision of the risen Christ but the fact that his vision occurred, that it corresponded to the experience of those who had followed Jesus during his lifetime, and that it resulted in his special divine commissioning as the primary apostle to the Gentiles. Paul's conversion was a vision, as the three different, evidently romanticized accounts in Acts (in chapters 9, 22, and 26) demonstrate by their disparities. Following this vision, Paul withdrew to "Arabia," by which he meant the territory controlled by Aretas IV of Nabatea in his time, and then returned to Damascus (Galatians 1:17). Only after three years did he confer with Peter ("Cephas," as it is

CLAUDIUS

After the emperor Gaius Caligula was assassinated by his own Praetorian Guard in 41 C.E., Claudius assumed power as the fourth of the Roman emperors. Suetonius, in his *Lives of the Twelve Caesars* (25.4), reports that a disturbance among the Jews in Rome reached such intensity that Claudius decided to expel them all from the city, probably in 49. The instigator of this struggle is said to have been Chrestos – a common name among slaves, and probably an incorrect reference to Christos, whose gospel would have reached Rome about this time, with resultant divisions within the Jewish community there. This incident is also referred to in Acts 18:2 and resulted in the move of some Jews who had converted to Christianity to places like Corinth, as was the case with Priscilla and Aquila (1 Corinthians 16:19; Romans 16:3).

transliterated in English from the Aramaic *Keypha'*) and James (Jesus' brother) in Jerusalem. According to Paul they acknowledged that he and they were preaching a common faith, and they "glorified God" that their former enemy had become a co-worker (Galatians 1:18–24), although they did not include Paul in their ministries. Paul describes his activities following his initial visit with James in Jerusalem as having taken place in the "regions of Syria and Cilicia," and he specifies that he is unknown to the churches in Judea, the district where Jerusalem was located.

When did this fateful conversion occur? From the few chronological details that Paul offers in his letters (three years until the first visit to Jerusalem; fourteen years later another) we can deduce that he had spent a considerable period in Nabatea, Syria, and southern Asia Minor by the time he launched his wider work in Asia, Greece, and to the west. The fact that when he reached Greece there were already Christians there who had been driven from Rome by the decree of Claudius provides a highly probable date: around the year 50 C.E. This means that Paul must have been converted in the early thirties, shortly after Jesus' crucifixion, which requires us to assume that there was a church in Damascus at that early date that was large enough and diverse enough to attract the hostile attention

Emperor Claudius, from a Roman house in Rabat. The fourth emperor of Rome ruled from 41 to 54 C.E. Following the assassination of Gaius Caligula, Claudius was virtually forced into the imperial office, and his reign was hampered by constant conflicts with the Senate, which debated restoring the Republic. Although he is reported by Josephus (*Antiquities* 19.290) as having made a decree granting Jews the right to carry out their religious practices, he later expelled some or all the Jews from Rome, as noted by Suetonius (*Life of Claudius* 25.4) and by the author of Acts (18:2), probably in response to mounting friction with Christians in Rome. His rule was plagued by the schemes of his four wives, of his children, and of freedmen who exploited their relationship with him for their own advantage. (BiblePlaces.com)

of the dedicated Pharisee Paul. This conclusion supports the indication in Mark's Gospel that the message of Jesus reached the cities of the Decapolis during his lifetime (Mark 5:20, 7:31).

Paul was persuaded that all who considered themselves to be God's people Israel through Christ truly became Israel, but that God had previously disclosed to the family of Jacob his purpose for covenant community. In this regard, Paul's outlook was thoroughly apocalyptic: he saw Jesus as the agent through whom God had disclosed his plan and through whom it would be accomplished. Jesus' death on the cross and his resurrection were the foundation of Paul's assurance that, through the faithful suffering of his people, God would sustain and ultimately vindicate them. This program of redemption was already in process and would soon come to conclusion. What was new about Paul's outlook is that there were no ritual or ethnic prerequisites to participation in the people of God: Jews and Gentiles together became "new creation" and "the Israel of God" (Galatians 6:15-16). Paul saw the death of Jesus as the divine sacrifice through which the purification of God's people was being accomplished, and we shall see how this theology is developed in Paul's letters.

Although Paul's primary concern is Jesus' redefining of the covenant people, the Hellenistic influence on him is apparent in both the literary structure of his writing and in several characteristic aspects of his thought. When Paul describes what the Spirit produces in the moral life of the believer (Galatians 5:22–3), he begins with qualities that are based in the biblical tradition: love, joy, and peace. But he then shifts to terms that come out of Stoic ethics: patience, kindness, goodness, faithfulness, gentleness, self-control. The argument of the Letter to the Romans builds on the assumption that, just as Jews have the Law of Moses given to them by God, so the Gentiles have the law within, what Stoics would call the law of nature, which provides them with norms by which they should live. Paul goes on to show that both Jews and Gentiles disobey the law they have received in a manner consonant with Stoicism. Far from finding any conflict between his convictions as a devout Jew and the insights he has gained from pagan culture, Paul draws on both to make his arguments. Similarly, Paul's style in his letters shows affinities with Jewish modes of interpretation of Scripture, while at the same time he also utilizes the rhetorical style of his Greco-Roman contemporaries. For example, he poses questions that would be raised by his opponents and then goes on to answer them – a method of argument characteristic of Hellenistic culture.

Paul's cultural mix in background and outlook helps explain his effectiveness in reaching out to a wide Gentile audience. As is evident from his letters, he was articulate – even eloquent – in Greek, although he always eschewed the kind of classical allusions of a writer (such as Philo of Alexandria) who had more thoroughly embraced Hellenistic culture. Acts' scheme of "missionary journeys" imposes an almost sedate degree of organization on his activities that Paul's letters contradict; we can infer from those letters – unique in the New Testament in that they are firsthand accounts of events by one of the principal participants – where Paul carried on his work, how his successes sporadically relieved evident failures, and the degree of effectiveness he had in bringing together Christian communities that bridged ethnic, cultural, economic, and social distinctions. References in his letters link him to the district known as Galatia in Asia Minor, as well as to Ephesus, one of the chief cities of the eastern Aegean area dominated by Greek culture, and the center of the worship of Artemis, the fertility goddess. Once he crossed to mainland Greece we hear of his connections and activities in Philippi and Thessalonica in the northern district of Macedonia, as well as in Athens (1 Thessalonians 3:1) and especially in Corinth, in the southern part of Greece known as Achaia. He mentions in writing to the Romans that his missionary activity has

The fertility goddess Artemis, as portrayed in a statue from first-century Ephesus. Known in classical Greek times as the daughter of Zeus and Leto, and the twin sister of Apollo, Artemis served several roles: she was a huntress, and the goddess of the moon and of birth. The Romans saw her as identical with Diana, who punished the wicked but could sustain and renew the lives of the faithful. In Asia Minor, Artemis became identified with the mother and fertility goddess Kubale (or Cybele, a spelling that can lead to confusion with the great mantic prophetess), who had been worshipped for centuries at a temple in Ephesus. This huge temple was 180 feet wide and 360 feet long, with more than one hundred 50-foot-high columns. With the pyramids of Egypt and the hanging gardens of Babylon, it was one of the most admired structures in the ancient world. The public uprising against Paul in Ephesus (Acts 19) was instigated by the silversmiths, whose business in making and selling miniatures of the temple or of Artemis declined because so many Ephesians became followers of the Christ whom Paul preached. Her statue depicts her as surrounded by bulbous appendages, variously identified by scholars, whose suggestions run from breasts to bull testicles. (BiblePlaces.com)

taken him as far west as Illyricum, on the west coast of what is now Bosnia and Croatia, and that he intended to complete the evangelization of the northern half of the Mediterranean world by going beyond Rome to Spain (Romans 15:24, 28).

In his Letter to the Romans Paul gives the most complete and systematic statement of his understanding of Christ and of the new community of faith. Although tradition has long linked the launching of Christianity in Rome to Peter, we have no firm literary or historical evidence from Peter's time for that claim. But the fact that for some years there had been a church there and that some of its members had been driven out along with other Jews under Claudius in 49 C.E. (Acts 18:1–2) shows that its founding was very early, prior to the activity of Paul. The high mobility of some of the early Christians is apparent in that Priscilla and Aquila, expelled from Rome by Claudius and whom Paul first met in Corinth and who later opened their house as the meeting place of the church in Ephesus (1 Corinthians 16:19), had apparently returned to Rome by the time Paul wrote his letter to that church (Romans 16:3). Paul wanted to visit his friends and the community of faith there, and he apparently did so.

Ancient tradition reports that both Peter and Paul were martyred in Rome in the time of Nero (54–68 C.E.). Some scholars have suggested that Paul, after reaching Rome, went on to Spain or that he returned to the eastern Mediterranean, but these are merely conjectures. All we can be certain about is that he did return to Jerusalem with the offering he had taken up among the Gentile churches of Greece and Asia Minor, as he explains in Romans 15:25–9. According to Acts 21–8, he was awaiting trial in Rome, having been sent there by the Roman authorities in

The theater at Ephesus. Settled by Greeks in the tenth century B.C.E., Ephesus was a major city on the western coast of Asia Minor and home of the renowned temple of Artemis, the fertility goddess. Ephesus boasted several synagogues, lecture halls, and theaters; temples for Hellenistic deities; a famous brothel; splendid baths and houses; giant tenements; and by the second century C.E., a spectacular library. An earthquake in 23 C.E. makes the population estimate of one hundred thousand hazardous, but there is no doubting the importance of the city. The theater [pictured here] seated twenty-four thousand and may have been the setting for Paul's fight "with beasts at Ephesus" mentioned in 1 Corinthians 15:32 and where Paul's co-workers were dragged in to confront the people (Acts 19:21–41). (BiblePlaces.com)

Jerusalem, so that the allegations of his having performed acts against the peace of the empire could be weighed by the emperor himself, based on Paul's own appeal (Acts 25:10–12). He last appears in Acts under house arrest, pending the hearing before Caesar (28:30).

Fire broke out in Rome in 64 C.E. and decimated the city. Rumor said Nero had ordered the arson, and had forbidden efforts to fight the flames. The cliché of his "fiddling" while Rome burned understates his depravity: he floated down the Tiber on a barge with his prostitutes (Tacitus, *Annals* 15.37). The prospect that he could rebuild Rome along any lines he wanted enhanced his pleasure. He even had building plans ready to go. All he needed – to complete his enjoyment and avoid carping criticism – was to find someone else to blame for the fire.

The emperor deflected suspicion from himself by pinning responsibility for the disaster on Christians. Their marginal status must have seemed to him a gift from the gods. They were rounded up, interrogated, often subjected to elaborate torture, and then slaughtered.

St. Peter's Basilica and the Tiber River. Although the main part of Rome lay east of the Tiber, Nero (54–68) finished a circular sports arena begun by Caligula west of the river in the section known as the Vatican. Since excavation fifty years ago of Constantine's basilica, built there in honor of Saint Peter in the midst of pagan graves and sarcophagi, the tradition that Peter was executed there has seemed more plausible. A Church tradition that developed after the period of the New Testament lists fourteen of the leaders of the church in Rome – including Peter – who are said to have been buried in a chamber beneath the Vatican. A report by Caius from around 200 C.E. says that Paul was martyred farther west, on the main road to Ostia (quoted in Eusebius, *Ecclesiastical History* 2.25). (BiblePlaces.com)

Nero's excesses were obvious even to those who despised Christianity. Tacitus, the first-century Roman historian, represents an aristocratic perspective on these atrocities (see his *Annals* 15.44): "But neither humanitarian aid, nor imperial largesse, nor propitiations to the gods, removed the scandalous suspicion that the fire had been an order. To put an end to this rumor, Nero found likely suspects, and inflicted contrived tortures upon people detested for their disgraces, whom the crowd called Christians. This name came from one Christus, who was put to death in the reign of Tiberius by the procurator Pontius Pilate; but though checked for the time, the pestilent cult broke out again, not only in Judea, the origin of the disease, but even in the capital, where all things heinous and shameful pour in from every which way and are celebrated."

Tacitus's description of the torture, therefore, owes nothing to any a priori sympathy with Jesus' movement: "First those who avowed were arrested; and upon their information a vast number were condemned, not so much on the charge of arson as for their hatred of the human race. Their

Emperor Nero, marble head from Athens. A son of Emperor Claudius by his fourth wife, Nero reigned from 54 to 68 C.E. He murdered his mother and his wife Octavia so he could marry another woman, Poppea; he then murdered Poppea, as well. Early in his reign his counselor, the famous Stoic philosopher Seneca, influenced him but any moderation in the emperor's habits soon gave way to cruelty and a sensuous way of life. He launched a campaign to have himself honored as divine during his lifetime and spent huge sums of money to entertain the masses and to rebuild the city of Rome after a disastrous fire, which he blamed on the Christians. Finally, he left Rome and took his own life, but the legend arose that he would return. (BiblePlaces.com)

death was turned into a diversion. They were clothed in the skins of wild beasts, and torn to pieces by dogs; they were fastened to crosses, or set up to be burned, so as to serve the purpose of lamps when daylight failed. Nero gave up his own gardens for this spectacle; he provided also circus games, during which in the garb of a charioteer he mingled with the populace, or took his stand upon a chariot. But guilty as these men were and worthy of extreme penalty, pity arose, since they were being destroyed not for public good, but for one man's savagery." It seems unlikely that Paul would have survived this campaign of systematic extermination.

B. Paul's Purpose and Strategy

Voluntary groups, based on shared occupational, religious, or other interests, featured centrally in the social life of the Roman world. Many of these gatherings consisted of devotees of a god or goddess, such as Isis, Asklepios (the god of health and healing), or Dionysus (the god of wine). Some of these groups indulged in ecstatic group experiences, while others fostered personal devotion and dedication of one's life to the deity. The increasing mobility of the population, brought about by military conflicts as well as by the need for relocation on economic grounds, gave many people a sense of breaking with their own heritage. For such people, the development of a local shrine to a familiar deity helped them regain a sense of purpose and identity. In a port city like Ostia (down the Tiber from Rome), for example, vestiges have been found of altars and shrines of divinities from many parts of the empire. Among Jews, the voluntary gatherings (i.e., synagogues) provided a setting in which to celebrate and maintain their identity as children of the covenant.

Not surprisingly, Paul's strategy on arriving in a new city seems to have been to go first to the synagogue, where he could offer his distinctive interpretation of the Jewish Scriptures, especially the prophetic writings. Gentiles who attended the synagogue were natural candidates for Paul's inclusive redefinition of the covenant, especially since Paul did not require circumcision of Gentile converts. Circumcision was regarded as barbaric in most of the Greco-Roman world, so that Paul's vision of a new Israel in Christ that included Jews and "Greeks" alike (see Romans 3:28–30, a stunning example of Pauline inclusiveness) appealed practically and aesthetically, as well as in intellectual terms. His message reached other non-Jews, who admired the monotheism and lofty ethics of Judaism, and found in Paul's recasting of the people of God new possibilities for their own adherence and participation. When such groups formed, they tended to use as their self-designation a Greek term, *ekklesia*, which refers to a public meeting "called out," or "called together": they were called into union from Jewish or pagan backgrounds to be the people God, his "saints," as Paul called all the members of the congregations to which he wrote.

This approach exerted an impact across the whole socioeconomic spectrum of urban Roman society. In 1 Corinthians, for example, Paul indicates that most of the members of the church in Corinth were poor and socially undistinguished (1:26). Yet as his greetings from the church at

Asklepios, god of healing, in a copy of a fourth century B.C.E. statue (made around 160 C.E. and found at Epidauros). Earlier identified as a human who had been taught medicine, Asklepios was later seen as the son of Apollo and as the god of healing, whose presence was visible in sacred serpents clustered at his shrines. Major shrines honoring him were at Pergamum, on the island of Cos, where a school of medicine developed in his name, and at Epidaurus, on the coast of Argolis, southwest of Corinth. His cult was later brought to Rome; the Latinized form of his name is Aesculapius. Those seeking healing slept in a grotto where they awaited a visit from the god. Found by archaeologists at his shrine at Epidaurus were signed testimonies to the god's healing power and descriptions of the process of cure. (BiblePlaces.com)

SAINTS

The two Hebrew words often translated as "saint" have different connotations. One, *chasid*, expresses faithful commitment to others with whom one has a covenant relationship (as in Genesis 21:22–4, 24:27–49), including God's fidelity to his covenant people (Exodus 20:2–6, 34:6–7; Jeremiah 33:11). The other term, *qadosh*, means "set apart for God," in service and obedience, as when the priests approach the presence of the Lord (Exodus 19:22–3) or when David and his associates are sanctified in preparation for his anointing as king (1 Samuel 16:1–6). The faithful community who remain obedient to God despite pressures and threats from the pagan ruler are called "the holy ones [saints] of the Most High" (Daniel 7:22, 27).

In the New Testament the Greek equivalent term for "saint" (*hagios*) is a favorite designation for the people of God. Paul addresses his readers as saints in his letters (Romans 1:7; 1 Corinthians 1:2; Philippians 1:1), and it is a frequently used term for the Church as a whole, as when the Spirit intercedes with God for God's people (Romans 8:27), or when several churches (Philippians 4:21–2) or all the churches are addressed (1 Corinthians 14:33). The future destiny of God's people involves the prospect of martyrdom (Revelation 13:7, 16:6) and oppression of the "saints" (Revelation 20:9), although they will have a say in the final judgment of the world according to Paul (1 Corinthians 6:2). The major connotation of "saint" is the special role and relationship of the covenant people to God, and eventually – and long after the period of the New Testament – its meaning became very specialized.

Corinth to the church at Rome show, church membership also included such a central figure in urban life as the city treasurer (Romans 16:23). Some believers in Corinth and Ephesus had houses large enough to serve as gathering places for the entire community (1 Corinthians 16:19; Romans 16:23). Christianity's appeal across a wide spectrum of socioeconomic and cultural groups and classes, rather than its dominance within any one of them, probably best explains its survival during the first century and its eventual embrace by the Roman Empire during the fourth century after successive centuries of steady growth.

Membership seems to have grown in large increments by the conversion of entire households, including children and slaves (1 Corinthians 1:16). The problem of a community in which both slave and master were members is addressed in Paul's Letter to Philemon. The need to foster some sense of unity and commonality among such a socially and economically diverse group of people is a pervasive theme in Paul's letters, especially those to the Corinthians. His favorite term in addressing the members is "saints," which means, basically, "holy," "sanctified," or "set aside," "dedicated" to God.

Paul's own letters, unlike those later written in his name, are not concerned with defining offices in the church, but rather with describing the range of functions appropriate for the life of the community. He does mention men and women deacons (Philippians 1:1; Romans 16:1; 1

A street and civic agora in Ephesus. (BiblePlaces.com)

Thessalonians 3:2 [variant reading]), but the usage (which simply means "servants" in the Greek of the period) seems to refer to "one who serves [the other members]" rather than to someone appointed to a formally hierarchical role. In a later letter he once uses the term *episkopos* (Philippians 1:1), which is elsewhere often translated as "bishop" and which thus may indicate the emergence of a degree of hierarchy of official functions, as is emphatically the case in the later letters written in Paul's name (1 and 2 Timothy, and Titus) and in Acts. Paul's primary concern, however, is with the *ekklesia* as a whole, identified as the people of the covenant in all of Paul's letters, but most comprehensively in Galatians and Romans. Instead of defining offices, Paul takes care to indicate the range of activity that members of the community fulfill for the benefit of the whole (1 Corinthians 12). These include the utterance of wisdom and prophecy, the performance of healing or other miracles, addressing the community in ecstatic speech ("tongues"), and the interpretation of what is thus uttered. All these activities are made possible by the work of the Spirit of God among the members. The community in its entirety is the place where God dwells among his people by the Spirit, permeating them individually and collectively.

This community of Spirit is to see itself in three tenses: in the past, founded in God's act of love, when he chose Israel and sent his son Jesus as the sacrifice that ratifies the covenant and thereby brings all people into right relationship with God; in the present, when God is active among his people by the Spirit, calling new members into fellowship through the reconciling work of the preaching and through the sharing of bread and wine in anticipation of the fulfillment God will bring to all things; in the future, the time for God's purpose to be achieved, in which all his people will be brought into fellowship, the powers of evil will be defeated, and God will be fully sovereign over his people and the whole creation. Paul's letters make it clear that his work is the announcement of God's act in Jesus to set things right and to reconcile the world to himself (2 Corinthians 5:19).

Despite the assumption that is sometimes made, that Paul was the first Christian messenger to preach the gospel to Gentiles, there were in fact precedents for his mission to the Gentiles. Paul's determination as a Pharisee to destroy the church in Damascus is one likely indication of that. What would have troubled Paul as a Pharisee was not merely that a rival group had emerged claiming to be heirs of the covenant promises, but that those who claimed to be the true heirs of God's promises to his covenant people included in their membership ritually impure persons, possibly Gentiles, and that they prophesied a completely new order in the Temple. Yet as a result of his vision near Damascus he had become convinced that God had called him to preach to precisely such people: the Gentiles and those marginal to Judaism. We may conclude, therefore, that the Gentile mission implied in the Gospels had already begun in cities like Damascus.

Acts describes the outreach of the apostles to Gentiles and to those on the fringes of Judaism as taking place before Paul's conversion. In particular, the activities of Peter in the house of the Roman centurion Cornelius (like Paul's conversion, detailed three times in Acts, in chapters 10, 11, and 15) represent a programmatic outreach to Gentiles prompted by visionary experience. Although Acts may have a special reason for setting this precedent before Paul comes on the scene (to show that the policy of Gentile inclusion was reached by the Jerusalem-based apostles), even Paul attests Peter's involvement with non-Jews in Antioch, as well as Barnabas's (Galatians 2:11–13). Where Paul differed from Peter and Barnabas was not in his contact with non-Jews, but in his refusal to require non-Jews to observe regulations of purity and in treating them as belonging to Israel by virtue of their baptism into Christ. Peter is described in Acts as reaching out to Gentiles who acknowledged and respected the Torah of Moses without accepting the covenant of circumcision, which was binding on Jews; in addition to insisting that circumcision could not be required of Gentiles who turned to Christ, Paul also rejected the proposition that they should subject themselves to other demands of purity in the Torah.

We have already observed the evidence for Christian activity in Rome before Paul even reached Corinth. The fact that Acts notes the Spirit's resistance to Paul's going into the northern parts of Asia Minor (Acts 16:6–7) may indicate that others had already begun to preach about Jesus there – possibly Peter, as 1 Peter suggests (1:1). Paul, however, eventually takes the lead in bringing the message about Jesus to the Gentiles and does so by agreement with the leaders of the church in Jerusalem, which remained more closely oriented to Judaism (Galatians 2:1–10).

C. Paul's Letters: Context, Intent, and Content

It seems likely that Paul wrote many more letters to churches that he had founded or where he had been active than those that have been preserved. The letters included in the New Testament date from the period beginning

---

PROBABLE CHRONOLOGY OF PAUL

Birth in Tarsus, into a family of Jewish tentmakers	7 C.E.
Conversion, after the stoning of Stephen, and therefore Paul's vision of the risen Jesus and his call to preach to the Gentiles took place during the summer	32
Retreat into Nabatean Arabia and escape from the agents of Aretas IV, king of Nabatea (2 Corinthians 11:32–3)	32–35
Initial introduction to Peter and James, Jesus' brother, in Jerusalem	35
Invitation from Barnabas to Antioch	40
Trajectory through Cyprus and south Galatia	42–44
Council in Jerusalem (Galatians 2:1–10)	46
Meeting in Corinth with Priscilla and Aquila and during the rule of Gallio	50–51
The confrontation at Antioch, occasioned by the decree of James that had been issued in Paul's absence (Galatians 2:11–21; and Acts 15:19–23)	53
Paul's period in Ephesus (with a retreat to Macedonia and Troas at the end); the composition of Galatians, 1 Corinthians, and 2 Corinthians	53–56
Letter to the Romans, written from Miletus off the coast from Ephesus, and final arrangements for the Sacrifice of the Nations, Paul's offering on behalf of Gentiles in the Temple. Paul's arrest in Jerusalem and detention in Caesarea, with Philemon composed the following year	57
Festus's tenure, following that of Felix and the high priest, Ananias (Acts 25–6). Paul's appeal to the Philippians for help in his letter to that city, written with Timothy from Myra in 60 and later expanded by Timothy	59–62
The death of James; Paul's release and final period in Rome; the composition of poetry later incorporated by Timothy into the Letter to the Colossians	62
Paul's death in Rome under Nero. Paul's followers, Timothy most prominently, began to collect and edit his works in Ephesus, Troas, and Miletus	64

---

almost twenty years after his conversion and extend to a time including his imprisonment in Rome. Only one is addressed to an individual (Philemon).

1. First and Second Thessalonians

The first Letter to the Thessalonian church, which Paul wrote with Silvanus (also referred to as Silas, a key figure connected with the church in Jerusalem) and Timothy, represents the earliest example of Paul's preserved correspondence. Paul takes the lead in 1 Thessalonians, because it was addressed principally to Gentile Christians in Thessalonica. In the way of first efforts, there is a tentative quality here compared to Paul's later letters. Nonetheless, the three teachers say that their message comes from God's own Spirit (1:5) and focuses on Jesus as divine Son, who alone can deliver humanity from the rapidly approaching end of the ages (1:10).

This eschatological tenor is typical of primitive Christianity and characterizes Paul's letters as a whole. Time is truly short, because the day of the Lord comes as a thief in the night (5:2), at a time that cannot be reckoned. In view of this impending judgment, the Thessalonian Gentiles had put their idols aside (1:9), and that also meant (as Paul is never slow to point

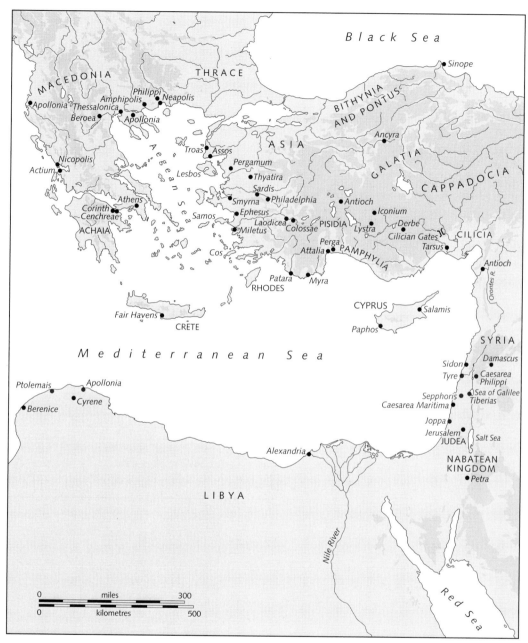

Map XVII. Greece, Asia Minor, and Syria during the first century C.E.

out) that sexual sanctification had to follow. Lust was a reflex of idolatry:
now was the time for "every one of you to keep one's own vessel in sanctification and honor, and not in the passion of lust just like the Gentiles
who do not know God" (4:4–5). The three teachers agreed that turning
from idolatry and perversion to serve the Living God was the only means
of human salvation in the short time before the Day of Judgment.

They also fiercely stated that the Pharisaic teachers from Judea who had
tried to prevent contact with Gentiles formed an obstacle to the gospel

TIMOTHY

Timothy features in the New Testament as Paul's companion and co-worker and as a symbolic figure for the generation of leadership in the Church following the death of the apostles. In Paul's earlier letters, Timothy participated with Paul and Silvanus in the work of the gospel (1 Thessalonians 1:1; 2 Corinthians 1:19). He was sent by Paul back to Thessalonica to see how the Church was faring under the persecution Christians were experiencing (1 Thessalonians 3:1–5) and brought back a hopeful report (3:6–13). First Corinthians 16:10–11 indicates Paul's expectation of sending Timothy to the Church in Corinth, when Paul pleads for acceptance of his emissary. Other details are found in Acts, some of which remain difficult to reconcile with Paul's letters. Some scholars doubt the claim in Acts that Paul circumcised Timothy (Acts 16:1–3). But Timothy's circumcision is described on the basis of the young man's identity as a Jew, and Paul himself bragged that "to the Jews I became as a Jew" (1 Corinthians 9:20), so that Acts cannot be dismissed just because it may seem surprising. Acts 17:10–15 offers further details of Timothy's relations with Thessalonica in Paul's behalf, suggesting that Timothy may have been one source used in the composition of the Book of Acts. The two Letters to Timothy clearly represent a period in the life of the Church decades after the time of Paul and reflect formal developments in doctrine, leadership, and Church administration. That was a major dimension of Timothy's contribution, along with his increasing editorial role in the letters to the Philippians, the Colossians, and the Ephesians.

(2:14): "For you, brothers, became imitators of the churches of God that are in Judea in Jesus Christ, because you also suffered the same things from your kinspeople as they did from the Jews." This refers back to deep contention in Jerusalem. Paul, Silas, and Timothy are using the word "Jews" (*Ioudaioi* in Greek) to mean the people back in Judea that wished to "forbid us to speak to the Gentiles" (2:16). But the same term could also be used during the first century (and later, of course) to mean any practitioners of Judaism anywhere, and that is the sense of the term "Jew" in common usage. So the three companions, writing to Thessalonica and dealing with local issues and recent history, spoke in a way that has encouraged anti-Semitism. Had they known they were writing for something called the New Testament, and how their words would be used to justify the persecution of Jews, they obviously would have spoken differently.

The Christians of Thessalonica, the capital city of Macedonia, seem to have been converted mostly from paganism rather than from Judaism (1 Thessalonians 1:9). They were subjected to severe hostility from their fellow citizens and were praised by Paul for their fidelity despite persecution (1 Thessalonians 1:6–8, 2:13–15). After he left their city, Paul was concerned about how they would survive the opposition and so sent his younger companion, Timothy, to observe them and report to him. The news was good, and the letter is one of praise and encouragement for their perseverance (1 Thessalonians 3:6–9). Paul urges them to continue to live in a way that is pleasing to God, to be faithful in marital relationships, and to maintain the respect of outsiders by their high moral standards (4:1–12).

Paul advises the Thessalonian community on two closely related matters. Its members are to live each day with the awareness that the appearance of Christ in triumph (*parousia*) is to take place in the near future (1 Thessalonians 4:9–12), even though the exact time cannot be predicted (5:1–11). Meanwhile, however, they are to take care to maintain their moral purity as God's people. Hence there is recurrent use of such terms as "holiness" and "saints," which indicates the importance of the community's achieving and exemplifying the life of obedience to which God has called them.

PAROUSIA

Parousia is the term used in the New Testament for the appearance of Christ in triumph at the end of the present age. Although it is usually translated as "coming" (Matthew 24:3; 1 Corinthians 15:23; 1 Thessalonians 2:19; James 5:7), its basic meaning is "presence," "appearing," or, for a monarch, "public manifestation." The *parousia* of Jesus Christ was understood to be God's presentation of Jesus as the triumphant agent who would defeat the evil powers of this world and vindicate God's faithful community. The earlier New Testament writings expect this event to take place within the lifetime of the first generation of Jesus' followers (Mark 9:1; 1 Thessalonians 4:15). In what is probably the latest New Testament book, 2 Peter, there is discussion of those who scoff at the promise of the *parousia* and a reminder that God does not calculate time as humans do: "With the Lord one day is like a thousand years, and a thousand years are like one day" (3:3–8).

Second Thessalonians purports to have been written shortly after the first letter, but there is considerable doubt among scholars that Paul is truly its author. It assures the members of the community that the end of the age is near, but that there are certain divinely determined events that must precede the end. These events – following the apocalyptic tradition – include the effort by the powers of evil to seize control and to mislead God's people (2 Thessalonians 2:1–12). But through Jesus, God will defeat the agents of evil and will vindicate his people (1:3–12). Accordingly, as in 1 Thessalonians, the second letter exhorts the Thessalonians to fulfill their role as God's holy people by continuing in faithfulness and obedience (2:13–15, 3:1–13). But the detailed apocalyptic scenario in 2 Thessalonians reflects the tendency of eschatological literature after the destruction of the Temple in 70 C.E., both in Judaism and Christianity, to specify the timing of the apocalypse by means of symbolic calendars.

Yet in both these letters there is evidence of the emergence of a struggle for power among those who aspire to leadership roles in the Thessalonian church (1 Thessalonians 4:9–10). The letters are cast as instruments of authority (1 Thessalonians 5:27; 2 Thessalonians 3:14–17) and remind their readers of their obligation to respect and obey those who have been given positions of responsibility within the community (1 Thessalonians 5:11). In view of the expectation of a speedy end of the age, there is no necessity for an ongoing organization, but the structures of authority that exist in the interim and those that point the way to the future should be respected.

2. Galatians

The Letter to the Galatians seems to have been written in haste; its sometimes reckless style also reveals the emotional pressure Paul felt. The result is that it lacks the organized structure of 1 Corinthians and Romans, as well as the formal introductory and concluding features that characterize Paul's letters. In passing, Paul gives the most important chronological clues that we have concerning the span of time that his public activity lasted: three years after his conversion until his first visit with the Jerusalem apostles; and fourteen years until his formal consultation with them and other leaders of the emerging church (Galatians 1:18–24).

Paul's purpose in mentioning these details is to strengthen his claim that his conversion, his apostolic activity among the Gentiles, and the gifts of the Spirit that are evident through him were entirely and directly from God, rather than mediated through the Jerusalem-based apostles or their aides. It is highly significant that he uses the language of *apokalypsis* ("revelation," "disclosure," a breakthrough that is literally apocalyptic), to describe his original vision of the risen Christ (Galatians 1:16), his having been commissioned with the gospel for the nations (Galatians 1:12), and his decision to check in with the apostolic leaders in Jerusalem (Galatians 2:2). He sought to collaborate with them, but they were not the source of his conversion, his commissioning, or his ministry to the Gentiles; only God could have been the source of those revelations.

GALATIANS

Galatia was a region in north central Asia Minor where the dominant inhabitants were Gauls, a Celtic tribe. The Romans gave the name Galatia to a province that included this district and territory to the south. Scholars have debated without firm conclusions whether Paul's missionary activities were concentrated on the Gauls to the north or included the ethnically more mixed region to the south, as indicated by Acts 13 and 14. In either case, Jews would have been a minority in this part of Asia Minor, although Paul's experience reflects how powerful an influence they could become.

The central issue for Paul in Galatians was the question about the ethnic and ritual requirements that other leaders of the church insisted on, even from Gentiles, for participation in the people of God. His address of this question, rooted in his own conversion, proved radical and dramatic. As he says (1:13–14), he had excelled before his conversion to Christ as a Pharisee in his devotion to the traditions of that movement within Judaism, which was primarily concerned with defining the people of God based on criteria that arose when the Pharisees transferred the ritual purity requirements from the Temple and its priesthood to the voluntary gatherings of the pious in their homes or public halls for worship and table fellowship. This resulted in an increase of ritual criteria – both in number and in kind – for God's covenant people as such. Paul's conversion brought about a reversal of this position, because he saw the revelation of God's presence, not preeminently in the Temple, in whose name he had persecuted followers of Jesus, but in the revelation within him of Christ, the Son of God who offered sonship to those who trusted in him. So powerful was this revelation that Paul set aside even the basic practice of circumcision as a requirement for covenant membership (1:6–10, 5:7–12). The sole requirement that Paul established for entrance into the community of faith he insisted on calling Israel was that one should see in Jesus God's agent whose sacrifice conveyed forgiveness of sins and whose resurrection was the guarantee of God's triumph over death and the powers of evil for all who joined Christ. The original nucleus of Jesus' followers whose horizon (like Jesus') was historic Israel and who had themselves been circumcised, naturally conceived of circumcision as a requirement universally binding on any male converts to Christ, as it was on Gentiles who converted to Judaism. Indeed, Jesus' movement prior to Paul's conversion does not show any sign of engaging in a programmatic outreach to non-Jews.

Paul insisted on this outreach to Gentiles as part of the meaning of his own conversion, and claimed that Peter and James, the principal Church leaders in Jerusalem when he conferred with them, endorsed his position (2:1–10). Moreover, Peter had accepted a policy of contact with Gentiles (albeit limited to those who had acknowledged the God of Israel and withdrew from the worst impurities of the pagan world, such as polytheism, promiscuity, and consuming blood) when his vision at Joppa caused him to offer baptism to the house of Cornelius (Acts 10). But the issue inevitably arose: did baptized Gentiles have to accept at least those rules of purity that would permit them to eat with Jewish disciples of Jesus?

In Paul's opinion, in the face of this fraught choice Peter vacillated. When he visited the Christian community in Antioch, he ate with Gentiles without prior restrictions. But under pressure from Judean Christians who acted under the authority of James, Peter then withdrew from table fellowship with uncircumcised Gentile Christians (Galatians 2:11–13). This argument between Peter and Paul in Antioch, which probably occurred in 53 C.E., turned on whether those who joined themselves to Christ from a background of Gentile religion and culture had to obey the Jewish law, whether in whole or in part. Paul's Letter to the Galatians presents a forceful case for his position on the issue, historically and biographically, but he also takes care to ground his law-free principle on biblical precedent and principle.

The Galatians' own experience of the Spirit of God should have shown them that the gifts of God are not earned by human achievements, Paul said, but derive solely from the outpouring of divine grace. Some people in the Galatian community felt bound to obey at least a minimum of Jewish ritual requirements, even if they had accepted baptism as Gentiles. Paul insists that even in the biblical tradition of the origins of God's covenant people, the first requirement for participation was trust in God, not ritual performance. The prime example of this for Paul is the story (cited in Galatians 3:6–18) of Abraham's becoming the father of the covenant people, even though up to that moment in his life he had been incapable of having a child by Sarah, his wife. God directly gave Abraham's son Isaac, the father of Jacob and the ancestor of those for whom the twelve tribes of Israel are named, to his parents. Further, the gift of the son was the means of fulfillment for the blessing for all the nations (Genesis 12:3) – not for Israel alone – that was to come through Abraham. The people of God are defined in one of two ways: through obedience to the law, under threat of a curse for failure to conform (Deuteronomy 27:26); or through the gift of God's grace, received by trusting in God and resulting in those who trust being placed by God in a right relationship to himself (the principle of Habakkuk 2:4, Paul says in Galatians 3:11). Because of the death of Jesus, whose execution as a criminal absorbed the punishment that curses disobedience (Leviticus 18:5), all the promises to Abraham of covenantal participation are now open to those who, through their faith, show themselves to be Abraham's true offspring (Galatians 3:7).

The Law of Moses, which Paul the Pharisee had regarded as normative, he now sees to be a late, temporary instrument to keep God's people in line morally until God's ultimate solution of the human problem could be disclosed through Jesus (Galatians 3:17). Paul depicts the function of the Law as temporary, like that of a child-minder (*paidagogos*), whose services are not needed when maturity is attained (3:24–9), because maturity brings freedom and the promise of one's inheritance (4:1–7).

To insist on circumcision or legal conformity would be to abandon one's freedom (Galatians 5:2–12). Yet this freedom does not endorse indulgence; instead, it carries with it responsibility toward all other members of the new community, taking into account their differing backgrounds and sensibilities (5:13–15). As Jesus did in the Gospels (Mark 12:31; Matthew 22:39; Luke 10:27), Paul quotes from Leviticus 19:18, the commandment to love one's neighbor as oneself (Galatians 5:14; Romans 13:9). The powerful new factor that transforms the lives of the people of faith is the Spirit, according to Paul. As long as they live out of their own weak and fallible human resources without reliance on grace, they will be characterized by religious, moral, social, and personal failings (Galatians 5:20–1). But when they live by the power of the Spirit of God, they will display the virtues enjoined by both the Jewish and the Hellenistic traditions (5:22). Such a life of free obedience through the power of the Spirit will be characterized by fulfillment of the proper demands of both the Jewish law and the natural law; Paul characterizes the spiritual virtues of this new way of life in the phrase "Against such there is no law" (5:23). The Spirit at work in the members will result in a community life that is characterized by mutual responsibility for the erring and the weak (6:1–5), by sharing insights with others (6:6), and in dedication of time and energy for the work of God and the welfare of the community (6:7–10). Underscoring the personal nature of this appeal to the Galatians, Paul added to the letter that he had just dictated final words, some written in his own hand (6:11–17), and concluded with a formal, liturgical farewell (6:18).

3. First and Second Corinthians

Commercially and strategically, Corinth was a vital center in first-century C.E. Greece. Located on the narrow neck of land that joins the Peloponnesus to the mainland, it provided overland commerce in Greece and for the movement of people and cargo by sea, since ships regularly stopped at one of the two ports (one east and one west) of the city and had their cargo transported over the peninsula to the other side for reshipment. The city had been destroyed in 146 B.C.E., but the Romans rebuilt it about a century later, bringing in people from various lands and cultures in the eastern Mediterranean. Although Greek was its official and commercial language, the population was diverse, even by the standards of the teeming port cities of the Mediterranean. The Isthmian Games and other major athletic events brought thousands of visitors, as did such religious sites as the shrines of the healing god, Asklepios, located in Corinth and in nearby Epidaurus. By the time of Paul, the once famous Corinthian shrine of Aphrodite, the goddess of love, was probably being restored.

Corinth was a lively, cosmopolitan city, though it lacked the rich intellectual traditions of Athens. Presumably, the original core of converts to Christianity there were Jewish, as is suggested by the fact that two of the leaders, Aquila and Priscilla, had come from Rome when Claudius's decree had expelled the Jews after the disturbance arose among them with the arrival of the Christian message about Jesus and the resultant divisions within the Jewish community. The Christians of Jewish background in Corinth were soon joined by Gentiles, who came to dominate the membership of the churches there.

From the two letters called "to the Corinthians" in the New Testament we may infer that Paul had an ongoing correspondence with congregations in Corinth, particularly those with predominantly or exclusively Gentile members. Both personally and conceptually, Paul's relationship with them was fraught. These letters provide the modern reader with insight into the nature of the multiple Christian communities that had

PAUL'S CORRESPONDENCE WITH THE CORINTHIANS

Although there are only two letters to the Corinthians in the New Testament, it is clear from these writings that Paul wrote other letters to congregations of Corinthian Christians, and that the members of the church in Corinth wrote to Paul as well. The following sequence may be inferred from the preserved correspondence:

A letter to Paul from the Corinthian Christians (1 Corinthians 7:1)

A letter from Paul, which the Corinthians seem not to have heeded (1 Corinthians 5:9)

1 Corinthians, which includes Paul's responses to the question raised by the Corinthians' letter to him

An anguished letter from Paul, which caused pain among the Corinthians (2 Corinthians 2:4)

2 Corinthians 1–7, in which Paul seeks to restore a relationship of mutual understanding with the congregations in Corinth.

In addition, there is the possibility that 2 Corinthians 6:14–7:1 is part of yet another letter: the anguished letter mentioned in 2 Corinthians 2:4. This has been proposed because this passage in 2 Corinthians seems to break the flow of the letter from 6:13 to 7:2. A more plausible explanation, however, involves the theory that Paul was interrupted as he was dictating this section of what we know as 2 Corinthians and therefore did not neatly follow his original line of argument. The letter that nearly broke Paul's relationship with the congregations in Corinth is probably represented in 2 Corinthians 10–13.

started to appear in major cities of the Roman world two decades after the death of Jesus.

Paul indicates that letters had been passing back and forth for some time and that the Jesus salons he wanted to see started had prospered in the city. His principal informants were people from the congregation that met in the house of a woman named Chloe. By letter and personal contacts through trade, they kept Paul abreast of developments.

Paul wrote 1 Corinthians to deal with just the kind of divisions one would expect in a culture of small, disparate congregations (1 Corinthians 1:11–12): "Because it has been made clear to me about you, my brothers, by Chloe's people, that there are contentions among you. I mean this, that each of you says, 'I belong to Paul,' 'I belong to Apollos,' 'I belong to Cephas,' 'I belong to Christ.'" Each salon claimed to be smarter than the next. Its members identified themselves by their favorite hero – Paul or Apollos or Peter. Salons are talking shops. They are often competitive and love their reputations as much as they love ideas; for them being in intellectual fashion is life's greatest pleasure, and being out of fashion as painful as sin itself. They try to trump each other. In Corinth, some upwardly mobile warriors in the art of rhetoric got to saying – our hero is Christ.

First Corinthians, after an introductory section (chapters 1–4) in which Paul discusses his apostolic role in relation to that of other apostles and Christian leaders, turns into a virtual checklist of problems in the Corinthian churches that had been reported to him: gross immorality condoned by some believers (chapter 5); internal dissension (6:1–8); moral laxity and involvement with immoral persons (6:9–19); disputes concerning sex and marriage (chapter 7); participation in idol worship, including eating food that had been offered to idols (chapter 8); controversies connected with the celebration of the Eucharist (11:17–34) and with the exercise of charismatic gifts, such as prophecy and ecstatic speech (chapters 12, 14); and deep disagreements about the resurrection and the end of the age (chapter 15). As he deals with these divisive issues, Paul interjects personal claims and appeals concerning his freedom (e.g., to marry or to remain single), his authority to enjoy the support of communities or to work to support himself (chapter 9), and a solemn warning about disobedience, based on Israel's judgment by God in the wilderness of Sinai (chapter 10).

The letter concludes with instructions about the Corinthians' contribution to the offering that is being taken up among the Gentile churches for the benefit of the church in Jerusalem (chapter 16).

Second Corinthians, by contrast, is not written in a topical style and most probably combines at least two original documents, out of chronological order. Second Corinthians 1–7 was probably a letter in which Paul seeks to challenge the growing impact on the church in Corinth of a group of rivals to his apostolic authority and style, and it represents an attempt at reconciliation that includes reference to a letter written "through many tears" (2 Corinthians 2:4, 9; 7:8) that Paul had sent earlier. That letter, an extraordinary, uncontrolled outburst of passion, is reflected in the latter part of 2 Corinthians (chapters 10–13), a response to a group that scorns Paul for regarding his trials, sufferings, and imprisonment as evidence of God's support for his apostolic role. In between these letters are two communications about a collection on behalf of the church in Jerusalem, representing Paul's attempt during this period to build up the offering. The chronological order of the fragments would be: 2 Corinthians 8, 2 Corinthians 9, 2 Corinthians 10–13, 2 Corinthians 1–7. Some scholars hold that 2 Corinthians 6:14–7:1, which seems to interrupt the flow of thought between the verses that precede and follow it, may be a fragment of yet another letter of Paul to the Corinthians.

The treatment of theological issues in both 1 and 2 Corinthians is always intermingled with and complicated by social and cultural tensions, between Jews and Gentiles, and between Paul and his critics, between those faithful to one apostle and those who looked for guidance to other leaders. There is evidence throughout this correspondence of the dual influences on Paul: his Jewish heritage and the Hellenistic environment in which he was reared and trained.

Paul's role as apostle and founder of the churches in Corinth he writes to features centrally in the correspondence. If, as Acts claims and Paul himself appears tacitly to admit (Acts 18:1–4; 1 Corinthians 1:17, 16:19), Priscilla and Aquila had founded Jewish congregations in the city prior to Paul's arrival there, his claims appear valid only as applied to Gentile congregations. In any case, the authority he claimed was under steady attack from unnamed detractors of various types. Some scoffed at what they considered to be his lack of rhetorical and intellectual sophistication (1 Corinthians 1:17, 21–5), to which he replied that wisdom is a gift of God, not a human attainment. He notes in passing that the Corinthian Christians themselves were not an impressive group in terms of education, wealth, or noble birth (1 Corinthians 1:26–31). Yet believers in Corinth did include a few prominent people in the city who were of sufficient means to be able to hold the gatherings of the entire church in their own homes. To his detractors Paul responds with accounts of his own divine call, including visions of the risen Christ (1 Corinthians 15:5–10) and of the throne of God (2 Corinthians 12:1–10). He recalls the miracles and other apostolic signs he performed in their midst (2 Corinthians 12:12).

Paul also claims that he has authority from God that he is willing to assert when necessary in settling moral issues or internal disputes, even to the point of expelling an unworthy member from the community, and therefore from the enjoyment of salvation (1 Corinthians 5:3–5; 2 Corinthians 10). On specific issues he makes binding pronouncements (1 Corinthians 7:12, 25, 37–40), supplementing those that had come down through the Jesus tradition. He regards these regulations as commonly agreed to by all the churches (1 Corinthians 11:16). His authority is also represented by his aides, such as Timothy, who arranges for the collection on Paul's behalf (1 Corinthians 16:10–11), and by those he has endorsed in their positions of responsibility, such as Stephanas (1 Corinthians 16:15–16).

Paul's major concern, expressed throughout this correspondence, is for the churches to understand and experience their identity and unity as the covenanted people of God. This is to be achieved despite the tendency of the members to identify with one of the leaders (as they say, "I belong to Apollos," "I belong to Cephas"; 1 Corinthians 1:10–17) or to exploit for purposes of self-gratification or ostentation the particular spiritual gift (*charisma*) that God may have granted them for the benefit of the community as a whole (1 Corinthians 12–14). The dominant quality and dynamic of their common life is love, which Paul describes in 1 Corinthians 13, a justly celebrated passage that evidences Paul's theological acumen, pastoral insight, and growing tendency to break from prose into poetry. Love in his overall vision goes beyond feeling and should be expressed concretely for the benefit of Christians elsewhere in the form of the collection for the church in Jerusalem (1 Corinthians 16; 2 Corinthians 8–9). Love is also the major factor in considering how outsiders will react to the church (1 Corinthians 14:20-5). The motivating power that is creating the people of God is the Spirit of God, manifest for the common good (1 Corinthians 12:3–7). The elaborate image of this new identity is that of the human body, with its diversity of members and its commonality of function and destiny (1 Corinthians 12:14–26). This represents a new creation, not merely an amelioration of the old (2 Corinthians 5:17–20).

Although Paul uses religious terms derived from the biblical tradition in describing this new community, such as "saints" or "holy ones" (1 Corinthians 1:2, 8; 6:11; 7:14; 2 Corinthians 1:1), he goes on to show that the formation of the covenant people in the light of Christ involves radically redrawing or abolishing sociocultural distinctions: non-Jewish membership in the church is endorsed (1 Corinthians 12:2), cultic requirements are set aside (1 Corinthians 7:19), and social gaps transcended (1 Corinthians 7:22–3). Only in the future will the purpose of God for his people be fully disclosed (1 Corinthians 15:12–58); the form of this world is passing away (1 Corinthians 7:31). Although Paul throughout quotes Scripture or refers to scriptural precedents to illustrate the continuity between what God promised earlier and what has now occurred through Jesus, he also makes a radical break with the conventional norms within Judaism for covenantal identity. This is clearest in his dismissal of circumcision as of no ultimate significance (1 Corinthians 7:19), although it had been the crucial rite for Israelite covenantal participation

(Genesis 17:1–17, 34:13–25; Exodus 12:44–8; Leviticus 12:3; Joshua 5:2–8). It seems likely, therefore, that in 2 Corinthians 6:14–7:1, which uses the language of ritual separation, Paul is discussing moral responsibility within the Christian community and the need to preserve moral purity among its members. It is not that he has abandoned his basic point of view throughout his letters: that trust in God's reconciling work in Jesus Christ is the primary basis for human acceptability to God. Rather, he is reaffirming his earlier statements that, once one is within the community, it is essential to observe and maintain moral purity by avoiding marital or other intimate associations with those who are not members of the community. But as noted earlier, this passage does not fit its present context in 2 Corinthians and may originally have been part of one of the other letters of Paul. In either case, Paul here shows that the fundamental category of purity remains a controlling factor in the life of faith, although he redefines the sectors of conduct in which it is a legitimate concern.

Paul's advice for both faith and practice in the Corinthian community rests in part on tradition, but tradition as modified by insights that he believes God has given him. The gospel message, and especially the assurance of the resurrection of Jesus, is part of the tradition that Paul himself received (1 Corinthians 15:1–11). The practice of the Eucharist is also patterned after a tradition traced back to the Jesus' actions (1 Corinthians 10:14–22, 11:23–6). But the ground of his apostolic call was personal: Paul's having seen Jesus after God had raised him from the dead. This vision was, however, recognized and confirmed by the other apostles as a resurrection appearance of Jesus. On some issues, Paul quotes a Jesus saying handed down in the tradition, but on others he offers his own opinion (1 Corinthians 7:2, 5). Paul's views on these matters assume authority as a "command of the Lord" (1 Corinthians 14:37).

For Paul, although the functioning of the Christian community in the world is not socially egalitarian, there is complete theological equality in Christ (see Galatians 3:28). Hierarchy and leadership roles are not assigned in terms of titles of formal offices, but are listed in 1 Corinthians 12:27–30 according to their authority and their impact within the community: apostles, prophets, teachers, workers of miracles, healers, helpers, administrators, those with the gift of ecstatic speech, and interpreters. Each of these roles has value as a contribution to the life of the entire community, and none is to be used for personal power or gratification. The welfare of the whole is the prime concern for those who serve in each of these roles.

Paul's language throughout the Corinthian correspondence reflects the deep influence of the Hellenistic intellectual environment in which he was evidently educated. This is the case even if one takes as historically reliable the report in Acts 22:3 that Paul studied under Gamaliel, the famous Jewish interpreter of the law, or if one allows – as seems more plausible – that the young Saul was influenced by Gamaliel's teaching. Educated people among the populace in Syrian cities and Tarsus above all – whether Jew or Gentile – were strongly influenced by Stoic philosophy, with its appeal to the universal human capacity (conscience) to know the law of nature that was inherent in all the universe. The Stoics called for people to persevere in conformity to this inner law, despite suffering and in confidence that in the future they would be called to account for their way of life and rewarded for their conformity to the divine law. This point of view had been readily assimilated to the Jewish understanding of the Law of Moses, as the extensive writings of Philo of Alexandria and books such as *4 Maccabees* demonstrate. It is not surprising, therefore, that Paul often refers to conscience (a term for which there is no precise equivalent in Semitic language or thought) and appeals to his readers to exemplify fidelity, self-control, and discipline (1 Corinthians 7:9, 8:7–10, 9:25–7, 10:29; 2 Corinthians 1:12). In his references to the future Day of Judgment (2 Corinthians 5:10), Paul unites elements of this Stoic tradition with the essentially apocalyptic outlook that he takes over and modifies from his Jewish heritage. Similarly, when Paul is enumerating the Christian virtues, some of his terms are drawn from the Bible and others from Stoicism (2 Corinthians 6:4–5). Yet the prime examples to which he points are the experiences of Israel in the past (1 Corinthians 10), which are to serve as warnings to the covenant people in the present that obedience, holiness, and endurance are essential for the maintenance of status, now and in the age to come. But unlike the reliance on obedience to the Law of Moses, which proved a broken reed, these new qualities are made possible through the death and resurrection of Christ and through the power of the indwelling Spirit of God.

4. Romans

The Letter to the Romans is unique among Paul's surviving writings in that it was written by Paul to communities he had not founded and had never visited, although he hoped to visit them after he offered sacrifice in Jerusalem (Romans 15:15–16, 23–5). His association with Priscilla and Aquila, first in Corinth and later in Ephesus, made the churches in Rome known to him. Now, these two co-workers had returned to Rome, where they had apparently been part of the original core of believers (Romans 16:3). Although no direct evidence exists concerning the founding of the Christian community in Rome, it appears from the fact that its members were expelled by the decree of Claudius against the city's Jews that most of the original converts were Jewish. This would help to explain why Paul takes such an extensive section of the letter to deal with the question of God's future purpose for his historical people Israel (Romans 9–11).

The identity of the original apostle(s) who took the gospel to Rome is unknown, although tradition and legends from later centuries identified Peter as the one who carried out that mission. Paul gives no hint of this in his letter to the Romans, yet the very fact that he does not regard the capital of the empire as a place where his own brand of preaching can be planted on fresh ground (as in 1 Corinthians 3:6) shows that others had been there and had established churches before his planned journey. His

GAMALIEL

The name Gamaliel appears in Numbers 1:5–10 as one of the leaders of the clan of Joseph, descended from Manasseh, who is to assist Moses in conducting a census of Israel. According to Acts, Gamaliel is also the name of a Pharisee who warns the Jewish council in Jerusalem against taking harsh action to destroy the movement launched through the apostles (Acts 5:17–40), the same man whom Paul in Acts identifies as having been his teacher in Jerusalem (Acts 22:3). Rabbinic sources represent Gamaliel as one of the patriarchal figures in the rabbinic movement. Gamaliel is identified as part of the patriarchal chain of tradition that begins at Sinai and culminates in the Mishnah. What became the patriarchate is embodied in Hillel, Gamaliel I, Simeon his son, Gamaliel II (after 70 C.E.), Simeon ben Gamaliel II (of the mid-second century C.E.), and the Mishnah's own sponsor, Judah the Prince (ca. 170–210 C.E.). Gamaliel's prominence makes it unlikely he was Paul's personal teacher, but the same consideration makes it likely that Gamaliel's thought influenced Paul through the Pharisaic movement.

Speaking specifically of his Pharisaic formation, Paul said, "What was gain to me I regarded as loss because of Christ" (Philippians 3:7). As Paul saw his life in retrospect, his conversion to Christ put everything else in its shadow. But that followed Paul's *first* conversion – to the Pharisees. That conversion, from Diaspora Judaism to Pharisaic practice, made him change his clothing, behavior, and associates; give up his native city for Jerusalem; and make the Temple the center of his zealous devotion. He could no more shake off the effects of his Pharisaic

conversion than he could conceal his origins in Tarsus, although at the time no one could have predicted the kind of zealot he would ultimately become.

Paul's letters show that he sometimes shadowboxed with his past. Gamaliel wrote letters to the Diaspora; so eventually did Paul. It cannot be sheer coincidence that the apostle who pioneered the art of writing personally to particular communities had studied in Jerusalem as a Pharisee during Gamaliel's time. Gamaliel deliberately tried to get the recipients of his letters to keep the calendar of Judaism, while Paul tried just as hard to *stop* Gentiles from observing that practice (Galatians 4:10–11). Even when he rebelled against his Pharisaic formation, Paul betrayed his knowledge of its strengths.

Gamaliel's influence was so great that he could enforce his teachings – even in the Temple – by means of his devoted disciples (his *talmidim*). When he gave the annual half-shekel tax in the Temple, Gamaliel had a member of his household throw it right in front of the collector, to make sure his money went for public sacrifices (Sheqalim 3:3 in the Mishnah), rather than to general maintenance. If the collector needed prompting to pick up the shekel and put it in the right container, a little gang of Pharisees loyal to the patriarch gathered, yelling, "Take up, take up, take up!" It did not take long for the collector to get the point and set aside Gamaliel's shekels for sacrifices alone. Gamaliel's followers also insisted on their own rules for determining when an animal should be excluded from sacrifice because of a blemish (Bekhorot 6:9). To do that,

they deployed themselves in the area where animals were brought in on the north side of the Temple, to make any Levite or owner who disagreed with them back off.

Gamaliel had developed the same sort of eschatological fervor that had motivated Jesus to enter Jerusalem in the last year of his life. A major difference between them was that Gamaliel had exactly the kind of local knowledge, influence, and finesse in Jerusalem that Jesus lacked. The prophet Zechariah had predicted that all the nations of the earth would stream into Jerusalem to offer worship there. The rabbi from Galilee tried to realize that prophecy directly, even organizing his followers in a raid to throw merchants out of the Temple, because Zechariah said in the very last words of his book, "There shall no longer be a trader in the house of the LORD of hosts on that day" (Zechariah 14:21). There is no room to doubt the passion of Jesus' commitment, but that does not mean he was unique in that passion. The followers of Gamaliel cherished Zechariah's injunction to insist on just and peaceful judgments in Jerusalem (Abot 1:18, citing Zechariah 8:16). God's apocalyptic plan centered on justice, so that all the nations of the earth would converge on Jerusalem (Zechariah 8:23). Gamaliel did not share the rustic program of direct action that Jesus committed his life to, but that did not make him any less committed in his own way to the prophetic vision of how all humanity would one day flow into Mount Zion.

In fact, Rabbi Gamaliel's affinity with Rabbi Jesus caused Paul to shift his own allegiance within the Pharisaic movement. Gamaliel had no problem in contradicting the high priest Caiaphas when it suited him. After all, Caiaphas had moved merchants into the Temple. That was his innovation, and the Pharisees did not take well to the high priests' habit of changing arrangements on their own authority. In addition, Caiaphas had pushed the Sanhedrin, the local council in which the Pharisees' influence was important, out of the Temple and onto the Mount of Olives. That is why Jesus found so many ready participants for his raid on the Temple.

Caiaphas had hoped following Jesus' execution to put down the remnants of a troublesome challenge to his authority. Gamaliel gave him no support, even though that meant expressing tacit sympathy with Jesus' movement. When some of Jesus' followers claimed God had raised him from the dead, Caiaphas wanted to ban them and their teaching from the Temple. He even arrested some of them and kept them in the custody of his police (Acts 5:12–26). But Gamaliel resisted Caiaphas (Acts 5:34–41), arguing that no one could yet discern whether Jesus' followers were deluded or not. The Sanhedrin prevailed on Caiaphas to release Peter, James, and John, the triumvirate among Jesus' apostles. Gamaliel's opposition undermined the high priest's already waning power, even as Saul, a young Pharisee, aligned himself with Caiaphas.

apostolic role of preaching the message about Jesus as the Christ where it had not been heard before had already taken Paul around the entire northeastern quadrant of the Mediterranean world: from Jerusalem to Illyricum, which included parts of Asia Minor, Greece, and other lands as far west as the shores of the Adriatic (Romans 15:18–19, 23). Now he plans to pass through Rome to the next region where his primary missionary work could be carried out: Spain (15:24). This seems to indicate that not only Rome and Italy but also perhaps even southern Gaul had already heard the gospel and that some had believed in it, although that area does not really come into the history of Christianity until the second century. In any event, Paul hopes to see the Roman Christians as he passes through their city. But first he must take to the leaders of the Jerusalem church the collection he has arranged to gather from the Gentile churches of Asia Minor and Greece (15:24–9).

From the opening lines of this letter to the Romans, Paul makes clear that the gospel is in accord with the Scriptures of Israel and that God has from the beginning of human history had a special place in his purpose for ancient Israel as the covenant people (Romans 1:2). He repeats a liturgical formula concerning the human and divine sonship of Jesus (1:1–4), which some scholars think was in use in Rome and is quoted here by Paul to help him establish rapport with a Christian community largely unknown to him. That effort is surely evident in the personal remarks in 1:8–15, where he draws attention to mutual concerns and his hopes for enriched common understanding. The fact that he refers to the Roman believers as being "among the rest of the Gentiles" (1:13) indicates that the church is now predominantly Gentile, but that there are tensions in the relationships between pagan and Jewish converts to the Christian faith (1:16), both within individual congregations and between congregations.

His goals of introducing himself and easing tensions within the Roman community are both addressed by Paul's focus on what is usually translated as "the righteousness" or "justification" of God. The concept must be understood against its background in the Hebrew Bible and the Judaic tradition in which Paul was steeped: the primary reference is to the work of God whereby he sets his people in a right relationship to himself. Paul emphasizes that this divine goal is achieved by God's own gracious action, not by human merit or moral achievement (Romans 1:17). The only appropriate human response is to "rely on" or "trust in" what God has done through Jesus. ("Believe" is an inadequate translation, because it can imply merely intellectual assent.) Paul then proceeds to show that this is the way to a right relationship with God for both Jews, who were given the Law of Moses and the prophetic insights, and Gentiles, who lacked both.

The Gentiles should have been able, from the order and splendor of the universe, to infer the majestic nature of the God who created all things. But instead, they turned to worshipping images of created things, animal or human (1:18–23). The refusal to acknowledge God disorders all human relationships. The sinful and corrupt condition of the human race is ultimately not the cause of its estrangement from God, but comes from its refusal to honor God. Because the basic pattern of relationship with the Creator has been warped by human attitudes and actions, all human relationships are misshapen (1:24–32). Drawing on the traditions of the Stoics, Paul declares that the conscience of all human beings makes them aware of what their moral responsibilities are, and he reminds the Roman Christians of the future day when God will call them to account for their behavior in life (2:1–16). Jews assume that they have a special relationship to God because they were given the law of God through Moses, but even if that were the basis of their status as God's covenant people, they in fact "dishonor God by breaking the law" (2:17–29). The ground of human relationship to God is an inward commitment of trust, not outward conformity to a set of rules or to such religious rituals as circumcision.

It is true that those who stand in the Jewish tradition have an advantage over the Gentiles, in that the former have received the oracles of God and therefore have a special insight into his purpose for his people. Yet many Israelites have not been faithful to God. Does this show that God's plan has failed? No, it demonstrates that a right relationship with God is not attained by human performance, not even by those specially favored with the gift of the Law of Moses and the words of the Prophets (3:1–8). The result is that all humanity, whether Gentiles informed by conscience or Jews instructed by the Scriptures, stands condemned before God because of their failure to meet their moral and religious obligations. All that law does, whether natural law or Mosaic Law, is provoke disobedience and remind humans of their failings (3:9–20). But through Jesus, God has provided a remedy: it is God's way of setting his people in a right relationship to himself on the sole ground of their trust in what he has done (3:21–6). Christ saves people from the estrangement consequent upon human sin by excluding pride, showing God's demands and divine wrath to be just, and providing a new foundation – trust

CONSCIENCE

In Stoic philosophy, and among the many thinkers (both expert and popular) influenced by Stoicism, conscience featured as the innate human capacity to be aware of the natural law – and especially the moral law – inherent in the universe. Morality was the product of the human will and humanity's decision to recognize these moral standards and to live by them. Paul, influenced as he was by Stoicism, describes the moral condition of Gentiles, who, though they have the inner possibility of living in accord with natural law ("what the law requires is written on their hearts"), do not obey it and therefore stand condemned on moral grounds (Romans 2:12–16).

empowered by the Spirit of God – on which human beings can gain their proper standing before God (3:27–31).

This divine program is not, according to Paul, an innovation: the pattern of salvation goes back to Abraham, whose role as the father of the covenant people rested solely on his trust in God's promise, and to David, who saw that God forgave rather than hold humans responsible for their moral failures. But the covenant community emerging in the light of Christ's revelation will include "many nations" – people who did not know and could not have conformed to the Mosaic ritual or moral commandments. The proof that God has accomplished this through Jesus is seen in his having raised Jesus from the dead (4:1–25).

In describing the moral consequences of this relationship to God by faith, Paul notes that the full realization of God's purpose for humanity – to share the glory of God (Genesis 1:26; Psalm 8:3–5) – lies in the future. The difficulties and sufferings that his people undergo in the present age purify and prepare them for the final goal of sharing the glory of God (5:1–11). Paul develops a series of contrasts between two modes of human existence: in Adam, according to which human disobedience forfeited the right to share the glory of God and led to estrangement and death; and in Christ, through whom God's people are reconciled and enabled to become obedient (5:12–21). The rite of baptism is the means and instrument of participation in the death and resurrection of Jesus, which both empowers and impels God's people to live a life of faithful obedience and service (6:1–23).

Paul sees sin as a subtle, pervasive agent that perverts the law and its reminders of human obligations, compelling men and women to disobey law's moral demands. Apart from Jesus, humans would live lives of hopeless ambivalence, aware of the consequences of sin, yet unable to avoid committing it (7:1–25). Believers have a new place in which they can live and enjoy the benefits of God's provision for them: "in Christ" (8:1). Not only is Jesus the agent through whom new life is made available to the people of faith; he is also the prime model of that mode of life and the source of divine Spirit that empowers a life of righteousness. He came in human form and yet triumphed over the powers of evil by his life of total obedience to the will and purpose of God. For those who live by the Spirit, which is the enabling, transforming force at work within this new community, the moral demands of the law are indeed met. To live out of one's own human resources ("according to flesh," Paul literally says) is to preclude a life of obedience to God. To live by the power of the Spirit is to experience true life and peace – and this new life will know no end (8:2–11).

This life will by no means be free of suffering, however. The creation itself will continue to undergo strife and struggle, just as a woman in childbirth endures pain in order that new life may be born. God's people live in the hope that God, who triumphed over evil and death in raising Jesus from the dead, will complete the final and full deliverance of all his people – and of the whole creation – from the power of sin and death. Jesus is the pro-totype for God's people; all will be conformed by God to his image. Nothing on earth and no force in the superhuman realm will be able to thwart the achievement of God's purpose for his covenant with all people (8:12–39).

Both logically and autobiographically, Paul feels obligated to explain, as much for himself as for his Roman readers, the connection between the promises God made through Jesus and those he made historically to Israel. Three chapters of his letter (Romans 9–11) are devoted to wrestling with this issue. Paul begins by spelling out in detail what the privileged position of historic Israel is: God has given the Israelites a special relationship as "son"; the sanctuary in their midst radiated the divine cloud of glory; they were given the covenantal relationship, the Law, the proper service and worship of God, the divine promises; God worked on their behalf through the patriarchs and promised to send his anointed to accomplish his purpose (9:1–5). For all this, Paul can only praise God. Yet why has not the right relationship of this people to God been maintained? From the outset of Israel's history, it was clear that genetic or ethnic links with the patriarchs did not guarantee participation in the life of the covenant, since not all the descendants of Israel live within the community of faith. Human relationship to God happens by divine choice, rather than human effort or attainment (Exodus 33:19). The offspring of Isaac are either the object of love (Jacob) or the object of hate (Esau; Genesis 25:23; Malachi 1:2–3).

Yet God, in his sovereignty, can use the wicked to accomplish his objectives (Romans 9:17–30). Paul cites examples from the Scriptures of Israel. Pharaoh's hostility toward Israel in Egypt resulted in events that proclaimed the name and power of Israel's God throughout the nations of the world (Exodus 9:16). Some hearts are unresponsive to the word of God because he has hardened them (Exodus 4:21, 7:3, 9:12, 14:4, 7). God's sovereignty will nonetheless be evident because although not all historic Israel will be included in the ultimate covenant people, many who are historically "not my people" will be included (Isaiah 10:22–3; Genesis 22:17; 2 Kings 19:4; Hosea 1:10, 2:23). The members of the people of God will be gathered from among all the nations (Isaiah 11:10–16).

Why does Israel fail to understand and accept the message about what God is doing through Jesus to reconstitute his people (Romans 9:30–3)? The answer lies, Paul says, in their involvement with their own method of obtaining a right relationship with God – through their conformity to the Law of Moses; they have tripped up on the rock that God had set down as the foundation of the renewal of the covenant – Jesus Christ (Romans 10:1–4). They have not been enlightened, as Paul claims he has been, about how God is achieving his purpose. Christ has shown that the law can never be the ground for human achievement of a right relationship with God. It is easy to understand how Israel would have taken this mistaken route to God. It seemed to be laid down in the Law of Moses (Leviticus 18:5) and confirmed in the later Jewish writings (Nehemiah 9:29–31), including the

Prophets, such as Ezekiel (Ezekiel 20:11–26), who describes Israel's exile as the consequence of its failure to obey the Law, especially with regard to the Sabbath and sacrifices.

Against this, Paul sets forth the true ground of human relationship with God: trust in what God has done through Jesus to set his people right (Romans 10:6–10). Nothing more needs to be done to achieve this: the word that Paul preaches about Jesus' death and resurrection is already at hand, to be heard, believed, and publicly confessed. That message is already spreading throughout the earth for all to hear and, for all who are willing, Jew or Gentile, to trust in as the basis of human relationship to God. The quotations from the Scriptures in 10:18–20 serve to make Paul's point that this is no innovation, but has always been foundational to God's purpose.

This inclusive definition of the covenant people does not mean that historic Israel no longer has a place in God's purpose, as passages such as 1 Samuel 12:22, Jeremiah 31:37, and Jeremiah 33:24–6 make clear (Romans 11:1–2). Yet as Elijah had recognized, only a remnant of Israel will ultimately share in the ongoing life of God's people (1 Kings 19:10; 2 Kings 19:4; Isaiah 11:11; Psalm 94:14). This remnant has been chosen by the grace of God, not as a reward for its achievements (Romans 11:3–6). Even the hostile attitude that Israel has taken toward Jesus is a part of the divine plan, whereby the hardening of Israel's heart (Isaiah 29:10; Deuteronomy 29:4; Psalm 69:22–3) has resulted in the gospel being preached among the Gentiles (Romans 11:7–12). Using a play on words in Greek, Paul notes that Israel's gross mistake (*paraptoma*) in rejecting Jesus will result ultimately in Israel's fullness (*pleroma*) in the life of the covenant people. He uses two analogies to show the long-range effect of what God has begun to do in reconstituting his people. First, Paul observes that dough, part of which is offered as a sacrificial first fruit, eventually transforms the whole of the lump. Then, through the image of a vine (or tree) and branches, which appears in the prophetic writings and the Psalms (Psalm 80; Isaiah 5:1–7, 11:1; Jeremiah 5:10, 11:16, 17:5–8; Ezekiel 15, 17, 19, 31; Daniel 4; Joel 1; Zechariah 3, 4, 6), Paul portrays Israel as the natural branches of God's people, who have now been replaced by the Gentile believers, who are the branches grafted onto the original vine (Romans 11:17–24). To this extended metaphor Paul adds the warning that the Gentile Christians must be faithful in this relationship, or like historic Israel, they may be cut off as well. The result of these divine actions is that, in the time of the end, "all Israel will be saved" (Romans 11:26), by which Paul means that the elect and faithful, from among both Jews and Gentiles, will be brought to the fulfillment of God's plan through and for them as his covenant people. This section of the letter ends, appropriately, with an ascription of praise to the sovereign God and an acknowledgment of the inability of the human mind to grasp these divine ways (11:33–6).

In the remainder of the letter, Paul addresses more practical matters, such as the need for mutual concern and purity of life by the members of the new community, and the appropriate attitudes toward outsiders, including one's enemies and the Roman government. This concluding section of the letter begins with imagery drawn from the worship traditions of Israel: the transformed worship of God in Christ (12:1) involves the community's presentation of their whole beings as a living sacrifice. Their values and norms are not to derive from those of the evil age in which they live, but from the transformation of attitude and expectation that enables them to perceive and to fulfill God's will for his new people (12:2). The result of this will be their seeing themselves as instruments of God rather than as proud achievers. They will recognize that the capacities they enjoy are not for fostering their own self-esteem, but for the shared welfare of the whole community (12:3–8). These responsibilities range from mutual love to sharing goods with those in need (12:9–13). They are also required to show grace and forgiveness toward those outside the community, including their enemies. Here the influence of the Jesus tradition is evident (12:14–21).

Paul is persuaded that the pagan Roman state is not a threat to the young church, but is to be honored as the instrument of maintenance of social order, and Christians are to pay the required taxes in its support (Romans 13:1–7). Up to this point in Paul's career, Roman authority made possible his safe travel and the sure delivery of his letters, and protected him against attack by his opponents. As 2 Corinthians, Philippians, and Acts indicate, Paul was seized and imprisoned by civil authorities as a disturber of the peace, but the Roman powers did not find him guilty of political subversion or prohibit him from carrying on his work. Even when he is sent from Palestine to Rome for a hearing before the emperor, the regional Roman authorities can find nothing subversive or contrary to Roman law in his activities as far as Acts is concerned (Acts 26:32). If the tradition that Paul was martyred under Nero is correct, then some formal political charge might have been brought against him, which could have led him to a changed perspective on Rome by the end of his life. In fact, by the time he wrote Philippians, Paul thought of his true citizenship as being in heaven (3:20) rather than in the Roman Empire. But in most of his letters, his conviction that the present age and world order were soon to come to an end prevented him from mounting any politically subversive movement.

The rest of Romans is largely taken up with detailing what it means for members of the community to accept responsibility for others within the group, despite basic differences in insight and conviction. Thus, those who have brought into their lives as Christians beliefs about food that is unclean, after the manner of Judaism, are to be respected by those who do not share their views (14:1–23). The fundamental rule is to seek to please one another, so that there can be mutual support, peace, and harmony among the membership (15:1–6).

Before turning to his personal notes about his travel plans and the long list of greetings that he conveys from the Christians with him to those he hopes soon to see in Rome (Romans 15:14–16:23), Paul underscores the

Claudian aqueduct. Among the major public works carried out by Claudius during his reign as emperor (41–54 C.E.) were two great aqueducts and a new harbor at Ostia, the port of Rome. The Appian Way, described by the first-century C.E. historian Statius as "the queen of the long roads," stretched southward 350 miles from Rome to the major port of Brundisium. The arches of the Claudian aqueduct that runs beside the Appian Way as it nears Rome are more than 110 feet in height. The Forum of Appius, where Roman Christians came to meet Paul (Acts 28:15), was 43 Roman miles (39.5 English miles) south of Rome. (BiblePlaces.com)

LOVE COMMAND

Jesus' reply to the question of a scribe (Mark 12:28–34) or Pharisee (Matthew 22:34–40) about which is the most important (the "first") of God's commandments to his people is a combination of two texts from the Law of Moses: the command to love God with all one's capabilities ("heart . . . soul . . . mind"), from Deuteronomy 6:5, and the call to love one's neighbor as oneself, from Leviticus 19:18. Luke links this command with the parable of the Good Samaritan, which defines who one's neighbor is: a person in need, regardless of ethnic origin or physical condition (Luke 10:25–37). Paul shared Jesus' dedication to the principle of the love of one's neighbor (Romans 13:8–10).

---

authority of the mission to the Gentiles in which he is engaged by quoting from several Scriptures (Psalms 18:49, 117:1; Deuteronomy 32:43; Isaiah 11:10) that anticipate the inclusion of the Gentiles in the covenant people (Romans 15:7–13). The final paragraph of the letter emphasizes that the work of preaching Christ is the outworking of the divine mystery, which is now being made known to all the nations in order to lead them to faith and thus into the fellowship of the new people of God (16:25–7).

5. Philemon and Philippians

Both the letter to Philemon and the letter to the Philippians were written while Paul was in custody; the legal wrangling at the end of his life, the likely period of Philemon and Philippians, involved his staying in several locations. A possible imprisonment in Ephesus is frequently discussed, in view of its proximity to both Colossae in Asia Minor and to Philippi in mainland Greece. More plausible proposals for the place of Paul's imprisonment from which he wrote these letters include Caesarea Maritima, where he was in Roman custody for an extended period (Acts 23:23–27:2), and Myra, the port that Paul's ship put into so that the centurion could seek passage for Paul to Rome (Acts 27:3–6). It is notable that in Philemon Paul resignedly describes himself as a prisoner, whereas in Philippians he speaks of the possibility of his release. That would accord with the prolonged custody in Caesarea and the transit toward Rome that followed. Other scholars have assumed that Paul was writing from a prison in Rome, since he mentions the Praetorian Guard, which was an imperial unit. But elements of this guard were found wherever major Roman

CAESAREA

Two cities named Caesarea are featured in the development of earliest Christianity: Caesarea Philippi and Caesarea Maritima. The former, which is located in northern Palestine near one of the sources of the Jordan River, was the site of a pagan shrine named for the god Pan and was called Paneas. Philip, one of the sons of Herod the Great, rebuilt the city along Hellenistic lines. It was near here, according to Mark 8:27, that Jesus first discussed with his disciples the link between his messiahship and his impending death and resurrection.

The other Caesarea, with the added designation of Maritima, was located on the Mediterranean coast north of Jaffa. Herod the Great built it on the site of a tiny port city and greatly improved its harbor. Its elaborate buildings and extensive port facilities made it well suited to serve as the capital of Palestine during the Roman period, and the Roman governors and troops had their primary base there. The gospel was preached early in this city, according to Acts 8:40 and 10:1–33, and the city was the point of departure and arrival for several of Paul's journeys (Acts 9:30, 18:22, 21:8, 27:1–2), as well as the setting for his imprisonment and initial judicial hearings by the Roman authorities (Acts 23–6).

officials were stationed, and thus Caesarea would have had such units, and the centurion who conducted Paul from Caesarea to Myra belonged to a unit named after Augustus.

More important than the specific place of origin for these letters from prison is their unequivocal evidence that the Christian mission had now come into direct conflict with the Roman Empire, a harbinger of the conflict that was to come in succeeding centuries. Paul is not sure whether he will be released from prison, and so be able to return to his mission, or whether he will be executed. He is prepared for either alternative (Philippians 1:19–26).

The shortest of Paul's surviving letters, Philemon, is the one purely personal communication from him that has been preserved. Paul's whole concern in the mere twenty-five verses of this letter is with a slave, Onesimus, whom Philemon had loaned to him. (Onesimus is mentioned in Colossians 4:9 as a member of the church in Colossae.) Onesimus had stayed on in Caesarea with Paul longer than originally

Caesarea harbor. On the shore of the Mediterranean midway between Joppa and Ptolemaïs, Caesarea Maritima was originally a small town called Strato's Tower. Emperor Augustus added this area to the kingdom assigned to Herod the Great, who renamed it Caesarea in his honor. It served as the official seat of Roman power in Palestine for more than half a millennium. The Roman troops declared Vespasian emperor there after his success in crushing the Jewish revolt of 66–70. The city had all the typical features of a Greco-Roman center: temple, hippodrome, theater, aqueduct, sewers, and palaces for the Roman authorities. (BiblePlaces.com)

PHILIPPI

Philip II of Macedonia (who ruled from 359 to 336 B.C.E.), the father of Alexander the Great, offered his protection to a city called Krinides and eventually named the city for himself. The site was developed because of the proximity of gold and silver mines on the northwest coast of the Aegean Sea, and the city became important as a major Roman military and commercial location near the eastern end of the highway, the Via Egnatia, that served as a main route across northern Greece from the Aegean to the Adriatic. The deities worshipped there included major Roman gods and others whose cults developed in the region. Acts 16:11–15 mentions a "place of prayer" outside the city. These were gathering places for Jews and proselytes who met for social and religious purposes in the period before the institutional and architectural development of the synagogue; of course, even after a building was dedicated in a city for purposes of prayer, other congregations could continue meeting in different locations.

agreed, and Paul wants to spare the man punishment from an irate Philemon (vv. 8–14): Paul praises Philemon for his love for his fellow members of God's people (Philemon 4–7) and urges him to accept his former slave as a brother in the community of faith. If Onesimus owes anything to his former owner, Paul himself promises to repay (Philemon 15–20). Here we have dramatic evidence of the way in which the relationships within the new people of God transformed the social and economic patterns of the day.

The immediate occasion for writing to the Philippians is to thank them for the contribution that they have once more made to Paul's support (1:3–11). His being in prison has given him opportunity to preach to members of the imperial guard (1:12–14). The opposition that resulted in his imprisonment did not end his mission activity but instead provided him further opportunities to preach his version of the message of Christ (1:15–18). It leads him to remind his readers of the importance of total commitment to the gospel, even when that results in suffering or death (1:19–30). He then goes on to either repeat or rephrase an early Christian hymn that depicts Jesus as the prototype of complete obedience to God, which leads beyond death to divine vindication (2:5–8). This is the pattern according to which God will vindicate the faithful, and Jesus' example will lead them on until the universal proclamation of the gospel has been accomplished (2:9–11).

Meanwhile, however, Paul must advise the Philippians about the guidelines for individual and corporate life within the community, in the confidence that God is at work among them (2:12–13). They are to beware of those who want to enforce circumcision, as though it were a badge of merit (3:2–3). Paul says he has plenty to boast about in regard to his

Philippi, forum from the south. Founded in honor of Philip II of Macedonia, father of Alexander the Great, Philippi became important in Roman times because of its location on the Via Egnatia, the Roman highway that joined ports on the Aegean Sea with those on the Adriatic, thereby serving as a vital military and commercial link between Rome and its eastern provinces. Worshipped there were the local Greek deities, as well as those imported from Rome (Jupiter and Mars), Egypt, and Asia Minor (Cybele, the mother goddess). (BiblePlaces.com)

heritage if he thought any of it was important – including his origins, training, and Pharisaic zeal – but he dismisses these things as worthless dung or refuse (3:4–8). The sole ground of his relationship with God is trust in what God has done on behalf of his new people; Paul places no value on legal conformity or moral achievement as such (3:9). He wants to follow the example of Jesus through obedience to divine vindication (3:10–11). He sees his life as a process of growth toward maturity, which will culminate in the call to meet the triumphant, returning Christ (3:12–15).

Further, the community must purge itself of those false teachers who consider Christian freedom to be a license for self-indulgence (3:17–19). Instead, Christians are to regard themselves as members of God's perfect society, *politeuma* – a term that Paul borrows from the Stoic tradition of a humanity obedient to natural law, but which he perceives to be the new community in the process of transformation by God until corporately it conforms to the image of the risen Christ (3:20–1). In the interim, the members are encouraged to promote mutual understanding and to live lives free from anxiety and filled with joy and peace (4:1–7). The body of the letter closes with Paul's repeated expression of thanks for the financial support that the Philippians have provided him (4:10–20).

The concluding greetings are extended from the entire body of "saints" (wherever Paul may have been at the time), including "those of Caesar's household." This would fit the circumstances in Rome, but it could also refer to members of the imperial establishment assigned to Ephesus, Caesarea, Myra, or wherever Paul was imprisoned, who had become members of the covenant people. This detail gives the modern reader an indication of the astonishing speed with which the gospel found its way from a fringe group in rural Palestine to a movement with an impact on the upper levels of Roman society. Philemon and Philippians also reflect the deep, passionate attachment among Christians, when Paul repeatedly refers to his connection to his readers "in the viscera of Jesus Christ" (see Philippians 1:8, for example). The "body of Christ" was not merely an abstract image, but an emotional connection that made believers into a community whose mutual care set them apart from most other voluntary groups.

D. Toward Organization and Orthodoxy: Later Pauline Traditions

Among the Christian Scriptures, five writings identify Paul as their author, but their form, style, and content all indicate they came from a later period and that they were written by people who saw themselves to be carrying forward the traditions linked with Paul. These documents are

> Colossians
> Ephesians
> 1 Timothy
> 2 Timothy
> Titus

The first two of these writings stand closer to Paul in style and in their approach to the needs of the churches, but all of them evidence significant shifts toward a formalization of faith and Church organization as compared to the letters written directly by Paul. As noted throughout our analysis of the biblical writings, the practice of writing in the name of an earlier prophet or leader of the community was seen as a way of extending the work of the former leader.

The factors that contributed to this move toward consolidation within the churches founded by Paul typify the social forces that influenced the movement as a whole. At first, the leadership of the churches was *charismatic*, as sociologists have labeled spontaneous leaders – self-appointed in the view of external observers, divinely commissioned in their followers' understanding – who launch initiatives such as the Church's inclusion of Gentiles. This resulted in different, sometimes conflicting styles and strategies for carrying out various missions, as the letters of Paul amply illustrate. With the passing of the original apostolic generation, however, their successors in leadership roles saw to the stability of the churches that the pioneer apostles had formed. This natural need was intensified to the point of crisis by the fact that the movement was beginning to come to the attention of the Roman authorities. Organization and assignment of specific responsibilities were required if the church was to survive.

Paul was willing to tolerate certain differences in the understanding of what Christians should believe and practice: for him the most important thing was to convert both Jews and Gentiles to trust in Jesus as God's Son, revealed within them, in view of the shortness of the time before the coming of the new age. But as Paul's generation passed, it became increasingly clear that the churches must prepare for a possibly extensive period of expectation of the end. It was inevitable that the earlier contrast between this age and the next would be gradually replaced by a contrast between the realm of time and that of eternity, following a familiar distinction in Greek philosophy. We shall see that in these later Pauline writings there is a significant shift away from expectation of a speedy end in the direction of portraying Jesus as the agent of the eternal world in the present life of humanity. Faith, like the leadership of the Christian communities, will no longer be spontaneous but increasingly formal and unified, representing a consolidation of belief and practice.

1. Colossians: Jesus as Cosmic Redeemer

The saints in Colossae, a small city in the orbit of Ephesus in Asia Minor, are addressed in a letter that follows the general pattern of Paul's letters: identification of the writer and the recipients, prayers and thanksgiving for the church in Colossae (Colossians 1:1–14), statements about the role of Christ in God's plan (Colossians 1:15–23), expression of the writer's concerns for church members (Colossians 1:24–2:15), advice and exhortations (Colossians 2:16–4:6), personal greetings from the writer's companions and to specific members of the church at Colossae (Colossians 4:7–17), and a final personal greeting (Colossians 4:18).

This letter displays important differences from the letters of Paul in the vocabulary used for depicting Jesus as God's redemptive agent, in the writer's view of the present state of the Church, in his use of Hellenistic terminology for portraying Christ, and in the tactics he employs for guiding behavior in the Church. Certain philosophical distinctions are made that have no parallel in the letters of Paul, such as the contrast between "shadow" and "substance," which sounds nearly Platonic. Terms that appear in Paul's letters, such as "truth," "faith," and "knowledge," are all given intellectual connotations that are not found elsewhere in Paul's writing and that do not depict the basis of the personal relationship to God in the same way as these terms do when used by Paul. In contrast to Paul's scorning of human wisdom in 1 Corinthians 1, in Colossians the writer contrasts human wisdom and divine wisdom in principle but then uses technical philosophical terminology, speaking of Christ as the one in whom are hidden all the treasures of wisdom and knowledge (2:3) – a synthesis of secular and sacred wisdom. The writer seeks to place the Christian faith in competition with human "philosophy" – a term otherwise never used by Paul (Colossians 2:8). It seems clear that by the time Colossians was written, Christian faith, with its claim to offer divine wisdom, had to engage in debate with other intellectual systems.

In contrast to Paul, who links statements about what God has already done through Jesus with the hope of his still-to-come defeat of the powers of evil (1 Corinthians 15; 1 Thessalonians 4), the writer of Colossians here describes Christ as having already achieved victory over the worldly powers and the forces of evil (2:15). The effect of this shift is to remove, or at least soften, the problem of the nonfulfillment of the hope of Christ's return in triumph. Instead of depicting the people of God as meeting Christ when he returns to earth in victory at the end of the age (1 Thessalonians 4:17; 1 Corinthians 15), the writer of Colossians expects Christians to appear with Christ enthroned in heaven (3:14). In Paul's letters, the image of the body illustrates both differentiation of roles and mutual dependence among members of the Church (1 Corinthians 12–14). In Colossians, however, the emphasis falls on Christ as the head of the body, the Church, as well as master of all powers, earthly and heavenly (2:10, 19).

Life within the Church as described in Colossians is significantly different from what one sees in Paul's letters. Instead of focusing on roles within the community – such as prophecy, performing miracles, speaking in ecstatic language, and teaching (1 Corinthians 12:27–31) – the writer makes social distinctions in terms of husbands and wives and of masters and slaves within the community (Colossians 3:18–4:1). This contrasts sharply with Paul's declaration in Galatians 3:28 that in Christ neither sexual nor racial or social distinctions have any meaning. It appears that church membership in Colossae has developed through household rather than individual conversions and that the traditional hierarchical roles of the household have been transferred to and confirmed in the Christian community.

One of the major concerns throughout Colossians is what the author regards as the perversion of faith through two kinds of false teaching: speculation about the nature of Christ; and the attempt to force Christians to adopt an ascetic mode of life, with strict requirements about diet and observance of holy days (2:16–23). Instead of denouncing this as a return to being enslaved by the Law, as Paul does in Romans and Galatians, the author of Colossians urges his readers to divert their attention from earthly to heavenly matters (3:1–4) and to put on a new nature (3:5–11). This interest in otherworldliness, which the writer is calling for, would come to full realization in the second century in the movement known as Gnosticism.

Although Paul's letters make frequent personal references to his associates, in Colossians there is a sense of authority's being delegated by Paul to these co-workers, who are to serve as guides and to develop the life of the church (4:7–17). This change reflects, and helps to achieve, the transition between the first generation, when the apostles claimed their authority based on their having seen Jesus risen from the dead (1 Corinthians 9:1), and the period after their passing. Significantly, there is mention here of Mark and Luke (Colossians 4:10, 14), whose authority was to be attached to the Gospels that came to bear their names. Also, the authority of Paul's letters is evident in the reference in Colossians 4:16 to another (otherwise unknown) letter from Paul, which is to be read in the church, along with other authoritative letters sent to other churches. Clearly, Colossians evidences the beginning of a formal collection and transmission of the Pauline letters – which demonstrates how important it was that this letter was itself written in the name of Paul. Colossians names Timothy as well as Paul as its author (1:1), and Timothy may have been the conduit of Paul's thinking near the end of his life, as well as of the growing concerns of churches confronting a very different situation in the years after Paul's death.

Despite the silence of Acts after Paul's arrival in Rome, Paul evidently pursued an interior journey during the last two years of his life. As he visited friendly congregations in Rome, freed of the imperative to raise resources for his massive offering, Paul refined the poetic idiom he had pioneered in his correspondence with Corinth and dedicated himself to in his letter to Philippi. Timothy continued – both at a distance and during his sporadic visits to Rome – to connect his withdrawn teacher to the world around him and to coax Paul's words onto papyrus. Even after Paul's death, Timothy wrote as Paul's agent on the basis of what he could remember his teacher had said, the written work he could squeeze out of Paul, and his own authority.

Writing in his own name and Paul's years later, Timothy addressed this letter to Colossae. It includes reference to Paul's time in Rome (Colossians 4:7–18) and represents the outcome of a visit Timothy must have made to that city a year or so prior to Paul's death. Colossians includes some of Paul's best poetry, which without Timothy would probably have remained purely oral.

In the vacuum of leadership after the deaths of James, Peter, and Paul during the sixties — blows exacerbated by the disastrous revolt that resulted in the destruction of the Temple that had been at the center of Jesus' movement — Paul's letters survived. Until the Gospels were produced and circulated, these were the only written sources distinctive to Christianity. That is why they rose to prominence in Christian usage, despite the controversy surrounding Paul, and formed the nucleus of what the second century Church called the New Testament. What we read about Jesus today in Matthew, Mark, Luke, and John circulated only in oral form during the sixties C.E., and took decades to be consigned to writing. The Bible of Christian worship was the Septuagint, Christianity's inheritance from the Diaspora synagogue. Posthumously, Paul filled the vacuum of leadership that plagued Christianity through his letters. They were at the right place and at the right time in a way he never managed personally.

Many hands copied these letters and got them to congregations sympathetic to Paul and his memory. Amanuenses and assistants had been with Paul when he composed them; these old entourages — in Ephesus, Troas, and Miletus — formed a natural cadre of editors that could correlate their work with copies of correspondence kept by churches in Galatia, Corinth, Rome, and Philippi. Wherever Paul had written from, wherever he had written to, salvaging his words offered guidance to a generation of believers that was battered and disoriented after the catastrophes that unfolded in Rome and Jerusalem.

Timothy played a key role in disseminating the letters in the decades after Paul's death. He had already worked with Paul in the composition of 1 Thessalonians, 2 Corinthians, and Philemon, becoming increasingly influential throughout that progression. Without Timothy's encouragement, support, and editorial initiative Philippians might not have been written and the poetry of Colossians would have been lost. He was the personal link between the author and the letters that circulated in Paul's name.

With Timothy's growing influence, these letters addressed issues closer to his heart than to Paul's. The beginning of Philippians, for example, includes special greetings to "bishops and deacons," part of the hierarchy that emerged as a result of

BISHOP

The English word "bishop" derives from the Greek term *episkopos*, which means "overseer." In Philippians 1:1, Paul extends greetings to the leaders of the church in Philippi, whom he designates as "bishops and deacons." The distinction in roles seems to be between those who serve the group (deacons) and those who oversee and safeguard the common life of the community (bishops). The post-Pauline writing 1 Timothy contains an impressive list of qualifications for those who aspire to the major leadership in the community: "the office of bishop" (3:1–7). Titus 1:7–9 also specifies requirements, including fidelity to "sound doctrine" in preaching. A pastoral role for the elders (singular *presbuteros*, from which the English word "priest" derives) as outlined in Acts 20:17–28 to be overseers of the flock; shepherds of the church of God is assigned by the Holy Spirit. In Acts 1:20, the replacement of Judas among the twelve apostles is justified by an appeal to Psalm 109:8, and the Greek term in Acts for the "position" or "office" is *episkope*. Clearly, in the New Testament the terminology for church leadership roles is fluid. Written near the end of the first century (and not included in the New Testament), the *First Letter of Clement* presents the office of an *episkopos* as authoritative and insists that due process must be observed in replacing the bishop when he dies (1 *Clement* 42:2–4 and 44:1–2). Yet even in 1 *Clement*, the bishop is also spoken of as elder (*presbuteros*), indicating that distinctions are not yet categorical.

Timothy's work to consolidate the influence of his teacher. Paul's own characteristic worries did not include Church officials, but Timothy had a particular concern for them as the years went on. His influence on the Book of Acts is as obvious as the anachronism involved when Paul and Barnabas ordain men to be clergy (Acts 14:23) just after Paul had been stoned.

Timothy was a young man when Paul circumcised him in 47 C.E. (Acts 16:1–3); by 90 C.E., when the collection of Pauline letters was virtually complete, Timothy was probably in his sixties. By then most of the letters written up until the time of Paul's imprisonment had been circulating. Timothy consolidated and arranged the fragments that make up 2 Corinthians to enhance the collection. His success in that emboldened him to edit and enlarge the Letters to Philemon, to the Philippians, and to the Colossians for general reading: the equivalent of publication.

Yet Colossians also represents a poetic achievement that probably reflects more of Paul than of Timothy. The Christ of Colossians projects his cosmic, divine body into the human experience. Solidarity with this body had long been a theme of Paul's, but in Colossians Christ is the center of the cosmos – natural, social, and supernatural – that created the world and makes the world new each day (Colossians 1:15–20):

> He is the invisible God's image, firstborn of all creation,
>   because within him everything was created,
>   in heaven and on earth, visible and invisible:
>   thrones, dominions, principalities and authorities.
>   Everything through him and for him has been created.
> He is personally before all things, and all things exist in him,
>   and he is personally the head of the body: the Church.
> He is the beginning, firstborn from the dead,
>   so he becomes in all things precedent.
> For in him all the fullness pleased to dwell,
>   and through him – and for him –
>   to reconcile all things (whether on earth or in heaven),
>   as he made peace through the blood of his cross.

The range of Paul's thinking was literally cosmic, and metacosmic, because the viscera of Christ, the mind of Christ, wove all things into the primordial whole that had been their source. To Paul's mind, the fulfillment of all things had already been accomplished. Christ had mended the world, and an attuned heart and mind could join in that victory.

Paul – master preacher, oral poet – was welcomed in many Christian communities in and around Rome, albeit not in synagogues (Acts 28:17–29). He still encountered resistance, but he rejoiced in that. He said it was the purpose of the believer to join Christ in suffering (Colossians 1:24), "to fill up what is lacking in the tribulations of Christ." Every drop of a martyr's blood flowed from the veins of Jesus and was shed to reconcile human divisions as decisively as Christ had already reconciled the forces of heaven to the all-consuming love of God. Paul at the end of his life became the first great mystical teacher of union with Christ, the fusion of divine Spirit and human spirit.

The Appian Way linked Rome with the port of Brundisium and is probably the route by which Paul went north from Puteoli (Acts 28:13) and entered Rome. (BiblePlaces.com)

2. Ephesians

The oldest existing copies of Ephesians do not include the name of a particular church to which it was addressed; only later copies specify the communication as "to those in Ephesians" (1:1). That the document now known as "Ephesians" was indeed sent to a group of churches, rather than to a specific congregation, is apparent from the fact that this letter – unlike Paul's letters that we have already examined – does not address the issues of a specific situation. Instead, the structure of the letter is twofold: an extended introduction, with an elaborate form of prayer (announced in 1:15–16; taken up in 3:1 and again in 3:14) that culminates in the blessing of God (3:20–1); and the concluding exhortations, instructions (with only the briefest personal note in 6:21–2), and prayers that end the letter (4:1–6:24). A middle section dealing with specific problems and concerns, such as we find in Paul's letters, is simply not there in Ephesians. It seems clear, therefore, that this letter was intended to be circulated widely among various churches, with the aim of promoting unity among them in faith and in practice.

The writer does develop Pauline themes. Jesus is referred to as Lord, as he is with great frequency in Paul's letters. At times the word for Lord, *kurios*, could refer to Jesus or to God, just as is the case with Paul. Only once, however, is Jesus spoken of as "Son of God" in Ephesians (4:13), although that is also an important term in the letters of Paul. The Spirit is referred to as the guarantee of the fulfillment of God's promises (Ephesians 1:13; 2 Corinthians 1:22). What is more significant, however, is the distinctive meaning that this letter gives to certain terms found in Paul's other letters. The term "heavenly" is used by Paul in contrast with things that are of earthly origin (1 Corinthians 15:40, 48). But Ephesians uses the word in the plural to refer to the sphere of eternity, where Christ is and where his followers have already entered (Ephesians 1:20, 2:6).

This is part of a shift in Ephesians, which reduces the expectation of a future fulfillment to an ancillary feature, emphasizing instead the cosmic, *timeless* transformation of the human situation that God has accomplished in Christ. The new reality is not the age to come, awaited in the near future, as in Paul, but rather the cosmic change that has already taken place (2:5–6, 11–13; 4:10). This new reality is also internalized: Christ dwells in the hearts of the faithful (3:17), and they have the possibility of being "filled with all the fullness of God" (3:19). The term *pleroma* (fullness) is used by Paul to refer to the divinely determined time of the birth of Jesus (Galatians 4:4), but in Ephesians 4:13, as in Colossians 2:9 and John 1:16, it seems to mean the fullness of the divine nature, which Jesus possesses and which he shares with his people.

The goal of God's redemptive program through Jesus, according to Ephesians, is to create a new and transformed humanity (Ephesians 2:13–18). That idea is implicit in Paul's statements in Romans about the contrast between being in Adam and in Christ (Romans 5:12–21), but here the emphasis is on the participation in the divine nature (Ephesians 4:24). An important feature in Ephesians is the unity of this new humanity that God has established in Christ. The old split between Jew and Gentile, which had practical implications in Paul's time, is now pictured as no longer significant, because through Christ, God has created "one new humanity" (2:11–19).

Ephesians represents the capstone of the collection of Paul's letters, together with writings attributed to him. Here the sweeping image of the cosmic Christ in Colossians is used to address the particular tensions between Gentile and Jewish Christians in Ephesus at a later period (Ephesians 2:11–14): "Therefore remember that you were once Gentiles in flesh, those called foreskin by those called circumcision in flesh – made by hands – because you were in that time apart from Christ, estranged from the citizenship of Israel and foreign to the covenants of the promise, not having hope and godless in the world. But now, in Jesus Christ you who were once far have become near in the blood of Christ. For he personally is our peace: he made the two one and looses the dividing barrier. . . ."

Timothy probably crafted these words for a community in which Gentiles had become dominant, so they would appreciate that it was only God's gracious inclusion of them within Israel that permitted them to inherit the covenantal promise. Christ's aim was to produce "one new man," joined in "the body of God" (Ephesians 2:15-16). By the time Ephesians was written, the body of Christ had indeed become the body of God for Pauline Christians, so completely had they incorporated Paul's revelation that Jesus was not only God's Son but also the cosmic reality of divine nature itself. Timothy is not named at the head of the letter. As a result, other candidates have been proposed for authorship, including Onesimus (the slave for whom Paul had appealed for mercy to Philemon) and

Harbor remains at Troas. Taking its name from the nearby ancient city of Troy, Troas was an important port city on the north-western coast of Asia Minor since it was the major access point for the Romans to the northern provinces there. The district was designated by the Romans as a Roman colony, and the Roman historian and geographer Strabo refers to it as "one of the renowned cities." According to Acts, Paul departed from Troas for the mainland of Europe (Acts 16:8–10) and passed through there again on the way to his final visit to Jerusalem (Acts 20:5–12). (BiblePlaces.com)

Tychichus (referred to in Ephesians 6:21). During this period, when the Church generally looked to its apostolic past for guidance, it is extremely difficult to specify authorship. But the affinity between Colossians and Ephesians points back to Timothy, writing from Troas, as their common author.

Then the image shifts from the creation of a new society of God's people to the building of a new sanctuary in which God is present (Ephesians 2:19–2). In this newly structured society, Christ is the foundation (as he is for Paul: 1 Corinthians 3:10), but the apostles and prophets are the building material from which the Temple of God has been constructed, and where God dwells in the Spirit. There is now a hierarchy of roles in the church: apostles, prophets, evangelists, pastors, teachers (Ephesians 4:11). These are less the charismatic gifts that Paul describes in 1 Corinthians 12 than ecclesiastical functions essential for the development of the Church in its institutional forms. The goal of this leadership pattern is to enable the Church to "attain to the unity of the faith." This is explained to mean fullness of knowledge, maturity of Christian living, and, above all, orthodox doctrines. These qualities alone will make possible the proper growth in faith within the community (4:13–16).

The members of the church are to seek to exhibit the very nature of God (Ephesians 5:1), with purity of life and thought, avoiding associations with any who might corrupt their morals or their doctrine (5:3–14). The sanctity of the life of the community is to be evident not only in the community's moral performance but also in its common life of devotion to God in worship (5:19–20). Ephesians 5:14 is perhaps a portion of an early Christian hymn, based on Isaiah 60:1. The concrete expression of the unity of the faithful is to be seen in their willingness to be subject to one another (5:21). In tone, what Ephesians says to its community is similar to Paul's

own message to the Romans. In the case of Rome in 57 C.E., Gentile preponderance had been occasioned by the imperial exclusion of Jews from
the *pomerium* (i.e., the sacred boundary of the city) in 49 C.E.; by contrast,
Gentile Christians had increased in Ephesus by 90 C.E. as a result of shifting demographics within the movement itself.

There follows a list of social roles and responsibilities within the community, as in Colossians. Rules are given for wives and husbands, children,
slaves, and masters (5:22–6:9). The final exhortation describes the cosmic
conflict in which the people of God are now engaged against the hosts of
evil (6:10–20). This may well point to the beginning of general hostility
toward the Christian movement in the later first or even early second century, as it began to penetrate the upper levels of Roman society and to
arouse suspicions concerning its social and political implications. Appropriately, the writer identifies himself as "an ambassador in chains," which
was very likely the actual fate of Paul. Presumably by the time Ephesians
was written, the final conflict of Paul with the Roman authorities and his
execution – which would not have been anticipated in view of his positive
attitude toward what he regarded as a benign political power – had
become a paradigm of the subsequent Church–state struggle and the
threat of martyrdom that is reflected here and in later writings of the New
Testament, such as 1 Peter and the Revelation.

3. First and Second Timothy, and Titus: The Pastoral Epistles

With the exception of the brief Letter to Philemon, the genuine letters of
Paul are addressed to churches rather than to individuals. The Pastoral
Epistles, however, are written to individuals: Timothy and Titus. Both the
addressees are mentioned elsewhere in the New Testament writings as
associates of Paul in his missionary work: Timothy in Acts 16:1 (as well as
in Paul's letters, sometimes as a coauthor) and Titus in Galatians 2:1–3.
More important than the difference in the address of these writings, however, is the divergence in vocabulary and attitude between these documents, commonly known as the Pastorals, and the letters of Paul.

When Timothy edited the core of Paul's letters, adding material of his
own, that spurred some Christians to continue writing in Paul's name.
They produced these new missives as personal letters of Paul to Timothy and Titus, but scholarship is nearly unanimous in rejecting these
attributions. Someone who tried to pass off such works today would be
called a forger, but antiquity provides many examples of intellectual
enthusiasts who wrote in a great master's name. We only know Socrates
from Plato's rosy scenarios, and the *Genesis Apocryphon* from Qumran
freely embellishes on what the patriarchs of Israel said and did. The biblical Book of Daniel is pseudepigraphal, written during the second century B.C.E. but attributed to a Jewish sage who lived centuries earlier.
Paul had stated openly during his lifetime that he could project his spirit
from one place to another (1 Corinthians 5:3–5): he practically invited

later disciples to claim his spirit for their own time, as well. The Pastoral Epistles (1 Timothy, 2 Timothy, and Titus) took this invitation up, and they deal explicitly with the pastoral imperative to organize, order, and care for congregations. In this, their tone and language is unlike Paul's, and also unlike those letters that have come to us in which Timothy had a hand.

The Pastoral Epistles are nonetheless extremely valuable for our knowledge of development and change within the Christian movement, since they document basic shifts in the inner life of the Church and in the Church's relationship to the wider Greco-Roman culture. Although the exact date of their writing cannot be determined, it is likely that they were written about the year 100 C.E. The continuity of the Pastorals with the Pauline tradition is also evident: however, since they not only mention Paul and his associates but also include some of the characteristic themes of Paul's letters: grace toward sinners, Jesus' coming into the world to save them, and Jesus' death for the redemption of believers (1 Timothy 1:12–16, 2:6).

Each claims to address Timothy or Titus personally, but the affectionate language of Philemon and Philippians is missing. Timothy and Titus in the Pastoral Epistles are not presented as coauthors with Paul; instead, they receive categorical, often stern advice. These alleged communiqués are unlike Paul's letters to particular churches (or to a person, in the case of Philemon). Rather, these are epistles, literary productions that try to crystallize Paul's wisdom for the Church at large.

They address the issues of their time, not Paul's. First Timothy emphasizes the necessity for prayer on behalf of rulers (1 Timothy 2:1–8), somewhat in the manner of Romans, but against the grain of Paul's proud rejection in Philippians of any citizenship but heaven's. It is particularly concerned to keep women in their place, which this epistle thinks of as bearing children (1 Timothy 2:13-15): "Because Adam was first fashioned, then Eve. And Adam was not deceived, but the misled woman came into transgression. But she will be saved through childbearing, if they remain in faith and love and sanctification with prudence." This was just the argument from Genesis that Paul had once started to make in a letter to Corinth, then stopped himself (1 Corinthians 11:8–12) because he realized that it contradicted his own principle of equality in Christ. Compunctions of that sort did not distract those who composed the Pastoral Epistles; the agenda of maintaining order overrode the subtleties of Paul's own thinking.

The vocabulary of the Pastorals demonstrates the changes that had taken place in the Christian community since the time of Paul. For example, instead of using the term "faith" as a description of the relationship of trust that God expects from humans, the Pastorals speak of "*the* faith," by which the writer means the correct doctrines that are to characterize the Christian religion. There is a "pattern of sound words" (2 Timothy 1:13) or of sound "doctrine" (Titus 2:10) that the leadership of the Church is to entrust to those who will teach it faithfully and accurately (2 Timothy

EPIPHANY

Derived from a Greek word (*epiphane*), meaning "to show (oneself)" or "to manifest (one's) presence," "epiphany" is a term for the appearance or self-disclosure of a divinity to human beings. It may take the form of a vision or of a divine action, such as a healing. Although in one New Testament text the word is linked with the *parousia* (which refers to Jesus' appearing in triumph at the end of the age), it is found in nonbiblical texts that describe mystical experiences in which a divinity is revealed to humans. These revelations are private and personal, and timeless in nature. The preference for "epiphany" (instead of *parousia*) as a way of describing the awaited revelation of Jesus as the triumphant Christ fits well with the outlook of the later Christian Scriptures, in which interest in the continuing personal revelation of Christ replaces the hope of his imminent public coming as victor over the powers of evil.

2:2–7). Significantly, this body of correct beliefs is referred to as "religion" (1 Timothy 3:16), a usage never found in the letters of Paul to describe Christian faith but widely used among the religions with which Christianity was in competition as it spread throughout the Mediterranean world. It is not surprising that the author of these pastoral letters substitutes terms that were in common religious use in his era, but which Paul does not employ, such as "epiphany" (*epiphane*, divine disclosure) and *palingenesia* (rebirth). Respectively, these words replace Paul's terms for the coming of Christ at the end of the age and believers' admission by faith into the covenant community.

Related to these changes in terminology and perspective is the shift to a more abstract representation of Jesus as God's agent for the redemption of his people. When the author speaks of "God our Savior," as he does in 1 Timothy 2:3, he seems to be referring to what Paul would have called "the Father." But in Titus 2:11–13, the "God and Savior" is identified as Jesus Christ. The role of Jesus in salvation is called mediator and ransom (1 Timothy 2:5–6), but there is no direct reference to suffering, crucifixion, or death. Similarly, in 2 Timothy 1:9–10, the purpose of God is said to have been manifested through the appearing ("epiphany") of Christ Jesus, who abolished death and brought immortality to light. Once again there is no allusion to the historical events of Jesus' birth, suffering, and death, such as we find in Paul's letters. Titus 2:13–14 is similar to these two descriptions of Jesus' role as redeemer, but "epiphany" is used in this text for what Paul would call the *parousia*, or the coming of Jesus in triumph at the end of the present age.

The truth of the Christian religion is set out in contrast to false teaching, different doctrines, myths, speculations, and vain discussions proclaimed by those who have "swerved from the truth" (1 Timothy 1:3–7). The gross immorality of their adherents demonstrates that they are not following "sound doctrine" (1 Timothy 1:8–11). The greed, conceit, envy, wrangling, arrogance, gluttony, and deceit with which they go about their religious endeavors match the corruption and wild irresponsibility of their teachings (1 Timothy 6:3–10; 2 Timothy 3:1–9; Titus 1:10–16). Christians are to avoid involvement in these "stupid controversies, . . . dissensions and quarrels, which are unprofitable and futile" (Titus 3:9–11). It is evident from these passages that some who claim adherence to the Christian faith are promoting elaborate mythical speculations, some of them based on emerging Gnostic traditions. The author denounces these notions as "godless chatter and contradictions" and disputes the claim of those who peddle these ideas that they have access to true "knowledge" (*gnosis*).

The proper pattern of life is expressed in a term that was common to religions in the Greco-Roman period: *eusebeia*, which means "proper behavior" or "piety" as well as "religion." The life of true piety is to be characterized by a pure heart, a good conscience, and sincere faith (1 Timothy 1:5; 2 Timothy 1:3–5). This way of life is handed down from one generation to the next (2 Timothy 1:5). It will manifest itself in gentleness,

GNOSIS

Gnosis, one of several Greek words for "knowledge," came to be used during the second century C.E. to refer to a mode of religious insight that claimed to convey exclusive information about the origin and destiny of the universe and its inhabitants. In many cases, Gnostics taught that the physical world is the work of evil powers that operated in defiance of the God of light, the true and beneficent sovereign ultimately behind the universe. Human beings were caught in material existence, helpless to escape until the agent of divine knowledge came into the world to explain and enable liberation from material corruption. Some of the followers of this movement (which came to be known as Gnosticism in modern discussion) thought that they could display their ability to rise above the material world by living in a strictly ascetic manner, whereas others took the route of unbridled self-indulgence as a way of showing that the material world and its conventions were of no significance.

Knowledge of this movement in its various forms was limited until modern times. Much of the information about the Gnostics came from attacks on them in the writings of defenders of the faith that came to be called "catholic" (i.e., "universal," distinguishing it from the local, often private traditions and customs on which Gnostics insisted). But in 1945 an entire library of Gnostic documents was found at Nag Hammadi in Upper Egypt. Written on papyrus (a writing material made from reeds) in thirteen volumes, some of which are not complete, the documents are in Coptic, a form of late Egyptian used by Christians in Egypt and written in Greek characters. They include gospels (the *Gospel according to Thomas*; the *Gospel of Truth*); acts (*Acts of Peter and the Twelve Apostles*); apocalypses (*of Paul, of Peter, of Adam*, and two *of James*); and dialogues (the *Sophia of Jesus Christ*; the *Dialogue of the Savior*). These documents provide primary evidence of Gnosticism.

Although scholarly opinion is divided, it seems probable that Gnostic teaching about the cosmos and human destiny had antecedents in Jewish wisdom speculation as well as in philosophical and religious currents in the early Roman period. Some Christian thinkers during the second century developed this approach further and identified Jesus as the agent of divine knowledge whose followers could escape from the material world and regain union with the truly divine. It is likely the beginning of this movement that is being attacked in passages from later New Testament writings such as 1 Timothy 6:20, where false teachers and their false claims to knowledge are denounced. The Gnostic documents expand and modify the Jesus tradition in order to make Jesus fit the role of an agent of secret knowledge and a liberator from the material world.

courtesy toward others, freedom from quarreling, and avoidance of slavery to passions and pleasures (Titus 3:1–3). Just as household vessels in the Jewish tradition were to be kept ritually pure, so members of the church are to exhibit purity of heart and act. The pious include wealthy men and women (1 Timothy 6:17–19) as well as slaves (1 Timothy 6:1–2; Titus 2:9). All are to exhibit this peaceable, gentle, respectable style of life. Their obedience to the Roman civil authorities, combined with the peace and quiet of their lives, will help to enhance the reputation of Christians as respectable citizens (1 Timothy 2:2).

Considerable attention is given in these books to outlining the leadership roles within the community. Specifically mentioned are the offices of bishop and deacon (1 Timothy 3:1–13, with women included in the latter function in v. 11; Titus 1:5–9). What is called for is gentleness, efficiency of management, and a good reputation among outsiders. There are also assignments of roles to those identified as presbyters (male and female) and to widows. The Greek term *presbyteros* could refer simply to older members of the community, but it is at times used to identify certain persons

THE GNOSTICISM THAT NEVER WAS

The word "Gnostic" seems to beg for misunderstanding, being easily confused with being "agnostic," the modern position that human beings cannot know whether there is a God. In fact, ancient Gnosticism directly contradicts appeals to uncertainty. Yet for all the clarity of Gnostic thought, recent fashion has made it into the mirror image of allegedly progressive Christianity.

In Greek, the term for knowledge was *gnosis*; people who pursued knowledge intently could be called *Gnostikoi*. If the word "knowledgist" existed in English that would be a good translation, because Gnostics claimed to be in the know about the most fundamental realities. Gnostics between the first and the fourth century of the Common Era searched for a single, integrating insight into the divine world amid the conflicting religious traditions of ancient society, apart from parochial requirements, peculiar customs, and ethnic preferences. Traditional religions often spoke of transcendence, but restricted the delivery of their truths to their different constituencies, which were limited and often mutually exclusive, defined by race, history, family, or status. Gnosticism claimed to smash through those barriers, making it the most potent cultural force in this period of the Roman Empire and the most successful effort at the intellectual reform of religion there has ever been.

Many people in the ancient world – some of them educated, all of them intellectually curious – resented the welter of religions around them, each often in open conflict with the others.

From one city to another, the civic god changed; new rites and obligations were required. Civic offerings – a requirement of citizenship, for those lucky and rich enough to be citizens – were costly.

The power of Gnosticism transformed the face of Greco-Roman religion: virtually every religious movement was influenced by it. Gnostic questers pioneered a philosophical approach to religious truth that was based on knowledge rather than faith, practice, or formal organization. The Christian church, the Jewish synagogue, the guild of adepts in the Mysteries find no real counterpart among the Gnostics.

Gnosis was not just reasoned argument or a collection of data, but insight into the celestial realm that transformed the Gnostic seeker. The true Gnostic transcended the shackles of the fallen, physical world and became inured to suffering and pleasure in his or her total dedication to the spiritual world. Each person who found *gnosis* lived thereafter in the assurance of divine favor, saved from the predations of the flesh, incarnated within the realm of Spirit.

Scholars still debate whether Gnosticism predates Christianity, but it is plain that both Paul and the Gospel according to John see true knowledge of God as liberating people from their corrupt passions. They probably did not originate Gnosticism, but they existed near its time of origin, when diversity in the Roman Empire seemed bewildering. By the second century, however, some Gnostic groups, named after teachers such as Carpocrates, Marcion, and Valenti-

nus, claimed that they alone had the true knowledge that Jesus conveyed. Tension inevitably emerged between them and the claim that the church at large (or, as a whole, *katholikos* in Greek) possessed saving *gnosis* within its faith.

Christian writers of the second century, including Irenaeus in Gaul, Clement of Alexandria, and Tertullian in North Africa, called these groups "schools." This is what gives us the term "heresy" in English, because *hairesis* refers to a school of thought in Greek. Obviously, "heresy" carries with it implications of violating established orthodoxy and being subject to punishments that did not apply during the second century, when the pagan Romans persecuted Christians, whether Catholic or not. As a result, scholars have tended to call the self-proclaimed specialists in divine knowledge Gnostics rather than heretics.

Whatever they are called, during the second century, a divide opened up between Catholic thinkers and those who produced private gospels within their communities that claimed unique access to the truth of God. Some of them were openly anti-Semitic, taught that the physical world was the hopelessly corrupt product of a false god, and insisted that only the predestined elect could know the divine truth. These are persistent tendencies, rather than a set of precise ideas that all the schools repeated.

The discovery of a whole library of writings at Nag Hammadi in Egypt in 1945 opened up a fresh interest in these private gospels and related writings. Perhaps inevitably, this interest

(continued)

THE GNOSTICISM THAT NEVER WAS *(continued)*

sometimes tipped into uncritical enthusiasm. It is frequently said, for example, that scholarship never had direct access to such sources before the discovery, but only to what their opponents (Irenaeus, and Clement and Tertullian above all) had to say. In fact, the *Pistis Sophia* (which means "Faith-Wisdom") has been known since the eighteenth century, and the *Gospel of Mary* since the nineteenth century.

This enthusiasm is part of the rise of neo-Gnosticism, a modern revival greatly encouraged by the discovery at Nag Hammadi. In embracing these ancient sources, however, the neo-Gnostics are unlike their ancient counterparts. They want to embrace the earth, not subjugate it; they do not

wish to be elitist. Above all, they want to insist on the gender equality of women with men. Gnostic sources need to be used very selectively to make that picture work as an account of the Nag Hammadi library.

In the *Gospel according to Thomas*, for example, Peter tells Jesus to make Mary Magdalene depart from the disciples because "women are not worthy of the life." Peter appears in the Nag Hammadi library more often than Mary does, and in an unequivocally positive light as a hero of the Gnostic quest. He is much more than a straw man to represent Catholic authoritarianism. Gnostic Christians were not about to cede the rich inheritance of Peter to their Catholic counterparts.

In *Thomas*, Jesus rebukes Peter's attempt to exclude Mary, but in terms that are the antithesis of some feminist readings of the text, and are all the more dramatic for being the book's last words: "Every female who makes herself male will enter the kingdom of heaven" (saying 114). The Coptic text of *Thomas* leaves no doubt about the meaning of these words, because "female" and "male" are the particular words for sexual difference, as in English. This gospel and the other documents found at Nag Hammadi, and sources like them, will reveal their secrets only when read in their ancient context, not as part of a modern agenda.

who have leadership functions (1 Timothy 5:1–2, 17–18). For example, since presbyters as a group were to bestow the gift of prophetic utterance by laying their hands on the head of candidates, they convey spiritual power, not merely sage advice on the basis of experience (1 Timothy 4:14). Obviously, the community by this time had the equivalent of modern processes of ecclesiastical ordination by an official body. The extended discussion of the place of widows in the community (1 Timothy 5:3–16) implies that the community will take care of destitute, solitary older widows, but it encourages the younger widows to remarry. Yet the use of what seems to be a technical term, "enroll" (5:9), may indicate that some widows were assigned roles of service within the community.

Paul himself was interested in seeing to some of the functions these terms refer to, but the Pastoral Epistles consolidated them into hierarchical offices. In all probability, Paul had designated some people as bishops. The term *episkopos* means "overseer," like the term *mebaqqer* in Hebrew (used at Qumran). Paul needed administrators, especially for his collections, and it made good sense to name them with the same title that James bore in Jerusalem. When a local elder from the synagogue (a *zaken* in Hebrew, a *presbuteros* in Greek) sympathized with him, Paul no doubt embraced this rabbi. And Paul freely used the word "servant," *diakonos* (in Greek, corresponding to *'eved* in Hebrew), to speak of anyone who helped in the spread of Jesus' message. All the major terms used in the Pastoral Epistles to speak of offices in the church had their precedents in the life of the synagogue as well as in Paul's life.

According to the writer of the Pastorals, the primary responsibility of the Church leaders is instruction. Although the roles of apostle and

ASSIGNED ROLES IN THE CHURCHES ACCORDING TO COLOSSIANS AND THE PASTORALS

Within the household:

Wives (Colossians 3:18)
Husbands (Colossians 3:19)
Children (Colossians 3:20)
Fathers (Colossians 3:21)
Slaves (Colossians 3:22–5)
Masters (Colossians 4:1)

Within the leadership of the churches:

Bishops (1 Timothy 3:1–7)
Deacons (1 Timothy 3:8–13); these instructions may include women who are deacons (1 Timothy 3:11; Romans 16:1)
Elders, both men and women (1 Timothy 5:1–2, 17–20)

It is likely that the widows described in 1 Timothy 5:3–16 are not simply women members of the church who have lost their husbands, but women who have special roles now that they no longer have obligations toward a husband and children. They would resemble the women who in more modern times were members of religious orders.

preacher are mentioned (1 Timothy 2:7), the chief function of the writer, who assumes the place of Paul, is that of teacher of the Gentiles. Timothy is portrayed here as the prime example of someone who has been reared in such a process of instruction (2 Timothy 3:14–15). It is wholly appropriate, therefore, that the author's instruction to Timothy, which begins as advice about preaching, shifts into counsel and warning about his role as a teacher (2 Timothy 4:1–4). Titus is given similar advice about teaching sound doctrine (Titus 2:1–9), where what is important is not only the content of his instruction but also his own mode of life as exemplifying the sound teaching. To characterize the lifestyle that he sees as fitting for Christians, the author uses throughout these letters terms never found in Paul but related to Greek philosophical concepts, such as *sophrosune*, which implies rationality, decency, and orderliness. This approach to instruction in the Church fits perfectly with what we have already observed about the stress on and definition of piety.

The epistles conclude with some personal remarks and greetings, as do the letters of Paul (2 Timothy 3:10–13, 4:6–13, 19–21; Titus 1:5–9, 3:12–13). In the course of these, reference is made to Paul's imprisonment and possible martyrdom, and there is mention of several of the associates of Paul known from Acts and from his letters. These are probably included to lend a sense of continuity between the historical Paul and later developments, as we find them embodied in these letters. Further links with earlier New Testament tradition appear in 2 Timothy 4:11, where Mark and Luke are mentioned. But at times the attempt at a personal note fails. Who could imagine the author of Galatians or 1 Corinthians or Philippians saying that he served God "from ancestral origins with clean conscience" (2 Timothy 1:3) – without mention of his career as a persecutor of Christians? And where is Paul's complex relationship with Moses in this unqualified assertion (2 Timothy 3:16): "All Scripture is God-inspired and useful for teaching, for reproof, for correction, and for training in righteousness"? Clearly, the farther the community moved from its origins in the first generation of Jesus' followers, the more important it became to affirm the continuity of the tradition. That continuity is dramatically demonstrated in the observation that Timothy, following in the tradition of his mother and his grandmother, is now a third-generation member of the Christian faith (2 Timothy 1:5).

III. CHRISTIANITY RESPONDS TO FORMATIVE JUDAISM

After the destruction of the Temple, the annihilation by Roman armies of many cities in addition to Jerusalem, and the eclipse of any semblance of Israelite political autonomy, Judaism underwent profound changes that proved to have enduring effects. With the fall of Jerusalem in 70 C.E., at least three major groups within Judaism headed toward extinction,

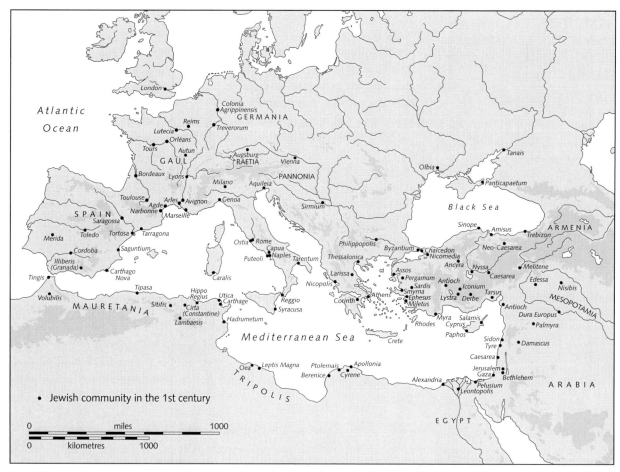

Map XIX. Major Jewish communities at the beginning of the second and third centuries C.E.

although at different rates: (1) nationalists with their programs of unsuccessful revolt, who resurfaced dramatically during the second century, only to be definitively obliterated by the Romans; (2) priestly coalitions, including the Sadducees and the aristocratic families that dominated Palestine politically through their collaboration with Rome; (3) the Essenes, whose community center at Qumran (together with their neighborhoods in other cities) was ruined by the Roman armies as they passed through that area. The Romans came to support the Pharisees as the one surviving group that could maintain Judaism as a legal religion without fomenting the tendency to revolt against Rome. Evidence for this development is late and largely inferential, but the pattern seems clear: the Pharisaic movement, with its transfer of ritual purity from the Temple to the voluntary gatherings in homes and public halls, was ideally suited to provide Jews with an ongoing structure of social and religious identity following the destruction of their priestly and political leadership.

Leaders of the Pharisees after the destruction of the Temple are reported in later tradition to have had an extended series of meetings at Yavneh (or Jamnia, as it is called in Greek) on the seacoast not far from modern

Tel Aviv. Whatever precise events lie behind this tradition about a council at Yavneh, beginning around 85 C.E. the patterns for Judaic piety began to be formulated and the increasingly powerful Rabbis (as Pharisees turned guides for the community of faith came to be called) even determined which of the sacred writings of Judaism were to be considered authoritative. During the second century C.E., after the failure of the second Jewish revolt against the Romans in 132–5 and the subsequent rebuilding of Jerusalem as a pagan capital, named Aelia Capitolina, the center for this formative movement shifted to Galilee. Meanwhile, a comparable development began among Rabbis who fled from Judea and Galilee to Babylonia in the wake of the failed revolts and their consequences; Jewish communities that had remained in Babylonia instead of returning to Judea from the Babylonian exile enriched the development of Babylonian Judaism. This process of rethinking and adapting Pharisaic tradition, the Scriptures, and the Torah of Moses, which the Rabbis believed both the Scriptures and their own teaching conveyed, continued for the next five centuries, reaching its climax in the development of patterns for instruction and worship that gave structure to and direction for the emergence of the synagogue in its institutional forms. That achievement included the creation of the Mishnah, the teaching of the sages of Rabbinic Judaism, and two Talmuds or commentaries on the Mishnah, one composed in the land of Israel and one in Babylonia. This formative process of Judaism seems to have been in frequent contact and competition with the emergent Christian church. The Gospel according to Matthew evidences the development of competing claims of Jews and Christians about the nature of, and requirements for, identity as God's covenant people.

At the same time, responses to the tensions that Jews throughout the Greco-Roman world had long felt between their traditions and the host cultures within which they lived continued to be articulated. In strongly Hellenized centers, such as Alexandria and Antioch, Jewish thinkers developed ways of synthesizing their biblical and cultural traditions with the most congenial products of pagan philosophical thought, especially the Platonic view of the structure of reality and the Stoic view of moral responsibility. Christians were attracted to this synthetic approach, as the letters of Paul show; that attraction is also clearly evident in the Letter of James and the Epistle to the Hebrews. On the other hand, some Jews continued to hold the apocalyptic view that the world and political power (whether the Hellenistic monarchs or Rome) was an agency of Satan. They believed God would soon intervene in human history, destroying the powers of evil and vindicating the faithful remnant of his people. The writings known as 2 Esdras and the *Book of Enoch*, which were not included in the Hebrew canon of Scripture but remained popular in the Diaspora as well as in territorial Israel, incorporate this outlook, as did such New Testament writings as Jude, 2 Peter, and Revelation. We begin our analysis of Christian responses to Judaism in the first century C.E. with a survey of the Gospel according to Matthew.

MISHNAH AND TALMUD

By 200 C.E. the Rabbis had developed a sophisticated understanding of the Torah, both as written in the Scriptures and, more characteristically, as evolved through a tradition of oral law they said also went back to Moses on Sinai. Their authoritative interpretation enabled their form of Judaism to survive after the destruction of the Temple, where worship had been an axiom in the Hebrew Bible, and to adjust to the often dislocating changes that came after 70 C.E. Rabbi Judah the Prince organized these legal materials into sixty-three tractates, grouped within six major divisions: agricultural laws, feasts, women and marriage, violations of the rights of others, sacrifice at the Temple, and ritual purity. This written distillation of oral law was known as the Mishnah. Regulations concerning the Temple, for which any practical hope of rebuilding perished with the collapse of the Bar Kokhba revolt in 135 C.E., became increasingly theoretical over time, but since so much of the Mosaic

Law dealt with the Temple cult, it had to be treated in any comprehensive discussion of the legal tradition. In effect, meditation and discussion of the laws of sacrifice took the place of sacrifice itself. This adjustment to the circumstances after 70 C.E. fed the growing Rabbinic conviction that, whatever conditions on the ground might look like, the Torah of Moses remained eternal and inviolate in heaven.

The Talmud was a later development and interpretation of the Mishnah; in fact, it is arranged as a commentary on the Mishnah. Two concurrent projects of Talmudic commentary were launched, one in Galilee and one slightly later in Babylonia. (Some Jews had continued to live in Babylon after others had begun to return from exile there during the sixth century B.C.E., and, much later, Babylon became increasingly attractive to Jewish settlers, as Roman policy became stricter, especially after the rise of Christianity.) These collec-

tions consist of detailed discussions of the same and related materials presented in the Mishnah, together with comparisons among the differing points of view and disparate perspectives. Although most of the Talmud was written in Aramaic, parts of it are in Hebrew, and some elements in either language may claim great antiquity. The Palestinian Talmud (fifth century C.E.) consists of discussion of the first four themes of the Mishnah, and the Babylonian Talmud (sixth century C.E.) offers interpretations concerning feasts, women, rights violations, and sacrifices. Since the Mishnah and Talmud emerged centuries later than the New Testament, and since they picture a Judaism with structures and concepts for which there is no evidence in the first century C.E., only a small proportion of the material from them is appropriate as a basis for comparison between Jewish and early Christian interpretation of the Law of Moses.

A. The Gospel According to Matthew

The Gospel according to Matthew is anonymous except for the title ("According to Matthew") that was added after its composition, as in the case of the other Gospels. When the Church of the second century sought to accord authority to its Gospels, it assigned each of them to an apostle or an associate of an apostle. In about 130, Papias attributed this Gospel to Matthew (who seems also to have been known as Levi; cf. Matthew 9:9 and Mark 2:13) and claimed that the author wrote it in Hebrew (or in Aramaic, as the Greek text of Papias might also mean). But Matthew's author (or authors) used the Greek Gospel according to Mark – or material virtually identical to Mark – as a source, and its many scriptural quotations are from the Greek translation (the Septuagint) rather than directly from the Hebrew Bible. Although we cannot determine who the author was, careful analysis shows what Matthew's concerns were, and on what basis this Gospel modified and expanded earlier traditions. The issues that prove central for this Gospel reflect the developments

Early manuscript of the Gospel according to Matthew. This manuscript dates from the third century and is an example of papyrus, a writing material made from a type of reed that grew abundantly in the Nile Delta. Cut into thin strips and pressed together, papyrus was readily available and surprisingly durable in the dry climate of Egypt. Containing parts of the first chapter of Matthew, this is one of the oldest surviving copies of that book. (University of Pennsylvania)

described earlier that were taking place in Judaism after 70 C.E. Those concerns can be grouped under three themes: how God has reconstituted his covenant people; the correct interpretation of the Law and the Prophets; and how Jesus is God's agent to establish divine rule over the earth. This Gospel emphasizes both the continuities between Jesus and the biblical tradition, and the radically new dimensions of covenantal identity and obligation that God has introduced through Jesus. For convenience we refer to all the authors involved in the process of composition of his Gospel as "Matthew."

1. The Structure and Method of Matthew

More than the other Gospels, Matthew seems to have been consciously structured. An introductory section sets forth the origins of Jesus and his links with Judaic tradition. A climactic concluding section describes Jesus' historic fate and divine destiny. In between are five main sections, each of which begins with a narrative account of Jesus' words and works and ends with a cluster of his teachings, unified in each instance by style and content and ending in the stylized phrase: "When Jesus had finished . . ." These phrases appear at 7:28, 11:1, 13:53, 19:1, and 26:1. The resulting structure is as follows:

Chapters 1–2	The divine origins of Jesus
Chapters 3–25	The words and works of Jesus in preparation for the covenant community:

Narrative	Discourse
Chapters 3–4	Chapters 5–7 (Sermon on the Mount)
Chapters 8–9	Chapter 10 (commissioning of the twelve disciples)
Chapters 11–12	Chapter 13 (parables of the kingdom)
Chapters 14–17	Chapter 18 (rules of the community)
Chapters 19–22	Chapters 24–5 (apocalyptic instruction)

Chapters 26–8	The divine destiny of Jesus and his followers

The fivefold structure of the middle section recalls the five books of Moses. This impression is strengthened by the explicit contrast between Jesus' rules for his people and those given by Moses in the first discourse (Matthew 5:21, 27, 31, 33, 38, 43). Just as Moses went up on the mountain to give instruction to God's people (Deuteronomy 8:1–2), so Jesus repeatedly in Matthew ascends a mountain to inform God's people and to manifest his divine authority (Matthew 4:8, 5:1, 14:23, 15:29, 39, 17:1, 28:19–20). In Jesus' sketch of his people's responsibility to God in this Gospel there is a distinctive emphasis on true righteousness, in contrast to that of the Pharisaic tradition (3:15; 5:6, 10, 20; 6:1, 33). That theme is most fully developed in a discourse section that does not fit the pattern sketched in our outline and seems to have been added to earlier traditions of the Gospel as the hostility between Matthew's community and the Pharisees (or Rabbis) intensified (Matthew 23).

The opening section of the Gospel stresses the divine purpose at work through Jesus; Jesus' genealogy is traced back to Abraham (the progenitor of the covenant people) through David (both Israel's king and the model for the future rule of God) and the exile (Matthew 1:2, 6, 12). The claim that Israel's history developed in a sequence of epochs covering fourteen generations in each stage (1:17) is presented as further evidence of a divine scheme. As in Daniel 2:2, the divine purpose is disclosed to the characters in the drama through dreams – not only to Mary, Joseph, and the wise men (1:20; 2:12, 13, 19, 22) but, in the concluding section, to Pilate's wife, as well (27:19). A second mode of communication of God's purpose for his people takes the form of the private explanations that Jesus offers to his followers about his teachings.

Confirmation that God's plan is being achieved through Jesus is offered to the faithful by Matthew's pervasive allusions to, or quotations from, the Scriptures of Israel. A formula of fulfillment frames the events portrayed as having taken place "in order to fulfill what was spoken . . ." (or similar phraseology: 2:15, 17–18, 23; 4:14–16; 8:17; 12:17–21; 13:14–15, 35; 24:4–5; 27:9–100). At times Matthew shapes the quotation to fit the event or circumstance in Jesus' life, as in the claim that the Scriptures predicted Jesus' living in Nazareth, whereas the Hebrew Bible never predicts a redeemer from Nazareth but presents two nonlocal terms: *nazir*, or "Nazirite" refers to a special consecration to God (Numbers 6:2–21; Leviticus 21:12), and *netzer*, which means "shoot" (Isaiah 11:1, 53:2). Elsewhere Matthew shapes the events reported in order to make them fit the Scriptures, as when Jesus is described riding into Jerusalem on *two* animals, since the mount is referenced by two different expressions in Scripture (Matthew 21:7; Zechariah 9:9). In this example, Matthew may show a certain ignorance of the basic structure of Hebrew poetry, parallelism. Nonetheless, the aim is clear, and the method similar to that of Jewish interpretation in the period: the interpreter of Scripture focuses on what it means in his own situation rather than in what it meant in the time of the writer.

2. The New Law for the People of God (Matthew 4–7)

Building on both the Markan narrative and features from the Q source, Matthew portrays Jesus as the authoritative Son of God, whose identity is publicly affirmed at his baptism (Matthew 3:17). Gentile participation in

Today a city, Nazareth in the first century was a tiny hamlet of several hundred people that lay high in the hills near Sepphoris, a garrison and seat of government in Galilee. Crossing the more level land below were the major highways connecting with Damascus in the north, the cities along the Sea of Galilee and farther east, the seaports to the west, and Jericho and Jerusalem to the south. (BiblePlaces.com)

God's people is shown to have scriptural precedent in the prophecy of Isaiah (4:13–16). According to Matthew 4:23–5, Jesus' reputation as a healer spread at the outset of his ministry throughout the whole of Galilee, Judea, and the Hellenistic cities east of the Jordan (the Decapolis). Yet the first instructions are addressed, not to the crowds that flocked to him to see and experience his healings, but to his disciples as the original core of the people of God (5:1). Instead of the direct, immediate address of the Q tradition – "Blessed are you poor" (Luke 6:20) – Matthew portrays Jesus as teaching from a more spiritual perspective: "Blessed are the poor in spirit . . ." (5:3). For Matthew the emphasis also shifts from the expectation of future fulfillment ("Blessed are you who hunger now: you shall be satisfied"; Luke 6:21) to the promise of entering now into a share in the blessings of God's rule. As a result, we have the picture of a community hoping for future fulfillment but prepared for an extended period in its present mode of existence.

Meanwhile, the community is given a series of interpretations of the biblical law on subjects that continued to be important for Jews but that are now redefined for the members of Matthew's community. Matthew contrasts the norms of Pharisaic piety with those binding on the Christian community in an array of subjects: basic relations with others, sexual behavior and divorce, oaths, nonretaliation, love of enemies, almsgiving, prayer, fasting, possessions, anxiety, judging others. Jesus approaches these moral issues in Matthew not only in terms of what is legally required or permissible but also with a view to responsible, caring ways of relating to God and one's fellow human beings. This constitutes for Matthew the true and greater righteousness, which fulfills the intention of God for his people through the Law and the Prophets (5:17–20).

3. Preparing the Disciples for Their Mission (Matthew 8–10)

Building on the Markan tradition about the sending out of the twelve disciples (Mark 3:13–19, 6:1–11), Matthew has used the Q source, as well as its own distinctive material, to give an extended picture of Jesus commissioning his followers to carry his purpose forward. Matthew 8–9 present a mixture of private instruction for the disciples and demonstration that those who by the standards of Pharisaic piety are outsiders have access to the healing and forgiving power of God through Jesus. A transition passage (Matthew 7:28–9) announces that, in contrast to the Pharisaic scribes, who quoted authorities to back up their interpretations of the law, Jesus had authority in himself. This authority is evidenced dramatically in his stilling the storm, when his followers address him as "Lord" (kurios), which already as early as the time of Paul had become a confessional title for Jesus (Philippians 2:9–11). Yet he also is seen as having taken on the authoritative role of teacher, since his critics object to his setting aside ritual custom in order to eat with outsiders (Matthew 9:11).

The disciples are to carry out their mission exclusively among "the lost sheep of the house of Israel" (Matthew 10:6). This phrase does not mean that all historic Israel is lost, but that there is a place among God's people for those Jews unbounded by Pharisaic strictures of religious acceptability. These people are portrayed consistently in Matthew as the special objects of Jesus' concern. The advice to the messengers is that they are to carry forward the work that Jesus had begun: heal the sick, raise the dead, cleanse the "lepers," cast out demons (10:8). They are to go out dependent solely on the hospitality that is offered them in the cities and villages they visit in the course of their mission. The destiny of the inhabitants of each place will depend on their response to Jesus' messengers (10:9–15, 40–2). The disciples are to be prepared for opposition, suffering, martyrdom, and violent hostility, even from the members of their own families (10:16–39).

4. Defining the New Community (Matthew 11–13)

The next narrative section depicts Jesus engaged in his healing activity, encountering opposition from the Pharisees as he opens his fellowship in a way that will allow the inclusion of Gentiles after the resurrection. His inclusiveness is defended by a quotation from Scripture (Matthew 12:18–21 = Isaiah 42:1–4) and by an appeal to examples of Gentile faith in the time of Jonah and Solomon (Matthew 12:38–42). Drawing on a tradition also in Mark (Mark 3:31–5), Matthew quotes Jesus as redefining membership in the family of God in such a way as to eliminate ethnic or ritual requirements (Matthew 12:46–50).

Even though Jesus is pictured as presenting his parables to the "great crowds" (13:2), it is only to the inner circle of his followers that he gives the essential interpretations of them (13:10–17). In addition to the basic point of the Markan parables about the mixed but ultimately astounding results of the proclamation of the gospel, Matthew adds parables that make a different point: that the new community that is in process of formation will include among its members both those who are worthy and those who are not. There is good and bad seed (13:24–30), weeds and wheat (13:36–43), choice fish and unfit fish (13:47–8), as Jesus' private explanation makes clear (13:49–50). The point is that the Christian community will include both suitable and unacceptable members, but the process of sorting them out is God's business at the end of the age.

5. Guidelines for the New Community (Matthew 14–18)

After the characteristic transition passage ("when Jesus had finished . . ."; 13:53), Matthew presents additional examples of how the message will reach outsiders (14:1–15:39) and of ensuing conflict with the Jewish leaders (16:1–4). These are followed by Peter's confession of Jesus as the Messiah, which is expanded significantly compared to the Markan presentation (Mark 8:27–33; Matthew 16:13–23). Peter's messianic identification of Jesus includes the phrase "the Son of the living God" (16:16) and elicits from Jesus an indication of the divine source of this belief. But Matthew then goes on to speak of Peter's confession as the rock on which the church will be built and to promise that this new community will prevail despite opposition from the evil powers. Further, Peter will be given the crucial authority to include or to exclude those within the community (16:18–19). Peter's insight is confirmed within the week (17:1) by the experience Jesus' Transfiguration with heavenly testimony to him as God's Son (17:5). Unlike in Mark (9:6), there is no comment in Matthew that the disciples did not understand the significance of these events. Meanwhile, there is to be no hostility toward Rome: Christians are to meet the demands of the state, whether for assistance in providing transportation (5:41) or in paying the tax that had been collected for support of the Jerusalem Temple but that now (after the Jewish revolt and the destruction of the Temple) supported the shrine to Jupiter built in its place in Rome (17:24–7). God will provide what is necessary to meet these human obligations. Paying taxes to Caesar is confirmed later in Matthew (22:15–22), as well.

The discourse that brings this section of Matthew to a close includes instructions for the members of the new community: the model of being like children (18:1–4); the need for nurturing these childlike members (18:5–6); the avoidance of temptation (18:7–9); the necessity of restoring those who stray (18:10–14); and informal (18:15–16) and formal (18:17–20) procedures for settling disputes within the church. The section ends with advice (18:21–3) and a parable (18:23–35) about the importance of forgiveness for the health of the community.

Only in Matthew is the "church" (*ekklesia*) referred to as such. The new community is also spoken of in Matthew (as in the other Gospels) by means of metaphors, such as "flock" (Matthew 26:31; Luke 12:32; John 10:16), but Matthew alone quotes Jesus as referring to the new community as a "church," with indications of its growth and structure ("on this rock I will build my church"; Matthew 16:18) and of the decision-making process that will go on in this new institution (Matthew 18:15–18). These passages show that this Gospel is meant to serve as a guidebook for the Church as it develops institutional form and function, enabling it to understand its origins and its ongoing responsibilities.

6. Vindication for Jesus and the New Community; Judgment on Israel, the People of God (Matthew 19–25)

Related concerns occupy the next section, following the transition in Matthew 19:1: attitudes toward sex and marriage, including divorce and remarriage as well as abstinence (19:1–12). Attitudes toward children (19:13–15) and wealth (19:16–30) appear once more. A parable unique to Matthew (20:1–16) deals with the church's problem with the seeming inequality of responsibility and reward among its members by declaring flatly that God's sovereign decisions are not subject to human review. The disciples are shielded by Matthew from appearing to vie for positions of power in the new age (as they do in Mark 10:35–45) by having the mother of the sons of Zebedee make the request for places of special honor for them (Matthew 20:20–8). As occurs in Matthew 8:28–34 and 9:27–31, Matthew increases the miraculous feature of Jesus' activity by reporting that he healed not one but two blind men as he passed through Jericho (20:29–34; cf. Mark 10:46–52).

The issues about Jesus' claim to be king are much more explicit in Matthew than in Mark, as is the prediction of God's judgment on historic Israel. The formula quotation ("this took place to fulfill what was spoken by the prophet") from Zechariah 9:9 and Isaiah 62:11 in Matthew 21:4–5 is followed by the direct identification of Jesus as king and son of David (21:5, 9) and as the prophet (21:11) – presumably the one expected at the end of the age (Deuteronomy 18:15–18), who, like Moses, performs signs and wonders (Deuteronomy 34:10–12). Matthew returns to the issue of the source of Jesus' authority in cleansing the Temple (21:12–13), in healing the blind and the lame (21:14–17), and in cursing the fig tree (i.e., the Temple; 21:18–22). The basic question here is, Who authorizes and empowers Jesus to carry out his work: God or some evil power? A corollary question is, Who are the true heirs of God's promises to his covenant people?

These issues become explicit in the interchange reported in Matthew 21:23–7. Its implications for reconstituting God's people are evident in a series of parables, including the parable of the two sons, where the climax comes in the prediction that tax collectors and harlots will enter the kingdom (21:28–32), and the parable of the vineyard workers, which insists explicitly that the kingdom will be taken from its traditional heirs and given to a new nation, that is, the Church (21:43). Matthew offers a different version of the Q-source parable of the guests invited to a feast (Matthew 22:1–14; Luke 14:16–24), in which Israel is depicted as rejecting and killing God's messengers, with the result that the king (God) destroys their city (Jerusalem) and now invites all manner of people to enjoy the feast. Yet when the feast takes place, those who are not properly attired (i.e., clothed in true righteousness) will be expelled and brought under judgment.

Beginning at Matthew 22:23 and extending through chapter 23, we find a series of controversies between Jesus and Jewish teachers on such subjects as resurrection (22:23–33), the priority among the commandments (22:34–40), and the identity of the Messiah (22:41–5). In these Matthew largely follows Mark. But from 23:1–36 a series of bitter attacks on the Pharisees appears, in which they are denounced as religious show-offs (23:1–12), as more zealous in making converts to Judaism than in living in true obedience to God (23:13–15), and as evading the clear import of the Law by subtle tactics (23:16–28). The climax of this section comes in the charge that the Jewish people have always rejected and even put to death the messengers of God, from the beginning (Genesis) to the end (2 Chronicles) of their Scriptures (Matthew 23:29–36). God is about to judge them for their refusal to hear his messengers, including Jesus, who is seen by Matthew as the fulfillment of the messianic hope expressed in Psalm 118:26 (quoted in Matthew 23:39).

The details of these impending judgments are spelled out in Matthew's extended version of the Markan apocalyptic discourse (Matthew 24–5), which (as in Mark 13) is spoken on the Mount of Olives overlooking Jerusalem. Here we find predictions of the difficulties within the community caused by the emergence of false prophets and of lawlessness, hatred, and indifference among the members of the group (24:9–14). Similarly, Matthew adds to the Q-source parable about the servants who misbehave when their master delays his return (Luke 12:42–6) the prediction of the weeping and gnashing of teeth that the unfaithful will experience in the Day of Judgment (24:45–51). In addition to the Markan tradition about the certainty that the end of the age is near (Mark 13:28–32; Matthew 24:32–6), Matthew has the distinctive parable of the ten maidens (25:1–13), with its point about the need for being prepared for the bridegroom's delayed return, and the parable of the talents (adapted from Q; Luke 19:12–27), which shows that responsible stewardship is necessary when the master at last returns (Matthews 25:19) and calls his servants to account (25:14–30). The discourse ends with the pageant-like depiction of the judgment at the end of the age, when the nations of the world are accepted or condemned by one criterion: how they responded to the messengers ("the little ones") whom Jesus had sent to work and witness among them. In accepting or rejecting these representatives of Christ they had accepted or rejected him (25:31–46).

7. The Destiny of Jesus and God's New People (Matthew 26–8)

The final transition (Matthew 26:1) brings the reader to Matthew's account of Jesus' experience of human rejection and divine vindication (chapters 26–8). The basic pattern of the narrative is like that of Mark 14–16, but there are significant supplements and changes in detail, many of which reflect the tensions between the Church and Judaism. Matthew 26:2 and 53–6 directly predict Jesus' death and his impending vindication by God, in accord with Scripture (possibly Psalm 91:11 or the vision of Elisha in 2 Kings 6:17). Judas' gruesome death and the payment he received for his betrayal fulfill the Scripture according to Matthew (27:3–10; cf. Zechariah 11:12–13; Jeremiah 32:7). The judgment on Judas, the earthquake that occurs at the moment of Jesus' death (27:51–3), and the descent of the angel and the earthquake at the tomb of Jesus (28:2) are for Matthew signs of God's direct involvement in the passion of Jesus and the outworking of the divine purpose through him. Pilate's washing his hands in public (27:24–6), combined with the Jewish acceptance of responsibility for the death of Jesus, shifts the blame from Rome to the Jews. The report of the disciples' having stolen the body of Jesus is also attributed to the Jewish leaders (28:11–15).

Matthew alters the Markan story of the women disciples' visit to Jesus' tomb (Mark 16:1–8) and provides details of the promised appearances of Jesus to his followers. Matthew heightens the supernatural features of traditions it shared with Mark, and the instructions for the disciples are more explicit than in Mark. Both these elements reflect the growing sense in the

TALENTS AND MINAS (POUNDS)

Two different kinds of coins are mentioned in the two versions of the parable usually called the parable of the talents in Luke 19:12–27 and Matthew 25:14–30. According to Luke, the money given to the slaves by the nobleman was a *mina*, which was equal to 100 drachmas (in Greek coinage) and has been estimated as three months' wages for a skilled laborer. The *talent* in Matthew's account amounted to better than seventy pounds of precious metal, the unit in which a region would pay its taxes to Rome, rather than a household measure, so that the responsibility placed on the slaves in this version is far heavier.

Obviously, a talent was not something the people Jesus spoke to had ever encountered in their lives. Matthew's Jesus deliberately referred to talents to convey the idea of unimaginable wealth. In a similar vein, the parable of the unforgiving debtor in Matthew 18:23–35 speaks of owing a myriad of talents. Compare that to the annual revenue paid to Herod Antipas by Galilee and Perea together: that was only two hundred talents. Jesus was speaking here, almost as a child would, of an astronomical sum.

Why use these outlandish numbers? It was to refer to an overwhelming reality, whether the debt we owe to God (in the parable of the unforgiving debtor) or the riches God bestows on us (in the parable of the talents; Matthew 25:14–30). In the Aramaic language, "debt" was the usual way to refer to sin, and the parable of the unforgiving debtor extrapolates from that metaphor. Then, in the parable of the talents, the image is pushed further: we owe God not only the deficit we have

incurred, but an account for the wealth he has given us in trust.

Jesus' deliberate hyperbole, his surrealism about money, is more easily understood when his own economic background is remembered. The economy of the small villages and hamlets Jesus frequented did not function day to day on the basis of currency. Currency indeed featured prominently when regions paid their tax to Rome, and in the great cities that grew up under Roman hegemony in Galilee and Judea. But what is stunning about Jesus' itinerary is that it did *not* center on the great cities that recent archaeological work has taught us much about: Tiberias, Sepphoris, or Caesarea. Jesus avoided those places in favor of Capernaum about as easily as he dismissed Caesar's coin as of small importance compared to what is God's (see Matthew 22:21; Mark 12:17; Luke 20:25).

In the rural Galilee that was the primary focus of Jesus' movement, currency was not the ordinary medium of survival. That kind of moneyed transaction, which grew up in urban environments and now dominates our daily practice and thinking, was simply not the rule. Indeed, not even barter was the norm. A person from one village might barter with a person from another village occasionally and trade with currency might happen within a city, but within the village or hamlet the exchange of goods and services would occur based on people's status in that place. The status of belonging to a community entitled people, with their various abilities and weaknesses, to the living that community was capable of. That is one reason Jesus focused on such places: in a small village, the policy

of giving freely and taking freely was already established (see Matthew 10:8). Part of his purpose was, in the name of God's kingdom, to supplant the economy based on currency with an economy based on exchange. Instead of making the city the model of Israel, the village was to show the way.

For that reason, when Jesus does speak of currency, the imagery is surreal (and Matthew probably appreciates and enhances that surrealism). He is not talking about actual amounts in the experience of the people he is addressing, nor is he advocating any action they could expect to imitate. Rather, the currency is symbolic of the unimaginable wealth involved when we owe God, because humans have no resources to repay God apart from what he has already given them.

People of wealth – and that includes most people living in the West today – understand that they do not need encouragement to make yet more money. Their problem is the eye of the needle and how to get through it (see Matthew 19:23–6; Mark 10:23–7; Luke 18:24–7). When Jesus speaks of "talents" he does not refer only to monetary investment; his target is the divine endowment that has been bestowed on us. The worst thing, the only bad thing, that can be done with that trust is not to expand on it. Just keeping it safe and hidden is precisely what Jesus does not want; in this regard again, the investment he speaks of is strange, because risks are not to be avoided. Stagnation is worse than risk, because the aim of what we do with God's talents should be their extension so as to magnify rather than reduce forgiveness.

PILATE, THE POLITICS OF ROME, AND EVANGELICAL POLITICS

Controversy regarding Jesus' death and the responsibility for his execution comes with the regularity of spring, prompted by the Christian calendar of worship that recollects Jesus' passion at the end of Lent. The issue of Jewish culpability – often pitched in terms of the guilt of Jews, sometimes as a people – features as the starting point.

Yet in first-century C.E. Judea Rome alone exercised authority to carry out crucifixion. By beginning with the perspective of Pontius Pilate, we can better assess the presentation of the Gospels, and counteract a prominent cause of anti-Semitism in the Christian West. Pilate confronted a difficult situation on two fronts in the autumn of 31 C.E. The first problem must have seemed routine at the outset. A rabbi named Jesus had disputed with the high priest Caiaphas concerning commercial arrangements inside the Temple. Given the number of times Josephus refers to Galilean disturbances there during the first century, one more incident like the others can hardly have daunted Pilate.

Yet Jesus' incursion had temporarily halted the conduct of sacrifice in the Temple (Mark 11:15–17), and that kind of interference directly engaged the interests of Rome. To the Romans, one potent symbol of their rule over the Jews was that the high priest accepted offerings that the emperor paid for every day, in effect interceding with God on the emperor's behalf and on the behalf of the Roman hegemony. The fact that many people in Jerusalem resisted Caiaphas's efforts to centralize power in his own hands – as Rabbinic sources show – did not concern Pilate directly. The fact that someone went into the

Great Court with enough force – amounting to between 150 and 200 men – to evict traders, drive out animals, and break up the cages for birds, most obviously did.

While Jesus pursued his dispute about arrangements in the Temple, events in Rome had altered the political landscape around him in ways that he himself could not begin to fathom. Emperor Tiberius sent a letter from Capri, which he ordered read before the Senate in the presence of Sejanus, the strong man of Rome. Sejanus had overreached himself. This apparently invincible regent, prefect of the nine-thousand-soldier Praetorian Guard, had become the target of several ambivalent messages from the emperor. Writing from his Villa of Jupiter on the island of Capri to the Senate, Tiberius expressed trenchant criticism of Sejanus's policy of arrogating judicial power against his detractors in Rome, while flattering Sejanus personally. Speculation grew in Rome that Sejanus's days were numbered.

Any concern Sejanus himself may have felt was overcome by recent rumors he had heard that Tiberius was about to promote him, making him second in command to the emperor himself within the empire. The Senate assembled on 18 October in the temple of Apollo on the Palatine and listened to the sort of long, rambling missive Tiberius had acquired the habit of sending. But the message became increasingly pointed in its criticism of Sejanus and at last accused him of treason.

At the end of the reading of the imperial letter, the *Vigiles* (local police) bound Sejanus and marched him to the Mamertine dungeon. A

crowd had gathered in the street, and they screamed in hatred as Sejanus was bullied past them. Tiberius had thrown them a scapegoat, someone to attack for all the dissatisfaction and hardship they knew. They ran wild, smashing the statues of himself that Sejanus had erected, and the forces of order in Rome did nothing to stop them. In his confinement, Sejanus might have hoped for a sentence of exile, rather then death, but the Senate knew to act quickly, before Sejanus could attempt to resort to the nine thousand crack troops of the Praetorian Guard under his command.

By the end of that same day, the Senate ordered Sejanus strangled, even for Rome a gruesome form of execution. Later, Pilate would learn of these events from traders and Roman functionaries recently arrived from Rome. The arrest of a high official on the charge of treason was enough to strike fear into any heart. But the gruesome tale went on and on. Sejanus's uncle and son were also killed, as were many of his friends and collaborators. His divorced wife, Apicata, committed suicide. Even his two young children were executed, the girl gang-raped by soldiers before she was dispatched. Livilla, to whom Sejanus was engaged, found little mercy, although she was a member of the imperial household. Her own mother, in a demonstration of fealty to the emperor, starved her daughter to death. The emperor's whims were as capricious as his power was boundles. As a well-known Jewish proverb (see Matthew 26:52 and Isaiah Targum 50:11) said, those who lived by the sword died by it. That applied especially to those who served the empire.

A strong working relationship with the high priest was now imperative for Pilate, like it or not, although earlier he had followed Sejanus's tendencies in pursuing a provocative policy toward the Jews and their leaders. He had no choice but to make common cause with Caiaphas. Through that redefinition of a vitally important alliance, Pilate showed himself a consummate politician. He bided his time. He would not appear weak in the sight of the people he ruled. The city was winding down for the winter in any case; the prefect was not going to act unless it was necessary, and then only when action was most clearly to his own benefit.

As if Jesus was not already in enough danger from the prefect and high priest, his old foe Antipas, tetrarch of Galilee and Perea, was also taking a keen interest in events in Rome and the tightening of the alliance between Pilate and Caiaphas. After all, it was Antipas's Galilean subjects who had been killed in Jerusalem during the riot of 30 C.E. (see Josephus, *Jewish War* 2.175–7; *Antiquities* 18.60–2; and Luke 13:1–3); Antipas felt that Pilate owed him a favor after the prefect's ruthless action and that this was a propitious moment to press the claim. More important, Antipas wanted to show himself both in command of his own territory and cooperative with other agents of Rome and local religious leaders in the uncertain circumstances after Sejanus's execution. Might he use his Roman colleague and priestly coreligionist to rid himself of Jesus at long last and solidify his position? Unless Antipas, Caiaphas, and Pilate together showed that they could effectively rule their

Jewish subjects, each of them was in danger of being stripped of his title, position, and power.

The nuances of the new common interest shared by the high priest, the prefect, and the tetrarch eluded Jesus as much as did the recently changed complexities of power in Rome. Politically, Jesus was now out of his depth. Jesus' action in the Temple was focused on the issue of sacrifice, but what he did unleashed a perfect storm of political opposition from Tiberius's Rome and Antipas's Galilee, as well as from the Jerusalem of Pilate and Caiaphas. Later interpretation has also shown itself naïve in treating Jesus' execution as if it were caused by objections to his teaching within Jewish opinion.

The best point of departure for understanding what the present generation of scholarship has made of Jesus' execution is Raymond E. Brown's monumental work *The Death of the Messiah*, Anchor Bible Reference Library 7 (New York: Doubleday, 1999), a nearly comprehensive treatment of the passion of Jesus. Brown proceeds pericope by pericope, analyzing both exegetical and historical issues in discrete sections within the context of the secondary literature. He correctly portrays events as centering on Jesus' confrontation in the Temple, which he sees as "prophetic dramatic action against improprieties in the Temple" (p. 458).

At the level of historical reconstruction (more prominent here than elsewhere in his book), Brown proposes that the Sanhedrin met concerning Jesus sometime before the arrest, much as the Gospel according to John (11:47–53) would suggest. Then the malefactor was brought before

Caiaphas immediately before he was denounced to Pilate. The entire scenario is developed within the framework of Brown's judicious discussion of the political realities in Jerusalem at the time (pp. 328–97). He is well aware of the objections to the historicity of the account of Jesus' trial: "The conflicts between the Gospel accounts of the trial and later rabbinic procedure . . . have sometimes been estimated at twenty-seven" (p. 358). He realizes that "the Sanhedrin" is not as described in Mishnah, that it had no capital jurisdiction, that it would not have convened at night or during Passover. In his reading, the Gospels reflect an "interrogation" of Jesus (rather than a trial) before two competent authorities, a council of elders and the high priest.

Brown summarizes his scheme in the following way (pp. 425, 557–60):

a Sanhedrin session was called to deal with Jesus

an issue in that session was the threat Jesus posed to the Temple

the one who urged the others to decide Jesus' death was the high priest

there was a judgment equivalent to a death sentence

there was an investigation of Jesus by the high priest on the night that he was arrested.

In short, Brown abstracts from the Gospels' account material he believes to be historical, recognizing that the bulk of the passage is pulled together for dramatic purposes.

Brown's concluding sentence may help us to assess his analysis overall:

The clarity and force of the unified trial presentation has moved and been remembered by hundreds of

(continued)

PILATE, THE POLITICS OF ROME, AND EVANGELICAL POLITICS *(continued)*

millions; the awkwardnesses have bothered a handful of scholars subjecting the narrative to microscopic examination.

In the very act of writing his book, Brown proved that he is one of the bothered few, but he also writes with a sense of responsibility for the outline of faith as presented in the Gospels. That dual loyalty involved him in some inconsistency.

Brown's analysis wisely accords much more weight to the issue of the Temple itself than had been conventional in writing until his time. He devotes an extensive section of his commentary to that general issue, but his overall concern is whether Jesus would have *said* anything against the Temple (as in Mark 14:58). He concludes that he would have, but the form of Brown's concern leads to a lack of focus about what Jesus *did*. Prophecies against the Temple had been traditional from the time of Jeremiah, and even under disturbed conditions much later (four years before the war against Rome), Jesus son of Ananias was scourged for his prophecy, not executed (see Josephus, *Jewish War* 6.300–9). Jesus of Nazareth evidently constituted a more pointed threat, both to the cultic authorities and to Pilate, whose chief interest was public order.

Brown, oddly, does not cite the contributions that address the arrangements in the Temple that Caiaphas innovated and that resulted in Jesus' occupation. Brown refers to some of the relevant Talmudic passages (Bavli Sanhedrin 41a; Shabbat 15a; Abodah Zarah 8b), but not in relation to the issue of Caiaphas's growing power. He does not refer to the evidence of Pharisaic actions akin to Jesus' (see Bavli Besa 20a–b and Mishnah Keritot 1:7), nor to the strong tradition of a failure in the efficacy of the Temple forty years prior to its destruction (Bavli Yoma 39b):

> Forty years before the destruction of the house, the lot did not come up in the right hand, the crimson strap failed to turn white, and the western light would not burn, and the gates of the Temple opened on their own . . .

In a commentary that is nearly comprehensive in its reach, these omissions are striking.

Because Brown does not develop an adequate understanding of the issue that divided Caiaphas and Jesus, he falls back on the argument that Jesus' "blasphemy" was that he spoke with authority and out of turn. Here Brown joins a tendency of pious scholarship that has been evident since the 1950s. While Brown concedes that Jesus made no direct messianic claim, the matter of Jesus' identity eclipses the issue of the Temple, although Brown had already shown that the Temple was the historical pivot of events. That is an example of the triumph of Christian apologetics over sound historical sense. No one can read the Talmudic episodes of Rabbinic actions in the Temple, including driving animals into the place and changing sacrificial requirements in order to control prices of offerings, and conclude that cultic arrangements were anything but contentious, or that claiming authority for oneself presented the biggest offense imaginable within that setting. Instead of exploring why Jesus appeared more threatening to the cultic authorities than his contemporaries did, Brown reverts to the picture of Jesus' "authority" causing the Sanhedrin to turn against him, with Caiaphas signing on at the last moment out of annoyance about something Jesus said in the Temple. The implicit assumption that inappropriate speech would automatically result in execution is implausible.

The same sort of implausibility afflicts the assertion that Jesus was put to death for claiming to be the Messiah or having people make that claim on his behalf. Brown's distortion is extended, when some scholars argue that Jesus' messianic claim provoked his death at Pilate's hands. Brown would probably not have agreed with those who extend his work in that way. The portrayal of the messianic issue reflects the perspective of those who told the story, rather than the perspective of Jesus, Caiaphas, or Pilate.

But that early Christian perspective is as important to appreciate as the perspective of Jesus, if we want to understand the Gospels (all of which were composed after 70 C.E.). Christians, as partisans of Christ, claimed that Jesus was the Son of God, and they therefore denied that Caesar was *divi filius*. That is what lead to their persecution and the pogroms against them at Roman hands from the time of the fire in Rome in 64 C.E. until Constantine's edict of Milan in 313 C.E. During that long period, the best that Christians could hope for was a Roman policy the equivalent of "don't ask, don't tell." In the correspondence between Pliny the Younger and Trajan during the second century, that is just what they got, and Tertullian rejoiced in the irony of that precedent.

The Gospels are in part designed to encourage that policy. We can see that in the unique additions each Gospel offers to get Pilate off the hook of the political responsibility he alone bore. In John, Jesus tells Pilate, "My kingdom is not of this world" (18:36). This exchange regarding political theory is not plausible. Luke alone among the Gospels has an acquittal pronounced at the moment of Jesus' death (Luke 23:47–8):

> The centurion standing by opposite him saw what happened and glorified God, saying, "In fact this person was righteous." And all the crowds that came upon this sight, observing what had happened, returned beating their breasts.

Mark is unique in having a befuddled Pilate "utterly astounded that he had already died" (15:44), as if he had not known that Jesus had been flogged prior to crucifixion. Matthew's Gospel is the most inventive, in passing on the legend of Pilate's wife (27:19), although prefects of Pilate's rank were not authorized to bring their wives on posting. In any case, Pilate and his entourage resided in Caesarea, not Jerusalem. Matthew is sensitive to the latter fact and has the wife "send" a message to Pilate.

By means of such embellishments and legends, early Christians supported the Roman "don't ask, don't tell" policy and deflected blame for Jesus' crucifixion as best they could from the Romans. In doing so, they wound up repeating a version of what Paul, Silvanus, and Timothy said in 1 Thessalonians. Those writers fiercely asserted that the Pharisaic teachers from Judea who had tried to prevent contact with Gentiles formed an obstacle to their preaching (2:14): "For you, brothers, became imitators of the churches of God that are in Judea in Jesus Christ, because you also suffered the same things from your kinspeople as they did from the Jews."

This refers back to the deep contention in Jerusalem among Jewish followers of Jesus. Paul, Silas, and Timothy are using the word "Jews" (Ioudaioi in Greek) to mean the people back in Judea who wished to "forbid us to speak to the Gentiles" (2:16). They had some disciples of Jesus in mind, teachers such as those Pharisees who believed in Jesus' message but insisted that circumcision was a requirement of salvation (Acts 15:5). But the same term could also be used during the first century C.E. (and later, of course) to mean any practitioners of Judaism anywhere, and that is the sense of the word "Jew" in common usage. The lineal descendant of 1 Thessalonians 2:16 is the Wagnerian crowd in Matthew 27:25 that declares, "His blood is on us and on our children."

So the three companions, writing to Thessalonica and dealing with local issues and recent history, spoke in a way that has encouraged anti-Semitism. Matthew's encouragement of that attitude is more extreme.

Church of the importance of divine confirmation of the claims made concerning Jesus as the Messiah and divine agent of renewal of God's people. The women who go to prepare the body of Jesus experience an earthquake, and the message they hear about Jesus' having been raised from the dead is not from a "young man," as in Mark, but from an angel who comes down to them from heaven (28:2–8). This is confirmed by an appearance of Jesus to the women on their way back to the city from the tomb (28:9–10) and then by his meeting the disciples (significantly, on a mountain) in Galilee (28:16–20). In this postresurrection encounter between Jesus and the disciples, the emphasis is on two themes: (1) the authority with which Jesus sends forth his disciples, and (2) the disciples' obligation to carry out a worldwide program of instruction in the commandments that Jesus has given them. The members of this new community of disciples from all nations are united by the rite of baptism, by the Trinitarian confession with which that rite is performed, and by the members' obedience to Jesus' commands. The combination of community definition over against emergent Rabbinic Judaism, of regulations for members' behavior and for the internal processes of the organization, and of prescriptions for liturgical practice provide clear evidence that the Gospel according to Matthew was intended to serve as a constitution for an emerging institution: the Church.

B. The Epistle to the Hebrews: Interpreting the Covenant for the Hellenistic Church

In the last century B.C.E. and the first century C.E., many Jewish thinkers in the Diaspora sought to make connections between the philosophical and literary traditions of the Hellenistic culture and their tradition. The *Fourth Book of Maccabees*, with its retelling of the struggle of the Jews for freedom from the Seleucids, pictures these events as exercises in the Stoic virtues of courage and perseverance. Using Platonic ideas of God, and assuming compatibility between knowledge of God as set forth in Scripture and as gained through human insight in Greek philosophy, the Jewish philosopher and interpreter of Scripture Philo of Alexandria describes in allegorical terms the experiences of the patriarchs and the establishment of the central cult of ancient Israel. It is not surprising, therefore, that the Christians of the later first century should take their cue from this intellectual precedent in Judaism and conceive their own heritage as a synthesis of biblical tradition and Hellenistic philosophy. A prime example of this development within early Christianity is the Epistle to the Hebrews.

Although this document has often been called "Paul's Letter to the Hebrews," Paul clearly did not write it, and it was not addressed primarily to Hebrews. Rather, this literary epistle, an artful reworking of the letter form, recast the Christian tradition along lines that made possible its communication to intellectually trained minds in the Roman world. The Epistle to the Hebrews builds throughout on the biblical tradition and contrasts

---

PHILO OF ALEXANDRIA

Philo, a wealthy and learned Jew of Alexandria, lived from ca. 25 B.C.E. until ca. 45 C.E. Philo came from a family of aristocrats; his brother served the Romans as a treasury official in Egypt and enjoyed excellent relations with Herod Agrippa. Philo's own vast, erudite corpus of work flowed from a cosseted life whose ornament was well-spent leisure. In all the ornate twists and turns and genuine complexity of his thought, Philo was committed to the fundamental Diaspora principle that the best that Greek philosophy had to offer and the Torah of Moses together attested the power and the moral character of one God, the God of Israel. His energies were devoted to interpreting the five books of Moses (Genesis through Deuteronomy) in such a way as to show by allegorical method the basic compatibility of Greek philosophy and biblical understanding. The migration of Abraham from Ur of the Chaldees to Hebron in what became the land of Israel, for example, he interpreted as an allegory of the seeking soul who moves from the realm of shadowy perceptions of reality to direct encounter with an illumination by the light of God. This corresponds to the Platonic vision of the flight of the soul from the physical world, which is subject to decay and misperceptions, through the world of the forms (or ideas), where the fundamental principles of the universe are discerned, to the direct vision of the divine. Philo believed that Plato had these insights into truth and the proper mode of apprehending it because of Plato's access to the writings of Moses. Philo's method of interpreting Scripture and his striving to correlate philosophical wisdom and the truth contained in the Scriptures set the pattern followed chiefly by Christian scholars in Alexandria in the second and third centuries C.E.

THE AUTHORSHIP OF HEBREWS

The Epistle to the Hebrews has long stood as an enigma within the New Testament. "Who knows who wrote the Epistle?" asked Origen in the third century; he answered the question himself, "God knows!" But the enigma of Hebrews goes beyond the question of who wrote it; when and where it was written and to whom are also issues of lively debate.

It is natural to wish to answer such questions as clearly as possible, but it is even more vital not to permit them to obscure the essential clarity of Hebrews' contribution. Origen himself valued the Epistle as the work of a follower of Paul's (such as Luke or Clement of Rome). In North Africa a common view was that the Epistle was written by Barnabas, not Paul; nevertheless, Tertullian reported it was "more widely received among the Churches than the *Shepherd* [of *Hermas*]," one of the most popular works among Christians of the second century. B. F. Westcott, perhaps the greatest commentator in English on Hebrews, provides the key to why the Epistle was accepted as canonical, doubts regarding its authorship aside: "no Book of the Bible is more completely recognised by universal consent as giving a divine view of the facts of the Gospel, full of lessons for all time, than the Epistle to the Hebrews." "A divine view of the facts of the Gospel" is just what Hebrews purports to deliver, and when we understand its purpose and achievement, the Epistle comes into a clear focus.

The Epistle has been compared to a homily, and it calls itself a "word of exhortation" in 13:22. "Word" here (*logos*, as in John's Gospel) bears the meaning "discourse," and the choice of diction declares Hebrews' homiletic intent. It is a sustained argument from authoritative tradition that intends to convince its readers and hearers to embrace a fresh position and an invigorated sense of purpose in the world. Hebrews engages in a series of scriptural identifications of Jesus: both Scripture (in the form of the Septuagint) and God's Son are the authoritative point of departure.

what God has done and is doing through Christ for his new people with the events recounted in the Scriptures of Israel. Because from the beginning of the Church all Christians used the biblical tradition, this line of argument was probably not directed especially toward Jews or even Jewish Christians, but served to provide a framework for valuing Judaic tradition while showing that in Christ, God has transcended the old covenant and transformed his covenant people.

This elegant post-Pauline epistle is also the last associated with Paul in the New Testament, and it deliberately presents Christian faith as independent of Judaism. Hebrews explains that the Temple on earth (which by this time, 95 C.E., had been destroyed) was only a copy – a shadow or Platonic type of the heavenly sanctuary. Moses had seen the very throne of God, which was then approximated on earth in the Temple. That approximation is the "first covenant," and its time has passed. But the heavenly sanctuary offers us a "new covenant" (9:1–15).

Christ entered that true sanctuary when he died a sacrificial death (9:24); its truth, palely reflected in Israel's institutions, is accessible to all who believe in him. Divine vision, the sanctification to stand before God, is in Hebrews the goal of human life, and the only means to such perfection is loyalty to Jesus as the high priest who completes the sacrifice that the practices of Israel could foreshadow but not accomplish.

The Epistle to the Hebrews deliberately emphasizes the finality of a perfection from which one must not defect, the heart's only sanctuary (12:22–4): "But you have come up to Zion, mount and city of the living God, heavenly Jerusalem, and to myriads of angels in festal gathering, and to a congregation of first-born enrolled in heaven, and to a judge – God of all, and to the spirits of righteous people made perfect, and to Jesus the mediator of a pristine covenant, and to sprinkled blood that speaks better than the blood of Abel."

Jesus is the single focus of revelation in Hebrews, and this Epistle – unlike Paul's letters – relegates Israel to a thing of the past (8:8–13) because the Son's authority is greater than that of the Scripture. Once, God spoke in many and various ways through the prophets; now, at the end of days, he speaks to us by a Son (Hebrews 1:1, 2). Scripture is only authoritative to the extent that it attests the salvation mediated by the Son (1:3–2:4). The argument that animates the whole Epistle derives directly from the conviction of the prior authority of the Son of God in relation to Scripture.

For Hebrews, Christ replaces every major institution within the Judaism of its time. There is a single center within the theology of Hebrews. It is not Christ with Moses, Christ with Temple, Christ with David, Christ with Abraham, Christ with Scripture, or Christ with Israel. Christ is the beginning, middle, and end of theology in Hebrews, just as he is the same yesterday, today, and forever (Hebrews 13:8). Everything else is a provisional and expendable type that is consumed in the fire that is God (12:29).

The fact that this is not a letter is apparent from the absence of the conventions of letter writing (identification of the writer and the recipients, personal greetings), except for a brief and evidently artificial note at the end (13:22–5). Throughout the writing there are references to speaking and hearing (2:5, 5:11, 6:9, 9:5, 10:25, 32; 12:4), and in 13:22 the author describes what he has presented as a "word of exhortation." It is possible, therefore, that what we have in this "letter" is a model of a formal speech, to which the personal greetings were later appended under the influence of familiarity with Paul's writings. The Epistle probably achieved its present form in the late first or even early second century.

The strategy of the work is that of Greco-Roman oratory; the speaker alternates between providing information or insights to his hearers and exhorting them to change their way of life. The first example of this tactic is evident when we compare the affirmations of 1:1–14 with the exhortations of 2:1–4. The basis of the moral appeal is a mixture of lessons from the past activity of God in the world and among his people, and reminders of the new network of relationships that God has created among his new covenant people. This method of reinterpreting the biblical tradition closely resembles what Jewish writers of the Hellenistic–Roman period were doing – most notably Philo of Alexandria, who employed basic insights from Platonic and Stoic philosophy to reinterpret the Law of Moses and the experiences of the patriarchs of Israel. Similarly, the author of the Wisdom of Solomon retells the story of creation and the history of Israel by the use of philosophical categories adapted from the Hellenistic culture. Basic to the argument of Hebrews is the language commonly used by philosophically oriented writers of the period – for example, *hypodeigma*, "pattern" (4:11, 8:5, 9:23); and *hypostasis*, "substance" (1:3, 3:14, 11:11).

The primary claim of Hebrews is that the patterns of worship and the laws that God has given to Israel offer valuable but imperfect copies of the ideal modes and principles by which he is working to accomplish his purpose for his people and for the whole of the creation through Jesus Christ. The philosophy of Plato contrasted the earthly, temporary, imperfect copies of objects, ideas, and experiences with their heavenly, eternal models or ideals. Embracing a similar view of reality, the author of Hebrews contrasts the imperfect copies of the instruments and procedures for approaching God and gaining right relationship with him in historical Israel with the eternal mode of access to and acceptance by God as revealed and accomplished through Jesus. The full disclosure of the timeless model of the sanctuary is yet to occur, but true faith is able to see in Jesus the heavenly reality. The author has combined basic aspects of the Platonic contrast between the eternal realm of the ideal and the transitory nature of human existence with the Jewish concept of eschatology, which contrasts the divine disclosure of purpose in the past and the future achievement of that purpose. Without abandoning the traditional orientation of the biblical writers, the author has been able to incorporate this perspective on the purpose of God for his people into a philosophically sophisticated framework. The later intellectual leaders of the church, such as Origen of Alexandria (186–253 C.E.) and Augustine of Hippo (354–430 C.E.), developed in their own ways this method of combining biblical insights and philosophical understanding.

The first claim made concerning Jesus is that as Son of God, he is superior to the angels (Hebrews 1:2–2:18), and even worshipped by them (1:4–5); they are servants of God, but Jesus is God's anointed Son, the agent of creation and redemption of the world. They pass away; he remains forever (1:6–11). Yet for a little while, Jesus was made lower than the angels, in order for him to identify fully with human beings in suffering and death; now he has been crowned with glory and honor (2:5–9; cf. Psalm 8:4–6). He is the leader, the prototype of the people of God, and through him the unity and the sanctity of God's people will be accomplished (2:5–11). In the midst of this new community (*ekklesia*) Jesus proclaims the name of God (2:12; cf. Psalm 22:12). The psalms are quoted here from the Greek version, which in the passage quoted in Hebrews 2:7 differs considerably from the Hebrew original ("you have made them a little lower than God"), yet in proof of the sophistication of the author, Hebrews 2:12–13 reflects closely the Hebrew original of Psalm 22.

Before continuing with his demonstration of Jesus' superiority to other agents and persons in the biblical tradition, the author turns to exhortation: how are the new people of God to act in this new situation? The answer, given in various ways, is that they are to hold fast what they have received, the message first spoken by Jesus and his way of life, which have now been confirmed by those who heard him (Hebrews 2:1–3). Thereby they can avoid the punishment that befell the disobedient angels.

The second aspect of Jesus' superiority is his role as high priest, which occupies the central section of the work: Hebrews 3:1–6, 4:14–5:10, 7:1–10:17. Exhortations and warnings to the people are interspersed throughout. Moses foresaw that God would build a house; Christ is the

MELCHIZEDEK

Melchizedek is identified in Genesis 14:17–20 as king of Salem (Jerusalem) and priest of "God Most High" when Abraham was dwelling in Hebron (Genesis 13:18). Melchizedek's blessing of Abraham is understood in Psalm 110:4 as the model for the dual role of the kings of Israel as monarch and priest. They rule as God's chosen agents, and they serve as the intermediary between God and his people. The passage from Psalm 110 is quoted in Hebrews 5:6, where the promise of an eternal priesthood is interpreted in a Platonic mode: the lack of mention of ancestors or descendants of Melchizedek is understood to mean that he is from the realm of eternity (Hebrews 7:3). This eternal priesthood becomes the model for the royal priesthood of Jesus in this epistle (Hebrews 7:11–28).

Son given authority over the "house," which is the new covenant people (3:1–6). With full understanding of human frailty, Jesus has already entered the presence of God on behalf of his people (4:14–16). He has no need to offer sacrifice for himself or to seek appointment as priest, since he was appointed by God and will serve in this role forever, as both king and high priest, like Melchizedek (Psalm 110:4), in total obedience to the will of God.

The inadequacy of the Levitical priesthood is evident to the author, in that they had to repeat their offerings continually, which could never bring their people to holiness and perfection. Jesus' self-offering is the perfect sacrifice, once and for all (Hebrews 7:15–28). And it was presented in the *true* tent; that is, in the ideal, or archetypal, dwelling place of God in heaven rather than in the earthly tent, which is an imperfect copy of that eternal reality of God's presence (8:1–2, 9:11–28). It purifies, not the externals, but the *conscience* – a concept that the author has taken over from Stoicism (as we have seen that Paul did in explaining how those who never knew the Law of Moses are aware – through the law of nature – of what human behavior should be). This is the new reality of which Jeremiah spoke in his prophecy of the new covenant (Hebrews 8:3–13; Jeremiah 31:31–4). Jesus' perfect sacrifice has ratified the new covenant; his appearance at the end of the age will attest the completion of his covenantal work in the presence of God (Hebrews 9:1–28). Once more the author presents contrasts between the inadequate old covenant (10:1–4) and the perfect, true covenant that has been established through the death and exaltation of Jesus (10:5–14). This marks the emergence of the language of "new covenant" (or "new testament," because the Greek *diatheke*, unlike *berit* in Hebrew, could be and was understood either way) as compared to an "old" version, which the author believes God had rendered antiquated (8:13).

Under the new covenant a whole series of new resources are open to God's new people, as well as some solemn warnings (Hebrews 10:19–39):

10:20	A new way to God
10:22	The conscience made clean
10:23	The hope of ultimate deliverance from sin
10:24	The new commandment, to love one another
10:25	The ongoing practice of community meeting, for mutual encouragement in light of the coming Day of the Lord
10:26–31	The necessity to avoid the fate of the apostates, who failed to repent
10:32–9	The necessity to persevere in the face of mistreatment, confident in the words of warning and promise from the prophet Habakkuk (2:3–4).

Faith, therefore, is not only confidence in the unseen realm of the ideal, heavenly reality; it is also enduring trust as the ground of daily living.

Chapter 11 of Hebrews lists the great figures of the biblical tradition of Israel who are paradigms of faith, including Noah, Abraham, Jacob, Joseph, Moses, and the Israelites at Jericho. The summary statement about the faith of the people in the biblical narratives appears in Hebrews 11:32–8, where the confidence in God that characterized his people and their leaders was sustained, not only in times of triumph but also in periods of severe testing through which they passed. In the face of threats and painful trials, they sometimes experienced deliverance, but at other times martyrdom. But whether confronted by joy or by suffering, they all displayed confidence in God and his promises. That trust remained even though the ultimate promise was not fulfilled for them, since God had a future agent by whom his purpose for his people was to be achieved: Jesus, the primary agent and guarantor of faith (12:1–2). God has already vindicated him, by seating him at his right hand in glory.

It is this Jesus who is to be the model for the people of God (Hebrews 12:3). But the author warns about incurring divine judgment if there is rebellion or disobedience in response to the disciplinary trials that the people are called to endure prior to their final deliverance (12:3–29). Further, he presents a series of moral injunctions that the people are to obey (13:1–22):

13:1–3	Mutual love and concern
13:4	Integrity in marriage
13:5	Avoidance of greed
13:7	Remembrance and emulation of the faith of former leaders
13:9	Avoidance of unnecessary rules, such as food laws
13:10–13	Preparedness to accept rejection and scorn
13:15–16	Making the appropriate offerings of praise to God and generosity to others
13:17	Obedience to leaders, who are accountable to God
13:18	Praying for the author (= "us")
13:19	Praying for his speedy return to the hearers or readers of his message
13:20	Heeding his message of encouragement.

Interspersed through these exhortations are reminders of the basis for what the author regards as true faith: the eternal, unchangeable Jesus Christ (13:8) and the promise of the "city" that is to come (13:14). In conclusion, there is the solemn prayer, in developed liturgical form. The ultimate source of action in all this is God, who is working to achieve true peace in the creation. The agent whose self-sacrifice ratified the new covenant is Jesus, whom God attested by raising him from the dead. God is now at work among his people, enabling them to do what is pleasing to him, and again the agent of this saving activity is Jesus Christ, who is to be glorified forever (13:20–1).

THE CITY

Throughout the history of the ancient Middle East, cities rose and fell as centers of political and military power and as symbols of civilized life, for which divine authority was claimed. As a nomadic people, the early Israelites had no significant urban center until David and Solomon established Jerusalem as the royal capital of Israel, with its Temple as the earthly dwelling place of Yahweh. In the Hellenistic period the Greek concept of polis (city) became a major factor in the shaping of human existence. Each city dominated its region and was characterized by a diversity of roles and institutions essential for common life: food supply, crafts, marketplace, municipal authorities (including a council of leading citizens), public entertainment in theaters, and central places of worship. Impressive colonnades, temples, towers, and gates gave the city the image of wealth, power, and stability. Greek and Roman philosophers, most notably Plato (in the Republic) and Aristotle, regarded the city in its stability and diversity as a symbol and model for human existence, with the hope for achievement of enduring beauty and justice. The early Christians utilized this model of the city in diverse ways: the author of Revelation developed this vision of the ultimate hope for God's people in terms of a city conceived in apocalyptic terms; the author of Hebrews projected a model involving the philosophical distinction between temporal and eternal, with the city of God as image for the fulfillment of God's purpose.

The Epistle as we have it concludes with personal greetings to the members of the community and to their leaders, with special mention of Timothy, who has allegedly just been released from prison, and with special greetings from "those from Italy," which may mean that the writer is in Italy or that a group of Italian expatriates are sending greetings back to the recipients of this message. On the other hand, the Italian setting may be as artificial as the claim of Pauline authorship.

Whatever the date and specific circumstances of this letter, the Church is confronted with the prospect of suffering persecution and expects to undergo trials similar to those experienced by the faithful in historic Israel, and at the same time, it faces intellectual challenges concerning what it proclaims as the truth. These challenges arise not only from Jewish thinkers, who were developing interpretations of Scripture confirming the move toward what was to become Rabbinic Judaism, but also from Greco-Roman intellectuals, who were scornful of the Christian claim concerning possession of the truth about the nature and purpose of God. In response to this configuration of issues, the author's prescription for the needs of the readers/hearers is faith: focus on the unchanging, eternal realities of the sacrifice of Christ; the true sanctuary, where Jesus is with God; and the true covenant people, who are thereby brought into existence as the new "house of God." This will enable them to challenge their conceptual critics and to remain firm while enduring hardship, hostility, even martyrdom. By persevering they can be sure of sharing one day in the life of the eternal city of God (Hebrews 11:10, 13–16).

C. Jude and Second Peter: The Continuing Influence and Development of Apocalyptic

1. Jude

Among the characteristic features of apocalyptic literature are (1) a sense of urgency about warning the faithful concerning the error and corruption that are rampant in the larger, ambient community, (2) advice on how they are to endure until the end of the age comes, and (3) reassurance of God's continuing support. All these elements are compacted in the little letter of Jude.

The authority of this pseudepigraphal writer from late in the first century is reinforced by his being linked with James – presumably the brother of Jesus who had presided over the Jerusalem church from the time of Paul (Galatians 1:19, 2:9). In some parts of the church, hereditary links with Jesus were important for leadership roles – in contrast to Paul's view; for Paul the single requirement was to have been commissioned by the risen Jesus (1 Corinthians 9:1). In the case of Jude, it is intriguing that he is identified as James' brother, yet not as Jesus' brother. The emerging doctrine of Jesus' birth from a virgin no doubt played a part in this form of identification, but it also shows that James was the supreme authority within much of the ancient church, even after his death in 62 C.E.

The main body of the letter consists of a series of warnings about those who have abandoned the true faith, together with a string of vivid characterizations of these apostates. Analogies are pointed out between various groups in the Scriptures who forfeited their place as God's people: the first generation of Israelites who escaped from Egypt in the Exodus but whose disobedience led to their death in the desert (Jude 5); the angels who exploited their powers and fell from favor with God (Jude 6); the inhabitants of Sodom and Gomorrah, whose indulgence in immorality and sexual perversion brought down destruction on the people and their land (Jude 7). Like these horrible examples of self-indulgence and disobedience, those who have now fallen away from the faith have defiled themselves, dishonored God and the angels, and taken authority to themselves in a way that not even the archangels would dare to do (Jude 8–10). They follow the example of the self-willed and rejected of Israel's past – Cain, Balaam, and Korah (Genesis 4:3, Numbers 22–4; Numbers 16) – and they will share similar destruction at the hand of God. The assurance that God will render to them the punishment they deserve is given through a quotation from the *Book of Enoch*, which deplores the irreligion of these people. They are described as "grumblers, malcontents, passion-driven, loud-mouthed boasters, flattering people to gain advantage" (Jude 14–16). The fact that *Enoch* is quoted as Scripture reminds us that this book was highly regarded in Jewish as well as in Christian circles during the first century, as the discovery of quantities of fragments of the *Enoch* literature among the Dead Sea Scrolls also attests. Its use here in Jude also indicates that the decisions as to which of the Jewish writings were to be considered authoritative by Jews and by Christians had not yet been firmly reached.

The author notes that there should be no surprise that the ranks of God's people have been infiltrated by the unworthy and disobedient: the apostles had given warning of this (Jude 17–19). This appeal to apostolic authority is an indication that Jude was written a generation after the apostles, when the Church needed to ground its authority in the past. Meanwhile, the leaders of the church are to build up their members in the true faith, urging them to pray in the Spirit, to manifest the love of God, and to await the ultimate manifestation of God's mercy and the entrance into eternal life that will bring to a close the present age (Jude 21). The best that can be hoped for is that some of those who waver on the border between the faithful and apostates may be kept from the fires of destruction. Yet even as the true believers act with a mix of fear and mercy, they need to despise the corruption that the borderline cases have been carrying with them (Jude 22–3). The letter ends with a beautiful liturgical ascription of glory to God, who through Jesus Christ is able to preserve his people from disobedience and apostasy (Jude 24–5).

2. Second Peter

One of the most remarkable features of 2 Peter is that it paraphrases or quotes thirteen verses from Jude (cf. Jude 4–16 with 2 Peter 2:1–18), an index of the widespread practice of pseudepigraphy within the Church at the close of the period of the New Testament. The author, writing in the name of Peter, shares the basic apocalyptic outlook of Jude, but he modified Jude in significant details. He deals directly with the problem of the delay in the fulfillment of the expectation expressed by Paul and others of the first generation of Christians that Jesus would quickly return to gather his people and establish on earth God's rule. His description of the defecting from Christian faith and practice goes far beyond the sketch in Jude, so that those who formerly "escaped the defilements of the world through the knowledge of our Lord and Savior Jesus Christ" end up in a worse condition than prior to their conversion (2 Peter 2:20). Clearly, defection from the faith is a major problem for the author of 2 Peter.

In several essential ways, however, the author of 2 Peter differs from the outlook of the first-generation apostles. First, he deals with the delay in the triumphant return of Christ to earth by telling his readers that God has a different way of calculating time than human beings do (2 Peter 3:8) and supports this point by quoting Psalm 90:4 in such a way as to claim that people simply cannot calculate the divine timetable. Second, depicting those events when God subdues the wicked and renews the creation, he uses terms derived from Hellenistic culture, such as the reference to the pits of gloom where the fallen angels are incarcerated in a form of Tartarus (2:4), a technical term in Hellenistic mythology for the realm of the dead. Similarly, when he describes the destiny of the faithful, he uses terms from the mystical tradition of Hellenistic religion, such as *eusebeia* (1:3, 6; 3:1; a term for piety never used by Paul or in the Gospel tradition). What constitutes true piety is spelled out in a passage in which a string of virtues are linked in a style familiar in Hellenistic moral treatises. In 1:16, the technical term *epoptes* (eyewitness) is used, which is a central element in Hellenistic mystical religion. It claims to offer divine illumination to the initiates or devotees of a god. In 1:19, the mythical image of the morning star is employed to point to the fulfillment of prophetic expectations.

Along more intellectual lines, faith – which has been central for both Paul and the Gospel tradition – is increasingly replaced by knowledge. *Knowing* the truth is an essential feature throughout this writing: 1:2, 3, 8; 2:20–1; 3:18. Using language and concepts that have counterparts in

THEODICY

One of the conceptual problems in any religious system is that of justifying those actions of God or the gods that bring suffering or harm to humans. Such a defense is called theodicy. The effort to discern a reason and a greater good than the obvious fact of human pain takes a variety of forms in religious systems of thought. For early Christians, the suffering and death of Jesus and the persecution and martyrdom suffered by his followers called for a theological explanation that would enable the members of the community to see these seemingly senseless events in the context of a universal divine plan for the benefit of the creation and of God's people.

Hellenistic philosophy (such as that of Epictetus, ca. 55–135 C.E., a contemporary of the author of 2 Peter), the author deals with such questions as, Why does God allow the suffering of the righteous to continue? And how and when will God call to account the wicked, as the Stoics were asking? In the Jewish tradition, Philo of Alexandria deals repeatedly with the issue of theodicy. The issue of the justice of God in dealing with humans is touched on elsewhere in the New Testament in passages such as the address on the Areopagus in Athens attributed to Paul in Acts 17: "God has fixed a day on which he will judge the world in righteousness" (17:31). But on the whole, throughout the New Testament, God's freedom in dealing with evil and with justice for human beings is simply assumed. Second Peter, however, treats the theme extensively in his short letter. This confirms the impression that the writer and his readers are from a cultural setting significantly different from that of the readers of the Pauline letters and the Gospels.

Further evidence from 2 Peter for changes within the Church comes in the form of references to and attitudes toward the authority and interpretation of the Scriptures. From 1:17, there is an extended excerpt from the Gospel tradition describing the scene of the Transfiguration of Jesus, at which Peter was present. It would seem that the Gospels are known and appealed to here as evidence. There is a reference in 3:1 to an earlier letter of Peter, which implies that letters by (or in the name of) the apostles are known and are accepted as authoritative. With regard to the letters of Paul, 3:15–16 refers to them as "Scripture," ranking them along with "the other Scriptures," thereby attributing authority for the Church to some of the writings that later were brought together to form the New Testament. In a frank acknowledgment of

Athens, Stoa of Attalos. The public marketplace and gathering place in Athens, the agora, was lined with colonnaded structures in which took place informal social encounters, business transactions, and addresses to the public who chose to listen. The columns, called by the Greeks *stoa*, provided the name for the followers of the Greek philosopher Zeno. They chose to address and challenge listeners in these public places rather than in the more formal lecture halls where the followers of other philosophers gathered for instruction and discussion. On the eastern side of the agora stood a large colonnade that has been reconstructed as here pictured. (BiblePlaces.com)

MARCION

In the mid-second century C.E., Marcion became the leader of a group in Rome that made a radical distinction between the God of Jesus Christ and the God proclaimed in the Law and the Prophets of the Hebrew Scriptures. They also rejected many of the New Testament writings, limiting their canon of Scripture to an edited edition of Luke-Acts and the letters of Paul. They were ascetic in mode of life, frowned on marriage, and did not eat certain kinds of food. Marcion's ideas are best known through a refutation of them by Irenaeus (130–ca. 203 C.E.) in his treatise *Against Heresies*.

how different the writer's views are from Paul's, he stresses the difficulties involved in interpreting Pauline letters and the distortions of their meaning that are current, although there is no indication in 2 Peter of the specific problems that had arisen in interpreting Paul. Even though the acceptable interpretive process is not detailed, the author declares that there are to be no private interpretations of Scripture: all instruction is to be given within the context of the Church by its authorized leaders. This serves as a solemn warning not to heed the "false teachers" who deny "the Master who bought them" and thereby bring upon themselves eternal destruction.

Clearly, the issues of correct doctrine and authorized interpretation of the Scriptures are interrelated at this stage in the life of the Church and are of paramount concern. The availability and wide use among the churches of the range of writings with their diverse perspectives that came to constitute the New Testament required the development of overarching creedal and theological formulations that would offer conceptual unity in the midst of the evident diversity among the documents. Some leaders tried to solve the problem of diversity by choosing a smaller group of writings and establishing them as normative. A major example of this was Marcion, the second-century Gnostic who rejected the Scriptures of Israel and reduced the New Testament to his own expurgated versions of Luke, Acts, and the letters of Paul. The church as a whole rejected this kind of solution, however. The final warning and exhortation of 2 Peter are to avoid being "carried away with error" and to seek to "grow in grace and knowledge" (3:18). The Church has entered a stage – probably at the dawn of the second century – where the norms of right doctrine and right behavior are the central issues.

IV. CHRISTIANITY RESPONDS TO ROMAN CULTURE AND IMPERIAL POLICY

A. Luke-Acts, Program for World Mission: The Church's Internal and External Relations

The Gospel according to Luke and the Book of Acts, now separated in the Christian canon of Scripture by the Gospel according to John, were composed as a two-volume work, which begins with the divine preparation for the birth of Jesus and ends with Paul in Rome, symbolizing the worldwide mission of the Church. The similar opening lines of each, the dedication to the same person (named as Theophilus), and the reference in Acts 1:1 back to "the earlier book" all strongly indicate a common author. The similarity in editorial style and overall point of view confirms this conclusion, which is taken for granted by scholars across the spectrum of stances, from the most conservative to the most radical.

From the second century to the present, the author has been identified as the Luke who is mentioned as a co-worker of Paul in Philemon 24 and

2 Timothy 4:11 and described as a "beloved physician" in Colossians 4:14. Some scholars have inferred from the occasional shifts in the narrative of Acts from "they" to "we" (cf., e.g., Acts 16:1 with 16:11, 20:1 with 20:5) that the author was a companion of Paul on part of his journeys around the Mediterranean Sea. But the change from third person to first person plural is found in historical writings of that epoch, and in any case appears in connection with Timothy in Acts, rather than Luke.

More likely, the author, as he states openly in Luke 1:1–2, was not an eyewitness of the events he reports, but based his account on reports he had heard or read from those who were. For convenience, we refer to him as Luke, but as with the other Gospels, the identity of the authors is simply unknown, probably has been from the earliest years of the document's existence, and many sources – oral and written – and authors fed into the final product.

The author is nonetheless remarkably skilled and fluent as a writer. This is apparent in the ability to modify the Gospel's style in ways that are appropriate to the material presented. In the opening section of the Gospel (Luke 1–3), for example, his writing sounds "like the Bible" – that is, he effectively mimics the style of the Septuagint (which was, of course, the version of the Bible that he was using) and gives the reader a sense of continuity between the characters from biblical history and the events the Gospel recounts. Some of these connections are implicit, such as the parallels between the divine gift of a son, John, to the childless couple Zechariah and Elizabeth (1:5–25, 57–80) and the story of the birth of Samuel in 1 Samuel 1. The exultant hymns that celebrate these miraculous births are similar (cf. 1 Samuel 2 and Luke 1:67–79). Other connections are explicit, such as the angelic voice that links the birth of Jesus to the divine assurance to David that he will have an enduring royal line (2:10–11). The care with which the ritual requirements are fulfilled for

Shepherds' fields near Bethlehem in Judea. In Luke's account of the events that occurred in connection with the birth of Jesus, shepherds tending flocks in fields near Bethlehem visit the newborn child (Luke 2:8–20). The terrain in this picture is typical of the open land surrounding Bethlehem in modern times. "Bethlehem" in Hebrew means "house of bread," a name as common as settlements with mills capable of producing fine flour, rather than the coarse grade most Israelites used for their daily needs. There was another Bethlehem in Galilee just seven miles from Nazareth, and archaeological excavations show that Jews had settled there during the first century. Joseph may well have been among them. (BiblePlaces.com)

both the boys and the testimony of the pious men and women around the Temple strengthen this sense of continuity within the history of God's covenant people. Luke's depiction of the new community's outreach to the humble and to outsiders is anticipated in the coming of the shepherds at Jesus' birth (Luke 2:8–20).

Although the Gospel relied on Mark, or Mark-like tradition, and on Q as its basic sources, Luke adapts them to his own purposes, rearranging the sequence and adjusting the details. In his editorial additions, the final writer (or writers) shows familiarity with literary conventions of the period, such as the dating of events by reference to several concurrent rulers (Luke 3:1–2) and the composition of extended speeches by leading characters in his story. In the overall narrative of Acts, where we learn how the Gospel moved from Jerusalem to Rome, the style resembles that of a popular literary genre of the second century C.E. and later, known as the romance. But Luke's work also displays the methods and features of Greco-Roman historical writers. He has remarkably accurate knowledge of details of urban life in the eastern Mediterranean, such as the distinctive

LUKE AS HISTORIAN

Since the nineteenth century, scholars have continued to debate the degree to which Luke's accounts of Jesus and the apostles (especially Paul) are historically reliable. Careful studies in the earlier part of the present century, such as H. J. Cadbury's *The Making of Luke-Acts*, have shown the extent to which Luke used the historical-literary methods of his time, and the impressive amount of historically reliable detail that he includes, especially in Acts. In more recent years, the use of early sources within Luke and Acts has also been acknowledged. It must be noted, however, that both ancient and modern historians are not interested merely in reporting facts, but in placing what was said and done by the historical figures in a larger framework of meaning. Luke makes clear to his reader what that historical framework is when he contrasts in Luke 16:16 the earlier epoch of "the Law and the prophets" that ended with John the Baptist with the new era inaugurated by Jesus, which will culminate in the evangeliza-

tion of the world (Acts 1:8) and the triumphant return of Christ (Acts 1:11).

In setting out his story of Jesus and the work of the apostles in preparation for the completion of God's purpose for the world, Luke uses a popular literary style of the early second century C.E. and subsequent centuries, known by classical scholars as "the Hellenistic romance." The title is misleading, however, since the romance is not a love story or merely an entertaining narrative (although some romances do have erotic passages), but is rather an engaging tale, filled with human-interest details, describing a life of devotion to a divinity, with vivid accounts of the resulting trials and rewards. Examples of this genre include Xenophon's *Ephesiaca* and Apuleius's *Metamorphoses*, both of which depict the lives of devotees of the Egyptian goddess Isis and their resulting transformation. Luke-Acts employs features of this narrative style in the interest of setting out a historical view of what God has done through Jesus and the apostles

to accomplish the renewal of his people and the establishment of his rule in the world. In the process, the tensions that often divided earliest Christianity are muted, and events known to us from earlier literature (Mark and Paul, chiefly) are conflated, confused, or passed over in silence.

The first two chapters of Luke, for example, provide what may seem to be circumstantial reports concerning Jesus' birth. But at many points, the Lukan chapters contradict the opening chapters of Matthew. For example, when Jesus' family is fleeing to Egypt in Matthew (2:13–15), they are in Luke (2:22–4) circumcising the child and bringing him to Jerusalem to present him at the Temple. In addition, of course, Luke has the characters speak in psalmic arias, which are still used as part of Christian worship, and which probably originated in that setting. The point about such material is not that it is a simple matter of legend. Rather, circumstantial material speaks to the theological meaning of Jesus' divine sonship.

titles of the civic leaders in Thessalonica (Acts 17:6) and the names of the various rulers and authorities in Palestine during this period. At some major points, however, there are tensions between his account of Paul's career and the apostle's own biographical notes in his letters. For example, Luke reports that Paul's consultation with the leaders of the Jerusalem church resulted in his agreeing that even Gentile Christians were to observe some minimal Jewish dietary laws (abstaining from food offered to idols and from blood; Acts 15:20; cf. Leviticus 3:17; 17:10–14). Paul, however, declares that no ritual or dietary requirements were placed on Gentile Christians by an agreement reached with James and the other leading apostles (Galatians 2:7–10). It appears that Luke's account reflects one of the developments in the later situation of the church, such as we have seen in Matthew and the later Pauline tradition, as it moved toward rules for regulating the life of its membership. In Acts 15, Luke presents James' teaching as if it were articulated during a meeting Paul had with James (Jesus' brother), Peter, and John in 46 C.E., when Paul was accepted as apostle to the Gentiles. But Acts 15 in fact reflects two meetings. One came to a decision about circumcision that Paul agreed with. But a later meeting, in 52 C.E., while Paul was far away in Corinth, stipulated rules of purity that Gentile believers had to observe to demonstrate their loyalty to the Torah. The simple facts are that Paul was not at that second meeting, never agreed with the decree James issued, and never mentioned in his letters the rules involved – except to contradict them! In this case, Luke is not concerned with detached, objective reporting, but with showing the importance of this tradition for Christian readers in his own time – probably at the very end of the first century.

The major objective of Luke in both volumes of this work (Luke and Acts) is to show that, from the beginning, the covenant people of God have had the divinely intended potential to become a universally inclusive community. Both volumes acknowledge that not all will be persuaded by God's message through Jesus, but everyone has the possibility of responding in faith to this gospel. For example, when Simeon blesses the child Jesus in the Temple (Luke 2:28–32), he declares that Jesus' coming is intended as "a light to reveal your will to the Gentiles, and to bring glory to your people Israel." Similarly, in the extended quotation from Isaiah before Jesus' baptism, we read, "All humanity will see God's salvation" (3:6; cf. Mark 1:3). That aim is apparent in the special material that Luke has included, as well as in the modification of sayings and narratives taken over from earlier sources. Before examining some of this special or modified material in detail, it is essential to see how Luke-Acts structured this account of God's work in the world, and especially its perception of the unfolding of the career of Jesus.

The direct connection between the ascension of Jesus, reported only by Luke, and the coming of the Spirit to launch the world mission of the Church is explicitly stated in Acts 2:33 and 3:19–1. After he has been taken up to God, his people will not see Jesus until he returns (Acts 1:11). But God's presence with his people in the extended interim of Jesus' absence from them will be powerfully evident through the work of the Spirit, which will enable them to carry out their mission "to the ends of the earth" (Acts 1:6–8).

The author of Luke-Acts conceives of this divine plan for world evangelism in three historical epochs:

1. Israel from ancient times until the ministry of John the Baptist
2. The coming of Jesus, his ministry and message, and his death and resurrection
3. The ascension of Jesus and the commissioning of the apostles for their mission to the world.

The Gospel according to Luke describes the end of the first epoch and the whole of the second epoch. Acts recounts the launch of the third epoch.

After Jesus' anointing by the Spirit at his baptism (Luke 3:21–2) – the key to his messianic identity – and his time of testing (4:1–15), he begins his public ministry in the midst of his own townspeople in Nazareth (4:14–30), choosing as the basis of his address a passage from Isaiah 61:1–2. Jesus' interpretation of this text makes clear the first phase of his activity in Luke, to invite "the poor" – that is, those who are considered impure or unworthy or outside the boundaries of the covenant – to share in the blessings of God's people. The prophets of Israel foreshadow this divine outreach: the Syrian widow from Sidon, whose child was healed by Elijah (Luke 4:26; 1 Kings 17:1–16), and the Syrian "leper" who was cured by Elisha (Luke 4:27; 2 Kings 5:1–14).

The Spirit of God poured out upon Jesus commissions him to carry out this work of healing and renewal on the margins of Israel. The preaching and healing activity in which Jesus engages for the next four chapters reaches out to precisely this kind of person, as Luke 6:17–19 makes clear. Jesus pronounces the blessedness of "the poor" in his (Q) version of the Beatitudes (6:20). The term "poor" does not mean simply the economically deprived, but includes those who by the standards of conventional piety were excluded from participation in the life and benefits of God's people by reason of birth, physical condition, ritual impurity, or occupation. Jesus' love of "the poor" is explicit in his response to the questioners sent to him by John the Baptist, which is framed in Luke by stories of the healing of the slave of a centurion (7:1–10), the cure of a widow's son (7:11–17), and the acceptance of and justification for direct contact with a sinful woman (7:36–50). Jesus calls attention to his reaching out to the socially and ritually rejected people and then accepts the characterization of himself as "a friend of tax collectors and sinners" (7:22–3, 34).

To extend his work among those marginalized within Judaism, Jesus sends out the twelve apostles, that number symbolizing the twelve tribes of Israel. The spectacular results of their work are described in symbolic form in Luke 5:1–11, where the Markan story of Jesus' calling fishermen to be his disciples (Mark 1:16–20) is replaced by a miracle story of the astounding catch of fish, which is the result of direct obedience to the command of Jesus.

LUKE-ACTS AND THE CHALLENGE OF PROPHECY AT THE END OF THE FIRST CENTURY C.E.

During the time Luke-Acts came into being, some Christians were disturbed by the phenomenon of prophecy. The Letter to Titus refers to a Jewish group ("the circumcision," Titus 1:10–11) and uses their own words against them (Titus 1:12): "One of them, their very own prophet, said, 'Cretans are always liars, evil beasts, lazy gluttons.'" Such are affairs in Crete; the author of Titus actually agrees, "This testimony is true" (Titus 1:13)! Aside from being among the most politically incorrect statements in the New Testament, the reference to the Jewish prophet in Crete is remarkable for several reasons. The Holy Spirit was understood among some Rabbis to have ceased its direct operation in Israel (see Sotah 48b in the Babylonian Talmud). So how could a person be acclaimed a prophet among Jews in Crete?

That question cannot be answered simply by observing that Rabbinic literature is, generally speaking, later than the New Testament. In 1 Maccabees 4:42–6, priests loyal to the revolt store the desecrated stones of the Temple that had been defiled in 167 B.C.E., until a prophet should arise to explain what should be done with them. So there was a sense, at least in some circles (highly official, influential circles), that classical prophecy had come to an end. Still, Josephus refers to movements of prophetic pretenders, who claimed divine inspiration for their efforts to free the land of the Romans (War 2.258–65; 7.437–46). Prophecy continued as a movement (or movements) within both Judaism and Christianity in the first century C.E. and proved to be a disruptive influence.

On the Christian side, the passage from Titus shows that Judaic prophecy in Crete had a particular profile: antilocal (1:12), insistent on circumcision (1:10), skilled in myths as well as in the Torah (1:14), dedicated to issues of purity (1:15). It seems to bother the author especially that this prophetic enterprise is profitable (1:11). Prophetic identity, which had been a major strength within the practice of Jesus, was seen soon after the destruction of the Temple to be a threat to the stability of the household church. That is shown not only by the Letter to Titus, but in the warning against "false prophets" in what is known as the "little apocalypse" in the Synoptic Gospels (Matthew 24–5; Mark 13). That is an eschatological prediction based on the events of the disastrous siege of Jerusalem, which resulted in the burning of the Temple. Part of that disaster – and particularly to be avoided in the understanding of this apocalypse – are the false prophets and false christs (Matthew 24:24; Mark 13:22).

Luke-Acts, together with the Pastoral Epistles, permits us to see how Christianity attempted to meet the challenge of fresh prophetic activity loyal to Judaism. It is notable that Luke's version of the little apocalypse (Luke 21:5-36) does not mention the false prophets and false christs, although there is a warning about not being led astray (Luke 21:8). The reason for that is that Luke claims that Judaic prophecy – in its recent and contemporary form – actually attests the truth of Christ. At the beginning of Luke the Spirit of God is portrayed as being as active as it is at the beginning of Acts. And that portrayal in the Gospel results in Zechariah (the father of John the Baptist 1:67), Simeon (2:25–6), and Anna (2:36–7) all being identified in prophetic terms. Instead of denigrating false prophets, the Gospel according to Luke co-opts Judaic prophecy – along with the Judaic Scriptures – to attest the coming of Christ.

The reason the Gospel can depart from the policy of Matthew and Mark, and embrace prophecy, is that some prophets are understood to act in the interests of Jesus' movement. That is the case even when their actual identification with the movement is uncertain. Anna, for example, is simply said to give thanks and to speak "concerning him" to all who were awaiting the redemption of Jerusalem (Luke 2:38). Although "concerning him" (peri autou) apparently refers to Jesus, without the sequencing that places the prophecy of Simeon beforehand, little the Gospel says would seem to make of Anna a prophetess of Christ. The situation is sometimes much the same in the Book of Acts, where the prophet Agabus predicts a famine and the arrest of Paul, but his relation to the apostles as a whole remains unclear (see Acts 11:27–30, 21:10–11). On the other hand, Acts is quite clear about the prophetic and Christian identity of Judas and Silas (Acts 15:22–33) and the daughters of Philip (Acts 21:8–9), as well as about the group in Antioch (Acts 13:1–3).

By the time of Luke, it appears, Christians in Antioch were confident about their ability to provide true

(continued)

LUKE-ACTS AND THE CHALLENGE OF PROPHECY AT THE END OF THE FIRST CENTURY C.E. *(continued)*

prophecy with a home. Indeed, Syrian Christianity as a whole was to develop a psalmic tradition of song and praise by means of the Holy Spirit (see the *Odes of Solomon* from the second century), and the opening of Luke – with its songs of Mary and Zechariah and Simeon – includes probably the earliest texts of this prophetic form of worship. Part of that incorporation of prophetic worship is that the leaders of the church, the bishops who emerge in the Pastoral Epistles as the successors of the apostles, and the Holy Spirit available to them are conceived to be endowed "through prophecy with laying on of hands by the eldership" (1 Timothy 4:14).

In Luke 10:1 uniquely, however, a whole new stage in the outreach to the wider world is depicted: Jesus sends out *seventy* people to spread his message about sharing in the life of God's people. The number seventy represented the number of the nations of the world within ancient Judaism. That the transition to the wider field of mission is in view is made evident by 9:51–3, where the prospect of Jesus' rejection by his fellow Jews is asserted and the confrontation with the authorities in Jerusalem is implied. Many of the stories and sayings found in Mark and Matthew appear in Luke as well, but at several points Luke emphasizes or introduces the element of Jesus' outreach beyond Judaism, although that inclusive policy will only be realized during the extension of the mission recounted in Acts. Examples of this anticipatory reference to the non-Jewish mission within the Gospel include the story of the Good Samaritan (10:29–37), which commends the generosity and human concern shown by a member of a group despised by the Jews despite their devotion to Mosaic tradition, and the teaching from Q in regard to the sign of Jonah (11:29–32), which reminds the hearer or reader that Jonah's preaching and Solomon's wisdom were heeded by non-Israelites. The Lukan form of the parables makes the same point: that God intends to reach out to the outsider. The parables Jesus tells in response to the charge of the religious leaders that he is having fellowship with impure people (15:1–2) makes this especially plain: the joyous shepherd, who rejoices at the restoration to the flock of a lost sheep (15:3–7); the joyous housewife, who rejoices at the recovery of a lost coin (15:8–10); and the joyous father, who rejoices at the recovery of a runaway son and rebukes the unforgiving older brother (15:11–32). Preceding this triad of parables is one with a similar point: the parable of the supper guests from Q (14:15–24), where the original invitees are too preoccupied with their own affairs to accept the invitation, which finally goes out to, and is accepted by, the society's outcasts. The same point is made in such uniquely Lukan stories as the rich man and Lazarus (16:19–31) and Jesus' visit to the home of Zacchaeus, the tax collector in Jericho (19:1–10), which ends with the assertion that the purpose of Jesus' having come into the world is "to seek and save the lost." This leads to the third stage of Luke's account of Jesus' career: the encounter with the authorities – civil and religious – in Jerusalem, which occupies the rest of the Gospel until the transitional chapter (Luke 24), which prepares for the launching of the world mission in Acts.

SAMARITANS

The city of Samaria was the luxurious capital of the northern kingdom of Israel from the ninth century B.C.E. until 722 B.C.E., as the prophet Amos attests in his description of its aristocrats (Amos 6:4–6) and as the excavation there of such luxury items as ivory-inlaid furniture confirms. In 722–721 B.C.E. the Assyrians invaded the territory and carried off the inhabitants into captivity in their own land. By the Hellenistic period, Samaria was rebuilt with public buildings and temples typical of Greek-style culture. Herod the Great developed it in grand style and renamed it for the Roman emperor: Sebastos, the Greek equivalent of "Augustus." To the east of the city of Samaria was Shechem, which had been the first location of the shrine of Yahweh when Israel entered the land (Joshua 24). In the Hellenistic and Roman periods, those who wanted to recover the traditions of Moses built a temple on nearby Mount Gerizim and produced an edition of the Pentateuch that they claimed was the authentic version of the Scriptures of Israel, in contrast to the expanded and edited version of the Law of Moses produced during and following the return of the Jews from exile in Babylon. These northern people, the Samaritans, asserted that the priesthood that carried out the cult in their temple was legitimate, in contrast to the unholy priesthood and practices of the Jerusalem Temple. So fierce was the hostility of other Jews toward the Samaritans that they avoided even journeying through that district lest there be some inadvertent contact with these Samaritan people, whom they regarded as perverters of the legal and priestly traditions of Israel.

The rejection of Jesus is anticipated in the concluding words of Luke's version of the parable of the pounds (Luke 19:11–27). Unlike Matthew's version (Matthew 25:14–20), where the issue is investing the wealth of an absentee owner, for Luke the major factors are the granting of royal power to a nobleman (19:12, 27) and the refusal of the people to accept that nobleman as king. The point for Luke is Israel's rejection of Jesus as God's agent who will establish the divine kingdom on earth. Jesus' rejection by the Jewish leadership is foretold in the Lukan version of what follows. When the disciples acclaim Jesus as he descends the Mount of Olives on his way to the Temple, their words echo the song of the angels at his birth (19:38, 2:14; cf. Psalm 118:25–6). When the Pharisees challenge his acceptance of this acclamation, he predicts the destruction of Jerusalem, including details of the methods the Romans will use to besiege the city and starve its inhabitants. Unlike Matthew, Luke follows closely Mark's account of Jesus in the Temple and the series of subsequent controversies with the Jewish religious leaders, culminating in the apocalyptic discourse, to which Luke adds only a brief additional warning about the unpredictability of the return of Christ (21:34–6). Luke does omit the Markan account of the cursing of the fig tree, but affirms themes of judgment and reformation of the covenant people in other ways. As a transition to the story of Jesus' arrest and execution, Luke notes that Jesus continued to teach in the Temple and that "all the people" came to hear him. The testimony to Jews continues despite the impending official rejection of him.

The Lukan account of the Last Supper differs in both order and content from Mark in so many ways that scholars have proposed that Luke had access to an independent tradition for this section of his Gospel. Luke's version emphasizes that Jesus' final meal with the disciples includes the

Eastern slope of the City of David and Mount of Olives. East of Jerusalem, the Mount of Olives stretches for nearly a mile north and south. This ridge is part of the main range of mountains running through central and southern Judea. From the crest of the ridge is a superb westward view across the Kidron Valley to the central part of Jerusalem. Towns located on the southeast side of the Mount of Olives are Bethpage and Bethany, which are linked in the Gospels with Jesus and his followers (Mark 11:1; Luke 19:21; John 11:1, 18). (BiblePlaces.com)

prediction of the fulfillment of God's purpose for his people. This is high-lighted by placing at the outset the reference to the establishment of the kingdom of God (22:15–16) – that is, the new age in which God's rule is established on the earth – and the appearance here (from the Q source; cf. Matthew 19:28) of the reward the disciples will receive for their fidelity to Jesus in his time of testing (22:28–30). But Luke's language also includes the use of the Greek verb *dietheto*, when he says "I have appointed you, just as the father appointed me, a kingdom," which is linked with the noun *diatheke*, meaning "covenant" or "testament." Thus the force of this state-ment is to promise that the Twelve will have a central role when God ful-fills his purpose for the covenant people of Israel. Meanwhile, the Eucharistic meal is an anticipation and a reminder of what God is set to do for his people. During the time of transition from the present situation to the coming age of peace, disciples are to expect conflict and hostility. Luke 22:35–8 seems to envisage a temporary, emergency setting aside of Jesus' earlier instructions (9:3, 10:4) about traveling unencumbered, dependent solely on local hospitality.

The hearing before Pilate begins with the explicit charge by the coali-tion of Jewish leaders that Jesus is "perverting our nation," forbidding the payment of taxes to Rome, and claiming to be the messianic king (Luke 23:2). Pilate states directly that he finds Jesus guilty of no crime (23:4). Then Pilate sends Jesus to Herod Antipas, within whose jurisdiction in Galilee Jesus lived and had first carried out his work of preaching and healing (23:6–16). Herod and his soldiers treat Jesus mockingly as a king, but even he does not find Jesus guilty of the accusations the authorities have brought against him. This motif is of great apologetic importance for the Book of

Acts, where Jesus' followers are repeatedly brought before the civil authorities of Rome, who are unable to find them guilty of acts against the state.

On the way to the crucifixion in Luke's account (23:26–32), Jesus turns to tell the women who are following him with lamentations that their sorrow should be for themselves and for their offspring, who will suffer when divine judgment falls on the city. This special attention to women is characteristic of the whole of Luke's Gospel. Women are prominent in the infancy stories; among those who herald the birth of Jesus is a prophetess, Anna (2:36–8). Women are frequently among the beneficiaries of Jesus' acts of grace and healing – more so than in the other Gospels. Examples are the healing of the widow's son (7:11–17); the expanded version of the woman with the ointment (7:36–50); the women who provide financial and other support for Jesus (8:1–3); the story of Mary and Martha's response to Jesus (10:38–42); the blessedness of Jesus' mother (11:27–8); and the healing of the woman with the infirmity (13:10–17). In Acts women also play a significant role, although they are excluded from the company of the apostles in a way that establishes a pattern of male hierarchical dominance.

The inclusiveness of the community of faith is indicated in other distinctively Lukan material: Jesus' compassion for the Samaritans, despite their initial rejection of his message (9:51–6), the healing of the man with dropsy or edema (14:1–6), the healing of ten "lepers" (17:11–19), and the story of the Pharisee and the tax collector (18:9–14). Other themes include the necessity for persistence in prayer (11:5–8, 18:1–8), the folly of trusting in material possessions to guarantee one's well-being (12:13–21, 16:14–15), the need to fulfill one's responsibilities in the service of God (17:7–10), and the certainty that God will call all humanity to account for their deeds (12:47–8, 13:1–9). Then there are specific assurances that God is already at work through Jesus to accomplish his plan for his people (13:31–3) and that the powers of the new age are already present and active in the words and works of Jesus (17:20–1).

Details of the story of the crucifixion of Jesus and the discovery of the empty tomb are unique to Luke as well. Instead of the cry of abandonment (Mark 15:34), Jesus commits himself to the Father (Luke 23:46); the women who witness his death and who hear the word of the angel at the empty tomb are specifically said to have been with Jesus in Galilee (23:49, 55; 24:10). Unlike in Mark, where the disciples are instructed to return to Galilee after the announcement of Jesus' resurrection, and in Matthew, where they do so, in Luke all the appearances of the risen Lord take place in the vicinity of Jerusalem. Jerusalem symbolizes Christian unity in Spirit for Luke; accordingly, this Gospel portrays the resurrection in its own way, placing all Jesus' resurrection appearances in Jerusalem and ignoring any appearances in Galilee. Although Luke does make room for visionary appearances to disciples – preeminently Paul – far from Jerusalem, the dominant conception of resurrection here is every bit as materialist as Matthew's, but for a different reason. Luke localizes revelation, and the authority revelation brings, in Jerusalem, which is depicted as the unique locus of Jesus' physical presence after his resurrection. Luke is the first

Gospel to have Mary and her companions (whose names change yet again as compared to Mark and Matthew) search the tomb and find it empty (Luke 24:2–4): "But they found the stone had been rolled away from the memorial, and entering did not find the body of the Lord Jesus. And it happened while they were at a loss concerning this, and look: two men stood opposite them in gleaming apparel."

Luke produces a certifiably empty tomb, because the women go in and inspect it. Likewise, Luke has the risen Jesus insist on his own physical reality: only in this Gospel does Jesus explicitly say (24:39-43): "See my hands and my feet, that I am myself. Feel me and see, because a spirit does not have flesh and bone just as you perceive I have." Jesus even eats some fish to make his point – and Luke's: the resurrection is substantial and material, more physical than in any of the other Gospels. In Luke, Mary and her companions do not succeed in convincing the other disciples that their vision was authentic; the men reject their testimony as "nonsense" (*leros*; Luke 24:9–12), idle tales from women. Apart from tangible, physical substance, Luke dismisses vision and women's testimony with a single word. For Luke's Gospel, only Jesus personally, raised from the dead in flesh and bone (Luke 24:39), can explain his resurrected presence among his disciples. The Book of Acts (1:3) sets aside a period of forty days during which the risen Jesus teaches his followers in and around Jerusalem, not Galilee.

When Luke's male apostles, who go on to see the risen Jesus, write off Mary Magdalene's vision, that is no idle dismissal. Luke does accept another visionary appearance, involving only men. A stranger joins two disciples (one named Kleopas) when they are on the way to Emmaus from Jerusalem after the crucifixion. At first they do not recognize him, but he reveals himself to them as Jesus during a meal – and then becomes invisible (Luke 24:13–35). In Luke this male-only account supersedes the story about Mary and the other women at the tomb. Jesus' death and resurrection are here shown to be in fulfillment of Scripture (24:13–27), but it is in the breaking of bread (told in language that uses the technical Eucharistic terms "took, blessed, broke, gave") that he was "made known to them" (24:28–35). The disciples' resources for understanding and interpreting to others the significance of Jesus are the Scriptures, the experience of the risen Lord, and the shared meal (24:36–47). This message is to go out to all nations, once his followers have been endued with power from God – an event that is to occur in Jerusalem (24:48–53). The Book of Acts realizes that program.

Acts pictures three major stages in the development of the church's transitions from a primarily Jewish to a primarily Gentile outreach, and in its encounter with the imperial power of Rome. Acts 1–8 depicts the empowering of the apostles and the constitution of the new community; Acts 9:1–21:26 describes Paul as the primary agent of outreach to the Gentile world; and Acts 21:27–28:31 presents Paul as the prototype for Christian confrontation with Roman authority.

Following Jesus' ascension into the presence of God (Acts 1:1–11; cf. Luke 24:50–1), the apostles – who have witnessed Jesus' life and work, death and resurrection – receive the outpouring of the Spirit (Acts 1:8) to enable them to fulfill their new mission. Significantly, this testimony is to begin in Jerusalem, which was seen as the dwelling place of God among his people, and which featured so centrally in the career of Jesus. In preparation for that event, a twelfth member of the apostolic circle is chosen to replace the traitor, Judas. With the selection of Matthias (1:12–26), the circle of apostles is complete.

The outpouring of the Spirit takes place on an Israelite holiday commemorating the promise of a new beginning for God's covenant people: Pentecost. The experience of wind and fire recall Elijah's experience when God spoke to him on Mount Sinai (1 Kings 19:11–12), commissioning him to challenge the leadership of Israel. In Acts 2, all the apostles were gathered in a house when the wind and fire came from heaven, and they all began to speak in other languages, which were immediately understood by the throng of Jews and the devout, God-fearing Gentiles who had come to Jerusalem from all over the known world of the time. Peter's explanation of this astounding event is based on allusions to and quotations from the Scriptures, especially the Book of Joel (Acts 2:17–21, cf. Joel 2:28–32), and he links the public outpouring of Spirit with the death and resurrection of Jesus (Acts 2:25–8, cf. Psalm 16:8–11; Acts 2:34, cf. Psalm 110:1). About three thousand people were persuaded by this event and its meaning according to Acts; they submitted to the public rite of baptism in Jesus' name (rather than immersion in the conventional sense) and joined the community, into which they were integrated through the instruction and fellowship led by the apostles (2:41–2).

The apostles' ability to perform miracles confirmed God's support for their claims about the significance of Jesus and the divine origin of the Spirit. Those who joined the movement gave their support tangibly in the resources they pooled for the benefit of the group (2:43–7). Peter's healing of the lame man in the Temple by appealing to "the name of Jesus of Nazareth" (3:6) explicitly connects the work of the apostles with the work of

---

PENTECOST

Originally an agricultural festival at the time of harvest (Exodus 23:16), and earlier known as the Feast of Weeks (Exodus 34:22), Pentecost was the occasion required by the law of Israel for thanking God for the grain just harvested. It was to take place fifty days (seven weeks plus one day) after the Feast of Passover (Leviticus 23:15–16). ("Pentecost" is derived from the Greek word for "fifty.") The agricultural focus of Weeks was so emphatic that there is no precise connection made within the Bible between that festival and an event in the history of Israel in a way comparable to Passover. Still, the Book of Deuteronomy makes the association between Weeks and remembering that one was a slave in Egypt: that remembrance, in turn, was to motivate one to observe and perform the statues (Deuteronomy 16:12). By the

time of the *Book of Jubilees* in the second century B.C.E., the feast is associated with the covenant and the Torah as mediated by Moses (see *Jubilees* 1:1–26), as well as with the covenants with Noah (*Jubilees* 6:1, 10–11, 17–19) and Abraham (*Jubilees* 15:1–16). At a later stage, certain Rabbinic traditions (but by no means all) would make the giving of the Law in Exodus 19 the lectionary reading of Weeks (see Megillah 31a in Bavli, departing from Exodus 19:1), and would recall that the word of God was split into the seventy languages of the nations (Shabat 88b). Although the specific association with the giving of the Torah cannot be established as a controlling sense by the time of the New Testament, that meaning grew out of the generative connection between Weeks and divine covenant that had been made long before.

Jesus. This healing is followed by another sermon preached by Peter (3:11–26). Its thematic structure is similar to most of the sermons attributed to the apostles throughout Acts:

1. Jesus stands at the culmination of the line that runs from Abraham (the source of the covenant people) through Moses (the agent of the law), David (from whom came promise of renewal of God's rule), and the prophets.
2. God approved what Jesus did, as is evident from the great deeds he performed through the power of the Spirit.
3. The Jewish leaders put Jesus to death, or arranged for his death, without realizing what they were doing, and thereby fulfilled prophecy.
4. Gentiles should be aware that God is also concerned for them and has promised through the prophets their inclusion in God's people.
5. God has vindicated Jesus and his message by raising him from the dead; he is now exalted at God's right hand.
6. All humanity, Jews and Gentiles, are called to repent and to receive God's deliverance in the name of Jesus, whom God has designated to be the final judge of the human race.

Not all these themes are present in every sermon in Acts, but they are recurrent motifs.

The religious authorities attempt to silence the apostles but fail to intimidate them (Acts 4:1–4). At the hearing before the local council, Peter delivers yet another speech (4:8–12), in which he makes the claim that in all the world there is no one else whom God has given who can save us. Despite further warnings, the apostles continue to tell about Jesus, gaining large numbers of followers (4:4, "about 5,000") and renewed conviction and commitment from the members of the community (4:13–37). Already, however, there are those who are not totally committed, as is evident when Ananias and Sapphira are struck dead for their failure to give all that they had to the community (5:1–9). As the group grows in numbers (5:12–16), the official opposition mounts (5:17–33) – even though an occasional cautionary voice is raised, such as that of Gamaliel, a leading Pharisee (5:34–9), who suggests that God might be behind this new movement.

Barnabas, a Levite who appears to have been a respected member of the Jewish community in Jerusalem with long-standing ties to Jesus' movement, joins the communal life of the apostles, making a public commitment of himself and his tangible resources. He proves a key figure in Paul's ministry to the Gentiles, with the result that he too becomes a victim of the persecution of Christians by those who see the movement as a betrayal of the covenant with Israel (Acts 13:44–51).

The apostles continue their associations with the Temple, even while carrying on meetings in their homes, somewhat as the Pharisees are doing in this period. The work of caring for the community becomes so demanding that the apostles have to look to others for assistance in the administration of funds for the group. Chosen for this task are Greek-speaking Jews, which signals to the reader the move the group is to take toward inclusion of the Gentiles. The names of all seven chosen for this role are Greek (Acts 6:1–6). One of the seven, Stephen, is accused by the Jewish leaders of subverting the Temple and the Law of Moses in the name of Jesus of Nazareth (6:8–15). His defense traces the founding of the covenant with Abraham, its renewal through Jacob and his twelve sons, the giving of the Law through Moses, the movement of the portable shrine of God's presence from Egypt to Canaan, and the shrine's replacement by the Temple in the time of Solomon (7:1–47). But Stephen declares that God does not dwell in houses built by human hands, and he quotes Scripture to make his point (Acts 6:48–50 = Isaiah 66:1–2). With that revolutionary statement, he turns to a denunciation of the leaders for their rejection of God's Messiah (7:51–3). Understandably, given his blasphemy against the Temple, his opponents put Stephen to death by stoning, even while he is claiming to see Jesus at God's right hand (7:54–60). From this point on, the work of the apostles increasingly moves across the boundaries of the Jewish people and out toward the wider Roman, Gentile world.

Despite the beginning of severe persecution of the church (Acts 8:2–3), the inclusive movement continues with successful preaching among the Samaritans, the conversion of a magician named Simon (8:4–25), and Philip's providential encounter in the desert with an Ethiopian eunuch (an official of

---

STONING

The legal traditions of Israel authorized execution by stoning for a range of offenses, including the worship of gods other than Yahweh (Deuteronomy 13:6–10, 17:2–7), participation in child sacrifice to the Canaanite god Molech (Leviticus 20:2–5), breaking the Sabbath law (Numbers 15:32–6), and female promiscuity (Deuteronomy 22:20–1). Even certain forms of disobedience of a son to his father were to be punished by stoning the guilty son. The procedure is not described in the Bible, but it usually took place outside the city (Leviticus 24:14; Deuteronomy 17:5; 1 Kings 21:13) and was a corporate act by multiple members of the community rather than the task of a single executioner.

It is likely that more was involved than throwing fist-sized rocks from a dozen yards away, as some Bible illustrators have pictured this action. The stones were probably large and heavy, so that the guilty one was simultaneously crushed to death and hidden from sight under the mound of rocks that were hurled at and heaped on the culprit. According to the Mishnah (Sanhedrin 6:4), the victim was thrown from a cliff or wall, head first, the apparent procedure in the attempt to kill Jesus in Luke 4:29. If that did not kill him, first the witnesses against him and then all Israelites present were to heave large stones on him from above until he died. The Mishnaic procedure is only slightly adjusted for women, and

then only to avoid their appearing naked in public. Jesus must have had sympathizers in Nazareth, because he escaped. But not even his family could (or would) shelter him any longer. Jesus' reference to his followers (Mark 14:22) about his own impending death in terms of his body's being broken may mean that he expected to be executed by stoning rather than by the Roman mode of crucifixion. This interpretation is confirmed by Jesus' perceiving the hostility that was mounting against him as leading to mass action that would result in his being denounced as "a glutton and a drunkard" and then suffering the group execution ordered in Deuteronomy 21:18–21.

the queen) who visited the Temple in Jerusalem and was puzzled by the Jewish scriptural reference to someone who will be killed like a slaughtered lamb (8:26–40, cf. Isaiah 53:7–8). Someone named Saul, later to be known as Paul (8:1–3), joins the persecution, supported by those Jews who are enraged by the apostles' inviting impure and non-Israelite people to enter the covenant community, as well as by the claim by Jesus' disciples that God will radically change the Temple, or destroy it (as some claimed Stephen had said). The movement nonetheless continues, as is manifest in the preaching activity of Philip along the Hellenized coast from Azotus to Caesarea (8:40).

The transition to the second major part of Acts begins with the account of Saul's conversion. While in the process of persecuting the new community, Saul has a vision of the risen Jesus, is struck blind, healed, and baptized, and then begins to preach Jesus as the Son of God (9:1–20). After escaping a plot to assassinate him and visiting the Jerusalem apostles, Paul moves back to Tarsus. The Acts narrative marks the transition by a summary statement of the growth and strength of the Church in "Judea, Galilee, and Samaria" (9:31), but excludes reference to the three years Paul said he spent in Nabatea (Galatians 1:17–18).

This second major phase of the Acts account gets under way with Peter's shift of evangelistic operations to the coastal cities of Lydda, Joppa, and Caesarea, cities dominated by Hellenistic culture that served as centers for Roman military control. After the apostle achieves spectacular success in healing a lame man and restoring to life a faithful and generous Christian widow (9:32–43), Cornelius (a Roman military officer who is attracted to the God of the Jews) is told by an angel to contact Peter. A vision also comes to Peter – and is repeated twice – instructing him to overcome his ritual and ethnic prejudices against Gentiles. The messengers from Cornelius arrive with an invitation to Peter and his associates to spend the night with him – which would result in their violating Pharisaic purity laws. He accepts the invitation to visit this Roman officer. The result of Peter's explaining the message to these Gentiles is that Cornelius and his associates believe, are given the gift of the Spirit, and are baptized. Peter also reaches a key insight for his fledgling movement: "that God treats everyone on the same basis," so that "everyone that trusts in Jesus will receive forgiveness of sins" (10:1–48). These events are reported to the Jerusalem apostles, whose natural prejudices are overcome, and who conclude, "God has also given the Gentiles the opportunity to repent and live" (11:1–18).

Once the precedent has been set for preaching to Gentiles and for their inclusion in the community, the challenge to extend the scope of the gospel to predominantly Gentile territories leads the Jerusalem apostles to commission Paul to take the initiative in this new phase of the church's work (Acts 11:19–30, 13:1–3). Persecutions continue (12:1–5), but God acts to set free his messengers (12:6–18) and to punish those rulers who oppose his purpose (12:20–4). The details vary, but the pattern is consistent: Paul and his associates in the Gentile mission seize the opportunity in each place as it presents itself:

Ashdod-Yam, a Crusader castle, from the west. References in ancient texts to Ashdod proper, which is three miles northeast, go back to the fourteenth century B.C.E., and in the Bible to the time of Joshua (Joshua 11:21–2). The city was a major center of the Philistines, and the ark of the covenant was taken there after its capture (1 Samuel 4–6). Ashdod expanded during the Persian and Hellenistic periods and shrank under Herod. The Romans destroyed the city during the Jewish revolt of 66–70 C.E. A port lay two and a half miles away at the mouth of the Lachish River. (BiblePlaces.com)

On Cyprus, they confront a magician and strike him blind, which leads to the conversion of the governor (13:4–12).

In Asia Minor, in Pisidian Antioch (not to be confused with Antioch in Syria), they preach in the synagogue, at first with spectacular results (13:13–43) and then with mounting resentment from the synagogue leaders because of their insistence on the inclusion of the Gentiles (13:44–52).

In Iconium, the same responses are evoked from Jews and Gentiles (14:1–7). In Lystra and Derbe, the Gentiles are so dazzled by the apostles' ability to heal a lame man that they acclaim them gods, to which Paul and Barnabas respond by preaching the gospel. Opposition from the Jews continues to follow them to the point that Paul is nearly killed by stoning (14:8–20).

Nonetheless, Paul and his colleagues complete their circuit of cities in Asia Minor and return to Antioch, where they report on the results of their mission (14:20–27). (Acts has Paul just pick himself up after being stoned, to retrace his steps with Barnabas through the same places where people had all but killed him. That strains credibility to the breaking point and betrays the strong tendency toward legendary embellishment in Acts.) Hostile

Roman aqueduct at Pisidian Antioch. The central region of what is now called Turkey is a vast plateau, which shows evidence of occupation back to Paleolithic times and a rich mixture of cultural influences. After Alexander drove out the Persians, Greek and then Roman culture became dominant. The Romans built or extended such cites as Ephesus, Sardis, Pergamon, and Pisidian Antioch, a crucial place in the emergence of Paul's message. (BiblePlaces.com)

reporters brought word of their work to the leaders of the church in Jerusalem, and a council is convened to settle the issue of the status of Gentiles within the Church, as Paul recalls in his Letter to the Galatians. As we noted, the results of the conference as told in Acts differ significantly from Paul's report (Galatians 2:1–10), according to which there were no ritual or legal obligations for Gentiles to become members of God's people. Here, however, the agreement is that Gentiles are to abstain from eating food made ritually unclean by being offered to idols, from sexual immorality, and from eating any animal that had been strangled or any meat containing blood. All these are forbidden in the Jewish law (Exodus 34:15–17; Leviticus 18:6–23; 17:10–13) and are here in Acts represented as binding on Gentile Christians. It is not at all likely that Paul would have agreed to such ritual obligations for Gentiles. Yet as Gentile Christians became increasingly steeped in the Jewish Scriptures, they were willing to adopt certain ritual norms for differentiating themselves from non-Christians.

According to Acts, Paul and Barnabas, following disagreement about their associate named John Mark, part ways (15:36–41), with Paul revisiting the cities of Asia Minor en route to the mainland of Europe (16:1–10). There among his first converts is a businesswoman named Lydia, in Philippi, the capital of Macedonia, named in honor of the father of Alexander the Great. The purple dye in which Lydia deals is a luxury item in the Roman world, which implies that she is a wealthy woman. The Acts account (16:11–15) suggests that she owns a sizable house and presides over a household that includes servants: they are baptized and join the community along with Lydia. The activities of Paul are centered at the "place of prayer" (16:13, 16), which was a common designation of the gathering places of Jews in predominantly Gentile towns and cities. The exorcism of an evil spirit from a slave-girl prophetess results in Paul and his companion,

THE APOSTOLIC COUNCIL

Prophecy proves key to Luke-Acts' presentation of the relationship between Israel and the community of the Church. In Acts 15, James speaks within a specific context, not only in Jerusalem but also within international Christianity, as it then existed. A controversy erupts because "some had come down from Judea, who were teaching the brothers, If you do not circumcise by the custom of Moses, you are not able to be saved" (15:1). The result is a dispute with Paul and Barnabas, which is not surprising, since they have just returned to Antioch after successful completion of the work that the prophets and teachers there, by the direction of the Holy Spirit, had sent them out to do (Acts 13:1–14:28; see 13:2 and 14:26 for the framing of the section in terms of the "work" they completed). They announce that by means of their ministry God has "opened a door of faith for the Gentiles" (Acts 14:27).

That, of course, is the most positive way of relating their experience of preaching in Asia Minor. In the same section of Acts, a pattern is developed in which Paul and Barnabas announce that they "turn to the Gentiles" because they have been rejected, even persecuted, by Jews (see Acts 13:46, and the whole of vv. 42–51; 14:1–5, 19). Indeed, that is the providential pattern of the whole of Luke-Acts, in which even Jesus is rejected by his own – to the point of being prepared for stoning – and speaks of the extension of the work of the prophets to those outside of Israel as a consequence of that rejection (so Luke 4:14–30). The rejection of Jesus and his message by the Jews is a piv-

otal motif in Luke-Acts, in that it permits of the transition in the narrative to the emphasis on the Gentiles that is a signature concern. But the relationship between Israel and the Gentiles in Acts is actually more than a matter of the apologetic explanation of how Gentiles came to predominate in the Church. The mention of the issue of circumcision in Acts 15, and the emphasis that the council in Jerusalem met to address that issue first of all, reflects a profound awareness that the very identity of the Church in respect of Israel is at stake.

Because the question of circumcision has already been dealt with in Acts 11, as a consequence of Peter's baptisms in the house of Cornelius, the mention of the issue in Acts 15 can only be read as a deliberate resumption of what was a genuinely contentious concern within primitive Christianity. The extensive narrative in Acts 10 has already confirmed, by vision and the coming of the Holy Spirit upon those in that house, that non-Jews are indeed to be baptized, and Peter in Acts 11 personally rehearses those events for "the apostles and brothers who were in Judea" (11:1). Having heard his response to "those of the circumcision" in Jerusalem, who taxed Peter for visiting and eating with those who were foreskinned (11:2–3), Peter's hearers are reported to accept that "God has granted even the Gentiles repentance for life" (11:18).

By dealing with circumcision and other issues of purity together, Acts 15 conflates not only the particular topics and different meetings but also the leaders who settle both questions.

The representative function of Paul and Barnabas (along with others) for the church in Antioch is underlined, because they bring news of the conversion of the Gentiles to Phoenicia and Samaria on their way to Jerusalem, to the "great joy" of all (Acts 15:4). These *apostles* of Antioch are then received by both *the apostles and the elders* of the church in Jerusalem (Acts 15:4), with Peter named as the leading figure, only to be trumped by James. When the gathering gets down to business, apostles and elders are again named as the participants (Acts 15:6). So the usual reference to this meeting as "the Apostolic Council of Jerusalem" is amply warranted. In fact, it would be better to speak of the "Council *in* Jerusalem," since apostles from other places are included. In addition, the "elders" are emphatically a part of the proceedings, within a document in which elders and bishops together are understood to function within the apostolic succession (see Acts 14:23, 20:28). The council is both apostolic and episcopal, and the latter aspect is especially reinforced by the later appearance of James, who was known as the first bishop in Jerusalem (Eusebius, *History of the Church* 2.1.1–6).

The key to James' position, in not requiring circumcision of Gentiles but requiring an acknowledgement of purity from them, was brilliantly provided by Kirsopp Lake in his study of the Council in Jerusalem. Scholarship since his time has provided a striking confirmation of his suggestion. Lake uses the proscriptions James insisted on – of food sacrificed to idols, of the consumption of blood or meat

(continued)

THE APOSTOLIC COUNCIL (continued)

from an animal that had been strangled, and of fornication – as a way of describing how James and the council identified believing Gentiles in relation to Israel. He observes the affinity with the rules in Leviticus 17 regarding non-Israelites who reside in the land: they are to desist from making offerings to other gods and from the usage of any altar but that in the Temple (Leviticus 17:7–9), they are to abstain from blood (Leviticus 17:10–13), and they are to avoid the type of sexual relations described in chapter 18 (Leviticus 18:24–30). By the time of the Talmud (Sanhedrin 56b), such prohibitions were elaborated into the so-called Noachic commandments, binding upon humanity generally, but Lake rightly observes they are formulated too late to have influenced Acts.

Lake also called attention to the requirements made of Gentiles within a work of Hellenistic Judaism, the fourth book of the *Sibylline Oracles* (4:24–34):

> Happy will be those of earthly men who will cherish the great God, blessing before eating, drinking and having confidence in piety. They will deny all temples and altars they see: purposeless transports of dumb stones, defiled by animates' blood and sacrifices of four-footed animals. But they will behold the great renown of the one God, neither breaking into reckless murder, nor transacting what is stolen for gain, which are cold happenings. They do not have shameful desire for another's bed, nor hateful and repulsive abuse of a male.

What is especially striking about this prophecy is that it is directed to the people of Asia and Europe (*Sibylline Oracles* 4:1) through the mouth of the Sibyl (*Sibylline Oracles* 4:22–3), the leg-endary oracle of mantic counsel. Her utterance here is explicitly backed up by the threat of eschatological judgment for all (*Sibylline Oracles* 4:40–8).

The emphasis on prophecy in Luke-Acts accords with the perspectives of Hellenistic historians such as Diodorus Siculus and Dionysius of Halicarnassus. The place of Sibylline prophesies is prominent in both. But while Luke-Acts invokes the motif of prophecy (literary and contemporary), the Sibyl makes no appearance in a work that is, after all, the largest in the New Testament. That suggests that the way for the synthesis of Hellenistic oracles and Hebrew prophecy had been prepared, especially by works such as the *Sibylline Oracles* of Hellenistic Judaism, but then that Luke-Acts insists on the attestation of Jesus' coming (directly or indirectly) as an indispensable criterion of true prophecy.

Silas, being imprisoned, but the outcome is their miraculous release from their bonds, the conversion of the jailer and his household, and the liberation of Paul and Silas by the Roman authorities (16:16–40). The author wants to show that Christianity is not a politically subversive movement and that its claims are credible, as various Roman officials (such as the centurion in Caesarea and this jailer and the local magistrates) recognized from the outset of the apostles' mission to the Greco-Roman world.

In Thessalonica and in Berea, Paul and Silas have remarkable results from their preaching about Jesus as the anointed of God, but Jewish opposition tries to discredit them as anti-Roman (Acts 17:1–15). In

PURPLE DYE

A rare and costly dye shading from red to purple was produced from a fluid secreted by a shellfish (*Murex*) that flourishes on the coast of Syria and Palestine. Only royalty and others of great wealth could originally afford it. Second Chronicles 2 reports the negotiations of King Solomon with the king of Tyre to obtain the services of a craftsman who could produce this purple dye for him. The sacred tent described in Exodus was to be decorated abundantly with purple (Exodus 35–6, 38), as were the garments of the priests (Exodus 39:1–3). In the gospel tradition, purple is the sign of wealth (Luke 16:19), as well as of royalty. Jesus, in mockery of his claim to be king, is robed in purple (Mark 15:17–20; John 19:2–5). The evil monarch of the end time is pictured in Revelation 17 and 18 as a harlot clothed in purple. The fact that purple dye was such a luxury item suggests that Lydia, whose business was selling it and who was Paul's first convert in Europe (according to Acts 16), was a woman of considerable means.

PLACE OF PRAYER

The Greek term *proseuche* is used for places where Jews gathered, not only for prayer but also for community assemblies of a more general nature. The group that gathered there referred to itself as a *synagoge*, which means "gathering" or "assembly." Only much later did this latter term come to be used for the buildings where the group met. Archaeological analysis of ancient synagogue buildings, a few of which date from the first century C.E., shows that originally most were private homes or similar structures where the members assembled. As the groups grew in size and self-confidence, they incorporated adjacent courtyards into their meeting places. Eventually they began to construct distinctive buildings for their religious meetings, later adding facilities for more formal instruction as well. The firmly dated Jewish meeting place (second century B.C.E.) that has been excavated in Delos was originally a private house, but it was later altered to serve as an assembly hall. The largest such structure adapted to function as a Jewish place of worship is a vast public hall (third century C.E.) excavated at Sardis in Asia Minor. The destruction of the Jerusalem Temple in 70 C.E. and the failure of the second revolt in 135 C.E. led Jews in Palestine and elsewhere to begin to construct special buildings as places of worship and instruction. Prior to this, these "places of prayer" served local and traveling Jews as somewhere they could study, meet and enjoy meals with others of similar convictions.

Athens, however, following some discussions in the synagogues, Paul is invited by the civic authorities responsible for the moral life of the city – the council of the Areopagus – to explain to them his teaching (17:16–31). His message to the Athenian intellectual leaders takes a very different approach from the themes he and the apostles use in the other sermons in Acts. Here, he begins by affirming certain aspects of universal natural law as taught by Stoic philosophers of the time and by noting the essential unity of the human race under the Creator. He even quotes Greek poets to make his point. But when he claims that God will judge the world by the resurrected Jesus – rather than by Stoic natural law – his hearers think he has lost his mind. Only a handful of men and women are persuaded by his message. One of them, Dionysius, was associated with mystical teaching in Church tradition centuries later.

In Corinth and Ephesus – two leading cities of the Greek world – Paul's strategy is to begin his work in the synagogues, until the Jewish opposition mounts (Acts 18:1–28, 19:1–10). In addition, in both cities he is brought before the civil authorities (18:12–16, 19:21–41). In this series of accounts several details give us important information about the spread of Christianity. Two tent makers, Priscilla and Aquila, have Paul live and work with them in Corinth, where they fled from Rome when Emperor Claudius expelled the Jews, who were in turmoil as a result of the coming among them of Christian messengers. This couple were already converted when Paul meets them; later they move to Ephesus, where they also have leadership roles in the young church, which meet in their home there (1 Corinthians 16:19). Gallio, the Roman governor in Corinth, refuses to accept the charges brought against Paul by the Jews. After a return visit to Syria and Caesarea, Paul goes to Ephesus, where he meets Apollos, a convert from Judaism and a native of Alexandria, who is apparently skilled in the Jewish Wisdom tradition and in the style of biblical interpretation best known from Philo of Alexandria. Paul gives him further instruction about Jesus, and, consequently, Apollos is effective in both Ephesus and Corinth in persuading Jews about Jesus as God's Messiah (18:24–8).

The healings and exorcisms performed among the Christians in Ephesus attract vast public attention, but also opposition from those who make their living as priests and attendants in and around the world-renowned temple of Artemis located in this city. The result is a riot, and Paul departs for Macedonia (Acts 19:1–20:1). His announced intention is to return to Jerusalem before sailing west to Rome (19:21–2). On his journey to Jerusalem, he meets with the elders from the church at Ephesus and tells them that they will not see him again: a clear indication of his impending martyrdom (20:13–38). In Jerusalem the religious and political authorities seize him. In reporting these events, the author of Acts recounts Paul's description of his life, including a defense of himself as not guilty of violating religious or civil regulations – a judgment that is confirmed by all the authorities who hear his defense (22–6). In his final hearings at Caesarea, the official seat of Roman rule in Palestine, he appeals to Caesar, which is his right as a Roman citizen, and is sent off to Rome as a prisoner (27:1). The voyage is interrupted by a shipwreck, from which the crew and passengers are saved (27:13–44). The narrative style is similar to romances of the second century, which have influenced the author's mode of telling this story. After another sign of divine deliverance – a deadly snake bites Paul but he is unharmed (28:1–6) – and other indications of God's favor upon him (28:7–10), Paul lands at Puteoli (near Naples). When he reaches Rome, he is placed under house arrest. This enables him to be visited by Jewish leaders, whom he tries to convince through his interpretation of the Law and the Prophets that Jesus was God's Messiah (28:16–23). Some are persuaded, but others he consigns to the people spoken of by Isaiah who lack an understanding of God and his purpose (Isaiah 6:9–10, cited in Acts 28:26–7). The message has been sent to the Gentiles, and they will give heed. The story ends with Paul carrying forward his work of preaching and teaching, even though the earlier narrative has already informed the reader of Paul's impending death in the service of the Gospel.

Acts emerges as a major document for the early Church; its style provides a contact with the literate Gentile world, and its content is both a justification for the claim that the Church has become the covenant people and a rebuttal to those who see in the Christian Gospel either a threat to the political status quo or a perversion of the Scriptures of Israel. Since the emphasis is on the worldwide mission to be performed by the apostles and their successors, the issue of when the new age will come is of secondary importance. Of primary importance is carrying out the commission to spread the news about Jesus to the ends of the earth, as was articulated when the Spirit was poured out at Pentecost. Greco-Roman writers in the second century C.E. told stories of divine visions and intervention of the deities in behalf of humans devoted to them or searching for them. Prime examples of this type of literature are the *Metamorphoses* of Apuleius, which details a young man's search for the goddess Isis, and the *Sacred Discourses* of Aristides, whose devotion to the god Asklepios led to transforming mystical experiences. Such popular literary styles were employed in the second and subsequent centuries by Christian writers to surround what they saw as significant for the life of the Church with an aura of the miraculous as a sign of contact with God.

B. The Gospel According to John: Mystical Participation in Divine Life

Two major cultural factors influenced the reworking of traditions in the Gospel according to John. The first derives from the Wisdom tradition of the Hellenistic age, especially as developed in Judaism. The second is manifest in the keen interest among both Jews and Gentiles of the first century C.E. in forms of religion that offered the possibility of a direct experience of God, especially through visions and hearing sacred messages. With a growing sense of the vast difference between God and human beings — "As high as the heavens are above the earth, so high are my ways and thoughts above yours" (Isaiah 55:9) — and of the awesomeness of God's presence (Ezekiel 1) came a yearning for some instrument or agent by which mere humans could benefit from contact with the sovereign, holy God. For some, this mediating agency was found in Wisdom, viewed as the first of God's creations and even as his co-creator (Proverbs 8) and as the channel through which knowledge of God comes to human beings (Sirach 1). Others hoped for a direct vision of God, on the model of the experiences of Moses, Elijah, Ezekiel, and Daniel, whose very appearances were altered as a consequence of their having contacted God. In the Gentile world of this time, there was a similar striving for religious experiences that would bring together the hallowed traditions of divine wisdom with a direct and immediate experience of the deities.

One of the most effective forms of these aspirations developed during this period in relation to the goddess Isis. In older Egyptian tradition she had a role as the one who restored to life her husband, Osiris. His death at the hands of his enemy and return from the dead symbolized the annual cycle of fertility caused by the rise and fall of the Nile. By the Hellenistic period Isis had taken over the role of goddess of wisdom and was believed to appear to those seeking her help or insights, with the result that the lives of her devotees were renewed and fulfilled by sharing in the divine life. In his portrayal of Jesus, the author of the Gospel according to John combines such factors of human participation in the divine life and understanding of the divine purpose.

1. The Prologue to John's Gospel

The prologue to the Gospel according to John (1:1–18) speaks of the Word, or *Logos*, of God as the instrument of creation and of divine self-disclosure. In a way that recalls the roles of Wisdom, but at the same time is significantly different, the Word enables human beings to become members of God's own people (1:12–13). This admission to the new

LOGOS

Two traditions, each from a separate culture, merge in the meaning of *logos* in the Gospel according to John. (1) In Greek philosophy, this term was used with reference to the rational process, seen as characterizing the universe and its ongoing functions. Humans, by perceiving this *logos*, can gain understanding of the inherent order that pervades all reality. The term, which may have taken on these connotations with Heraclitus, the sixth-century B.C.E. philosopher who sought to discern order in the universal processes, was employed by the Stoics in connection with their similar concept of the law of nature, which dominates all that is. (2) The other tradition is the biblical understanding of creation through the *word* of God, which in the Septuagint is translated as *logos*. In the Jewish Wisdom tradition, the instrument through which God called the world into being and rules it is "wisdom" – in Greek *sophia*. This role of wisdom is described in such passages as Proverbs 8:22–31 and the Wisdom of Solomon 9:1–2. For Philo of Alexandria, the *logos* was both the means by which God communicated his purpose to his people – the Word of God – and the agent by which the world was created and sustained. Further, this understanding of divinely ordered reason in the universe was fully compatible with the insights of the philosophers of that period, and at the same time resonates with the significance of the term *memra* in Aramaic, which refers to God's word of command.

In the prologue to the Gospel according to John, however, another crucial dimension is added to the *logos*: the creative, reasoned purpose of God has been disclosed in a human form: "The word became flesh" and dwelt among human beings, so that they can come to discern the divine purpose and to see themselves as God's children (John 1:1–18).

community of faith differs completely from natural birth into an ordinary human family or race. Indeed, the Word's own people did not receive him (1:11). This unique Son of God is the source of the light of the knowledge of God (1:4) and of the radiance of God's glory (in contrast to the Temple, where God's glory once shone) and is the channel of God's grace and truth (1:14, 16, 18). The requirement for becoming God's child is to trust God's Son (1:12). John the Baptist prepared for Jesus' coming (1:6–9, 19–27), denying that he was himself the Light, and acclaiming Jesus of Nazareth as the Lamb of God, who takes away the world's sin (1:29, 36), and as the Spirit-anointed Son of God (1:32–4). At the outset of his public career, Jesus begins to rally around him the core of his followers, who acclaim him as Messiah, Son of God, and King of Israel (1:41, 49). He responds by promising them that they will see his ultimate vindication by God's angels as son of man (1:51). Paradoxically, John's Gospel pictures Jesus as fully human ("son of Joseph"; 1:45) but also as sharing the very nature of God (1:18, 8:58, 17:21).

Although we do not know who wrote this anonymous work, frequent references in John to "the disciple whom Jesus loved" (13:23–5, 19:26–7, 20:2–8, 21:7, 20) and his identification as the one who remembered or recorded this Jesus material led many in the early Church to the conclusion that the Gospel was written by John, the son of Zebedee (Mark 1:19), although he is never mentioned by name in the Gospel. The reference in 21:22 to the possibility that this disciple might live until Jesus returned to earth led some to suppose that he was writing at a greatly advanced age, perhaps late in the first century. No matter how attractive, these are no more than ancient guesses, and in any case the Gospel itself refers to a group of people who received the testimony of the beloved disciple and who took responsibility for the text (21:24). What is clear is that this Gospel is not directly dependent on the other Gospels and that its composers and writers were more interested in symbolic meaning than in historical narrative. Indeed, John shows delight in using words with double

JOHN

"John," a shortened form in Greek (*Ioannes*) of the Semitic name Yohanan, was a commonly used name in the centuries before Jesus. In the New Testament, those with this name include John the Baptist (John 1:19–34); John, the father of Simon Peter (John 1:42); John, from the family of the high priest (Acts 4:6); John Mark (Acts 15:37); John, the son of Zebedee (Mark 1:19); and John, the author of the Book of Revelation (Revelation 1:4–10). The authorship of the fourth Gospel was traditionally assigned to John the disciple (the son of Zebedee and the brother of James), who was with Jesus at the Transfiguration (Mark 9:2) and during the struggle of Jesus in the garden of Gethsemane

(Mark 14:33). John and his brother James were called by Paul "pillars" in the Jerusalem church (Galatians 2:6–10). This John was identified as the unnamed "beloved disciple" mentioned repeatedly in John, and assumed to be the author, but scholars have proposed many alternatives, including Nathaniel, John Mark, a disciple unidentified except in association with the fourth Gospel, and even Lazarus, none of whom has won widespread agreement.

The language of John's Gospel is disarmingly simple. But the symbolic strategy of the author, with the focus on timeless meaning rather than literal reports of what happened, and the fact that in many narratives and teachings

this Gospel differs widely from the other Gospels, suggest that it was written by someone who later became a follower of Jesus, not someone who was an eyewitness. In sharp contrast to the Gospel according to John, the Revelation of John is written in thoroughly apocalyptic style, and its major interest is never touched on in the Gospel according to John: the political and cosmic conflict between the Roman Empire and the people of God, which is soon to culminate in the final battle between God and the powers of evil. The confrontation that is shaping up between the Church and the empire, with their incompatible claims to the divinity of Christ and of the emperor, is the distinctive focus of the author of Revelation.

---

meaning, intent that the audience grasp both meanings rather than choose between them. For example:

> "be born again" – "be born from above" (3:3–7)
> "living water" – "running water" (4:13–15)
> "born of wind" – "born of the Spirit" (3:8)
> "lifted up" – exalted or crucified (3:14, 8:28, 12:32).

As is evident throughout the material included in this Gospel, the strategy of John is evocative rather than primarily informational. In addition to a unique account of Jesus' arrest, execution, and postresurrection appearances (18–24), the Gospel focuses on two quite different kinds of material: the narratives of Jesus' miraculous acts, or "signs," and the extended discourses uttered by Jesus according to John, most of which include the characteristic expression "I am . . ."

2. The Signs of Jesus

John highlights the *signs* of Jesus throughout, commenting near the conclusion on their meaning (John 20:30–1), and even mentioning them by number at certain points (2:11, 4:54). Like the English word "sign," the Greek term *semeion* indicates an experience or event pointing beyond itself to some greater reality. For John the miracles of Jesus are not only acts of mercy and healing but also indicators of Jesus' relationship to God and of God's unique purpose at work through him. John tells the reader that he has chosen to report this selection of Jesus' signs to evoke trust that Jesus is the Messiah, the Son of God, and that those who thereby trust in him attain new life among God's new people (20:30–1). From the outset, Jesus' signs disclosed his glory and confirmed his disciples' faith in him (2:11).

The first of the signs is Jesus' exchanging water for wine, which he did after the wine supply was exhausted at a wedding feast to which he and his followers had been invited. Jesus ordered that water used *for purification* be served up as wine, and the manager of the feast tasted and distributes what is explicitly called in John "water become wine" (2:9); an exchange rather than a physical alteration is implied. It is understandable that, in John's Gospel, written at the end of the first century in the cosmopolitan environment of Ephesus, Jesus would have been portrayed as a new Dionysius, who was associated with the miraculous provision of wine, in order to compete with that perennially popular Hellenistic god. Two chapters later in the text, the Gospel refers to what happened in Kana as a miracle: when wine ran out, Jesus "made" water into wine (see John 4:46). That is not the story's conception, but the take on it that John's Gospel attempts to develop.

Archaeologists have discovered the kind of stone jars described at Kana (in John 2:6) in first-century Jewish settlements in Galilee. How Jesus used those peculiar emblems of Jewish identity was, in the symbolic language of early Judaism, even more radical than changing water into wine: by imbibing waters of purification during the festivities, and having others join him, he insisted that the purity of Israel was indeed to begin *from the inside* (see Mark 7:15), and from Galilee. This concept of a new purity, enacted in Galilee but out of reach of Herod Antipas, was powerfully attractive to Galilean sensibilities. This sign, for Jesus not a miracle in the modern sense, but an enacted parable of Galilean integrity, galvanized the sort of zealous pride that had made Galileans repeatedly dare to try to take over the Temple in Jerusalem. John beautifully exploits the symbolic dimensions of the story, including the facts that it was a wedding (a symbol for God's completion of his purpose for his people; see Hosea 3), that the receptacles for the new wine are the jars containing water for ritual purification, and that the best has been kept until the last (2:1–10).

Although it is not included among John's numbered list of the signs, Jesus' action in the Temple (which occurs at the end of his career in the other Gospels) is interpreted here in signlike fashion (2:19–22) as pointing to his resurrection and the establishment of "his body," the Christian community, where God now dwells. Similarly, the story of Jesus' debate with Nicodemus symbolizes the contrast between Pharisaic and early Christian understandings of how one becomes part of God's people. For John that happens not by ethnic descent but by the new birth through faith, with a new understanding of the Scriptures of Israel as pointing to their ultimate fulfillment in such events as the lifting up of Jesus on the cross as the remedy for human sin (3:1–17). The discussion between Jesus and the Samaritan woman (4:1–41) demonstrates God's welcome of those regarded as outsiders from Israel and leads to the dismissal of the question whether God dwells in the temple in

Samaria or in the one in Jerusalem, because for John the true worship of God is not in some sacred earthly place but in the Spirit.

The next sign (by John's listing) is Jesus' healing of the son of a governmental official (4:43–54), which points once again to access by outsiders to the healing power of God through Jesus. The healing of the lame man at the pool called Bethesda in Jerusalem (5:1–18) is presented as a violation of the Sabbath law and reaches its climax in the explicit claim by Jesus to be the Son of God – both of which factors are sufficient to convince the religious authorities to seek to have Jesus put to death. The feeding of the five thousand and the associated account of Jesus crossing the water (6:1–21) are the only miracle stories reported by both John and the other Gospels (cf. Mark 6:30–52; Matthew 14:13–33; Luke 9:10–17). The feeding of the throng recalls the miraculous supply of food to Israel in the desert (Exodus 16), but its wording ("he took, he gave thanks, he broke, he gave") points to the Christian Eucharistic meal. The crossing of the water recalls God's control of the waters of chaos in the creation story (Genesis 1:1–10) and the miraculous passage of the liberated people of Israel across the sea from Egypt to Sinai (Exodus 14). But it also points to the Christian experience of being buried and raised to new life in the baptismal waters (John 3:5; Romans 6:2–4).

The story of Jesus healing the man born blind (John 9) is pictured as an unprecedented event (9:32) and implicitly as the fulfillment of prophecy about the new age (Isaiah 35:5). Two immediate issues emerge: Jesus' alleged violation of the Sabbath and the official decision among the Jewish leaders that those who confess Jesus to be the Messiah are to be expelled from the synagogue (9:22). Both these issues are anachronistic, because healing as such was not forbidden on the Sabbath in Jewish law, and the attempt to prevent Christians from worship in synagogues came well after the destruction of the Temple in 70 C.E. These are examples of the polemics between Jewish and Christian communitities in John's Ephesus, rather than primitive tradition regarding Jesus. The concluding paragraph of the chapter (9:35–41) makes clear that what is at stake is not merely physical ability to see but spiritual insight as to who Jesus really is.

The last in the series of signs is the story of Lazarus being raised from the dead by Jesus (11:1–44). Lazarus's sisters believe in the eschatological resurrection of the dead but are not prepared for Jesus the Messiah to demonstrate in person the triumphant power over death. As with the healing of the lame man on the Sabbath, Jesus' act consolidates the opposition that seeks to destroy him (11:45–57). The authorities plot to seize him when he comes to Jerusalem to take part in the Passover ceremonies, which are seen by John as symbolic of the death of Jesus, the Lamb of God, who takes away the world's sin.

3. The "I Am" Sayings of Jesus

In John's account of crossing the water (6:20), Jesus' response to the terror of the disciples is to address them with the words, "It is I" – in Greek, *ego eimi*. This is an emphatic form of the ordinary first-person singular of the verb "to

"I AM"

The distinctive name of the God of Israel used in the Hebrew Bible, *yhwh*, was considered so holy that it should not even be pronounced except by the high priest on the Day of Atonement. From the Middle Ages until the present day, pious Jews when reading the Scriptures substitute a different designation for God, *'adonai* (Lord), instead of trying to pronounce the Hebrew word in the text (which is spelled without vowels), Yahweh according to the current scholarly reconstruction. (In fact, it is also a convention to refer to God in print as "G-d," to avoid even approaching an unauthorized or frivolous reference to the divine being.) In the Greek translation of the Bible, the Septuagint, references to God occasionally appear as *ego eimi*, meaning "I am" or "it is I." This usage comes from the incident in Exodus 3:13–14 in which Moses asks how he is to identify to his people who this God is who has commissioned him to lead them out of slavery into the land of promise. God replies that his name is "I Will Be Who I Will Be." Since the hallowing of the name of God by abstaining from pronouncing it is very ancient, Jesus' practice according to the Gospel according to John of referring to himself as "I am" could have been understood by ancient Jews in the Diaspora as an audacious, even sacrilegious claim to identity with God, and this phrase in Greek also appears in association with magical practice within the Hellenistic world.

THE STORY OF THE ADULTEROUS WOMAN

The moving story of the adulterous woman and Jesus' compassion toward her, which appears in many late manuscripts of the Gospel according to John (7:53–8:11), is not found in the oldest witnesses. In some manuscripts the whole vignette appears in Luke, following Luke 21:38 or 24:53, rather than in John. The story evidently did not originally feature as part of the Gospel according to John, but circulated orally within the Church and eventually found its way into the manuscript tradition of the Gospels at different points. Although it generally comports with the topic of this section of John's Gospel (disputes with Jewish religious leaders), this passage also breaks the flow of Jesus' confrontation with the authorities in Jerusalem.

be": "I am." It is also the exact phrase found in Exodus 3:13–14, where in response to Moses' inquiry as to who is sending him to lead Israel out of Egyptian slavery, God gives his name (in the Greek version) as "*ego eimi*." The "I am" declarations of Jesus in John's Gospel concern not only Jesus' relationship to God but also the response to Jesus from the people of God.

The first of these sayings appears in John 6, following the story of the miraculous feeding, when Jesus announces, "I am the bread of life" (6:35). There is a vital distinction to be made between bread (even miraculously supplied bread such as Moses provided for Israel in the desert) that can sustain life in the ordinary sense and "the bread of life." All who partake of the true bread from heaven (6:32–5) will share in eternal life. They constitute the true people of God, who are called into new life by Jesus, who has come down from heaven, as the *manna* did in the days of Moses. Those who share in his flesh and blood will live forever. "Flesh and blood" symbolize both his true humanity and the Eucharistic elements by which his people are united and nurtured (6:53–8).

In the following chapter (John 7), Jesus goes up to Jerusalem for the Feast of Tabernacles (or Booths), which had acquired strong associations in the traditions of Israel: with the years in the wilderness when God journeyed with his people on the way to the land of promise; with the time of the dedication of the Temple of Solomon, where God dwelled among his people, and – in a Sabbath year – with the reading out the Torah (Deuteronomy 31:9-13). Jesus' words and actions link these themes, in that Jesus appears in the Temple teaching and challenging the received view of God's people and even the claims of those who worship God in the Temple that they know God or the one he has sent among them (John 7:28–9). Jesus builds on the symbol of Moses' having provided water for thirsty Israel in the desert (Exodus 17:6) when he states that he provides the Spirit, which renews and sustains human life as God intends it to be (7:37–9). Even though the phrase "I am" is not used, Jesus asserts that his teaching is from God (7:17), that he comes from God (7:28), and that he is going to be with God (7:33–6).

In some ancient copies of John, the second "I am" saying is preceded by the story of the woman caught in adultery (8:1–11). But the best texts indicate that the original version of John went directly from 7:52 to what we know now as 8:12–30, where Jesus proclaims his oneness with the God whose name is "I am" (8:24, 28, 58). In the process of these declarations, Jesus claims to have existed prior to (or to have precedence over) Abraham, the founder of the covenant people, and he denounces as unfit for membership in God's people all who fail to see in him the true Son of God, who truly honors God and conveys God's truth to those who are ready to receive it. The third "I am" saying builds on scriptural images of God as shepherd and of Israel as God's flock (Psalms 23, 80:1; 1 Kings 22:17; Isaiah 14:30; Micah 7:14). Expanding the image, Jesus claims to be both the door of access to the true flock (10:7) and the good shepherd (10:11, 14–15), who is willing to die for the sheep. His giving up his life will result in God's raising him from the dead (10:17–18). The response of his hearers is mixed: some see him as crazy (10:20), while others are persuaded that only God could give anyone the capacities that Jesus possessed (10:40).

In the course of actions and statements connected with his raising Lazarus from the dead, Jesus declares that he not only makes possible resurrection but also *is* "the resurrection and the life" (John 11:25–6). Jesus' power to renew life is not automatic, however, but is realized through trust in him as God's agent for human transformation. The religious authorities recognize that these astounding claims cannot be ignored: many people believe them, and the developing movement has implications for the future of the entire nation. Accordingly, the priestly and Pharisaic leaders form a coalition – despite their own differences – in order to be rid of Jesus

LIFE AFTER DEATH

In the Jewish tradition, *she'ol* was a place below the surface of the earth to which the dead departed from this life, as though the grave provided access to a dark and inescapable territory. The richest possibilities for life appeared in what one made of earthly existence, especially in having offspring, rather than looking for life beyond the grave. Children were produced so that one's heritage might be continued beyond death. The grave and *she'ol* were regarded with despair in much of the Wisdom tradition (Job 17:1; Ecclesiastes 9:10; Proverbs 30:16). Although *she'ol* is in some texts regarded as the special destiny of the wicked (Proverbs 5:5; Psalm 9:17), the faithful are confident that God will be with them, even in *she'ol*. In other later texts, however,

there is an expectation and hope of renewal and restoration of the righteous dead (Psalm 16:10; quoted in Acts 2:27, 31, in connection with the resurrection of Jesus). At times, resurrection seems to refer to the restoration of the whole faithful community, as in Ezekiel 37. But in Isaiah 26:19 and Daniel 12:2, faithful individuals among God's people are given personal assurance that their fidelity to God will be rewarded when they are raised up from among the dead.

This hope was given concrete expression in the early Christian assurance that God raised Jesus from the dead and that his people will share in the resurrection of the faithful and in the age to come (1 Corinthians 15). In passages like John 11:25–6, however, the benefits of the resurrection life are

seen as already being enjoyed by God's people in the present age. In Hellenistic tradition there was a belief that the human soul would be released from the body at death and might ascend to the realm of the eternal and divine. That notion was taken up by some Jewish thinkers in the Hellenistic period, as the Wisdom of Solomon 3:1–4 attests. But when Paul describes the state of the faithful in the new age, it is not in terms of a disembodied soul but as a transformed human body – the spiritual body (1 Corinthians 15:35–49). Similarly, in Revelation 20:11–22:5, the righteous find their ultimate joy and fulfillment – not as souls ascending to heaven – but in the new order, the new city, and the new temple, which come down out of heaven to a renewed earth (Revelation 21:10).

LIFE

Three common words for "life" appear in the New Testament. (1) *Bios* refers to the basic functions of ordinary human life: its duration, its means of subsistence, and its patterns of conduct. Examples include Mark 12:44 and Luke 15:12, 30. (2) *Psuche* means the breath of life, as in Luke 12:20 and Acts 20:10. In Mark 10:45 Jesus speaks of giving up one's *psuche* for the benefit of others. Similar uses of this term occur in Philippians 2:30 and John 15:13. In some contexts, this word implies the quality of life in its potential for love of God or love of fellow humans (1 Thessalo-nians 2:8; Matthew 22:37; Ephesians 6:6). In Greek philosophical usage *psuche* is the soul, a dimension of human existence that transcends death. It is possible that the word carries these connotations in such passages as Mark 8:35, Matthew 10:39, and 1 Peter 1:9, 22, but it is more likely that here also the issue is, What are you going to do with the life that is at your disposal? God will fulfill, reward, or judge individuals according to the way in which that responsibility is discharged. (3) *Zoe* is occasionally used with the same connotations as *bios* for ongoing physical existence (Luke 16:25; 1 Corinthians 15:19; Hebrews 7:3), but more often it appears contrasted with life under ordinary conditions of human limitations and despair. *Zoe* refers to the transformed life that will be available in the age to come through trust in Christ. Sometimes it is identified with Christ himself, as in John 6:35, 11:25, and 14:6. More often it concerns the life of the believer, either now (Romans 6:13; 2 Corinthians 2:16; 1 John 5:12) or in the future (Mark 10:30; Galatians 6:8; 1 Timothy 6:19; Revelation 2:7, 22:1–2).

and to preserve what they see as the integrity of Israel (11:45–57). The reactions of the people are varied: uniquely in John's Gospel, Mary of Bethany (portrayed as the sister of Lazarus) shows that she understands Jesus' destiny by anointing him for his death (12:1–8); the crowds turn out for his entry into the city in fulfillment of the prophecies about Israel's future king (Psalm 118:25–6; Zechariah 9:9). Even some Greeks (i.e., Gentiles) come seeking Jesus, which leads him to declare that the way will shortly be opened for all of humanity to respond to him and his message (12:20–2). At this point Jesus begins to speak directly of his impending death (12:23–32). Yet most people cannot grasp his message or the significance of his death. In rejecting him and his word, they reject the life of the age to come (12:35–50).

Chapters 13–17 of John mingle promises and instructions for the new community with additional "I am" declarations by Jesus. Two other "I am" statements bear on the role of Jesus and the response of the covenant people. In 14:1–14 Jesus announces that he is going away to the dwelling place of the Father to prepare a place for his followers. His disciples do not know the way to reach God. Jesus announces that he is the way to God, the embodiment of the truth about God, as well as the life that God intends for human beings to enjoy (14:6). It is through seeing him that men and women can see God, through remaining faithful within the community that his followers can do God's work and grasp God's truth. While Jesus is gone from them, preparing for them to enter and remain in God's presence, he will provide the Spirit, who will teach them God's will and fill them with God's peace (14:15–31). Modifying the biblical image of Israel as God's vineyard (Isaiah 5:1–7), Jesus pictures himself as the true vine

(15:1–7), with God as the gardener who cares for and prunes the branches (i.e., Jesus' followers) and enables them to produce the appropriate fruit (deeds of love and mercy). Those who adopt this way of life will experience hatred from the world, which rejects and crucifies Jesus (15:18–16:4). But by the Holy Spirit, God will guide them, enable them to persevere, and reveal to them the truth about God and his purpose in the world (16:5–23). Despite the seeming defeat represented by the impending death of Jesus, his crucifixion and resurrection are God's triumph over the world and its hostile powers (16:25–33).

Jesus' farewell messages conclude with a series of self-declarations: eternal life means to know God and Jesus, whom God has sent (John 17:3); Jesus and the Father are one (17:11); his people share in this divine unity (17:21); that unity is to be expressed in and to the world (17:23); love is the bond that binds together God, Jesus, and the people of the covenant (17:26). Promises and guidance run through these farewell discourses. The sole commandment that Jesus gives is for the members of the community to love one another (13:34, 15:12–13). That forgiving, accepting love is to be expressed to the point of washing of one another's feet (13:14). The most important public witness that the members of the community bear is their love for one another (13:35). The Spirit provided by God guides them into the wider reaches of knowledge of God (16:12–14). Spirit's presence and power will give assurance of God's ultimate victory over the world and its evil forces (16:33). Meanwhile, the experience of unity among the faithful enables them to be sustained in their reliance on God (17:9–12) and bears testimony to the essential unity of God's people (17:20). Throughout this Gospel, symbolic actions and declarations of Jesus point to God's purpose: to convey the unity in love and trust that is to characterize the people he has called into being through Jesus.

Unlike the letters of Paul or the Gospel according to Matthew, John's Gospel sets forth no guiding principles for the life of the Church other than the commandment to love one another (13:34–5). There is not even a command to love one's neighbor, as in the other Gospels. Clearly, the primary concern in John is for mutual love within the community, symbolized by the washing of one another's feet (13:12–15). Issues such as the appropriate attitude toward the Roman government are not addressed in John. The prime focus is on the common life within the community.

4. The Death and Resurrection of Jesus

Although the structure and content of John's story of Jesus' arrest, trial, and execution resemble the general pattern of the other Gospels, John also appears unique in several ways. When a large number of soldiers come to seize Jesus (18:5–9), and he identifies himself with the words "I am," they fall to the ground before him, obviously (for the believing reader, but unknowingly for the soldiers) overwhelmed by the presence of God. The preservation of the eleven from arrest or trial is seen as fulfillment of Jesus' prediction about their being kept by God's power (John 6:39, 10:28, 17:15).

CAPITAL PUNISHMENT

John 18:31 quotes the Jewish authorities as declaring that they could not put anyone to death, but prior to the fall of Jerusalem in 70 C.E., the Jewish council (*sunedrion*) did have the theoretical right to execute those non-Jews who transgressed into the area of the Temple reserved for Israelites (Josephus, *The Jewish War* 6.124–6, *Antiquities* 15.417; Philo, *Embassy to Gaius* 212; and an inscription on a stone slab discovered in 1871). The council needed the approval of the Roman authorities to carry out any such sentence, however, since taking human life was the prerogative of Romans. Executions were ordinarily carried out by Roman hands, and by the time of Jesus crucifixion could be carried out only under Roman order. Those whose misdeeds were seen as threats to the public order had to be turned over to the Roman authorities for judgment and appropriate action. The decision by the Jewish council leading to the death of Stephen in Acts appears to be a case where a group hostile to Jesus' movement influenced at least some members of the council to act unofficially (Acts 6:12–15; 7:54–8:1), and the Roman authorities turned a blind eye to the execution. Further, early Rabbinic sources report executions carried out by authority of the Jewish council according to their laws.

His own impending death is pictured metaphorically as his drinking the cup that God has prepared for him (18:11) and theologically as taking place in behalf of all his people (18:13–14).

From this point on, references are made to the special relationship to Jesus and his mother reserved for "the beloved disciple," whose name is not given but who is reported to have a special connection with the high priest, making possible his admission to the courtyard where the hearing is to occur (John 18:15–18). Jesus commends his mother to the care of this disciple, who remains as a witness of the crucifixion (19:25–7); the beloved disciple – rather than Mary Magdalene – is the first person to understand the significance of the empty tomb (20:1–10) and is said to have the possibility of surviving until Jesus' triumphal return (21:20–4). As we have noted earlier, it is the special role assigned to this disciple throughout this Gospel that led to its being assigned to John the son of Zebedee, who, according to the common testimony of the Gospels, was from the outset part of the inner circle of Jesus' followers.

John narrates Jesus' confrontation with the religious authorities in a distinctive way. When Jesus declares before the high priest that his testimony to God and his purpose have been wholly public, rather than a hidden plot, he is struck for his audacity in challenging the high priest (18:19–24). Although the religious leaders will not enter Pilate's courtyard lest they defile themselves for the Passover, which begins at sundown (18:28), they urge that Jesus be executed as a threat to Roman imperial rule, because they had no right to perform capital punishment themselves. Later they continue to press the point that Jesus is a threat to Roman rule and that the only sovereign they acknowledge is Caesar (19:15).

In contrast to the accounts of Jesus' death in the other Gospels, John reports no agony or struggle on the cross but only a word to the beloved disciple concerning the new relationships within the community ("Here is your mother," 19:27). His cry of thirst results in his being offered wine, which John notes is in fulfillment of Scripture (Psalm 69:21). At this point the symbolic meaning of his life and death is complete for the disclosure of God's purpose to and for his people, and Jesus says simply, "It is finished," and dies (John 19:30).

In conformity to the commandment prohibiting exposure of a corpse on the Sabbath (Deuteronomy 21:22–3, a regulation also mentioned in the

Qumran *Temple Scroll*), the authorities ask Pilate to give orders to assure that Jesus and the other victims of crucifixion are dead, so they may be buried (John 19:31–7). Jesus' side is pierced, thus fulfilling both the law against the breaking of the bones of a sacrificial victim at Passover (Exodus 12:46; Numbers 9:12) and the prediction of the wounded victim (Zechariah 12:10). Two details found only in John's account of the burial of Jesus are the note that Joseph of Arimathea was a secret disciple of Jesus (19:38) and that Nicodemus, who had come to Jesus at night (John 3), assisted in the preparation of his body for entombment. Clearly, these two individuals, although part of historical memory, represent for John that segment of Judaism that was to recognize Jesus as God's Messiah. That the burial was *in a garden* (19:41) is perhaps both a backward look to the garden of Eden, where humans are pictured in Scripture as first assigned responsibility by God (Genesis 2), and a forward look to the restoration of God's new covenant people in the future garden of abundance as depicted by the prophet Jeremiah (Jeremiah 31).

Mary Magdalene figures prominently as a witness to the risen Lord (John 20:1–2, 11–18), whereas the disciples as a whole – with the notable exception of "the beloved disciple" – are slow to understand what has happened (20:3–10, 24–29). When they see Jesus' pierced hands, they are certain that he is the one who had been crucified, now risen from the dead. The risen Christ, like the "Word become flesh" in the prologue of John, is present in fully human form and is not merely a spirit or an apparition. He commissions the disciples to "cast the net" (21:6) and to "feed my sheep" (21:15–17) – that is, to accept responsibility for drawing new members into

"Garden Tomb." The place of Jesus' burial (now known as the Church of the Holy Sepulcher) as identified during the fourth century C.E. lies *within* the walled Old City of Jerusalem, which would have prohibited its use as a cemetery. It has been argued that during the first century the wall ran south and east of this church, but that is suppositious, and in any case the area does not seem to have been used for more than an occasional burial at that time. During the nineteenth century a rocky hill outside the present city wall was identified as Calvary, and a nearby rock-hewn tomb (pictured here) was designated as the burial place of Jesus. In 1990, however, an extensive cemetery was discovered a mile and a half south of Mount Zion, which held the remains and epitaph of Caiaphas, the high priest at the time of Jesus' crucifixion. That would have been a likely place (among the thousand tombs identified from the Second Temple period around Jerusalem) for the burial chamber owned by Joseph of Arimathea, who was also a member of the council in Jerusalem. (BiblePlaces.com)

the fellowship and for nurturing the members of the community. Jesus' final words to Peter are interpreted by John to be a prediction that this disciple who recently denied him will one day follow Jesus to a martyr's death at the hands of the civil authorities. The question of whether some of his followers will live until his return is left open (21:20–3). There are no direct indications of organization or distribution of authority within the community.

C. The Letters of John: Toward Unity of Faith and Authority

There is an analogy between changes that become apparent as one moves from the Gospel according to John to the letters of John, and from the genuine letters of Paul to the later writings in his name. The spontaneous, loosely organized group bound together by mutual love that is reflected in the Gospel seems not to have been able to survive on those terms. The letters of John reflect a process of developing a social structure that includes expectations for remaining within the group, maintenance of good standing, and even departure from the community. Further, these letters refer to established agents with authority to enforce conformity on matters of teaching and practice, and they direct their message to the church at large (sometimes by means of symbolic recipients), so that they are ranked among the "Catholic Epistles."

The urgency of these changes was heightened by intellectual developments in the Roman world and by forms of speculation that were developing within Judaism. Among pagan philosophers, the thought of Plato was being recast along lines now known as Neoplatonism, which saw the goal of existence as the union of the human spirit with divine spirit. It disdained the physical universe as transitory and subject to decay, while affirming the eternal nature of pure spirit. Among Jewish speculative thinkers, wisdom was defined as the divinely provided instrument by which individuals could be liberated from their involvement in the material world (which had come to be regarded by some as inherently evil) and ascend into the presence of God.

Among some Christian groups, therefore, by the first half of the second century C.E. a style of religious thinking arose that claimed that the created world had been made by an evil divinity. Even the human body seemed a tomb from which the human spirit had to be freed. The body of Jesus was depicted as a kind of costume behind which the real Jesus was concealed, and which he could set aside at will. To many people of this persuasion, moral behavior was a matter of indifference because it involved the worthless, illusory mode of bodily existence. The only worthy goal of life was to rise above the material world, including life in the material body. These conceptual trends within Christianity (along with those that utilized Christian traditions only tangentially) have been known as Gnosticism among scholars, and produced an extensive literature. These notions contradicted the biblical beliefs in the goodness of God's creation and in God's call to his people for purity of life in this age and the age to come.

NEOPLATONISM

Although what historians designated as Neoplatonism did not develop into an elaborate system until the time of Plotinus (early third century C.E.), important anticipations of this philosophical system can be found in the writings of the Jewish philosopher and biblical interpreter Philo of Alexandria in the first century C.E., and of both Plutarch and Numenius of Apamea in the second century C.E. Central to this developing philosophical view are (1) a system of hierarchical principles by which the universe is ordered and sustained; (2) the identification of a supreme principle, which is transcendent and designated as "the One," or "the Mind," in which all the Platonic ideas or forms are located; (3) the necessity of the mind or soul to escape from the body in order to ascend for contemplation and understanding of the One; and (4) the understanding that evil is an inherent feature of the material world. This system contributed to Gnosticism and to the increasingly otherworldly outlook of many later Christian writings, both Gnostic and Catholic.

The three letters attributed to John evidence how the Johannine community, in and for which the writings were produced, attempted to come to terms with the twin problems of order within the group and the appeal of incipient Gnosticism. The letters are anonymous, although the writer refers to himself at the beginning of 2 and 3 John as "the Elder." But since the style and point of view most nearly resemble those of the Gospel according to John, they have been from earliest times linked with that – also anonymous – Gospel. Contemporary scholarship agrees in linking these writings and assigning them to what is called for convenience "the Johannine community," or "the Johannine school."

The issue of the true humanity of the earthly Jesus is asserted at the outset in 1 John 1:1–2, in the declaration that he was seen *and touched* by his followers. This affirmation responded to those influenced by the movement that would become Gnosticism in the later second century, who wanted to regard Jesus as a divine being who masqueraded in human form in order to convey his sublime truths. Those who held that Jesus merely seemed to have a physical body were denounced by major thinkers of the early church as *docetists*, a term that comes from the Greek word for "seem" (*dokeo*). This letter, like the Gospel according to John, insists on the full and true humanity of Jesus as the one through whom God's renewal of humanity was disclosed and through whom it is being accomplished. Purity of life is affirmed, which is realized by the hope that, when Jesus appears again, his followers will be made as pure as he (3:2), with recognition of the need for confession (1:8–9) and the forgiveness provided through the death of Christ (1:7, 2:1–2). The life of full obedience makes possible the perfection of human existence through the love of God (2:3–6), which calls to mind the single commandment from the Gospel: to love one another (2:7–11). Parents and children are given instructions, as they are in the later Pauline and post-Pauline tradition (Colossians 3:18–22; 1 Timothy 5). To love this corrupt and cruel world system is incompatible with love of the Father (1 John 2:15–17). These themes are repeated throughout the letter (4:7–21), where God's very nature is said to be love.

Meanwhile, there are enemies within the church: not some satanic figure of past or future, but those who deny that Jesus is the Christ (1 John 2:18–29). The resources to combat this evil are readily available: the Spirit within the community (2:27) and the hope of Jesus' coming again, when his people will be made like him (2:28–3:3). Now his people must maintain their purity, living in love rather than sin, despite the hatred that God's people always have experienced and continue to experience (3:11–15). True love manifests itself in actions, not merely in words (3:16–24), and is dependent on God, not on one's inner feelings. The guideline for testing the faith and action of others is their stance on the question of the true humanity of Jesus (4:1–6). It is the Spirit that conveys to God's people the love and the conviction of God's support. The themes of love of God, obedience to God's commands, life in union with God, and victory over the world are repeated in 1 John 5. There are warnings about false gods (5:21), about sins so gross that they are not forgiven (5:16–18), and about the

DOCETISM

Derived from the Greek word *dokeo*, meaning "seem," the term "docetism" has been used by modem scholars for the belief of certain early Christian thinkers that Jesus transcended his physical body or did not have ordinary human limitations. Influenced by Greco-Roman stories about deities who masqueraded as humans, appearing and then vanishing into the heavens, docetic Christians portrayed Jesus' suffering and death as described in the Gospel tradition as a ruse to deceive his opponents. For example, in the later apocryphal *Gospel of Peter*, Jesus does not die on the cross but leaves his body there and ascends to heaven. Later, a voice from heaven asks a question, and an answer comes from the cross, even though the body of Jesus has been removed.

power of the Evil One in this world (5:19). In addition to continuing reference to the Spirit, there is also an allusion to ritual practice in the mention (5:7–8) of water and blood (probably metonyms of baptism and the Eucharistic cup). There are not only final warnings concerning continuing in sin (5:18) and the worship of false gods (5:21) but also assurance of true understanding about and vital union with God (5:20).

Second John is addressed to a particular church under the title of "the Lady" (in Greek, *kuria*, which is the feminine equivalent of the basic Christian title for Jesus, *kurios*, "Lord"). In this letter there is even greater emphasis on knowing the truth and on living by obedience to God's love commandment. There is also strong condemnation of those who deny that Jesus truly became human. Both false teaching and false teachers are to be avoided, and the latter are not even to be offered the hospitality of the community (8–10). The Elder closes with a statement of his intention of visiting the members.

Third John conveys the delight of the Elder on hearing the report of the community's fidelity to the truth in faith and practice, and of the members' extension of hospitality to the teachers of the truth who have visited them. At the same time, he denounces one Diotrophes, who has questioned and threatens to displace the authority of the Elder. Clearly, we have the emergence within an early Christian community of ecclesiastical disciplinary action. These doctrinal and structural regulations stand in sharp contrast to the atmosphere of mutuality and the simplicity of belief and standards of behavior apparent in the Gospel according to John.

D. The Letter of James: Pure and Peaceable Wisdom

When the writer of the Letter of James identifies himself as "James," he presumably means the brother of Jesus, although this attribution has been questioned. But in any case, the author was not a former Galilean fisherman, such as James the son of Zebedee (Mark 1:19–20), since it is highly unlikely that someone from that background could write such smooth Greek, with effective use of Greco-Roman rhetorical style and the technical terminology of Hellenistic philosophy. Further, we should expect a disciple of Jesus to evidence more interest in the Jesus tradition than is apparent in this writing, which mentions the name of Jesus only twice (1:1, 2:1) and never quotes his teachings. There are no references to the cross or the resurrection of Jesus, to baptism or the Eucharist. Although the love commandment is quoted, it is given in its form from the Bible of Israel (James 2:8 = Leviticus 19:18). There are also brief references to commandments against adultery and murder (James 2:11; cf. Exodus 20:13–14; Deuteronomy 5:17–18), but references to the law depict it as universal law, binding on all humanity, and describe it in language akin to that of Stoic natural law. The way of life that is laid out for the reader is also identified as the word (*logos*) of truth (1:18) and is depicted as wisdom that comes "from above." It is peaceable, gentle, open to reason, full of mercy and good fruits, and free of uncertainty or insincerity (3:17). The author perceives a close correspondence between this wisdom

JAMES

"James" is the English equivalent of the Hebrew name Yaqov, or Jacob. It has obviously been a common name among Jews in every era, including the first century C.E. There are at least five men with this name mentioned in the New Testament:

James, the son of Zebedee, brother of John, disciple of Jesus (Mark 1:19–20, 3:17)

James, the son of Alphaeus, disciple of Jesus (Mark 3:18; Acts 1:13)

James, the brother of Jesus, initially hostile to Jesus' message and activity (Mark 3:21, 31–5); later a witness to the risen Jesus (1 Corinthians 15:7) and a major leader in the Jerusalem church (Galatians 2:1–12)

James, the father of Jesus' disciple Judas (Luke 6:16)

James, the author of the New Testament writing that bears his name (James 1:1)

The Letter of James in the New Testament appears to be attributed to Jesus' brother of that name, although the Hellenistic character of the document makes the attribution unlikely.

and the Stoic notion of universal reason, which communicates to receptive human beings the rational law that pervades and orders the universe.

James's presentation of his case for this wisdom is offered in the literary and rhetorical style that is known from Cynic and Stoic philosophers of the first centuries C.E., such as Seneca and Epictetus. Many of the arguments of the Letter of James, such as the emphasis on divine accountability and judgment of human behavior, correspond closely to features in the writings of Seneca, a major Roman philosopher, while the style of posing questions and then offering answers is a feature of the Stoic diatribe. In James, at least one example of this style appears in every chapter: 1:26, 2:18, 3:13, 4:13, 5:13. Similarly, many of the metaphors used in the popular philosophy of the period are found in James: seeing oneself in a mirror (1:23); reining in the tongue, with comparison to guiding a ship with a rudder (3:3–12); the divine nurturing of growth in human beings (5:7–8). Where references to other New Testament material occur, such as the familiar prayer "lead us not into temptation" (Matthew 6:13) and Paul's teaching about being made right with God by faith apart from works (Galatians 2:16), James takes an opposing position (cf. James 1:13, 2:14–26). The goal of the Christian life for James is the attainment of wisdom, which makes possible peace and perseverance in obedience to God. We become his children through the word of truth, James declares (1:18).

Much of James is occupied with practical ethics:

Be aware that wealth is transitory (1:9–11)
Avoid anger and unworthy conduct (1:19)
Put God's wisdom into practice (1:20–5, 3:13–18)
Refuse to give preference to the rich (2:1–6)
Avoid conflicts over possessions (4:1–6)
Avoid judging others and boasting (4:11–16)
Beware of riches (5:1–6)
Pray when difficulties come (5:13)
Pray for and anoint the ill (5:14–15)
Confess one's faults and pray for each other (5:16–18) (examples of effective prayer are those of Elijah, Abraham, and Rahab the harlot; Joshua 2:1, 6:17)
Bring the wanderers back to the truth (5:19–20)

Counsel of a more strictly religious nature includes resisting the devil (James 4:7), purifying the self (4:17), and expecting the coming of Christ, who will appear as judge (5:7–9). Using a word for religion (*threskeia*) that appears once in Acts (26:5, where it is used by a Roman official describing the conflict between the apostles and the Jews) and once in Colossians (2:18, where it refers to the forbidden practice of worshipping angels), James describes the Christian faith as "pure and genuine *religion*" (1:26–7), thereby placing it in the larger framework of religions in general. He also incorporates into his letter concepts that are peculiar to pagan philosophy, such as speculative teaching regarding the fate of the soul (3:6) and the contrast between the heavenly bodies, which cast changing shadows, and "the Father of Light," who does not change (1:17). At one point (4:5) he claims to be quoting Scripture, but there is no such text in any known canonical or other document – which suggests that he is employing a wide range of traditions and literature in the shaping of wisdom in which he is engaged. He sees himself primarily as a teacher (3:1), and his major task as fostering wisdom among Christians, so that they may live consistent and virtuous lives. His grounding in the earlier Christian tradition is perhaps most clearly evident in his reference to "our Lord Jesus Christ, the Lord of glory" (2:1), and he still distills his wisdom for "the twelve tribes which are scattered abroad" (1:1).

E. First Peter: A Community for Concord, Holiness – and Survival

First Peter is written in the name of Peter and is linked with the names of companions of the apostles (Mark and Silas; 1 Peter 5:12–13; cf. 2 Corinthians 1:19; 1 Thessalonians 1:1–2; Colossians 4:10; Acts 12:12, 25; 13:13, 15:37), but many features of the writing show that it comes from a time after the age of the apostles, perhaps during the last decade of the first century C.E. Its relatively smooth, quasi-literate Greek, its use of technical terms from Hellenistic philosophy and mythology, and its quotations from the Greek version of the Bible indicate that it was not written or dictated by the former Galilean fisherman named Simon Peter. The circumstances of the community and the document's absorption of Hellenistic culture suggest that it originated some decades after the death of the apostles. It is possible that Peter did in fact carry on evangelism in the provinces along the southern coast of the Black Sea, where the Christians to whom this letter is addressed lived. This would account for Paul's reported decision not to go into this territory (Acts 16:6–7), based on his conviction (learned from unpleasant experience) that he should evangelize only those areas where no one had done so before (Romans 15:20). If this inference is correct, then perhaps Peter or some of his associates had already preached the gospel and established Christian communities in these southern Black Sea coastal districts. The issue that had caused conflict between Peter and Paul – the application of Jewish law to Gentile Christians (Galatians 2) – is wholly absent from 1 Peter, however. For 1 Peter the Church appears to be the successor of Israel, consisting of "exiles" in "the dispersion" (1:1), and it considers non-Christians to be "Gentiles" (2:12). In this part of the world, heated conflict between Jews and Christians (as reflected in Paul's letter to the Galatians, for example) seems to have cooled down.

A paramount issue for this community was the prospect of their "suffering as Christians" (4:16). Roman sources show that the imperial policy toward the growing Church was first explicitly formulated in the early second century in precisely this region. At that time the newly arrived local governor, Pliny, wrote Emperor Trajan asking how to cope with the surge of Christianity in these provinces. The issue was not new, but although there had been local persecutions of Christians as early as the reign of Nero (especially after the fire of 64 C.E.), the movement had been too small to require official action. But by the beginning of the second century it could no longer be ignored. Punishment was to be given to those who, in response to official inquiry, persisted in identifying themselves as Christians (Pliny, *Letters* 10.96; Trajan's response, 10.97). The pattern was set for direct confrontation between Roman authority and Christian confession of faith, and the issue was the refusal of Christians to participate in ceremonies honoring the emperor as divine. The writer of 1 Peter reflects an apocalyptic point of view (1:5): the end of the age will come quite soon; meanwhile, Christians should expect to suffer (1:6, 5:9–10); they must persevere, awaiting God's vindication of them (4:7); meanwhile, they are not to oppose the state (2:13–14, 5:4). During this interim they are to live as holy pilgrims, in anticipation of the transition to the new age (1:1, 2:11).

The cultural background of the writer reflects both Hellenistic and Jewish features. He speaks of rebirth (1 Peter 1:3), as do the Mystery religions, and calls for his readers to prepare to offer a formal, logical defense (in Greek, *apologia*) for their convictions (3:15). The imagery he employs elsewhere, however, echoes speculation in Judaism about divine messengers exhorting the evil spirits and the souls of the dead (3:18–4:6), as well as the more familiar notion of the Devil as seeking to subvert God's people (5:8–9). Out of this spectrum of cultural features, the author has fashioned a coherent view of the Church and its perilous place in the Roman world toward the end of the first century.

The major image of the Church is that of a living structure (1 Peter 2:5–9). Its base is the conviction that God raised Jesus from the dead (1:3), that Jesus died as the sacrificial lamb (1:19), and that God has disclosed his purpose to his people through his message (1:25). Those believers are the living stones in this structure (2:5). The author employs a skillful variant of the image of the rock: Christ is for outsiders the stone of stumbling (1 Peter 2:7; Psalm 118:22; Isaiah 8:14–15), but for those inside the community, he is the foundation of their existence. The members as a whole – rather than those assigned as a clergy – are the priests that offer the appropriate sacrifices to God. The community is called "a royal priesthood," which indicates that the royal and national aspirations of Israel are transformed and find fulfillment in the leadership and sacrificial roles that Church members carry out (2:9–10). Their lives are to manifest the holiness that God enjoined on his people of old (1 Peter 1:16; Leviticus 11:44–5). They are to bear witness to their faith before the Gentiles (2:12, 3:17), and they are not to retaliate when attacked or accused (2:21, 3:15). Prepared for suffering (4:12–16), they await God's ultimate vindication (5:10).

Meanwhile, they are bound together by their union with Christ and their unity in the Spirit (1 Peter 3:18). The leaders of the group are given the title of "elder" (5:1–15). Each of them is to be concerned for the welfare of the whole, and each will be rewarded appropriately when the Chief Shepherd appears (5:4). The only one to whom the title *episkopos* (bishop, or guardian) is assigned in this letter is Christ himself (2:25). Even though

PETER IN ROME

Although there is no contemporary evidence directly linked to the events, it is probable that Peter was martyred in Rome in 64 C.E., when Nero made the Christians the scapegoats for the arson of Rome, which he himself seems to have instigated. The clear implication of John 21:15–18 is that Peter is to die a martyr's death. In *1 Clement* 5:1–6:1 this tradition is confirmed and consolidated. Modern excavation of the ruins of the ancient structure beneath the present Saint Peter's Church in Rome remain inconclusive as to a connection with Peter. The evidence is substantive for the flourishing in Rome of a tradition linked with Peter, of which 1 Peter is a prime example. Written from Rome (or as if from Rome), for which

"Babylon" is the cryptic designation as the center of power threatening God's people, 1 Peter demonstrates that Rome has become a major center for the life of the Church. As the language and style of this letter demonstrate, the clientele of the church include those at an impressively high cultural level. The production of an abundance of material attributed to Peter in the subsequent four or five centuries (*Acts of Peter and Paul; Passion of Peter and Paul; Letter of Peter to Philip; Acts of Peter; Apocalypse of Peter*) shows how important he became for that segment of the Church that wanted to exalt him as the chief among the apostles and as the major figure in the church at Rome.

this title is not to be given to any leader in this community, there are ranks and levels of responsibility within the organization (3:1–7), along lines similar to those developed in Pauline communities after Paul's death (1 Timothy; 2 Timothy; Titus). A particular problem is the ostentation of the wealthy and their tendency to ignore the poor (3:3–5). Baptism is described as the agent of human salvation – just as Noah's ark saved him and his family from the Flood (3:20–1). Yet its effects are not automatic, since the transformation of the believer is linked with personal purification and "a good conscience." The ultimate ground of its effectiveness is the resurrection of Jesus Christ and his exaltation at God's right hand (3:22). It is the death and resurrection of Jesus that provide the essence of the call to share in this new community (2:4), just as it is his example that provides the paradigm for the life of its members. The letter synthesizes biblical tradition with Jesus tradition and incorporates conceptual and organizational structures from the Roman culture.

F. The Revelation of John: The Community of the Faithful in Conflict with the State

The problem of the appropriate attitude toward the Roman state, which under Emperor Trajan (98–117 C.E.) moved toward autocracy encouraged by military expansion, intensified in direct proportion to the incumbent

Colosseum, Rome. Some years after the death of Paul, the emperors Vespasian (69–79 C.E.) and Titus (79–81 C.E.) erected this enormous elliptical stone structure. In it many Christians died as martyrs, torn to pieces by wild animals or shot with arrows, as was Saint Sebastian during the great persecution of Christians by Diocletian (284–305 C.E.). (BiblePlaces.com)

DIVINE HONORS TO THE ROMAN EMPEROR

On his formal accession to the office of emperor in 27 B.C.E., Octavian accepted the designation of himself as "Augustus," and the Senate affirmed the divinity of his deceased predecessor (and adoptive father) Julius Caesar. The pattern was set from the beginning of the empire for the deification of dead emperors and the offering of appropriate divine honors to them. Gaius Caligula (37–41 C.E.) and Nero (54–68 C.E.), however, sought to promote the notion of their divinity while they were alive and ruling; Domitian (81–96 C.E.) actually demanded that he be addressed as lord and god (*dominus et deus*). Nearly all the subjects of the empire were willing to take part in the rites of the imperial cult because such rituals were regarded as essential to the maintenance of the stability of the empire and the continuing favor of the gods. Jews, however, were excused from participation in these rites, and until the Jewish revolt against the Romans in 66–70 C.E., Jews throughout the empire were permitted to pay an annual tax for the support of the Jerusalem Temple and its priestly establishment. As long as Roman officials regarded Christians as a sect of the Jews, the issue of their taking part in the divine honors to the emperor seems not to have arisen. Both Jesus (Mark 12:13–17) and Paul (Romans 13:1–7) taught that their followers should meet the legitimate demands of the Roman state, although the question of divine honors is not raised and was probably not yet a problem.

Even when Nero tried to place the blame on the Christians for the fire in Rome, the question of the imperial cult was not raised. But it may lie behind the puzzling fragmentary evidence that Domitian executed some of his imperial staff on the charge of lapsing into "Jewish customs" and "atheism," which may have been an indirect reference to the discovery of Christian converts within the imperial establishment. The fact that Flavius Clemens and Flavia Domitilla were put to death on this charge by Domitian (Dio Cassius, *Roman History* 67.14), and that the name of the latter is linked with one of the catacombs in Rome where Christians were buried, seems to support this inference about persecution of Christians under Domitian. As the correspondence between Trajan and Pliny (in Pliny's *Letters* 10.94) indicates, by the early second century, Christians were expected to take part in divine honors, and failure to do so was criminal.

emperor's demand to receive divine honors from his subjects. Around the turn of the second century John, the author of Revelation, addressed that problem in direct and radical form. He was convinced that the only solution to the situation of the Church in the world, including the mounting imperial opposition, was the appearance or disclosure (in Greek, *apokalupsis*; Revelation 1.1, 19:11–16) of Jesus Christ on earth.

In developing his dramatic sketch of the way in which God will defeat the powers of evil, will call to account the disobedient human race, and will vindicate his own people, the author of Revelation draws on the imagery of older apocalyptic writings: the fantastic portraits of the world empires (Daniel 7), the majesty of God's dwelling place (Ezekiel 43), and the symbolic use of numbers as indicators of God's having predetermined the events of human history (Daniel 12:11–12; cf. Revelation 12:6, 13:18). The overall view is that the universe is approaching the end of the age-long conflict between God and the Adversary (i.e., Satan, or the Devil). The dominant political power of the world, Rome, is the instrument of Satan, who seeks to force the faithful to abandon God and serve him. The community addressed is a small segment of humanity, scorned and dismissed as worthless by the major religious and political powers. To this brave band of the faithful God has given special insight as to his purposes for the world. Their most severe treatment at the hands of the evil powers lies in the near future and will serve as a time of divine testing of their ability to endure. Beyond this impending period of unparalleled difficulties lies their vindication by God through Jesus Christ.

The literary approach of the author differs in some ways from that of Jewish apocalyptic writers in that the author identifies himself and is apparently well known to his readers. In other apocalypses the author adopts a

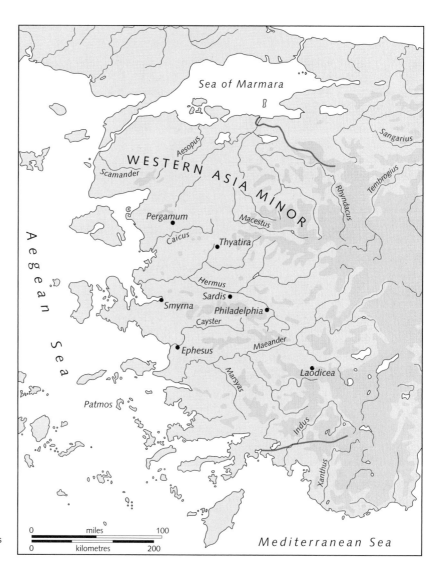

Map XX. The island of Patmos, with churches addressed in Revelation

pseudonym – usually of someone from a much earlier era, such as the time of Moses (*Testament of Moses*), the age of the patriarchs (*Enoch*), or the time of Israel's exile in Babylon (Daniel). The Book of Revelation is addressed to Christians living in the writer's own time, and he speaks to their immediate situation: the churches of Asia Minor threatened by pressure from the empire to conform to requirements that all subjects of Rome perform ceremonies honoring the emperor as divine. The book is not to be sealed (Revelation 22:10; cf. Daniel 12:4), but is to be read by the community (1:3) until the end of the age comes. The symbolic use of the number seven pervades the book:

Seven churches are addressed (2:1–3:22)
Seven seals are on the scroll containing God's plan (6:1–8:1)
Seven trumpets announce the divine plan (8:2–9:21, 11:14–19)
Seven bowls of God's wrath will be poured out on the wicked (15:1–16:21).

In ancient Hebrew, Babylonian, and Persian numerology, seven represents totality – the eternally reverberating rhythm in Genesis of creation and repose. Israelite fascination with this number represents a version of Babylonian wisdom, rooted in the observation of the heavens. In the lunar calendars of the ancient Near East, the seven-day week marked the phases of the moon: four quarters waxing and waning during the month. Israel embraced this calendar, and Genesis embeds the seven-day week in the structure of nature itself (1:3–2:3), while apocalyptic thought developed its own perspective on numerological fulfillment.

Although specific details of the triumphs and failures of the seven churches cannot be recovered by modern interpreters, the central concern is very likely enunciated in 2:13, where Pergamum is described as "where Satan dwells." This is a reference to the great altar of Zeus there, which was the major center in the eastern Mediterranean world of the divine cult of the Roman emperors. As we have observed, Asia Minor yields the earliest documentation for the conflict between Church and state over this issue. The characteristics of each of the seven churches seem to have spanned the whole range of conditions and responses of churches everywhere in this period. In each case (except the Laodicean church) the faithful remnant is implicitly or explicitly described and differentiated from the wider professing group, which will renounce the faith when the pressure is applied by the state:

Ephesus (2:2–4)	Patience, fidelity, suffering are present, but also the need to renew love
Smyrna (2:9, 10)	The prophet gives encouragement to accept suffering, and warning against those who claim to be God's people ("Jews") and against the imperial cult
Pergamum (2:13–16)	Most have remained faithful, but some have participated in idolatry
Thyatira (2:19–20)	Patience, fidelity, and suffering are here also, but they tolerate a false prophetess (cf. 1 Kings 16:31)
Sardis (3:4)	Only a few remain pure; the rest have lost their place or have died
Philadelphia (3:9)	They have endured and are faithful, and are promised vindication
Laodicea (3:17–18)	Utterly self-satisfied, they are wholly disqualified from sharing in God's new age.

The letter section ends with a series of final warnings to the churches (3:20–1).

The main section of Revelation opens and closes with visions of the throne of God, on which the Lord of creation and Savior of the faithful community is seated in triumphant majesty. The first such vision (4:1–11) recalls the visions of Ezekiel and Daniel and emphasizes in symbolic language the brilliance, power, and purity of the divine presence. The cry of

Remains of the Altar of Zeus at Pergamum. After the regional monarch Attalus (241–197 B.C.E.) allied himself with the Romans as they were extending their power over Greece and Asia Minor, his chief city, Pergamum, became a center of major political, cultural, and intellectual significance. Two of its chief attractions were the shrine of Asklepios, the god of healing, and the Altar of Zeus, built by Eumenes II (197–159 B.C.E.), which became a central focus for divine honors to the Roman emperor – hence the reference in Revelation 2:13 to this city as "where Satan's throne is" and "where Satan dwells." (Bible-Places.com)

adoration is led by a group of twenty-four elders – that is, twice the number of the twelve tribes of Israel (4:10).

Unlike earlier biblical visions of the throne of God, the agent of God – through whom the redemptive purpose for the creation is achieved – is presented in Revelation as an intrinsic part of this celestial scene: he is both Lion and Lamb (5:5–6). To him is given the scroll, which is the embodiment of the divine purpose for the creation and for God's people. He alone is worthy "to take the scroll and open its seals" (5:9). This means that he alone is qualified to know God's plans for the future of the world and to be God's agent in carrying them to fruition. Universal honor is given him (5:9). His people combine the two traditional Jewish messianic functions: they are both a kingdom and priests (5:10).

As the details of the redemptive scenario unfold in the successive series of sevens (seals, trumpets, bowls), periodic interludes in the literary flow offer reassurance to the faithful in the midst of cosmic and social disturbances:

7:1–17 depicts the faithful community, first in symbolic form as the twelve tribes of Israel multiplied, 12 × 12,000 (= 144,000), and then as an innumerable throng from every nation on earth.

10:1–11:14 gives a symbolic picture of the angels making available the divine plan in the form of a scroll to be eaten (10:9–10). The measuring of the Temple in Jerusalem symbolizes its destruction (11:1–2). The two witnesses represent the final opportunity for humanity to hear and respond to the gospel before the end of the age comes. This is to occur three and one-half years after they begin their testimony, which will end in their martyrdom at the hand of the satanic agent (11:4–10) and their resurrection, which signals the final outpouring of divine judgment.

14:12–13 offers a brief encouragement to those who face martyrdom. They will obtain rest and their works on behalf of the gospel will endure forever.

15:2–8 depicts the heavenly sanctuary in the time just before the final judgments of God are poured out on the world. In contrast with the disasters that are to follow, John here describes the joy and serenity shared by those whose trust is in God.

Five of the seven seals, whose sequential opening represents the unfolding of the divine plan, symbolize the fearful catastrophes that are to come upon the disobedient human race and the diabolically controlled world:

Absolute political control (6:2)
Slaughter (6:3–4)
Famine (6:5–6)
Widespread death (6:7–8).

The fifth seal, however, symbolizes the fidelity of the martyrs, who remain true in the face of death (Revelation 6:9–11), and their endurance opens the way to the cosmic destruction of the sixth seal (6:12–17). The seventh seal (8:1–5) serves as a transition to the next series of seven, the trumpets, which introduce:

Scorching of the earth (8:7)
Destruction in the sea (8:8–9)
Pollution of the springs and rivers (8:10–11)
Dimming of the sun, moon, and stars (8:12)
Stinging by locusts of those not sealed by God (9:1–11)
Destruction of one-third of the human race by 200,000 horrendous horses (9:13–19)
Final defeat of the evil powers (11:15).

Despite these fearful judgments that befall the earth and its inhabitants, the majority of the human race continues to worship idols and demons and to participate in murder and magic (9:20, 21). Following the seventh trumpet, however, elders (whose number again represents twice that of the ancient tribes of Israel: $12 \times 2 = 24$) join in the worship of God, in the celebration of the fulfillment of God's promises, and in the opening of access to the heavenly sanctuary where God dwells (11:16–19).

Two contrasting visions follow: the woman and the child (Revelation 12:1–6), representing God's people and the Messiah; and the war in heaven between the angels, led by Michael, and the demonic forces, led by "the dragon" (Satan), which seek to destroy the woman and her child (12:7–18). Assurance is given of the triumph of God over these enemies through the Messiah (12:10–12). Similarly, Revelation 13 describes a vision of two Beasts: the first claims divine honors (= the emperor), and the second is his chief publicity and enforcement agent, who requires all to honor the first Beast as divine. The first Beast's symbolic number, 666, probably derives from the name of Emperor Domitian (81–96 C.E.): the numerical equivalents of the letters of his name add up to that number. (Nero is also a possible reference, if the numerical equivalent of his name is taken from its Hebrew spelling.) Domitian was the first to insist that he be addressed as *dominus et deus* (Lord and God). In contrast to these symbols of idolatry in the Roman culture is

MICHAEL

The angel Michael – whose name means "Who is like God?" – had a special role as messenger and agent in the fulfillment of God's purpose for his people in apocalyptic writings, beginning with Daniel (10:13, 21; 12:1) and continuing in many apocalypses and testaments, including *Enoch*, the *Sibylline Oracles*, the *Testament of Moses*, the *Testament of Solomon*, and the *War Scroll* from Qumran. In the New Testament, Michael's name appears in two apocalyptic contexts, Jude 9 and Revelation 12:7, which says he is waging war against the dragon (Satan).

the portrait of the Lamb of God and his people, who number, symbolically, twelve times the sacred tribal number 12 multiplied by 12,000 (= 144,000; Revelation 14:1–12). The angels of God summon this throng to honor God alone (14:6–7) and to refuse to worship the Beast, while announcing the fall of "Babylon" (Rome), which is the captor and oppressor of the new Israel as ancient Babylon was of Israel in the days of the exile.

From Revelation 14:14 to 19:4 there is a string of images of the unleashing of divine wrath on the wicked earth and its inhabitants. The angelic harvest symbolizes God's calling humanity to account (14:14–20) and is followed by the pouring out of the bowls of God's judgment (15:5–16:20). The effects of these resemble the effects of the seven trumpets on the whole, but the new feature is the emphasis on the destruction of "the great city" (16:19)—that is, Rome, the symbol and center of the evil, idolatrous, diabolical empire, and the embodiment of human schemes that corrupt or combat God's purpose for human life in the created order. The theme is expanded in 17:1–5, where the city is called a prostitute; in 17:9, where Rome's seven hills are mentioned; and in 17:18, where the city's dominance over all the kings of the earth is noted. Its successive emperors are symbolized as "horns," whom ironically God will use to bring about the destruction of the city and finally their own defeat (17:12–16). Wicked as the city is, a voice from heaven utters a dirge in which both the wickedness and the impressiveness of the city are marked (18:1–24). Only God's people rejoice at Rome's ruin (18:20, 19:1–4).

The final group of visions represent the new age and God's new order. The wedding feast of the Lamb builds on and modifies the older biblical image of Israel as the wife of Yahweh to indicate the fulfillment of God's plan for his new people (19:5–10). The rider on the white horse (19:11–21) pictures the Messiah (Word of God) as triumphing over God's enemies, destroying the Beast and the False Prophet and inviting the world's birds of prey to come and gorge themselves on the dead bodies. Before the ultimate conclusion of God's triumph and renewal, there is an intermediate period during which the faithful share in the Rule and during which Satan and his agents are chained for a thousand years (20:1–6), although this is followed by a period during which the powers of evil exercise control prior to their final defeat and eternal destruction (20:7–15). The wicked, and even death itself, are consumed in an eternal fire. The sequence reaches its grand climax in a series of new things:

New Heaven and New Earth (21:1)

New City of God (21:2–21), for which 12 is the key symbol: 12 gates = 12 tribes, each consisting of a single pearl; 12 foundation stones = 12 apostles

New Presence of God (21:22), for which no Temple is needed, since God and the Lamb are present always and forever; all the faithful may enter their presence, and no impurity or deceit are allowed in their presence

New Tree of Life (22:2), which bears fruit 12 times a year
New Light of the World (22:5) and thus no more day and night.

All these transformations are linked with the coming of Jesus in triumph at the end of the present age (Revelation 22:6–7, 12–13, 16–17, 20). In preparation for these glorious events, the faithful are called to worship God alone (22:8–9), to strive for purity (22:10–11), and to denounce those whose actions exclude them from God's people: magicians, the immoral, idolaters, and those who lie by word and deed (22:14–15). The book ends with a warning against adding to or subtracting from the prophetic words of John (22:18–19). Like the heavenly scroll in which are recorded the pre-determined acts of God to defeat the powers of evil and redeem his people (5:1–14), so this revelation of God's purpose for his people is to stand unaltered, awaiting its fulfillment.

V. DIVERSITY IN THE CHURCH

A. Revisions of the Traditions about Jesus and the Apostles

The attempt to establish a uniform teaching for all the churches was not successful until the time of Constantine in the fourth century. At the beginning of the second century there was a range of understandings of Jesus, of interpretations of the New Testament writings, and of which writing should be considered Scripture; those who called themselves Christians affirmed widely different models of faith and practice. Prominent teachers in different churches sometimes wrote to correct or criticize others, seeking to combat perceived error. In other instances, writers undertook to supplement the New Testament with new, expanded accounts of the stories of Jesus and the apostles. Some of these latter writings were quickly accepted as authoritative in segments of the early Church, equaling or even surpassing the authority of the documents that came to be included in the official canon of the New Testament.

Many supplementary writings have featured centrally in study of the New Testament, especially those produced by groups commonly called Gnostic and those that have come to be known by modern scholars as the New Testament Apocrypha. Recently, some scholars have argued that among the writings classified by the mainstream of the Church as "Gnostic" and "apocryphal" are works that are older and more authentic than some included in the canon. What is more likely, however, is that these documents were written in the period that overlaps with the writing of the later books of the New Testament; that is, supplementary works were produced during the early decades of the second century at the earliest. We shall examine first two Gospel-type writings preserved by the Gnostics that consist entirely of sayings attributed to Jesus. Then we shall analyze several apocryphal narratives. Some are Gospels and others are accounts of the activities of the apostles.

CONSTANTINE AND EUSEBIUS

Born in 273 C.E., son of the emperor Constantius from his concubine Helena, Constantine was in the vicinity of York in England, after having subdued the Caledonians, in the year 306 when his father died. Five others competed with him for power in the empire, including Galerius, who had shared the title of Augustus with Constantius. Internal conflicts among the competitors, in addition to the intelligence and leadership skills of Constantine and his support from the Christians (who had been outlawed and persecuted by Diocletian), led to Constantine's eventual attainment of supreme power in the empire. His decision to side with the Christians was encouraged by a vision he reported having seen in which he was urged to take the sign of the cross as his imperial standard, with the promise that he would thereby conquer his enemies. By 323 Constantine was sole ruler, and he later transferred the seat of power to Byzantium, which was renamed Constantinople. His edicts outlawed idolatry, restored the property of Christians, and reorganized the empire in such a way as to foster the Church and its institutions. His friend Eusebius, a native of Palestine, served Constantine as adviser on churchly and doctrinal matters, including convening the very important Council of Nicea in 325, which made critical deci-

sions about terminology for describing the nature of Christ and his relationship with God.

The beginning of Christian history as a way of looking at the world came with Eusebius (260–340), bishop of Caesarea. Through Pamphilus, his martyred teacher and model, Eusebius had been deeply influenced by the thought of Origen. So even before there was a consciously Christian history, we are confronted with an irony of history: from the least historical perspective there was provided the first comprehensively historical account of the meaning of Christ. Eusebius's prominence in the ecumenical church at various councils from Nicea onward, as well as his friendship with Constantine, go a long way toward explaining why Eusebius should have made the contribution that makes him to ecclesiastical history what Herodotus is to Greco-Roman history.

As Eusebius attempted to express the startling breakthrough of Christianity under Constantine, he portrayed the new emperor as chosen by God himself. The most famous result of his meditation on the significance of the new order in which Christianity was vindicated is his *History of the Church*, a vitally important narrative that takes up the Christian story from the time of Christ. The settlement

under Constantine is Eusebius's goal, however, and his glowing portrayal of the emperor is most vividly conveyed in his *Praise of Constantine*. After speaking of Christ as the word of God that holds dominion over the whole world, Eusebius goes on to make a comparison with Constantine (*Praise of Constantine*, 1.6): "Our Emperor, beloved of God, bearing a kind of image of the supreme rule as it were in imitation of the greater, directs the course of all things upon earth." Here the old pagan idea of the rule of the emperor as commensurate with the divine rule is provided with a new substance: the emperor who obeys Christ, himself imitates Christ's glory.

Eusebius was inclined to describe himself as moderately capable (*History of the Church* 1.1, 10.4), and that may be an accurate assessment of him as a theologian and historian. But as a political theorist, Eusebius is one of the most potent thinkers in the West. He provided the foundation on which the Roman Empire could later be presented as the Holy Roman Empire, and the grounds for claiming the divine rights of rulers. At the same time, his reference to the conditional nature of those rights, as dependent on the imitation of Christ, has provided a basis on which political revolution may be encouraged on religious grounds.

1. Gnostic Gospels

The library found in 1945 among the ruins of an ancient library in Upper Egypt at a place called today Nag Hammadi includes the *Gospel according to Thomas* and the *Gospel of Truth*. The first of these presents 114 sayings of Jesus (by modern count), many of which approximate to passages in the canonical Gospels, but others that are striking and original. On the basis of quotations from the *Gospel according to Thomas* found in other early Chris-

NEW TESTAMENT APOCRYPHA

Many texts were produced by various Christian groups from the second to the ninth centuries that supplement, and in some cases contradict, what is found in the writings recognized as the New Testament. These works seem on the whole to have been a popular literature, produced for the most part by and for pious imagination rather than authoritative tradition. But they provide rich insights into what many Christians in those centuries after the New Testament were interested in: how did God confirm the claims of Jesus and the apostles that God was at work through them? How should Christians deal with their opponents? How should they face the prospect of martyrdom? What are the proper attitudes toward wealth and sex?

The writings can be grouped according to literary type: (1) Gospels, including stories of Jesus' birth and childhood; (2) Acts of various apostles; (3) alleged correspondence between Jesus or Paul and their followers or with prominent public figures; and (4) apocalypses, including secret revelatory letters. This material has been supplemented by the discovery in the middle of the twentieth century of a library from a Gnostic community in fourth-century C.E. Egypt.

tian documents, it is probably to be dated to the middle of the second century C.E. The *Gospel of Truth*, on the other hand, contains few references to material found in the four canonical Gospels and, in each case, interprets it in a metaphorical fashion and likely emerged somewhat later.

The *Gospel according to Thomas* Many images and parables familiar from the New Testament Gospels appear in *Thomas* as well. Examples include the parable of the sower and the seed (9), the mustard seed (20), the city on a hill (32), good and bad seed (57), the feast (64), the pearl (76), the tenant farmers (65), the persecuted and hated are blessed (68), the harvest and workers (73), and foxes and holes (86). Many sayings are unique to *Thomas* in form and content. One of the most famous of them is likely authentic: "Who is near to me is near the fire; who

THE GOSPEL ACCORDING TO THOMAS

The *Gospel according to Thomas* is an anthology of aphorisms and parables originally from the second century C.E. It was first compiled in the Syriac language in the ancient city of Edessa in Syria, a kind of oriental Ephesus in terms of its cultural patterns and vibrant intellectual life. But Gnosticism was an international movement, and *Thomas* was also embraced in Egypt and translated into Coptic, the first-century inheritor of the language of the hieroglyphics. The Coptic language itself is key to Gnosticism's success in Egypt. The hieroglyphics of ancient Egypt were difficult to write and read, but Coptic put that language into the phonetic system of the Greek alphabet (with four extra characters).

That innovation enabled people with leisure in rural Egypt to read and hear recitations of the world's wisdom in their own tongue. They became avid for philosophy, religion, and esoteric knowledge, and Gnosticism packaged them all in a way that assured its advance on Egyptian soil.

In *Thomas*, the "Living Jesus" – the eternal personality whom death could not contain – speaks wisdom that promises immortality. The Coptic text includes material presented in the canonical Gospels as well as teaching culled from oral traditions. *Thomas* focuses so completely on the wisdom spoken by the Living Jesus in response to questions from his disciples that it does not include any sto-

ries about Jesus. As the Living Jesus responds to his disciples' problems, doubts, and entreaties, his epigrammatic wisdom becomes a rich, rhythmic chant – a guide for Gnostic meditation complete with oral cues.

The Gnostics who lived near Nag Hammadi in Egypt, away from cities in their rural enclaves, used the *Gospel according to Thomas* as well as other texts deposited there to deepen their *gnosis*. *Thomas* clearly states its purpose, and the aim of Gnosticism as a whole: "The one who finds the interpretation of these sayings will not taste death" (saying 1). *Thomas* promises to convey the reality of resurrection to the attentive Gnostic, whose goal is to cheat death itself.

is far from me is far from the kingdom" (87). Many other sayings are out-wardly similar to those in the canonical Gospels but differ significantly in meaning. For example, the need to become as a child in order to enter the kingdom is not a call for simple trusting acceptance, as in Mark (10:15), but a demand to transcend one's sexual identity (*Thomas* 22, 37). This is an important feature of the overall emphasis in *Thomas* on achieving *unity*, which is variously described as being solitary (75) or as two becoming one (11, 16, 61, 75, 106). This means that the divided nature of human exis-tence (body and soul, flesh and spirit, male and female) is overcome and surpassed as one enters a new realm of spiritual unity. This is a basic con-cept within Gnostic thought, which commonly regarded the material world, including bodily existence, as inherently evil. Through the disclo-sure of the divine knowledge that God provides through Jesus, the ulti-mate individual unity is attained. Anyone who gains this status is free of human limitations and liberated from the body, which *Thomas* regards as a corpse (15, 60, 71, 80, 111).

These insights are gained only through the divine knowledge that God has provided, which includes true knowledge of the self (*Thomas* 3, 5, 6, 13, 17, 18). Divine knowledge exists as inner light (24, 70) and is already within the elect individuals, waiting to be recognized (61, 62, 70). It is through Jesus that this divine awareness comes (77, 108): he enables men and women to overcome their sexual separateness and thus to achieve divine androgyny (114). Those who receive this new knowledge will be free from the body and its enticements (27, 28, 56, 87) and will become detached observers of the passing world (42). In this Gospel, redemptive significance is not attached to the death of Jesus, which is mentioned only as an instance of spirit triumphing over the body. There are no references to the sacraments and no mention of covenant or com-munity responsibilities, either within the group or toward outsiders or the state. Issues concerning community identity and relationships were central for both Judaism and Christianity in the period following the return of Israel from exile until the early second century C.E.; *Thomas* took a different direction.

The *Gospel of Truth*

The Gnostic library at Nag Hammadi includes the *Gospel of Truth*, which is referred to by Irenaeus in about 185 C.E. in his work *Against Heresies* (3.11.9). It presents an extended discourse in which the themes of inner divine knowledge and freedom from the body and earthly involvements, such as are set out in the *Gospel according to Thomas*, are developed more fully. References to Gospel material found in the New Testament are fewer than in *Thomas*, and more metaphorical: Jesus is said to have been nailed to a tree "because Error was angry at him" (18.20, 20.25); from that situation symbolizing a threat from evil (the cross) Jesus published the edict of the Father, which consisted of letters written by the Unity (23.15). The primary role of Jesus throughout the text is to enlighten those in conceptual darkness, thereby making visible the Invisible Father.

The goal of human existence is to know one's origin and destiny (*Gospel of Truth* 22), the latter of which is the attainment of unity by self-purification through knowledge (25). The parable of the lost sheep is a metaphor for achieving the completeness (*pleroma*) of being. The Son is the Name of the Father (38) and came from the depths of the Father to explain him and to disclose secret things (40). None of the issues, aims, or values of the original Jesus tradition – the renewal of the created order; the transformation of the covenant people; God's offer of reconciliation to an estranged, disobedient humanity – are evident in this Gnostic document, which claims to offer the secret clues to understanding Jesus and his role as renewer of the covenant.

The quest for knowledge by itself, even knowledge of the divine, is not the same thing as Gnostic thought. Gnostic thought, rather, represents a popular Platonism with an antimaterialist bias, a development that successfully competed with Catholic Christianity, even as it adopted (and transformed) elements of Christian teaching. The emergence of Gnosticism reflects the appeal of dualism within the period. Dualism refers to any bifurcation of experience into two distinct realms. Gnostics typically made a radical distinction between the present, material world and the ineffable nature of God. This world is subject to decay and the rule of evil forces; only release from it can bring the spiritual awakening and freedom of *gnosis* ("knowledge"). Although appeals to the power of *gnosis* were commonly made during the first century, Gnosticism proper with its dualistic emphasis emerged somewhat later.

Attempts have been made in the past to explain the emergence of Gnosticism on the basis of the apocalyptic literature of Judaism. Apocalypses such as Daniel and *4 Ezra* represent a clear separation between those who are to be saved in a final judgment and those who are to be punished. Similarly, one of the documents found at Qumran, the *War of the Sons of Light and the Sons of Darkness*, provides a clear example of dualism. The whole of Gnosticism – particularly its appeal to Platonic thought and its antimaterialism – cannot be explained simply as an inheritance of apocalyptic thought, but its ethical dualism, the hard distinction between the saved and the doomed, does emerge just after the period of the most intense production of apocalypses.

Works such as *4 Ezra* and *2 Baruch* are examples of apocalyptic dualism, and they are joined on the Christian side by the Revelation of John. These works were produced after the destruction of the Temple in Jerusalem, which was an incentive to explain how recent history could possibly fit within the overall plan of God. To this list, we should also add the *Testaments of the Twelve Patriarchs* (treated in Part Two of this *Companion*), a composite Judaic and Christian document, reflecting an interest in adding new dimensions of meaning to previously existing text. That is also a characteristic of Gnosticism.

The *Gospel of Truth* provides a good example of a Gnostic text from the second century, beginning as it does:

> The gospel of truth is a joy for those who have received from
> the Father of truth the gift of knowing him, through the
> power of the Word that came forth from the fullness – the one
> who is in the thought and the mind of the Father, that is,
> the one who is addressed as the Savior, that being the name of
> the work he is to perform for the redemption of those who
> were ignorant of the Father, while the name of the gospel is
> the proclamation of hope, being discovery for those who
> search for him.

What is useful about that initial statement is that it simplifies characteristic precepts and assumptions of Gnosticism.

Knowledge here comes only as a gift of the Father, and is mediated by the "Word," a designation for Jesus taken from the first chapter of John's Gospel. But that Word comes forth from "the fullness," emanations outward from the Father. The complexity of the divine world around the Father is often emphasized in Gnostic texts, and developed to a bewildering degree of detail. The fascination with schemes representing the generation of the world is probably an inheritance from Greek and Roman mythology. The mastery of that detail is held to mean that one has successfully become one who knows, a Gnostic.

A firm distinction is made in the *Gospel of Truth* between those who are spiritual, capable of receiving illumination, and those who are material, ignorant of what is being offered (see *Gospel of Truth* 28–31). Failure to attain *gnosis*, then, is a mark of one's incapacity to be rescued from the conditions of this world. The assumption throughout is that the material world is a pit of ignorance and decay, from which the Gnostic must be extricated and in which all others must perish.

2. Apocryphal Gospels and Acts

The *Gospel according to Peter* is in part a composite of the canonical Gospels and in part an expansion of them along lines that further two of the writer's major concerns: (1) the conviction that everything that happened to Jesus in connection with his death and resurrection was in fulfillment of Scripture; (2) the determination to put the blame primarily on the Jews for the death of Jesus. This Gospel has survived only as a Passion story that depicts Jesus' arrest, trial, crucifixion, suffering, and death. Whether it once included accounts of Jesus' earlier activities and teachings cannot be determined. The writer depends in general on Mark, but many of the details are adapted from Matthew and John. The minor role of Herod in the trial and crucifixion of Jesus as described by Luke (Luke 23:6–12) has been considerably expanded in the *Gospel according to Peter*, and the author has confused Herod the Great, who was king of Judea at the time of Jesus' birth, with Herod Antipas, who was governor of Galilee during Jesus' ministry

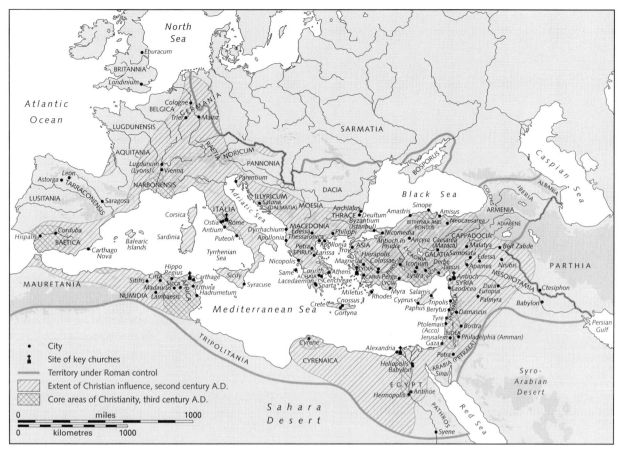

Map XXI. The expansion of Christianity during
the second and third centuries

(Luke 3:1) and would therefore have had no immediate authority in
Jerusalem over judicial matters. Yet this Gospel reports Herod as having
direct responsibility for Jesus' crucifixion. It also describes the Jews as coming in large numbers to wait at Jesus' tomb on the Sabbath, which would
have been unthinkable in terms of first-century C.E. Jewish piety. The
author is obviously writing at a time and in a culture in which first-century Jewish practices are not accurately known.

The *Protoevangelium of James* sets out, as the title (with the prefix
"proto") suggests, to give an account of the birth and childhood of Jesus.
It includes details of the miraculous circumstances of Mary's virgin birth,
of her alleged part in the preparation of the veil of the Temple that was
torn at the moment of Jesus' death, and of the virginal conception of Jesus
– that is, without human sexual activity. Both Joseph (who had no intercourse with Mary) and Mary (who had no extramarital sex) have their testimony vindicated by a supernatural test, in which they are given to drink
"the water of conviction" and are unharmed by it. The work is a combination and expansion of the infancy stories in both Luke and Matthew and
was written at a time when the Church was concerned to defend the
purity of Mary and the miraculous nature of Jesus' birth.

The *Infancy Gospel of Thomas* seeks to enhance the canonical Gospels' portrait of Jesus as a miracle worker. Building on oral traditions and pious imagination, it pictures Jesus as putting down his opponents, performing healings, and helping his family, even to the point of correcting some of his father's carpentry errors by stretching pieces of wood. At the same time, he displays supernatural knowledge, as in his allegorical interpretation of the alphabet.

Similarly, the apocryphal Acts embody imaginative developments of traditions concerning the apostles, modeled on those in the canonical Acts of the Apostles, especially in connection with divine affirmation of them in public scenes and in the presence of religious and political authorities. These writings range in date from the *Acts of Peter* and the *Acts of Paul*, which were written in the latter half of the second century, to the *Acts of John*, which may be as late as the fourth century. Gnostic influence is evident in the third-century *Acts of Thomas* and the *Acts of Andrew*. A dominant concern in the older apocryphal Acts is abstinence from sex, as in the case of two young women in the *Acts of Peter* who are kept by Peter in a state of impaired health to prevent them from being sexually exploited.

In the *Acts of Peter*, Peter's preaching and healing activity in Rome, following Paul's alleged departure for missionary activity in Spain, consists mainly of spectacular public performance of miracles. Some of these involve only Peter and his listeners, as when he makes a fish swim after it has been removed from a display in a fishmonger's shop. Others are more showy events in which Peter's miracles not only outdo those of the legendary magician Simon (*Acts of Peter* 13:6–8) but also bring the latter under divine judgment.

A major section of the *Acts of Paul* consists of a travel narrative, modeled after Hellenistic romances that were popular in the second and third centuries C.E., in which the devotees of a divinity travel around the Mediterranean world, taking advantage of opportunities to bear witness to their religious convictions in public gatherings and in the presence of religious and political authorities. Dramatic displays of divine deliverance feature in the Hellenistic romances, as do direct communications from the deity that confirm the travelers' convictions and commitments regarding the purpose and power of the deity. This is precisely what happens to Paul and his female companion, Thecla, as they carry forward their journey for Christ. It may be inferred from the writer's use of this literary medium in the *Acts of Paul* that the Christian movement has made its way into the wider reading public of Roman society, offering its own equivalent of the popular religious romances of that epoch.

The *Acts of John* is taken up with more speculative features of the Jesus tradition and transforms aspects of them so as to heighten the supernatural identity of Jesus. The cross is not so much the symbol of death or atoning suffering as it is the focus of the divine light, the intersection of divine disclosure and human response, equated with the *Logos* (cf. the

"Word" in John 1), by which God communicates with human beings. In the *Acts of John*, when John describes his experience with Jesus during his lifetime and after the resurrection, he indicates that Jesus' appearance and even the tangibility of his body varied considerably. Yet like the other apocryphal Acts, the *Acts of John* includes delightful stories of miracles, such as one about the bedbugs that had been keeping John awake at an inn but then cooperatively withdrew to enable him to get a good night's sleep. Other miracles include the destruction of the temple of the pagan goddess Artemis, and divine judgment – in the form of a deadly snakebite – on someone who first comes to the true faith and then defects from it.

These writings motivated believers with enticements and solemn warnings alternately. At the same time, they show by the examples of the apostles that fidelity to the will and purpose of God may lead to martyrdom. They represent both the internal and the external pressures – social, moral, doctrinal, and political – under which the Church was living in the larger Roman society in the centuries prior to its establishment as the religion of the emperor in the time of Constantine.

VI. ATTEMPTS TO UNIFY FAITH AND PRACTICE

A. The Apostolic Fathers

By the end of the first century, Christianity had taken root in widely scattered areas and diverse cultures, stretching from western Europe to Iran and across the Mediterranean coast of Africa. It was under pressure from a variety of sources: Roman political authorities, Greek and Roman philosophy, various popular religions, and the competing modes of organization and belief that had developed within Christianity. In such circumstances, how was the Christian movement to survive as a coherent entity?

The primary strategy of leading thinkers in this situation focused on three areas where unity could emerge: conformity to proper norms of behavior, acceptance of authoritative leadership, and adherence to the doctrine and ritual of the Church as a whole. Indications of the development of these strategies are evident in the later New Testament writings, but they became more urgent, explicit, and central early in the second century. Scholars have designated Church leaders of that time as the Apostolic Fathers, because they were in some sense the successors of the apostles, who had been the original leaders of the Christian movement. Appeal is frequently made in the works of the Apostolic Fathers to the earlier documents that came to be known in Christian settings as the Old and New Testaments. There was no effort on the part of ancient scholars (as there has been none by modern scholars) to have the writings of the Apostolic Fathers included in the canon of the New Testament. Indeed, the basic

THE *DIDACHE*, OR THE *TEACHING OF THE TWELVE APOSTLES*

A copy of the *Didache* (which means "teaching") was recovered in the later nineteenth century from a monastery in Constantinople. The text preserves a version of a document called the Two Ways, apparently a widely used late-first-century manual of discipline for the Church. The tradition of the Two Ways is found in a more primitive form in the *Epistle of Barnabas*. The material from the *Epistle* in *Didache* 1:1–6:2 has been reworked in light of the mounting tensions between Christianity and emergent Rabbinic Judaism – a development that began to gain momentum in the late first and early second centuries. The place of origin of both the original document and of this adaptation of it is impossible to determine. The *Didache* reflects a simple organizational structure of the Church, with no clear indication, for example, whether a single bishop presided over the churches of a city or a region.

question as to which of the books in the biblical tradition were to be considered authoritative (i.e., canonical) was not yet resolved or even fully addressed in the early second century.

1. Standards for Ethics and Worship

A late-first-century document, probably known as the Two Ways, was incorporated into two early-second-century writings: the *Teaching of the Twelve Apostles* (or the *Didache*) and the *Epistle of Barnabas*. These works attempt to influence the behavior of members of early Christian communities. They have a choice between the Way of Life and the Way of Death – a theme that appears in Matthew 7:13–14, and is akin to Jesus' identification of himself as "the Way" to the Father in John 14:4–6. In the *Didache*, the instruction begins with quotations and paraphrases of Jesus' words about the first commandment: to love God and neighbor (*Didache* 1). But it then expands on the moral obligations of both Church members (*Didache* 2) and those under instruction for membership (*Didache* 3). Among the things to be avoided are love potions, magic, omens, enchantment, and astrology – all of which were flourishing among the upper classes of Roman society in this period. These practices were included among the works that lead to divine punishment by death (*Didache* 5). The same basic pattern is repeated in the *Epistle of Barnabas*.

The *Didache* offers detailed advice along liturgical lines: how baptism, prayers, fasting, and the Eucharist are to be performed within the life of the community (*Didache* 7–10). The Church's program of instruction, especially for baptism, is of major importance, as is evident from the counsel to accept orthodox teachers and prophets, who teach the truth, even though no details are offered here as to what constitutes truth or orthodoxy (*Didache* 11). Members are to accept as well as to offer hospitality, and

EPISTLE OF BARNABAS

The *Epistle of Barnabas* is attributed to Barnabas, the apostle and co-worker of Paul mentioned frequently in Acts and also in the letters of Paul (1 Corinthians 9:6; Galatians 2:1–13; Colossians 4:10). The document refers to the Temple in Jerusalem as lying in ruins, which would imply that it was written after 70 C.E., when that catastrophe took place, but probably before 135 C.E., when Emperor Hadrian ordered that a shrine of Jupiter be built on the site of the Jewish Temple. The *Epistle* uses the allegorical method of Scripture interpretation, which suggests that it may have originated in Alexandria, where that method was widely used by Jewish and early Christian scholars. Yet it also exhibits features of apocalyptic thought and style in expressing the author's expectations about the imminent end of the present age. Apocalyptic shows up in a variety of settings, and thus the presence of this characteristic offers no direct clue as to the work's place of origin although it has frequently been associated with Alexandria in modern scholarship.

CLEMENT OF ROME AND *FIRST CLEMENT*

Clement was the third bishop of Rome according to Eusebius's *Ecclesiastical History* (1.4.10) and thus would have been the second to succeed Peter in that office (if Peter is counted first). Clement's term lasted from 92 (in the reign of Emperor Domitian) until 101 (in the reign of Emperor Trajan). Later tradition claims that he was consecrated for the office by Peter and that he is the Clement mentioned by Paul (in Philippians 4:3). His surviving writing (if he truly is the author) came to be known as *1 Clement*, to distinguish it from *2 Clement*, an anonymous sermon attributed to Clement but different from *1 Clement* in style and perspective, probably written in Alexandria in the latter part of the second century.

IGNATIUS

Ignatius was bishop of Antioch in Syria during the reign of Trajan – probably until 107 C.E. He saw himself as the central authority for the church in this important city and wrote in that capacity to churches and individuals in Rome and cities in Asia Minor; his letters to the churches of Ephesus, Magnesia, Trallia, Rome, Philadelphia, and Smyrna, as well as his *Letter to Polycarp*, have been preserved. His primary concern was to preserve the church by unifying its organizational structure and doctrine. Taken to Rome by imperial authority, Ignatius was martyred there by being thrown to wild beasts in the amphitheater.

they should provide financial support for itinerant prophets who offer instruction to communities. Although their roles are not sharply defined, the leaders of the church are also mentioned: apostles, bishops, and deacons (*Didache* 11, 15). The work ends with solemn warnings about being prepared for the end of the age, which will be preceded by corruption within the Church and by oppression from without. The members are called to persevere, in expectation of the resurrection of the dead and vindication by the returning Christ (*Didache* 16). The final exhortations of *Barnabas* similarly call for faithful obedience in view of the coming Day of Judgment and deliverance (*Barnabas* 21).

In other Christian writings of this period, the basis of the moral appeal is not only the words of Jesus as preserved in the New Testament tradition but also the philosophical insights of the time, especially from Stoicism. In *1 Clement*, written at the end of the first century by the bishop of Rome, there is an appeal for unity within the communities based on the letters of Paul and various parts of the Old Testament, especially Psalms. Yet when the virtues are specified, the list includes such Stoic terms as "piety," "self-control," and "sobriety." Similarly, in his *Letter to the Ephesians* (10, 14–17), Ignatius (the early-second-century bishop of Antioch in Syria) extols virtues also expressed in Stoic terminology, although the larger framework of Christian moral responsibility includes quotations from the sayings of Jesus and warnings of the coming judgment.

In a highly allegorical writing, the *Shepherd of Hermas*, one of the visions described is of seven women who represent the seven virtues, including the biblical virtues of faith and love but also philosophical counterparts: simplicity, intellectual knowledge, purity, reverence, and godliness. This appropriation of terms from the contemporary philosophical traditions is evident to a limited degree in the letters of Paul (especially Philippians 4:8–9; Galatians 5:22–3) but has been considerably developed in these later Christian writings. *First Clement* (25) goes so far as to claim that the Greek myth of the phoenix was a sign of the Christian belief in the resurrection. In this case, the myth was not denounced; this Christian writer transformed it.

An important feature of Greco-Roman culture that Christian writers of the second century adapted for their own purposes was the allegorical interpretation of classic literature. Allegorical renderings of the Scriptures of Israel already appear in the New Testament, the use of Isaiah 5:1–7 in Matthew (21:33–46), Mark (12:1–12), and Luke (20:9–19) being obvious examples. The transformation of narratives into abstract and even philosophical concepts flourished in the early centuries C.E., as is shown by the writings of the Jewish scholar Philo of Alexandria and by such Greco-Roman writers as Livy and Plutarch. Through allegory *Barnabas* explains the symbolic meaning of the sacrificial system and food laws of ancient Israel (*Barnabas* 7–10). For instance, he writes that permission in the Law of Moses for Israelites to eat the meat of certain animals that chew the cud (Deuteronomy 14:6) refers to the virtue of meditating on the word of God. The parables section of the *Shepherd of Hermas* contains an elaborate allegory (9) of twelve mountains,

PHOENIX

In Greek mythology the phoenix is sacred to the sun, famed for its splendid plumage and musical voice, and mentioned by writers from the fifth century B.C.E. on. The bird, which was always male, was said to live for a long time – from five hundred to thirteen thousand years – and then to burn itself alive in its nest of twigs. From the ashes emerged its successor, which when it could fly, transported the remains of its predecessor to the temple of the sun at Heliopolis in Egypt. Serious discussions of the country of origin of the phoenix appear in such works as the *Natural History* by Pliny (23–79 C.E.).

which represent the twelve tribes of the earth. Some are blessed; some are cursed for rejecting the message of God. Those accepted include innocent babies, suffering believers, Church leaders and those who contribute to their support, the simple, the guileless, and the blessed. The rejected tribes range from apostates and blasphemers to misbehaving deacons and rich believers preoccupied with their own affairs. In the visions section of this same document, the Church is pictured first as a great lady and then as a tower, into which some stones fit, some are reworked, and some are rejected (Vision 3). The allegorical details give the modern reader a vivid picture of the social situation of the Church in the second century, including the problems of diversity of membership and the ways in which the Church appropriated features of the contemporary culture for its own purposes.

2. Leadership in the Churches

First Clement and Ignatius's *Epistles* evidence the growing necessity to enforce acceptance of the Church leadership. The picture that emerges is one of bishops presiding over churches, some in the major city of the region and others in smaller cities or rural areas. Chapters 41–3 of *1*

THE *SHEPHERD OF HERMAS*

Attributed to the brother of Pius, who was bishop of Rome from 139 to 154 C.E., the *Shepherd of Hermas* is a mix of prophetic, apocalyptic, and allegorical styles. It is in three sections: visions (communications from heaven), mandates (requirements for members), and parables (images and lessons drawn from them concerning present values and future hopes). One major concern is how to deal with church members who have lapsed into sin after baptism. On the question of whether or not such persons could be restored and renewed in the community, Hermas emphasized grace and forgiveness.

Written in Rome almost a hundred years after Mark, *Hermas* set aside Jesus' rejection of family ties. The family became the sphere of first recourse in working out the behavior that God required, a haven from persecution whose prudent conduct was a recommendation of Christianity to the overlords of the Roman Empire.

Hermas, a recently freed slave with a rich visionary life, is told by an angel in his vision that keeping women in check within the domestic household is a principal Christian duty, crucial for salvation (the *Shepherd of Hermas* 1.1–2.4):

But make these words known to all your children and to your wife, who shall in future be to you as a sister. For she also does not refrain her tongue, with which she does evil; but when she has heard these words she will refrain it, and will obtain mercy. After you have made known these words to them, which the master commanded me to be revealed to you, all the sins which they have formerly committed shall be forgiven them, and they shall be forgiven to all the saints who have sinned up to this day, if they repent with their whole heart, and put aside double-mindedness from their heart. For the master has sworn to his elect by his

glory that if there be still sin after this day has been fixed, they shall have no salvation; for repentance for the just has a limit; the days of repentance have been fulfilled for all the saints, but for the nations repentance is open until the last day.

A man, even a low-class man in control of his household, will win salvation despite sin, and that means he needs to keep his women in check.

Demands for mastery of one's family became a rhetorical strong-arm tactic of Christians, despite their weak political and social position. Everyone in the empire complained of the debauchery of the elite, and Christians could join in that critique, holding themselves above such practices even during periods when they were persecuted. The servility of women became an emblem of the harmony that derived from following Jesus as one's true lord and master.

PLUTARCH

Plutarch was a philosopher and prolific writer who lived from 46 to 122 C.E. Born in central Greece at Chaeronea, he studied philosophy at Athens and then lived for an extended period in Rome, where he lectured on philosophy and, according to later tradition, tutored the emperor Hadrian. He is best known for his *Lives*, in which he presents comparative biographical studies of twenty-three figures from Roman history and twenty-three from Greek tradition. Plutarch also wrote speculative and metaphysical essays.

SECOND CLEMENT

Although *2 Clement* is written in the outward form of a letter, it is actually a discourse, intended to be read aloud to congregations, probably composed in Alexandria or Corinth after 150 C.E. The emphasis in *2 Clement* is on the full deity of Christ, as well as on the claim that human flesh (and not merely the human spirit) will take part in the life of the age to come. There is warning of future judgment and an appeal to live by the power of the Spirit, thus overcoming the temptations that beset God's people.

Clement make the case that the pattern of having God's people ruled by bishops, with the aid of deacons, is foretold in the Old Testament and goes back to Moses. Military organization, in which soldiers obey their generals, is commended (37). In Ignatius's *Letter to the Magnesians* (5) he declares that the bishop presides in the place of God and that presbyters have the same role as the council of the apostles. That deacons are commissioned to perform services for the community is affirmed in this letter (7), as well as in that *to the Trallians* (2), where subjection to the bishop is compared to submission to Jesus Christ. The people of God are defined in Ignatius's *Letter to the Philadelphians* as those who stand with or submit to the bishop (3). The bishop, together with the one Eucharist and the one altar, represents the unity of the church (4). Similar appeals to submit to the bishop appear in his *Letter to the Smyrneans* (8–9) and *Letter to Polycarp* (6).

3. Basis for Proper Beliefs

Second-century Christian writings affirm the principle of doctrinal truth, without much specification of what those doctrines are. One of the latest of the writings included among the Apostolic Fathers is *2 Clement*, in which "the truth" of Christianity is described as "knowledge." Such terms show that faith is not primarily trust in God and what he is doing for his people through Jesus, as it is in the Gospels and in Paul, but that the emphasis is on the content of faith, now perceived as conceptual in nature, so that authentic faith means sound doctrine. In the later New Testament books and in what is often called the subapostolic period (from the late first century onward), the writers were content to call for sound doctrine without defining what it included. But from the middle of the second century on, such intellectual leaders of the church as Irenaeus and Clement of Alexandria devoted their energies to the definition of true doctrine in detail.

Similarly, writings from the first half of the second century often assume the truth and the authority of a body of sacred Scriptures that are in some sense normative for the Christian Church, even though they do not state the principles by which scriptural authority is to be established or specify which books compose the Old and New Testaments and are therefore to be considered as Scripture. In Acts 20:35, for example, Paul is reported as basing his appeal to the Ephesian elders for generosity on an otherwise unknown saying of Jesus. In 2 Peter 3:1–16 the author's call for purity and patience is grounded in "the Scriptures," which include the letters of Paul. The authority of these writings is taken for granted. Similarly, Ignatius, in his *Letter to the Ephesians* (19), refers to the mystery of the nativity as God's way of overcoming magic and death, although he does not quote the Gospels that speak of Jesus' birth. *First Clement* appeals to precedent from the Scriptures of Israel and the letters of Paul in his effort to overcome schisms that are dividing the churches (45–56). The images of the tower and the stones developed by the *Shepherd of Hermas* (Vision 3 and Parable 9) presuppose such biblical passages as Mark 12:10–11 and

IRENAEUS

Appointed bishop of Lyons in what is now France in 178 C.E., Irenaeus (130– ca. 203) in the succeeding years produced writings that provided an approach to a reasoned understanding of the Christian faith, as well as a thoughtful basis for rejecting such offshoots of the faith (as he saw them) as Gnosticism. His basic view was that the human race had been in process of maturation since creation, so that Adam was the prototype of immature, erring humanity, and Christ was both teacher and exemplar of mature human existence. In the future, that divine plan for humanity would be achieved in the new age that the coming of Jesus had made possible. Irenaeus shared with Marcion (who taught a dualist form of Christianity in Rome during the second century) the conviction that one must designate an authoritative list of biblical writings, but unlike Marcion, he chose and gave reasons for choosing the four Gospels, the Acts, the Epistles, and Revelation that make up the New Testament as the foundation for God's ongoing disclosure of his cosmic purpose. He ruled out both the allegedly secret supplements on which the Gnostics were basing their teachings and the other apocryphal works that were being presented with claims of authority. Irenaeus's work stands as a model of reason and as a coherent theological scheme that considered divine revelation to be a reasoned process.

In his treatise *Against Heresies*, Irenaeus countered Gnostic understandings of the gospel with what was called by his time a "catholic" faith. Faith as catholic is "through the whole" (*kath holou*) of the Church. It is faith such as one would find it in Alexandria, Lyons, Rome, Ephesus, Corinth, Antioch, or wherever. That construction of Christianity was designed to avoid any particular requirement (such as one of the metaphysical cosmologies of Gnosticism) being made upon Christians as such.

Irenaeus's attempt to join in establishing a generic, or catholic, Christianity called attention to four aspects of faith that have remained constant in classic definitions of Christianity. First, faith was to be expressed by means of the Scriptures as received from Israel; there was no question of eliminating the Hebrew Bible. Second, faith was grounded in the preaching of the apostles, as instanced in their own writings and the creeds. Third, communities were to practice their faith by means of the sacraments that were universally recognized at that time, baptism and Eucharist. Fourth, the loyalty of the Church to these principles was to be assured by the authority of bishops and priests, understood as the successors of the apostles. Taken together, these were the constituents of "the great and glorious body of Christ." They made the Church a divine institution: "Where the Spirit of God is, there is the Church and all grace, and the Spirit is truth."

Although Irenaeus's conception was designed to be inclusive, it also was at odds with emerging Gnosticism. The issue was not only the authority of the Hebrew Bible (which was typically contested by Gnostics). Gnostics also cherished writings that were not apostolic, sacraments of initiation that were not universal, and leaders who were set up privately. The sort of tensions involved might be compared to the relations between adherents of one of the "New Age" movements and of Presbyterianism. Although formal exclusion is not in question, neither is one group truly comfortable with the other.

Irenaeus's concern to establish this fourfold definition of the Church is consonant with one of his most vivid observations. Just as there are four quarters of the heavens, four principal winds that circle the world, and four cherubim before the throne of God, he says, so there are four Gospels. Indeed, the number four corresponds to the four universal (or catholic) covenants between God and humanity: those of Noah, Abraham, Moses, and Christ. The Gospels belong to the order of the very basics of life, and – what is equally important to appreciate – the basics of life belong to the Gospels. The power of God is not to be abstracted from the terms and conditions of the world in which we live. In insisting on that, teachers such as Clement of Alexandria and Irenaeus opposed the popular dualism that was a principal appeal of the Gnostics. Instead, Catholic Christians insisted on the incarnation as the key to the revelation of God's truth to humanity.

CLEMENT OF ALEXANDRIA

Clement was a Christian Intellectual who flourished in Alexandria until the persecution under Septimus Severus (202 C.E.). In addition to his extensive knowledge of Greek philosophy, he studied Hebrew with a Jewish scholar, who introduced him to Stoic thought. Clement drew on Platonism for his theory of the universe and on the Stoics for details of his ethical concepts. His major writings were (1) *Stromata*, a collection of insights on a range of religious and philosophical issues; (2) *Protrepticon*, in which he sought to persuade pagans of the truth of Christianity; (3) *Paedagogos*, a book of instruction for new Christians; and (4) *Can a Rich Man be Saved?* a tract warning about the moral danger of wealth. Another writing, the *Hypotyposes*, is now lost, but it was denounced by early critics as incompatible with the Scriptures.

Matthew 21:42–3, as well as Psalm 118:22–3, which is quoted in the Gospels, yet no explicit reference to a Gospel or Old Testament passage is given.

Direct quotations from the Gospels occur in some documents of this period, however. *Didache* 1 quotes phrases from Matthew 7:12, Luke 6:31–3, Matthew 5:44–7, and later (9) from Matthew 7:6. Similarly, Polycarp's *Epistle to the Philippians* (ca. 140 C.E.) repeats words from Matthew 7 and Luke 6 that are part of their respective versions of Jesus' Sermon on the Mount/Plain. Through direct quotation and especially by allusion to the narrative and instructional content, these writers build on the New Testament without specifying their sources or providing authoritative lists of the writings. The ambivalence of the Church in this period toward the Scriptures of Israel is evident in that they are appealed to repeatedly for precedent or authorization – by either direct reference or allegorical interpretation – and yet a writer like Ignatius in his *Letter to the Magnesians* insists that Christians should not adopt Jewish doctrines or laws; not the Sabbath, but the Lord's Day, should be their obervance in their independence from Judaism. Complicating this definitional process was the concurrent move within Judaism to set the limits of its recognized Scriptures and to draw a sharp line between themselves as the true people of God and the Church and its growing Gentile constituency. That the Christians had not yet drawn up a universally accepted list of their own is apparent in that *2 Clement* 12 quotes as authoritative the *Gospel according to Thomas*, which the Church was soon to discount. On the other hand, around the middle of the second century, Marcion asserted that Christians should reject all the Jewish Scriptures and all of the New Testament except the letters of Paul and an expurgated (i.e., de-Judaized) version of Luke-Acts. Marcion's radical proposal seems to have stimulated the leaders of the Church to define formally what they understood to be the scriptural authority for Christians. That process of deciding which writings were to be regarded as normative or canonical was of major importance for the subsequent development of the life and thought of the Church.

B. The Bible Assumes a Normative Function

1. Stages in the Selection of the Biblical Books

By the beginning of the Common Era there was emerging agreement among Jews as to which books in the biblical tradition were to be considered authoritative, but the Diaspora and territorial Israel went their different ways. Jesus and his movement clearly recognized the traditional grouping of the Hebrew canon into the Torah, the Prophets (often distinguished between the Former Prophets [Joshua–2 Kings] and the Latter Prophets [Isaiah–Malachi]), and the Writings. That grouping is cited in almost so many words in Luke 24:27, 44. But the Gospels themselves were written in Greek, and the Bible of the Church was also Greek in language and

POLYCARP

Bishop of Smyrna in Asia Minor, Polycarp lived from about 69 to 156 C.E. He is mentioned by Irenaeus, bishop and scholar from Gaul (130–ca. 203), and was addressed by Ignatius in a letter that has been preserved. Polycarp's major concerns were to uphold what he saw as true doctrine and to oppose heresy, which was infiltrating the Church. As a guarantee of the truth of his views of faith and practice, he appealed to associations he claimed to have had with the apostles. His leadership was so effective and so many pagans converted to Christianity through his efforts that he was attacked and martyred by Roman authorities, who considered him to be undermining the traditional religious roots of the Roman order. The story of his martyrdom is itself a major contribution to Christian literature.

Hellenistic in conception. A great deal of work has been done in recent years on the Greek text of the Septuagint; less attention has been given to the actual structure of the rendering, which amounts to a radical revision of the significance of the Hebrew Bible. The Septuagint truly creates an Old Testament by the time of the first extant manuscript of the whole, the Codex Vaticanus, dated in the fourth century C.E.

As Henry Barclay Swete, the British biblical and patristics scholar, showed a century ago, the ordering of books – the sequence and structure of the canon – follows a pattern in the Septuagint significantly different from that of the Hebrew Bible. In the Codex Vaticanus, an order is followed that is as foreign to the Hebrew Bible as it is to the English Bible:

1. Genesis, Exodus, Leviticus, Numbers, Deuteronomy, Joshua, Judges, Ruth, 1–4 Kings, 1–2 Chronicles, 1–2 Ezra
2. Psalms, Proverbs, Ecclesiastes, Song of Songs, Job, Wisdom of Solomon, Wisdom of Sirach, Esther, Judith, Tobit
3. Hosea, Amos, Micah, Joel, Obadiah, Jonah, Nahum, Habakkuk, Zephaniah, Haggai, Zechariah, Malachi, Isaiah, Jeremiah, Baruch, Lamentations, Letter of Jeremiah, Ezekiel, Daniel.

This grouping is by no means fixed, and even the content of the Greek Bible famously deviates, not only from the Hebrew canon (producing the academic category of the "Apocrypha," works of the Septuagint without apparent Hebrew originals), but in the text being used as one moves from manuscript to manuscript, ancient commentator to ancient commentator. Still, Swete was able to show that Vaticanus attests to a representative order, in which the first category was "historical," the second "poetical," and the third "prophetic."

Swete argued that this grouping was initially literary, derived from the reception of the Greek Bible in Alexandria, but he also suggested at the close of his discussion that "it may have seemed fitting that the Prophets should immediately precede the Evangelists." That is a remarkable insight, which helps us to understand the sequence within the third category, that of Prophecy (which also departs signally from the Hebrew Bible). The Septuagintal order, by commencing with the minor Prophets, is able to finish off with the greatest of the literary Prophets: Isaiah, Jeremiah (with the additions of Baruch, Lamentations, and the Letter), and Ezekiel. Even more strikingly, the canon closes with Daniel, now emphatically and climactically one of the Prophets (rather than one of the Writings, as in the Hebrew Bible). Its references to the resurrection (12:2) and to the son of man (7:13, 9:21, 10:16) make it an ideal transition into the story of Jesus. It is interesting that the canon of the New Testament, which was also solidifying during the fourth century, closes similarly on a strong note of prophecy, with the Revelation of John.

When Latin grew in usage as a common language of the Mediterranean world in the second and third centuries C.E., Latin translations of the Bible included variants and additions to the Scriptures. These Latin versions have provided the canon for Roman Catholics down to the present day. But how and why were the authoritative lists of books drawn up, and how did they come to be incorporated in the standard versions?

With the destruction of the Jerusalem Temple in 70 C.E. and the crushing of the Jewish nationalist movement by 135, the significant and enduring option was what became Rabbinic Judaism, which began taking shape around the end of the first century C.E. For this movement, the interpretive tradition replaced the Temple as the major focus of the life of the religious community. It was essential, therefore, not only to set the limits of what members of the community were to consider as sacred Scripture but also to differentiate this movement from another that was at the same time claiming to have the true and authoritative interpretation of these Scriptures: the early Christians. The Rabbis reportedly formulated their official list at Yavneh on the Mediterranean coast of Palestine by the last decade of the first century C.E., although no documentary evidence confirms this tradition. An extended consultation appears to have resulted in the production of the standard text of the Hebrew Bible, which has been normative ever since.

For the early Christians this issue of an authoritative scriptural basis for their identity as covenant people was more complicated. They chose the longer list of Jewish Scriptures (the Septuagint) as their "canon" (from a Greek word meaning "rule" or "guideline"). But they had also been producing writings of their own, which soon came to be regarded as in some sense authoritative as well.

THE OLD TESTAMENT APOCRYPHA AND PSEUDEPIGRAPHA

The following books are included in the Septuagint and the Roman Catholic canon of the Old Testament but not in the Hebrew Bible or the Protestant canon. These writings are known as the Old Testament Apocrypha. They include additions to the books in the Hebrew canon and writings similar to the Hebrew Scriptures but extant only in Greek. They can be classified as (1) historical, (2) prophetic (or apocalyptic), (3) wisdom, and (4) writings, but the historical and writings books contain prayers and exhortations that cause them to resemble the other two types.

1 and 2 Esdras (1)
Tobit (4)

Judith (4)
Additions to Esther (also called the Rest of Esther) (4)
Wisdom of Solomon (3)
Wisdom of Ben Sira (or Sirach) (also called Ecclesiasticus) (3)
Baruch (2)
Epistle of Jeremy (or Jeremiah) (2)
Additions to Daniel: Prayer of Azariah; Song of the Three Jews; Susanna; Bel and the Dragon (2)
Prayer of Manasseh (4)
1 Maccabees (1)
2 Maccabees (1)

Other similar writings, called Old Testament Pseudepigrapha, were never included in the canon by the great majority of Jews or Christians.

These writings include apocalypses and testaments. Typical are the following:

Apocalypse of Enoch
Sibylline Oracles
Fourth Book of Ezra
Apocalypse of Baruch
Testaments of the Twelve Patriarchs
Testament of Moses
Testament of Solomon
Letter of Aristeas
Jubilees
Joseph and Aseneth
3 and 4 Maccabees
Psalms of Solomon
Prayer of Joseph
Odes of Solomon
Ezekiel the Tragedian
Artapanus

2. Supplementing the Biblical Writings

Rabbinic discussion from the late first century C.E. onward began pro-grammatically to interpret the Torah of Moses as developed in their oral tradition, applying it to the radical new circumstances that followed the destruction of the Temple. The outcome of this process was the Mishnah and the Talmud, which continue to the present day to serve as a normative approach to the interpretation and application of the Hebrew Scriptures. In the same period, the Christians were having to come to terms with the Scriptures that they had taken over from Judaism and claimed to have the keys to interpret properly, but they also had produced their own writings depicting the origins and destiny of their movement: the Gospels and Acts. Writings such as the letters of Paul, which had originated in or were sent to various centers of early Christianity, were understandably highly regarded in the places where they first appeared, but then they also began to be circulated from region to region and came to be accepted as inter-esting, important, and even authoritative throughout the Christian com-munities worldwide. Yet well into the second century, some Christians, like Papias of Hierapolis in Phrygia (western Asia Minor), preferred the oral reports transmitted through those who had heard the disciples of Jesus as having greater authority than the written accounts. The question could not be avoided as to which of these writings, diverse in origin and content, were to be regarded as authoritative for the churches of different cultural orientations spread across the Mediterranean world and the Middle East.

3. Establishing the Christian Biblical Canon

By the middle of the second century C.E., the leaders of the Church known as the Apostolic Fathers recognized the importance of having accounts of Jesus and the apostles that were available and accepted as authoritative throughout the churches across the civilized world. In a con-scious or unconscious attempt to lend authority to these writings, the accounts of the life and teachings of Jesus, although preserved in anony-mous documents known as the Gospels, came to be associated with disci-ples of Jesus (Matthew and John) or with associates of the disciples or apos-tles (Mark, said to be Peter's companion, and Luke, associated with the apostle Paul). The place of origin of the Gospels cannot now be deter-mined with certainty, and in any case, by the second century they came to be embraced by Christianity as a whole (i.e., in its catholic form).

In contrast, Tertullian in North Africa reflected the strict attachment to divine Spirit, and the imminent expectation of judgment, that character-ized much of Christianity during the second century. He addressed his *Apology* to those who might be called on to judge Christians, but in fact it was intended to counter the common prejudice that Christianity encoun-tered. It is as effective an example of rhetoric as one will find, and at the same time it illustrates the legal situation and the popular reaction to the

TATIAN

In the second century C.E., Tatian, who was widely regarded as a distinguished interpreter of Greek philosophy, was converted to Christianity by Justin Martyr (who died in 167 C.E.). He became an effective intellectual champion of Christianity, offering a challenge to the concepts of Greek philosophy in his treatise *Against the Greeks*. Later he became the leader of a rigidly ascetic Christian sect, which substituted water for wine in the Eucharist. Tatian's most enduring contribution, albeit highly controversial, was his synthesis of the four Gospels into a single sequential account of the career of Jesus: the *Diatessaron* (meaning "Through the Four" [Gospels]).

new religion. The *Apology* was written in 197 C.E., shortly after Tertullian's conversion to Christianity. The uncompromising stance is characteristic of the climate of the movement in Carthage and may explain why, around 207 C.E., Tertullian himself became a Montanist, attracted by the asceticism that comported with the conviction that each believer was a vessel of the Holy Spirit.

The apostolic link was crucial to the authority of writings, to some extent to counter claims of charismatic authority: later documents were written in the name of an apostle (such as the later letters attributed to Paul) and anonymous writings were attributed to an apostle (as Hebrews was assigned to Paul). Since there were no official copies of these writings – either Jewish or Christian – it was inevitable that they would be modified by those who copied or used them. Additions and adaptations were made, such as harmonizing differences in the Gospel accounts of Jesus. A painstaking and brilliantly successful effort to unify the Gospel accounts of Jesus' words and works was undertaken by Tatian, who harmonized the four Gospels into a consecutive account that included most of what was in each of them. It was called the *Diatessaron* (Through the Four [Gospels]) and helped to set the pattern for other Gospel harmonies and for the weaving together of the narratives and sayings of Jesus from all the Gospels. Furthermore, insertions from one Gospel to another were made in copying the documents, and passages were added in some copies of a Gospel, such as the story of the adulterous woman in John 8.

As their respective communities were taking shape in the early centuries of the Common Era, both Jews and Christians were struggling with the issue of which writings concerning the origins of their movements were to be regarded as authoritative, including historical, prophetic, and Wisdom books. For example, some wanted to add to the traditional Hebrew canon of Scripture such later writings as the Wisdom of Solomon, the Wisdom of Ben Sira, the later books attributed to Ezra (Esdras), and the various Books of Maccabees. The decision by some Jews to limit the authoritative Scriptures to those of Hebrew origin was probably reached by the end of the first century C.E., but the Christians by the middle of the second century had not yet drawn up a definitive list of their Scriptures. Two kinds of pressures provoked their decisions. One factor was the claim by Marcion, who came to Rome from Pontus on the Black Sea, that the contradictions between the Hebrew Bible and the Christian Scriptures were to be seen as evidence that the God of the Jews and the creator of the material world was an inferior being, whereas the sovereign and just Lord was the God whose messenger Jesus was. Accordingly, by the middle of the second century, Marcion had rejected the Old Testament and purged the Gospels and apostolic letters of all features based on the Old Testament, thereby creating what he regarded as the proper canon of Christian Scriptures. The second factor was the production in this period of Gospels and Books of Acts by Gnostics and others that claimed to supplement, to interpret, or even to correct what was in the more widely accepted Christian writings. During

MONTANUS

Around 157 C.E., a native of Phrygia named Montanus claimed that he was filled by the Spirit and had come as the comforter promised after Jesus in the Gospel according to John (see John 14:16, 26; 16:7). Associated with two prophetesses, Prisca and Maximilla, Montanism's "new prophecy" became extremely influential far outside Asia Minor, despite the resistance of leaders such as Apollinarius, bishop of Hierapolis. Its most famous convert was Tertullian, the great writer of North Africa, who became a Montanist in 207. In the environment of persecution that Tertullian addressed, the rigorism of the Montanists, which derived from their conviction that each believer was a vessel of the Holy Spirit, attracted him. Compromise is the first victim of persecution, and Montanism offered the prospect of continuing guidance directly from the Spirit during a period in which the viability of the Church as a well-ordered household was seriously brought into question by the policy of the Romans.

the second half of the second century an ecstatic visionary named Montanus from Phrygia in western Asia Minor claimed to have had a revelation about the detailed fulfillment of the Revelation of John concerning the coming of the end of the age. His claims spread westward, and many were convinced by his predictions, which expected the consummation to occur in his native territory. The leaders and scholars of the churches had to make decisions about which of the proliferating Christian claims and writings were to be considered normative for Christians as a whole.

Since there was no central agency to make such decisions, steps toward drawing up an authoritative list were made by various regional leaders of the Church. Justin, a Christian philosopher who found his way from his native Samaria to Rome, where he was martyred in about 167, noted in his *Apology* (1.67–3) that preaching and instruction in the churches were based not only on "the writings of the prophets," by which he seems to have meant the Scriptures of Israel, but also on "the memoirs of the apostles," by which he referred to what came to be known as the writings of the New Testament. Since he quotes from Matthew 16:4 as a "memoir," it is clear that the Gospels were being used as Scripture in the churches by the middle of the second century. A more explicit claim was offered by Irenaeus, bishop of Lyons in the second half of the second century, in his *Against Heresies* (3.11.8): there are four Gospels because of the way the universe is structured, with its four winds and four points of the compass. In his writings Irenaeus indicates his admiration also for the letters of Paul and for 1 Peter, 1 John, and the Revelation of John. He includes as authoritative the Wisdom of Solomon and the *Shepherd of Hermas*, both of which would have attracted him by their philosophical orientation and method. Not named by him are 2 and 3 John and 2 Peter.

By the early third century, Clement of Alexandria was more specific about which writings were to be considered authoritative by Christians: the four Gospels, the letters of Paul (among which he included Hebrews), and what he called the "catholic letters" (from the Greek phrase *kath holou*, "through to the whole"), since they were addressed to a general audience rather than to a specific community. These included James; 1, 2, and 3 John; 1 and 2 Peter; and Jude. But he also listed among the authoritative writings *1 Clement*, the Wisdom of Solomon, the Wisdom of Ben Sira, the *Epistle of Barnabas*, and the *Apocalypse of Peter*.

By the third century, lists of "canonical" books also came to be cited, thereby implying their authority and official status. For example, Origen of

Alexandria, one of the leading biblical scholars of the early church, includes in his canonical list the four Gospels, fourteen letters of Paul (although he thinks Hebrews is not really by Paul), 1 Peter, 1 John, and Revelation; he omits 2 and 3 John, 2 Peter, Jude, and James. Of uncertain date (second to fourth century) is an anonymous canonical list discovered by a librarian named Muratori in Milan in the later nineteenth century and hence known as the Muratorian Canon. The first part of the list is lost but must have included Matthew and Mark, since it takes up with Luke and John. It goes on to Acts, thirteen letters of Paul (excluding Hebrews), Jude, 1 and 2 John, Revelation – but also the Wisdom of Solomon and the *Apocalypse of Peter*. The *Shepherd of Hermas* is said to be worthy of being read to the church but is not to be considered authoritative.

In the early fourth century, Eusebius, whose *Ecclesiastical History* is our most important source of information about early Christianity apart from the New Testament, gives the same basic canonical list as Origen. But it is only in the second half of the fourth century, in an episcopal letter sent by Athanasius, bishop of Alexandria, that we find a list of canonical writings identical with what is now called the New Testament. Although Athanasius reports the list of disputed works mentioned by other writers and notes that these may be profitable reading for Christians, he is clear that they are not to be considered part of the canon.

4. Criteria for Canonicity

The judgments offered about the authoritative status of these early Christian writings ultimately were not based on scholarly decisions or ecclesiastical decrees, but derived instead from the functions these writings had been serving over the centuries in the communities for whom they were produced. The Gospels and the Letters had initially been written to help the communities understand who Jesus was and how he had disclosed what was to be their place in the purpose of God. These writings enabled early Christians to discern the purpose of their movement and provided guidelines for the ongoing life of the group. Decisions about canonicity rested on three factors: (1) what had proved useful in Christian communities throughout the Greco-Roman world; (2) what could be traced back to the earliest times of the Church; and (3) what could be shown to have been written by an apostle or an apostolic associate. Eusebius noted that one could determine by their style and vocabulary the authenticity of documents that claimed to come from the apostles (*Ecclesiastical History* 3.25.6–7). This powerful interest in affirming links with the traditional past is evident not only in the Church at that time but also in the wider Roman society, where strong and effective literary and cultural enterprises were seeking to regain access to the life and thought of classical Greece and Rome.

The primary considerations in assembling the canon, therefore, were the needs, the experience, and the corporate judgments of the early Christian

SYRIAC

Syriac is a dialect of Aramaic, the Semitic language spoken by Middle Eastern Jews and Christians in the Hellenistic and Roman periods. Unlike Aramaic, which uses the same alphabet as Hebrew, Syriac has a more flowing script and was widely used in Syria and Mesopotamia until Arabic became the dominant Semitic language after the eighth century. Ancient versions of biblical writings have been preserved in Syriac manuscripts and must be taken into account in establishing the original version of the Hebrew text of the Bible.

communities. The decisions did not derive from objective criteria offered by detached observers. In the process of deciding what writings would constitute the Bible, both Jewish and Christian decision makers demonstrated the conviction held by the biblical writers themselves: that God addresses his people, calling them to account and disclosing his purpose for and through them, and that this takes place in the living context of social and cultural crisis and change.

C. Ancient Copies and Ancient and Modern Translations

Until the invention of printing in the fifteenth century, all copies of documents were handmade and thus subject to all sorts of copyist errors. No two ancient copies of biblical texts agree in every detail, although an effort was made by scholars over a period of centuries to determine an official text and to provide the Hebrew (which was originally written only in consonants) with the appropriate vowels for easier reading. Scholarly opinion varies as to the date when this normative text was established, but the oldest copy available is from the ninth century C.E. (although the biblical scrolls at Qumran attest to its accuracy). Since the eighteenth century, scholars have worked to reconstruct what they consider to be the original of the Hebrew text and have done so through detailed comparison of this text with the translations, especially those in Greek, Latin, and Syriac, taking into account scribal errors and fragments of various portions of the Bible that have been found in Egypt and Palestine.

Similar efforts to reconstruct the original text of the New Testament writings began about three hundred years ago, when scholars noted the differences among the established texts of the New Testament in use among churches, which had preserved this material in Greek, Syriac, Latin, Armenian, Ethiopic, Georgian, and other languages into which it had been translated in the early centuries. The text of the Greek New Testament that was accepted as normative was analyzed through comparison with ancient copies that were discovered or seriously studied in the sixteenth century and subsequently. The standard edition of the Greek text, or Received Text as it was called, was shown to contain tens of thousands of errors or questionable readings, some of them deriving from simple, obvious mistakes by the copyists, and many from the effort to harmonize passages in the Gospels with each other or to incorporate within the text later theological ideas or liturgical practices (such as the ending to the Lord's Prayer in Matthew 6:13).

The process of analyzing these divergences with the aim of reconstructing something closer to the original text was launched in the nineteenth century and continues to the present day. In 1831 serious efforts to reconstruct the Greek text of the New Testament began with the work of Karl Lachmann, who recognized that the so-called *Textus Receptus* (Received Text) was late and composite and that a few older manuscripts from the eastern Mediterranean more likely preserved something closer to the original. A major step in this analytical process was made when in the middle of the nineteenth century C. Tischendorf discovered a fourth-century manuscript in the library of Saint Catherine's monastery on Mount Sinai in Egypt. He developed a method of listing and classifying the alternative readings from various manuscripts and on this basis decided which of the variants was more likely to be the original. After his death, this approach was carried forward by two British scholars, B. F. Westcott and F. J. A. Hort, who analyzed by this method both Codex Sinaiticus and Codex Vaticanus, as well as other ancient copies of the New Testament in various languages (especially Syriac) and quotations from the New Testament in the writings of the early Church fathers. As a result, the method of classification and evaluation of the textual variants was better informed, and the results more persuasive. This work is still being carried on by an international group of scholars. The resultant text of the Greek New Testament has established a wide circle of usage. Yet such editions have also been criticized, on the grounds that they mix together readings from many different times and periods, when it is perfectly possible to base work on complete fourth-century manuscripts, and only deviate from them as a result of the fragmentary evidence of earlier manuscripts.

Some of the oldest known manuscripts of the Bible are ancient translations, such as the Septuagint or the Latin and Syriac versions of the New Testament. The sixteenth and seventeenth centuries saw the rise and spread of the practice of making the Bible available in contemporary languages. That policy has continued to the present day, with a current surge of activity worldwide to make the Bible available in local languages. At present, translations of all or portions of the Bible exist in more than two thousand languages, and work on translations into more than six hundred new languages is currently in process. Clearly, the significance of the Bible has transcended the cultural and linguistic worlds in which it originated. Yet study of its worlds and of the social and linguistic contexts out of which it came are essential for understanding it today.

BIBLIOGRAPHICAL ESSAY

1. Jesus and the New Covenant People

A good summary of developments within Judaism in the Greco-Roman period is provided in William Scott Green and J. Andrew Overman, "Judaism (Greco-Roman Period)," in the *Anchor Bible Dictionary* (New York: Doubleday, 1992), 3:1037–54, and Oskar Skarsaune, *In the Shadow of the Temple: Jewish Influences on Early Christianity* (Downers Grove, IL: Inter-Varsity, 2002). An overview of the changing methods and historical approaches to the study of Jesus is offered in S. C. Neill and N. T. Wright, *The Interpretation of the New Testament, 1861–1986* (Oxford: Oxford University Press, 1988). For analyses of the issues involved in the historical study of Jesus, see A. E. Harvey, *Jesus and the Constraints of History* (London: Duckworth, 1982); Bruce Chilton and Craig A. Evans, *Studying the Historical Jesus: Evaluations of the State of Current Research,* New Testament Tools and Studies 19 (Leiden: Brill, 1994 and 1998); *Jesus in Context: Temple, Purity and Restoration,* Arbeiten zur Geschichte des Antiken Judentums und des Urchristentums 39 (Leiden: Brill, 1997); *Authenticating the Activities of Jesus,* New Testament Tools and Studies 78,2 (Leiden: Brill, 1999); and *Authenticating the Words of Jesus,* New Testament Tools and Studies 78,1 (Leiden: Brill, 1999).

In *Jesus in History*, 3d ed. (Fort Worth: Harcourt Brace, 1995), Howard Clark Kee offers a sketch of the rise of questions about the historical knowledge of Jesus and an analysis of the evidence from the Gospels and other ancient sources. This consideration is developed in narrative terms in Bruce Chilton, *Rabbi Jesus: An Intimate Biography* (New York: Doubleday, 2000). For a study of John the Baptist as the organizer of a protest movement against the priestly establishment and as the prophetic voice of renewal of the people of God, see Joan E. Taylor, *The Immerser: John the Baptist within Second Temple Judaism,* Studying the Historical Jesus (Grand Rapids and Cambridge: Eerdmans, 1997), and the essay on John by Paul Hollenbach in the *Anchor Bible Dictionary* (New York: Doubleday, 1992), 3:887–99. In the latter volume are two perceptive essays on Jesus: (1) Ben F. Meyer sets out the historical methods and results for reconstructing the figure of Jesus that come from critical analysis of the Gospels and the Letters of Paul, with a comprehensive bibliography (pp. 773–96); (2) N. T. Wright gives a useful survey of the ways in which the question of historical knowledge of Jesus has been addressed in scholarly circles since the eighteenth century (pp. 796–802), including recent efforts to picture Jesus as a mouthpiece for popular wisdom.

The Q source behind the Gospels of Matthew and Luke is reconstructed in Richard A. Edwards, *A Concordance to Q* (Missoula, MT: Scholars Press, 1975). A detailed analysis of the contents of Q is David R. Catchpole, *The Quest for Q* (Edinburgh: T. & T. Clark, 1993). The hypothesis that Q originally was a collection of wisdom sayings of Jesus to which other elements were added is presented in John Kloppenburg, *The Formation of Q* (Philadelphia: Fortress Press, 1987). See James M. Robinson, Paul Hoffmann, John S. Kloppenborg, and Milton C. Moreland, eds., *The Critical Edition of Q: Synopsis Including the Gospels of Matthew and Luke, Mark and Thomas with English, German, and French Translations of Q and Thomas* (Minneapolis: Fortress Press; Leuven: Peeters, 2000). Sociological approaches to Mark are offered in Herman Waetjen, *A Re-ordering of Power: A Socio-political Reading of Mark's Gospel* (Minneapolis: Fortress Press, 1989); J. D. Kingsbury, *Conflict in Mark: Jesus, Authorities, Disciples* (Minneapolis: Fortress Press, 1989); and Howard Clark Kee's *Community of the New Age: Studies in Mark's Gospel* (Philadelphia: Westminster; London: SCM Press, 1977). A study of the Gospel tradition in terms of the historical background of the Jewish revolutionary movements during the first century is offered by Richard A. Horsley, *Jesus and the Spiral of Violence* (San Francisco: HarperCollins, 1987).

Studies of Jesus' titles, and beliefs in Jesus as the Christ include James D. G. Dunn, *Christology in the Making* (London: SCM Press, 1980); Ben Witheringon III, *The Christology of Jesus* (Minneapolis: Fortress Press, 1990); and Reginald H. Fuller and Pheme Perkins, *Who Is This Christ? Gospel Christology and Contemporary Faith* (Philadelphia: Fortress Press, 1983). A survey of the models for the covenant community found in the literature of postexilic Judaism and of early Christianity is offered in Howard Clark Kee, *Who Are the People of God? Early Christian Models of Community* (New Haven: Yale University Press, 1995).

Jesus' practice of fellowship at meals is analyzed with regard to emerging Christian practice in Bruce Chilton, *A Feast of Meanings: Eucharistic Theologies from Jesus through Johannine Circles;* Supplements to Novum Testamentum 72 (Leiden: Brill, 1994); *Jesus' Prayer and Jesus' Eucharist: His Personal Practice of Spirituality* (Valley Forge, PA: Trinity Press International, 1997); and Bernhard Lang, *Sacred Games: A History of Christian Worship* (New Haven: Yale University Press, 1997).

2. Paul: The Jesus Movement Launched in the Roman World

Albert Schweitzer produced a classic survey of Pauline studies in *Paul and His Interpreters: A Critical History*, trans. W. Montgomery (London: Black, 1912; New York: Macmillan, 1951). An important analysis of Paul that helped to recover understanding of the apocalyptic aspects of his thought is J. C. Beker, *Paul the Apostle: The Triumph of God in Life and Thought* (Philadelphia: Westminster, 1980). Fine studies of the chronology of Paul's life are available in Robert Jewett, *A Chronology of Paul's Life* (Philadelphia: Fortress Press, 1979); Gerd Lüdemann, *Paul. Apostle to the Gentiles: Studies in Chronology,* trans. F. S. Jones (London: SCM Press, 1984); and Rainer Riesner, *Paul's Early Period: Chronology, Mission Strategy, Theology,* trans. D. Stott (Grand Rapids: Eerdmans, 1998). Information about the authenticity of letters attributed to Paul and the circumstances of their origin is provided by W. G. Kümmel, *Introduction to the New Testament,* trans. H. C. Kee (London: SCM Press, 1975), and more recently by Raymond E. Brown, *An Introduction to the New Testament,* the Anchor Bible Reference Library (New York: Doubleday, 1997). More accessible treatments of Paul and the Pauline letters are offered in Marion L. Soards, *The Apostle Paul: An Introduction to His Writings and Teachings* (New York: Paulist Press, 1987), and in Bruce Chilton, *Rabbi Paul: An Intellectual Biography* (New York: Doubleday, 2004). Important studies of aspects of Paul's thought include Ernst Käsemann, *Perspectives on Paul* (London: SCM Press, 1971); Victor P. Furnish, *Theology and Ethics in Paul* (Nashville: Abingdon, 1968); and Richard B. Hays, *Echoes of Scripture in the Letters of Paul* (New Haven: Yale University Press, 1989).

A good survey of interpretive questions relating to Paul's Letter to the Romans was edited by K. P. Donfried, *The Romans Debate*, revised ed.

(Peabody, MA: Hendrickson, 1991). Substantive commentaries on the letters of Paul include W. F. Orr and J. A. Walther, *First Corinthians*, Anchor Bible (New York: Doubleday, 1976); V. P. Furnish, *Second Corinthians: A New Translation with Introduction and Commentary*, Anchor Bible 32A (New York: Doubleday, 1984); and Frank J. Matera, *Galatians*, Sacra Pagina (Collegeville, MN: Liturgical Press, 1992). An important study of letter writing in the time of Paul is Stanley K. Stowers, *Letter Writing in Greco-Roman Antiquity* (Philadelphia: Westminster, 1986).

3. Christianity Responds to Formative Judaism

The term "formative Judaism" was coined by Jacob Neusner as a counter to the phrase "normative Judaism" employed by George Foot Moore in his widely influential study *Judaism in the First Centuries of the Christian Era*, 3 vols. (Cambridge, MA: Harvard University Press, 1927–30), where Moore constructed a picture of Jewish rabbinical orthodoxy built on the Mishnah and the Talmud, although this literature was produced only between and the second and the sixth centuries C.E. Neusner's incisive approach has shown that Judaism in the postexilic and post-Maccabean period was in a complex process of formulation and self-definition that continued into the Rabbinic period. See, for example, Jacob Neusner, *Introduction to Rabbinic Literature,* Anchor Bible Reference Library (New York: Doubleday, 1994), and his *The Theology of the Oral Torah: Revealing the Justice of God* (Montreal: McGill-Queen's University Press, 1999). The often-neglected role of women in early Judaism and Christianity is developed in Bruce Chilton, *Mary Magdalene: A Biography* (New York: Doubleday, 2005).

Using this historical reconstruction of Judaism in the time of Jesus, advances have been made in understanding how these developments related to the origins of Christianity; see Bruce Chilton and Jacob Neusner, *Judaism in the New Testament: Practices and Beliefs* (London and New York: Routledge, 1995; London: Taylor & Francis, 2002); Lars Hartman, *"Into the Name of the Lord Jesus": Baptism in the Early Church,* Studies of the New Testament and Its World (Edinburgh: Clark, 1997); Bruce Chilton, *Jesus' Baptism and Jesus' Healing: His Personal Practice of Spirituality* (Harrisburg, PA: Trinity Press International, 1998). Two important works considering this factor as central to the writing of the Gospel according to Matthew are J. Andrew Overman, *Matthew's Gospel and Formative Judaism: The Social World of the Matthean Community* (Minneapolis: Fortress Press, 1990), and Anthony J. Saldarini, *Matthew's Christian–Jewish Community* (Chicago: University of Chicago Press, 1994). A pioneering approach to Matthew on this basis is that of W. D. Davies, *The Setting of the Sermon on the Mount* (Cambridge: Cambridge University Press, 1964); see W. D. Davies and Dale C. Allison, *A Critical and Exegetical Commentary on the Gospel according to Saint Matthew* (Edinburgh: T. & T. Clark, 1997). An important shift in method is represented by the analysis of the adaptation of the Gospel tradition evident in Matthew by G. Bornkamm, G. Barth, and H. J. Held in *Tradition and Interpretation in Matthew's Gospel* (London: SCM Press, 1963). This basic method is adopted by Georg Strecker in an analysis that assumes that Matthew pictures Jesus as calling for obedience to his understanding of Torah, in *The Sermon on the Mount: An Exegetical Commentary*, trans. O. C. Dean (Edinburgh: T. & T. Clark, 1988).

Raymond E. Brown has prepared illuminating analyses of the birth narratives in Matthew and Luke in his *The Birth of the Messiah: A Commentary on the Birth Narratives in Matthew and Luke* (New York: Doubleday, 1977). A fine study of Matthew is offered by Graham N. Stanton in *A Gospel for a New People: Studies in Matthew* (Edinburgh: T. & T. Clark, 1992).

Recent commentaries on Hebrews include those of Harold W. Attridge, Hermeneia Series (Philadelphia: Fortress Press, 1989), and William L. Lane, *Hebrews* (Waco, TX: Word, 1991); they include a comprehensive analysis of the text, its cultural background, and the scholarly literature on this unusual early Christian writing. Briefer and less technical commentaries are those of Donald A. Hagner (San Francisco: Harper, 1983; repr., Peabody, MA: Hendrickson, 1990) and of R. M. Wilson, New Century Bible Commentary (Basingstoke: Marshall Morgan & Scott; Grand Rapids: Eerdmans, 1987). Wilson takes into account the influence of middle Platonism, which accounts for the modification of the earlier eschatological expectation of a new age by means of a contrast between the temporal and the eternal spheres. John Dunnill's study *Covenant and Sacrifice in the Letter to the Hebrews* (Cambridge: Cambridge University Press, 1992) employs a structuralist method of interpretation that seeks to find the meaning inherent in the text as distinct from the conscious aim of the author.

Recent analyses of the Letters of Jude and 2 Peter, with good bibliographies, include those in the Word Biblical Commentary by Richard Bauckham (vol. 50) and in the Anchor Bible by Jerome H. Neyrey (vol. 37C). Bauckham notes the pervasive influence of apocalyptic on Jude and describes its distinctive mode of interpretation of Scripture. As Neyrey shows, 2 Peter mingles features of Jewish apocalyptic and Hellenistic philosophy, as well as alluding to the letters of Paul as Scripture and showing direct dependence on the Letter of Jude. The social conditions that influenced the post-Pauline production of Ephesians are analyzed in L. Michael White, "Urban Development and Social Change in Imperial Ephesos," *EPHESOS, Metropolis of Asia: An Interdisciplinary Approach to Its Archeology, Religion, and Culture*, Harvard Theological Studies 41, ed. Helmut Koester (Valley Forge, PA: Trinity Press International, 1995), 27–79.

4. Christianity Responds to Roman Culture and Imperial Policy

Luke-Acts

Current studies of Luke and Acts continue to be influenced by the monumental five volumes in the series *The Beginnings of Christianity*, part 1, launched by F. J. Foakes-Jackson and Kirsopp Lake and brought to completion by H. J. Cadbury (London: Macmillan, 1920–33). The most enduring volumes are vol. 4 (a commentary on Acts) and vol. 5 (a collection of critical essays). Cadbury also wrote a review of older critical studies of Acts in *The Book of Acts in History* (London: A. & C. Black, 1955). A more recent useful survey of critical studies of Acts is by W. Ward Gasque, *A History of the Criticism of the Acts of the Apostles*, revised ed. (Peabody, MA: Hendrickson, 1989). Charles H. Talbert proved to be a central figure in fresh analysis of Acts through the Society of Biblical Literature seminar that he led, published as *Perspectives on Acts* (Edinburgh: T. & T. Clark, 1978), and in *Luke-Acts: New Perspectives* (New York: Crossroad, 1983). Literary studies of Luke and Acts include Robert Maddox, *The Purpose of Luke-Acts*, Studies of the New Testament and Its World (Edinburgh: Clark, 1982); Robert C. Tannehill, *The Narrative Unity of Luke-Acts* (Philadelphia: Fortress Press, 1986); the Luke-Acts section of David E. Aune, *The New Testament in Its Literary Environment* (Philadelphia: Westminster, 1987), 77–157; Colin J. Hemer, *The Book of Acts in the Setting of Hellenistic History*, ed. C. H. Gempf (Tübingen: Mohr, 1989); a collection of essays on Acts, M. C. Parsons and J. B. Tyson, eds., *Cadbury, Knox, and Talbert: American Contributions to the Study of Acts* (Atlanta: Scholars Press, 1992); and John T. Squires, *The Plan of God in Luke-Acts*, Society for New Testament Monograph Series 76 (Cambridge: Cambridge University Press, 1993).

Important among studies of historical and sociological issues for the understanding of Acts are Wayne Meeks, *The First Urban Christians: The Social World of the Apostle Paul* (New Haven: Yale University Press, 1983) and Gerd Lüdemann, *Early Christians according to the Traditions in Luke-Acts* (London: SCM Press, 1989). Four volumes in the Society for New Testament Study Monograph Series of importance for the study of Acts are P. F. Esler, *Community and Gospel in Luke-Acts* (Cambridge: Cambridge University Press, 1987); John C. Lentz, Jr., *Luke's Portrait of Paul* (Cambridge: Cambridge University Press, 1993); W. A. Strange, *The Problem of the Text of Acts* (Cambridge: Cambridge University Press, 1992); and Paul Trebilco, *Jewish Communities in Asia Minor* (Cambridge: Cambridge University Press, 1991). A series of volumes of essays on Acts has been edited at Tyndale House in Cambridge under Bruce Winter: vol. 1, *The Book of Acts in Its Ancient Literary Setting* (Carlisle: Paternoster; Grand Rapids: Eerdmans, 1993); vol. 2, *The Book of Acts in Its Graeco-Roman Setting* (Grand Rapids: Eerdmans, 1994); vol. 3, *The Book of Acts and Paul in Roman Custody* (Grand Rapids: Eerdmans, 1994). An innovative study that incorporates textual criticism and interpretation has been developed in Josep Rius-Camps and Jenny Read-Heimerdinger, *The Message of Acts in Codex Bezae: A Comparison with the Alexandrian Tradition*, vol. 1, *Acts 1.1-5.42: Jerusalem*, Journal for the Study of the New Testament Supplement Series 257 (London and New York: T. & T. Clark, 2004)

Commentaries on Luke include Joseph A. Fitzmyer's two-volume contribution to the Anchor Bible (New York: Doubleday, 1981–5); Luke T. Johnson, *The Gospel of Luke*, Sacra Pagina 3 (Collegeville, MN: Liturgical

Press, 1991); Ernst Haenchen, *Acts of the Apostles* (London: Blackwell, 1971); and I. Howard Marshall, *Acts of the Apostles*, Tyndale New Testament Commentaries (Leicester: Intervarsity Press, 1980).

The Gospel and Letters of John

Two of the major perspectives dominating study of the Gospel according to John for decades were the historical approach of C. H. Dodd, in his *Historical Tradition in the Fourth Gospel* (Cambridge: Cambridge University Press, 1963), and the existentialist interpretation of Rudolf Bultmann, *The Gospel of John* (1950; Oxford: Blackwell, 1971). Literary analytical theory was employed for the study of John by Robert Fortna in his *The Gospel of Signs: A Reconstruction of the Narrative Sources Underlying the Fourth Gospel* (Cambridge: Cambridge University Press, 1970), and later in his *The Fourth Gospel and Its Predecessor* (Edinburgh: T. & T. Clark, 1988). Alan Culpepper used an analogous approach in *Anatomy of the Fourth Gospel: A Study in Literary Design* (Philadelphia: Fortress Press, 1983). D. Moody Smith's earlier contribution in this field, *Composition and Order of the Fourth Gospel: Bultmann's Literary Theory* (New Haven: Yale University Press, 1965), was followed by his *Johannine Christianity: Essays on Its Setting, Sources, and Theology* (Columbia: University of South Carolina Press, 1984) and *John among the Gospels: The Relationship in Twentieth Century Research* (Minneapolis: Fortress Press, 1992).

A masterful two-volume commentary on John was written by Raymond E. Brown for the Anchor Bible (Garden City, NY: Doubleday, 1970). Less technical are those of Barnabas Lindars for the New Century Bible (London: Oliphant, 1972); Robert Kysar for the Augsburg Commentary on the New Testament (Minneapolis: Augsburg, 1986); and Gerard S. Sloyan for the Interpretation Commentary (Atlanta: John Knox Press, 1988).

The Letters of John have been analyzed as sources for theological and community development in the early Church by Raymond E. Brown, *The Community of the Beloved Disciple* (New York: Paulist Press, 1979), and by Urban C. van Wahlde, *The Johannine Commandments: 1 John and the Struggle for the Johannine Tradition* (New York: Paulist, 1990). Commentaries on the Letters of John include Raymond E. Brown in the Anchor Bible (New York: Doubleday, 1982); Judith Lieu, *The Second and Third Epistles of John* (Edinburgh: T. & T. Clark, 1986); D. Moody Smith, *First, Second, and Third John*, Interpretation Commentary (Louisville: John Knox Press, 1991); Robert Kysar, *First, Second, and Third John* (Minneapolis: Augsburg, 1986); and J. L. Houlden for Black's Commentaries (London: A. & C. Black, 1994).

The Letter of James

The Letter of James, as well as the Letters of Peter and Jude, received a learned analysis by Bo Reicke in his commentary for the Anchor Bible, *The Epistles of James, Peter, and Jude* (New York: Doubleday, 1964). A study of James that takes into account the influence of Stoic philosophy is Sophie Laws, *The Epistle of James*, Black's Commentaries (London: A. & C. Black, 1980). For comprehensive analyses of the historical James, his relationships and followers, see Bruce Chilton and Craig A. Evans, *James the Just and Christian Origins*, Supplements to Novum Testamentum 98 (Leiden: Brill, 1999); Bruce Chilton and Jacob Neusner, *The Brother of Jesus: James the Just and His Mission,* (Louisville: Westminster John Knox, 2001); and Bruce Chilton and Craig A. Evans, *The Missions of James, Peter, and Paul: Tensions in Early Christianity*, Supplements to Novum Testamentum 115 (Leiden: Brill, 2005).

First Peter

John H. Elliott's work *A Home for the Homeless: A Sociological Exegesis of 1 Peter, Its Situation and Strategy* (Philadelphia: Fortress Press, 1981) is equally important for its analysis of this writing and as a prime example of sociologically based exegesis of the text. F. W. Beare wrote a substantive study of the Greek text of 1 Peter, *The First Epistle of Peter*, 3d ed. (Oxford: Blackwell, 1970). Another useful commentary on 1 Peter is that of Ernest Best, *First Peter*, New Century Bible (London: Oliphant, 1971).

Revelation of John

Commentaries on Revelation include those of Gerhard A. Krodel, Augsburg Commentary on the New Testament (Minneapolis: Augsburg/Fortress, 1989); M. E. Boring, *Revelation*, Interpretation (Louisville: Westminster, 1989); Wilfrid J. Harrington, *Revelation*, Sacra Pagina (Collegeville, MN: Liturgical Press, 1993); and Richard Bauckham, *The Theology of the Book of Revelation* (Cambridge: Cambridge University Press, 1993).

5. Conceptual and Organizational Diversity in the Church

The expansions and revisions of the canonical traditions about Jesus and the apostles flourished in the second and subsequent centuries. The entire body of extant works of this type was brought together by E. Hennecke and W. Schneemelcher in two volumes that have been translated, edited, and expanded by R. M. Wilson in *New Testament Apocrypha*, 2 vols., revised ed. (Cambridge: J. Clarke; Louisville: Westminster, 1991–2).

Some scholars have advanced the theory that apocryphal Gospels actually include texts and traditions that are older and more reliable than those in the canonical New Testament writings. For example, Helmut Koester claims in *Ancient Christian Gospels: Their History and Development* (Philadelphia: Trinity Press International, 1990) that the *Gospel according to Thomas* is the oldest of the Gospels and that an earlier version of the Q source than the one used by Matthew and Luke did not include references to judgment, to apocalyptic expectations, or to the conflict between the followers of Jesus and those of John the Baptist (pp. 162–71). John Dominic Crossan, in *Four*

Other Gospels: Shadows on the Contours of the Canon (Sonoma, CA: Polebridge, 1992), likewise claims that the *Gospel according to Thomas* and the *Secret Gospel of Mark* are older than the canonical Gospels and that the *Gospel of Peter* is based on a narrative account of the Passion of Jesus that is older than that used in the canonical Gospels. The *Secret Gospel of Mark* was published by Morton Smith in *The Secret Gospel of Mark: The Discovery and Interpretation of the Secret Gospel according to Mark* (New York: Harper & Row, 1973). Smith claimed to have found a very late copy of this document on a sheet pasted inside the cover of an old book in a Palestinian monastery. Recently, this alleged source has been discredited; Stephen C. Carlson, *The Gospel Hoax: Morton Smith's Invention of Secret Mark* (Waco, TX: Baylor University Press, 2005). These opinions are purely circular arguments, since the investigators have found material that they prefer to what is in the canonical Gospels and, in support of their preferences, attribute this material to more ancient sources. No ancient evidence confirms these theories, but the theories have been welcomed and widely publicized in the popular press.

6. Christianity Seeks to Unify Faith and Practice

The text of the New Testament is analyzed in Bruce Metzger, *The Text of the New Testament: Its Transmission, Corruption, and Restoration* (New York: Oxford University Press, 1992), and Bart Ehrman, *The Orthodox Corruption of Scripture. The Effect of Early Christological Controversies on the Text of the New Testament* (New York: Oxford University Press, 1993).

The Greek text and a translation of the writings of the Apostolic Fathers may be found in the two volumes by Kirsopp Lake in the Loeb Classical Library (London: Heinemann; Cambridge, MA: Harvard University Press, 1925–6). Translation and commentary of this material are also available in a series of volumes edited by Robert M. Grant, *The Apostolic Fathers*, vol. 1, *Introduction*, by R. M. Grant (New York and London: Nelson, 1964); vol. 2, *First and Second Clement*, by R. M. Grant and Holt H. Graham (New York and London: Nelson, 1965); vol. 3, *Barnabas and Didache*, by Robert A. Kraft (New York and London: Nelson, 1965); vol. 4, *Ignatius of Antioch*, by R. M. Grant (London and Camden, NJ: Nelson, 1966); vol. 5, *Polycarp, Martyrdom of Polycarp, Fragments of Papias*, by Willam R. Schoedel (London and Camden, NJ: Nelson, 1967); and vol. 6, *Hermas*, by Graydon F. Snyder (London and Camden, NJ: Nelson, 1968). See also Bart D. Ehrman, *The Apostolic Fathers* (Cambridge, MA: Harvard University Press, 2003).

Standard studies of the development of the canon include those of Hans F. von Campenhausen, *The Formation of the Christian Bible* (Philadelphia: Fortress Press, 1972), and Julio Trebolle Barrera, *The Jewish Bible and the Christian Bible* (Leiden and Grand Rapids: Brill and Eerdmans, 1998). Analyses of the canon of Scripture and the processes by which it developed include James Barr, *Holy Scripture: Canon, Authority, and Criticism* (Oxford: Clarendon Press, 1983); James A. Sanders, *Canon and Community: A Guide to Canonical Criticism* (Philadelphia: Fortress Press, 1984); and Eugene

Ulrich, "Origen's Old Testament Text: The Transmission History of the Septuagint to the Third Century C.E.," in *The Dead Sea Scrolls and the Origins of the Bible* (Grand Rapids and Leiden: Eerdmans and Brill, 1999), 202–23.

Studies focusing on the canon of the New Testament include David G. Meade, *Pseudonymity and Canon: An Investigation into the Relationship of Authorship and Authority in Jewish and Early Christian Tradition* (Tübingen: Mohr, 1986), and Bruce M. Metzger, *The Canon of the New Testament: Its Origin, Development, and Significance* (Oxford: Clarendon Press, 1987).

INDEX OF BIBLICAL REFERENCES

GENERAL INDEX

Note: b = boxed material, f = figure,
 m = map

Aaron, 80, 81, 97, 98, 99, 143, 264
Abdon, 128
Abegg, Martin G., Jr., 36
Abel, 60, 256, 470–1
Abijam, 176
Abimelech, 127, 128, 134
Abiram, 99. *See also* Korah
Abner, 148, 290
abomination, as theme in Hebrew Bible,
 200, 201, 208–209, 300, 350. *See also*
 condemnations; idolatry
Abot, 467–8
Abraham: and ancestors of Israelites, 39, 69,
 70, 71; and Babylonian exile, 28; and
 Egypt, 21; in Galatians, 546; God's
 covenant with, 2b; and justice "in the
 gate," 91b; and oral tradition, 40, 46, 47;
 and Patriarchs, 63–4, 68, 69, 70; Paul on
 story of, 547, 557; as prophet, 143; and
 sacrifice, 256, 261, 263. *See also Apocalypse
 of Abraham*; *Testament of Abraham*
Absalom, 90, 148, 251, 388
Achaia, 33
Achan, 117b, 123–4
Acts of Andrew, 658
Acts of the Apostles, 383, 390, 423b, 428,
 489, 495–6, 531, 532, 541, 544b, 569, 606
 –27, 677–8
Acts of John, 658
Acts of Paul, 658
Acts of Peter, 658
Acts of Thomas, 658
Adam, 57, 174, 574
'*Adonai* (Lord), 632b
Adonis (god), 351b
adoption, and ancient Israelite life, 61–3
adultery, 215–16, 258, 632b. *See also* marriage
Aemilius Sura, 370b
afterlife, in Hellenistic Jewish literature, 365b
Agabus, 611b

Against Apion (Josephus), 454
Against Celsus (Origen), 14b
Against the Greeks (Tatian), 669b
Against Helvidius (St. Jerome), 494b
Against Heresies (Irenaeus), 654, 664b, 670
agnosticism, 577b
agriculture: and ceremonial calendar of ancient
 Israel, 252; and early Israelite technology,
 120–1b; and Feast of Weeks, 617b; in
 Leviticus, 96; and taxation during Roman
 period, 423, 425. *See also* livestock; shepherds
Agrippa I, 420b, 421b, 435, 437b
Agrippa II, 421b, 425–6, 445b
Ahab, 48–9b, 158, 185, 264
Aharoni, Yohanan, 35
Ahasuerus (Xerxes), 302
Ahaz, 48b, 190, 193, 265
Ahijah, 180–1, 185
Ahikam, 107. *See also* Shaphan
Ai (city), 113f, 117b
Akiva, Rabbi, 462
Akkadians, 41b, 57. *See also* Babylon
Akra, 348, 349b
Albinus, 444
Albright, William F., 62b, 117b, 323–4
Alcimus, 352b, 356
Alexander Balas, 357
Alexander the Great, 6, 13b, 20, 327
Alexander Jannaeus, 358m, 362, 381, 382,
 383, 388–9
Alexander Polyhistor, 340, 341
Alexandria, 13b, 14, 20–21, 206b, 328, 339f,
 340b, 435, 449
Allison, Dale C., Jr., 477, 676
alphabetic script, 42b
altar, and worship in early Israel,
 260, 262–9
Amalek, 304
Amalekites, 147
Amel-Marduk, 194
Amenophis IV (pharoah), 75
Ammi, 215. *See also* Hosea
Ammon, 22–3, 71, 224, 240

Ammonites, 22, 63b
Amon, 158
Amoraim, 465b
Amorites, 24, 64b
Amos, 222–6, 229, 264
Amos, Book of, 12, 49b, 91b, 145, 156, 178,
 183, 185, 219–26, 613b
amphictyony theory, 127, 132b, 136
Amurru, 64b
Ananus (Annas), family of, 421b, 422, 444, 493
Anatolia, 30–1
ancestors, stories of in Genesis, 69–71
Anchor Bible commentaries, 319
"Ancient of Days," 370b
Anderson, Bernhard W., 36, 316
angel(s), 313b, 379, 521b, 599, 603, 650b
Angelic Liturgy, 393, 394b. *See also* Dead Sea
 Scrolls
Animal Apocalypse, 372, 373, 374. *See also
 Enoch, Book of*
animal imagery, in apocalyptic literature,
 312b
Anna, 610b
Antigonus, 327, 406
anti-Jewish literature, in Egypt of third
 century B.C.E., 341b. *See also* anti-Semitism
Antioch, 23, 26, 329b, 493f, 542b, 611–12b,
 621
Antiochus III, 332, 333b, 397b
Antiochus IV, 16, 311, 312, 314, 347–8, 350,
 355, 361, 363, 364–5, 371
Antipater, 395, 396, 397
Antiquities of the Jews (Josephus), 374b, 436b,
 454, 490b
anti-Semitism, 474, 480, 592b, 595b, 577b. *See
 also* anti-Jewish literature
antithetic parallelism, in poetry, 271
Antonia fortress, 443b
Antoninus Pius, 27f
Apamea, peace of, 333
aphorisms, and *Gospel According to
 Thomas*, 653b
Aphrodite (goddess), 33, 351b

709